Handbook of EDP Auditing

SECOND EDITION

MICHAEL A. MURPHY, CPA, CISA (Certified Information Systems Auditor), is a partner of Coopers & Lybrand. As Director, Audit Practice Support in the National Auditing Directorate, his responsibilities include technology-based guidance materials and software. He also directs development of advanced technology audit, control, and security materials for the firm's Information Technology Audit Services (ITAS) unit and is Chairman of the Information Technology Subcommittee of C&L's International Accounting and Auditing Committee. Prior to assuming his current position in 1987, he was the ITAS Mid-Atlantic Regional Managing Partner.

XENIA LEY PARKER, CISA, is a manager in Coopers & Lybrand's National Auditing Directorate, with responsibility for a wide range of information technology-oriented projects. She is Co-Chair of the C&L-sponsored Internal Audit Steering Committee, and coauthor of audit guides and monographs published by the Institute of Internal Auditors (IIA), Bank Administration Institute, and EDP Auditors Foundation. She directs C&L's technical communications department. A member of the IIA's International Advanced Technology Committee, she is an adjunct Assistant Professor of Information Systems at New York University, specializing in information systems auditing.

Handbook of EDP Auditing

SECOND EDITION

Michael A. Murphy

Xenia Ley Parker

COOPERS & LYBRAND

WG&L

WARREN, GORHAM & LAMONT

Boston • New York

ISBN 0-7913-0411-6

Library of Congress Catalog Card No. 89-51645

PERMISSIONS

Published by

WARREN, GORHAM & LAMONT, INC.
210 SOUTH STREET
BOSTON, MASSACHUSETTS 02111

PRINTED IN THE UNITED STATES OF AMERICA

PREFACE

IT IS AN INTERESTING EXPERIENCE to create the second edition of a book, especially one that deals with the dynamic and accelerating changes in information technology. After working diligently on the original, it is fascinating to update its contents and improve its design. For this handbook, the task was made particularly challenging by the retirement from Coopers & Lybrand (C&L) of Stanley D. Halper, lead author of the original volume. In a career spanning more than forty years, Stan's vision helped shape the profession of EDP auditing. As he moves on to new personal challenges, those who had the good fortune to work with him wish him the best. We will miss him, and hope he likes the new version of "his book."

Revising a book while adding new technical information and folding in a 600-page supplement means making hard decisions about what can stay and what should go. We made those decisions and restructured the book to be more responsive to readers' needs. It will move with us into the 1990s as we continue responding to changes in information technology. We hope this volume proves as useful to its readers as did the first. The response to that book was so favorable that we felt a special sense of pride and commitment to making the new one even better.

This is the first complete revision since C&L and Warren, Gorham & Lamont published the first edition of *Handbook of EDP Auditing*, in 1985. That book allowed us to share our knowledge with the profession. We are pleased to maintain that tradition with this edition, updated for important developments in technology. The impact of those developments was demonstrated at C&L when the Computer Audit Assistance Group (CAAG) became Information Technology Audit Services (ITAS) to describe the broader role and responsibilities of our IT audit professionals as they deal with audit, control, and security issues faced by client organizations of all sizes. Our response to technology is reflected in this book.

Acknowledgments

This book would not exist without Stan Halper, so we thank him first.

The material is developed on an ongoing basis through the daily efforts of too many people to list. We would like to thank C&L people in all areas of practice who made special contributions: Thomas Barrett, Frederick Beal,

Jr., Douglas R. Bean, Neil Bebbington, Timothy J. Botts, M. Constance Brown, Marilyn M. Bruneau, Jayne Burke, Vincent A. Campitelli, John W. Cassella, Albert H. Decker, Lynn Edelson, Raymond W. Elliott, Thomas F. Farrell, James S. Gerson, Leonard Gilbert, Lynford E. Graham, Jr., Geoffrey H. Hamway, George A. Hermann, Murray B. Hirsch, Susan E. Johnson, John E. Koretz, Brian J. Morse, Bradley J. Oltmanns, William R. Robinson, Richard M. Steinberg, Andrew B. Zimmerman, George Brucato, Thomas Carver, Joseph J. DiMuro, Thomas Flanagan, Michael Ford, John F. Garry, Stash Jarocki, Henry R. Jaenicke, Richard Jun, John McNamara, Kurt Meiser, Gunnar Myhre, Jacqualine R. Rushing, Russell Sapienza, David Schemel, Fred Shuback, Thomas Sisson, Fred Umbach, Lynn Veatch, Judy Ward, Peter Wild, Jan Wilkins, and Nurit Zanani; and C&L National technical communications staff members: Marianne Agius, Sherry Beck, Larry Bernstein, Lucille Borelli, Erving DelPilar, David Frawley, Brenda Gibbons, Adam Goldson, Patrick Peyton, and Jon Wettingfeld.

We thank the following external contributors: Robert W. Boyd, Internal Auditing Manager, American Brands; Frederick Gallegos, Michael P. Cangemi, Gerald Fee, John Lainhart IV, Kenneth Pollock, EDP Auditors Association (EDPAA); Richard Kusserow, Inspector General, and the Department of Health and Human Services, for allowing us to excerpt the report "Interviews With Perpetrators of Computer Fraud"; and Leslie Wharton, Attorney, Mathew & Branscomb, for the section "Copyright Protection for Computer Programs and Data Bases."

We would like to thank the EDP Auditors Foundation (EDPAF) for allowing us to share our report case studies, funded by MITI (Japanese Ministry of International Trade and Industry). C&L conducted the research and wrote the report *Advanced Computer Assisted Audit Techniques* under the direction of Dr. Dan C. Kneer, Arizona State University, Director of Research, EDPAF, and retired C&L Partner Stanley D. Halper. As project manager, Xenia Ley Parker had the invaluable assistance of Akira Matsuo, C&L, Tokyo, and Edwin Cheung, C&L, Hong Kong. We thank case study participants at Manville Corporation: John Leasher, General Auditor; Dennis A. Dallas, Manager, Audit Operations; and C&L Partner Frederick M. Beal, Jr. At Manufacturers Hanover: William J. Duane, Senior Vice-President and General Auditor; Thomas A. Johnson, Vice-President and Deputy General Auditor; Ivan Brass, Vice-President; Fred Mistretta, Mike Lapelosa, and Steve Doherty, Audit Manager; and C&L Partner William R. Robinson. At Johnson & Johnson: John Begley, CFO Hospital Services; John Marchwinski, Audit Director; and C&L Partners, Vincent A. Campitelli and Neil Bebbington.

We acknowledge with thanks permission granted by the American Institute of Certified Public Accountants (AICPA), the Institute of Internal Auditors (IIA), and EDPAF to quote or paraphrase passages from their publications. The complete documents can be obtained from those organizations.

At Warren, Gorham & Lamont, we thank Eugene Simonoff, Senior Vice-President; and Paul Donnelly, Vice-President; Kathleen Peterson, Managing Editor; and Linda Reiman, Senior Editor.

We hope that this second edition will become a constant reference as a source of useful information for your own work.

MICHAEL A. MURPHY
XENIA LEY PARKER

New York
August 1989

SUMMARY OF CONTENTS

TABLE OF CONTENTS

PART I
EDP Auditing

1 The Impact of Changing Technology

2 The Auditing Profession

3 The EDP Auditing Profession

PART II
Information Technology Concepts

4 MIS Organization

5 Computer Concepts

6 Computers

7 *Telecommunications Networks and Systems*

PART III
Information Systems

8 Introduction to Information Systems

9 Revenue Systems

10 Disbursement Systems

11 Production Systems

12 General Ledger Systems

PART IV
Control Concepts

13 Information Technology Controls

14 Application Controls—I

15 *Application Controls—II*

PART V
Systems Audit Approach

16 The Risk-Based Audit Approach

17 *How to Document Systems: Using Flowcharts*

18 Interviews and Transaction Reviews

19 The Control Risk Assessment Process

20 *Control Reviews and Tests of Controls*

21 Substantive Procedures

PART VI
Auditing System Development

22 System Development Trends and Practices

23 System Development Methodology and Auditing

24 End-User Computing

25 Implementation Reviews

PART VII
Auditing Advanced Systems

26 Testing Techniques for Computer-Based Systems

27 System Software

28 Data Base

PART VIII
Information Security

29 Computer Abuse

30 Security Reviews

31 Logical Access Controls

32 Access Control Software

APPENDIX A

Internal Control Reference Manual—Information Technology Controls

APPENDIX B

Internal Control Reference Manual—Application Controls

APPENDIX C
Computer Assisted Audit Techniques: Case Studies

APPENDIX D

Interviews With Perpetrators of Computer Fraud

PART I

EDP Auditing

CHAPTER **1**

The Impact of Changing Technology

KEY CHANGES TAKING PLACE IN TECHNOLOGY

As evolutionary changes in technology pick up their pace, it becomes all the more important to understand the key concepts. Many new words, acronyms, and buzzwords are being used in the current literature as new ways to do things are developed. (See the Glossary for basic definitions.) The concepts listed here are those most likely to have a major impact on the widest area over the next several years.

Networking

Networking provides the ability to communicate data between parties, such as supplier to customer, customer to supplier, between computers, possibly worldwide. Global telecommunications networks that support the systems of large banks and other organizations have become commonplace, as other organizations are in the process of developing new systems.

Distributed Data and Computer Power

This concept involves distributing data and computer power to departments and/or operating centers to allow them to do their own processing within the network. Although this idea is not new—distributed processing has been around since the 1970s—the ways in which it is being done may have changed. For example, when confronted by the proliferation of end-user systems, some of the more experienced information technology (IT) auditors liken end-user computing (EUC) to the old distributed processing concept, using new machines and user-maintained systems rather than centrally developed software as in the past. The audit challenges are similar.

Seamless Architecture

Seamless architecture gives software the ability to run on various-size computers, usually from the same manufacturer, without requiring reprogramming. Organizations are coming to expect the same software and hardware to run on all of their computers. An example of planned seamless architecture can be seen in IBM's SAA (Systems Application Architecture), designed to be used to create systems that will run on all their machines, from PCs to minicomputers to mainframes.

As IBM describes it in one of their advertisements, "SAA will allow everyone in an organization to access information, regardless of its location." An added benefit to users is that software written to SAA specifications gives similar menus and screen layouts. The terminology is also similar, allowing people to learn how to use different-size computers more easily. As it is now, the use of different-size systems often requires complete retraining. Other manufacturers, such as DEC, are planning, or already have, similar architectures.

Connectivity

Connectivity is the ability of devices from different manufacturers to talk to each other. A greater degree of connectivity lessens the amount of difficulty in making different machines communicate with each other. As the technology develops, more and more computers will be able to communicate without requiring separate, elaborate software interfaces, which are needed in many current applications.

Real-Time Systems

In real-time systems, transactions are executed as they occur, and necessary information is immediately updated. Provisions are usually made for an automatic record to be kept of the previous version of the data, to provide for recovery or startup. Having an audit trail of these transactions is critical.

Many people use the term real-time systems when they are really talking about on-line systems. On-line systems provide immediate responses to queries of information, but do not normally change the data file at that time.

The distinction between on-line systems and on-line real-time systems is still worth making and indicates, for the most part, when the update or change to data on file actually takes place. In on-line real-time systems, that change is immediate, and old data on the file is updated with the new transaction date. In on-line systems, the actual update often takes place in batch, overnight or at another specified time. A shadow or memo update—to a copy of the file—takes place immediately, to allow for reference to the most current information during the day, before the actual update occurs.

Software Packages

Software packages are third-party, prewritten computer programs to accomplish specific tasks. Many people credit packaged spreadsheet software with spurring the microcomputer explosion of the early 1980s. Most of the widely used applications for business are available as packaged software, since packaged software is usually more cost-effective than in-house development of software programs to accomplish common tasks. Packaged software is so widely used that considerations for its acquisition have been added as a procurement portion to many system development methodologies, to provide control over the selection and implementation process.

Operational Systems

The ability of systems to help in the day-to-day running of businesses increases as standard processes are automated and linked together within the system. Operational systems, for example in manufacturing, can include processes from managing inventory and the shop floor to providing strategic information for planning a business's future. Accounting information generally is a by-product of these systems, and its processing often takes place within them. Most operational systems are real-time.

Artificial Intelligence

As currently defined, artificial intelligence (AI) is the ability to use software to bring the knowledge of experts to a particular task. Today, people tend to use the term somewhat loosely. They use AI to refer to systems that are really expert systems, or even decision support systems, which rely on the data and rules people have developed and employed within the software. As such, these systems can make seemingly intelligent choices, since they have been given the rules and data needed to make those choices. However, this is not true artificial intelligence, which would require that they have the ability to perform original thought. There is not yet a computer that can really think, in the sense of imagining new concepts, although computer scientists are working on it.

Because of the growing availability of ready-to-use AI shells—systems that are ready for users to insert their own rules and knowledge—and other development tools, AI concepts are becoming commonplace. End users will be able to incorporate AI into their own operational systems.

The benefits of such "intelligent" software will lead to its use in many kinds of systems—on the shop floor, in warehouses, and so forth. In the future, these systems will be embedded in many applications, whether purchased or developed by formal management information systems (MIS) or end users.

Possible Effects of Key Changes on Business

The impact of the widespread use of computer technology offers the opportunity for significant changes in the way we work. Looking at those significant changes just discussed, there are some predictions that can be

FIG. 1-1
Possible effects of key changes on business

		Fortune 1000 (Large)	Middle	Small
1.	NETWORKING	X	X	X
2.	DISTRIBUTION OF DATA/ COMPUTER POWER	X	X	
3.	SEAMLESS ARCHITECTURE	X	X	
4.	CONNECTIVITY	X	X	X
5.	REAL-TIME SYSTEMS	X	X	X
6.	SOFTWARE PACKAGES	X	X	X
7.	OPERATIONAL SYSTEMS	X	X	
8.	ARTIFICIAL INTELLIGENCE	X	X	X

made about their potential to change ways of doing business. Like any predictions, these are open to modifications due to unforeseen circumstances, but, looking over the last 30 years of computer use, some assumptions seem plausible. Figure 1-1 presents areas of greatest impact.

Networking. Networking will affect all U.S. business over the next five years. The driving force behind this will be the large companies that will network with their suppliers through private or public carriers. In turn, the larger companies will network with their customers, often small companies, to provide them with an easy and flexible way to buy the large companies' products. An example is Johnson & Johnson (J&J) Hospital Supply. In this use of networking, healthcare centers are connected through J&J terminals to J&J's computers so that they can order their supplies directly. Many automobile dealerships are connected to their manufacturers to order parts. Similarly, the automobile manufacturers are linking to their suppliers in the United States and Europe. In a recently announced move, an automobile manufacturer is linking its European suppliers to supply invoices and delivery schedules through an EDI (electronic data interchange) system provided by a large network provider and a systems house. The change is planned to help reduce errors on input, to help reduce slowdowns caused by using the mail, and to eliminate hard copy.

Another networking trend is the growing use of EDI to transmit standard business documents over the telecommunications networks. The benefits to organizations obtained by the speed, accuracy, and relatively low cost of EDI are such that its use is growing faster than anyone predicted.

Controls over the telecommunications network will become crucial to businesses. Loosely controlled networks can allow much trouble.

Distribution of Data and Computer Power. In the Fortune 1000 companies, often the companies that set the trends for others to follow, the trend to distribution of data and computer power will continue at an increased pace. The large central computer will be used to house the corporate data bases. Much of the information in those data bases will result from processing at various sites throughout the company. Those results will be communicated to the central machine over the network.

The large machine can provide the additional computing power for massive "number crunching" when a site requires it, but for the most part, processing will be local. The large central computer will continue to hold and provide the corporate accounting information, but the processing to develop that information will be at the various sites where computing power has been distributed. The size of computers at the sites will vary, based upon local requirements. In some cases, the end-user systems, developed and running on microcomputers, will be enough to satisfy local needs. In others, minicomputers, and possibly mainframes, will be required.

Like the Fortune 1000 companies, medium-size companies will also distribute data and computer power. While the size of their data bases and computers may be smaller and their sites fewer, they will have many of the same requirements and resulting uses of the technology as large companies.

To those concerned with controls, these systems will point out the need to ensure that local processing areas have the same understanding of controls and their value as the traditional data centers do. Corporate policies will mandate that control be established and maintained at all local sites.

Seamless Architecture. In order to take maximum advantage of distributed processing, companies will expect their computer vendors to allow the same software and data bases to be run at all of their various sites on different-size machines without reprogramming. This will ensure both uniformity and efficiency in the initial design and implementation of software as well as its subsequent maintenance. It will also bring an end to years of confusion over the various types of machines and overapplicability of software to different business situations. Today, it is still common for an organization to have numerous vendors, with completely different packages performing similar tasks on microcomputers, minicomputers, and mainframes, without any ability to share the software, or even the data in many cases.

Connectivity. Connectivity will affect companies of all sizes as they link to each other through networks, as described previously. True connectivity will allow different devices to communicate with each other; therefore, one device at each site will be able to do multiple tasks in addition to communicating with outside parties. Controls over access to the system will become all the more important as systems are linked together.

Real-Time Systems. The availability of efficient computing power and communications, together with software packages, will allow all aspects of American business to use this type of real-time system. (Most microcomputer systems process in this manner.) Many of the new packaged software systems are real-time in nature. Controls over who can enter data and how it is prepared will become critical as the systems update the information immediately. Backup and recovery procedures must be provided.

Software Packages. Independent software vendors are creating many new application packages for all computers, in addition to the application packages now available, which number in the thousands. Computer hardware vendors rely on software to help sell their hardware. The major advantage of purchasing software is the economy it can offer, compared to designing and implementing systems internally. Further, software maintenance can be assigned to the vendor, helping to lessen the expense incurred by many organizations that keep a staff of programmers to maintain their systems. The increasing availability of quality application software will dramatically expand computing on all levels of American business. In particular, it will ease the entry of new users into the computer era.

Operational Systems. Initially, business computing was used primarily for accounting systems. Where it was used for operational purposes, as in, for example, governing a process flow on the shop floor, it was usually totally separate from the computer for accounting systems. Results of the operation were entered separately into the "accounting computers." Today, an integration of operational systems and accounting systems is starting to take place. One example of this is a just-in-time (JIT) inventory system. Another example will be the tying in of a reservation system with the revenue system, as might exist in a hotel.

This will affect the large company and the middle-size company. Smaller companies entering computing will use their computer initially for accounting purposes. As they grow larger, the smaller companies will follow in the large companies' tracks by using their computers primarily for operational purposes.

Artificial Intelligence. AI is likely to become a major part of operational systems. The ability to bring expertise to users through computer software will show considerable advances over the next five years. AI will have the most dramatic effect on large companies with many employees and high turnover. The use of such systems will allow retention of the knowledge pool, even when key employees leave the organization.

Medium-size companies will also make considerable use of such systems once they are within affordable range. They are ideally suited for organizations that usually cannot attract experts to work for them. Through acquisition of expert systems, these companies will have access to experts.

Smaller businesses, especially in professional areas, will make considerable use of these systems to maintain a high quality of work. Albeit with different motives, all segments of American business will take advantage of this technology.

GENERAL OBSERVATIONS

Obviously the pace at which these changes occur depends on competitive forces and the desire to achieve efficiencies. Although this technology can produce computing power at significantly decreasing costs, the power may exceed American organizations' ability to use it unless they can also provide abilities in the eight areas cited above.

It appears that all parts of the computer industry are now focused to marry raw computing power to those eight areas. The business strategies of major players in hardware and software—as well as of those in data, voice, and image transport—now recognize the necessity for all eight areas to work together for customers to increase their use of the technology.

Skill Requirements to Implement the Technology

As noted previously, the eight areas will have varying effects on organizations of different sizes. Adoption of the technology depends on particular driving forces. In some industries, such as financial services, there is little choice. An individual company in this segment can hardly afford to ignore technological advances. They must adapt to remain competitive. In other industries, implementation of the technology may be slower. Nevertheless, over the next five years advances will be made in most of the business world. A continuing assessment of the technology will become critical, both to survive and to position products and services better.

To employ the technology, businesses will need skills in the areas shown in Figure 1-2. Note that there are no skill requirements listed for the seamless architecture area. It is assumed that these will be provided by equipment vendors. In each of the other areas, however, while the equipment or other vendor will provide the tools (for example, AT&T provides the network), it will be up to the organization to implement these tools in a timely and cost-effective manner.

OVERALL IMPACT

When considering the skill sets in relation to an organization's needs, it is important to note that the competition for people with skills in many of these areas is already severe. As the technology continues to trickle down to the medium-size companies, the competition for skilled personnel will become even more acute.

Decisions about whether to use outside resources in certain of these areas may be colored by the fact that an organization is unable to get that particular kind of assistance. For example, in the area of advanced system design and implementation, many organizations will need to change their requirements to fill their jobs. There may be a resulting decline in in-house design and programming of systems and a shift to packaged software selection and integration. In many places, this shift is already quite evident. Another logical result is the increasing activity by large computer manufacturers to provide much-needed consulting services in networking, data base, and system integration.

Clearly, organizations that can afford it will be increasingly forced to use outside resources to obtain skill sets not available internally. For some time, larger organizations have relied on training and growing skills internally. Owing to timing, today's competitive pressures may no longer allow this course of action. Conceivably, these organizations will move toward

FIG. 1-2

Skills required to implement the new technology

	Fortune 1000 (Large)	Medium	Small
1. NETWORK MANAGEMENT	X	X	
2. DATA BASE DESIGN AND DISTRIBUTION	X	X	
3. PACKAGE SOFTWARE SELECTION	X	X	X
4. OPERATIONAL SYSTEMS CONCEPTS, DESIGN AND INTEGRATION	X	X	
5. ARTIFICIAL INTELLIGENCE DESIGN AND INTEGRATION	X	X	
6. CONNECTIVITY IMPLEMENTATION	X	X	
7. EQUIPMENT SELECTION		X	X

(Note that the equipment vendor will provide skill requirements for the "seamless architecture" area. It is assumed that in each of the other areas, the equipment vendor (or others) will provide the tools (e.g., AT&T provides the network); it will be up to business to implement these tools in a timely and cost-effective manner.)

facility management by a third party for certain systems, until they can "grow their own."

The medium-size organization will have even less choice. It will be pursued by vendors offering a combined software-hardware solution. Manufacturers such as IBM and DEC are increasing their efforts in their Independent Software Vendor (ISV) and Value Added Resellers (VAR) programs to meet those requirements and capture the market. A medium-size company may even have to go to other third parties for assistance in system selection. It will not, except in unusual situations, be designing and implementing its own software.

A small company will be far more unlikely than the medium-size company to attain its own skills. It will be pursued by vendors offering software-hardware solutions and will likely accept those solutions as they are, as it has been doing for some time. Much of this will be done through retail computer stores, as well as through small consultants who are VARs. It will need assistance in selection and implementation similar to today.

Whatever happens in the various-size organizations, it is clear that an abundance of computer power will be available at the intelligent workstation and that the distinction between a microcomputer and a minicomputer will blur. This availability will have a profound effect on software vendors in the products they will offer, and on consultants in the field.

In reviewing the effects of the technology, it is apparent that it affects not only systems developers but auditors as well. Auditors cannot choose to ignore the technology, because they cannot perform their function without understanding how their organization is using the technology to run the business.

The business generates the numbers that appear on the financial statements. The audit will change significantly as business changes because of technology such as networking and real-time systems. Use of both of these technologies, among other effects, minimizes or eliminates historical paper audit trails and, therefore, how audits are performed.

The use of software used to assist in the audit function will have to respond to changes in technology to maintain high-quality work. Vendors are likely to expand their efforts to supply the necessary software, particularly in areas such as security and micro-based tools. At the same time, equipment and software vendors will make advanced software available to query data bases and generate reports.

There is a growing need for investments to be made on a careful but rapid basis. The computers of several years ago had a life cycle of at least five years. Today, that has been reduced to three years. The product acquisitions or development cycle must recognize this changing landscape. Similarly, human skill sets will have to be upgraded for the technology. For example, a very powerful intelligent workstation may be equivalent to yesterday's large central computer in capability, so that software designed to run on yesterday's large central computer can now run on the workstation. The market potential for software will increase dramatically because of the delivery vehicle.

IMPACT ON THE AUDITOR

From an attest viewpoint, there will no longer be the traditional paper trails used to audit around the computer. Indeed, many major vendors now consider paper an option. As the industry trend moves toward a transaction-processing facility or real-time mode, more screen displays will give up-to-the-minute status reports.

To retain data, it will be moved into archiving in a machine-sensible mode through magnetic tape or optical disk. The auditor will have to understand access routines that give system entry, thereby governing authorization and division of duties, in addition to understanding how the system does computation.

Audit Implications of Networking

Understanding systems becomes especially important in networking and connectivity. Computer vendors describe new systems that allow processing of data from anywhere in the network. Visualizing the network as a series of telephones that can call each other through a number of switches, it is possible to gain an understanding of how a network operates, except that in this case the switches are governed by a network manager.

In a large IBM system, most often the software that generally does the routing is VTAM (Virtual Telecommunications Access Method). The network manager knows who can connect to whom by using the VTAM routings. What each of the nodes can do can be defined in the CICS (Customer Information Control System) resource definitions. For example, a transaction originates at a terminal and is forwarded to a processor that does an edit and validation. It is then forwarded to another processor that updates a master file and prepares a bill. The updated master data base and bills are routed to local smaller processors. Through the originating terminal, the user may not know which machine the transaction is processing on or whether there are appropriate controls over that processor. If one processor is busy, the system may move the transaction to another processor to do the work. The auditor must be able to identify the resource and how it is controlled.

The auditor is concerned with the completeness, accuracy, and existence of transactions and related results. For example, where should security be exercised to authorize the transaction? What kind of security should be exercised at each processor?

The auditor will need an understanding of the network and the various resource definitions of what each processor can do and who can access each processor. The auditor must understand the applications on each processor and the controls to ensure accuracy and authorization.

Audit Implications of Distributed Processing

When looking at networking and connectivity, auditors are really examining a newer method of providing distributed processing. Typically, auditors see three-tier processing: mainframe to mini to micro. Each is becoming more powerful in relation to the areas of distribution. Distribution can occur in many different modes.

What is important are the controls to ensure completeness, accuracy, and existence at each of the distributed nodes. In some areas only object code is distributed to the nodes, as is done by large companies concerned that uniform controls are applied at the various procession nodes. Such distribution is typical of companies with uniform operations throughout. In this case, auditors using the network facilities can compare the object code loaded at the distributed facility to the authorized version maintained at the headquarters or development site.

In a similar manner, access control software at the nodes can be tested by auditors electronically from those nodes and analyzed for propriety at a location. Very often, the central site retains summary records, or even detailed backup, of what is at the nodes. The auditor may do testing of the data centrally, or test the data at the node through the network.

The auditor may download selected data to an audit workstation as a node on the network, for analytical review or other purposes. Networks and connectivity will allow this to be done more easily.

The auditor will encounter a more difficult situation when diverse operations are on a network. Often, programs are developed locally, and access control software is selected on a local basis. While the central computer on the network may assemble summary data for consolidation and analytical purposes, the auditor will have to satisfy himself that the locally developed software includes proper controls. Auditors can use the network to sample data and perform appropriate analytical reviews.

Audit Implications of Seamless Architecture

As suggested previously, the ability of software to be processed on any node has significant advantages to organizations. It also offers significant advantages to auditors. When they develop or use software that conforms to the standards, it can be used throughout the network with no change, limited only by machine capacity. Combined with SQL (structured query language) and data bases, it will take maximum advantage of software for selection and analytical purposes.

Audit Implications of Data Base Systems

Central to the architecture of advanced computing is the use of data bases throughout the network. For example, IBM's DB2 is a relational data base. IBM plans a distributed version to run on its three levels of computers: the mainframe 30XX and 9300, the minicomputer System 3X, and the microcomputer PS-2 series. It will include SQL, which is now an ANSI (American National Standards Institute) standard for data base query.

The ability to have the same view of data throughout the network is critical and is part of IBM's SAA. Other vendors, such as DEC and Hewlett Packard, have similar strategies. Independent software vendors will have to provide their proprietary data bases for various-size machines to allow such transparency.

What does this mean to the auditor? Currently, many retrieval software packages require "flattening" of the data base and/or reformatting records to be able to foot files, select data, and so forth. Usually, the file is frozen at a given point in time. With the expanded use of SQL, the auditor will be able to perform many of these tasks dynamically across the entire network from a central point without special coding and with only limited training. Standard SQL shells can be generated to allow routine audit tasks. The auditor can browse the data bases and transfer data in the same format to the workstation to allow further analytical work.

Audit Implications of Real-Time Systems and Connectivity

For many years, there has been discussion about the ability to record and process transactions as they occur, in real time. To trace the history of real-time systems, consider the earliest airline reservation systems. They processed a transaction (a seat request) against seating availability of a flight.

Such a system cost many millions of dollars and had no effect on the financial records. It required massive computers and had limitations on the number of terminals. In the same system today, thousands of terminals located at travel agencies, airports, and so forth have access. Although there is still no direct entry into financial systems, this will come in time.

To increase the use of such systems, easy-to-use software had to be available at relatively low cost. The cost of computer power and storage also had to become cheaper. As this happens, businesses are becoming increasingly dependent on their systems to carry out corporate strategy and compete better.

Other examples of real-time systems that use these building blocks of networks, connectivity, and data bases are automated teller machines (ATMs), stock trading and claim settlement systems, and optical scanners used to process purchases in retail stores. The list is growing daily because the building blocks are there. Arguments now rage about the best hardware and software for these systems, including "fault tolerant machines and parallel processors" designed to ensure continuous servicing of customers with little or no down time.

The effect of these systems on auditors is significant. There may be elimination of batch totaling and more reliance on computer matching to ensure completeness. Authorization will be directed more by the computer, with heavy reliance on access controls for the approval to proceed.

The traditional paper that allowed a historical audit will disappear. Auditors will be auditing on a continuous basis from terminals. Relying heavily on computer-based controls, auditors must have an understanding of the various general controls, such as maintenance and computer operations. Security, and the application systems, and how security is applied will be critical to the audit.

Why is this important? Given a lack of paper, auditors will be unable to reperform programmed procedures manually over the entire period under review. Using the auditor's node on the system, auditors will monitor the flow of transactions and use such techniques as interactive test facilities.

Understanding controls over system changes will require testing the maintenance controls. To ensure that changes are not made in an unauthorized manner will require understanding of the program security controls. Recoverability will be key to these systems; auditors must understand computer operations.

Networking and connectivity increase the importance of understanding where transactions can be routed and which nodes on the network can do what. In batch systems, auditors tended to rely on manual controls and review of reports to determine whether a significant error or irregularity had occurred. Batch controls ensured completeness: Although individual details could be changed in an unauthorized manner, the total could be controlled manually. For computer-generated transactions, major reliance was on the maintenance controls, computer operations, and program security. Now, with real-time systems, auditors must rely on the data file security controls as a primary method to enforce division of duties, to prevent irregularities, and, if irregularities occur, to detect them. Preventive control is crucial in real-time systems.

From an audit perspective, auditors will have to understand the system development life cycle to evaluate whether appropriate controls are built into the system, maintenance controls to understand whether changes are made properly, computer operations for access and recoverability, and program and data file security for validity.

Audit Implications of Software Packages

Many of the applications that formerly were written in-house are now acquired from software vendors. These packages range from large mainframe systems with elective options that change the way accounting transactions are recorded and controlled to the now-endemic spreadsheets.

The auditor must have a detailed understanding of a package and of how it is implemented. Often, vendors offer courses in their packages and how to implement auditability. Many packages have report generators or other utilities that can help the auditor foot files and select items for further investigation or analytics. The auditor must understand the package and its controls.

Audit Implications of Operational Systems

It is difficult to talk about operational systems separately from real-time systems. They go hand in hand. The effect on audit procedures is dramatic, as seen by a JIT inventory system. The system affects audit work with respect to inventory valuation and existence. If the system is not working, audit risk in those areas increases significantly. To understand whether the system is working or not, auditors must know the system and its terminology.

Newer computer systems will be integrated, such as real-time systems often are now. As part of the process, accounting records are updated automatically. For example, in an insurance company, claims are settled online between the adjustor and the claimant. The adjustor uses a terminal to query the system as to limits on a particular type of damage, to find out whether the claimant is insured for the particular damage, and has a check cut on the terminal for the claim. At the same time, the claim file, claim statistics, and other files are updated.

In a manufacturing environment, the router is on a screen. As it passes each workstation, a function key is depressed, to remove the appropriate parts, inventory, and debit work in process for parts and appropriate labor. The finished goods are debited and work in process credited.

In retailing, the process begins with scanning the uniform product code. The SKU inventory is updated and entered into the buyer's records for automatic reordering. The open-to-buy books are updated, as are the sales plans for the sites. Accounting records are by-products of this system.

The point here is that the business process results in the accounting records automatically. To understand how this is done by an operational system is crucial to auditing those systems.

Audit Implications of Artificial Intelligence

The growth of expert systems or AI to help accomplish work has become more of a reality. In the future, more of these systems will be developed for personal computers. For smaller organizations without expertise in certain areas, AI will be a boon. Such systems for accountants, for example, will appear initially in specialized areas such as Financial Accounting Standards

Board (FASB) interpretations and income taxes, gradually expanding into wider areas such as internal control evaluations for complex computer systems.

The whole idea behind expert systems is to bring the knowledge of experts to people's fingertips—not to make decisions but to help make decisions. These expert systems will be extremely useful in staff training. At Coopers & Lybrand (C&L), these techniques are being used now. For example, the ExperTAXsm package assists in tax planning and calculating tax accruals. This system is used by general practice and tax personnel, not computer-oriented people. It holds the tax expertise of many leading tax practitioners and significantly helps the engagement team do its work.

The real potential of expert systems is the ability to learn and build rules files as new situations are encountered and solved. Although not yet available, it is believed that these "thinking machines" will be a reality before the end of the century. Real AI will allow businesses to have the brains of experts customized to individual needs.

Combined with networking, connectivity, transparent data bases, and an audit node, access to data can be combined with expert systems to help auditors do their work.

Auditors and End-User Computing

The advent of powerful microcomputers and intelligent workstations offers the auditor an unparalleled opportunity to bring yesterday's mainframe power into the auditor's office. Proposed systems under OS/2, according to IBM and Microsoft's latest announcements, are powerful multi-tasking machines with up to 160-MB disks. Current costs may be out of reach for most end users, but such systems will become available at more economical costs with new types of storage media for data. Optical disks can store large amounts of data at low rates. Data ranging from 800 megabytes to 4 gigabytes will be available on personal computers.

Such a system might work as follows:

1. Data would go from tape (print image or other) to optical disk, off-line from the computer.
2. The system would build indexes to find the data.
3. Next, the system would search the data on the optical disk and process it against software packages: accounts receivable, 1-2-3, graphics, and so forth.
4. Last, the system would print, or do further processing of, results.

This process would keep away from the mainframe for audit work, avoiding downloading and connect time. It would bring greater masses of data to PCs for detailed audit or analytical work. The increasing availability of data bases on optical disk allows greater use of analytics. (Time-sharing networks used to be the only way to gain access to such data.) Optical disks used in this way combine mainframe power on a micro with tremendous availability of data, which may revolutionize auditing through micros, using the technology in a network or stand-alone environment.

Implications for Management

When looking at how technology will affect audits, it is important to consider how management will run business using the technology. What sort of reports will they have to control the business? The quality of the information will govern their ability to detect material error or irregularity from numbers being generated by the system. It is critical that these reports contain the appropriate data to allow such detection to take place. This top-down approach will be important to understand.

Auditors must view such management reports in terms of audit objectives: completeness, accuracy, existence, and valuation. To the extent that management provides the necessary controls in these systems, the more auditors can rely on them and their consistent application.

The risk is that errors or irregularities will not be discovered on a timely basis. With all this system complexity, how rapidly would an error or irregularity be discovered? Audit teams will require skills to assess that risk. Knowledge of microcomputers alone will not qualify an individual to audit complex computer-based systems.

SUMMARY

This may well be the auditing world of the 1990s. All will feel the impact of these changes, small firm as well as large. Small companies will use technology, more often than not as part of a large network of customers or suppliers. Auditors of smaller companies will see on-line real-time systems, using purchased software packages. Micro-based, the systems may well use local area networks with gateways to other larger networks.

Often, auditors of smaller companies will need a similar level of knowledge as their colleagues in larger companies. The same analytical tools and expert systems will be available throughout the profession. Auditors must be able to use them to be successful.

CHAPTER **2**

The Auditing Profession

INTRODUCTION

Auditing has changed considerably over the years as EDP techniques have had an enormous impact on the way in which management information is processed. Although fundamentals of the profession remain the same, the need to develop and maintain up-to-date knowledge of computer systems is growing. EDP auditors provide special skills and an understanding of computer technology. Although many of the same control questions are involved, EDP audit specialists in computer-based systems provide invaluable assistance to the organization and to other auditors regarding controls over those systems.

The audit functions naturally are related. Many of the professional ethics and requirements for internal, external, and EDP auditors are similar. Some differ only because of the specific job-related activities that each type of auditor performs. This chapter discusses some of the major pronouncements of the Institute of Internal Auditors (IIA), the American Institute of Certified Public Accountants (AICPA), the EDP Auditors Association (EDPAA), and other organizations relevant to the internal auditor or, in some cases, to external and internal auditors. For more about the EDP auditing profession itself, see Chapter 3, "The EDP Auditing Profession."

PROFESSIONAL STANDARDS FOR THE PRACTICE OF INTERNAL AUDITING

Statement of Responsibilities of Internal Auditors

Internal auditing is an independent appraisal activity within an organization that reviews operations as a service to management. It is a managerial control that functions by measuring and evaluating the effectiveness of other controls. Particularly in today's computerized environment, controls over MIS systems can be essential to an organization's conduct of business.

The "Statement of Responsibilities of the Internal Auditor" was issued originally by the IIA in 1947. The continuing development of the profession has resulted in four revisions of that statement. The current statement embodies the concepts established previously and includes such changes as are deemed advisable for the present status of the profession. "Standards for the Professional Practice of Internal Auditing," as shown in Figure 2-1, were adopted by the IIA in 1978. EDP auditors, as part of internal audit, operate under the same statement of responsibilities, standards, and code of ethics.

FIG. 2-1

Professional standards for the practice of internal auditing, adapted from *Standards for the Professional Practice of Internal Auditing* (Institute of Internal Auditors: Altamonte Springs, Fla., June 1978)

INDEPENDENCE — Internal auditors should be independent of the activities they audit.

- **Organizational Status** — The organizational status of the internal auditing department should be sufficient to permit the accomplishment of its audit responsibilities.
- **Objectivity** — Internal auditors should be objective in performing audits.

PROFESSIONAL PROFICIENCY — Internal audits should be performed with proficiency and due professional care.

The Internal Auditing Department

- **Staffing** — The internal auditing department should provide assurance that the technical proficiency and educational background of internal auditors are appropriate for the audits to be performed.
- **Knowledge, Skills, and Disciplines** — The internal auditing department should possess or should obtain the knowledge, skills, and disciplines needed to carry out its audit responsibilities.
- **Supervision** — The internal auditing department should provide assurance that internal audits are properly supervised.

The Internal Auditor

- **Compliance With Standards of Conduct** — Internal auditors should comply with professional standards of conduct.
- **Knowledge, Skills, and Disciplines** — Internal auditors should possess the knowledge, skills, and disciplines essential to the performance of internal audits.
- **Human Relations and Communications** — Internal auditors should be skilled in dealing with people and in communicating effectively.
- **Continuing Education** — Internal auditors should maintain their technical competence through continuing education.
- **Due Professional Care** — Internal auditors should exercise due professional care in performing internal audits.

SCOPE OF WORK — The scope of the internal audit should encompass the examination and evaluation of the adequacy and effectiveness of the organization's system of internal control, and the quality of performance in carrying out assigned responsibilities.

- **Reliability and Integrity of Information** — Internal auditors should review the reliability and integrity of financial and operating information and the means used to identify, measure, classify, and report such information.
- **Compliance With Policies, Plans, Procedures, Laws, and Regulations** — Internal auditors should review the systems established to ensure compliance with those policies, plans, procedures, laws, and regulations which could have a significant impact on operations and reports, and should determine whether the organization is in compliance.

(continued)

FIG. 2-1 *(continued)*

- **Safeguarding of Assets** — Internal auditors should review the means of safeguarding assets and, as appropriate, verify the existence of such assets.
- **Economical and Efficient Use of Resources** — Internal auditors should appriase the economy and efficiency with which resources are employed.
- **Accomplishment of Established Objectives and Goals for Operations or Programs** — Internal auditors should review operations or programs to ascertain whether results are consistent with established objectives and goals and whether the operations or programs are being carried out as planned.

PERFORMANCE OF AUDIT WORK — Audit work should include planning the audit, examining and evaluating information, communicating results, and following up.

- **Planning the Audit** — Internal auditors should plan each audit.
- **Examining and Evaluating Information** — Internal auditors should collect, analyze, interpret, and document information to support audit results.
- **Communicating Results** — Internal auditors should report the results of their audit work.
- **Following Up** — Internal auditors should follow up to ascertain that appropriate action is taken on reported audit findings.

MANAGEMENT OF THE INTERNAL AUDITING DEPARTMENT — The director of internal auditing should properly manage the internal auditing department.

- **Purpose, Authority, and Responsibility** — The director of Internal auditing should have a statement of purpose, authority, and responsibility for the internal auditing department.
- **Planning** — The director of internal auditing should establish plans to carry out the responsibilities of the internal auditing department.
- **Policies and Procedures** — The director of internal auditing should provide written policies and procedures to guide the audit staff.
- **Personnel Management and Development** — The director of internal auditing should establish a program for selecting and developing the human resources of the internal auditing department.
- **External Auditors** — The director of internal auditing should coordinate internal and external audit efforts.
- **Quality Assurance** — The director of internal auditing should establish and maintain a quality assurance program to evaluate the operations of the internal auditing department.

Objectives and Scope

The basic objective of internal auditing is to assist all members of management in the effective discharge of their responsibilities. The internal audit department provides this assistance by furnishing management with analyses, appraisals, recommendations, and comments concerning the activities reviewed. Internal auditors can be concerned with any phase of business activity in which they can be of service to management. Frequently, this involves going beyond accounting and financial records to obtain a full understanding of the operations under review. As well as reviewing MIS systems that process financial data, internal auditors are frequently called on to monitor computer systems of all kinds within an organization. To attain this overall objective, activities include the following:

- Reviewing and appraising the soundness, adequacy, and application of accounting, financial, and other administrative controls, and promoting effective control at reasonable cost, including controls over MIS.
- Ascertaining the extent of compliance with established policies, plans, and procedures.
- Ascertaining the extent to which company assets are accounted for and safeguarded from losses of all kinds, including security of MIS systems.
- Ascertaining the reliability of management data developed, and systems producing that information within the organization.
- Reviewing MIS systems that record and process financial or management data.
- Appraising the quality of performance in carrying out assigned responsibilities.

Responsibility and Authority

Management policy should clearly establish the responsibilities of the internal auditor within the organization. Management's express authority should provide the internal auditor with full access to all of the organization's records, properties, and personnel that could be relevant to the subject under review. The internal auditor should be free to review and appraise policies, plans, procedures, and records.

Responsibilities of the internal auditor include:

- Informing and advising management and discharging this responsibility in a manner that is consistent with the IIA's Code of Ethics.

- Coordinating internal audit activities with others to achieve both the audit objectives and the objectives of the organization.

Internal auditors have no direct responsibility or authority over any of the activities reviewed. Therefore, the internal audit review and appraisal does not in any way relieve other people in the organization of the responsibilities assigned to them. For example, if internal EDP auditors review the phases of the system development life cycle (SDLC), the responsibility for following the steps required still rests with the MIS department and others designated as users or systems developers. (See Chapter 22, "System Development Trends and Practices," and Chapter 23, "System Development Methodology and Auditing.")

Independence

Independence is essential to the effectiveness of internal auditing. This independence is obtained primarily through organizational status and objectivity:

- The status of the internal audit function within the organization and the support accorded to it by management are major determinants of its range and value. The head of the internal audit function, therefore, should be responsible to an officer whose authority is sufficient to assure both a broad range of audit coverage and the adequate consideration of, and effective action on, the audit findings and recommendations.
- Objectivity is essential to the audit function. Therefore, an internal auditor should not develop and install procedures, prepare records, or engage in any other activity that he would normally review and appraise and that could reasonably be construed to compromise his independence. The internal auditor's objectivity need not be affected adversely by determining and recommending standards of control to be applied in the development of the systems and procedures being reviewed.

CODE OF ETHICS OF THE INSTITUTE OF INTERNAL AUDITORS

The IIA's Code of Ethics, as revised in July 1988, applies to all members and Certified Internal Auditors (CIAs). Its provisions cover basic principles in the various disciplines of internal auditing. (See Figure 2-2.) Members should realize that individual judgment is required in the application of these

FIG. 2-2

Articles of the Code of Ethics of the Institute of Internal Auditors

I. Members shall have an obligation to exercise honesty, objectivity, and diligence in the performance of their duties and responsibilities.

II. Members, in holding the trust of their employers, shall exhibit loyalty in all matters pertaining to the affairs of the employer or to whomever they may be rendering a service. However, members shall not knowingly be a party to any illegal or improper activity.

III. Members shall refrain from entering into any activity which may be in conflict with the interest of their employers or which would prejudice their ability to carry out objectively their duties and responsibilities.

IV. Members shall not accept a fee or a gift from an employee, a client, a customer, or a business associate of their employer without the knowledge and consent of their senior management.

V. Members shall be prudent in the use of information acquired in the course of their duties. They shall not use confidential information for any personal gain nor in a manner which would be detrimental to the welfare of their employer.

VI. Members, in expressing an opinion, shall use all reasonable care to obtain sufficient factual evidence to warrant such expression. In their reporting, members shall reveal such material facts known to them, which, if not revealed, could either distort the report of the results of operations under review or conceal unlawful practice.

VII. Members shall continually strive for improvement in the proficiency and effectiveness of their service.

VIII. Members shall abide by the bylaws and uphold the objectives of The Institute of Internal Auditors, Inc. In the practice of their profession, they shall be ever mindful of their obligation to maintain the high standard of competence, morality, and dignity which The Institute of Internal Auditors, Inc., and its members have established.

principles. Members are responsible for conducting themselves in a manner that does not leave their good faith and integrity open to question. While understanding the limit of their own technical skills, members should promote the highest possible internal auditing standards toward advancing their own organizations.

AICPA PRONOUNCEMENTS

Over the years, the AICPA has become increasingly specific in its Statements on Auditing Standards (SASs), which concern the external auditor's responsibilities. Logically, as more organizations computerized their financial accounting recordkeeping, many of the SASs needed to be revised. In the past several years, important SASs have been superseded by new pronouncements that reflect the effects of technological developments on the audit function.

PLANNING AND STRATEGY CONSIDERATIONS

SAS No. 47, *Audit Risk and Materiality in Conducting an Audit:* Audit Risk Model

Business failures, economic uncertainty, congressional hearings, court decisions, and the changes wrought by technology have all combined to increase the profession's attention to audit risk. Differences in the nature of both business and audit risk due to complex, often paperless, computerized systems are of particular concern to auditors.

Controls over access to computerized systems become critical as the potential for fraud by technologically knowledgeable users increases. If these users can get into the system at will, fraud can be hard, if not impossible, to detect. Access controls and timely follow-up on exception reports produced by programmed procedures become all the more important. Checking the performance of programs themselves is usually the job of auditors, since users can no longer do so.

As a result of these concerns, the need to assess and control risks, and the need for a better process for doing so, have become essential to an effective audit. SAS No. 47 defines audit risk and its components, explains the relationship of those component risks, and provides a risk-assessment framework, which is the basis of modern auditing.

The discussion of audit risk in SAS No. 47 is not directed specifically to the MIS environment. It is relevant to EDP auditing, however, as it becomes more and more unlikely that an audit of a major organization could be conducted without attention to this basic auditing standard and, within that framework, to the special risks in EDP processing.

SAS No. 47 helps provide answers to crucial questions, such as:

- How much audit work is enough?
- What is the link between tests of controls and substantive tests?
- How can cost-effective audits be planned?

SAS No. 47 also addresses audit risk in the context of planning an audit and evaluating audit findings. It provides broad guidance for achieving a low level of overall audit risk, a central objective of an audit. "Audit risk" is defined by SAS No. 47 at the financial statement level as "the risk that the auditor may unknowingly fail to appropriately modify his opinion on financial statements that are materially misstated." Since it is most practical to assess risk at the level of individual balances or classes of transactions, when addressed at the statement level, audit risk is referred to as overall audit risk. Overall audit risk results from audit risk assessments for a number of individual account balances.

At the account balance or class of transactions level, audit risk has two major components:

1. The risk that the balance contains material error[1] (or may aggregate to material error).
2. The risk that the auditor will not detect an error that has occurred (detection risk).

These elements can be related to the principal types of audit procedures—tests of controls and substantive procedures—and to their purpose. Tests of controls help assess the first element: the risk that material error exists. Tests of controls do not alter that risk (because material error either exists or it does not); they are tools to assess that risk. Tests of controls are seldom used to identify and quantify specific errors; substantive procedures are more suitable for that purpose. Substantive procedures, such as inventory pricing tests and confirmation of accounts receivable, address and reduce the second element: the risk that error will not be detected.

The risk that material error exists is further divided into two component risks, defined by SAS No. 47 as follows:

1. *Inherent risk*—"The susceptibility of an account balance or class of transactions to error that could be material, when aggregated with error in other balances or classes, assuming that there were no related internal accounting controls."
2. *Control risk*—"The risk that error that could occur in an account balance or class of transactions and that could be material, when aggregated with error in other balances or classes, will not be prevented or detected on a timely basis by the system of internal accounting control."

Auditors assess, but cannot control, inherent and control risk. Audit detection risk, however, can be controlled by the auditor by determining an appropriate audit strategy. In doing so, the auditor decides the relative re-

---

[1] As used in SAS No. 47 and in this discussion, the word "error" includes both unintentional mistakes and deliberate fraud (defalcations and financial statement misrepresentations).

FIG. 2-3
Components of audit risk

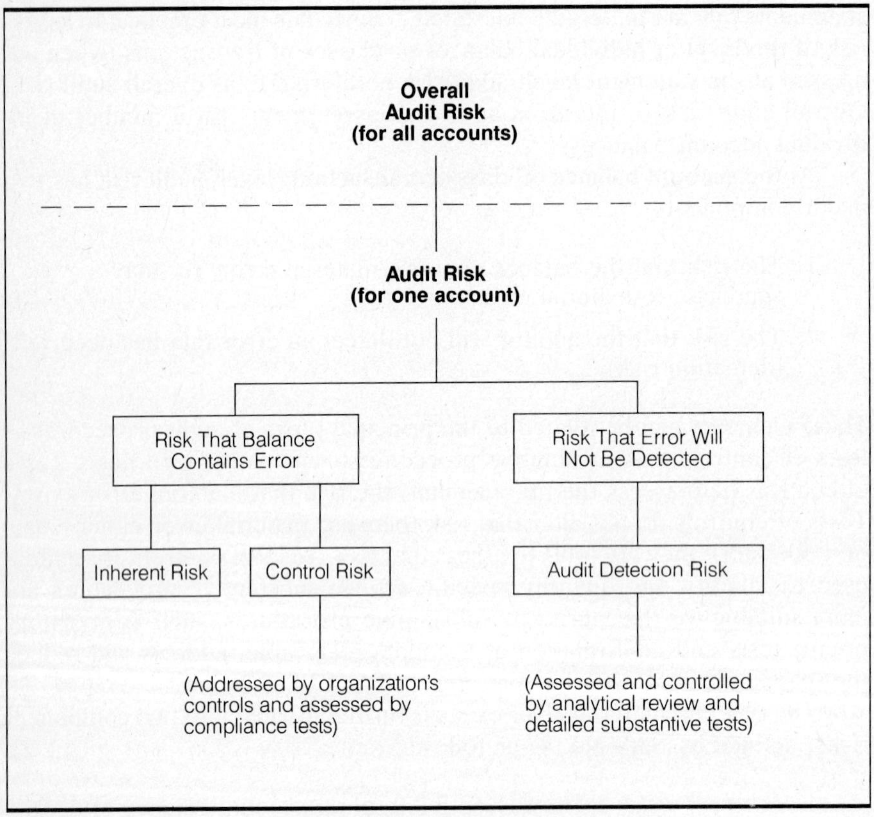

liance to place on analytical procedures, and their potential effectiveness, as opposed to substantive tests of details. Sometimes procedures such as analytical comparisons may be more useful than tests of details to detect possible material error, as is often the case in collusive fraud, where detailed documentation may support rather than refute the reported figures. The extent of procedures and their timing (year-end versus interim) are also considered. This hierarchy of components of audit risk is shown in Figure 2-3.

For external auditors, audit risk assessment is an informed judgment about the risk that (cumulatively) material errors and misstatements can reach the financial statements. During the planning stage, inherent risk and internal control risk, as well as materiality and other factors, are considered to determine the audit strategy (the nature, timing, and extent of audit procedures). Once analytical and other substantive procedures are done, the chance that cumulatively material errors and misstatements have escaped detection is reconsidered. When an audit is designed and executed properly, those assessments ordinarily lead to the conclusion that overall audit risk is acceptably low.

Inherent Risk. Usually, auditors have considered inherent risk factors to set the nature, timing, and extent of audit procedures, but with little emphasis on documenting inherent risk assessments formally. SAS No. 47 recommends that auditors consider documenting inherent risk, such as the greater risks associated with estimates (e.g., the allowance for uncollectible accounts) as opposed to risks associated with routine factual data (e.g., daily product sales) or the special audit considerations arising from a recession or a technological upheaval in the economy (as a whole or in part).

The control environment and system affect inherent risk assessments, since auditors consider the presence and effectiveness of controls before setting the audit strategy (e.g., tests of controls versus substantive tests) and the nature, timing, and extent of those procedures. Where an account balance is inherently risky—a number of key audit objectives are susceptible to misstatement—management is more likely to have instituted appropriate controls. The auditor can consider the inherent risks and the controls simultaneously to determine the most effective and efficient audit strategy.

Some aspects of inherent risk are characteristic of a specific transaction or account. The risk of errors or irregularities is greater for some types of transactions or accounts than for others. Some assets are more susceptible to theft in the absence of strong physical controls (for example, a microcomputer is more prone to misappropriation than a mainframe).

Account balances derived from accounting estimates or that require considerable accounting judgment (e.g., valuation allowances for high technology components or programming contracts that are partially completed) are more likely to be misvalued than account balances composed of factual data (e.g., cash transactions). Generally, such risks remain the same in an organization until changes come when the nature of the business changes. Thus, the auditor can carry forward the assessment of those unchanged inherent risks to future years.

A knowledge of the business and an understanding of its transactions, their flow through the system, and the accounts that they generate are fundamental to identifying inherent risks related to characteristics of specific types of transactions and accounts. Factors that help identify these risks include:

- The susceptibility of an asset to misappropriation or misvaluation.

- The complexity and volume of transactions processed.
- The extent to which the balance results from judgments as opposed to factual data.
- The control environment. (It may provide clues as to which inherent risk characteristics have been addressed, in part, by management.)

External factors or conditions in inherent risk relate to one of three levels: (1) macroeconomic, (2) industry, or (3) organization. At the macroeconomic level, these conditions may result from government policy or pending legislation, international situations, or the level of interest rates. At the industry level, they include technological change, government regulation, or lessening consumer demand. At the organization level, conditions can be unique to a particular business, such as unusual material transactions (e.g., a merger or sale of a segment of the business), ineffective management, pending litigation, absence of quality control, symptoms of financial distress, or performance-based executive incentive plans. Since internal controls usually are not designed to address those conditions, internal control assessments may not address the attendant risks adequately.

Understanding inherent risks related to conditions, as opposed to characteristics, is based on an understanding of the business, its industry, and the economic environment. Conditions, rooted in diverse areas, can be more difficult to identify than characteristics. To assess inherent risk conditions, the auditor should:

- Look beyond the internal information system to identify conditions such as those already suggested, as well as others at the macroeconomic, industry, or organization level that might increase the likelihood that the financial statements contain material error.
- Reassess those conditions each year because they are subject to change.
- Consider ways in which substantive tests should be modified to assess or address those conditions.

An audit approach is needed to assess and respond to inherent risk, to help identify risk factors, and to employ procedures that address them efficiently. One approach suited to external audits is:

- For new engagements, seek and document both inherent risk conditions and characteristics.
- For continuing engagements, seek and document new conditions and update the status of previously identified conditions and characteristics.

- Identify the balances or accounts affected by an identified inherent risk condition or characteristic.
- Identify the relevant audit assertions in each affected balance or account.
- Determine the nature, timing, and extent of tests of controls, detailed substantive tests, and analytical procedures, sufficient in total to provide high assurance that the financial statements will not be materially misstated.
- Reconsider those assessments as the audit proceeds and respond to changed assessments appropriately, so that at completion there is a high level of assurance that the financial statements will not be materially misstated.

Internal Control Risk. To assess internal control risk, the auditor estimates the effectiveness of the control system. The basic objectives of any internal accounting control system are to provide assurance that all valid transactions of the entity are processed completely and accurately and that the records are updated and maintained properly. The auditor needs to know how and whether the system prevents and detects incomplete, inaccurate, or invalid transactions and improperly maintained or updated records, files, and reports. The auditor reviews and evaluates the internal control system in large organizations, usually including EDP controls, to determine whether controls exist to accomplish those objectives.

Internal control procedures address the risks associated with both routine processing and some factors described previously as characteristics of an account. Internal controls may also provide some protection against the risks due to certain conditions, but it may be too expensive to design control systems to address risks associated with all possible conditions.

No affordable system of internal control can completely eliminate the risk that misstatements will be reflected in the financial statements. Therefore, some risk is normally associated with every system. Effective systems carry a relatively lower risk; less effective systems, relatively higher. Assessing that risk is a basis for determining the extent to which the system can be relied on when setting the nature, timing, and extent of substantive tests.

As indicated previously, it is often impossible to evaluate internal control risk independent of inherent risk because of the relationship of inherent risk characteristics and internal controls. The inherent risk assessment provides the auditor with an indication of areas where controls are most desirable and likely to be significant. It facilitates evaluation of the controls in place and determination of substantive procedures to detect material error that might exist. The inherent risk assessment may lead the auditor to a preliminary judgment that:

- The controls do not address the inherent risks; thus further review and testing of the controls may not be effective.
- The controls address the risks, but are unlikely to be reliable enough, so that further review and testing of the controls may not be efficient.
- The controls address the risks and appear sufficiently reliable to warrant testing, but it is not efficient to do so.
- The controls address the risks and appear sufficiently reliable and economical to test, thus warranting an audit strategy that includes assessment and tests of them when determining the program of substantive procedures.

In many internal audit environments, tests of controls and systems evaluations are done to meet management objectives. Such evaluation may not play a central role in the auditor's strategy for concluding that the risk of significant error is low.

As a practical matter, assessments of the effectiveness of internal controls in addressing inherent risks usually are made at the audit objective, audit assertion, account balance, or other such level. Assessment of internal controls as a whole are difficult to relate to specific audit procedures. Control systems often vary in effectiveness between accounts, transaction cycles, or locations.

In an MIS environment, certain elements of control risk may be evaluated at one time for all accounts or balances that are part of the MIS system. Examples are risks of unauthorized changes to key programs or risks created by access of unauthorized personnel to the files or programs. Typically, these risks are addressed by general information technology or IT controls. Other risks may be related to the specific account under examination, and the account balance and audit objective become the focus for identifying and assessing them. Examples are the risk that invalid transactions will be entered into the system or the risk that valid transactions will not be summarized properly. These risks typically are addressed by application controls, and tests of controls of the system of internal control within a segment of the overall system.

To determine whether testing internal controls will be efficient, the auditor identifies:

- The control objectives and corresponding audit objectives addressed by the controls.

- The audit objectives that still must be addressed, by performing substantive tests, after the tests of controls have been completed satisfactorily.

Controls over an account balance or class of transactions should be tested for compliance with the prescribed system. If the auditor decides not to test the control system for an account or class of transactions, those controls are not considered in setting the scope of audit procedures. Instead, the auditor designs sufficient substantive tests of details and analytical procedures to reduce audit risk to an acceptable level.

After performing tests of controls, the auditor may be able to draw conclusions about the risk of error occurring, but may not be able to draw separate conclusions about inherent risk or control risk. That is because it is rarely possible to assess independently the reason that tests of controls did not disclose errors. For example, it is often unclear whether satisfactory tests of controls results reflect the effectiveness of the control system (low control risk) or the lack of errors entering the system (low inherent risk). Usually, auditors cannot, or do not, determine whether a properly processed transaction represents a correct transaction that entered and flowed through the system or an erroneous transaction that entered the system and was detected and corrected subsequently by the proper operation of a control.

Inherent risks associated with some transactions and balances may not be addressed—either intentionally or otherwise—by the existing control system and procedures. In addition, management override of controls is always a possibility. For identified inherent risks not addressed by specific controls or addressed by controls that will be tested, inherent risk and the risk of error occurring are the same from an auditor's perspective (when designing substantive procedures to reduce audit detection risk). Where the risk of error occurring cannot be assessed as negligible, extensive analytical procedures and/or substantive tests of details are necessary.

Detection Risk. "Detection risk" is defined by SAS No. 47 as "the risk that an auditor's procedures will lead him to conclude that error in an account balance or class of transactions that could be material, when aggregated with error in other balances or classes, does not exist when in fact such error does exist." Audit detection risk is, therefore, the possibility that neither analytical review procedures nor substantive tests of details will reduce undetected errors and misstatements to a cumulatively immaterial amount.

The auditor relies on substantive tests, including analytical procedures, for sufficient assurance that material error, if present, will be detected. Accordingly, those procedures are tailored to assess risk of error occurring. For example, when determining the inventory value of high technology products, the auditor may perceive a high risk of material error occurring due to potential product obsolescence, or pricing errors resulting from the imposition of new government regulations over the product. More reliable substantive procedures (tests of details) performed close to year-end and of a significant extent (perhaps sufficient to assess an appropriate revised value for the inventory) may then be warranted. If the auditor assesses the risk of error to be relatively low, as when extensive security controls established over electronic funds transfers have been assessed as effective, the auditor may select limited, early detailed tests combined with analytical procedures.

By varying the nature, timing, and extent of audit procedures and providing sufficient supervision and safeguards over the examination, the auditor can better control the risk that cumulatively material errors and misstatements will not be detected. The auditor designs a substantive audit strategy based on the assessments of inherent and internal control risks for particular accounts. Each account may first be grouped into the following classifications:

- Items of particularly high inherent risk, such as a potentially material adjustment to a loss or an expense account, nonrecurring transactions, sensitive transactions that either occur frequently or involve a single material amount, and material contingencies.
- Items requiring special consideration, such as the introduction of new accounting principles, changes in accounting principles and estimates, and questions about proper accounting treatment.
- Other items that may be individually material.
- All other items taken as a whole.

Items in the first three categories should be addressed separately, according to priority, in designing substantive procedures. Remaining "other" items may be subjected to routine audit procedures.

Factors that auditors should consider when assessing the level of assurance obtained from substantive procedures applied to a specific balance or relevant to particular audit objectives (e.g., completeness, valuation) include:

- The quantitative and qualitative results of each test.
- Whether substantive test results agree with other audit evidence and prior experience. The auditor has a greater degree of assurance that material error is not present when audit procedures corroborate each other than when each test result is considered separately or when some test results appear contradictory.
- The number of independent procedures applied and the contribution of each procedure toward a specific audit objective.

- The confidence in the underlying data. A higher level of assurance is achieved from tests performed on data generated in a well-controlled environment than from tests of data generated in an environment where controls are limited or applied inconsistently.
- The nature and timing of the procedures and their perceived relative strength in addressing certain types of error as indicated by inherent risk assessments. Substantive tests of details performed at, or near, year-end often are considered to give the most assurance and to be most effective in detecting material errors or misstatements in the financial statements. However, where fraud or collusion is suspected, the examination of underlying evidence of a transaction in a detailed test may do a poorer job of detecting error than a well-designed analytical procedure. An analytical procedure designed to reveal unusual patterns of account activity or unusual relationships may be more effective.

Overall Audit Risk. "Overall audit risk" is the combination of the individual audit risks assessed for each account balance or class of transactions. A primary objective of audit management is to limit the audit risk in individual balances or classes of transactions so that overall audit risk is limited to a sufficiently low level at the completion of the examination. Another objective is to assess and control those risks to achieve the desired level of assurance as efficiently as possible.

Various audit strategy options are available to control overall audit risk. They can result in significant differences in audit efficiency. They are an outgrowth of the relationship of components of overall audit risk. For example, if the preliminary assessment of internal controls indicates that they are weak, the risk of error occurring is therefore high. The nature, timing, and extent of audit procedures should then be designed so that detection risk is low. This can be accomplished either by performing detailed substantive tests on year-end balances alone, or in combination with in-depth analytical procedures. The best choice among alternate strategies for controlling detection risk usually depends on the relative cost of performing the procedures.

SAS No. 48, *The Effects of Computer Processing on the Examination of Financial Statements*

SAS No. 48 was issued to integrate guidance on the effects of computer processing on audits with auditing standards on planning and supervision, analytical review procedures, the auditor's study and evaluation of internal control, and evidential matter. In the planning area, it states:

.09 The auditor should consider the methods the entity uses to process accounting information in planning the audit because such methods influence the design of the accounting system and the nature of the internal accounting control procedures. The extent to which computer processing is used in significant account applications, as well as the complexity of that processing, may also influence the nature, timing, and extent of audit procedures. Accordingly, in evaluating the effect of an entity's computer processing on an examination of financial statements, the auditor should consider matters such as—

a. The extent to which the computer is used in each significant account application.

b. The complexity of the entity's computer operations, including the use of an outside service center.

c. The organizational structure of the computer processing activities.

d. The availability of data. Documents that are used to enter information into the computer for processing, certain computer files, and other evidential matter that may be required by the auditor may exist only for a short period or only in computer-readable form. In some computer systems, input documents may not exist at all because information is directly entered into the system. An entity's data retention policies may require the auditor to request retention of some information for his review or to perform audit procedures at a time when the information is available. In addition, certain information generated by the computer for management's internal purposes may be useful in performing substantive tests (particularly analytical review procedures).

e. The use of computer-assisted audit techniques to increase the efficiency of performing audit procedures. Using computer-assisted audit techniques may also provide the auditor with an opportunity to apply certain procedures to an entire population of accounts or transactions. In addition, in some accounting systems, it may be difficult or impossible for the auditor to analyze certain data or test specific control procedures without computer assistance.

.10 The auditor should consider whether specialized skills are needed to consider the effect of computer processing on the audit, to understand the flow of transactions, to understand the nature of internal accounting control procedures, or to design and perform audit procedures. If specialized skills are needed, the auditor should seek the assistance of a professional possessing such skills, who may be either on the auditor's staff or an outside professional. If the use of such a professional is planned, the auditor should have sufficient computer-related knowledge to communicate the objectives of the other professional's work; to evaluate whether the specified procedures will meet the auditor's objectives; and to evaluate the results of the procedures applied as they relate to the nature, timing, and extent of other planned audit procedures. The auditor's responsibilities with respect to using such a professional are equivalent to those for other assistants.

SAS No. 48 superseded SAS No. 3. Two other statements affected by SAS No. 48 directly, SAS No. 1 and SAS No. 23, have been superseded by SAS No. 55 and SAS No. 56, respectively. Portions of both are discussed in the following sections, as are relevant portions of other statements affected by SAS No. 48.

SAS No. 55, *Consideration of the Internal Control Structure in a Financial Statement Audit*

SAS No. 55 provides guidance concerning the auditor's consideration of an entity's internal control structure in a generally accepted auditing standards (GAAS) audit of the financial statements. It describes the three elements of an internal control structure—the control environment, the accounting system, and control procedures—and explains how the internal control structure should be considered in planning and performing an audit.

SAS No. 55 requires the auditor to obtain, for all audits, "a sufficient understanding of each of the three elements to plan the audit by performing procedures to understand the design policies, procedures relevant to audit planning, and whether they have been placed in operation." An assessment of control risk, made in terms of financial statement assertions, is identified as the auditor's primary consideration for evaluating the internal control structure's effectiveness.

The statement defines those elements as follows:

> 9. The control environment represents the collective effect of various factors on establishing, enhancing, or mitigating the effectiveness of specific policies and procedures. Such factors include the following:
> - Management's philosophy and operating style
> - The entity's organizational structure
> - The functioning of the board of directors and its committees, particularly the audit committee
> - Methods of assigning authority and responsibility
> - Management's control methods for monitoring and following up on performance, including internal auditing
> - Personnel policies and practices
> - Various external influences that affect an entity's operations and practices, such as examinations by bank regulatory agencies
>
> The control environment reflects the overall attitude, awareness, and actions of the board of directors, management, owners, and others concerning the importance of control and its emphasis in the entity.
>
> 10. The accounting system consists of the methods and records established to identify, assemble, analyze, classify, record, and report an entity's transactions and to maintain accountability for the related

assets and liabilities. An effective accounting system gives appropriate consideration to establishing methods and records that will—

- Identify and record all valid transactions.
- Describe on a timely basis the transactions in sufficient detail to permit proper classification of transactions for financial reporting.
- Measure the value of transactions in a manner that permits recording their proper monetary value in the financial statements.
- Determine the time period in which transactions occurred to permit recording of transactions in the proper accounting period.
- Present properly the transactions and related disclosures in the financial statements.

11. Control procedures are those policies and procedures in addition to the control environment and accounting system that management has established to provide reasonable assurance that specific entity objectives will be achieved. Control procedures have various objectives and are applied at various organizational and data processing levels. They may also be integrated into specific components of the control environment and the accounting system. Generally, they may be categorized as procedures that pertain to—

- Proper authorization of transactions and activities.
- Segregation of duties that reduce the opportunities to allow any person to be in a position to both perpetrate and conceal errors or irregularities in the normal course of his duties—assigning different people the responsibilities of authorizing transactions, recording transactions, and maintaining custody of assets.
- Design and use of adequate documents and records to help ensure the proper recording of transactions and events, such as monitoring the use of prenumbered shipping documents.
- Adequate safeguards over access to and use of assets and records, such as secured facilities and authorization for access to computer programs and data files.
- Independent checks on performance and proper valuation of recorded amounts, such as clerical checks, reconciliations, comparison of assets with recorded accountability, computer-programmed controls, management review of reports that summarize the detail of account balances (for example, an aged trial balance of accounts receivable), and user review of computer-generated reports.

12. The applicability and importance of specific control environment factors, accounting system methods and records, and control procedures that an entity establishes should be considered in the context of—

- The entity's size.
- Its organization and ownership characteristics.
- The nature of its business.
- The diversity and complexity of its operations.
- Its methods of processing data.

- Its applicable legal and regulatory requirements.

SAS No. 55 includes extensive guidance on the linkage between understanding the control structure and assessing control risk:

- The procedures for understanding the internal control structure and assessing control risk can be performed concurrently.
- The auditor may be able to assess control risk as less than 100 percent based on the minimum required understanding of the control structure, if that understanding provides evidence as to the effective operation of a control structure element.
- For some assertions, the auditor may decide to obtain additional evidential matter to support an assessed level of control risk that is lower than that supported by the assessment made by the auditor in obtaining an understanding of the internal control structure.

Numerous factors should be considered when obtaining evidential matter, including its type, source, timeliness, and the existence of other evidential matter related to the conclusions to which it leads. These affect the degree of assurance the evidential matter provides. They also affect the nature, timing, and extent of the tests of controls applied to obtain evidential matter about control risk. Testing techniques include inquiry, observation, inspection, and reperformance of a policy or procedure pertaining to an assertion.

Other issues discussed in the SAS No. 55 include:

- The approach the auditor should take in identifying internal control structure policies and procedures relevant to specific financial statement assertions.
- Procedures and tests of controls directed toward the operating effectiveness of an internal control structure.
- Considerations in determining the evidential matter needed to support a conclusion (i.e., assessed level of control risk) at below the maximum level.
- The inverse relationship between control risk and detection risk.

It also contains an appendix of some basic concepts that are implicit in an internal control structure, but are not addressed explicitly (e.g., management's objectives in establishing and maintaining an internal control structure).

More specific recommendations regarding the implementation of the standards set forth in SAS No. 55 will be covered in the audit and accounting guide being prepared by the AICPA, "Guide for Consideration of Internal Control Structure in the Financial Statement Audit." SAS No. 55 is effective for audits on or after January 1, 1990, although early application is permissible.

SAS No. 56, *Analytical Procedures*

SAS No. 56, superseding SAS No. 23, *Analytical Review Procedures*, requires the use of analytical procedures in the planning and overall review stages of an audit. It also provides guidance on the use of analytics and offers examples used in the planning, substantive testing, and overall review stages.

Analytical procedures are stated as being "an important part of the audit process and consist of evaluation of financial information made by a study of plausible relationships among both financial and nonfinancial data." The statement describes factors that affect the influence of analytics on an audit.

SAS No. 56 introduces the required use of analytical procedures in the planning and overall review stages of an audit.

> 6. The purpose of applying analytical procedures in planning the audit is to assist in planning the nature, timing, and extent of auditing procedures that will be used to obtain evidential matter for specific account balances or classes of transactions. To accomplish this, the analytical procedures used in planning the audit should focus on (*a*) enhancing the auditor's understanding of the client's business and the transactions and events that have occurred since the last audit date, and (*b*) identifying areas that may represent specific risks relevant to the audit. Thus, the objective of the procedures is to identify such things as the existence of unusual transactions and events, and amounts, ratios and trends that might indicate matters that have financial statement and audit planning ramifications.
>
> 22. The objective of analytical procedures used in the overall review stage of the audit is to assist the auditor in assessing the conclusions reached and in the evaluation of the overall financial statement presentation. A wide variety of analytical procedures may be useful for this purpose. The overall review would generally include reading the financial statements and notes and considering (*a*) the adequacy of evidence gathered in response to unusual or unexpected balances identified in planning the audit or in the course of the audit and (*b*) unusual or unexpected balances or relationships that were not previously identified. Results of an overall review may indicate that additional evidence may be needed.

The statement previously discussed, SAS No. 48, mentions the importance of computers in providing the data used for analytical procedures:

> .07e. *The increased availability of data prepared for management's*

> *use when computer processing is used.* Computer systems have created an ability (which may not be practical in manual systems) to store, retrieve, and analyze data for use in achieving broader management objectives. These data and analyses, although not necessarily part of the basic accounting records, may be valuable sources of information for the auditor to use in applying analytical review procedures, other substantive tests, or compliance testing.

SAS No. 56 became effective January 1, 1989.

PERFORMING AND COMPLETING THE AUDIT

SAS No. 53, *The Auditor's Responsibility to Detect and Report Errors and Irregularities*

SAS No. 53 requires the auditor to assess the risk that errors and irregularities may cause material misstatements and to design the audit to provide reasonable assurance that material errors and irregularities will be detected.

It defines errors as "*unintentional* misstatements or omissions of amounts or disclosures in financial statements." Irregularities are defined as:

> *Intentional* misstatements or omissions of amounts or disclosures in financial statements . . . [and] include fraudulent financial reporting undertaken to render financial statements misleading, sometimes called *management fraud,* and misappropriation of assets, sometimes called *defalcations*.

SAS No. 53 goes on to distinguish errors from irregularities thus:

> 4. The primary factor that distinguishes errors from irregularities is whether the underlying cause of a misstatement in financial statements is intentional or unintentional. Intent, however, is often difficult to determine, particularly in matters involving accounting estimates or the application of accounting principles. For example, an unreasonable accounting estimate may result from unintentional bias or may be an intentional attempt to misstate the financial statements.

An appendix on the characteristics of errors and irregularities that influence the auditor's detection ability is included in the statement.

SAS No. 53 emphasizes that a GAAS audit should be planned and performed with an attitude of professional skepticism. The statement also provides guidance regarding the effect of irregularities on an auditor's report and the responsibility to communicate detected irregularities both inside and outside the entity.

> 8. The auditor should exercise (*a*) due care in planning, performing, and evaluating the results of audit procedures, and (*b*) the proper degree of professional skepticism to achieve reasonable assurance that material errors or irregularities will be detected. Since the auditor's opinion on the financial statements is based on the concept of reasonable assurance, the auditor is not an insurer and his report does not constitute a guarantee. Therefore, the subsequent discovery that a material misstatement exists in the financial statements does not, in and of itself, evidence inadequate planning, performance, or judgment on the part of the auditor.
>
> 12. The auditor should assess the risk of management misrepresentation by reviewing information obtained about risk factors and the internal control structure. Matters such as the following may be considered:
>
> - Are there known circumstances that may indicate a management predisposition to distort financial statements, such as frequent disputes about aggressive application of accounting principles that increase earnings, evasive responses to audit inquiries, or excessive emphasis on meeting quantified targets that must be achieved to receive a substantial portion of management compensation?
> - Are there indications that management has failed to establish policies and procedures that provide reasonable assurance of reliable accounting estimates, such as personnel who develop estimates appearing to lack necessary knowledge and experience, supervisors of these personnel appearing careless or inexperienced, or there is a history of unreliable or unreasonable estimates?
> - Are there conditions that indicate lack of control of activities, such as constant crisis conditions in operating or accounting areas, disorganized work areas, frequent or excessive back orders, shortages, delays, or lack of documentation for major transactions?
> - Are there indications of a lack of control over computer processing, such as a lack of controls over access to applications that initiate or control the movement of assets (for example, a demand deposit application in a bank), high levels of processing errors, or unusual delays in providing processing results and reports?
> - Are there indications that management has not developed or communicated adequate policies and procedures for security of data or assets, such as not investigating employees in key positions before hiring, or allowing unauthorized personnel to have ready access to data or assets?
>
> 16. An audit of financial statements in accordance with generally accepted auditing standards should be planned and performed with an attitude of professional skepticism. The auditor neither assumes that

> management is dishonest nor assumes unquestioned honesty. Rather, the auditor recognizes that conditions observed and evidential matter obtained, including information from prior audits, need to be objectively evaluated to determine whether the financial statements are free of material misstatement.
>
> 23. The auditor's objective is to reach a conclusion on whether the financial statements, taken as a whole, are materially misstated. The auditor should accumulate potential audit adjustments during the audit and summarize and evaluate the combined effect. In this regard, the auditor may designate an amount below which potential audit adjustments need not be accumulated. This amount would be set so that any such adjustments, either individually or when aggregated with other adjustments, would not be material to the financial statements.
>
> 26. If the auditor has concluded that the financial statements are materially affected by an irregularity, the auditor should insist that the financial statements be revised and, if they are not, express a qualified or an adverse opinion on the financial statements, disclosing all substantive reasons for his opinion.
>
> 28. . . . However, irregularities involving senior management of which the auditor becomes aware should be reported directly to the audit committee. Irregularities that are individually immaterial may be reported to the audit committee on an aggregate basis, and the auditor may reach an understanding with the audit committee on the nature and amount of reportable irregularities.

SAS No. 53 supersedes SAS No. 16, *The Independent Auditor's Responsibility for the Detection of Errors or Irregularities.*

SAS No. 22, *Planning and Supervision*

SAS No. 22 (AU Section 311.03), with SAS No. 48 integrated, has the required planning considerations expanded.

> .03*c* The methods used by the entity to process significant accounting information (see paragraph .09), including the use of service organizations, such as outside service centers.

Additional paragraphs (AU Sections .09 and .10—quoted earlier in the section "Overall Audit Risk") summarize those aspects of computer processing that may affect planning and examination of financial statements. They also describe how the auditor might consider the need for using a professional possessing specialized skills to determine the effect of computer processing on the examination.

SAS No. 9, *The Effect of an Internal Audit Function on the Scope of the Independent Auditor's Examination*

Although the work of internal audit cannot be substituted for the work of the external (independent) auditor, particularly as to judgments on audit matters, the external auditor can, and indeed should, consider the procedures performed by the internal auditors. If the external auditor decides that the internal auditor's work may have a bearing on his own procedures, the standard set forth in SAS No. 9 (AU Section 322) requires that he also review the competence and objectivity of the internal auditor and evaluate his work.

To review competence, the external auditor is required by SAS No. 9 to inquire about the qualifications of the internal audit staff, including, for example, consideration of the practices for hiring, training, and supervising the internal audit staff, especially in relation to their technical EDP capabilities. Regarding the objectivity of internal auditors, the external auditor considers the organizational level to which internal auditors report the results of their work and the organizational level to which they report administratively. One suggested method for judging internal auditors' objectivity is to review the recommendations made in their reports.

To evaluate the work of internal auditors, the external auditor examines, on a test basis, documentary evidence of the work performed by internal auditors and considers such factors as whether:

- The scope of the work is appropriate.
- Audit programs are adequate.
- Working papers adequately document work performed.
- Conclusions reached are appropriate in the circumstances.
- Any reports prepared are consistent with the results of the work performed.

The external auditor also performs tests of some of the work of internal auditors, and may make use of internal auditors to provide direct assistance in performing an examination in accordance with GAAS. Internal auditors may assist in performing audit tests or, for example, getting computer processing time for tests to be run using audit software, when testing has been automated. When the external auditor makes use of internal auditors in these ways, the competence and objectivity of the internal auditors must be considered and their work supervised and examined to the extent appropriate under the circumstances.

Many internal auditors have derived benefits from collaborating with external auditors. Particularly in EDP, many companies find auditing resources scarce. Cooperation can lead to a more effective and efficient use of these scarce resources. From the internal auditor's view, the first step to an effective relationship is often establishing a properly trained professional department that produces working papers that document work adequately. Two common areas of cooperation are audit documentation and audit testing techniques (particularly when using software). Sharing the audit documentation of systems and control evaluations can help avoid unnecessary repetition of work. When using software, cooperation permits the internal auditor to get on-the-job training while the external audit specialist installs and executes these more sophisticated audit tests. The internal auditor is then better placed to re-execute the software (run it again) on a periodic or surprise basis. The knowledge gained can also be used to install and execute the software for other purposes whenever necessary. In more advanced internal auditing departments, the auditors can be proactive and offer suggestions to the external auditors. (Note that as this book went to press the Auditing Standards Board was in the process of revising SAS No. 9.)

SAS No. 31, *Evidential Matter*

SAS No. 31 (AU Section 326.12), as amended by SAS No. 48, makes it clear that audit evidence is not affected by the use of computer processing. Only the method by which the auditor gathers that evidence can be affected.

> .12 The auditor's specific audit objectives do not change whether accounting data is processed manually or by computer. However, the methods of applying audit procedures to gather evidence may be influenced by the method of data processing. The auditor can use either manual audit procedures, computer-assisted audit techniques, or a combination of both to obtain sufficient, competent evidential matter. However, in some accounting systems that use a computer for processing significant accounting applications, it may be difficult or impossible for the auditor to obtain certain data for inspection, inquiry, or confirmation without computer assistance.

SAS No. 57, *Auditing Accounting Estimates*

SAS No. 57 provides guidance to auditors on obtaining and evaluating sufficient competent evidential matter to support significant accounting estimates in a GAAS audit of financial statements. An accounting estimate, defined as "an approximation of a financial statement element, item or account," introduces additional risk of material misstatements.

Accounting estimates used in historical financial statements measure the effects of past business transactions or events, or the present status of an asset or liability. They are used when:

- The measurement or valuation of some amount is dependent on the outcome of future events.
- Relevant data regarding past events cannot be accumulated timely or cost-effectively.

Examples include net realizable values of inventory and accounts receivable, property and casualty insurance loss reserves, revenues from contracts accounted for by the percentage-of-completion method, and pension and warranty expenses. SAS No. 57 cites numerous others in its appendix.

It is the subjective nature of accounting estimates that led to SAS No. 57 and the distinction between management's responsibility to make estimates and the auditor's responsibility to evaluate the reasonableness of those estimates.

> 3. Management is responsible for making the accounting estimates included in the financial statements. Estimates are based on subjective as well as objective factors and, as a result, judgment is required to estimate an amount at the date of the financial statements. Management's judgment is normally based on its knowledge and experience about past and current events and its assumptions about conditions it expects to exist and courses of action it expects to take.
>
> 4. The auditor is responsible for evaluating the reasonableness of accounting estimates made by management in the context of the financial statements taken as a whole. As estimates are based on subjective as well as objective factors, it may be difficult for management to establish controls over them. Even when management's estimation process involves competent personnel using relevant and reliable data, there is potential for bias in the subjective factors. Accordingly, when planning and performing procedures to evaluate accounting estimates, the auditor should consider, with an attitude of professional skepticism, both the subjective and objective factors.
>
> 6. An entity's internal control structure may reduce the likelihood of material misstatements of accounting estimates. Specific relevant aspects of that structure include the following:
>
> *a.* Management communication of the need for proper accounting estimates
>
> *b.* Accumulation of relevant, sufficient, and reliable data on which to base an accounting estimate
>
> c. Preparation of the accounting estimate by qualified personnel
>
> *d.* Adequate review and approval of the accounting estimates by appropriate levels of authority, including—
>
> 1. Review of sources of relevant factors
> 2. Review of development of assumptions
> 3. Review of reasonableness of assumptions and resulting estimates
> 4. Consideration of the need to use the work of specialists

5. Consideration of changes in previously established methods to arrive at accounting estimates

e. Comparison of prior accounting estimates with subsequent results to assess the reliability of the process used to develop estimates

f. Consideration by management of whether the resulting accounting estimate is consistent with the operational plans of the entity.

SAS No. 57 establishes that the auditor should determine that all material accounting estimates:

- Have been developed.
- Are reasonable.
- Conform with generally accepted accounting principles (GAAP).
- Are disclosed properly, in accordance with SAS No. 32, *Adequacy of Disclosure in Financial Statements.*

SAS No. 57 suggests procedures for the auditor to use to evaluate the reasonableness of estimates. These include:

- Concentrating on key factors and assumptions, such as deviations from historical patterns, areas sensitive to variations, and areas susceptible to misstatement or bias.
- Obtaining an understanding and evaluation of management's process, an independently developed estimate, and a review of subsequent events or transactions.

Finally, SAS No. 57 acknowledges that the difference between an estimated financial statement amount and what the auditor believes is reasonable should be treated as an error and aggregated with other likely errors. (See SAS No. 47, *Audit Risk and Materiality in Conducting an Audit*, paragraph 29.)

COMMUNICATING AUDIT RESULTS AND FINDINGS

SAS No. 58, *Reports on Audited Financial Statements*

SAS No. 58 revises the language of the auditor's standard report that is issued in pursuance of a GAAS audit. It also includes guidance on these reporting responsibilities as they are affected by the revisions:

- Reporting on comparative financial statements.
- Reporting on accounting changes.

- Reporting on loss contingencies, subsequent events, material uncertainties, and departures for GAAP.
- Wording of modifications to the report in the form of additional explanatory paragraphs. Circumstances that might require comments independent of the auditor's unqualified opinion include:
  - — Opinion based in part on report of another auditor.
  - — Departure from a promulgated accounting principle.
  - — Emphasis of a matter.
  - — Uncertainties.
  - — Consistency.

Generally accepted auditing standards include four standards of reporting. SAS No. 58 is concerned with the relationship of the fourth reporting standard to the language of the auditor's report. This standard, quoted in the following paragraphs, is meant to prevent misinterpretation of the auditor's assumed degree of responsibility in relation to the entity's financial statements.

> 4. The fourth standard of reporting is as follows:
> The report shall either contain an expression of opinion regarding the financial statements, taken as a whole, or an assertion to the effect that an opinion cannot be expressed. When an overall opinion cannot be expressed, the reasons therefor should be stated. In all cases where an auditor's name is associated with financial statements, the report should contain a clear-cut indication of the character of the audit, if any, and the degree of responsibility he is taking.
>
> 8. The auditor's standard report identifies the financial statements audited in an opening (introductory) paragraph, describes the nature of an audit in a scope paragraph, and expresses the auditor's opinion in a separate opinion paragraph. The basic elements of the report are the following:
>
> *a.* A title that includes the word *independent*
> *b.* A statement that the financial statements identified in the report were audited
> *c.* A statement that the financial statements are the responsibility of the Company's management and that the auditor's responsibility is to express an opinion on the financial statements based on his audit
> *d.* A statement that the audit was conducted in accordance with generally accepted auditing standards
> *e.* A statement that generally accepted auditing standards require that the auditor plan and perform the audit to obtain reasonable assurance about whether the financial statements are free of material misstatement
> *f.* A statement that an audit includes—

FIG. 2-4
Revised standard auditor's report

We have audited the accompanying balance sheet of X Company as of December 31, 19XX and the related statements of income, retained earnings, and cash flows for the year then ended. These financial statements are the responsibility of the Company's management. Our responsibility is to express an opinion on these financial statements on our audit.

We conducted our audit in accordance with generally accepted auditing standards. Those standards require that we plan and perform the audit to obtain reasonable assurance about whether the financial statements are free of material misstatement. An audit includes examining, on a test basis, evidence supporting the amounts and disclosure in the financial statements. An audit also includes assessing the accounting principles used and the significant estimates made by management, as well as evalulating the overall financial statement presentation. We believe that our audit provides a reasonable basis for our opinion.

In our opinion, the financial statements referred to above present fairly, in all material respects, the financial position of X Company as of December 31, 19XX, and the results of its operations and its cash flows for the year then ended in conformity with generally accepted accounting principles.

(1) Examining, on a test basis, evidence supporting the amounts and disclosures in the financial statements
(2) Assessing the accounting principles used and significant estimates made by management
(3) Evaluating the overall financial statement presentation

g. A statement that the auditor believes that his audit provides a reasonable basis for his opinion
h. An opinion as to whether the financial statements present fairly, in all material respects, the financial position of the Company as of the balance sheet date and the results of its operations and its cash flows for the period then ended in conformity with generally accepted accounting principles
i. The manual or printed signature of the auditor's firm
j. The date of the audit report

Usually, the auditor's report is issued in connection with an organization's basic financial statements and "states that [those] financial statements present fairly an entity's financial position, results of operations, and cash flows" and conform with GAAP. Such an opinion can be expressed only when a GAAS audit has been performed by the auditor on those financial statements.

Figure 2-4 is an example of a revised standard auditor's report. In addition to this example, SAS No. 58 also includes examples of reports for comparative financial statements, division of responsibility, opinions affected by scope limitations, and other circumstances that need explanatory paragraphs.

SAS No. 58 includes guidance on appropriate circumstances for issuance of various audit opinions. Opinions described and illustrated include:

- Unqualified opinions (i.e., the standard report).
- Qualified opinions.
- Adverse opinions.
- Disclaimers of opinions.
- Piecemeal opinions.

SAS No. 58 was effective for reports issued or reissued on or after January 1, 1989.

SAS No. 60, *Communication of Internal Control Structure Related Matters Noted in an Audit*

SAS No. 60 provides guidance on identifying and reporting conditions, discovered during an audit, that relate to an entity's internal control structure. It requires reporting those "reportable conditions," defined as "significant deficiencies in the design or functioning of the internal control structure that could adversely affect the organization's ability to record, process, summarize, and report financial data," to the audit committee or other "appropriate recipient of the communication." Such deficiencies may involve aspects of these internal control structure elements:

- The control environment
- The accounting system
- Control procedures

The auditor is not required by SAS No. 60 to search for or identify reportable conditions beyond those encountered in the normal conduct of a GAAS audit. It is also recognized that determining which matters are reportable conditions is a matter of judgment.

However, the auditor and client may establish agreed-upon criteria for identifying and reporting additional matters. Agreed-upon arrangements may include the "reporting of matters of less significance, the existence of conditions specified by the client, or the results of further investigation of matters noted to identify underlying causes."

Timely communication of the findings can be important. As a result, the auditor may choose to communicate matters he deems significant during, rather than after, the audit. In accordance with SAS No. 60, the auditor's findings report should:

- Be written, preferably, although oral communications are allowed, as long as they are documented in working papers and memoranda.
- Be restricted for use solely by the audit committee, management, and others within the organization. The restriction should be stated in the report.
- Indicate that the audit's purpose was to report on the financial statements, not the internal control structure. The report also should use cautionary language regarding the nature and extent of involvements with the internal control structure.
- Define reportable conditions.
- Differentiate between reportable conditions, material weaknesses, and other comments.

Figure 2-5 is an example of an auditor's report. Based on the potential for misrepresentation of the limited degree of assurance associated with the report, SAS No. 60 prohibits the issuance of "no reportable conditions" letters.

SAS No. 60 supersedes SAS No. 20, *Required Communication of Material Weaknesses in Internal Accounting Control*, paragraphs 47 through 53 of SAS No. 30, *Reporting on Internal Accounting Control*, and related auditing interpretations. It does not affect the reporting of material weaknesses in an entity's internal control structure as noted in an engagement report.

SAS No. 61, *Communication With Audit Committees*

SAS No. 61 requires the auditor to determine that certain matters related to the conduct of an audit (in addition to the current requirements of SAS No. 53, SAS No. 54, and SAS No. 60) are communicated to those who oversee for the financial reporting process generally—that is, an audit committee or other formally designated group. SAS No. 61 also applies to all SEC engagements.

> 2. This Statement requires the auditor to ensure that the audit committee receives additional information regarding the scope and results of the audit that may assist the audit committee in overseeing the financial reporting and disclosure process for which management is responsible. This Statement does not require communications with management; however, it does not *preclude* communications with

FIG. 2-5

An example of an auditor's report containing reportable conditions

In planning and performing our audit of the financial statements of the ABC Corporation for the year ended December 31, 19XX, we considered its internal control structure in order to determine our auditing procedures for the purpose of expressing our opinion on the financial statements and not to provide assurance on the internal control structure. However, we noted certain matters involving the internal control structure and its operation that we consider to be reportable conditions under standards established by the American Institute of Certified Public Accountants. Reportable conditions involve matters coming to our attention relating to significant deficiencies in the design or operation of the internal control structure that, in our judgment, could adversely affect the organization's ability to record, process, summarize, and report financial data consistent with the assertions of management in the financial statements.

[Include paragraphs to describe the reportable conditions noted.]

A material weakness is a reportable condition in which the design or operation of one or more of the internal control structure elements does not reduce to a relatively low level the risk that errors or irregularities in amounts that would be material in relation to the financial statements being audited may occur and not be detected within a timely period by employees in the normal course of performing their assigned functions.

Our consideration of the internal control structure would not necessarily disclose all matters in the internal control structure that might be reportable conditions and, accordingly, would not necessarily disclose all reportable conditions that are also considered to be material weaknesses as defined above. However, none of the reportable conditions described above is believed to be a material weakness.

This report is intended solely for the information and use of the audit committee (board of directors, board of trustees, or owners in owner-managed enterprises), management, and others within the organization (or specified regulatory agency or other specified third party).

management or other individuals within the entity who may, in the auditor's judgment, benefit from the communications.

Items communicated by the auditor can be written or oral. If oral, the communication must be documented in the working papers. Written communication should contain indication that it is intended solely for use by the audit committee, board of directors, and, at times, management. It is important for audit committees to be informed about:

- The auditor's responsibility under GAAS (level of responsibility assumed for internal control structure reasonable, but not absolute, assurance).
- Significant accounting policies (initial selection and changes, and method used to account for significant unusual transactions).

- Management judgments and accounting estimates (process used by management in formulating sensitive accounting estimates and basis for the auditor's conclusion about the reasonableness of such estimates).
- Significant audit adjustments (adjustments arising from the audit that could have a significant effect on the entity's financial reporting process)
- Other information in documents containing audited financial statements (the auditor should discuss with the audit committee his responsibility for other information in documents containing audited financial statements).
- Disagreements with management (over the application of accounting principles, scope of audit, or disclosures).
- Consultation by management with other accountants. Major issues discussed with management prior to retention.
- Difficulties encountered in performing the audit (in dealing with management, such as unreasonable delays or timetable, or the unavailability of personnel).

The communications required by SAS No. 61 are incidental to the audit; therefore, they need not occur prior to issuance of the auditor's report on the financial statements. However, they should be timely and, based on the auditor's judgment, may be given before the report.

SAS No. 59, *The Auditor's Consideration of an Entity's Ability to Continue as a Going Concern*

An auditor may detect risk during an audit that can lead him to question an organization's ability to continue as a going concern (i.e., have the ability to continue operation and meet obligations). SAS No. 59 states that "continuation of an entity as a going concern is assumed in financial reporting in the absence of significant information to the contrary."

> 2. The auditor has a responsibility to evaluate whether there is substantial doubt about the entity's ability to continue as a going concern for a reasonable period of time, not to exceed one year beyond the date of the financial statements being audited (hereinafter referred to as *a reasonable period of time*). The auditor's evaluation is based on his knowledge of relevant conditions and events that exist at or have occurred prior to the completion of fieldwork. Information about such conditions or events is obtained from the application of auditing procedures planned and performed to achieve audit objectives that are related to management's assertions embodied in the financial statements

being audited, as described in SAS No. 31, *Evidential Matter* (AICPA, *Professional Standards*, vol. 1, AU sec. 326).

5. It is not necessary to design audit procedures solely to identify conditions and events that, when considered in the aggregate, indicate there could be substantial doubt about the entity's ability to continue as a going concern for a reasonable period of time. The results of auditing procedures designed and performed to achieve other audit objectives should be sufficient for that purpose. The following are examples of procedures that may identify such conditions and events:

- Analytical procedures
- Review of subsequent events
- Review of compliance with the terms of debt and loan agreements
- Reading of minutes of meetings of stockholders, board of directors, and important committees of the board
- Inquiry of an entity's legal counsel about litigation, claims, and assessments
- Confirmation with related and third parties of the details of arrangements to provide or maintain financial support

SAS No. 59 provides guidance to the auditor on:

- How to evaluate whether there is substantial doubt.
- The procedures that should be performed when there is believed to be substantial doubt.
- The impact on the auditor's report when it is concluded that there is substantial doubt.

Effective January 1, 1989, SAS No. 59 superseded SAS No. 34, *The Auditor's Considerations When a Question Arises About an Entity's Continued Existence*. One significant change was expanding the consideration of a going concern beyond its effect on the recoverability and classification of assets and the amounts and classification of liabilities to encompass the ability to continue operation.

SAS No. 54, *Illegal Acts by Clients*

SAS No. 54 describes the nature and extent of the auditor's required consideration of possible illegal acts in a GAAS audit. Illegal acts are defined as "violations of laws or government regulations."

SAS No. 54 provides guidance on the auditor's duties when a possible illegal act is detected. It establishes the auditor's responsibility to detect and report misstatements resulting from illegal acts that have a direct and material effect on the financial statement as is also cited in SAS No. 53. Auditor responsibility for "other illegal acts," or those illegal acts that do not have a direct or material effect on the financial statement, are also described.

> 3. Whether an act is, in fact, illegal is a determination that is normally beyond the auditor's professional competence. An auditor, in reporting on financial statements, presents himself as one who is proficient in accounting and auditing. The auditor's training, experience, and understanding of the client and its industry may provide a basis for recognition that some client acts coming to his attention may be illegal. However, the determination as to whether a particular act is illegal would generally be based on the advice of an informed expert qualified to practice law or may have to await final determination by a court of law.
>
> 17. The auditor should assure himself that the audit committee, or others with equivalent authority and responsibility, is adequately informed with respect to illegal acts that come to the auditor's attention. The auditor need not communicate matters that are clearly inconsequential and may reach agreement in advance with the audit committee on the nature of such matters to be communicated. The communication should describe the act, the circumstances of its occurrence, and the effect on the financial statements. Senior management may wish to have its remedial actions communicated to the audit committee simultaneously. Possible remedial actions include disciplinary action against involved personnel, seeking restitution, adoption of preventive or corrective company policies, and modifications of specific control procedures. If senior management is involved in an illegal act, the auditor should communicate directly with the audit committee. The communication may be oral or written. If the communication is oral, the auditor should document it.
>
> 23. Disclosure of an illegal act to parties other than the client's senior management and its audit committee or board of directors is not ordinarily part of the auditor's responsibility, and such disclosure would be precluded by the auditor's ethical or legal obligation of confidentiality, unless the matter affects his opinion on the financial statements. The auditor should recognize, however, that in [certain] circumstances a duty to notify parties outside the client may exist . . .

SAS No. 54 superseded SAS No. 17, effective January 1, 1989.

THE DEVELOPMENT OF COMPUTER-RELATED GUIDANCE

The AICPA's Computer Auditing Subcommittee provides guidance on the effect of computers on the audit process and advises the Auditing Standards Board (ASB), other AICPA committees and task forces, and the AICPA membership on matters relating to audits that involve computerized systems. Several smaller task forces, under the direction of the Computer Auditing Subcommittee and the ASB, develop nonauthoritative guidance on computer-related matters in the form of audit guides and auditing procedure studies.

Guidance Related to the Computer Environment

Several AICPA publications discuss EDP auditing.

Computer Services Guidelines. Computer services guidelines are issued for the information of AICPA members and other interested parties and do not represent official positions of an AICPA senior technical committee. A number of computer services guidelines have been issued on various aspects of EDP auditing. A guideline entitled *Management, Control, and Audit of Advanced EDP Systems*, issued in 1983, describes the characteristics of advanced EDP systems and discusses control mechanisms as they relate to the management and auditing of such systems. The study also identifies certain hardware and software features that enhance control of advanced MIS systems.

Another 1983 computer services guideline, *Audit and Control Considerations in an On-Line Environment*, describes the variety of environments that are encompassed by on-line systems and identifies the impact of the on-line environment on the auditor's study and evaluation of the system of internal accounting control.

A guideline issued in 1981, entitled *Audit and Control Considerations in a Minicomputer Environment*, is intended to assist the auditor in planning and conducting an audit in an environment where a minicomputer is used to process significant data. This guideline defines a minicomputer environment and addresses audit and control considerations in that environment.

The 1980 computer services guideline, *Audit Approaches for a Computerized Inventory System*, is intended to help auditors understand computerized inventory systems. It identifies techniques to satisfy control objectives and possible compliance and substantive tests for a computerized system.

A guideline entitled *Controls Over Using and Changing Computer Programs*, issued in 1979, provides guidance on controls to ensure that computer programs are processed as authorized by management and that changes to computer programs are authorized and implemented properly. This guideline includes a case study that demonstrates the appropriate audit considerations for these controls.

A computer services guideline entitled *Audit Considerations in Elec-*

tronic Funds Transfer Systems, issued in 1978, describes electronic funds transfer (EFT) systems, addresses their status in government and the legal community, and contains an initial assessment of the audit impacts of EFT systems. The guideline was designed to present issues for further research and professional deliberation.

An audit guide, *Computer-Assisted Audit Techniques*, issued in 1979, describes audit tools and techniques appropriate when an organization uses a computer to process accounting data, and relates EDP tools and techniques to auditing procedures.

Report of the Joint Data Base Task Force, issued in 1983, resulted from a study conducted by a task force formed by the AICPA, the Canadian Institute of Chartered Accountants, and the IIA. It describes the effects of a data base environment on control and audit procedures. (Note that copies of these publications are available from the AICPA, 1211 Avenue of the Americas, New York, NY 10036. Request the most current printing.)

A related development with implications for evaluating controls in MIS systems is an auditing interpretation published by the AICPA in May 1985 on compliance test procedures. The interpretation states that reperformance of an accounting control is not always required to obtain reasonable assurance that accounting control procedures are being applied as prescribed. Inquiry, observation, and inspection are also valid compliance tests. In selecting the appropriate compliance testing procedure, the auditor should consider factors such as the following:

- The nature of the control procedure being tested.
- The related audit evidence available.
- The ability of the compliance testing procedure to identify control deviations.
- The auditor's planned degree of reliance (e.g., high, medium, or low) on internal controls.

An audit and accounting guide entitled *Audits of Service-Center-Produced Records*, issued in 1974 and revised in 1987, addresses the special problems of auditing an organization that uses a service center, and provides guidance on related aspects of auditing MIS systems. The revised guide incorporates the general guidance in SAS No. 44, *Special-Purpose Reports on Internal Accounting Control at Service Organizations,* as well as other relevant auditing pronouncements.

The revised guide is directed to both independent auditors of organizations that use services provided by EDP service centers and independent auditors who are engaged to report on certain aspects of control systems that relate to accounting data processed by EDP service centers. It provides detailed guidance to the auditor who is engaged to prepare a report on certain aspects of the service center's control system and also discusses the use of such a report by the auditor of the entity that uses the service center.

The guide has three chapters, which cover the following aspects of service center use:

- *The effects of an organization's use of an EDP service center on the auditor's study and evaluation of internal control.* The guide describes how the use of an EDP service center can affect the user organization's system of internal accounting control and the user auditor's study and evaluation of that system. It describes the circumstances in which the user auditor should include control procedures at an EDP service center in the study and evaluation of the client's system of internal accounting control. The guide also describes other matters a user auditor may wish to consider in providing services to clients that use EDP service centers to process significant accounting applications.
- *Reporting on reviews of EDP service centers.* EDP service centers that process accounting data for clients of several different auditors may find it excessively time-consuming to cooperate with each user auditor's separate review of accounting applications and related controls at the service center. A reasonable alternative may be for one auditor (the service auditor) to perform a review at the service center and report the results to the service center or the other auditors (the user auditors). Under this approach, the service auditor would be engaged to perform a review at the service center and report results in the manner described in the guide; user auditors would use the report of the service auditor, but would retain responsibility for evaluating internal accounting control at service centers as it affects their examinations.
- *Using reports on internal control at EDP service centers.* The guide discusses how a user auditor can use service auditors' reports in examining financial statements of clients that use EDP service centers to process significant accounting data. The nature, timing, and extent of the user auditor's audit procedures depend on several factors, including the significance of the transactions processed by the service center and the accounting control procedures of the client's organization relating to those transactions.

Auditing Procedure Studies. Auditing procedure studies are non-authoritative; they are issued by the AICPA to provide practical assistance in carrying out auditing procedures.

In April 1985, the AICPA issued an auditing procedure study entitled

Audits of Small Businesses. This study discusses auditing standards for small business engagements and covers topics such as engagement planning, internal accounting control, audit risk and materiality, and timing of audit tests. A small business is characterized in the study as having concentration of ownership or operational control in one or a few individuals, with limited separation of duties and functions in the accounting system. The study also discusses the increasing use of microcomputers by small businesses to process accounting applications. It notes that although audit procedures may be different in a computer environment than in a manual environment, audit objectives and auditing standards do not change when an entity uses a computer to process significant accounting applications.

Five separate task forces within the Computer Auditing Subcommittee have developed or are developing auditing procedure studies on computer-related matters. These studies may update or supersede several computer services guidelines. The studies are as follows:

- *Auditors' Use of Microcomputers.* This study guides auditors in the use of the microcomputer as an audit tool. It was published in early 1986.
- *Auditing in a Paperless Environment.* This study will provide guidance to auditors on inherent risk when there is no paper trail to substantiate transactions and on the effect of a paperless environment on the audit approach.
- *Audit Impact of Small (Micro/Mini) Computer Systems.* This study will provide guidance when clients use a microcomputer or minicomputer in a small business where reliance on computer controls is unlikely.
- *Audit Impact of Mid-Size (Mini/Mainframe) Computer Systems.* This study will guide auditors when clients use a noncomplex computer where some reliance on computer controls is likely.
- *Audit Impact of Large (Complex) Computer Systems.* This study will provide guidance on planning the engagement and evaluating inherent and control risks when the client uses a complex computer and significant reliance on controls is likely.

Attestation Standards. The ASB has approved issuance of a set of general standards, called attestation standards, that affect some computer-related engagements. The attestation standards provide a framework for performing and reporting on attest engagements that provide users with various levels of assurance on diverse types of assertions.

Until recently, the attestation function was generally limited to reporting on financial information, primarily historical financial statements. This function has been expanding, however, to encompass many other types of information, including prospective financial statements, supplementary information accompanying historical financial statements, systems of internal accounting control, the accuracy of assertions made in connection with counting ballots, and even the validity of claims made by computer software manufacturers.

The attestation standards are similar to the 10 generally accepted auditing standards in that they deal with the need for technical competence, due care, adequate planning, sufficient evidence, and appropriate reporting. However, they are written broadly enough to apply to any attestation service in which a certified public accountant (CPA) examines or reviews an assertion and issues a report containing a conclusion on that assertion.

Prospective Financial Statements. Accountants' services with respect to prospective financial statements, which to a large extent are attestation services, have expanded greatly in recent years, and this is likely to continue. The increasing abilities of microcomputers and easy-to-use spreadsheet packages have contributed significantly to this trend, since managements can now prepare forecasts and "what if" projections efficiently and effectively. In late 1985 and early 1986, the ASB issued two documents—a statement and a guide—that apply to this area of practice. They require accountants to perform a compilation, an examination, or an application of agreed-upon procedures whenever they assemble, or assist in assembling, prospective financial statements for third-party use.

A compilation of prospective financial statements is similar to a compilation of historical financial statements in that it consists of limited procedures and the accountant expresses no assurance on the prospective financial statements. An examination of prospective financial statements is similar to an audit of historical financial statements in that it requires the accountant to obtain appropriate support for the expression of a positive opinion on the reasonableness of the assumptions underlying the prospective financial statements. The application of agreed-upon procedures to prospective financial statements is an engagement tailored to the needs of specific users who agree on the procedures to be performed by the accountant. Distribution of the accountant's report in an agreed-upon procedures engagement is restricted to those who agreed to the accountant's procedures. The guide also provides flexible guidance for engagements involving prospective financial statements for internal use only.

The guide defines a financial forecast and projection, sets forth preparation and presentation guidelines for managements that issue forecasts and projections, and describes their appropriate uses. A financial forecast consists of prospective financial statements that present an entity's expected financial position, results of operations, and changes in financial position. It is appropriate for general use. A financial projection consists of prospective financial statements that present an entity's expected financial position, results of operations, and changes in financial position, given one or more hypothetical assumptions. A financial projection is sometimes referred to as a "what if" presentation. Because it does not portray expected results, it is a limited use presentation and is not appropriate for general use. A financial projection should not be distributed to anyone who is not negotiating directly with the responsible party.

CHAPTER **3**

The EDP Auditing Profession

THE BEGINNING OF THE EDP AUDITING PROFESSION

Beginning in the late 1960s, the rapid development of automated systems led management to demand a sophisticated response from their management information systems (MIS) support staff. Interrelated files, high-speed transactions, concealed information, data base management systems, communication networks, distributed processing systems, minicomputers, and, soon, microcomputers changed the way financial and operating results were recorded and reported.

As accounting and operational data was calculated and stored increasingly on computers, management's control and auditing needs became more complicated. Management was confronted with the question of how to perform effective reviews of EDP activities. One frequent response to this question was—and is—to establish a staff of EDP auditors.

THE ROLES OF THE EDP AUDITOR

The auditing profession can be divided into two major divisions: external auditing and internal auditing. The EDP auditor may function in either environment. To understand the EDP auditor's role, the differences in the functions of external and internal auditors must be examined briefly.

Role of the External Auditor

External auditing is an independent appraisal function, external to the organization being examined. Most enterprises, either voluntarily or in accordance with regulations, such as those for registrant corporations of the Securities and Exchange Commission (SEC), have an annual audit of their financial statements conducted by an independent certified public accountant (CPA). In this context, the independent CPA is an external auditor.

The principal objective of an external audit is to be able to express an opinion about the quality of an organization's financial statements. Therefore, the external auditor is concerned primarily with the reliability of financial information.

Role of the Internal Auditor

Like external auditing, internal auditing is also an independent appraisal function. It exists, however, within an organization under management sanction to examine and evaluate the entity's activities. The internal auditor's primary function is to assist management in meeting its responsibilities to ensure:

- Safeguarding of company assets.
- Accuracy and reliability of accounting records.
- Promotion of operational efficiency.
- Adherence to company policies and compliance with regulatory and legal obligations.

The internal auditor is almost always concerned with the adequacy of the controls over MIS and, in most cases, with the cost-effectiveness of the procedures used.

Role of the EDP Auditor

The EDP auditor supplies technical EDP skills and expertise to the audit function, whether internal or external.

As technologically advanced computer systems are used by organizations to manage their resources and to record, monitor, and report activities and financial conditions, those technological advances affect the procedures and techniques used to achieve audit objectives. Thus, whether the audit function is internal or external, the audit function's need for EDP expertise increases as the technological sophistication of the financial and operational environment increases.

In many organizations, the auditor's emphasis has shifted from evaluating and testing processing results to evaluating and testing controls. Many of those controls are incorporated into computer programs or exercised within the organization's MIS function. This controls approach usually requires a degree of EDP expertise commensurate with the EDP technology used in the area or organization being reviewed.

The EDP auditor evaluates and tests the more technically complex EDP controls and procedures and develops and applies computerized audit techniques, including the use of audit software. In many cases, it is no longer possible to verify manually the computer procedures used to summarize, calculate, and categorize data. As a result, audit software and other computer-assisted techniques must be used.

One way to ensure the availability of EDP knowledge is to include EDP audit specialists in the audit function. Where internal audit does not include a full-time EDP auditor, the expertise can be provided from the organization's MIS department.

THE RESPONSIBILITIES OF THE EDP AUDITOR

EDP auditors' efforts to maintain, develop, and apply advanced methodologies in EDP auditing have important implications. These implications affect the accounting profession and financial management, internal auditors, and EDP specialists, in the public and private sectors.

The following are among typical EDP audit tasks, often grouped into four main categories:

1. Reviews of systems under development.
2. Data center reviews.
3. Application system reviews.
4. Support to non-EDP auditors.

A brief description of these tasks follows. Subsequent chapters of this book address the issues, concerns, and performance of these tasks in greater detail.

Reviews of Systems Under Development

Pre-implementation reviews and reviews of planned enhancements to existing systems are performed increasingly by both EDP and general or financial auditors. These reviews should include an examination of the systems design to ensure the presence of adequate controls in the new or modified application. Auditor participation in the design and development process can help eliminate the need to retrofit controls after the new system has been implemented. Retrofitting controls can be difficult and expensive, and perhaps impossible.

While participating in the systems development process, the auditor should maintain objectivity and independence from any operational responsibility for system development. This remains outside the audit department.

A review must include proper testing of the system and should also check compliance with the organization's development procedures. Whether this check is done can depend on management's requirements and how they are met in a particular organization. In addition, the auditor may monitor project management for efficiency and effectiveness.

Data Center Reviews

Data center audits are an increasingly important function, almost always performed by EDP auditors. Typically, data center reviews include evaluation of the data center's organizational structure, staffing practices, system development standards, operating procedures, security, program and data library control procedures (the information technology (IT) or general controls), communications network, backup, and disaster recovery procedures.

The review may also include evaluation of administrative or operational effectiveness and efficiency. Although the scope of a data center review is determined partially by management directive, the auditor may suggest a broader scope where circumstances indicate.

Application System Reviews

Application system reviews are usually performed by general auditors in consultation with EDP auditors, who address two primary areas:

1. *Programmed procedures*—These are the parts of processing that are performed within the computer, i.e., the ''logic'' of the application. Programmed control procedures, such as input edit checks and exception report production, are of particular significance.

2. *User control procedures*—These are the portions of application processing duties undertaken by the people responsible for the correct performance of the application. These procedures include appropriate segregation of duties, existence of proper management approval procedures, and timely performance of job responsibilities. Many user control procedures depend on the user taking timely, appropriate action in response to conditions reported in computer output, for example, the investigation and correction of exceptions reported by the program. Without the user follow-up, these usually can be no real control.

Audit procedures applied to application system reviews include:

- Evaluating computer system controls to determine whether they are adequate to
  - — Ensure the accuracy and completeness of processing results and the proper maintenance of programs and data files.
  - — Prevent errors and omissions from going undetected.
  - — Ensure the continuing reliability of data processing results.
  - — Ensure that only properly authorized transactions are processed.
- Testing to determine that controls are applied properly and consistently.
- Testing to ascertain that the results of processing data files and reports are accurate and complete.

- Evaluating the effectiveness of the system in achieving users' and management's objectives.

Support for Non-EDP Auditors

An EDP auditor may provide audit assistance to general internal auditors within the organization or to external auditors who come into the organization to perform a review. The assistance provided may include any of the tasks mentioned above.

Assistance to Internal Non-EDP Auditors. An EDP auditor may assist the general internal auditor in technical areas, such as performing an evaluation of some phase of operations or in arriving at a judgment in areas related to computer processing. In this regard, the EDP auditor functions as an adviser. Such assistance and advice can provide the best use of time and the most efficient use of software in completing the audit. Among the types of assistance normally provided are:

- Gathering and analyzing data.
- Creating report formats and analyzing reports.
- Testing a computer system's internal controls.
- Extracting data from existing files using audit software.
- Investigating inconsistencies or omissions in output generated by the computer system.
- Assisting the audit function in determining the nature, timing, and extent of required audit procedures.

Assistance to External Non-EDP Auditors. Today, most external auditors include EDP specialists whose role within the external audit organization closely parallels the role in an internal audit function. Coordination of efforts between the internal audit function and the external auditor may result in increased audit efficiency. The internal EDP auditors will often assist the external auditors in the same ways that they serve their own function, including arranging for the use of computer time and processing capabilities.

Additional Assistance. Because of their skills and experience, EDP auditors are often asked to take on other responsibilities, including:

- Training EDP and non-EDP auditors in EDP procedures and EDP audit methods.
- Coordinating the audit function's use of EDP for administration and performance of work (e.g., staff scheduling, report writing, workpaper processing). An EDP auditor may manage the hardware and software used for such processing.

THE DEVELOPMENT OF PROFESSIONAL STANDARDS

Among the basic guidelines for the auditing profession as a whole are the materials prepared by the American Institute of Certified Public Accountants (AICPA). The AICPA has published technical literature to be used as guidance for the accounting and auditing profession since 1917. Currently, the Auditing Standards Board (ASB) of the AICPA furnishes this guidance to the external auditing profession through the issuance of Statements on Auditing Standards (SAS). These statements define the nature and extent of the auditor's responsibility, and provide a course of action to follow in carrying out professional duties. An outline of statements particularly relevant to EDP auditing is presented in Chapter 2.

The Institute of Internal Auditors (IIA) provides guidelines for the practice of internal auditing and the certification of internal auditors.

The EDP Auditors Association (EDPAA) is the only professional membership association dedicated solely to EDP auditing. It fosters professionalism by:

- Facilitating the free exchange of audit techniques, practices, and problem-solving methods.
- Supplying current information on developments in the field of information systems auditing (ISA).
- Providing seminars, conferences, and professional forums.

Its seminars, conferences, and professional forums educate and provide for the exchange of audit techniques, practices, and problem-solving methods among members. Special publications that address current developments in information systems auditing and control and research also promote growth of the profession. The EDPAA has become influential in EDP auditing.

The EDPAA membership reflects a multiplicity of backgrounds and skills. Since many members come from outside the EDP audit profession, a typical EDPAA chapter meeting brings together experts and novices, programmers and accountants, technicians and statisticians, quality assurance specialists, internal and external auditors, and representatives of both the public and the private sectors, including a diversity of industries. They all share two interests:

- The establishment of information systems in a controlled and manageable environment.
- The development of audit techniques to assure management of the effectiveness and efficiency of system controls.

Shortly after its formation in Los Angeles, the EDPAA became an international organization when chapters were formed in Canada, Mexico, and Israel. The leaders of these chapters recognized the need to provide for the different languages and cultures and to communicate over distances. Today, EDPAA publications are produced in several languages.

At the EDPAA's regularly scheduled conferences and meetings, leaders in EDP auditing and control discuss new ideas and techniques for resolving problems. A number of special EDPAA international conferences are held annually, in addition to the annual EDPAA membership meeting in June. Each year, a "Computer Audit, Control and Security Conference" is held, as well as special national, regional, and local conferences and seminars. At each event, qualified professionals in EDP and EDP auditing speak on topics such as "Telecommunications and EDP Auditing," "The Nature of Computer-Related Crime," and "Organizing and Managing the EDP Audit Function." Programs are geared toward practitioners at all levels of experience.

Aided by EDPAA efforts and encouragement, a growing number of colleges and universities are including information systems auditing in their curricula. Association members also work within their communities to teach information systems auditing courses. Members of the EDPAA have helped develop accredited degree programs on the university level and have been active in developing college courses in EDP auditing.

The EDPAA publishes *The EDP Auditor Update,* a journal, to keep EDPAA members informed of chapter, regional, and international activities.

The EDP Auditors Foundation (EDPAF), established by the EDPAA in 1985, develops and promulgates official audit standards applicable to EDP auditing. Its objectives are to:

- Develop and maintain professional standards.
- Provide credentials as Certified Information Systems Auditors (CISA) to individuals whose competence meets the organization's standards.
- Provide education in EDP auditing.
- Conduct research in EDP auditing and controls.

- Assist qualified individuals in the study of EDP auditing.

The EDPAA also undertakes other activities, including:

- *Research.* Funding and administering research in EDP auditing to develop state-of-the-art auditing and control techniques.
- *Publications.* Providing professional books, guides, and periodicals of interest to EDP auditors and the control community including
  - *Control Objectives.* A regularly revised handbook of EDP auditing principles and techniques.
  - Many special audit guides and publications.
  - *The EDP Auditor Journal.* The quarterly publication of the EDPAA.
  - Study aids and practice questions for the certification program.
- *Education.* Sponsoring seminars and conferences on timely issues of technology, management, auditing, and controls.

EDPAF publications and activities are provided or sold at a substantial discount to members of the EDPAA.

CERTIFICATION

In any area of technology, techniques change continually. EDP auditors must maintain current skills to ensure that audit and control techniques remain appropriate in an EDP environment. The EDPAF, as the research and education arm of the EDPAA, oversees the issuance of credentials as CISAs.

Certification by the EDPAF as a professional CISA indicates a high level of achievement. A CISA must pass a rigorous examination and must have at least five years of EDP audit work experience and education. To retain certification, a CISA must participate in continuing education programs, or retake the examination.

Certification is granted to candidates who complete successfully the CISA examination and meet educational and work experience qualifications. The examination is open to all individuals who have an interest in the field of EDP auditing. It was developed by CISA-holders under the sponsorship of the EDPAF and the direction of the Educational Testing Service (ETS), an independent testing organization. The CISA examination has a multiple-choice format. It consists of two four-hour sessions administered on a single day, once a year.

A Certification Board is appointed by the EDPAF to oversee the program and ensure that the examination content is current. Testing dates and locations are announced in the *Bulletin of Information* available from the EDPAF. Certification is independent of membership in the EDPAA.

ETHICS AND STANDARDS

The EDPAF has established the following Code of Professional Conduct for CISAs:

- CISAs shall promote the establishment of and compliance with appropriate standards, procedures, and controls for data processing systems and operations, consistent with generally accepted professional practices.
- CISAs shall promote the need for adequate data processing controls to senior management and to the general public.
- CISAs shall perform their assigned responsibilities in a loyal and honest manner and not knowingly be a party to any illegal or improper activity.
- CISAs shall promote the education and understanding of the interrelationship between data processing and auditing.
- CISAs shall develop and communicate their opinions in an objective manner. Sufficient documentation and evidence should support their professional judgments.
- CISAs shall maintain the confidentiality of privileged information obtained during their normal duties.
- CISAs shall maintain their competencies in data processing and auditing through participation in professional development activities.
- CISAs shall uphold high standards of conduct, character, and morality in both their professional and their personal activities.
- CISAs shall not participate in activities that may be, or that appear to be, in conflict with policies of their employers or clients. Activities that threaten the independence or perceived independence of the CISA also should be avoided.

CURRENT ISSUES IN EDP AUDITING

Current issues confronting the EDP auditing profession are found in several areas.

Lack of Trained, Experienced EDP Auditors

The EDP auditing profession still enjoys the seemingly enviable position of the demand for EDP auditors exceeding the supply. There are not enough qualified personnel who have both audit and data processing skills. Combined with organizational budget constraints, this situation frequently leads to inadequate staffing and high turnover. These factors have had an impact on the ability of EDP audit groups to satisfy their objectives.

Need for Practitioners to Keep Up With Technological and Auditing Developments

For the EDP auditor to remain current, continued technical training and reading, such as review of technical journals, are necessary. Unique problems are emerging in relation to distributed data processing, microcomputers, teleprocessing, and data base systems. Such areas must be addressed by practitioners who understand the concepts and business impact of the technology.

Insufficient Support From Upper Management

Because EDP auditing is a relatively new function, it is rarely as well understood as the more traditional areas of an organization. The absence of understanding sometimes leads to poor communication between EDP audit and upper management or audit committees. A large gap is often found between what management says EDP audit is doing and what EDP audit is doing. Good communication skills are important for an EDP auditor, who must bridge the gaps that can exist between EDP audit, MIS, and management.

Misconceptions by the Public of the Auditors' Role

Public concern regarding the uses (and abuses) of data processing technology, the proper role of government, and the conception (or misconception) of the auditing profession raises serious issues. Legislation enacted partly in response to some of these issues has become a part of the environment. Examples include the Freedom of Information Act, the Fair Credit Reporting Act, the Privacy Act, the Foreign Corrupt Practices Act of 1977, the Electronic Funds Transfer Act, the Right to Financial Privacy Act of 1978, the Software Protection Act, and the Counterfeit Access Device and Computer Fraud and Abuse Act of 1984.

Addressing Current Issues

The current issues facing the profession can be addressed in several ways.

Need for Trained Professionals. The establishment of good training programs can provide an incentive for people to stay in an organization. It can also solve the problem of inexperienced, untrained staff. External training is one answer. The reputation of the course sponsor, as well as the sponsor's practical EDP audit and educational skills, should be considered. In addition, where possible, the course materials should be reviewed prior to enrolling in the course.

Using the data processing department training (such as manufacturers' training courses) or organizing seminars to use in-house expertise are other solutions. Joining professional associations (such as the EDPAA, Bank Administration Institute (BAI), and the IIA) is an excellent way to communicate with professionals working in the same areas. These organizations are also a resource for course information, publications, and the like.

Rotation of staff, such as with the MIS department, can also help develop skills. Development of standardized or automated workpapers may be particularly helpful where there is high turnover. Finally, use of decision support systems, expert systems, and artificial intelligence (AI) can provide less experienced staff with the skills of more knowledgeable, highly experienced auditors.

Need for Practitioners to Keep Up With Technological and Auditing Developments. Many of the suggestions listed above regarding establishment of a good training program can also help fulfill the need for continuing education among EDP auditors. Particularly important is involvement with the EDPAA, the IIA, and other professional associations relevant to the auditors' areas of responsibility. This might include industry associations as well as EDP-related groups such as the Computer Security Institute (CSI).

All auditors should ensure that they are well acquainted with the findings, reports, and studies of the various groups that examine the role of the auditor in public policy matters. Maintaining an awareness of current major issues under study by professional associations such as the EDPAA, the IIA, and the AICPA can help the EDP auditor gain a better understanding of and sensitivity to the public interests inherent in some accounting, auditing, and financial presentation issues.

Included in this book are summaries of selected reports that can provide the EDP auditor with background on some of these sensitive issues. These include:

- Report of the National Commission on Fraudulent Financial Reporting (often called the Treadway Commission Report)—in Chapter 2.
- The Foreign Corrupt Practices Act of 1977—in this chapter.
- The Institute of Internal Auditors—Systems Auditability and Control Report—in this chapter.

Finally, in their contacts with the public or media, auditors should strive to communicate facts and issues in a manner that will contribute to a greater outside understanding of the profession.

Summary of the Foreign Corrupt Practices Act of 1977

The Foreign Corrupt Practices Act (FCPA) had a major impact on the profession of auditing. The FCPA is divided into three sections. One section deals with illegal foreign payments. Another section deals with books and records and internal accounting control. The third section, dealing with regulating disclosure of information when a significant beneficial ownership interest is acquired, does not relate directly to EDP audit considerations.

Foreign Corrupt Payments. The FCPA prohibits any domestic company—or its officers, directors, employees, agents, or stockholders—from using any means of interstate commerce in furtherance of an offer, payment, promise, or authorization of payment of money (or anything of value) to a foreign official to act on the domestic company's behalf.

The section of the FCPA dealing with foreign payments applies not only to publicly held companies but also to other entities termed "domestic concerns," which, defined broadly, include any citizen, national, or resident of the United States, or any corporation, partnership, association, or sole proprietorship that has its principal place of business in the United States, or that is organized under the laws of a state, territory, or other entity of the United States.

Internal Accounting Control. The part of the FCPA that deals with internal accounting control had a much greater impact on U.S. business than the section on foreign payments and, simultaneously, had a greater impact on auditors and auditing. The FCPA requires all publicly held corporations to keep adequate records and to be properly controlled. The FCPA applies even if the corporation does not trade outside the United States.

Specifically, the law provides that publicly held companies must:

- Keep books and records that, in reasonable detail, accurately and fairly reflect their transactions.
- Maintain appropriate systems of internal accounting control.

These requirements, which amend the Securities Exchange Act of 1934, relate only to publicly held companies, not to "domestic concerns." The subject companies are primarily those whose securities are traded on the national stock exchanges or in the over-the-counter market.

The system of internal accounting control must be adequate to provide reasonable assurances that:

- Transactions are executed in accordance with management's general or specific authorization.
- Transactions are recorded as needed to permit preparation of financial statements in conformity with generally accepted accounting principles (GAAP) or any other criteria applicable to such statements, and to maintain accountability for assets.
- Access to assets is permitted only in accordance with management's general or specific authorization.
- The recorded accountability for assets is compared with the existing assets at reasonable intervals, and appropriate action is taken with respect to any differences.

Although the penalties for illegal payments do not apply here, failure to maintain appropriate books and records and systems of internal control would violate the Securities Exchange Act of 1934. Liability for failure to comply will not be imposed, however, when a person acts pursuant to a directive of a federal department or agency for national security purposes.

Action Plan. Companies are advised to adopt a comprehensive action plan to meet the requirements of the FCPA. This plan should contain a program for evaluating internal accounting control. The program should include the controls over the company's significant EDP accounting systems.

Amendments to the Foreign Corrupt Practices Act

As part of an omnibus trade bill passed in August 1988, the FCPA was amended. These recent amendments limit criminal penalties relating to FCPA internal control requirements to individuals who knowingly fail to comply with them, clarify what constitutes "bribery," and increase bribery penalties.

Elimination of Some Criminal Penalties. The amended FCPA still requires SEC registrants to maintain a system of internal accounting control.

(See this chapter for a description of those responsibilities.) However, the new amendments remove criminal liability when failure to comply with those accounting requirements is unintentional. As long as the individuals did not knowingly circumvent or knowingly fail to implement a system of internal accounting control or knowingly falsify any book, record, or account, no criminal penalties will be imposed.

The amendments also define the terms "reasonable detail" and "reasonable assurances" to mean a level of detail and degree of assurance that would satisfy prudent officials in the conduct of their own affairs.

Public companies that own 50 percent or less of an entity are required only to "proceed in good faith" to use their influence to cause the entity to implement and maintain a system of internal accounting control. However, the company must be able to demonstrate good-faith efforts to use such influence.

"Bribery" Definition Clarified. The original FCPA recognizes that in some countries payments to government officials are common and, indeed, necessary to conduct business. Thus, the original act allowed payments to foreign employees "whose duties are essentially ministerial or clerical." This has been interpreted to allow the payment of "fees" to foreign officials to obtain and/or to expedite routine governmental actions. The new amendment clarifies this interpretation by defining activities considered "routine governmental actions." (See this chapter for definitions of these activities.)

Bribery Penalties Stiffened. The new FCPA amendments retain both criminal and civil penalties for U.S. businesses and individuals guilty of bribery. The maximum criminal penalties were increased to $2 million from $1 million for companies and to $100,000 from $10,000 for individuals. It is illegal for any U.S. individual or business enterprise, public or private, to offer a bribe to a foreign official, foreign political party, party official, or candidate for foreign political office for the purpose of obtaining, retaining, or directing business to any person. Companies and individuals who violate any of the FCPA bribery provisions are also subject to civil penalties imposed by the SEC or the Attorney General.

Foreign Corrupt Practices Act Definitions

Accounting Requirements for SEC Registrants.

- Make and keep books, records, and accounts that, in reasonable detail, accurately and fairly reflect the transactions and dispositions of the assets of the issuer.

- Devise and maintain a system of internal accounting control sufficient to provide reasonable assurances that:
  - Transactions are executed in accordance with management's general or specific authorization.
  - Transactions are recorded as necessary to permit preparation of financial statements in conformity with generally accepted accounting principles (GAAP) or other applicable criteria and to maintain accountability for assets.
  - Access to assets is permitted only in accordance with management's general or specific authorization.

Routine Governmental Actions.

- Obtaining permits, licenses, or other official documents to qualify to do business in a foreign country.
- Processing governmental papers, such as visas and work orders.
- Providing police protection, mail pick up and delivery, and scheduling inspections associated with contract performance or inspections related to transit of goods across country.
- Providing phone service, power and water supply, loading and unloading cargo, or protecting perishable products or commodities from deterioration.
- Actions of a similar nature.

Actions Not Considered Routine.

- Any decision by a foreign official whether, or on what terms, to award new business to or to continue business with a particular party.
- Any action taken by a foreign official involved in the decision-making process to encourage a decision to award new business to or to continue business with a particular party.

These definitions help to clarify the actions that must be taken—or avoided—as a result of the FCPA. Organizations may want to consider changing their codes of conduct in response.

Systems Auditability and Control Report

IBM provided a grant to the IIA to fund a project on the audit and control of EDP systems. The study was conducted by Stanford Research Institute, now called SRI International. The results were published as a set of three reports

1. Executive Report
2. Control Practices Report
3. Audit Practices Report

Although published in 1977, many of the findings are still relevant to the audit and control of today's EDP systems. Copies of these reports are available from the Institute of Internal Auditors, 249 Maitland Avenue, Altamonte Springs, Fla. 32701.

The Executive Report. This report represents an overview of the audit of EDP systems. Some of the major topics covered are:

- Hazards of inadequate audit and control.
- Project methodology.
- Management responsibility.
- Need for improved controls.
- Participation by internal audit in systems development.
- Verification of controls.
- Need for improved internal audit involvement.
- EDP audit staff development.
- Need for improved EDP audit tools and techniques.
- Need for audit and control assessment.
- Cost implications of systems auditability and controls.

The general conclusion of the study is that although data processing systems and internal audit techniques are continuing to evolve, there has been little coordination between the two disciplines.

The Control Practices Report. This report states that EDP auditing is a rapidly developing field, beginning to fulfill many of the requirements for an effective level of control and proper evaluation of data processing systems. While discussing the general subject of controls within an EDP environment, the study arrives at the following conclusions:

- The primary responsibility for overall internal control resides with top management, while the operational responsibility for the accuracy and completeness of computer-based information systems should reside with users.

- There is a need for improved controls, because inadequate attention has been given to the importance of internal controls in the data processing environment.
- Internal auditors must participate in the system development process to ensure that appropriate audit and control procedures are designed and built into new computer-based information systems.
- Verification of controls must occur both before and after installation of computer-based information systems.
- As a result of the growth in complexity and use of computer-based information systems, the need exists for greater internal audit involvement relative to auditing in the data processing environment.
- An important need exists for EDP audit staff development to audit the data processing environment effectively.
- New tools and techniques are needed to test the accuracy and completeness of data processing activities and results.
- Many organizations are not adequately evaluating their audit and control functions in the data processing environment. Top management should initiate a periodic assessment of its audit and control programs.

The Control Practices Report discusses specific control techniques, classifying them under computer application controls and general controls. Auditors should encourage the pre-installation review of EDP systems recommendations of the report. When an EDP auditor who understands why controls should be built-in participates in the process, better systems result.

The Audit Practices Report. This report contains a list of 28 data processing audit tools and techniques, discussed in further detail in the balance of the report.

The section entitled "Audit Management Tools and Techniques" provides audit management with four overall approaches to take when applying EDP audit techniques.

1. *Multisite audit software*. This approach can be used by auditors involved with centralized system development and decentralized computer data centers. For this environment, the computer audit software programs are written centrally and run on a multisite basis. Presumably, only minimal variations are required from site to site; the computer centers are usually sufficiently similar in equipment configurations and applications systems for the audit programs to work with minor modifications.

2. *Competency center.* This concept can also apply to multisite locations. The competency center receives data from outlying locations and executes the computer audit software programs centrally. Resulting reports are then distributed to the auditors responsible for auditing the individual sites.

3. *Audit area selection.* This approach recommends applying computerized techniques to determine which locations to audit. Central to its use is the development of location profile material, providing key indicator information for each location. These indicators are evaluated by the computer to determine where audit emphasis is required. This method could be applied manually where the profile pattern or key indicator development is relatively simple.

4. *Scoring.* The scoring technique assigns a number of attributes to a computer application, with appropriate point values, to perform a risk analysis. The weighted characteristics of a system then develop its total score. Applications that contain the greatest number of points are those to which the auditor would give the most attention during the course of examination.

The Audit Practices Report describes specific techniques for examining EDP systems, often requiring the auditor to use the computer as an audit tool. Other techniques use review and/or manual testing of the system. Some of these techniques have stood the tests of time and practicality better than others, but they are all known to EDP auditors. A brief description of each follows:

- *Test data method.* The auditor creates special test input data, passes it through the computer programs that have been determined to be of audit significance, and compares the output to predetermined results.
- *Base case system evaluation.* This technique employs a standardized body of data for testing purposes, normally established by user personnel. It is used to validate production computer application systems. The data can be used to test the ongoing accurate operation of the system throughout its lifetime.
- *Integrated Test Facility.* The Integrated Test Facility (ITF) processes test data in the actual system. It usually represents a set of fictitious entities such as departments, customers, and products. The auditor can process any variety of transactions against the ITF in a live operating environment and get printed reports to confirm the correctness of the processing. This method is especially useful when it is not considered practical to test the system on a separate

processing cycle basis. It does not have an effect on processing of valid existing entities.

- *Parallel simulation.* In many cases, it is possible to confirm the accuracy of records of accounting significance by performing a process that is equivalent, but not identical, to the one employed by management. Normally this requires a smaller number of programs, since it limits the logic and calculations necessary to secure the equivalent results for areas of auditor interest. Many program types can be used for this type of simulation, such as generalized audit software, utility programs, custom-coded programs, and programs written by the EDP function under audit control.
- *Transaction selection.* The auditor uses a separate computer program to select transactions for further review and testing. Transaction selections can be made on a random or a statistical sampling basis, or by stratification using auditor-established criteria, such as dollar value and age.
- *Embedded audit data collection.* A screening process can be incorporated into regular production programs. Items that fulfill certain criteria established by the auditor are then selected during regular production runs. This requires that screening routines be specially coded and inserted within the production programs at those logic points where the selection is to occur. It also requires that the programs be designed that way to begin with, which means including EDP audit participation in their development.
- *Extended records.* Sometimes auditors need various different elements relating to an item from a number of different files. This method takes and combines these elements into a single record. This new record contains the total set of elements required, thus forming a work record that can be processed. The computer reviews the relationships of various elements in the new record to determine whether any conditions of audit significance exist.
- *Generalized audit software.* This technique employs computer software written to apply certain generalized processes to make selections, summarizations, reports, and the like. The generalized software user must prepare specification sheets, describing the contents of the file and the specific computer processes to be employed against those files. Whatever selections are to be made, or other processes applied, can be supplemented as directed by parameters for further actions that the auditor prepares at the time the program is run.
- *Snapshot.* It is sometimes desirable to determine precisely which elements of information were available to the computer at a given moment while performing a logic or decision-making process.

Through special coding, a triggering process can take place whereby all data that is pertinent to analysis of the specific situation is printed. This is a "snapshot" of that processing instant. This technique helps determine why a computer produced questionable results when the reasons are not readily apparent and cannot be determined otherwise.

- *Tracing.* This method is, in effect, a walk-through of a given transaction or other record through the computer process. It usually generates output used to determine exactly which computer instructions were executed by the computer program upon the transaction or record, as well as the sequence of execution.
- *Mapping.* Ordinarily, mapping is used to confirm the thoroughness with which test or production data has been applied against a given computer program. From an audit standpoint, mapping can be used to determine whether there is any unexecuted code within a computer program. Unexecuted code may be routines that are dormant at the moment but that might have been added to permit improper computer use. Or it may be there for authorized periodic or occasional processing. Any unexecuted code should be examined.
- *Control flowcharting.* In many cases, the auditor wants to gain a general understanding of a system while providing specific consideration of individual controls. An understanding can be achieved by flowcharting the process, placing narrative emphasis on the control points.
- *Job accounting data analysis.* Many computer systems create a log of system use. Software can analyze this log. The auditor can review the results of that analysis to determine the appropriateness of actions performed during a given period.
- *Audit guide.* An audit guide provides the internal auditor with an outline of the steps to perform when conducting an audit of an area or application system.
- *Disaster testing.* This technique makes use of a simulated disaster in the computer center to test the adequacy of the center's contingency planning and response.
- *Code comparison.* An auditor is often concerned with whether a program being executed in the production environment corresponds to a controlled, authorized copy of the program. To establish the validity of the production program, the auditor uses a version maintained under audit control and makes comparison tests of the two versions.

The Audit Practices Report also discusses the internal auditor's increasing role in the development and life of EDP systems. This involvement is covered under the following topics:

- System development life cycle.
- Control guidelines for use during system development.
- System acceptance and control group.
- Post-implementation audit.

The report emphasizes the internal auditor's involvement during the development process, to help ensure that:

- User requirements are properly satisfied.
- Adequate application controls are installed and maintained.
- Anticipated cost/benefit or procedural improvements are realized.
- Adequate acceptance testing occurs.
- Projects are completed as scheduled and within costs as budgeted.
- Administrative or operational controls are adequate to ensure a methodical and disciplined development process.
- Adequate application controls are incorporated into new or revised application systems to prevent undetected errors and omissions.
- Predictability is improved in system development.

THE FUTURE OF THE PROFESSION

Future Professional Tools and Techniques

Because the trend is toward more sophisticated technology to support the business environment, EDP auditors will need more sophisticated tools and techniques to deal with this technology effectively. Common sense and audit judgment will continue to have major roles in the auditor's approach. However, technology will assist in the identification, testing, evaluation, and reporting of audit work.

The use of computers for storing and processing large amounts of financial data has created the need to analyze the information within its own environment. For example, a manual approach to statistical sampling of accounts that reside on megabytes of disk space would require many hours of analysis and, for practicality, a reduction of the sample size, possibly reducing accuracy. However, automated techniques can pose serious problems if not approached using a sound basis in audit fundamentals.

Hardware Tools. Business systems of the future are likely to be on-line real-time systems (as opposed to batch processing) that can reduce the auditor's control over audit applications. Auditors' files stored in a multi-user mainframe environment may be open to alteration by an organization's personnel. Incompatible computer equipment in a company can create problems for auditors who must adapt their audit programs to the specifications of the various vendors' computers—micros, minis, and mainframes.

One promising solution to these difficulties has been the introduction of an audit workstation. Use of a secure microcomputer or super-micro facility allows the EDP auditor to download the data to be tested. In addition, through this method, a decrease in costs and training time, enhanced control over maintenance of an audit software library, and increased security may be realized. This tool allows the auditor many of the same advantages as auditing on a mainframe, and provides the additional benefit of greater independence. However, extensive use of this system does not mean that the EDP auditor should avoid using the organization's information system facilities totally, because discrepancies can exist that would be impossible to resolve through the use of file downloads.

Software Tools. Future audit software seems most likely to develop in the following general categories:

- *Modeling tools.* These allow auditors to process "what if" scenarios and assess recommendations.
- *Test support software.* This varies widely and includes testing facilities, data reduction programs, and statistical data collection routines, as well as a variety of audit-oriented software.
- *Software analysis tools.* These include compare utilities, complexity measures, graphics support, coverage measures, path flow analyzers, and even formal verification software.

EDP auditors of the future can expect these tools to be contained in microchips capable of being transferred to any architecture. For example, documentation and code analyzers might be activated via menus to operate at two levels, the program level and the system level.

At the program level, they would provide complete program documentation for any application language. The resulting reports might include a graphic representation of all files, records, and working storage used by the application. The length, picture type, and relative locations of each data name would be printed, and any initial values printed just below the data name. This report would also provide a reference index in the order of appearance in the files and the individual area used by the program, plus data flow analysis and paragraph tracing.

At the system level, the facility would permit analysis of multiple programs within a given system. Through this option, file analysis, data analysis, copy analysis, linkage analysis, and data set analysis reports might be generated. For example, the linkage analysis report would record all "entries" and "calls" and their linkage parameters within the system. This report would contain a program linkage section and a call/entry linkage section. These would be important to the auditor because they could help identify all of the computer programs used by the application, and vice versa.

Computerized data retrieval and analysis will be performed using generalized audit software packages. Such software of the future will probably include a series of enhanced computer programs with the power and flexibility of programming languages. They will permit auditors to perform the functions of programming languages, such as reading, manipulating, and sorting data, and printing reports.

AI and expert systems will have an impact as the auditor's emphasis continues to shift from evaluating processing results to evaluating controls. Many technologically advanced organizations will focus more closely on risk assessment. Future audit software is likely to include use of AI concepts to assist auditors in risk assessment.

Public policy concerns regarding the uses of data processing, financial reporting requirements, and the role of the auditor may influence future legislation on information technology and transborder data flow. All undoubtedly will have an effect on the practice of EDP auditing.

PREPARING FOR THE FUTURE

As system complexity increases, EDP auditors will need to develop specialized knowledge of computer-based information systems. System software, telecommunications, microcircuitry, computer law, advanced languages, and information security all require training beyond that necessary for current conventional audit practice. Keeping pace with technology is crucial in any audit training program. Approaches to the issue include on-the-job training, continuing education, seminars, cross-training, and use of outside educational resources. In addition, the EDPAA and the EDPAF will continue to support the profession in its commitment to the needs of EDP auditing.

PART II

Information Technology Concepts

CHAPTER **4**

MIS Organization

THE EVOLVING ROLE OF THE MIS FUNCTION

As computer use became widespread, organizations discovered that they needed more processing ability than one EDP department as the central processing area. In effect, lots of tiny EDP departments developed wherever user departments needed processing capability. This decentralization of processing was basically a sound concept, since many of the smaller processing tasks could be accomplished locally, at the source of transactions. One of the difficulties in this approach has been that the various small systems, because of ever-decreasing hardware costs, can be easily purchased without any thought about the larger organizational picture (e.g., whether the various systems are compatible). Their installation and use are similarly uncontrolled in many instances.

This proliferation of computer use without a concomitant plan for acquisition and subsequent implementation has caused concern in many organizations. A similar situation developed as local managers discovered microcomputers, which were frequently purchased without following EDP standards and procedures. Managers bought the system they thought best for their area, without considering whether the information they processed could be accessed by another system within the company. To solve this problem, standards were organized by a central management information system (MIS) department with responsibility for the development of a sound, overall corporate plan for the management of all information systems. Local management learned to follow the new procedures for implementation and maintenance of systems and data, and the new MIS planning area made sure that future computers in the company were compatible and ensured the integrity of programs and data in use in many locations.

Problems such as these are becoming less common as organizations realize how important it is to have a sound written policy to control computer system purchase, use, and maintenance. At the same time, having a well-organized MIS department to handle major processing for the organization and help implement policy for all users, no matter where they are located, is essential to its effectiveness.

Another invaluable, and sometimes overlooked, source of assistance in planning and controlling computer use in any organization is the internal audit department. This is particularly true when one or more of its members is an EDP audit specialist. Their participation in the system development life cycle can assure that the computers and software implemented in an organization will be the ones that fulfill the requirements of the users, MIS department, and management.

In the past, EDP strategy often developed on a "catch-as-catch-can" basis, with new computers purchased as old ones collapsed under the strain or new programs written in the middle of a crisis to meet present needs. Often there was no time to investigate and plan for the future. In today's rapidly moving world of computer technology, this kind of approach simply will not work.

There are many different ways to develop a sound MIS strategy. Their names are based on their methods, such as the "bottom-up" or "top-down" approach to planning, yet there is a common thread in all of them. They all involve the implementation of policy and procedures through the talents of people in the department most directly concerned: the MIS department. Data processing has become so important to the success of the organization itself that a well-structured, well-running MIS department should be high on the list of priorities for any organization.

Because organizational needs fluctuate according to the business cycle and economic conditions, the MIS department must be flexible enough to meet the changing demands for its services. To function successfully, it should take into consideration the peaks and valleys in demand for processing so that when there is a lot of work to be done, the system can do it without becoming overloaded. For most organizations, these needs are predictable enough that expected volume requirements can be designed into the system.

The MIS department and its systems also must be adaptable to integrate new software and hardware as needed. As technological advances occur naturally, MIS should be able to incorporate them, to grow and develop, rather than require replacement of entire systems in order for advances to be implemented.

This chapter discusses various aspects of department structure, operating procedures, and organization that can apply to any MIS department. This information can be used to ensure that an existing MIS department meets basic standards. Simultaneously, the checklist of MIS department functions, structure, and controls in the second half of the chapter can help ensure that an MIS department has appropriate procedures and controls in place.

DATA PROCESSING ENVIRONMENT, ORGANIZATION, AND CONTROLS

The MIS Department

Computer departments vary considerably from one organization to the next. The structure of the computer or MIS department obviously depends on such constraints as size and workload, but the structure generally reflects two basic divisions:

1. System development—Designing and programming computer systems (see Chapter 22, "System Development Trends and Practices," and Chapter 23, "System Development Methodology and Auditing").

2. Operations—Controlling and processing data.

It is becoming increasingly common in medium to large installations (more than 10 people) for other support groups, in addition to these basic areas, to exist.

An organizational chart of a typical medium-size installation is shown in Figure 4-1. This chart indicates the broad functional divisions that may exist within an MIS department. The extent of formalization, or lack of it, within those divisions depends largely on the size of the department. However, in any structure the operational aspects of the MIS department, the role of the data base section, and the role of the software support group are similar. What may differ is the number of people available to do those jobs. Figure 4-2 shows some of the areas in a company where MIS support is required.

Computer Operations

A typical medium-size computer used for batch and on-line applications, such as an IBM 4341, might have a data center manager in charge of operations, with the following functions reporting:

- Operations manager responsible for computer operations.
- Chief operator (responsible for senior operators in charge of each shift and other computer operators on staff).
- Security administrator.
- Data base administrator (DBA), if a data base management system (DBMS) is used.
- Technical support.
- Control section.
- Data preparation.
- Scheduling.
- Job assembly.
- Library.
- Output distribution.

FIG. 4-1

A possible organization chart for an MIS department

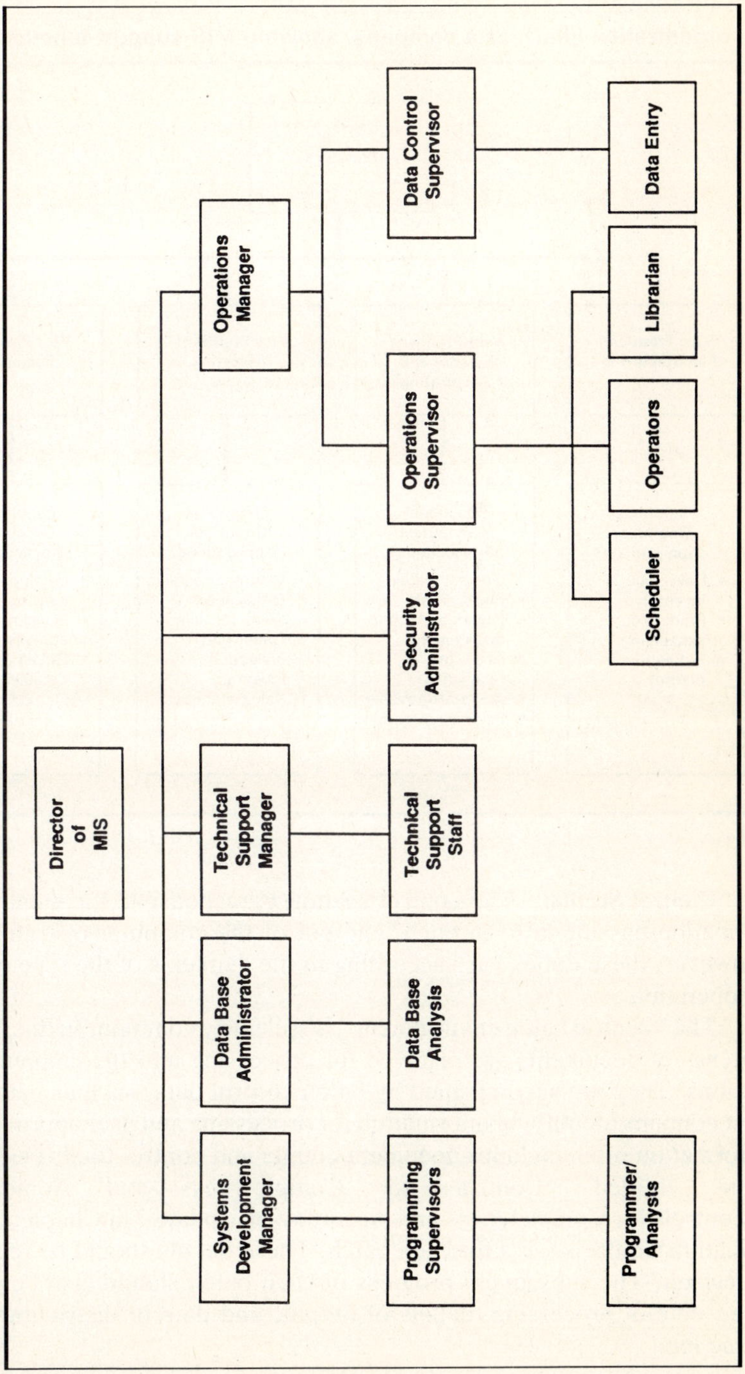

FIG. 4-2

An organization chart for a company, showing MIS support functions

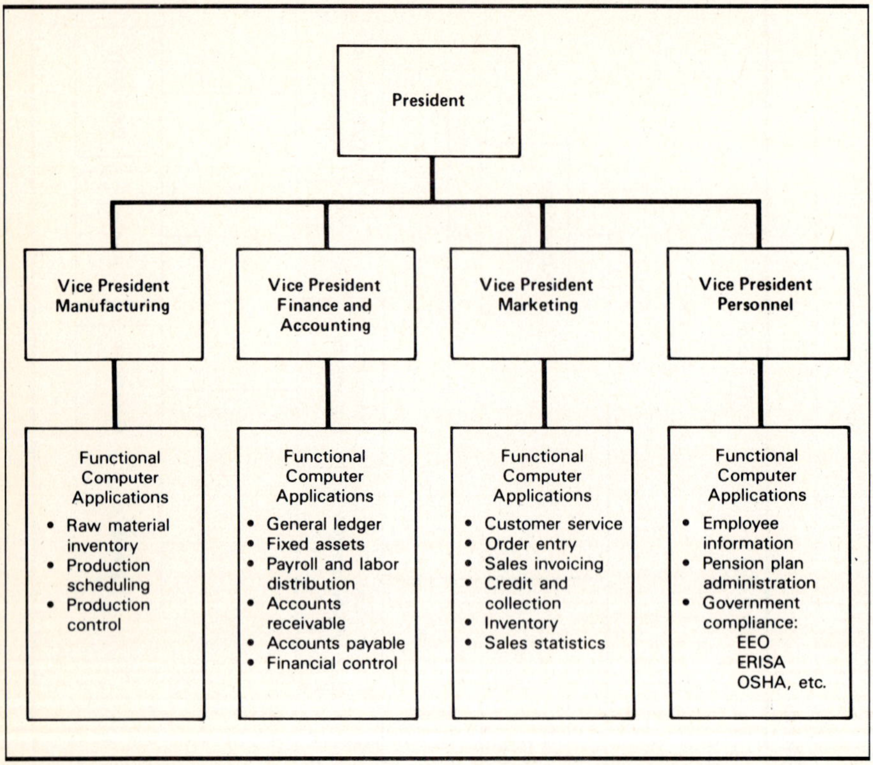

Control Section. The control section is responsible for monitoring information passing into, through, and out of the computer operations area. However, these duties vary according to the demands of the type of system in operation.

The "central batch environment" is still fairly common. In this situation, batches of documents are received for processing into the computer applications. They are accompanied by batch control data, such as batch totals, that contains identifying information for processing and user approval. Other information often includes document counts and control totals (see the sections entitled "Controls for Completeness and Acraot" and "Controls for Completeness and Accuracy of Update" in Chapter 14, "Application Controls—I") for each batch. These details should be recorded in a register. The subsequent progress of each batch should also be recorded (i.e., date of processing, details of output, and date of distribution) in the same log.

Where data is input at a location remote from the computer, control over transmitted data may be established at the central location by software. (See Chapter 7, "Telecommunications Networks and Systems.") The physical control of source documents, which is otherwise part of the central control section's function, will be carried out at the outlying (remote) location. Controls should be in place to ensure that only authorized personnel can gain access to the computer programs and files through remote terminals. These controls can consist of software checks, such as passwords or account codes, or hardware features, such as terminal locks.

Upon completion of each scheduled job, the control section should check for each program or series of programs run, that:

- Data specified as input was fully processed.
- Required output was produced in the correct form.
- Correct computer programs and control records were used.
- Correct tape, disk, and other files were used at every stage.
- Data files were correctly read or written.
- Correct action was taken by the computer operator following program halts, both scheduled and unscheduled.
- There is no evidence of unauthorized alteration of data or programs.
- Computer and associated procedures were completed without undue delay.

In the absence of a control section, these duties can be performed by users.

Data Preparation. Although considerable progress has been made in automating methods of preparing data for input (light pens, optical scanning, and the like), the most common form of off-line data conversion is still through a keyboard with a terminal to magnetic tape or disk. The staff involved in keying data in central locations normally is a section within the computer operations group. However, decentralized data entry environments are more prevalent today. Generally, the staff is responsible to local management for administrative reasons. For example, accounts payable clerks who perform data entry of customer invoices usually report to the accounting manager, not the MIS manager. On-line systems typically use terminals and direct keying, often by the user departments.

Keyed data should be verified. If possible, data should not be keyed and verified by the same operator. A separate subsection is often set up for verification by the more experienced operators.

A record is normally maintained in the data preparation area to monitor the progress of documents through the various stages of preparation and verification. Sufficient information should be recorded to indicate the present whereabouts of each batch of documents, together with the date and, if necessary, time of completion of processing for each stage.

Scheduling. For every job run on the computer, there should be a detailed schedule that sets the total time for the job to run, the sequence of events within the job, and the various peripherals and files involved. These schedules are used to determine each day's work for the computer. There should be a work scheduler, who has responsibility for preparing:

- A detailed schedule, divided if necessary into a schedule for each operating shift. (This is usually reviewed by the data control supervisor or operations manager.)
- Detailed schedules for the week or month ahead.
- Outlines of long-term forecasts of computer time requirements and other operating workloads, which may cover periods of six, twelve, or more months. The periods selected for long-term forecasts should extend far enough in advance for effective action to be taken to recruit and train additional operating staff, if needed. Cases where work volumes are expected to increase significantly may require the increase of computer or other equipment's capacity.

The daily schedule provides each shift of computer operators with the work to be done, the sequence in which programs are to be run, and, where possible, lower-priority work that can be introduced if time becomes available. At the end of a shift, each operator should pass to the work scheduler or to the next shift of operators (when the work scheduler is not on duty) a statement of the work completed and the reasons any scheduled work was not completed.

It is necessary to revise the detailed schedules if there are errors or failures that substantially delay the completion of the computer procedures or make it necessary for them to be repeated. The work scheduler should be kept informed of the progress of work and, in the event of delays or failures, should amend the schedules. The detailed schedules should also be revised when delays occur in the submission, to the operations group, of input documents or other media, or in input media preparation by operations group staff. As the relative importance of scheduled procedures may change because of the delay, the work scheduler may need to consult users before making these revisions. If it is necessary to repeat entire jobs or procedures, it is likely that there will be a conflict over the job priority between several users who expect their jobs to be completed. Such situations must be handled with care and might require the computer operations manager to step in to decide the sequence of jobs to be run and make the necessary arrangements with users. The MIS manager should be informed whenever significant delays occur or when extensive rerunning is necessary.

Many large companies that process a large number of batch jobs use automated job scheduling software to set up daily work schedules. Job scheduling software efficiently produces schedules that are more flexible and easier to control.

In the automated environment, the scheduler is responsible for the set-up of job processing information (e.g., processing frequency, job dependencies, and report distribution) on the schedules data base and subsequent maintenance of changes and jobs run on request.

Automation also allows for greater control over the scheduling process in the following ways:

- Job information is set up only once, reducing the possibility of an error, such as not listing all jobs to be run.
- Job dependencies are defined so that if a job fails, subsequent jobs relying on its output will not be processed.
- Software packages provide security over access to production data.

Job Assembly. Job assembly or job set-up is the physical assembly of the material necessary for processing. This material may include the tapes or other devices that hold the relevant programs and data, the job control statements, the run instructions, and the parameters. In more advanced systems, system software takes over some of these functions, and the programs and data files are often available in the on-line program library.

Job control statements contain the instructions for programs to execute in a particular sequence. Job control statements also define system resources (such as data sets, tape and disk drives, printers, and terminals). In more advanced systems, they are stored on disk and are usually called into operation through the master console terminal.

Run instructions, sometimes referred to as "runbooks" or "jobbooks," contain the program operating instructions. They give details of the action to be taken by operators before, during, and at the completion of the operation of the program. Run instructions also provide the current processing instructions, which give details of the programs and files to be used and the stationary requirements. These run instructions are specific to a job and complement the standard operating instructions that apply to all processing.

Runbooks usually are created by the application programmers during system development and then are revised by them to reflect program maintenance.

Some applications use parameters that contain the run information a program needs but that is variable in nature. The most common parameters are dates, which are used, for example, in the generation of data and the aging of accounts receivable and inventory balances. Parameters may also be used to indicate whether program steps used only periodically, such as production of customer statements, should be activated. Parameters are often stored as table files or can be entered as part of the job control statements.

The job set-up personnel are responsible for the maintenance of the job set-up instructions and the use of the proper instructions during processing. It is usual for the control section to match the job set-up instructions with the details of job control statements and the parameters that are actually used. Once the programs, files, run instructions, job control statements, and parameters requested on the daily, or shift, schedule have been assembled, they are passed to the computer operators for processing.

Library. For batch systems, programs and data files in use include tapes and disks that have been loaded for a specific processing run but are otherwise stored off-line in the production library. They are permanently loaded on disk or tape and available for inquiry or updating in on-line and real-time systems. (See Chapter 7.) Files organized as a data base (see Chapter 28, "Date Base") would normally be in the latter category. Off-line files and programs are held in a physical library and require an operator to mount or place them on the tape drive or other device, or the librarian may be able to mount them mechanically.

The physical library should be a lockable storage area, separate from the computer room. Preferably, the library should be supervised by a full-time librarian responsible for the issue, receipt, and security of all files. Where the installation is not large enough to warrant a full-time librarian, a member of the control section should have similar specific duties. Access to the library should be restricted to staff authorized to obtain and deliver programs and data files; even then, such activities should be in accordance with the authorized processing schedules prepared by the work scheduler.

The librarian should follow up on all issued tapes and disks in order to ensure their prompt return. The librarian is responsible for maintaining adequate records of all tapes and disks, either manually (in the form of a register or index card file) or through an automated library system (e.g., TLMS or Tape Management Library System) run on the computer. Other routine but extremely important, functions include the transfer of files and programs to "backup" for storage as a safeguard against destruction or loss of operational copies.

Output Distribution. The printed output from computer processing can be voluminous. Its decollation (i.e., separation into units) and distribution normally are the responsibilities of personnel within the control section. Output should be distributed only in accordance with current processing instructions and only after the control section is satisifed that processing was properly completed in accordance with those instructions.

Computer Operators. Computer operators are responsible for the accurate and efficient operation of the scheduled jobs on the computer. The computer operators report directly to the chief operator or, where shifts are worked, to the shift supervisor.

Operator procedures should be based on standing instructions. These instructions deal with the operation of the computer and its peripheral equipment, the actions to be taken in the event of machine or program failure, and the records to be kept. The standing instructions, when combined with the run instructions, provide rules for each step that need to be taken by operators. A responsible official, such as the operations manager, should review the operating instructions periodically and confirm that they are up-to-date. Except in the smallest computer installations, operators should not carry out work associated with:

- Job set-up
- Control procedures
- Writing application programs

After processing has been completed, the computer operators should distribute output according to the current instructions. Tape and disk files should either be retained for a subsequent operation or returned to the file library. Before being forwarded to the control section, printed output should be labeled to indicate the computer program that produced it, the processing cycle reference number (which may be the creation date or a unique reference number), and the time it was produced.

Normally, the computer records the start and stop times of computer runs, and operators report any delay times. Most computers have software that provides for this information to be logged and displayed on the console or master terminal by the operating system, but it is sometimes necessary for a separate report to be compiled by the operator regarding details of delays and problems, together with any actions taken to correct them. Where a delay occurred as the result of machine failure, a copy of any report prepared by the vendor's customer engineer should be filed with the chief operator's copy of the delay report.

Technical Support

In large operations, it is not unusual to find that the computer operations department has developed a specialist software support service, staffed by systems programmers. These programmers are responsible for such activities as:

- Obtaining detailed knowledge of the operating system and other system software.
- Using their software knowledge to resolve inquiries from development and operating staff.
- Controlling the incorporation of software amendments provided by the manufacturer or software house.
- If necessary, devising and incorporating additional amendments to the system software, usually to improve its efficiency and to tailor it to the organization's requirements and computer configuration.

Although considerable improvements to operating efficiency can sometimes be obtained from local amendments to generalized software, there is a risk to security, especially when the amendments are devised and controlled entirely within the computer operations department.

The size and complexity of data bases often lead to the appointment of specific personnel responsible for all aspects of data base administration. These personnel are collectively called the DBA. Their tasks include the design and maintenance of the schemas (description of all data in the data base) and subschemas (description of all data available to a particular program); the maintenance of the DBMS and related software; and liaison with users, other computer department staff, and outside suppliers. The DBA may thus combine responsibility for procedures and controls that would normally be carried out by separate people in conventional computer systems. (See Chapter 28 for a discussion of data base concepts.)

REVIEWING THE MIS DEPARTMENT

When organizations of all sizes seek to control costs, they often focus on MIS operations. Basically, they want to know how successful the MIS function is in supporting overall organizational objectives. But how does an organization go about determining the effectiveness, efficiency, and reliability of its MIS function?

One approach is an operational review, which is frequently performed by an outside organization, such as an accounting firm with EDP audit capabilities. The review encompasses user services, MIS management, technical development, operations, facilities, and contingency plans. This is a good way for management to get an independent assessment of its MIS function. (The chart in Figure 4-3 shows some of the questions in relation to access that would be assessed during such a review.)

Obviously, each entity's computer processing needs are different, but there are general questions that all types of organizations should ask themselves. An operational review can supply management with answers to such questions as:

- Is the organization getting an appropriate payback on its computing expenditures?
- Are users getting the processing results they need?
- Is the entire function managed effectively?
- Is the MIS function responsive to overall organizational objectives and plans?
- Are EDP resources being applied to the appropriate needs?
- Is the total MIS function performing productively?

Determining When a Review Is Needed

Apart from the broad questions above, how does an organization know it needs a review? If an organization exhibits some of the following symptoms, it may be time to investigate the feasibility of an operational review of MIS:

- Unfavorable user attitude toward the MIS department.
- Excessive costs.
- History of aborted or suspended development projects.
- Major budget overruns on development projects.
- Excessive staff turnover.
- Unsupported hardware/software procurement requests.
- Frequent computer errors or omitted processes.
- Insufficient processing abilities due to organizational growing pains.
- New requirements due to external growth or organization expansion.

Fig. 4-3

Specimen form to be used in the review of an MIS department regarding access to records, equipment, and files

Indicate who is responsible, or normally has access to, the following records, equipment, and files.

	RESPONSIBILITY/ACCESS											
RECORDS, FILES AND EQUIPMENT	Software Programmers	Systems Analysts	Applications Programmers	Data Control Clerks	Job Scheduler	Computer Operators	Key Entry Operators	Librarian	Data Base Administrator	Quality Assurance Officer	User Department Personnel	Vendor Personnel
System Software Documentation												
Application Source Programs and Documentation												
Data Control												
Job Set-Up Instructions and JCL												
Operator Instructions												
Enter the Computer Room												
Operate the Computer System												
Operate Terminals												
Files Stored in the Physical Library												
Files Stored in the Back-Up Store												
Negotiable Instruments												

The objectives and outcome of such an operational review can differ according to the organization's needs and even the industry it is in.

Internal Growing Pains. As an example, a research and manufacturing company was concerned with the rapid growth of both staff and functions in its MIS operation. They wanted a review to evaluate strengths and weaknesses, develop a corporatewide definition of future requirements, establish a basis for developing an action program to deal with deficiencies, and formulate a long-range MIS plan, among other things. The review resulted in recommendations, with accompanying detailed work plans, that:

- Senior management become more deeply involved in directing, planning, and funding MIS operations to better achieve corporate goals.
- MIS organization, standards, and procedures be examined.
- Existing technical expertise be enhanced.
- Security and contingency plans be developed.

If implemented, the recommendations would lead to a more effective MIS operation with increased productivity.

External Growth. A major utility wanted to assess how the merger of three subsidiaries would affect the MIS function. The review focused on organizational requirements, existing MIS plans, the planning process, equipment, data communications, applications consolidation, data base consolidation, and staffing.

A short-range action program was suggested, concentrating on the consolidation. A financial forecast projected program cost and the ultimate possible savings. Note, however, that operational reviews are not necessarily performed with cost-cutting in mind.

REVIEWING AN MIS FUNCTION—CHECKLISTS

The following checklists show some of the issues to be considered during an internal or external review of an MIS department.

1. **Applications.** Develop a list of the major computer-based applications that are both in production and proposed for the future. (See Figure 4-4 for a sample questionnaire used to review applications.)

FIG. 4-4

Specimen chart to be used in review of application programs run by the MIS department

APPLICATIONS

Client________________ Date________________

Engagement #________________ Prepared by________________

Location________________ Review________________

Fiscal Year-End________________ Review________________

APPLICATION (Enter actual name)	FOR APPLICATION IN USE: Is documentation up-to-date and in accordance with current standards	FOR PROPOSED APPLICATIONS: Approximate Implementation Date	PROGRAMMING LANGUAGE	Batch	On-line	Data base
Order Entry						
Billing/Invoicing						
Accounts Receivable						
Cash Receipts						
Sales Analysis						
________________						
________________						
Raw Material Inventory						
Work in Progress						
Bill of Materials						
Finished Goods						
Cost Accounting						
________________						
________________						
Purchase Orders						
Goods Received						
Accounts Payable						
________________						
General Ledger/ Budgets						
________________						
Fixed Assets						
________________						
Investments						
________________						
Payroll						
Labor Distribution						
Pensions						
________________						
Cash and Bank						
________________						
________________						
________________						
________________						

2. Equipment:

- ☐ Create a list or diagram of EDP equipment at each location, including service bureaus.
- ☐ Describe plans for equipment purchases or enhancements and their intended use. (Figure 4-5 shows a sample of a chart used to help assess equipment during a review.)
- ☐ Create a list or diagram of the network.

3. System Software:

- ☐ Make a list of the software prooucts and packages in use, including vendor-supplied and specially developed system software.
- ☐ Specify the type of documentation available that records the particular software features and any adaptations. (Figure 4-6 is a sample of a chart used to help assess system software during a review.)
- ☐ Is vendor-supplied system software reviewed for security exposure prior to implementation?

  Note: System software is software not particular to any one application (e.g., the operating system, utilities, sorts, compilers, file management systems, librarian packages, time-sharing software, communications software, job accounting software, DBMS, security software, scheduling software, 4GLs (fourth generation languages), and in-house system software).

4. Personnel:

- ☐ Obtain an organization chart of the MIS function.
- ☐ Attach job descriptions of MIS department functions.
- ☐ Review job descriptions for proper segregation of duties (especially in small departments).
- ☐ Do any EDP personnel have responsibilities outside the MIS department? If so, list the individuals, their MIS functions, and their external responsibilities.
- ☐ Develop a list of those personnel who have access to particular documentation, files, and equipment.
- ☐ Describe special procedures, if any, for segregating and reviewing EDP personnel's own records and accounts (e.g., payroll data, retail sales account, bank account).

FIG. 4-5

Specimen chart to be used to record the equipment in the MIS department as part of a review

INSTALLED EQUIPMENT

This schedule may be used if the client does not already have an equipment inventory or diagram.

Location: ______________________ Type: ______________________

CPUs: Quantity: ______________________ Memory: Real ______________

Virtual ______________

Peripheral Devices	Quantity	Type
Magnetic Tape Drives		
Disk Storage Drives		
Scanner		
Printer		
System Console		
Display Console		
Other: (List) including terminals RJE stations Point-of-sale devices optical scanner, etc.		

Operating System Employed Version Name ______________________________

Version No.____________ Release Date______________ Memory Req.______________

FIG. 4-6

Specimen chart to be used in review of system software

SYSTEM SOFTWARE

(include both vendor supplied and specially developed software)

Location(s) or System(s)__________

System Program, software product, or utility	Titles of manuals describing the software	Describe the documentation setting out the options and adaptions of the software actually in use	Group responsible for software support
Operating System________ Version #________ Release Data________			

5. Personnel Policies:

- ☐ What are the MIS department policies with respect to delegation of duties when staff are absent because of illness, vacation, or other reason?
- ☐ What are the MIS department policies for obtaining references before hiring new employees?
- ☐ What are the MIS department policies for continuous assessment of personnel performance and provision of necessary training?
- ☐ What are the termination procedures for relieving personnel of sensitive duties and retrieving keys and invalidating their system ID?
- ☐ Who is responsible for reviewing and approving organization charts, job descriptions, and policies to determine that they are up-to-date?

6. Installation Standards:

☐ Is there an installation standards manual (attach a summary or table of contents) for the following?

- Selection of purchased or leased hardware, software, and other computer services.
- System development life cycle methodology for application and system software.
- Computer operations.
- Quality assurance.
- Security of software and data stored on computer media.
- Privacy and confidentiality of documentation, output, and information stored in computer files.
- Procedures for DBA and DBMS support.
- Procedures for teleprocessing support.

☐ Is conformity to standards mandatory, or are they considered guidelines that can be varied in individual cases?

☐ Describe procedures for developing and changing installation standards and who is responsible for preparing, reviewing, and approving the standards.

7. Backup and Disaster Recovery:

☐ Describe the procedures for determining the need for backup and rerun arrangements (such as by estimating the mean time between failures).

☐ Describe the backup arrangements, both on-site and off-site, for:

- Data processing and transmission equipment.
- Date, programs, and systems information stored on computer media.
- Documentation instructions and source data.

☐ Review retention periods of backups for adequacy (for example, ensure the ability to recreate a year-end general ledger).

☐ Describe arrangements for alternative processing facilities in the event of equipment failure (contingency plans).

☐ Describe the procedures for periodically testing and reviewing the effectiveness of the backup arrangements for the following:

- Data processing and transmission equipment.
- Data, programs, and systems information stored on computer media.

- Documentation, instructions, and source data.

8. Insurance:

☐ Describe the insurance coverage for hardware and software, and for recreating data and files.

☐ Describe the fidelity bond coverage for MIS personnel.

☐ Describe the insurance coverage for business interruptions.

9. Contracts:

☐ Describe the procedures for reviewing contracts for computer services, hardware, and software before they are signed.

☐ Attach a copy or a summary of any significant current contracts (such as for service bureau services).

REVIEWING IMPLEMENTATION AND MAINTENANCE OF SYSTEMS—CHECKLIST

1. System and Program Documentation:

☐ Does documentation in accordance with the installation standards exist for all applications and programs developed or modified:

- In the current financial year?
- In previous years?

☐ Describe any system and program documentation aids or documentation software products in use.

☐ Do the source programs conform to the installation programming standards for all programs written:

- In the current financial year?
- In previous years?

☐ How and where are the documentation and source listings filed?

☐ Where modifications have to be made to old programs that have not been developed in accordance with the current standards, what procedures are followed to bring the documentation of the applications up-to-date?

2. Access to System and Program Documentation:

☐ Describe how and where source statement listings, flowcharts, file layouts, sign-on procedures, passwords, and other system documentation are held.

☐ Who is responsible for the custody and issue of documentation?

☐ Who has access to the documentation?

☐ How are unauthorized persons prevented from gaining access to the documentation?

☐ Describe the procedures for the issue and return of documentation.

3. Approval of System Specifications:

☐ Who has the authority to approve system specifications for proposed new applications in the following?

- User department(s).
- System development function.
- Computer operations function.
- Quality assurance function.

☐ What documentation is presented to the above for approval?

☐ How are the approvals evidenced?

☐ When the system specifications are modified during the development process, how are the approvals for the change documented?

☐ How and where are system specifications and approvals filed?

☐ Describe any variation in the above procedures for new systems implemented or under development in the past year.

4. Testing New Applications:

☐ For new applications, describe the involvement in program and system testing of:

- Analyst(s) who specified the programs.
- Programmer(s) who wrote the programs.
- Computer operations function.
- Users.
- Quality assurance function.
- Others (such as a separate testing group or the internal audit department).

☐ Describe the use made of system and program documentation in designing the tests.

☐ What documentation is produced in the process of program and system testing?

☐ What is the policy for the retention of testing documentation and test data files?

☐ When system software (such as utilities, interrogation packages, sorts, or routines incorporated by the linkage editor) is incorporated into applications, is its proper functioning always covered by the normal application testing?

☐ Describe any variations in the above procedures for new systems that were tested in the past year.

5. Approval of Modifications to Production Programs:

☐ How are modifications to production programs requested?

☐ How is the nature of the required change documented?

☐ Who has the authority to approve program modifications in the following:

- User department(s).
- Systems maintenance function.
- Computer operations function (if appropriate).
- Quality assurance function.

☐ How are the approvals evidenced?

☐ How and where are the records of program modifications filed?

☐ Describe any variations in the above procedures (such as for minor modifications or as a result of changes in standards during the year).

6. Control of Approved Program Modifications:

☐ How are all approved modifications controlled to ensure that they are subsequently implemented as authorized?

☐ What are the procedures for reviewing modification requests to ensure that they are implemented within the required time frame?

☐ How are the results of this review documented?

7. Testing Program Modifications:

☐ What documentation is produced in the process of program and system testing?

☐ What is the policy for the retention of testing documentation and test data files?

☐ When program modifications are tested, what procedures are used to ensure that the modification does not affect unchanged parts of the programs or system (for example, when retained system test data is rerun)?

☐ When system software (e.g., utilities, interrogation packages, sorts, or routines incorporated by the linkage editor) is incorporated into applications, is its proper functioning always covered by the normal application testing?

☐ Have all modifications made during the current financial year been tested in accordance with the installation standards?

☐ Under what circumstances, if any, may the normal testing procedures be waived?

☐ When the normal testing procedures are waived, what alternate steps are taken to ensure the proper operation of the modified systems?

☐ Who may approve the waiving of testing, and how is this approval evidenced?

8. Urgent Modifications:

☐ Under what circumstances may urgent modifications that bypass the normal procedures be made to production programs or job control language (JCL) procedure libraries?

☐ Describe the procedures for making such modifications and recording their occurrence.

☐ What procedures are in force, either at the time the modification is made or at a subsequent time, to ensure that the modification is properly documented, tested, and approved?

9. Acceptance by Users of New Applications and Program Modifications:

☐ How are users notified of the effective date when new systems and modifications to systems are to become operational?

☐ Who in the user department(s) is responsible for givng the final approval of new systems and modifications for production use? How is this approval evidenced?

☐ Are there any types of program modification to which the users are not required to give approval?

☐ When users give their approval, how do they ensure that:

- Programs and systems have been adequately tested with respect to the methods used and scope of testing?
- Satisfactory results were achieved from testing?
- Instructions for user procedures have been appropriately prepared or amended?

10. Final Approval for New Applications and Program Modifications by the MIS Function:

☐ Prior to implementation of a new application, who is responsible for checking that the following are complete, up-to-date, and in accordance with the installation standards?

- System and program documentation.
- Job set-up and operating instructions.

☐ How are the results of this check documented?

☐ In the case of program modifications, who is responsible for checking that the following have been amended to be brought up-to-date and in accordance with the current standards?

- System and program documentation.
- Operating instructions.

☐ How are the results of this check documented?

☐ Who is responsible for checking that system and program testing of new applications and program modifications has been properly carried out before programs are made operational, and how are the results of this check documented?

☐ Who is responsible for checking that user approvals have been received, and how are the results of this check documented?

☐ Who is responsible for giving the final approval to make new applications and program modifications operational, and how is this approval evidenced?

11. Cataloging Approved New Applications and Program Modifications:

☐ Describe the procedures for segregating programs being amended from normal production programs.

- ☐ Describe the procedures that ensure that only authorized changes are made during programming (such as program comparison software being run on the before-and-after versions to identify all code that has been changed, or accumulations of changes, in a file that updates the previous version in the library in batch mode and that can be reviewed through an update utility or supervisory review of the source code after programming).
- ☐ Describe the procedures that ensure that:
  - The correct version of the program is transferred to production status.
  - Unauthorized changes are not made to approved programs between the time they are approved for implementation and the time they are taken into production libraries.
  - Changes made to source statement libraries are also made to executable program libraries or vice versa.
- ☐ Who is responsible for carrying out the work?
- ☐ How is this work evidenced?
- ☐ How is the work supervised, reviewed, and approved?

REVIEWING JOB SET-UP, SCHEDULING, AND DATA CONTROL—CHECKLIST

1. Scheduling:

- ☐ Is job scheduling software used?
- ☐ Describe the procedures for scheduling production work (batch and on-line).
- ☐ Who authorized the schedule, and where are the authorized schedules stored? (If job scheduling software is used, are these files protected from unauthorized changes?)

2. Data Control (Application Controls):

- ☐ Describe the responsibilities of data control and associated personnel for preparing and correcting input data (such as a result of rejections).
- ☐ What procedures are in force to ensure that no authorized changes are made to input data?
- ☐ Who has access to the data control records?

☐ How is control over access to the data control records enforced?

☐ Who is responsible for supervising, reviewing, and approving data control activities?

3. Job Set-Up and Execution:

☐ Are there adequate procedures for setting up batch jobs and loading on-line systems (application and system)?

☐ Are there controls to prevent or detect and investigate unauthorized changes to approved job set-up instructions?

☐ Are there controls to ensure that control statements and parameters used in processing are in accordance with the approved procedures?

☐ Is there appropriate written approval, including user involvement, when parameter and control statements are updated (including emergency departures from normal job set-up procedures)?

4. Use of Correct Files:

☐ What controls are there to ensure that correct data files are used in production processing (e.g., use of generation data sets, manual review of system logs, all volumes of a multi-volume file are used, or reliance on an automated tape management system)?

☐ When these controls rely on automated procedures, can such procedures be overridden (e.g., overriding label checks)?

☐ What procedures are in effect to report any incorrect use of data files?

☐ Are the results of the action taken on reported, incorrect use of files reviewed and approved, and, if so, by whom?

☐ How are the results of the reviews and approvals documented?

5. Review of Processing:

☐ To what extent are the results of processing (such as the job execution log or production output) reviewed to ensure that:

- The established production schedule is adhered to and no unauthorized processing has occurred?
- No unauthorized changes were made to production JCL and parameters after job set-up?
- Production jobs are completed successfully?
- The output appears reasonable?

☐ How is the review of processing documented?

6. Variations in Normal Procedures:

☐ Describe any variation in the job set-up and review of processing procedures during the following periods:
- Second and third shifts (if any).
- Weekends and holidays (if applicable).
- Periods of nonproduction processing (such as program testing).

REVIEWING COMPUTER OPERATIONS—CHECKLIST

1. Computer Room Access:

☐ Who is permitted access to the computer room?

☐ Under what circumstances may others be permitted access?

☐ How is control over computer room access enforced?

☐ How does this control operate during the following periods?
- Second and third shifts (if any).
- Weekends and holidays (if applicable).
- Periods of nonproduction processing (such as application and system software testing).

☐ Is a card-key system in place? If so, how is it maintained?

2. Operation of Computer Equipment:

☐ Who is permitted to operate computer equipment for the following?
- Production processing.
- Application testing.
- System software development and testing.
- Third-party processing. (Is there processing for outsiders?)

☐ Under what circumstances may others be permitted to operate computer equipment?
- How is control over the operation of computer equipment enforced?
- How does this control operate during the following periods?
  a. Second and third shifts (if any).
  b. Weekends and holidays (if applicable).
  c. Periods of nonproduction processing (such as hardware maintenance).

3. Operating Instructions:

☐ Do the installation standards require the operating instructions to contain the following?

- Operating instructions for system software (where applicable).
- Operating procedures for applications.
- Restart and recovery procedures.
- Procedures for labeling and disposition of input and output tapes.
- An application system flowchart or run instructions for each run.
- An identification of all input and output forms and media.

☐ Have operating instructions been prepared for all applications in accordance with these standards?

☐ Who has the authority to approve operating instructions (or changes thereto) in the following?

- Applications development and maintenance functions.
- Computer operations function.
- Quality assurance function.

☐ How are the approvals documented?

☐ What procedures are adopted to ensure that the operating instructions remain correct and up-to-date?

4. Operator Actions:

☐ Are there controls over:

- Loading and using system software?
- Amendments to parameters while the system is running?
- The execution of application programs (if operators are involved)?
- Compliance with standard operating procedures?

☐ Is there adequate identification and reporting of system failures, restart and recovery, emergencies, and other unusual situations?

- Are operator actions reviewed for appropriateness and assurance that the results of processing are not adversely affected?

☐ Is there appropriate supervision of operators at all times, including shifts outside the usual working periods?

5. Program and Data File Security:

☐ What are the procedures (such as librarian packages and password access systems) for preventing unauthorized access to the following files?

- Source statement libraries.
- Object program modules.
- Executable program libraries.
- Procedure libraries (JCL).
- Sign-on procedures and passwords.
- Production data.
- System files (such as those containing system software programs and utilities).
- Log files (such as SMF, or System Management Facility).

☐ Who is authorized to access these files, and what level of access is permitted (such as read-only or write access)?

☐ In the event that an unauthorized access occurs, are control procedures exercised to detect such an access?

☐ When password protection is used to prevent unauthorized access to program and data files:

- Describe the procedures adopted, including maintaining secrecy.
- Who is responsible for setting and distributing passwords?
- Are passwords changed periodically and, if so, how often?
- Are accurate records kept of authorized user access levels?

☐ When comparison of independently controlled copies of authorized programs to those in the production library is used to detect any unauthorized access:

- How often and by whom are such comparisons made?
- Describe the software used to make the comparison.
- Are comparisons made on a surprise basis?
- Where are records of the results of the comparisons filed?

☐ Who supervises, reviews, and approves the work described above?

☐ How are the results of the reviews and approvals documented?

6. Logs of System and Operations Activity:

☐ What manual and automated logs are produced that provide the following information? (*Note:* include job accounting information, control logs, DBMS logs, or other.)

- Operator commands entered on the system console.
- Jobs and programs executed.

- Abnormal termination of jobs and programs.
- Jobs and programs rerun.
- Program and data files accessed.
- Utilities used.
- Operating problems encountered and action taken.

☐ In the case of any automated logs, what software was used to generate them? Indicate the information recorded in each log (such as by attaching a copy of the output or record layout or by referring to the relevant sections of the software manuals).

☐ When vendor-supplied software is used (such as SMF), what amendments, options, or user exits have been used and for what purpose?

☐ How is the completeness and accuracy of the manual and automated logs ensured? By whom and to what extent are these logs reviewed and approved? How are the results of the review documented?

☐ If, for any reason, this review was not properly carried out, how would the lack of review be detected?

7. Emergency Program Modifications:

☐ Under what circumstances can operators make urgent modifications to production programs or JCL procedure libraries that bypass the normal procedures?

☐ Describe the procedures for making emergency modifications and recording their occurrence.

☐ What records are kept of emergency modifications that have been made?

☐ What procedures are in force, either at the time the modification is made or at a subsequent time, to ensure that the modification has been properly documented, tested, and approved?

8. Utilities:

☐ What records are kept over the use of utilities and other similar programs that can do the following?

- Dump data.
- Change production programs, data files, or memory at execution time.

☐ What controls are in effect over the use of these utilities?

- ☐ Who must authorize the use of utilities?
- ☐ What procedures are in effect to ensure that only duly authorized use occurs?

9. Supervision of Operators:

- ☐ Who is responsible for reviewing and supervising the action of operators?
- ☐ If, for any reason, operators do not adhere to installation operating procedures, how would this fact be detected?

REVIEWING STORAGE OF PROGRAMS, DATA FILES, AND FORMS—CHECKLIST

1. Access to Files:

- ☐ When program and data files are not being used for processing, where are they held (on-site and off-site)?
- ☐ Normally, who is permitted access to these files?
- ☐ Are there adequate controls to log or save activity so that the status of data files can be determined?
- ☐ Under what circumstances may others be permitted access?
- ☐ How is control over access to files enforced?
- ☐ How does this control operate during the following periods?
  - Second and third shifts (if any).
  - Weekends and holidays (if applicable).
  - Periods of nonproduction processing (such as application and system software testing).

2. Issue and Return of Files:

- ☐ Who is responsible for the custody and issue of files (tape librarian)?
- ☐ Describe the procedures for the external labeling of files and for organizing the storage of files (such as through the use of labeled racks) in the:
  - Computer room.
  - Main file libraries.
  - Backup or disaster storage.
- ☐ Describe the procedures for requesting, recording, and authorizing

issue and prompt return of files (including files containing software).

- ☐ Who is responsible for supervising, reviewing, and approving the activities of librarians and the security and issuing procedures?
- ☐ Describe any variation in the procedures during the following periods:
  - Second and third shifts (if any).
  - Weekends and holidays (if applicable).
  - Periods of nonproduction processing (such as application and system software testing).

3. Storage and Issue of Forms (Job Control):

- ☐ Develop a list of computer forms that require special security. (Normally these will only include checks or other potentially negotiable instruments.)
- ☐ Where are stocks of these forms stored?
- ☐ Who is normally permitted access to these stocks?
- ☐ How is access to the stocks restricted?
- ☐ Is the restriction effective outside the normal working period during the following periods?
  - Second and third shifts (if any).
  - Weekends and holidays (if applicable).
- ☐ Who authorizes the use of such forms?
- ☐ Describe the procedures for controlling the inventory of forms.
  - What are the procedures for issuing forms from, and returning forms to, stock?
  - Are inventory records maintained?
  - Is actual form usage reconciled to inventory issues?
- ☐ Describe the procedures for controlling spoiled and canceled forms.

REVIEWING SYSTEM SOFTWARE PROGRAMMING—CHECKLIST

1. System Software Documentation:

- ☐ Has documentation in accordance with the installation standards been prepared for all system software implemented or modified:

- In the current financial year?
- In previous years?

☐ Does the documentation describe the functions, options selected, user exit changes, and specially designed routines?

☐ When reliance is placed on documentation provided by the software supplier, what records are kept of the particular options, versions, software reviews or fixes, and changes implemented by the company?

☐ When enhancements have to be made to old system software that has not been developed in accordance with the current standards, what procedures are adopted to bring the documentation up-to-date?

2. Access to System Software Documentation:

☐ Describe how and where documentation of the functions of the system software, including system generation reports, suppliers' manuals, documentation of options selected, fixes applied, descriptions of security features, and documentation of system software designed or modified by the company, are held.

☐ Who is responsible for the custody and issue of system software documentation?

☐ Who is authorized to have access to the documentation?

3. Approval of System Software Enhancements:

☐ Describe the procedures for selecting new system software, evaluating the different options provided by the software, and designing the operating procedures for its use.

☐ How are necessary enhancements to existing system software identified?

☐ How are repairs to software (fixes) provided by the software supplier reviewed for applicability?

☐ Who has the authority to approve new system software, enhancements, and fixes in the following?

- Department(s) that will make use of the software (unless covered by computer operations below).
- Computer operations function.
- Quality assurance function.

- ☐ What documentation is presented to the above functions for approval?
- ☐ How are the approvals evidenced?
- ☐ How are the records of enhancements controlled to ensure that all required enhancements are made within the required time frame?

4. Review of Vendor-Supplied System Software Enhancements:

- ☐ What procedures are used to review or test enhancements and ensure that the enhancement does not affect other system software?
- ☐ Describe the involvement in system software review or testing of:
  - System programmer(s) who implemented the software enhancement.
  - Computer operations function.
  - Department(s) that will use the software (if not covered by computer operations above).
  - Quality assurance function.
  - Others (such as a separate review or testing group or the internal audit department).
- ☐ What documentation is produced in the process of supervising, reviewing, or testing the enhancement?
- ☐ What is the policy for the retention of testing documentation and test data files?
- ☐ When enhancements are made to system software (such as utilities, interrogation packages, sorts, or routines incorporated by the linkage editor) that are incorporated into applications, what procedures are used to ensure that the enhancements do not adversely affect the results produced by the application programs?
- ☐ Have all enhancements made during the current financial year been reviewed or tested in accordance with the installation standards?

5. Testing of System Software Designed or Modified by the Company:

- ☐ What procedures are used to test the system software and ensure that the enhancement does not affect other system software?
- ☐ Describe the involvement in system software testing of:
  - System programmer(s) who implemented the software enhancement.
  - Computer operations function.

- Department(s) that will use the software.
- Quality assurance function.
- Others (such as a separate review or testing group or the internal audit department).

☐ What documentation is produced in the process of testing the enhancements?

☐ What is the policy for the retention of testing documentation and test data files?

☐ When enhancements are made to system software (such as utilities, interrogation packages, sorts, or routines incorporated by the linkage editor) that are incorporated into applications, what procedures are used to ensure that the enhancements do not adversely affect the results produced by the application programs?

☐ Have all enhancements made during the current financial year been tested in accordance with the standards?

6. **Unauthorized Enhancements.** How are unauthorized amendments made to system software detected?

7. **Urgent Modifications:**

☐ Under what circumstances may urgent modifications, which bypass the normal procedures, be made to system software?

☐ Describe the procedures for making such modifications and recording their occurrence.

☐ What procedures are in force, either at the time the modification is made or at a subsequent time, to ensure that the modification is properly documented, reviewed or tested, and approved?

8. **Acceptance of System Software:**

☐ Who in the department(s) that will use the system software (usually the computer operations department in the case of system software) is responsible for giving the final approval to software enhancements for production use?

☐ How is this approval documented?

☐ Are there any software enhancements for which the users of the software are not required to give approval?

☐ When users give their approval, how do they ensure that:

- The methods and scope of the reviews or tests are adequate?

- The results of the reviews or tests are satisfactory?
- Instructions for using the software have been appropriately prepared or amended?

☐ How are users notified of the effective date when the system software enhancements are to become operational?

9. Final Review and Approval of System Software Enhancements by the Data Processing Function:

☐ Prior to implementation of a system software enhancement, who is responsible for checking that the following are complete, up-to-date, and in accordance with the installation standards?

- System software documentation.
- Job set-up and operating instructions.

☐ How is this check documented?

☐ In the case of vendor-supplied software enhancements:

- Who is responsible for checking that proper review or testing of the enhancement has taken place?
- How is this check documented?

☐ In the case of system software designed or modified by the company:

- Who is responsible for checking that testing has been properly carried out?
- How is this check documented?
- Who is responsible for checking that the department(s) that will make use of the software has approved it?
- How is this check documented?

REVIEWING QUALITY ASSURANCE—CHECKLIST

The following reviews a quality assurance (QA) function. When a separate review of the QA function is undertaken, the checklist can be completed for QA areas. QA can be included in an MIS review by making a separate entry when QA is involved in the activities.

1. Organization of the MIS Function:

☐ Which personnel are involved in QA?

☐ What personnel policies are in place for this function?

- ☐ Are there written installation standards?
- ☐ Are there contracts?

2. Implementation and Maintenance of Systems:

- ☐ Are system and program documentation subject to QA?
- ☐ Is approval of system specifications subject to QA?
- ☐ Does testing of new applications meet QA requirements?
- ☐ Is approval of modifications to production programs involved?
- ☐ Is there control of approved program modifications from a QA standpoint?
- ☐ Is there testing of program modifications to meet QA standards?
- ☐ Are urgent modifications subject to the same requirements?
- ☐ Is final approval of applications and program modifications by the MIS function involved?
- ☐ Does cataloging of approved new applications and program modifications fall under QA?

3. Job Set-Up, Scheduling, and Data Control. Is QA concerned with data control and job set-up instructions?

4. Computer Operations:

- ☐ Are operating instructions in conformance with QA standards?
- ☐ Does update of production program libraries fall under this area?

5. System Software Programming:

- ☐ Does system software documentation have to be submitted to QA?
- ☐ Is there QA approval of system software enhancements?
- ☐ Does control of approved system software enhancements include QA?
- ☐ Does review of vendor-supplied system software enhancements include QA?
- ☐ Is testing of system software designed or modified by the company subject to QA?
- ☐ Do urgent modifications have to meet the same QA standards?

- ☐ Does acceptance of system software come into this category?
- ☐ Does final approval of system software enhancements by the MIS function have to meet QA requirements?

REVIEWING TELECOMMUNICATIONS SUPPORT—CHECKLIST

1. **Implementation and Maintenance of Telecommunications Applications.** Telecommunications systems and applications should be subject to the same types of procedures for implementation and maintenance as are batch or other systems. Describe any differences in the authorization and control of program development and maintenance compared with the rest of the MIS department (see above). In particular, what are the procedures for the following?
   - ☐ Authorization of changes to the network or terminals.
   - ☐ Authorization of changes to telecommunications-related system software.
   - ☐ Authorization of changes to any password or security software.
   - ☐ Notification to users of any changes affecting their applications.
   - ☐ Describe how telecommunications-related application programs are tested and how test results are reviewed.
   - ☐ Describe any differences in the procedures for updating program libraries.
   - ☐ Are those application programs maintained on a separate program library?

2. **Applications:**
   - ☐ List and describe the use of the network for processing financial accounting applications. For each application, record the following:
     - Software used (such as CICS or Customer Information Control System).
     - Types of communication lines used (such as leased or dial-up).
     - Data base software used.
     - Numbers and type of terminals used (such as remote job entry or RJE).
     - Use made of terminals (such as for inquiry or input).
     - Location of the host computer.

- Whether any edits, conversions, or other processing is carried out at the terminal.

☐ List and describe the use of telecommunications for program development and maintenance. Note especially:

- Type of software used (such as TSO or Time-Sharing Option, CMS or Conversational Monitor System).
- Number and location of terminals used.

☐ Are there any master or administrative terminals that can modify controls or data that regular terminals cannot access?

☐ How is the use of the terminals controlled?

☐ Is there an approved schedule of transactions and applications that may use the system?

☐ Describe the procedures for ensuring that only authorized transactions and applications are processed.

3. Error Detection and Recovery Procedures:

☐ Describe the procedures for error detection and error recovery during transmissions to and from the host computer.

☐ How do the terminals and network account for all messages sent to and from the host computer?

☐ Does the network provide for a way to inform the terminal operator and/or the master terminal operator of possible lost messages?

☐ Do the terminals provide for a way to store messages from the terminal in the event of network or host computer failure?

☐ Is there a method of retransmitting these messages when the network is restarted?

☐ Is there a log of all messages sent to and from the terminals and the host computer?

☐ Are there adequate restart and recovery procedures in the event of the network or the host computer failure?

☐ Are the users notified of a network failure so they may re-enter any messages lost by the failure?

4. Use of Terminals:

☐ Are terminals and other communication equipment located in one area to prevent access by unauthorized individuals?

- ☐ Are terminals equipped with locks or other protective devices to prevent their use by unauthorized individuals?
- ☐ Are terminals equipped with multiple locks to control the transactions that may be authorized (such as master keys)?
- ☐ Describe the controls within the software that prevent unauthorized users from accessing the system.
- ☐ Are all terminals given a unique identification that is recognized by the system as the authorization for that terminal to access the network?
- ☐ Describe the procedures for setting or changing the definition of which terminals are authorized for use in each application. Where is that definition maintained? How is the definition protected against access by unauthorized persons?
- ☐ Are passwords or other authorization codes used to limit access to the system?
- ☐ Describe the procedures for adding, changing, and deleting passwords and/or other authorization codes enabling access to an application from a terminal.
- ☐ Where is the computer file of passwords maintained?
- ☐ How is the file protected?
- ☐ Is the password or other authorization code printed out or displayed when used?
- ☐ Who has access to the list of valid passwords?
- ☐ How often are passwords changed?
- ☐ Describe any special or additional passwords required for updating critical data elements or gaining access after normal business hours.
- ☐ How are passwords constructed?
- ☐ What controls exist within the software to prevent one authorized user from accessing the data files and programs of another authorized user?
- ☐ What action is taken when unauthorized users attempt to gain access to the system or when other violations are attempted/committed?
- ☐ Are terminals disabled if they are inactive for a predetermined period of time?
- ☐ Is the authority of the user periodically reverified?

☐ Where passwords are not used, describe the controls that:
- Restrict file access to authorized users, terminals, or jobs.
- Restrict users, terminals, or jobs to the functions they are authorized to perform.

☐ How is access to important files restricted during periods when they are not under the control of the terminal or security software?

☐ If dial-up lines are used:
- Are phone numbers changed periodically?
- Are phone numbers listed on the terminals?
- Are special "restricted" telephone numbers used to limit allowable terminal functions?
- Is "call back" used to verify origination of calls?

☐ In relation to programmer terminals:
- Can the terminals be used to obtain access to live programs or data files, either via interactive processing or by submission of batch jobs through the terminal?
- Describe the procedures used to prevent programmer terminals from accessing live programs or data files.

5. Logging and Review of Network Activities:

☐ Is all significant network activity recorded in a log?

☐ Are the following significant activities recorded?
- Successful and unsuccessful attempts to access the network.
- Disabling or disconnection of terminals.
- Reverification of user authorization.

☐ Is a responsible official, outside the MIS department, responsible for the security of the network?

☐ Does this official change passwords and other authorization codes periodically?

☐ Does the same official ensure that the list of valid passwords is protected from disclosure to unauthorized individuals?

☐ Does this official periodically review the log of network activity to ensure that:
- Unauthorized attempts to access the network are investigated?
- Successful attempts were by authorized users?
- Other unusual activity is properly investigated?

6. Distributed Processing:

☐ Obtain or prepare a description of the distributed processing network showing sites at which:

- Remote processing may be performed.
- Data files are maintained.

☐ Regarding each remote processing site and the central processing facility, obtain or prepare a list of:

- System software and application software in use at the site.
- Date files maintained and the transactions/applications processed.

☐ How does the system determine the site at which a particular transaction and/or application is to be processed?

☐ If data redundancy exists, how does the system or the user ensure that data is synchronized and reported only once in consolidated financial reports?

☐ In relation to processing carried out at remote sites, are application programs the same at each site?

- If so, describe the procedures to ensure that programs at different sites are and remain identical (such as distribution of load modules only or no remote compiler facilities).
- If not, describe the procedures to ensure that local programs interface properly with other processing sites in the network and operate in accordance with management's intentions.

☐ From an audit planning viewpoint, do either of the following require special arrangements?

- Ownership of remote processors by other than the organization.
- Location of any processing facilities across international boundaries.

REVIEWING DATA BASE ADMINISTRATION—CHECKLIST

1. Organization of the Data Base Function:

☐ Indicate which major computer-based applications use a data base system (such as IMS or Information Management System from IBM—examples here relate to IMS).

☐ Indicate the data base support products and packages in use.

☐ Include the particular features and adaptations in use of:

- Information Management System Virtual Storage (IMS/VS).
- Application Development Facility (IMS/ADF).
- Data dictionary facilities.
- Report generators and inquiry facilities.

☐ Describe the organization of the data base support function.

☐ Include organization chart, job descriptions, and the division of responsibilities.

☐ Show who is responsible for the following:
- Data base administration and control.
- Maintenance of the data base data dictionary.
- Maintenance of the data base system or IMS libraries.
- Maintenance of the data base or IMS systems.
- Coding of program specification blocks (PSBs) and data base definitions (DBDs).

☐ Indicate any differences in the personnel policies relating to the data base support function.

☐ Indicate the installation standards regarding data base administration and support.

☐ Indicate the specific backup and recovery procedures applied to the following:
- System libraries
- Data bases

2. Data Base Documentation:

☐ Does documentation exist in accordance with the installation standards for all data bases, components, generating (GEN) options, dictionaries, and other DBA and system support functions?

☐ Describe any IMS documentation aids or documentation software products in use.

☐ Indicate whether there are any differences in the procedures for controlling the access to this documentation.

3. Implementation and Maintenance of Data Base Applications. Describe the following:

☐ Any differences in the authorization and control of data base application program development and maintenance.

☐ The role of the data base support function in the maintenance of those applications.

☐ How the applications are tested, and how the results of the tests are reviewed.

☐ Any differences for updating these application program libraries.

☐ The data base generation (IMS GEN) options in use.

4. Controls:

☐ Describe the DBA's participation in the development of program specification blocks (PSBs) and data base definitions (DBDs) for data base (IMS) applications.

☐ Does the DBA approve all the processing options (PROCOPTs) for the various segments and fields within the data bases?

☐ When logical relationships are used, does the DBA explain to all affected user departments the effects of the various processing options (such as PROCOPTs) on the physical data involved in the logical relationship?

☐ Are separate production and test libraries maintained for DBD and PSB (and ACB or access method control block—when used) libraries?

☐ List the names of the libraries used for the following:

- PSB
- DBD
- ACB (when used)

☐ Who has access to the above libraries?

☐ Who has access to the data base system (IMS) macro library?

☐ Are application programmers permitted access only to the PSBs required for testing their programs?

☐ Are there adequate procedures to ensure that only authorized programs, with authorized PSBs, are used to access production data bases?

5. Cataloging:

☐ Describe the procedures for segregating PSBs and DBDs in a test status from those being used by production programs.

☐ Describe the procedures that ensure that:

- Correct PSBs and DBDs are transferred to production status.
- Unauthorized changes are not made to approved PSBs and DBDs between the time they are approved for implementation and the time they are placed in production libraries.

☐ Is a log maintained of all production PSBs and DBDs?

☐ Does this log include details about:
- Which data bases the PSBs use?
- Which program uses which PSBs?
- Program communications blocks (PCBs) contained in the PSB?
- PSB sensitivity to segments and fields in the data base?

☐ Are the PSB and DBD (and ACB when used) libraries periodically reviewed in order to ensure that no unauthorized changes have been made?

6. Standards:

☐ Describe the standards for the use of data language (DL/1) to access the data bases.

☐ Describe the procedures for handling the DL/1 status codes for application programs accessing the data bases.

7. Log:

☐ Are there any log records (IMS or SMF) maintained that record accesses to the data bases:
- By programs not executing under the control of the data base (IMS) system?
- By programs executing under the control of the data base (IMS) system?

☐ Are there procedures to prevent or detect unauthorized accesses to the data bases?

☐ Are the system logs (IMS or SMF) controlled to prevent unauthorized access?

8. Utilities:

☐ What records are kept on the use of utilities and other similar programs such as the following?
- DL/1 test program.
- Data base system file select and formatting programs.
- Data base system (IMS) reorganization/load utilities.

- Data base system (IMS) recovery utilities.
- System log recovery program.
- Data base mapping program.
- The program that builds DBDs (DBDGEN).

☐ What controls are in effect over the use of these utilities?

☐ Who must authorize such use?

☐ What procedures are in effect to ensure that only duly authorized use occurs?

9. Libraries:

☐ Who is authorized to access the data base system (IMS) production libraries and what level of access is permitted to the following?

- PSB library.
- DBD library.
- Data base (IMS) macro library.
- Data base system (IMS) library.

☐ What are the procedures for preventing unauthorized accesses to the above libraries?

☐ Are there control procedures to detect unauthorized access?

☐ When password protection is used to prevent unauthorized access to programs and data files:

- Describe the procedures adopted.
- Who is responsible for the establishing and distributing of passwords?
- How is password security maintained?
- Are passwords periodically changed and, if so, how often?

☐ Who supervises, reviews, and approves the above? How are the results of the reviews and approvals documented?

SUMMARY

The MIS function usually is a major cost center, with an effect on most operating groups and management areas of an organization. It is often possible to improve controls over MIS operations, important for the organization as a whole. Weak or improper controls over MIS can mean misapplication of financial, computer, human, and physical resources. An inadequate response by the MIS department to user needs is also possible. Using the information obtained from an MIS operational review, management can allocate and redirect resources to build on the strengths of its MIS operation, addressing control weaknesses and thereby helping the entire entity.

CHAPTER **5**

Computer Concepts

INPUT, OUTPUT, AND PROCESSING CONCEPTS

Data Flow and Processing Concepts

It is extremely helpful for an auditor to be able to identify the processing features that are common to computer systems and to define terms that are used frequently. When dealing with computer applications, one should be able to distinguish among:

- *Input*—The initial recording of a transaction and the subsequent activity until the transaction is written to a file in the computer.
- *Processing*—All the work carried on within the computer.
- *Output*—The printing, or presentation on a screen, of information processed by the computer.

Input

The flow of data can be divided into three stages:

1. Recording transactions.
2. Converting the data into input media.
3. Writing the input to a magnetic file.

Recording Transactions. In many cases, the methods of recording transactions are the same as in noncomputer systems. All the information for a transaction has to be obtained prior to the transaction being processed. For example, a customer purchase requires recording the transaction quantity, product number, description, price, customer name, date, and any terms. A computer can also be programmed to initiate or generate data for a transaction. This happens, for example, when a computer program reaches a condition that indicates it will call on another program to produce a report or other document.

There are a number of methods that can be used to convert data such as transactions into the form in which data is acceptable to the computer. In general use, those methods include the use of display screen terminals (cathode ray tubes—CRTs) and devices for entering data directly onto magnetic tape or disk. The latter are often arranged as a number of operator stations using terminals that are linked to a small computer. (See Figure 5-1.) The computer can be programmed to check the data to some extent before submission to the main computer. This can be a great advantage in detecting errors and identifying queries at an early stage. (See Figure 5-2 for a sample screen format for data entry through CRTs.)

FIG. 5-1

Simplified overview flowchart depicting basic configuration of a computer.

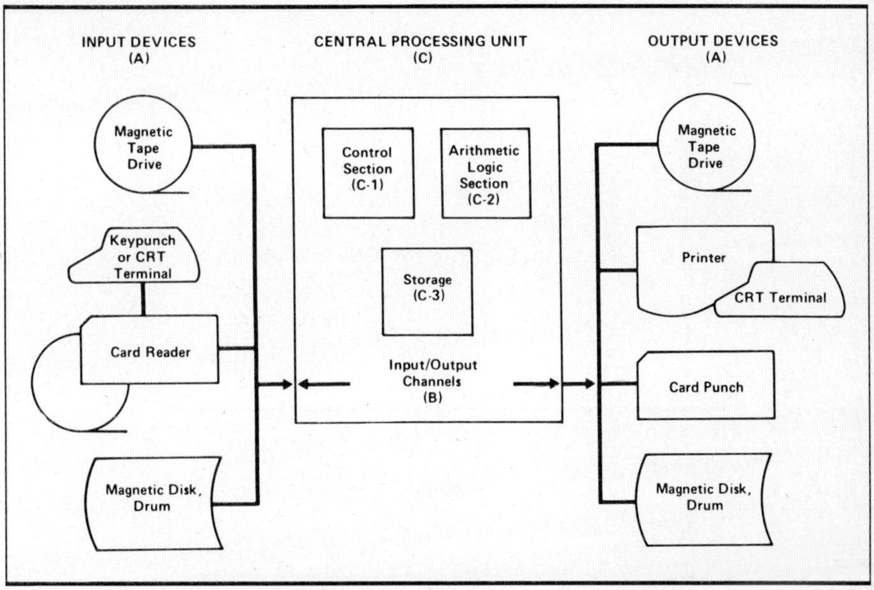

In older systems, punched cards were the prevalent input media. Some of these systems are still in use today.

Data Conversion for Input. A number of devices can be used to enter data by reading source documents. This avoids the manual keying or entry of information, which is the principal source of data error. Magnetic ink character readers (MICRs) read special characters preprinted or keyed into the document by a special machine. These characters can be seen along the bottom of checks, where the account and check number are preprinted to be read when the check is processed. These documents are also used as hard copies, so when prepared this way, they do not need to be rekeyed.

Optical character recognition (OCR) scanners read special characters preprinted or typed on documents. Examples are electric or telephone bills. Pre-printed documents are also called turnaround documents, since they can be sent back with payment and entered into the system. Optical scanning devices or optical mark readers (OMRs) read special marks preprinted on documents. The best known of these is seen in the common use of bar codes on grocery products.

Another input technology that is becoming commercially viable is image

FIG. 5-2

Typical display screen format for direct data entry (courtesy of International Business Machines Corporation).

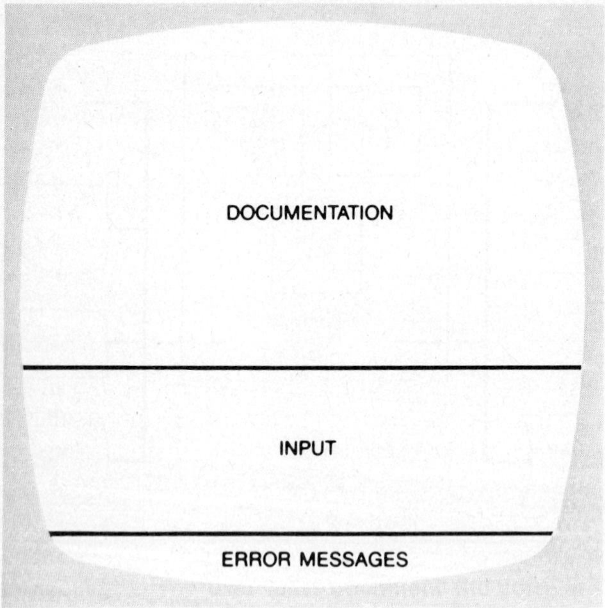

processing. In image processing, entire documents are scanned, converted into digital codes, and stored on computer media, normally on laser disks or high-density magnetic disks.

Input devices can be operated at a distance from the main computer using telecommunications. Telecommunications is the process of transmitting data over telephone lines or via microwaves. Data entered at a remote terminal is converted into a form suitable for transmission, transmitted, and then reconverted. (See Chapter 7, "Telecommunications," for more information on this process.)

Writing Input to a File. The third stage of flow of input data is writing input to a file. This occurs when the data—converted into some form of input medium—is presented to the computer, usually by an application program, together with appropriate internal instructions for creating or updating a file.

Processing

Processing includes all the functions performed within the computer. Although not all-inclusive, the following is a synposis of the significant processing stages.

Editing. Editing is system checking of data that has been entered. It usually consists of validity, accuracy, and reasonableness checks. These checks can include tests such as whether alpha or numeric data is required in a field, or whether a number is within a predefined range. Editing can also include matching input with data already on file. When terminals are used in an on-line processing system, editing functions usually are carried out at the time data is entered. (See Figure 5-3 for a sample screen used to enter data in an on-line system.)

Calculating. Calculating is the use of arithmetic computation on data, such as multiplying hours by rate to produce pay. Typically, the process consists of matching standing data, in this example, the wage rate that is stored on a master file, with transaction data (input and processed only once), here, the hours worked.

Summarizing. Summarizing is the process of accumulating all transactions (often after calculation, as explained previously) and generating a total. Using the previous example, the amount of the weekly payroll is the total.

Categorizing. Categorizing consists of analyzing and grouping individual components of a summarized total. For example, categorization would occur to analyze payroll expense by department. Categorizing is usually achieved by reference to a code included in the data input for each transaction.

Updating. Updating is the process of adding, changing, or deleting data in the system.

Initiating Transactions

Computer systems can be programmed to generate transactions and reports automatically. Computer initiation of transactions can be done in a number of ways, two of which are:

FIG. 5-3

Display screen for writing input to a file in an on-line environment (courtesy of International Business Machines Corporation).

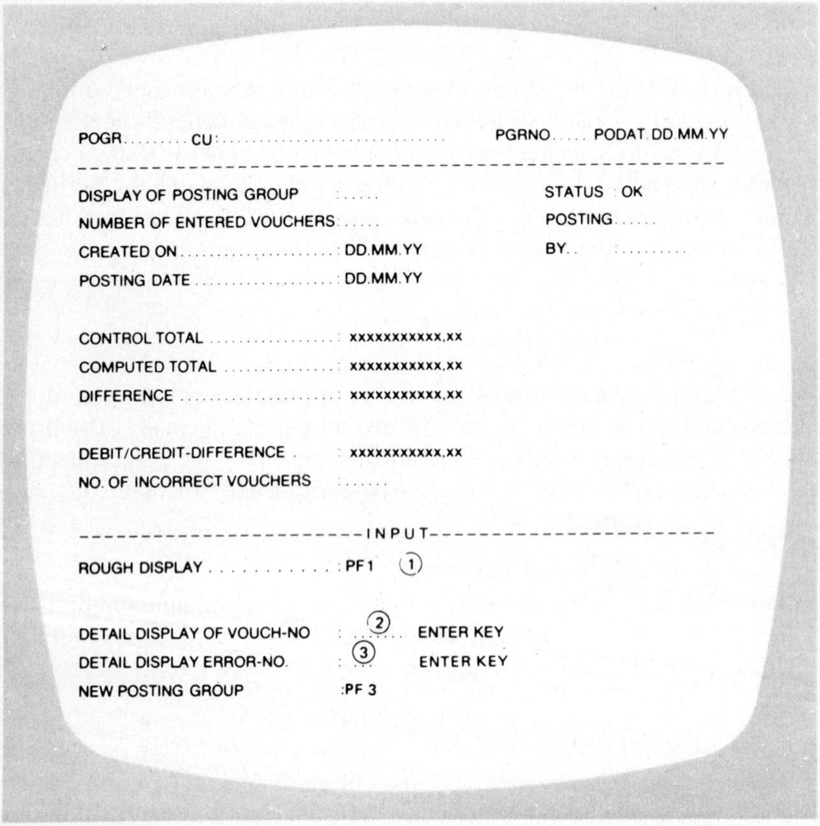

1. The processing of one transaction may trigger initiation of another transaction. This occurs, when, for example, the processing of a sales order that reduces inventory below the minimum triggers a replacement purchase order. In such cases, the trigger condition is recognized through a comparison with master file data. In this example, the trigger would be the predefined minimum stock level.

2. A request to initiate transactions may be input. For example, a requisition code to generate a parts listing can be input.

Files

Computer files are similar to the files in any manual system. Their organization can be compared to the folders in a well-organized cabinet. They can hold financial and reference data of importance to more than one processing run (such as sales and stock ledgers or price files). These are called master files. Suspense files are similar to suspense accounts in a manual system and normally hold only transaction data (such as outstanding orders or records of goods received). Records are individual groups of data, somewhat like a page in a manual file system. Individual items within the records are called fields or data elements.

Files are updated by adding, changing, or deleting data (e.g., in the case of accounts receivable, adding invoices and recording cash receipts to the open invoice file or deleting dormant customer accounts from the customer master file). The method of updating depends on the file organization. Tape files are updated by sequentially reading the old master file and the current transaction file to create a new master file (merging). Disk files can also be processed in this manner. However, direct access on an item-by-item basis, as in disks, is faster than reading the whole file, as is required in tape, when only the records affected by current transactions need changing.

Output

The most important output of a computer program is often the updated master file, which may or may not be printed out. Generally, information from the updated master file is printed only when it is requested or updated and may consist of listings, analyses, exception reports, or accounting documents, such as invoices and checks. Information for third parties is sometimes transferred directly to magnetic tape or disk (e.g., transfer of credit details from a bank to its customer, or sales statistics from branches to head office for consolidation). Output may also be displayed on a terminal screen.

COMPONENTS OF A COMPUTER SYSTEM

Computer system components are similar whether in microcomputers, minicomputers, or mainframe computers. Since microcomputers are familiar to so many, their components are described here to provide an example.

Central Processing Unit

The central processing unit (CPU) is the brain of any computer configuration. Within the processor, in addition to the input/output (I/O) control channels, the CPU is composed of three sections: (1) the control section, (2) the arithmetic-logic section, and (3) storage.

1. The control section directs all operations in the computer system, including:
   - Execution of program instructions in the proper sequence.
   - Transfer of data between storage and the arithmetic-logic section and between storage and I/O devices.
   - Control of I/O devices.
2. The arithmetic-logic section (also called the arithmetic logic unit or ALU) performs:
   - Mathematical operations, such as addition, subtraction, division, multiplication, rounding, and so forth. Essentially, the ALU does all of the operations by adding or subtracting the 0's and 1's of binary digits as many times as required to reach an answer. It can do thousands or millions of operations per second. Even for extremely large numbers, the answer is determined quickly.
   - Logical operations, such as comparisons and the resulting decisions about the appropriate sequence of operations.
3. Storage or memory is where the computer keeps the information it is going to use, the results of its work, and the programs that tell it what to do.

A microprocessor can be contained on a single integrated chip in the CPU of a microcomputer. To perform processing, systems software programs serve as "traffic controllers" to tell the computer what to do and when. (Ths is discussed in the later section "System Software and Operating Systems" in Chapter 27, "System Software.")

Internal Memory

A microprocessor has a limited number of places to store information at one time. To execute programs or process large amounts of data, the CPU must have a place to store instructions and data. Memory (also called internal storage, to distinguish it from external storage on a recording device) consists of microchips on an integrated circuit board or card that can store a certain number of bits, maintaining each bit as an electrical signal. The memory size is the number of uniquely addressable memory locations, and the unit of measurement is the byte (eight bits, or binary digits). Size is expressed in kilobytes or megabytes. A kilobyte is not 1,000 bytes but 1,024 (two to the 10th power), and a megabyte is 1,024,000 bytes.

The amount of memory available depends on the microcomputer's architecture: construction, interconnection, and organization of the internal circuitry. Microcomputers usually are classed according to their maximum addressable memory. Older microcomputers, such as the Apple II and CP/M machines, had eight-bit architectures; their maximum addressable memory was 64 kilobytes, although some "memory swapping" tricks allowed the illusion of 256 kilobytes or more. The first significant business computer, the IBM/PC, was a 16-bit computer limited by an eight-bit data path microprocessor. The effective result was that it had an addressable memory of one megabyte, which was further limited to 640 kilobytes by the software. More advanced 16-bit machines, such as the PC/AT, have 16-megabyte memories. The recently released 32-bit machines also operate with up to 16 megabytes, although their theoretical memory sizes exceed one gigabyte (1,024,000,000 bytes).

Basically, all internal memory is random access, which means that any bit usually can be addressed in the same amount of time, no matter where it is located physically in the memory. There are three classes of internal storage:

1. Random access memory (RAM) is read/write memory. RAM can have data stored in it and extracted from it; data can be written to and read from it. RAM contents are altered as new data is stored, overwriting what was there. RAM is usually volatile. It loses its contents when the power to the processor is shut off. Some computers have batteries to maintain the contents.

2. Read-only memory (ROM) can have its contents read, but data can only be written to it once by the manufacturer (or later "burned in" using a special ROM-writing device). Once data is stored in ROM, it is permanent. ROM is nonvolatile. When the power is off, its contents remain intact (although it can possibly be affected by power surges and electromagnetic interference). ROM often gives the CPU initial start-up, to hold a specific computer language or to store frequently used routines. In some lap-top and portable computers, whole application programs (such as LOTUS 1-2-3) can exist in the computer's ROM.

3. Virtual memory is a common memory type on mainframes and larger minicomputers. As microcomputers grow in speed, power, and sophistication (see Chapter 6, "Computers"), it can be expected that virtual memory will become available in desktop machines. Virtual memory is a software and hardware method that gives the illusion of greater addressable memory by swapping data to and from the storage devices.

External Storage. The internal memory of a computer is limited and relatively expensive. To store large quantities of data, external storage is required, such as the following:

- Magnetic tape drives are used in minicomputers and mainframes (and with increasing frequency in microcomputers) to store large amounts of data inexpensively. All tape drives have sequential access, which means the machine must search through the entire sequence of data on the tape to find the data requested. Today, tape drives are more commonly used to back up the fixed disk drives.
- Until recently, floppy disk drives were the most popular storage medium for microcomputers. They come in a variety of sizes—8 inches (known as floppy disks), 5¼ inches (the most common size), and the newer 3½ inches and 3 inches. They may be single, double, or quad-density, and single- or double-sided. Floppy disks store data in direct access format; the machine goes directly to the location of the requested data. Although floppy disks are much faster than tape drives for securing information, they are not as fast as fixed disk drives.
- Fixed disks have much greater capacity than floppy disks. Although most business microcomputers have 20-megabyte or 40-megabyte fixed disk drives, the major limitation on the size of a fixed drive is in the operating system.
- New storage technologies are becoming available for microcomputers. Removable cartridge drives combine the convenience of a floppy disk with the storage and speed of a fixed disk. CD-ROM drives offer high capacity and read-only capabilities based on laser technology. The WORM drive allows writing once to the disk, but is not erasable. Erasable CD-ROM drives are becoming available. The greatest problem of CD-ROMs now, however, is their speed. Although faster than a floppy disk, they cannot match most fixed disks.

Keyboards

Usually, there is a keyboard to enter data into the system. Most keyboards have keys similar to a typewriter; some have additional numeric keypads like an adding machine. Programmable function keys are found on many keyboards and simplify using menu-driven software. Key touch and arrangement varies.

Monitors

The monitor, which is similar to a television screen, displays the data typed in and the computer's output. The quality of the image depends on the resolution, or number of pixels or tiny dots that create the images on the monitor screen. The monitor can display different numbers of characters in columns across the screen (e.g., 80 characters equals a normal business letter width of 8½ inches). The display monitor can be one color (monochrome), but a black background with green characters is thought to be easiest to read. Black and white or sometimes amber on black are also used. Color monitors for graphics are available, which look even more like a television screen.

To indicate where data will be entered, the screen displays a cursor, usually a rectangle or an underline that blinks on and off. As data is entered, the character is displayed at the cursor position, which moves with the entry.

Terminals

Terminals are used when several users share a microcomputer or for access to the systems of minicomputers or mainframe computers.

Terminals are differentiated in terms of their "intelligence." Intelligence in a terminal allows changes to be made in the data that was keyed in before sending it to the processor. These facilities are called editing functions, such as tabulation, clearing or erasing the screen, deleting a line or character, or inserting a line or character.

"Dumb" terminals use conversational operation, where data travels from the terminal to the processor one character at a time. Editing functions may be limited.

"Smart" terminals use message operation, where data generally travels to the processor one line at a time. Smart terminals have a full complement of editing functions, located on separate keys, that allow cursor control functions (arrow keys) to move the cursor up and down, left and right, and HOME (the top lefthand corner of the screen). Smart terminals may have several visual attributes, such as inverse video (the color of the characters can be reversed with the color of the background), highlighting (designating portions of the screen in different intensities of light), and scrolling (the ability to move the display up or down, and sometimes left or right).

"Intelligent" terminals, which have a built-in microprocessor, use page operation, where data generally is transmitted to the processor a screenful or page at a time. They may include graphics, which enable simple block or line drawings to be produced; special character sets, such as mathematical symbols or foreign alphabets; protected fields or the facility to "freeze" a given area of the screen so that no changes can be made to the data in that area; built-in memory, which provides storage of data before transmission to the processor; and soft keys, also known as user-definable keys or function keys (often labeled F0, F1, F2, and so on), which can be assigned a particular task or sequence of other keystrokes. For example, using a soft key, the steps needed to request that a program be loaded can be activated using one keystroke.

Peripherals

For actual use, a processor must be connected to peripherals, which are the I/O devices (such as magnetic tapes, disks, diskettes, and printers) that provide the means of getting data into the processor and also for seeing or recording the results of processing.

Interfaces. The connection or channel between a processor and a peripheral is called an interface, which takes binary data from the processor and arranges it for the peripheral device to accept and act on, and vice versa. Interfaces may sometimes be built into the processor itself; if not, they are usually available in the form of a small printed-circuit board or card that plugs into the processor and is connected to the peripheral via a cable. Interfaces have been standardized to a large extent, so that various types of equipment from different manufacturers can be used together. These standards govern the way the data is transmitted and received, the signal types and levels, and the way sockets, plugs, and wires are interconnected. Each standard is known by the name of the governing body that set the standard and by a number, such as EIA RS232 (Electronics Institute of America) and IEEE 488 (Institute of Electrical and Electronic Engineers).

Some peripherals also have a built-in buffer or a temporary storage area for data. It is used to hold data passed between the processor and other devices, such as a printer, which operate at much slower speeds. The buffer compensates for a difference in the rate of data flow.

There are two widely used interfaces: serial and parallel. Serial interfaces like the RS232, allow data to flow along a wire as a sequence of bits, one after the other. Parallel interfaces, like the IEEE 488, enable data to flow along several wires, with bits parallel to each other, at the same time. The channel path along which the data flows from one or more sources to one or more destinations is referred to as a "bus," which is a circuit of parallel wires. A computer with one of the common bus standards has more growth potential than one without. Additional peripherals with the appropriate interfaces can enhance the computer's abilities. Each interface requires a port or an entrance and exit for data from the processor. The more ports a processor has (determined by the bus structure) the more peripherals that can be connected to it.

Emulators. Some peripherals have built-in emulators, which eliminate the need to obtain a separate attachment. Emulators are, in effect, translators that convert data presentation as defined by one of the international standards such as Extended Binary Coded Decimal Interchange Code (EBCDIC) or American Standard Code for Information Interchange (ASCII) into the presentation of a specific manufacturer, or vice versa, so that the peripheral imitates and behaves like another peripheral from a different manufacturer.

Printers. The peripherals that are used most often include a printer that produces hard copy output similar to that produced by a typewriter.

Some points about printers are:

- Dot matrix printers create characters that are composed of many dots produced by a printing head made up of a number of pins that strike the paper independently. Dot matrix printers are called utility printers, since they are used to produce documents that do not need a finished appearance. Some may emulate the finished appearance of more expensive printers by a larger number of pins in the printing head (24 pins can produce a near letter-quality appearance) or by a double pass of the printing head.
- Laser printers produce a high-density dot matrix output that closely resembles expensive professional typesetting. Laser printers usually print at up to 300 dots per inch (dpi), which is about twice as dense as a dot matrix printer, although only about one fourth the density of professional typesetting. Lasers are now becoming available in 400- and 600-dpi capabilities.
- Letter-quality printers use typing elements, such as daisy wheels, thimbles, or balls. They are expensive, rather hard to maintain, and gradually being replaced by laser printers.
- Plotters are graphics output devices used to print charts and graphics. They are available in a wide range of prices and styles and must be compatible with systems and applications software.

SOFTWARE

Software allows a computer to perform work. The term "software" applies to all programs used as instructions for the operation of general and specific tasks and applications performed by the computer. Three types of software perform the overall programming functions that are needed for the operation of a computer system: (1) system software, (2) utility software, and (3) applications software.

The availability of inexpensive, high-quality software that is designed to handle most standard business applications has contributed to the rapid growth in the use of microcomputers. However, software that works on one machine does not always work on another. When implementing a system, it may be advisable first to choose the software that meets application needs and then choose the hardware that is compatible with that software.

SYSTEM SOFTWARE AND OPERATING SYSTEMS

Each CPU uses a certain operating system that is part of the system software. System software works with the computer, not the user: It controls and coordinates the running of the computer and its many functions. The operating system is the most important component of this software category. It is a set of programs, usually written in machine code or assembly language, that acts as an intermediary between the user, the processor, and the applications software. The operating system informs the user of any errors that occur with the processor, I/O devices, or programs. It also provides a repertoire of simple commands for otherwise complicated functions. The operating system (or portions of it) may come installed in ROM and is, therefore, permanently stored. This software, unalterable by the user, is often referred to as "firmware." In microcomputers there is more user interaction with the system software than in larger computers, where system software is usually "off limits" to all but the MIS personnel who run the system. (System software for mainframes is discussed in Chapter 27.)

Operating Systems

Most business microcomputers use a disk operating system based on Microsoft's Disk Operating System (MS-DOS, also known as PC-DOS when used on IBM machines). DOS is responsible for reading and writing data from and to the disk; it tells the disk drive's read/write head to move to the appropriate track/sector on the disk and reports any errors that may occur during access. DOS is also responsible for program and file management. It creates files on the disk by allocating space, giving file names, erasing or deleting files from the disk, and keeping a directory, or catalog, of the disk's contents (the File Allocation Table, or FAT). To find a file on the disk, DOS checks the directory in the same way a person would check the index of a book. The DOS also initiates and formats the disks and moves programs into memory so that they can be used.

Besides MS-DOS, other popular business operating systems are OS/2 and UNIX. A program written on one computer can usually be used on or adapted for use on another, provided that both use the same version of the same operating system and the same disk format.

Utility Programs

Another type of system software is the utility program. Utility programs are used for maintenance and other functions only when needed and may not be an integral part of the operating system. Two common utilities are the copy program (which is used to make duplicate copies of disks for backup purposes) and the sort program (which uses a key or a field within a record to sequence the contents of a file, e.g., putting names in alphabetical order).

Application Software

The most critical type of software for the accounting profession, as with any highly specialized profession, is the application software. There are two types of application software:

1. Generic programs
2. Application packages

Generic programs perform general tasks, such as data base management (organizing, searching, and retrieving records), word processing (preparing text), and electronic spreadsheets and graphics. Application packages, on the other hand, perform specific functions, such as general ledger, payroll, and inventory management.

Software Packages

Application software is often called packaged software, providing the computer user with prewritten programs for generic or specific applications. Each package comes with software and instruction manuals, which are designed to help users work with and tailor the package to particular system needs. Many software vendors provide implementation assistance along with their package sales. Among the most widely used software packages are accounting applications, word processing, data base management and other file and data storage and manipulation packages, graphics packages, and programs for preparing spreadsheets and spreadsheet analysis.

As the variety of potential uses of application software grows, the number of vendors increases dramatically. Once software is selected and purchased for use in a business application, the data contained within the system that uses it becomes a reflection of the organization. It is important to ensure that it be treated like any asset purchase, suited to organizational needs as specifically and accurately as possible. (See Part III, "Information Systems," for discussions of major applications.)

COMPUTER SHARING AND PUBLIC DATA BASES

Service Bureaus

The most widely used computer-sharing arrangement is the service bureau, which usually has one or more large computers and its own programming and operations staff. A computer user who cannot justify the expense of an in-house computer, or who needs additional capacity, can go to a service bureau and buy the use of the computer and the assistance of bureau support staff for operations. Service bureaus frequently make the same programming services available as do software vendors, tailoring applications software packages to the specific needs of the customer.

One such specialized service provides a specific application, namely payroll processing. When a business subscribes to such a service, its data processing for payroll can be maintained externally. This is helpful, since payroll applications always require annual maintenance, or updating, to keep abreast of changes in the tax laws. This kind of service provides an additional level of security by removing the payroll functions from the MIS department. When an application with such potential for abuse is physically removed from an organization's general user computer, there is far less opportunity for unauthorized access from within. Naturally, there is a need to ensure the safety and integrity of data at the service bureau itself. To this end, a third-party review of the processing services can be done. (For further discussion of third-party reviews, see Chapter 25, "Implementation Reviews.")

Public Data Bases

There is an ever-growing number of public data bases accessible to users via telephone and modem or, soon, through cable or satellite distribution. These include videotex, an interactive information service that provides transaction services as well (e.g., banking and shopping), and information-only services, which may have abstracts or full text of newspapers, magazines, and books, or other business information, such as stock prices.

SOFTWARE PROGRAM DEVELOPMENT

The steps involved in developing the software instructions or programs are:

- *Request for system design*—Analysis and possible solution of situations that the system program will address.

- *Detailed system specifications*—Written requirements in detail.
- *Program development*—Using computer language to express program instructions and source program logic. High-level languages like COBOL or Common Business Oriented Language and FORTRAN or FORmula TRANslation are frequently used and require subsequent conversion to machine-readable form.
- *Testing*—Running the program with test data to compare output results with predetermined results. This allows verification of the proper operation of the program and correction of any errors found as a result of this procedure.
- *Storing the program*—Maintaining the final authorized version of the program for production.

Only those steps that relate to the execution of a program are discussed here. (See Chapter 22, "System Development Trends and Practices" and Chapter 23, "System Development Methodology and Auditing" for detailed discussion of the creation of programs.)

Preparing the Program for Processing

To code a program, it must be entered in a form, or language, the computer can read. The program is usually printed out to make human interpretation and handling possible.

A set of instructions written in a high-level language comprises what is referred to as a source language program. In a business-oriented environment, COBOL is the usual source language used. FORTRAN, RPG II (report program generator), and PL/1 (a programming language developed by IBM), among others, are also used. Other forms of programming include BAL (Basic Assembler Language), ADA, decision support or expert systems languages, such as LISP and PROLOG, and data base languages, such as those used by FOCUS and ORACLE.

Compilers

Compilers are actually language translator programs because they translate a source language program into an object language program meaningful to the computer. Separate compilers are used for each source language. In mainframes, compilers are part of the system software.

The compiler edits the source program for syntax errors, which are any errors in spelling, errors in sequencing the commands that tell the computer what to do, or errors in applying the rules of the language.

FIG. 5-4
Language flow using a compiler.

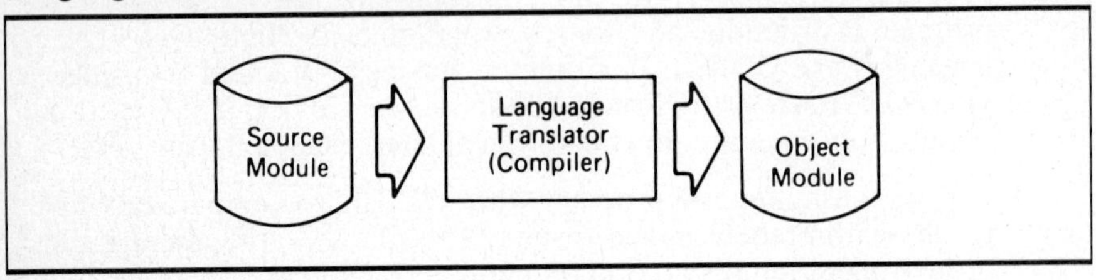

Some of the basic rules or syntax for using the languages are the following:

- All data fields must be defined.
- Only valid commands can be used.
- Correct format and sequence of instructions must be followed.
- Spelling of data fields must be consistent in all instructions.

Once the compiler has made sure that there are no syntax errors, it converts the source program to an object program. This is accomplished by translating the high-level statements into the bits of machine code. Then the program is in machine language that the computer can understand. (See Figure 5-4.) For microcomputers, programs normally come compiled, ready-to-run, and only development environments will acquire compilers for PCs.

Source Statement Conversion

MACRO commands can also be included in programs. They are then included in the machine-language instructions. A MACRO is a stored, single word or mnemonic instruction that refers to a previously written set of instructions for frequently used operations. The compiler converts all the required source statements into machine-language instructions. This means that the compiler can convert either single-source statements or MACRO-source statements. DIVIDE is one example of a MACRO command; in machine or assembly language, division is carried out by repetitive subtraction, using a number of commands. MACRO commands make it possible to use such commonly required functions without having to write their steps into a program each time they are needed, since the system stores the relevant steps for each MACRO and the compiler inserts those steps where indicated.

To perform the conversion of source statements to machine-readable language, the compiler also carries out two related functions:

1. The compiler assigns a storage location (address) to each of the commands in the program so that when the program runs, the commands and data items will be available in the specified location.
2. The compiler assigns a storage location (address) to each data name created in the program. Collectively, this is known as a name table and is referred to throughout the processing of the program.

Testing

After the program has been written, syntax errors have been corrected, and the program has been compiled, it should be tested. Sometimes the results of the test data have been predetermined manually. If the processing results in different output, the programmer must investigate to discover the cause of each error and make any necessary corrections. This process is sometimes called debugging. There are programming aids that can be used, but often the programmer must make a painstaking search for such logic errors.

Storing the Program

After the program has been tested and all errors are corrected, it must be stored in machine-readable form for future use.

The computer stores the program in the medium specified by the user, depending on the system's I/O devices. Generally, the user retains three copies of each program as follows:

1. A working copy on magnetic tape or disk, from which it can be loaded or executed.
2. Additional copies of the source and object language programs on tape or disk, kept in case of problems with the working copy; also used to make subsequent changes to the programs.
3. A printed copy, or print image, of the source program for future reference, or as an aid in planning later revisions.

Loading and Running the Program

Before a computer can use a program, it must be entered into the storage area of the CPU. As part of the compilation process, each command is assigned to a specific location or address in a specific part of the storage area.

To start, the address of the first command is entered into the control section. After the CPU is instructed to process the program, the first command is executed and the address of the second command is entered into the control section. When the first command has been executed fully, the second command is performed and the address of the third command enters the control section. This process, which is handled automatically by software, is repeated until all steps have been carried out for all data involved. Production programs are run repeatedly to process the organization's data.

CONTROL PROCEDURES

A computer system cannot be effective unless there are adequate application control procedures, designed to ensure the accuracy, completeness, and validity of information stored in the system. Information technologyy (IT) controls help ensure the security and integrity of the system and its operation. Controls should prevent, detect, and help investigate errors and unusual situations. The auditor should be able to understand and test the controls, often making use of the "management trail" or "information trail" (also known as the audit trail).

Many computer systems are adequately controlled without detailed listings of transactions, and instead provide totals and analyses. The ability to trace individual items through the system is provided by the audit trail, which retains information about how transactions were processed.

Exception reports are widely used and provide information on unusual transactions, or on those that were not processed, to allow for investigation and follow-up on those items. For example, an exception report for a wire funds transfer system may be designed to report all transactions over $25 million for examination. Obviously, this would not report a transaction for a $10 million transfer that might, in fact, merit closer scrutiny. The programmed procedures and criteria used for such exception reports must be evaluated carefully to make sure that the appropriate levels of exceptions are being reported. Responsible management at a high level should be involved in setting criteria for reporting.

Loss of Audit Trail

In computer systems, data is usually stored only as long as it is in use, for backup and recovery, or to meet regulatory requirements. The problems of destruction of data may be compounded by a lack of visible evidence, sometimes referred to as the "loss of audit trail." In this context, the audit trail implies the existence of information at every stage of the processing cycle that can be used to check on the operations carried out. However, the term audit trail also refers to visible evidence (as when every programmed operation on every transaction is recorded on a computer report). It may also refer to systems designed in such a way that the auditor can use conventional audit tests. For those reasons, the term "loss of audit trail" is often replaced with "loss of visible evidence" when discussing computerized operations.

SUMMARY

Understanding basic computer concepts is necessary to use and incorporate computer technology into the auditor's professional operations. This technology is changing rapidly. To keep up with a constantly evolving field, it is a good idea to discuss with MIS personnel how they are adapting to changing needs. Have they installed the latest computers, and what is their experience with them? Are they experimenting with new equipment and systems? Have they gotten any reaction and feedback from users of new software or hardware? The hardware and software aspects of microcomputers, workstations, minicomputers, and mainframes are discussed in greater detail in Chapter 6.

CHAPTER **6**

Computers

INTRODUCTION

The division of computers into three system classes—mainframe, minicomputer, and microcomputer—still retains some validity, although the lines have blurred as the power of small systems has increased dramatically. Descriptions of the differences may also not apply in all cases. Some problems are so complex that one program can use the resources of a mainframe supercomputer completely for a period. Minicomputers can serve as many as 300 users at one time. The power of top-of-the-line 32-bit microcomputers rivals that of current mainframes for certain applications, and certainly surpasses that of earlier ones.

Despite the difficulties in making distinctions, a general classification into big (mainframe), medium (minicomputer), and small (microcomputer) is useful. It shows some descending level of complexity in the environment faced by the auditor, as well as an ascending level of responsibility. Mainframes are among the most complex machines and can pose a challenge to an auditor. At the same time, auditors can rely on technical support staffs and many years of experience in dealing with those machines. Minicomputers are less daunting, but these facilities have fewer on-site support staff and less sophisticated controls. Although most auditors are acquainted and comfortable with microcomputers, their experience with microcomputer-based accounting systems may be recent. Often those systems have only limited controls. Auditors are dealing with small systems in increasing numbers. This chapter describes hardware and software aspects of computers, with most attention on minicomputers and microcomputers; mainframe concerns are addressed throughout this book.

MAINFRAME SYSTEMS

Computer development was pioneered by manufacturers whose original directions were in the scientific and educational fields. In essence, original computers were huge calculating engines. Today, these machines are smaller in size and relative price, while growing exponentially in power.

The term "mainframe" refers to both the central processing unit (CPU) of a large computer (peripheral or remote devices are classified separately) and to the large traditional computer that is used for commercial or scientific processing. In general, the addressable memory capacity and physical dimensions of a mainframe computer are likely to be much larger than those of minicomputers and microcomputers. Organizations with huge processing needs maintain their own mainframe operations. Mainframe computers may be used by several organizations through cost-sharing systems, which access and use the capacities and power of one mainframe. Service bureaus, which do processing for others, usually employ mainframes for their processing.

Mainframe computers continue to have the greatest variety of system software. They have been used by organizations for several decades now, so that traditional systems of control, often based in large part on that variety of system software, normally exist. Although those controls can be complex, many auditors are comfortable in the mainframe environment because it is known and often well-controlled by the organization.

Hardware Characteristics

In the 1950s, mainframes were first used for business processing of data. They occupied entire rooms with special environmental requirements. They also required a large technical support staff. Although current mainframes may not be as large physically as their predecessors, they still can be distinguished from other computers by their special needs and supporting staff requirements.

Central Processing Unit. The CPU is the brain of the computer configuration. Usually, it is housed in its own physical unit. The main system unit ranges in size from that of a refrigerator to several thousand cubic feet. As with any computer, the CPU has three sections: the control section, the arithmetic-logic section, and internal storage.

Control section—The control section of the CPU directs all operations in the computer system, including:

- Execution of program instructions in the proper sequence.
- Transfer of data between storage and the arithmetic-logic section and between storage and input/output devices.
- Control of I/O devices.

Usually, a mainframe's control section is vastly more sophisticated than a minicomputer's or microcomputer's. As a rule, mainframes execute faster and can control more I/O devices and data access paths.

Arithmetic-logic section—The arithmetic-logic section (also called the arithmetic logic unit or ALU) is the actual computer within the computer. It performs mathematical operations, such as addition, subtraction, division, multiplication, and rounding. Essentially, the ALU operates by adding or subtracting the binary digits 0's and 1's as many times as required to reach an answer. A mainframe's ALU includes special coprocessing devices for floating point arithmetic. These auxiliary processors are also available in minicomputers and as add-on devices in microcomputers. Modern mainframes have at least 32-bit addressing space in their machine logic (although some 24-bit IBM 360s and 370s are still in use). Currently, mainframes are the only computers able to address 64-bits. Some supercomputers now in development have theoretical addressing spaces of 128 bits; however, at this time such processing power would only have theoretical applications.

Internal storage—Internal storage or memory is where the computer stores its information, saves the results of its work, and keeps programs. Usually, mainframes require at least 16 megabytes of memory, although older machines with one megabyte still exist, and newer machines with 256 megabytes or more are available.

Mainframes have another significant advantage over minicomputers and microcomputers: The high speed of the processors and the I/O devices allow a mainframe to create "virtual memory" where data is passed back and forth between external storage and internal storage so rapidly that the computer can treat the data as if it were all in internal storage.

Input/Output. A major distinction between mainframes and smaller computers is their capacity to support I/O devices. Mainframes have the processing power to drive many peripherals. For example, an airline reservation mainframe system supports thousands of terminals around the country simultaneously.

Mainframes can manage a variety of external storage devices. Because mainframes are often used as central depositories of data for business, storage capacity requirements are high. Laser and magnetic disks with capacities in excess of 4 gigabytes (400 million words) are now available. Seemingly unlimited amounts of data can be kept off-line on tape drives.

Environmental and Personnel Considerations. Although not as temperamental as their predecessors, today's mainframes still have special requirements. Except for a few machines on the minicomputer borderline, mainframes continue to require customized physical conditions. The machines operate best in a controlled climate and are kept in specially prepared, climate-controlled rooms, with guards against smoke and static electricity. Special power lines and uninterrupted power supplies are also necessary.

Mainframes also require an extensive technical and other support staff. Because they are such complex mechanical and electronic engines, they have continual maintenance requirements. Most mainframe systems require an on-site or on-call system operator. Scheduling, administrating, and programming a mainframe requires several staff people. There are few systems without at least one full-time "keeper," and some systems involve hundreds of staff members. There are also numerous technical software people who support the data base management system, the telecommunications network, security administration, and so forth.

MINICOMPUTER SYSTEMS

Auditors need to understand how data is processed in any computerized information system. Organizations handle different systems differently; the size of the system can affect the auditor's concerns. The growing use of minicomputers makes it particularly important for auditors to know more about these small but powerful machines.

Beginning in the 1960s, companies such as DEC (Digital Equipment Corp.), Data General, and Hewlett-Packard developed a range of processors, lower in cost than those used in mainframes. These machines were geared to multiple users working via terminals that were simple to operate and required few, if any, special environmental conditions. They were refrigerator-size and were called minicomputers, to distinguish them from the room-filling mainframes. Their value in commercial data processing soon became apparent, and the early experimental models were quickly repackaged for business use.

Minicomputers usually are designed to offer:

- Simplicity in system development and operation.
- Direct entry and checking of data, immediate update of files, and easy inquiries of files.
- Operation in an office with user staff entering data and controlling operations, rather than special computer operations staff.
- Ability to form part of a computer network that communicates with remote terminals and a large central, or other, computer.

Hardware Characteristics

A popular minicomputer, for example, the IBM System 36, in its smallest configuration is indistinguishable in many respects from a microcomputer with a hard disk, such as an IBM PC/AT. At the other extreme, an IBM System 9370 may run in a normal office environment (no special air conditioning or raised floors as are needed for a large mainframe), but still uses a mainframe operating system.

Main System Unit. The main system unit of a minicomputer usually includes the CPU, disk storage, system console with keyboard and display, and sometimes an auxiliary storage device, such as a diskette or tape drive. Main memory can range from 256 kilobytes to 256 megabytes, although 32 megabytes is typical. The addressing space in the machine logic is from 16 to 48 bits; this should increase to 64 bits in the near future. This can be compared to the earlier IBM 369 and 370 mainframes' 24-bit limitation and the current microcomputer limitation of 32 bits.

Disk storage can go as high as 20 gigabytes. This upper end is available on the new large IBM AS/400 models.

Input/Output. A minicomputer can support anywhere from two to several hundred terminals, depending on the system. These can be attached locally and via communications lines. Peripheral tape and disk drives can be acquired to supplement the storage devices that come with the main system unit.

Environmental Considerations. Minicomputers are designed to operate in a normal office environment. For example, an IBM System 38 can tolerate temperatures between 12 and 38 degrees celsius and relative humidity between 10 and 90 percent. However, a computer system may provide unpredictable results if the climate varies too much or remains at an extreme for too long.

Software Characteristics

The operating system software for minicomputers is powerful. This software promotes a user-friendly environment and almost eliminates the need for large in-house technical support staff. In addition, the operating software itself may contain features that would be available only from separate packages on a microcomputer or mainframe.

Here are some features of operating system software on the new IBM AS/400:

- *Menu-driven screens.* The operating system includes standard, easy-to-use menus and can design custom menus (e.g., the Screen Design Aid).
- *Programming support tools.* These help create and modify source programs (e.g., the Source Entry Utility).
- *Interrogation.* Operating software can print data file information, make selections, and perform simple calculations (e.g., the Query Utility).

- *Data manipulation*. These utilities can create or modify data files (e.g., the Data File Utility).
- *Data base functions*. Built-in data base capabilities.

Physical and Logical Files. The AS/400 stores data in physical files. These are flat files with only one record format or layout per file. Physical files can be accessed by application programs.

To achieve greater data independence, logical files can be used. Logical files are built over one or more physical files and can contain more than one record layout. Logical files can also be a subset of a physical file or can combine fields from several physical files.

Within applications, files can be described externally. External files are described to the system using Data Description Specifications (DDSs). These specify file name, type of file, field description, record format names, physical files used (for logical files), key fields, and logical files. The DDSs are input as source statements and compiled into objects.

Security Software. At a minimum, minicomputer operating software should require users to log onto the system with a user identification code (user ID) and a password that is not displayed on the screen when entered. Sometimes these features are activated only when management selects the appropriate system options.

Beyond simple password protections, each minicomputer brand offers different security levels and subsystems. In the IBM AS/400, available security options include:

- Individual users or groups of users can be granted authority to perform special functions, such as access to all system resources, save and restore files, etc.
- Users can be routed to initial menus and programs, and their abilities can be restricted to those available on the menus.
- Access to system resources (also known as objects—data files, libraries, terminals, and so forth) can be granted restrictively to users.

In some cases, third-party application packages have additional security features, and companies will attempt to limit users to the menus provided within the packages. Note, however, that although menu security may limit applications users' abilities, it is not foolproof. Also, it rarely restricts the access of MIS department users or other sophisticated personnel.

Application Software. Application software performs the specific tasks of a functional area, such as general ledger, payroll, and inventory management.

Some companies that process with minicomputers have their own staff of programmers to develop applications programs. In many smaller companies, where a single minicomputer is used for all company processing and there is no in-house programming staff, packaged software is used for applications.

Packaged software provides the computer user with programs for generic or specific applications. The package comes with software and instruction manuals, which are designed to help users work with and tailor the package to particular system needs. Many software vendors provide implementation assistance along with the package sale.

Once software is selected and purchased for use in a business application, the data contained within the system that uses it becomes a reflection of the organization. It is important to ensure that it be treated like any asset purchase, suited as specifically and accurately as possible to organizational needs.

Using the Minicomputer

There is no "best way" to use a minicomputer. A company may use several techniques to connect machines at various locations, or it may use a single machine as a standalone.

Minicomputer as a Central Machine. In a smaller company, the minicomputer can be the main processor. All company processing is run on this machine, and terminals access its information.

Minicomputer as a Distributed Processor. In larger companies, often a mainframe does the primary company processing, usually including nightly batch update processing. Remote minicomputers are used to perform the following activities:

- *Initial data gathering*. Minicomputers record transactions and transmit activity to the main computer. For example, warehouse minicomputers record incoming orders and shipments; every night, the minicomputers transmit this activity to the central office.
- *Inquiry and editing*. Depending on the complexity of the minicomputer tasks, mainframe data may be sent daily to the minicomputer for appropriate editing. For example, the central office mainframe updates the orders data base every night. In the

morning, the data base (or relevant portions of the data base) is sent to the warehouse minicomputers so that outgoing shipments can be compared with the appropriate orders.

- *Report processing.* After processing, mainframe data is transmitted to minicomputers at remote sites, where the reports for appropriate groups are prepared and printed.

Minicomputer as a Special Applications Processor. Specialized applications may be processed on a minicomputer, separate from the main processor. Some examples include scientific applications and telephone answering, voice mail, and switching operations.

Minicomputer as a Network Server. In addition to connecting with mainframes, minicomputers can be linked with other minicomputers, microcomputers, and workstations. The central minicomputer can serve as a central repository of information, either through remote hook-up or through a Local Area Network (LAN). Data is uploaded and downloaded, and the minicomputer does "central" processing of the information.

MICROCOMPUTER SYSTEMS

Microcomputers are the fastest growing and developing segment of the computer marketplace. Many surveys have plotted the rapid growth of installations, the dramatic improvements in cost-performance ratios, the variety of new entries to the market, and the ever-broadening base of applications. In many respects, this growth parallels the earlier expansion of sophisticated electronic calculators, except that the scale and ability of microcomputers are far greater. Nonetheless, development has followed a similar path of technological advances, miniaturization, and falling costs.

In 1981, IBM's Personal Computer (PC) spearheaded the microcomputer invasion of organizations throughout the country. However, many people credit the success of microcomputers to the somewhat earlier development of spreadsheet software packages.

The range and power of these small machines and associated software packages continue to increase rapidly, at an ever-decreasing cost. Microprocessors with more and more powerful microchips are among the latest developments in the electronics industry. They are being rapidly introduced into computing equipment of all types. Microcomputers are suited to a wide variety of tasks. A typical system covering order entry, stock control, sales analysis, and ledger accounting can be implemented for a distributor with

5,000 stock items, 500 customers, and 500 order lines a day. The equipment can also be used as a terminal, providing not only local processing ability, but linked via modem and telephone lines to a larger minicomputer or mainframe. Microcomputers are also linked together in LANs.

The attraction of microcomputers (and minicomputers) is that they bring the facilities of powerful computers into daily use. Consider the case of processing at a remote office location. Instead of user staff completing input forms, sending them in batches to a central computer department for processing, and receiving an error report many hours—or even days—later, the users use a local computer to enter data and check for errors immediately. Once the data has been checked, the processing of individual transactions can take place and an immediate response can be received. In this way, systems can, for example, take an order for goods entered by a sales clerk and create packing and dispatch instructions to be printed immediately on a printer in a separate storage area.

The multiplicity of small computer environments presents the auditor with some practical difficulties in determining the most appropriate audit strategy. Implementing that strategy at reasonable cost is another consideration. The approach to be taken should be based on the sensitivity/criticality of the application and the associated risk.

Hardware Characteristics

A typical business microcomputer consists of:

- A 16-bit address space (32 bits are becoming common where processing power and speed are critical).
- At least 640 kilobytes of memory (some systems are as large as 16 megabytes).
- Fixed disk storage from 20 to over 100 megabytes.
- A laser printer capable of printing from eight to 12 pages per minute at a resolution of 300 dots per inch.
- A color monitor with high-quality resolution.

Many business installations also have sophisticated peripheral devices such as tape drives, laser disks, high-speed modems for connecting with other computing devices, and special customized devices for workstations.

Current Hardware Limitations. Microcomputers have limitations that become apparent with use. These include:

- The main memory size or disk storage may be insufficient for the growing needs of a business. The more advanced microcomputers based on 16- and 32-bit architectures have large potential memories (16 megabytes) and can handle large disk storage systems easily.
- Except for a few high-end systems, performing calculations, moving data, and printing are usually slower with microcomputers than with mainframes and newer minicomputers.
- The hardware buses, or data pathways internal to the system (and associated operating systems), have limits on the number of peripheral devices that can be attached.
- Incompatible hardware concerns surface when several different microcomputers and devices are present in the same organization. (See Chapter 25, "Controlling End-User Computing.") Programs for one machine may not work on a competitor's machine, or even on an earlier-generation machine from the same manufacturer.

Other Hardware Problems. Microcomputers are subject to many of the same problems as mainframes and minicomputers. They are sensitive to power fluctuations and static electricity. For comfortable use, microcomputers require appropriate, ergonomic furniture. Diskettes and hard disks are sensitive to dust and cigarette smoke. When a system has been assembled with parts from different vendors, the source of a problem may be difficult to find or to resolve once located.

Typical microcomputer problems may become evident long after first use. Power surges and dust take their toll slowly. Intermittent failures or errors may appear randomly.

Diskettes. Diskette quality is also important; careful handling of diskettes even more so. Frequently, backup is overlooked or ignored, when it is essential to maintaining data. When mailing diskettes, they should be placed between layers of corrugated cardboard at right angles or in specifically designed mailers.

Diskettes can fail for several reasons. Dropouts, which are bits missing from the data, can occur and stem from various causes. The diskettes may have surface defects, caused by poor quality control. A weak read/write signal may be caused by the computer program, whereas a dirty read/write head on the diskette drive can also cause such errors. Drop-ins, which are bits added randomly, can be added by electromagnetic interference (EMI), a malfunctioning disk drive, or bad software. Bit shifts are bits moved to incorrect locations, and may be caused by physical distortion, EMI, normal wear, or high temperatures.

Backups. At all times, there should be backup copies or duplicates of programs, data, and equipment. When it comes to using microcomputers, backup is the only certain protection for hardware or software failure. Diskettes are still the principal method of backup, but tape drives and replaceable hard disks are becoming popular.

Software Characteristics

The system software, including the operating system, is the master director controlling the flow of programs and events in the computer. Software for a microcomputer must be compatible with its operating system. The most widely used operating system for IBM-compatible business microcomputers is MS-DOS from Microsoft, known as PC-DOS for IBM machines. Other popular systems include OS/2, and Unix.

Operating systems include standard utility programs, to:

- Copy files to other disks, tape, or the printer.
- Delete files.
- Protect files.
- Check storage space available.
- Rename files.
- Verify files.
- Initialize or format storage devices.
- Save and loan files.

Application programs operate under the direction of the operating system. Such applications include spreadsheets, which automate "what if" analyses and modeling to reduce effort and improve accuracy in projections. Other applications include typical business functions. Software applications can also integrate divisional information for optimization of report capabilities.

Since management reports used in decision-making are often produced on microcomputers, these applications can be critical to an auditor. Data base packages allow storage and retrieval of data, search by criteria, report of results, and information access control. Data bases also allow modification to include new data elements. Many mainframe- and minicomputer-based data base programs have derivative programs for microcomputers.

Word processing may rival spreadsheets as the most popular microcomputer software applications. It eliminates repetitive typing and reduces the cost of form letters and repetitive presentations. Packages usually allow global word changes, movement of paragraphs within the text or between texts, and mailmerge or computerized linkage of two or more documents (such as a mailing list and a form letter).

Applications software can be off-the-shelf, customized, or do-it-yourself. Sometimes programs can be modified with special development tools or original programming. Most programming languages available on mainframes have complete (or nearly so) implementations on microcomputers.

Desirable Software Features. Software can run on different computers; for example, if they are all MS-DOS, the same software should run successfully. Well-written software takes advantage of a computer's special features. User-friendly menus include single-key, easy-to-remember commands. Good software should request confirmation of dangerous operations; for example, when exiting a program without saving new data, the software should require confirmation that the user does not want to save the new data. "Help" should be available to describe on-screen commands. Software should trap errors and give clear error messages. It should also provide choices of input source and output disposition.

Microcomputer Software Limitations. The limitations of microcomputer software include operating system differences, such as those found between two release versions. A newer release may have desirable enhancements, but cannot be implemented in place of the existing release on a smaller microcomputer. There may be disk-format differences within a family of operating systems. Following are some limitations of microcomputer software:

- Microcomputer programming languages may use a subset of the full language and therefore have fewer abilities.
- Users may find that there are frequent revisions.
- Microcomputer core limitations can cause problems when handling extremely large numbers and rounding.
- It usually is not possible to move software from copy-protected diskettes to hard disk.

Good Microcomputer Software Documentation. Good documentation should be included with purchased software, and include hardware and operating system requirements. The installation instructions are very important. User manuals should include the meaning of all menu choices and error messages. It is also helpful to have samples of all output reports with explanations of columns, totals, and breaks. New users should receive tutorial examples of typical operations. Definition of formulas and calculations can also be extremely useful.

Software and Hardware Obsolescence. Software can be rendered obsolete when the user outgrows the maximum space in a particular microcomputer, and processing speeds become too slow when a system receives heavy demands. Hardware becomes obsolete as technological evolution continues. As more flexible, integrated, or specialized software packages become available, users cannot run them because of memory limitations unless they replace their existing equipment. Business environment changes often require new software. As more applications are employed, the user needs to integrate functions so that repetitive entry and data redundancy are lessened. This integration of functions may not be possible within the existing configuration.

Customized Software Concerns. High development costs tend to keep the use of customized software out of reach of many organizations. There is also a great risk of customization failure, even after great expense, and, unfortunately, it is often the user who discovers all the errors. Then, users must also maintain the programs, not the software vendors who normally maintain the packages. The user must document the software, which may only work on the existing computer for which it was written. Documentation of source code and technical documentation may not be developed adequately, making maintenance of the software difficult once the original programmer is no longer available.

WORKSTATIONS

Workstations are a recent development in computer engineering, uniting the size and flexibility of a microcomputer with the power of a minicomputer processor. These machines were developed originally for the scientific and engineering communities. Many applications in those fields, such as graphics and publishing, demand the speed and raw power of the minicomputer processor, but do not require the minicomputer's extensive support for multiple users and a variety of I/O devices.

Several trends are moving the workstation into the business office. Highly sophisticated financial planning and development tools have been developed to take advantage of the 32-bit architecture in the top-of-the-line microcomputers. Workstations, too, have 32-bit architecture and usually more power than even the best microcomputer. Reduced Instruction Set Chips (RISC) are now becoming available to workstation manufacturers. Those chips duplicate minicomputer performance in a smaller size and with less heat, making them more suitable to the uncontrolled conditions of the business office. Finally, the workstation market has become highly competitive, and a group of manufacturers see business as a new world to conquer.

Hardware Characteristics

Workstations have roughly the same physical dimensions as microcomputers, but they are substantially more powerful. Processors used in some current workstations include:

- Micro-VAX chip, roughly comparable in power to a low-end VAX minicomputer manufactured by DEC.
- Several processors built on the Motorola 68030 chip, a 32-bit processor.
- Several processors built on customized RISC, with speeds in excess of 25 million instructions per second (MIPS).

The more powerful processor in a workstation also allows the use of larger and more flexible peripheral devices than those used by ordinary microcomputers. Workstation processors can drive high-density, high-resolution monitors at speeds considerably higher than those available on even top-of-the-line microcomputers. Specialized RISCs can work in tandem with the main processors to yield even better performance.

Software Characteristics

The availability of software is the greatest impediment to business development of workstations. Several workstations have been designed to work with a UNIX operating system, and many applications have been written for UNIX. However, these programs still require some modifications to work with the different hardware configurations.

The workstation's greatest hardware advantage, the RISC machines with their tremendous power, is also its greatest software disadvantage. These specialized chips require special modifications and, often, reprogramming of standard applications. At this time, there are few application programs for RISC workstations, except for compilers.

LOCAL AREA NETWORKS

LANs are growing in popularity. They allow a group of microcomputers, workstations, and intelligent peripherals to communicate with one another directly, without passing all their signals through a central mainframe or minicomputer server. Businesses are finding LANs attractive because they are flexible and easily expanded or adapted to new circumstances or applications.

LANs must have full connectivity among stations. Each station in the network, except for peripheral devices, should be able to contact any other station to which it has the right of access. LANs also, by definition, are fully administered by their owners and run on a single set of cables. The latter eliminates cable television networks or telephone companies. In fact, some telephone companies are now referring to themselves as "Wide Area Networks" (WANs) in recognition of the growing importance of LANs and connectivity.

Current LANs are classified according to their physical configurations. The first configuration resembles a star, where a central hub device services the orbiting stations. This form is well known to computer workers, because it resembles the older system of a mainframe with its terminals. However, in a star LAN, it is the network hardware and software, not the mainframe or central minicomputer, that controls the flow of data.

Star LANs are now being replaced with state-of-the-art bus and ring networks. Bus networks send data to a retransmitter that makes the data available simultaneously to all other stations on the network. Ring networks circulate messages in a constant loop through the system. (IBM's LAN is a token ring network.)

The division of hardware and software characteristics is not applied easily to networks, because there is an interaction and relationship between hardware and software at several levels in LANs. A model may help explain the relationship on each level or layer.

In the early 1970s, the International Standards Organization (ISO) developed a model of a data communication system. Like any standards organization, including its American member the American National Standards Institute (ANSI), the ISO developed its model so that equipment from different manufacturers could conform to design standards and communicate with each other. The ISO's model is called Open System Interconnection (OSI). Both IBM and DEC had earlier developed models, known as System Network Architecture (IBM's SNA) and DEC Network Architecture (DNA). This discussion will focus on the ISO model, because both IBM and DEC systems are compatible with OSI.

It is easiest to think of the ISO model as a series of seven layers, much like a layer cake. Each layer can be examined independently, but remember that layers are built on lower layers and support higher ones.

Physical Layer

This is a strictly hardware layer. It includes a description of the physical connections between the stations and the network, both the mechanical aspects (cables and connectors) and the electrical aspects (voltage, signal strength, amplifiers, and modulators). The physical configuration of the network (star, bus, or ring) is part of the physical layer.

This layer carries the signals of the higher layers. Any error, defect, or software incompatibility at this layer is fatal.

Data Link Layer

The data link layer is also a hardware layer, although some systems software and application programs can address this layer directly. It defines the protocols that computers must use to transmit and receive messages. The layer protocols put characters together into message packets, check them before transmission, transmit the packets, check the received messages, and, in some situations, reconstitute a corrupt or garbled packet. Errors in the data link should be self-correcting.

Network Layer

The network layer is a close link between the system software and hardware. The network layer controls the physical path the message packet takes when going through the network. An analogy may help explain this layer. When dialing from a telephone in New York to a number in Los Angeles, the long-distance carrier can route the call in a number of ways, depending on physical conditions of the phone network, priorities of service, and volume of traffic. The call might be first transmitted by ground line to Atlanta, then beamed via satellite to San Francisco, and again linked by ground line to Los Angeles. The call might be switched in and out of a dozen locations before arriving in Los Angeles. Similarly, the network layer in the LAN may send the message packet through various routes, depending on network conditions. The network layer's software usually resides in switches out in the network.

Transport Layer

The transport layer functions similarly to the network layer, but at the local level. The same software drivers control both levels. The transport layer backs up the network layer, retransmitting, rerouting, or storing messages in case the network goes down. It also checks the messages to make sure they are in the right form and correct order. The transport layer functions are most critical when connecting different types and brands of machines in the same LAN.

Session Layer

At the higher layers, software control becomes more pervasive. The session layer is very important for microcomputer applications. It provides functions that allow two applications to communicate across the network. The functions include security, recognition of names, logons, and so on.

The session layer is important to software writers, because it is the lowest level that allows devices to be addressed by name rather than by network address. Consequently, programmers can write software that controls functions at this layer on any installation of a particular network.

Presentation Layer

The presentation layer controls the on-screen appearance of data, as well as encryption and special file formatting. The programmer uses the presentation level to format screens and files so that the final product looks the way the programmer intended.

The presentation layer is the first layer that allows the user some direct control. The software may allow the user to select special graphic and character sets. Printers, plotters, and other peripherals can be accessed or modified at this level. The user may even choose to change the appearance by using emulation protocols that make an IBM PC "think" that it is a DEC TV-100 or IBM 3278 terminal.

Application Layer

At the application layer, the user is in full control. This layer is where the network operating system and application programs reside. The application layer includes most functions available to a user of a stand-alone microcomputer or workstation, as well as functions available on a network: file sharing, print spooling, and electronic mail, among others.

SUMMARY

LANs are flexible and cost-effective tools that greatly expand the variety of services that can be performed by microcomputers and workstations. A model based on the International Standards Organization's Open Systems Interconnection (OSI) helps explain the software and hardware characteristics of LANs. The OSI model describes the seven layers of activity for LAN communications.

CHAPTER **7**

Telecommunications Networks and Systems

INTRODUCTION

Telecommunications is the electronic transmission of any kind of information by radio, wire, fiber optics, microwave, laser, or any other electromagnetic system. It can be evaluated along several lines, including:

- Type of system (e.g., voice, data, integrated, facsimile).
- Geographical organization (e.g., local, domestic, national, or international).
- Service environment (e.g., intercompany, intracompany, third-party).

While all telecommunications systems have similar components and are advancing essentially in the same direction, the characteristics noted above can affect risk levels, costs, and reliability.

Data Transmission

Data characters in computer systems are represented by strings of bits or binary digits, the 0's and 1's of machine code. To represent characters, these conform to coding conventions developed for consistency within the industry, such as EBCDIC and ASCII. These codes were developed to achieve compatibility in the transfer of data between different data devices. Information in this format is known as digital data, which consists of off and on signals that represent the 0's and 1's.

Digital transmission is used to send data between devices in a computer room, such as from the computer to the line printer, or between terminals and the computer in a local network. When the terminal and the computer are connected in a remote network, the method of transmitting data depends on the type of communication channel being used and the protocols in existence. Today, extensive public digital transmission systems are in place and provide worldwide connectivity.

However, the majority of the telephone systems use analog transmission, as opposed to digital transmission. Analog transmission is the modulation of electromagnetic waves (the sine or carrier waves) sent over the transmission line. There are three forms of modulation: amplitude, frequency, and phase. In all three forms the wave is continuous, which makes the method ideally suited to transmitting voice over the phone, or sound over a radio.

Messages are indicated by varying the amplitude (height) of the signal (amplitude modulation), varying the frequency of occurrence of the signal (frequency modulation), or varying the direction of the cycle (phase modulation).

Amplitude modulation is generally used for slower speed data transmission due to its high distortion factor. Frequency modulation is used for lower bit rate transfers. Phase modulation over different amplitudes is used for higher rates of data transfer.

For a remote terminal to communicate with a central computer, its digital signals must be converted to analog form in order to be transmitted through existing telephone lines. The communication must then be converted back to digital signals before it can be processed by the computer. A modem (which stands for modulator-demodulator) at each end of the transmission line translates the data from digital form to analog form (and vice versa) to allow sending data over the phone lines.

Transmission Modes

Following is a definition by example of the different modes of transmission:

- *Full- and half-duplex.* Transmission lines can be used to transmit data along a given channel in:
  - — One direction only (simplex).
  - — Both directions, but not at the same time (half-duplex).
  - — Both directions at the same time (full-duplex).

  Full-duplex transmission allows the transmission of data in both directions, or the sending of data in one direction and control signals in the other. Full-duplex transmission can be achieved on lines that have four wires or on a two-wire line by splitting the band width of the line into two separate frequency bands.
- *Parallel and serial transmission.* In parallel transmission, multiple wires simultaneously transmit the component bits that make up a data character, and the control bits that indicate various things, such as the end of a particular message. In this method, there is one bit sent on each wire. Parallel wire transmission is often used to transmit digital data over short distances (e.g., in a local network to connect terminals to a central computer). Serial transmission is the transmission of a series of data characters as strings of bits sent along the same wire. Serial transmission is used on analog lines, since only one bit can travel over the line at a time.
- *Asynchronous and synchronous transmission*
  - — With asynchronous transmission, start and stop bits are used to signal the beginning and end of a character. This form of transmission is used for character-oriented transmission, and ranges from 7.5 bits per second (bps) to 9600 bps. It is the major mode of transmission used by microcomputers.
  - — With synchronous transmission, characters are transmitted in blocks. Typically, the bit string starts with a unique synchronization bit pattern that the receiving machine understands. The block ends with an end-of-message character, followed by an error-checking character that is compared against the error-checking pattern accumulated by the receiving device. This is widely used for terminals that transmit large quantities of data at one time, such as those in distributed processing networks or computers communicating with other computers.

In practice, there are a variety of protocols used to regulate the transfer of data. This tends to limit the possibility of system interchanges among different manufacturers' products. Recent developments include devices that can automatically translate the information from one system so that it can be understood by another system.

Accuracy of Data Transmission

Errors in data transmission are different from those caused by erroneous data or errors in data input. Transmission errors often occur as a result of line noise or erratic impulses of sufficient magnitude to damage or garble the data being sent. They also occur when equipment controlling the transmission fails.

A number of control techniques can be used to help detect transmission errors. Some of these are:

- *Redundancy bits/characters.* These bits or characters are additional information included in a message by the sending unit. They enable the receiving unit to perform an error check on the data received. Examples are:
  - — Parity bits (less reliable at high transmission rates).
  - — Polynomial checking.
  - — Cyclic redundancy check (CRC) (a check character calculated using polynomial cyclic code on the bits in a block of data).
- *Loop checks (echo check).* The receiving unit sends messages back to the sending unit to make it possible to check the transmission against the stored message.

If an error is detected, the following techniques can be used to correct it:

- *Automatic retransmission.* The most common method in transmission systems, automatic retransmission, uses special characters that are defined by the transmission protocol in effect. An example is IBM's Binary Synchronous Communication (BSC) protocol. The sending unit waits for an acknowledgment (ACK) or negative acknowledgment (NAK) from the receiving unit. If ACK is received, the next block is sent; if NAK, the last block is retransmitted.
- *Forward error correction.* As well as enabling the receiving unit to detect errors, sufficient redundant data is included to allow the receiving unit to reconstruct the correct message using special codes. Thus, the sender does not need to retransmit the data.
- *Operator retransmission.* The terminal operator is informed of the error, and the message is either retransmitted (if held in a buffer) or reentered.

Completeness of Data Transmission

There is always a possibility that messages will be lost in transmission. When the data being transmitted is significant, as in an on-line transaction, it is particularly important to be able to detect the loss of messages. If there is no method to check on whether a message is lost, there is no way to know for sure that all messages sent were received.

In some systems, messages are numbered so that their sequence can be checked. For example, in IBM's Synchronous Data Link Control (SDLC) protocol, each message frame or unit forwarded by a secondary station is numbered sequentially. The primary station can check that all messages were received in the correct sequence.

Transfer Rates

The capacity of a communication channel is measured in terms of the bit rate, which is the number of bps. The speed of a transmission line is measured by the baud rate, which is the number of times the line condition (on or off) changes per second. In a series of binary signals, 1 baud is 1 bit per second; the baud rate will equal the bit rate.

The bit rate is equal to the baud rate multiplied by the number of bits per state. For example, on a 1600 baud-carrier line, eight-state modulation will achieve a data transfer rate of 4800 bits per second.

Line Switching

Line switching involves the creation of a physical path or circuit between incoming and outgoing lines (e.g., the switched public telephone system) in order to provide linking for distant locations. Private line-switching systems are not common; private organizations use message-switching systems, which may use the public switched networks.

Message Switching

Message switching involves the storing of messages from remote terminals or concentrators by another concentrator or minicomputer in the network. Each message is subsequently routed to the destination address on the message header as soon as a line becomes available. Incoming messages are always accepted, even if they cannot immediately be transmitted to their destinations (e.g., messages for terminals on a multidrop line or for terminals that are busy).

Packet Switching

Packet switching is designed to transfer data through a network. Data from terminals or other computers in the network is formed into "packets" (often blocks of fixed length) by an interface computer (node) and sent to its destination via a high transmission (wide band) communication line. Alternate communication paths are designed into the system to provide different paths that can be used in the event of line congestion or failure. A particular message may be broken up into a number of packets, and each packet may be transmitted via a different path.

COMPONENTS OF A TELECOMMUNICATIONS NETWORK

The relationship of terminals and computers to each other when they communicate is called a network. Networks can be constructed with different configurations and services, depending on the users' needs. The network can also be part of a global transmission facility that allows users to communicate from anywhere in the world. This is accomplished through the use of building blocks described below.

Terminals

Terminals are the input and output devices in a teleprocessing network. These include teletype terminals, video terminals, remote job entry (RJE) terminals, transaction terminals, and intelligent terminals. The features of each of these terminal categories are shown in Figure 7-1.

Modems

As discussed previously, when analog transmission is used, a modem is needed to encode digital signals from sources in the computer network into the range of frequencies required to transmit data along the communication channel. When the modem receives incoming analog signals, they are decoded back into digital signals so that the data can be processed by the receiving point in the computer network. There are different varieties of modems: Some require a telephone, others take the place of a phone, and some terminals have modems built in.

Multiplexers and Concentrators

A multiplexer is a hardware device that connects several communications devices to the same communications channel. A multiplexer typically links

FIG. 7-1

Features of various terminal categories

Type	Characteristics
1. Low-speed teleprinter	■ 0–1,200 bits/second ■ Generally unbuffered ■ Asynchronous transmission ■ Limited intelligence ■ Mostly dial-up lines used ■ Examples: a. TI Silent 700 (acoustic coupler) b. TTY–Texas 745
2. Visual display terminals (VDTs, also called CRTs)	■ 100–9,600 bits/second ■ Generally unbuffered, linked to cluster controller ■ Limited intelligence ■ Synchronous or asynchronous transmission ■ Dedicated, dial, or lease lines ■ Example: a. IBM 3278's linked to IBM 3274 buffered controller
3. Remote job entry (RJE) terminals	■ 2,400–9,600 bits/second ■ Card reader, printer, operator console (CRT and diskette options in configuration) ■ Buffered, often programmable ■ Normally synchronous transmission ■ Dial or lease lines ■ Examples: a. IBM 3770 b. IBM 3780
4. Transaction terminals	■ 2,400–9,600 bits/second ■ Buffered ■ Dial or lease lines ■ Examples—Special industry application: a. IBM 3600 series (banking) b. IBM 3650 series (retail) c. Diebold Tabs ATM (banking)
5. Intelligent terminals	■ 2,400–9,600 bits/second ■ Buffered ■ Programmable; can control a number of peripherals; can handle data entry, editing ■ Often used as cluster controllers ■ Dial or lease lines ■ Examples: a. Four-Phase System IV b. IBM 8100

several low-speed lines to one high-speed line in order to enhance transmission capabilities. In time-division, or time slot, multiplexing, there are successive scans of the connected transmission lines; messages that were found as a result of the scanning are retransmitted. For example, one message might be a block of data composed of one character that is scanned from each terminal for transmission to a host computer. Frequency division multiplexing involves the assignment of a separate frequency range, on a high-speed line, for each low-speed line. Thus, each terminal has its own frequency range on its line. In these methods the time slots or frequencies are fixed.

A concentrator is used to group several low-speed lines to a high-speed line in much the same way as a multiplexer. In addition, it is capable of certain processing functions. The shared channels can be used by terminals on a demand basis. For example, terminals may transmit to the concentrator in asynchronous mode; the concentrator stores and formats the message into a block or segment, adds the necessary address and control characters, and retransmits the data on a higher speed line in synchronous mode. The concentrator can be programmed to handle devices transmitting at different speeds automatically, while a multiplexer can only handle a preset speed or preset group of speeds. On the whole, the concentrator is more flexible and can deal with a variety of circumstances.

Communication Lines

Computer systems can be linked to other systems and users by various transmission facilities. These can take many forms, such as:

- Private, single-use networks.
- Private networks interlinking systems.
- Private shared networks.
- Limited public networks.
- Nationwide public networks.
- International public networks.
- Integrated Services Digital Network (ISDN).

The choice of communication links depends on the cost and performance of the available lines and the requirements of the applications using the network.

Front-End Communications Processor

A front-end communications processor is a hardware device that connects all of the network data communication lines to a central computer. It is used to relieve the central computer of the overhead of network control and message handling. In an IBM system, for example, the hardware unit might be a 3705 communications controller, directed by the Network Control Program. The IBM 3705 is a key component of IBM's System Network Architecture (SNA), which connects devices using their SDLC protocol. Typical functions of such devices are:

- Polling and addressing of remote units.
- Dialing and answering stations on a switched network.
- Determining to which remote station a block is to be sent.
- Character code translation.
- Dynamic buffering.
- Transmission rate selection.
- Control character recognition and error checking.
- Error recovery and diagnostics.
- Activating and deactivating communication lines.

Central Processing Unit

The central processing unit (CPU) carries out the major processing tasks of the computer and is the heart of any system. Binary data from the front-end communications controller is accepted via a designated channel. The access method (such as VTAM, or Virtual Telecommunications Access Method) is used to manage the allocation of resources and the flow of data within the central system. Communications software, such as Customer Information Control System (CICS) or Information Management System/Data Communication (IMS/DC), provides the interface between users and applications.

Teleprocessing Equipment in Data Communication Networks

Typical uses of teleprocessing equipment in networks include:

- *Cluster controller.* Figure 7-2 illustrates a cluster control mode, which is a communications terminal control unit controlling a number of CRTs (cathode ray tubes). In such a system, all

FIG. 7-2

Configuration of a cluster controller

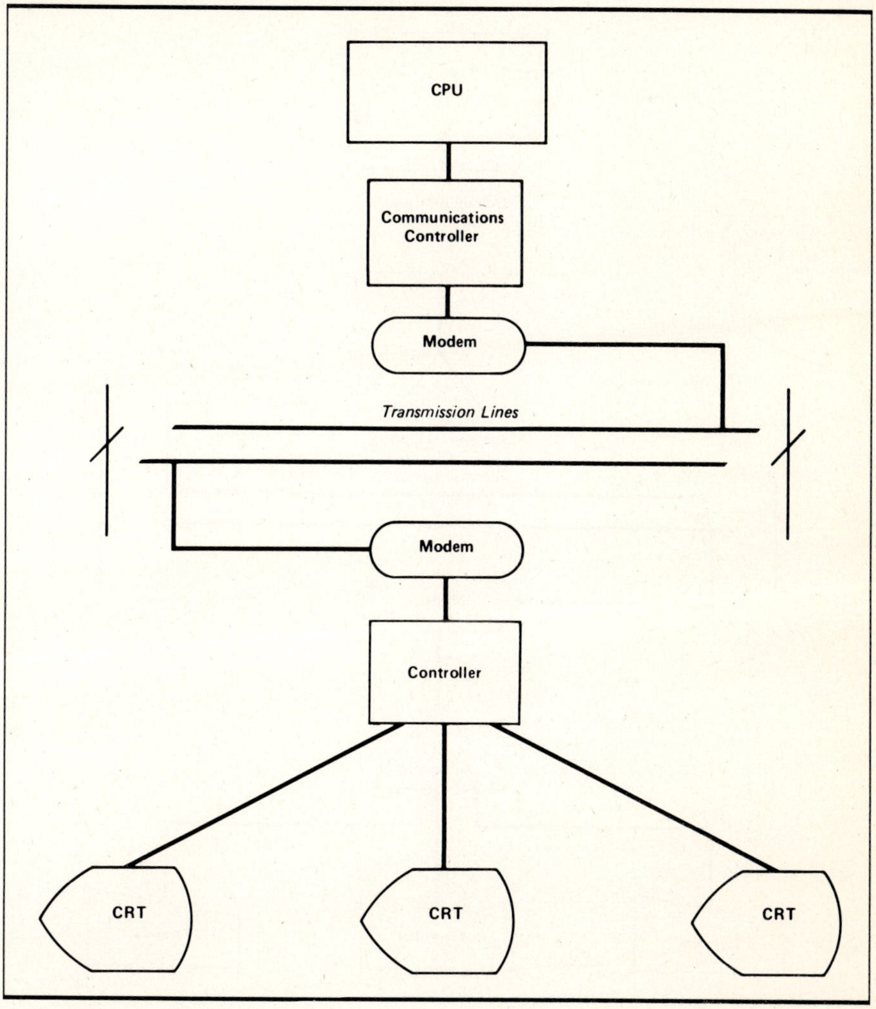

messages are buffered by the terminal control unit and forwarded. The communications terminal can be partitioned, so that the first partition controls the cluster and the second acts as a concentrator.

- *Multiplexer*. Figure 7-3 illustrates a multiplexer linking several terminals. It can also be used to link several cluster controllers. The outward-bound line is generally a high-speed line. If the linked terminals are in remote locations, modems are required to convert

FIG. 7-3
Example of a multiplexer configuration

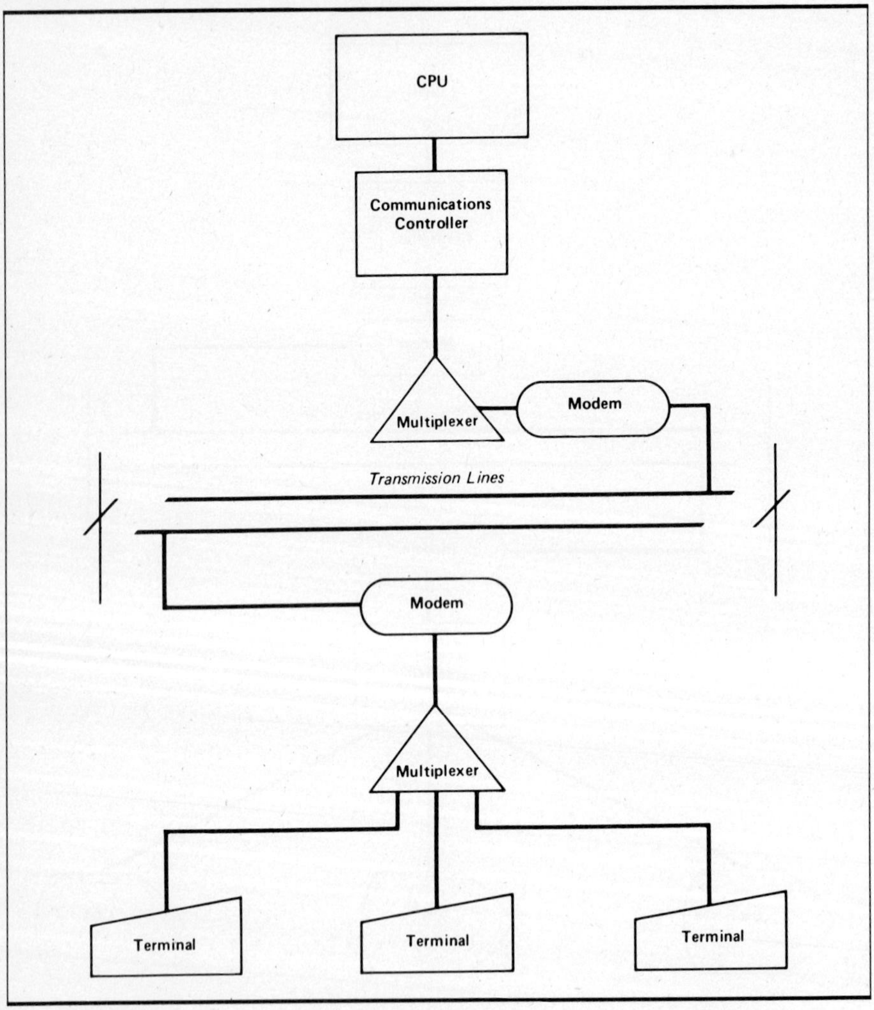

analog signals to digital form before multiplexing. (This is a dial-up line, since the modem is used to call into the host computer.)

- *Multidrop or multipoint connection.* Figure 7-4 illustrates a number of terminals linked to a multidrop line. Only one message can be transmitted or received on the line at any one time, since it is a single line with multiple connections. Multidrop connections are only used on dedicated lines (lines reserved for a single device,

FIG. 7-4

Example of a multidrop line connection

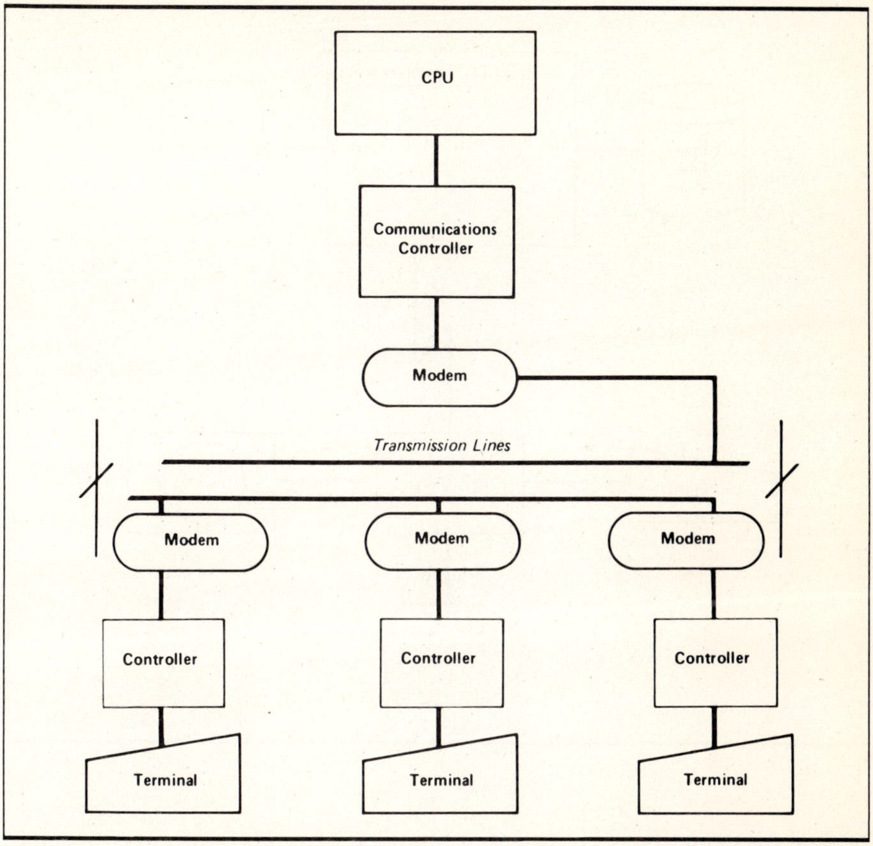

terminal, or user). In a switched network, the lines are not dedicated.

KINDS OF TELECOMMUNICATIONS SYSTEMS

All teleprocessing systems include some form of remote computer activity. For example, a simple activity might be the remote logging of transactions and subsequent transmission of a batch to a central computer for processing. On the other hand, fairly complex processing capabilities may be distributed to centers remote from a host computer. When this is done, the maintenance

FIG. 7-5
Configuration of a remote job entry system

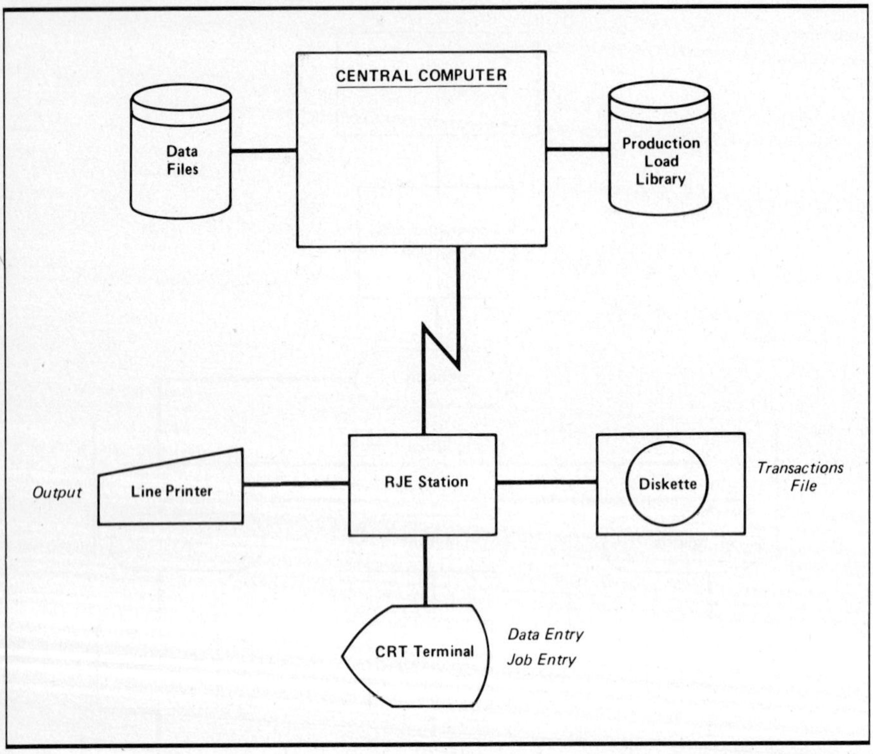

of data files, and possibly program libraries, at remote locations becomes necessary.

To audit computer systems with teleprocessing features, the auditor must understand those systems and their features. This knowledge enables the auditor both to classify accounting systems in use throughout an organization and to perform preliminary surveys of general or integrity controls.

Remote Job Entry

An RJE configuration is illustrated in Figure 7-5. RJE systems normally include the following features:

- In batch-oriented systems, data capture is usually through key-to-disk or key-to-tape at remote locations; the data is transmitted in a batch mode to the host computer.

- Data is spooled to disk or tape at the host computer to await processing.
- A remote user initiates jobs (via terminal, card reader, or diskette reader), which are entered into the job queue by the host computer.
- Job requires little operator intervention other than loading required files.
- Output is returned to the remote user and printed on the remote printer when the job is finished, unless it is specifically routed to another printer or screen.

The method of data capture may vary from system to system. Essentially, RJE gives remote users access to a central computer in a remote batch-entry mode.

An example of an RJE application is a divisional payroll system where time sheets and other data are keyed to diskette on a daily basis and accumulated for each week. At the end of the period, the RJE operator initiates the weekly edit runs. After the edit report is received and all errors are corrected, the divisional paymaster authorizes the payroll production run. This run is done in the remote batch-entry mode.

On-Line Systems Abilities

An on-line system accepts data from the source, where it is created, and may involve immediate processing of the data. An on-line system may have the following abilities:

- On-line inquiry.
- On-line data entry.
- On-line update (add, change, or delete).

However, a given application may not use all of the above abilities.

On-Line Inquiry. On-line inquiry, which is a common feature of computer systems in a teleprocessing environment, enables a remote user to retrieve data directly from the computer files. Since this access may create problems if it is unrestricted, the system software should control what data is available to be read by remote terminals. Access to data should be regulated rather than unlimited.

On-line inquiry situations are common in banks. A bank teller can confirm that a customer has sufficient funds to cover a check via a terminal at the teller's station. No transaction actually takes place at the terminal, but the use of the inquiry feature provides an important control step.

On-Line Data Entry. With on-line data entry, a terminal is used to enter data for transmission to a host computer. The data can be held for intermediate storage (batch processing mode) or sent for immediate processing (transaction processing mode). In transaction processing mode, a number of transactions may be processed concurrently on different remote terminals. These transactions may be the same type or of different types. For example, several sales orders and cash receipts can be processed concurrently. In order for this to work, the computer must be programmed to:

- Recognize the transaction type and select the appropriate program (including programmed format) for that type.
- Queue the messages received concurrently from different terminals and handle situations where different terminals wish to access (or update) the same data files at the same time.

In transaction processing mode, on-line processing normally includes:

- Matching to master files to check the existence of data on which the transaction will act (e.g., customers, suppliers, or products) or matching to related transaction data (e.g., as purchase invoices to records of goods received). This matching may include interactive checks and controls. For example, the computer may retrieve the full customer name based on the reference field input; visual verification by the terminal operator ensures that the correct customer name has been entered.
- Temporary storage of data keyed in on a work file during the edit and validation stages. Then, if the data is accepted, it is written to a transaction file for subsequent batch updating.

On-Line Update. Transaction processing systems may perform on-line updating of relevant master files or data bases (to add, change, or delete data) on a transaction-by-transaction basis. An on-line transaction processing system is illustrated in Figure 7-6. Location No. 1 is processing all the payroll details based on daily employee time records. A limited amount of validation is performed on-line so that the operator can make immediate corrections. Transactions are written to a transaction file. The actual payroll production is run in batch mode each week using the relevant data on the transaction file.

At Location No. 2, various inventory movement transactions, such as

FIG. 7-6
An on-line processing system

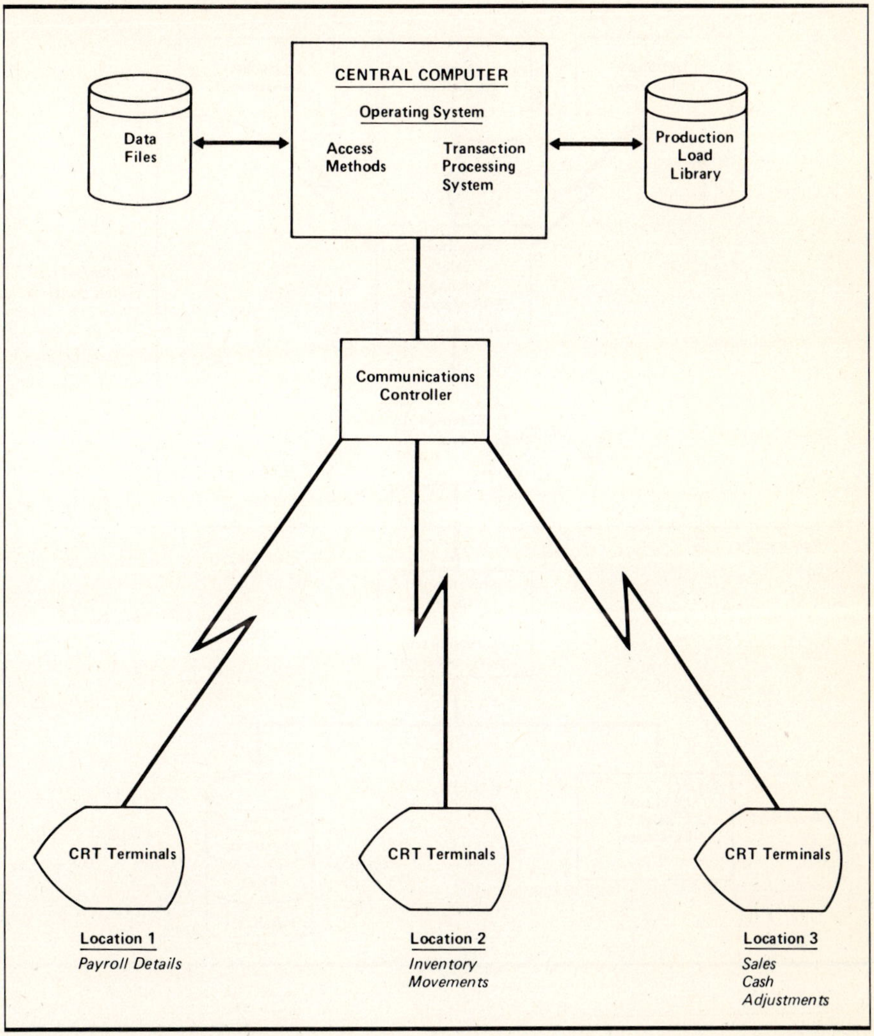

stock count adjustments, are being entered and updated to the inventory master file, which is always on-line.

At Location No. 3, sales orders are processed on-line. At the time of input, each order is compared to information on the updated inventory file to ensure that sufficient inventory is on hand to fill the orders. Accounts receivable balances are updated overnight from a file of invoices and ad-

FIG. 7-7
Input and output of an on-line processing system

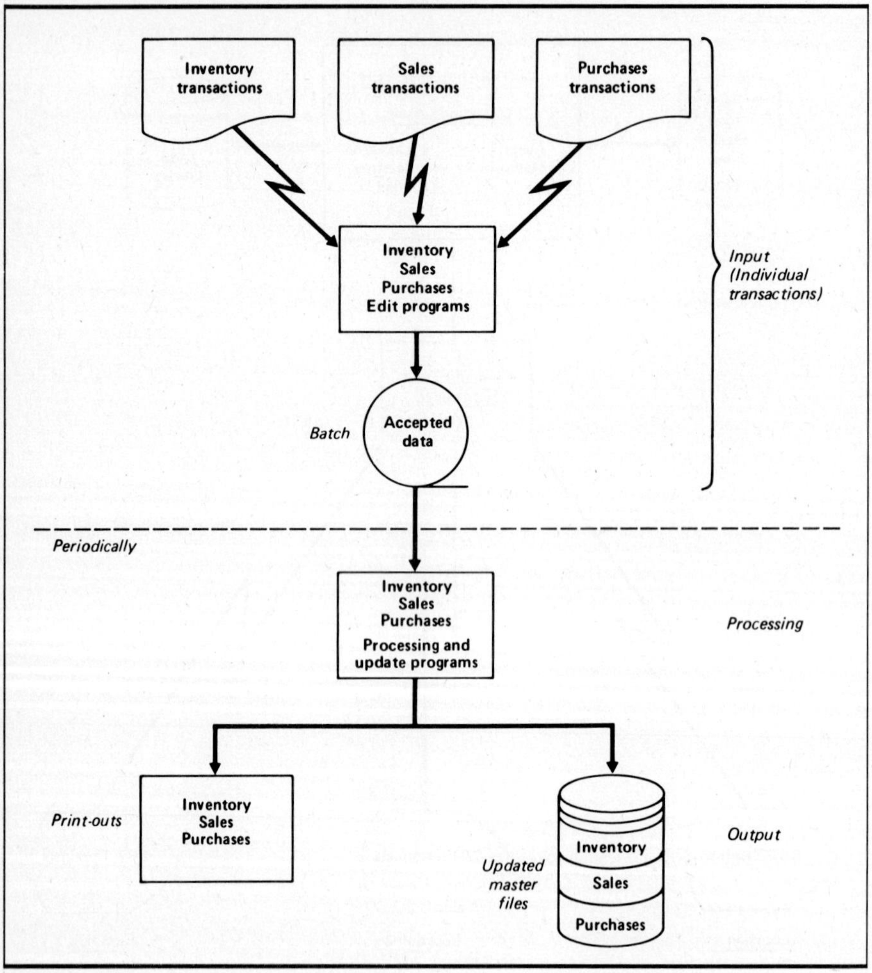

justments created during the day's processing of accepted sales orders. Figure 7-7 shows the input and output of an on-line sales and inventory system.

Time-Sharing Systems and Public Data Bases

Time-sharing systems are terminal-oriented. They are designed to handle the processing requirements of a number of different users at the same time. Each user acts independently using individual data files stored by the time-sharing system and the programs available on that system. Time-sharing systems are interactive: They are designed for conversational situations where the application system and terminal operator send instructions and data back and forth. Use of computer resources is controlled by the time-sharing system, which limits the time that any one program may control processing on a time-slice basis (i.e., the amount of time the computer resources can be used for a particular process). Once the slice is used up, the computer goes to the next task. For this reason, time-sharing systems are not suited to running large batch jobs, which may take too long to execute efficiently. In such a situation, processing would be constantly interrupted each time a time slice was completed.

Time-sharing services to process application data are provided by a large variety of time-sharing bureaus; one of the largest is General Electric Information Services (GEIS). From the user's viewpoint, time-sharing has many of the characteristics of an RJE system.

In-house time-sharing systems, such as TSO (Time-Sharing Option), normally are used for on-line program development and maintenance rather than for application processing.

Public data bases are an expanding area of on-line system use. These systems permit business and individual use, for a fee, of the data base of information maintained by the service provider. Users access the computer, usually through the telephone lines using a modem, to receive text-only or text and graphics information (videotex). Text-only videotex is popular for business use, such as the legal data provided by LEXIS or news provided by NEXIS. Text and graphics videotex, a growing area, provides information and, frequently, transaction services, such as banking and ordering capabilities.

Distributed Data Processing

The term "distributed data processing" (DDP) refers to the decentralization of computerized data processing functions through the interconnection of computers and terminals. These are arranged in a network designed to meet the user's processing and information needs.

Unlike most of the preceding types of systems, in DDP certain functions are off-loaded or sent from the central computer to the remote processing sites. This improves the overall information and processing system, since some of the demands on the central computer are reduced. Obviously, the economic assumption underlying such a transfer is that it can be done relatively cheaply, which is now possible due to technological developments and decreasing hardware costs.

DDP refers to the existence or creation of a teleprocessing network structure. The following functions may be scattered throughout the system:

- Data collection.
- Data editing and correction.
- File creation and maintenance.
- Transaction processing.
- Data base management.

These functions are located at remote sites and are performed and controlled by a local processor. This differentiates distributed processing systems from terminal networks, which are under the control of a central processor.

Any number of different DDP network structures can exist in practice. A typical network structure in a manufacturing company with large divisional offices is illustrated in Figure 7-8. In this example, each division is responsible for processing and maintaining its own data. Certain information is transmitted to the central computer for further processing, such as sales details, costing, and so forth. New versions of application programs and systems software are sent to the divisions as load modules.

Sometimes, DDP is structured so that a node (usually a mainframe or a minicomputer) performs a certain type of processing for the other nodes. This is called centralized distribution.

More complex network structures are used by organizations that adopt an even more decentralized approach. In these systems, multiple communication paths might exist with work nodes linked to various other work nodes in the network. In many organizations, microcomputers are linked together and into networks that communicate with mainframes or minicomputers. When the microcomputers are linked locally, it is called a local area network (LAN). When they are also linked to remote sites, it is called a wide area network (WAN).

CONTROL ASPECTS OF ON-LINE TELECOMMUNICATIONS SYSTEMS

The large number of possible, different telecommunications system configurations creates a broad spectrum of security and other control considerations. There are, however, certain basic control features that are important in any telecommunications environment, and are of particular concern to auditors, including:

- Security of terminals and access.
- Control over data.

FIG. 7-8

Example of a typical distributed processing system in manufacturing

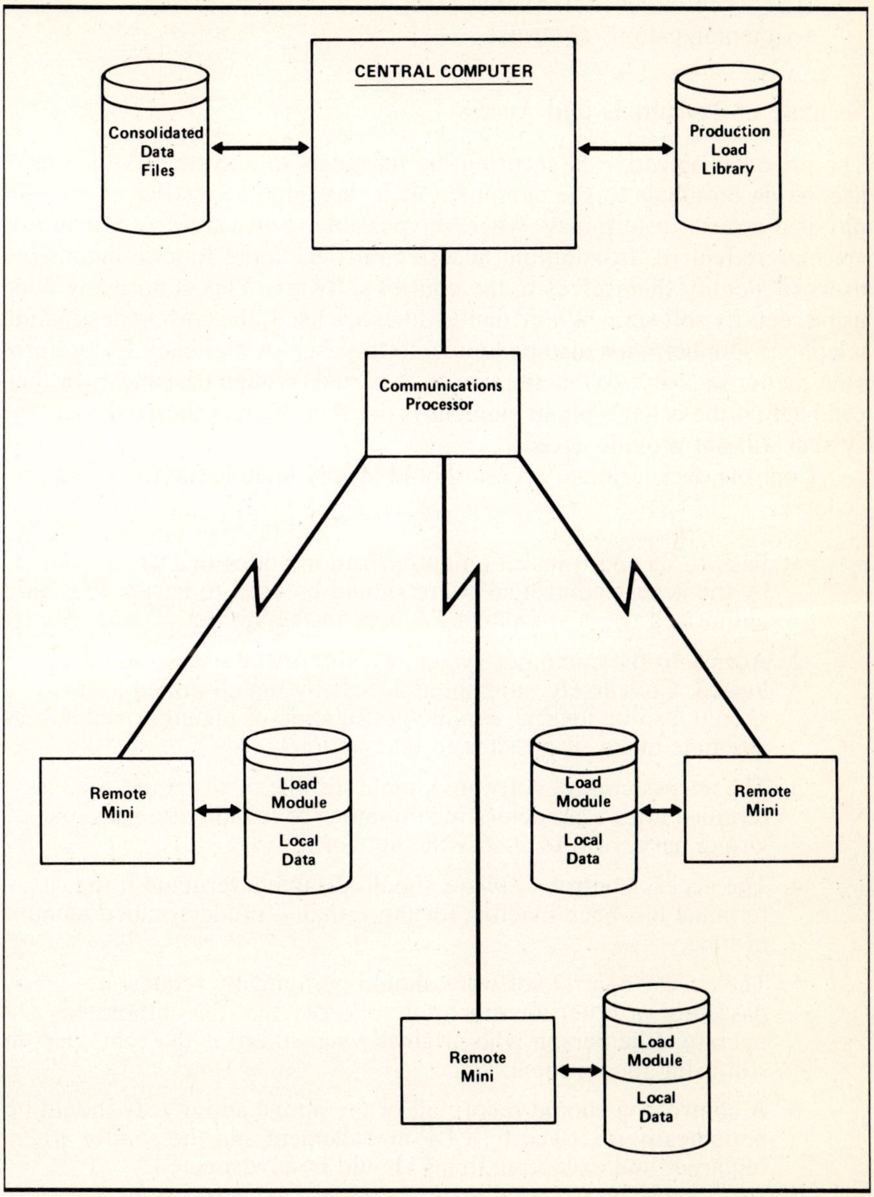

- Backup and recovery of the system.
- Information technology (IT) control considerations.
- Communications controls.

Security of Terminals and Access

The principal objective in securing the terminals in a system is to control access via terminals to the computer. It is desirable to restrict or monitor physical access to terminals wherever possible. Software access controls are more effective. In addition, access controls should require authorized users to identify themselves to the control software. This is normally done using security software. Where dial-up lines are used, the correct destination telephone number must also be known to the user. A dial-back feature provides better security, so that numbers uncovered through trial and error then call back; if the caller's phone number is not that of an authorized user, the system will not provide access.

Controls over terminal access should ideally include the following procedures:

1. Passwords and transaction authorization codes that are validated by the access control software should be used to ensure that only authorized users are allowed access to the system.
2. Access to the computer system by authorized users should be logged. Conversely, attempted access by unauthorized users should also be logged. On-line notification of unauthorized access attempts makes it possible to take action.
3. The access control software should disable or disconnect a terminal after a predetermined number of invalid attempts (use of wrong password) to access the network.
4. The access control software should disable a terminal if the terminal has been inactive for more than a predetermined amount of time.
5. The access control software should periodically request a password or other identification to verify that the authorized operator (the person who originally signed on) is the same person still using the terminal.
6. A control log should record all of the above activity. It should be periodically reviewed by EDP management and the auditor when required, and exception items should be investigated.
7. Critical information, such as passwords and other authorization codes, should not be displayed on the terminal. (Password software is part of security software that is part of, or can be added to, system software.)

8. Lists of valid passwords should be secured against unauthorized access, with additional password protection or data encryption.
9. Passwords should be easy to change, should be changed periodically, and should be disabled immediately for separated users.
10. When dial-up lines are used, phone numbers should be changed periodically. Phone numbers should not be listed on the terminals.
11. Entry of system commands that affect the status of terminals should be restricted to master terminals.
12. System commands should be logged, reviewed, and restricted.

Where possible, terminal security control procedures should enforce an adequate separation of duties. Operators and terminals should be restricted to the particular functions that should be performed within each application and only as required for the particular job responsibility. For example, a terminal in a warehouse, used to track inventory, should not have access to the customer master files.

Many of the terminal control procedures described above will not necessarily detect successful attempts to use terminals in an unauthorized manner. Rather, they are intended to prevent such unauthorized attempts from succeeding in the first place. The presence of terminal security controls in itself does not provide conclusive evidence that unauthorized use of terminals did not, in fact, occur. Their actual use must be reviewed for the auditor to place reliance on these controls.

Control Over Data

Application controls are defined as those controls built into each application to ensure the complete and accurate input, update, validity, and maintenance of the application data.

On-line teleprocessing systems differ from document-oriented batch processing systems because transactions may be originated at a terminal instead of on a controllable document. If source documents are available, user controls similar to those commonly used in batch systems may also be present. If, however, the initial transaction record is on the terminal screen, such user controls may not be feasible. The correct operation of the system will depend largely on the appropriateness of programmed procedures built into the application programs and system software. The key concerns in control of data are discussed in the following sections.

Transaction Authorization. In an on-line system, transaction authorization is largely a function of security software. Terminals can be limited to certain types of transactions, and codes required to enter transactions. If an operator is allowed unlimited access to the system, unauthorized browsing through the files can occur; it may even be possible to create a transaction that will update the data files. That is why it is so important to make sure that only authorized use is permitted. Access to the system must be controlled, as discussed earlier, in the section "Security of Terminals and Access."

Transaction Accuracy and Validity. In on-line systems, it is possible and helpful to check the validity of data fields before a transaction is accepted. Tests for transaction validity should ensure that:

- Data is in the correct format, through on-line prompting or questioning of the user and format checks.
- Account or reference keys are accurate and valid. In particular:
  - The operator should be notified of invalid keys so corrections can be made. An invalid account number, for example, may mean that the account does not exist and could mean that the transaction is unauthorized.
  - The selected key should be correct. By introducing an interactive check that provides the operator with the description of each account key entered, it becomes possible to visually check that the correct key or information was entered.
- Transaction data is reasonable and within defined limits, such as a sales order should not exceed the available credit limit or balance for an account.

To reduce the likelihood of updating files with erroneous data, a transaction should not be accepted until the required operator and computer subsystem message exchanges (such as responses to the prompts) have been completed. Suspense files may hold unaccepted transactions or, alternately, the transaction can be terminated. The follow-up action taken will depend on the nature of each application.

In situations where incoming data is validated by reference to data fields that will themselves be updated once the incoming data is accepted, it is important to ensure that other, subsequent incoming data is not validated until the previous transaction has been completed. For example, incoming sales orders are often subject to a credit availability check: The credit limit must exceed all unpaid sales transactions for that account by at least the value of the new order. If the order is accepted, it increases the amount of unpaid sales and decreases the credit availability by an equal amount. If the system allows a second order for the same customer to be validated before the update of the previous order has been completed, the credit check becomes invalid, since it will not take the first order into account.

Completeness of Transactions. Ensuring completeness of input can be a problem in on-line systems whenever accountable documents are not used as a basis for entering transactions. In some applications, such as on-line banking systems, transactions are logged and/or totaled at each terminal. Transaction totals can be subsequently reconciled to cash balances to provide a completeness of input control.

In other applications, where transactions are created on-line, an interactive feedback check may be relied on. For example, a sales clerk taking orders over the telephone enters a transaction without having a physical document on hand. The application program sends an acknowledgment that the order has been accepted and permits the next sales order to be entered. It is critical that the application program logs the accepted transaction on a transaction history file and adds it to a control total as part of the acknowledgment routine. The allocation of sequence numbers by the application program is not in itself a control over completeness of input. It may, however, facilitate subsequent control procedures, such as computer matching or control over completeness of update.

File Updating. Control over file or data base updates in full on-line update applications is usually achieved by reconciling the control totals of the transaction history file to the totals from the updated files. This reconciliation is normally performed at the end of the day's on-line processing. In this way, the day's transactions are grouped for processing and reconciliation in a manner similar to one batch. If the reconciliation process finds that the totals disagree, further processing is required to find the errors.

Another technique involves taking copies of the master file at selected checkpoints in processing. These copies are subsequently updated in batch mode by the transactions recorded on the history file. Such updates are often processed using a technique called memo updates, in which the system issues a memo to temporarily update a copy of the file (important so that, for example, cash withdrawals from an automated teller machine do not exceed the available balance) and then actual update is performed in batches overnight. Matching the updated copy file against the master file used during actual on-line processing then provides assurance of both the completeness and the accuracy of the update process.

Backup and Recovery of the System

Adequate procedures should be built into the system to handle either a complete system failure or the failure of a system component. The purpose of recovery procedures is to allow normal operations to resume as quickly as possible, without the introduction of errors.

Recovery procedures should include the following:

- The ability to identify the status of all processing in the computer subsystem so that a cutoff can be established. A checkpoint facility may be incorporated where before-and-after images of the master file fields being updated are written to the transaction file, allowing the computer to reinstate the records it held prior to the failure.
- The ability to status check and account for all messages in transit, such as numbering, time/date identification, and logging of messages at switching centers and communication controllers. This is important to ensure that messages are neither lost nor processed twice as a result of system failure.
- Provision for maintaining security copies of transaction history files and other log files needed for restarts or reruns.
- The safe storage of critical system information, such as current network configurations.
- Dynamic back-out of partially processed transactions.

Cutoff procedures following system recovery are simplified if the user terminals can be advised of the last transaction accepted. Then the users can resume processing by entering the next transaction in sequence. If users do not know the last transaction accepted, they may reprocess accepted transactions.

For long delays caused by major failures, alternate processing facilities may be required to permit normal business to continue. The alternatives may include manual processing or use of backup computer facilities for situations where manual processing is not practical or possible. In a large-scale network, it is possible to designate one of the remote sites to take over processing on an interim basis.

Depending on the nature of the system and the adequacy of its application controls, many backup and recovery procedures may be essentially administrative or operational in nature. This possibility should be taken into consideration when reviewing the controls.

Information Technology Control Considerations

On-line teleprocessing systems often involve programmed procedures that cannot be checked in detail by the user. Such systems cannot be readily controlled or audited solely by examining output. Therefore, all aspects of IT controls over such processing environments are likely to be important.

Implementation Controls. System design and implementation procedures are critical in on-line teleprocessing systems. This is due to the operational and control complexities involved and the high level of reliability required. Auditors should be involved in the design stages to ensure that appropriate control procedures are incorporated. (See Chapter 22, "System Development Trends and Practices," and Chapter 23, "System Development Methodology and Auditing.")

Program and Data File Security Controls. Some of the major data file security considerations were addressed earlier in the section "Security of Terminals and Access." Adequate data file security within the computer system itself is also essential. On-line programming facilities available via telecommunications and other links require that program files be protected by the same sort of terminal security controls that have been discussed for use with data files. Principally, the production source and load libraries should be protected against unauthorized access either through the on-line programming system or through jobs entered from the programmers' terminals.

Computer Operations Controls. There are various considerations that need to be made regarding adequacy of operations controls:

- To the extent that processing (either batch or on-line) can be initiated from locations outside the computer room, there should be procedures to ensure that only authorized processing occurs. Procedures should ensure that only authorized jobs are processed using the correct data files and programs.
- In a centralized processing environment, one security technique is limiting access to the computer. When computer operations hardware or software, such as the master terminals, are located outside the environment, similar restrictions should be placed on access as would normally be enforced in a centralized processing environment.
- When possible, development systems should be segregated from production systems by electronic separation (separate systems).

System Software. Controls over system software (including communications software and security software) are necessary to ensure the correct operation of the system, its software, and the controls that rely on that software. (See Chapter 27, "System Software.")

Communications Controls

To consider the significance of communications controls, it may be useful to limit the examination to the following areas of concern to an auditor:

- A message may be lost from the system.
- A message may be routed to the wrong address in the system.
- A message may contain errors.
- An unauthorized message may be introduced into the system.
- Messages may be monitored by unauthorized methods.

One technique used to provide error control in transmission links is the automatic request for repetition (ARQ) technique. This technique is a feature of almost all data transmission systems that provide for error control and involves attaching an additional sequence of bits, called check bits, to a block of data. This sequence of bits is computed from the contents of the block. Then, at the receiving terminal, the check sequence is recomputed. If the computed sequence does not match the check bits that were received, a request to retransmit the data block is automatically sent to the transmitting terminal.

IBM's SDLC and BSC protocols provide this capability. This type of line-error protocol detects transmission errors between a sending and a receiving point that employ the protocol.

Routing verification procedures, such as checks of message addresses in headers, are also necessary to ensure that:

- The message destination is valid and is authorized to receive data.
- Unbroken message sequences are received.

The communications network makes it difficult to control physical access to transmission lines. This creates a risk of unauthorized monitoring, unauthorized modifications to messages, or both. As a result, security software often provides alternate methods to restrict access. Encryption of messages reduces the chances that unauthorized intervention will produce any useable information, but this is not generally employed in accounting applications. Multiplexing messages with others increases the difficulty of understanding messages through monitoring.

As discussed previously, full end-to-end control includes the use of acknowledgments between the terminal and the application program. When this level of control is built into application programs, it may provide assurance that transmission is complete and accurate. Controls over the system of communications, however, may be viewed as helping to ensure the reliability of the communications environment rather than the accuracy of the application data, so that even where controls over communications are adequate, the application data controls must still be reviewed, evaluated, and tested.

CONTROL ASPECTS OF DISTRIBUTED DATA PROCESSING SYSTEMS

Impact of Distributed Data Processing

Computer resources are decentralized to varying degrees in DDP systems, as was described previously. This decentralization can include:

- Distributed data.
- Distributed software.
- Distributed system development and maintenance.

Distributed Data. In distributed processing systems, the creation and maintenance of data by remote network users results in distributed data. Since these users are not in the central location, particular data may be collected and processed only at their remote location. It may be retrieved from, and transmitted to, other points in the network. Data may be stored locally, either in standard file structures or as a data base.

Distributed Software. In order to permit processing at sites outside the central computer facility, the system software and application programs required to process the data must be located at the remote site. In many cases this occurs as part of a computer configuration that includes microcomputers or minicomputers, or both, with local processing abilities.

Distributed System Development and Maintenance. Software located at remote sites may be developed centrally. In other cases, the remote users are responsible for the design, implementation, and maintenance of the systems running at their location. When this is true, it is necessary to make sure that there are standards and controls over these procedures. The same types of controls over program maintenance and development, such as procedures to ensure that only authorized changes are made to programs and that those changes are properly tested and implemented, are required.

Audit Considerations in Distributed Processing

For the purpose of an audit, distributed processing is usually viewed as a configuration where application systems are processed in whole or in part at locations other than the central computer. This frequently includes the use of financially significant data files and programs at sites outside the central computer facility. Important considerations in understanding and evaluating such systems are:

- Extent to which application systems are processed outside the central computer facility.
- Extent to which program and data files are located outside the central facility.
- Means by which the systems are controlled; in particular, the effectiveness of IT controls at the various points in the network where significant processing is performed and significant computer files are used.

Areas of Concern in Distributed Data Processing Environments—Checklist

Evaluation of controls in a DDP environment involves similar audit concerns and control objectives as in a centralized processing environment. However, there are frequently many more exposures. Ideally, application controls should be implemented to ensure the complete and accurate input and update of data, its validity, and the proper maintenance of data held on computer files. Also, programmed procedures are usually not controlled by the user, so that IT controls should exist. Problems arise because the controls that are typically found in centralized computing systems may not be implemented in smaller remote sites associated with DDP environments. Another concern is that when microcomputers are used in such systems, it is rare to find adequate IT controls. Similar difficulties arise in installations that use minicomputers, since the staff is usually too small to implement an adequate division of duties, for one example. Some factors that have resulted in unfavorable control characteristics in distributed systems are outlined below.

1. Access to Microcomputers and Other Intelligent Nodes:

☐ Security software adequate to prevent unauthorized access to computer files or to the network may not be implemented at the microcomputer or minicomputer levels.

☐ The size of main storage may preclude the use of available security software that requires a substantial memory area for installation and takes up much of the processing capability.

☐ Use of security software may degrade the performance of the microcomputer or minicomputer systems so much that the overall performance of the distributed system is no longer acceptable. In this case, it is often decided not to employ the security software.

☐ In the absence of adequate security software, physical security procedures (e.g., locks, voice-activated mechanisms, etc.) may be the only means of protecting access both to the network and to files maintained at the remote site. The local user may be unwilling or unable to implement such physical security procedures, when they are expensive or impossible due to space constraints and such.

2. Application Controls at Local Sites:

☐ The local user may not understand the need to implement application controls, or they may be inadequate even when understood.

☐ Depending on the nature of the system, strong central supervision of locally operated controls may be necessary to ensure that controls are properly coordinated throughout the remote sites.

☐ If there are redundancies in the distributed data, centrally monitored controls may be necessary to ensure that data is not included more than once in any financial information prepared from the distributed data. The data must also be synchronized so that it does not become out of date and/or vary from one remote site to the next.

3. Local System Development:

☐ Local system development usually suffers from lack of enforceable standards, such as controls to ensure that programs are satisfactorily tested.

☐ Documentation of locally developed systems is often insufficient or nonexistent.

☐ Documentation of program changes is often insufficient or inadequate.

☐ Small numbers of local staff may result in an inadequate separation of duties at the remote site.

☐ It is less likely that adequate controls will be included when systems are developed. Provision for audit information and control reports are two items that are frequently overlooked.

Ways to Achieve a Controlled Environment—Checklist

There are many ways to control remote and distributed data processing, including:

1. Centralization of System Development:

☐ All new systems and enhancements should be developed by a central software support function.

☐ Only the load modules should be distributed to remote user locations. Those locations should not be permitted to have compiler facilities. Unique version numbers should be used that will identify the copies of the same programs when they are distributed to different locations.

2. When Remote Users Are Directly Responsible for the Development of Accounting Applications:

☐ A centrally controlled quality assurance function should be established to ensure adherence to minimum control standards.

☐ The actual network configuration and communications system should be controlled by a central teleprocessing software administrator.

3. Access to the System via Remote Terminals:

☐ Software controls over access to the computer, data files, and remote access to the network should be implemented.

☐ The physical control environment should be as secure as possible, such as having lockable terminals and computer room.

☐ Supervisory controls should be established over terminal and computer operations at the remote locations.

☐ Opportunities for unauthorized people to gain a knowledge of the system should be limited, such as by implementing controls over access to system documentation and manuals.

4. Applications Controls:

☐ Controls should exist over data transmitted between locations, such as sales in one location that update accounts receivable files at another location. The sending location should transmit control information, such as transaction control totals, to enable the receiving location to control the update of its files. When practical, central monitoring of controls should ensure that all remotely processed data is correct.

☐ When replicated files exist at multiple locations, controls should ensure that all files used are correct and current and, when data is used to produce financial information, that no duplication arises.

On the whole, telecommunications has made the efficient processing from remote locations possible for many organizations. When the proper controls are built in, the benefits of computer networks far outweigh any negative aspects such as security risks. In a well-designed and controlled environment, such risks can be kept to a minimum.

AUDITING TELECOMMUNICATIONS NETWORKS

The increased use and dependence on telecommunications technology dictate the need for active audit involvement. Threats and risk to sensitive and critical data accessed and transmitted through these networks have grown exponentially because of newly affordable communications equipment and an increase in the number of potential users. Therefore, a primary security issue is to ensure that access to and use of telecommunications resources are appropriate and authorized.

Setting Audit Scope

An initial step in the audit of a telecommunications network is to determine the scope of the audit. Depending on the network and its purpose, processing environment, and stage of development, there are as many as four perspectives from which it should be reviewed:

- *Operational*—An audit of a network's operating characteristics.
- *Development*—An audit of a network during planning or development stages.
- *System*—An audit of a network system design under development or in operation.
- *Compliance*—An audit of a network's compliance with the law, industry and company standards, and good business practices.

Applications used in a telecommunications environment introduce their associated risks into the network in which they operate. User requirements, based on the applications used, affect performance requirements and, therefore, the access demands and security risks of the network. Depending on the type of audit conducted, the auditor should determine if the network is performing properly and as designed. For example, what effect would the malfunction of a network component (e.g., a switching node) have on the system, the user, and the application? Controls to ensure the proper security performance and reliability of all network components need to be assessed. (Risks and controls for the network and each component are discussed later, in the section "Risks and Control Techniques by Network Component.")

The following considerations should be addressed during a telecommunications network audit:

- Is the network cost-effective? Is its operation and design consistent with its expected life cycle?
- Is physical security sufficient to safeguard equipment, users, and information?
- Is critical data protected from loss of damage? Is sensitive data protected from unauthorized exposure?
- Is network management providing the appropriate direction, policies, and standards for effective network service?
- Are appropriate hardware and software techniques being used to ensure network reliability?
- Are controls sufficient to ensure that access to the network is limited to authorized users?
- Is network utility use accounted for?
- Is the system meeting user requirements? Are there facilities available to measure performance?
- Are there operational procedures to ensure that system availability is maintained?
- Does system design allow revisions to the network without disruption to existing links? Does backup exist in case of media failure?

An entity's policies, organizational structure, and needs, as they relate to the network, have an impact on the audit. Identifying these elements helps the auditor define audit objectives:

- *Corporate policies and standards*—Review the corporate policies and standards that apply to the network service function.
- *Network management*—Review the management structure of the network service organization. Does that structure provide effective service?
- *Network function/requirements*—Review the network's functions in terms of applications, types of data, and importance to the company.

- *User requirements*—What are the user requirements for existing and future services? If these are not defined clearly or are based on estimates of current use patterns—not growth—strategic planning for the future cannot be done effectively. Network failure can result if monitored improperly.

Individuals responsible for the network and its elements need to be identified. Areas of responsibility include:

- Design
- Operations and maintenance
- Interface with:
  - MIS
  - Users
  - Telecommunications
- Security

These individuals should receive the report at the conclusion of the audit.

Audit Objectives and Conduct

Audits need to be tailored individually because some network components will receive more or less attention than others, depending on the type of audit and the complexity of the network and operating environment. For example, in a development audit, the auditor may recommend security provisions and performance parameters that should be incorporated during the network's development, whereas in an operational audit, the auditor may address the adequacy of those features. In a compliance audit, the auditor will determine whether the installed network complies with the original design.

Every network should meet a set of functional requirements based on these factors:

- End users' needs.
- The processor's specifications.
- Governmental requirements (federal, state, and local).
- Corporate requirements (standards, policies, and procedures).

One audit objective is to determine whether the network functions as it was designed and meets requirements. The auditor also should identify the network components and how well they perform. The auditor should also determine what security, preventive, corrective, and recovery provisions exist. Finally, but perhaps most important, the auditor must assess threats to the network, and the controls in place to reduce risk. To accomplish those objectives, the auditor must gather data by reviewing the network, its components, and its documentation, and by communicating with the individuals responsible for network operations.

Data Gathering. Data gathering can be the most difficult task of the audit because documentation and records may be maintained poorly, hard to find, or nonexistent. Well-planned interviews of responsible individuals should be conducted to supplement documentation. Ideally, the auditor should collect and review:

- The original network requirements definition based on:
  - The feasibility study.
  - The proposed design and alternatives.
  - The trade-off study and decisions.
- Design standards, criteria, approach, and documentation.
- Development and implementation plans.
- Network operations and maintenance plans and procedures.
- Testing criteria, plans, procedures, and results.
- The original and current configurations and configuration change controls.
- Performance standards, reports, history, trends, and the applied measurement techniques.
- Identification of critical or vulnerable network elements and controls to lower risk.
- Audit trails in the network.
- Contingency and disaster recovery plans.
- Inventory of applications and network users.
- Analysis of security requirements for current and proposed applications.
- Inventory and analysis of current and proposed circuits.
- Network personnel training program.

Review. A thorough understanding of the network environment can be helpful to the auditor. This includes an understanding of the network's life cycle and any completed or planned changes, integrations, consolidations, or expansions. For example, if the network is to be replaced, the auditor would perform a development audit of the new network rather than an operational audit of the existing network.

The analysis phase can be time-consuming, but it also can be the key to a successful audit. The auditor should ensure that the design meets all communication requirements and complies with any applicable regulations. The development and implementation plan should satisfy requirements as well. Testing should be performed to ensure both.

The network's configuration must be accurate, current, and readily available to the authorized operations and maintenance personnel. No changes should be permitted without ensuring that they will not affect current capabilities. Provisions for reverting to the prior configuration should be available in case it is needed.

Standards. Once a network is operational, a set of standards is needed against which performance can be measured and reported. These standards must be understandable and upgradable. They must be strict enough to ensure user satisfaction, but not so much so that they damage morale or incur excessive costs. Performance standards can satisfy users and corporate management, but still not provide for ease of use, auditability, security, or versatility of the network. A network can perform effectively and efficiently, yet be extremely vulnerable to security breaches.

Analysis of Weaknesses. Review is likely to raise questions on suspected weaknesses. If data gathering was inadequate or key points were missed during review, this stage is the time to conduct other interviews to see if there are additional data sources that can be accessed. As usual, risks should be matched against controls to see if controls are missing or inadequate.

Backups or Workarounds. In addition to controls, many networks have provisions for temporary backups or workarounds. These should be assessed to determine:

- Whether they have been tested recently.
- Whether they can be implemented quickly.
- Whether they provide full or partial backup.
- How long they might serve the need.
- What other service might be affected, and how severely, if the backup is implemented.

For some components, the auditor should look within the network to reduce risks. For example, if the mean time is great to restore service after interruption, the auditor may want to consider the adequacy of maintenance contracts and procedures. Also, since all companies are relying more on communications and data processing, it is imperative to have contingency and disaster recovery plans which are tested and maintained under the jurisdiction of qualified professionals.

Documentation of Findings. This should describe the audit and identify:

- The target network, or portions thereof.
- The responsible parties, and specify those interviewed.
- The purpose, scope, and objectives of the review.
- The general audit approach.
- The documentation reviewed.
- Key findings.
- Good areas that might be useful to other networks.
- Weaknesses and recommendations.

The findings should then be reviewed with the responsible individuals, preferably prior to release to management. A cover letter to the audit report should schedule when management should respond.

Risks and Control Techniques by Network Component

Four network components support processing and switching needs, or "traffic," between hosts (i.e., mainframe or minicomputer) and remote nodes (i.e., user terminals). The components are:

- *Switching nodes*—The equipment that processes and routes the data based on the message's destination and the network's configuration.
- *Trunk lines and user access lines*—The media that connect switching nodes and transmit data signals along the specified path.
- *Modems and concentrators*—A modem is a modulation/demodulation device used to transmit data signals from an originating source to its destination via the communications link. A concentrator is an intelligent device that combines several data signals, sent simultaneously from independent stations, into one data stream.

- *Network control center (NCC)*—A diagnostic center with privileged access to provide operational and maintenance support to the network. It monitors the status of all network components, and includes:
  - — Fault prediction and identification.
  - — System processing restoration.
  - — Event reporting.

Each component has function-specific risks that require control consideration. Vulnerabilities and control techniques for the four components are discussed in the following sections.

Switching Nodes. Processing and routing the data in a network are subject to numerous risks, including:

- Omissions, accidental or otherwise, and errors in the transmission to or from the switching node. To control this risk, documentation should be maintained and referenced, including acknowledgments for all messages sent. Also, detection/correction software should be implemented.
- Inadequate capacity to handle traffic. Controls to avoid this problem include:
  - — Analyzing, trending, and predicting traffic volume during development based on design specifications.
  - — Prioritizing messages for transmission once the network is operational.
- Misrouting messages. Incorrectly transmitted data can be addressed by:
  - — Software that validates destination.
  - — Sequence number checks.
  - — Node edits of destination address.
- Component failure. To avoid malfunctioning, the network should have:
  - — Redundancy and sufficient power supply.
  - — Adequate backup of high-risk components.
  - — Sufficient vendor maintenance for switching nodes.
- Switching node software error. This can result for any number of reasons. To ensure proper procurement, review:
  - — Software change and modification control procedures.
  - — Utilities used to validate changes.
  - — Software design and default options.

- Poor vendor support. Consider maintenance adequacy by reviewing maintenance contracts, service response time, and software and hardware documentation.
- Unauthorized access to switching room facilities. Physical controls should include equipment rooms with alarms, locks, and good personnel practices (e.g., bonding, rotation practices).
- Unauthorized access to network system. Control options include:
  - —Call-back capability on sensitive dial-up access facilities.
  - —Identification by user password, terminal, and sequence numbers.
  - —Operator logon passwords and security levels.
  - —Assurance that the software does not cycle access to other users if communications circuit fails.
- Unauthorized access to data files. Access should be secured:
  - —Centrally for downloading to distributed sites.
  - —By monitoring access by programs and data base files (tables should be protected in memory).
  - —By software security controls.
- Power failure. Contingency plans should ensure that adequate backup of environmental supports; heating, ventilation, and air conditioning (HVAC); and power supply exists. Separate paths for communication gear on recovery generators provide additional assurance of accurate processing resumption.
- Operator error. Human mistakes can be minimized if training is adequate and system interface is controlled. It is imperative that documentation of operations procedures be maintained.

Trunk Lines and User Access Lines. The lines that carry data signals along a path are vulnerable to:

- Loss of continuity. Adequate link redundance of a backup access channel should be designed into the network to avoid such a breakdown or ensure access for correction.
- Errors associated with line degradation and interference. Use of digital transmission over analog transmission can help to reduce the risk of such interruptions. However, if analog is used, consider phased conditioning.
- Power loss. Typically, installation of redundant power supply, where feasible, is an effective contingency plan. In addition, a reverse channel capability for controlling signals can be used.
- Unauthorized access to links (e.g., tapping). To reduce this risk,

media circuits should be physically secured and public switchboard pathing avoided.

- Unauthorized physical access to circuit switching room. Physical controls should be implemented to ensure adequate protection from unauthorized access and restrict bypass security. Documentation for circuit assignment changes should be reviewed, as well as updates to installations and trend circuits paths to detect tapping and duplication.
- Inadequate vendor support. As with the switching nodes, maintenance agreements and response time for new service, maintenance, and equipment installation should be considered.

Modems and Concentrators. Risks vary depending on which device is used. Modems should be designed to handle network line degradation. The following controls help ensure the proper functioning of a modem:

- Diagnostic indicators on the device to indicate circuit malfunctions.
- Adequate design specifications.
- Secondary channels and alternate voice capabilities.
- Reverse channel capabilities.
- Adequate "mean time between failure" (MTBF) ratio.
- Automatic equalization to compensate for transmission errors.

Because concentrators combine several data signals simultaneously, sequence number checking is important. For effective control the auditor should:

- Ensure message reports indicate messages processed, illegal messages, and the like.
- Verify tables and transaction journals for updates, additions, and deletions.
- Consider two-level reviews—one of items for messages, rerouting, addressing, and party checks, and another of transactions that enter the system per application program.

Network Control Center. NCC, as the communication center of the network, is subject to an array of control considerations. A variety of vendors and technologies can make it difficult to collect and assimilate control point information. Often, operators are service—and not security—oriented. On the other hand, technical personnel are so technically oriented that they may lack cross-training (with operations) and avoid documenting procedures. Finally, operator and technician privileges are difficult to control, since their access is broad and changes frequently.

Other weaknesses the auditor should look for include:

- Lack of adequate network change control procedures.
- Inadequate or inaccurate network documentation. Are there established standards and procedures for daily documentation maintenance and periodic review of documentation and tests of compliance to standards?
- Ineffectively controlled test equipment. Physical security and adequate training in the correct use of test equipment can help reduce this risk. In addition, an inventory of test equipment should be maintained and reviewed periodically.
- Ineffective operating procedures. Procedures for recording and connecting each class and type of problem and operating function should be established. This includes setting standards for the development and maintenance of those procedures in order to locate problems and facilitate response.
- Inadequately trained personnel and undue reliance on individual expertise. To reduce this likelihood, ensure that adequate training is provided for network employees. Rotation can improve cross-training between operations and technical personnel.
- Failure to monitor and resolve network problems. If this is found in the NCC, the auditor should:
  - Ensure that adequate problem identification and resolution procedures are in place (e.g., prediction, identification, determination, bypass, and resolution).
  - Consider the effects of installing an automated system to track and record all problems.
  - Determine if maintenance of problem areas is coordinated.
  - Recommend implementation of shift turnover procedures and summaries of shift activities.

ELECTRONIC DATA INTERCHANGE

Electronic data interchange (EDI) is the electronic transmission of standard business documents in machine-readable format between corporate trading partners' computers. It replaces the physical exchange of common paper documents, such as purchase orders or invoices.

In the late 1960s, the transportation industries developed EDI to help alleviate delivery delays that resulted from large volumes of paper documentation. Today, approximately 50 industries worldwide use EDI, including transportation, automotive, and pharmaceutical. Others include:

- Chemical
- Retail
- Manufacturing
- Utilities
- Health care
- Financial services
- Government

Standards

Most EDI transactions are formatted following predetermined standards. These specify data format so that both partners handle data the same (e.g., each data element in a document always occupies the same field in a file). Uniform standards facilitate trade with multiple EDI partners using the same format.

Standard X.12, developed in the late 1970s by the Accredited Standards Committee of the American National Standards Institute (ANSI), is currently the most prevalent EDI standard in the United States. It is a uniform, interindustry format used by EDI trading partners. Strong international support also exists for the United Nations-backed EDI for Administration, Commerce, and Transport Standard that would unite all standards around the world.

Communications Options

Various methods are used to transmit data via EDI, each affecting the control considerations discussed later in this chapter. Two data transmission methods are discussed in the following sections.

Point-to-Point Connection. EDI partners can establish a direct link between their computers to transmit electronic documents from one computer into another. This point-to-point connection raises scheduling and compatibility concerns when dealing with multiple trading partners.

FIG. 7-9
Inbound EDI transaction

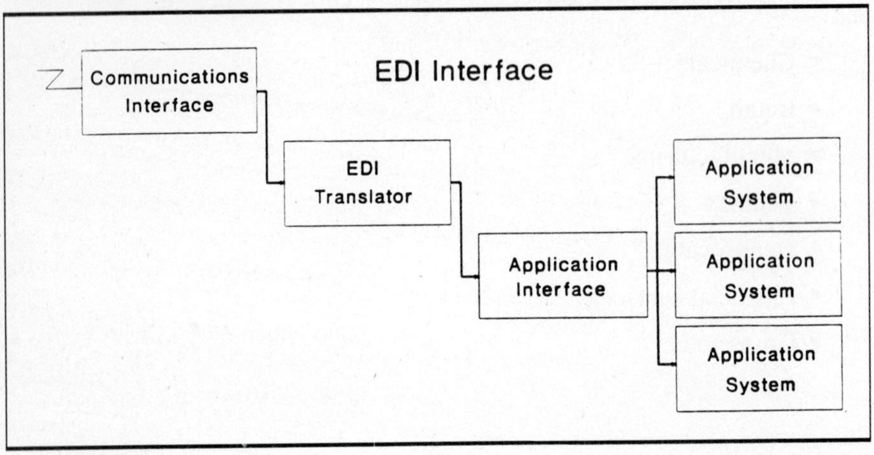

Value Added Networks. Value added networks (VANs) are third-party networks that store and forward EDI documents for trading partners. Additional services performed include format checking and translating. The sending partner links electronically with the VAN and transmits a document. Upon receipt, the VAN determines the recipient and places the data in an "electronic mailbox" (i.e., a file on the VAN's computer system) where it remains until the recipient connects with the VAN, accesses the file, and retrieves the document. As always with a third party, the appropriate controls should be assessed for design and continued operation.

System Architecture

Typically, EDI transactions are processed by three elements: the communication interface, the EDI interface, and the application system. Whether being sent or received, the transaction is processed by those three system elements and demands appropriate control techniques to monitor transmissions. (See Figure 7-9, which illustrates an inbound transaction).

Communications Interface. The communications interface transmits or receives the electronic document. It has controls to ensure that the data is received properly, especially in the event of transmission error or interruption. In addition, routing verification procedures ensure that the destination is valid and the system is authorized to send or receive data. Many control techniques are performed by hardware and system software and, typically, are time-tested by organizations' normal teleprocessing procedures.

EDI Interface. The EDI interface serves two functions: one performed by the EDI translator and the other by the application interface. The EDI translator translates between standard format and the trading partners' proprietary format. It can generate functional acknowledgments (FAs) that are transmitted to a sender when a document is received. FA matches can be performed to ensure that all transactions sent were received and vice versa.

The EDI translator can also perform authorization checks of transactions received against a trading partner master file to verify the partner and its authorized transactions.

The application interface passes electronic transactions to or from the application system. This entails either distribution of inbound transactions to appropriate systems or collection of documents from those systems.

Controls Impact

EDI processing has an impact on application and IT controls. The controls discussed in the following sections relate solely to the processing of EDI transactions in preparation for delivery to an application system. Note that regular application controls remain in effect when EDI transactions are processed by an application system. (See Chapter 13, "Information Technology Controls," Chapter 14, "Application Controls—I," and Chapter 15, "Application Controls—II," for definitions and descriptions of controls in the computer environment.)

Application Controls

EDI processing involves recording transaction data as part of input or output to an application system. The control objectives affected are discussed in the following sections.

Completeness of Input. The following control procedures ensure that all EDI transactions are sent or received, input, translated, and processed only once by the application.

- Maintain and check control totals, such as batch totals, sequence numbers, and "line item counts" to:
  —Track missing transmissions.
  —Validate completeness.
  —Ensure one-time-only receipt of a transaction.

- Match functional acknowledgment reports.
- Review exception reports to ensure correction of problems.
- Review VAN reports. (Typically, they include information that allows EDI transmissions to be tracked and provide an audit trail.)
- Review system software controls that verify completeness.
- Review error recovery procedures.

Accuracy of Input. The following control procedures ensure that EDI transactions are sent or received, translated, and input accurately for application processing. They also should identify errors in initial recording, transcription, computation, and transmission of data.

- Perform application interface edits of transactions passed to the system (similar to those performed against on-line transaction entry, such as reasonable and matching checks).
- Review system software controls that verify accuracy.
- Review transaction syntax edits that occur during the translator phase against EDI standards.
- Review exception reports to ensure correction of differences or omissions.
- Review recovery procedures.

Note that EDI processing typically does not involve calculations or overriding of standing data; therefore, the associated risks are not issues.

Authorization of Transactions. Inbound transactions should be checked to ensure that they are from partners authorized to send. The following control procedures ensure that only valid and authorized EDI transactions are received and processed by the application system.

- Maintenance of a list of partners (i.e., a trading partner master file) and the transactions they are authorized to send.
- Communication about exceptions or failures, and subsequent actions, between users and MIS.
- Review documentation (e.g., the trading partner agreements to support authorization).
- Build authentication schemes into transmissions.

Once in the application system, EDI transactions are subject to the standard application controls over master file updates. Therefore, control objectives discussed in the following sections are not affected by EDI processing.

File Continuity. These controls are not affected because EDI deals with input to or output from the application system—not stored data. Master files are updated with EDI data after it is passed to or from the application system; therefore, it is subject to the same controls as other transactions.

Asset Protection. EDI processing does not affect the custody of physical assets. If a transaction causes an asset (e.g., inventory) to be moved, authorization controls verify the interface to the EDI translator and standard application controls ensure that assets remain secure, and movements are controlled properly.

Generation of Transactions. EDI does not generate financially significant transactions automatically. However, the application system controls are in effect when transactions are processed.

Update of Data. EDI does not affect the regular updating process that takes place in the application system because EDI transactions are merged with regular transactions prior to the update. Note that while these controls are not affected by EDI processing, when an application system is modified to integrate an EDI system, the controls should be reassessed.

Information Technology Controls

EDI processes are similar to those of any application system in that IT controls support processing. Most of a company's existing IT controls apply to EDI processing. However, some new control procedures for computer operations and security control may be necessary to ensure integrity.

Implementation Controls. Implementation controls are important when an EDI processing system is implemented as a standalone system, or as a function integrated into an existing application system. In either instance, control concerns are similar to those that apply to any application system. Usually, file conversion controls are not affected unless converting from an existing EDI system.

When implementing an independent EDI system that will interface with an application system, implementation procedures and control considerations are the same as for any system. However, if an existing application system is modified to integrate EDI processing, then the entire application system must be reevaluated for implementation controls. (See Chapter 13 for a discussion of implementation controls.)

Maintenance Controls. Like an application system, an EDI system, specifically the translation and interface software, must be maintained properly to remain effective. For example, organizations must ensure that new or most current revisions of EDI standards are used. In the EDI environment, maintenance control concerns may be expanded to include:

- Maintenance over new standards or new releases of existing standards.
- Exception capture and reporting control techniques for the translator and interface phases.
- Change management over trading partner relationships and VANs (i.e., adding the new and deleting the old).

Computer Operations Controls. EDI affects computer operations controls because it involves the operation of a separate system with controls unique to electronic transaction processing. The computer operations controls should be reviewed to ensure that:

- Authorized programmed procedures are applied consistently.
- Proper data files are used.
- Contingency plans exist for the resuming processing in the event of failure or stoppage.
- Programs, transaction files, and trading partner master files are backed up and work.
- Operation procedures are revised to address EDI processing in MIS.

Security Controls. Through prevention and detection, security controls should ensure that EDI data files, program files, and networks are not at risk from unauthorized changes. Security should be assessed at these levels:

- Transaction files:
  - —Existing techniques (where applicable).
  - —Controls available within the EDI transmission (such as passwords or data encryption).

- The internal EDI processing system, including existing access controls over data, program files, and transaction initiation facilities.
- The network that transmits the data via VANs or directly to a partner.
- The VAN, especially if transaction data is confidential.

System Software Controls. Like application systems, EDI processing relies on system software, especially telecommunications software that facilitates inbound and outbound transmissions. Typically, these procedures are established within MIS. Basically, system software issues relate to:

- Controlled implementation and maintenance of EDI processing software.
- Adequate security over system software.

Operational Controls and Issues

EDI processing raises operational control issues that relate to efficient use of resources and achievement of objectives and goals. Considerations that should be addressed include:

- *Trading partner agreement*—This contract between partners should define "written" and "signed" electronic documents, discount periods, accountability, timing issues, and general terms and conditions of the relationship.
- *File retention*—The issue of how long EDI transaction files are retained for audit, security, and management purposes should be addressed.
- *User education*—All users and MIS personnel should be well-informed about operations and responsibilities in the EDI environment.
- *Documentation*—EDI policies and procedures should be documented adequately.
- *System availability and reliability*—Procedures should exist to monitor and report system availability and reliability. Is the EDI function structured effectively and efficiently? As more transactions are processed using EDI, this issue becomes increasingly critical.
- *Policy compliance*—Policies regarding EDI must be understood and complied with consistently. Policies may address network access, addition of VANs and trading partners, and processing standards.

PART III

Information Systems

CHAPTER **8**

Introduction to Information Systems

INTRODUCTION

In considering the kinds of things that computers do best, it almost seems that they were invented to allow business to automate accounting systems. Seemingly endless streams of numbers, details, and transactions that once were recorded painstakingly in longhand can be tracked on an up-to-the-minute basis if that is what a business requires.

Of course, the people involved in making sure that all that data was not only on hand, but accurate and complete at the same time, were quick to appreciate the obvious. To have a machine that not only followed orders to the letter, but could rapidly calculate to a precision beyond that of the finest mathematicians, is something that an organization could only dream about a few short decades ago. Some of the most repetitious and tedious work—footing and refooting sets of numbers, backtracking of transactions from first order through getting paid for same, performing "what if" calculations—can be done in seconds. It is not surprising that the value of computers to business was recognized at the outset. It is thought that the first business data processing on a computer occurred in the mid-1950s when General Electric acquired the UNIVAC-1, the first commercially marketed computer.

Accounting's manual procedures have not changed much since people figured out why they needed debits and credits to make a system of bookkeeping work. The only difference is that over time they have become increasingly complex. More descriptive names have been developed for the same procedures. The data processing (DP) department has become management information systems (MIS).

Whatever it is called, DP is still responsible in part for the same number-crunching, sorting, and reporting of information from accounting. Even after "accounting" has become "financial information systems," it still has to make sure that its trial balances balance.

ACCOUNTING PROCEDURES' RELATIONSHIP TO SYSTEMS

To apply the principles of accounting to organizations, there is a standard set of systems and procedures to be followed. These systems consist of a set of records that are filled out in a specific series of steps. These records are the basis of all accounting systems, regardless of whether they are manual or computerized, and include ledgers, journals, and registers. All the financial activity in an organization is recorded in these records so that there is a physical place where the information is available for reference, the actual numbers can be reconciled, and the material is available for use in the creation of reports and financial statements.

To enter this data, or "keep the books," the following procedures are generally the same, both for computer and for manual recordkeeping:

- Creating and processing documents, the basis of business transactions, such as invoices or purchase orders, and ensuring the accuracy of those documents and transactions.
- Keeping records of all transactions in the appropriate place, such as sales orders in the sales journal or payroll data in the payroll register. These primary sources are usually called books of original entry or subsidiary ledgers.
- Posting all transactions to a subsidiary ledger and to the general ledger.
- Preparing general ledger balances and making sure that they agree with the subsidiary ledgers.
- Preparing the trial balance from the general ledger.
- Preparing financial statements using the trial balance. These statements include the balance sheet, income statement, statement of cash flow, and any other statements that may be required to depict an organization's position or operating results. (Figure 8-1 shows the financial reports created by the IBM Interactive Financial System 1-2 (IFS 1-2).)
- Creating reports and projections for management, based on existing financial data.

FINANCIAL INFORMATION SYSTEMS

The significance of computer systems in providing financial information may be best understood in terms of three elements that can be ranked according to their potential impact on financial statements. Usually they are ranked under the following headings:

- Transaction data
- Master file data
- Programmed procedures

Transaction Data

Transaction data is the data that is specific to each transaction. It may be held in its original form (such as by invoice number, invoice date, or invoice amount) or in a summary form (such as current inventory stock on hand).

FIG. 8-1

Main data flow of Interactive Financial System 2 (IFS-2) showing reports produced (courtesy of International Business Machines Corporation)

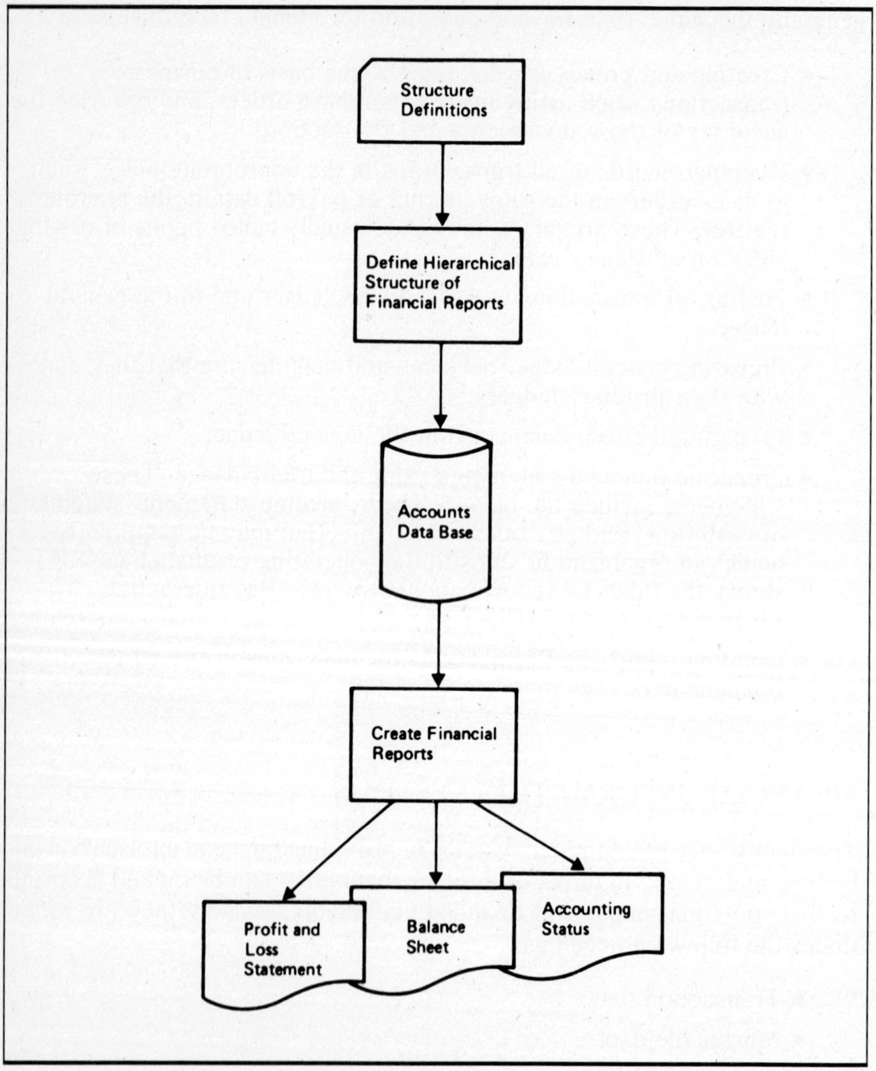

Errors in transaction data have a limited impact. Errors are limited to one transaction at a time and often are detected by subsequent manual or programmed procedures. However, a significant error may result from a single wrong transaction. There is also a danger that bogus transactions will be entered into a poorly controlled system.

Master File Data

Master file data is data of a permanent or semipermanent nature, such as customer number, sales price, employee name, and depreciation rate. Frequently, master file data operates on transaction data for purposes of control, such as customer credit limits on orders, or bookkeeping, as when inventory cost prices are used to calculate inventory value. (This master file reference data is sometimes called standing data.)

Errors in master file data may affect many transactions or all transactions for a particular account, such as the customer, employee, product line, vendor, and so forth. Furthermore, the error may not be detected by manual procedures, since master file data is not frequently printed out and checked. Programs are less likely to be designed to detect errors in low-volume master file data (such as a customer credit limit entered once) than in high-volume transaction data (such as sales to that customer). As an example of such an error, imagine what the repercussions would be if a customer credit limit was entered as $1,000,000 instead of as $1,000.

Programmed Procedures

Program errors have the potential to affect all transaction and master file data that is processed. The errors may not be detected by manual procedures because of a lack of visible evidence and user assumptions that the system is functioning properly. Programmed procedures that do not function properly and other related errors have a way of mounting up over time. They may not be noticeable at first, but eventually they can cause a major difference in the financial records. For example, an erroneous calculation of interest on savings accounts at a large bank of only one cent per account could mean a difference of thousands of dollars over a long period.

FINANCIAL SYSTEMS PROCEDURES

Manual Procedures

Manual procedures in a computerized financial systems environment are sometimes similar to those used in noncomputer systems. They differ in the following ways:

- Specific procedures are required both to prepare data for computer processing and to act on the results of computer processing, as shown by printed reports or by displays on a terminal screen. As an example, to prepare an item for an inventory system there must be a special inventory number scheme that is related to the item descriptions. Those numbers have a specific meaning to the computer and are the key to how it stores the information.
- There is a decrease in the number of manual procedures, with the result that data receives less manual scrutiny and review. For example, invoice extension and calculation are done by the computer, not by hand.

Note that manual procedures are frequently described in written instructions, similar to written procedures of the programs. However, manual procedures are not usually followed as closely as the computer follows the programmed procedures.

Programmed Procedures

Programmed procedures can be used to perform many of the routine calculations, information storage, and decision functions of an accounting system. For convenience, these procedures may be divided into the following categories:

- Bookkeeping functions such as calculation, summarization, categorization, and updating procedures that are applied to the data. For example, an upgrade in an employee's salary requires an update of the payroll master file to arrive at an accurate calculation of the paycheck.
- Procedures relating to control over the completeness, accuracy, validity, and maintenance of data. These normally consist of edit tests, accumulation of totals, reconciliations, and the identification and reporting of incorrect, exceptional, or missing data. Just as automated teller machine customers must use valid transaction codes for cash withdrawal and all inventory items in a retail establishment require inventory numbers, procedures must ensure an accurate, complete, and effective data control system.
- The automatic generation of accounting data or paperwork following the occurrence of another transaction, such as the automatic creation of purchase orders when inventory is reduced below prescribed levels.

Obviously, these programs must contain, in specific detail, all the processing steps required for the computer to be able to accomplish the desired results.

The relative mix and importance of manual and programmed procedures varies, depending on the complexity and type of system in use.

Nature of Data

Traditionally, accounting information is recorded on visible accounting documents (such as invoices, purchase orders, and checks) and in the ledgers and journals of the company. Even when techniques such as microfilm and microfiche are used, the nature of the data and its accessibility do not change.

Lack of Visible Evidence

In a computer system, data is recorded and held in machine-readable form; as such, it is an "invisible" record. Furthermore, not all data held in the computer is printed; summaries and exception reports may be all that is output until the data is required for a particular function. The data that makes up the financial records may not be fully available. Intermediate results of computer processing may be unavailable as well.

For example, detail transactions may be available for a certain period (such as a month). Then, at the end of the period, a total figure summarizes all the detail transactions that occurred within that period. Sales history by product is often maintained in detail for one month and then totaled to sales for the month. This technique is used as an effective way to save on the cost of computer storage. However, this may also mean that a detailed analysis beyond the stored totals may not be readily available.

Data Storage

Data is stored in computer files or data bases. Files are organized sets of data, each with a common subject. Five types of files are generally used:

1. *Temporary files*. These files hold transactions during job processing. They are not usually of major concern to an auditor when considering controls, since the transaction data ends up on master files (see item 3) at the completion of each job. An example of a temporary file is the open invoices file from accounts receivable, often sorted in sequence by date. In the master file, the same information is probably stored in sequence by invoice number. Normally, the open invoice file is stored in sequence of customer number, account number, and invoice number.

2. *Suspense files.* These files contain transactions held in suspense, pending some further action. Examples of these are erroneous transactions held back from further processing and awaiting correction, such as an invoice with an invalid customer number, or orders awaiting shipment.
3. *Master files.* These files represent the subledgers or books of account. They contain all permanent information for each account as well as the current balances (such as accounts receivable master with customers and balances, payroll master with employees and payroll history, general ledger chart of accounts with account descriptions and current month's activity). Master files contain both transaction data and more permanent reference data (also called standing data):
   - *Transaction data.* This is the data unique to each transaction (such as invoice number, invoice date, invoice amount), held in its original form or in a summary form. It represents the current balance, status, or cumulative history of each account.
   - *Reference data.* This is data of a permanent or semipermanent nature such as customer number, sales price, employee name, depreciation rate. Frequently, this master file data is referenced for purposes of control (such as customer credit limit on orders) or accounting computations (such as inventory cost price used to calculate inventory value).
4. *Table files.* These are files of reference data, often used to convert codes and indicators to values. Common table files are a stock price table and a currency conversion rate table.
5. *System files.* These files are used by the system. They can contain system software, application programs, tables that control processing, and activity logs.

The most sophisticated type of file is a data base. Data base concepts are discussed further in Chapter 28, ''Data Base.''

Data Parameters

Parameters (values that restrict or determine the specific form of the instructions) are entered for a job each time it is to be run on the computer. These values may change each time the program is executed (such as date, file generation number, batch number, batch control total). Parameters may also be variable data that could otherwise be coded into the program but is entered separately to allow for flexibility in modifying the system. Examples are a code indicating whether the program is executed daily or monthly, and the dollar value above which sales credit memoranda are reported as exceptional.

Data Retention

In noncomputer systems, there is normally complete retention of all financial records, at least for the period being audited and for the period required by government regulation. Nothing is destroyed until after year-end, and many files are retained for five to seven years.

In computer systems, the cost of storage on magnetic tape or magnetic disk is high. Thus, it is economically impractical to retain all versions of all data files ever created. Older copies of computer files are destroyed as data is summarized and updated into current versions.

Although the cost of computer storage has dropped dramatically and this trend is expected to continue, it is still not economically feasible to store all financial records. However, government requirements force many companies to retain data related to tax reporting, personnel, safety, and so forth for prolonged periods.

Transaction Processing Systems

Accounting systems relate to business transactions. The systems exist to record and analyze these transactions within a set of defined categories. They are used to record the past activity or history of an organization, portray the current state of its financial affairs, and make forecasts of its future.

One of the best ways to think about these systems is to consider the related transaction groups that are usually found together in an organization. These sets of transactions occur cyclically and in reaction to each other, in a chain of cause and effect. As a result, there are specific procedures to be followed in specific sequences.

Some typical transactions for various industries are:

- Financial services industry
  a. Securities, bought and sold
  b. Loans, billing and accounts receivable
  c. Mortgages, billing and accounts receivable
  d. Lease accounting
  e. Insurace premiums and claims
- Wholesale and retail businesses
  a. Purchases and cash disbursements
  b. Billing and cash collections

- Manufacturing companies
  - a. Purchases and payments
    - — Purchase orders and receiving reports
    - — Purchase and expense distribution
    - — Accounts payable
    - — Cash disbursements
  - b. Sales and collections
    - — Sales orders
    - — Customer credit control
    - — Shipping
    - — Billing and accounts receivable
    - — Cash receipts
  - c. Production and costs
    - — Production orders
    - — Inventory control
    - — Cost accounting
  - d. Payroll
    - — Employee recordkeeping
    - — Timekeeping
    - — Distribution of labor
    - — Payroll disbursements

Often a monthly operating statement is produced for each set of transactions. It should be completed within a few days of the close of the month and contain the information required to run the organization. These statements yield a picture of how the business is doing from a financial standpoint. They are created by using the data from various transaction processing systems, so the systems must be able to produce this material on a timely basis and in a format that is readily usable.

Transaction Size and Volume. Individual transactions are rarely significant to a business, but when a transaction is spectacular, everyone takes notice. One example is the takeover of a major company. In 1988, Philip Morris Companies, Inc. acquired Kraft, Inc. for $12.9 billion. This was not a routine task for Philip Morris' daily accounting system.

Routine accounting systems are designed to handle the usual transactions, not the exceptions; common, everyday items are the ones these systems handle best. In fact, one of the guidelines in determining whether a manual procedure is ready for automation is if there is an adequate stream of routine transactions. Another consideration is whether these transactions have become so complex that it is no longer cost-effective to process them by hand.

Accounting Transactions. Transactions are categorized into major groups, which are commonly found in many organizations. These are also accounting systems categories:

- Sales accounting
- Inventory control
- Purchase accounting
- Payroll
- Fixed asset
- General ledger

To understand a general overview of the systems most often used in large organizations, remember that the various transactions drive their particular system. The transactions can affect more than one system, but not necessarily at the same level of detail. For example, the payroll check created for work done by an employee this week is processed initially in the payroll system and eventually becomes part of a summary total posted to the general ledger system.

It is also important to remember that, with few exceptions, an organization's business flow has peaks and valleys. As a result, its systems must be able to deal with inconsistent volume. Many businesses are cyclical, and this is reflected in the volume of transactions per cycle. One such industry is toy sales.

It is essential that department store retailers have systems that can absorb the volume created by the Christmas rush. The system must be able to process the sale while verifying that the customer's credit limit covers all purchases made. If the system cannot do this, it can cost the organization a lot in terms of lost sales or sales over credit limit that should not have taken place.

It can hurt a store if its system is slow or inefficient, causing a customer perception of inordinate time spent making a purchase. If customers have to wait for a sale to go through, they may consider shopping where purchases are faster. This perceived speed and ease is one factor that has kept more expensive stores in business, since many people tend to think of long lines and slow service in connection with discount operations. The degree to which these perceptions—whether true or false—affect customer decisions is something a retailer must consider when choosing a system.

When automated accounting systems do not perform properly in the time required some organizations can be brought to the brink of disaster. This happens when systems are not properly designed and developed to suit the organization. There are systems that never got past the design and approval phases because the process took too long. By the time acceptable systems designs were completed, management had changed, business needs had changed, and the proposed systems were out of date before they could be programmed.

Management Influence on Systems

Another factor complicating the selection and design of accounting systems is the general volatility of the business climate. Huge companies that did not even exist 40 years ago have become national presences. These changes reveal the need for new accounting systems and a fast response to changing conditions.

The particular focus or management style of any organization is often the key factor in determining which systems are chosen and automated for use. As a result, accounting systems are strongly influenced by management and by its perception of the needs of that organization. For example, an organization that stresses the control and careful negotiation of purchases is likely to have an excellent purchasing system. One that is service-oriented, based on a labor-intensive operation, will have a well-run payroll system that relates closely to the billing system.

Addressing Management Concerns

Although accounting systems are mainly used to record transactions, they are usually designed with the capacity to answer other kinds of management questions. One such response to management's need for information is the production of monthly financial reports. These usually take the form of a balance sheet, an income statement, and a statement of cash flow. When systems are designed to provide the right kind of information, such information can be obtained without having to develop additional programs. In well-designed systems, the basic data for reports is there when it is needed.

For the most part, special management reports focus on particular areas of concern. Among these are:

- *Profit by area*. These reports analyze potential problem areas where profits may not match expectations, and can also detect areas where profits are large and can be used to finance new products or expansion. Management can use such an analysis to find ways to improve production, change marketing strategy, increase prices, or perhaps decide to expand or drop a particular line.

- *Production reports*. These reports focus specifically on production issues, such as identifying unfinished jobs and determining how far behind schedule they are. Production reports can be used to help manage resources more efficiently and to address the demands of the organization.
- *Cost variance reports*. These reports show the difference between projected costs and actual costs. They reveal whether a product or project is being handled efficiently or inefficiently.
- *Payroll analysis reports*. These reports can range from reports on projected versus actual payroll, to comparisons of payroll within the industry or at different locations within the geographic area. They can also analyze the efficiency of a workforce by comparing cost of productivity and are widely used to do internal trend analysis.
- *Inventory reports*. These reports are critical to the success of an organization, since management of inventory can have widespread implications for a company. For example, aging of inventories yields reports that distinguish between fast- and slow-moving items or back-ordered items and can be analyzed to set effective production schedules, purchase materials, and control inventory. An inventory analysis usually includes a balance of inventory levels, to help management decide whether to increase, decrease, or maintain the current levels of inventory.
- *Accounts receivable analysis*. Aging of receivables to analyze patterns and trends can provide management with the information it needs to decide whether the problem is with the product itself, as indicated by a general trend toward late or nonpayment for goods received, or with a specific customer.
- *Cash flow*. Consistent reporting on the cash position of any organization is another critical area. Future cash needs should be analyzed, as well as the availability of surplus cash for which an investment strategy should be planned.
- *Sales reports*. These reports analyze sales trends and sales by grouping (area, product line, division, salesperson, etc.). These reports can help to ensure that production schedules are being met and that purchasing required to be able to produce the goods takes place on schedule.
- *Employee reports*. These reports can include the degree of turnover in the organization as a whole or in only one department. Since high turnover rates can have a negative impact on

productivity, reports comparing turnover with past years, and possibly with the industry as a whole, can be significant.

- *Projection reports*. These reports try to predict how the business will do in coming months, based on the months just past and on seasonal fluctuations. They may also analyze what would happen if certain changes were made. The production of projection reports has been greatly accelerated by the use of "what if" financial modeling software packages. Microcomputers with this software can provide spreadsheet analysis of changes in different variables in seconds, as opposed to the days it used to take to create them by hand.

Here are some examples of useful reporting capabilities:

- Certain information can be used to evaluate the effect or performance of management itself. For example, assume that one management goal is to reduce by 25 percent the total value of accounts receivable balances more than 30 days past due. Reports can measure whether this goal is achieved.
- Another goal might be to raise the average value of each invoice by 5 percent and reduce the number of line items by 10 percent. This means a bigger dollar volume for less paperwork, thereby reducing operating expenses.
- Customer *A* places four orders a month, one each week. Suggesting that the customer place the order twice a month in order to save time and take advantage of a volume discount would increase the size and reduce the number of transactions.

Here are some examples of poor use of reporting capabilities:

- Sometimes the information presented to management has such broad implications that a precipitous reaction to it can hurt the business. For example, a security and casualty company decided that, because of losses in its direct insurance business (mostly automobile insurance), it should increase rates. Lacking adequate data to determine which groups of policyholders were causing the losses, an across-the-board rate increase was made. Policyholders with a good risk profile went elsewhere. The insurance company was left with the poor risks who could not obtain insurance otherwise. The system should have been able to provide the information necessary for determining an appropriate rate structure.
- Another issue is the transaction flow through various systems. One type of transaction is rarely sufficient to build the kind of system that is needed to provide useful management information.

- In one organization, there was a strong desire to avoid stock-outage situations. To avoid them, there was aggressive purchasing, often in railcar-size lots. Somehow the paperwork for an entire railcar full of seasonal merchandise was not processed on a timely basis. The goods were received in the warehouse and began to be disbursed to the stores to meet the demands of the summer season. As shown by the computer reports, the inventory quantity was substantially below the reorder point. Without checking further, the purchasing department placed a rush order for another railcar full of goods. As a result, the second lot sat in the warehouse for a full year as the company waited for the season to roll around again. Management had relied completely on the reports in its ordering. Although there could have been several reasons for the problem, including operator error, it may also have been indicative of a pervasive defect in the system itself.

Timeliness of System Response

Management frequently worries about the availability, timeliness, and accuracy of information on which important decisions are based. The rapid development and implementation of the immediacy of response from online, interactive systems were stimulated by management's desire to have faster results than those provided by the older batch processing. Since batch processing was done either at set intervals or when there was a sufficient quantity of work to be processed, results were not available as fast as desired. In response to these demands, second and third EDP shifts began to do overnight batch processing. Even this was not timely enough, since the data was only current when delivered at the start of the business day.

In a high-volume transaction system, three hours of transactions can have a substantial impact. During the early 1970s, the New York Stock Exchange discovered that its systems could not handle the volume of trading. History almost repeated itself during a disastrous week late in 1987, when the same problem brought down the systems in several brokerages. The maximum volume for both the stock exchange and the brokerage houses had been reached earlier than expected. Business had to close early to catch up on the transactions. Although these problems are exceptional cases, it is important to provide for the "worst case scenario" when designing any system.

Interaction Between Accounting Systems

When transactions are processed, they frequently go through more than one system. In a department store a sale is first processed in the sales accounting system, then processed by the accounts receivable system (if the purchase was by credit card), and for either cash or credit sales, through the inventory system (when they are linked). In yet another system, that same sale might trigger the purchase accounting system to replace depleted inventory. Eventually, the transactions become part of the general ledger system, as all transactions are recorded somewhere in that system. For the integration of systems to be effective, processing of transactions must be complete, accurate, and timely. If it is not, a ripple effect impairs the integrity of the data.

Figure 8-2 is a view of the transaction flow in relation to all the accounting applications in a manufacturing system. This flowchart depicts how transactions proceed from vendor (the manufacturer, in this case) to customer. This order can also be presented in reverse, from customer to vendor.

The system should be designed to cope with the peaks and valleys in a processing cycle. In service-related businesses where there are a number of repeat customers, processing loads can be evened out by staggering the billing—a technique used by the telephone company or any large department store with a large volume of charge account customers.

From the manufacturer's point of view, the customer is involved directly with three of its systems: the sales accounting system, which processes sales orders; the accounts receivable system, which processes invoices for payment by the customer; and the system in which receipts are processed. The other accounting systems shown in this chart are internal to the manufacturer: the purchase accounting system; the inventory system (including goods received and those on hand, as well as work-in-progress systems); the accounts payable system, which includes payments made; the general ledger system, into which all transactions involving dollar amounts are entered eventually; and a payroll system, which processes pay for all the people who work for the manufacturer.

System Accuracy

Management is also concerned about the accuracy of the system response and data on which important decisions are based. Data may be inaccurate due to weaknesses in control or flaws in the system's ability to catch erroneous transactions, but it can also be in error due to a lack of security over the data. If anyone can access data, then there is nothing to stop someone from changing the information. This can be equated to the idea of leaving files of data open for anyone to look through. Systems should demonstrate that they restrict access to data to only authorized users of the data. This means that the data elements processed by the systems have to be categorized by:

FIG. 8-2

Integration of accounting applications overview flowchart

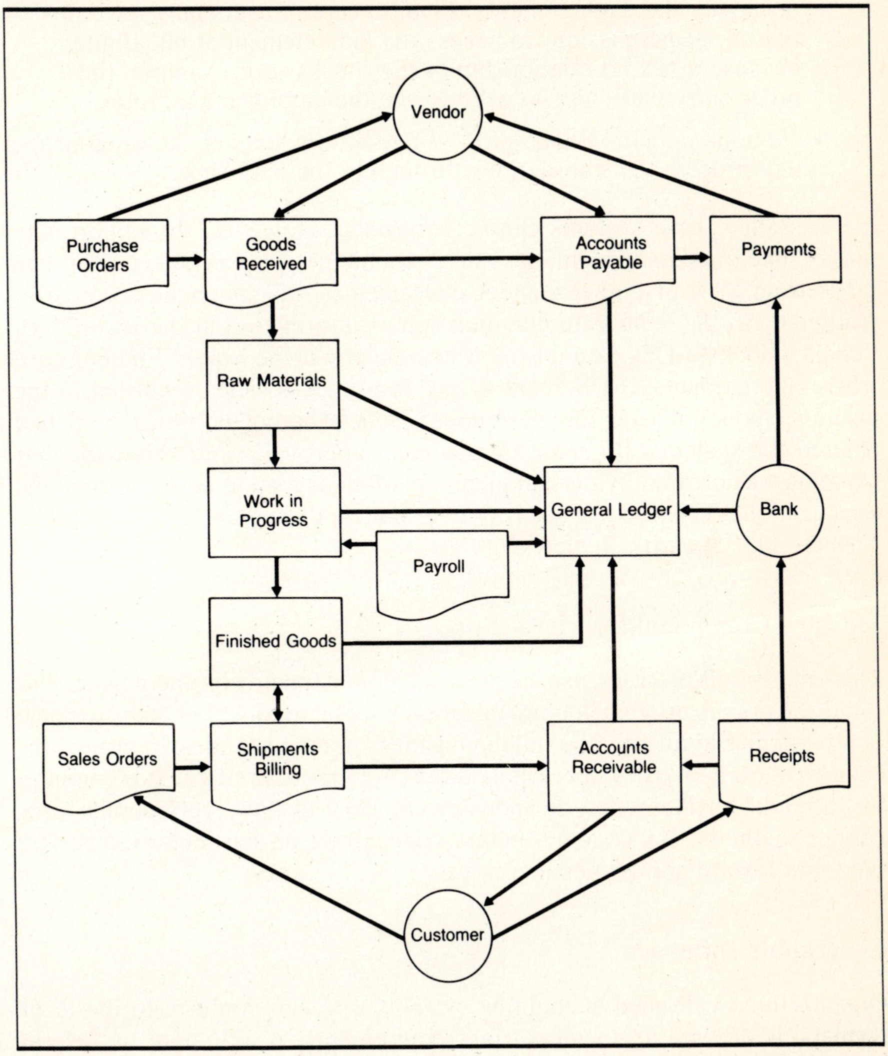

- *Data independence*. How the organization's data is structured so that it can be made available to the various accounting applications.
- *Data sharing*. The organization's data elements are no longer owned by specific applications. Individual data elements may be used by many applications, and the users and providers of the data

may be different. For example, certain users may only retrieve data elements, while others may have the authority to add, delete, or modify the data elements. Finally, certain users may have no reason, or permission, to access the data element at all, simply because it has no relationship to their tasks. For example, the order entry clerk has no need to see the employee pay rates.

- *Data manipulation.* The processing requirements of the programs that process the transactions through to the data base.

Certainly these systems can be controlled. However, the opportunity for possible fraud in accounting systems should not be overlooked. This can range from theft or embezzlement concealed by changing the records intentionally to the deliberate manipulation of information in the records, or "cooked books." One example of system misuse is the Equity Funding case where approximately 65 percent of the insurance policies recorded in the insurance policy master file were nonexistent. The bogus transactions had entered the system with some management approval, since this particular situation was created by certain members of management acting against the organization. (The issue of security over data is discussed in more detail in Chapter 30, "Security Reviews.")

Industry Commonality

The needs of different industries place specific demands on the people who run these organizations. One organization may be involved in many aspects of a particular industry. The unique business practices and accounting procedures of each industry necessitate different types of systems. It is common for different businesses in an industry category to have very similar processing methods. As system vendors concentrate on particular industries, the trend toward similarities increases.

Geographic Influence

Organizations will need accounting systems that can conform to the local regulations as well as the reporting requirements of any state or federal government agencies that might be involved. Within the United States, the accounting system most affected by geographic location is probably payroll, due to different local, state, and federal tax requirements. Other kinds of taxes are handled by sales accounting systems in many areas.

Multinational organizations need systems that can deal with currency conversions and possibly with the tax requirements of several different countries. Routines that perform currency conversion and can be adapted for changes in rates are built into the systems that need them.

Influence of Growth

An organization that has set a goal to achieve a certain level of growth each period needs systems that measure the growth and provide quick feedback as to whether the growth was achieved in the last or prior period. A growth-oriented organization must have systems that can grow as rapidly and be as flexible as required for expansion. Furthermore, the systems must have appropriate controls to ensure that the growth is real, according to generally accepted accounting principles (GAAP), and not merely creative bookkeeping, derived from management's need to achieve. The need to build in the kinds of controls that can prevent this distortion of information deserves special emphasis.

PACKAGED ACCOUNTING SYSTEM SOFTWARE

Accounting systems, although they may be tailored to suit an industry's specialized functions, apply to many industries. This is the reason that packaged accounting software systems have been developed and are so popular: They are flexible enough to meet many needs.

The DATAPRO[1] Directory of Software lists and describes the kinds of accounting system software packages under the following headings:

- Accounts Payable
- Accounts Receivable
- General Ledger
- Fixed Assets
- Contractor/Construction Accounting
- Petroleum and Gas Accounting Systems
- General Accounting
- Professionals Accounting/Billing Systems
- Tax Accounting Systems
- Utility Billing/Municipal Accounting Systems
- Special Application Accounting Systems

Other major headings describing available packaged software are:

- Banking and Finance

[1] DATAPRO Research Corp., N.J., November 1988.

- Education
- Engineering and Scientific
- Finance
- Health Care
- Insurance
- Management Services
- Manufacturing
- Payroll and Personnel
- Sales and Distribution
- Utilities

In over two decades of software development, the accounting function software has, for the most part, been developed to be generic and usable in a variety of industries, often by making the packages flexible with options to satisfy the different users' needs.

THE SYSTEM AND DATA AS ASSETS

Most organizations realize the value of their computer systems and resident software simply because they know how much they cost to buy and put in place. Like other assets, they need to be maintained and are updated as organizational requirements change. Many organizations are beginning to realize that the data within the system is itself an asset. This realization has spawned vaults that guard backup tapes of data for businesses.

Some kinds of data have been recognized as an asset for a long time, such as customer master lists, which can be used as an excellent source of mailing lists for special-interest groups. In some industries, the data itself is made all the more valuable by lack of source documents. An example is electronic funds transfers. The funds transfer systems, as a group, have been subjected to very strict controls, since the data itself literally represents an asset. As systems of this sort become widespread, the need for controls and proper authorization procedures is also becoming more apparent.

INTEGRATED FINANCIAL SYSTEMS

Since computers were first used to record financial information, a variety of successful systems have been developed. However, until the appearance

FIG. 8-3

Applications in a typical manufacturing or selling environment

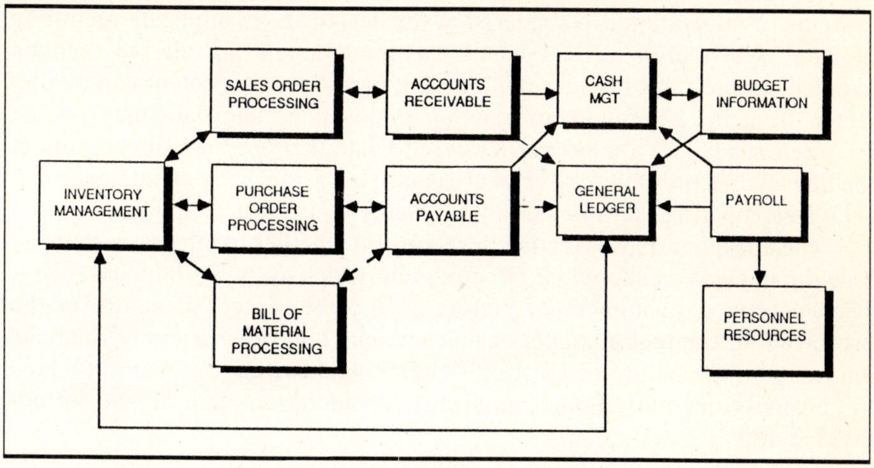

of very fast and powerful computers, most systems functioned independently of each other. The increase in computing capacity and emphasis on improved data management have resulted in the integration of many previously "stand-alone" systems to share common data and resources. This integration of systems has provided organizations with more meaningful and up-to-date information, which, in turn, has allowed for more efficient and effective management. This development has been encouraged by the widespread use of financial applications offering integrated systems for microcomputers, making it possible for even the smallest organizations to benefit from these advances.

Planning Considerations

An analysis of financial systems shows that in most cases a definite relationship exists between the data used by different applications. This relationship can be used as a basis for integrating those systems. Figure 8-3 illustrates this relationship in a typical manufacturing or selling environment.

A similar analysis is helpful in considering the integration of financial systems. The analysis should include both those applications currently operating and those planned for future development. Any further decisions can then be made with a clear understanding of which applications should be integrated and of the impact that such integration may have.

The integration of existing stand-alone systems normally entails different considerations than the integration of completely new systems. Generally, integration is more efficient and effective if it is planned as part of the development of new systems than when done by combining existing systems. If integration is considered at the design stage, duplicate recording of data, which often occurs when existing systems are altered, can be avoided. In the same manner, all data required by management can be collected from the beginning; in existing systems, certain data may not be recorded at all. This applies particularly to data that does not directly affect the financial records but may be of great assistance in management decisions, such as comparing the timeliness and quality of various suppliers.

The considerations affecting decisions on whether to integrate systems, how the integration should be effected, and which systems to include vary. They depend on a number of factors such as the size and nature of the organization, the requirements of management and other users of financial information, the nature of existing systems, and the environment in which the business operates. Some important considerations that should be addressed are:

- *Resources.* What software and personnel are required to develop, operate, and maintain the integrated system?
- *Need.* Is integration essential for providing critical management information or is it only a desirable improvement?
- *Efficiency.* Integration of which systems will provide the greatest benefit relative to the effort required?
- *Costs.* What are the costs involved in achieving integration?
- *Existing information.* How reliable is the existing data held by the affected applications?
- *Time.* Are there any particular timing constraints or considerations?
- *Security.* What impact will integration have on the security of data and programs?

Packaged Software and In-House-Developed Software

As in the development and implementation of all software, there are two principal methods of achieving integrated financial systems: They can be purchased as a package from a vendor or they can be developed by the organization. Although packaged software was initially used almost exclusively on microcomputers and minicomputers, it is now available and being implemented by many organizations on mainframe computers.

The numerous advantages and disadvantages of both approaches are beyond the scope of this discussion. However, the extensive integration between systems in most purchased software packages has been one of the major reasons for the rapid growth of their use. The packages normally divide the information recording system into a number of applications or modules (as shown in Figure 8-3) that can be used either individually or as part of an integrated system. This allows users the flexibility to implement the systems that meet their particular requirements while still enjoying the advantages of integration.

In-house-developed sophisticated integrated software systems have been implemented by many organizations. These systems require thorough and careful planning, especially in evaluating both current and long-term requirements. A major advantage of these systems is that they can be designed to meet the exact specifications of the user. Although packaged software normally has many options, features, and combinations, it seldom meets all of the users's specifications. Organizations with very specific data and system integration requirements are therefore more likely to develop their own software. This trend may change in the future as packaged software becomes more tailored to specific requirements. The decision to use packaged software or in-house-developed software is important when planning the integration of financial systems and should be made only after giving due consideration to all of the other planning criteria previously discussed.

Figure 8-4 presents a brief description of the type of integrated financial system presently being used by some retailers on a test basis. This type of system is expected to become common in the 1990s. Throughout the system, numerous reports are produced that allow the users to monitor the data flow within the computer. Although it is greatly simplified, this example clearly illustrates how each transaction processed automatically affects the records in a number of different applications and how the transactions are recorded on computer files instead of paper. The integration could also be done using computers of different organizations. Such integration, if well planned, should provide management and users with the required information accurately and on a timely basis, allowing the organization to operate more effectively and efficiently.

ASSESSING FINANCIAL SYSTEMS

The accounting systems that are in widespread use range from relatively simple and straightforward to complex and integrated. Simplicity is actually a desirable feature, since the more complex a system becomes, the more difficult it is to catch errors, follow the transaction logic, and detect operational weaknesses. When a system is unnecessarily complex, it can even be hard to detect unauthorized activities. Following the proper evaluation

FIG. 8-4
Specimen integrated financial system

Stage 1

Daily, the computer reviews the inventory levels shown by the records. For all items where the level on hand is below the predetermined reorder level, a purchase order is automatically generated. The order is not printed on a document but is transmitted directly to the supplier's computer, which is linked to the retailer's computer. The file of outstanding orders, which records all orders transmitted for which the goods have not yet been received, is updated.

Stage 2

When the goods are received from the supplier, the details are immediately processed on the computer and matched to the details on the original order. If this matching is accurate, the following processing occurs: The details on the outstanding order file are deleted; the accruals file, which maintains details of goods received but for which no invoice has been processed, is updated; the inventory levels are updated; the general ledger is updated nightly with the necessary entries to record the transactions processed during the day.

Stage 3

The invoice details are transmitted from the supplier's computer to the retailer's computer. These details are matched to the goods received details. If this matching is accurate, the following processing occurs; The details on the accruals file are deleted; the accounts payable file is updated with the details, including the date the invoice is due for payment; the general ledger is updated nightly, as explained in Stage 2.

Stage 4

Weekly, the computer reviews the accounts payable file and extracts all the information for invoices that are due for payment. These details are recorded on a magnetic tape, the details are deleted from the accounts payable file, and the general ledger is again updated. The magnetic tape is sent to the bank or other financial institution for processing, resulting in the necessary transfer of funds to the suppliers.

procedures to select and implement an accounting system produces a basic system that does just what it needs to, with the appropriate degree of control over its use.

When a system is up and running, it is still possible to make sure that it is performing in the way it should be and to make any corrective measures that are required. The following questions raise issues that are basic to the functioning of a financial information system. They can be used to make a broad assessment of a system that is already running (or, for that matter, to assess one that is to be purchased or designed):

- Does the system provide the kind of reports and information the organization needs from the data that is available?
- Is the information available within a reasonable time frame?
- When the information is obtained, is it accurate?
- Can the system provide the kind of information needed to make forecasts and projections?
- Can the system provide information needed to make analyses of components (such as product performance by region)?
- If a system handles billing, are the transactions taking place on a timely basis? Does it provide adequate information on outstanding and past-due items? Can these be analyzed by time period?
- If a system handles inventories, does it provide an accurate picture of what is on hand? Can it do aging analyses? Can it track work-in-progress information or track merchandise and stock transfer between warehouses?
- If the system handles payables, does it establish priorities for them? Does it ensure that it processes items on time for vendor discounts? Are payments made on a timely basis?
- Are erroneous transactions flagged or rejected and shown on exception reports?
- Are there controls to ensure the integrity of data?
- Can income statements and other financial statements be generated on a timely basis, feeding off data already in the system?
- Can the cash position of the organization be readily discerned whenever this information is necessary?
- Is a lot of manual work required to complete tasks that the system does not finish on time?
- Are there any major reports that still have to be created from scratch whenever the financial information they contain is required?

Of course, this is a brief overview of the functions and controls in computerized financial systems, but it provides some of the basics to consider when working with these systems.

CHAPTER 9

Revenue Systems

INTRODUCTION

Revenue systems are those systems that process transactions that bring money into an organization. As such, they are obviously vital to the financial health of the organization. There are several different systems that fall into this category.

The development of a suitable system to meet the needs of an organization depends on the computer processing facilities and technology available. It is important to spend some time reviewing typical computerized accounting systems in order to become familiar with their operation. In the sales accounting systems and the purchase accounting systems discussed in this chapter, the complexity of the computerized accounting system depends on the number of different applications incorporated in the system. When systems such as this were developed in-house, they frequently started with one application and were built on as the need arose. Now that software packages are so widely available, it is more common for an organization to acquire a system that does the applications required.

SALES ACCOUNTING SYSTEMS

Applications

Most sales accounting systems perform three basic accounting functions:

1. *Accounts receivable processing.* Recording transactions in the accounts receivable records or ledgers.
2. *Billing.* Calculation of invoices from shipping notes in order to bill customers, and processing details of goods shipped to generate sales figures.
3. *Order entry.* Processing customer orders resulting in the shipment of goods and generation of shipping documentation.

Some aspects of the system may be computerized, while some can remain manual. The following list of the systems described here is presented in the usual sequence in which computerization takes place as a growing business evolves:

- Accounts receivable systems
- Billing systems
- Order entry systems

ACCOUNTS RECEIVABLE SYSTEMS

In the simplest accounts receivable systems, the computer processes the accounts receivable records while order entry and billing functions remain manual operations.

Accounts Receivable Master File

Records are maintained on the accounts receivable master file for each customer with which the company has business. The accounts receivable records hold both:

- *Master file data.* The permanent reference data required to be held (e.g., customer's name, address, and credit limit).
- *Transaction data.* Information about the transactions processed against that account (e.g., outstanding transactions).

Information on the accounts receivable files is used for:

- *Financial accounting.* Outstanding balance; unmatched cash and adjustments; goods on consignment; back orders; contract details; special terms, prices, or discounts; prepayments; standing charges such as rents, dues, and subscriptions; and salespeople's and agents' commissions.
- *Credit control and collections.* Name and address, reports of credit investigations, and reports by credit agencies, bankers, and employers, often converted into a credit limit or other summary form; doubtful debt, stop shipment, and delinquent indicators; an analysis of amounts due by age; a history of previous late payments and any dunning notices sent.
- *Marketing.* Sales region; delivery/shipment information; sales history; main product interest; statistical information.

An example of an accounts receivable master file layout is illustrated in Figure 9-1.

Accounts Receivable Functions

The main types of transactions processed in accounts receivable functions are:

- Sales invoices.
- Adjustments.

FIG. 9-1

An accounts receivable master file layout (courtesy of International Business Machine Corporation)

CUSTOMER MASTER FILE

Record:	Customer Master	File Organization:	Index Sequential
Disk File:	CUSTMTR	Key Length:	6
Record Length:	160	Key Location:	4

Field	Description	From	To	Length	A/N/P	Decimal Position
RECCD	* Record Code (CM)	1	2	2	A	
DELCD	* Delete Code Blank-active,'D'-deleted	3	3	1	A	
CUSNO	* Customer Number	4	9	6	N	0
CUSNM	* Customer Name	10	34	25	A	
CUSA1	* Customer Address	35	59	25	A	
CUSA2	* Customer City and State	60	79	20	A	
ZIPCD	* Zip Code	80	84	5	N	0
SLSNO	Salesman Number	85	89	5	N	0
STCDE	State Code	90	91	2	N	0
CUSCL	Customer Class/Status	92	96	5	A	
TXCDE	Customer Tax Code - user defined	97	97	1	A	
TRDCT	Customer Trade Discount Percent	98	99	2	P	3
TERMS	Cash Discount Terms - user defined	100	100	1	A	
PHNER	* Customer Phone Number	101	110	10	N	0
SMTCD	* Statement Code - N=No Statement	111	111	1	A	
CRLAM	* Credit Limit Amount	112	114	3	P	0
DLTPM	* Date of Last Payment	115	118	4	P	0
DUEOO	* Amount Due - Current	119	122	4	P	2
DUE30	* Amount Due - Over 30	123	126	4	P	2
DUE60	* Amount Due - Over 60	127	130	4	P	2
DUE90	* Amount Due - Over 90	131	134	4	P	2
CURSL	$ Sales Current Month	135	139	5	P	2
YTDSL	$ Sales Year-to-Date	140	144	5	P	2
CURCT	$ Cost Current Month	145	149	5	P	2
YTDCT	$ Cost Year-to-Date	150	154	5	P	2
	Not Used	155	160	6	-	-

* Required For Accounts Receivable

- Cash received from customers.
- Master file data amendments.

Charges to Customers. Sales invoices are prepared manually for details of goods shipped or services rendered, and are then entered into the system.

The invoices are updated to the customers' accounts on the accounts receivable file, and the total value of transactions is summarized for posting to the general ledger. The total may be categorized for financial reasons (e.g., providing a basis for the payment of commissions), or for operational reasons (e.g., classification of sales by geographic region). Exception reports may also be produced, such as balances over credit limits as a result of updating invoices.

The summaries of transactions may be printed on a report or written to a file for direct input into a computerized general ledger application. In more advanced applications, the updating of the accounting receivable records and general ledger records may take place simultaneously.

Adjustments. Adjustments will always be necessary to account for returns, cash discounts allowed, allowances for defective products or partial shipments, reversals of mispostings and other errors, and writeoffs of bad debts. Different input codes are often used to indicate the type of adjustment.

Adjustments are usually processed in the same way as the invoices. In more advanced systems, certain adjustments, for which the entry of documents is required in simpler systems, may be initiated by a computer program. For example, the program may identify and write off small balances outstanding for longer than a certain specified time.

Adjustments are updated to the accounts receivable records and are summarized and categorized for posting to the general ledger in the same way as for invoices.

Cash Receipts. The method of updating details of cash received usually depends on the way in which the transaction data is stored in the accounts receivable file.

In a balance forward system, details of individual invoices are not retained. The amount outstanding is summarized into either a single balance or a series of balances for various age categories. Cash receipts may be applied against the outstanding balance or may be allocated against specific age categories, such as the oldest. The true aging of the file may be distorted if specific invoices are in dispute or otherwise remain unpaid.

In an open item system, the file contains a separate record of each uncleared transaction. Individual invoices are cleared by matching them with the relevant cash receipt. Unmatched cash receipts are posted as new open items. The matching operation may be performed either by manual allocation prior to processing or by programming the computer to allocate cash receipts to the relevant items. The second method is especially useful when only one periodic charge arises, as in the case of utilities and insurance companies, since separate records can be matched and cleared. Cash received that cannot be matched is normally reported for investigation.

Master File Data Amendments. Amendments to master file data are processed to alter the data held on the customer's accounts receivable record. Such amendments are needed to:

- Open new accounts.
- Change master file data on an existing account.
- Close accounts.

Master file data amendments may be entered on documents in batch mode or by using entries into terminals.

In some systems, the computer programs may initiate amendments to master file data. Examples of this are discounts based on historical records of sales, or increased credit limits, based on payment history and sales volume. A listing of master file data amendments is normally produced.

Periodic Output. Apart from the reports resulting from the processing of transactions, it is usual for the accounts receivable master file to be read periodically to:

- Produce statements.
- Categorize open items or balances by age, and summarize these categories to provide an age analysis.
- Summarize balances and provide a listing of balances.
- Provide information for control purposes, such as summarized details of movements on the accounts receivable records.
- Produce exception reports, such as lists of credit balances or balances over the customer's credit limit.

Figure 9-2 is a flowchart for an on-line sales accounting system. When only the accounts receivables processing is computerized:

- Accounts receivable master file is updated by transaction data and master file data amendment.
- Transaction data includes sales invoices to customers, cash received, and adjustments.
  - —Charges are entered in the form of invoices.
  - —Cash received is entered depending on the manner in which transaction data is stored on the accounts receivable file (balance forward or open item).
- Master file data amendments are necessary to open new accounts, to change data on file, and to close old accounts.

FIG. 9-2

A sales system overview flowchart for a real-time system

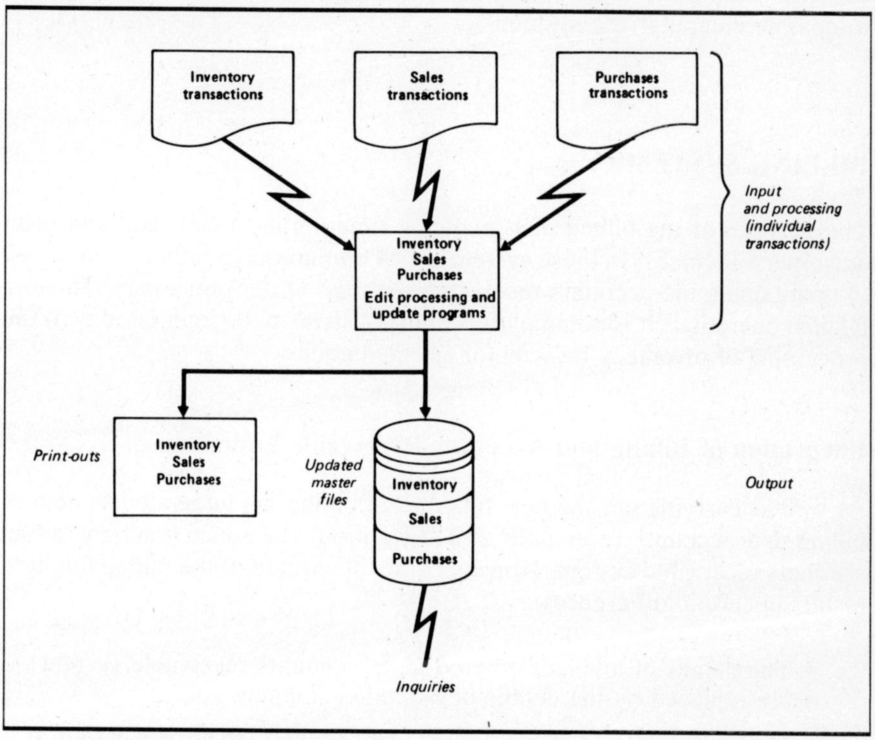

- Accounts receivable master file information includes reference data and transaction data for financial accounting, credit control and collections, and marketing.
- Output from the sales accounting system with one application—accounts receivable processing—would typically include the following:
  - —Statements for customers, showing the monthly activity for each account.
  - —Age listing, reporting the current status of the accounts.
  - —Sales analysis, detailing sales results by region, salesperson, product, and so forth.
  - —Master file movements summary, showing changes to the master file data.
  - —Reference data amendments, showing the change to the data.

In a system with just one application—accounts receivable processing—billing and order entry are manual operations or are performed by a separate computerized system.

BILLING SYSTEMS

The purpose of the billing and invoicing function is to calculate and print customers' invoices. In these systems, the computer is usually also involved in maintaining the accounts receivable records. Order entry may remain a manual operation. It is common for billing systems to be integrated with the processing of inventory records for finished good.

Integration of Billing and Accounts Receivable Functions

As well as carrying out the new function of billing, an integrated system of billing and accounts receivable also carries out the same functions as an accounts receivable system. However, the integration of the billing function results in certain differences:

- The details of invoices entered in an accounts receivable system are replaced by the details of extended shipping notes.
- Many of the details for posting to the general ledger are output at the billing stage rather than as part of the accounts receivable processing.

Figure 9-3 shows a system of this type. In this installation, the billing or invoicing applications are part of the system. In the configuration:

- Quantities are matched with the relevant selling prices held on the inventory master file in order to calculate the invoice amounts.
- Quantity discounts, taxes, freight charges, and special prices are calculated as necessary.
- Special term/prices may require that the accounts receivable master file be accessed for that information.
- Individual customer accounts may be updated at the same time that the invoices are prepared.
- Or, the system may produce a file of evaluated shipping notes that would be used later to update the accounts receivable file.

FIG. 9-3

An integrated billing system

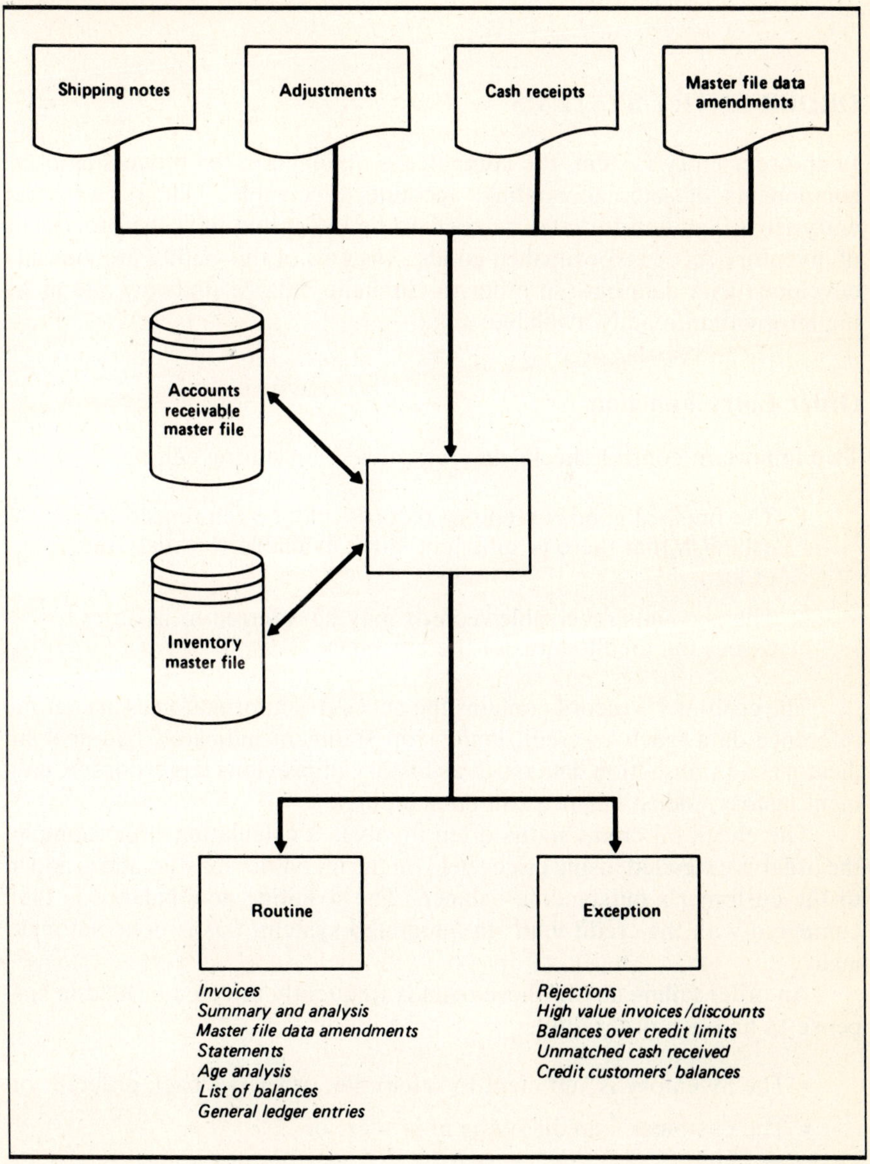

- Additional output might include invoices and possibly inventory issues.

ORDER ENTRY SYSTEMS

In an order entry system, the computer is involved in the processing of all components of sales accounting: accounts receivable, billing, and order entry. It is common for such systems to be integrated with the processing of inventory records for finished goods. Systems of this nature are logically developed as a data base in order to eliminate data redundancy and make the information readily available.

Order Entry Function

Two important control checks may be carried out during editing:

1. The finished goods inventory records may be referenced to establish that there is sufficient stock available to satisfy the order.
2. The accounts receivable records may be referred to in order to assess the credit status of the customer.

The customer's record contains the necessary information as master file reference data (such as credit limit, stop shipment indicator, bad-debt indicator) and transaction data (such as history of previous largest order, payment history, oldest balance still outstanding).

The check on credit status often involves a calculation. For example, the order is extended, using prices held on the inventory master, and is added to the customer's outstanding balance. The resulting new balance is then compared with the credit limit. In integrated system, this is done automatically.

An order failing any of these tests is frequently rejected or held in suspense as an open order until:

- The inventory is sufficient to satisfy the order (a "back order"); or
- The customer's credit status improves; or
- The shipment is authorized by the credit manager despite the customer's poor credit status.

Accepted orders are written to an accepted orders file, which usually shows both quantity and value. Then picking tickets and shipping notes are produced. The production of shipping notes may be carried out in real time as each order is accepted, or in batch mode at a later stage. A summary of all orders processed and their shipping notes produced is printed out periodically. Subsequent processing varies according to the type of order entry system in operation. The two types of order entry systems are referred to as postbilling and prebilling.

Postbilling Systems. In postbilling systems, customer charges are prepared from shipping notes returned from the warehouse after the goods have been shipped. The shipment details are reentered and matched with the accepted orders file. Matched items are either deleted and written to a goods-shipped file, or their status on the order record is changed to indicate that they are now matched. In either case, a summary of the matching process is normally accumulated and printed for control purposes. Duplicate or mismatched items are normally either reported or rejected for investigation. In on-line systems, a duplicate or mismatched item usually cannot be accepted.

The accepted order record, at any time, contains details of shipping notes produced but not yet reentered. These records are read periodically, and records remaining unmatched for a given period are printed, providing details of outstanding shipping notes. It is necessary to be able to process adjustments to the accepted order records so that entries on the records can be amended (e.g., if the goods actually shipped differ from those ordered) or eliminated (e.g., when the order is canceled by the customer).

Matched shipping records are passed through to the billing function and, when integrated, to inventory applications, as described for billing systems.

Prebilling Systems. In prebilling systems, accepted sales orders are treated as matched shipping records and passed directly into the billing and accounts receivable functions. Invoices are printed and a picking ticket sent to the warehouse to initiate shipment. A shipping note is produced and the goods are shipped. The customer is therefore charged before actual shipment.

Prebilling systems depend on an accurate system of inventory control. Unexpected lack of stock in the warehouse when attempting to pack the shipment can cause major problems. It is difficult to reverse the chain of accounting entries; therefore, only companies with few stock lines or with vigorous systems of inventory control can operate effective prebilling systems. This point is sometimes overlooked by designers of such systems.

To ensure that all amounts billed to customers reflect shipments actually made, it is necessary to establish methods of control. This may be accomplished by reentering the shipping note and matching it against the order record. This matching operation determines the need for adjustments for incomplete deliveries and provides a control over the dispatching of orders.

Integration of Order Entry and Billing

As well as carrying out the new function of ordering, an order entry system also carries out the same functions as a billing system. However, the integration of the ordering function results in certain differences:

- The shipment details entered in a billing system are replaced by the details of matched shipping notes (in a postbilling system) or orders (in a prebilling system).
- The calculation of the sales and cost-of-sales values of transactions may be carried out as part of the processing of the original order and not as part of the processing of invoices.

An integrated order entry system is illustrated in the overview flowchart in Figure 9-4.

When the order processing application is present, the system can do the following:

- Sales orders become the initial input. Two important checks may be performed during editing:
  - —The inventory master file may be referred to in order to determine that the goods are available.
  - —The accounts receivable master file may be referred to in order to establish credit status.
- Orders failing these tests are either rejected or held in a suspense file until the reason for the rejection has been cleared, as by manual checking ending in improved credit status.
- Accepted orders are written to an outstanding orders file and the shipping notes are produced.
- Order entry applications are often combined with invoicing and accounts receivable applications in one of two ways: either as a prebilling system or as a postbilling system, depending on whether the invoice is produced before or after shipment of goods.

Industry Variations

Variations peculiar to a particular industry are often found in these systems, as discussed in the following paragraphs.

FIG. 9-4

An overview flowchart for an integrated order entry system

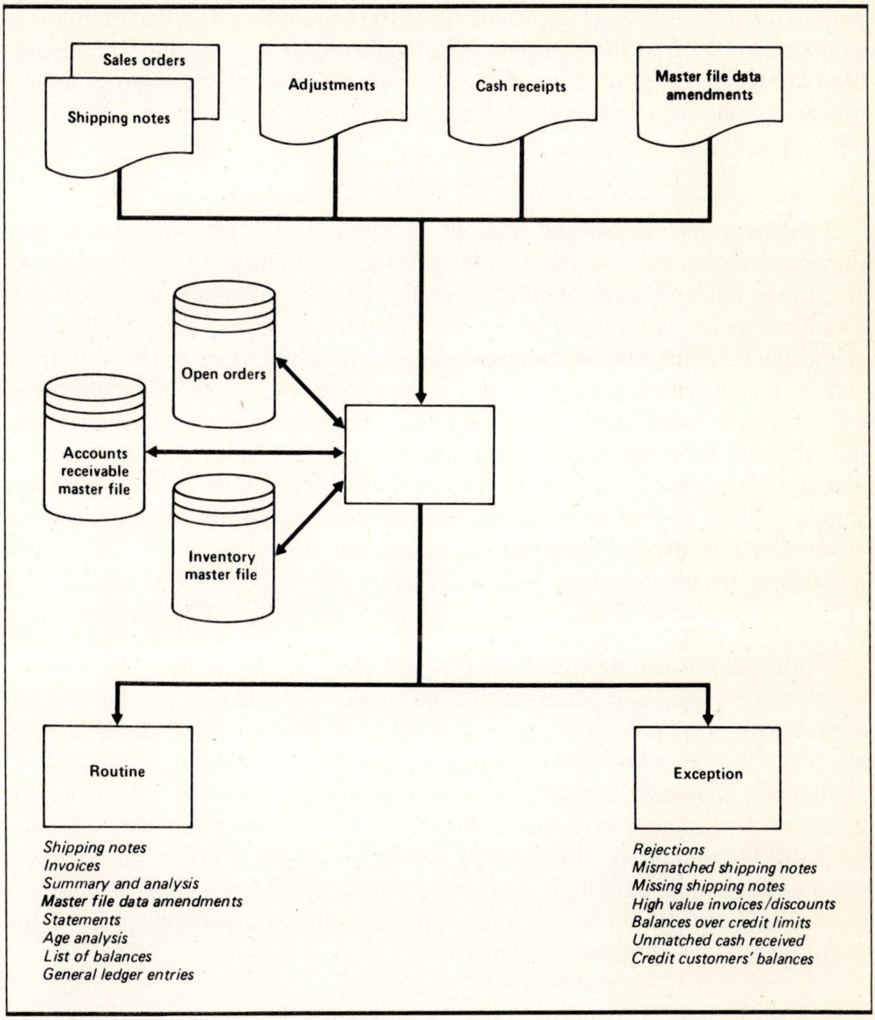

Service Industries. Service industries do not have a shipping transaction to initiate invoicing; instead, a completion report or order may start the billing cycle. Billing in service-related industries is often more complex, since the services rendered can vary from month to month and may require documentation to prove accuracy of charges. A billing file may be used to accumulate costs in the same way as a work-in-process inventory file. Payroll costs, purchase costs, and other costs may be recorded, at their selling price, on the file. Such invoicing files are used, for example, by hospitals, advertising and public relations agencies, lawyers, accountants, and temporary employment agencies. At a suitable time, the accumulated costs are invoiced to the customer and the charges are transferred to the accounts receivable file. These applications do not always use a separate computer accounts receivable file, in which case cash received may be recorded directly on the billing file.

Subscriptions, Dues, and Rentals. Systems where revenues are related to subscriptions, dues, or rentals have no input to initiate the billing cycle. The cycle starts processing automatically on an anniversary date, which is usually held as reference data on the master file. With some of these applications (such as rents or magazine subscriptions), sales must be prepaid and the actual sale does not take place (the goods or service are not provided) until payment is received. The computer therefore ensures that benefits are not received by nonpayers (rental applications may automatically issue an eviction or repossession notice, or magazine applications may stop issuing shipping labels so that no more magazines are sent). Many book and record clubs ship and invoice the goods automatically unless a "no order" notice is returned by the customer before a certain date.

Utilities. In utilities such as gas and electric companies, the date on which a meter-reading sheet should be initiated is held as master file reference data. Current dates are entered as parameters, and the computer produces the relevant meter-reading sheets or renewal notices. Details of documents produced are written to a suspense file awaiting reentry of the meter-reading sheets or renewal notices. This file operates like an order suspense file in a postbilling system, which awaits details of goods shipped. Sometimes billing combines transaction data (meter reading), master file reference data (rental or minimum charge), and transactions from other sources (sales of appliances or repairs).

Banking. In customer service financial institutions, transactions involving checking, savings, or credit card data are initiated by individual customer activities (such as by writing a check). Periodic processing through an update program can match or adjust master file records according to this input. Final processing of updated master files creates output that accurately reflects transactions and permits customer inquiries as well as cyclical record output for customer references. This process can often access information from the reference field for visual checking by the terminal operator, providing effective control over accuracy of input and master file data.

System Description: A Sample Accounts Receivable Data Base

Cash flow is important for any organization, and control over the accounts receivable contributes to this end. The amount of money owed to a company by its customers for merchandise sold or services rendered can be tracked and used to provide management information. When it runs efficiently, this process can increase the flow of cash back into the company. Prompt and accurate accounts receivable recordkeeping and processing are essential to any organization.

The IBM Accounts Receivable System software described in this section facilitates recordkeeping for customer invoices from data entry to receipt of total payment. In the sample system described here, transactions, including charges, cash receipts, credits, and adjustments, are recorded and posted to the customer accounts, as would be expected.

Customer invoices and credit memos must be coded with the correct customer number and invoice number so that they can be entered into the system. The system edits each transaction as it is entered and flags error situations. An invoice/credit memo batch edit listing is produced with batch totals, error messages, and cumulative totals. Data that passes the edit checks is saved in a temporary disk file. Cash receipts and adjustments are input separately and subjected to the same controls.

The two temporary files (invoice/credit memos and cash receipts/adjustments) are then merged and combined into a single input. A proof totals listing is produced, showing totals that include any discounts taken.

The combined input is then sorted in sequence by customer number. This combined input is used to update the open item master file.

The transactions are applied to the open item master file and, as a result of the update, a new open item master file is created. A report is produced that shows open item previous totals and then the new open item totals resulting from this run.

Customer statements can be produced either selectively or for all customers on demand. Final totals are printed after the last statement for control purposes. At the top of each statement, provision is made for the addition of a printed message. The actual text of messages is entered through the input device and can be changed. It is possible to produce statements selectively or for all customers, without updating the customer master file.

An aged trial balance can be produced on demand in either a detailed or summary format. It offers information about a customer such as:

- Date of last payment.
- Credit limit, flagging any customer who exceeds the limit.
- Total outstanding amount due.

- Amounts due (current, 30, 60, and 90 days and over).
- Totals for this information (outstanding amounts due—total and by age) for all customers.

Having this information on a timely basis assists a sales or credit manager to make suitable business decisions. It can help answer such questions as:

- Should we not sell anything more to this customer until the outstanding invoices are paid?
- Should we increase a customer's credit limit?
- Should we change our discount policies to encourage earlier payment?
- Should we investigate why a customer has not purchased anything recently?

The customer master file can be printed on demand, either in total or for selected customers by inquiry, to show pertinent information about each customer.

Invoice summary and credit memos are entered with two-digit preassigned batch numbers. As each enters the system, totals are accumulated for each field in the record. These totals are printed on the batch edit report for each batch. They should be balanced against totals accumulated on an adding machine. For invoices, the customer number is checked against the customer master file for validity.

The open item master file is checked for duplicate records. Credit memos are also checked against the open item master file for duplicate records.

Cash receipts and adjustments are processed in a similar manner as invoices and credit memos. They are grouped together in batches, batches are printed on the batch edit report, and the report is balanced against totals. The system also matches each transaction against the open item file to verify that it is being processed against a valid open item.

One or more times a day, the invoice/credit memo file and cash receipt/adjustment file are combined to form a daily activity file. This file is used to print the daily transaction report and to update the open item master file and customer master file.

AUDITING REVENUE SYSTEMS

To audit revenue systems, an understanding of the system can be obtained using the following methods:

- Create or obtain overview flowcharts, often so useful that they may become a required piece of documentation in many EDP audits.
- Review audit or user documentation and/or procedure manuals.
- Analyze detailed flowcharts for a more thorough understanding of the system.
- Follow processing through both computer and manual portions of the system.
- Interview management and staff.
- Observe system operations.

Testing Accounts Receivable

Generalized accounts receivable audit software packages were developed to increase audit efficiency by automating some of the common substantive testing procedures. When these functions are precoded into the software, it can be installed quickly. The auditor should retain flexibility in choosing parameters and in the generation of computer reports. Audit software can be used to assist in the audit of most open item and balance forward accounts receivable systems. Software is particularly effective when there are a large number of open items or balances.

Many common accounts receivable substantive testing procedures, such as the following, should be performed by an audit software package:

- Adding, aging, and stratifying account balances. (See Figure 9-5.)[1]
- Selecting accounts for positive and/or negative confirmations. (See Figures 9-6, 9-7, and 9-8.)
- Producing confirmation letters and control working papers. (See Figures 9-7 and 9-8.)
- Testing transactions dated after audit testing date. (See Figure 9-9.)
- Identifying cash received after audit testing date. (See Figure 9-10.)

Thus, the accounts receivable audit software can assist the auditor in achieving the following substantive testing objectives:

- Determining whether recorded accounts receivable represents amounts due to the company.

---

[1] Reports illustrated in Figures 9-5 through 9-10 are from Coopers & Lybrand's Accounts Receivable Audit Software package.

FIG. 9-5
Stratification histogram

REPORT NO. ARCAAG04 | SPECIALTY MFG CO | PAGE NO. 1
REPORT DATE.11/05/79 | STRATIFICATION HISTOGRAM | PERIOD ENDED 04/30/79

LOGARITHMIC METHOD
CREDIT REPORT

SEQ #	INTERVAL----BOUNDARIES		# ITEMS	VALUE	% OF TOTAL	CUM %	MEAN	STANDARD DEVIATION	DISTRIBUTION SCALED 1 FOR 27
1	-699.99 TO	-600.00	1	682.47-	22.33	22.33	682.47-	.00	*************************
2	-599.99 TO	-500.00	0	.00	.00	22.33	.00	.00	*
3	-499.99 TO	-400.00	0	.00	.00	22.33	.00	.00	*
4	-399.99 TO	-300.00	1	307.94-	10.08	32.41	307.94-	.00	***********
5	-299.99 TO	-200.00	2	460.22-	15.06	47.47	230.11-	20.10	*****************
6	-199.99 TO	-100.00	4	658.64-	21.56	69.03	164.66-	20.49	************************
7	-99.99 TO	-90.00	1	97.60-	3.19	72.22	97.60-	.00	***
8	-89.99 TO	-80.00	1	87.61-	2.87	75.09	87.61-	.00	***
9	-79.99 TO	-70.00	0	.00	.00	75.09	.00	.00	*
10	-69.99 TO	-60.00	1	66.23-	2.17	77.26	66.23-	.00	**
11	-59.99 TO	-50.00	2	104.19-	3.41	80.67	52.09-	1.90	***
12	-49.99 TO	-40.00	6	261.62-	8.56	89.23	43.60-	2.26	*********
13	-39.99 TO	-30.00	3	109.39-	3.58	92.81	36.46-	1.84	****
14	-29.99 TO	-20.00	3	66.00-	2.16	94.97	22.00-	2.12	**
15	-19.99 TO	-10.00	7	100.19-	3.28	98.25	14.31-	1.73	***
16	-9.99 TO	-.01	9	53.52-	1.75	100.00	5.94-	2.04	*
** TOTALS **			41	3,055.62-			74.52-	120.51	

- Determining whether material amounts due to the company have been omitted from the books of account.
- Determining whether shipping cutoffs have been performed satisfactorily.
- Determining whether the allowance for doubtful accounts is adequate.

Use of the software may also reveal breakdowns and weaknesses in internal controls requiring management report comments. Figure 9-11 illustrates how audit software can be used to meet some of the important objectives.

Microcomputer Audit Packages

Audit software can be used when auditing accounts receivable. Microcomputer audit packages can provide field and internal auditors with computer

FIG. 9-6
Selection criteria totals—accounts receivable report

REPORT NO. ARCAAG05 | SPECIALTY MFG CO | PAGE NO. 2
REPORT DATE 11/05/79 | SELECTION CRITERIA TOTALS - ACCOUNT RECEIVABLE | PERIOD ENDED 04/30/79

TS	NAME	REL	CRITERIA CONST	JN	CD	RAN	INT	P/N	NUMBER	TOTAL SELECT
BG	CUSTOTAL	BG	000000000500000			0000	0000	P	1	29,174.20
01	CUSTOTAL	GT	000000000300000	A	S	0001	0002	P		
01	CUSTOTAL	LT	000000000499999		S	0001	0002	P	2	7,443.36
02	CUSTOTAL	GT	000000000100000	A	I	0001	0001	P		
02	CUSTOTAL	LT	000000000299900		I	0001	0001	P	12	19,940.37
03	CUSTOTAL	GT	000000000010000		S	0004	0015	N	7	23,782.15
						TOTAL SELECTED			22	80,340.08
						NOT SELECTED			170	45,133.92
						FILE TOTAL			192	125,474.00

FIG. 9-7
List of customers confirmed

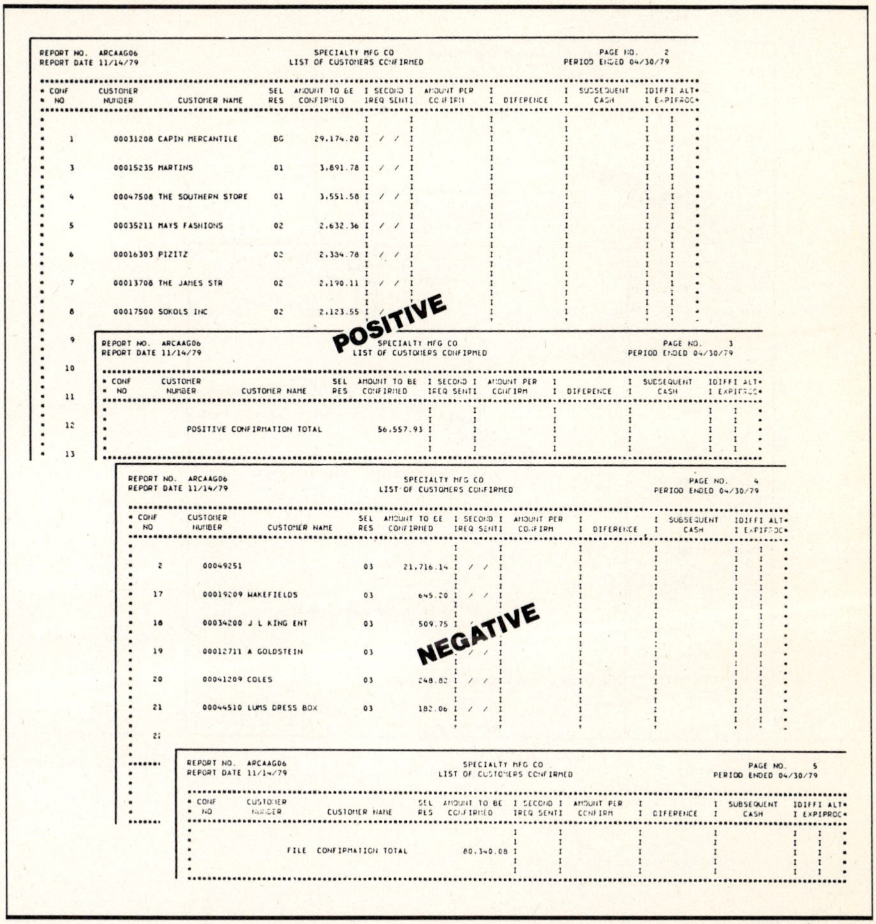

REPORT NO. ARCAAG06 SPECIALTY MFG CO PAGE NO. 2
REPORT DATE 11/14/79 LIST OF CUSTOMERS CONFIRMED PERIOD ENDED 04/30/79

CONF NO	CUSTOMER NUMBER	CUSTOMER NAME	SEL RES	AMOUNT TO BE CONFIRMED	SECOND REQ SENT	AMOUNT PER CONFIRM	DIFERENCE	SUBSEQUENT CASH	DIFF	ALT EXPIPROC
1	00031208	CAPIN MERCANTILE	BG	29,174.20	/ /					
3	00015235	MARTINS	01	3,891.78	/ /					
4	00047508	THE SOUTHERN STORE	01	3,551.58	/ /					
5	00035211	MAYS FASHIONS	02	2,632.36	/ /					
6	00016303	PIZITZ	02	2,334.78	/ /					
7	00013708	THE JAMES STR	02	2,190.11	/ /					
8	00017500	SOKOLS INC	02	2,123.55	/					
9										
10										
11										
12										
13										

REPORT NO. ARCAAG06 SPECIALTY MFG CO PAGE NO. 3
REPORT DATE 11/14/79 LIST OF CUSTOMERS CONFIPMED PERIOD ENDED 04/30/79

CONF NO	CUSTOMER NUMBER	CUSTOMER NAME	SEL RES	AMOUNT TO BE CONFIRMED	SECOND REQ SENT	AMOUNT PER CONFIRM	DIFERENCE	SUBSEQUENT CASH	DIFF	ALT EXPIPROC
		POSITIVE CONFIRMATION TOTAL		56,557.93						

REPORT NO. ARCAAG06 SPECIALTY MFG CO PAGE NO. 4
REPORT DATE 11/14/79 LIST OF CUSTOMERS CONFIRMED PERIOD ENDED 04/30/79

CONF NO	CUSTOMER NUMBER	CUSTOMER NAME	SEL RES	AMOUNT TO BE CONFIRMED	SECOND REQ SENT	AMOUNT PER CONFIRM	DIFERENCE	SUBSEQUENT CASH	DIFF	ALT EXPIPROC
2	00049251		03	21,716.14	/ /					
17	00019209	WAKEFIELDS	03	645.20	/ /					
18	00034200	J L KING ENT	03	509.75	/					
19	00012711	A GOLDSTEIN	03		/ /					
20	00041209	COLES	03	248.82	/ /					
21	00044510	LUMS DRESS BOX	03	182.06	/ /					
2:										

REPORT NO. ARCAAG06 SPECIALTY MFG CO PAGE NO. 5
REPORT DATE 11/14/79 LIST OF CUSTOMERS CONFIRMED PERIOD ENDED 04/30/79

CONF NO	CUSTOMER NUMBER	CUSTOMER NAME	SEL RES	AMOUNT TO BE CONFIRMED	SECOND REQ SENT	AMOUNT PER CONFIRM	DIFERENCE	SUBSEQUENT CASH	DIFF	ALT EXPIPROC
		FILE CONFIPMATION TOTAL		80,340.08						

audit capabilities that, until recently, were available only on mainframe systems. These packages perform many useful substantive test procedures and produce customized reports that show the results of the tests.

Microcomputer Accounts Receivable Audit Package.[2] This package can assist with auditing both open item and balance forward accounts receivable systems. Many useful standard accounts receivable substantive test procedures can be performed, including:

---

[2] Id.

FIG. 9-8
Confirmation letters

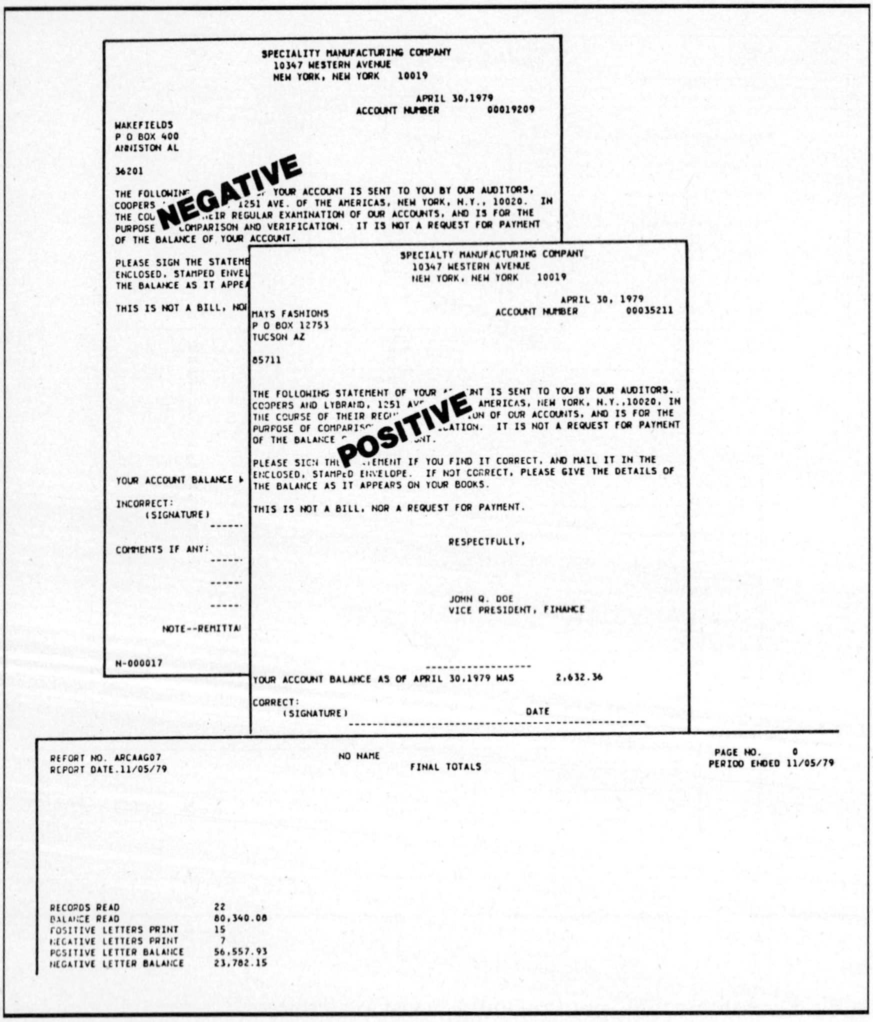

SPECIALITY MANUFACTURING COMPANY
10347 WESTERN AVENUE
NEW YORK, NEW YORK 10019

APRIL 30,1979
ACCOUNT NUMBER 00019209

WAKEFIELDS
P O BOX 400
ANNISTON AL

36201

THE FOLLOWIN... YOUR ACCOUNT IS SENT TO YOU BY OUR AUDITORS, COOPERS ... 1251 AVE. OF THE AMERICAS, NEW YORK, N.Y., 10020. IN THE COU... EIR REGULAR EXAMINATION OF OUR ACCOUNTS, AND IS FOR THE PURPOSE ... COMPARISON AND VERIFICATION. IT IS NOT A REQUEST FOR PAYMENT OF THE BALANCE OF YOUR ACCOUNT.

PLEASE SIGN THE STATEME... ENCLOSED, STAMPED ENVEL... THE BALANCE AS IT APPE...

THIS IS NOT A BILL, NO...

YOUR ACCOUNT BALANCE ...

INCORRECT:
(SIGNATURE)

COMMENTS IF ANY:

NOTE--REMITTA...

N-000017

SPECIALTY MANUFACTURING COMPANY
10347 WESTERN AVENUE
NEW YORK, NEW YORK 10019

APRIL 30, 1979
ACCOUNT NUMBER 00035211

MAYS FASHIONS
P O BOX 12753
TUCSON AZ

85711

THE FOLLOWING STATEMENT OF YOUR ...NT IS SENT TO YOU BY OUR AUDITORS. COOPERS AND LYBRAND, 1251 AV... AMERICAS, NEW YORK, N.Y.,10020, IN THE COURSE OF THEIR REG... ION OF OUR ACCOUNTS, AND IS FOR THE PURPOSE OF COMPARIS... CATION. IT IS NOT A REQUEST FOR PAYMENT OF THE BALANCE ... UNT.

PLEASE SIGN TH... TEMENT IF YOU FIND IT CORRECT, AND MAIL IT IN THE ENCLOSED, STAMPED ENVELOPE. IF NOT CORRECT, PLEASE GIVE THE DETAILS OF THE BALANCE AS IT APPEARS ON YOUR BOOKS.

THIS IS NOT A BILL, NOR A REQUEST FOR PAYMENT.

RESPECTFULLY,

JOHN Q. DOE
VICE PRESIDENT, FINANCE

YOUR ACCOUNT BALANCE AS OF APRIL 30,1979 WAS 2,632.36

CORRECT:
(SIGNATURE) DATE

REPORT NO. ARCAAG07 NO NAME PAGE NO. 0
REPORT DATE.11/05/79 FINAL TOTALS PERIOD ENDED 11/05/79

RECORDS READ	22
BALANCE READ	80,340.08
POSITIVE LETTERS PRINT	15
NEGATIVE LETTERS PRINT	7
POSITIVE LETTER BALANCE	56,557.93
NEGATIVE LETTER BALANCE	23,782.15

- Adding, aging, and stratifying account balances.
- Identifying doubtful debts.
- Reporting items for cut-off testing.
- Selecting accounts for detail testing.
- Producing confirmation letters.

These programs are an improvement over their mainframe counterparts be-

FIG. 9-9

List of transactions after closing date

REPORT NO. ARCAAG08 — SPECIALTY MFG CO — PAGE NO. 2
REPORT DATE 11/12/79 — LIST OF TRANSACTIONS AFTER CLOSING DATE - — PERIOD ENDED 04/30/79

CUSTOMER NUMBER	CUSTOMER NAME		CONFIRMED AMOUNT	TRANSLATED DATE	TRANSACTION NUMBER	CODE	DATE	JULIAN NUMBER	SUBSEQUENT PAYMENT
00010617	BARKETTS	AL	1,130.01	053079	01074A	9	053079		124.97-
00010617	BARKETTS	AL	1,130.01	050579	01127I	9	050579		662.88-
00010617	BARKETTS	AL	1,130.01	COUNT	2	* TOTAL *			787.85-
00012711	A GOLDSTEIN	AL	355.33	052479	01286A	9	052479		150.15-
00012711	A GOLDSTEIN	AL	355.33	COUNT	1	* TOTAL *			150.15-
00013708	THE JAMES STR	AL	2,190.11	052079	01373I	9	052079		31.35-
00013708	THE JAMES STR	AL	2,190.11	052879	01375C	9	052879		45.00-
00013708	THE JAMES STR	AL	2,190.11	052879	01374A	9	052379		33.00-
00013708	THE JAMES STR	AL	2,190.11	050579	0135[illegible]	9	050579		172.04-
00013708	THE JAMES STR	AL	2,190.11	052879	01393I	9	052879		231.00-
00013708	THE JAMES STR	AL	2,190.11	053079	01395D	9	053079		256.88-
00013708	THE JAMES STR	AL	2,190.11	COUNT	6	* TOTAL *			769.27-
00015235	MARTINS	AL	3,891.78	051779	01528	9	051779		45.50-
00015235	MARTINS	AL	3,891.78	051079	01525E	9	051079		20.55-
00015235	MARTINS	AL	3,891.78	051079	01522D	9	051079		49.82-
00015235	MARTINS	AL	3,891.78	051779	01522D	9	051779		47.40-
00015235	MARTINS	AL	3,891.78	053079	01531D	9	053079		79.20-
00015235	MARTINS	AL	3,891.78	051079	01531F	9	051079		81.51-
00015235	MARTINS	AL	3,891.78	051079	01531H	9	051079		83.05-
00015235	MARTINS	AL	3,891.78	051079	01533D	9	051079		149.59-
00015235	MARTINS	AL	3,891.78	052479	01531C	9	052479		78.76-
00015235	MARTINS	AL	3,891.78	051979	01532C	9	051979		86.06-
00015235	MARTINS	AL	3,891.78	052479	01531C	9	052479		78.75-
00015235	MARTINS	AL	3,891.78	052679	01551F	9	052679		261.51-
00015235	MARTINS	AL	3,891.78	051079	01563	9	051079		395.40-
00015235	MARTINS	AL	3,891.78	COUNT	13	* TOTAL *			1,479.99-
00015901	NEW IDEAL	AL	1,881.72	052279	01599I	9	052279		98.83-
00015901	NEW IDEAL	AL	1,881.72	052379	01595I	9	052379		58.76-
00015901	NEW IDEAL	AL	1,881.72	051079	015[illegible]G	9	051079		46.76-
00015901	NEW IDEAL	AL	1,881.72	052479	0159[illegible]	9	052479		47.55-
00015901	NEW IDEAL	AL	1,881.72	052879	01603E	9	052879		134.50-
00015901	NEW IDEAL	AL	1,881.72	051079	016[illegible]D	9	051079		151.59-
00015901	NEW IDEAL	AL	1,881.72	052679	01677I	9	052679		878.00-
00015901	NEW IDEAL	AL	1,881.72	COUNT	7	* TOTAL *			1,416.07-
00016303	PIZITZ	AL	2,384.78	052879	01624F	9	052579		57.00
00016303	PIZITZ	AL	2,384.78	052379	0162[illegible]	9	052379		42.75
00016303	PIZITZ	AL	2,384.78	052579	01631A	9	052579		8.99-
00016303	[illegible]								
00016303									
00016303									
00016303									
00016303									

REPORT NO. ARCAAG08 — SPECIALTY MFG CO — PAGE NO. 8
REPORT DATE 11/12/79 — LIST OF TRANSACTIONS AFTER CLOSING DATE - — PERIOD ENDED 04/30/79

CUSTOMER NUMBER	CUSTOMER NAME	CONFIRMED AMOUNT	TRANSLATED DATE	TRANSACTION CODE NUMBER	DATE	JULIAN NUMBER	SUBSEQUENT PAYMENT
GRAND TOTAL		80,215.23	COUNT	234			58,766.23-

cause the auditor is not required to know the operating procedures necessary to generate reports from mainframe data.

To use the microcomputer audit packages, client data must be transferred (downloaded) from the client's mainframe or minicomputer to the auditor's microcomputer. By downloading client data, the auditor can reduce intrusion into the data center. In the past, customized software would have to be installed and operated by the auditor at the data center location. Downloading data to a microcomputer audit package makes the audit less disruptive, since the auditor can perform much of the work away from the data center. The auditor can use any available method to download data.

Audit Program—Sequence of Events

The following sample audit program illustrates the use of an accounts receivable audit software package. Software reports[3] generated by this audit software package are listed as events.

---

[3] Id.

FIG. 9-10

Accounts confirmed with subsequent payments

REPORT NO. ARCAAG09-1
REPORT DATE 11/12/79

ACCOUNTS RECEIVABLE
ACCOUNTS CONFIRMED WITH SUBSEQUENT PAYMENTS

PAGE NO. 1
PERIOD ENDED 04/30/79

CONFIRM NUM	P N	WHY	CUSTOMER NUMBER	CUSTOMER NAME		TOTAL	SUBSEQUENT PAYMENTS	DIFFERENCE	ID
2	N	03	00049251			21,716.14	18,047.18-	3,668.96	
17	N	03	00019209	WAKEFIELDS	AL	645.20	393.84-	251.36	
18	N	03	00034200	J L KING ENT	AZ	509.75	509.75-	0.00	
19	N	03	00012711	A GOLDSTEIN	AL	355.33	150.15-	205.18	
20	N	03	00041209	COLES	AR	248.82	203.51-	45.31	
21	N	03	00044510	LUMS DRESS BOX	AR	162.06	165.81-	3.75-	
22	N	03	00015229	S L MESSER MERC	AL	124.85	0.00	124.85	
						23,782.15	19,490.24-	4,291.91	L1
1	P	BG	00031208	CAPIN MERCANTILE	AZ	29,174.20	16,190.19-	12,984.01	
3	P	01	00015235	MARTINS	AL	3,891.78	1,479.99-	2,411.79	
4	P	01	00047509	THE SOUTHERN STORE	AR	3,551.53	2,833.17-	713.41	
5	P	02	00035211	MAYS FASHIONS	AZ	2,632.11	1,041.28-	1,591.08	
6	P	02	00016303	PIZITZ	AL	2,384.75	1,171.65-	1,213.10	
7	P	02	00013708	THE JAMES STR	AL	2,190.11	769.27-	1,420.84	
8	P	02	00017500	SCHOLS INC	AL	2,123.55	1,806.20-	317.35	
9	P	02	00015901	NEW IDEAL	AL	1,881.72	1,416.07-	465.65	
10	P	02	00010201	THROWER DRY GOODS	AL	1,537.72	842.47-	695.25	
11	P	02	00040611	BUSTER BROWN STR	AR	1,524.40	3,080.82-	1,556.42-	
12	P	02	00030002	AJO VARIETY DPT ST	AZ	1,409.04	5,939.86-	4,450.82-	
13	P	02	00010617	BARKETTS	AL	1,130.01	787.85-	342.16	
14	P	02	00045218	HYATTS	AR	1,039.52	896.35-	143.17	
15	P	02	0003530[illegible]	PHELPS DODGE MERCA	AZ	1,007.19	912.59-	94.60	
16	P	02							

REPORT NO. ARCAAG09-Z
REPORT DATE 11/12/79

END OF JOB STATISTICS

PAGE NO. 1
PERIOD ENDED 04/30/79

				• S E L E C T E D •				• P O P U L A T I O N •	
JOB NO.	DATA NAME	ITEM ID	STATISTIC TYPE	ITEM COUNT	ITEM PERCENT	VALUE	VALUE PERCENT	ITEM COUNT	VALUE
1	CUSTOTAL		POSITIVE	22	100.0	80340.08	100.0	22	80340.08
			NEGATIVE	0	0.0	0.00	0.0	0	0.00
			ZERO	0	0.0			0	
			NET TOTAL	22	100.0	80340.08	100.0	22	80340.08
1	SUBSPAY-MS		POSITIVE	0	0.0	0.00	0.0	0	0.00
			NEGATIVE	21	100.0	58766.23-	100.0	21	58766.23-
			ZERO	1	100.0			1	
			NET TOTAL	22	100.0	58766.23-	100.0	22	58766.23-

Events	*Auditor's Actions*
Planning	• Develop plan and budget. • Decide on confirmation strategy. • Collect the information concerning the accounts receivable system. Prepare planning working papers. • Determine desired report options. • Agree to create reports within the audit time requirements. Keep audit staff informed as to progress and any reasons for additional time. • Inform audit staff of the following dates: —Year-end or audit date. —Aging categories. —Confirmation mailing date. —Subsequent payments period. • Before the due date, install the package, execute the edit program, and review the results for exceptions.

Events	*Auditor's Actions*
Report	
List of Open Transactions After Closing Date	• Review the accounts receivable file total. • Edit the accounts receivable file and agree the totals.
Audit review	• Reconcile totals to books of account. Select the stratification method and supply the necessary parameters.
Reports	• Prepare reports and agree the totals.
Aged Open Transactions File—Summary	
Aged Accounts Receivable Listing	• Use aging reports for audit tests.
Stratfication Histogram	• Determine selection criteria for confirmation.
Selection Criteria Total—Accounts Receivable	• Check that the correct number and value of accounts have been selected. • Code selection criteria onto parameter cards and prepare reports. Review results of selection.
List of Customers Confirmed	• Provide wording for positive and negative confirmation letters.
Confirmation Letters	• Arrange for controlled mailing of letters and follow-up responses.
List of Transactions After Closing Date	• Confirm the period for examining subsequent payments. Select the required report detail option.
Accounts Confirmed With Subsequent Payments	• Use the report to update the list of customers selected for confirmation but for which a reply was not received.
Second Aging After Validation	• Use reports to determine the effect of subsequent transactions on long overdue amounts.
Completion	• Summarize time costs and expenses. Document any reasons for changes from original budget. Provide suggestions for the coming audit year.

FIG. 9-11

Accounts receivable audit objectives

Audit Objectives	Software Capabilities
Determine whether recorded accounts receivable represents amounts due to the company at year-end or early substantive testing date.	■ Performs additions of account balances. ■ Produces a stratification of account balances to assist in selecting accounts for confirmation or other audit tests. ■ Selects accounts for positive and negative confirmations. ■ Produces confirmation control working papers. ■ Produces positive and negative confirmation letters using format and wording designed by the auditor. ■ Identifies and lists subsequent payments for accounts selected for confirmation.
Determine whether material amounts due to the company at year-end or early substantive testing date have been omitted from the books of account.	■ Performs a second aging of accounts receivables at a date subsequent to year-end or early substantive testing date. ■ Selects accounts with credit balances or unapplied credits for confirmation. ■ Identifies and reports transactions after the audit date.
Determine whether shipping cutoffs have been performed satisfactorily.	■ Selects accounts based on date of last debit or last credit. ■ Identifies and reports transactions after the audit date.
Determine whether the allowance for doubtful accounts is adequate.	■ Performs an aging of accounts receivable at year-end, early testing date, or any other date. ■ Identifies and lists accounts with irregular customer information. ■ Identifies and lists subsequent payments of accounts selected for confirmation.

Implementing Revenue Systems

Auditors often participate in the design, selection, and implementation of new systems. One function that is important is to ensure that controls are built in and that proper procedures for purchasing, programming, testing, and installing the new system are followed. (See Chapter 22, "System Development Trends and Practices" and Chapter 23, "System Development Methodology and Auditing.") The following checklists can be helpful in determining the initial requirements for such systems.

ORDER ENTRY

Location ______________________________

1. How many customers do you do business with? ____________
2. How many of these customers are considered active? ____________
3. What is your customer file growth rate? ____________
4. How many orders are processed on the average day? ____________
   Peak day? ____________
5. What is the average number of line items on each order? ____________
6. Do you use back order processing? ☐ Yes ☐ No
7. If so, how many individual back order entries are written per day?
   ____
8. How long (in days) before a back order is filled? ____________
9. On what basis do you fill back orders? ____________
10. Do you have a customer number scheme? (Describe) ____________
    ____
11. How many invoices are processed on the average day? ____________
    Peak day? ____________
12. Do you handle over-the-counter sales? ☐ Yes ☐ No
    Number daily ____________
13. Do you require separate ship-to information? ☐ Yes ☐ No
14. Do you have multiple ship-to addresses for each sold-to address?
    ☐ Yes ☐ No

15. If so, how many additional ship-to addresses in total? ____________

16. Do you have a commission plan for your salespeople?
☐ Yes ☐ No

17. Briefly explain sales commission processing. ____________

____

18. What is the largest quantity sold? ____________

19. How many prices do you use per product? ____________

20. Do you use any special pricing formulas? ☐ Yes ☐ No

21. What is the largest unit price? ____________

22. Do you give discounts (e.g., quantity discounts, item discounts, or chain discounts)? ☐ Yes ☐ No

Explain. ____________

23. Do you distinguish between exempt or nonexempt sales for tax purposes? ☐ Yes ☐ No

24. Is freight included on invoices? ☐ Yes ☐ No

25. If yes, how is it determined? ____________

____

26. Are there any other miscellaneous charges included (labor, deposits, handling, etc.)? ☐ Yes ☐ No

27. What type of sales analysis reports are now being maintained from your order-writing and/or invoice systems? ____________

____

28. Is there any other information that you feel is pertinent to your system?

____

____

SALES ANALYSIS

Location ____________

1. Are you currently compiling sales analysis information?

☐ Yes ☐ Manual

☐ No ☐ Automated

2. How are your sales analysis reports compiled?

Category	*Yes*	*No*	*Frequency*
By customer	☐	☐	____________
By customer class	☐	☐	____________

By product	☐	☐	________
By product class	☐	☐	________
By state or region	☐	☐	________
By supplier	☐	☐	________
Other	☐	☐	________

3. Indicate if information is compiled in:
   - ☐ Detail (by line item), or
   - ☐ Summary only (total of detail items)
4. Do you perform comparison to prior statistics?

☐ Yes	☐ Last month	☐ Year to date
☐ No	☐ Last quarter	☐ Last year (by month)

5. Please indicate the number of:

Customer classes	________
Product classes	________
Active states or regions	________
Salespeople	________

6. Indicate any other sales analysis information that may be helpful to us.

____

____

____

SUMMARY

In practice, computerized revenue systems may begin with one simple computer-based application, gradually adding and linking others to provide the total system. The principal control considerations are that reliable software is used and that manual procedures do not, by error or otherwise, interfere with or affect normal processing.

A sound, practical knowledge of these types of computer systems is an important factor that enables the auditor to use, evaluate, and test the revenue systems developments discussed in this chapter. Although computer systems differ depending on the system requirements and design, their features are often similar enough to provide a knowledge base.

CHAPTER **10**

Disbursement Systems

INTRODUCTION

Disbursement systems are those systems where goods and services are purchased and paid for. They lend themselves to misuse, since use of these systems results in payments. It is important to ensure that their use and results—payments—are controlled, accurate, and timely. There are several systems that can be categorized as disbursement systems, including:

- Payroll
- Purchase accounting
- Accounts payable
- Goods received processing
- Order processing

PAYROLL SYSTEMS

Overview

The payroll system processes the cost of the labor force that supplies the products and services an organization produces. The payroll system must be accurate, since there is no quicker way for an EDP department to lose credibility than by errors and delays in the payroll.

Payroll systems are sometimes developed by an in-house programming staff. If a system is not already in place, it is usually faster to implement one by buying a package. Packaged payroll systems have been available for a number of years, since they are common to all industries. An outside service bureau that does the entire payroll processing can also be used.

Whatever type of payroll processing system is in place, it should be audited to ensure control of both the system and its input. The payroll system is the way to track how much the labor force is costing a business. This information is especially valuable when performing sales analysis, profit analysis, and forecasting.

Although it is not always critical from an overall financial statement perspective, payroll is one of the most important computer applications for an organization. Good employee relations depend on an accurate and timely payroll system.

Because checks are often printed automatically, authorization and data security are also needed to provide adequate protection against fraud. Figure 10-1 shows the processing flow for part of a typical payroll system, and Figure 10-2 shows the related disk files.

There are two major types of payroll systems:

1. Salary systems, where employees are paid a fixed amount per pay period.
2. Hourly pay systems, where employees are paid for hours worked. Similar systems exist for piece work (employees are paid for work done) or commission systems (employees are paid a percentage of sales).

In practice, most systems combine the two types, because salaried employees may still be paid for overtime, or the organization may employ both types of worker. Conversely, it is also common for organizations to run separate payroll systems for different classes of employee. Confidentiality often requires that executives be handled by a different system. The special system of executive incentives, bonuses, and stock option plans also argues for such a split.

The Payroll Master File. The main file is the payroll master, which is sometimes integrated with the personnel data base. The latter contains profiles of employees, including qualifications, employment history, training completed, and employment health records.

Research shows that within many companies today, payroll and personnel data is fragmented. A modern and efficient human resource system calls for that data to be integrated. Six benefits are cited for the integrated approach:

1. It limits or eliminates redundant data.
2. It improves data accuracy by defining responsibilities more clearly.
3. It provides data more promptly.
4. It establishes single sources for obtaining data.
5. It eliminates the effort needed to keep and maintain multiple data bases.
6. It reduces the need for overall system maintenance.

FIG. 10-1

Payroll system overview flowchart (courtesy of International Business Machines Corporation)

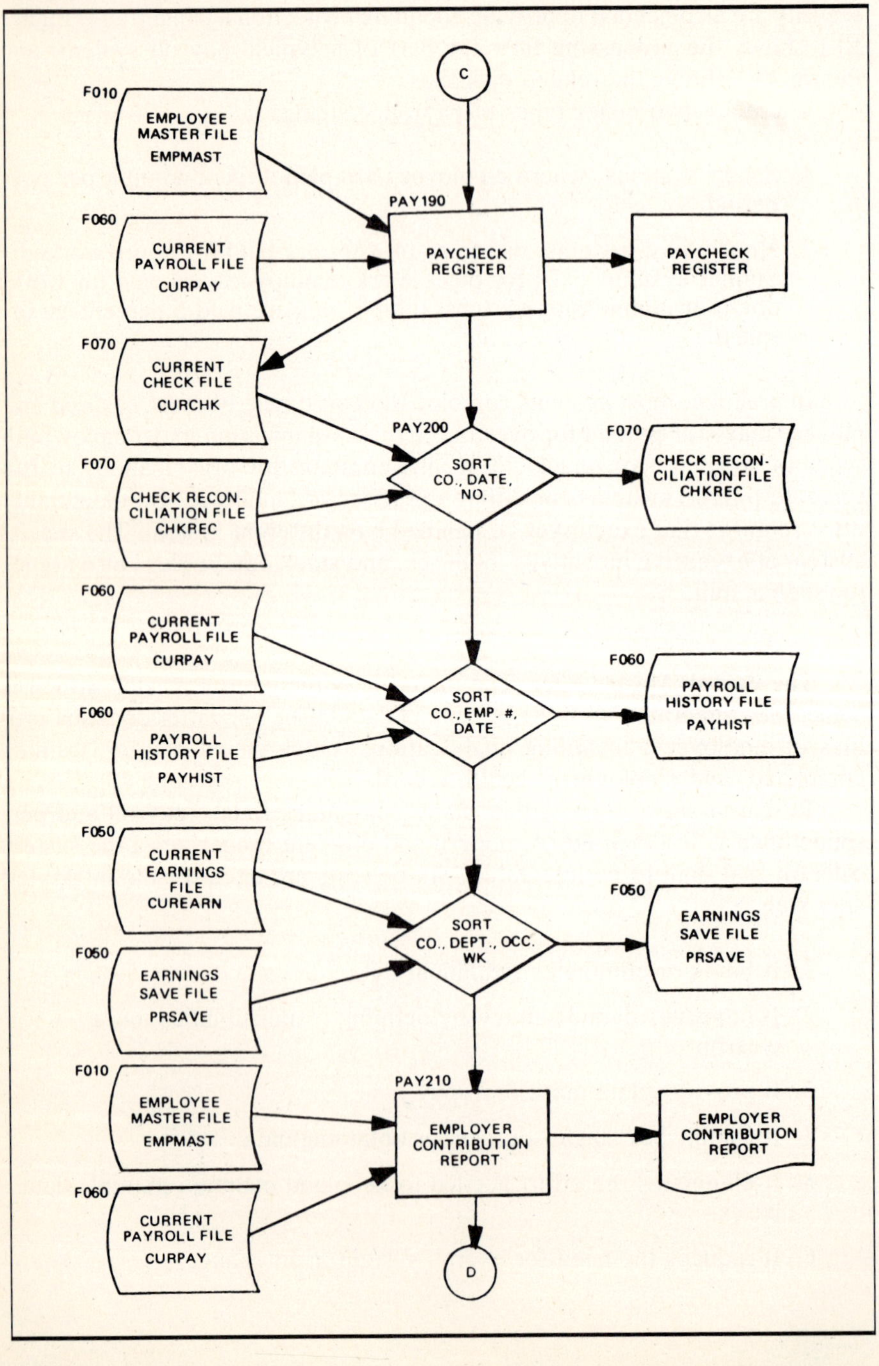

FIG. 10-2

Payroll system disk files (courtesy of International Business Machines Corporation)

File Name	File ID	File Orgn.	Record Size	Block Size	Format No.
EMPMAST	Employee Master File	VSAM	384	1152	F010
EMPLOAD	Load File	SAM	96	960	F020
TIMEWRK	Time Card Work File	SAM	38	380	F030
TIMECRD	Time Card File	VSAM	38	380	F030
TIMDATA	Time Card Data File	SAM	96	960	F040
CUREARN	Current Earnings File	SAM	120	960	F050
CURPAY	Current Payroll File	SAM	175	875	F060
CURCHK	Current Check File	SAM	18	504	F070
CHKREC	Check Reconciliation File	SAM	18	504	F070
PAYHIST	Payroll History File	SAM	175	875	F060
PRSAVE	Earnings Save File	SAM	120	960	F050
DEDREC	Deduction File	SAM	24	480	F090
CANCHK	Cancelled Check File	SAM	14	280	F080
TCHECK	Temporary Check File	SAM	18	360	F070
HISTREQ	History Request File	SAM	80	80	F120
WKCOMP	Workmans Comp. File	SAM	16	320	F100
UNION	Union File	SAM	120	960	F050
UNPREM	Union Premium File	SAM	28	560	F110
SUNION	Selected Union File	SAM	120	960	F050
NEWMAST	New Employee Master File	VSAM	384	1152	F010
JOBCLAS	Job Class Table	SAM	80	80	F130
FEDTAX	Federal Tax Table	SAM	80	80	F140
CALTAX	State Tax Table-California	SAM	80	80	F150
OCCGRP	Occupation Group Table	SAM	80	80	F160
UNRATE	Union Premium Rate Table	SAM	80	80	F170
EMPMASB	Double Definition of EMPMAST				
BEMPMAS	Backup Employee Master File	VSAM	384	1152	F010
BCURPAY	Backup Current Payroll File	SAM	175	875	F060
BPRSAVE	Backup Current Earnings File	SAM	120	960	F050
BPAYHIS	Backup Payroll History File	SAM	175	875	F060
BCHKREC	Backup Check Reconciliation File	SAM	18	504	F070

The payroll master file itself contains:

- *Master file data.* Pay rates, deduction rates, and the necessary minimum of personnel data needed for payroll purposes (social security number, employee number, name, address, department, job classification, etc.).
- *Transaction data.* Most of which is held for tax or other reporting purposes, including year-to-year figures for pay and deductions. Some systems also hold current, month-to-date, quarterly-to-date, or quarterly historical figures as well.

Input and Output. Input to a payroll system includes:

- Master file data changes—e.g., a change in pay rate.
- Time cards or time sheets.
- Vacation pay, bonuses, manually processed checks, and other unusual events.

Output includes:

- Payment to employees, usually by check.
- Information trails—regular and exception reports.
- The distribution of expense to the appropriate general ledger code.

Master File Data. Amendments to master file data are processed to:

- Record new employees, terminations, and employees on leave in the employee master file.
- Alter rates of pay, pay status, or details of allowances.
- Change deductions or other data (such as change in tax status or department number).

A part of a file layout for the employee master file, illustrating the variety of data that such files can hold, and for which amendment routines may be necessary, is shown in Figure 10-3.

In some systems, the computer may be programmed to:

- Calculate changes to master file data on the basis of input, such as increments to rates of pay as a result of changes in personnel details (such as passing of examinations).

FIG. 10-3

Payroll master file layout (courtesy of International Business Machines Corporation)

EMPLOYEE MASTER FILE - EMPLOYEE RECORD

Format: FØ1Ø

Field Description	Field Name	Field Length	Dec Pos	Format	Positions	Comments
RECORD CODE	MRECCD	2		A	1-2	'EM' in all cases
DELETE CODE	MDELCD	1		A	3	'D' = Deleted 'I' = Inactive/ Terminated Blank = Active Employee
COMPANY CODE	MCOMPY	2	Ø	N	4-5	Two digit designator for each unique company
EMPLOYEE NO.	MEMPNO	6	Ø	N	6-11	Includes five digit employee number with check digit (modulus 10)
UNUSED		2			12-13	
DEPARTMENT NO.	MHDEPT	3	Ø	N	14-16	
SOCIAL SECURITY NO.	MSOSEC	9	Ø	N	17-25	
EMPLOYEE LAST NAME	MLSTNM	15		A	26-40	Employee last name, if JR, SR, III etc place after last name
EMPLOYEE FIRST NAME	MFSTNM	9		A	41-49	
EMPLOYEE MIDDLE INITIAL	MMINIT	1		A	50	
STREET ADDRESS	MSTRAD	25		A	51-75	
CITY ADDRESS	MCITY	16		A	76-91	
STATE ADDRESS	MSTATE	2		A	92-93	

- Initiate amendments to master file data, such as increases in rates of pay on anniversary of starting date.

Payroll Production

In hourly payroll systems, it is usually necessary to enter details of time worked. The input can be all hours worked or variances from the standard hours held as master file data. Variances include overtime, holidays, and absences. The computer is often programmed to report cases where the hours entered exceed a defined norm.

For the system to act on the payroll input, it has to reference other files of standard information. Among these are:

- Overtime rate multiple.
- Premium rate multiple.
- Report options selected.
- Pay rate table.
- Valid bank code table.
- Valid state code table.
- Valid local code table.
- FICA rate table.
- FUTA rate table.
- Vacation entitlement table.
- Sick pay entitlement table.
- Bank number and name table.

These provide the rest of the data needed to calculate meaningful output.

The system matches transaction data with the relevant employee details on the master file. Unmatched input or erroneous data is usually rejected (such as duplicate input) or reported (such as no time report received), whichever is appropriate to the system.

The computer then:

- Calculates the pay details for each employee.
- Updates the transaction data on the master file.
- Summarizes the accounting total for posting to the general ledger.

The totals are often categorized. This is done as a basis for posting work-in-process or cost accounts.

In salary systems it is normal for the monthly or annual salary to be held as master file data. The only transaction data entered is any adjustments or overtime details. The computer is programmed to select or calculate the salary and take account of any additional input.

Sample System Overview

A software aid for payroll systems is IBM's COBOL (Common Business Oriented Language) Payroll Management System. It includes a basic payroll system and additional subsystems, which may or may not be implemented. The basic system provides employee file loading and maintenance, tax and other table loading, time and attendance processing, payroll processing, file backup, personnel reporting, quarterly statements (941s), and year-end W-2 forms. The additional subsystems, not interrelated, are the check reconciliation system, time card preparation, employer contributions report, vacation/sick pay report, labor distribution, payroll history, deduction report, union reporting, and worker's compensation report. Implementation of all components of the payroll management system makes comprehensive reporting to management—with strict controls, edits, and information or audit trails—possible.

Time Card Preparation System

A time card preparation system produces employees' time cards on the computer's printing device. The system prints employee details on card-stock continuous forms. Time cards are usually printed in company number, home department, and employee name sequence. Upper and lower limits are input to the time card printing program so that groups may be printed selectively. Programs included in this optional system are:

- Select time card data.
- Load time card file.
- Print time cards.
- Build deduction file.
- Deduction report.
- Pay period vacation/sick pay report.

Upon completion of this processing, the payroll cycle associated with the pay period is complete except for backing up critical files.

AUDITING PAYROLL SYSTEMS

Among the procedures for auditing payroll systems are common payroll substantive procedures such as:

- Identifying duplicate social security numbers.
- Comparing current period's payroll figures with a previous period's payroll figures.
- Identifying employees with "unusual" payroll records (such as those with excessive overtime).
- Identifying possible excessive increases in an employee's salary.

As a result, an auditor can achieve the following substantive objectives:

- Determining whether the net income for the year and the individual items of income and expenses that are disclosed in the income statement are fairly stated.
- Determining whether production in relation to cost is appropriate, where pay is related to production.
- Determining whether liabilities for accrued liabilities and other accounts payable have been recorded and fairly stated.

Using Audit Software to Analyze Payroll

Audit software packages exist to assist the auditor by automating many of the tasks associated with payroll substantiation. Additional audit work required is sometimes beyond the scope of most payroll audit packages. For example:

- Recalculation of federal, state, and local taxes.
- Verification of accruals for vacation pay.

Many common payroll substantive tests or procedures can be performed using audit software. Since the data is maintained on computer files, it was natural to develop audit software that analyzes this information. The auditor can thus be assisted in analysis of data and controls.

A number of data elements can be analyzed to determine whether there are any weaknesses in the controls and whether there has been any breakdown.

Duplicated Data. Whenever there is a possibility of duplicated data (inappropriate for processing), there is usually a way for the computer to

FIG. 10-4

Duplicated data report

REPORT NO. PR05CAAG-1 COMPUTER MFG CO PAGE NO. 1
REPORT DATE 02/28/81 DUPLICATE SOCIAL SECURITY NO. PERIOD ENDED 01/31/81

SOCIAL SECURITY	EMPLOYEE NUMBER	DEPT. NO.	EMPLOYEE NAME	START DATE	STOP DATE	PAY TYPE	PAY RATE	DEP.	GROSS PAY	TOTAL DEDUCTIONS	NET PAY
011-21-8765	416	1017	HARDY, KENNETH	01/21/75		A	15,000.00	2	15,000.00	4,000.00	11,000.00
011-21-8765	416	1122	HARDY, KENNETH	01/21/75		H	5.25	1	10,920.00	3,920.00	7,000.00

*** TOTAL RECORDS PROCESSED 22,000 ***

RECORDS PRINTED ABOVE 2

EMPLOYEES WITH DUPLICATE SS NO. 1

deal with it. For example, using the master file, the program can sort by social security number to locate any duplicate social security numbers. (See Figure 10-4 for an example of a report.[1]) Once the report has been obtained, the reasons for the duplicate numbers should be investigated to ensure that they represent valid employees.

No Match and Excessive Increases. Another technique to analyze the data is to obtain the payroll master file from two periods (usually two calendar years). Then each employee's current information can be compared with the corresponding historical information to identify excessive increases in pay rates, changes to number of dependents, date of birth, and date of hire. It is also possible to determine who has been hired and terminated during the period. (See Figure 10-5 for a sample report.)

The report totals are subsequently agreed to payroll master file report totals, highlighting any unusual or unsubstantiated results. All reasons for employee information that does not match the previous period data can then be investigated.

Large Increases. An organization may have a standard guideline for pay increases. Using this as a guide, employees can be reviewed to determine how many received pay increases that were above the guideline. Once selected, the pay increases can be checked to see that they agree with authorized documents. It is possible that such an increase is warranted and was duly authorized.

---

[1] Coopers & Lybrand.

FIG. 10-5

No match/excessive increases report

REPORT NO. PR07CAAG-1 — COMPUTER MFG CO — PAGE NO. 1
REPORT DATE 02/28/81 — NO MATCH AND EXCESSIVE INCREASES — PERIOD ENDED 01/31/81

SOCIAL SECURITY	DEPT NO.	EMPLOYEE NAME	PERIOD	BIRTH DATE	DATE HIRED	STOP DATE	DEP	PAY RATE	TYPE	GROSS PAY	TOTAL DEDUCTIONS	NET PAY	REASON
101-25-1011	1211	JONES, THOMAS	CURR	012245	050180		0	60,000.00	A	45,000.00	13,950.00	31,050.00	NEW
121-16-8011	1212	SMITH, FRANK	CURR	061354	021578		2	30,000.00	A	30,000.00	8,500.00	21,500.00	TYPE CHG.
			PREV	061354	021578		2	2,000.00	M	24,000.00	6,000.00	18,000.00	

REPORT NO. PR07CAAG-1 — COMPUTER MFG CO — PAGE NO. 212
REPORT DATE 02/28/81 — NO MATCH AND EXCESSIVE INCREASES STATISTICS — PERIOD ENDED 01/31/81

DESCRIPTION:	EMPLOYEES	RECORDS	GROSS PAY	DEDUCTIONS	NET PAY
NEW EMPLOYEES	2,000	2,000	30,000,000	7,500,000	22,500,000
TERMINATED EMPLOYEES	500	500	7,500,000	1,875,000	5,625,000
EXCESSIVE PAYRATE	100	100	5,000,000	1,000,000	4,000,000
PAYTYPE CHANGE	200	200	10,000,000	2,000,000	8,000,000
BIRTHDATE CHANGE	10	10	100,000	25,000	75,000
DATE OF HIRE CHANGE	20	20	100,000	35,000	65,000
NO. OF DEPENDENTS CHANGE	600	600	20,000,000	5,000,000	15,000,000
TOTAL PRINTED - CURRENT FILE	2,930	2,930	65,200,000	15,560,000	49,640,000
TOTAL NOT PRINTED -CURRENT FILE	20,194	20,194	275,316,711	14,555,000	260,761,711
*** GRAND TOTALS - CURRENT FILE	23,124	23,124	340,516,711	30,115,036	310,401,685
TOTAL PRINTED - PREVIOUS FILE	1,330	1,330	42,000,000	9,935,000	32,065,000
TOTAL NOT PRINTED - PREVIOUS FILE	20,270	20,270	288,425,675	20,174,804	268,250,000
*** GRAND TOTALS - PREVIOUS FILE	22,000	22,000	330,425,675	30,109,804	300,315,871

Operational Audits. This analysis might also be very effective for operational audits. To evaluate a particular department, this type of payroll information gives a perspective of how well the department is functioning.

Analysis can be made of:

- Number and frequency of pay increases.
- Department turnover. Excessive new hires and terminations reflects on the department business. Too many terminations may indicate an overzealous ''mean and lean'' operation that could affect future production. A combination of too many new hires and terminations indicates heavy employee turnover, which could have a serious impact on the department's ability to achieve its business objectives.

Along these lines, a report such as the one in Figure 10-6, can be produced showing a comparison of current-year information to previous-year information.

Department hours, overtime hours, regular pay, gross pay, and number of people with percentage of change in gross pay can be analyzed. Where

FIG. 10-6
Annual comparison by department report

REPORT NO. PR10CAAG-1 COMPUTER MFG CO PAGE NO. 1
REPORT DATE 02/28/81 ANNUAL COMPARISON BY DEPARTMENT PERIOD ENDED 01/31/81

CURRENT YEAR INFORMATION							PREVIOUS YEAR INFORMATION				
REGULAR HOURS	OVERTIME HOURS	REGULAR PAY	GROSS PAY	NO. OF PEOPLE	DEPT NO.	NO. OF PEOPLE	GROSS PAY	REGULAR PAY	OVERTIME HOURS	REGULAR HOURS	PERCENT CHANGE
10,400	500	104,000	114,000	5	211	4	89,880	74,880	1,000	8,320	27 ***
				23,124	*TOTALS*	22,000					
		RECORDS IN CURRENT FILE		23,124		22,000	RECORDS IN PREVIOUS FILE				

there are large changes in percentages, the auditor ensures that they are valid and that they are properly reflected in the costing of products and services.

High and Sample Reporting. An analysis based on gross pay can be made by sorting master file year-to-date gross pay in descending sequence. The ranking by pay is then shown. Of course, sample data should be taken in different ranges. (See Figure 10-7 for a report example.)

FIG. 10-7
High and sample report display

REPORT NO. PR04CAAG-1 COMPUTER MFG CO PAGE NO. 1
REPORT DATE 02/28/81 HIGH AND SAMPLE REPORT PERIOD ENDED 01/31/81

SOCIAL SECURITY	EMPLOYEE NUMBER	DEPT. NO.	EMPLOYEE NAME	START DATE	STOP DATE	PAY TYPE	PAY RATE	DEP.	GROSS PAY	TOTAL DEDUCTIONS	NET PAY
101-25-1011	1211	1016	JONES, THOMAS	05/01/80		A	60,000.00	0	45,000.00	13,950.00	31,050.00
127-44-5601	843	1016	SMITH, GEORGE	02/16/78		M	1,014.50	1	12,174.00	3,165.24	9,008.76
079-46-6403	844	1017	KNIGHT, JR., CARLTON	01/10/78		H	5.25	2	10,920.00	2,948.40	7,971.60
111-16-6021	1016	211	RUSH, ANNE	02/01/80	02/15/80	H	4.00	0	8,320.00	1,913.60	6,407.00

REPORT NO. PR04CAAG-1 COMPUTER MFG CO PAGE NO. 27
REPORT DATE 02/28/81 HIGH AND SAMPLE STATISTICS PERIOD ENDED 01/31/81

CRITERIA	RECORDS	EMPLOYEES	GROSS PAY	NET PAY	DEDUCTIONS
SELECTED BY GT-TEST	15	15	175,000.00	127,750.00	47,250.00
TOTAL ABOVE CUTOFF VALUE	10	10	385,612.00	285,353.00	100,259.00
SELECTED BY LT-TEST	40	40	120,000.00	90,000.00	30,000.00
TOTAL BELOW CUTOFF VALUE	500	500	282,614.42	209,134.68	73,479.75
SELECTED BY BT-TEST	22	22	1,621,817.16	1,216,362.89	405,454.27
TOTAL BETWEEN RANGE VALUES	618	618	2,112,819.80	1,593,230.26	519,589.54
TOTAL SELECTED	215	215	3,225,000.00	2,418,750.00	806,250.00
TOTAL NOT SELECTED	21,785	21,785	327,200,675.12	297,102,879.00	30,029,179.00
*** TOTAL IN FILE ***	22,000	22,000	330,425,675.12	300,315,871.00	30,109,804.12

Analyzing the Effectiveness of the Controls

Using the software and the data stored in the files, it is possible to obtain the results of system processing and determine how effectively it was controlled by seeing what was recorded, as in the following:

- Garbage, or garbled transmissions or data, may mean that the computer system is not operating properly.
- There may be undetected errors in the programs. For example, FICA deductions that exceed the limit may indicate that the program was not changed appropriately.

Inappropriate changes that were requested but not made usually means that there is poor control over programmed procedures.

These are not all the analyses that can be performed on payroll data, because different organizations have different needs. However, they indicate the many ways that data processed by the computer can be analyzed. Many payroll audit procedures currently performed manually can be automated in this way.

Audit Program—Sequence of Events

The effective use of an audit software package requires cooperation between the auditor and an EDP auditor. The EDP auditor can explain the package capabilities and can implement and execute the package. However, the auditor has overall responsibility for properly performing the audit.

This section describes the typical sequence of tasks using a payroll audit software package; the title of each report is listed as an event.[2]

Events	*Auditor's Actions*
Planning	• Develop plan and budget. • Collect the information concerning the payroll system. Prepared planning working papers. • Determine desired report options and assist in preparing the appropriate parameters (e.g., what is the maximum acceptable pay rate). • Agree to provide reports within the audit time requirements. Keep audit staff informed about progress and any reasons for additional time.

[2] Coopers & Lybrand.

Events	*Auditor's Actions*
Planning (*cont'd*)	• Inform audit staff of the following: a. Year-end or test date. b. The exception profile applicable to the edit report. • Before the due date, install the package, execute the edit program, and review the results for exceptions.
Report	
Payroll Master File Edit and Exceptions and Statistics	• Obtain the relevant payroll totals. • Edit the payroll file (edit current-period file as well as prior-period file as two processing steps), resolve error messages, and agree the totals.
Audit review	• Review any error messages to determine significance and make any adjustments that may be required. Check records printed as exceptions against employee personnel records. Decide, based on errors, whether the "Employee Master File Printout" is required. Provide information on the high and low values and the sample rate to be used for producing the "High and Sample Report."
Report	
High and Sample Report	• Assist in determining significance of error messages. • Review the report and agree the totals.
Audit review	• Review the report for unusual pay. Check sample to personnel records to verify accuracy of data.
Report	
Duplicate Social Security Numbers	• Use the report to identify duplicate social security numbers.
Audit review	• Follow up any duplicates, determine audit significance, and make any adjustments required.

Events	*Auditor's Actions*
Report	
Employee Master File Printout	• Use this report in place of "Payroll Master File Edit" when that report discloses significant errors. • Prepare report and agree the totals.
Audit review	• Compare selected employees with personnel information.
Report	
No Match and Excessive Increases and Statistics	• Prepare report and agree the totals.
Audit review	• Check new hires, terminations, amendments, and increases to appropriate authorizations.
Report	
Annual Comparison by Department	• Prepare report and agree the totals.
Audit review	• Agree the totals to departmental cost figures. Consider whether movements in period indicate that further audit testing is required.
Completion	• Summarize time and expenses. Document any reasons for changes from original budget. Provide suggestions for the coming audit year.

Implementing Payroll Systems

The following material provides an example of documentation for questions that can be answered to develop a payroll system when an auditor participates in the system development. (Figure 10-8 provides a completed matrix to analyze this application.)

PAYROLL

Location ______________________________

1. How many employees are on your payroll? ______________
2. What is your yearly turnover? ______________

3. How many companies do you process payroll for? ______________
4. What type of payroll do you have?
   - ☐ Hourly and salaried
   - ☐ Piecework
   - ☐ Special distribution to job cost
   - ☐ Manufacturing (other)
   - ☐ Special (explain)

   Special: ____

   ____

   ____
5. What is your employee numbering scheme? ______________

   ____
6. By what method are they paid?
   - ☐ Weekly
   - ☐ Biweekly
   - ☐ Semimonthly
   - ☐ Other (specify) ______________________________
7. What factors are used in calculating gross pay (salary, hourly rate(s)), overtime (O.T.), bonus, commission, sickpay, expense reimbursement, piecework performance, etc.?

   ____

   ____
8. Is there more than one state involved in calculating state taxes? ____

   ____
9. Do you process city taxes? ☐ Yes ☐ No
10. If so, what cities? ______________________________
11. What types of deductions are used in your payroll and in what frequency are these deductions taken (medical insurance, life insurance, union bonds, credit union, stock purchase, etc.)?

    ____
12. If union deductions are taken, how many are involved and how are they calculated? ______________________________
13. How many union reports are processed? ______________
14. Do you generate any special reports (insurance deductions, etc.)? ___

    ____

FIG. 10-8

Information systems Control Matrix—payroll application

Transaction	Completeness	Accuracy	Authorization	Maintenance	Programmed Procedures
Time cards Daily Weekly Pay Period	Manual: Review and reconciliation of total hours to Transmission Control and Error (TCE) Report and Labor Distribution Report.	Manual: Review of pay detail on Payroll Register.	Manual: Authorization of vacation, holiday, and sick time based on earned accrual by supervisory personnel.	Manual: Review and reconciliation of Quarter-to-Date and Year-to-Date Listings to previous Quarter-to-Date and Year-to-Date Listings and current pay period Payroll Register.	Calculation of overtime based on overtime data and method in employee master file. Calculation of pay based on time card hours and master file data elements.
	Programmed: Based on salary status code on employee master file.	Programmed: Edit numerics, pay date, and status codes. Validity check of employee number.	Programmed: Based on employee master file data.	Programmed: Employee master file crossfoot.	
Supplemental time cards	Manual: Review and reconciliation to TCE and Labor Distribution Reports.	Manual: Review of pay detail on Payroll Register.	Manual: Authorization of vacation and other advances based on earned accruals by supervisory personnel.	Manual: Same as maintenance of regular time cards.	Calculation of pay based on time card hours and master file data elements.
	Programmed: Exception code reported. Batching on hours.	Programmed: Same as regular time cards.	Programmed: Valid pay period check performed.	Programmed: Employee master file crossfoot.	
Deduction refunds	Manual: Review and reconciliation of gross deduction refund from payroll register to manual log of deduction refunds.	Manual: Same as completeness.	Manual: Determination of validity of refund and amount to be refunded by supervisory personnel.	Manual: None.	

15. Do you produce a departmental expense report? ☐ Yes ☐ No
16. Is your payroll system going to be interfaced with any other applications (job cost, manual checks, wage accrual)?

____

____

17. What control totals do you keep on your present payroll?

____

____

18. Is there any other information that you feel is pertinent?

____

____

PURCHASE ACCOUNTING SYSTEMS

Purchase accounting systems process the data for purchases and payments. Since purchases automatically lead to payments, if purchases are properly contracted, control over payment should be effected, but not entirely. Controls over payments are still needed to ensure that every payment was made for goods and services received, that the same purchases were not paid for twice, and that they were indeed paid. Analysis of how purchases and payments were made can be done as well; for example, were they timely so that the benefit of discounts was received?

Purchase accounting systems can handle various types of purchases, including:

- *Trade*. Those that are bought to sell or convert before reselling.
- *Other*. Expense-type items such as supplies, assets, and equipment.

Applications

Most purchase accounting systems perform three basic accounting functions:

1. *Accounts payable processing*. Recording of transactions in the accounts payable records.
2. *Goods received processing*. Recording of details of goods received, but not yet invoiced.

3. *Order processing.* Recording of goods ordered, but not yet received.

The computer may be involved in each of these activities, and the extent to which they are computerized determines the complexity of the purchase accounting system. The various types of systems are described under the following headings:

- Accounts payable systems.
- Goods received processing systems.
- Order processing systems.

Payment of creditors can also be carried out by the computer. This is considered a separate function, which can be integrated with any of these systems.

ACCOUNTS PAYABLE SYSTEMS

Accounts payable systems are appropriate systems for the auditor to review. When the system is computerized, the auditor's task can be that much easier: The data can be analyzed more quickly and effectively to find the exceptions that could be unauthorized payments.

The larger the volume of transactions being processed by the system, the greater the opportunity for bogus transactions to be entered, processed, and easily paid. A faulty accounts payable system can also result in poor vendor relations and loss of favorable payment terms. Likewise, if the accounts payable transactions are not properly posted to the cost of doing business, this can be easily misstated, making the organization appear to be either more or less profitable, depending on how the error has occurred.

In these systems, the computer processes the accounts payable records. Order processing and goods received functions are manual operations. An example of this type of system is illustrated in the overview flowchart in Figure 10-9.

Accounts Payable Master File

Records are maintained for each of the vendors whose transactions are processed by the system. The accounts payable records for each vendor hold the following information:

FIG. 10-9

Accounts payable data base system overview flowchart (courtesy of International Business Machines Corporation)

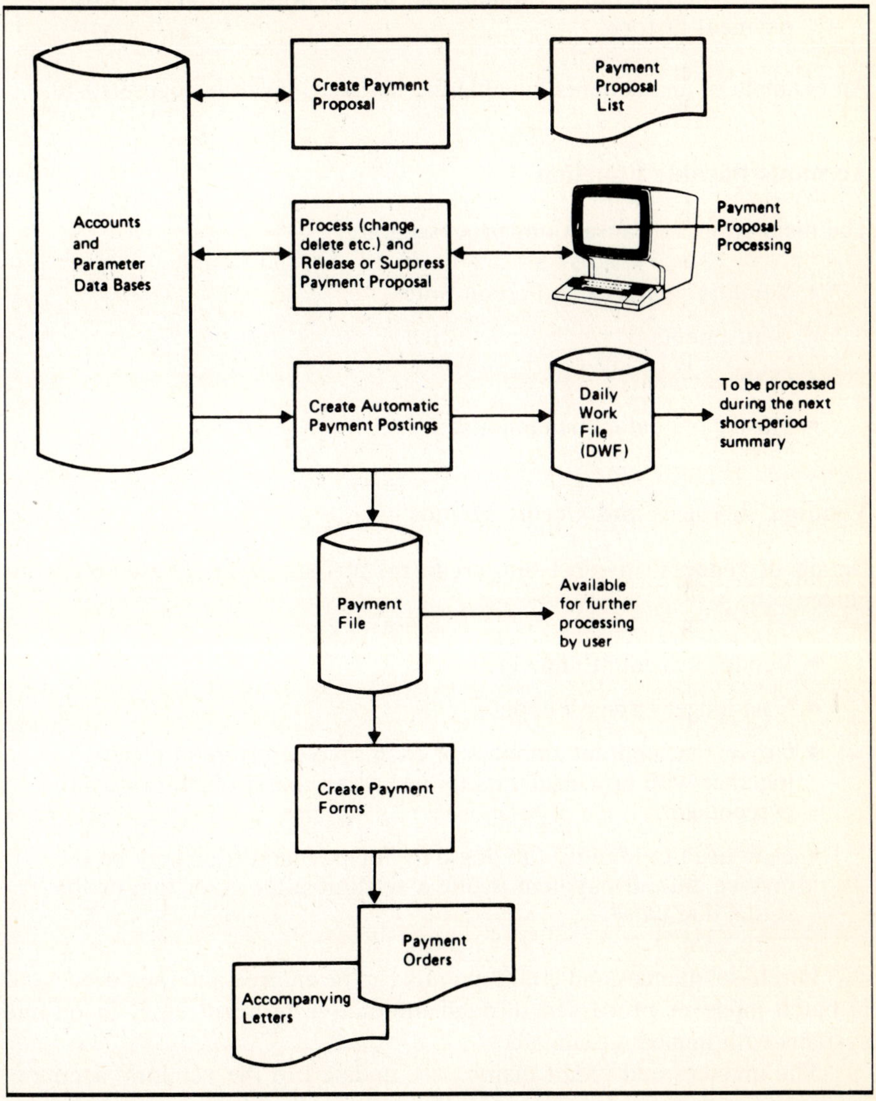

- *Master file.* Vendor's name and address, payment terms, vendor's bank account details, special terms.
- *Transaction details.* Outstanding transactions, invoice history, payment history.

An example of an accounts payable file layout is given in Figure 10-10.

Accounts Payable Function

The main types of transactions processed are:

- Vendors' invoices and credit notes.
- Adjustments.
- Cash payments.
- Master file data amendments.

Vendors' Invoices and Credit Memos

Details of vendors' invoices and credit memos are input. These details include:

- Vendor's account number.
- Cost ledger expense codes.
- Gross, tax, and net amounts of each invoice or credit memo, together with any discounts (either as a separate figure or as a percentage).
- Date used to identify the due date for payment (this may be the invoice date, if payment is due a set time after invoicing, or the actual due date).

Purchase invoices and credit memos can be entered and then processed in batch mode or processed through interactive terminal entry in on-line systems with immediate update.

The invoices and credit memos are updated to the vendors' accounts on the accounts payable master file. The total value of transactions is summarized and categorized for posting to the general/cost ledgers.

During updating of the accounts payable records, the computer normally summarizes the items or balances and produces information for control purposes. Lists of balances and exception reports (such as debit balances) may also be produced.

FIG. 10-10

Accounts payable files (courtesy of International Business Machines Corporation)

The Accounts Payable Package uses three permanent files and thirteen temporary work files. The records in each file contain a unique Record Code as the first two characters of the record. They also contain a Delete Code as the third character of the record; a blank means a valid record, a "D" means a deleted record.

WHERE USED LIST

FILE NAME	RECORD CODE	DESCRIPTION	WHERE USED
VENDOR - SYS010	01	Vendor Master File	AP30, AP01, AP02, AP05, AP07, AP10, AP17, AP20, AP21, AP31, AP40, AP41
PAYABL - SYS012	02	Payables File	AP31, AP02, AP03, AP04S AP06, AP12, AP20, AP22, AP42, AP43
CHECKS - SYS014	03	Check File	AP31, AP09, AP10, AP13, AP15, AP16, AP23, AP44, AP45
DETAIL	20	Distribution File	AP03, AP17S
CASHED	21	Cashed Checks	AP13, AP13S
OCHECKS	03	Outstanding Checks	AP16
WORKA	20,02	20 Invoice Line Item 02 Invoice Total	AP02, AP02S

Adjustments

Adjustments will always be necessary to input corrections to entries in the accounts payable records. The principal purpose of adjustments is to correct mispostings or change invoice values. Adjustments may also be needed for other purposes, such as to adjust for a payment discount after processing a "quick" payment to take advantage of cash discount terms offered by a vendor. Adjustments are summarized and categorized in a similar manner to invoices and credit memos.

Cash Payments

Cash payments are normally dealt with separately. This is discussed later in this chapter in the section entitled "Payment of Creditors."

Amendments to Master File Data

Amendments to master file data are needed to open and close vendors' accounts and alter the various data fields. A listing of master file data amendments made is normally produced.

GOODS RECEIVED PROCESSING SYSTEMS

In these systems, the computer is involved in goods received processing, but the order processing and accounts payable may remain a separate manual operation. It is common for such systems to be integrated, such as with the processing of the raw material inventory records. The goods received details are used not only to process purchases but also to update the inventory records for raw materials at the same time or in a subsequent run.

Goods Received Function

Goods received details are prepared and entered, and the following processing is carried out:

- *Valuation of goods received.* The value of goods received is calculated by reference to costs (such as standard costs) held as master file data.
- *Recording of outstanding invoices.* Goods received details are entered and stored as suspense records of goods received but not invoiced. A summary of movements in the suspense records is normally produced for control purposes.

Amendments to Master File Data

Amendments to master file data are needed to open and close vendors' accounts and alter the various data elements or fields. A listing of master file data amendments is usually produced.

The main effect of computerization on the accounts payable system is that the manual matching of purchase invoices with goods received details is replaced by a programmed matching with the suspense records of details of goods received. The following procedures are performed:

- *Invoice matching.* Goods received records remain in suspense until matched with the vendors' invoice details; invoices may be matched on quantities and/or price. Matched items are deleted.
- *Calculation of price variances.* Performed at the time of matching, provided the goods received details are held at standard cost value. The computer may calculate the cost variances.
- *Follow-up of invoices not received.* Periodically, the suspense records are read, and the goods received that have not been matched with vendors' invoices for a given period are printed.
- *Liability for goods received not invoiced.* Where the goods received records are held in dollar amounts or can be valued by reference to a costs file, the total accrued liability with respect to goods received can be periodically summarized and printed.

A capability must be incorporated in the system to ensure that invoices relating to items other than inventory can be processed. This may be achieved by the entry of dummy goods received details. Another method is to include an indicator on the relevant invoices that the program recognizes as an instruction to bypass the matching of that item with the goods received suspense file.

Audit procedures are similar to those for an accounts payable system, as discussed previously in this chapter.

ORDER PROCESSING SYSTEMS

In these systems, the computer may be involved in processing all components of purchase accounting—accounts payable processing, goods received processing, and ordering. As with goods received processing, systems of this type may be integrated with the processing of raw materials inventory records.

Order Processing Function

The order processing function is illustrated in Figure 10-11. The initial processing in this application relates to purchase orders: Purchase orders are either entered or initiated by the computer.

FIG. 10-11
Order processing system overview flowchart

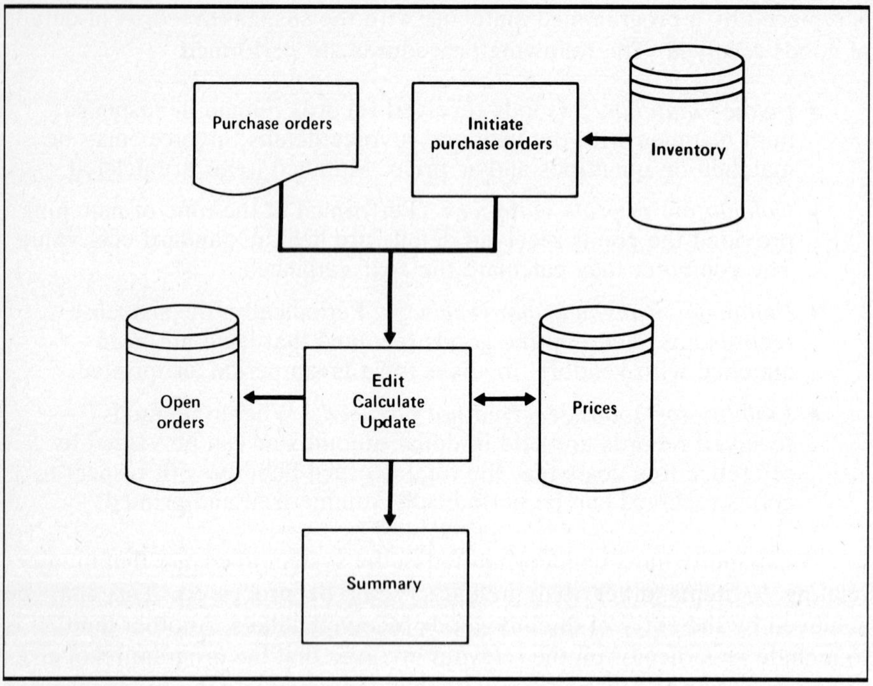

When orders are entered manually, on-line data entry techniques are often used. The computer then produces the order document to send to the supplier.

The computer initiation of orders may be triggered by:

- Comparing current stock balance with minimum stock levels held as data on the master file.
- Using more complex modeling programs, taking into account historical usage, current orders, marketing forecasts, seasonal trends, carrying cost, safety factors, future scheduled deliveries, lead times, and economic order quantities.

Computer-produced orders are often manually scrutinized prior to being sent to the vendor.

Once purchase orders are manually entered or generated by the computer, they are written to an open order suspense file to await the receipt of the goods and the processing of the goods received note. Open orders may be recorded in terms of both quantity and estimated purchase value of each order.

In some systems, when the order is written to the open orders file, the computer produces a goods received note that is used later to enter details of the goods actually received.

Integration of Order Processing and Goods Received Functions

When the goods are received, the order of processing is as follows:

- The goods received note is entered and matched with the appropriate open order record. In addition to matching on the order number field, the computer may also be programmed to match on the inventory reference field, quantity field, and/or value field.
- Matched items are either deleted from the open orders file and written to a new suspense file of goods received awaiting invoices, or their status on the order record is changed to indicate that they are matched. In either case, a summary of the matching process is normally accumulated and printed for control purposes. Mismatched items are usually reported or rejected. In on-line systems, mismatched items usually cannot be accepted by the computer.

The open order suspense records, at any given time, contain details of orders placed for which a goods received note has not been processed. These records are read periodically and those remaining unmatched for a given period are printed. The printed records may be used to follow up on old orders and to ensure that goods received notes are being processed upon receipt of goods. Totals of the open order suspense records, where they are maintained in dollar amounts, may also be produced, and these figures provide details of the purchase commitments not yet fulfilled.

A capability is usually necessary to process adjustments to the open order suspense records so that entries can be amended. Examples of these adjustments might be amendments to orders or canceled orders.

Once goods received notes have been matched against outstanding orders, the receipt and the related invoice are processed in the same manner as described for the accounts payable processing and goods received processing systems.

PAYMENT OF CREDITORS

The method used to process details of cash paid to creditors depends on whether items are selected for payment manually or by the computer, as described in the following paragraphs.

Manual Selection

When items are selected manually, the details of items paid should be entered and updated in the same manner as vendors' invoices. The computer usually matches on either the account number alone, or the account number, invoice number, and value.

Computer Selection

A purchase accounting system may include computer selection of items for payment. Normally the computer updates the account for payment details and prints remittance advices showing the makeup of the payments. As a result of the selection, the computer may produce the following:

- Details from which checks are prepared.
- Checks for manual or mechanical signature.
- Presigned checks.

The normal selection criteria are date and, less frequently, the discount indicator. The computer may be programmed to recognize an indicator on invoices for which a discount is available if payment is prompt. The computer may also be programmed to calculate the discount by reference to discount terms held as master file data. However, the processing of invoices of this nature is often diverted for separate manual payment.

Manually produced checks may also be required for other purposes. Details of such manual payments would be entered as adjustments.

Some systems can also produce cash requirement forecast reports to assist in the management of the company's cash flow. If so, there may be a capability to delay payments when funds are low and to speed up payments (such as to take advantage of discounts) when excess funds are available.

USING AUDIT SOFTWARE TO ANALYZE ACCOUNTS PAYABLE

A major concern for the auditor is the potential for understatement of liabilities and overstatement of assets. In this regard, four specific areas of accounts payable merit special attention: (1) cutoffs, (2) debit balances, (3) duplicate payments, and (4) confirmations. Inaccuracies in any of these areas can significantly affect the financial statements. Therefore, it is especially important that they are examined comprehensively. There are various ways in which this can be done.

Generalized accounts payable audit software helps the auditor to analyze the data for these vital areas, as well as automating many of the common substantive procedures encountered in the audit of accounts payable. An overview flowchart of accounts payable audit software is shown in Figure 10-12.

To determine whether receiving cutoffs have been performed satisfactorily, an accounts payable audit software package can furnish the following different reports.[3]

- *Last five days of period.* Lists transactions in vendor sequence that were processed during the last five calendar days of the validation period.
- *New items before closing date.* Lists those transactions that were recorded after the test date but should have been recorded on or before the closing date.
- *First five days after closing.* Lists all transactions dated in the first five days following the test date.

In the area of debit balances, there are other reports:

- *Debit accounts payable balances.* Lists those accounts that have a debit balance and quantifies the total for possible reclassification as receivables.
- *Detailed debit accounts payable balances.* Lists the individual transactions that make up each vendor account having a debit balance.

Another report, possible duplicate payables, identifies possible duplicate payment transactions based on the same vendor number and the same amount.

To facilitate an efficient confirmation process, the software usually furnishes two levels for confirmation reports (one summary and one detailed). The following are other reports produced by this audit software:

- *Edit report.* Lists data errors encountered on vendor master and transaction files.

---

[3] Coopers & Lybrand.

FIG. 10-12

Audit software flowchart for accounts payable

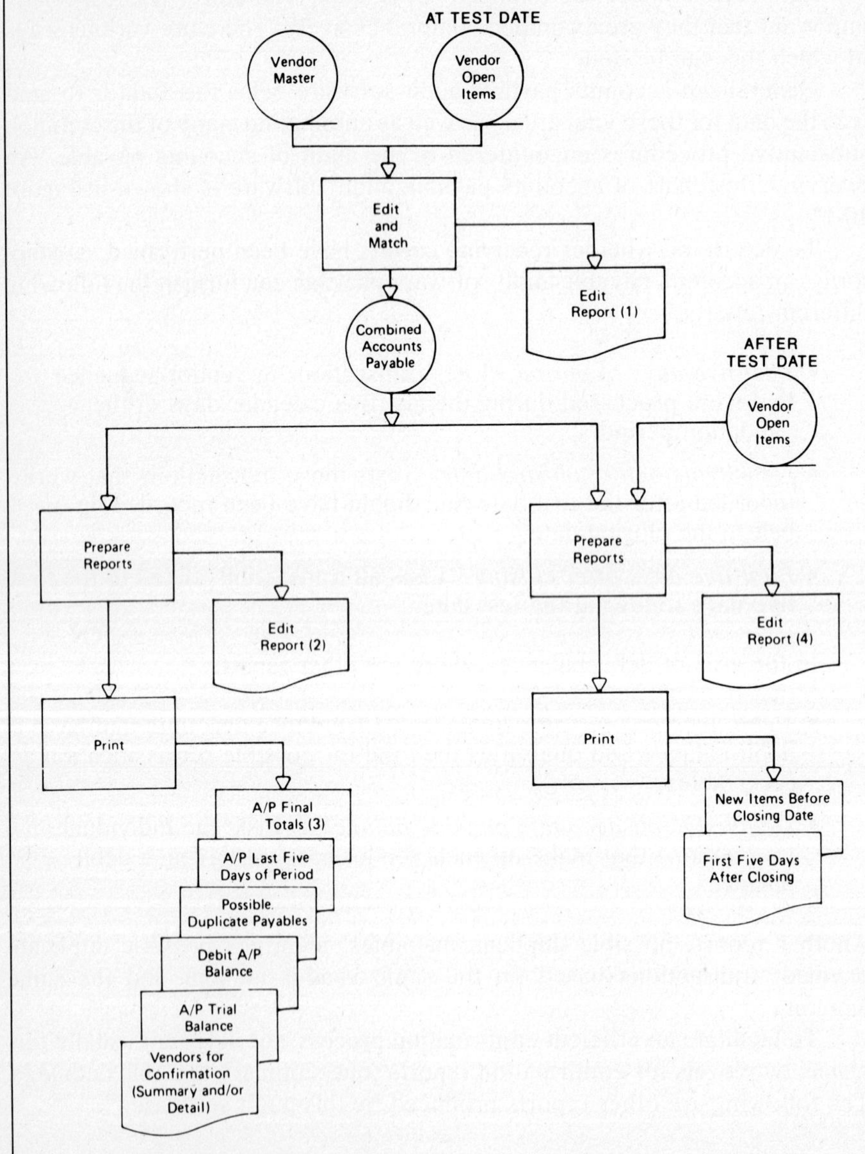

NOTE: Disk files may be substituted for tape files.

- *Trial balance.* Represents summarization of year-to-date purchases and accounts payable outstanding for each vendor.
- *Detailed trial balance.* Lists the individual open item transaction amounts for each vendor, as well as totals by vendor.

Use of audit software can assist the auditor in achieving the following substantive objectives:

- Determining whether all material liabilities for trade accounts payable existing at the balance sheet date have been recorded.
- Determining whether recorded liabilities for trade accounts payable represent valid liabilities and are fairly stated.
- Determining whether receiving cutoffs have been performed satisfactorily.

In addition, an analysis of the reports generated by the software may reveal breakdowns and weaknesses in internal controls. The auditor can communicate these problems to management for follow-up.

Two distinct phases are included in this software:

1. The analysis and reporting of the accounts payable at the test date.
2. The optional reporting of relevant transactions after the audit date.

There is also flexibility in varying guidelines (parameters) on the processing of data and selecting those reports that satisfy the audit objectives for a particular situation.

Audit software is particularly effective where there are a large number of accounts payable transactions or balances.

An example of this software in use occurred when a large discount retail company found that it did not have adequate controls within its accounts payable system to detect debit balances with sufficient accuracy. Accounts payable audit software was implemented during a recent year-end audit of the company. The debit accounts payable balances report indicated over $1 million in debit balances. Nearly $3 million in unrecorded liabilities was detected during the same audit, using the software report on new items before closing date.

Many common accounts payable substantive tests or procedures, such as the following, can be performed using audit software:

- Adding and listing transactions and account balances.
- Selecting accounts for confirmation or statement reconciliation.

- Identifying transactions pertaining to the audit period but recorded after the test date.
- Identifying transactions with a date immediately before or after the test date.
- Identifying possible duplicate payments.
- Identifying transactions not pertaining to valid vendors.

Accounts Payable Audit Objectives

An accounts payable audit software package can help the auditor meet the following audit objectives.

Audit Objectives	*Package Capabilities*
Determine whether all material liabilities for trade accounts payable existing at the balance sheet date have been recorded.	• Identifies and reports transactions processed after the test date that should have been processed before. • Selects accounts for confirmation or statement reconciliation. • Selects accounts with debit balances for confirmation or statement reconciliation.
Determine whether recorded liabilities for trade accounts payable represent valid liabilities and are fairly stated.	• Performs additions of accounts balances • Identifies and reports accounts with irregular vendor information. • Lists accounts payable balances in optional sequence and at various levels of detail to assist in review for unusual accounts. • Identifies and reports possible duplicate transactions. • Reports all vendors with a debit balance and optionally includes all open file items for these vendors.
Determine whether receiving cutoffs have been performed satisfactorily.	• Identifies and reports transactions with a date after the test date.

Audit Objectives	*Package Capabilities*
	• Reports all transactions processed during the five days preceding the test date. • Reports all transactions processed during the first five days after the test date.

Audit Program—Sequence of Events

The effective use of audit software packages requires cooperation between the auditor and the EDP auditor. An EDP auditor who knows the software can explain the package capabilities to the audit staff and can implement and execute the package. Overall responsibility for properly performing the audit belongs to the auditor, as usual.

This section describes a typical sequence of tasks necessary to use such software. The title of each report[4] is listed as an event.

Events	*Auditor's Actions*
Planning	• Develop plan and budget. • Collect the information concerning the accounts payable system. Prepare planning working papers. • Determine desired report options. • Obtain the following dates: a. Test date of accounts payable. b. Subsequent transaction examination period. • Complete reports within the time requirements. Keep audit staff informed as to progress and any reasons for additional time. • Before the due date, install the package, execute the edit program, and review the results for exceptions.
Report	
Accounts Payable—Edit Report	• Obtain the accounts payable total. • Edit the vendor master file and accounts payable open item file and agree the totals.

---

[4] Coopers & Lybrand

Events	*Auditor's Actions*
Audit review	• Reconcile report totals to books of accounts. • Confirm the reports to be produced and supply the necessary confirmation selection parameters.
Reports	
Accounts Payable—Edit Report	• Examine report for records identified as unusual. Compare items with hard-copy documentation to ensure that no further audit response is required. • Ensure that report requirements and confirmation selection parameters have been confirmed. Agree processing totals to totals from planning report.
Vendors for Confirmation	• Examine the report and agree calculated balance for each selected vendor to the detailed accounts payable records. Perform appropriate confirmation procedures. • Ensure that all reports required have been printed.
Accounts Payable Trial Balance	• Use the report to indicate the accounts tested and the procedures used.
Accounts Payable—Last Five Days of Period	• Review accounts listed to ensure that activity levels are not unusual. Test cut-off procedures.
Debit Accounts Payable Balances	• Reveiw accounts listed to determine reclassification or to ensure that there are no unrecorded liabilities.
Possible Duplicate Payables	• Review transactions listed to determine possibility of duplicate transactions.
Accounts Payable—Edit Report	• Examine report for records identified as unusual. Compare items with hard-copy documentation to ensure that no further audit response is required.
New Items Before Closing Date	• Check reported results by comparing items to hard-copy documentation and ensuring that cutoff was adequate.

Events	*Auditor's Actions*
First Five Days After Closing	• Use selected items on the report to test cutoff procedures.
Completion	• Summarize time, costs, and expenses. Document any reasons for changes from original budget. Provide suggestions for the coming audit year.

Microcomputer Audit Packages

Audit software that is microcomputer-based is available for accounts payable. Microcomputer audit packages provide field and internal auditors with computer audit capabilities that, until recently, were available only on mainframe systems. These packages perform many substantive test procedures and produce customized reports that show the results of the tests.

A microcomputer accounts receivable audit package can assist with auditing both open item and balance forward accounts receivable systems. Many useful standard accounts receivable substantive test procedures can be performed, including:

- Adding, aging, and stratifying account balances.
- Identifying doubtful debts.
- Reporting items for cut-off testing.
- Selecting accounts for detail testing.
- Producing confirmation letters.

These programs are an improvement over their mainframe counterparts, because the auditor is not required to know the many different operating procedures.

In order to use the microcomputer audit packages, data must be transferred (downloaded) from the mainframe or minicomputer to the auditor's microcomputer. By downloading data, the auditor reduces the disruption of the data center. In the past, customized software had to be installed and operated by the auditor at the data center location. Downloading data to a microcomputer audit package is less disruptive, since the auditor performs much of the work away from the site. The auditor can use any method available to download the data.

CHAPTER **11**

Production Systems

INTRODUCTION

The pressure of a competitive business environment underscores the need for comprehensive controls over the organization, its product, and its production systems. Monitoring systems that are not linked together can unintentionally cause conflict with internal and overall management goals, as when they track only a single department. Ideally, production system monitoring must be part of an integrated, comprehensive control approach.

The framework to prepare such a comprehensive monitoring plan includes the following elements of production systems planning:

- Inventory control system.
- Raw materials movements and balances.
- Fixed assets systems.

These components are discussed in this chapter, including production controls, cost and sales auditing, operational controls, and overall audit objectives.

INVENTORY CONTROL SYSTEMS

Applications

Inventory control systems are designed to record the purchase, manufacture, and sale of a company's inventory. Such systems may vary substantially in operation, but they can be divided into three main applications:

1. Raw materials
2. Work-in-process
3. Finished goods

Each application can be considered in the context of the following functions: inventory recording, inventory valuation, and inventory counting.

Inventory Recording Function

The raw materials, work-in-process, and finished goods inventory records are updated by entering updates or adjustments to master file data and transaction data, such as inventory movements. Adjustments are also made to correct mispostings and inventory differences when these are discovered. Summaries and analyses of movements and adjustments are produced from these updates. Amendments to master file data are also made in order to open and close records of stock items and to alter the various master file data fields. In most systems a list is normally produced of all master file data amendments that have been made.

An example of an inventory file layout, depicting the data elements included follows:

Inventory Details	*Number of Characters*
1. Part number	14
2. Product group	6
3. Stock description	30
4. Unit of measure code	1
5. Made in/bought out indicator	2
6. Store location	5
7. Latest purchase price	9
8. Reorder level indicator	1
9. Reorder level	7
10. Reorder quantity	7
11. Safety (minimum) stock	7
12. Maximum stock	7
13. Production reserve	7
14. Lead time	3
15. Average weekly demand	7
16. Standard cost	9
17. Current selling price	11
18. Price-effective date	6
19. New price increase percentage	5
20. New selling price	11
21. Stock on hand	7
22. Allocated stock	7
23. Shipping stock	7
24. Outstanding sales orders	7
25. Outstanding purchase orders	7
CURRENT WEEK DETAILS	
26. Transfers	7
27. Receipts	7

Inventory Details	*Number of Characters*
28. Outstanding orders	7
29. Shipments	7
30. Adjustments	7
CURRENT MONTH DETAILS	
31. Transfers	7
32. Receipts	7
33. Outstanding orders	7
34. Shipments	7
35. Adjustments	7
WEEKLY AVERAGES	
36. Transfers	7
37. Receipts	7
38. Outstanding orders	7
39. Shipments	7
40. Stock on hand	7
41. Last year's standard cost	9
42. Physical inventory check count	3
43. Physical inventory check frequency	2
44. Beginning inventory this year	7
45. Outstanding purchase requisition indicator	1
46. Outstanding purchase requisition quantity	7
47. Latest purchase quantity	7
48. Latest issue date	6
49. Date of latest purchases	6
50. Forecast total demand	7

Raw Materials

The main transaction types that are entered for raw materials records are:

- Receipts of inventory (or materials coming into the warehouse or store that increase inventory). Data entered from goods received records will also be processed for purchase accounting if the systems are integrated.
- Issues to production (or materials required for production to start that reduce or decrease inventory)—usually made before computer processing details are entered from production schedules or requisitions. (Details are listed on a bill of materials.)

In more advanced systems, materials issued to production from the warehouse or store may be generated by the programs in the following ways:

- The computer generates issues to production on the basis of low finished-goods stock or the receipt of sales orders.
- The computer generates issues to production based on entries in the work-in-process application, of a production number or stage in processing reached. This is common with bill-of-materials or list of materials issued processing systems.

In the preceding cases, information about the material necessary for the relevant job is held as master file data. The computer prints out the issue documentation, including the production schedule, and updates the raw materials file. Occasionally, computer processing is carried out prior to the actual issues from the stores. The details generated are sometimes held in suspense until they can be matched with details of the actual quantities issued to production. Raw materials recording is illustrated in Figure 11-1.

Work-in-Process. Work-in-process recording is often the most complex part of the inventory system. Figure 11-2 is an overview flowchart for inventory control work-in-process recording. The main transaction types of input for this category or records are:

- *Issues to production.* These are based on production schedules or requisitions. Work-in-process records are often updated at the same time as the raw materials file.
- *Labor charges.* These are usually entered manually prepared input documents or from details produced during the payroll production. The computer categorizes labor charged by referring to an input code. In some cases, standard labor charges are held as master file data and the computer may be programmed to calculate variances.
- *Overheads.* Overhead rates are normally held as master file data, and the computer calculates how much to charge the appropriate jobs.
- *Transfers to finished goods.* These are usually entered from manually prepared documentation. In advanced systems, the computer may be programmed to initiate details of the transfer when a completion request is entered, while transfer details are held on the inventory file as master file data. Variances between actual and standard quantities produced may be reported.

Finished Goods. The main transaction types entered for this category of records are as follows:

FIG. 11-1
Raw materials inventory control flowchart

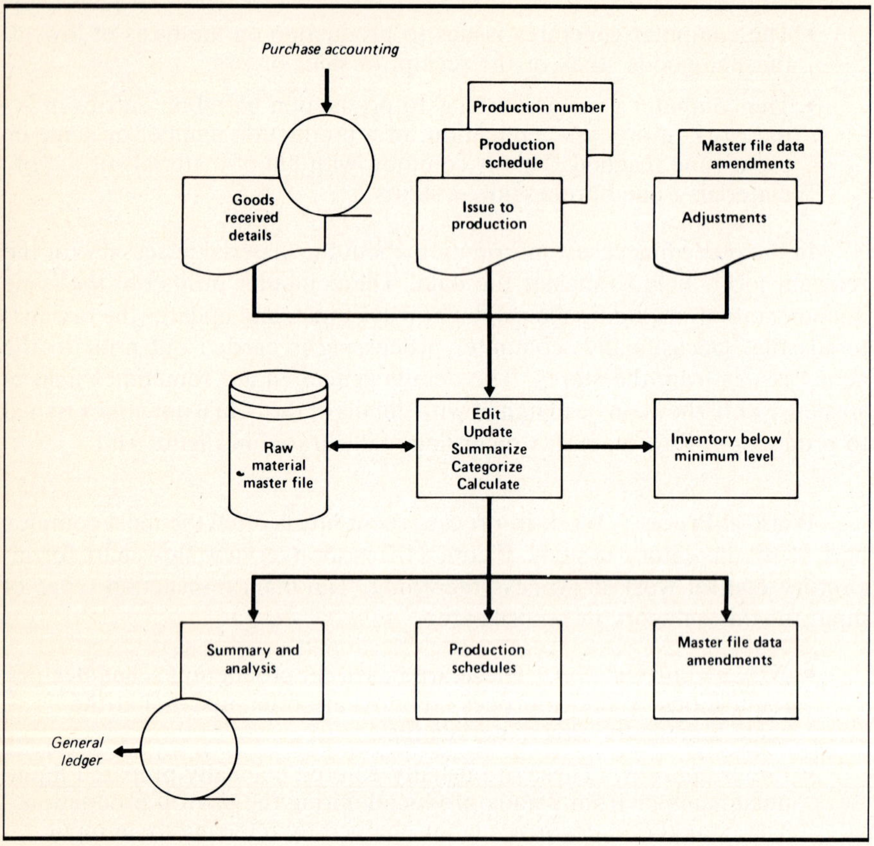

- *Receipts.* As described previously, this input includes details of completed work prepared manually for processing or initiated by the computer. The finished goods file is often updated simultaneously with the work-in-process file.
- *Issues.* Details of shipments made are entered. Updating of the finished goods file is often integrated with billing and sales accounting. If the cost of finished goods is recorded, the cost of sales will be summarized.

Finished goods recording is illustrated in the overview flowchart in Figure 11-3.

FIG. 11-2
Inventory control work-in-process overview flowchart

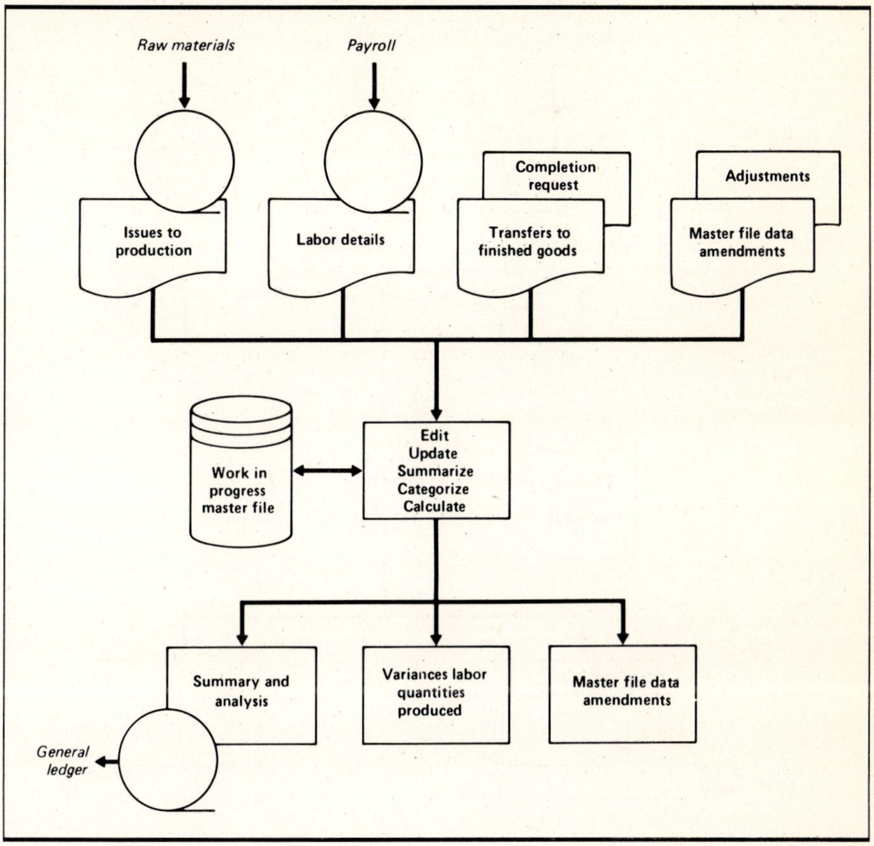

Inventory Valuation Function

Although it is common for the inventory movements and balances to be recorded in item quantities, costs are normally available in the form of master file data. In this way, the value of inventory can be calculated regularly.

Computer systems also offer the ability of holding several costs of inventory, used for different purposes. Examples of this are average cost for accounting, standard cost for determining variance, and replacement cost sometimes used for calculating future sales prices.

FIG. 11-3
Finished goods inventory control flowchart

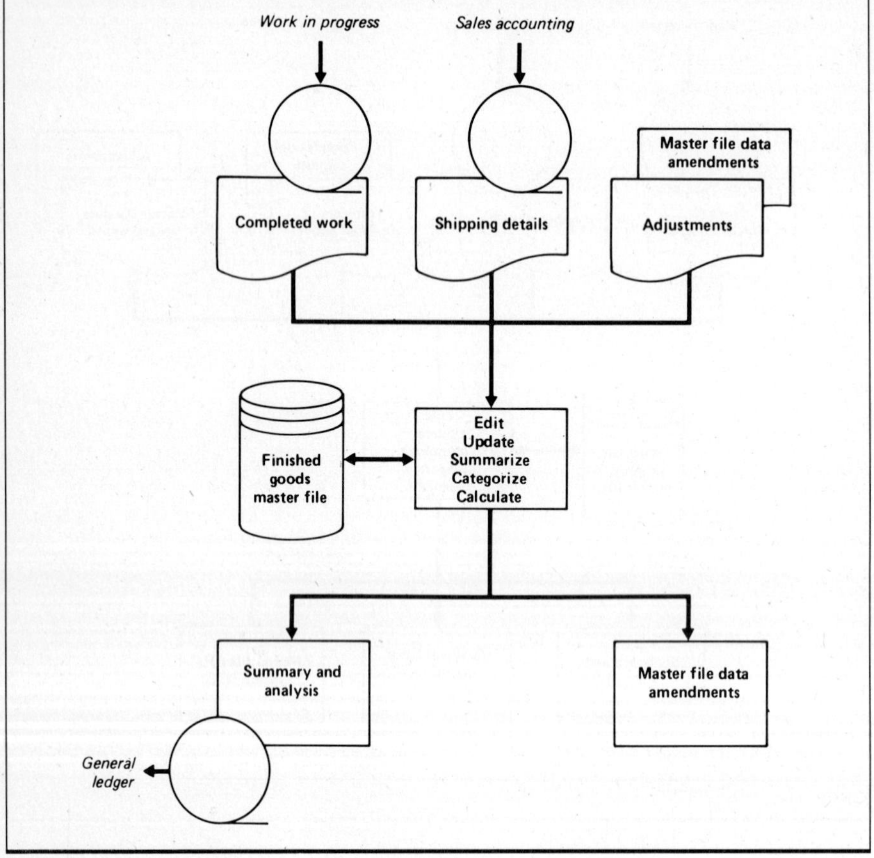

Raw Materials Movements and Balances. It is common for the computer to calculate the value of raw materials movements and balances by one of the methods listed here:

- *Reference to a standard cost price.* The computer is also programmed to report variances if actual costs are entered in this method.
- *Reference to the ordered price.* If goods received reports are matched manually to orders before entry, the price may be recorded manually on the goods received report. If matching is done by computer, the price can be picked up by the matching program.

- *Reference to actual invoiced costs.* There is usually a need to book receipts into inventory immediately, for operational reasons. To maintain an accurate inventory, the booking cannot wait for the arrival of the invoice to be processed. Therefore, many systems based on actual cost use one of the two preceding methods as an approximation until the invoice is received. Then the approximate cost is replaced by the actual invoiced cost; this temporary approximation seldom distorts the value of inventory materially.

When determining actual costs, most computer systems calculate an average figure. The computer can easily be programmed to compute the changes to the average cost price each time a purchase is made.

The booking of movements under FIFO (first-in, first-out) or LIFO (last-in, first-out) is more complicated to program, since each shipment may have a different cost price. (Therefore, they are used less frequently.) One obvious exception to this rule is the inventory systems that treat each purchase as a separate inventory item (such as automobile sales).

Most systems using actual costs (FIFO, LIFO, or average) are programmed to identify and report receipts whose cost price is significantly different from that of previous receipts, or whose actual cost is different from the standard or normal values.

Work-in-Process Movements and Balances. Materials used in production are charged out at the rates at which they are held as raw materials. Labor and overhead may be charged at standard predetermined rates, at actual rates, or at a combination of the two (e.g., labor hours at actual rates with predetermined overhead charges). Predetermined rates are held as master file data.

Labor Hours. Labor hours may be charged at standard or actual hours. If standard hours are used, the hours are normally taken from the bill of materials or otherwise held as master file data.

Actual hours may be charged by manually prepared documents or may be produced as output from the payroll application. The payroll application would then include some means of identifying the cost centers to be charged, either from employees' time reports or from information permanently kept as master file data on the payroll master file. If standard hours are also held, the computer may be programmed to report variances.

Labor and Overhead Rates. Hourly labor rates are usually held as master file data within the payroll or inventory records. The labor costs are calculated by multiplying hours (at actual or standard) by the rate.

Overhead may be included in the labor rate. It may also be held in another way, such as a separate charge on each bill of materials. Whatever method is used, the overhead rate is effectively held by the computer as master file data and is applied automatically to each production job.

Finished Goods Movements and Balances. Finished goods may be held at actual cost (such as the costs transferred from the work-in-process application), average actual cost, or standard cost price. Variances or abnormal price changes are normally identified and reported.

Inventory Provisions. The computer may be programmed to periodically calculate and report other information relevant to the value of inventory. Depending on the system, this may include details of excess stock, obsolete stock, and slow-moving stock.

- Excess stock is usually calculated by comparing inventory on hand with past usage or future requirements.
- Obsolete stock may be calculated by referring to usage or by setting an indicator (e.g., a component of a finished product that is no longer in production).
- Slow-moving stock may be calculated by referring to the date of last movement.

Inventory Counting Function

Procedures will always be needed to adjust any differences between what is shown in the books and the actual inventory by count. The differences may result from a periodic count of all inventory. However, if records are processed by computer it is easier to ensure their reliability, so that continuous cycle counts are more likely. If a continuous inventory count is carried out, one of the following three methods is normally used:

1. The inventory is counted and compared with the most recent report of the balance on the file adjusted for outstanding issues and receipts. The adjustments can be made manually or by the computer. A manual record is kept of items to be counted.
2. Inventory is counted and compared, and adjustments are processed as above. At the same time as the adjustments are processed, the date of the inventory count is entered. The

FIG. 11-4

Integrated inventory control system overview flowchart

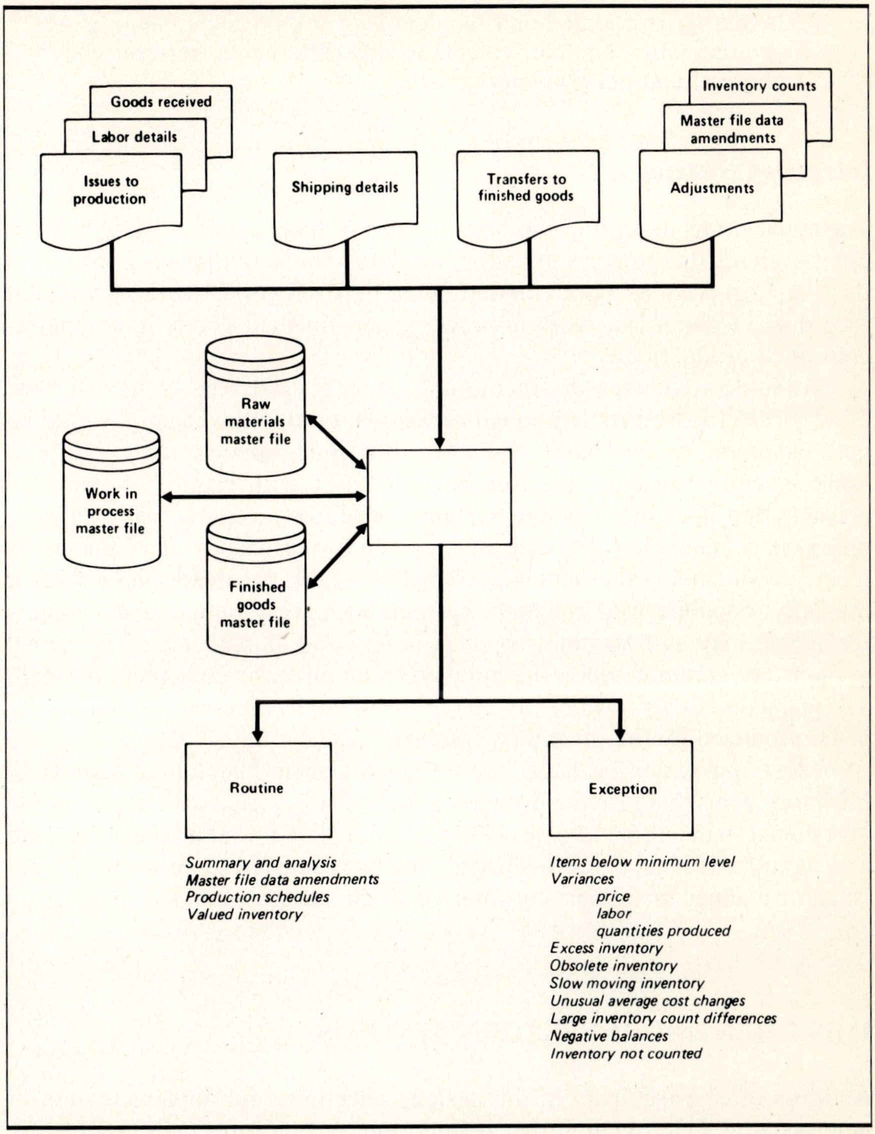

computer records the date and produces a regular report of items that have not been counted for a specified period.

3. Inventory is counted and the details of the physical balances are entered. The computer calculates any differences between the physical and book inventory.

Integrated Systems

The applications described can be combined to form a wide variety of computer systems that process inventory activity. The activities may vary from the simple recording of raw materials or finished goods to the integrated recording of materials, work-in-process, and finished goods in computer-controlled production.

An integrated inventory recording system is illustrated in the overview flowchart in Figure 11-4. Although not shown on the flowchart, it would be quite common for purchases and sales to be integrated in such a system. Some inventory systems are used in conjunction with manual accounts receivable and accounts payable systems. Inventory systems without computerized accounts payable may still account for purchase orders and goods received—including the matching of orders, goods received, and invoices. Similarly, computerized inventory systems with noncomputerized accounts receivable may still account for sales orders and shipments; such manual systems are common when the number of suppliers or customers is small. The manual systems rely heavily on reports of goods received and shipments made produced by the inventory systems.

Most application packages are designed to help maintain a quantity of inventory items that provide the maximum level of service with the minimum investment in inventory. Some systems responsible for maintaining on-hand and on-order balances plus historical data are designed to be used with existing or planned customers, or internal stock status systems.

IMPLEMENTING INVENTORY SYSTEMS

Auditors often participate in the design, selection, and implementation of new systems. One function that is important is to ensure that controls are built in and that proper procedures for purchasing, programming, testing, and installing the new system are followed. (See Chapter 22, "System Development Trends and Practices," and Chapter 23, "System Development Methodology and Auditing.") The following checklist can be helpful in determining the requirements for an inventory system.

INVENTORY

Location ____________________

1. How many individual inventory items do you stock? ____________
2. Do you sell nonstocked items? ☐ Yes ☐ No
3. What is your inventory file growth? ____________
4. What is the largest quantity (individual units) of inventory units on hand?
____
5. Do you have multiple warehouses? ☐ Yes ☐ No
6. How many product classes do you have? ____________
7. Do you have an existing inventory numbering system?
☐ Yes ☐ No
8. If yes, what is the maximum length of your inventory code number?
____
9. How comprehensive is the description of your products? ____________
10. Is more than one vendor involved when purchasing any particular inventory items? ☐ Yes ☐ No
11. Do you give quantity dicounts or price breaks to particular types of buyers (price matrix)? ☐ Yes ☐ No
12. Do your prices change frequently? ☐ Yes ☐ No
13. How are your pricing changes made? ____________

	Yes	*No*
On a percentage basis	☐	☐
Individual items only	☐	☐
By product class	☐	☐

Other ____________

14. What is the costing method of your inventory? ____________
____
15. What types of reports are being produced from your inventory? ______
____
16. Is there any other information that you feel is pertinent? ____________
____

OPERATIONAL AUDITING

Slow economic growth and high interest rates can force management to focus on controlling operational expenditures. In today's manufacturing environment, effective management of inventory, financing, carrying costs, purchase material costs, direct labor efficiency, overhead, human resources, and office systems has never been more important.

To meet these concerns, operational auditing for manufacturing helps auditors and consultants to identify management problems, as well as the financial and general control weaknesses.

Operational audits require that technical, audit management, and supporting documentation be developed to conduct a comprehensive review of a company's manufacturing function and related organizational activities. Important considerations are manufacturing's direct responsibilities and relationships with other organizations within the company.

The objectives of a diagnostic review approach are to:

- Review the manufacturing executive's direct and related responsibilities.
- Develop key findings and analyze the manufacturing operation's strengths and weaknesses.
- Identify and set priorities for key problem areas.
- Report the diagnostic results in a well-organized summary.
- Establish a transition between current procedures and an improved operating environment.

Such an approach is usually based on interviews and reviews of reports, systems, the decision-making process, and the policies and organizations that have guided manufacturing.

What is done in an operational audit varies widely, depending on the audit's scope, complexity, and purpose. In general, all such efforts require a set of standardized audit tasks, which can be preplanned and integrated to use audit software, as for any audit. Overall audit management and control are essential to perform a diagnostic review. As a result of a diagnostic or operational review, an audit report is issued to management. The final report may include these components:

- Performance profile for each function and area, indicating areas of risk and the significance of problems.
- Description of each problem area, further detailing and supporting the performance profile.
- Definition of corrective action and alternatives.

- Documentation of the approach for corrective actions, supported by conceptual systems design where appropriate.
- An action program structured by priority for management consideration.
- A work program indicating the specific tasks, resource requirements, and schedule for implementing a corrective action program.

Inventory Analysis Software

Inventory analysis software is a system of computer audit software programs that can quickly and economically diagnose how well a company is managing its inventory. Most such software can be used with manual and computerized recordkeeping systems, in a time-sharing mode, or on the organization's computer.

The objectives of inventory analysis are to:

- Provide the auditor with a quantitative diagnosis of inventory performance.
- Identify and quantify performance problems that indicate inadequate planning and control.
- Measure the potential for improvement.
- Provide a technique to establish and monitor inventory performance goals, in aggregate and in detail.
- Quantify the need for reserves for inventory obsolescence.

Inventory analysis software can produce various reports,[1] including the following:

- *Usage Distribution Report.* Classifies inventory items by dollar value of usage and corresponding levels of inventory.
- *Inventory Turnover Report.* Shows the investment in slow-moving stock, a quantification of shortages, and a stratified analysis of turnover.
- *Management Report.* Synthesizes the software output reports into a management summary.

Recently, using inventory analysis software at a $1 billion multi-industry manufacturing firm, auditors found $16 million of slow-moving inventory

---

[1] From the Coopers & Lybrand package.

that had not been identified as such; two thirds of the inventory was concentrated in five slow-moving product groups, and a correlation of high stock outs and excess inventories. Auditors discovered, at the same company, that responsibility for inventory and customer service functions was not identified, sales forecasting was inadequate, and inventory decisions were not supported by economic evaluations.

A program of reorganization was recommended that would lead conservatively to a reduction in inventory of $30 million, about 15 percent. The entire program was financed on a cash-flow basis after six months, and a discounted cash-flow analysis showed a return in excess of 200 percent.

INVENTORY AUDITING

Facing a rapid rise of interest rates and other expenses, management strives to keep costs at a minimum. This means making sure that inventory is maintained at normal, or even reduced, levels. If inventory has crept up substantially, it is a more significant factor on the balance sheet and, hence, an increasing concern for the external auditor.

Auditing inventory may be particularly time-consuming where there is an unusually large number of items in the inventory. Generalized audit software can increase audit efficiency by automating some of the common substantive procedures. It is especially effective for a large inventory.

Counting the Inventory

Audit software for testing the counting of inventory often includes reports,[2] such as the following, furnishing data that assists the auditor in performing an accurate physical count:

- Stratification histogram furnishes a stratification of inventory values (extended cost). With this data, the auditor is able to specify the most appropriate selection criteria, thereby facilitating a scientific selection of items for physical count. (See Figure 11-5.)
- Selection for physical count is a worksheet showing the parts selected for the auditor's independent count.
- Selection by part shows the parts selected for the auditor's further testing procedures.
- Auditor's physical comparison compares the auditor's independent count with the company's physical count. (See Figure 11-6.)

[2] From the Coopers & Lybrand package.

FIG. 11-5

Stratification histogram

REPORT NO. IN02CAAG-2 — COMPUTER MFG CO — PAGE NO. 1
REPORT DATE 12/04/79 — STRATIFICATION HISTOGRAM PLANT 00200 — PERIOD ENDED 12/31/79

ARITHMETIC METHOD

SEQ #	INTERVAL----BOUNDARIES		# ITEMS	VALUE	% OF TOTAL	CUM %	MEAN	STANDARD DEVIATION	DISTRIBUTION SCALED 1 FOR 6,192
1	41.40 TO	10,000.99	26	41,674.42	8.89	8.89	1,602.86	2,568.16	******
2	10,001.00 TO	20,000.99	0	0.00	0.00	8.89	0.00	0.00	*
3	20,001.00 TO	30,000.99	0	0.00	0.00	8.89	0.00	0.00	*
4	30,001.00 TO	40,000.99	0	0.00	0.00	8.89	0.00	0.00	*
5	40,001.00 TO	50,000.99	1	50,000.00	10.66	19.55	50,000.00	0.00	********
6	50,001.00 TO	60,000.99	2	120,000.00	25.58	45.13	60,000.00	0.00	*****************
7	60,001.00 TO	70,000.99	0	0.00	0.00	45.13	0.00	0.00	*
8	70,001.00 TO	80,000.99	2	154,815.56	33.01	78.14	77,407.78	2,592.21	************************
9	80,001.00 TO	90,000.99	0	0.00	0.00	78.14	0.00	0.00	*
10	90,001.00 TO	100,000.99	0	0.00	0.00	78.14	0.00	0.00	*
11	100,001.00 TO	102,543.02	1	102,543.02	21.86	100.00	102,543.02	0.00	***************
	** TOTALS **		32	469,033.00			14,657.28	28,270.99	
	CREDITS		0	0.00					
	LOWEST VALUE ON FILE			41.40					
	HIGHEST VALUE ON FILE			102,543.02					

REPORT NO. IN02CAAG-2 — COMPUTER MFG CO — PAGE NO. 1
REPORT DATE 12/04/79 — STRATIFICATION HISTOGRAM PLANT 00300 — PERIOD ENDED 12/31/79

FIXED INTERVAL

SEQ #	INTERVAL----BOUNDARIES		# ITEMS	VALUE	% OF TOTAL	CUM %	MEAN	STANDARD DEVIATION	DISTRIBUTION SCALED 1 FOR 636
1	0.00 TO	99.99	14	690.09	2.58	2.58	49.29	26.85	*
2	100.00 TO	499.99	13	3,047.63	11.39	13.97	234.43	118.76	****.
3	500.00 TO	999.99	0	0.00	0.00	13.97	0.00	0.00	*
4	1,000.00 TO	1,999.99	5	7,085.78	26.49	40.46	1,417.15	245.83	***********
5	2,000.00 TO	4,515.00	5	15,924.33	59.54	100.00	3,184.86	868.19	*************************
	** TOTALS **		37	26,747.83			722.91	1,120.26	
	CREDITS		0	0.00					
	LOWEST VALUE ON FILE			0.00					
	HIGHEST VALUE ON FILE			4,515.00					

- Physical comparison with book or inventory as recorded compares the company's physical count with the book or recorded quantity. The auditor uses this data to investigate discrepancies and to determine their effect on the total inventory valuation.
- Missing tag report lists all possible tag numbers, distinguishing those present from those missing. Duplicate tags are also identified. (See Figure 11-7.)
- Physical inventory lists the company's physical counts, either in part number sequence or in tag number sequence.
- Cyclical count procedure lists each item not counted within a specified period, together with the current book quantity and the calculated value.

Evaluating Costs

Evaluation of cost is another key concern in the audit of inventory. It is often addressed by reports, such as the following, that are produced by this software:

FIG. 11-6

Auditor's physical comparison report

REPORT NO. IN04CAAG-1 — COMPUTER MFG CO — PAGE NO. 1
REPORT DATE 12/04/79 — AUDITORS PHYSICAL COMPARISON — PERIOD ENDED 12/31/79

PART NO	PLANT	LOCATION/TAG	C&L COUNT	CLIENT COUNT	BOOK QTY	UNIT COST	CALC VALUE	CLIENT PHYS VAL DIF
MTF3601	00100	00105104A330130	101.0200	101.0000	101.0000	2.5000	252.55	252.50 ***
MTW3601	00100	00100000A330135	190.0000	190.0000	190.0000	2.6666	506.65	506.65
MTW3603	00100	00100000A330137	120.0000	125.0000	125.0000	25.8000	3,096.00	3,225.00 ***
MT3601	00100	00105001A330125	200.0000	200.0000	200.0000	4.0000	1,600.00	1,600.00
MT3602	00100	00105001A330126	2,000.0000	210.0000	210.0000	3.0000	18,000.00	1,890.00 ***
MT3603	00300	001050018B	301.0000					***
MT3604	00100	00105001A330128	120.0000	150.0000	150.0000	0.8500	1,020.00	1,275.00 ***
MT3604	00100	001050019B	30.0000					***
RB1212	00100	00100101A330101	305.0000	300.0000	300.0000	1.5000	457.50	450.00 ***
RB810	00100	00100101A330106	30.0000-	105.0000	105.0000	1.2000	36.00-	126.00 ***
WB22	00100	00100000A330119	30.0000-	125.0000-	125.0000	1.5000	45.00-	187.50-***

TOTALS

SELECTED ITEMS	VALUE	NUMBER
CALC VALUE:	24,851.70	9
CLIENT PHYS:	9,137.65	9
DIFFERENCE:	15,714.05	9
NON SELECTED ITEMS		
CLIENT PHYS:	1,423,195.22	149
TOTAL FILE	1,432,332.87	158 (CLIENT PHYS)

FIG. 11-7

Missing tag report

REPORT NO. IN05CAAG-1 — COMPUTER MFG CO — PAGE NO. 1
REPORT DATE 12/04/79 — MISSING TAG REPORT — PERIOD ENDED 12/31/79

PRESENT FROM	PRESENT TO	MISSING FROM	MISSING TO	AUDITORS FOLLOW-UP
A 330101				
		A 330102		
A 330138				*DUPLICATE*
A 330103	A 330138			
		A 330139	B 9130199	
B 9130211				*DUPLICATE*
B 9130200	B 9130242			
		B 9130243	C 772499	
C 772503				*DUPLICATE*
C 772500	C 772538			
		C 772539	D 934700	
D 934701	D 934702			
		D 934703	D 934704	
D 934705	D 934722			
		D 934723	X 7900499	
X 7900500	X 7900515			

TOTALS

TOTAL RECORDS PROCESSED 158

DUPLICATES 3

Interpretation of sample report:

- The starting tag number is A 330101.
- Tag number A 33102 is missing.
- Tag number A 330138 is duplicated.
- Tag numbers A 330139 through B 9130199 are missing.
- The last tag number is X 7900515.

FIG. 11-8

Cost compared with selling price report

REPORT NO. IN06CAAG-1 — COMPUTER MFG CO — PAGE NO. 1
REPORT DATE 12/04/79 — COST COMPARED TO SELLING PRICE — PERIOD ENDED 12/31/79

PART NO	DESCRIPTION	CLASS	CUMUL QUANTITY	U/M	UNIT COST	COST VALUE	MAR	CALC SALES VAL	UNIT SELL PRICE	SALES VALUE	OVERVAL SZ
CAB0500	COMP'T CABINETS	FN500	112.0000	1.0000	80.0000	8,960	1.00	8,960	0.0000	0	8,960
FB1212	MFG 12X12 COP-BRD	FN500	212.0000	1.0000	5.0000	1,060	1.00	1,060	0.0000	0	1,060
FB1416	MFG 14X16 COP-BRD	FN500	55.0000	1.0000	4.9560	272	1.00	272	0.0000	0	272

REPORT NO. IN06CAAG-1 — COMPUTER MFG CO — PAGE NO. 3
REPORT DATE 12/04/79 — COST COMPARED TO SELLING PRICE — PERIOD ENDED 12/31/79

PART NO	DESCRIPTION	CLASS	CUMUL QUANTITY	U/M	UNIT COST	COST VALUE	MAR	CALC SALES VAL	UNIT SELL PRICE	SALES VALUE	OVERVAL SZ
RECORDS											
24	TOTAL PRINTED ABOVE					67,939.00		115,669.88		28,497.35	87,172.53
14	NOT PRINTED NEGATIVE					..131,976.39		1,133,776.39		2,500,730.50	1,366,954.11-
0	POSITIVE					0.00		0.00		0.00	0.00
38	TOTAL TESTED					1,199,915.39		1,249,446.27		2,529,227.85	1,279,781.58-
0	DUPLICATE COST RECORD										
34	EXCLUDED RECORDS										
3	RECORDS WITH NO COST										

- Cost compared with selling price reports items that are overvalued based on a comparison of calculated cost and sales values. This report assists the auditor in ensuring that the cost values of the parts in inventory do not exceed their net realizable values. (See Figure 11-8.)
- Individual invoice price comparison compares the sales value recorded on the current book cost file with selling prices used on sales invoices. The report prints the difference between the standard unit selling price (USP) and the invoice USP.
- Current costs compared with previous costs shows the percentage of cost increase from one period to another.

Reporting on Sales

Sales history is important, not only to verify revenue from sales, but to use as a basis for judging whether items are valued correctly. Software reports

FIG. 11-9

Inventory aging report

REPORT NO. IN08CAAG-2 COMPUTER MFG CO PAGE NO. 1
REPORT DATE 12/04/79 INVENTORY AGEING PERIOD ENDED 12/31/79

PART NO	DESCRIPTION	QUANTITY SOLD	QUANTITY ON HAND	VALUE	NOT AGED	UP TO 1 MTHS	2 TO 2 MONTHS	3 TO 3 MONTHS	4 TO 4 MONTHS	5 TO 5 MONTHS	OVER 5 MTHS
CAB0500	COMP'T CABINETS	0	112	8,960		0	0	0	0	0	8,960
CD96	96 COLUMN CARDS	1,000	60	450		450	0	0	0	0	0
CMP4000	COMP'T 4000	2	4	160,000		20,000	20,000	20,000	20,000	20,000	60,000
CMP5000	COMP'T 5000 COM	4	2	100,000		50,000	50,000	0	0	0	0
CMP6000	COMP'T 6000 COM	2	2	120,000		30,000	30,000	30,000	30,000	0	0
DDF100	DISK DRIVES	0	15	301,500		0	0	0	0	0	301,500
DDM100	MINI PACK DISK	4	23	437,000		19,000	19,000	19,000	19,000	19,000	342,000
FBF1416	COMP'T 14X16 B	14	28	129		16	16	16	16	16	49
FBF22	COMP'T 2X2 BRD	9	30	1,155		89	89	89	89	89	710
FBF35	COMT' 3X5 BRD	2	15	518		17	17	17	17	17	433
FBF44	COMP'T 4X4 BRD	2	40	1,560		20	20	20	20	20	1,460
FBF46	COMP'T 4X6 BRD	11	26	838		93	93	93	93	93	373
FBF810	COMP'T 8X10 BRD	0	20	600		0	0	0	0	0	600
FBF816	COMP'T 8X16 BRD	5	45	1,440		40	40	40	40	40	1,240
FB1212	MFG 12X12 COP-B	0	212	1,060		0	0	0	0	0	1,060
FB1416	MFG 14X16 COP-B	0	55	273		0	0	0	0	0	273
FB22	MFG 2X2 COP-BRD	0	52	154		0	0	0	0	0	154
FB35	MFG 3X5 COPPER	5	46	315		9	9	9	9	9	270
FB44	MFG 4X4 COPPER-	0	103	671		0	0	0	0	0	671
FB46	MFG 4X6 COP-BRD	0	51	247		0	0	0	0	C	247
FB810	MFG 8X10 COP-BR	0	34	170		0	0	0	0	0	170
FB816	MFG 8X16 COPPER	0	71	287		0	0	0	0	0	287
FDD92	DUAL DENSITY PA	4	19	2,850		150	150	150	150	150	2,100
FSD46	SINGLE DENSITY	0	23	2,990		0	0	0	0	0	2,990
MDD23	MINI-DUAL DENSI	3	15	1,800		90	90	90	90	90	1,350
MSD18	MINI-SINGLE DEN	2	18	1,260		35	35	35	35	35	1,085
MTF3601	METAL SIDING	0	564	1,410		0	0	0	0	0	1,410
MTF3602	FRAME AND BASE	0	238	14,597		0	0	0	0	0	14,597
MTF3603	LOGIC SUPPORT C	0	273	13,726		0	0	0	0	0	13,726
MTF3604	INTERIOR FRAME	0	397	13,950		0	0	0	0	0	13,950
MTF3605	BRASS SCREWS	0	470	186		0	0	0	0	0	186
TD100	TAPE DRIVE	7	12	6,786		969	969	969	969	969	1,941
TD81	800BPI TAPE 100	10	50	661		33	33	33	33	33	496
TD815	800BPI TAPE 150	7	30	419		25	25	25	25	25	294
TD818	800BPI TAPE 180	2	40	582		7	7	7	7	7	547
TD824	800BPI TAPE 24	6	50	863		26	26	26	26	26	733
TD918	900BPT TAPE 18	11	18	264		38	38	38	38	38	74
TD924	900BPT TAPE 24	15	13	244		81	81	81	1	0	0

REPORT NO. IN08CAAG-2 COMPUTER MFG CO PAGE NO. 2
REPORT DATE 12/04/79 INVENTORY AGEING PERIOD ENDED 12/31/79

PART NO	DESCRIPTION	QUANTITY SOLD	QUANTITY ON HAND	VALUE	NOT AGED	UP TO 1 MTHS	2 TO 2 MONTHS	3 TO 3 MONTHS	4 TO 4 MONTHS	5 TO 5 MONTHS	OVER 5 MTHS
015	TOTALS DO NOT EXCEED LIMIT			0.00	0.00	0.00	0.00	0.00	0.00	0.00	0.00
000	TOTALS NEW ITEMS			0.00	0.00	0.00	0.00	0.00	0.00	0.00	0.00
038	TOTALS PRINTED			1,199,915.28	0.00	121,187.92	120,737.92	70,737.92	70,656.66	40,656.65	775,938.21
053	TOTALS FILE			1,199,915.28	0.00	121,187.92	120,737.92	70,737.92	70,656.66	40,656.65	775,938.21

can furnish information that assists the auditor in determining inventory usage and possible obsolescence:

1. *Sales history edit listing.* Designed to detect and report various types of errors in sales history data.

2. *Inventory aging.* Presents an aging of the current book quantity sold. The report indicates slow-moving merchandise and inventory turnover by part number, based on historical sales. (See Figure 11-9.)

3. *Sales by month by item.* Sales summary report by part number. This report is useful in identifying whether the company's

explanations of apparently slow-moving items are correct and can also be used to verify the total turnover for a month.

4. *Sales by month by product class.* Produces sales totals for each product class (or group).

Audit software may be implemented in the organization's management information system (MIS) environment or at a service bureau. Three distinct phases are involved: (1) the company's inventory-related files are edited and combined; (2) the information is analyzed and selections made based on the criteria specified by the auditor; and (3) the various reports are produced. The software has been designed so that the first phase is required but the other two phases are optional, depending on the requirements of the auditor. Flexibility is usually provided by the report options or alternatives available.

In the recent audit of inventory at a major retailer in the Southwest, an automated package was needed to process data for an exceptionally high volume of inventory items. Consequently, an inventory audit software package was implemented. Using data generated by the package's stratification histogram, the auditors were able to identify that, out of an inventory of over 30,000 items, 1,500 represented 80 percent of the inventory's dollar value. This finding was invaluable in ensuring the proper and efficient selection of items for substantive testing.

The computer manufacturing division of a large company had an inventory count of 17 million items, valued at approximately $42 million. The inventory audit software package assisted in identifying several discrepancies within the division's financial reporting system. The information listed in the missing tag report helped highlight items that were included in one of the reports but missing in another. The physical comparison with book report assisted the auditors in determining that several items in inventory had been incorrectly valued. Adjustments were subsequently made to the division's records.

Microcomputer Audit Packages

Microcomputer audit software can be used when auditing inventory. Microcomputer audit packages provide field and internal auditors with computer audit capabilities that, until recently, were available only on mainframe systems.

Microcomputer Inventory Audit Package.[3] This package is designed to audit client inventory computer systems. Many useful standard inventory

---

[3] From the Coopers & Lybrand package.

substantive test procedures can be performed, including:

- Reperforming inventory valuation.
- Reporting negative on hand.
- Identifying slow-moving inventory items.
- Identifying excess inventory items.
- Selecting items for detailed testing.

These programs are an improvement over their mainframe counterparts because the auditor is not required to know the operating procedures necessary to generate reports from mainframe data.

To use the microcomputer audit packages, data must be transferred (downloaded) from the mainframe or minicomputer to the auditor's micro. By downloading data, the auditor can reduce intrusion into the data center. In the past, customized software would have to be installed and operated by the auditor at the location. Downloading data to a microcomputer audit package makes the audit less disruptive, since the auditor performs much of the work away from the data center site. The auditor can use any available method to download data.

Inventory Audit Objectives

Many common inventory substantive test procedures, such as the following, can be performed by the use of appropriately selected inventory audit software:

- Adding and stratifying inventory valuations.
- Recalculating extended costs.
- Selecting items for an independent count of inventories.
- Selecting items for detailed substantive tests, including verification of costs.
- Identifying uncounted items where cyclical counts are used.
- Comparing audit counts with organization's physical counts.
- Identifying missing or duplicate inventory tags.
- Comparing organization's physical inventory with perpetual inventory records.
- Comparing current period's cost prices with a previous period's cost prices.
- Comparing selling prices with cost prices.
- Detecting decreasing cost prices.

- Identifying items sold at other than standard selling price.
- Identifying slow-moving inventory items.
- Identifying unusual inventory items.
- Determining whether the inventory quantities are reasonably stated.
- Determining whether slow-moving, damaged, or obsolete inventories have been appropriately identified and valued.
- Determining whether the inventory summaries are arithmetically accurate.
- Determining whether pricing of inventory quantities as to cost is appropriate.
- Determining whether appropriate net realizable values have been used in making any required inventory writedowns.
- Determining whether the net income for the year and the individual items of income and expense that are disclosed in the income statement are fairly stated.

Figure 11-10 is an audit software overview processing flowchart.

Sequence of Events

The effective use of the packaged audit software in an inventory audit requires cooperation between the non-EDP auditor and EDP auditor. An EDP auditor who know the software can explain the package capabilities, implement, and execute the package. However, the auditor naturally has overall responsibility for properly performing the audit tests.

This section describes a typical sequence of tasks that can be followed to use an audit software package of this kind. The column headed "Auditor's Actions" includes actions that the auditor should perform and assumes the inclusion of the EDP auditor. The title of each report[4] is listed as an event.

Events	*Auditor's Actions*
Planning	• Develop plan and budget. • Collect the information concerning the inventory system. Prepare planning working papers.

[4] From the Coopers & Lybrand package.

FIG. 11-10
Audit software inventory overview flowchart

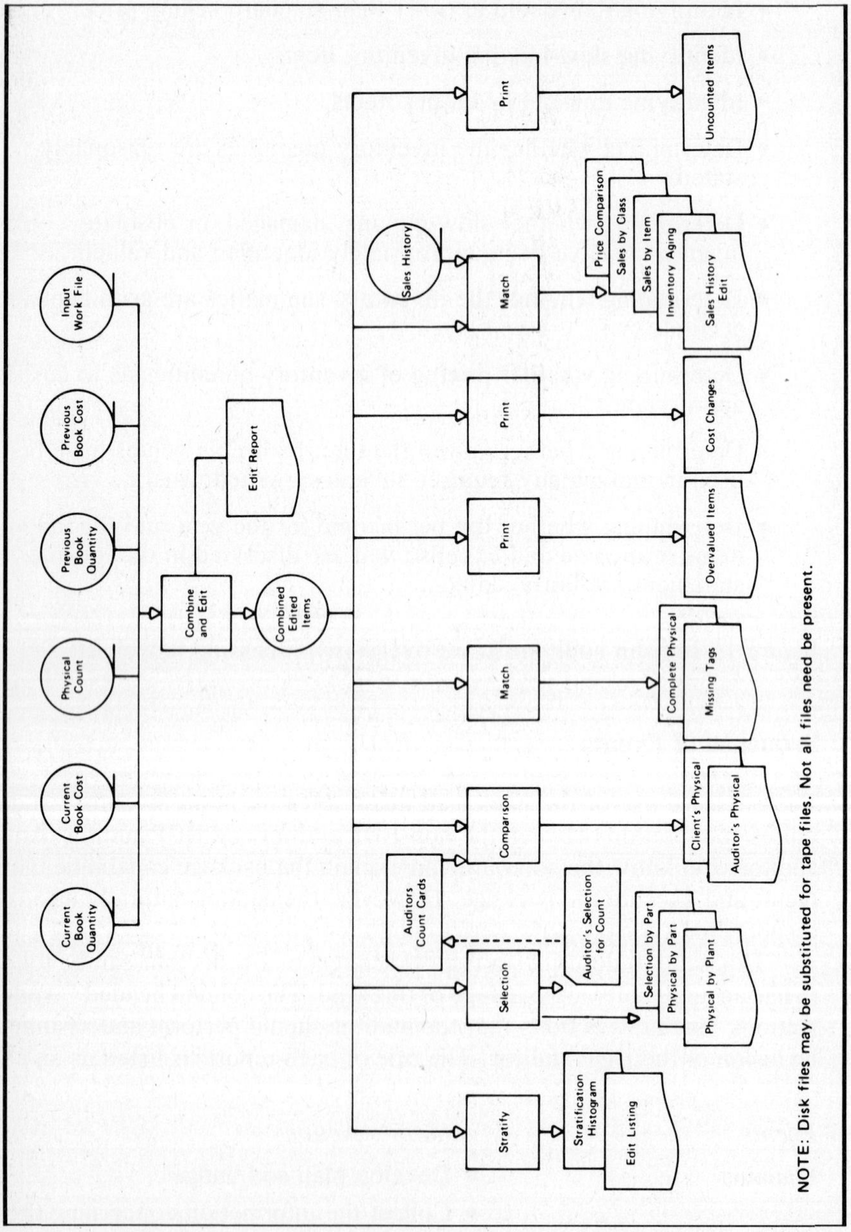

NOTE: Disk files may be substituted for tape files. Not all files need be present.

Events	*Auditor's Actions*
Planning (*cont'd*)	• Determine desired report options and prepare the appropriate parameters (such as margin for net realizable value tests). • Complete reports within the audit time requirements. Keep audit staff informed of progress and any reasons for additional time. • Inform audit staff of the following: —Year-end or test date. —Aging categories. —Sales history periods. —Physical count date. —File date for stratification. • Before the due date, install the package, execute the edit program, and review the results for exceptions.
Report	
Input File Edit Errors	• Edit the inventory files, resolve error messages, and agree the totals.
Audit review	• Review any error messages to determine significance and corrections. • Assist in determining significance of error messages.
Report	
Work File Edit Listing	• Obtain the inventory valuation total. Review the edit report for accuracy of data. • Review the edit report and agree the totals.
Audit review	• Reconcile report totals to books of account. Select the stratification method and supply the necessary parameters. • Determine stratification method.
Reports	
Stratification Histogram	• Use the report to determine selection criteria for auditor's count. • Prepare reports and agree the totals.

Events	*Auditor's Actions*
Reports (*cont'd*)	• Check that the correct number and value of items have been selected.
Selection for Physical Count	• Code selection criteria onto parameters and prepare report. Review results of selection.
Selection by Part	• Check that the correct number and value of items have been selected. • Code selection criteria onto parameters and prepare report. Review results of selection. • Perform independent count.
Auditor's Physical Comparison	• Use the report to investigate discrepancies and to review inventory valuations. Use report to determine the effect of discrepancies on total inventory valuation.
Physical Comparison With Book	• Use the report to investigate discrepancies and to determine their effect on the total inventory valuation.
Missing Tag Report	• Use the report to identify missing or duplicate tags.
Physical Inventory	• Use the report for audit tests.
Cost Compared to Selling Price	• Use the report to detect inventory overvaluation.
Current Costs Compared to Previous Costs	• Use the report to identify unusual cost increases and/or items where the cost did not increase.
Sales History Edit Listing	• Review any error messages to determine significance and corrections. • Assist in determining significance of error messages.
Inventory Aging	• Use aging report for audit tests.
Sales by Month by Item	• Use the report to review seasonal fluctuation of parts. Agree to sales figures for the period.
Sales by Month by Product Class	• Confirm product mix and slow-moving product analysis.

Events	*Auditor's Actions*
Reports (*cont'd*)	
Individual Invoice Price Comparison	• Review transactions listed to determine possibility of erroneous recording.
Uncounted Items	• Check that all items have been counted during the period.
Completion	• Summarize audit time costs and expenses. Document any reasons for changes from original budget. Provide suggestions for the coming audit year.

SUMMARY

Ultimately, the steady stream of information presented by a computerized monitoring system can start to approach the ideal of "continual audit." Recent implementation plans for monitoring systems are recognizing this fact, as seen in one plan developed for a major telecommunications corporation. Auditors involved in the system development recognized that this booming industry, along with other high-technology sectors, is extremely vulnerable to constantly and rapidly changing markets and economics. Industries in the high-tech market must be able to rely on a comprehensive, competent audit approach to inventory control and overall systems management.

The auditors supported the need for comprehensive audit systems by providing examples of manufacturers whose systems were unable to match control capabilities with the needs of high-volume sales environments. More than one of the companies cited used inventory control systems that were unable to distinguish between sales to distributors' inventories and those to end users. The results in a highly competitive market were, of course, disastrous.

The auditors proposed a comprehensive production system and monitoring plan that would ultimately provide an overall "management system." Such a system relies on the integration of information from the entire range of sectors responsible for development, production, marketing, and sales. This type of development in audit procedure—comprehensive system of inventory control, auditing, and analysis—provides an integrated tool to meet the demands of a constantly shifting economic and marketing picture.

CHAPTER **12**

General Ledger Systems

INTRODUCTION

In a rapidly changing economic environment, an organization must have accurate, comprehensive financial information, and ready access to it. The accounting department should be able to deliver up-to-date information to help management in organizational decision-making. The exchange of information between different departments should be fast and complete. Financial accounting is the foundation of an information system for the entire financial and accounting area. Conducted efficiently, according to generally accepted accounting principles (GAAP), financial accounting can be a great asset in producing timely, useful reports of an organization's transactions, whether they are needed for the annual summary, financial statements, tax accounting, or other informational purposes.

For their functioning, general ledger systems depend on the generation of separate records for each debit and credit posted. In a computerized general ledger, the debits and credits are then grouped and printed in accordance with the general ledger account codes.

Major functions of a general ledger system are shown in the overview flowchart in Figure 12-1.

Simple Ledger Systems

The simplest computerized general ledger systems duplicate the manual functions of posting journal vouchers: The account code from the chart of accounts is often entered manually on journal vouchers, along with the amount to be posted. At the end of each month, the debits and credits are separately sorted by account code and printed out with a new balancing total. The balancing total is carried forward to the next month, together with a permanent header record for each account. The header record generally contains the account description, the format in which it will be printed, and perhaps certain summary information from previous months.

Journal entries arise from many sources, some of which are other computer applications (such as sales, payroll, or accounts payable systems). These other applications will, when necessary, summarize the journal entries required. When designed that way, they can feed the general ledger system directly.

The following is an example of a general ledger file layout, illustrating the kind of data elements that make up a general ledger record, including data elements and the number of characters each element uses in this particular format.

FIG. 12-1

General ledger system overview flowchart

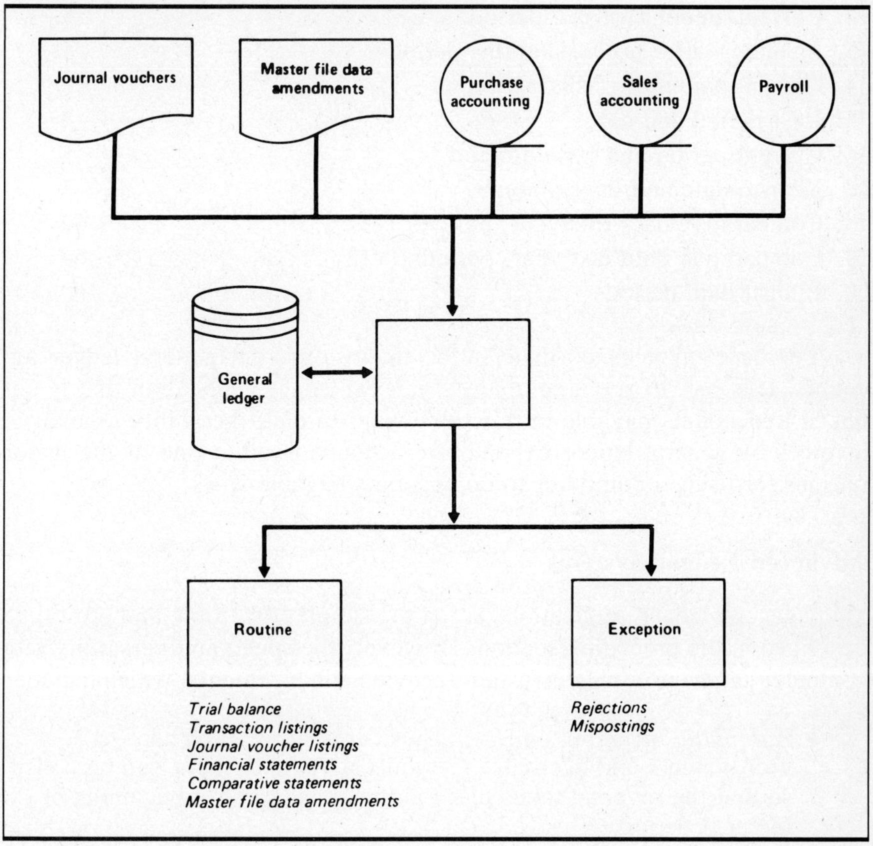

Details	*Number of Characters*
1. Transaction type "5"	1
2. Company	4
3. Account number	5
4. Department number	4
5. Subsidiary account number	4
6. Budget code	5
7. Account code	1
8. Account title	30
9. Print control characters and various flags	10

10. Balance—beginning of year	5
11. Balance—end of last period	5
12. Current amount for last period	5
13. Balance—after processing this period	5
14. Current amount for this period	5
15. Last period end date	4
16. Current period and base amount	5
17. Year-to-date and base amount	5
18. Comparative data this year, periods 1–12	60
19. Comparative data last year, periods 1–12	60
20. Budget data periods	60

Purchase invoices normally affect many different general ledger accounts. It is rare to see a company's general ledger application that is not linked to accounts payable in this same way. In fact, the ability to analyze invoices by general ledger expenditure account is often one of the major reasons for using a computer to do accounts payable work.

Advanced Ledger Systems

Many general ledger applications are of the simple sort, total, and print type described in the preceding section. However, the speed and versatility of a computer can be used when systems provide enhancements, which include:

- *Automatic reversing entries.* These are entries such as prepayments and accruals. The journal voucher input can be coded so that the reversal takes place automatically at the beginning of the next period.
- *Automatic repeating entries.* Some entries must be made each period (e.g., to allocate $\frac{1}{12}$ of the yearly rent to each month).
- *Budget figures.* Budget figures are often incorporated into general ledger systems for actual versus budget comparison purposes.
- *Standard costs.* These costs can be used in the same way as budget figures, but actually form part of the accounts.
- *Other statements.* General ledger figures may also form part of other financial statements, such as cash flow projections, departmental budgets, cost ledgers, consolidations, and financial statements themselves. Therefore, one set of financial records can serve many purposes.

Occasionally, the debits and credits on a journal voucher do not balance. Such vouchers may be:

- Rejected.
- Held in suspense within the computer.
- Posted, despite the error, along with a balancing figure to force the whole ledger into balance.

Obviously, users must correct such errors as soon as possible, especially when they are posted with the errors.

INTERACTIVE FINANCIAL SYSTEM SOFTWARE

Facilitating access to timely and accurate financial accounting information is one goal of appropriately designed and developed computer software. An example of the input and output of such a system is shown in Figure 12-2.

The system provides financial processing, including a general ledger function, with the following capabilities, as described by IBM:

- The accounting data base organization and management functions.
- Posting in conversational or batch mode.
- Creation of the journal and the general ledger.
- System documentation and restart functions.

The Interactive Financial System's (IFS) programs make it possible to do accounting functions in conversational mode. This means that any account and any voucher can be entered, displayed, and, if necessary, processed at CRT terminals, using a question-and-answer format. Such interactive, on-line processing helps the accounting department do financial processing independently of lists and account cards, as shown in Figure 12-3. Advantages to such computerized processing, as described by IBM, include the following:

- Transactions on prime documents can be entered directly at the terminal, avoiding the need to transfer documents to intermediate recording media (magnetic tape, diskette, or punched card). Transactions are immediately validated or verified, corrected, and then entered.
- The storage and processing capacities of the computer can be accessed directly by the terminal. Operating procedures and daily processing can be controlled in the department as a result. (There is no need to work through the EDP department.)

FIG. 12-2

Financial information System/Budget Accounting Information Subsystem (FIS/BACIS) overview (courtesy of International Business Machines Corporation)

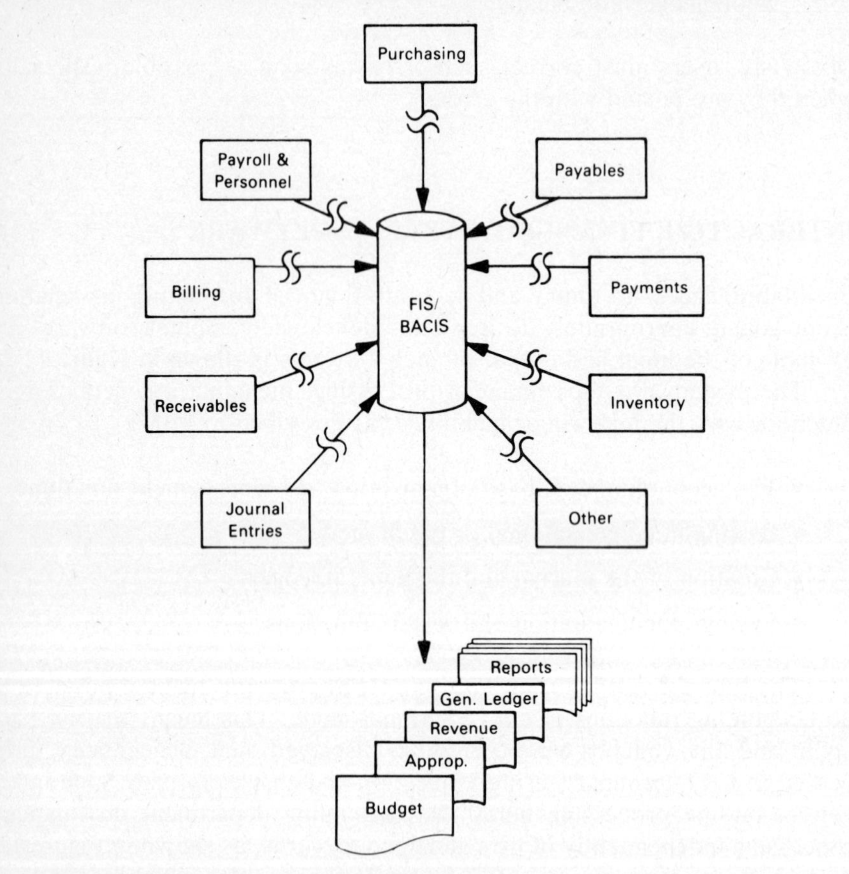

- Posting is performed from the transaction's prime document, directly into the system.
- The system labels postings that are entered incorrectly and stores them in a suspense file for later correction, eliminating the need to reenter postings after correction.
- Transaction entry and its subsequent posting time span are considerably reduced. Transactions posted immediately update the

FIG. 12-3

Interactive Financial System 1-4 (IFS 1-4) overview (courtesy of International Business Machines Corporation)

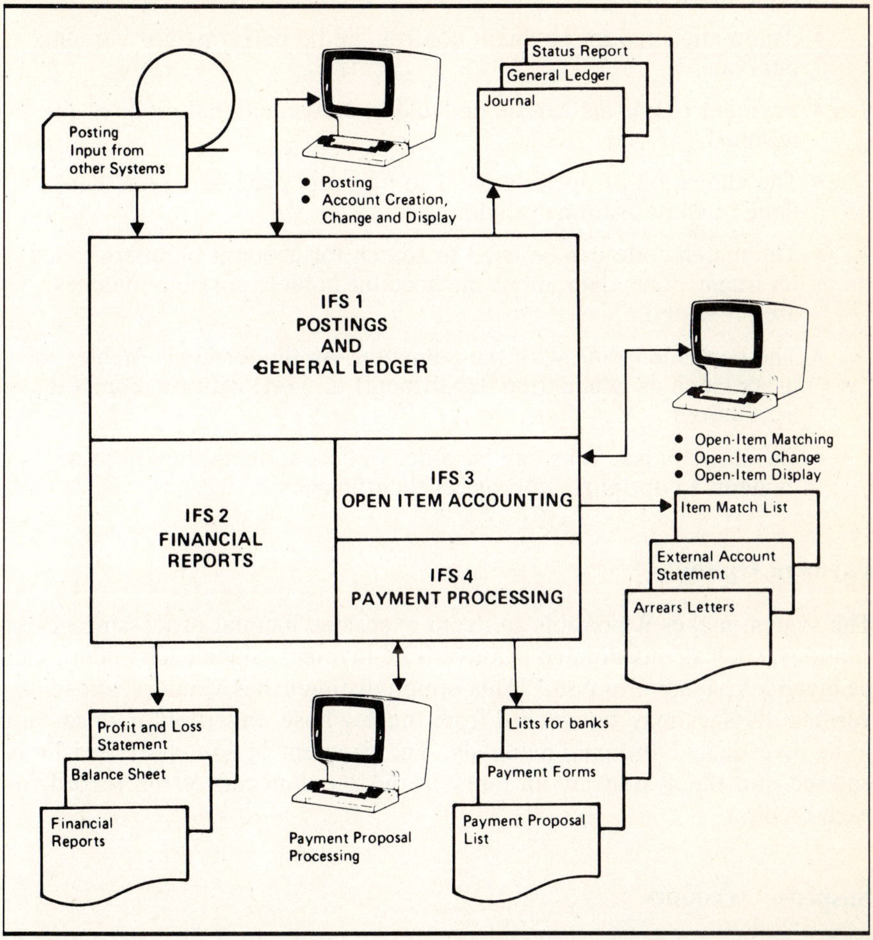

master files, which are then available for any other accounting activity, so that little processing time is lost.

- Special reports can be created and printed on short notice.

There are other advantages to an integrated accounting system; in IFS these include the following:

- Open-item allocation and matching, including discount posting and sales tax adjustment, are possible.

- Specific open-item information can be displayed and updated.
- An automatic arrears letter procedure writes individually worded reminder notices.
- Automatic account payment control can be performed at variable intervals.
- Payment proposals can be updated in conversational mode at the terminal.
- The allocation of open invoices to payment processing and banks is done in conversational mode.
- The match code can be used to search for account numbers based on fragmentary data about the account holder; possible matches are presented.
- The permanent link with the computer via the terminal enables the users (such as accounting department) to work with the computer as required.
- Business transactions can be processed as soon as they become evident, to optimize working cycle efficiency.

Payment Option

The system makes it possible to avoid excessive manual processing of exceptions, such as unvalidated or unverified invoices, since each vendor can be given a "payment option." This option distinguishes vendors whose unverified invoices may be entered from those whose unverified invoices are to be investigated and paid manually. The payment option characteristic is entered into the system by an entry in the account master file record for each creditor.

Suspense Accounts

In an interactive financial system suspense accounts (or accounts that hold items requiring further investigation and/or processing) are often used to process unverified invoices. The suspense account usually operates in an open-item mode.

SECURITY ASPECTS AND DATA INTEGRITY

Financial data base systems contain financial accounting data of great significance to an organization. Accessing and updating this data, especially in an interactive or conversational mode, require that controls protect the data base from unauthorized access, from unintentional changes or errors, and from destruction. This is particularly important in such a system because the master files are updated immediately by transactions entered at terminals. An unauthorized user could create much damage in a short period of time.

Following is an overview of the security measures provided by the application programs of IBM's IFS 1-4. They are presented here to depict how such systems can be controlled by programmed procedures. They provide four types of security:

1. Preventing posting errors.
2. Protecting updating or posting data.
3. Protecting account master file data.
4. Preventing unauthorized access.

Preventing Posting Errors

Two main procedures serve to prevent updating or posting errors: (1) validation of posting data and (2) rejection of posting groups containing unvalidated data.

Validation of Posting Data. The IBM programs, like other systems of this kind, provide comprehensive edit checks and validation tests of posting data as it is entered. In this case, entered data does not actually update the file until the items of the posting group have been successfully balanced. The following balance checks can be carried out as an option for each voucher and are mandatory for the total number of vouchers collected as a posting group:

- *Voucher balancing.* Before entering a group of transactions, the user can specify whether the system should check the debit/credit equality of each voucher within the group. An incorrect voucher can be corrected either immediately or later during the correction phase of the posting program.
- *Posting group balancing.* Two checks are always carried out on the vouchers of the posting group as a whole: (1) that there is an overall debit/credit balance, and (2) that the total posted agrees with a previously entered control total. Entered data can be finally posted only if these two checks are satisfactory.

Rejection of Unvalidated Data. The program ensures that entered transaction groups are not posted if they contain unvalidated data or data that for some reason is subject to correction. It also ensures that once a posting group is posted, it cannot be changed. To effect this, entered posting groups here are classified into two subgroups:

- *In progress (HOLD status).* Posting groups with HOLD status may be changed, completed, and corrected. They are not posted during short-period summary (processing completed to a certain time or date), but are retained until they have OK status.
- *Posted (OK status).* Posting groups with OK status are assumed posted; that is, their data is final and cannot be changed. The actual posting of the data occurs during the next short-period summary.

A posting group cannot be given OK status unless the posting group balance check is satisfactory. If voucher balancing was also to be carried out, the posting group can be given OK status only if all vouchers in this posting group are balanced. Posting groups with OK status will be entered in the data base and in journals during the next short-period summary.

Protecting Posted Data

In addition to the checks described previously, further checks are carried out during and after storage of the postings in the data base. These checks are carried out during short-period summary, monthly summary, and when account statements are requested.

To prevent falsification of stored data, the accounting date (determined only by selected personnel) accompanies all entries. Deletion of stored data is always accompanied by a report of the stored data (which shows the data as it was just before deletion).

Short-Period Summary. Posting groups with OK status are transferred to the data base during short-period summary for storage. During short-period summary all postings are printed in the general journal of the organization. At the time the postings are transferred to the data base, a further debit/credit equality check is made. (At this point, discrepancies can have been caused only by a program defect or by unauthorized manipulation of posting data.)

Journal discrepancies or exceptions are reported in a special printout that indicates whether program errors or unauthorized attempts at data manipulation have occurred between the time the postings were entered and the printing of the journal.

Account Statements. When account statements are produced as non-periodic reports, they are checked by the system. Differences between the total stored in the individual account and the sum of the separate items are shown in the statements, with an indication that the difference was due to a program error or unauthorized data manipulation.

Monthly Summary. The monthly summary is carried out for each account. The system ensures that no further postings can be made for a particular month, once it has been subject to the monthly summary.

The checks carried out during monthly summary are:

- Debit/credit balance checks of monthly and annual turnovers for all the accounts.
- The amount shown in the journal must match the accumulated monthly turnovers of all appropriate accounts.

Discrepancies are indicated so that they can be investigated. Only if the summary balances can the month be finally closed.

Accounting Date. The accounting date is entered at the beginning of a session by selected personnel. Usually only one person with authority can enter the date, to prevent the falsification of accounts by the entry of data under an incorrect date. (Note that this authorization should be checked as part of controls.)

Controlled Manipulation of Stored Data. To limit the amount of posted data stored in the system, the user must decide for how many closed months posting data should be retained in the data base. Data for the preceding months is deleted and the program provides a report of all of the deleted posting data. The deleted data can be stored on magnetic tape, according to the requirements of the organization. In this way, past data is retained for auditing purposes and later analysis. To delete data from the data base, the following conditions must be fulfilled:

- The posting month must have been closed.
- In the case of open-item accounting, items must be balanced and printed on an item matching list.
- Postings must have the status "verified," meaning that they have been appropriately checked and are ready for deletion.

Protecting Account Master File Data

When account master file data is created, changed, or deleted, the system verifies that the user is authorized and that the data is reasonable. A report of the data concerned is then produced.

Creating and Changing Account Master File Data. In order to create or change account master file data, users must first identify themselves to the system. In addition, the system allows the user to carry out only those functions for which that user is authorized. Plausibility checks are carried out by the system on all changes to master file data, and the changes are recorded. Similar plausibility checks are carried out for data entered by batch processing.

Deleting Account Master File Data. Accounts that are no longer in use may be deleted from the data base to release storage capacity for other purposes. It is possible to delete master file data created before a certain selection date for a given account. In order to delete master file data, the following conditions must be met:

- No subaccounts may exist for a main account being deleted.
- The amount balanced from the account brought forward, the turnovers of the previous and the current year, as well as the turnovers of posting months 1 and 2, must be zero.
- The turnovers for posting months 1 and 2 and for the thirteenth month of the previous year must all be zero on both the debit and credit sides of the account.
- In the case of an account being used more than once, the debit and credit turnovers for the current year must be zero, and no accounts may have been posted after the selection date.

Deleted accounts are printed and can also be stored on magnetic tape. Users can write programs that extract or combine data for statistical or financial reports. In this format, deletion of account master file data can be executed only in batch mode.

Preventing Unauthorized Access

A well-designed financial data base system ensures that unauthorized users are denied access to the system; authorized users are permitted to carry out only predetermined authorized functions. In general, the system first checks the identity of the user for authorization. Authorized users are then checked for the accounts they can access and whether they have authorization to change (post) or only to view or display data.

User Identification. The system is programmed to respond to users who identify themselves by means of an authorized name and password; unauthorized users are denied access to the system. So that the password cannot be observed by onlookers, it does not appear on the screen when it is entered. Three unsuccessful attempts at identification by a user causes the terminal to be deactivated. It can be reactivated only by the master terminal.

User Authorization. The user name (or USERID) is designed and implemented to indicate and permit a predetermined level of authorization. Only certain users can carry out master terminal functions, such as initiating or terminating sessions or activating or deactivating terminals. For bookkeeping functions, the user name has two categories of authorization: (1) the accounts to which access is allowed, and (2) the functions that can be processed using those accounts.

As an example, the accountant responsible for creditors may be authorized to have access to all creditor accounts and expenditure accounts to post items: This is the "update" or "write" permission. For information only, the "read" or "inquiry" permission allows display of debtor accounts. An attempt by a user with only read or inquiry permission to enter new debtor account postings would be unsuccessful and would cause an error message to be displayed.

The various levels of authorization should be determined by a person with appropriate authority in the organization.

USING AUDIT SOFTWARE FOR GENERAL LEDGER AUDITS

General ledger audit software is designed to increase audit efficiency by automating some of the common substantive procedures. Because many functions are precoded into the software, it can be installed relatively quickly. The auditor has flexibility in choosing parameters and in the generation of computer reports. Audit software can be used to assist in the audit of most computerized general ledger systems. Such a package is particularly effective where there are a large number of transactions and accounts comprising the general ledger. Some financial information systems have their own built-in report capabilities that can be useful to the auditor.

Testing Facilities

Many common audit substantive procedures can be performed by an audit software package:

- Analyzing data for consistency and accuracy of information.
- Identifying new accounts.
- Identifying closed accounts.
- Identifying abnormal account conditions.
- Comparing current, prior, and budget figures for all accounts in the trial balance.
- Identifying transactions comprising the account balances.
- Identifying accounts comprising the financial line.
- Preparing financial line analysis, including current- and prior-year balances.
- Selecting transactions for detailed validation tests.
- Detecting different transaction dates within the same journal entry.
- Checking journal entries to ensure that debit and credit entries balance.
- Checking that transaction details correctly sum to the account total.
- Selecting journal entries for detailed validation tests.
- Comparing current, prior period, and budget account totals for selected accounts on financial lines.
- Comparing financial line totals over a five-year period.
- Plotting movements in selected accounts for financial lines in graphic form (see Figure 12-4).
- Calculating financial ratios for two to five accounting periods.
- Calculating a vertical consolidation or a consolidation worksheet of multicompany and/or multisubsidiary accounts (see Figure 12-5).
- Reprinting the general ledger trial balance and preparing a trial balance worksheet.

Many audit objectives are achieved more easily as a result of using general ledger audit software. Figure 12-6 is an overview of processing[1].

[1] From the Coopers & Lybrand package.

FIG. 12-4

Plot by month report

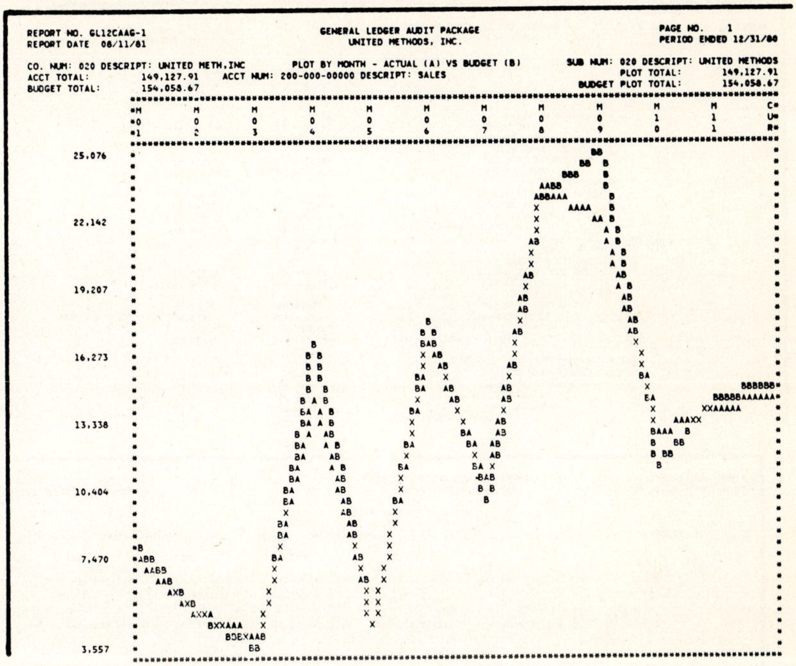


```
REPORT NO. GL12CAAG-1                GENERAL LEDGER AUDIT PACKAGE               PAGE NO.    3
REPORT DATE  08/11/81                    UNITED METHODS, INC.                   PERIOD ENDED 12/31/80

                                             - TOTALS -

               RECORDS                                     DEBIT               CREDIT

                 2,278   RECORDS READ      CURRENT    771,710,915.79      774,609,794.78-
                                           BUDGET     807,569,687.33      810,513,251.53-

                     2   ACCOUNTS PLOTTED
```

The extent of the assistance obtained from use of the software package is affected by:

- The capabilities of the package in use.
- The nature of the organization's general ledger system—in particular, the extent of the information relating to individual transactions.
- The audit approach adopted for a particular situation.

FIG. 12-5
Vertical consolidation report

REPORT NO. GL16CAAG-2 — GENERAL LEDGER AUDIT PACKAGE — PAGE NO. 1
REPORT DATE 08/26/81 — UNITED METHODS, INC. — PERIOD ENDING 12/31/80

VERTICAL CONSOLIDATION

	CURRENT PERIOD	PRIOR PERIOD
001 CASH IN BANK		
020 UNITED METH.INC		
020 UNITED METHODS	4,971,477.09	3,238,468.48
TOTAL COMPANY	4,971,477.09	3,238,463.48
050 UNITED COMM.INC		
050 UNITED COMM.INC	404,804.88	259,102.00-
TOTAL COMPANY	404,834.88	259,102.00-
060 UNITED METH.INT		
060 UNITED METH.INT	618,604.89	103,967.39
TOTAL COMPANY	618,604.89	103,967.39
- SUBTOTAL -	5,994,885.66	3,033,333.87
TOTAL FINANCIAL LINE	5,994,836.86	3,003,333.87
002 CASH ON HAND		
020 UNITED METH.INC		
020 UNITED METHODS	12,494.60	8,550.00
TOTAL COMPANY	12,494.60	8,550.00
060 UNITED METH.INT		
060 UNITED METH.INT	558.00	558.00
TOTAL COMPANY	558.00	558.00
- SUBTOTAL -	13,052.60	9,108.00
TOTAL FINANCIAL LINE	13,052.60	9,108.00
003 MARKETABLE SEC.		
020 UNITED METH.INC		
020 UNITED METHODS	489,000.00-	0.00
TOTAL COMPANY	489,000.00-	0.00
- SUBTOTAL -	489,000.00-	0.00
TOTAL FINANCIAL LINE	489,000.00-	0.00

REPORT NO. GL16CAAG-2 — GENERAL LEDGER AUDIT PACKAGE — PAGE NO. 25
REPORT DATE 08/26/81 — UNITED METHODS, INC. — PERIOD ENDING 12/31/80

VERTICAL CONSOLIDATION
- TOTALS -

RECORDS		CURRENT PERIOD DEBIT	CURRENT PERIOD CREDIT	PRIOR PERIOD DEBIT	PRIOR PERIOD CREDIT
258	020 UNITED METH.INC	666,286,327.32	666,286,327.32-	571,843,299.41	571,843,299.41-
24	050 UNITED COMM.INC	9,793,738.48	9,798,738.48-	47,979,264.01	47,979,264.01-
39	060 UNITED METH.INT	44,209,730.22	44,209,730.22-	44,647,518.18	44,847,518.18-
321	ALL COMPANIES	720,294,796.02	720,294,796.02-	664,670,081.60	664,670,081.60-
85	020 UNITED METHODS	198,600,932.15	385,446,040.56-	140,407,642.13	197,235,764.75-
24	021 UNITED COMM.INC	9,798,738.48	9,798,738.48-	47,979,264.01	47,979,264.01-
39	022 UNITED METH.INT	44,209,730.22	44,209,730.22-	44,847,518.18	44,847,518.18-
52	023 NUTS DIVISION	323,481,199.14	131,136,740.98-	379,087,931.11	322,101,729.39-
22	024 N.E.W.S.	22,410,048.99	14,269,348.64-	22,529,132.76	18,620,509.72-
18	025 MILLING DIV.	0.00	0.00	126,722.49	87,399.41-
2	026 LATHE DIVISION	0.00	0.00	0.00	0.00
27	027 EDUCATIONAL DIV	3,930,581.36	4,211,473.64-	7,944,296.90	8,469,163.40-
28	050 BOLT DIVISION	12,535,744.01	14,533,691.67-	21,747,574.02	25,328,732.74-
24	060 U.M.ELECTR. DIV	105,327,821.67	116,688,431.63-	0.00	0.00
321	ALL SUBSIDIARIES	720,294,796.02	720,294,796.02-	664,670,081.60	664,670,081.60-
14	CONSOLIDATING JES	39,974,000.13	39,974,000.13-		
335	GRAND TOTAL	760,268,796.15	760,268,796.15-	664,670,081.60	664,670,081.60-

The results obtained from using the software when a system is particularly well-suited for it may be sufficient to warrant an extended substantive approach when it would be otherwise impractical or unwarranted.

Substantive audit objectives typically are split up according to major balance sheet headings. The general ledger, by its nature, contains information relating to all of these headings and also to the income statement itself. Thus, a general ledger audit software package can assist the auditor in many of the different substantive audit objectives. For example, the procedures usually include, as a minimum, the requirement to prepare a detailed

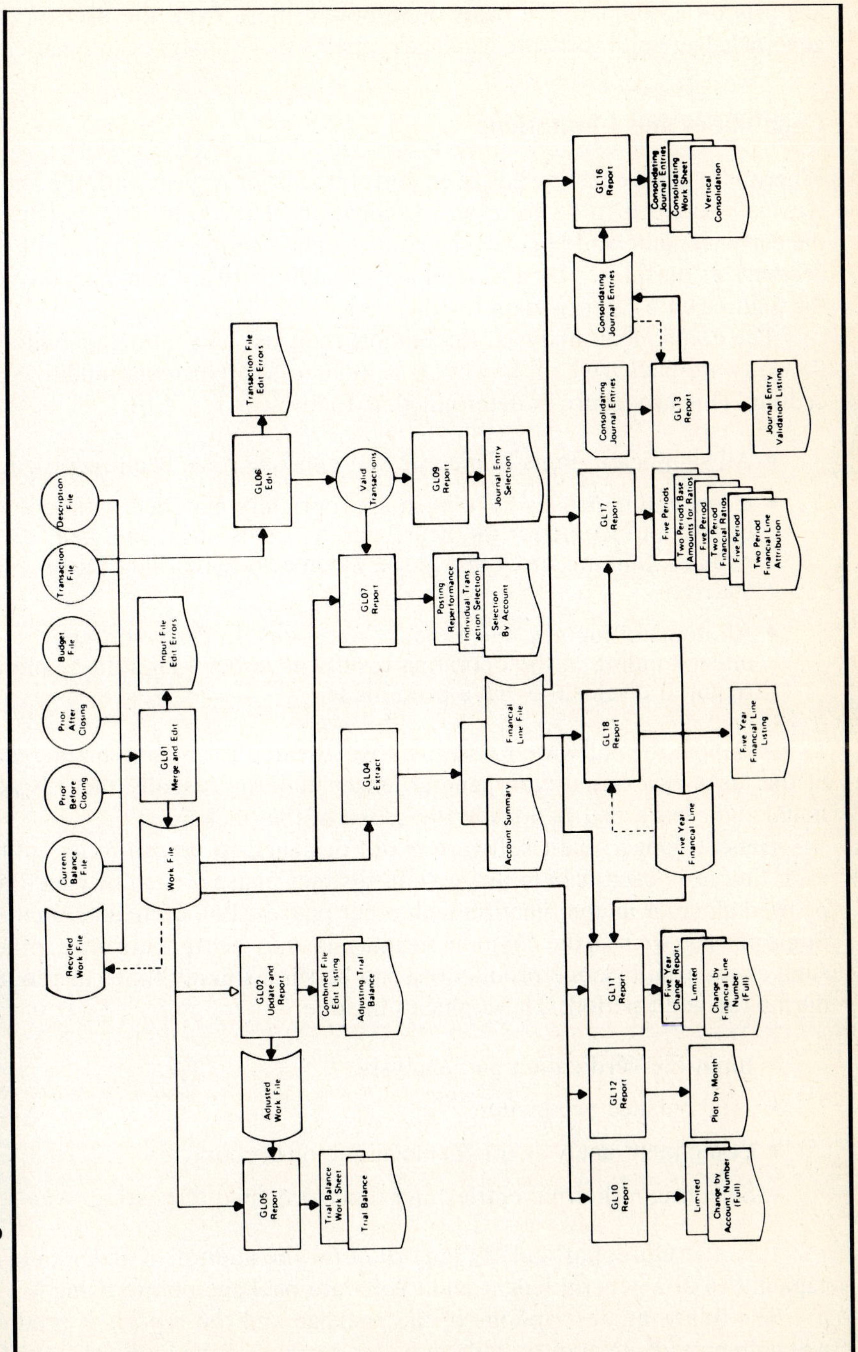

FIG. 12-6
General ledger audit software processing flowchart

analysis on a comparative basis or to obtain these from the user. A good general ledger audit software package prepares these analyses automatically.

Capabilities and Limitations

Where substantive testing has been performed prior to year-end, the auditor is usually obliged to perform an examination of the transactions between the early test date and balance sheet dates. The component analysis of each account, as performed by a general ledger audit software package, provides the auditor with the raw data for this task.

The component analysis, fluctuation analysis, and ratio capabilities of the software package can, however, be related to a particular auditing procedure. This procedure is determined as follows:

- All significant items of income and expense have been recorded.
- Costs and expenses have been appropriately matched with income or the net income for the year, and the items of income and expense that are disclosed in the income statement are fairly stated.
- All items of income and expense necessary to give a proper understanding of the operating results have been identified, and all required disclosures have been made.

Although the software package assists the auditor by automating many of the tasks associated with general ledger auditing, usually there is additional audit work that is outside the scope of the package.

General ledger audit software is not designed to be run in its entirety each time it is used. There are several distinct phases, each of which may be used alone or in combination with other phases, in a particular situation. Some phases, such as the component analysis, may be run only once; others, such as the trial balance production, can be run as many times as required during the audit period. These phases include:

- Input file verification and analysis.
- Trial balance production.
- Component analysis for financial line or account.
- Selection of journal entries and reperformance of posting.

It is, therefore, particularly important for the auditor to understand the capabilities of a general ledger audit software package before using it.

The following descriptions of the package and the reports it produces will help provide an auditor with an understanding of the kinds of tasks that can be automated by using software. Additional information is also given to aid the auditor in becoming aware of options and reports that can be selected.

Audit Procedures

Using general ledger audit software, the following audit tasks can be accomplished. The names of reports[2] generated are shown in parentheses.

Audit Procedures	*Package Capabilities*
Review of general ledger trial balance	
Determine that the general ledger trial balance contains all necessary accounts.	• Provide a comparative trial balance showing current, prior, and budget figures (Trial Balance).
Determine that all of the accounts in the general ledger trial balance are valid.	• Provide a comparative trial balance showing current, prior, and budget figures (Trial Balance). • Select transactions from the cumulative transaction file on the basis of their deviation from a predefined norm or on a random basis for manual follow-up (Individual Transaction Selection).
Determine that all necessary entries, reclassifications, or adjustments are reflected in the trial balance, and that all necessary consolidating journal entries are reflected in the consolidated balances.	• Prepare a trial balance showing current figures with columns for auditor's adjustments (Trial Balance Work Sheet). • Provide a mechanism for the auditor to adjust the trial balance amounts and produce a new trial balance. This process can be performed many times (Adjusting Trial Balance). • Prepare a schedule of all transactions making up an account balance (Selection by Account). • Select transactions from the cumulative transaction file on the basis of their deviation from a predefined norm or on a random basis for manual follow-up (Individual Transaction Selection).

[2] From the Coopers & Lybrand package.

- Provide a mechanism for the auditor to process consolidating journal entries to the financial lines and produce either a vertical consolidation or a traditional horizontal worksheet. This process can be performed many times.

Determine that all entries in the general ledger are proper and valid.

- Prepare a trial balance showing current figures with columns for auditor's adjustments (Trial Balance Work Sheet).
- Provide a mechanism for the auditor to adjust the trial balance amounts and produce a new trial balance. This process can be performed many times (Adjusting Trial Balance).
- Prepare a schedule of all transactions making up an account balance (Selection by Account).
- Select transactions from the cumulative transaction file on the basis of their deviation from a predefined norm or on a random basis for manual follow-up (Individual Transaction Selection).
- Ensure that, in a multiple company file, the component debits and credits of each journal entry stay within one company (Journal Entry Selection).
- Ensure that within journal entries the effective dates of application of transactions are identical for all transactions (Journal Entry Selection).
- Ensure that all journal entries balance to zero (Journal Entry Selection).
- Provide for selection of total journal entries based either on their total magnitude, or on some exceptional characteristic applicable to the entire journal entry (Journal Entry Selection).

Determine that the classifications of accounts are proper and consistent with prior years.

- Analyze the input files for consistency and accuracy of information (Input File Edit Errors).
- List new accounts (new; not on old file) (Combined File Edit Listing).

- Provide a comparative trial balance showing current, prior, and budget figures (Trial Balance).
- Prepare a schedule of all transactions making up an account balance (Selection by Account).
- Select transactions from the cumulative transaction file on the basis of their deviation from a predefined norm or on a random basis for manual follow-up (Individual Transaction Selection).
- Compare account totals for current period, prior period, and budget for selected accounts; provide differences between periods in both amount and percentage (Change by Account Number).

Determine that the general ledger and the trial balance are mathematically accurate.

- List abnormal account conditions, such as bad footings within records (Combined File Edit Listing).
- Verify the mathematical accuracy of the general ledger trial balance (all reports, but in particular Trial Balance).

Review of financial statements (external auditor)

Identify areas that, as a result of unusual activity, unexpected fluctuations, or ratios, appear to involve a higher audit risk and therefore warrant detailed validation.

Determine that the financial statements contain all of the proper accounts.

- Provide a mechanism to attribute a financial statement line number to each account for financial line correspondence (Input File Edit Errors).
- Summarize accounts into a financial line and provide the lead schedule showing each account with the comparative prior year for figures (Account Summary).

	• Compare financial line totals between current, prior, and budget; provide difference between amounts in dollar value and percentage (Change by Financial Line).
Determine that the accounts listed on the financial statements are valid and properly classified.	• Provide a mechanism to attribute a financial statement line number to each account for financial line correspondence (Input File Edit Errors). • Summarize accounts into a financial line and provide the lead schedule showing each with the comparative prior-year figures for financial line analysis (Account by Summary). • Select transactions from the cumulative transaction file on the basis of their deviation from a predefined norm or on a random basis for manual follow-up (Individual Transaction Selection). • Compare financial line totals between current period, prior period, and budget; provide difference between amounts in dollar value and percentage (Change by Financial Line Number). • Calculate the 24 ratios commonly used for financial statement analysis for current period, prior period, and budget (Two-Period Financial Ratios).
Determine that the grouping of accounts included in the financial statements is proper and consistent with prior years. Furthermore, an important part of "analytical review" is to determine those areas of audit risk by identifying large or unusual activity in particular areas.	• Summarize accounts into a financial line and provide the lead schedule showing each amount with comparative prior-year figures for financial line analysis (Account Summary). • Select transactions from the cumulative transaction file on the basis of their deviation from a predefined norm or on a random basis for manual follow-up (Individual Transaction Selection). • Compare financial line totals between current period, prior period, and budget; provide difference between amounts in dollar value and percentage (Change by Financial Line Number).

- Calculate the ending balance for each financial line amount for five-year period showing movement between each period in percentage (Five-Year Change Report).
- Calculate the 24 commonly used ratios for financial statement analysis for current period, prior period, and budget (Two-Period Financial Ratios).
- Select accounts and plot movement in graphic form with comparative budget amounts (Plot by Month).
- Summarize financial line amounts in the base amounts used for calculating the ratios (Five-Period Financial Line Attribution).

Determine that consolidated journal entries are correctly processed and that the consolidating process is accurate and proper (both internal and external auditors).

- Within a multicompany or multisubsidiary file, summarize company and subsidiary amounts by financial line to provide a traditional horizontal consolidated worksheet (Consolidation Work Sheet).
- Within a multicompany or multisubsidiary file, summarize all accounts by financial line to produce a vertical consolidation (Vertical Consolidation).

Additional audit information

- Provide totals of each amount used within the ratio calculations for subsequent analysis. Reference information required if any ratios need more detailed analysis (Five-Period Base Amount for Ratios).

Audit Program—Sequence of Events

The effective use of a general ledger audit software package requires co-operation between the non-EDP auditor and the EDP auditor. An EDP auditor who knows the software can explain the package capabilities and can implement and execute the package. However, as usual, the auditor has overall responsibility for analyzing results and properly performing the audit tests.

Because the events involved in using software vary depending on the extent and timing of the auditor's substantive tests, an assumption has been made for convenience that a substantive audit approach has been adopted and that early testing is not being performed. The title of each report[3] is listed as an event to show relative timing of procedures.

Events	*Auditor's Actions*
Planning	• Develop audit plan and budget. • Collect the information concerning the general ledger system. Prepare planning working papers. • Determine desired report options and prepare the appropriate parameters (e.g., validation date, five-year comparison option). • Create reports within the time requirements. Keep audit staff informed as to progress and any reasons for additional time. • Finalize the following: — Audit date. — Exception profile applicable to the edit report. — Any other information needed in respect to those phases of the package to be executed. (This package has numerous options available for the auditor to specify.) • Before the due date, install the package, execute the edit program, and review the results for exceptions.

PHASE 1 — INPUT FILE VERIFICATION AND ANALYSIS (RECOMMENDED)

Reports	
Input File Edit Errors	• Ascertain relevant general ledger details.
Combined File Edit Listing	• Edit the general ledger files, agree the totals, and create reports.

[3] From the Coopers & Lybrand package.

Transaction File Edit Errors

Audit review	• Review any error messages to determine significance and corrections. • Review new accounts and old accounts that existed in prior periods for reasonableness or for justification.

PHASE 2 — REPERFORMANCE OF THE TRIAL BALANCE PRODUCTION (OPTIONAL)

Reports

Trial Balance	• If the trial balance does not have comparative figures, produce the reports prior to starting the audit.
Trial Balance Work Sheet	• If adjusting journal entries are required, prepare entries.
Adjusting Trial Balance	• Prepare reports and agree the totals.
Audit review	• Agree totals and selected details to the trial balance. Use reports as a basis for audit tests including the general ledger. Identify unusual accounts for later extraction for audit review.

PHASE 2A — TRIAL BALANCE PRODUCTION (RERUN) (REITERATED AS REQUIRED)

Reports

Adjusting Trial Balance	• Discover any adjusting journal entries required as a result of audit tests.
Trial Balance	• Prepare reports and agree the totals.

PHASE 3 — COMPONENT ANALYSIS FOR FINANCIAL LINE OR ACCOUNT (OPTIONAL)

Reports

Selection by Account	• Review the accounts that require details of all the period's transactions.
Account Summary	• Prepare reports and agree the totals.

Audit review

- Agree the totals and selected details to the trial balance. Review for unusual account classification. Identify unusual variations from budget for further follow-up. Use reports as lead schedules.
- Use information for detailed audit tests, including checking to source documentation.

PHASE 3A — COMPONENT ANALYSIS FOR FINANCIAL LINES (RERUN)

Report

Account Summary

- If adjusting journal entries have been processed as a result of Phase 2, request rerun of this report.
- Prepare reports and agree the totals.

Audit review

- Ensure all journal entries appear to be taken up in final lead schedules.

PHASE 4 — SELECTION OF JOURNAL ENTRIES AND REPERFORMANCE OF POSTING (OPTIONAL)

Reports

Selection by Account

- Choose dates and accounts for selection.
- Prepare report and agree the totals.

Individual Transaction Selection

- If auditor prefers selection by transaction, decide characteristics of transactions to be selected, and whether transactions are to be selected using a random start and interval sampling.

Posting Reperformance

- Select dates and accounts for reperformance posting.

Journal Entry Selection

- Select characteristics for journal entry and decide whether journal entries are to be selected using a random start and interval sampling.

Audit review	• Review any posting errors to determine significance and corrections. Use information in detailed audit tests of transactions.

PHASE 5 — FLUCTUATION ANALYSIS (OPTIONAL)

Reports

Change by Account Number (Full or Limited)	• Make the special selection criteria for comparing accounts: Current-period balance to prior periods or current-period balance to budget (monetary or percentage). • Prepare report and agree the totals.
Change by Financial Number (Full or Limited)	• Formulate special selection criteria for comparing financial lines: Current-period balance to prior periods or current-period balance to budget (monetary or percentage).
Five-Year Change Report	• Decide that the five-year comparison report is to be produced.
Plot by Month	• Choose accounts or ranges of accounts to be plotted. If no accounts are specified, then all financial lines will be plotted.
Audit review	• Use reports as basis of analytical review procedures to identify those areas requiring detailed audit tests.

PHASE 6 — RATIOS FOR FINANCIAL STATEMENT ANALYSIS (OPTIONAL)

Reports

Two periods

Financial Line Attribution	• Obtain any extra information required for report production.
Financial Ratios	• Prepare reports and agree the totals.

Base Amounts for Ratio Calculations

Five periods

Financial Line Attribution (Five Years)

- Obtain any extra information required for report production (e.g., extract years for producing five-year reports).

Financial Ratios (Five Years)

Base Amounts for Ratio Calculations (Five Years)

Audit review

- Use reports as part of analytical review procedures to determine areas for detailed audit test and investigation.
- Review financial line attributions and base amounts used to produce ratios. Review ratios for trends and unusual changes. Where necessary, specify individual transactions for follow-up.

PHASE 7 — CONSOLIDATIONS (REITERATED AS REQUIRED)

Reports

- Prepare considating journal entries needed.
- Arrange for journal entries to be key entered, prepare report. Assist in determining significance of error messages.

Consolidating Journal Entries

- Resolve any journal entries not properly processed.

Vertical Consolidation

- Prepare report and agree the totals.

Consolidation Work Sheet

Audit review

- Agree or reconcile to the organization's totals. Review for reasonableness and possibly omitted eliminations. Use consolidation report in preparing consolidated financial statements.

PHASE 8 — CONSTRUCTION (OPTIONAL)

Reports

Five-Year Financial Line Listing	• Provide information for combining prior periods with current-period data to create five-year data. • Input the prior year's file to construct a new updated five-year financial line file. • Prepare report and agree the totals. • Check report to ensure that data appears to be correct. Give clearance for data to be filed for next year's use.

COMPLETION

Reports	• Provide brief written comments on use of package (e.g., effect on audit, user acceptance, ease of use, suggested enhancements, staff evaluation). • Summarize time, costs, and expenses. Document any reasons for changes from original budget, provide suggestions for the coming audit year.

OPERATIONAL CONSIDERATIONS

General ledger audit software packages usually consist of many separate programs designed to provide an easy-to-use tool to assist in auditing a computerized general ledger. The software can be used in the organization's MIS environment or at a service bureau.

Total Transaction System

Automated general ledgers generally fall within the range between a total transaction system and a master file balance-forward system. A total transaction system is one where each transaction is added to a cumulative file that is kept for a period of time. Each journal entry is made up of multiple transactions, since under this system it is necessary to add up all transactions on the file to determine an account balance at any point in time. The opening balance at the beginning of the period is usually known as a dummy transaction. Some systems maintain only the transactions for the current month, and all prior transactions are summarized into one brought-forward entry. This type of system may be modified to create a separate file containing account numbers, descriptions, and budget amounts.

Master File Balance-Forward System

In a master file balance-forward system, one record is kept for each account, and this record is updated by any transactions that occur during the period. In most such systems, a total by month of all transactions is kept within the record for a minimum of 12 months and often for up to five years. Transactions are applied to each account (record) as their effective date falls due. These transactions are archived to a historical file either on a cumulative or monthly basis.

Journal Entries

Regardless of the method used to maintain an account balance, there are differences in the way in which journal entries originate, depending on the computerization of the system. In the highly developed data processing system, movements in the subsidiary applications, such as sales, accounts payable, and inventory, may result in automatic journal entries at month-end that summarize the movement for the period and debit and credit the correct accounts. Journal entries that do not originate in an automated system may be of two types: (1) a standing journal entry or (2) an adjusting journal entry. Standing journal entries typically relate to such items as depreciation and are set up either as a semiautomated procedure or as their effective date falls due. Adjusting journal entries are prepared manually and generally relate to the correction of errors and year-end movements. In a more basic system, all journal entries may be manually prepared and entered. The characteristics of the particular general ledger system therefore affect the way in which general ledger audit software can be used.

MICROCOMPUTER AUDIT SOFTWARE

Microcomputer audit software can automate many of the routine and labor-intensive tasks associated with an audit. As an example, Coopers & Lybrand's PRE-AUDIT will:

- Create an opening balance from prior-period totals.
- Summarize the monthly totals into account balances.

- Group accounts into line items for the financial statements.
- Sequence the line items into appropriate headings and subheadings.
- Calculate net income for the period under review.
- Post journal entries to the account balances.
- Accumulate unadjusted differences (scoresheet entries) and provide schedules to help in analyzing the materiality of these items.
- Convert the unadjusted differences into journal entries, with a flowthrough to the financial statements.
- Prepare analyses of fluctuations between periods on a percentage or amount basis.
- Calculate standard and nonstandard ratios.
- Calculate a common size for a series of accounts, financial lines, or subheadings.
- Group interperiod changes into categories appropriate for statement of cash flow.
- Post reclassification entries to the financial statement line amounts for presentation purposes only.
- Produce a set of financial statements in either working paper format or tailored exactly to the client's requirements.
- Produce account, financial line, ratio base, or ratio result data in the format required for input to SuperCalc3, Lotus 1-2-3, or standard ASCII format.
- Reconstruct files and data damaged by a computer failure during processing.
- Consolidate subsidiary files into a parent company's file.

In addition, the software can produce, on request, more than 100 different reports, either printed or displayed on the screen. Here are some of the more significant ones:

- Posting summary details in either account or summary number sequence.
- Comparative trial balance with the percentage of period-to-period fluctuation.
- Account detail showing original balance, posting summaries, and journal entries.
- Trial balance worksheet showing adjusting journal entry total by account.

- Comparative financial statement summary with the fluctuations at various levels shown as percentages or amounts.
- Charts of accounts.
- Lead schedules for each financial statement line, or custom-designed.
- Common size report.
- List of ratio results and schedules of underlying data.
- Adjusting journal entries in journal entry number, account number, or financial line sequence.
- Scoresheet entries in scoresheet entry number or financial line sequence.
- Reclassification entries in reclassification entry number or financial line sequence.
- Financial statements in two formats, including notes and auditor's reports.
- Statement of cash flow.

Using software automates many of the routine, repetitive tasks that are part of the compilation, review, or audit processes.

IMPLEMENTING GENERAL LEDGER SYSTEMS

Auditors frequently participate in system development. (See Chapter 22, "System Development Trends and Practices" and Chapter 23, "System Development Methodology and Auditing.") The following is a sample of the kinds of questions an auditor may ask when assisting in the planning, design, selection, and implementation of a general ledger system. These questions can help determine initial requirements for such a system.

GENERAL LEDGER SYSTEM

Location ______________________________

1. How many ledgers (separate companies) do you have? __________
2. How many divisions/profit centers do you have on each ledger? ____
3. Are the following reports produced by divisions/profit centers?

	Yes	*No*
a. General Ledger	☐	☐
b. Trial Balance	☐	☐
c. Profit and Loss	☐	☐
d. Balance Sheet	☐	☐

4. If there is more than one ledger, are consolidated reports produced?
   ☐ Yes ☐ No
5. Is your accounting period other than monthly? ☐ Yes ☐ No
   If yes, give details. ______________________
6. Do your fiscal year and calendar year coincide? ☐ Yes ☐ No
   If no, give details. ______________________
7. Is a comparison of this year versus last year made?

	Yes	*No*
a. Month-to-date	☐	☐
b. Year-to-date	☐	☐

   Does your consolidated report also reflect this? ☐ Yes ☐ No
8. Do you do budgeting on your income and expenses?
   ☐ Yes ☐ No
   If so, is it a:
   a. Monthly budget ☐
   b. Quarterly budget ☐
   c. Yearly budget ☐
9. What is the total number of accounts in your chart of accounts?
   (real and nominal accounts) ______________________
10. Do you have subaccount numbers to identify your profit center's operations? ☐ Yes ☐ No
    If yes, how many? ______________________
11. How many of the account numbers indicated in Question 9 are affected by profit centers? (total number) ______________________
12. What is the length of your account number (taking into consideration subnumbers for profit centers)? ______________________
13. What is the approximate number of transactions (sum total of transactions from different journals)? ______________________
14. Are quarterly and yearly ledgers prepared? ☐ Yes ☐ No
15. Is there additional information that may be of use? ______________________
    ____

PART IV

Control Concepts

CHAPTER **13**

Information Technology Controls

INTRODUCTION

In a computer-based application system, numerous accounting and control procedures are performed by computer. In addition, much of the company's data is stored in and manipulated by the computer. Just as those in management are concerned about controls within an application system, they are equally concerned about the controls over: maintenance and operation of those systems; programmed procedures; and how the stored data is protected.

In most complex systems it is impractical, and sometimes impossible, to reperform the programmed procedures for computer applications manually. For example, when a computer checks the sequence of prenumbered shipping documents, it may be programmed to print only an exception report. There is no logical way that a user can reperform every intermediate step that the computer considers for all prenumbered documents. A set of controls must be established over programmed procedures to ensure their consistency and proper operation. These controls, known as information technology (IT) or general controls, are the controls over data processing as a whole.

IT controls are procedures within the MIS department which ensure that the programs operate properly and that unauthorized changes are prevented. They include controls over the design, implementation, security, and use of computer programs and files. Those controls consist of a combination of programmed and manual procedures.

IT controls are similar to application controls. The following points should be noted:

- IT controls are controls over the entire MIS environment.
- Application controls are controls over specific applications; IT controls apply to all applications.
- Application controls are made up of both manual and programmed procedures.
- IT controls regulate the MIS environment to ensure that programmed procedures continue to work properly.
- If there are weaknesses in IT controls, there is no assurance that programmed procedures will continue to work properly, even if they have not been changed.

Typically, IT controls are implemented when the control risk warrants an associated control procedure. Improperly controlled MIS environments can disrupt an organization's operations by:

- Requiring multiple reruns of applications to correct errors, thereby causing delays.

- Affecting data used by management to operate the business.
- Allowing fraud to occur, such as unauthorized altering of computer records.
- Allowing trade secrets to be exposed.

THE SEVEN PRIMARY INFORMATION TECHNOLOGY CONTROLS

IT controls can be divided into seven major areas:

1. *Implementation controls.* Designed to ensure that programmed procedures for new systems are appropriate and are implemented effectively.
2. *Maintenance controls.* Designed to ensure that changes to programmed procedures are designed, tested, approved, and implemented appropriately.
3. *Computer operations controls.* Designed to ensure that authorized programmed procedures are applied consistently and that correct versions of data files are used.
4. *Program security controls.* Designed to ensure that unauthorized changes cannot be made to programmed procedures.
5. *Data file security controls.* Designed to ensure that unauthorized changes cannot be made to data files.
6. *System software controls.* Designed to ensure that suitable system software is implemented and protected effectively against unauthorized changes.
7. *File conversion controls.* Designed to ensure that data is converted from an old to a new system completely and accurately.

An important factor that influences the nature of IT controls in an organization is the structure of the MIS department. Department organization depends largely on the extent of computer processing, the number of employees, and the control techniques used. The larger the department, the greater the opportunity to install a satisfactory system of IT controls. Such a system can make use of the software features that are available in a large installation and can provide better disciplines over the basic controls. These disciplines are easier to create and enforce when there is a larger staff, since an appropriate division of duties can be arranged.

IMPLEMENTATION CONTROLS

Implementation controls help guard against errors in new applications. They include controls over the design of new computer applications, testing of new application programs, and procedures for putting approved application programs into use. They apply to both internally developed and vendor-supplied applications.

Usually, the work undertaken by an organization from the time it completes a feasibility study for a proposed computer system (see Chapter 22, "System Development Trends and Practices," and Chapter 23, "System Development Methodology and Auditing") to the time it implements that system successfully is significant. It can take a considerable amount of time to translate users' requirements from an overall statement into a series of detailed production programs and related instructions for both the MIS and the user departments.

The procedures involved with new system development are:

- System development management.
- System design and program preparation.
- Program and system testing.
- Cataloging.

System Development Management

Generally, requests for new applications are submitted to MIS by application owners. Feasibility study reports, general system designs, test plans, and results usually are reviewed and approved by the application owners and MIS management (e.g., data base and network administrators) who will be affected by the new applications, technical support group management (for compatibility with existing system software), and application programming management (for program conformity with application design specifications, correctness and compatibility with existing application software). Often, a quality assurance or internal audit function is involved in the process.

Data processing installations usually control the scheduled implementation of new applications with a project management log or other method that tracks the project's progress. Normally, the progress of each module (program or group of closely related programs) within a new application is tracked.

System Design and Program Preparation

Typically, new application requests are initiated by users, through application owners, based on business needs, changes in legal or regulatory requirements, or a desire to increase processing efficiency. Application owners, designated users, or systems analysts also can present requests at meetings of MIS personnel.

Users and MIS personnel perform feasibility studies, including cost-benefit analyses, technical analyses to determine effects on existing hardware and application software, and operational analyses to measure the applications' impact on operations.

The general design of the system is documented, including both programmed and manual procedures. Control points and interfaces with system software and other computerized applications are defined. Prototyping can help users refine their specifications for new applications. Management of each department involved in data flow reviews the plan to ensure that they understand and agree with it before development progresses.

On approval of feasibility studies and the general system design, detailed specifications are developed. Typically, detailed design specifications for new applications include narratives and/or flowcharts of activities, flow diagrams of data gathering, data entry and report reconciliation processes, and expected completion and implementation date.

The involvement of users and MIS personnel in developing general and detailed design specifications ensures that appropriate control features are incorporated into the applications. Control features, such as run-to-run balancing and review of JCL (job control language) streams, are included in detailed specifications to enable control over completeness, accuracy, and authorization of processing.

Program and System Testing

Normally, MIS policies require development of test plans for all new applications. Those policies specify the level of detail for test plan documentation, parties to be included in the development process, and approvals that must be obtained.

Test plan documentation includes a description of the tests, the data to be used or the methodology for developing that data, and expected test results. Generally, test plans are joint user-MIS efforts, reviewed and approved by application owners and programming and MIS management.

The test plan identifies these testing stages to be performed: (1) program testing, (2) system testing, and/or (3) parallel testing.

1. *Program testing* involves checking the logic of individual programs. The principal methods used are desk checking and test data. Desk checking entails analyzing the logical paths in the program and confirming that the program code meets specifications. Wherever practical, desk checking should be

carried out by a programmer other than the one who designed and wrote the program. The original programmer is likely to think the logic is correct and try to prove it rather than to really check it.

Normally, desk checking is performed in conjunction with the use of test data. Test data is fictitious data prepared according to the system specifications for entry into the system. It should be designed to cover all possible processing, including periodic and/or error conditions. Formal procedures should be set up to identify and correct any errors discovered during testing. All results of running the test data should be documented and retained as evidence that the tests were performed. The same data can also be used to test future changes to the system.

2. *System testing* involves checking that the logic of the various individual programs is consistent and links together to form a complete system that meets the requirements of the detailed system specifications. The principal technique used is test data. The test results should be scrutinized carefully. The test data should be rerun and redesigned, if necessary, until all failures in logic are detected. In addition to common situations that the system is designed to handle, the tests should also measure the effects of unusual conditions. Wherever possible, system testing should be performed or checked by people other than those responsible for detailed programming.

3. *Parallel testing* means operating the new system at the same time, or in parallel, with the existing system. The results obtained from the dual processing can be checked to identify and investigate any differences. Parallel (or pilot) testing is a way to test the complete system during operation, including all user procedures. Unlike system testing, the purpose of parallel running is to test the system's ability to cope with real, rather than test, data and to handle actual volumes, rather than individual transactions. The new system should not be accepted, nor should the existing system be dropped, until the full processing cycle has been run successfully, as far as practical, on the new system. In addition, recovery procedures—the ability of the system to recover from an abnormal termination—should be tested and documented. The results should be reviewed by people other than those responsible for the detailed programming.

Cataloging

Cataloging is the set of procedures necessary to transfer the tested programs into operation. Important procedures are those that ensure that all testing and documentation have been completed satisfactorily before the programs go into production, and that the manual procedures for the new or modified system are already in place in both the user and the MIS departments.

Normally, programs are moved into production libraries on the basis of approved program move requests. Typically, program move requests for new applications are approved by the management of the group responsible for system and final testing.

There are two ways to move programs into production libraries. Either the source code is moved to production source libraries and recompiled into production executable (load) libraries, or both the source and the executable code are moved directly into the production source and load libraries. Although both practices are common, recompiling source code into production load libraries allows production control or computer operations management to obtain a copy of the source code (compilation listing), to be retained for control purposes.

Normally, production control or computer operations management ensures that the correct program versions are updated to all relevant operational libraries by manually checking the names (and, if relevant, version numbers) of programs listed in the directories of those libraries against logs of current programs.

Library management software can help prevent or detect erroneous changes to software in test libraries. Some packages raise the version number of programs in a library automatically each time they are updated. Consequently, changes to programs after they have been tested will be detected when operations management tries to transfer the version into production libraries and finds that it is not in the test library.

MAINTENANCE CONTROLS

Maintenance controls are intended to ensure that modifications to programmed procedures are designed and implemented effectively. They cover the same areas as implementation controls, but relate to program amendments rather than new applications. Controls should ensure that changes are designed, tested, approved, incorporated, and updated properly and that change requests are handled appropriately.

The procedures concerned with the maintenance of existing systems are the following:

- System change management
- Program testing
- Cataloging

System Change Management

Users and MIS management follow specific procedures to request changes. For example, one individual in each department can prepare requests or represent application owners at meetings with MIS personnel to discuss the need for changes and the methods by which they will be accomplished. A manual or computerized management system, or regular status meetings of MIS management and application owners, or both, ensure that all change requests are addressed and their status tracked.

Program changes should be documented as thoroughly as new systems. System, program, operations, and user documentation should be updated to reflect all changes. Inadequate documentation can result in system errors, unnecessary maintenance time, and inordinate dependence on individual technical staff members. To ensure that the documentation has been updated satisfactorily, it is reviewed and approved by either a quality assurance department or MIS management and application owners.

Testing

A well-controlled organization has policies that require test plan development for every program change and that specify the level of detail, necessary plan approvals, and who should perform the tests. Test plan documentation should include tests to be performed, expected results, and how test data will be developed. Normally, the test plan is reviewed and approved by application owners and MIS management.

Depending on the complexity of the change and its impact on the application system, both users and MIS personnel will determine the appropriate testing techniques: (1) program testing, (2) system testing, and/or (3) parallel testing. Most changes require program and/or system testing. (See earlier section "Implementation Controls" for testing technique descriptions.)

Cataloging

Generally, the transfer of tested programs to production libraries is the same for system implementation and subsequent maintenance. (See earlier section "Implementation Controls" for a description of cataloging procedures.)

COMPUTER OPERATIONS CONTROLS

Computer operations controls are designed to ensure that systems function as planned on an ongoing basis. They include controls over the use of the correct data, programs, and other resources, and the proper performance of this function by operations, particularly when a problem occurs.

Usually, the computer operations department controls the day-to-day functioning of MIS hardware and software. In many organizations, it is assisted by a production control department. Computer operations is responsible for the physical running of the computer system (e.g., mounting files and printer forms and making decisions about computer hardware, such as whether to discontinue the use of a device in the event of a failure). Production control is responsible for job scheduling and set-up.

Computer operations controls consist of the following:

- Scheduling.
- Job set-up and execution.
- Use of correct data files.
- Logs of activity.
- Backup and recovery procedures.

Scheduling

Scheduling entails recording when jobs are to be processed and which data files are to be used. In many data processing installations, scheduling software is used to submit jobs for processing on a predetermined basis (e.g., every day at 3:00 P.M., or the 15th and last day of the month). Other installations use a manual scheduling system. In either case, the job processing schedule is approved by the application owners and operations management when systems are implemented. The schedule is provided to computer operators.

Normally, production control or operations management requires written approval from application owners to run jobs or programs in another sequence. Application owners are required to submit written requests for the scheduling of jobs run "on request only," such as periodic updates to standing data files, and special processing, such as year-end closing routines.

MIS management uses logs (either automated or manual) to monitor computer operators' adherence to the approved schedule. Those logs report jobs scheduled for execution, their scheduled and actual start and completion times, and any abnormal conditions that occurred during execution. When abnormal conditions occur, computer operators prepare problem determination forms for use in investigating the problems and authorizing the appropriate reruns.

If on-line application systems are in operation, scheduling is relevant only to regular batch jobs, end-of-day or period-end runs, and backup and housekeeping activities. The control considerations are whether the jobs are run at the appropriate point in time and in the correct sequence.

Job Set-Up and Execution

Job set-up is the preparation of an application for processing. Programs and data sets must be defined and loaded onto the system, the sequence of events specified, and the devices allocated. Job set-up is an important aspect of computer operations controls primarily because it helps to ensure that the job control statements and parameters are prepared properly and that the correct data files are used.

Typically, operators have written procedures and instructions for all applications and system software. Those instructions are developed and approved by application owners and production control when the system is implemented or modified.

Set-up and execution instructions (e.g., job run books) specify the required job control statements, parameters, data files, and so on. Normally, when an automated job scheduling system is used, it provides for the set-up and submission of batch jobs for processing and prompts the operator for the required files, and so forth. When job set-up is controlled manually, production control provides computer operators with job run books or checklists covering each operator action required.

Typically, production control reviews system-generated or operator-prepared logs to ensure that proper parameters and control statements were used. Special processing or reruns may require temporary departures from approved parameters or control statements, or the use of nonproduction programs. Production control authorizes all such changes and obtains required approvals from application owners and MIS management.

Use of Correct Data Files

In many cases, the normal updating and maintenance controls, described as application controls, ensure that the correct data files are used. However, specific controls over the use of correct files are still necessary. This is true particularly for files that contain tables referred to in processing (e.g., the lists of numbers when sequence checks are used).

Typically, controls over data files require that each file have a unique internal header label that is read by system software and checked by the computer against information in job control statements or a tape management system. Corresponding external labels are affixed to removable storage devices and read by file librarians and computer operators when submitting files to the system. When a data file is larger than one physical tape volume (a multi-volume file), system software checks the internal label of each volume to ensure that all are mounted in the correct sequence.

When a data file requested by a job is incorrect (that is, the requested data file was not on the specified volume), normally the operating system or computer operator will cancel the job. Production control determines the cause of the problem and has corrective actions taken (i.e., rerun a previous job to recreate the correct file). Those actions are reviewed and approved by production control and, where appropriate, by application owners.

Some operating systems allow internal label-checking to be bypassed in emergency situations or to allow the system to copy files being transmitted from an outside source with a different labeling scheme. Bypass label processing (BLP) is specified in JCL. JCL use is specified and monitored by production control or computer operations management. Consequently, production control or computer operations management approves all BLP.

Monitoring Activity

Usually, computer processing and operations are controlled by programmed and manual procedures. In more advanced systems, these procedures are increasingly carried out by software, while manual functions are restricted to actions required or requested by the software. The principal control considerations are that the system software used is reliable and that the manual procedures do not, because of error or other reasons, interfere with or affect normal processing.

In large installations, the computer operations staff often is divided into teams, or shifts, each with an experienced operator designated to supervise operations and approve other operators' actions. Usually, smaller installations do not have supervisors on all shifts, placing greater emphasis on subsequent reviews performed by computer operations management.

A review of operator actions is based on either a computer-produced or manual report, such as a problem log. The system software records, on a file called the system log, details of all activity during processing. Unusual activity, such as hardware malfunction, reruns, the use of utilities, abnormal endings (abends), and the resulting operator actions, can then be investigated. However, the information recorded on system logs is voluminous and technical in nature, so that a full review often is impractical. Packaged audit software is available, or audit software can be created, that will analyze the entries as an aid to audit investigation.

Backup and Recovery Procedures

Backup procedures and arrangements should exist. In the event of a computer failure, the recovery of production programs, system software, and data files should not introduce any erroneous changes into the system. Procedures may involve both MIS and users. Principal techniques used are:

- A facility for restarting at an intermediate stage of processing. This applies to programs terminated before their normal ending and avoids the need to reprocess the whole run.
- A system to copy and store master files and associated transactions files independently, based on how frequently the files change. This makes it possible to restore any files lost or damaged during the disruption.
- Similar procedures to ensure that copies of operating instructions, run instructions, and other essential documentation are available, if the originals are lost.
- Formal instructions for the restoration of processing or transfer to other locations.

(See the section ''Disaster Recovery and Contingency Planning'' in Chapter 30, ''Security Reviews.'')

PROGRAM SECURITY CONTROLS

Program security controls are designed to ensure that unauthorized changes cannot be made to the production programs that process data. They ensure that the only changes are those made through the normal program change procedures. Program security is of special concern to an auditor when an unauthorized change to a program might benefit the person making the change (e.g., a change made in a system processing wages and cash payments that could result in unauthorized payments).

The procedures concerned with security over programs are:

- Software access controls
- Physical access controls
- Division of duties

Software Access Controls

An organization may use system software (e.g., operating system options, security package, program library management package, communications software) to restrict access to program libraries or specific programs in program libraries. Generally, the control techniques used include:

- User identification codes (user IDs) and passwords.
- Restricted menu options.
- Restricted user access levels (e.g., read-only access).
- Restricted terminal or other input/output (I/O) device capabilities.

In modern computer systems, programs can be accessed and altered in a variety of ways. Most organizations use access control software to restrict both on-line and batch processing access. (See Chapter 31, "Logical Access Controls.") Access is restricted not only to specific programs or libraries, but also to:

- Procedure libraries (JCL).
- Access control software files (password and user information).
- System software libraries (system options and parameters and sensitive utilities).
- Log files.

Complete access security requires that all user accesses are logged by the system and monitored by an independent security administration function. Problem situations (e.g., deactivated users and access denials) are identified and followed up on a timely basis. Privileged actions (e.g., the definition of new users, changes to users' privileges, changes to resource definitions and access rules, and security bypasses) are logged by the system and reviewed on a timely basis by security administrations. Daily or weekly reviews of security log data are preferable, but monthly reviews can be adequate for low volumes of activity. Typically, the security administration functions:

- Maintain suitable controls over the design, maintenance, and issuance of users IDs and passwords, and ensure that user IDs and passwords cannot be obtained by unauthorized staff.
- Define and maintain access rules to authorized users.
- Control, issue, and amend password tables.
- Immediately revoke user IDs and passwords when staff leave or are transferred.

All access control systems need users with special system privileges for administration and other important tasks, such as:

- Establishing and changing user IDs.
- Resetting passwords or other secret codes.

- Bypassing access controls (i.e., unrestricted access attributes).
- Changing the security system's status (i.e., from "on" to "off") and access control software options.

Security administration should implement and monitor those special privileges. Normally, a special change request form is used to authorize special privileges. Other techniques used to secure programs include:

- Review of a comprehensive computer report of jobs processed. By comparing this report with the authorized job schedules, any unauthorized accesses of production programs can be identified and investigated. This report should be reviewed and approved by a responsible official.
- Comparison of the production programs with independently controlled copies on a regular basis. These copies, and the software executing the comparison, normally are held in either a permanent, supervised physical library, or off-site at a remote location.
- Periodic running of test data by responsible officials.

Physical Access Controls

Physical controls, together with software access controls, provide extensive control over programs. Control procedures of concern include:

- Restricting physical access to terminals or the access privileges of specific terminals and users. For example, in a warehouse, restricting terminal (and related user IDs) access to physical stock records and enforcing strict time limits on terminal usability.
- Restricting computer room access (via card key or key lock on the door).
- Restricting access to hardcopies of programs.
- Controlling and restricting access to backups of programs and documentation.

Division of Duties

With sufficient technical skill and detailed knowledge of file contents, users can circumvent security and make changes in production programs. Normally, protection against this is enhanced by segregation of duties. When duties are separated, users cannot obtain a detailed understanding of the programs. In addition, those responsible for program development and maintenance cannot gain unsupervised access to production programs. It is important to maintain segregation of duties at all times, even outside normal working hours.

DATA FILE SECURITY CONTROLS

Data file security controls are controls designed to ensure that unauthorized changes cannot be made to data files. The need for data file security controls is likely to be greater for master file data than for transaction data because not all significant master file data elements are subject to regular reconciliation procedures. Any cyclical checking of data on files may not be done often enough to provide timely identification of unauthorized changes.

Data file security controls also are important from an operational standpoint. Considerations include protecting data from destruction or erasure, both accidental and intentional, and from theft or other misuse.

Controls are required for data files both while they are on-line and while being held off-line. On-line data includes tapes and disks that have been loaded for a specific processing run but are otherwise stored off-line, as in batch systems. Data files may also be on disks permanently loaded and available for inquiry or updating, as in on-line and real-time systems. Off-line data files are those held in a separate library.

Software Access Controls

A particular threat to data is unrestricted access that can allow unauthorized change. In batch systems, where data files have been loaded for a specific processing run, the problem is limited to controlling the action of operators during the particular run. On-line and real-time systems, however, require a combination of control techniques, including restricting the access paths into the system and the activities permitted to users. Dial-up systems require particularly high levels of security due to the risk of access by hackers. The appropriate level of access control is determined by the sensitivity of the data, users' divisions of duties, and the resources available.

Access by Users. The control procedures to protect data files from unauthorized access by users during processing are similar to those for programs and can be executed simultaneously. These procedures include system software functions such as library packages, security software, passwords, communications software, and data base management systems.

Access to On-Line Data. When data is entered through a terminal, as it is in on-line and real-time systems, it is essential to protect against unauthorized entry that subsequently will update the data.

The entry of invalid data might be made to either transaction or master file data. Normally, it is entered to alter the effect of a transaction already on file. For example, a fictitious credit note would alter the status of a matching sales invoice on file. Invalid master file data might consist of a complete record, such as a fictitious supplier's account, or a data element, such as a pay or an interest rate.

When data files are on-line, there should be a suitable combination of system software, such as restricting terminals to particular transactions, programs, or files. Only authorized personnel should have access to the files to obtain information or enter alterations.

Access by Production Programs. In addition to user and terminal access controls, procedures should be established to restrict data access by various programs. Access can be restricted through the use of software, including which data elements a program can access, read, and/or update. Reports, generated by the software, of all accesses of the programs can be produced. They should be reviewed and investigated as necessary.

Physical Access Controls. The control procedures related to physical access to data files are similar to those for programs. To secure off-line files from unauthorized access, there should be a lockable storage area separate from the computer room and, preferably, supervised by a librarian responsible for the issue, receipt, and security of all files. Access to the library should be restricted to staff authorized to obtain and deliver files.

Procedures are needed to ensure that files are issued only for authorized processing. Processing schedules that specify the files required for processing should be prepared for all applications and approved by a responsible official. Specific authorization should be required to move files off-site or to another computer.

Each removable storage device, such as a tape, should be given a unique identity number that is recorded permanently on the device. Then, a record of devices can be maintained to account for and control files issued from the library and those created during processing. Records of devices and files can be maintained manually or by system software.

Division of Duties

Just as with program security controls, suitable segregation of duties should be established and maintained for data file security controls. This protects against users circumventing security and making changes in master file or transaction data.

SYSTEM SOFTWARE CONTROLS

System software is the set of computer programs that control the functions of the computer itself, and that make the use of application programs possible. It consists of programs that are not specific to any particular application but which can be used to design, process, and control all applications. It includes operating systems, librarian packages, security packages, data base management systems, and communications software. (See Chapter 27, "System Software.")

System software controls ensure that system software is implemented, maintained, and protected from unauthorized changes properly. The auditor is concerned with system software because programmed procedures within applications, such as access to a data base, involve its use. Many IT controls, such as data file and program security, depend on system software.

The system software that may be relevant to control includes programs that relate to:

- Cataloging.
- Reporting of jobs processed.
- File handling.
- Data communications.
- Reporting of operations.
- File set-up.
- Security protection.
- Library records.
- Data bases.

The controls over system software are discussed in the following sections.

Implementation

The controls required for the successful implementation of system software are similar to those for the implementation of applications programs, except that work is performed by the technical support group (i.e., system programmers), not by application programmers. Specific considerations relating to system software are discussed here.

All vendor-supplied system software should be subject to review and approval by a person who is able to determine the software's impact on existing systems and operating procedures, and whether the software will meet the company's needs and objectives. This review should encompass both basic software packages and available options.

It is imperative to test new system software using the proven application programs with which it will interface. Any anomalies can then be identified as resulting from the system software.

Instructions and other documentation for system software and options supplied by an outside vendor should be reviewed by technically competent personnel. Personnel should make sure that the documentation properly describes the procedures necessary to use and operate the software correctly.

Access to system software should be restricted to authorized users. For example, the technical support group may need to use some utilities and service aids that should not be available to operators or dial-up users.

Maintenance

Maintenance of system software includes changes made by users and vendors. Users' modifications include internally developed routines and changes to options selected within vendor-supplied software. All such modifications to system software are controlled in much the same way as changes to application programs.

Vendor-supplied system software is modified periodically by the vendor and introduced as new programs or amendments to existing programs. New or amended system software is tested to ensure that it operates as intended within an organization's unique MIS environment.

In many organizations, neither the technical expertise nor the tools exist to make amendments to system software. In those circumstances, the risk of unauthorized amendments to the system software is minimal. Where the technical expertise and tools do exist, an organization should establish controls similar to those over application programs. Normally, organizations enforce a division of duties to prevent technical support personnel from obtaining a detailed understanding of the applications processed and of user controls over key files and transactions in those applications. Finally, the work of technical support staff should be closely supervised by technical support management.

Security

Controls similar to those previously described (see earlier section "Program Security Controls") should be applied to ensure that unauthorized changes are not made to system software. Password and security tables, and the means by which they can be changed, require the highest possible level of protection on the system.

FILE CONVERSION CONTROLS

File conversion controls address the conversion of existing data files to new data files for new application systems. They are designed to ensure that the conversion process does not cause data file errors.

To ensure that new or converted data files contain the correct data, a conversion plan should be developed and approved by users and MIS management. The plan should include:

- Design of the conversion process.
- Documentation of any data conversion programs to be written.
- Techniques to be used to validate the results of conversion (e.g., file balancing, one-to-one comparisons).
- Conversion timetable.
- Assignment of user and MIS responsibilities.

The file conversion plan should ensure that the conversion process results in data files that are:

- *Complete*—All data has been converted in the appropriate format to records on the new system.
- *Accurate*—All data is carried forward to the new records, unchanged.
- *Cutoff properly*—Converted data is recorded in the proper time period.

The final results of the conversion process should be reviewed and approved by appropriate users and MIS management.

THE EFFECT OF GENERAL CONTROL WEAKNESSES

To determine whether significant errors can arise, an auditor must consider the effect of a weakness on the programmed procedures or data elements at risk. At-risk are any programmed procedures and data identified as not being checked in detail by the user. Weaknesses in the different areas of IT controls have different effects on the programmed procedures and data, as follows:

- Weaknesses in the implementation or maintenance controls generally cause new or modified systems to function incorrectly. Often, such errors are embedded in the system and erroneous processing continues until errors are identified and corrected.
- Weaknesses in the computer operations controls can cause random errors in the system. Some errors, such as those in master file data, have lasting consequences. The main effect of such weaknesses is similar to the effect of weaknesses in a noncomputer system: Most processing is correct, but occasionally it is not.
- Weaknesses in the program security controls can mean that unauthorized changes can be made to the systems. These are changes that are not subject to normal implementation controls. The organization may not be sure which systems have been changed and which have not. As a result, opportunities for the misappropriation of assets increase.
- Weaknesses in the data file security controls can mean that unauthorized changes can be made to stored data. How long it takes to discover those unauthorized changes depends largely on the structure of the application controls. Some errors in transaction data may be discovered fairly quickly through the operation of control accounts, the mailing of statements, and so forth. In a payment system, the error may never be noticed—particularly if it involves an incorrect overpayment. Usually, errors in master file data take longer to detect. Weaknesses in data file security controls combined with weaknesses in program security controls provide particular opportunities for almost undetectable misappropriation of assets. Weaknesses in data file security controls coupled with weaknesses in the application controls over continuity of the data increase the likelihood that undetected errors will occur.
- Weaknesses in system software controls usually do not have a direct effect on the applications. However, since other IT controls rely on system software controls for proper functioning, weaknesses may mean existing controls are not appropriate. As a result, one or more of the other IT control areas may be weak.

FIG. 13-1
Control deficiencies

Description	Possible Audit Comments	Recommended Audit Procedures
Limited size of staff means that there may be: ■ No segregation between EDP and users. ■ Poor segregation between user departments. ■ Limited number of technical EDP personnel so that there is a poor segregation of duties within EDP. ■ Lack of disciplines over basic controls.	■ For all deficiencies noted evaluate risk areas and design or modify to improve compensating user controls. In addition: a. Implement segregation of duties where possible. b. Review user and operation logs where possible. c. Rotate duties.	■ Extended testing of data with more emphasis on cash systems (such as controls over cash receipts and payments). ■ Evaluate control procedures. ■ Spread tests through year.
A lack of experience in computerized environments may result in a lack of adequate completeness and accuracy controls being built into the system or considered when purchasing package systems.	■ Institute controls over completeness and accuracy. ■ Modify systems to create edit check processing at input time (such as comparison of counts, totals, etc.), range tests, verification of part numbers, display of vendor/part name in response to input of number. ■ Screen design could include use of menus, prompts for missing data, and production of meaningful diagnostics.	■ Extended testing of data to include manual reconciliation of input and update totals and to ensure that data files are footed. ■ Reperformance of input and update transactions.
■ Poor systems, programs, and operations documentation.	■ The organization should review requirements for standards and then develop and adhere to those documentation standards.	■ Gain understanding by discussion with EDP and user departments and, if necessary, with vendor.

(*continued*)

FIG. 13-1 (*continued*)

Description	Possible Audit Comments	Recommended Audit Procedures
	■ Ensure that vendor-supplied systems are documented in accordance with contract terms.	
■ Program and system development may be undertaken on an ad hoc basis with few development standards — or none at all.	■ Establish controls over program development, which will include: a. Review the need for controls. b. Ensure that users are involved. c. Ensure that responsible officials have no conflicting duties.	■ Extended testing of data can include direct tests of significant programmed procedures.
Controls over program data and data file security may be weak due to:		
■ A lack of system software controls over program libraries.	■ Develop and implement controls over program libraries so that all program changes are logged and approved.	■ Copy programs at beginning of year and do comparison with programs at the end of year; investigate differences. ■ Testing of data on data files can be spread throughout the year.
■ Where interpretive languages are used (such as BASIC), the source code is available to the user on execution.	■ Replace interpreters with compilers if possible and restrict use of compilers to authorized program development.	■ Increase tests of data.
■ No notification of unsuccessful log-on attempts; only one level of use.	■ Employ physical security over terminals, such as use of terminal key locks. ■ Change passwords regularly. ■ Review and make full use of the security features available for the particular machine.	

Description	Possible Audit Comments	Recommended Audit Procedures
	■ Restrict terminals as to functions. ■ Inactivate or otherwise restrict special keys. ■ Log access to files and assign file passwords. ■ If secure password system does not exist, program or obtain one.	
■ No restrictions on users entering data and making inquiries using screens.	■ Restrict access to computer and data files.	
■ Utilities are available for entering, changing, and interrogating data, bypassing application controls.	■ Remove data alteration utilities from the system (may be easier said than done) or disable the functions or log their use if the utility cannot be removed.	
■ Destructive program updates so that no program history exists (very common).	■ Manually document program amendments.	
■ Vendor-supplied utilities that may be used to make program patches.	■ Disable functions or restrict their use to exceptional authorized circumstances.	
There may be: ■ Few system software controls to ensure only authorized use.	■ Restrict access to computer.	■ Testing of data can include reperformance of any significant programmed procedures.
■ No controls to ensure that only tested and approved programs are executed against data files.	■ Catalog only tested and approved programs (manual control). ■ Data librarian should not be same individual as operator, and duty may be rotated periodically.	

(continued)

FIG. 13-1 (*continued*)

Description	Possible Audit Comments	Recommended Audit Procedures
Typically, the console log is either nonexistent or too voluminous.	■ Develop adequate system log procedures.	■ Audit software can be used to examine voluminous systems logs.
Inadequate backup and contingency planning.	■ Develop and test backup and contingency plans including design of good recovery method. ■ Performance of backup should be logged (including date of performance, as-of date, and use of file labels). ■ The adequacy of backup and contingency plans should be regularly reviewed.	■ However, this may affect "going concern" consideration.
There may be little or no control over amendments made to vendor-supplied system software.	■ Develop controls over modifications to system software. ■ If possible, ensure that system software programmers are not allowed access to application programs or documentation.	■ Assess risk (there may be none) and increase levels of tests, or extend testing if appropriate.

- Weaknesses in file conversion controls generally mean that the master file data used in the operation of the application may not be correct. This can go undetected by system users.

Reporting General Control Weaknesses

When control weaknesses or deficiencies exist in a system, they may fall into the categories shown in Figure 13-1. These weaknesses are grouped by type of control, possible deficiency, possible audit comments, and recommended audit procedures.

CHAPTER **14**

Application Controls—I

COMPLETENESS OF INPUT

Control Objectives

A well-designed computer system has built-in controls for all of its functions and for all aspects of its operations. One of the most fundamental of these application controls is completeness of input. This is the control designed to ensure that every transaction to be processed is recorded and then entered for processing.

This control is concerned with the actual number of documents and items to be processed. Control is created to meet the following criteria:

- Is every transaction recorded?
- Is every recorded transaction entered into the computer?
- Is every transaction accepted?
- Which items are rejected by the computer?
- Is every transaction entered once and only once?
- Are duplicate items identified?

Those are the objectives. To help achieve them, various control techniques exist that can be used either in batch or on-line systems. These techniques accomplish essentially the same thing, but the way they do it, and their effectiveness, varies.

Controls for completeness are not concerned with the correctness of any details of a transaction, but merely with the act of recording and entering the transaction. Completeness simply means that all of the transactions arrived and were processed as specified. Accuracy relates to the control of the individual data elements that make up each transaction. The reason for the distinction is that the techniques used to control completeness are often different from those used to ensure accuracy, which is also discussed in this chapter.

As an example of how this distinction operates in a payroll system, completeness of input means that every employee who was supposed to be paid was paid, and accuracy of input means that every employee who was paid received the right amount.

There are two parts to these control objectives. The first is to make sure that all transactions are:

- Recorded initially.
- Entered into the computer for processing.
- Accepted by the computer.

Once the transactions are in the computer, the second part of the controls should check the following aspects of completeness:

- All rejected transactions should be reported.
- Each transaction should be processed only once.
- Duplicate transactions should be reported.

All Rejected Transactions Should Be Reported. For example, if a payroll system rejects an employee's time sheet from further processing because the employee number is invalid, the program has discovered and rejected an invalid number, as it should. There are several possibilities why this might occur: The number could be recorded incorrectly on this particular time sheet (which can happen if the numbers are entered by hand each time); the program doing the edit check of valid numbers may be in error; the master file data being matched may be incorrect; or, least likely, the employee does not exist and has been entered on the payroll fraudulently. Whatever the answer, the situation must be resolved and the time sheet reentered. If this is not reported as an exception, it could be that erroneous employee numbers are paid automatically and, as a result, employees could be paid twice, enter false time sheets, and so forth.

Each Transaction Should Be Entered Only Once. The importance of transactions being entered only once is obvious on consideration of the problems a company could experience if, for example, vendor invoices are paid twice. And, of course, the difficulties that can result from duplicate billings may have an adverse effect on customer relations. They can also distort the picture created in the entire system by showing more income potential than actually exists and by indicating that twice as much material was sold, thereby prompting the purchase of more inventory when it is not warranted.

Duplicate Transactions Should Be Reported. If there is a weakness in the reporting of duplicate transactions, they may recur. Once the system properly identifies duplicates, it is important to discover how the duplicates made it that far in processing and to strengthen the controls to ensure that duplicates are not processed in the first place.

Controls for completeness should also include controls designed to ensure that rejected data is resubmitted after the problem has been resolved.

Control Techniques

Various techniques are available to control the completeness of input. The most commonly encountered techniques are:

- Computer sequence check of serially numbered documents.
- Computer matching with previously processed data.
- Agreement of manually established batch controls.
- One-for-one checking of reports.

These techniques, together with tasks that need to be done in the case of rejections, are discussed in the following sections.

Computer Sequence Check

In computer sequence checking, the computer checks the preassigned serial numbers of input transactions and reports missing or duplicate numbers for manual investigation. Ideally, transactions should be recorded on serially prenumbered documents. They can also be sequenced after preparation. The first method is preferred, but is not possible if a document originates outside the organization (e.g., a supplier's invoice).

Computers also record transactions on serially prenumbered documents. For example, when checks have been preprinted with serial numbers, it is necessary to record the actual use of these otherwise blank preprinted checks. The numbers are used by the bank and by the issuer, but they are also entered in a control register in the organization as they are actually used. Before the checks can be filled out by the computer's printer, the check forms must be aligned within the printer, and this almost always means that at least the first, and maybe the second, check is voided because the operator has to set up the top-of-form. The operator then enters the preprinted number of the first check actually used into the check-writing program via the operator's console. As each check is printed, it contains both the preprinted number and the number printed by the computer (if any), which helps control the use of blank check forms. Those numbers should be the same (in some systems they are not) to make control easier. When the computer operator returns any unused forms to the control point, those voided for form alignment also should be returned so that they can be accounted for. In many systems, all of the check numbers are recorded in the computer's check register file by the computer. It can easily tell whether a number has been skipped, which indicates an unrecorded check, or, perhaps less likely in a modern system, whether a number has been used twice. Handwritten checks can also be entered into the system by using a check number sequence. The program must have this routine built in as a way of tracking manually processed checks. In this way both manually prepared and computer-printed checks have an appropriate serial number to enable the checks processed at the bank reconciliation stage to be controlled for completeness of input.

FIG. 14-1

Cumulative sequence check (input)

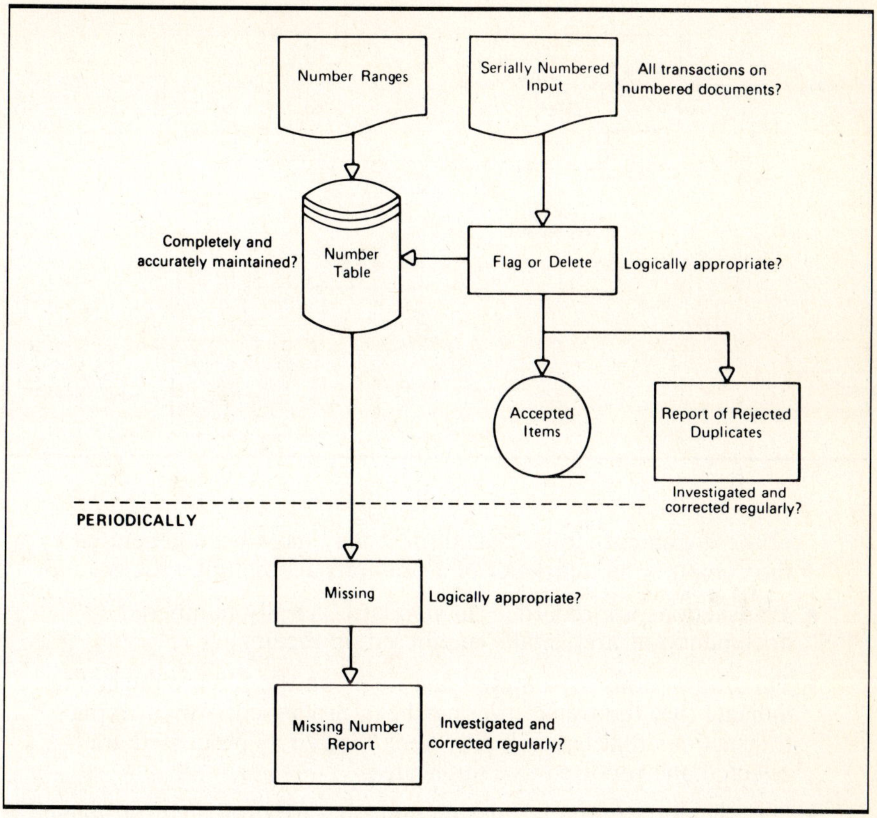

In an on-line system, the transaction may be assigned a sequence number by the edit program upon entry. Computer-assigned sequence numbers can be highly effective in tracing the exact point of cutoff after a processing failure. If such a failure necessitates a restart further back in the processing cycle, it is easier to locate the right place for the restart.

There are different ways to carry out a sequence check. Two of the most widely used are described in the following sections.

Cumulative Sequence Check. A cumulative sequence check, shown in Figure 14-1, typically operates in this way:

- A file is created containing a table of all document numbers that have been issued. This file may be created by entering the numbers

FIG. 14-2
Sequence check on batches (input)

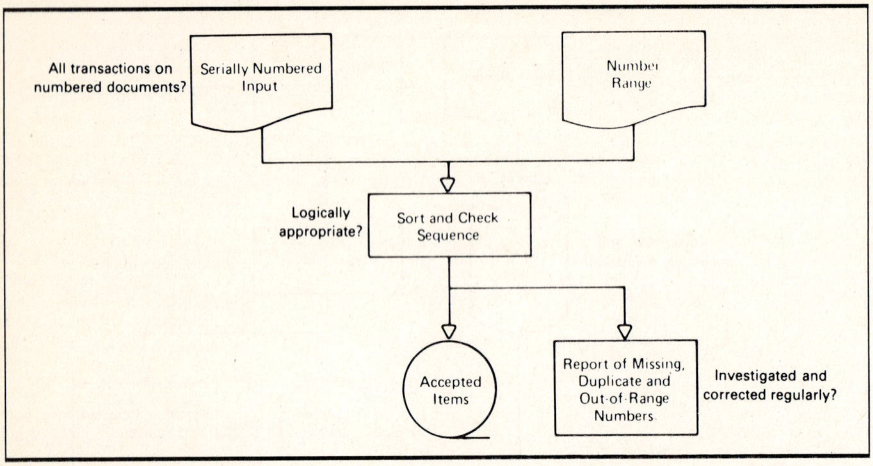

of the documents to be issued, or it may have been generated by the computer as a product of a previous accounting process.

- Transactions are recorded on standard, serially numbered documents, or are serially numbered on receipt.
- The transactions are entered and items on the file are flagged to indicate that the transaction has been processed. Any arriving transactions that have already been flagged as processed are rejected and reported as "duplicates."
- Periodically, reports of missing numbers are produced for manual follow-up.

Batch Sequence Check. In a batch sequence check, shown in Figure 14-2, the sequence of transactions within a batch or file is checked as follows:

- The serially numbered transactions are entered together with the range of the numbers to be checked (the range is the first and last numbers in the particular sequence).
- The computer program first sorts the transactions into numerical order, then checks the documents against the sequence number range and reports missing, duplicate, and out-of-range transactions.

For computer sequence checking to be effective as a control technique, the following user controls and programmed procedures must be present:

- There must be adequate procedures to ensure that all forms are indeed numbered after completion or, if practical, that all transactions are recorded on serially prenumbered forms.
- The method used in the program for checking the numerical sequence must be logically appropriate and understood by the user department. In this context, procedures are required to deal with:
  - —Changes or breaks in sequence.
  - —More than one sequence running concurrently (such as when different locations use different blocks of numbers).
  - —Identification and reporting of duplicate numbers.
- When a suspense file of missing numbers is maintained, there should be adequate controls to ensure that unauthorized adjustments are not made to this file.
- Reports of missing and duplicate numbers must be produced frequently to allow for prompt follow-up action to correct the error.
- There must be adequate manual procedures to investigate missing numbers. Any rejected duplicates must be manually checked. Then they are cancelled or reentered, depending on the outcome of the investigation.
- A cumulative sequence check is easier to operate, since it rejects all duplicates and keeps reporting overdue items. If the sequence check is not cumulative, then specific manual procedures are needed to check for duplicates in different runs and to ensure that each item reported as missing is followed up.
  - —Changes or breaks in sequence for the batch-type sequence check ranges should also be verified, manually or by a computer program, to ensure that sequence continuity is maintained from computer run to run, subject only to new sequences issued.

Computer Matching

The computer matching technique is shown in Figure 14-3. It consists of the computer matching of input data with information held on master or suspense files. Unmatched items are reported for manual investigation.

As an example, the computer might match an employee's time sheet details, as entered, against a payroll master file. Then it would identify and report missing or duplicate time sheets. Or, the computer might match suppliers' invoices with a file of goods received details and report invoices for which goods have not been received. In these examples, the matching process is an effective control over the completeness of input. As a result of the first, all time sheets and employees will be accounted for, and in the

FIG. 14-3
Computer matching (input)

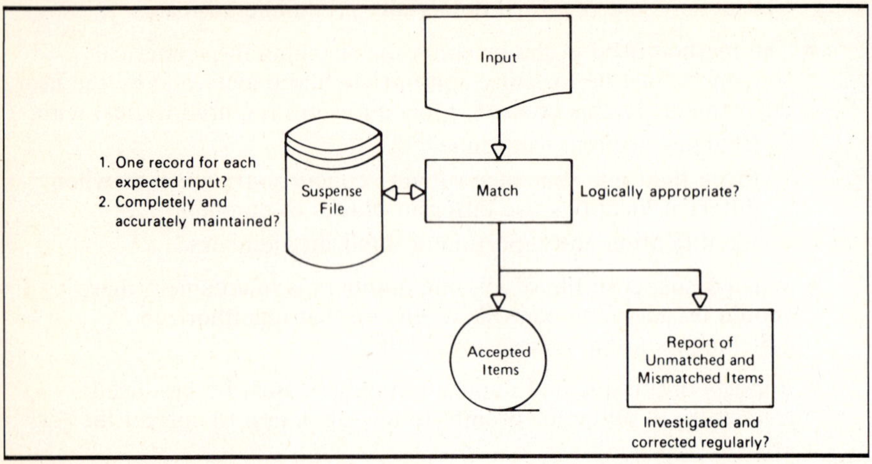

second, invoices for goods not received will not be processed for payment until the goods have been located.

Computer matching is especially useful in on-line systems because the system has the ability to match with up-to-date master or suspense files during editing.

For this control technique to be effective, the following user controls and programmed procedures must be present:

- There must be adequate controls over the file holding details of items to be matched. This is usually achieved by a regular agreement of file totals with an independent control account.
- All adjustments to the data on file should be properly authorized. For example, partial shipments in an accounts payable system need special authorization.
- The method used in the program for matching must be logically appropriate and approved by the system users. The number of data elements matched must be sufficient to make the transaction unique. For example, matching a date is usually inappropriate, since many transactions can have the same date. Matching an invoice number may also be inappropriate if there are many branches, all of which use the same range of invoice numbers. In this case, to make them unique, a possible solution is to add the branch number to the invoice number, creating a unique transaction number.

- The matched items must be appropriately indicated on the reference file to permit production of a report listing unmatched items.
- Manual procedures must be adequate to follow up outstanding and mismatched items. If reports contain a cumulative list of outstanding items, control over investigation is easier.
- The current generation of file holding details of items to be matched must be used. If an older file were used, many mismatches would turn up, merely because the file would be out of date.

Batch Controls

The batch control technique involves manually grouping transactions at the input stage and establishing a control total over the group. This control total can be based on document count, item count, dollar totals, or hash totals.

For totals of transactions, the methods used may be one or more of the following:

- *Document counts*—A simple count of the number of documents entered, which is agreed to the number of documents processed. A count is normally the minimum level required to control completeness of input. It is not sufficient if more than one transaction can appear on a document.
- *Item or line counts*—A count of the number of items or lines of data entered (such as a count of the number of items or lines on a sales invoice). The number of items or lines is agreed to the number processed.
- *Dollar totals*—An addition of the dollar value of items in the batch, which is agreed to the dollar value of items processed.
- *Hash totals*—An addition of any numeric data existing for all documents in the batch, which can be checked against the total of the same numeric data fields for items processed (such as total of quantities, total of part numbers, total of all numeric fields entered).

The use of batch totals is a common control technique in batch processing systems. It has also proven effective in on-line systems where documents are entered as received. A batch concept is created by choosing a time frame in which transactions are entered and treating it as a batch. There are a number of different ways batch totaling may be carried out.

FIG. 14-4

Batch totals and batch register—Manual reconciliation (input)

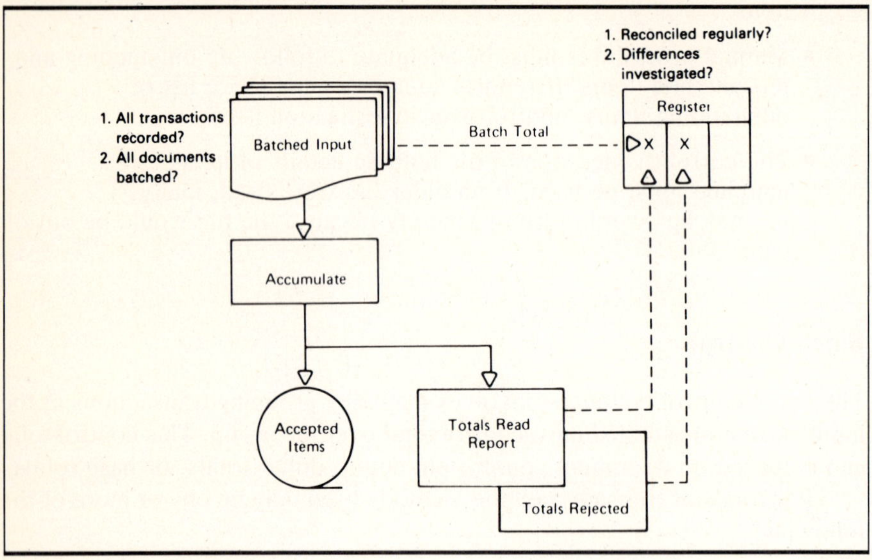

Manual Agreement of a Batch Register. This technique, illustrated in Figure 14-4, is used in the following manner:

- The batch total is established manually and recorded in a register or batch control book.
- The batch is entered to the computer, accumulated, and the batch total printed.
- The total printed is agreed manually to the total recorded in the register or control book.
- Procedures are required for adjusting the batch totals in the register or control book for rejected items.

Computer Agreement of Batch Totals. This technique, illustrated in Figure 14-5, is used in the following manner:

- The batch total is established manually and entered on a batch header slip with the batch.
- The application program accumulates the batch total and compares it with the total entered. (This technique is sometimes referred to

FIG. 14-5
Batch totals—Computer batch balancing (input)

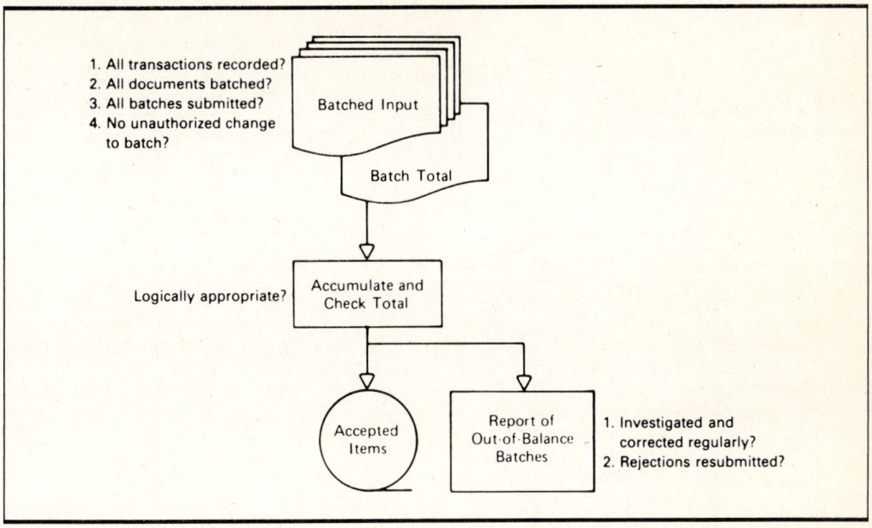

as zero-batch balancing, since the total of the batch minus the total on the batch header should be zero.)

- A report is produced that normally contains details of each batch, together with an indication of whether the totals agreed or disagreed.
- Batches that do not balance are normally rejected. Some applications write the batch to a suspense file pending the reentry of corrected items.

Manual Agreement of a Control Account. This method, which is illustrated in Figure 14-6, is a variation on the use of a batch register and works in the following manner:

- Totals of all types of transactions that update the master file (such as invoices, credit notes, cash, and adjustments) are established during an initial edit program prior to the program that would update the master file. These totals are established in the same way as for manual agreement of a batch register.
- The totals are recorded in a control account.
- Transactions are entered and processed in the master file.
- Periodically, the balance on the control account is agreed manually

FIG. 14-6

Manual agreement of a control account (input and update)

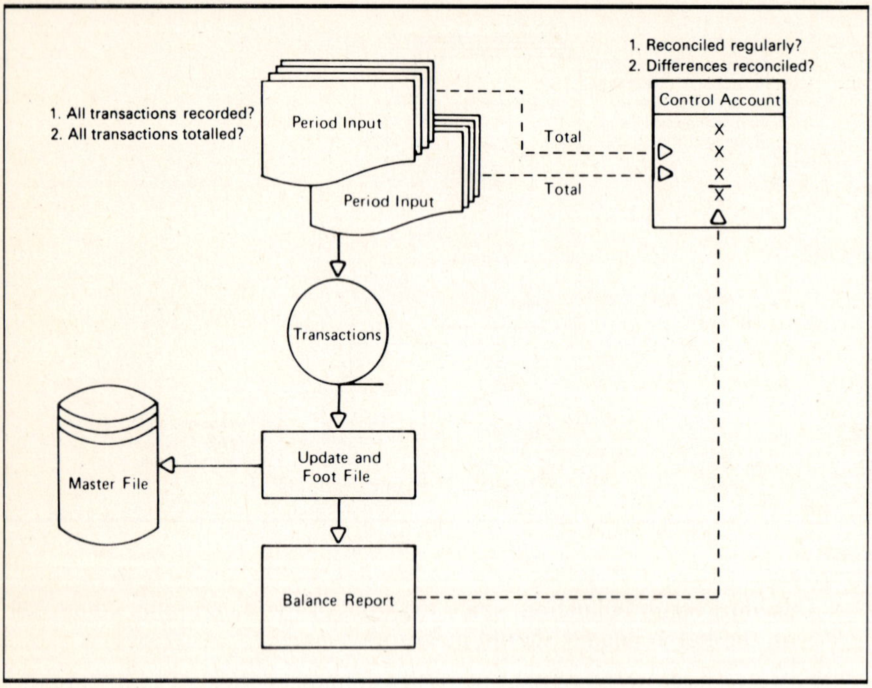

to an accumulation of all individual balances on the master file. For example, in an accounts payable system, each vendor on the vendor master file might have a data element designated as month-to-date payments. A total of all the vendor month-to-date payments should agree to the total paid to all vendors, calculated from each batch of checks written during that month.

This method, as well as ensuring completeness of input, also ensures completeness of update (discussed in Chapter 15, ''Application Controls—II,'' under the heading ''Completeness of Update'').

Batch totaling is effective as a technique when the following user controls and programmed procedures are present:

- There should be adequate controls to ensure that a document is created for each transaction.
- There should be adequate controls to ensure that all documents are batched.

FIG. 14-7
One-for-one check (input)

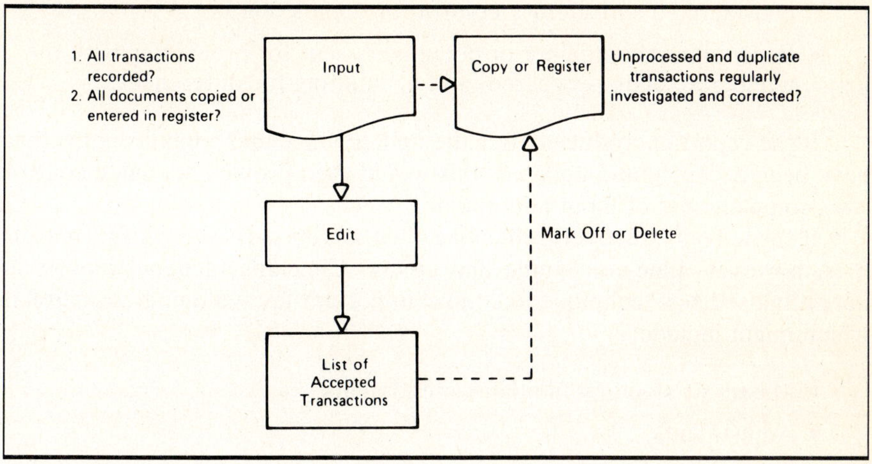

- There should be adequate controls to ensure that all batches are submitted for processing (such as a manual or computer sequence check on batch numbers).
- The user should determine that all batches have been accepted by the computer.
- When computer agreement of batch totals is used, there should be adequate evidence printed that the checking was carried out.
- There should be adequate procedures for the investigation and correction of differences disclosed by the input reconciliations. These procedures must be performed on a timely basis.
- There should be adequate procedures for the resubmission of all rejections.

One-for-One Checking

This technique, illustrated in Figure 14-7, consists of checking each individual document or source document with a detailed listing of items processed by the computer. To rely on this technique, it is necessary to ensure that all documents are submitted for processing. This is usually achieved by one of the following methods:

- Retaining a copy in the originating department of all documents sent for processing. The report is then checked with the retained copy, and missing items are followed up. Checking against copies returned from data processing does not guard against forms being mislaid before they are entered, and therefore cannot be considered a satisfactory control for completeness.

- Reconciling the number of documents sent for processing with the number actually processed, and accounting for differences.

If the report is produced after the update stage and contains items that have been accepted and updated, this would then provide adequate control over completeness of input and update.

If carried out effectively, checking of detail reports is a powerful control; it is, however, time-consuming and costly. Checking of detail reports is normally used as a technique to control important low-volume transactions, which might include:

- Master or standing file data amendments.
- Adjustments.

For checking of reports to be effective as a control technique, the following user controls and programmed procedures should be present:

- There should be adequate controls to ensure that all documents are submitted for processing (such as checking output with retained copies by sequence checking or by document counts).
- There should be regular review of source documents to detect unprocessed items.
- Missing or duplicate items disclosed by the checking process should be identified and followed up promptly.

Rejections

The data entered for processing in a computer system often contains incorrect items. Particularly in batch processing, it is not possible or practical to investigate and adjust each incorrect item as it occurs during processing. It is usually faster to have the computer continue processing the batches on hand as it handles input errors. This is frequently done in two ways:

1. The computer rejects the items or particular batch from further processing, with no record other than a report of the rejections.
2. The computer rejects the items or particular batch from further processing, but maintains error suspense files within the computer system of items awaiting correction. It then produces cumulative reports of all uncleared items on the error files. This is illustrated in Figure 14-8.

FIG. 14-8
Error suspense files for rejections (input)

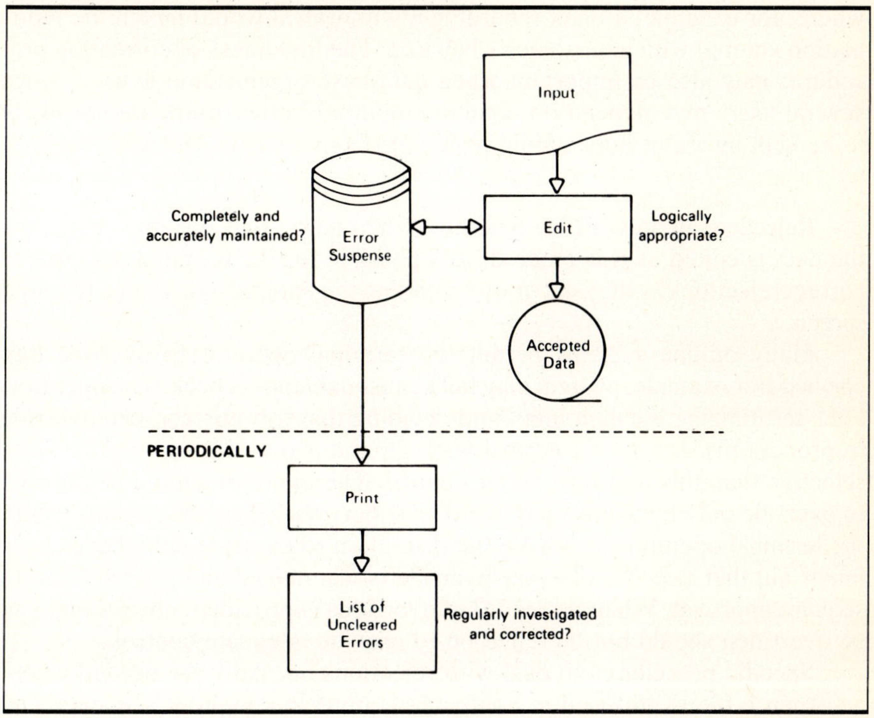

When data is not rejected but is identified, reported, and carried through processing in the normal way, the report must be investigated. Corrective action is necessary only if the transaction was in fact wrong. However, this method is not preferred. It is usually not good system design to identify problems and continue processing unless the problems are minor in nature. If there is a real problem, then another transaction has to be entered to back out the transaction in error before reentering the correct transaction. Detailed procedures are required to ensure that:

- Rejection reports and items held on error files are promptly investigated, and rejections are corrected and resubmitted.
- Previously established control totals are adjusted in relation to the rejected data.

The timely correction of rejections is important in real-time systems where input data is matched with master files for validity. If rejections were left uncorrected, the master files would not be up-to-date when the validity of subsequent input is checked. This would be of particular importance where, for example, a bank recording a withdrawal would match the information entered with a customer's balance. The timeliness of correction procedures may also be important when data base organization is used, since several users may depend on common input and other users are not likely to be kept aware of outstanding rejections from a particular user's area.

Rejections in an On-Line System. When an on-line system is used and the data is edited as it is entered, it is possible for the terminal operator to correct rejections as they occur by amending the entered data on the terminal screen.

Many on-line systems permit the terminal operator to override edit checks. For example, an item may fail a reasonableness check. The operator, after scrutinizing the data input and deciding that it is correct, can override to process the data in the normal way. Operator overrides should be more selective than this to afford better control. The operator should be allowed to override only by using a password or supervisor's key. In systems where the terminal operator does have the discretion to override edit checks, it is important that a record of every override is maintained and printed for subsequent approval. When no record of overrides is provided, checks that can be overriden should not be relied on to provide adequate control.

Specific procedures to deal with rejections normally are needed where a suspense file is not used to control rejections in computer sequence and matching techniques, or where batch totals form the input control. Checking of detail reports, computer sequence checking, or computer matching techniques that use a suspense file of accumulated rejections serve as adequate controls over rejections because these techniques usually continue to identify items that are unprocessed, missing, or unmatched. This may not be the case when other techniques form the control, because the computer may not store, or report details of rejected items or batches.

ACCURACY OF INPUT

Control Objectives

There is a difference between controls designed to ensure completeness of input and those designed to ensure the accuracy of that data. Controls for accuracy of data are concerned with the data on the transactions being processed. Controls for completeness are mainly concerned with whether a transaction is processed at all.

FIG. 14-9
Controls over accuracy of input

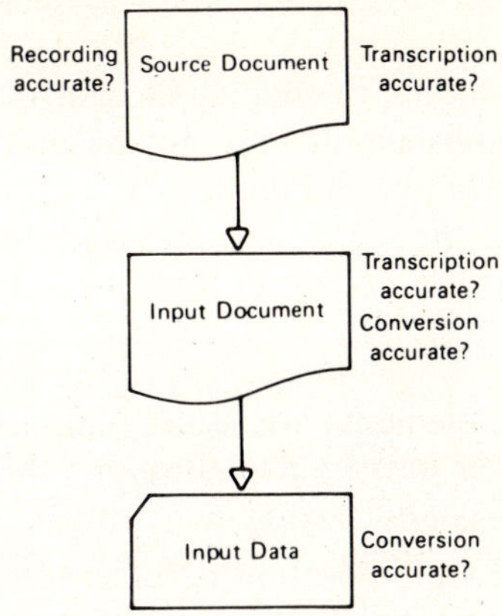

Controls over accuracy of input, shown in Figure 14-9, are designed to ensure that:

- The initial recording of data is correct.
- Where applicable, the data from source documents to input documents is transcribed accurately and the data is converted accurately into machine-readable form.

The requirement to control accuracy is greater at the data entry stage than during processing and updating, since data typically does not become corrupted or unintentionally changed during processing. For example, during key entry, an employee number might be erroneously recorded. It should be rejected during subsequent edit checks because it fails to match any employee number on file. Another example might be the inclusion of an alpha character in an all-numeric employee number. Or perhaps a keystroke error transposes two digits in an employee number, inadvertently matching it to another number in the master file. This type of error, which might be caught by an edit program looking for duplicate time sheets, might escape detection if one of the employees had not worked that week. A review by the payroll clerk to ensure that each time sheet processed produced a paycheck is one manual control that would catch such a compounded type of error that the computer might not catch.

Data to Be Controlled

All important data elements or fields should be controlled to effect real accuracy. Initially, therefore, it is necessary to decide which data elements are the important ones.

After that has been done, the degree of control necessary for each element must also be established. It may not be practical to achieve an exhaustive degree of control over all data.

Which elements are the important ones and the degree of control necessary for each element are not necessarily obvious. To find out, use the following guidelines:

- All financial data elements are usually important (such as values or elements that enter into a calculation of value, such as hours, quantities, and discount codes).
- Less obvious but still important is reference data, such as account numbers, dates, and indicators. Examples of the importance of reference data fields are:
  - — Reference numbers. The accuracy of reference numbers such as those for personal accounts, inventory lines, and general ledger codings is important to ensure that the correct accounts are updated. The accuracy of inventory line numbers is likely to be particularly important to ensure that pricing is carried out on correct balances, incorrect orders are not automatically generated, and unnecessary physical count adjustments are not created.
  - — Dates. The accuracy of dates can obviously be important. Dates held as master file data may initiate a computer accounting process. For example, the discount date may trigger a check to be produced as payment for a bill prior to the time the discount would be lost. Failure to enter dates accurately may lead to loss of revenue or inability to successfully carry out control procedures. Dates entered as part of transactions may also be important. For example, in the case of sales or inventory transactions, computer aging of customers and inventory balances is an essential part of controlling the revenue flow.
  - — Indicators. The accurate entry of indicators (such as special codes to indicate transaction types to the program) can also be important. The type of transaction is often identified by an indicator. An error could lead to an effect that is the opposite of the one intended. For example, in wage and salary or payroll systems it is common for the same form to be used for new hires and for terminated employees. A different indicator shows whether the person is a new hire or a termination. Indicators can also be important from a control point of view. For

example, where an inventory item is defined as a high-risk or high-security item, it is entered with an indicator, so that the program will select it to be counted more frequently than low-security items.

Control Techniques

Various techniques are used to control the accuracy of data input. The most widely used are as follows:

- Completeness control techniques used for accuracy.
- Programmed edit checks.
- Prerecorded input.
- Key verification.

Completeness Control Techniques

Although the objective of controlling accuracy of input is different from controlling completeness of input, some of the techniques used are identical. The applicable completeness of input controls described earlier are listed here, together with a description of the circumstances in which they can control accuracy.

- *Computer matching.* Computer matching can be effective as a control for accuracy, but it establishes the accuracy of only those elements matched by the program. Often several fields are matched by the program, each of which is therefore controlled in this way.
- *Batch totals.* The agreement of manually established batch totals can control the accuracy of those data fields that are totaled and agreed. This does not, however, guard against the possibility of compensating errors in one or more individual items. It is unusual, because of the time that would be involved, to establish batch totals over a large number of fields. Batch totals of numbers of documents or line items do not control for accuracy.
- *Checking of detail reports.* The checking of detail reports can control the accuracy of those fields covered in the detailed checking. Often several data fields are covered by the checking and can be controlled in this way. Data should be checked with the original input documents retained by the user department. This provides the only adequate control over accuracy of input and/or update.

Programmed Edit Checks

As seen in the preceding list, it is unusual for completeness control techniques to cover all important data elements. Programmed procedures are often used to check the accuracy of other data.

Programmed procedures of this kind are usually called edit checks. Edit programs often include several checks, which can be ingenious and powerful. At the program specification stage, it is important to ensure that all appropriate checks are included in the program and that the logic of the checks is correct. Powerful editing is usually easier to achieve in on-line systems, since a variety of data is available for reference at the data entry stage.

In many cases, edit checks cannot provide conclusive proof that only accurate data is accepted. However, a suitable combination of edit checks may be very helpful in reducing the likelihood of error.

Sometimes data may be entered on-line by an operator who is not from the originating department. Under these circumstances, there is a danger that the operator may incorrectly adjust a transaction that fails an edit check, so close supervision is required.

It may also be possible to override edit checks. In such cases, the system should be designed to ensure that all instances of override are suitably reported for investigation by users. The reasons an override was used should be included in the system's documentation.

For reasonableness checks to be effective as a control for accuracy, the following user controls and programmed procedures should be present:

- The method used in the program for relating data and identifying exceptional items should be logically sound.
- Where data referred to in the edit check is entered by means of parameters, adequate controls are required to ensure that the correct parameter data is used each time.
- Periodically, any parameters used should be reviewed by the user department. This is particularly true when the parameters are variables.

For existence checks to be effective as a control, the following user controls and programmed procedures should be present:

- The allocation of codes to transactions should be checked.
- The method used in the program for validating the input data should be logically appropriate.
- The file holding any referenced standing data should itself be adequately controlled.

- Reports of transactions failing the edit should be produced at regular intervals. Positive reporting methods should be employed so that the user knows that all such reports are received.
- There should be adequate procedures for the investigation of the exceptional items reported.

The most common types of programmed edit checks are the following:

- Reasonableness checks
- Dependency checks
- Existence checks
- Format checks
- Mathematical accuracy checks
- Range checks
- Check digit verification
- Document reconciliation
- Prior data matching

Reasonableness Checks. These are checks to test whether the contents of the data entered fall within predetermined limits. The limits may describe a standard range or may be determined in relation to previous input. Data that fails such a check is not necessarily wrong but is considered sufficiently suspicious to require further investigation.

Reasonableness checks can often be applied to data fields (such as dates and indicators) that are difficult or impractical to control in any other manner.

An example of the use of a standard range is frequently encountered in payroll applications where the input is the number of hours worked. The computer program identifies and reports employees who have worked more than a given number of hours and, less frequently, fewer than a given number of hours.

Following is an example of a reasonableness check by reference to previous input. A computer program identifies new items taken into stock in instances where the price of the stock item is unusually high or low in relation to previous prices. The data referred to for the reasonableness check may be held on a file (as with the price example discussed previously), included in the computer program (as in the range limits possibly used in the preceding wages example), or input at run time (the more likely approach in the wages example). Reasonableness checks are illustrated in Figure 14-10.

FIG. 14-10

Examples of programmed validity and edit checks: reasonableness, dependency, and existence checks

	Input Data	Reasons for Failing Validity Check	Stored Data
REASONABLENESS CHECK	Date received: 021183 (MMDDYY)	Must be received today or before.	System date: 021282
	Hours worked: 72	Hours exceed normal maximum.	Maximum hours: 55
	Stock cost $/unit: 010.25	New inventory cost exceeds previous price by more than 10%.	Previous cost $/unit: 001.25
DEPENDENCY CHECK	Date received: 81067 (YYDDD)	Expiration date exceeds date received by more than the shelf life of 4 months.	Shelf life: 00120 (YYDDD)
	Expiration date: 83159 (YYDDD)		
EXISTENCE CHECK	Department numbers:		Valid department numbers:
(Matching)	169		169
	224	Department 224 is invalid.	214
	598		598
	624		624

Note: 1. Stored data must be correct.
2. Program must be logically correct and must report all failures.

Dependency Checks. These are checks to test whether the contents of two or more data elements or fields on a transaction bear the correct logical relationship. Considerable ingenuity can be required in devising checks of this nature. They can provide a strong control over the accuracy of the fields concerned when properly designed and implemented.

As an example, when entering details of a loan agreement, there should be a logical relationship between the amount advanced, the number of repayments to be made, and the repayment installments. As with reasonableness checks, dependency checks are often applied to dates and indicators. Dependency checks are also illustrated in Figure 14-10.

Existence Checks. These are checks to test that the data codes entered agree with valid codes held on the file or in the program.

As an example, when purchase invoices are processed, they require the allocation of a general ledger code and an accounts payable code. On input, the program checks that the codes allocated exist as valid account numbers in the general and accounts payable ledgers. Items that do not match are reported.

Existence checking is usually limited to the control of reference numbers or, occasionally, indicators. It is not, on its own, a complete control, since it does not detect the entry of an incorrect but valid code. Further controls are required. Careful construction of codes can reduce the possibility of erroneous but valid codes being entered. The code should be sufficiently complex. The use of check digits (see the section entitled "Check Digit Verification") or alphanumeric codes can assist in adding the needed complexity. The use of check digits often occurs in conjunction with existence checks. In this case, the use of the check digit complements the existence check by making the number more complex. It is therefore more likely that an incorrect number will be identified, especially when the error is a transposition of numbers. Existence checks are also illustrated in Figure 14-10.

Format Checks. These check the format (existence of expected numeric or alphabetic characters) of a transaction. They ensure that all required data is present. Checks of this nature are often included for operational reasons and may assist in ensuring that reference data, such as dates and indicators, is present.

All numeric data should be properly subjected to format checks. However, since format checks usually only determine that data complies with certain wide general rules, it is unlikely that they will be of much help in the control of the accuracy of data. Format checks are illustrated in Figure 14-11.

Mathematical Accuracy Checks. These check the calculations performed, as shown in Figure 14-11.

Range Checks. These check to see whether a number falls within a predefined set of numbers, or the range, as shown in Figure 14-11.

Check Digit Verification. This technique is used to control the accuracy of input of reference numbers. A check digit is designed to prevent an incorrect, but valid, match. The numbers are constructed in such a way that the last digit bears a mathematical relationship to the preceding digits. As transactions are entered, the computer checks that the reference number contains this relationship. This is especially useful if the table of valid codes,

FIG. 14-11

Examples of programmed edit checks: format check, mathematical accuracy check, range check, check digit verification, and document reconciliation

			Input Data	Reasons for Failing Edit Check
FORMAT CHECK	Reference number:		122 476	Embedded blank.
	Dollar value:		00013A4	Nonnumeric.
	Name:		______	Must enter (cannot be blank).
MATHEMATICAL ACCURACY CHECK			$ Value	
	Invoice:	Goods	2000.00	
		Tax	10.00	
		Total	2100.00	Does not foot.
RANGE CHECK	Date:		131381	Month 13 is illegal (out of range).
CHECK DIGIT VERIFICATION	Employee numbers:		046176	*Modulus 11 check digit* 6 × 1 = 6 7 × 2 = 14 1 × 3 = 3 6 × 4 = 24 4 × 5 = 20 0 × 6 = 0 Total is 67, not divisible by 11. Should be 046167.
DOCUMENT RECONCILIATION	Document number:		1394	
	Code:		17	
	Value:		1732.59	
	Hash total:		2144.59	Hash total does not foot.

Note: Program must be logically correct and must report all failures.

against which existence is checked, is not available on-line. Check digit verification is also illustrated in Figure 14-11.

Alphanumeric codes, which are combinations of letters and digits, can function in a manner similar to check digits, since alphabetic characters have a numeric value in the system. When these, or numbers edited with existence checks as described previously, are constructed with check digits, it avoids the possibility of a number in error matching with a valid code. If existence can be checked on input, it is not necessary to also apply these computational checks.

Document Reconciliation. This technique, which is common in on-line systems, involves checking the mathematical accuracy of the entry of the numeric data on transactions.

In effect, each transaction is treated as a batch. Prior to entry, a hash total is established of all, or all important, numeric data elements on the document. The total is recorded on the document and the document entered, usually through a terminal.

Then, the program totals the data and checks the result with the hash total. Transactions that do not balance are not accepted. The terminal operator can see on the terminal screen if an input error was made and, if so, correct it. If the error is the result of an incorrect hash total, the document should be returned to the originating department for correction. Document reconciliation is illustrated in Figure 14-11.

Prior Data Matching. Neither existence checks nor check digit verification can tell when an incorrect but valid reference number has been entered. To overcome this drawback, prior data matching is used. This technique is commonly used for the control of master file data amendments and works in the following way:

- The new data to be processed is entered, together with the old data, which is to be superseded. For example, if the price of an inventory item is to be amended, the product reference number is entered with both the new price and the price to be replaced.
- The computer matches the product number and the old price as entered with those held on the file. If a match is obtained, the new data is updated to the file.
- If a match is not obtained, the item is reported for investigation.

This technique ensures that the correct product number is updated. It controls the accuracy of which reference field is entered, but not the accuracy of the new information being put on the file. For example, in this case it cannot ensure that the new price is accurate, only that the correct item received a new price. Prior data matching is illustrated in Figure 14-12.

Prerecorded Input

Errors frequently arise during the initial recording of a transaction. By preprinting certain information fields on blank document forms, these errors can be reduced. Of course, there should be strict control over the accuracy of the initial design of prerecorded data included on the documents.

Another approach is to use optical character recognition (OCR), mark

FIG. 14-12
Prior data matching

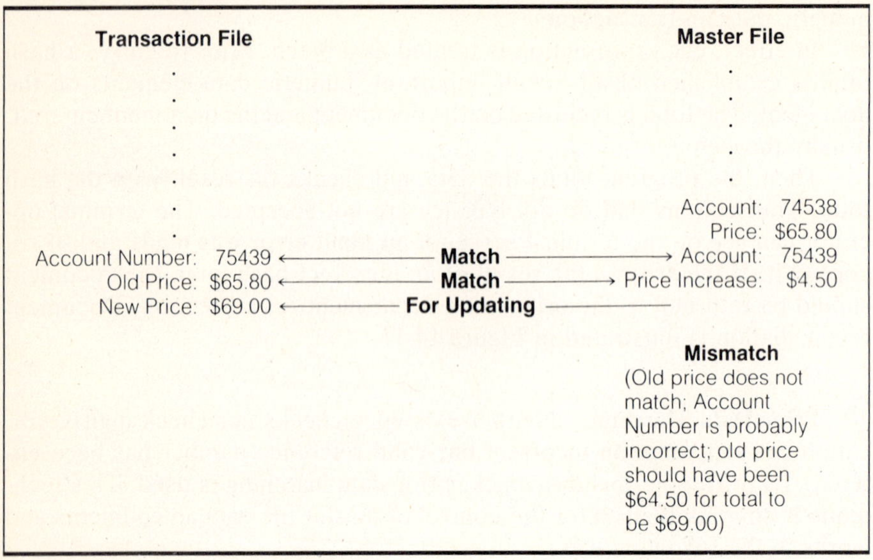

sensitive (OMR), or magnetic ink character (MICR) forms. These make the input form itself machine-readable and avoid the errors inherent in keying.

Control over both initial recording and conversion to machine-readable form will be adequate for the above types of prerecorded input, as long as:

- The particular edit software used is appropriate to identify, report, and reject any incorrect input forms from further processing.
- User procedures include the investigation, correction, and reentry of rejected data. If documents are damaged, which precludes use of the original input technique, there must be alternate procedures readily available to ensure the accuracy of such input.

Examples of prerecorded information include:

- Preprinted serial numbers used in a computer sequence check.
- Preprinted MICR customer numbers on bank checks.
- Preprinted transaction-type indicators, identifying different document types.
- Preprinted department, branch, depot, division indicators, and so on, on all documents used by that department.

FIG. 14-13
Using prerecorded input

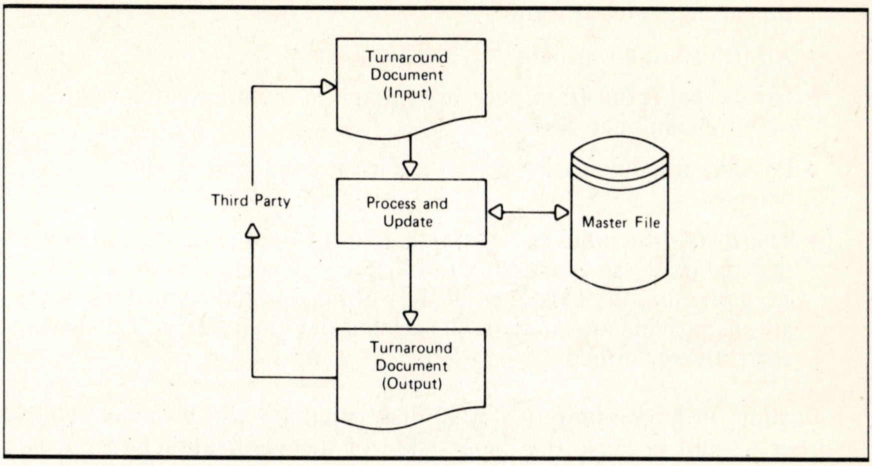

- Magnetically encoded credit cards used to identify customers at bank terminals or retail point-of-sale (POS) terminals.
- Preprinted payment advice forms, which are sent to customers with the request that they return the form with the payment. When the payment amount is preprinted, the payment requires special handling if a different amount is in fact paid.

Turnaround documents can also be used as input documents. The payment advice form sent to customers is a familiar example of what is often called a turnaround document. This is a document that is produced by the computer for subsequent entry to its own or a related system. The use of turnaround documents is illustrated in Figure 14-13.

Key Verification

Key verification is a common technique for controlling the conversion of information from input documents into machine-readable form. It is normally used for key entry, and involves a repetition of the keying-in process by a separate individual using a machine that checks the results of the keystrokes with what was originally keyed. (In some on-line systems, the equivalent of key verification is performed on-screen.) The technique usually is of limited use in the absence of the other techniques discussed previously because:

- The technique checks only the actual keying process. Errors at other stages of the input cycle are not covered (such as errors in preparing the input form).
- All fields are not usually key verified.
- Errors that result from poor interpretation of handwritten figures often remain undisclosed.
- Possibly fraudulent changes to the input document are not detected.
- There are difficulties in supervising verification personnel to ensure that the process is carried out effectively. Experience shows, for example, that the existence of the verification indicator does not always provide adequate evidence that the keying-in process was correctly performed.

Verification on key-to-tape or key-to-disk machines can be more reliable than key-to-card because the supervision of the verification process is a programmed procedure, which can be more effectively controlled.

Rejection Handling

The procedures for handling rejected transactions are usually the same for transactions reported for completeness or for accuracy. The rejection procedures are discussed in the earlier section entitled "Rejections."

CHAPTER **15**

Application Controls—II

VALIDITY OF TRANSACTIONS

Control Objectives

It is essential that only valid transactions, authorized by management and representing economic events that actually occurred, be written to master files, printed on reports, or incorporated in records. Thus, all data should be appropriately authorized or checked.

Control Techniques

It is the controls over validity that are so important in preventing fraud that could occur because of unauthorized transactions being entered into the system. These transactions include any transaction that is not properly authorized, never occurred, or is otherwise not genuine. Certainly, with a computer system that does not question the validity of transactions, it is simple to enter unauthorized transactions. The possibility also exists for the computer to be used to create fictitious transactions that, when processed, look very real.

Possibly the largest detected computer fraud involved the Equity Funding Corporation of America, where millions of dollars' worth of false transactions were entered into the system. More than 20 officers of the company were involved in the case, in which invented insurance policies with fictitious documentation were entered into the regular system as if they were real and then sold to reinsurers. Claims for "deaths" were entered to collect cash. As any premiums came due, more policies were invented and sold. This pyramid grew to incredible proportions; in the 19733 annual report, Equity claimed almost 100,000 policyholders and over $730 million in assets. Only a third of the policies were real. Yet, these transactions were processed as valid because many company people were involved and whatever controls existed were circumvented.

A validity control can be built into a computer application system to test transactions against predetermined conditions, often established as a result of reviewing historical data. For example, an insurance company may decide to monitor the premiums for all policies falling into a certain category. It is important to ensure that they are valid by matching them with the expected increase for the policy type. If it is not within the expected range, the policy should be rejected.

Sometimes validity of transactions can be ensured by matching an organization's data to other data. An example of this technique is when a store that accepts bank credit cards checks a transaction with the bank systems.

The most difficult transaction to detect is the transaction that appears genuine and passes all of the checks and controls. Historical information can assist in determining whether transactions are really valid. An example is a last-in, first-out (LIFO) inventory system, where inventory is costed out at the most recent purchase price. The inventory application programs can compare the current cost to previous cost, looking for stock with an abnormal increase or decrease in purchase prices.

Validity controls can also help ensure that all assets are fairly represented. Although a transaction may be valid, sometimes the computer programs, due to established criteria, conclude that a transaction is invalid. A familiar example is that an inventory system may refuse to allow the balance-on-hand (BOH) to go to a negative quantity. This is based on the fact that a quantity that does not exist cannot be shipped. Logically, this is not possible; however, if the paperwork is in error or out of date, then it is entirely possible that the stock indeed exists and the transaction is indeed valid.

In many cases, the authorization procedures are similar to those used in a noncomputer system. There are, however, the following important differences in authorizing data in computer systems:

- Data is often authorized at the time it is entered into the computer system rather than at the time the resulting output is used.
- Instead of authorizing data manually prior to processing, the computer may be programmed, in accordance with management's specifications, to identify and report defined items for manual authorization (e.g., in a payroll system, excessive overtime). This focuses attention on important items likely to be incorrect, making manual checking more efficient and effective.
- In some cases the ability of the program to test an item's validity is so precise that manual authorization is no longer required.

The significance of these differences is discussed in the following paragraphs.

Timing of Authorization. The authorization of data at the time of entry, rather than when the resulting output is produced, occurs both with master file data and with transaction data. For example, sales prices may be authorized when they are written to the file. Thereafter, the price is not normally authorized again when sales invoices are produced. Another example is that credit given to customers may be authorized at the time the claim is input and not when the credit note is produced.

When data is authorized at the time of input, it is important to ensure that the authorization remains effective and that changes cannot be made after authorization, during the subsequent processing.

In some cases, the controls for completeness and accuracy of input and update indicate the presence of unauthorized data. For example, processed output is sometimes checked in detail with authorized input using one-for-one checking of master file data amendments. Input is matched with authorized data held on file, such as goods received details being matched with a file of purchase orders.

In other cases, specific procedures are required. These normally consist of either authorizing the data after controls for completeness and accuracy of input and update have been established (such as authorizing items in batches after batch totals have been established and recorded) or checking that all items have been authorized after control has been established (such as checking that all items on serially numbered documents have been authorized). These procedures are illustrated in Figure 15-1.

Selective Manual Authorization. Selective manual authorization is used when the computer is programmed to identify and report defined items for manual authorization. This involves the program matching the input with criteria stored as master file data or tables (e.g., matching hours worked with a standard, and reporting excessive overtime). For this form of authorization to be effective, the criteria must be correct and reasonable, the matching process must be logically sound, and all items reported as exceptional must be checked.

An example of the preceding procedure occurred when an EDP system for sales orders was developed. All sales orders over $10,000 had to be approved and signed off by the sales manager before the order was sent to the warehouse. Every day, all the sales orders over $10,000 were extracted from standard processing and placed in a suspense file for approval. The sales manager believed that all sales were good and would authorize the entire batch with his signature at the end of the day. In this case, the control procedure existed, but was being improperly used. It appeared that the pro-

FIG. 15-1
Authorization and validity of data processed flowchart

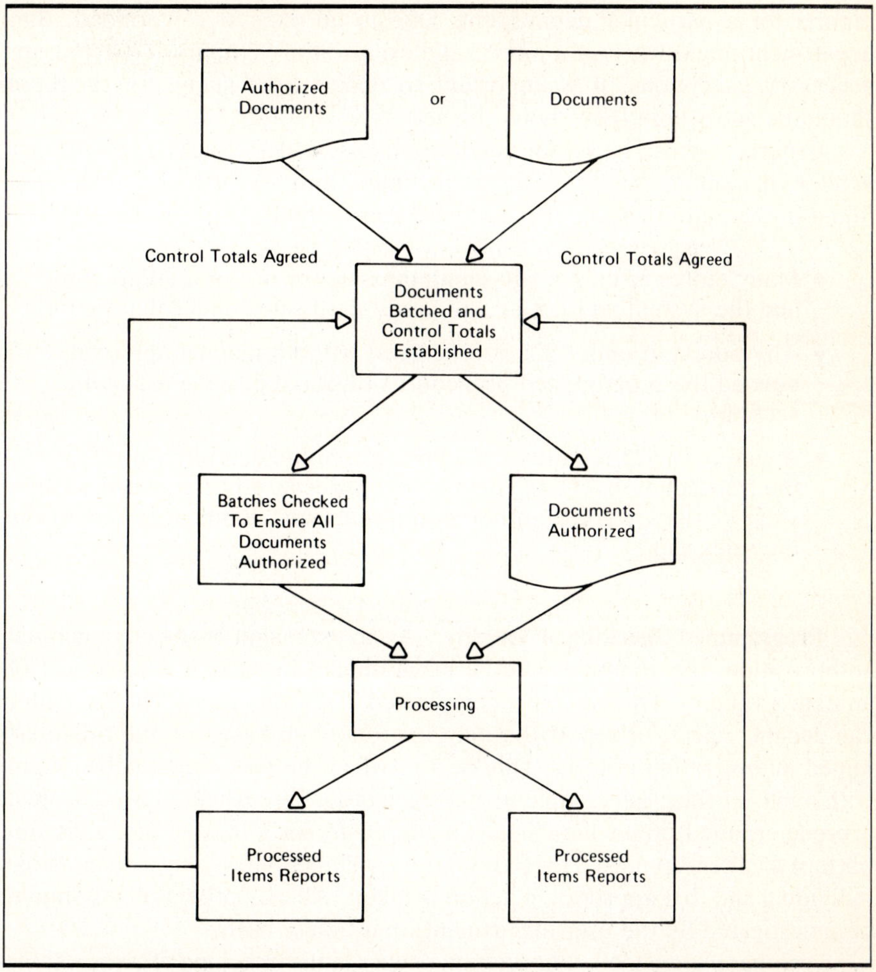

cedure was being followed, since the routine of having the sales authorized was acted out. The authorization function was taken away from the sales manager after the controller reported difficulty in collecting for these large sales. The authorization function was given to the accounts receivable department manager, who actually checked up on every exception.

The concept of authorization criteria is not so rigid that it must apply to all transactions. For example, in a payroll system the criterion might be that since a 40-hour work week is the norm, no employee should ever work more than 60 hours a week. This would be the standard criterion for all payroll transactions. Rigid application might result in frequent exception reports for a particular department. Due to an excessive workload, that department might warrant a more valid criterion of 72 hours. To avoid unnecessary exceptions, it is important to decide how many criteria there should be and where they should be set.

Criteria can also be set for vendor purchase orders, such as amount per vendor, maximum sales tied to credit limits, and so forth. Examples are found in the authorization of credit card transactions:

- Many stores require a $10 minimum sale for use of a credit card, and the system will not accept credit card sales under that figure.
- Any purchase under $25 is processed without manual approval beyond the programmed procedures (discussed in the following section).
- A sale over $25 requires a telephone credit check to ensure that the transaction is valid. This manual procedure is evidenced when store clerks are given authorization reference numbers to record on the sales slip.

Programmed Checking of Validity. As an extension of selective manual authorization, the computer can be programmed to make a precise test of an item's validity. This can be accomplished in various ways. The computer can accept, reject, or report the item for follow-up based on the predetermined authorization criteria. This occurs when the program matches input with a master file. An example is that sales orders are usually tested against a predetermined credit limit held on the customer's master file. It is important that items reported for follow-up are in fact reviewed by a responsible individual and that appropriate action is taken. All exception reports should be investigated by the user department on a timely basis.

Another example of authorization occurs in the matching of transactions to another file. An open purchase order is often authorization for a receipt of merchandise. The validity control might be the existence of a valid purchase order number. If a particular order does not exist as an open purchase order, it can be for one of the following reasons:

- Merchandise was shipped without a valid purchase order number.
- Duplicate shipments of merchandise took place against one purchase order. In times of low inventory turnover, this might be a deliberate "error" on the part of the supplier to help clear out excess stock. The supplier can then claim a clerical error and

subsequently ask the organization that received the overshipment to keep it for a reduced price.

It is not enough for the system to match the purchase orders. It must also ensure that individual items received match individual items ordered. Vendors sometimes make substitutions for higher-priced merchandise, claiming stock outage, without adjusting the price.

Output is generated under certain conditions. For example, it is common to find inventory systems that generate reports of recommended economic buying quantities, or even the purchase orders themselves, based on predefined order quantities, when a minimum stock level is reached. This represents a standard management decision, activated according to management design when the computer establishes that a particular set of circumstances exists. Controls should exist over this output to determine that reports are distributed to the appropriate management personnel for checking and that the reports are useful to management in their current format.

When minimum stock level quantities control whether a purchase order is issued, the minimum stock level quantities have to be reviewed periodically. This review ensures that correct quantity figures are being used, by analyzing inventory turnover. A low inventory turnover may indicate that the minimum stock level should be changed. This analysis can be performed by a computer program, with authorization for a change being made by management.

In both these methods, the programmed procedures are based on predetermined management criteria, leaving people out of the day-to-day decision-making process for these items. Even more control, however, is required over the original authorization used as the criteria in the system. It is very important that adequate controls exist over the amendment and maintenance of master file data used by the program (such as credit limits or minimum stock levels). These procedures are illustrated in Figure 15-2.

Rejected Transaction Reports. Rejected transactions usually require the investigation and correction of all transactions reported as in error. This may mean that previously authorized data can be subject to authorized or unauthorized changes.

For example, a sales order is processed and falls within the credit limit for the customer. The customer sends in a check to pay the previous balance and the check is returned marked "insufficient funds." The accounts receivable clerk immediately updates the customer's record, putting a hold on future shipments and sales. Meanwhile, the previously authorized sales order is being processed in the warehouse for shipment. As a control, the

FIG. 15-2
Programmed checking of validity flowchart

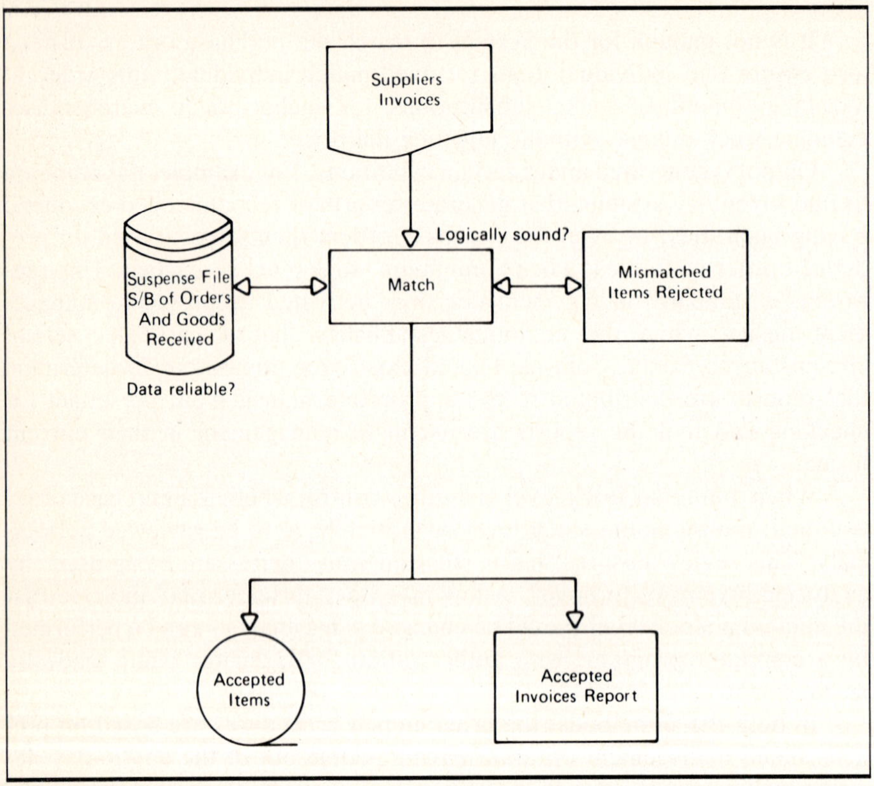

organization runs a prebilling program after staging the merchandise but prior to its delivery. During the prebilling processing, that customer's order would be rejected. This is an example of an authorized change.

Of course, a transaction can be in error, subsequently corrected, and sent for processing. Depending on the type of error (if in fact rejected for validity), any additional change would have to be authorized.

For example, in a payroll validity error, an employee's time sheet may be rejected because it shows 80 hours of overtime when the standard is 20 hours of overtime. The transaction is investigated and found to be in error. Since all overtime went into an overtime bank that was paid quarterly, there was no real need to report the overtime in a timely fashion. The employee had recorded overtime for two periods into one period, and had also been late turning in the time sheets. The employee was automatically paid for 45 hours every week unless otherwise reported. The records were adjusted, and a call made to the employee about the error; the supervisor was asked to authorize the change after correction. To prevent such situations, adjustments should be authorized by the supervisor after review, and corrective action taken.

The extent to which authorizations need to be repeated or checked after correction of errors is an important consideration. The sequence of events is also significant. The presence of an authorizing signature on a source document may not in itself be sufficient, since people frequently sign things out of habit.

COMPUTER-GENERATED TRANSACTIONS

Control Objective

The previous sections have dealt with transaction data that is entered for processing. A computer can also be programmed to initiate data, as illustrated in Figure 15-3.

Transaction data can be generated in the following ways:

- The processing of a transaction may create the condition that triggers generation of data. For example, processing a stock issue reduces stock below minimum level and a purchase order is produced. In these cases, the conditions that cause the new data to be generated are normally identified by a comparison with master file data: in this instance, the minimum stock level.
- A signal to initiate transactions may be entered. For example, the entry of a certain date initiates the production of checks for all suppliers' invoices prior to that date; entering a particular stage of production that has been reached generates the appropriate charges to work-in-process; the entry of a requisition code generates a list of the components to be issued.

From a control perspective, the stored data in the transaction should be complete, accurate, and authorized. The parameters, conditions, or programs used to imitate the transaction should be appropriately set up and maintained.

Control Techniques

Generated data requires controls over completeness and accuracy. These controls should cover the generation process and, at times, the updating of the data produced. All generated data does not update a file. For example,

FIG. 15-3
Computer-generated transaction

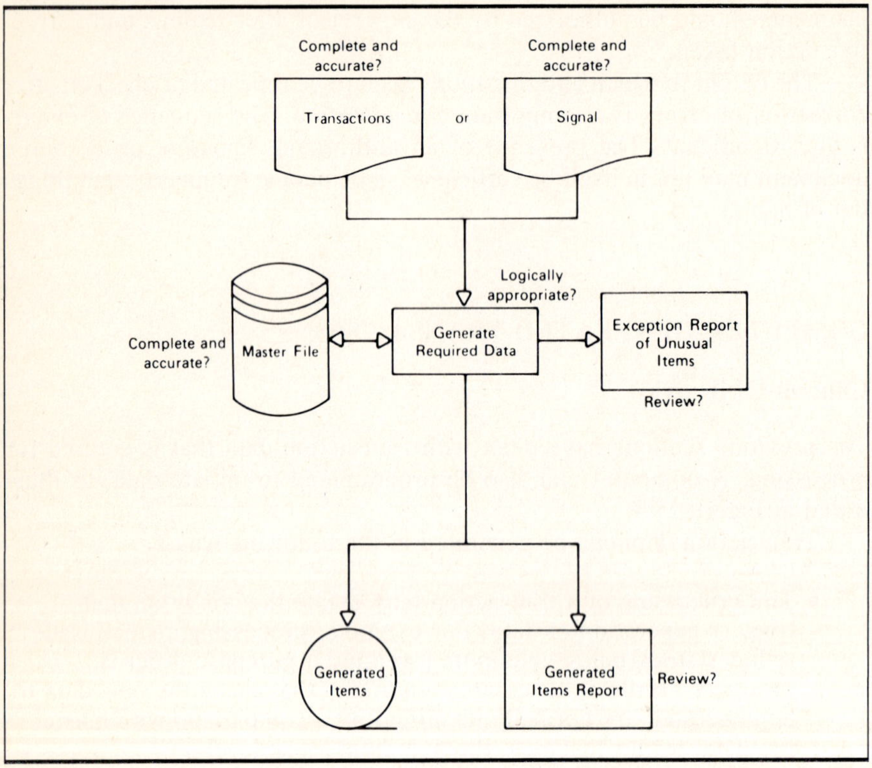

a computer can generate premium renewal notices that are sent to customers. If data is to be produced by the computer completely and accurately, the following user controls and programmed procedures are necessary:

- The data (such as dates or stages of production reached) that triggers the generation of other data must be entered completely and accurately.
- The steps carried out by the program in generating the data must be logically sound.
- The master file data that is referred to (such as the minimum stock level) or used as the basis for generating the new data (such as reorder quantity) must be reliable. This involves all the controls over the amendment and maintenance of master file data on the file because the master file data may not be manually checked on the documents as it is in manual systems.

- The generated data should be controlled for accuracy, either by a manual review (such as a scrutiny of purchase orders before dispatch) or by programmed procedures (such as reporting all checks over a certain dollar amount so that they can be investigated).

After the data is produced by the computer, it may need to be subjected to update controls. These are similar to the controls already outlined for entered data. They are based on the control totals accumulated while the data is being generated. In practice, updating often takes place prior to, or at the time of, production of the data.

COMPLETENESS AND ACCURACY OF UPDATE

A major concern of any organization is ensuring that data already in the computer is completely and accurately updated. Chapter 14 describes how important it is to make sure that all data is complete and accurate when it is entered; that is the beginning of the processing of data by the computer. Inside the computer, the data is handed off to the next processing stage.

The data may go through a series of processing steps, such as:

- Sorting and calculation by programmed procedures.
- Analysis and accumulation.
- Updating a master file.

Several things can go wrong with the data once it has been entered into the computer for processing. Problems can result from the following:

- *Programming errors.* Program procedures do not perform as expected or desired. For the most part, programs are designed, written, tested, and then put into production to handle common types of transactions in a particular system. Consequently, these procedures are usually well tested. It is when unforeseen errors or exceptions occur that the programmed procedures may not be able to process the data correctly. And it is possible for programs to have logic errors that escape detection in testing. A program can be accurate when implemented, but errors may be introduced when new procedures are added. Since such errors may occur in the way the data is processed, the errors can go undetected for long periods of time.
- *Operational errors.* During the operation of standard computer procedures, the operator may do something wrong, such as

selecting an out-of-date master file for processing current transactions. Computer operating manuals may become out-of-date or erroneous; computer operators may have to be re-trained; and, of course, they can—and do—simply make mistakes. Equipment failure is another possible cause of error.

Some examples of problems that can occur due to both types of errors are:

- *Wrong record updated.* A transaction to update information on the vendor record for one company instead updates the next record, which is for another company. Such an error occurs when the program selects the wrong record for updating, and it happens because the programmer did not build in a check to see which record was selected for updating. A control for completeness would not necessarily catch an error of this sort, but a control over accuracy, such as one-for-one checking, should show the error in processing.

- *Wrong calculations.* Either the formula for the calculations is in error or the variable and table data used in the calculation are incorrect. Calculations that include the date commonly fail to consider that in a leap year transactions can be dated "2/29." A program may disregard the fact that payroll is variable; errors in table data can result when the payroll department forgets to have the program that handles payroll calculations updated with the most current information on withholding deductions.

- *Analysis and accumulation errors.* Incorrect programmed procedures can produce these errors. If data analysis is based on matching data to another file and the wrong file is selected, then the resulting analysis would be incorrect. For example, if purchases are recommended by analyzing year-to-date information and the operator is running purchase recommendations for December, he should use the file containing year-to-date for November but instead uses year-to-date for October. The analysis has been performed correctly, but the wrong data has been used.

  Accumulation errors do not usually occur when columns can be added to a total. They usually take place when the numbers are selected and categorized into accumulations that are not easily footed.

These are some of the examples of how things can go wrong even when the data is complete and accurate at the input stage.

A well-controlled system ensures that data is complete and accurate when it is entered and updates files with equal completeness and accuracy.

FIG. 15-4
A comparison of the appropriateness of application controls

	Completeness of Input	Completeness of Update	Accuracy of Input	Accuracy of Update	Validity	Maintenance
One-for-One Checking	X	X	X	X	X	X
Batch/Control Totals	X	X	X	X		X
Computer Sequence Check	X	X				
Computer Matching	X	X	X	X		
Programmed Checks			X	X	X	X
Prerecorded Input			X			

Completeness and accuracy of update is the way that data is controlled through every stage, including the internal computer processes carried out by programmed procedures. Only when these steps are followed can all data entered into the computer be processed without being garbled or lost during its passage through the computer.

COMPLETENESS OF UPDATE

Control Objectives

Completeness of update controls are designed to make sure that all data entered into, and accepted by, the computer is updated to the proper master file. Not just the actual act of updating but all stages of processing must be controlled, from acceptance of items through to the updated master file. (See Figure 15-4.)

Essential to ensuring the completeness of update are the controls over the correction and resubmission of items that are rejected at the update stage. When these items are reprocessed after being corrected, they become new update items in the next round of updating.

Control Techniques

There are two basic ways to assure that files are updated completely:

1. Introduce controls for completeness of input that can also apply to update.
2. Institute specific update controls.

Sometimes controls over the completeness of input also control the completeness of update. When controls can do both, the input controls described earlier are reviewed, with a description of the circumstances in which they can be used to control updating.

Computer Sequence Check. Normally, a computer sequence check is performed when data is entered; however, it does not ensure completeness of update. The following situations are found in some systems, particularly in on-line and real-time environments:

- A sequence check and identification of missing and/or duplicate transactions are carried out on the updated master file after the transactions have updated the file.
- The file that maintains the sequence numbers is not flagged until after the master file has been updated.

As a result, in the cases described previously, computer sequence checking provides a control over the completeness of update.

In on-line systems, the sequence check often operates along with procedures to update the master file. This ensures the completeness of input and update. No duplicates can be entered; they would probably be rejected at the input stage, as the computer does not allow the terminal operator to reuse a previously entered number.

Some systems carry out the sequence check by flagging the sequence number file, as the last step prior to actually updating the master file. This does not normally provide sufficient control over updating of the master file, so it is important to know how the particular system operates before deciding to rely on this control. The use of a computer sequence check to control completeness of update is illustrated in Figure 15-5.

Computer Matching. As with sequence checking, computer matching is normally carried out as data is entered. In certain circumstances the matching process also provides a control over the completeness of update. Matching is then conducted against:

FIG. 15-5
Computer sequence check (input and update)

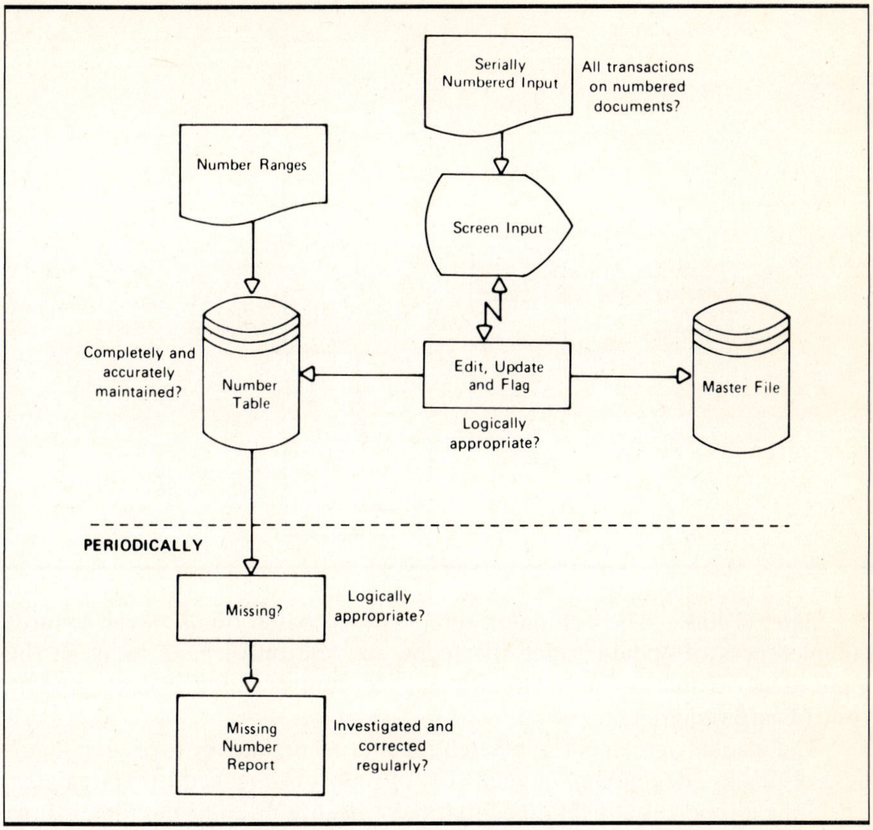

- A master file (as opposed to a suspense file). The missing data report is produced by reading the master file after the matching process has been completed.
- A suspense file that is not updated until after the master file has been updated. As with sequence checking, care is required, since some systems update the suspense file immediately before updating the master file. In the latter case, the matching does not normally provide control over updating of the master file.

The use of computer matching to control completeness of update is illustrated in Figure 15-6.

FIG. 15-6

Computer matching (input and update)

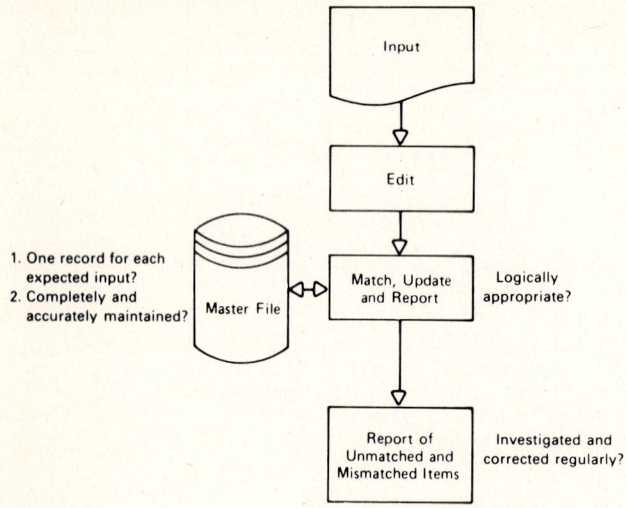

Batch Totals. The computer agreement of batch totals never ensures completeness of update, since the technique can only check totals at the input stage. If this is the technique used to control input, specific update controls are required.

The manual agreement of a batch register sometimes ensures completeness of update, depending on what sort of report is checked to the register. Checking a report that lists items that have been written to the file ensures completeness of update; checking batch totals against reports produced at the edit stage, however, does not, so specific update controls are required. The use of a batch register to control input and update is shown in Figures 15-7 and 15-8.

Manual agreement of a control account usually ensures completeness of update, because the control account is checked against an accumulation of the balances on file.

Manual agreement of a batch register and of a control account can usually be applied only where there is little or no intermediate processing and the data updating the file is identical in form with the data originally entered (such as processing details of cash received).

More often, the data entered is subject to further processing before updating. During this time the form of the data may change (for example, figures for quantities shipped are converted to sales invoice values). When

FIG. 15-7
Reconciliation of batch register (input and update)

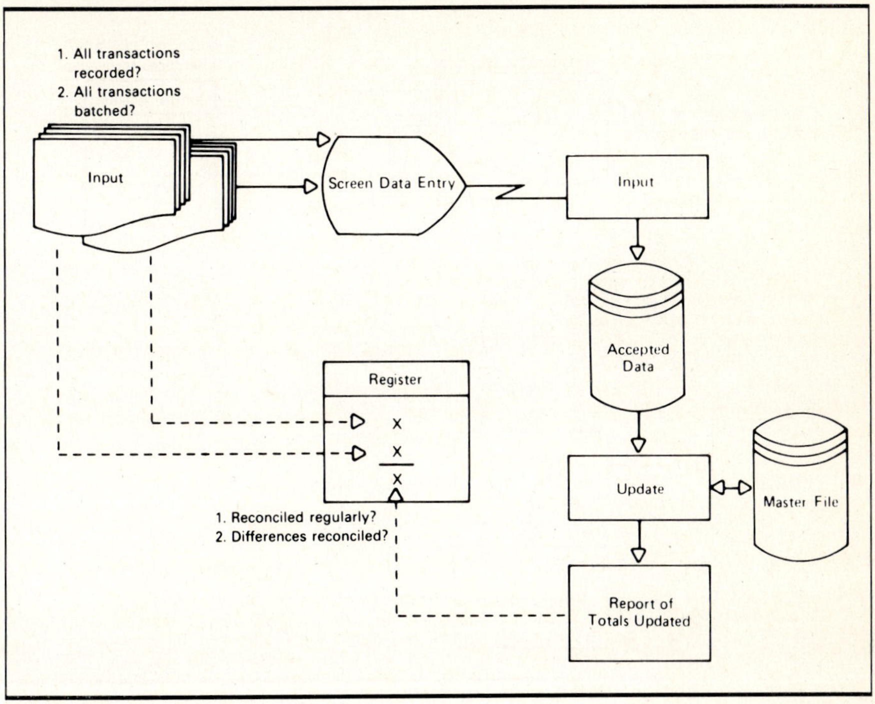

this happens, batch totals cannot be checked manually against the updated totals, so specific updating controls are required.

One-for-One Checking of Detail Reports. This technique ensures completeness of update in cases where the report checked contains items that have been used to update the file. If such reports are produced only at the edit stage, they will not control updating.

Checking of reports is not an effective control technique unless the appropriate method is used in the program that updates transactions to a master file. If the user checks the source documents for a report that shows the record after update, this check will also control the reliability and logic of the programmed procedure. The user must clearly understand this method for it to work effectively. The use of this technique to control updating is illustrated in Figure 15-9.

FIG. 15-8
Using a control account (input and update)

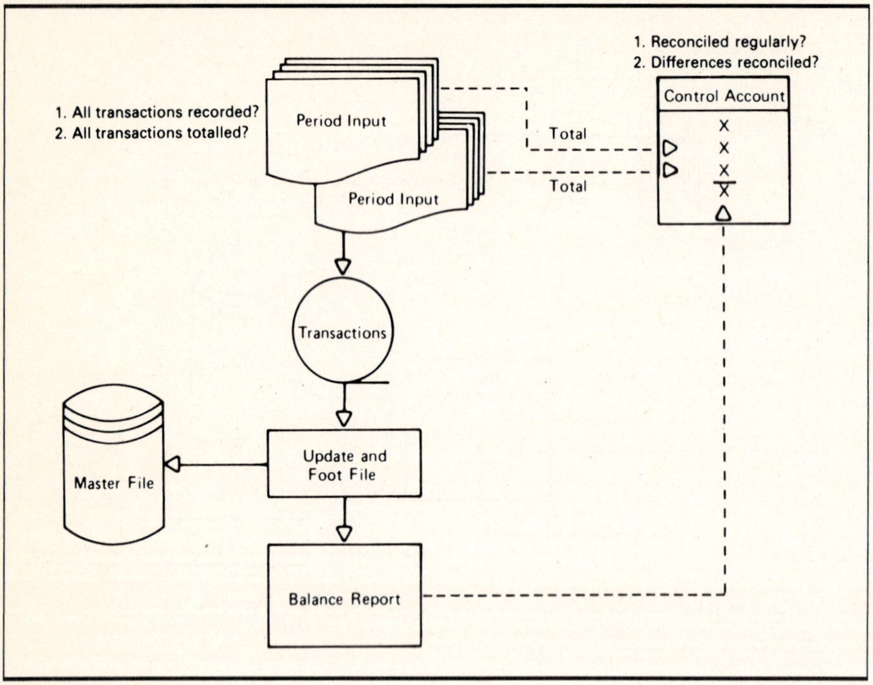

SPECIFIC UPDATE CONTROLS

Whenever an input control does not also apply to completeness of update, updating is usually controlled by the agreement of control totals. These control totals are generated by the computer programs during, or prior to, applying the input control. This control uses the totals of items that have updated the file.

Totals cannot always be checked directly to see that they agree. To rely instead on reconciliation procedures, consider the following:

- Control totals may be summarized (such as when several input batches are combined for subsequent processing).
- The type of control total used may change as a result of a particular intermediate processing step (for example, a hash total of quantities may change to an invoice currency value total as a result of pricing).
- Items may be, or may have been, rejected at an intermediate step.

FIG. 15-9

One-for-one check (update)

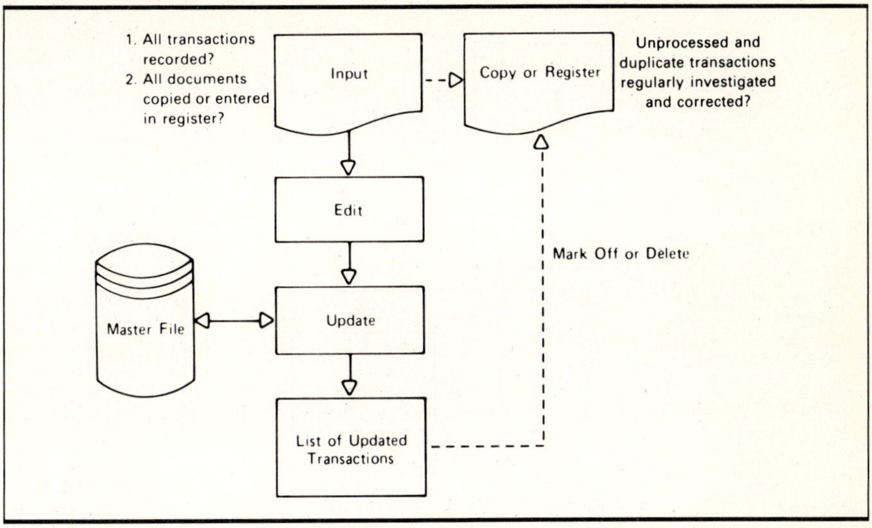

The totals of accepted items can be reconciled either manually or by the computer.

Techniques that can be used to control updating are described in the following sections, and different methods for accumulating the totals of accepted items are explained.

Manual Reconciliation of Accepted-Item Totals

The manual reconciliation of accepted-item totals is illustrated in Figure 15-10. This method works as follows:

- The computer program accumulates and reports the total of items accepted when the input control was exercised.
- The computer then processes items onward through a series of programs. Reports that include the relevant control totals are produced, usually at the conclusion of each program in a series.
- When totals are summarized or changed, the new control totals are printed at the end of the computer run. The old totals are usually printed and may be carried through all later processing.
- After updating, the totals of items updated to the master file are reported.

FIG. 15-10

Accepted-item totals—manual reconciliation (update only)

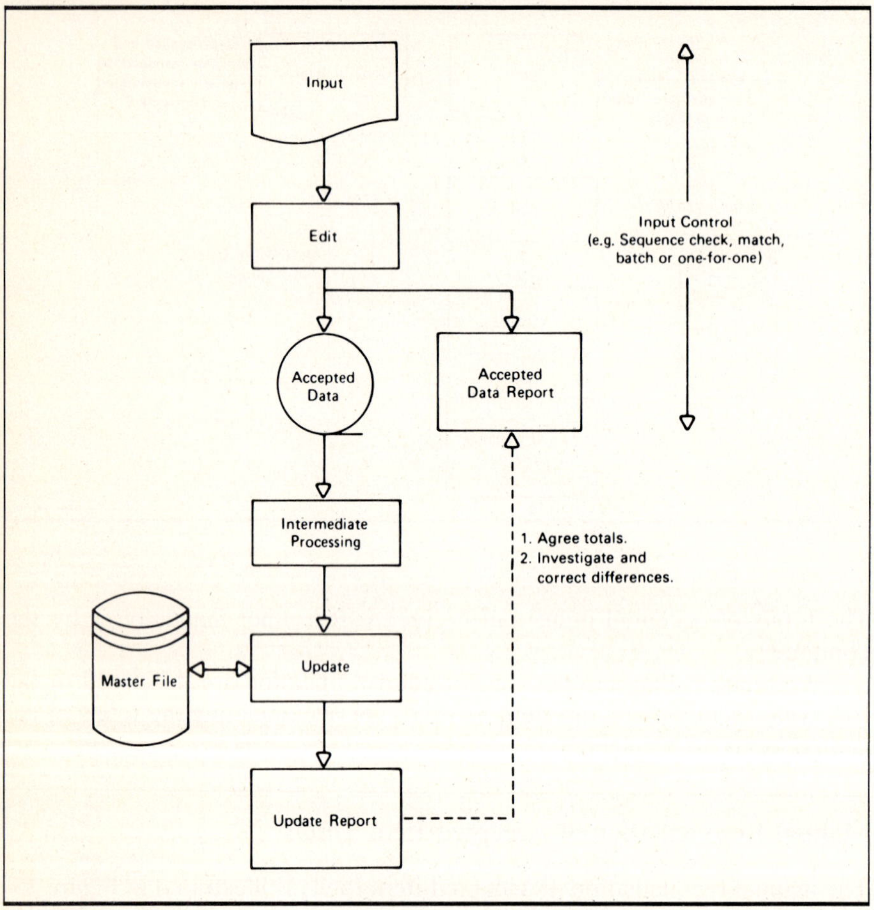

- The totals of accepted items are manually reconciled to the updated totals, using any summarization or change in totals that has taken place. Any rejections are also taken into account.

When there is no change in the totals, the accepted-item totals may be recorded in a manual control account or cumulative register. The balance on the control account or register can then be periodically agreed to an accumulation of the total balances on file to prove completeness of update.

FIG. 15-11

Accepted-item totals—computer reconciliation (update only)

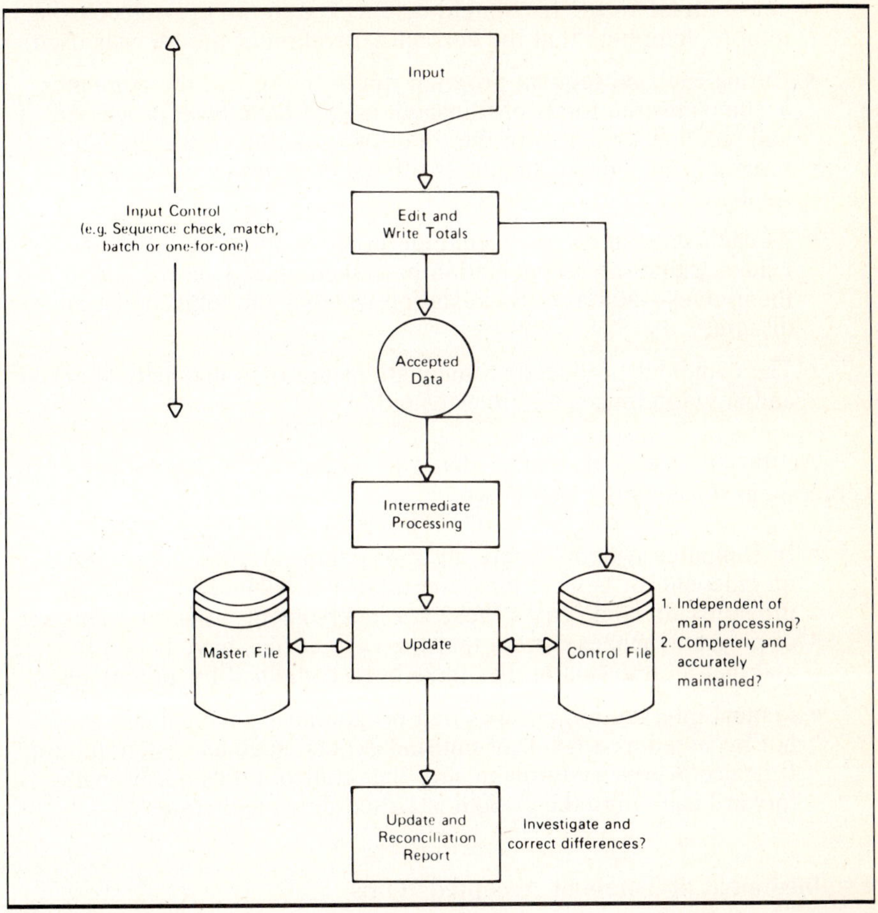

Computer Reconciliation of Accepted-Item Totals

Computer reconciliation of accepted-item totals is illustrated in Figure 15-11. This method of control works as follows:

- The computer program accumulates the totals of accepted items in the same way these totals are accumulated in manual reconciliation. After all data has been entered and processed, the control totals are recorded on a control record in the file of accepted items. In sequential tape files, the totals are added to the trailer label; in disk files that are indexed-sequential or managed by a data base management system (DBMS), the control record information is usually contained in a separate record. The opening control total on the file should be checked to the previous closing total to determine that the correct generation of the file was used.

- During each subsequent program run in the series, the computer accumulates the totals of transactions that have been processed and reconciles them with the total forwarded from the previous program run. This technique is often called run-to-run control totals.
- At each stage in the reconciliation process, the program produces evidence that the reconciliation has taken place—usually the totals themselves—and a message stating whether the totals agree or disagree.
- The computer-produced reconciliations are then manually checked and any differences are investigated.

Another mesthod of control that uses computer reconciliation of accepted-item totals works as follows:

- In computer systems where all transactions are first summarized on independent control files, the totals are balanced by a set of programs. In some cases these are independent programs. This set of programs makes certain that the correct files have been used and that all transaction files have been combined for processing.
- Manual intervention ensures that programmed reconciliations are not bypassed as a result of unusual events, such as system failure. It is also necessary to make sure that control totals are brought forward each time the system is closed down and restarted.

Establishment of Totals of Accepted Items

The way the total of accepted items is established depends on whether transactions are entered and processed in batches or individually, as is the case in many on-line systems. Depending on the method used, the following procedures are employed:

- *Batch systems*—The total of accepted items should be accumulated during or prior to the program run in which the computer sequence check, computer matching, or other input control is carried out.
- *On-line systems*—The concept of a program run or the complete processing of a batch of transactions does not exist. Transactions are entered one by one and trigger whichever programs are required to process them. Transaction totals are progressively

accumulated at intervals during processing and are periodically reported or reconciled by the computer. These totals can be done daily or more frequently when there are many transactions. It is important that accepted-item totals are accumulated during or prior to applying the input control for the input control to be effective.

Reliance on Controls Over a Previous Application

As systems become more integrated, a file produced by one application is often used for another application. When this happens, the completeness of input to the first application should be controlled to ensure completeness of input to the next application.

Specific update controls, described in this section, are necessary to ensure that all transactions accepted by the first application are passed through to the second. This is illustrated in Figures 15-12 and 15-13. In addition, if two or more files are updated at the same point in the processing cycle, the same input and update controls may be effective over each file.

On-Line Sequence

Another method of control, the on-line sequence check, is illustrated in Figure 15-14. It is organized as follows:

- Transactions are assigned a sequence number as they are entered.
- A report of missing and duplicate numbers is produced after all transactions have updated the master file.

On-line sequence control is similar to a batch sequence check. This type of control also helps to prevent unusual events such as the possible loss of transactions when the system fails to operate, since transactions can be identified and recovered at the proper point in processing.

Duplicate Processing

Duplicate processing is common in an on-line data base environment. When transactions are entered in this type of operation, a memo update is usually made to the data base. This memo update enables the current updated status to be checked at any time. The data base, however, is not actually updated until overnight processing is done. At the time the actual updating occurs, the transactions are rechecked against the memo update and a report is produced. This report lists the differences between the memo update and the overnight update. Duplicate processing is illustrated in Figure 15-15.

FIG. 15-12
Reliance on controls over another application

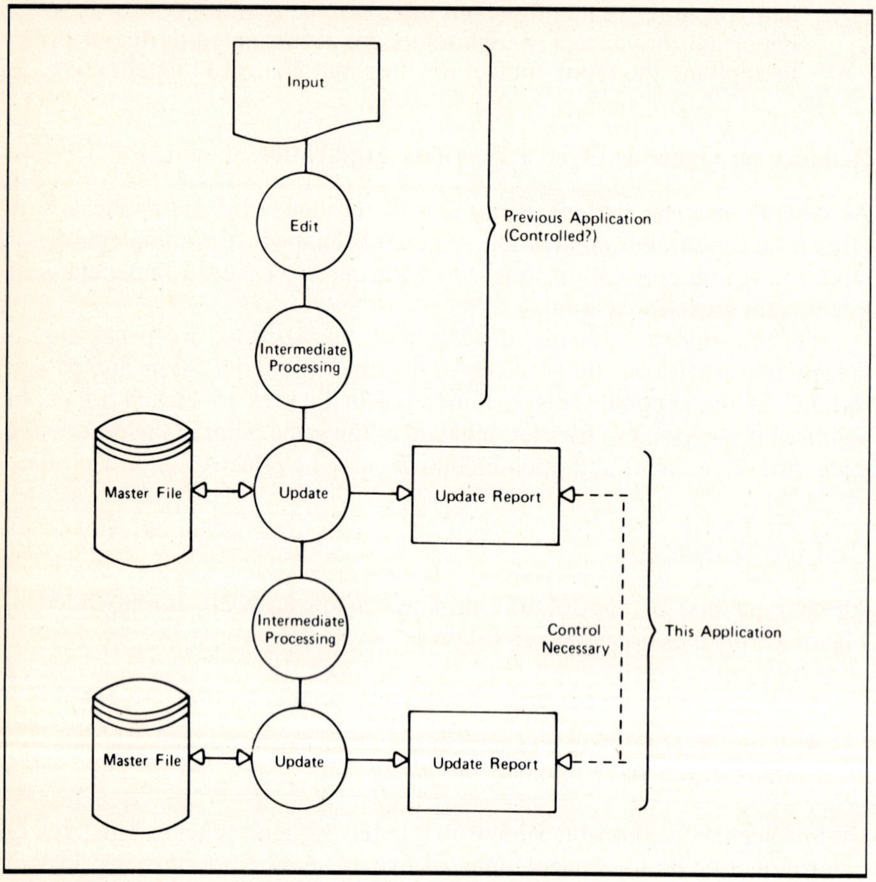

Rejections

Rejections may arise at the update stage as well as on input. Rejections at the update stage usually occur because a transaction cannot find a matching master file record.

In on-line systems such rejections are much less common, because the system can match the transaction against a master file record on entry and establish that a matching record exists.

The procedures and techniques required to control rejections arising at the update stage are similar to those required for rejections produced at the data entry stage.

FIG. 15-13
Input and update controls

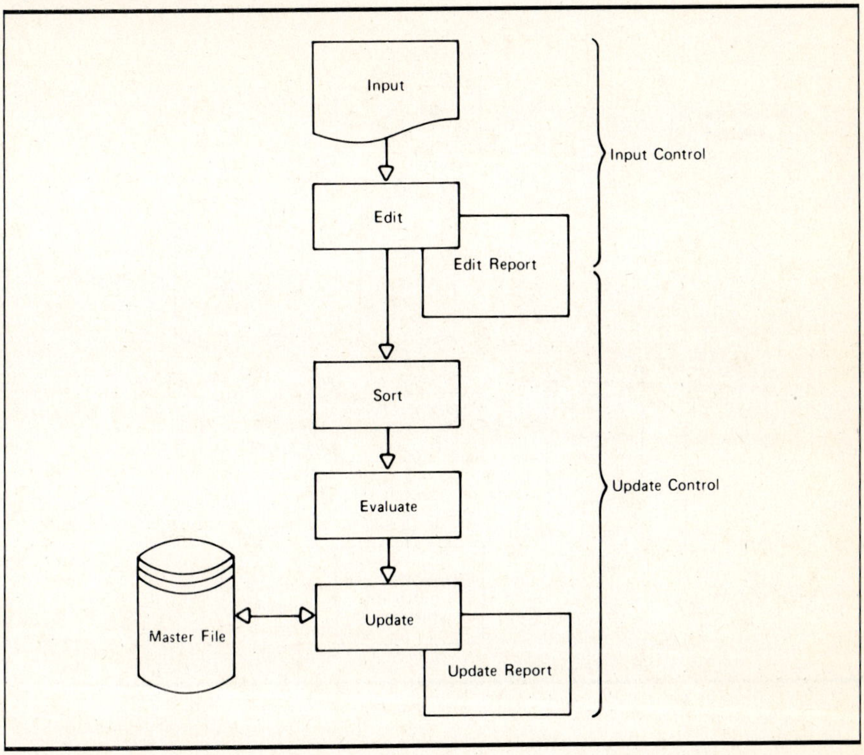

ACCURACY OF UPDATE

Control Objectives

When computer files are updated, controls are needed to ensure that the new input is accurately carried through intermediate processing and accurately updated to the correct data on the correct generation of the master file.

As with the control of input, both master file data and reference data must be accurately updated.

Control Techniques

Financial Data. Control techniques previously described can ensure the accurate updating of financial data. Control techniques that do this are:

FIG. 15-14

On-line sequence check (update only)

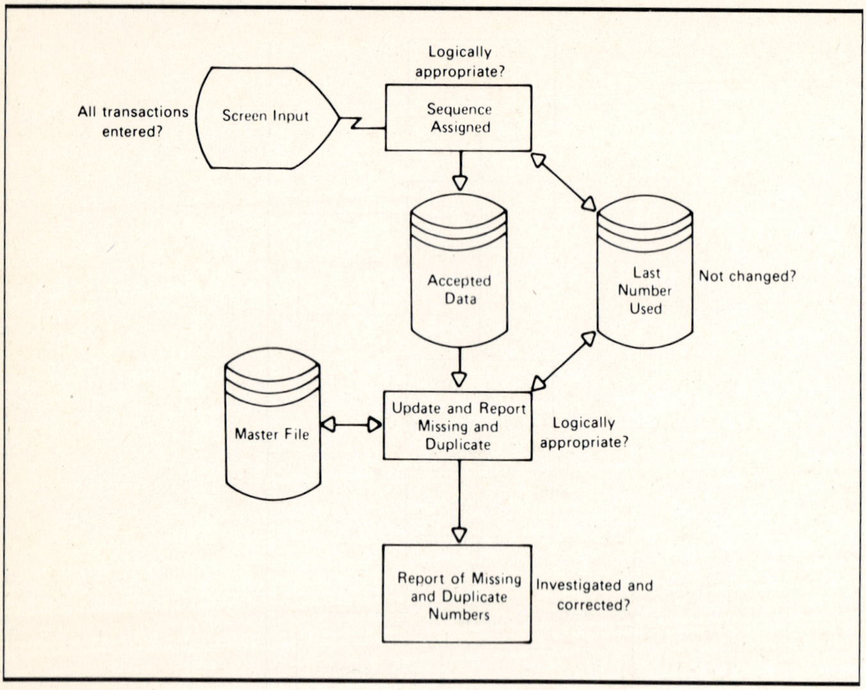

- *One-for-one checking of detail reports.* Checking a report of items that have updated the file ensures that financial data covered by the checking is accurate.
- *Manual reconciliation of accepted-item totals and computer reconciliation of accepted-item totals.* Both of these techniques ensure the accuracy of the data covered by the reconciliation.
- *Programmed edit checks.* Normally these checks are applied to data as it is entered and do not ensure accuracy of update. Occasionally a variation of the reasonableness and dependency checks may be encountered where the programmed editing is carried out on the master file after updating. In such cases, the reasonableness and dependency checks may also control accuracy of updating of the data involved.

In practice, it is likely that one or more of the above techniques will be used in batch or on-line systems. When this is the case, they serve as a control for accuracy of update.

FIG. 15-15
Duplicate processing (update only)

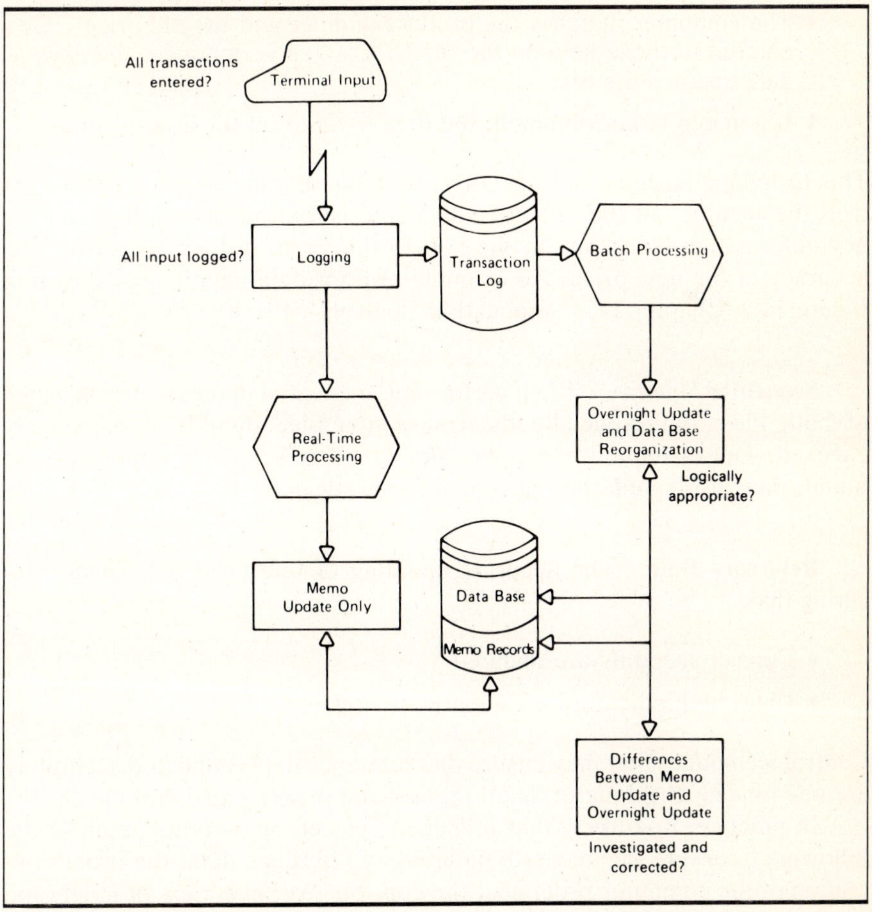

Not all significant financial data fields may be controlled in one of these ways. Often, only the primary financial data fields (such as the invoice value) are so controlled.

Prior Data Matching. This method controls accuracy of update as well as accuracy of input. It is commonly used for the control of master file data amendments and works in the following way:

- The new data that is to be processed is entered together with the old data to be superseded. For example, if the price of an inventory item is to be amended, the product reference number is entered with both the new price and the price to be replaced.

- The computer matches the product number and the old price entered to those held on the file. If a match is obtained, the new data updates the file.
- If a match is not obtained, the item is reported for investigation.

This technique ensures that the correct product number is updated. It controls the accuracy of the reference data entered but not the accuracy of the new information being put on the file. In this case, it does not ensure the accuracy of the new price. An example of prior data matching is shown in Figure 14-2 (Chapter 14, "Application Controls—I").

Sequential Updates. When performing sequential updates, the sequence of both files, but especially the transaction file, should be specifically checked. Out-of-sequence records should be rejected. If duplicates are found, they also should be rejected and investigated.

Reference Data. The accurate updating of reference data means ensuring that:

- Correct accounts are updated.
- Dates and indicators are accurately updated.

Control techniques that may ensure that reference data is updated accurately are one-for-one checking of detail reports and programmed edit checks.

In practice, it is likely that reliance is placed on a combination of the following to ensure the accurate updating of reference data: the proper operation of the computer programs; the controls over accuracy of input; and other procedures (such as checking of suppliers' statements and the dispatch of statements to customers).

These procedures do not cover all accuracy requirements. Generally, the accuracy of the programmed procedures is relied on to ensure that some or even all of the significant data fields are accurately updated.

Correct Master File Generations. Master files are processed according to generations. The previous master file is run with the input transactions to create a new master file. In subsequent runs, the new master file will become the old master file, and so on. If the most recent file is not used, all transactions processed since the last correctly updated master file will be lost.

Controls Over Master File Generations. When a control account technique is used at input, no additional control is necessary to ensure that updating has been performed on the correct generation of the master file. The control account technique records all types of transactions that should eventually reach the master file in a control account; the cumulative totals of these transactions are carried forward from period to period. The balance of the control account is compared at intervals with the accumulated individual balances on the master file to see if they are the same. If the wrong generation of the master file is used for an update, the control account and master file balance will disagree.

MAINTENANCE OF DATA ON FILE

Control Objectives

Once an organization ensures that data is completely and accurately processed onto the file, the stored data must remain properly on the file until amended, deleted, or added to during subsequent authorized processing.

This may not seem to present any special problems, yet it can. Remember that unless action is taken against the data, it will remain on file, untouched, and possibly unreviewed until something unusual happens.

Usually, every master data record should have a date mark to indicate when the record was first entered or last amended. Then guidelines can be set for review of any data not amended for a certain period of time (such as one year). It is easy to overlook reviewing data, forgetting that the data can be seriously out of date and create repercussions for the organization. Recently, an insurance company discovered that it was using a 1945 actuarial table to calculate the life expectancy and the reserves on hand. The life expectancy of Americans has increased since 1945, and coverage will be required for longer periods.

Not only is it important to ensure that the data remains accurate, but it must also remain complete. When data is untouched for long periods, it is important to make sure that records are not lost in the interim.

Controls that ensure that data remains correct are called controls for the maintenance of data. Maintenance controls are required for both transaction data and master file data. They are designed to provide controls over the following:

- *Currency of data*—To ensure that data is kept up-to-date and that unusual data requiring action is identified.
- *Correctness of data*—To ensure that the data stored on the file

cannot be changed other than through the normal, controlled processing cycle.

Currency of Data. A date mark is the best way to indicate when the data was last amended. However, if the system does not create date marks, master file data from a prior period can be matched to the master file data of the current period. Records that are identical for both periods may be the exceptions that require investigation.

In addition, maintenance controls should provide assurance that the correct generation of the file has been used each time it is updated.

Correctness of Data. Data can be changed by one-time fix-it programs, often called quick-and-dirty programs, written and processed to change data due to other program errors or operational errors.

For example, in a particular billing system, the invoice date was entered on a batch parameter for the day. At the start of the new year, the computer operator kept entering the month and date correctly but forgot to change the year. No one caught the error; they were not used to seeing the new year either.

The first aging for the year showed that accounts receivable over 90 days had increased dramatically. The clerk could not believe it, and an investigation uncovered the error. To have the invoices aged properly, the date had to be changed for all the invoices processed during the first four days of the year. The invoices themselves had already been mailed. To issue credits and reprocess all the invoices seemed like too much work, so the MIS manager suggested a quick-and-dirty program that would change only the last digit of the year. It seemed to be such a simple solution that the program was not even tested. Unfortunately, it had a logic error that is quite common in programming. The program forgot to write the last record read, dropping the last invoice on the file while still adding it to the totals. The invoice was deleted from the records. When the customer received a statement, only the amount shown was paid.

An EDP operation may use a utility program to change data already on file. Such an example could occur at year-end when the year-to-date balances are not set to zero. It is simple to use a utility to do this, but the utility must operate correctly, or it can zero out other valuable data by accident.

In both of the preceding cases, the examples are found in operations that were not daily occurrences. What a staff does every day, it usually does well; it is the procedures done infrequently in which errors often occur.

Control Techniques

The main techniques to control the maintenance of data stored on file are the following:

- Reconciliations of file totals.
- Exception reports.
- Detailed checking of data on file.
- Data file security controls.

Reconciliations of File Totals. A very effective maintenance control is the regular reconciliation of an accumulation of the records on a file with an independently maintained control total. The control total used may take one of the following forms:

- Manually maintained control account.
- Control record maintained as part of the file.
- Control record maintained as part of another file within the system (such as a receivables control account in the general ledger to control the detailed items on the outstanding receivables ledger).

Manually Maintained Control Account. The manual reconciliation of file balances with control accounts involves regular agreement of the accumulation of individual balances on the computer file to a manual control account. It is usually applied to transaction data but can also be used for master file data if a hash total control account is maintained. The most common example is the use of batch logs, in which the value of the batch and the total of all batches processed is recorded in order to check the accuracy of the data. For example, in a batch billing system, all invoices for all batches would be added to open accounts receivable, all receipts would be subtracted, and the new total then reconciled to the new weekly accounts receivable trial balance.

An example of applying this technique to master file data is frequently found in payroll applications. Often there is a data field on each record of the hourly rate of pay, which is used in the program to calculate gross pay. The payroll clerk maintains a manual record of the total of all pay rates. Periodically, this hash total of pay rates is agreed to the total of individual pay rates on the payroll master file. This technique helps to ensure that data in the fields totaled remains complete and accurate on the file. It does not guard against compensating errors between accounts (e.g., if the pay rates

FIG. 15-16

Manually maintained control account flowchart

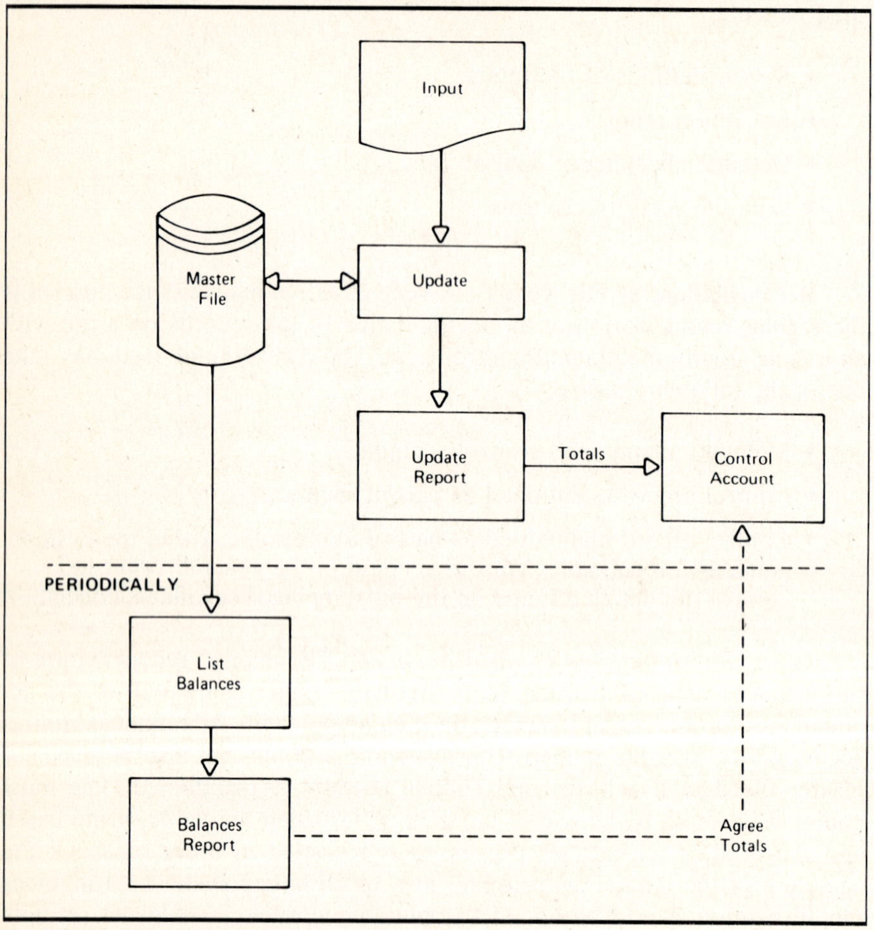

for two individuals were inadvertently transposed). The use of a manually maintained control account is illustrated in Figure 15-16.

File Control Record. Using this technique, a control record on file (usually the last record in a sequential tape file, or often the first record in an indexed-sequential disk file) contains a total, or totals, of items held on the file. Every time the file is updated, the control record is altered. Periodically, the relevant data fields on each record are accumulated and agreed to the control record. Out-of-balance conditions are reported and corrected.

The frequency of the reconciliation procedures should be sufficient to ensure that errors do not accumulate to the point that it is difficult to investigate and correct them. Because the total is stored in the same record as the data it controls, this technique would not detect the use of the wrong file. Each time the file is updated, a report should be printed showing the opening balance, transaction balance added, deleted, or changed, and closing balance on the file. The opening balance can then be agreed manually to the closing balance on the previous report.

The use of a file control record as a maintenance control is often encountered in data base and on-line systems where programmed reconciliations are relied on for updating purposes. (See earlier section entitled "Completeness of Update.") A file control record used in this way is illustrated in Figure 15-17.

Independent Control File. This method of control is similar to the reconciliation of a manually maintained control account. A typical case is when the general ledger system is integrated with the processing of subsidiary ledgers (such as receivables or payables).

The control technique consists of the maintenance of control totals in a separate file, which is updated each time transactions are processed to the master file. The control total is agreed to the total of individual items on the master file each time the file is updated. This agreement may be carried out manually or by computer program.

The technique can also occur when total balances for one file are kept as part of another file. For example, consider an accounts receivable open invoice file and a separate customer master file. The customer master file contains one record for each customer, while the open invoice file has one record for each invoice—and there may be many invoices per customer. Therefore, the customer master usually has a total balance outstanding for the customer. This total acts as a control between the two files if it is reconciled regularly.

This method provides greater assurance as to the maintenance of data than the file control record method discussed previously, since the comparison of totals is from two separate files, not two records on the same file. For this control technique to be effective, there must be:

- Adequate controls over the file containing the control total, both to prevent unauthorized alteration and to ensure the use of the correct generation of that file.
- A reconciliation of the opening balance to the previous closing balance each time the system is stopped and restarted.
- Adequate procedures to identify and follow up differences arising from the reconciliation.

FIG. 15-17
File control record flowchart

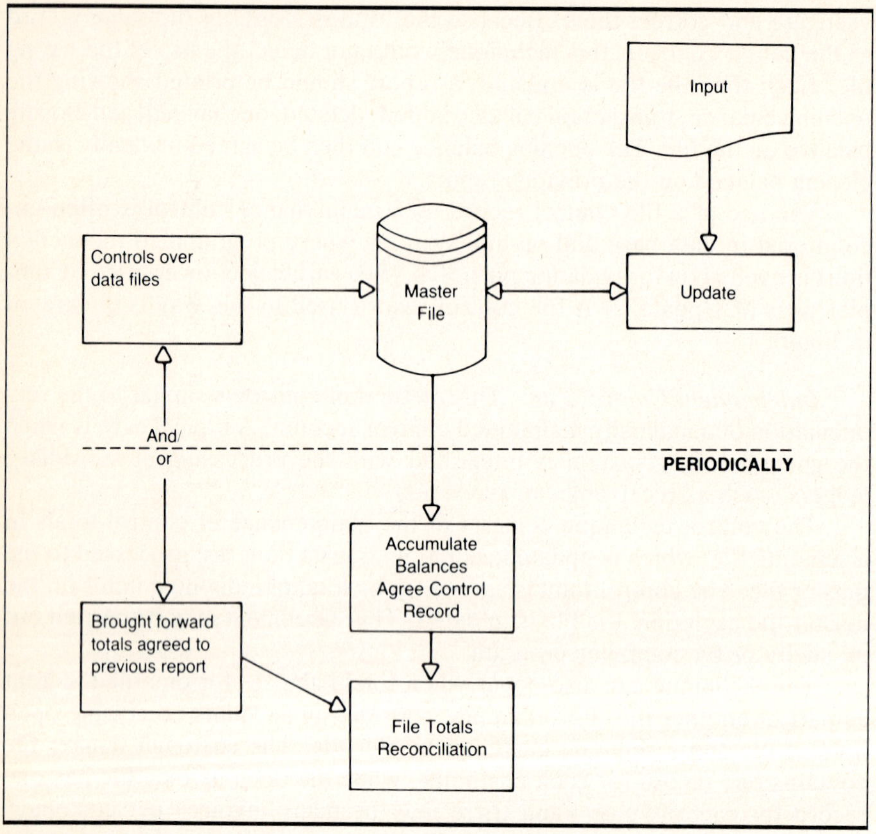

The use of an independent control file is illustrated in Figure 15-18.

Exception Reports. This technique involves using a computer program to examine the data on file and report items that appear incorrect or out-of-date. It is valid for both master file and transaction data. For example, with respect to master file data, this technique can be used to control the correctness and timeliness of inventory prices held on the file by periodically producing exception reports of:

- Prices that have not been amended for a certain period.
- Prices with an abnormal relationship between the cost and selling price.

FIG. 15-18
Independent control file flowchart

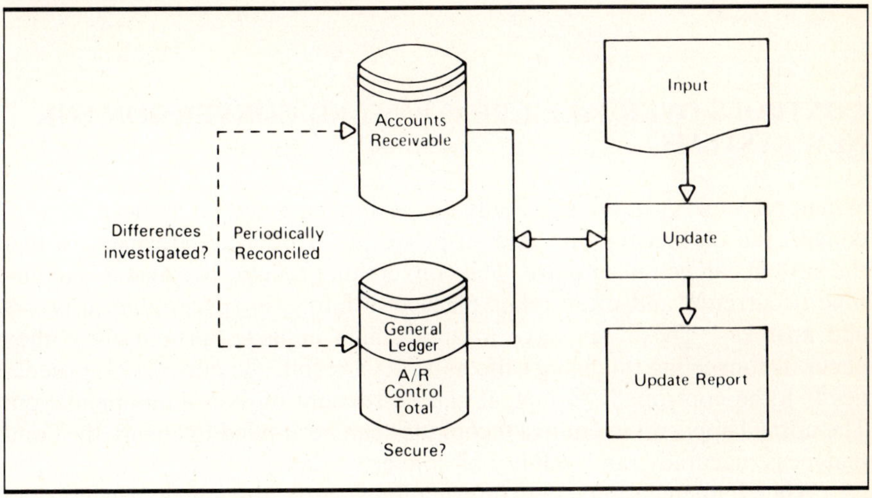

- Prices showing an abnormally high or low fluctuation.

For the exception reports to be relied on, the method used in the program for identifying exceptional items must be logically sound. This requires that careful consideration be given to the setting of parameters used.

Detailed Checking of Data on File. Controls for the maintenance of master file data can also be exercised by regularly checking data on the file against authorized source documentation. When this checking is done, it is usual to check only a portion of the file at a time. Thus, the whole file is regularly checked in cycles. As a result, the control technique is often referred to as "cyclical checking." The frequency of checking depends largely on the importance of the data and the existence and strength of other controls (such as the checking of suppliers' statements).

If checking is carried out on a cyclical basis, the selection of items for checking should preferably be made at random. It should not be predictable, which might inspire a manipulation of data just prior to the check.

Data File Security Controls. Data file security controls are required within the MIS department to prevent unauthorized access to, and use of, data files. The control provided relates only to the correctness of data, providing no assurance as to the currency of data. (These procedures are discussed in Chapter 13, "Information Technology Controls.")

CONTROLS OVER FILE CREATION AND CONVERSION FOR NEW SYSTEMS

Whenever new systems are ready to be implemented, it is necessary to convert the old master files and suspense files to the new formats so that the system can be put into use. The conversion process, because it is a one-time occurrence and often takes place in a hurry, is susceptible to errors and mistakes. These can have a far-reaching impact, particularly if they occur in converting the master file data. As a result, the conversion process needs to be controlled. In fact, it can be thought of as a mini-application. The normal application control techniques can be applied to ensure the completeness, accuracy, and validity of converted data.

When implementing a new information system, the master file data can be entered for the first time using the future system's normal data input procedures. The new system, of course, should have adequate application controls built into the data change process. Providing that these controls are adequate, the main problem is that the controls are being operated by inexperienced people for the first time and in volumes that are higher than normal. Therefore, the entire procedure is more susceptible to mistakes. The control procedures should be carefully monitored to ensure the correct conversion of the data. When existing systems are changed for new ones, it may also be necessary to enter new master file data. The same considerations apply when the new master file data amendment procedures are used.

It may not be practical to convert all the data using the new manual data amendment procedures. Account balances and other cumulative transaction data, as well as master file data from existing computer systems, are usually converted by computer programs that are written especially for this purpose. These programs may not always be developed and tested with the same care as the new system as a whole. Therefore, there is a particular need to ensure that the conversion process takes place correctly. It is always advisable to test the conversion programs thoroughly. Proper application controls over the conversion process are necessary; they are significant whenever, for any reason, the conversion programs have not been tested.

One-for-one checking is a common technique for data entered manually to the new files. It is also commonly applied to data transferred from one file to another, particularly when the data is sensitive and the volume is not too large.

As a minimum, when information is transferred from one file to another, control totals should be used on all significant fields. A program should read the existing applications file and establish hash totals for each field on the file. After conversion, these totals should be independently reconciled to similar totals taken from the new file.

Programmed edit checks are valuable control techniques, particularly for controlling the accuracy and the validity of data. Their disadvantage for controlling conversions lies in their complexity and the time necessary to program and test them. However, it is sometimes possible to pass the newly converted data through the edit programs in the new system. This technique should be applied wherever it is feasible. It is not possible to treat all data fields in this way, since the edits in the new system are usually designed to handle input transactions, whereas the conversion process is trying to convert existing master file data and balances. The use of edits is particularly valuable for data that is being collected and used for the first time; data coming from existing manual sysstems, which tend to be less accurate than well-controlled computer systems; or data that comes from an existing information system that is known to be inaccurate in some respects.

Whichever techniques are used, it is always desirable to manually review the data after conversion to ensure that it is valid. This process is similar to the authorization of transactions and should be carried out by someone with sufficient knowledge of the company's operations to be able to notice any substantial errors.

Parallel running can be used to test the operation of the new system. The comparison of the results produced by the new system with the results produced by the old system from the same input may expose some errors on the new master files. The longer the parallel tests are run, the more likely it is that errors on the new file will be picked up. Maintenance controls (those controls over the continued correctness and currency of stored data) may also detect errors on the new file. Although valuable in helping to detect errors, these controls cannot be used as a complete substitute for the types of detailed application controls described previously.

Because of the high risk of error and the potentially significant consequences of those errors, the conversion process is often checked or audited by supervisory personnel, the EDP auditor, a quality assurance group, or a similar function.

Techniques used to check the conversion process include:

- Test checking individual data and records on the new file to the source records.
- The use of audit software or verification programs to look for exceptional or unusual data on the new file.

- The use of audit software or specially developed programs to compare information on the new application files with that on the existing application files and to report differences.

File conversions are very rarely simple when, for every record in the existing format, the record will be reformatted for the new system. Often, conversions are no more than making the change from a nine-digit identifying number to a 10-digit number (such a change means that the entire organization will have to implement it at the same time). A more difficult conversion occurs when the data for the new application will be derived from the old data through the use of logic in programmed procedures. The programs, obviously, must be accurate.

ADMINISTRATIVE CONTROLS

Administrative or operational controls are designed to ensure that an organization's information structure functions as management intended. The application controls deal mainly with internal controls. Management's concerns are, of course, much wider in scope.

Administrative controls relate to the effectiveness of operations within an organization. They can be considered as the controls that ensure the timeliness of information and the efficiency of the control procedures and of the processing in general. They also relate to the effectiveness of management decisions. The reliability of the information on which management decisions are based and the procedures for implementing management decisions are inextricably linked. A review of administrative controls might also consider the appropriateness of management's decisions in relation to the objectives of the organization.

Efficiency

Efficiency relates to the cost incurred in processing and controlling the system. A review of administrative controls typically includes the efficiency of internal accounting control procedures as well as a consideration of efficiencies in all parts of the system. A knowledge of the most cost-efficient techniques is particularly valuable when designing or modifying systems. In some cases the more effective control procedures are also less costly. An example is when time-consuming, detailed clerical checks are replaced with accurate computer-based reporting procedures. These are usually more precise and less costly to operate, making a twofold contribution to efficiency.

Timeliness

A company can operate more effectively if its information is up-to-date. Some delays are inevitable, but timeliness can be enhanced.

Generally, the easiest ways to reduce the age of the information are to shorten the period involved, increase the frequency of the reports, or switch from batch processing to an on-line system.

The speed with which errors, exceptions, and control failures are detected should be considered. The timely detection of errors has the following advantages:

- Further errors, or a repetition of the same mistake, can be prevented by changing the procedures that allowed the error to take place.
- The investigation of the cause of an error is easier when checking transactions recently completed.
- Reversing the effect of an error is easier earlier in the transaction cycle before the error has had a chance to affect other information within the system.
- If the error is caught early in the transaction processing cycle, it will pass through only the early stages twice, avoiding duplicate processing at the later stages (once for the erroneous transaction, once for the correct one).

Management Information

Management needs far more than financial information. For this reason, many accounting information systems are part of management information systems. In such systems, accounting procedures are just one of the systems that exist within the overall system.

Much management information is derived from processing that is very similar to that occurring in a financial information system. One major difference is in the required precision of the results. Information accurate to within 5 percent may be sufficient for many management purposes. This is particularly true when more accurate information is more costly to prepare or would take more time. Other features of management information systems include:

- Need for up-to-date information.
- Greater need for specialized inquiry and reports, as opposed to the routine reports of financial information systems.
- Need to produce summary reports, exception reports, or graphic

representations of information in a form that is easily used by management.

- Power of senior management to request special information, which may take priority over much of the normal processing.
- Possible unfamiliarity of senior management with the capabilities of the management information system. This is particularly true when the EDP system is technologically advanced. Management may not realize, and therefore not specify, the detailed nature of the information available from the systems that would be of greatest assistance.

Management information systems naturally include many nonfinancial transactions and data. Control techniques for these are similar to those used in financial systems. They cover the same concerns of completeness, accuracy, authorization, and maintenance of data. In addition, the efficiency of processing, as well as the timeliness, quality, and usefulness of the management information, should be considered.

Quality of Information

Due to background and experience, the operational or EDP auditor is able to make suggestions that will improve the information received by management. This is particularly valuable when senior management is not intimately familiar with details of the management information system or the capabilities of MIS systems. Common suggestions could include:

- Adding information to a report that would make it more useful to management.
- Resequencing a report so that the most significant items appear at the front.
- Restructuring reports for clarity and ease of use.
- Producing better summaries and subtotals so that management can review information at an overview level.
- Greater use of exception reports, thereby decreasing the cost of producing the reports and making management more effective by concentrating attention on those items that require action.
- Suggesting additional reports that can be readily produced for management, since the data already exists within the system.

PART V

The Risk-Based Audit Approach

CHAPTER **16**

The Risk-Based Audit Approach

INTRODUCTION

Advances in computer technology and changing professional standards have encouraged development of significant enhancements to the audit approach presented in the original *Handbook of EDP Auditing*. The risk-based audit approach described in this chapter allows the auditor to take a broad look at the way a company controls its business. The approach is flexible, risk-sensitive, and makes maximum use of the auditor's intellect and judgment. It allows examination of the business from management's perspective, allowing auditors to make observations and recommendations that are responsive to management concerns.

Some of the more significant concepts in a risk-based approach are:

- More emphasis on using knowledge of the organization, which includes understanding its control environment, to assess risk and make testing decisions.
- Assessment of the control environment, identifying operating and control recommendations.
- A focus on assessment of the effectiveness of a combination of controls, instead of compliance testing of individual control procedures, as the basis for judgments about control risk.
- Flexible tools called Control Assessment and Record of Tests (CARTs) help in understanding and assessing internal control procedures in modern computer systems.
- A stronger linkage between risk assessments and testing decisions through an increased focus on audit objectives.

Figure 16-1 summarizes the principal steps in this risk-based approach. Each section of this chapter focuses on one of the steps depicted in the chart, highlighting major procedures and practical implications and benefits of applying the approach. While this chapter focuses on audits of financial systems, the concepts apply equally to reviews of all information technology-based systems. (See the glossary for key terms)

SUMMARY OF THE RISK-BASED AUDIT APPROACH

The audit approach emphasizes the assessment of risks relative to specified audit objectives to ensure an effective and efficient audit. The first step, perform initial audit activities, is to gather or update information about the organization to determine the audit strategy. Determining the audit strategy includes making judgments about materiality and assessing inherent and con-

FIG. 16-1

The risk-based audit approach

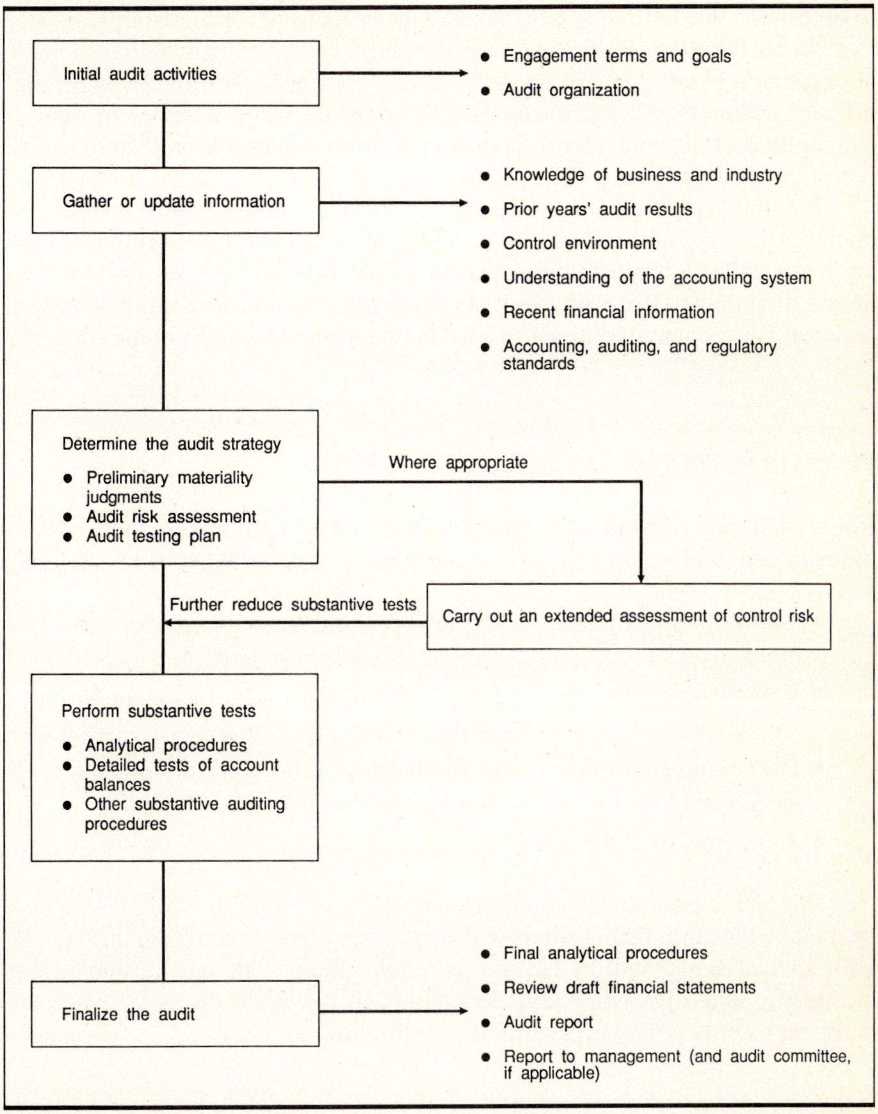

trol risks to develop the audit testing plan. Risk assessments are related to audit objectives for individual account balances and classes of transactions to determine the minimum level of assurance required from substantive tests.

As part of the audit testing plan, the auditor will decide whether to make an extended assessment of control risk for certain audit objectives for significant accounts. This decision is a basis for deciding whether to restrict substantive tests, and plan responses to other favorable and unfavorable factors identified during risk assessment.

Preliminary judgments about materiality and assessments of inherent and control risks may be revised as substantive tests are performed and the audit is finalized. Both risk assessments and substantive tests provide evidence to support the audit report and provide a basis for making operating and control recommendations to management and the audit committee.

PERFORM INITIAL AUDIT ACTIVITIES

Initial audit activities identify the requirements of audit acceptance and administration, and establish goals for the audit. Initial audit activities include:

- Gathering information as a basis for the decision to perform an audit.
- Establishing or confirming the terms of the current-year audit and establishing specific audit goals.
- Determining whether to use the work of other auditors and specialists (such as actuaries, appraisers, etc.).
- Assigning an audit team.

The risk-based approach emphasizes that initial audit activities be performed by the audit team leader, with appropriate assistance from individuals with special skills such as tax and computer audit. The nature and extent of specific activities will vary, depending on factors such as whether the audit represents a new or a continuing situation.

GATHER OR UPDATE INFORMATION ABOUT THE ORGANIZATION

The understanding and assessment of the control environment and the understanding of internal accounting controls should be documented. Information obtained about the entity in the current and prior years should be used to assess risk and make testing decisions.

The following information is important in assessing inherent and control risk and making appropriate audit strategy and testing decisions:

- Knowledge of an organization's business and industry.
- Review of prior years' audit results.
- An understanding of the accounting system.
- An analysis of recent financial information.
- Knowledge of applicable accounting, auditing, and regulatory standards.

Although a formal, documented assessment of the control environment (management's attitudes, abilities, perceptions, and actions in overseeing the effectiveness of the entity's accounting system and internal accounting control procedures) is not required, audit teams generally consider the quality of the control environment when making audit strategy and testing decisions. Documentation can make it easier to understand and assess the control environment and develop the audit strategy and testing plan.

The risk-based approach emphasizes a continuous audit process. All information obtained about the organization, in both current and prior years, is used to assess risk and make testing decisions. As a result, control risk does not necessarily have to be assessed as high even when there are no tests performed of internal accounting controls.

The remainder of this section discusses in more detail:

- Requirements, under a new Statement on Auditing Standards (SAS), to understand and assess the control structure on all external audits.
- How the control environment fits into the broader concept of the control structure.
- How to assess the control environment and use the assessment to improve the quality of the audit and accomplish broader objectives.
- More flexible methods of documenting internal accounting controls.
- The increased importance of understanding the accounting system and the key role of computer audit specialists in assessing risk.

Control Structure

A significant aspect of the audit approach is a broad view of controls, to include all elements of an organization's operations that are designed to prevent or detect material misstatements in the financial statements. SAS No. 55, *Consideration of the Internal Control Structure in a Financial Statement Audit* (which is mandatory for external audits of fiscal years beginning January 1, 1990), establishes the concept of the control structure and the requirement to obtain a sufficient understanding of its elements to plan the audit. The audit approach incorporates this standard.

The elements of the control structure are the:

- Control environment.
- Accounting system.
- Internal accounting controls.

Control Environment. The control environment encompasses the attitudes, abilities, perceptions, and actions of an organization's personnel, particularly its management. The "tone at the top" and active involvement of key members of management in monitoring financial and operating results are examples of factors that can contribute to the quality of an entity's control environment and to the fair presentation of its financial statements.

Accounting System. The accounting system is the set of methods and records established to identify, assemble, classify, analyze, and record an entity's transactions. Those methods and records assist in the effective operation of the business, permit the proper preparation of financial statements, and are important in preventing material misstatements in those statements.

Internal Accounting Controls. Internal accounting controls are specific procedures established by management to ensure that an entity's transactions are processed completely and accurately and recorded in accordance with management's authorization, and that assets are safeguarded.

Assessing the Control Environment

An assessment of the control environment should be made as part of gathering or updating information about the organization. This assessment provides a basis for:

- Determining to what extent the environment appears to encourage the maintenance of reliable accounting and control procedures.
- Determining the extent to which the environment reduces

incentives and opportunities for intentional misrepresentations by management in the financial statements.

- Identifying significant reports and procedures used by management to control the business that can be helpful in designing substantive tests.
- Identifying high-level control and operating issues of concern to top management, boards of directors, and audit committees.

Procedures and Documentation Requirements

Auditors assess the quality of the control environment by addressing factors such as:

- Organizational structure and key executive responsibilities.
- The role of the board of directors, audit committee, and internal audit.
- Management's judgments and financial statement integrity.
- Performance planning and monitoring.
- Availability and reliability of management information.
- Policies and procedures for control and accountability.
- Control of the MIS organization.

Some of these factors influence the entity's ability to maintain reliable internal accounting controls. Others influence management's ability to make the judgments needed to prepare financial statements, and still others influence the entity's ability to restrict opportunities for management fraud.

Effect of the Assessment on Audit Quality

After considering factors that either contribute to or detract from the quality of the entity's control environment, an overall conclusion is made and documented, reflecting:

- Whether the environment appears to be conducive to maintaining reliable internal accounting controls.
- The apparent quality of management's judgments and estimates.
- Whether sufficient, reliable information appears to be available for management to conduct and control the business effectively.

This conclusion should be considered, together with other information obtained about the organization, to assess control risk, determine the appropriate audit strategy and testing plan, and identify recommendations to management and the audit committee.

For example, a conclusion that an entity's control environment is extremely effective in contributing to the prevention or detection of material misstatements should be a key favorable consideration, along with other information, in designing the nature, timing, and extent of substantive tests. Individual factors or conclusions that indicate potential weaknesses in the control environment should be evaluated to ensure that all significant risks are addressed fully by substantive tests, and that appropriate recommendations for improvement are made to management and the audit committee.

Documentation identifying potential weaknesses in the control environment can assist in:

- Making recommendations on issues that management should focus on in the future (e.g., key employee succession planning).
- Promoting more meaningful discussions with management and the audit committee about control and operating matters.

Understanding the Accounting System and Internal Accounting Controls

The audit approach emphasizes understanding the accounting system and internal accounting controls, since they are critical to making appropriate testing decisions. Procedures in the approach provide:

- Flexibility in documenting internal accounting controls.
- Guidance on how to understand and document accounting systems and the computer environment.
- Clarification of how information obtained about the accounting system can be used in assessing risk and making testing decisions.

Documenting the Accounting System. Understanding the accounting system is documented by preparing an overview flowchart and completing the Computer Environment Form (CEF), shown in part in Figure 16-2. The overview flowchart should be in sufficient detail to facilitate planning and designing of substantive tests and to supplement detailed testing of internal accounting controls, if performed. If existing documentation of the system provides enough information to determine the audit strategy and plan and design substantive tests, it need not be redrafted.

FIG. 16-2

Computer Environment Form (partial)

INSTRUCTIONS TO PART 1: PROCESSING ENVIRONMENT

MIS organization

Identify main contact for appointments and obtaining technical support.

Record the size and structure of the MIS department. If possible, attach a copy of the MIS organization chart.

Hardware

Identify the computer manufacturer (e.g., IBM, Honeywell, DEC, etc.) and the Central Processing Unit (CPU) model number (e.g., 4341, System 38, HP 3000, VAX 11/780, PCXT, etc.). Check types of magnetic storage media used.

Software

Identify software, for example:

Operating system: DOS/VSE Release 4, MVS/XA, VM/CMS Release 5, etc.

Communications software: VTAM & CICS 1.8, IMS/DC, ACF/NCP, etc.

Major programming languages: COBOL, RPGII, Assembler, etc.

Inquiry/report writer packages available: Query, Quiz, DFU, Easytrieve, etc. (Identify application specific inquiry/report writer features in Part 2 under package details)

Network

Describe the network. List terminals, remote processors and dial-up lines, their approximate number and main purpose. (Alternatively, obtain a copy of the network overview diagram). For example:

Terminals/Processors/Lines	Number	Location	Purpose
PCs and 327X terminals	5	MIS	Programming and operations
327X terminals	10	Accounting	Accounting
	5	Warehouses	Shipping/Receiving
	5	Various	Non-accounting
DEC/VAX & 5 terminals	1	Houston	Local sales order processing and inventory control
Dial-up lines	3		Access by PCs. Mainly inquiries
PCs (off line)	approx. 40	Various	End-user computing. About 10 with modems

Documenting Internal Accounting Controls. On all audits, the auditor should obtain an understanding of internal accounting controls sufficient to assess control risk and design substantive tests. Audit teams can prepare File and Transaction Control Matrices and the Preliminary Assessment of Information Technology Controls form (PAIT) as part of gaining an understanding of internal accounting controls. The PAIT includes considerations such as data processing strategic plans and disaster planning.

Portions of the PAIT can be completed to identify matters to be reported to management or to assist in obtaining a general understanding of information technology (IT) controls for determining areas in which to make an extended assessment of control risk. These tools may be helpful in making audit strategy decisions and identifying management comments. (See Figures 16-3, 16-4, and 16-5 for examples.) The extent of the understanding of internal accounting controls necessary, and the nature of related documentation, will vary from audit to audit, based on the planned audit strategy, the organization's accounting systems, the characteristics of its account balances, and audit objectives addressed by substantive tests. (Figure 16-6 summarizes the documentation to be used in this phase of the audit.)

Documenting the Computer Environment. An understanding of the hardware and software used in significant applications should be obtained and documented by completing the CEF.

Using Information Technology Audit Specialists

Information technology audit specialists should participate in preparing accounting systems documentation to enhance information-gathering effectiveness. Joint participation of general and computer audit staff in the process of understanding the accounting system can improve the quality and efficiency of the risk assessment process, generate more in-depth recommendations, and improve the exchange of knowledge and ideas among auditors.

DETERMINE THE AUDIT STRATEGY

Information gathered or updated about the entity supports judgments about the audit strategy and testing plan. Decisions about the audit testing plan are made in terms of audit objectives for significant accounts.

The key to an effective audit strategy and audit testing plan is considering all information known about an entity, in terms of audit risk and audit objectives. The professional judgment and experience of the audit team are critical here. Documenting important strategy decisions in the strategy memorandum and more detailed elements of those decisions in the audit program provides effective direction to the staff responsible for their implementation.

FIG. 16-3
File Control Matrix (partial)

Coopers & Lybrand

File Control Matrix (AAM 33402)

Client/Location ______________________

Application/Class of transactions ______________________

Financial statement account name and value	Key file(s) and/or data elements	File continuity				
		Detail level	(Check (√) corresponding audit objective)			Total level
			Completeness	Accuracy	Existence	

Form 93-0588

FIG. 16-4

Transaction Control Matrix (partial)

Coopers &Lybrand

Transaction Control Matrix (AAM 33402)

Client/Location ____________

Application/Class of transactions ____________

Significant transactions/ key fields (Volumes)	Input/Generation			
	Completeness	Accuracy (specify fields)	Standing data used	Authorization

Form 94-0588

FIG. 16-5

Preliminary Assessment of Information Technology Controls (partial)

PRELIMINARY ASSESSMENT OF INFORMATION TECHNOLOGY CONTROLS

Part 1: Assessment of control risk

Questions	Yes	No	Comments
A. Organization of computer processing 1. In the context of the client's operations, is the number of people employed in the Management Information Systems (MIS) department sufficient to enable a proper division of duties to exist?			
B. Implementation 1. Where systems are developed internally, does the client have adequate procedures governing the review and approval of the design, testing and implementation of new systems by responsible user and MIS personnel? 2. Where systems are purchased from outside vendors, does the client have procedures governing the selection, testing and implementation of new systems by processing personnel? 3. Are there adequate procedures for transferring all new programs into production? 4. Are instructions for the following prepared and issued as part of the systems documentation: (a) Operation procedures? (b) Back-up requirements? (c) User clerical procedures? Do the answers to questions B. 1-4 above indicate that the implementation is likely to be adequately controlled?			
C. Maintenance 1. Are there procedures for making amendments to systems and programs, including modifications to purchased application packages, that govern the review and approval of the design, testing and implementation of amendments by responsible user and MIS personnel? 2. Are there adequate procedures for transferring all modified programs into production? 3. Are there procedures to ensure that the users of modified systems are instructed in their duties? 4. Where purchased software is used, is the source code secure from access by client's staff? Do the answers to questions C. 1-4 above indicate that the maintenance of applications is likely to be adequately controlled?			

FIG. 16-6
Documentation for understanding of accounting systems

Form	Use in Audit Approach
Overview Flowchart	Required
Computer Environment Form (CEF)	Required
File and Transaction Control Matrices	Optional
Preliminary Assessment of Information Technology Controls (PAIT)	Optional

Determining the Audit Strategy

Materiality judgments and risk assessments are the basis for audit strategy decisions. Preliminary judgments about materiality and assessments of inherent and control risk are used to focus on audit objectives and account balances with higher audit risk and to restrict tests of those with lower audit risk.

The audit testing plan is the plan of action for achieving the desired audit objectives for significant accounts. It considers the favorable and unfavorable factors identified from risk assessment activities. A key decision in the plan is whether to extend previous assessments of control risk for certain audit objectives as a basis for restricting substantive tests. Extending the assessment of control risk entails obtaining and recording a detailed understanding of internal accounting controls and determining whether they operate effectively through various tests of controls. These were formerly called compliance tests. Determining the most appropriate audit testing plan is always a matter of professional judgment.

Deciding Whether to Make an Extended Assessment of Control Risk

Similar to the concept of compliance testing of controls, making an extended assessment of control risk and performing tests of controls provide a basis for restricting substantive tests. (The process of making an extended assessment is discussed in detail in Chapter 19, "The Control Risk Assessment Process.") This strategy decision is based on the same factors that were considered in deciding whether to perform compliance tests. An extended assessment is normally made only for systems-derived accounts, which are considered part of a transaction cycle and are commonly subject to internal accounting controls. Examples of systems-derived accounts include accounts receivable, inventory, accounts payable, purchases, and sales.

Often, the audit team will decide that it is not efficient to make an extended assessment of control risk when:

- The prior year's audit or other information about an entity indicates that internal accounting controls are not effective.
- Transaction volumes are low or the nature of assets, liabilities, or operations makes substantive testing more efficient.
- The control environment appears to be unfavorable.
- The organization has manual systems, or computerized systems that are neither complex nor integrated.

In those circumstances, a program of substantive tests is designed to address relevant audit objectives for significant account balances and consider judgments about materiality and evidence already obtained from risk assessments.

When an extended assessment of control risk appears to be an effective testing option, the following factors should also be considered before a decision is made:

- Whether audit savings from reduced substantive tests will exceed the costs of performing an extended assessment.
- The organization's reporting deadline, which may make it impractical to perform only substantive tests.
- The organization's expectations and potential benefits from a more detailed assessment of controls.
- Benefits that could be derived from enhanced use and training of staff.

In large organizations with complex computerized systems, it may appear that an extended assessment of control risk would be appropriate. However, because organization operations and accounting systems vary widely, the decision is a matter of judgment on each audit.

Normally, an extended assessment of control risk is not an efficient strategy when IT controls are inadequate. In most systems, application controls depend on the proper operation of programmed procedures. When relevant IT controls do not ensure the continued proper operation of programmed procedures, an extended assessment of control risk may require a large amount of reperformance, and thus may not be an efficient strategy.

In small and medium-size organizations, the use of packaged software may mitigate weaknesses in certain IT controls, and those in place may not need to be formal and complex. Accordingly, the audit hours spent identifying and assessing relevant IT controls in packaged software environments may be reduced considerably. Provided that relevant IT controls are identified and assessed as satisfactory, the risk of improper operation of programmed procedures in this type of environment generally can be assessed as low, and an extended assessment of control risk may be an effective testing option.

Making Testing Decisions in Terms of Audit Objectives

When selecting and designing substantive tests, attention should be directed to specific audit objectives. These are completeness, accuracy, existence, cutoff, valuation, rights and obligations, and presentation and disclosure. (Figure 16-7 lists and defines those audit objectives and illustrates their application to trade accounts receivable and sales.)

The risk-based audit approach uses the framework of audit objectives to link assessments of inherent and control risk and substantive tests. Guidance and practice tools illustrated in this chapter are designed to focus on this linkage. This focus is critical because, although all relevant audit objectives should be considered when planning substantive tests, the degree of risk and concern is not usually the same for all objectives.

Audit Objectives With Lower Risk. The risk of material misstatement, and therefore the assurance required from substantive tests, will often be lower, even when an extended assessment of control risk is not made, for the completeness, accuracy, and, in some cases, existence and cutoff objectives because:

- Those objectives are often addressed by internal accounting controls.
- The degree of discipline necessary to process data by computer (particularly with the increasing use of packaged software) reduces the risk of material misstatement with respect to accuracy and, to a lesser extent, completeness.
- These objectives normally are not affected by management's subjective judgments and estimates.

When an extended assessment of control risk has been made, substantive tests directed to completeness and accuracy can often be restricted to analytical procedures. However, due to the risk of management override of controls, minimum levels of substantive tests of details for existence and cutoff may still be needed.

Control risk cannot be assessed as low unless an extended assessment

FIG. 16-7

Audit objectives and examples of application to trade accounts receivable and sales

Audit Objectives	Examples of Application to Trade Accounts Receivable and Sales
Completeness—All account balances and transactions that should be included in the financial statements are included.	■ Trade accounts receivable represent all amounts owed to the entity, with respect to sales transactions, at the balance sheet date. ■ All shipments or services rendered during the period covered by the financial statements are reflected in the financial statements.
Accuracy—Recorded transactions and account balances are mathematically accurate, are based on correct amounts, have been classified in the proper accounts, and have been accurately summarized and recorded in the general ledger.	■ Accounts receivable balances reflect sales transactions that are based on correct prices and quantities and are accurately computed and classified in the appropriate general ledger and accounts receivable subsidiary ledger accounts. ■ Invoice summarizations and postings to the trade accounts receivable subsidiary ledger and sales account are correct. ■ The trade accounts receivable subsidiary ledger is mathematically correct and agrees with the general ledger.
Existence—Recorded assets and liabilities exist as of the balance sheet date; recorded transactions have occurred and are not fictitious.	■ Recorded trade accounts receivable represent amounts owed to the entity at the balance sheet date. ■ Recorded sales transactions represent actual goods shipped or services rendered during the period covered by the financial statements.
Cutoff—Transactions are recorded in the proper accounting period.	■ Sales transactions are recorded in the proper period.
Valuation—Generally accepted accounting measurement and recognition principles are properly selected and applied.	■ Trade accounts receivable are stated at net collectable amounts (i.e., allowances for doubtful accounts, discounts, returns, and similar items are appropriately determined). ■ Revenue is recognized only when appropriate recognition and measurement criteria are met.

(*continued*)

FIG. 16-7 (*continued*)

Audit Objectives	Examples of Application to Trade Accounts Receivable and Sales
Rights and obligations—Recorded assets are rights of the entity and recorded liabilities are obligations of the entity at the balance sheet date.	■ Trade accounts receivable are legal rights of the entity at the balance sheet date (i.e., customer accounts that have been sold or factored are excluded from the trade accounts receivable balance).
Presentation and disclosure—Financial statement components are properly classified and described; appropriate disclosures are made.	■ Trade accounts receivable and sales are properly described and classified in the financial statements. ■ Trade accounts receivable pledged as collateral are properly disclosed. ■ Changes in the measurement and recognition of revenue have been properly presented and are disclosed.

of control risk is made. If this risk is not assessed as low, some substantive tests directed to those "lower risk" objectives should be performed.

Audit Objectives With Higher Risk. The risk of material misstatement associated with the valuation, rights and obligations, and presentation and disclosure objectives is usually higher than for other audit objectives because:

- Management's judgments and estimates affect those objectives significantly.
- An organization may not have the professional expertise to deal completely with some of the issues relating to those objectives.

Even in large, well-managed entities, rarely can the risk of material misstatement be assessed as low with respect to those objectives. Careful consideration should be given to inherent risk conditions and the control environment when designing and performing tests regarding those objectives. Particularly relevant aspects of the control environment include the:

- Role of the board of directors and audit committee in overseeing the selection of accounting principles and development of estimates.
- Circumstances in the business that may cause intentional misstatements.

- Adequacy of information available to make decisions and develop estimates.
- Competence of individuals responsible for developing estimates.

Testing Income Statement Accounts. Normally, it is not necessary to perform substantive tests of details directed to transactions in the income statement. Assurance about those transactions comes from:

- Audit work carried out on the balance sheet for unsettled transactions.
- Analytical procedures, which confirm the low risk of material misstatement associated with settled transactions in the income statement, and identify significant misclassifications or defalcations embedded in the income statement.

Substantive tests of details of income statement accounts are appropriate when the risk of material misstatement in a particular account is high, or because of specific disclosure requirements.

Documentation of the Audit Strategy

Audit strategy documentation requirements include the strategy memorandum, which should document important issues identified in initial audit activities, significant information gathered or updated about the organization, and the audit testing plan, including the rationale for deciding whether to perform an extended assessment of control risk. The strategy memorandum should be in sufficient detail to identify how audit objectives will be achieved, but should not duplicate details in the audit program.

CARRY OUT AN EXTENDED ASSESSMENT OF CONTROL RISK

SAS No. 55, *Consideration of the Internal Control Structure in a Financial Statement Audit*, which is mandatory for external audits of fiscal years beginning January 1, 1990, makes fundamental changes in professional requirements regarding the study and evaluation of internal control. The risk-based audit approach incorporates this standard through procedures and documentation for the assessment of the control environment, understanding the accounting system in assessing control risk, and making an extended assessment of control risk in appropriate situations.

Making an extended assessment of control risk, including tests of controls, replaces compliance testing in the risk-based approach. Examination of evidence, together with inquiry and observation, is recognized as an acceptable alternative to testing controls by reperformance.

Similar to the concept of compliance testing control procedures, making an extended assessment of control risk provides a basis for restricting substantive tests. However, the two approaches differ in a number of important ways:

- Compliance testing focuses on *control procedures* within *transaction cycles*. In an extended assessment of control risk, the focus is on *audit objectives* for *account balances*, which helps to relate tests of controls to substantive testing.
- Examination of evidence and reperformance are the primary techniques used to perform compliance tests; reperforming control procedures ordinarily involves sampling. The risk-based approach recognizes that examination of evidence, coupled with in-depth inquiry and observation, often provides sufficient evidence about the effective design and operation of controls without using sampling techniques.
- Compliance testing focuses on determining whether a control procedure is reliable by searching for evidence of exceptions in its operation. In an extended assessment, the focus is on whether individuals responsible for a control understand it and are diligent in its execution. For computerized controls, emphasis is on the control design and assurance that it is implemented, maintained, and operated properly.
- Formerly, the absence of a specific control procedure was addressed by identifying a compensating control or designing a substantive test procedure. In risk-based auditing, controls in place are identified and assessed to reach a conclusion about the risk of error for a particular audit objective. Conclusions about control risk are based on the effectiveness of a combination of controls, not on the presence and effectiveness of individual controls in isolation.
- In compliance testing, tests for evidence about the continuous operation of a particular control are usually spread. By contrast, in an extended assessment, other sources of evidence of the continuous operation of controls, in addition to tests of individual controls, are recognized. These include successful day-to-day use of system-generated data by third parties and others in the organization; management's use of, and reliance on, this data to monitor and direct the organization's operations; and secondary evidence from substantive tests directed primarily at other audit objectives.

These important features of control risk assessment should be supported by new procedures and tools. The CARTs tool provides for understanding and assessing control procedures concurrently, providing the flexibility necessary for carrying out an extended assessment of control risk in modern computer environments. (See Chapter 19 for information on making an extended assessment of control risk and examples of CARTs.)

PERFORM SUBSTANTIVE TESTS

Linking Risk Assessments to Substantive Tests

The assurance required from substantive tests, and thus the nature, timing, and extent of those tests, depends on the assessments of inherent and control risk made earlier in the audit. The risk-based audit approach makes that linkage clear by relating assessments of inherent and control risk to specific audit objectives and by indicating the audit objectives relevant to each substantive test.

Analytical Procedures

Analytical procedures should be used as substantive tests. The decision to use analytical procedures, substantive tests of details, or both, to provide assurance with respect to audit objectives is a matter of professional judgment, considering factors in designing and performing analytical procedures that should contribute to improved audit quality and effectiveness.

FINALIZE THE AUDIT

Procedure for finalizing the audit should address recent professional standards on communicating with management and audit committees. Those communications, their content and format, depend on particular organizational requirements.

Procedures for finalizing the audit (for an external auditor) consist primarily of:

- Reviewing subsequent events, including consideration of the organization's ability to continue operations (as an ongoing concern).
- Obtaining managements' and others' representations.

- Performing final analytical procedures on the draft financial statements.
- Reviewing the draft financial statements for appropriate presentation and disclosure.

The risk-based approach emphasizes the importance of performing final analytics as an overall check on the financial statements and preparation for discussions with management, boards of directors, and audit committees.

These procedures address SAS No. 60, *The Communication of Internal Control Structure Related Matters Noted in an Audit*, and SAS No. 61, *Communications With Audit Committees*. These new pronouncements change the external auditor's responsibility for communicating to management and the board of directors, or its audit committee, deficiencies in controls and other audit-related matters. Internal auditors will finalize their audits according to their organizational requirements, but should take the SAS requirements into consideration.

CHAPTER **17**

How to Document Systems: Using Flowcharts

DOCUMENTING THE SYSTEM

An auditor has to obtain an understanding of any system under review in order to plan a logical audit strategy. This means learning about the system. To do so, the auditor may review correspondence files, key business statistics, organization charts, internal audit reports, consultants' reports, procedural manuals, and external audit reports, including previous comments to management. Furthermore, the auditor may interview personnel at the location to be reviewed or tour the site to get first-hand knowledge of the operations under review. An important part of the audit is the documenting, or flowcharting, of systems under consideration.

It is also helpful for an auditor to review working papers from prior years. These reveal the type of work that was done in the past and the kinds of problems that were encountered. Finally, whenever possible, it is a good idea to interview the auditor who performed the review in the past. This can provide valuable insight into problem areas. In short, this is a research process the auditor performs in order to become familiar with the operation of the system.

FLOWCHARTING TECHNIQUES

There are several popular methods of flowcharting that are used to document, or put down on paper clearly, just what happens in a system. Flowcharts have become popular because their users find this special illustrative technique particularly effective.

Some of the major system-oriented flowcharting techniques and their principal characteristics are:

- *ANSI (American National Standards Institute)*—Uses standardized flowchart symbols and techniques.
- *PERT (Program Evaluation Review Technique) and CPM (Critical Path Method)*—Show precedence of activity, the relationships between events, and relative time sequence.
- *HIPO (Hierarchy: Input-Processing-Output)*—Depicts program or system elements in a hierarchical format, similar to a tree structure. This presentation can be quite helpful to an auditor in achieving an understanding of the purpose of the programs or systems. It subdivides systems into parts, and those parts are further subdivided into appropriate subparts.
- *Transaction flow diagrams*—Emphasize each transaction type and the procedures that affect each transaction. These are used frequently by auditors.
- *Microcomputer software packages*—Use fairly standard symbols.

There are a number of different graphic flowcharting techniques auditors use to structure their presentation of system information. The way the transaction flow itself is set out on the flowchart varies. Some of the more common techniques are:

- *Horizontal.* The transaction flow is shown from left to right on each page, with the far right of a page connecting with the far left of the following page.
- *Horizontal by organization.* The flow is depicted from left to right by organizational subunit. Within each subunit the sequential procedures or operations are shown vertically. The flowchart generally proceeds from top left to bottom right of a page.
- *Vertical.* A transaction flows down a single line, which shows the sequential operations that affect each transaction and the files or records that are needed at each operration. A key characteristic of this type of flowchart is that it shows final disposition of each transaction, file, or record on the flowline.

Each of these types of flowchart may employ its own set of unique symbols, as well as some fairly standard ones. The connecting line is the only universal feature of all flowcharting techniques.

An auditor interested in controls requires flowcharts that define clearly the point at which a control begins to exist and the range of operations or procedures covered by the control. In purely system-oriented flowcharts, the controls usually are depicted. A single flowline flowcharting technique (with a minimum of parallel functions) is very effective in documenting controls in both manual and automated systems. One such technique is presented here. Note that today's auditor often will use microcomputer packages to "draw" the flowchart.

FLOWCHARTING

Objective

Auditors flowchart systems to achieve the specific goal of documenting the system and its controls. To meet objectives, the following topics need to be reviewed:

- Summary of flowcharting principles and techniques to be used in documenting accounting systems of management information systems.
- Specific symbols and methods used in an audit-oriented flowcharting technique.
- Presentation of the flowcharting considerations unique to a computer-based system.
- Some of the more common errors encountered in flowcharts of computer systems.

Understanding the System

An understanding of the processing system for each transaction type and the controls incorporated is fundamental to an effective system evaluation. This understanding is the basis for evaluating internal controls and should be properly documented. Many auditors and system analysts use flowcharts for this purpose.

Advantages of Flowcharting

A flowchart serves two functions: comprehension and communication. By showing procedures in graphic form, flowcharts improve comprehension and provide a superior means for communicating information. Flowcharts allow the auditor to identify particular control features in the system. The significance of those features can then be evaluated to see whether they are meeting the objectives of the internal control system. Flowcharting promotes efficiency and uniformity in the preparation of working papers. For these criteria to be met, the charts must be prepared logically, concisely, and clearly.

When the right kind of flowchart is prepared, it also improves communication among those involved in the administration and evaluation of the internal control system, such as management, system development, and users.

Criteria for Flowcharting

The flowcharting technique shown here was designed specifically to depict control procedures. An auditor or system analyst should be able to determine which procedures are significant for purposes of meeting the internal control objectives of a system from these charts. This technique is shown because it has worked well for a wide variety of reviews and types of systems.

Flowcharts should meet the following criteria:

- Procedures should be shown in sequence.
- All copies of pertinent documents should be explained and accounted for.
- The maintenance of files and preparation of reports with control significance should be shown.
- The flow of transactions among the various departments of the business should be shown.
- Both manual and EDP operations should be shown.
- The title or position and, where practical, the name of people performing the procedures should be shown.

One Flowcharting Technique

This flowcharting technique meets the preceding criteria. Moreover, it provides a suitable basis for carrying out transaction reviews. The technique adapts standard flowcharting approaches to the special needs of the auditor (although it has also been found useful by others). Specifically, it:

- Identifies records, files, and reports.
- Provides descriptions of operations and related documents in the sequence of processing.
- Guides the auditor through all the processing steps leading to the disposition of copies of documents with internal accounting control significance.

Main Flowline. This flowcharting technique features a "main flowline" illustrating the flow of processing and the documents involved. The flowline runs from the beginning to the end of each system. It starts with the inception of transactions and ends with their recording in the financial or management records. It includes both manual and computer procedures. To depict a complete flow of transactions to their termination, flowcharts and/or narratives should show the posting to the general ledger. This helps to trace the flow of transactions into the accounting records and ensures that all principal documents in the system have been covered in the charts. Particular attention should be given to showing the steps in the flow of principal documents through the entire system, providing a suitable basis for carrying out transaction reviews. Figure 17-1 illustrates this concept of flowcharting.

Preparation of Flowcharts. The preparation or updating of flowcharts is an integral part of an internal control evaluation process. When possible, the same individual who obtains (or updates) an understanding of the system and related controls should develop the flowchart. The help of EDP auditors may be required in flowcharting computer systems. Flowcharts should be reviewed by supervisory personnel after they have been prepared.

Updating Flowcharts. Flowcharts or narratives should be reviewed and updated at scheduled intervals, preferably annually. When changes are necessary, the auditor may either draw new charts or correct the old ones. A complete redrawing of flowcharts is not usually required unless they have been entirely superseded or are no longer legible due to the number of changes. If the flowcharts require changes, photocopies of the old charts should be made beforehand so that there is a record of the procedures in force at a particular date.

Knowledge Required. Apart from providing the auditor with a general idea of how the procedures operate, the main audit use of flowcharts is to

FIG. 17-1
Concept of flowcharting

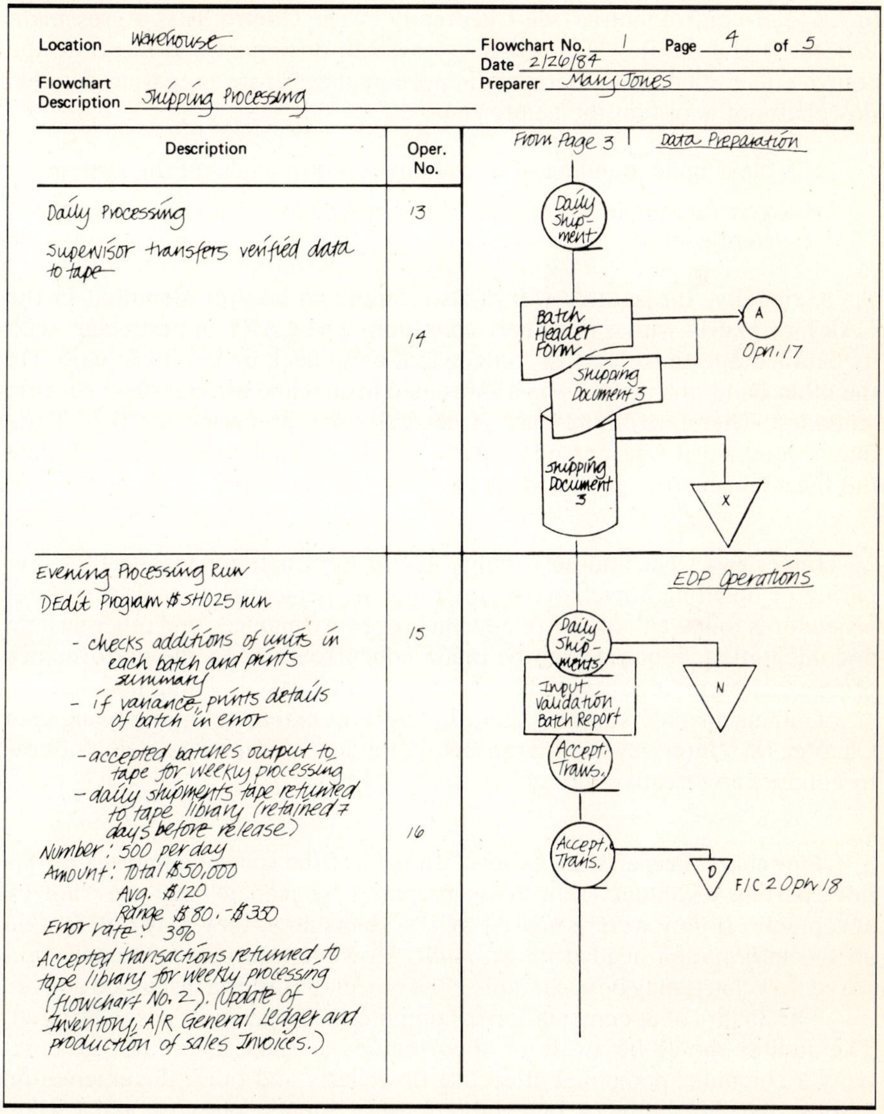

document controls. The evaluation of a system and the subsequent tests of that system are based on the Control Assessment and Record of Tests (CART) or control matrix (see Chapter 19, "The Control Risk Assessment Process") and the flowcharts that are used to document and illustrate the controls identified. It is therefore important that before preparing detailed flowcharts of a system the auditor has:

- A clear understanding of documents used to evaluate the system.
- A general idea of the nature of the procedures and controls in the system itself.

Generally, the auditor will cross-reference a control identified in the CART or matrix with a flowchart operation. The CART in particular, with its detailed questions, acts to some extent as a check on the flowcharts. On the other hand, the matrix is in a shortened format and provides less specific guidance. Therefore, more care is needed when preparing the flowcharts that accompany it. The person preparing the flowcharts should also complete the CART or matrix, in most cases.

Interviews. The auditor usually obtains information necessary for preparing or updating flowcharts by interviewing personnel at each site about procedures followed, and by reviewing procedure manuals and other system documentation. Inquiries can be made concurrently with the performance of transaction reviews, particularly when flowcharts are being updated.

Gaining an understanding typically involves extensive interviewing. See Chapter 18, "Interviews and Transaction Reviews," for a discussion of how to conduct an effective internal control inquiry.

Flowcharts Prepared by Others. In light of the special emphasis of this flowcharting technique, flowcharts prepared by management may not be acceptable. If they were prepared by a systems area, they may not contain all the information needed for an audit. However, certain previously prepared flowcharts may be acceptable if they meet the criteria discussed above.

The quality of documentation in computerized systems tends to be good. The auditor should be aware of opportunities to make use of it. The company's computer personnel often use flowcharts and other documentation to describe the sequence of computer runs, inputs, outputs, and certain processing details. This information may be particularly useful to the auditor obtaining an initial understanding of the computer applications and documenting programmed procedures. It is unlikely, however, that the material available will meet all the auditor's needs, particularly in relation to controls. Consequently, it usually cannot substitute for the kind of flowcharting described here. Nevertheless, the existing material may provide a useful supplement to the auditor's own flowcharts. The parts describing programmed procedures can be integrated with flowcharts of the manual procedures where possible.

The auditor must understand flowcharts prepared by others to use them. They must be suitable for the intended audit purposes and be adequately cross-referenced to other flowcharts that are being prepared.

Copies for Site Personnel. Copies of flowcharts prepared by the auditor can be given to the site personnel, who may find them useful for their own purposes. Since those who use a system should know it best, the auditor may find it helpful to ask site personnel to comment on and confirm the accuracy of the flowcharts.

Internal Controls

Flowcharting is appropriate for most of the procedures that have significant accounting implications. The flowcharts should reflect all operations having financial control significance. The flowcharting technique shown here makes it possible to integrate administrative controls. For example, the part of the payments cycle flowchart describing control procedures in the purchasing function may describe such administrative control procedures as the calculation of minimum economic order quantities, lead times, and buffer stocks, or the solicitation of competitive bids from vendors and maintenance of vendor evaluation files. If it is more efficient, those controls can be discussed in the narratives that supplement the flowcharts. Decisions about review of administrative controls and the extent of documentation to be done for such a review should be made before the system review starts.

Ordinarily, an auditor flowcharts procedures relating to document handling and retention only to the extent that they are relevant to internal (or certain administrative) controls. However, when management so desires, flowcharts can detail the handling and retention of all copies of documents as part of an evaluation of the effectiveness and efficiency of company procedures.

Flowcharts in Nonfinancial Systems

The flowcharting technique can be used to depict nonfinancial management information systems. The auditor can then evaluate the quality and reliability of the management information produced, and the efficiency of the procedures involved.

Amount of Detail

Flowcharts should not be elaborate; they should show only what is needed for understanding. Preparation time should be commensurate with the expected benefits. Accordingly, a lot of time should not be spent on charts with limited usefulness. It is rarely necessary to flowchart every process applied to every copy of every document in detail. The information should be confined to what is essential to understand significant aspects of the system and related controls. Flowcharts used to evaluate internal controls over financial systems may be less detailed than those used to assess administrative controls.

Properly prepared, detailed flowcharts are particularly helpful to people who subsequently perform the tests of controls. When the person responsible for documenting the system is not the one to carry out the tests, the control procedures should be described in some detail. Then, the location of documents and the names by which they are known to site personnel will be readily available to the auditor actually performing the tests.

Using Narratives

This approach to flowcharting can be applied to most businesses, regardless of size. Nonetheless, there are situations—such as when major changes will be made in the system or when control procedures seem to be nonexistent—when it may be more efficient for the auditor to prepare a succinct narrative explanation of the system. When narratives are used, the auditor should make sure that they contain the same information concerning the system that would have been shown in flowcharts. The reasons why narratives were used instead of flowcharts should be explained in the working papers.

Overview Flowcharts

Overview flowcharts are useful for outlining computer-based systems. They can also show the broad flow between departments. When flowcharting an application for the first time, it is often helpful to sketch a brief outline of the system as a prelude to preparing detailed flowcharts. In some cases, the overview flowcharts are suitable to describe a system.

Computer Overview Flowcharts

In computer-based systems, the auditor should prepare an overview flowchart for each important computer application. Normally these charts are prepared before detailed flowcharting to convey the scope of computer processing, which may best be done by an EDP auditor. The information is often useful in planning an evaluation.

The computer overview flowchart indicates significant input, master files, and output, in terms of both routine and exception reports. (See Figure

17-2.) In more complex systems, it is helpful to show the flow of data through the separate subsystems within the overall system, indicating the points in the process at which the various reports and files are generated. Figure 17-3 exhibits the vertical method of preparing a computer overview flowchart. The horizontal technique is exhibited in Figure 17-4.

Departmental Overview Flowcharts

When a system is especially complex, it is important for someone other than the original preparer of the detailed flowcharts to be able to obtain a broad view of the flow among the various departments of the organization. In this case, it is useful to prepare a departmental overview flowchart to serve as a summary or index to the detailed flowcharts. For an example of a horizontal departmental overview flowchart and its narrative, see Figures 17-5 and 17-6. When preparing a horizontal overview flowchart certain guidelines should be followed:

1. The sequence of procedures determines the order of the departments depicted on the flowchart. Sequential flow is from left to right with the right-hand column continuing onto the left side of the next diagram.
2. A vertical dividing line assists in separating departmental functions, both physically on the diagram and conceptually to the reader. Departmental names should be shown clearly across the top of the diagram.
3. All financially significant transactions should be addressed on the flowchart and their initiation shown with the proper symbol, i.e., manually prepared orders indicated with multiple copies shown versus orders entered on-line at a terminal and transmitted to a distributed or centralized computing facility.
4. The maintenance of files, including standing data, and the creation of reports with control significance should be shown.
5. The flow of documentation (i.e., reports) between the various departments should be identified and the control procedures performed at each step explained in the appropriate narratives.
6. The flowline of the diagram should start with the inception of significant transactions and end with their recording in the books and records of the company.
7. It is optional to include names and/or titles of department heads and personnel performing key control procedures.
8. Copies of input documents and sample reports should be included as supporting documentation.

FIG. 17-2
Computer overview flowchart

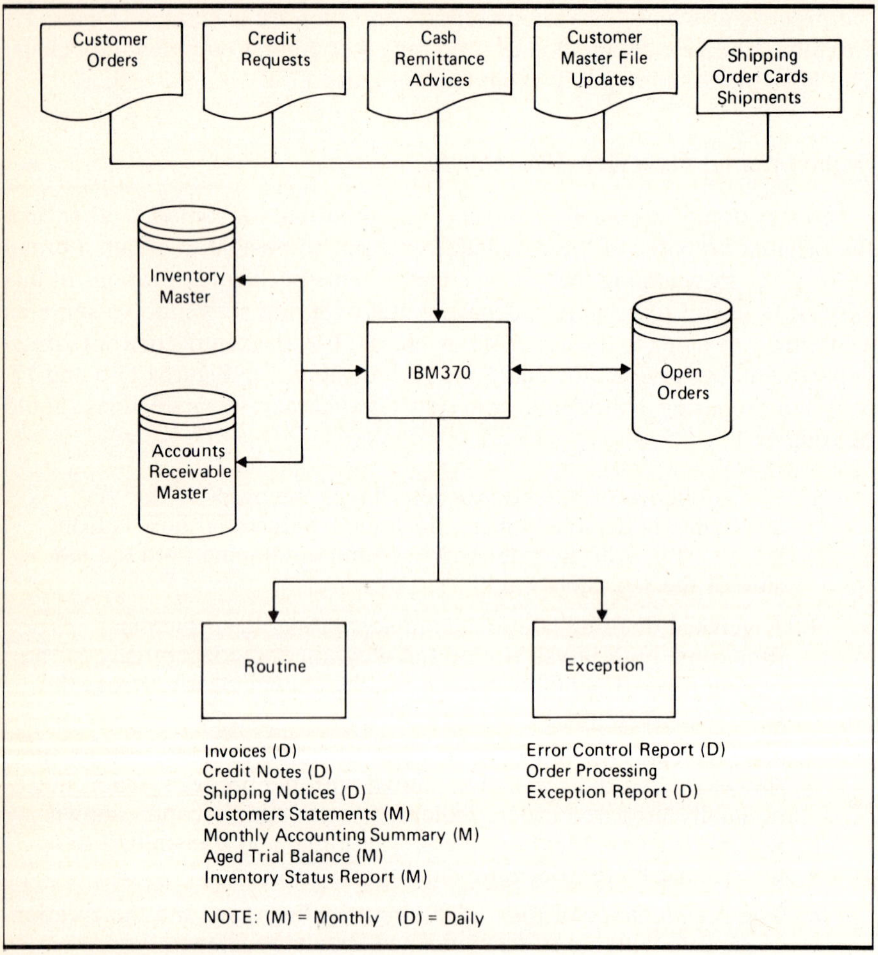

Preliminary Review

Sometimes an auditor starts with a preliminary review and evaluation of controls. This type of review provides an overview of the controls. This method may be useful in some circumstances, for example, when it would not be possible for the auditors to evaluate all the systems in depth or as a means of identifying those systems with major problems that require a detailed review as soon as possible. For those purposes, departmental overview flowcharting may be modified to show the major control points.

FIG. 17-3

Flow of subsystems

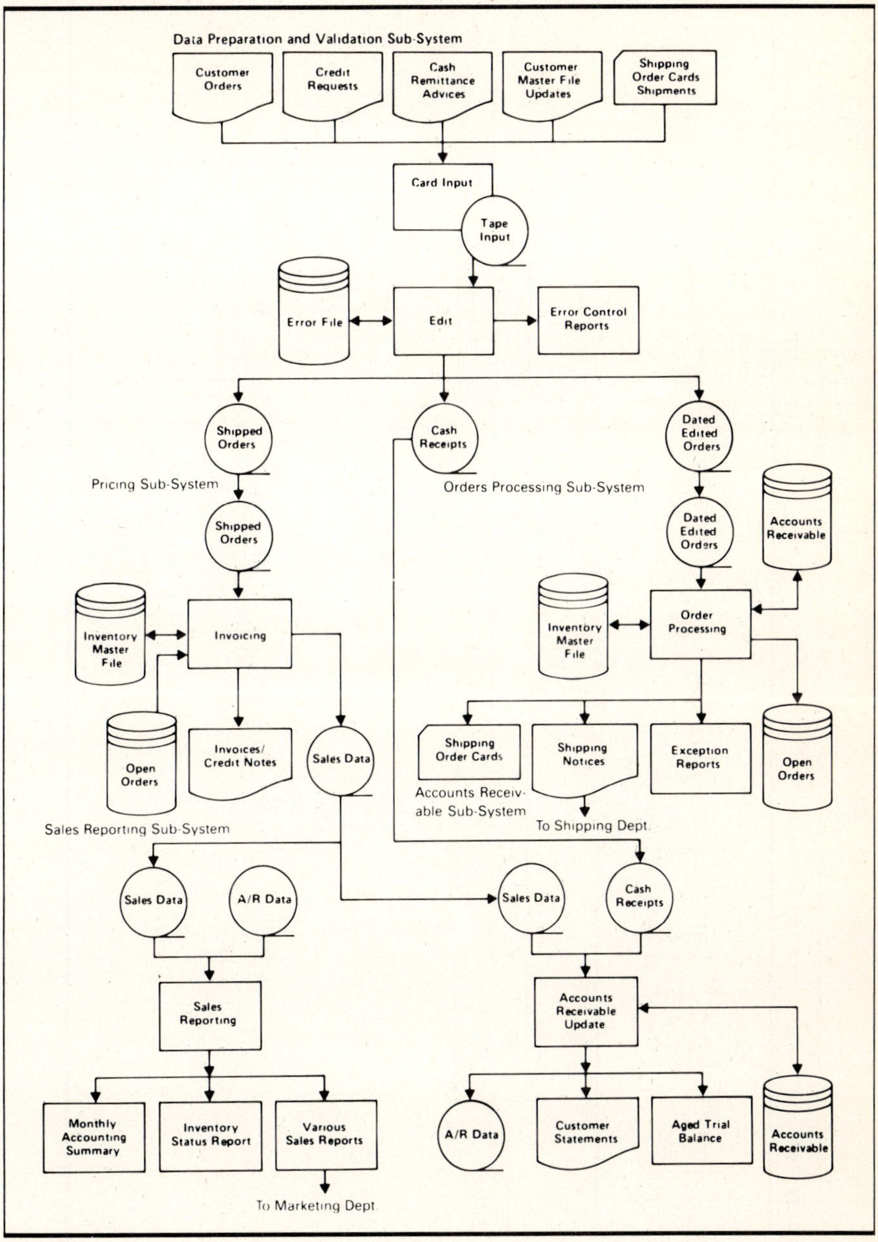

FIG. 17-4
Trading system

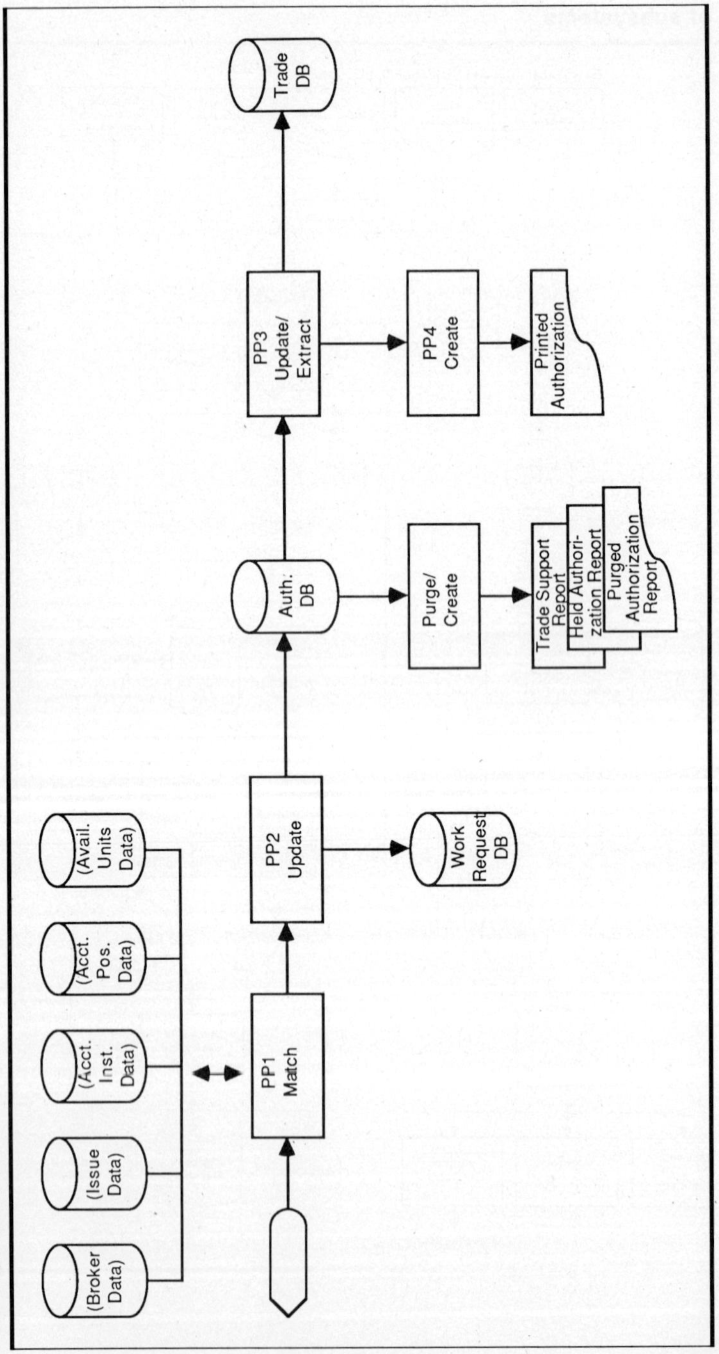

FIG. 17-5

Departmental overview flowchart

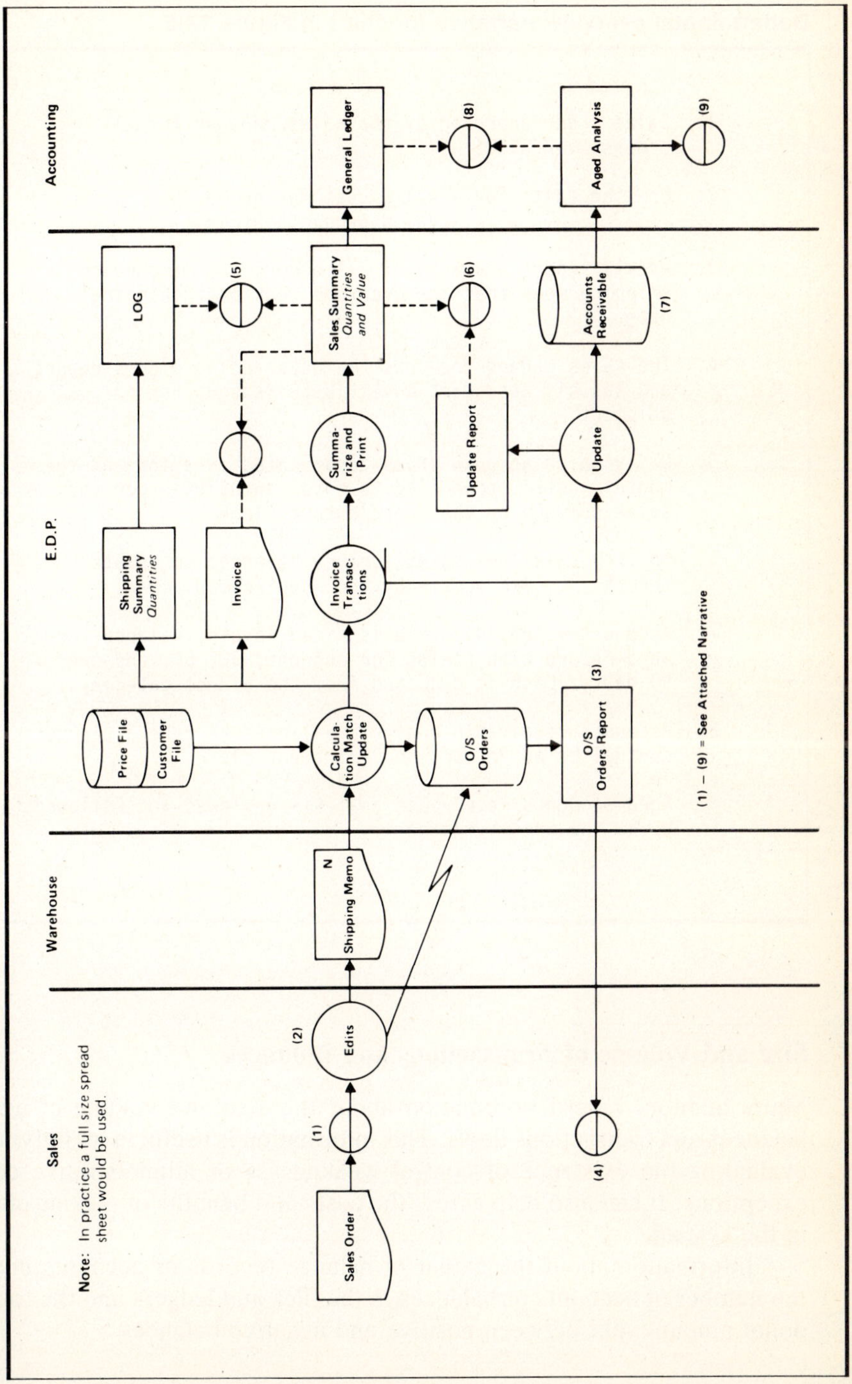

FIG. 17-6

Departmental overview narrative for chart in Figure 17-5

1. Sales order approved by the sales manager for all orders over $500.

2. On-line edits for - valid customer number
   - valid product number

3. Weekly report prepared of all orders not matched to shipping memo that are over one week past shipping date.

4. The sales manager reviews the outstanding orders report and has his assistant investigate reasons for no shipment.

5. Daily shipping quantities accumulated in a log and the monthly total reconciled to total quantities per the sales summary by the input/output clerk.

6. Monthly sales per sales summary balanced to update report from A/R update by the input/output clerk.

7. Accounts receivable file is fixed-length, balance-forward record with fields for current, 30, 60, and over 90 days. Cash is deducted from the oldest category.

8. Accounts receivable analysis balanced to general ledger control by an Accounting Department clerk.

9. Aged accounts receivable analysis reviewed and followed up by the credit manager.

Size and Volume of Transactions and Balances

Many auditors record information about the size and volume of account balances and transactions flows. This information is useful in identifying and evaluating the existence of control weaknesses or administrative control exceptions. It can also help assess the costs and benefits of making changes in the system.

Information about the extent of balance records or accounts includes the number of accounts or balances in the files and ledgers and the total net dollar amount split between positive and negative balances.

Information on transaction flows includes the following:

- The number of transactions flowing through a transaction processing system in a certain time period.
- The total dollar amount.
- The range of amounts.
- The average amount of transactions flowing through a transaction processing system in a certain time period.
- If available, error rates in transaction processing.

Since this information may not be available at sites, it is a good idea to give prior notification to the site personnel to allow time to develop the data. In addition, the auditor may find it useful to use structured interview techniques to obtain data when visiting the site. Chapter 18 gives examples of useful interview techniques, including procedures for obtaining estimates of error rates.

BASIC PRINCIPLES OF THE FLOWCHARTING TECHNIQUE

Preparing Flowcharts

Three major points should be kept in mind when preparing flowcharts.

1. The flow of transactions through a system must be charted step by step.
2. All relevant information relating to the transactions, such as completeness of documentation, establishment of control totals, and review of open files, should be recorded so that the controls can be properly evaluated.
3. Clarity and simplicity in presentation are the key.

Transaction Processing Systems

Flowcharts should follow the main flowline of transactions from their inception to their termination. Then a separate flowchart is prepared for each transaction processing subsystem or major part of the overall system.

Transactions Defined

A transaction is defined as a series of business activities related to an exchange involving money, goods, or services, or to any other change in an asset or liability that should result in an accounting entry. For example, all the activities that result in recording a purchase of raw materials in the accounts are part of a transaction. Those activities normally include:

- Preparing a purchase order.
- Recording the receipt of the goods.
- Matching the supplier's invoice with the record of goods received and the purchase order.
- Approving the supplier's invoice for payment.
- Paying the supplier (including, where applicable, preparing, signing, and mailing checks).
- Recording the purchase in the appropriate asset or expense account.
- Controlling the foregoing documents before and during the related processing activities. Controls over unmatched receiving reports and controls to ensure that all approved suppliers' invoices are recorded properly are examples.

Types of Transactions

Transactions are defined by the procedures followed and the controls applied, which differ from one transaction to another. For example, if purchases of raw materials are processed and controlled in the same manner as purchases of office supplies, then both purchases represent only one type of transaction. On the other hand, if purchases of raw materials are processed and controlled in a manner different from that followed for purchases of office supplies, then those purchases represent two different types of transactions.

To distinguish types of transactions, emphasis should be placed on differences in control. The fact that otherwise similar transactions are processed by different people, or in different locations, does not in itself mean that they are different types of transactions. If the control procedures are uniform and there is reason to believe that they are adequately supervised, the transactions can be considered to be the same type.

Standard Format

For consistency, it is a good idea to work with a standard format for flowcharting working papers. One possible format is illustrated in a specimen form in Figure 17-7.

FIG. 17-7

Standard format for flowcharting working papers

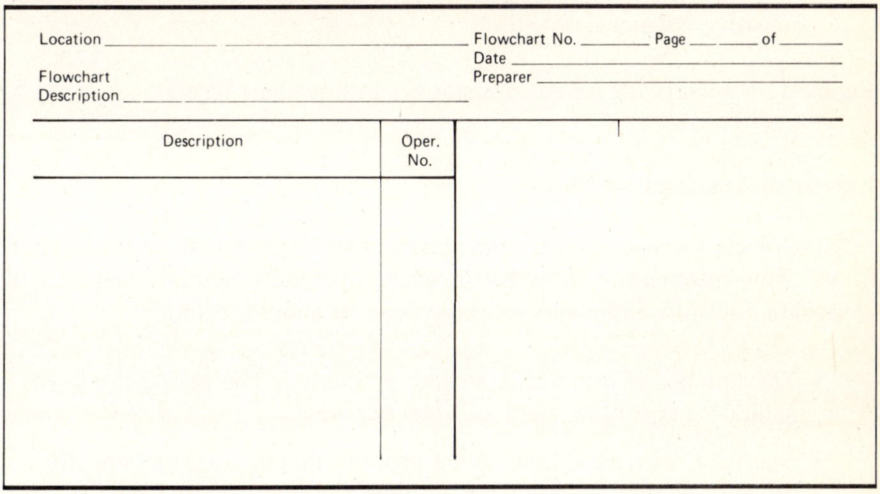

Location ______ Flowchart No. ______ Page ______ of ______

Date ______

Flowchart Description ______ Preparer ______

Description	Oper. No.	

Sign-Offs

It is important to know who prepared or updated a flowchart, and when. A standard form that provides space for signing off to show who prepared or updated the flowcharts and who performed the related transaction reviews can be used. Dates should always be included with sign-offs. Space can be allowed to show that the flowcharts were reviewed. The specimen form in Figure 17-7 includes these spaces with appropriate titles.

Exhibits

Copies of all relevant documents (such as copies of, or extracts from, pertinent procedure manuals; examples of filled-in forms; sample reports; computer file layouts; and descriptions of programmed procedures) should be cross-referenced to and filed with the flowcharts. These are particularly useful in explaining how a control operates, how a control is evidenced, what the document or form looks like, and where the relevant details of the control are located on a complex report.

Extent of Balances

It is often useful to collect information about the extent of balance records or accounts. This information can help place specific control procedures in a proper perspective. It includes:

- The number of accounts or balances in the files and ledgers.
- The total net amount of the file or ledger split between positive and negative balances.

Figure 17-8 depicts the extent of balances in flowchart format.

Extent of Transaction Flows

Many flowcharts also record information about the extent of transaction flows. This information is useful in evaluating the potential existence of identified control weaknesses or exceptions. It should include:

- The number of transactions being processed. The period involved should be specified, such as 1,000 per week.
- The value of transactions being processed. The total amount, the range of amounts, and/or the average amounts can be used.
- If available, error rates in transaction processing. This information is particularly useful for evaluating the efficiency of the system. For an example, see Figure 17-9.

More extensive statistics may be available in a computerized system, either from regular management reports or as a result of running audit software. The preparer may find it useful to use structured interview techniques to obtain this data when visiting the site. (See Chapter 18.)

FIG. 17-8
Extent of balances in flowcharting format

Description	Oper. No.
Inventory Master File Updated. Extent of Balances:	2

	$ Value	Count
Net:	100,000	10,500
Debits:	120,000	6,000
Credits:	20,000	800
Zero Balance:	–	3,700

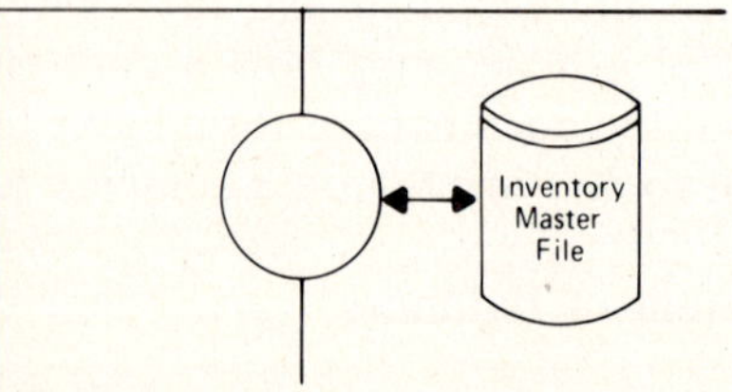

FIG. 17-9
Extent of transaction flows in transaction processing

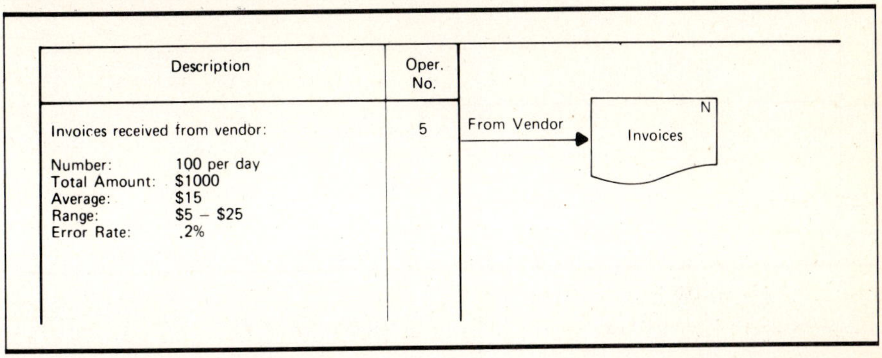

SYMBOLS AND DEFINITIONS

Form Heading

The location and a description of the transaction flow being recorded should be entered at the top of the form. Each flowchart should be given a separate flowchart number, and the individual pages within that flowchart should be numbered sequentially. The form usually provides space to record the name of the person who prepared or updated the flowchart and the date this was done. (See Figure 17-10.)

Organizational Units

The area of responsibility should be shown when the flow of transactions passes from one organizational unit to another, for example, from the purchasing department to the accounting department. Use a horizontal line or a separate page to indicate this motion. At this point, the name of the new organizational unit, the title, and, if desired, the name of the person in charge

FIG. 17-10
Flowcharting form heading

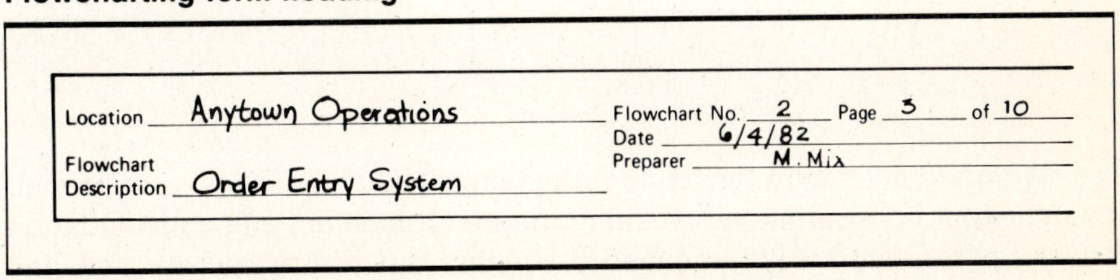
Location Anytown Operations
Flowchart Description Order Entry System
Flowchart No. 2 Page 3 of 10
Date 6/4/82
Preparer M. Mix

FIG. 17-11
Organizational unit

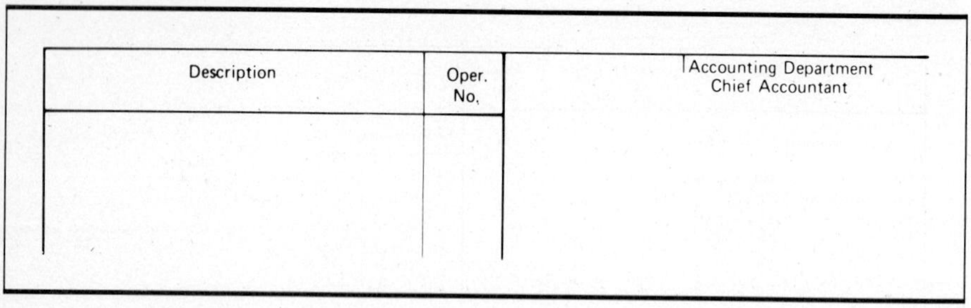

is placed on the right side of the flowchart. Repeat this information at the top of each page dealing with the same department. For flowcharting purposes, an organizational unit may vary from a large department, such as a sales department, to one individual, such as the credit manager. (See Figure 17-11.)

A choice must be made between starting a separate page or using a horizontal line on the same page to indicate when the processing flow enters a new department. If relatively few operations are performed, more than one department can be shown on a page, in line with the flow of processing. In other cases, the use of separate pages may be advantageous: The pages can be sorted by department and all activities within a particular department brought into perspective. The pages should be re-sorted into the actual processing sequence before being filed.

Operation or Process

The symbol that indicates processing is a circle. A process is an action performed by either a person or a programmed procedure. Examples of a process include recording batch totals in a control log and updating a transaction or master file.

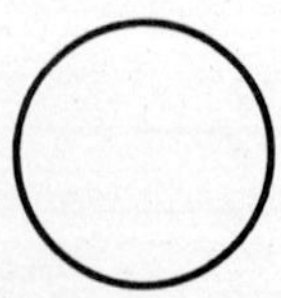

A horizontal line in the circle processing symbol indicates an approval, comparison, verification, or checking routine. It includes edit and validation checks performed by programmed procedures. If errors that are detected are cleared by the person performing the step, this need not be mentioned in the narrative and the correction process need not be charted. If correction involves re-routing of the documentation, the correction routine should be flowcharted or narrated, as appropriate. (See later section entitled "Rejections.")

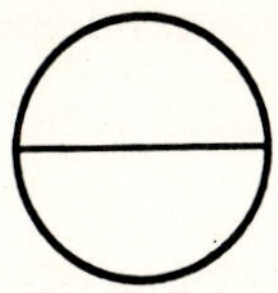

Descriptions

For each operation that appears on the right of the flowchart, a brief narrative description should appear at the corresponding location on the left. When applicable, the narrative includes authority limits, explanations of how controls are evidenced, and the frequency of operation of the control. These descriptions should enable a reader to understand the nature of processing and related controls. (See Figure 17-12.)

Operation Numbers

One operation number should be used for each process. The numbers should appear in a separate column between the narrative description on the left and the main flowline on the right.

FIG. 17-12
Descriptions of operations

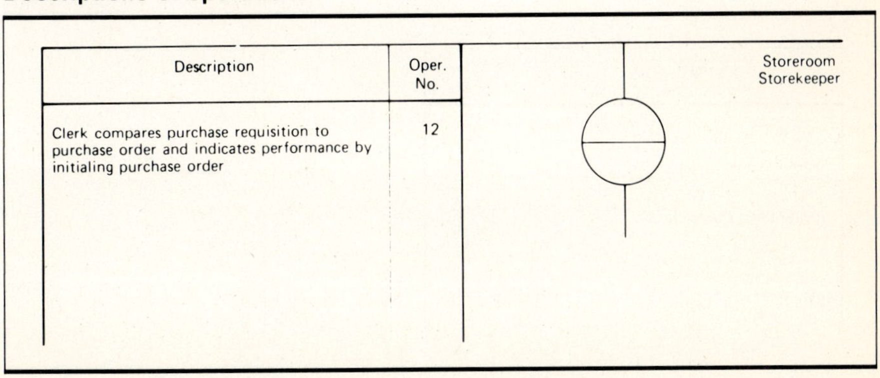

If the process produces a document or other information medium, only the medium symbol (as discussed subsequently) should be placed on the main flowline; it is not necessary to show it with an operation symbol. However, the operation is assigned its own number. If the activity involves a yes/no decision, the special diamond symbol (described subsequently in the section entitled "Decision and Branching") is used in lieu of the operation symbol. Again, a separate operation number is assigned.

Attached Narratives

If a separate flowchart is used to show the details of a particular operation, or if the narrative required is so long that it will not fit on the page, the operation shown on the main flowchart should be referenced to the detail by a single numbered operation set off by oblique lines. This method is particularly useful for cross-referencing flowchart operations to attached copies of programmed procedures extracted from the system documentation. (See Figure 17-13.)

Main Flowline

Processing within an organizational unit moves along a vertical line on the chart, its main flowline. (See Figure 17-14.) Symbols for documents or other information media needed for processing appear on the main flowline, as described subsequently, at the point those documents or media are created or received. The media are then presumed to flow along with the processing, from department to department, until their disposition is indicated. File/storage symbols and connector symbols, discussed subsequently, provide a

FIG. 17-13
Attached narratives

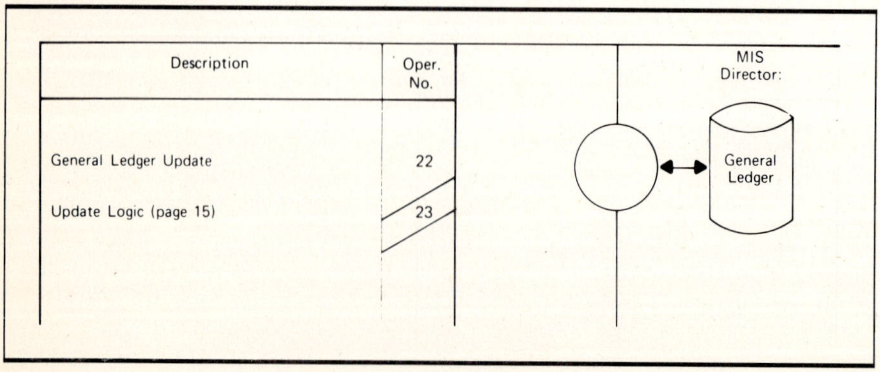

FIG. 17-14
Main flowline

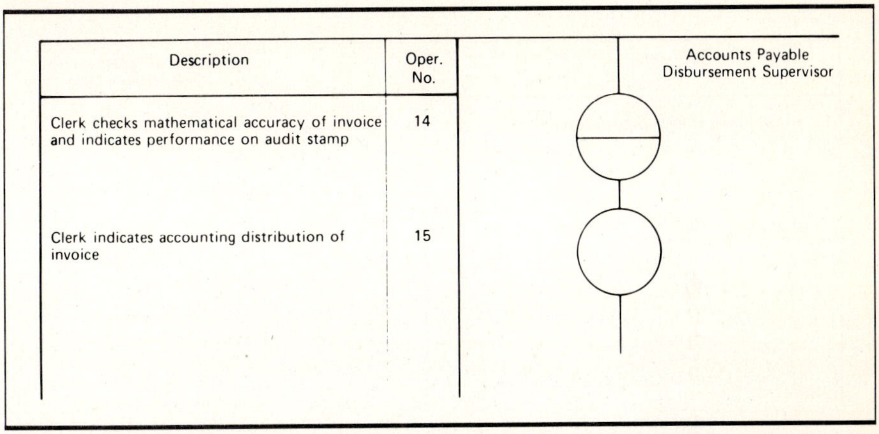

simple means for indicating the permanent or temporary removal of media from processing. Only documents and media that are directly related to the function being described normally remain on the main flowline. When the flowline is continued on another page, appropriate references should be entered at the bottom of the first page and at the top of the second page. (See Figure 17-15.)

FIG. 17-15
Continuation main flowline

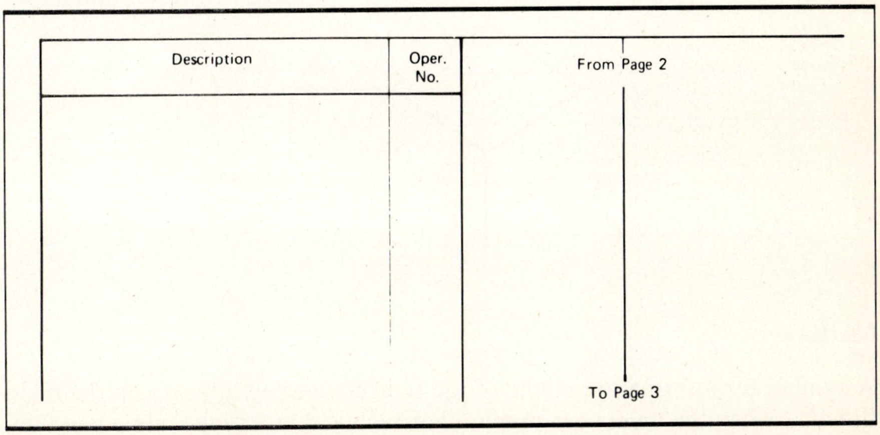

FIG. 17-16
Decision and branching symbol in flowchart

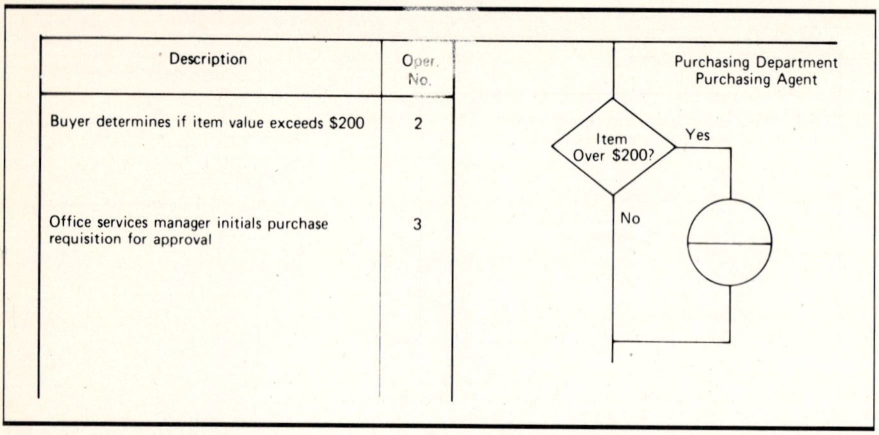

Decision and Branching

The decision and branching symbol is a diamond. This symbol represents a point at which alternate procedures come onto the flowchart. Processing along the main flowline is suspended until the branch condition has been accommodated. If alternative processing is significant and/or extensive, a separate flowchart can be made. (For an example of the decision/branching symbol used in a flowchart, see Figure 17-16.)

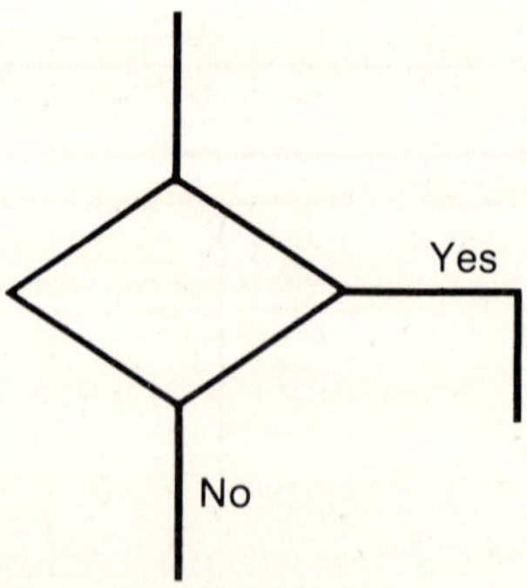

Media

A symbol for information media of the type concerned appears on the main flowline when the media are prepared or received and reappears when they are distributed, filed, or disposed of. They are assumed to continue in process in the interim. If their origin coincides with their disposition in a single (numbered) operation, the symbol appears only once. Individual media symbols used are described in the following paragraphs.

Document. The symbol for documents is used to designate items such as a purchase order, requisition, invoice, or voucher. The name of the document is inserted in the symbol.

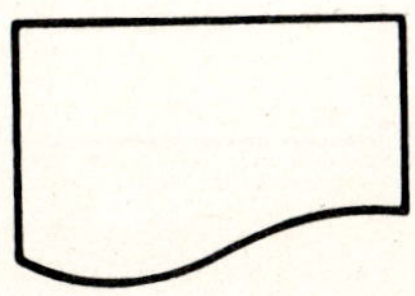

When more than one copy of a document is prepared and distributed, the multiple-copy overlapping symbols may be used or the number of copies may be indicated by a circled numeral placed within the single document symbol. Each copy that has accounting significance should be followed through from its origin to its disposition.

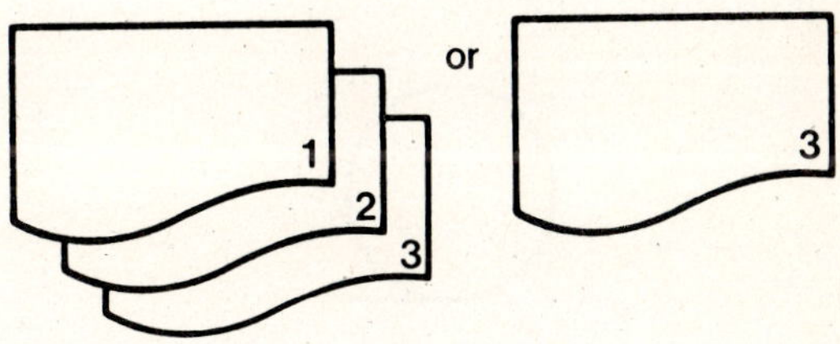

If a document, whether single or multiple copy, is numbered serially for accounting control purposes, the letter N is placed in the upper right corner of the document symbol. This treatment is useful in alerting the auditor to numerical control aspects. The disposition of the documents is flowcharted by showing the copy (or copies) with the identifying number.

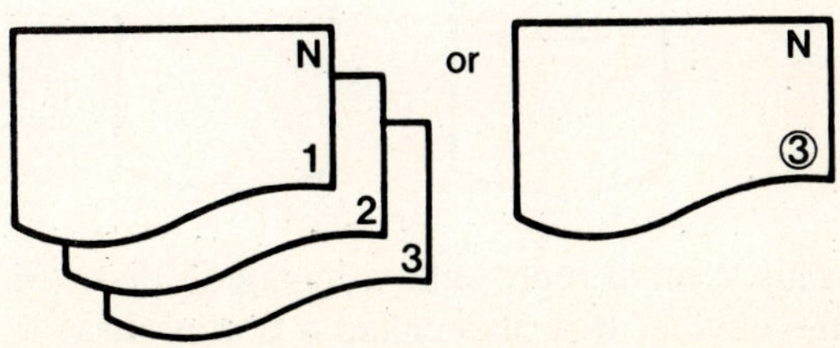

Report/Book. A rectangle is used to represent a report, journal, book, register, computer listing, or similar document, which may be machine-printed or completed by manual entry. Its title is inserted in the symbol. The symbol usually represents an output medium that is self-contained (such as a complete listing of selling prices) and that may be used as input for other processing (such as pricing customers' invoices).

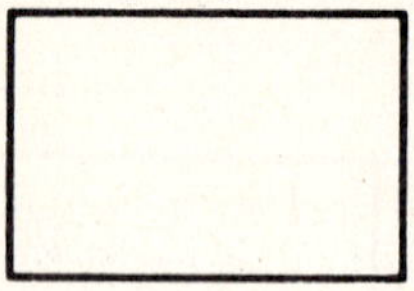

EDP Media

Electronic data processing systems also make use of machine-readable media. In batch processing systems, the conversion of source or input documents into machine-readable input media should be shown on the flowchart. The EDP media symbols are discussed in the following paragraphs.

Magnetic Tape. This symbol represents one or more reels or cassettes of tape containing a single data file.

Data Base Disk. This symbol is used in conjunction with electronic data processing to represent a single data file contained on one or more disk packs. As illustrated, this symbol may be used to represent more than one file.

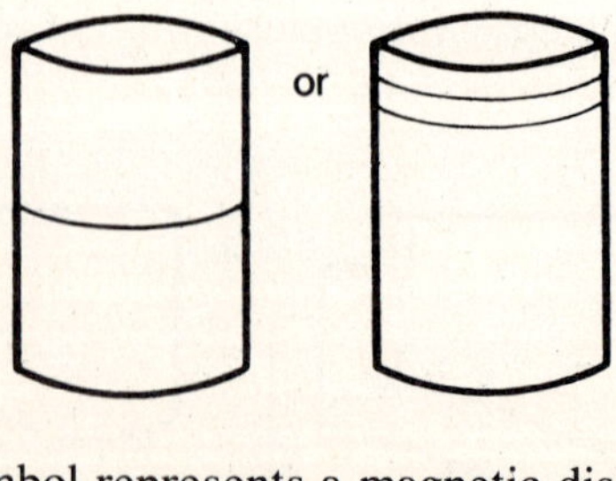

Diskette. This symbol represents a magnetic diskette that is used as a computer storage device. It is also called a floppy disk.

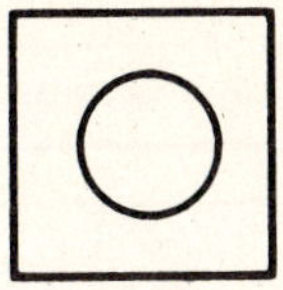

Terminal or CRT. These symbols are used, instead of an operations symbol, where data is entered through a terminal or CRT (cathode ray tube). The narrative should indicate whether the terminal is operating in an on-line or real-time (immediate update) mode. The narrative should include enough detail to make evaluation of the related control procedures possible. This is shown in Figure 17-17.

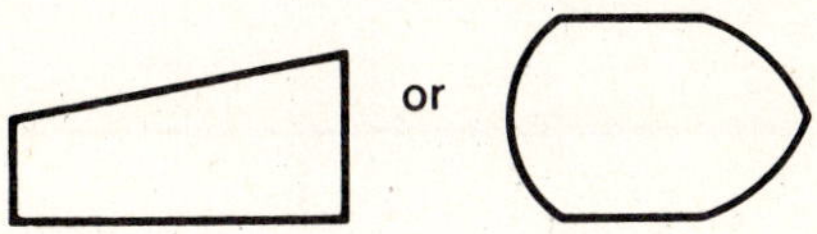

Communications Link. This symbol is used to represent the transmission of information by a telecommunications link, most typically via telephone lines. It is not used to show transmission through a hardwired terminal or device. Communications links between departments can either be depicted with this symbol or explained in the narrative. (An example is shown in Figure 17-18.)

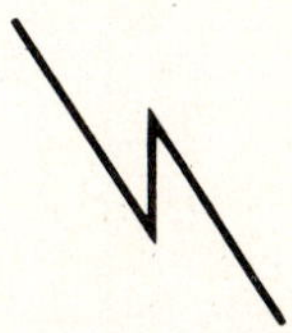

INFORMATION FLOW AND DISPOSITION

Referral Line

The symbol for referral line is a broken line. It is used when referring to information, for example, when reviewing a file to obtain information or when posting information. The referral line leads to a symbol depicting the media and content of the reference source. That source does not travel with the main flowline but remains in physical custody of, or is accessible to, the organizational unit indicated. A tape or file that simply supplies data, and

FIG. 17-17

Illustrative narrative to indicate how terminal (symbol) is operating

Description	Oper. No.
(On-Line, Batch) Password and transaction code are entered on CRT. Screen format is displayed if the password is appropriate for the transaction code. Invoice details input: • invoice number • customer reference • value (net) • value (discount) Details are displayed on the screen for visual confirmation	12

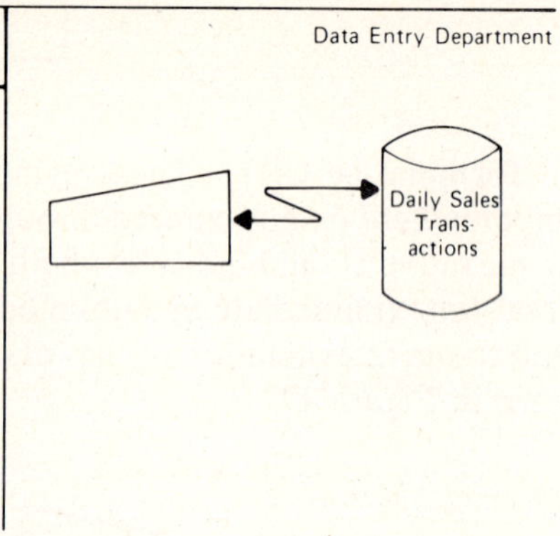

FIG. 17-18

Communications link between departments

Description	Oper. No.
Transaction tape transmitted to New York daily	24
Data received and recorded	25

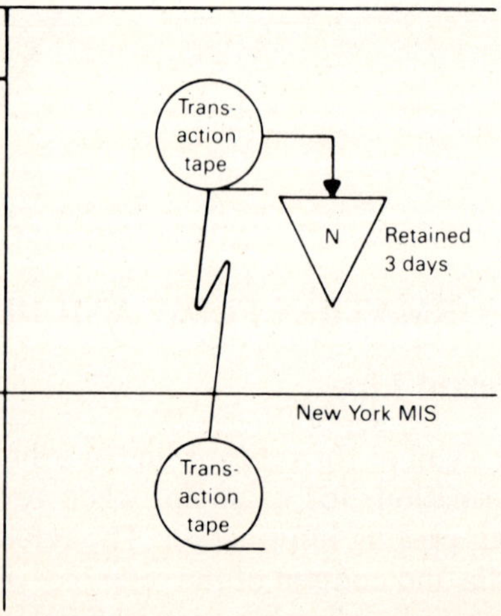

is not superseded, should be shown with a referral line. (An example is shown in Figure 17-19.)

Media Distribution Line

A solid line is used to indicate the media distribution line. The movement of all documents and other information media follows the main flowline from one organizational unit and process to the next. The movement of information media to or from the main flowline is indicated by a horizontal distribution line attached to the document or other media symbol.

Information media leaving or entering the system from outside or from an organizational unit and not charted with the origin or disposition explained are shown on a horizontal line. The line is marked with an arrowhead to show movement. Media may be brought onto the main flowline from either the left or the right. Normally, document disposition is shown moving to the right. (See Figure 17-20.)

Connector

The connector symbol, a small circle, is used in sets of two, one at each point that is being indexed. Each of the pair of symbols contains the same unique identification letter of the document distribution line. Connector symbols are used to cross-reference the continuation of a horizontal document distribution line. The horizontal distribution line joins the connector and the document or other media symbol. Note the operation number or page reference next to corresponding connectors, particularly those that do not appear on adjacent pages. If the reference is to another flowchart, that chart number should also be shown. The name of the organizational unit of destination or of origin should be written above the horizontal distribution line. (See Figure 17-21.)

If a document or other media come from or are sent to another organizational unit, the media symbols appear on the main flowline at the point

FIG. 17-19
Nonsuperseded tape showing data with referral line

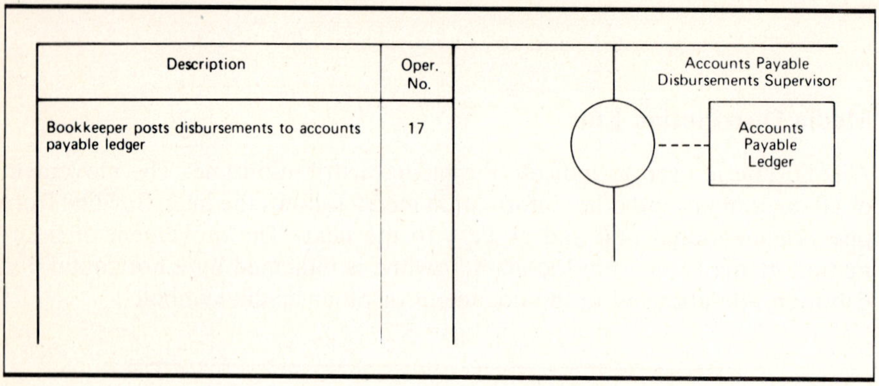

FIG. 17-20
Document distribution moving to right

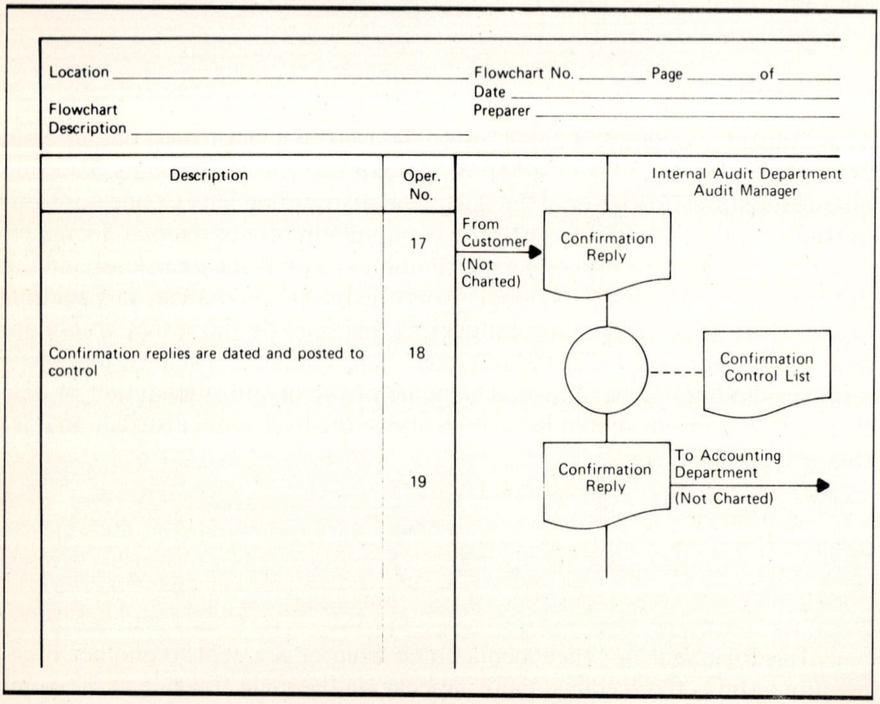

FIG. 17-21
Reference to another chart with connector

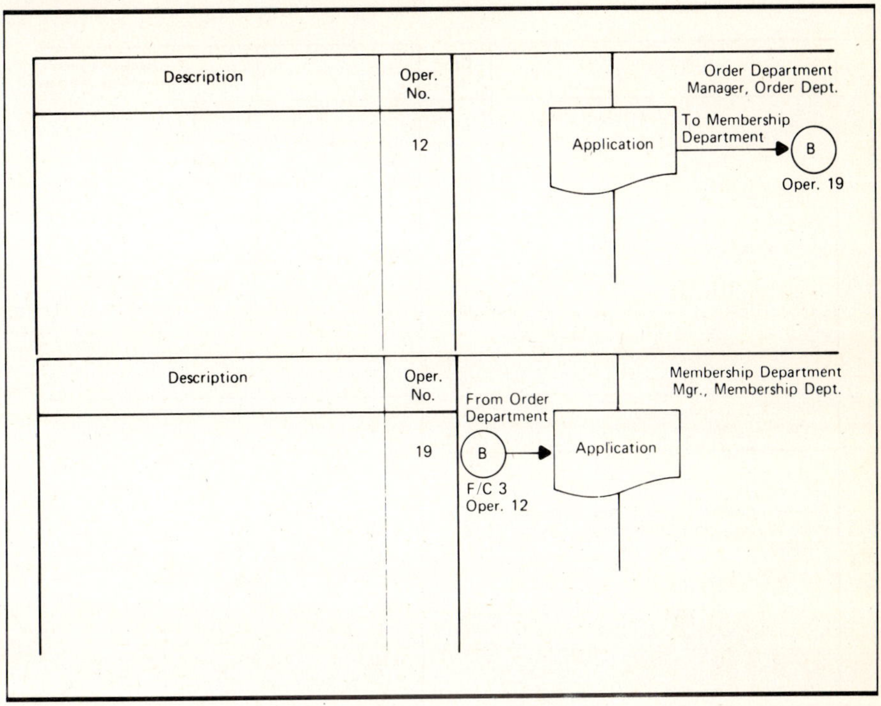

at which the media enter or leave the processing. Connector symbols, cross-referenced as described subsequently, are drawn at the end of the document distribution line (with arrowheads) to or from the media symbols on the main flowline. If the media are stored without immediate or further processing, the symbol on the main flowline carries a document distribution line connected with a file/storage symbol, to indicate that disposition. (An example is shown in Figure 17-22.)

References between narratives or other working papers and flowchart pages may cite the flowchart operation number in addition to the page.

Match and Update

The symbol for match and update is used in conjunction with electronic data processing. It represents the matching on a specified record key and the update of one or more data elements on the master file. The match and update logic should be explained, either in the narrative or as an additional item attached to the flowchart. The communications version of this symbol

FIG. 17-22

Document distribution with file/storage symbol

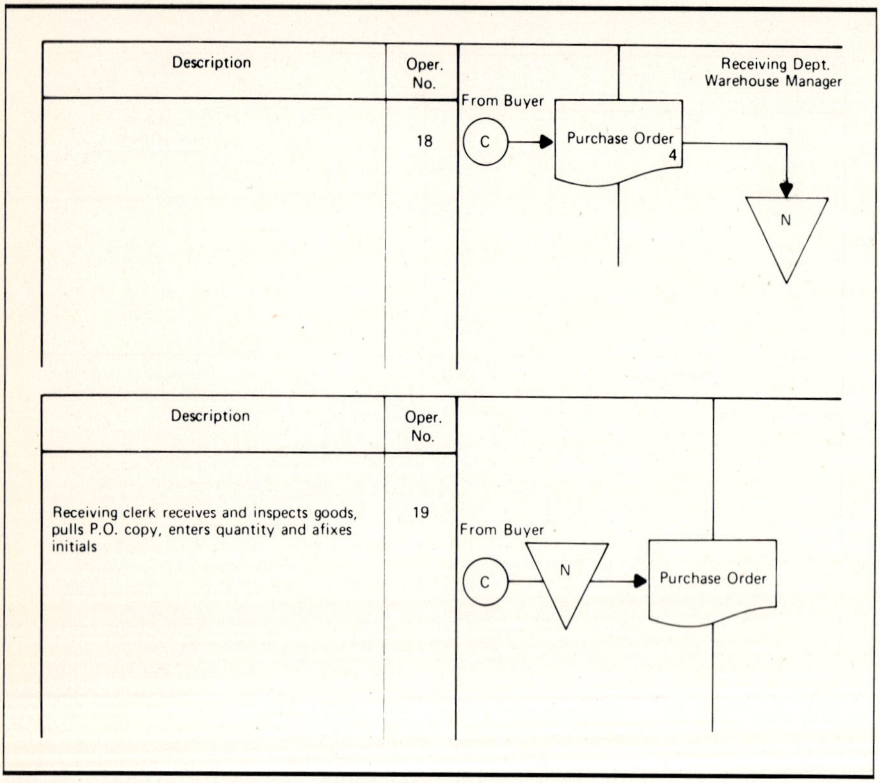

indicates that the file is in a remote department and accessed via a communications link. The straight line indicates an update within MIS. Figure 17-23 shows an example.

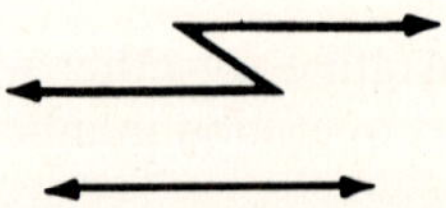

Note that a tape on the flowline must be removed after use in match or update to provide a visual indication that the tape will not be used for further processing. Also, it is not necessary to show both generations, old and new, in a sequential update process. The techniques for updating or referring to tapes or disks that are not shown on the flowline but are to be included in the flowchart are shown in Figure 17-24.

FIG. 17-23
Match and update symbol in use

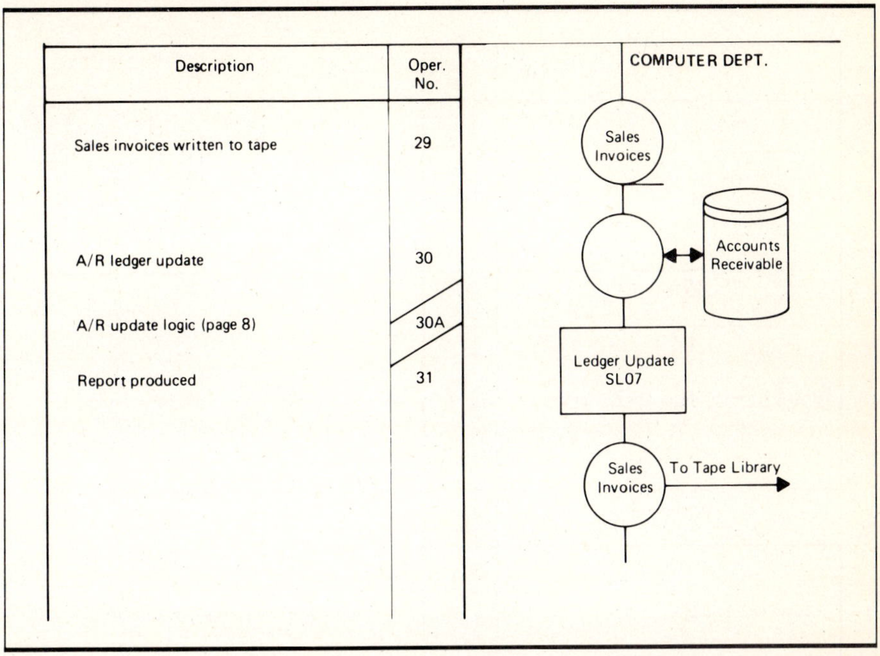

Ghosting

If the nature of documents or media remaining on the main flowline might not be evident to the potential flowchart reader, the symbols are shown surrounded by brackets on the main flowline as a reminder. This technique is referred to as ghosting. (See Figure 17-25.)

File/Storage

The file/storage symbol takes several forms. A large triangle (*a*) indicates a permanent file, while a small triangle (*b*) indicates a temporary file. A document, or equivalent recording media, that has temporarily been taken off the flowline for convenience in flowcharting may be indicated by a small triangle placed within a larger one (*c*). (Use of this symbol is optional.) An "X" in a triangle (*d*) indicates a file that is to be destroyed. A letter designation is used to indicate the manner of filing:

FIG. 17-24

Techniques for updating tapes not shown on flowline

Description	Oper. No.
Real-time update to disk	10
Description	Oper. No.
Update from punched cards to tape	11
Description	Oper. No.
Update tape to disk	12
Description	Oper. No.
Transaction checked for validity to product file. Updates the inventory balances.	13

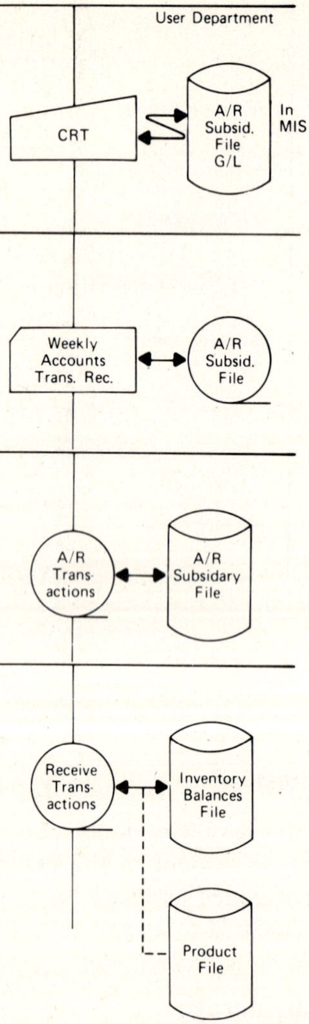

FIG. 17-25
Ghosting

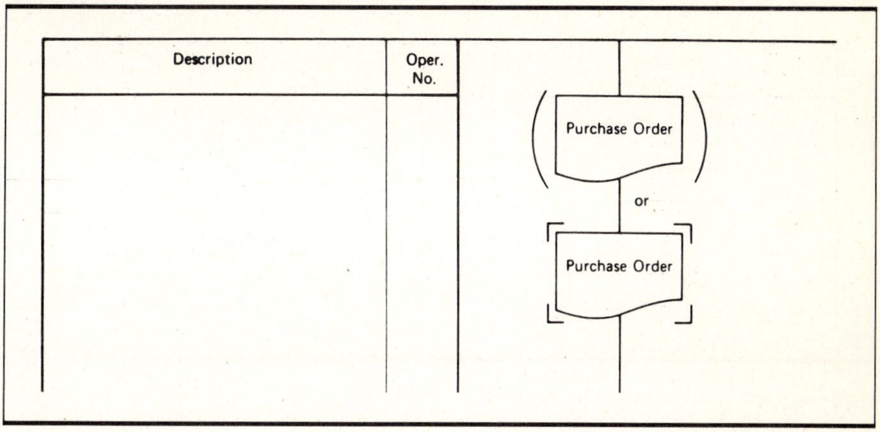

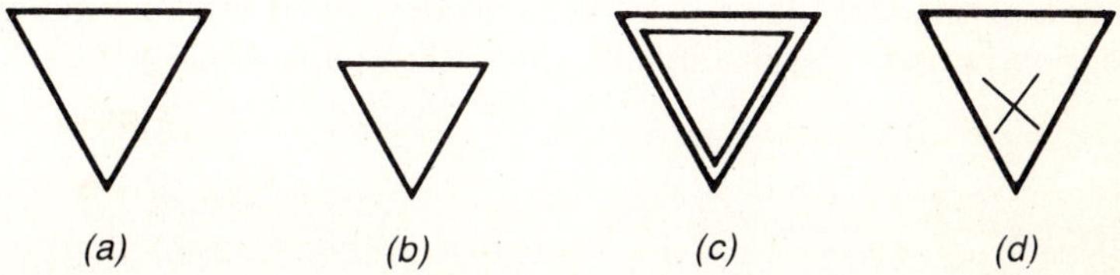

A—Alphabetic

N—Numeric

D—Date

S—Sundry

The file/storage symbol is used to indicate that a document or other information medium that has left the main flowline (via a horizontal document distribution line) is being held in the organizational unit under which the symbol appears.

The filing of information media is shown by placing the appropriate file symbols at the end of the horizontal document distribution line, drawn from the media symbols on a main flowline. The retrieval and restoration of a document or other media to the main flow of processing are shown in the same way. The direction of movement is indicated by arrowheads on the document distribution line. Or, the file/storage symbol can be entered at the top and exited at the bottom.

It is not usually necessary to show the tape library as a separate organizational unit. Library procedures are documented as part of the general

FIG. 17-26
Filing of information stored on magnetic tape

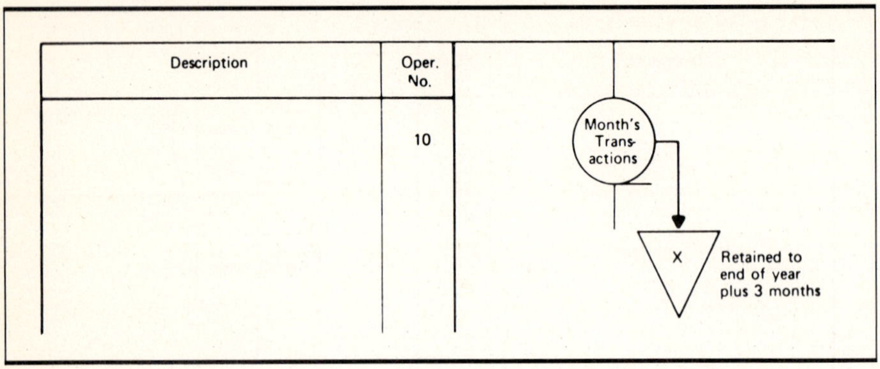

control review. The filing of information stored on a magnetic tape is shown by either a permanent file or by a file to be destroyed, with an indication of its retention period. (An example is shown in Figure 17-26.)

METHODS

Number of Flowcharts

It may not be practical, except in very basic systems, to prepare a flowchart covering an entire transaction processing system or systems cycle. For example, separate flowcharts may be required for the purchase of goods, the purchase of services, and the computation and payment of wages, when the control procedures are different for each. In those cases, separate flowcharts should be prepared for each process. If, at a point, common procedures are applied to these transactions, they are shown together. For example, a system that involves sales of finished goods and a procedure for leasing goods may both conclude with the same cash receipts procedures.

In computerized systems, usually it is most efficient to prepare a separate flowchart for each input-processing-output cycle.

Computer-Generated Data Flowcharts

Computer-generated data, transactions, or reports can be:

- Shown on the same flowchart when they are stimulated by input, for example, the generation of general ledger entries.

- Recorded on a separate flowchart when they are produced at the end of a period, for example, a monthly report.
- Divided into other convenient flowchart units according to processing.

An example is shown in Figure 17-27.

Overview Flowcharts

The detailed flowcharts of computer systems should be prepared after completing the overview flowchart. Unless a clear general understanding of the system is first obtained from the overview flowchart, it is hard to ensure that the detailed flowcharts will be relevant to the entire system.

Minor Deviations

Minor deviations from the system should be explained in the space provided in the flowcharts for narrative. If necessary, deviations can be explained in separate notes, thereby avoiding needless complications on the flowchart. This is true even when different transaction types are involved. For example, if purchases of goods and purchases of services are processed similarly except with respect to the initial authorization, both types of transactions can be covered in the same flowchart, with the deviation explained in the narrative column.

FIG. 17-27
Computer-generated report

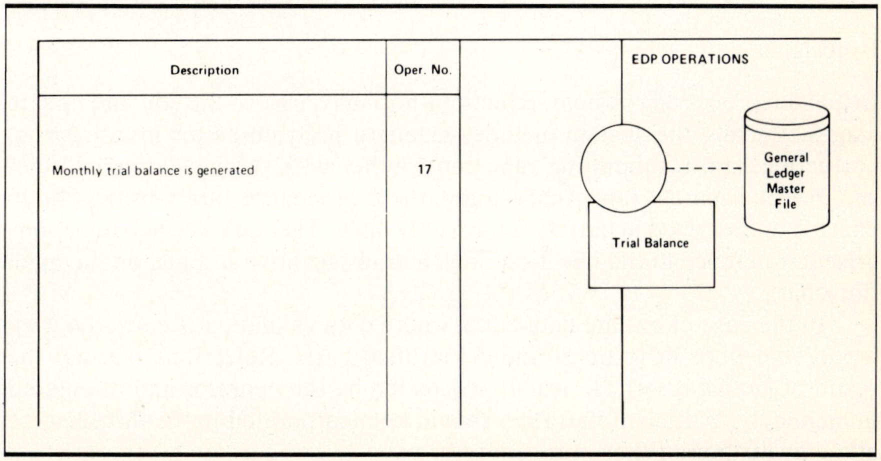

Periodic Processing

To avoid clutter, overall controls that operate on a periodic basis may be described in a separate narrative or flowchart form. Examples of such periodic processing are the monthly reconciliation of control accounts and the weekly production of a report that lists exception items on the file requiring action.

Data Conversion and Key Verification

The conversion of documents into machine-readable information media or the conversion of one form of machine-readable information media to another is shown on the flowchart. The creation of the new form of information media is indicated using the appropriate symbol on the main flowline. The old form of information media should be removed from the flowline and its disposition should be shown.

When an off-line keyboard device is used for key verification, the verification is shown as a separate step. It is indicated as a process involving approval, comparison, verification, or checking (a circle with a horizontal line). However, this is becoming less common in many of today's systems.

Similarly, when data is input by terminal, this is shown on the flowchart with an operation symbol. A narrative is included to indicate whether the terminal is operating in on-line or real-time mode. This narrative should be sufficiently detailed to make possible evaluation of the related control procedures.

Once the input medium has been written to a file, the input medium is removed from the flowline and its disposition is shown.

Data conversion and key verification are illustrated in Figure 17-28.

Rejections

In a batch processing system, rejections normally arise at the edit and update stages. Usually the system includes standard procedures for investigating, correcting, and resubmitting rejections, either with the next original input run or as a separate run. Accordingly, these procedures are normally flowcharted or described in narrative form only once. Thereafter, when rejections arise, a reference to the injection flowchart or narrative is made on the main flowchart.

In the case of on-line data entry where data validation is carried out on input, rejections arise on an individual item basis. Rejections that are the result of keying errors are usually corrected by the operator and re-entered immediately. Sufficient narrative should be incorporated in the flowchart to allow evaluation of these procedures.

FIG. 17-28

Data conversion and key verification

Location MICROS — Flowchart No. 1 Page 4 of 5

Date 12-31-82

Preparer M. SMITH

Flowchart Description DATA CONVERSION AND KEY VERIFICATION

Description	Oper. No.
Purchase invoices punched	20
Punching verified	21
	22
Purchase invoices written to magnetic tape	23
Punched cards held for 1 month; then destroyed	24

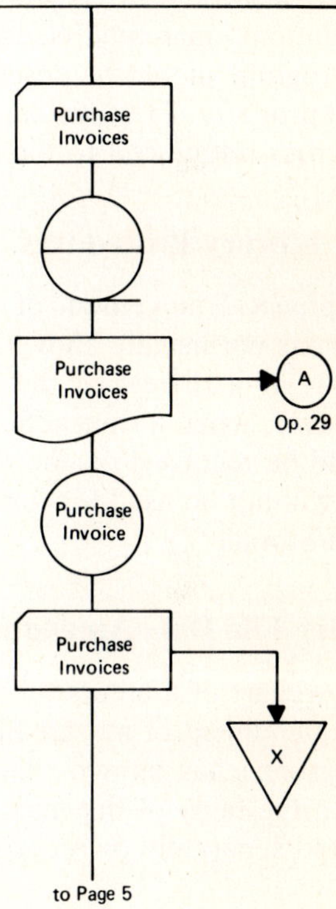

Rejections arising for other reasons require clearance by the originating department. In this event, the rejection flowcharting procedures for batch processing, discussed previously, are appropriate.

Programmed Procedures

Where operations are performed by a computer program, such as edit tests, calculations, matching checks, or exception reporting, the method used in the program should be described in sufficient detail to enable it to be evaluated properly. EDP system documentation, if available, should be attached and cross-referenced to the flowchart for this purpose.

EDP Library Procedures

The physical movement of tape or disk master files to and from an EDP library is not usually shown. Controls of this nature can be better assessed as part of a review of the general controls in the computer department. However, when a transaction tape finally leaves the system, its destination should be recorded on the flowchart to provide a visual indication that the tape will not be used for further processing. (See the earlier section entitled "File/Storage.")

Master File Data Amendments

A flowchart of a computer system should show the procedures relating to the amendment of master file data for each master file used in the system. Experience has shown that these procedures are difficult to incorporate within the body of the main flowcharts. These procedures should be flowcharted separately or recorded in narrative form.

General Controls

The general or integrity controls within MIS, while relevant to the consistency of processing, generally operate separately from the flow of data through the application systems. Accordingly, MIS department procedures should be flowcharted separately or recorded in narrative form.

Common Errors

Some of the more common faults encountered in flowcharts, particularly those of computer systems, include the following:

- Overview flowcharts have not been prepared for computer-based applications.

- When overview flowcharts have been prepared in advance, the overview and detailed flowcharts differ (for example, different master files are shown).

- Computer procedures are not flowcharted. Thus the flowchart shows documents sent to the computer department and a printout or report returned, without any indication that the master files have been updated. This is particularly common when processing is done at a service bureau or another remote location.

- Controls are shown on the flowcharts but evidence that they are operating is not described or explained.

- Programmed procedures are not described in sufficient detail.

- Master file data and transaction data are documented on a single flowchart. This error is common in payroll system flowcharts.

- Insufficient thought is given to planning the overall structure of the flowchart in relation to different transactions. A particularly common error is to flowchart computer processing procedures only once, covering all transaction types, so that a conglomeration of resulting output is shown at the same point on the flowline. The result is that procedures relating to a specific document type become difficult to follow, to say the least. This in turn makes it difficult to identify principal controls when these differ for various transactions. In order to maintain the general clarity of the flowchart and to assist in identifying the control procedures relevant to each transaction type, flowcharts should be structured chronologically in order of processing, and logically according to the sequence in which each transaction type occurs. For example, invoices that are processed weekly and adjustments that are processed monthly should be treated separately.

- Flowcharts are prepared without regard to the control questions to be answered. As a result there are gaps in the transaction flow, superfluous procedures are flowcharted, and critical control procedures are not shown.

- Attempts are made to flowchart procedures that either do not fit into the general movement of the flowchart processing or operate on a periodic basis. For example, a chart might show the maintenance of master files and data together with the reprocessing of rejections arising at the input stage. The resulting flowchart becomes confusing and difficult to understand. Where it is necessary to record controls of this nature, it is often clearer to record them in narrative form on a separate sheet to be filed behind the flowcharts.

FIG. 17-29
FLOWCHART II+™ commands

MAIN MENU

F1	EDIT	F2	PRINT CHART
F3	LOAD CHART	F4	SAVE CHART
F5	DIRECTORY	F6	CHANGE DRIVE
F7	CONFIGURE	F8	CHANGE DIRECTORY
F9	PRINT MULTIPLE	F10	QUIT

EDIT MENU

F1	SHAPE — SELECT FLOWCHARTING SHAPE TO USE
F2	LINE — DRAW CONNECTING LINES
F3	TEXT — ADD TEXT TO THE FLOWCHART
F4	DELETE — DELETE A RECTANGLE FROM THE FLOWCHART
F5	RELOCATE — RELOCATE A RECTANGLE TO ANOTHER AREA
F6	COPY — COPY A RECTANGLE TO ANOTHER AREA
F7	LOAD — LOAD SYMBOLS FROM AN IMAGE CHART
F8	SAVE — SAVE SYMBOLS TO AN IMAGE CHART
F10	QUIT
/	REPEAT LAST — REPEAT THE LAST COMMAND GIVEN
?	HELP — HELP SCREEN

HOT KEYS

^I	INSERT — INSERTS SYMBOLS, LINES, TEXT, ETC. . . .
^R	RELOCATE — SEE F5
^L	LOAD — SEE F7
^P	PAGE WIDTH — CHOOSE PAGE WIDTH (120/200 COLUMNS)
^D	DELETE — SEE F4
^C	COPY — SEE F6
^S	SAVE — SEE F8
^Z	ZAP — ERASE ENTIRE FLOWCHART
^Q	QUIT
B	BORDER MOVE — MOVE TO THE BORDER IN THE DIRECTION SPECIFIED
F	FAST MOVE — MOVE AT HIGHER THAN NORMAL SPEED IN A GIVEN DIRECTION
S	SHRINK SCREEN — SHOW ENTIRE FLOWCHART ON SCREEN
T	TEXT TOGGLE — HIDES TEXT WHILE IN SHRINK MODE
W	WINDOW CENTER — MAKE CURRENT CURSOR POSITION CENTER OF SCREEN

CREATING A FLOWCHART USING SOFTWARE

For many of today's auditors, microcomputers have become an important tool. One of the time-saving procedures that can be done using a micro is the creation of flowcharts. The packages available vary, but most provide a convenient way to "draw" charts that usually are easier for others to read since they are not handwritten.

To provide an example of how software can simplify this process, this section is an overview of how to use FLOWCHART II+™, a popular package. This example is specific to that product, but it gives an idea of how using flowchart software works.

Instructions

Install the software following the user manual, in a directory named **FLOW**. To start FLOWCHART II+™, first change into the **FLOW** directory by typing **CD\FLOW**. Then type **FLOW** to start the package. The main menu is presented. To create a new chart, select option **F1, EDIT** to get to the flowcharting screen. Once in the flowchart editing window, the **EDIT MENU** can be seen at the bottom of the screen and all of the **HOT KEYS** are accessible.

F1 SHAPE is used to select a flowcharting symbol and presents a list of shapes available. Once the generic shape is chosen, it appears on the editing window at the current cursor location. Now select the size of the shape with the left and right arrow keys and accept or reject the shape with the **RETURN** and **ESC** keys, respectively.

F2 LINE allows the connecting lines between symbols to be drawn. Once **F2 LINE** is selected, the arrow keys can be used to draw the lines or the defaults for line type and width can be edited as shown at the bottom

FIG. 17-30
Flowchart created using microcomputer software

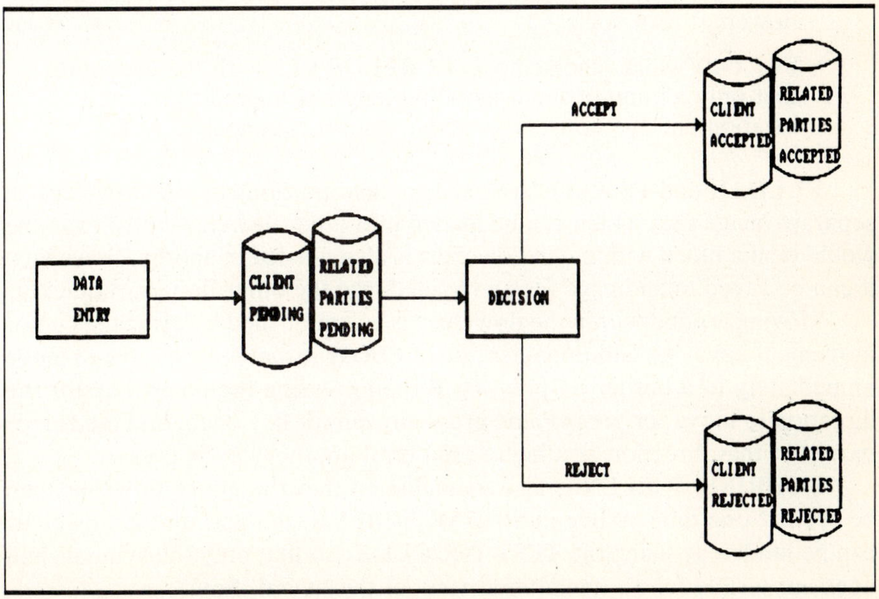

of the screen. Connectors, bypasses, and arrows are also available under this option.

F3 TEXT is used to add text to a flowchart, either within the symbols or as headers or narratives on the body of the flowchart. Once **F3 TEXT** is selected, the default options are displayed at the bottom of the screen and can be edited as needed. These options include font size and style, and auto-centering. The **INS** and **DEL** keys retain their normal functions within **FLOW** and can be used as in a word processor.

F4 DELETE, F5 RELOCATE, and **F6 COPY** all work in basically the same way. Once any of these three options are chosen, the user is prompted to select the first corner of the rectangle to be worked on. After the cursor is in position, press **RETURN** to mark the point. Then use the cursor keys to move to the opposite corner of the rectangle and press **RETURN**. At this point the function of the three options differ.

- **F4 DELETE** prompts the user to verify the deletion, after having hidden the rectangle to show the effect of the deletion. **RETURN** accepts the deletion and **ESC** cancels it.
- **F5 RELOCATE** also hides the rectangle, but allows the user to move to the relocation position. Pressing the **SPACE** bar shows what the relocation would look like and prompts the user to verify the relocation. Answering "no" allows movement to another location, again pressing **SPACE**, while "yes" makes the relocation permanent. Pressing **ESC** cancels the relocation and leaves the flowchart as it was.
- **F6 COPY** works the same as **F5 RELOCATE** with the exception that only a copy of the original rectangle is moved to the new location and the copy stays active until it is canceled by **ESC**.

F7 LOAD and **F8 SAVE** are used to save portions of the flowchart to separate image files which can be loaded into other flowcharts. An example would be if a block within one flowchart is also needed in another flowchart, it can be saved to an image file and loaded into the other flowchart quickly.

Moving around within the flowchart is accomplished by using the cursor movement keys. An additional feature of **FLOW** is that it is possible to move immediately to a border by pressing **B** then pressing the arrow key for the direction to move, or press **F** and press any cursor key once, and the cursor moves in that direction at a high speed until another key is pressed.

S SHRINK SCREEN is also available so that the entire flowchart can be seen at one time. While in **SHRINK SCREEN**, the text on the flowchart can be hidden by using the **TEST TOGGLE T**, so that only the symbols and lines are visible for an uncluttered view of the overall flow.

USING FLOWCHARTS IN AN AUDIT

Since overview flowcharts provide a summary view of systems, they are useful to outline and understand the overall flow in EDP systems. As already discussed, they can also show the broad flow between departments and indicate major control points. Thus, they are valuable to an efficient audit.

Computer overview flowcharts show the major input, output, and files used in a particular application. They can be used to show how the different parts of the system are linked. (See Figures 17-1, 17-2, and 17-3.)

Computer overview flowcharts illustrate the following:

- Relevant source documents that are entered into the system.
- Computer master files and suspense files that hold data of significance and are used in the system under review. When recording systems that use related data element file structures (such as a data base), it is necessary to indicate clearly the particular data within the data base that is affected by noting the input processed. For clarity, the data usually should be described according to the same system employed by the user.
- The type of computer used.
- A summary of computer-produced output or reports, divided into routine and exception. Routine reports are for transactions that were processed normally. Exception reports are the reports generated by the computer when data that does not fit into the routine is encountered. Examples are differences in stock count or abnormality reports, such as stock not counted within specific time limits and sales of products at abnormal gross profit (or loss) margins. Exception reports are also produced for transactions that cannot be processed further for any of a number of reasons.

Specific control techniques in overview can be identified in a computer overview flowchart. The flowchart can provide sufficient information for the following considerations to become apparent:

- The nature and type of the application, such as accounts receivable processing, invoicing, or sales order processing systems.
- The relevant control objectives.
- Whether detailed questions will be for computer or manual systems. It is common to use a combination of control objectives and detailed questions to evaluate a computer system. There are usually manual aspects in all computerized systems, such as follow-up on exceptions. For another example, the preparation and authorization of sales invoices in a computerized accounts

FIG. 17-31
MAPICS general ledger: interactive entry—batch update

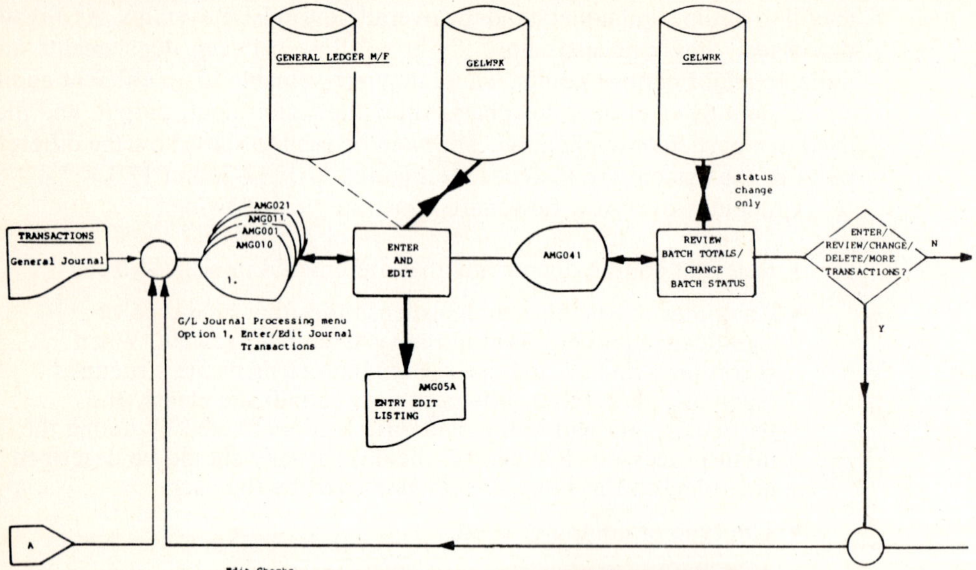

Edit Checks

- o Valid company number
- o Valid G/L debit account number
- o Valid G/L credit account number
- o Entered amounts greater than zero
- o Total debit amounts equal to the total credit amounts
- o Valid posting date or period

Other Significant Data Entered

- o Source (originating journal identifier)
- o Description of transaction

General

Journal transactions must be batched so that only one company and one accounting period are in one batch. The application edits the entered batch of transactions and produces the General Journal entry edit report. This report prints all transactions with associated error or informational messages. The operator should use this report as a basis for error corrections.

All transactions are written to a transaction file (including errors). Transactions in error must, however, be corrected before they can be updated to the relevant master files.

Batch totals over entered journal transactions' debit and credit amounts are displayed on the screen for verification by the operator. Also displayed is the calculated difference between the debit and credit amounts. Debit and credit amounts must be equal.

Batch status may be changed to:

- o "Deleted." Which marks the batch deletion;
- o "Suspended." In which case existing transactions can still be modified, deleted, or additional transactions can be entered. Suspended batches will not be included in the batch update run.
- o "Closed." Makes the batch available for update.

receivable processing system may still be a manual procedure. Therefore, detailed questions about manual procedures are also required.

- It is usually possible to obtain a good idea of the principal controls operating in the system from the types of input, the master files used, and the various routine or exception reports. For example, a

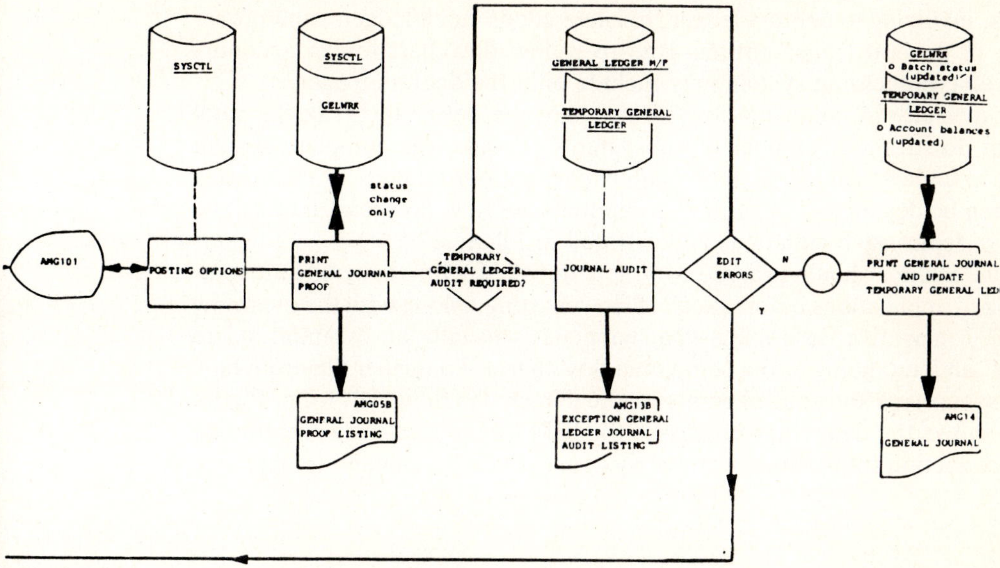

Batches of edited (error-free and closed) transactions are selected by accounting period and company, to be made available for journal posting.

In order to maintain the integrity of General Ledger, a further edit of transaction batches is performed by balancing the transactions by source of entry when printing the General Journal Proof listing. This report is similar to the General Journal Entry Edit Listing, but the entries are grouped based on the transaction source field. The debit and credit amounts associated with the source are totaled and checked to be sure that they are equal.

The General Ledger application audits (checks that all the debits equal the credits) the transactions received from AR, Payroll, or AP before posting General Ledger transactions. This audit is performed during the journal posting procedure. Should a procedure be run that uses the Temporary General Ledger file before it has been audited in the posting procedure, the Journal Audit from the Demand Reports menu will be requested to be run (by the system). The Journal Exception Aydit is not printed unless errors are detected in the Temporary General Ledger.

When the General Journal Proof and Journal Exception Audit are error-free the General Journal is printed and transactions are posted to the Temporary General Ledger.

file of unused goods-received note numbers suggests that a numerical sequence check can be used as the completeness of input control for goods-received note numbers; batch reports indicate that batching can be used as a completeness control, or as an accuracy control, or both.

Computer overview flowcharts may not provide a summary of all the procedures for a given application. While an overview flowchart for a sales order processing system often covers the entire revenue cycle—from sales orders, invoicing to debtors ledger, finished goods stock ledgers, and preparation of general ledger entires—the overview flowchart for an accounts receivable processing system may include only the debtors ledger.

Especially in complex situations, it may be better to break the total system down into a number of subsystems to make the complete system easier to understand. The relationship between different parts of the system can then be described. (A form of computer overview flowchart that can be used to depict such situations is illustrated in Figure 17-5.)

The auditor should prepare overview flowcharts for all significant computerized applications before detailed flowcharting. Along with the overview charts, a narrative describing what happens is usually an essential aid to others' understanding of the completed flowcharts. To further illustrate how processing steps and control points can be depicted in flowchart form, Figure 17-31 shows the data entry processes for IBM's Manufacturing Accounting and Production Information Control System (MAPICS) General Ledger system.

CHAPTER **18**

Interviews and Transaction Reviews

CONDUCTING AN EFFECTIVE INTERNAL CONTROL INQUIRY

Introduction

To document a system, the auditor must understand it. To obtain that understanding, gathering information from site personnel regarding the systems in use is an important and time-consuming part of the evaluation of internal control. Things the auditor can do to increase the reliability of this information and reduce the time required to obtain it are discussed in the following order:

1. Prepare adequately in advance.
2. Learn how to conduct interviews.
3. Become familiar with different types of questions.

Advance Preparation

Before discussing internal control matters with site personnel, the auditor should:

- Be as familiar as possible with the matters to be discussed. For example, any previously prepared flowcharts and transaction review working papers, internal control questionnaires and the like should be studied. Interviews always go better when the auditor is prepared and knowledgeable about the topic being discussed.
- Try to ensure meeting the appropriate individual, or the person best able to answer questions. For example, the management information systems director may be the appropriate person to interview for an overall understanding of the system, while the programmer/analyst may be the appropriate person if a detailed knowledge of the inventory management system is required. The auditor should try to figure out who is most likely to have the information needed.
- Formulate the questions to ask beforehand. The interview will proceed more smoothly and quickly, and the need for follow-up interviews should be reduced. When questions are not adequately prepared, relevant information that was overlooked in the initial interview may have to be obtained in a second meeting.
- Obtain as much information as possible from other company personnel about the personal characteristics of the individual to be interviewed. Knowing in advance that the person to be interviewed is quite busy can increase the likelihood of establishing rapport by getting right down to business. A busy person being interviewed may appreciate a no-nonsense approach.
- Consider scheduling carefully. The person to be interviewed should have sufficient time to answer questions and should know in advance how much time will be required.
- Consider the management level of the person to be interviewed. If

he is a member of senior management, a senior audit staff person should do the interview whenever possible.

The Interview

An auditor needs to learn how to apply a few simple methods to be more effective in obtaining information during a meeting with site personnel. The methods described in the following paragraphs are useful in interview situations. The steps include:

1. Telling the person about the purpose of the interview.
2. Establishing a basic rapport or common interest.
3. Emphasizing positive behavioral factors.
4. Choosing vocabulary carefully during the interview.

Most people being interviewed want to know the following:

- The reason for the interview.
- Why they were selected.
- How the information or data will be used.
- Whether they will be informed about any outcome.

These questions should be anticipated and dealt with early in the interview. The answers can provide positive motivation and make it easier to get the desired responses. If the relevance of the interview is unclear or the questions asked do not seem to relate to the stated purpose, unnecessary barriers may be created.

As interviewer, the auditor should provide the necessary motivation to continue the interview. If the interviewee identifies with the interviewer and enjoys the interaction, or sees the interviewer as someone who may help to effect some desired change in procedures, the interviewee will be more likely to respond. On the other hand, the interviewee may be unwilling to provide certain information because it seems to be potentially threatening or embarrassing. Sometimes information is forgotten or overlooked. An inability to respond may also result from repressed envy or hostility, as might the inability to ask meaningful questions.

The better the psychological forces at work during an interview are understood, the easier it is to minimize or control any negative forces. The interviewer should try to see the world as the interviewee sees it, through his particular set of experiences and background, to develop greater understanding on both sides.

The behavior of both parties in an interview can act as a positive or negative influence. The interviewer's role is to maximize the forces that enhance communication and minimize or eliminate the negative forces or barriers. Behavioral influences include physical, vocal, listening, and feedback behavior.

Physical Behavior. Physical behavior includes eye contact, facial expressions, and mannerisms. A pleasant and relaxed appearance creates a comfortable atmosphere. The initial impressions, conveyed in the first 30 to 60 seconds, will affect the remainder of the interview. As an expert in the field puts it, "You can't make a first impression a second time." Therefore, in most interviews it is important to try to establish rapport immediately. Taking notes during the interview, to some people, is a sign that the interviewer is listening and that what they are saying is important; to others, it seems threatening. Although thorough note-taking may be needed, do not become too intensely involved in writing.

Physical factors are somehow magnified during an interview. An interviewer must be particularly aware of any personal characteristics and mannerisms that can create a positive or a negative effect, as well as of other potentially distorting environmental influences.

Vocal Communication. Good vocal communication skills entail the following aspects:

- A pleasant voice
- Audibility
- Articulation
- Naturalness and spontaneity

Negative vocal factors, which can create barriers, include:

- Speaking too fast or too slowly.
- A brisk or impersonal speaking manner, in which little interest or enthusiasm is projected.
- Mumbling or "over-articulate" speech.

Physical and vocal communication are important. But what is most important, and can overcome both physical and vocal limitations, is conveying a feeling of genuine and personal interest in the interviewee.

Listening and Responding. Listening and responding concerns both the sensitivity and the willingness of the interviewer to behave according to different cues from the interviewee. The interviewer should listen and try to understand the interviewee, not simply conduct a monologue.

Restating the interviewee's response in his own words is an effective technique. This creates the impression that the interviewer is really listening. It can also increase the accuracy of the interchange, since people sometimes need help expressing their thoughts. A good interviewer should be sure to allow ample time for a response to questions and always encourage the interviewee to express things in the most natural way. The interviewer should be quick to sense when the interviewee wants to express or elaborate on a particular point but is unable to do so without some prodding or help. Some areas may be difficult to discuss, or there may be some question about their perceived appropriateness. The good interviewer senses these difficulties and tries to create an atmosphere where the interviewee feels free to discuss sensitive areas.

As interviewer, the auditor should have the flexibility to adjust and modify the interview in light of the responses, while making sure that the objectives of the interview are met.

Vocabulary

The vocabulary or choice of words used in an interview can be a major help or a major problem in the communication process. Words must be understood by both parties in the interview. This is very important for the EDP auditor, who usually understands EDP terms well enough to be able to use them. (The glossary provides definitions of many EDP terms and acronyms.) If the interviewee is unfamiliar with certain terms or concepts, the interviewer should notice this and try to establish a frame of reference; this could be called educating the interviewee.

Sometimes the interviewer may have to vary vocabulary used to include words chosen by the interviewee. For example, if the interviewer refers to the process of accounting for the numerical sequence of prenumbered documents as a completeness control, while the interviewee refers to it as "the number control," then the interviewer should remember to refer to the process as the number control. Using words chosen this way motivates the interviewee to communicate. However, chosen words should not be beyond the vocabulary level easily understood by the interviewee, nor should they appear to be deliberately oversimplified.

Another aspect of word choice is making sure that an appropriate verbal setting is established and followed. For example, if the interviewee is responsible for system security over both on-line and data base systems, the interviewer should ensure that questions and answers deal with the same aspect of the particular system under discussion. When discussing on-line systems, this aspect of system security should be referred to specifically, or the words that are particular to the process should be used.

Sometimes, including a question referring to possible extenuating circumstances indicates a nonjudgmental attitude and increases the likelihood of getting an accurate response. For example, assume that the person who receives exception or rejection reports does not follow up on all missing items or batches. To which of the following questions is that person likely to give an accurate answer: "Why don't you follow up on all the missing items or batches?" or "I can see that you're very busy. Do you always have a chance to follow upon on all the missing items or batches?" Ordinarily, most people are more likely to answer the second question accurately.

Types of Questions

The basic types of questions, discussed in more detail in the following paragraphs, are:

- Open-ended
- Direct
- Closed
- Yes/No
- Probes
- Restatement

Open-Ended Questions. These questions are broad and basically unstructured; they simply establish the topic and allow the interviewee to structure the answer. They let the person know that the interviewer is interested in their feelings, frame of reference, attitudes, and value system.

Open-ended questions establish good rapport and can often help maintain good communication. The degree of openness varies. Some examples are:

- Tell me about the organization's management information systems.
- What are the procedures to ensure that only authorized users access your system?
- How do you process program changes?
- How do you process transactions for the accounts payable system?

Although these questions are all open-ended, they are successively more specific, and therefore more limited in their degree of openness. Open-ended questions cannot be answered with a "yes" or "no"; they force the interviewee to really think about the answer, thereby giving the interviewer an insight into the interviewee's frame of reference.

Direct Questions. Many interviewing situations require that, once rapport has been established, certain questions be asked directly. Direct questions ask for explanations or further expansion on a particular point; they call for a specific reply on a specific topic. The following are examples of direct questions:

- How do you make sure that all transactions are processed?
- How do you ensure that programs in production have been properly tested and approved by management?

The advantage of asking direct questions indirectly is that they do not sound as much like questions, but it is obvious that a response is sought. They also leave a broader area for response.

Closed Questions. These are a form of direct question that greatly narrows the range of possible responses. The closed question is appropriate when the objective is to lead the interviewee to identify with a certain attitude or perspective, or to express agreement or disagreement with a stated viewpoint. For example:

- Do you restrict access to the system by using system software security, physical security, or a specific password identification method?
- Why don't you account for all users who have access to the system?

If the question does not seem threatening, it is usually answered easily (as in the first question). If, however, it is perceived as threatening, it may not be answered directly and can create barriers (as in the second question). The use of closed questions assumes that:

- The interviewer has substantial knowledge of the interviewee's information level.
- There are a limited number of known frames of reference, which are clearly presented in the question.
- The interviewer has information or an opinion on the matter.

Since closed questions assume considerable knowledge about the situation, they should be used with caution. When the interviewer's objective is to force the interviewee to consider or think through several factors or alternatives before coming to a conclusion, a series of closed questions can be effective. In this case, the interviewer should determine that all the conditions for use of closed questions are met.

Yes/No Questions. These are even more restricting than closed questions. They allow the interviewee virtually no latitude or response except "yes" or "no," or possibly "I don't know." This sort of question is most often used by an inexperienced interviewer. While it is useful for the purpose of filling out forms and obtaining specific facts, it also tends to limit the amount of information obtained. Since the "law of least effort" usually operates, the interviewee answers only what is asked. Even if some additional information is volunteered, interviewers who ask such questions are apt to pay little attention, since they are likely to be too busy formulating more questions and not really listening.

A major problem with yes/no questions is that they tend to turn the interview into an interrogation. The tendency to ask questions in rapid order often causes the interviewee to react defensively rather than to give frank, honest answers. Short-answer questions should be used to get needed factual data. They should be interspersed within the interview as needed. A long list of yes/no questions should generally be avoided.

Internal control questionnaires often employ a yes/no format. This does not mean that they must be asked in this manner, but rather that the answers are to be recorded in this format.

Probes. Probes are used to stimulate discussion and obtain more information. They motivate the interviewee to expand on, clarify, or explain reasons for information already given. Probes are ways of following up on partial or superficial responses. When done well, they direct the interviewee's thinking toward further aspects of the topic under discussion. Some examples of probes are:

- Why do you think this happens?
- Is there some way you would change the situation?
- Can you give me a reason for that?

Probing is one way to obtain specific, complete responses. Some interviewees have difficulty putting their thoughts into words, so that their answers are unclear or incomplete. Others may want to hide information they feel would be unacceptable to the interviewer. Probes can be used after any question to encourage the interviewee to think further about the topic. For example:

> INTERVIEWER: How does your organization process program amendments?
> DATA PROCESSING MANAGER: Haphazardly.
> INTERVIEWER: What makes you feel that way?
> DATA PROCESSING MANAGER: There are no established procedures in place so that some changes are put into production without proper testing.

As a result of this exchange, an inconclusive answer is turned into a useful piece of information.

Restatement. The purpose of restatement is to verify the interviewer's understanding of what the interviewee has said. It also allows the person being interviewed to hear what has been said as encouragement to go on speaking, examining, or looking deeper into the question. Good use of restatement communicates this impression to the interviewee: "I am listening to you very carefully. So carefully, in fact, that I can restate what you have said. I am doing so now to help you to hear yourself through me so that you may absorb your statement and consider its impact, if any, on you. For the time being, I am keeping my thoughts out of it." The most effective method of restating seems to be to restate that part of what has been said that the interviewer feels is most significant and worth having the interviewee hear again. To continue with the example from the previous paragraph:

> INTERVIEWER: What do you mean?
> DATA PROCESSING MANAGER: Joe has no control over those guys and they never fill out the control sheets anymore.
> INTERVIEWER: The programmers never make out control sheets and the program changes are processed for production without them?
> DATA PROCESSING MANAGER: Yes, that's right. We have to make so many changes and our programmers are so familiar with the system we rely on them to test the changes.
> INTERVIEWER: There are numerous changes made to programs and some of the general controls are not being implemented properly?

To use the restatement technique, interviewers should not state their own views. Instead, without making a commitment or evaluation, the restatement technique shows that the interviewer understands the interviewee's point of view. It also enables the interviewee to hear his or her own logic, possible biases, and assumptions that may be based on false information or doubts. Restatement should have a positive effect on the interviewee because it demonstrates that the interviewer is listening and trying to understand what is being said. Like all good things, however, restatement can also be overdone, resulting in an artificial and affected situation.

PROCEDURES ON ERROR RATES

Finding out about error rates can be tricky, since people tend to be defensive about any discussion of errors. In general, the auditor should take the position that what is going on is an attempt to gain information that might help to make the interviewee's job easier and better. It is important to avoid giving the impression that the auditor is looking for something wrong. If possible, it is helpful to take the position that all parties concerned are engaged in a mutual learning process.

Possible Questions to Ask About Error Rates

There are many questions that might be asked of an interviewee to try to get complete information about the error rate for a given process. Several assumptions should underlie these questions.

- It is desirable to avoid the use of terms such as "error rate," since frequently these put the interviewee on the defensive.
- In many cases, information about error rates may not be very precise because company procedures may not produce that information routinely. Accordingly, the auditor should realize that the information may be incomplete.
- The auditor should consider the types of errors as well as the rate of errors. Often, the only information available relates to types of errors. However, typically it is useful in evaluating weaknesses or exceptions and may also point to appropriate corrective action.
- It is usually preferable to determine error rates per error type. Information about the composite rate of all errors is also useful and should be documented if it is the only information available.
- Questions about error rates in a previous control process—that took place prior to the processes performed by the person being interviewed—are answered more readily.

Possible questions to use in investigating error rates include:

- "How could the task be done more easily or better?" There are two aspects to this question. First, responses can help to identify ways to improve efficiency and control. Second, responses often indicate whether errors are frequent and the type of errors involved. This information can then be pursued further.

- "What kinds of things cause you to take extra time in processing documents?" This question can elicit information about errors from two possible sources: first, errors that come up through the system to the interviewee and, second, errors that are identified later in the system and are sent back to the interviewee to be rectified.
- "What is the most common mistake that you see in documents you process?" While this question can usually identify types of errors, it is a more general question designed to get the interviewee to consider errors that are routinely encountered. The auditor should not stop here, but should use any response as a basis for pursuing further information. A follow-up probe might be: "Do any others come to mind?"
- "Who tells you when you've made a mistake?" This question can be used to initiate a discussion of what kinds of errors are returned to the interviewee for correction. It also identifies personnel farther along in the system who can be queried about errors.
- "Why do you think people keep making the same mistake?" This may identify possible improvements and may also provide a better understanding of why the error happens so often.
- "Do you keep track of errors that you correct?" This may provide information about the type and quantity of errors and logging procedures for them.
- "How often do you refer mistakes that you find back to the user departments?" Even if the person does not initiate such communications, he or she can often identify who does, and that person may be a useful source of information. If there is no communication of errors, the auditor may have uncovered a major problem area.

Other Ways to Detect Errors

When asking the preceding questions, an auditor should try to identify procedures that are in effect and that might be useful in detecting error rates. Some typical examples follow:

- *Computer rejects.* If error runs are made, or if input is frequently kicked back from computer processing, there may be a record of error rates. There may also be some indication of error types.

- *Manual listings.* In addition to the errors corrected by the interviewee, there may be listings of documents returned for additional information or correction, or listings of types of errors typically encountered. For example, there may be a list of program change requisitions returned to the users because there was no indication of proper approval.
- *Budget variance analysis.* A form of control over errors may exist as part of the investigation of budget variances. Whoever performs these investigations may be a useful source of information about the type and extent of errors found.

Recording Information

As described previously, a great deal of information the auditor receives is imprecise, and it may consist of rather subjective impressions. Whenever possible, the person being questioned should be encouraged to give a percentage estimate. This helps the auditor to understand the order of magnitude. For example, if somebody says there is "probably only a 2 to 5 percent error rate," the auditor gains a different appreciation of the range of the problem than if the interviewee says there is "a good chance that the stuff will be wrong." When personnel do not feel that they can give a percentage estimate, the auditor might try to get a better overall impression of the extent of error, for example, "appears to be low frequency of error" or "may be frequent errors." There is no set procedure for recording this kind of feedback; auditors are encouraged to use any means that they feel communicates the necessary information and can be accomplished reasonably. The objective is to help senior management identify trouble spots so they can reorder their priorities when necessary.

Types of Errors

An auditor will probably find that some errors are more important than others. As a result, it is likely that he will spend more time identifying the error rate for certain types of errors. For example, if the error type would permit the conversion of corporate assets or would not be caught and corrected at a subsequent point in the internal control system, further inquiry is warranted. Factors considered important enough to warrant a greater degree of inquiry should be noted, since feedback might be used to develop a questionnaire or design other procedures which will improve controls in these areas.

Questions About Irregularities

The preceding discussion focuses on errors, unintentional acts or failures to act that lead to mistakes. Auditors are also concerned about intentional acts, such as irregularities that may be fraudulent. When this is the subject being investigated, the auditor must know how interview procedures can elicit information about these acts.

This is an extremely delicate area. Any questions should be framed carefully and cautiously. One possible question is: "How do you know that everything that you are approving is OK?" A frequent answer is that the interviewee has confidence in the integrity of his or her personnel. There may also be occasional spot-checks. In most instances such interview responses taken alone provide very little assurance that irregularities do not exist.

Organizations normally employ a variety of other procedures for dealing with irregularities or possible frauds. For example, one general approach is establishing a code of corporate conduct, monitoring compliance, and taking necessary corrective action. These procedures are usually outside the scope of an internal accounting control system evaluation. Accordingly, separate consideration should usually be given to reviewing and evaluating such procedures.

Conclusion

Whenever frequent errors are found, the auditor should consider whether other controls compensate for or correct these errors. This is helpful in completing an internal control questionnaire or other documents and in reporting to senior management.

CONFIRMING THE UNDERSTANDING—TRANSACTION REVIEWS

Having completed the interviews and flowchart or narrative of the system, the auditor may choose to trace one transaction of each type through the company's accounting system in order to confirm the recorded understanding of the system. In some cases, depending on the audit approach for a particular system, tracing a transaction may also serve the dual purpose of testing the system.

In this regard, a transaction is defined as a series of business activities related to an exchange involving money, goods, or services, or to any other change in an asset or liability that should result in an accounting entry.

Normally, transaction reviews are performed after the flowcharts have been prepared or updated. However, it may be more efficient to perform the transaction reviews and prepare the related documentation at the same time an understanding of the system is obtained or updated. The auditor who prepares or updates the flowcharts should generally perform the transaction reviews.

Selection of Transactions

Each type of transaction identified at the time the understanding was obtained and the flowcharts were prepared should be considered for a transaction review. A transaction review should also be performed annually when updating the understanding.

If individual types of transactions are combined during processing and subjected to common procedural and reporting controls from that point forward, only one example of the combined type need be traced through subsequent procedures.

Nature of Transaction Reviews

The transaction review should cover each operation shown on the flowchart. The specific way in which this is done depends on the circumstances. When carrying out a transaction review, the auditor should be aware of the possibility that operations with internal accounting control significance have been omitted from the flowcharts. This is particularly true when using flowcharts prepared by others. If that is the case, the necessary additions should be made to the flowcharts. The starting point of a transaction review may be any stage in the flow where the type of transaction is readily identifiable. Normally, a transaction is traced all the way from its inception to its termination as an entry in the general ledger. However, the transaction review may begin in the middle of the flow providing that all steps in the process are covered at some time.

Documentation

Transaction review working papers should document the work performed. To minimize the time required in preparing these working papers, use of the following techniques is recommended:

- A worksheet should be prepared in a form that will accommodate several years' evaluations, whenever this is possible.
- A worksheet should be set up in columnar form, with the numbers

of the operations from the flowchart and supporting narratives listed on the left. The operation numbers listed on the worksheet indicate the procedures performed as outlined on the flowchart or narrative. When there are numerous or complex procedures indicated by a single operation number, it may be necessary to provide an explanatory note on the worksheet.

- The specific transactions reviewed should be identified in a column of the worksheet.

If the work performed is evident from the flowchart, and the document reference is shown on the transaction review working papers, no further documentation is required. (See Figure 18-1 for a sample transaction review worksheet.)

Results of Transaction Reviews

If the transaction reviews confirm the understanding of the system and that understanding has been correctly recorded in the flowcharts or narratives, no further work with regard to transaction reviews is necessary. If the transaction reviews indicate that the auditor's initial understanding of the system was incorrect, the next step is to find out the procedures actually in effect, revise the documentation of the system accordingly, and note this on the working papers.

If management contends that an exception revealed by the transaction review is an isolated instance, the auditor should perform a few additional reviews of the procedures that gave rise to the exception. This is done to determine whether the exception really is an isolated event before any revisions are made to the flowcharts or narratives.

Completion of the transaction reviews should be indicated in the space provided on a record of flowchart preparation and transaction reviews or another document being used for this purpose.

TRANSACTION REVIEWS IN COMPUTER SYSTEMS

Transaction reviews are carried out in computerized systems for much the same reasons as in noncomputerized systems. However, the characteristics of a computerized system may change the methods the auditor uses to confirm an understanding.

The application of transaction reviews to computer systems is dealt with in the following sections:

FIG. 18-1

Flowchart preparation and transaction review worksheet

Location ______________________________

Preparation/updating of flowcharts (F) and performance of transaction reviews (TR)

FLOWCHART		19				19				19			
		Prepared/Updated*				Prepared/Updated*				Prepared/Updated*			
NO.	DESCRIPTION OF SYSTEM	F	TR	Done By	Reviewed By	F	TR	Done By	Reviewed By	F	TR	Done By	Reviewed By

*Place ticks (√) in columns provided.

- *Manual accounting procedures* Accounting procedures carried out manually both prior to and subsequent to the processing of data by the computer.
- *Programmed procedures* Procedures carried out by the computer programs that relate to:
  - — The completeness, accuracy, validity, or maintenance of data.
  - — The calculation, summarization, categorization, updating, or generation of data.

Ideally, the auditor should be able to trace *one* transaction, or resulting information, through all key manual procedures *and* programmed procedures.

Manual Accounting Procedures Within Computerized Systems

A transaction review of manual accounting procedures within computerized systems is carried out in a manner similar to one in a totally noncomputerized system, except:

- It may not be practical to trace the same transaction through both input and output procedures because:
  - — The computer system may hold data for considerable periods of time on suspense or on master files before the transactions are processed further, such as orders awaiting shipment.
  - — There may not be sufficient evidence to easily trace input to output or vice versa.
- When input transactions are batched or grouped together prior to posting to a computer file, the batch, file, or control total should be traced, rather than the individual transaction.
- The output available for review may consist primarily of exception reports, depending on the type of information generated.

Programmed Procedures

Transaction reviews of manual accounting procedures are not adequate to confirm the auditor's understanding of a computerized system; the programmed procedures should also be confirmed.

Ideally, the auditor should carry out a transaction review to confirm an understanding of the programmed procedures. However, in practice it is not practical (or sometimes even possible) to confirm the program logic adequately by tracing transactions through the system. The following problems are encountered:

- Transactions are sometimes grouped into batches prior to computer processing. A summary of the procedures applied to the group is usually reported, but complete evidence about the effect of processing on each individual transaction may not be documented.
- A particular programmed procedure may consist of one or more complex programs and may involve several computer files. Each program may encompass many different logical paths (100 or so is not uncommon). Not all these paths are of accounting significance, so that the auditor may be required first to identify those that are.

As in manual systems, the auditor looks for evidence that may be used to confirm an understanding. Some methods to follow in performing transaction reviews of programmed procedures involve reperforming the programmed procedures, reviewing program documentation, and performing limited reviews of actual source code.

- If the computer prints out all the details of the transaction, such as quantity, unit price, and total, the auditor may reperform the programmed procedures manually. Here, the auditor would compare the quantity and unit price to the source data and reperform the "total" calculation. This would confirm the results of the operation of the programmed procedures. The technique generally provides sufficient confirmation only in the simplest computer systems, because all the information needed to reperform the calculation is readily available.
- Programmed procedures are often described in the system and program documentation. If the documentation is adequate, the auditor may review it to confirm the understanding. If program documentation is to be used, the auditor must be satisfied that:
  - The program documentation reflects the logic incorporated in the source programs.
  - The documentation corresponds to the production programs currently in use.
- The transaction review may also include a limited review of relevant portions of the source code.
- The auditor may sometimes find that the documentation does not adequately describe the programmed procedures. It may be incomplete, out-of-date, or prepared poorly, and thus cannot be used in confirming an understanding of the programmed procedures. In these circumstances, the auditor should:
  - Be sure that the program listing is current and up-to-date before performing reviews of program code.
  - Interview key data processing personnel to determine the accuracy of the recorded programmed procedures.
  - Reperform the programmed procedures, as stated previously. It should be noted that the methods used to confirm the understanding may also serve as audit tests when applied at a later stage of the audit.

Effects of Transaction Reviews

The effects of the transaction review of a computer system on the audit, and on the audit documentation, are as follows:

- It is important to time the transaction review carefully to obtain the maximum advantage. The work schedule should allow sufficient time for the controls to be evaluated before audit tests are begun.
- Much of the work of the transaction review, in particular parts relating to how the programs treat individual items, can be done at the time an understanding of the system is obtained, for example, by reviewing program documentation.
- For the preceding reason, and also because of the complexity of the work, it is especially desirable from an efficiency perspective that the person who obtains the understanding also carries out the transaction review.
- Transaction review working papers for computer application systems are similar to those for noncomputer systems. They show flowchart operation numbers down the page and transaction types across the page, and should be referenced to the transactions reviewed. Where the same transaction has not been traced through the system, this should be made clear on the transaction review working papers.
- It is apparent from the preceding discussion that the time spent on procedures included in the transaction review of a computer system may exceed the time spent on a transaction review of a manual system. This should be considered when planning for the audit.

Special skills and experience are necessary to carry out transaction reviews in a complex EDP system. The EDP auditor should have sufficient expertise in this area to be able to carry out the task.

CHAPTER **19**

The Control Risk Assessment Process

ASSESSING INTERNAL CONTROLS

To assess the adequacy of the internal controls in a system, it is helpful to use a methodical process. This process can include the use of flowcharts, forms, questionnaires, and guides. The discipline of the process and the tools used are integral parts of an assessment approach. This kind of approach has been adopted by management and by external and internal auditors in business, industry, and government. This chapter provides an overview of one such process, and of the documents that can be used.

Essentially, there are four phases to the process of assessing internal controls in a structured audit approach.

- Phase I—Gathering or updating information about the organization within which the internal controls of the system operate, assessing the overall control environment of the organization, and obtaining an understanding of the system itself.
- Phase II—Determining the scope of the assessment, the audit objectives, and how they will be attained.
- Phase III—Performing an extended assessment of control risk by defining the control objectives required, deciding on the presence or absence of control procedures, and testing the controls to determine whether they are operating as planned.
- Phase IV—Concluding the results of the extended assessment performed during Phase III, making appropriate recommendations, and following up on subsequent audits of the system.

PHASE I—GATHERING OR UPDATING INFORMATION

The following information is very important for the auditor to assess control risk properly and make appropriate audit strategy and testing decisions:

- Knowledge of the organization's business and industry.
- Review of prior audit results.
- An understanding of the system under review.
- Knowledge of applicable accounting, regulatory, and industry standards.

Assessing the Overall Control Environment

An assessment of the overall control environment should be made as part of gathering or updating information about an operation to be reviewed. This assessment provides a basis for:

- Determining the nature of the work or business of an organization, and the way it is conducted.
- Identifying any special legal or commercial requirements relevant to the organization.
- Identifying accounting principles and policies followed by the organization that are industry-specific.
- Identifying significant reports and procedures that management uses to control the business.
- Identifying high-level control and operating issues of concern to top management, boards of directors, and audit committees.

A questionnaire process should be used by the auditor to document and assess the control environment more easily. Internal audit management can have significant involvement in the preparation of this control environment assessment questionnaire. It has the overall organization knowledge, contact with senior management, and audit experience that are critical in evaluating the control environment.

A control environment assessment questionnaire is completed primarily through inquiry and observation, taking into account knowledge obtained on prior audits, if it exists. Its completion will help the auditor assess the quality of the control environment, and whether it is conducive to good internal control. Broad categories that should be covered in this questionnaire include:

- Organizational structure and key executive responsibilities.
- Role of the board of directors, audit committee, and internal audit function.
- Management's judgments and integrity.
- Performance planning and monitoring.
- Availability and reliability of management information.
- Policies and procedures for control and accountability.
- Management information system (MIS) organization and nature of EDP systems.

After considering factors that either contribute to or detract from the quality of the entity's control environment, an overall conclusion should be made. It is documented on the control environment assessment questionnaire, reflecting:

- Whether the environment appears to be conducive to maintaining reliable internal controls.
- The apparent quality of management's judgments and estimates.
- Whether sufficient and reliable information appears to be available for management to conduct and control the business effectively.

This conclusion should then be considered, together with other information obtained about the operation, to assess control risk, determine the appropriate audit strategy and testing plan, and identify recommendations to be communicated to management and the audit committee.

Understanding of the System

In conjunction with the initial assessment of the control environment, other tasks should be performed. The understanding of the accounting system should be documented by preparing an overview flowchart. This process should include interviewing key personnel and obtaining data file descriptions and other documentation of the system. The overview flowchart should illustrate the flow of significant types of transactions from initiation through processing, and to the ultimate reports from the system. The level of detail should be sufficient to supplement assessing the effective operation of internal controls.

PHASE II—SCOPE OF ASSESSMENT

Before assessing controls of a specific system, the auditor should consider initial audit activities and the results of gathering or updating information about the organization. These processes will assist the auditor in making preliminary judgments about assessing risks and developing the audit plan.

The audit plan is the auditor's plan of action for achieving the relevant audit objectives. It should take into account the favorable and unfavorable factors identified from the initial risk assessment activities. A key element of the audit plan is the decision about which audit objectives are to be addressed through an extended assessment of control risk, or evaluation of controls. The emphasis given to objectives for a system, and thus the nature, timing, and extent of auditing procedures used to achieve those objectives, varies according to the auditor's initial risk assessments. Extending the assessment of control risk entails obtaining and recording a detailed understanding of internal controls, and determining whether those controls have operated effectively. The process includes tests of controls.

PHASE III—EXTENDED ASSESSMENT OF CONTROL RISK

The approach to control risk assessment is supported by a tool—the Control Assessment and Record of Tests forms (CARTs)—that provides the ability to understand and assess control procedures concurrently. The CARTs provide the flexibility necessary for carrying out an extended assessment of control risk in modern computer environments.

The auditor should consider the effect of any significant control weaknesses encountered while recording and obtaining support for controls. Control weaknesses identified during completion of the CART may be classified as:

1. Those that are significant to the assessment of control risk and that also would require communication to management.
2. Those that do not affect control risk but should be communicated to management.
3. Those that are insignificant to both the auditor and management.

Making an Extended Assessment of Control Risk

Making an extended assessment of control risk comprises:

- Determining the accounts and audit objectives to be addressed by the assessment.
- Identifying and understanding key controls designed to reduce the risk of errors related to those audit objectives.
- Determining whether the individuals responsible for a control understand its purpose, how to exercise it, and how the control detects and resolves errors.
- Assessing a control's effectiveness through evidence of its operation and some tests of controls.
- Concluding whether the combination of control procedures relative to a particular audit objective is sufficient to reduce the risk of material misstatement to a low level.

Figure 19-1 illustrates the process of making an extended assessment. It starts with selection of the appropriate CART sections to be completed, based on the accounts and audit objectives to be addressed. Generally, an extended assessment is made only for systems-derived accounts.

Next, relevant application and information technology (IT) controls are identified and assessed, and conclusions are drawn from this work. Identification and assessment of IT controls are critical in today's computer

FIG. 19-1
Making an extended assessment of control risk

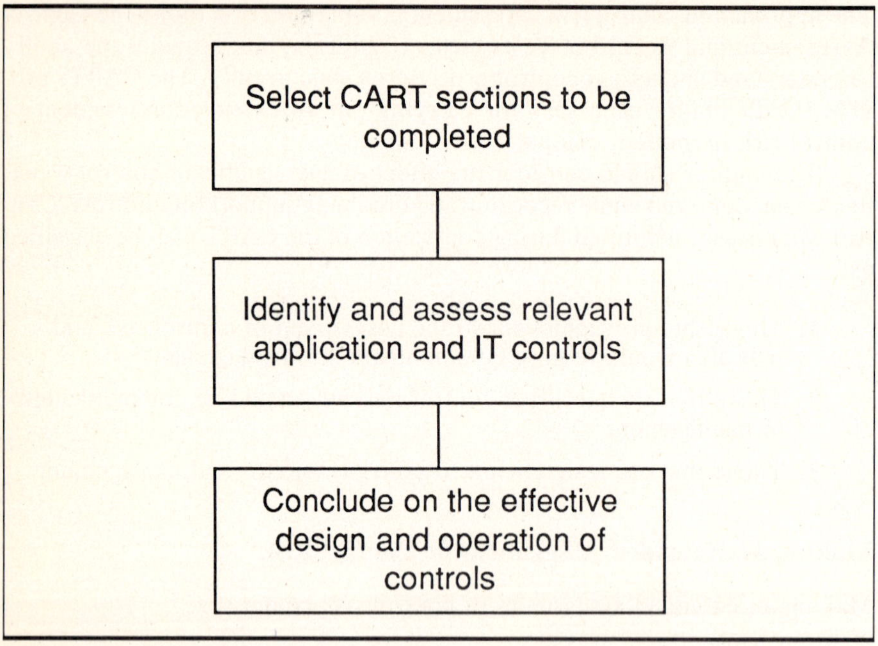

systems, since controls over files and transactions (application controls) depend on the proper development and maintenance of programmed procedures. Generally, selected IT controls are assessed whenever application controls are assessed. There is explicit recognition, however, that unless management expectations dictate otherwise, not all areas of IT controls need to be assessed in many situations.

Selecting CART Sections to Be Completed

The three CARTs developed for use in performing and documenting an extended assessment of control risk are the:

- Application Controls CART.
- Information Technology or IT Controls CART.
- Packaged Systems IT Controls CART.

Each CART is divided into sections by control objective. Since, under the audit approach, all work is directed toward achieving audit objectives,

FIG. 19-2

Application controls CART (partial)

Questions and control procedures	Yes	No	Tests
A.1 Are the packages used well established and in common use?			first year
			year 2
			year 3

the control objectives in each section of the CARTs are linked to audit objectives. Figures 19-2, 19-3, and 19-4 show examples of each type of CART.

Application Controls. In determining the audit testing plan, the audit team must decide the accounts and audit objectives for which an extended assessment of control risk will be made. Understanding the relationship between control objectives and audit objectives is critical in selecting the CART sections to be completed.

Figure 19-5 illustrates the likely relationship between control objectives in the Application Controls CART and audit objectives. These relationships are not absolute; the audit team must also consider the characteristics of the specific account and understand that additional audit objectives may be affected by controls. For example, certain controls over completeness and existence may also reduce the risk of cutoff errors at year-end. Additionally, information used to make valuation judgments may be subject to controls; if so, the extended assessment may provide evidence about the reliability of that information, thus reducing the evidence needed from other tests.

IT Controls. The IT Controls CART is designed for assessing IT or general controls in more structured and complex data processing environ-

FIG. 19-3
IT controls CART (partial)

Controls over program changes ensure that:
(a) new procedures are appropriate
(b) errors are not introduced as a result of the change.

	Questions	Applicable
Vendor maintained packages	1- 2	☐
Internally maintained applications	3- 9	☐
Cataloguing	10-12	☐
Back-up and recovery	13-15	☐

Identify libraries containing significant programmed procedures including program production libraries, source code libraries and programs held for back-up purposes .

____
____
____
____
____
____

Questions and control procedures	Yes	No	Tests
Vendor maintained packages Answer the following questions if vendors maintained the packages during the year. ***Validity and testing*** 1 Are there controls to ensure that: (a) the modifications are appropriate to the user's requirements (b) the amended systems are adequately tested (c) systems, operations, back-up and user documentation is appropriately updated?			first year
			year 2
			year 3

ments. The Packaged Systems IT Controls CART may be appropriate when an entity uses software developed and maintained by third parties. Even in those circumstances, however, a greater degree of IT control may be necessary. Therefore, the IT CART (rather than that for packaged systems) should be used where, for example:

- The client has considerable in-house programming expertise and makes changes to the package.

FIG. 19-4
Package systems IT controls CART (partial)

Questions and control procedures	Yes	No	Tests
Control totals 1.1 Is the total of the items on file regularly *reconciled* to an independently established total (e.g., agreement to a manual control account or computer agreement to a control record) on a suitably timely basis?			first year
			year 2
			year 3

- Extensive modifications are made to the software package for the organization by the supplier.
- The sophistication and flexibility of the software package itself and the degree of manual intervention needed in its operation require greater control.

Once the appropriate CART has been selected, the audit team decides which sections are to be completed. Figure 19-6 illustrates the likely relationship between sections in the IT CARTs and audit objectives. Those relationships are considered, together with other factors, in selecting CART sections. The following are factors to consider when selecting IT CART sections to be completed:

- Maintenance controls are usually assessed in all cases when an extended assessment is carried out.
- Computer operations controls are usually assessed when it is more efficient than assessing certain file continuity controls, and to evaluate client backup and recovery procedures.
- Data file and program security controls, even when not assessed for audit purposes, may be assessed on management request.

FIG. 19-5

Likely relationship between application controls CART and audit objectives

SELECTION GUIDANCE

Application CART Sections/Control Objectives	AUDIT OBJECTIVES		
	Completeness	Accuracy	Existence
File Continuity	X	X	X
Asset Protection			X
Completeness of Input	X		X
Accuracy of Input		X	
Authorization of Transactions			X
Generation of Data/Transactions	X	X	
Update of Data	X	X	X

- System software controls are usually assessed when program and data file security controls are assessed.
- Implementation and file conversion controls are usually assessed only when a new computer application or a major enhancement to an existing application is being implemented.

Identifying and Assessing Controls

The audit team should identify and document relevant key control procedures and assess their effective operation. CART questions are organized by control objective. Questions under each objective are adaptable to a variety of audit situations, since, unlike the Internal Control Questionnaire (ICQ) formerly used, they do not specify the control techniques or documents that should be used to accomplish the control objective. Figure 19-7 illustrates the difference between a question in the revenue cycle ICQ and a comparable question in the CART. Note that the ICQ describes a specific procedure; the CART provides more leeway in assessing the control. All procedures can be considered when they are related to the particular control.

FIG. 19-6

Likely relationship between IT controls CART and audit objectives

SELECTION GUIDANCE

Information Technology CART Sections	AUDIT OBJECTIVES		
	Completeness	Accuracy	Existence
Maintenance	X	X	X
Computer Operations	X		X
Data File Security			X
Program Security			X
System Software			X
Implementation	X	X	X
File Conversion	X	X	X

Identifying and Understanding Controls. To identify and understand specific controls, inquiries should be made of appropriate personnel about how a control objective is achieved and how a control procedure is performed. During this process, the inquiring auditor should consider how the particular control relates to other controls designed to achieve the control objective. The auditor should also observe the execution of the procedure and review reports or other documentation used in exercising the control, such as exception reports or control logs, to corroborate answers to inquiries. The use of inquiry, observation, and examination of evidence are the most often used tests in the extended assessment.

Through this process, a complete understanding of the control design and function is obtained. The understanding should be documented under applicable questions in the CART. This method of understanding and documenting controls is more flexible than the ICQ, which was based on a predefined "control model" and included a standard set of controls and documents. The CARTs provide a greater opportunity to focus on the controls that are most important to each organization in controlling financial information.

Assessing the Effective Operation of Controls. Once the understanding of a control has been obtained, evidence of its effective operation should be

FIG. 19-7

Comparison of question in the revenue cycle ICQ and a comparable question in the CART

Revenue Cycle ICQ - Completeness of Sales

31.8 Are unmatched records of goods shipped and services performed (31.6) reviewed on a regular basis (e.g., monthly) to determine the reasons for any such items that have not been matched within a reasonable period of time in respect of:
(a) goods;
(b) services?

Application Controls CART - Completeness of Input

3.5 Are there adequate procedures to investigate and if necessary correct:
(a) long outstanding items;
(b) all duplicates, mismatches, and rejections?

sought. In practice, these activities are often performed concurrently. To obtain support for the effective operation of a control, the inquiries should be more in-depth than those made to understand the control. These inquiries are intended to ascertain:

- How the control detects and resolves errors.
- Whether the person responsible for the procedure understands the purpose of the control and how to exercise it.

For example, if the control follows up on exceptions from a match of receiving documents and vendor invoices, some questions about the effective operation of that procedure might be:

- Is every exception report reviewed?
- How long does the review take?
- Are all exceptions investigated?

- How many and what types of problems do you normally find?
- Are steps taken to eliminate these problems?
- Are there ever any reports with no exceptions?
- Were there any times when the report was not reviewed?
- Who reviews the reports when you are not here?

Inquiries should be supplemented by examining exception reports for evidence of the individual's investigation and, in some cases, corroborating explanations with others, such as the individuals responsible for resolving exceptions. This assessment of the effective operation of a control provides a more in-depth understanding of how the control operates.

These inquiries, observations, and examinations of evidence are normally sufficient to assess whether the control is operating effectively. However, there may be instances where a control is so significant to the assessment that it should be reperformed (e.g., controls over updating interest rates to a standing data file used for interest calculations in a bank).

PHASE IV—CONCLUDING, REPORTING, AND RECTIFYING

Extended Assessment Conclusions

An extended assessment of control risk should be made when the audit team expects, on a preliminary basis, that the control risk for certain audit objectives will be low. The extended assessment either confirms or denies this expectation. When the control risk for a particular audit objective is not confirmed as low, planned substantive tests should be reconsidered.

These assessments are made on the basis of conclusions reached for applicable control objectives in the CARTs. Considering the combination of controls assessed for a particular objective, a conclusion should be reached as to whether the control objective has been achieved. Those conclusions are a matter of professional judgment, and the principal reasons for them should be documented.

Weaknesses in specific controls do not necessarily lead to a conclusion that a particular control objective has not been achieved. The significance of the weaknesses must be assessed in light of the effectiveness of the combination of controls. That combination may be sufficient to compensate for apparent weaknesses in specific procedures. Recommendations for improvements in controls should then be summarized and reported to management and the audit committee, as appropriate.

Control Weaknesses

A control weakness worksheet can be used to integrate the work performed in relation to any weaknesses found in the control system. The purpose of this document is to bring together in one document:

- All control weaknesses that were identified during the evaluation.
- The results of discussing those weaknesses with appropriate management.
- Any reporting to senior management.
- Any corrective action taken.

The enhanced audit approach emphasizes assessing the combination of application, IT, and management controls for a given audit objective. For example, if application controls, which depend on IT controls for the proper operation of programmed procedures, are assessed as good, but the IT controls are weak, the auditor might conclude that controls are not adequate and additional substantive tests must be performed.

Common Weaknesses in Computer Systems

Weaknesses often occur because of a failure to plan controls adequately during the early stages of system development. As a result, controls are developed on an ad hoc, after-the-fact, or unstructured basis. Consideration of the entire system, both computer and noncomputer, during the planning of controls is essential. However, this integrated approach is often overlooked, and manual controls frequently are not decided on until after the system has become operational. The need to restructure existing manual controls when computer processing is introduced may also be overlooked.

The more common weaknesses in relation to user controls and programmed procedures include:

- Failure to establish control over the maintenance of master file data.
- Failure to recognize the need to control reference data.
- Ineffective authorization procedures, particularly in relation to irregular entries, such as adjustments.
- Failure to recognize the importance of supervisory controls.
- Failure to check the accuracy of computer-generated data (e.g., interest charges), by either reasonableness checks or manual reviews of the generated data.

- Unrealistic criteria in programmed reasonableness and dependency checks, with the result that either too few or too many exceptional items are reflected or reported.

The more common weaknesses in relation to IT controls include:

- Failure to establish a proper segregation of duties within the MIS department to distinguish clearly the functions of systems analysts, programmers, and computer operators.
- Failure to produce easy-to-understand reports of computer use so that a meaningful review of computer operations can be carried out.
- Absence of control over modifications made to program libraries, particularly to ensure that only properly authorized amendments can be made to existing programs.
- Failure to safeguard data files against access by unauthorized personnel.
- Failure to ensure that restrictions over the operation of a computer and access to data files are enforced at all times, particularly during evening and weekend shifts.

The more common breakdowns that are encountered during testing of controls include:

- Failure to act promptly on exception reports.
- Buildup of uninvestigated rejections.
- Buildup of suspense items on files.
- Delays in the follow-up of outstanding and overdue items, such as follow-up letters for overdue bills.
- Failure to carry out reconciliation procedures because of time pressures resulting from processing delays.
- The low priority often given to cyclical checking of master file data.
- Inadequate enforcement of restrictions on the operation of the computer, in particular, permitting unsupervised programmers to operate the computer or to test programs.
- Amendments made to operational program libraries (such as APF or authorized program facility [APF] libraries) that bypass the normal control procedures and authorization requirements.

To assess the effect of breakdowns in controls over computer systems, the auditor should realize that an exception relating to failure of a programmed procedure is unlikely to be an isolated incident. At best, it indicates a breakdown in the general controls. At worst, it points to a fault in the program itself. In the latter case, the situation should be reported to management immediately, since the fault will remain until it is corrected.

ADDITIONAL EVALUATIVE CONSIDERATIONS

Management Reporting

When the audit is completed, a formal report is typically required, which includes an assessment of the system or area reviewed. This report should also discuss the internal controls. In addition, where deficiencies are noted, recommendations should outline whatever corrective action is needed to ensure that adequate controls are implemented.

With the passage of the Foreign Corrupt Practices Act (FCPA), corporate officers can be held accountable for the adequacy of internal controls that affect the organization's financial statements. Thus, merely identifying and reporting weaknesses and recommending corrective action to management may not be sufficient. Adequate follow-up procedures should exist to ensure that corrective action is taken on a timely, cost-effective basis, so that an adequate system of internal control results.

Alternatives to Low Control Risk Assessment

When the auditor determines the control risk is other than low, to ensure the operation of the programmed procedures or for reasons of efficiency, suitable alternative procedures should be adopted. For example, it may be appropriate to test the operation of the programmed procedures to a significant extent.

Controls in New Systems

When new systems are introduced, the auditor may decide that it is more efficient to perform an extended assessment of the implementation controls, especially if significant problems were encountered during the conversion or implementation process. The remaining IT controls should then be assessed to ensure the consistent and proper operation of the programmed procedures in the new system during the balance of the period under review.

It can be useful to assess the adequacy of the controls in an application system before the application becomes operational, for the following reasons:

- It is difficult and usually costly to make changes in a computerized system once it is operational. Therefore, the auditor should make any suggestions or recommendations at the relevant stage of development so that they can be incorporated without problems or great expense. Indeed, users often encourage or specifically request the auditor's assessment and comments prior to system implementation.
- The auditor needs to know the nature and extent of programmed procedures in order to decide whether to perform an extended assessment of implementation and conversion controls. Without adequate lead time before implementation, it may be impossible to plan and perform appropriate tests.
- The auditor may be able to arrange for additional control-related features to be included in the system that will assist in subsequent audit tests. For example, facilities may be arranged to obtain printouts or reports on request, or to include additional data elements on the master files so that the subsequent examination by a computer audit program will be easier (such as date of last interest bill).
- If, under exceptional circumstances, weaknesses cannot be covered by substantive procedures, the auditor may want to reconsider the extent to which the findings properly describe the control situation. In those circumstances, the auditor should ensure that subsequent auditing procedures give appropriate consideration to the weaknesses. If it is necessary to amend the nature, extent, or timing of substantive procedures, the amendments to the audit program should be recorded on the appropriate documentation.

Administrative Control Weaknesses

The auditor should consider whether the identified weaknesses could have financial or nonfinancial audit implications. If the weaknesses could result in an error that would be important to management, this possibility, together with the justification for the decision, should be documented.

When practical, the auditor should quantify the effect of a weakness (e.g., in terms of revenue losses or cost increases) in order to make the related control comments as meaningful to management as possible. Putting these effects in pragmatic dollars-and-cents terms helps readers of the report to understand it. If this is not practical, an effort should be made to determine the order of magnitude of the transactions, or of the operations affected by the control weakness. For example, if a failure to calculate economic order quantities leads to lost revenue or additional costs, the auditor may be unable to quantify the loss precisely. When this happens, the auditor should comment instead on the total volume of purchases, or purchased-goods inventory, or other amounts that can be quantified.

The overall purpose is to be able to provide management with useful, meaningful reports in specific terms that can be understood and addressed.

CHAPTER **20**

Control Reviews and Tests of Controls

INTRODUCTION

To ensure an effective and efficient audit, an auditor performs a control review to make a risk assessment of a system and its controls relative to specific audit objectives. The objective may be to write an audit report (a common objective of the internal auditor) or to determine the audit strategy by making judgments about materiality and assessing inherent and control risk as the audit test plan is developed. Risk assessments are related to audit objectives in determining the minimum level of assurance required from substantive tests.

The assessment of control risk resulting from the review often concentrates on the deficiencies or weaknesses in the control system. Those deficiencies are featured in the internal auditor's report as items requiring management attention. They are also communicated to management by the external auditor and, more important, are used as a basis for determining the level of substantive tests and other auditing procedures required. In spite of this apparent concentration on deficiencies in the results of the review, the control assessment in fact focuses mainly on control strengths. The auditor applies procedures designed to determine what risks the system might be subject to, what controls are in place that would reduce those risks, whether the controls are properly designed, and whether the controls continue to function through time. The auditor normally applies a variety of auditing procedures in performing these tasks, including:

- Interviews and inquiries.
- Observation and physical inspection.
- Documentation and analysis.
- Examination of evidence.
- Reperformance of manual or computer processes.

These audit procedures are clearly related; the typical control review includes most of these techniques, performed in appropriate sequence. The audit approach divides the control review into a number of steps, which are covered in different sections of this book:

- The documenting and analysis of the processing system is covered in Chapter 17, "How to Document Systems: Using Flowcharts."
- Inquiry techniques are covered in Chapter 18, "Interviews and Transaction Reviews," along with the audit procedures that can be used to confirm the documented understanding of the system.
- The documenting and analysis of control points are covered in Chapter 19, "The Control Risk Assessment Process," with further guidance for general controls in Appendix A, "*Internal Control Reference Manual—Information Technology Controls*," and for application controls in Appendix B, "*Internal Control Reference Manual—Application Controls*."

This chapter focuses on the next step of the audit approach, those audit procedures called tests of controls, the main purpose of which is to ensure that the controls operate as planned.

Scope of Tests of Controls

Auditors may test some of the controls, but rarely test them all. Which controls are selected for testing depends on the audit objectives. External auditors typically restrict their review and their tests to internal accounting controls and audit objectives for individual account balances and classes of transactions. Internal auditors sometimes test the operational or administrative controls to identify opportunities for system improvements that do not affect internal accounting controls. Internal auditors sometimes omit testing of controls altogether, preferring to rely on other control review procedures. They do this to use scarce internal audit resources best and get the maximum coverage from the resources available. Internal auditors may restrict their tests of controls to a single point in time. The external auditor more frequently extends the scope of the tests to a part or all of the period under review. The internal auditor concentrates on testing those controls most important to management. The external auditor, to determine the minimum level of assurance required from substantive tests, focuses on controls providing evidence that specific audit objectives are met by controls procedures for individual account balances and classes of transactions. Other factors that may affect the decision of whether or not to test specific controls include:

Materiality considerations

- The approximate volume or number of transactions that pass (or should pass) through the control point. An auditor can use a number of techniques to make a reasonable estimate of volume, such as inquiries of knowledgeable personnel, review of statistical records maintained by personnel operating the system, and review of use of serially numbered documents.

- The estimated monetary value of the transactions that pass (or should pass) through the control point and the approximate range of individual transactions. An auditor can use a number of techniques to make a reasonable estimate of the monetary value, such as inquiries of knowledgeable personnel, review of records maintained by personnel operating the system, and relating recorded monetary values to the company's known operating levels.
- The effect of an error resulting from a control weakness. An internal auditor may concentrate tests on areas where errors or late processing could have a significant effect on operations. An external auditor may seek other compensating controls to assess control weakness more accurately, or may broaden the nature, extent, or timing of substantive tests. For example, a control weakness that can lead to an overstatement of inventory is more likely to be significant if the offsetting erroneous credit is to income than if it is to accounts payable.

Risk factors—that is, the susceptibility of particular accounts and transactions to material or significant errors

- The amount of accounting judgment involved in the measurement and classification process.
- The susceptibility of an account to misappropriation.
- The extent to which account balances are derived from estimates.

Other considerations

- The risk that error may not be detected in later stages of processing.
- Any other indications of potentially significant errors.

Types of Tests of Controls

Normally, tests of controls include the following procedures:

- *Interviews and inquiries.* Make specific, detailed inquiries of organization personnel. For example, in an inquiry on a sales manager's review and investigation of a report of invoices with unusually high or low gross margins, only asking if discrepancies are investigated is not sufficient. Probing, in-depth questions should be asked on how the report and its items are reviewed, and how frequently.

- *Observation and physical inspection.* View organization personnel in their work environment. For example, physical security techniques can be observed and documented easily during a data center tour.
- *Examination of evidence.* Inspection of records, documents, reconciliations, reports, and the like for evidence that a specific control appears to have been applied properly. An example is the inspection of signatures or initials on a purchase invoice for evidence that the invoice was matched with a purchase order and record of goods received. Another method is by inspection of exception reports.
- *Reperformance.* The repeating, either in whole or in part, of the work processes performed by people or computers. For example, the matching of a purchase invoice with the corresponding purchase order and records of goods received.

In many situations, observation and/or inquiry are the principal tests of controls that can be performed. For example, control over counting and examining incoming goods and the physical security of inventory are tested by observation of the procedures used. Where observation is employed, an auditor should bear in mind the possibility that the observed control may not be performed when the auditor is not present. In addition, it is important to see evidence of the action taken as a result of the application of the observed control (such as follow-up on exception reports).

Tests of operational controls normally consist of examination of evidence and, to a lesser extent, observation of procedures. Unless there has been a specific decision by management, operational controls generally are not reperformed. The examination of evidence, coupled with in-depth inquiry and observation, is often sufficient to assess the effective design and operation of controls without using sampling techniques.

Compliance testing focuses on determining whether a control procedure is reliable by searching for evidence of exceptions in its operations. In a test of controls, the focus is on whether individuals responsible for a control understand it and are diligent in its execution. For computerized controls, emphasis is on whether the control is designed effectively and how the entity ensures that it is implemented, maintained, and operated properly.

The absence of a specific control procedure is addressed by identifying a compensating control or designing a substantive test procedure. Conclusions about control risk are based on the effectiveness of a combination of controls, not on the presence and effectiveness of individual controls in isolation.

CATEGORIES OF CONTROLS TO BE TESTED OR REVIEWED

Internal controls can be divided into two categories:

1. Internal accounting controls, which may be further divided into:
   - *Basic controls.* Those controls that are necessary for the completeness and accuracy of the accounting records.
   - *Disciplines over basic controls.* Those controls designed to ensure the continued and proper operation of basic controls and to safeguard assets.
2. Administrative or operational controls, which may also be divided as above.

Internal Accounting Controls

Basic controls cover a wide range of checks and procedures. Typical examples are:

- Checks on completeness (such as by means of sequential numbering of transactions or batch totals).
- Matching or comparison of documents or previously recorded records.
- Checks of addition, calculation, and extensions.
- Electronic monitoring and reporting of exceptions.
- Controls over groups of transactions (frequently by means of control totals).
- Controls over the recording of physical movements of goods.

Testing of basic controls generally includes examination of evidence, reperformance (when appropriate), and observation.

Disciplines over basic controls comprise the following:

- Custodial controls.
- Segregation of duties so that the work of one person checks that of another adequately.

- Supervisory control or adequate supervision of the work of people involved in the operation of the basic controls.

Testing of custodial controls and segregation of duties usually involves observation and inquiry and/or examination of signatures and initials on documents and records. These tests normally are carried out as part of the tests of the related basic controls, rather than as a separate operation.

Testing of the supervisory controls, on the other hand, is based largely on the examination of evidence. The primary evidence examined is the signature or initials of the person exercising the control on the relevant document or record. Particular attention should be given to other evidence (such as evidence that computer-produced exception reports have been investigated and follow-up action taken) that has been produced as a result of the supervisory control. In addition, the application of the supervisory control to current transactions can be observed.

Complete reperformance of a supervisory control usually is not possible. The auditor rarely has knowledge and experience of the supervisor concerned; the nature and extent of the checks carried out at the supervisor's discretion may not be evidenced clearly. Reperformance is limited to the tasks that are expected to be undertaken in the exercise of the supervisory control. It normally includes inspection of the supporting documentation that should have been seen by the person exercising the supervisory control, together with evidence of prior checks as required by entity procedures. Using the same items for examination of evidence of basic controls provides increased efficiency. The existence of errors in the application of the basic controls that were not detected by the supervisor may indicate that the related supervisory control is not being applied effectively.

Administrative Controls

Administrative or operational controls deal with the efficient use of resources. Tests of operational controls are based largely on the examination of evidence. Such evidence may consist of the items that form the basis for the control, including an organization chart or policy manual; a report or worksheet, such as technical performance specifications for goods to be purchased; a document, such as a purchase order containing routing, delivery date required, and other instructions; or exception reports or internal memoranda indicating that the control is being applied. Tests of some administrative controls may involve observation.

Reperformance of an administrative control is often not practical, primarily because of the large amount of time that may be required to reperform those controls. For example, an auditor normally does not take the time to recalculate economic order quantities or to check the accuracy of routing instructions for purchased goods. On the other hand, the auditor ordinarily examines evidence that economic order quantities are used and that routing instructions are provided to purchasing personnel.

Sometimes, however, the auditor can reperform an administrative control procedure with a limited expenditure of time. For example, the auditor may wish to reperform a calculation to determine whether a cash discount on a purchase invoice was performed correctly by a programmed procedure. Applying this test to a sample of the invoices permits the task to be done efficiently.

Controls in Management Information Systems

In a computer environment, internal controls are categorized as follows:

- *Application controls.* Those controls that are unique to individual user systems or applications.
- *General or information technology (IT) controls.* Those controls that ensure the effective operation of programmed procedures, including controls over design, implementation, security, and use and amendment of computer programs and files.

Both application and IT controls consist of basic and disciplinary controls.

Tests of application controls are similar to tests of controls in a manual system. The types of tests carried out are the same. However, the documentation being examined and the operations being reperformed may differ. Tests of user controls are sufficient in computer systems where the user checks all output and no reliance is placed on programmed procedures or data held on computer files. In most computer systems, the output is too voluminous and/or there is not adequate visible evidence to be checked manually. In those circumstances, it is necessary to rely on, and therefore perform tests on, the general controls. (See Chapter 13, "Information Technology Controls.")

It is often best to test the general controls before testing the related application controls. Even when application controls are adequate, the auditor may not be able to assess them properly if they are functioning in an environment of undependable general controls. For example, there is little point in testing the action taken on computer reports if the programs creating those reports are not reliable.

Sometimes the auditor does not believe that the results of testing application controls and general controls provide sufficient assurance as to the consistent and proper operation of programmed procedures. At that point, the use of other testing techniques should be considered. Those techniques, such as the use of audit software, can ensure that the programs are appropriate and operating consistently. Normally, they are considered substantive tests because the auditor is attempting to gain satisfaction with the programmed procedures by direct tests, rather than by evaluating and testing the general controls. Nonetheless, in this situation management may wish to consider such testing as a possible alternative to tests of controls.

Tests of general controls consist of inquiry of organization personnel, observation, examination of evidence, and reperformance. These tests are performed on program maintenance, computer operations, data file security, program security, system software, implementation, and file conversion controls.

Tests are prepared for many common internal control techniques (see examples later in this chapter). Tests can be segregated into types: tests of user controls in computer systems, tests of general controls, tests of programmed procedures, and tests of manual systems.

USING TESTS AND REVIEWS TO ASSESS CONTROL

Control procedures are evaluated and tested to provide evidence supporting an assessment of control risk. Control is evaluated by obtaining and recording an understanding of internal accounting controls and determining whether those controls have operated continuously throughout a period. The nature of testing is affected by:

- The accounts and audit objectives to be addressed.
- The key controls designed to reduce the risk of errors related to those audit objectives.
- Whether the individuals responsible for a control understand its purpose and how to execute it, and how it detects and resolves errors.
- The effectiveness of a control through evidence of its operation.
- Whether the combination of control procedures for a particular audit objective is sufficient to reduce the risk of error to a low level.

Levels of Tests

It is not possible to prescribe hard-and-fast rules for determining levels of tests (such as the number of items to be tested). The level to be selected in each case is a matter for judgment in the light of all relevant factors, including the audit objectives to be achieved as a result of the test of controls, the nature of the account balance, and considerations related to the coordination of work with other auditors. The goal of the test of controls, however, should always be to reach a conclusion about the risk of error for a particular audit objective, while testing to the minimum extent necessary. To make a judgment about an appropriate level of tests, all relevant factors should be taken into account, including the complexity of the transactions and experience of previous evaluations.

The levels of tests of administrative controls should consider the effort involved in performing a particular review procedure. When the additional time to review a control is small and the potential impact of a control breakdown is large, the level of test of the administrative control should be relatively high. Normally, this is the case when an administrative control is reviewed in conjunction with the testing of a related internal accounting control. On the other hand, where the effort to review an administrative control is great and the potential impact of a control breakdown is small, it may not be necessary to perform any tests of administrative controls.

Effective Operation of Controls

Observation, inquiry, and examination of evidence often provide information about the effective operation of a control. Use of those techniques must be broad enough to support a conclusion about risk, based on the effectiveness of a combination of controls, not on the presence and effectiveness of individual controls in isolation.

Inquiry procedures, to be effective tests of controls, must be detailed. By themselves, they will not provide sufficient evidence to support a conclusion about the effectiveness of control procedures. During the inquiry process, explanations should be supported by observations, examination of evidence, or both.

Situations may exist where a control is so significant that further evidence of its effectiveness is necessary. In such cases, it may be appropriate to reperform the control procedure. For example, to test the completeness and accuracy of the update of reference data in a master file, reperform the updating procedure a few times to gain additional evidence that the control is operating as designed. If reperformance is appropriate, sampling techniques may be useful, and possibly required. (See later section "Applying Sampling.")

If extensive reperformance is required, reconsideration should be given to the efficiency of testing controls in order to reduce the level of required substantive tests. If reperformance is considered appropriate, remember it is the performance of the control procedure that is being tested and not the existence or accuracy of specific transactions. For this reason, it is unnecessary to select high-value items or different types of transactions for testing. Any transaction subject to the control procedure may be tested.

In assessing whether a control procedure has operated continuously, consider the possible sources of evidence. Select the most efficient approach to obtaining the evidence required.

In testing control procedures related to a particular audit objective and account balance, consider the effectiveness of those procedures in combination. Consider whether the control procedures support a conclusion that control risk is low with respect to related audit objectives and accounts. The absence or weaknesses of individual procedures need not necessarily lead to a conclusion that control procedures are inadequate. Rather than focusing on individual control procedures in isolation, assess the effective operation of controls by considering the aggregate effect of all relevant procedures performed to meet the audit objectives being assessed.

Order of Performing Tests and Reviews

Internal controls need not be tested in the same order in which they appear in any control questionnaires used. Supervisory controls are often tested before the related basic controls. Controls over groups of transactions are tested because the results of tests of supervisory or group controls can help determine the levels of tests needed for underlying controls. It is acceptable to test the basic controls first, or the basic controls and the supervisory controls at the same time, if this is more efficient.

Administrative controls should be reviewed in the most efficient order. Review of an administrative control should be carried out in conjunction with the test of a related internal control procedure whenever efficiency is enhanced by doing so. For example, in testing controls over the matching of purchase orders with receiving reports and purchase invoices, the auditor usually determines at the same time whether routing and other instructions are on the purchase order and whether a cash discount was taken. Since these tests can be done simultaneously, it would be less efficient to make them separate tests.

APPLYING SAMPLING

When an audit performed by an external auditor requires use of sampling, Statement on Auditing Standards (SAS) No. 39 requires that items in the sample be selected from the population in a manner that allows them to be representative of that population. Although they are not required to do so, internal auditors will find that following the auditing standards of the American Institute of Certified Public Accountants (AICPA) improves their ability to coordinate their work with the work of external auditors.

To apply sampling, the auditor considers the sampling risk (the risk of incorrect acceptance or risk of over-reliance on a control); the tolerable deviation rate or error rate; and the attributes of the population, such as the deviation rate or error amount that might be expected (or the fact that items themselves may vary*).

When using nonstatistical sampling, also referred to as judgment sampling, such factors need not be quantified; the auditor can express the criteria used in qualitative terms.

Sampling Risk

Sampling risk is defined as the risk the auditor can accept that the results of a sampling application might be less than accurate. The test may indicate that a control can be relied on (or that an account balance is not significantly misstated*) when there is a chance that the control is unreliable (or the account is significantly misstated*). This risk can be seen as the complement of the desired level of assurance that the auditor seeks from a particular sample. When the auditor desires a test to provide a high degree of assurance, a low degree of sampling risk is required. Sampling risk also has a relationship to the size of the sample. The larger the sample is, the smaller the sampling risk, as long as other factors do not change.

The tolerable deviation rate (or error amount*) is the rate that management has specified as acceptable for a given control situation. When accepting a sample that is designed with an extremely high tolerable error rate, however, the auditor's procedures may become too imprecise to draw meaningful conclusions at a low level of risk.

The Attributes of the Population

The expected deviation rate (or error amount*) in a sample is based on the auditor's best estimate of the actual deviation rate (or error amount*) in the population as a whole. To make such an estimate, information from prior audits can be used, as long as any change in the controls or the circumstances of a particular test are considered. The characteristics of the population in this regard can affect sample size.

The sample size required to meet an auditor's acceptable degree of sampling risk for a given tolerable deviation rate (or error amount*) increases as the population's expected deviation rate (or error amount*) increases.

---

* Refers to substantive tests.

When using statistical sampling, this relationship—the increase in expected deviation rate or error amount and the increase in sample size—is not directly proportionate. (If an expected error amount comes close to the tolerable error amount, it may be necessary to use very large sample sizes.)

Selection of Representative Samples

In order for the sample items to be representative of a population, all items in the population should have a chance of being selected. When this is so, the sample actually chosen is more likely to be representative of the characteristics of the population as a whole. If a sample is selected from less than the entire population, or is composed only of items found in a particular area or unit (such as from one page in a report of a computerized ledger or from one period of time), it cannot be relied on to be truly representative.

When there are several attributes in a population, they may not all be represented in a particular sample. When selecting a sample, the auditor may determine which attribute is of major concern (such as the size of error) and make a sample selection designed to be representative of that concern.

Representative samples for nonstatistical sampling can be attained using various methods, including dollar-weighted (or value-weighted), unsystematic, and systematic selection. When an auditor makes sample selections based on "dollar weight," items are chosen according to the auditor's judgment, assigning more weight to items that have larger recorded values. Such dollar-weighted sampling is not the same as examining all items over a certain dollar limit and a sample of the rest of the items.

Unsystematic or haphazard sample selection is used to achieve a sample that is as random as possible from the population as a whole, avoiding the normal human tendency to favor particular items (such as never choosing the first or last item on a computerized ledger report). Once the auditor is assured that the complete population is available for selection (e.g., being satisfied that the computerized ledger report lists all of the items), a number of items can be selected unsystematically from the entire population. This selection should be as unbiased as possible under the circumstances, although there is always some possibility that bias in selection will exist without the auditor's awareness.

When an auditor is using statistical sampling, a random sample must be selected, no matter what impediments to doing so exist. Random number selection and systematic selection with a random starting point are two techniques that may be used. Computer-assisted techniques are useful particularly in using random number selection samples, since the machine can use random number generators and tables that are completely free from human bias and save time in the selection process. A random sample is not required in nonstatistical sampling, but an understanding of random sampling techniques can help an auditor select a representative sample.

Systematic sample selection is choosing items at an interval, based on a formula that divides population size by sample size. The answer is the interval used for item selection, starting at a single random point between the first item in the population and the interval size. The sample may also be selected using multiple random starting points to minimize the chance that an unexpected pattern in the population will be reflected in the sample. For example, in a sample designed for two random starting points, the computed interval would be twice the size of the interval computed for the single random starting point sample, and two random points within the enlarged interval would be chosen to begin the selection process. Using software, computerized selection can be used to select items at intervals specified from computerized ledgers, saving a lot of time and manual effort.

The main difference between using systematic sample selection in statistical and nonstatistical applications is that nonstatistical techniques do not require that the starting point be random.

Tests of controls and administrative reviews are designed to both test the operations and review the apparent existence and effective operation of specific controls. They are concerned primarily with the flow of transactions through individual control points, rather than the flow of transactions through the entire system. Accordingly, different documents within the same transaction processing system may be selected for examination to verify different control points. It is not necessary, although in some cases it may be more efficient, to test or review related controls using the same documents.

Obviously, in computer systems many programs and data files do not have accounting significance. When carrying out reperformance tests of general controls, the auditor should select control procedures carried out on programs and files that have accounting control significance, when this is what is being tested. For example, normally the auditor selects procedures relating to changes in programs in the inventory system rather than changes in programs in the personnel scheduling system. The auditor can identify appropriate programs and data when obtaining and confirming an understanding of the accounting system and completing or updating an evaluation of internal controls. On the other hand, when an auditor is reviewing a system itself or administrative controls, then controls that apply to all significant programs and files are covered.

If implementation controls vary from system to system, the auditor should test the different sets of controls separately.

Although there are two types of general controls dealing with program security and data file security, often the same controls may apply to both programs and data files. For example, both may be stored in the same physical library or both may be protected by the same software while on-line. When this is so, only one set of tests of controls is required.

DOCUMENTING TESTS OF APPLICATION CONTROLS

The auditor must document the control review and testing process, including control procedures, the audit tests performed and their results, and control assessment conclusions reached. This section describes an approach to documenting the process, using the Control Assessment and Record of Tests (CART) form developed by Coopers & Lybrand (C&L) as an example.

The assessment of application controls is documented on the Application CART. (See later section "Documenting Tests of General or IT Controls," for a description of the Information Technology CART.) The Application CART has two sections, which address the following control objectives:

- File section
  - —*File continuity* of stored data, ensuring that a file supporting an account balance remains correct.
  - —*Asset protection*, including the elements related to custody and security of key data.
- Transaction section
  - —*Completeness of input*, which guards against incomplete or duplicate inputs of data for key transactions.
  - —*Accuracy of input* and key transaction processing.
  - —*Authorization of transactions*, addressing controls used to ensure that key transactions are valid.
  - —*Generation of data* for transactions initiated and processed by the application system automatically.
  - —*Update of data*, addressing controls over the completeness and accuracy of key file updates.

Figure 20-1 shows a typical linkage between audit objectives and the Application CART sections. It is useful in determining which sections should be completed. The linkage can vary, depending on the facts and circumstances.

A separate Application CART is used for each systems-derived account balance subjected to a test of applications controls. Generally, the systems-derived accounts include accounts payable (payments cycle), accounts receivable (revenue cycle), and inventory (production cycle). Normally, one Application CART is sufficient to document and test the controls over all

FIG. 20-1
Audit objectives and Application CART sections

SELECTION GUIDANCE

Application CART Sections/Control Objectives	AUDIT OBJECTIVES		
	Completeness	Accuracy	Existence
File Continuity	X	X	X
Asset Protection			X
Completeness of Input	X		X
Accuracy of Input		X	
Authorization of Transactions			X
Generation of Data/Transactions	X	X	
Update of Data	X	X	X

types of key transactions in each cycle, such as purchases and cash disbursements in the payments cycle. If necessary, however, additional CARTs may be used for different transaction types within an account (cycle). In addition to one or more systems-derived accounts, the pertinent sections of an Application CART are completed to address trial balancing, adjusting general ledger entries, and bank reconciliation procedures (time cycle).

The process of testing application controls starts with selecting the appropriate CART sections to be completed, based on the accounts and audit objectives to be addressed.

Next, relevant key application and general or IT controls are identified and assessed, and conclusions are drawn from this work. Identification and assessment of IT controls are critical in today's computer systems, since controls over files and transactions (i.e., application controls) are dependent on the proper development and maintenance of programmed procedures. Therefore, selected IT controls will be assessed whenever application controls are assessed.

Normally, testing application controls is not reasonable when IT controls are not adequate, because in most systems, application controls depend on the operation of programmed procedures. When relevant IT controls do not ensure the continued proper operation of programmed procedures, an assessment of control risk may require a large amount of reperformance, and thus may not be an efficient strategy.

Application CART Cover Sheet

Figure 20-2 is an illustration of the Application CART cover sheet. It includes the following sections:

Application. Enter the name of the application (or class of transactions) in the space provided on the CART cover sheet.

Financial Statement Account, Value, Key Files and Data, Transactions, and Volumes. Record the financial statement accounts (e.g., accounts receivable, sales), the estimated values (using either the amounts at the preparation date, the previous year-end data, or anticipated current year-end), the key file(s) supporting the accounts, and the related key data elements in the spaces provided. In data base systems, it will not be possible to identify separate physical files for financial statement accounts, but it will be possible to identify the significant individual data elements. For example, the key data elements for an open-item trade accounts receivable file might include for each item its monetary amount, date, and reference number (such as sales invoice number). Master file or reference data significant to transaction processing should be identified. In addition, record each significant type of transaction updating the key file(s)—whether initiated manually, computer-generated, or amendments to master file or reference data—and estimates of the annual volumes of transactions processed. The same transaction types may update both a balance sheet account and an income statement account, in which case they may be referenced to both financial statement accounts.

Audit Objectives and Control Objectives. The decision regarding which audit objectives to address with the test of controls—completeness, accuracy, existence—should be indicated by placing a tick in the appropriate boxes. Indicate decisions as to which control objectives should be completed by placing a tick in the appropriate boxes.

Extent of Testing

The extent to which a particular control procedure should be tested is a matter of professional judgment and depends on the risk that its failure to

FIG. 20-2

Application CART cover sheet

Client ______________________________

Application ______________________________

Financial statement account	Value	Key files and/or data elements updated	Transactions	Volumes

Audit Objectives	Addressed
Completeness	
Accuracy	
Existence	

Year ended

______ 19____ ______ 19____ ______ 19____

Control objectives: File section	To be completed	Signature	Date	Signature	Date	Signature	Date
File continuity							
Asset protection							

Transaction section

Completeness of input							
Accuracy of input							
Authorization of transactions							
Generation of data/ transactions							
Update of data							

Reviewed by in-charge accountant						
Reviewed by engagement manager						

operate would result in an undetected material misstatement of the financial statements. Generally, this risk is a function of:

- The financial significance of the transactions subject to the control.
- Other control procedures that might detect a potential misstatement. Other factors also affect the risk of a potential undetected material misstatement and, therefore, affect the auditor's decision about the extent of tests of control procedures.

Normally, tests of controls begin with a complete inquiry of organization personnel. This is an interactive process with the answers to one question generating additional, follow-up questions. The inquiry process may be accompanied by observation, which can produce more assurance than inquiry and usually is accompanied by examination of evidence. The amount of evidence the auditor examines is dependent on the results of inquiry and observation. The more sound and credible the answers to the inquiries seem and the greater the extent to which observation of personnel supports the obtained information, the less necessary the examination of evidence becomes. It should be considered, however, that the observed application of a procedure might not be performed in the same manner when the auditor is not present.

When considering the extent of testing, recognize that a conclusion is reached with respect not to a particular control but to a control objective. Frequently, limited testing of a number of controls will provide sufficient support to form a conclusion on a control objective. In many instances, testing includes the examination of only one or two items. Extensive documentation, such as that normally required in sampling applications, would be unnecessary in such circumstances. Only the items selected and the findings of the test need to be documented.

The following paragraphs illustrate the relative extent of testing of control procedures that might be encompassed by a test of application controls in circumstances in which the initial risk assessment activities indicate that risk is low. Those activities include:

- Updating the understanding of the control environment and accounting system.
- Considering the results of the prior year's extended assessment of application controls and IT controls relevant to specific audit objectives.
- Considering other information gained in the initial audit activities.

The following illustrations are not standards or benchmarks, but are presented to provide some insight into the extent of testing that might be appropriate.

In assessing control risk relating to *accuracy of input* of sales orders, the reporting of entries that are not matched to approved lists (files) of customer numbers and product codes might be tested. Inquiries of the clerical supervisor and observations of clerks entering data on-line via terminals would be made. Observation of re-entries of initially mismatched items and examination of the supervisor's screen or printout of items failing a second attempt would be made as well. Considering the limited significance of a potential failure of this control, as well as tests of other controls (including discussions with sales, accounts receivable, and credit department personnel and tests of IT controls), no further testing of this control may be deemed necessary.

In assessing control risk relating to *completeness of input*, procedures related to the follow-up of long-outstanding purchase orders, receiving reports, and invoices might be tested. Conduct a complete inquiry of organization personnel. Consider a variety of factors, including the significance of the control. Examine the report for the current period (e.g., a month) being used for follow-up purposes and note that the employee marks each item acted upon. Request documentation used in the follow-up process and evidence as to the disposition of items. After examining such evidential matter for a few—perhaps five—items, request one or two reports from preceding months (assuming the reports are not cumulative) and scan them to ascertain whether all items are marked as having been resolved. Considering the soundness of the responses to the inquiries, the satisfactory results of the evidence examined, as well as tests of other controls that affect completeness of input, decide whether the extent of testing was sufficient.

The Intervening Period

The need to perform additional tests of controls in the period from the date the tests were performed to the end of the audit period should be considered. Although often it is not necessary to perform additional tests, consider whether the performance of tests of controls during the intervening period or of additional substantive tests is required as a result of:

- Significant changes in the organization's control environment, accounting systems, or control procedures. (Document any such significant changes.)
- Significant changes in the organization's use of related data in managing the business.
- The results of substantive tests.

Application CART Guidance Material

The CART is supported by guidance material for the common systems-derived accounts—accounts payable (payments cycle), accounts receivable (revenue cycle), and inventory (production cycle)—and for the time cycle, which covers trial balancing, general ledger entry, and bank reconciliation procedures. The guidance material provides information as to files and data that normally are significant to the particular cycle and, for each question, describes:

- Control procedures that typically will be performed to effect the control implicit in the question.
- Tests that might be used for those controls. This material may be referred to as necessary for assistance in recognizing relevant controls and deciding how to test them.

Similar information is presented in Appendix B, "*Internal Control Reference Manual—Application Controls*."

Recording Control Procedures

Beneath each question, space is provided to record a description of the control procedures. Each question in the CART is phrased so that it may be answered "yes" or "no," thereby indicating the presence or absence of a control procedure, respectively. Record the answer by placing a tick in either column, as appropriate. If a question does not apply, insert "N/A" in the "yes" column.

Only those control procedures to be assessed should be recorded. There may be instances in which more than one control procedure applicable to a particular question has been designed. In those instances, only the control procedure considered to be the primary control for the audit purposes need be recorded.

Control procedures should be described in sufficient detail to support a conclusion as to whether the control objective has been achieved. Typically, the following details should be recorded for each procedure:

- The name and job title of the person performing the procedure.
- A description of the procedure.
- The frequency with which the procedure is performed.
- The identification of reports used in performing the procedure.

If the space beneath a question is insufficient for recording this information, reference should be made to the supporting working paper where the information is documented. File the working paper directly behind the CART page with the related question.

Inquiries about changes in the entity's procedures should be made each year. The CART should be updated for such changes unless the system has changed to the extent that it is more practical to complete a new CART. The method of updating should follow the principles applicable to the initial preparation of the CART. Whenever amendments are made, the date of the amendment should be indicated clearly alongside the amendment. The previous answer should remain legible so that the procedures in force at a particular date can be ascertained.

Recording Tests of Controls

The support obtained for the proper design and operation of controls should be recorded in the space opposite each question. If the space is insufficient, reference the supporting working paper that contains such documentation. File the working paper directly behind the CART page with the related question.

The documentation should address each of the organization's control procedures documented in the CART, and should be described in sufficient detail to support the conclusion as to whether those procedures are operating as prescribed. (The proper operation of related programmed procedures is assessed in connection with IT controls.)

Typically, the following details should be recorded for each CART question:

- The name and job title of the person with whom the procedure was discussed or who was observed performing the procedure.
- The date of the discussion or observation.
- A description of the discussion or observation.
- Details of any documents, reports, or other evidence examined or other tests performed.

Usually, the recording of controls and related tests will be combined into one process. This avoids duplication of inquiries and can significantly reduce the time required to complete the CART.

The effect of any significant control weaknesses encountered while recording and obtaining support for controls should be considered. Control weaknesses identified may be classified as:

- Those significant to the assessment of control risk, and requiring communication to management.

- Those not affecting control risk, but which should be communicated to management.
- Those significant to both the auditor and management.

Recording Conclusions

After assessing internal controls, it should be concluded whether the procedures, taken as a whole, are designed to achieve the control objective appropriately and are operating as prescribed. Document the conclusion, along with a brief description of the basis for the conclusion, on the last page of the CART section. Because the assessment of control risk focuses on the identification of control strengths rather than weaknesses, a specific audit reaction is not needed for every "no" answer. Consider the controls that are present and form a conclusion as to whether the procedures, taken as a whole, are designed appropriately and operated to achieve the control objective.

For completion/updating of the CART, the cover sheet should be signed and dated in the spaces provided. That signature evidences completion and achievement of those control objectives and the related audit objectives. If, however, it is concluded that control risk for any of the control objectives or related audit objectives addressed is assessed as other than low, the signature on the cover sheet should indicate its completion and state clearly which control or audit objectives are assessed as having other than low control risk.

Review and Approval

Evidence of supervisory review and concurrence with the conclusions is indicated by signing and dating the cover sheet. The evaluation considers any control objectives or audit objectives with control risk assessed as other than low, and the effect on substantive tests. When control risk is assessed as other than low, reference should be made to the audit strategy memorandum, substantive test audit program, or other documentation reflecting the consideration of that assessment on substantive test procedures. The evaluation of management addresses the auditor conclusions in the CART. In making the evaluation, the manager also considers the assessment of control risk for relevant IT controls as documented in the IT CART.

Subsequent Years

The CARTs are designed for use over a three-year period. Once control procedures have been recorded under applicable questions in the CART, the descriptions should be reconsidered in subsequent years and modified as necessary. Space is provided for recording the tests performed and concluding about control objecctives in each year. Normally, a new CART should be used after the third year, although the number of periods it is used may be extended.

Payroll System Illustration

This section describes an illustrative payroll system (Figure 20-3) and a testing program that might be used for that system (Figure 20-4). The tests are based on information obtained while gaining an understanding of the company. The company's system is described, tests of controls determined to be pertinent are developed, and explanations are provided as to how those decisions were made and the types of controls that are tested. Obviously, the example shown is not the only one that could be developed and supported for this system. Auditing is a subjective process, and this example needs to be considered in that light. It is provided as an example of one testing approach that could be taken to this system.

The level (i.e., number of items to be examined) of the tests illustrated is not presented. The level of tests is dependent on the auditor's decision to use statistical or nonstatistical sampling, the relationship between the general EDP controls and those of the system under review, and other subjective factors not within the scope of this example. Note that whenever an external auditor uses sampling, whether statistical or nonstatistical, the methods and criteria employed must meet the requirements of SAS No. 39. This requirement pertains whenever the test program indicates that the auditor selected a sample to perform a test.

In addition, Figure 20-5 describes audit software referred to in the testing program, including its benefits from both a financial and an operational point of view.

DOCUMENTING TESTS OF GENERAL OR INFORMATION TECHNOLOGY CONTROLS

The assessment of IT controls is documented on the Information Technology Control Assessment and Record of Tests (IT CART) form. The IT CART has seven sections: program maintenance controls, computer operations controls, program security controls, data file security controls, system software controls, implementation controls, and file conversion controls.

Like the Application CART, the IT CART is supported by guidance

FIG. 20-3

Specimen payroll system

XYZ Company is a large manufacturing company in which payroll expense represents a very high proportion of the operating expenses. XYZ Company allows hourly employees to complete their own timecards by filling in a box on a card daily. The cards are collected by the foremen of the various departments and checked for completeness and accuracy. Once approved and initialed, the cards are read by a scanner device that reads the employee number, department, and hours worked. This information is written onto a magnetic tape that is processed weekly by the company's mainframe computer.

The following control procedures have been identified as a result of interviews conducted and documentation examined:

1. Employees use mark sensitive time cards to record time daily. Foremen review the cards and initial them as being correct. Time cards are read by a mark sensitive reader and written onto magnetic tape each day.
2. Magnetic tape is processed weekly by the company's mainframe computer. The following fields are edited and an error list is created for items not meeting the edit requirements:
   - *Man number* — matched to employee master file.
   - *Department number* — matched to internal table of valid numbers.
   - *Hours worked* — number cannot be greater than 75.

   The error report is reviewed by the payroll clerk and errors are investigated, corrected, and resubmitted. The payroll clerk initials each error corrected. The payroll supervisor reviews the error reports monthly and notes the initials next to each corrected item. The supervisor also initials the reports.
3. Each week, the payroll system calculates gross and net pay; prints checks, a payroll register, and a check register; and updates the payroll master file. Totals are provided for normal, overtime, sick, vacation, and other hours worked.
4. Control totals for both gross dollars and net dollars are produced by the payroll update process and are reconciled to manual totals maintained by the payroll clerk. The reconciliation consists of adding current dollars per the payroll register to ending dollars from the previous update and comparing the totals with the ending balance on the report. Periodically, the supervisor reviews and initials the reconciliation.
5. The checks are signed by a signature plate attached to the forms burster. The signature plate is kept locked in the desk of the payroll supervisor, who observes the bursting process. The blank check forms are kept in a locked cabinet in the computer room. The lead operator keeps the key to this cabinet.
6. A starting check number is supplied by the payroll clerk from a manual log and is printed on the check and the check register by the computer. This number must match the preprinted number already on the check form. The payroll clerk verifies that the numbers match.
7. Each month, the accumulated payroll expense is extracted from the payroll system and used to update the general ledger. There is no manual verification of this process.
8. Payroll master file changes are initiated by the personnel department after receiving proper authorization. They can make changes to:
   - Department
   - Pay rate

(*continued*)

FIG. 20-3 (*continued*)

- Marital status
- Withholding exemptions

A report of master file changes is produced by the computer and checked one-for-one against the authorized notification by the personnel supervisor, who initials and files the report.

The following general EDP controls have been documented within the data processing department:

1. The procedures for making changes to production programs appear to be adequate. They include written requests, appropriate approvals, proper testing procedures, and security over the program libraries.
2. The controls over computer operations appear to be adequate. They include approved schedules, reviews of results, reviews of problems, and security over data files.

material that describes common IT control procedures and illustrative audit test and review techniques.

Figure 20-6 shows the typical linkage between audit objectives and the IT CART sections, and is useful in determining which CART sections should be completed. The linkage on a particular engagement may vary depending on the facts and circumstances.

IT CART Cover Sheet

Enter the name of the location in the space provided on the CART cover sheet. (See Figure 20-7.) The decision by management regarding audit objectives to be addressed by the extended assessment of control risk—completeness, accuracy, existence—is indicated on the cover sheet of the Application CART. Indicate the decision as to which general objectives should be completed by placing a tick in the appropriate boxes on the IT CART cover sheet.

Program Maintenance Controls

Program maintenance controls are exercised over the maintenance of present systems. They ensure that appropriate programmed procedures are maintained adequately. The auditor tests these controls for changes to ongoing systems. The tests of program maintenance controls may include:

FIG. 20-4

Specimen payroll system program and record of tests

DETAILS OF TEST OR REASON FOR OMITTING TEST	REASON FOR TEST	CONTROL BEING TESTED
PRT 1		
1. EXAMINE DAILY TIME CARDS FOR FOREMEN'S INITIALS.	BY EXAMINING THE SUPERVISORY CONTROL OVER THE BASIC CONTROL, THE AUDITOR CAN ENSURE THE CONTINUED OPERATION OF THE BASIC CONTROL AND THEREBY REDUCE THE TESTING OF THE BASIC CONTROL.	AUTHORIZATION OF INPUT.
2. SELECT A SAMPLE OF TIME CARDS AND ENSURE THAT THEY ARE COMPLETELY FILLED OUT.	THE AUDITOR MUST DO SOME TESTING OF THE BASIC PROCEDURE. IF THE TEST OVER THE DISCIPLINE IS NOT CONCLUSIVE THE LEVEL OF THIS TEST MAY HAVE TO BE INCREASED.	COMPLETENESS AND ACCURACY OF INPUT.
3. USING AUDIT SOFTWARE, VERIFY THAT ALL MARK SENSITIVE CARDS ARE PROCESSED COMPLETELY AND ACCURATELY BY THE MARK SENSITIVE READER. (SEE AUDIT SOFTWARE PROJECT 1)	AUDIT SOFTWARE MAY ALLOW THE AUDITOR TO TEST MANY MORE CARDS OR EVEN THE ENTIRE PAYROLL. BOTH EFFICIENCY AND EFFECTIVENESS COULD BE ENHANCED.	COMPLETENESS AND ACCURACY OF INPUT.
PRT 2		
1. EXAMINE THE PAYROLL ERROR REPORT FOR EVIDENCE OF SUPERVISOR'S REVIEW.	BY EXAMINING THE SUPERVISORY CONTROL OVER THE BASIC CONTROL, THE AUDITOR CAN ENSURE THE CONTINUED OPERATION OF THE BASIC CONTROL AND THEREBY REDUCE THE TESTING OF THE BASIC CONTROL.	SUPERVISORY CONTROL OVER ACCURACY OF INPUT.
2. REVIEW WEEKLY ERROR REPORTS TO ENSURE THAT ALL ERRORS HAVE BEEN NOTED, CORRECTED, AND RESUBMITTED.	THE AUDITOR MUST DO SOME TESTING OF THE BASIC PROCEDURE. IF THE TEST OVER THE DISCIPLINE IS NOT CONCLUSIVE THE LEVEL OF THIS TEST MAY HAVE TO BE INCREASED.	ACCURACY OF INPUT.
3. USING AUDIT SOFTWARE, PROCESS WEEKLY TAPES AND PERFORM THE FOLLOWING INDEPENDENT EDITS: • MATCH MAN NUMBERS TO EMPLOYEE MASTER FILE. • VERIFY CORRECT DEPARTMENT NUMBER. • VERIFY THAT THE HOURS WORKED WERE WITHIN AN ACCEPTABLE RANGE. PRINT OUT ALL ERRORS WHICH WILL BE COMPARED WITH THE COMPANY'S ERROR REPORT FOR ANY DIFFERENCES. (SEE AUDIT SOFTWARE PROJECT 2)	THE COMPANY'S ERROR REPORTS PRINT OUT ERRORS ONLY. THEREFORE, THE AUDITOR NEEDS TO VERIFY THAT ALL ERRORS ARE PRINTED. THIS COULD POSSIBLY BE DONE MANUALLY, BUT THE TIME TO DO IT COULD BE PROHIBITIVE.	ACCURACY OF INPUT.

(continued)

FIG. 20-4 (*continued*)

DETAILS OF TEST OR REASON FOR OMITTING TEST	REASON FOR TEST	CONTROL BEING TESTED
PRT 3		
1. SELECT A SAMPLE OF EMPLOYEES AND MANUALLY REPERFORM THE GROSS PAY CALCULATION.	THIS IS A BASIC ACCOUNTING PROCEDURE THAT IS PERFORMED BY A COMPUTER PROGRAM, AND SOME COMFORT MUST BE GAINED AS TO ITS ACCURACY. SINCE THE INFORMATION IS AVAILABLE ON TWO REGISTERS, IT CAN BE DONE MANUALLY. AUDIT SOFTWARE COULD ALSO BE USED FOR THIS PURPOSE. FROM A FINANCIAL POINT OF VIEW, THE NET PAY CALCULATION IS NOT SIGNIFICANT; HOWEVER, FROM AN OPERATIONAL VIEW IT MAY BE.	PROGRAMMED ACCOUNTING PROCEDURE.
2. SELECT A SAMPLE OF PROGRAM CHANGE REQUESTS IN THE DATA PROCESSING DEPARTMENT AND VERIFY THAT THE PROPER APPROVAL AND TESTING WERE DONE. 3. TEST THE SECURITY OVER THE PAYROLL PROGRAMS AND OVER THE PAYROLL DATA FILES.	BY TESTING SOME OF THE GENERAL EDP CONTROLS, THE AUDITOR CAN GAIN ADDITIONAL ASSURANCE THAT THE PROGRAMMED PROCEDURE WAS PROPERLY DESIGNED AND IMPLEMENTED, AND THAT NO UNAUTHORIZED CHANGES HAVE BEEN MADE TO EITHER THE PROGRAMS OR THE DATA.	IMPLEMENTATION CONTROLS. PROGRAM SECURITY CONTROLS. DATA FILE SECURITY CONTROLS.
PRT 4		
1. EXAMINE THE RECONCILIATION REPORTS FOR THE INITIALS OF THE PAYROLL SUPERVISOR.	BY EXAMINING THE SUPERVISORY CONTROL OVER THE BASIC CONTROL, THE AUDITOR CAN ENSURE THE CONTINUED OPERATION OF THE BASIC CONTROL AND THEREBY REDUCE THE TESTING OF THE BASIC CONTROL.	SUPERVISORY CONTROL OVER COMPLETENESS AND ACCURACY OF UPDATE.
2. SELECT PAYROLL REPORTS AND RECONCILE THEM TO THE MANUAL TOTALS MAINTAINED BY THE PAYROLL CLERK.	THE AUDITOR MUST DO SOME TESTING OF THE BASIC PROCEDURE. IF THE TEST OVER THE DISCIPLINE IS NOT CONCLUSIVE THE LEVEL OF THIS TEST MAY HAVE TO BE INCREASED.	COMPLETENESS AND ACCURACY OF UPDATE.
3. USING AUDIT SOFTWARE, FOOT THE GROSS AND NET DOLLARS FOR SEVERAL PAY PERIODS. (SEE AUDIT SOFTWARE PROJECT 3)	EVEN THOUGH THE COMPUTER-PRODUCED TOTALS ARE COMPARED WITH MANUAL TOTALS, IT IS IMPORTANT TO RECOGNIZE THAT THE COMPUTER PRODUCES THE ENDING TOTALS THAT ARE USED AS BEGINNING TOTALS FOR THE NEXT PROCESSING CYCLE. AUDIT SOFTWARE PROJECT 3 DESCRIBES SOME ADDITIONAL BENEFITS THAT CAN BE DERIVED FROM USING THIS SOFTWARE.	PROGRAMMED ACCOUNTING PROCEDURE.

DETAILS OF TEST OR REASON FOR OMITTING TEST	REASON FOR TEST	CONTROL BEING TESTED
PRT 5		
1. OBSERVE THE BURSTING AND CHECK SIGNING PROCESS ON SEVERAL OCCASIONS AND ENSURE THAT PROPER SECURITY PROCEDURES ARE FOLLOWED WITH RESPECT TO THE SIGNING AND HANDLING OF THE CHECKS AND THE HANDLING OF BLANK FORMS.	SINCE SIGNED CHECK FORMS ARE NEGOTIABLE, THE AUDITOR MUST GAIN ASSURANCE THAT PROPER CUSTODIAL AND SECURITY CONTROLS ARE BEING EXERCISED.	PHYSICAL SECURITY AND CUSTODIAL CONTROLS.
2. OBSERVE THAT THE CHECK SIGNATURE PLATE IS KEPT SECURE DURING PERIODS WHEN IT IS NOT IN USE.	SECURITY IS JUST AS IMPORTANT DURING OFF-HOURS AS DURING NORMAL WORKING HOURS.	SECURITY AND CUSTODIAL CONTROLS.
3. OBSERVE THE SECURITY OVER THE CHECK FORM CABINET DURING ALL SHIFTS AND ON WEEKENDS. INQUIRE INTO PROCEDURES FOR ACCESS IF THE LEAD OPERATOR IS NOT AVAILABLE.	SECURITY IS JUST AS IMPORTANT DURING OFF-HOURS AS DURING NORMAL WORKING HOURS.	SECURITY AND CUSTODIAL CONTROLS.
PRT 6		
1. VERIFY THAT THE NEXT CHECK NUMBER IN THE CHECK FORM CABINET MATCHES THE CHECK NUMBER IN THE LOG KEPT BY THE PAYROLL CLERK.	IF THIS CONTROL IS EFFECTIVE, THE AUDITOR CAN REDUCE THE TESTING OF SECURITY OVER THE CHECK FORMS, SINCE THE CLERK WOULD KNOW IF BLANK CHECKS WERE MISSING.	SECURITY AND CUSTODIAL CONTROLS.
2. INQUIRE INTO THE PROCEDURE FOR HANDLING BROKEN NUMERICAL SEQUENCES IN THE CHECK FORMS AND THE PROCEDURE FOR ACCOUNTING FOR CHECKS USED FOR ALIGNMENT OF THE PRINTER.	SEQUENTIALLY NUMBERED FORMS DO NOT ALWAYS COME WITHOUT BREAKS IN THE SEQUENCE. THERE MUST BE A PROCEDURE FOR HANDLING MISSING NUMBERS AND ALSO FOR VOIDING THE CHECKS USED IN LINING UP THE PRINTER.	CUSTODIAL CONTROL.
PRT 7		
1. MANUALLY VERIFY THAT THE PAYROLL EXPENSE TOTAL FROM THE PAYROLL REGISTERS FOR A MONTH EQUALS THE PAYROLL EXPENSE AMOUNT POSTED TO THE GENERAL LEDGER.	THE AUDITOR MUST OBTAIN ASSURANCE THAT THE EXPENSES ARE ACCUMULATED AND PASSED ON ACCURATELY TO THE GENERAL LEDGER. SINCE NO ONE PERFORMS THIS VERIFICATION, THE AUDITOR IS NOT TESTING A CONTROL, BUT IS ACTING AS THE BASIC CONTROL. THE AUDITOR COULD ALSO USE AUDIT SOFTWARE TO TEST THIS PROGRAMMED PROCEDURE OR COULD PERFORM A PROGRAM ANALYSIS ON THE COMPANY'S COMPUTER PROGRAM TO ENSURE THAT IT IS WORKING ACCURATELY. THE TESTS OF THE GENERAL EDP CONTROLS OVER SECURITY AND PROGRAM CHANGE PROCEDURES PROVIDE COMFORT THAT THE PROCEDURE WILL CONTINUE TO OPERATE CORRECTLY. THE AUDITOR MIGHT WANT TO SUGGEST TO MANAGEMENT THAT SOMEONE IN THE ACCOUNTING DEPARTMENT MAKE THE RECONCILIATION MONTHLY.	COMPLETENESS AND ACCURACY OF UPDATE.

(continued)

FIG. 20-4 (*continued*)

DETAILS OF TEST OR REASON FOR OMITTING TEST	REASON FOR TEST	CONTROL BEING TESTED
PRT 8		
1. EXAMINE PAYROLL MASTER FILE CHANGE REQUESTS FOR PROPER AUTHORIZATION.	PERSONNEL SHOULD NOT MAKE CHANGES WITHOUT PROPER AUTHORIZATION.	AUTHORIZATION OF INPUT.
2. EXAMINE THE PAYROLL MASTER FILE CHANGE REPORT FOR EVIDENCE OF REVIEW BY THE SUPERVISOR.	BY EXAMINING THE SUPERVISORY CONTROL OVER THE BASIC CONTROL, THE AUDITOR CAN ENSURE THE CONTINUED OPERATION OF THE BASIC CONTROL AND THEREBY REDUCE THE TESTING OF THE BASIC CONTROL.	SUPERVISORY CONTROL OVER COMPLETENESS, ACCURACY, AND AUTHORIZATION OF INPUT.
3. AGREE THE DETAILS ON THE MASTER FILE CHANGE REPORTS TO THE AUTHORIZED DOCUMENTATION AND ENSURE THAT ALL DATA SUBMITTED WAS PROCESSED AND THAT ALL ERRORS WERE INVESTIGATED AND RESUBMITTED.	THE AUDITOR MUST DO SOME TESTING OF THE BASIC PROCEDURE. IF THE TEST OVER THE DISCIPLINE IS NOT CONCLUSIVE THE LEVEL OF THIS TEST MAY HAVE TO BE INCREASED.	COMPLETENESS AND ACCURACY OF INPUT.
4. USING AUDIT SOFTWARE, MATCH THE BEGINNING-OF-THE-YEAR PAYROLL MASTER FILE TO THE END-OF-THE-YEAR FILE AND PRINT OUT A SAMPLE OF MASTER FILE DATA CHANGES IN PAY RATE. TRACE THESE CHANGES TO AUTHORIZATION FORMS. (SEE AUDIT SOFTWARE PROJECT 4)	THE AUDITOR HAS ALREADY TRACED CHANGES FROM THE FORMS TO THE MASTER FILE. THIS TEST WILL ALLOW THE AUDITOR TO TRACE THE OTHER WAY—FROM THE MASTER FILE TO THE AUTHORIZATION FORMS. BOTH ARE NECESSARY FOR AN EFFECTIVE TEST. FROM A FINANCIAL POINT OF VIEW, THE OTHER MASTER FILE DATA FIELDS MENTIONED ARE NOT SIGNIFICANT. HOWEVER, FROM AN OPERATIONAL VIEWPOINT, THEY MAY BE VERY IMPORTANT AND COULD EASILY BE INCLUDED IN THIS SOFTWARE TEST.	AUTHORIZATION OF INPUT AND UPDATE. COMPLETENESS OF INPUT AND UPDATE. ACCURACY OF INPUT AND UPDATE.

FIG. 20-5

Use of audit software in the payroll test example

Audit Software Project 1

- **Purpose —** To verify independently that the magnetic tape containing the data from the mark sensitive time cards is processed completely and accurately by the mainframe computer.
- **Input —** One or more weeks of daily tapes created as a result of the daily processing of the mark sensitive time cards.
- **Output —** A report containing weekly totals of normal, overtime, vacation, sick, and other hours by employee.
- **Reconciliation —** Total hours for each day in the week should be manually calculated from the authorized time cards and should be reconciled to the totals on the output report above and to the totals produced as a result of the weekly processing on the company's mainframe computer. Any discrepancies should be investigated and traced to individual employees.

Audit Software Project 2

- **Purpose —** To verify independently that the edit and error logic in the company's program is reading and editing all available data and that the edits are functioning as designed.
- **Input —** One or more weeks of accumulated daily payroll input tapes.
- **Output —** A report containing:
  - — Employees unmatched to the payroll master file;
  - — Employees having an invalid department;
  - — Employees working more than X or less than Y hours; and
  - — Employees submitting duplicate time cards for the same day.
- **Reconciliation —** Errors should be matched one-for-one to the company's reports for the same week. Any errors on one report but not on the other should be investigated.

Audit Software Project 3

- **Purpose —** To foot the gross and net dollars on the payroll master file independently.
- **Input —** Payroll master file.
- **Output —** A report containing total gross pay and total net pay.
- **Reconciliation —** Totals should be compared with totals printed on the company's report for the same period. Any differences should be investigated.
- **Other Possible Benefits —** Many additional tasks could be accomplished in this software project. Most of them address operational concerns, and all of them could generate important information pertinent for reporting to management. Examples are:
  - — Whether anyone in the company received a raise greater than a predetermined amount.
  - — Whether anyone accumulated more overtime or vacation pay than seemed reasonable.
  - — Whether there was more than one employee with the same street address, which could indicate a duplicate employee.

(*continued*)

FIG. 20-5 (*continued*)

Audit Software Project 4

- **Purpose** — To select a sample of master file data changes that occurred during the year for verification of authorization.
- **Input** — Payroll master files from the beginning of the year and the end of the year.
- **Output** — A report containing a sample of employees that had a change in pay rate. The report should show the beginning pay rate and the ending pay rate.
- **Other Possible Benefits** — This project can provide additional benefits to the auditor. Some of these are:
  - — Identify employees hired during the year for verification with the personnel department.
  - — Identify employees removed from the file during the year for further investigation.

FIG. 20-6

Audit objectives and IT CART sections

SELECTION GUIDANCE

Information Technology CART Sections	AUDIT OBJECTIVES		
	Completeness	Accuracy	Existence
Maintenance	X	X	X
Computer Operations	X		X
Data File Security			X
Program Security			X
System Software			X
Implementation	X	X	X
File Conversion	X	X	X

FIG. 20-7
IT CART cover sheet

Client ______________________________

Location ______________________________

Control objectives	To be completed	Year ended ______ 19____ Signature	Date	Year ended ______ 19____ Signature	Date	Year ended ______ 19____ Signature	Date
Maintenance							
Computer operations							
Data file security							
Program security							
System software							
Implementation							
File conversion							

	Signature	Date	Signature	Date	Signature	Date
Reviewed by IT audit manager						
Reviewed by engagement manager						

- Examination of evidence to determine that programs are maintained, reviewed, and approved adequately.
- Examination of evidence and reperformance of system and program testing to establish that testing procedures are adequate to ensure the appropriateness of the programmed procedures.
- Examination of evidence to verify that tested programs are brought into use without subsequent alteration.
- Determination that users are involved sufficiently in program changes.

Maintenance. In testing controls related to the maintenance of computer programs, test the procedures for designing appropriate program modifications. After conducting a complete inquiry of relevant personnel, examine the log of program changes and, for several changes, examine program design specification, narratives, flowcharts, and logic diagrams, and related evidence of user and data processing supervisory personnel involvement and approval.

Other tests of maintenance controls include tests of the procedures for testing program changes. After conducting a complete inquiry of relevant personnel, use the log of program changes to select a number of programs changed during the period. Examine documentation evidencing the testing plans, use of relevant test data, execution of the tests, management's review of output reports, and acceptance by the test group and user departments. Because of the high level of significance of these controls (they can affect programmed procedures in any program modified), documentation for 10 program changes might be examined.

If program maintenance controls vary from system to system because different development groups are involved, the auditor should test each different type of control.

Computer Operations Controls

Controls over the consistency of computer operations ensure that jobs are set up properly and run in accordance with authorized instructions and procedures. The tests of control over the consistency of operations may include:

- Determination that adequate separation of duties exists (e.g., that computer operations personnel do not have programming responsibilities).
- Examination of processing schedules, operating instructions, and job control language (JCL) to determine if jobs were properly scheduled and set up in accordance with written instructions.
- Examination of job processing sheets, console log reports, problem log reports, and the like, reperforming the control procedures to verify that jobs were properly run in accordance with established procedures, and that any problems that arose did not affect the results adversely.
- Observation of controls over the restriction of access and exercise of supervision.

Computer Operations. In testing controls related to computer operations, activity logs maintained by operations management and the investigation of unusual situations may be tested. Conduct a complete inquiry of relevant personnel, including the manager of computer operations, and examine a recent activity log, noting evidence of the review. In addition, examine notations or correspondence, or obtain explanation for several items on the log. One other log might be examined, noting whether appropriate evidence of review by the manager of computer operations is present. Considering the soundness of the inquiries and the satisfactory results of the evidence examined, it may be decided that the extent of testing of that particular control procedure is sufficient.

Program Security and Data File Security Controls

Program security and data file security controls are designed to prevent unauthorized changes to programmed procedures and data files. Separate tests should be carried out for each of the following:

- Off-line programs protected by physical custody controls (such as supervised storage areas).
- On-line program libraries protected by software controls (such as passwords).
- Off-line data files protected by physical custody controls.
- On-line data files and other files protected by software controls.

The tests of program security controls may include:

- Examination of evidence to determine that production program libraries are maintained separately from test libraries.
- Examination of execution JCL listings, librarian listings of source program modifications, and standards manuals to determine that adequate procedures exist to ensure that the correct version of the program is transferred to the production program library.
- Examination of evidence to determine whether adequate procedures are in place to monitor consistency between source and object programs.
- Examination of evidence to determine that production program libraries are password-protected and that access violations are investigated.
- Examination of computer-generated output resulting from the production program library updating process for evidence of authorization and supervisory review.
- Observation of off-site backup storage area and examination of

operations schedule listing backup jobs run to ensure adequacy of program file recovery procedures.

The tests of file security may include:

- Examination and reperformance of the log of physical movements to determine whether they are recorded and whether files are returned promptly to the library.
- Observation to see whether overdue files remain in the computer room (they should not) and, further, that access to data files is restricted.
- Examination of the console log, or other report, of password protection messages to find evidence of the company's investigation of unauthorized attempts to access password-protected files.
- Determination by observation and examination of evidence that adequate backup files and recovery procedures exist.
- Examination of evidence of password changes to verify that they take place regularly and that the passwords of separated employees are removed promptly.
- Examination of evidence of supervisory review of output from tape and disk library management systems.

System Software Controls

System software assists in the control of both the programs that process data and the data files themselves. Therefore, although controls over system software do not affect the programs and data directly, they affect the other general controls. The auditor tests the controls over the implementation and security of the system software. The tests performed are discussed in the later section entitled "Implementation Controls" and in the earlier section "Program Security and Data File Security Controls." Security considerations are discussed in Chapter 30, "Security Reviews."

Implementation Controls

Implementation controls are designed to ensure that for new systems or major enhancements, programmed procedures are designed appropriately and implemented effectively. They apply to both internally developed and vendor-supplied packaged software, although control generally is achieved more easily where software is purchased from vendors. In the latter case, the principal concerns are the original selection of the package, any modifications required to the package, and the testing and implementation of the package in the organization's environment. Tests of implementation controls may include:

- Examination of evidence to determine that systems are designed, reviewed, and approved adequately.
- Examination of evidence and reperformance of system and program testing to establish that testing procedures are adequate to ensure the appropriateness of the programmed procedures.
- Examination of evidence to verify that tested programs or changes to programs are brought into use without subsequent alteration.
- Determination that users are involved sufficiently in system development, tests, and final approvals.

File Conversion Controls

When a significant new computerized system is introduced during the year, there is concern that data transferred from the old system and additional data used in the new system are set up on the new system properly. File conversion controls are designed to ensure that the conversion is performed properly. Tests of file conversion controls may include:

- Examination of evidence and reperformance of program testing to establish that testing procedures are adequate to ensure the appropriateness of the programmed procedures that provide control totals.
- Examination of evidence to determine that the use of control total techniques are adequate to control the completeness and accuracy of the data file conversion.
- Examination of evidence to verify that the detailed comparison of data on the new file with that on the previous file is adequate.
- Determination that users are involved sufficiently in file conversion procedures.

Extent of Testing

The extent of testing of particular controls is a cumulative process that results in forming a conclusion on a control objective. If test results disclose, for example, less than satisfactory user involvement in approval of program change design, additional attention is likely to be directed to user involvement in program design and implementation in connection with the procedures described previously for testing program changes. In those circumstances, focusing particular attention on the extent of user involvement in that testing process, deciding to use sampling techniques, and taking a judgmentally selected sample of program changes are likely.

SPECIMEN TESTS OF USER CONTROLS

1. **Review of computer-produced exception or rejection reports for completeness and accuracy of input and updating continuity (maintenance) of data and (Specimen Test):**

   ☐ When a computer sequence check or computer comparison of batch totals is relied on for the completeness and accuracy of input, test the initial recording on the input form as follows:

   - When the information is transcribed from another source document, one of the tests suitable for manual systems may be applicable.
   - When the first record of the transaction is the input form, or the transaction is first entered through a terminal, visit the appropriate departments and observe that there are adequate procedures to ensure that transactions are completely and accurately recorded.

   ☐ Review computer reports for evidence that items or batches reported (such as outstanding, mismatched, or missing) are checked and investigated regularly by people with no conflicting duties.

   ☐ When appropriate, determine that the results of the procedures in the immediately preceding step have been reviewed and approved by a responsible official.

   ☐ If necessary, reperform the control by selecting a sample of reported items or batches and seeing that they have been properly cleared.

2. **Manual agreement of predetermined batch totals for completeness and accuracy of input and updating (Specimen Test):**

   ☐ Test the initial recording of transactions on the input form as follows:

   - When the information is transcribed from another source document, one of the tests suitable for manual systems may be applicable.

- When the first record of the transaction is the input form, or the transaction is first entered through a terminal, visit the appropriate departments and observe that there are adequate procedures to ensure that transactions are completely and accurately recorded.

☐ Review computer reports, control registers, or other documentation for evidence that the predetermined batch totals have been regularly agreed with the totals printed on the computer report by people with no conflicting duties.

☐ Determine that differences have been investigated by people with no incompatible duties.

☐ When appropriate, determine that the results of the procedures in the two immediately preceding steps have been reviewed and approved by a responsible official.

☐ If necessary, reperform the control by selecting batches of source documents and

- Test the additions of the predetermined batch totals.
- Test the agreement of the predetermined batch totals with the computer report.
- Inspect the control register to ensure that all batches have been processed.
- Obtain satisfactory explanation for any discrepancies.

☐ When appropriate, determine that there are controls that ensure that rejections are properly corrected and then completely and accurately resubmitted. Reperform the control if necessary. The exact nature of the test will depend on the user department procedures and should be specified on the CART.

☐ When appropriate (such as in the case of batches of payments and credit memoranda), see that the input documents and supporting documentation have been effectively cancelled to prevent subsequent reuse.

3. Manual agreement of computer-established totals (run-to-run control) for completeness and accuracy of updating (Specimen Test):

☐ Review computer reports, control registers, or other documentation for evidence that the computer-produced totals have been regularly agreed with the totals printed out on the update report by people with no incompatible duties. (*Note:* Take into account any summarization of totals or any changes in the totals used.)

SPECIMEN TESTS OF GENERAL CONTROLS: IMPLEMENTATION AND MAINTENANCE OF APPLICATIONS

1. System and Program Documentation (Specimen Test):

☐ Examine system development and maintenance records for evidence that up-to-date system and programming documentation has been prepared for all programs and systems.

☐ Reperform control by reviewing system and programming documentation and source listings to confirm that:

- The applications conform to generally accepted accounting principles and to the company's own requirements.
- The documentation appears to be up-to-date.
- The documentation contains sufficient detail to form a suitable basis for making subsequent program modifications.
- The documentation agrees with source listing. (*Note:* The use of a flowcharting package, to help document and understand the source listing, may assist in carrying out this step.)
- The programs have been coded in accordance with generally accepted MIS standards

☐ When modifications have been made to programs that were not developed or maintained in accordance with generally accepted MIS standards, examine evidence that the documentation has been brought up to date as part of the process of making the modification.

2. Access to System and Program Documentation (Specimen Test):

☐ Observe that source statement listings, flowcharts, file layouts, and other system documentation of application programs are held securely and are restricted from access by computer operators, job controllers, and system programmers.

☐ Observe the access-granting procedures for the above documentation when it is given to applications programmers and programmer analysts in the course of their jobs.

☐ By observation and inquiry, ensure that operators, job controllers, and system programmers do not borrow application program documentation or write application programs.

☐ Observe that manually maintained records of the means of access to programs and data files (such as password listings) are held securely and restricted from access by unauthorized people.

3. Approval of System Specifications (Specimen Test):

- ☐ Examine system development records or other documentation for evidence that system specifications have been prepared for all new applications that have been implemented and for any new applications still under development.

- ☐ Examine system specifications for evidence that:
  - They have been reviewed and approved by a responsible official in the user department(s).
  - They have been reviewed and approved by responsible officials in the data processing function (such as the operations manager, applications programming manager, system programming manager, quality assurance manager).
  - Subsequent changes to the approved system specifications are properly approved.

4. Testing New Applications (Specimen Test):

- ☐ Examine the documentation and results of testing of new applications implemented to confirm that:
  - A test plan was prepared and executed for program and system testing.
  - The methods used in testing were appropriate to test the proper functioning of both the individual programs and complete systems.
  - The volume and variety of transactions used to test the program were adequate to ensure the proper operation of programmed procedures for all transaction types, both individually and in combination.
  - System software that is incorporated into the application programs has been adequately tested.
  - The programmers who wrote the program being tested either were not involved in the testing or were involved but their work was subject to review.

- ☐ Reperform control, as appropriate for the control techniques used, by:
  - Tracing dummy transactions through the source statement listing.
  - Checking test data results with predicted results.
  - Selecting a period from the parallel running and testing the results with the output from the previous system.
  - Selecting a part of the pilot run and checking the results.

5. Approval of Modifications to Production Programs (Specimen Test):

☐ Examine program change records for evidence that they have been approved by responsible officials in:

- The user department(s).
- The system maintenance function.
- The computer operations function (if appropriate).
- The quality assurance function.

☐ Reperform control by checking program change records against the program change requests.

6. Control of Approved Program Modifications (Specimen Test):

☐ Examine the register of program changes for:

- Evidence that entries therein appear to be up-to-date.
- Evidence that outstanding program changes are being reviewed regularly and investigated when appropriate.

☐ Reperform control by testing entries in the register with program change records to establish that the change has either been implemented or is a valid outstanding item.

7. Testing Program Modifications (Specimen Test):

☐ Examine the documentation and results of testing program modifications to confirm that:

- A test plan was prepared and executed for programs and system testing.
- The methods used in testing were appropriate to test the proper functioning of:
  - — The program modification.
  - — Other, unchanged, parts of the changed programs.
  - — Other related programs in the system.
- The volume and variety of transactions used to test the modification were adequate to test the proper operation of programmed procedures for all affected transaction types, both individually and in combination.
- System software that is incorporated into the application program has been adequately tested.
- The programmers who made the modifications being tested either were not involved in testing or were involved but their work was subject to review.

☐ Reperform control, as appropriate for the control techniques used, by:

- Tracing dummy transactions through the source statement listings.
- Checking test data results with predicted results.

8. Urgent Modifications (Specimen Test):

☐ Examine the records of urgent program modifications that bypass the normal control procedures for evidence that:

- The modifications made were documented and tested properly.
- The action taken was reviewed and approved by a responsible official in the data processing function. (*Note:* When the controls over the documentation and testing of urgent modifications consist of the retroactive application of the standard procedures for the documentation and testing of non-urgent modifications, in most cases further tests are not necessary.)

☐ When the controls over the documentation and testing of urgent modifications do not consist of the retroactive application of standard procedures, reperform the controls designed to ensure that:

- The modification made is logically valid.
- The system and program documentation is brought up-to-date.
- The modification is properly tested.

9. Acceptance by Users of New Applications and Program Modifications (Specimen Test):

☐ Examine evidence of user approval of new applications and modifications for production use.

☐ Reperform control by confirming that the documentation supporting the approval has been prepared, including:

- Results of testing.
- Computer department approvals.
- User instruction.

☐ Examine documentary evidence of the notification from the computer department to the user department of the effective date that the new system or modification is to become operational.

10. Final Approval of New Applications and Program Modifications by the Data Processing Function (Specimen Test):

☐ Examine evidence of computer department approvals of new systems and modifications for production use.

☐ Reperform control by confirming that the documentation supporting the approval has been prepared, including:
- System documentation.
- Program documentation.
- Operating instructions.
- Results of testing.

11. Cataloging of Approved New Applications and Program Modifications (Specimen Test):

☐ Examine evidence that the cataloged changes to the production libraries are being checked to ensure that:
- All authorized programs are being cataloged.
- The correct versions of the authorized programs are being cataloged.
- Suitable action is being taken when the cataloging process fails.

☐ Select a number of new or modified programs, and reperform the controls over cataloging.

CHAPTER 21

Substantive Procedures

INTRODUCTION

When controls are weak, or are assessed as not having an acceptably low risk of failure, substantive procedures are normally used to test computer systems. The main objective of substantive procedures is to determine whether errors exist in account balances. Using these procedures, the auditor can determine whether the computerized and manual accounting treatment of the related transactions (application controls) was appropriate. When this is so, the processing and account balances produced should not contain errors or irregularities. For example, substantive procedures (and related controls) check that:

- Assets and liabilities exist at a given date and recorded transactions have occurred during a specified period (existence/ occurrence).
- Transactions are recorded in the proper accounts at the correct amounts (accuracy).
- Transactions are properly authorized in accordance with management intentions (authorization and validity).
- All transactions and accounts that should be presented in the financial statements or management reports are included once, and only once (completeness).
- Assets and liabilities that appear on the balance sheet represent rights and obligations of the organization (rights and obligations).
- Components of financial statements or management reports are properly classified, described, and disclosed (presentation and disclosure).

Substantive procedures also include identifying and evaluating the accounting principles used and evaluating judgments used by management that affect valuation estimates. In addition, these procedures complement tests of controls or tests of transactions, since they provide further evidence as to whether the controls have continued to operate.

When Substantive Procedures Are Performed by an Internal Auditor

The internal auditor may find it necessary to perform substantive procedures under the following circumstances:

- When there are no relevant controls.
- When the internal auditor may be required to assist the external auditor in a cooperative effort during the annual examination of the financial statements.
- When required for regulatory agencies.

This section addresses the nature, extent, and timing of substantive procedures and how they constitute an integral part of a systems audit approach.

Substantive Procedures and a Systems Audit Approach by an External Auditor

An audit approach to systems can be flexible; it allows the external auditor to assess controls and possibly limit substantive testing when there is a low risk of control failure. It also permits the auditor to rely principally on substantive techniques for all or part of an audit when assessing controls appears impractical or less efficient.

There is a direct correlation between the level of internal controls and the amount of substantive testing required. If the results of testing controls reveal the presence of adequate internal controls, the auditor is justified in minimizing the substantive procedures. Conversely, if the testing of controls reveals weaknesses in control that may raise doubts about the completeness, accuracy, or validity of the accounts, substantive testing can alleviate those doubts.

In any decision on the extent of substantive procedures required by computer-based accounting systems, the following two general factors might justify a reduction in the levels that would be applied in noncomputer systems:

1. The increased satisfaction that usually can be obtained from the other auditing procedures, based on improved account analyses produced by computer.
2. The potential in computer systems for testing improved internal controls over the updating and maintenance of details of account balances and master file data held on computer files.

In computer systems where the auditor cannot, or prefers not to, assess or test the internal controls, it is necessary to perform extended substantive procedures. These extended substantive procedures include additional work on data, or tests to confirm that programmed procedures are operating properly. The additional work on data may include the following:

- Additional use of procedures already planned, such as verifying a greater proportion of the items that make up an account balance.
- Greater depth in the procedures already planned, such as seeking more complete documentary evidence in support of payments made.
- Using procedures not previously considered, such as confirming accounts payable with suppliers where this has not already been done.

The auditor is free to choose a methodology that provides the most effective and efficient approach. However, relying principally on substantive procedure techniques does not supply assurances that internal controls are adequate, although it may result in the identification of some control weaknesses.

Generally, the results of the various substantive tests can provide some insight into the system of internal controls. For example, if the system is operating properly:

- Subsidiary records should agree with, or be easy to reconcile with, control accounts.
- Confirmation exceptions should be few.
- Cutoff tests should indicate that transactions are recorded in the proper period.
- Book-to-physical inventory variances should be relatively small.
- Depreciation expense per the analysis of fixed assets should agree with the related expense accounts.

Audit Software Advantages

To perform substantive tests in a computerized environment, the use of audit software offers advantages. This is because computer files usually hold large volumes of accounting data. Each record may contain a great deal of information, such as the history of debtors' payments or the details of stock issues. In addition, detailed records of transactions processed during the year are often held on transaction files. This concentration of data allows the auditor to use audit software to carry out extensive substantive tests on the records with relative speed and ease.

The principal advantages of the use of computer audit software programs are:

- Test results are more conclusive when all data on a file is examined consistently and accurately, rather than only a sample. Reperformance can be much more extensive when computer programs are used, since it is relatively simple and less time-consuming to have the software subject all items in an account balance to the calculation and accumulation procedures.
- The ability to quantify precisely data that meets a particular condition is improved. For example, the software can quickly and accurately produce a total of all customer balances larger than twice their credit limits.
- The performance of sampling procedures, whether statistical or nonstatistical, is more cost-effective when software is employed, providing a time-saving alternative to work that would otherwise have to be done manually.
- It is only necessary for the program to print the results of tests on items that are selected for investigation. Clerical audit work can then be devoted to examining items defined by the auditor as

significant. Again, this is less time-consuming than the equivalent manual procedures.

- Because the programs can examine large volumes of data, in some cases it may be more efficient to carry out extended substantive tests rather than to evaluate and test the system of internal control.

Although the purpose of the substantive tests remains unchanged when an audit software program is used, the facilities the program provides make it possible to approach the work in a different way. In conventional audit work, conclusions are drawn from a thorough examination of a limited number of transactions. When an audit software program is used, every transaction can be examined thoroughly with a specific purpose in mind, and the results can be quantified. An example is producing analyzed totals of obsolete inventory.

Samples of the kinds of tasks performed by audit software programs are outlined in the following sections dealing with specific applications.

NATURE OF SUBSTANTIVE PROCEDURES

Substantive procedures can be divided into two categories: substantive tests that are direct tests of the account balances and their components, and other auditing procedures, such as analytical reviews.

The nature of the substantive procedures varies depending on the account balance being examined. Examples of these procedures include:

- Confirmation
- Inspection
- Reperformance
- Cutoff testing
- Vouching
- Analysis of fluctuations
- Analysis of financial trends and ratios
- Reconciliation
- Account analysis
- Observation

Such procedures can be performed manually or with the assistance of computer programs (audit software). Many are described in greater detail in the following pages. Analytical procedures are described in the next section.

Confirmation

Confirmation consists of obtaining verification of a fact or condition, such as account balances, through correspondence with a third party. This independent verification strongly supports the existence of the account balance. Confirmation often serves as the principal substantive test for accounts receivable and cash account balances. Audit software may be used to assist in the selection of items for confirmation; it also may be used to print confirmation letters and to identify missing returns, where a second request may be needed.

Inspection

Inspection involves physically counting and/or examining the items represented by the dollar balance in an account. Management normally has the count performed by staff people, while the auditor observes and tests the procedures used. At times, the auditor may actually perform the physical count. This substantive procedure is typically applied to inventory; less often, it is applied to fixed asset account balances. EDP audit assistance may be used for the following:

- Selecting the items for physical inspection.
- Providing lists of duplicate or missing tags.
- Performing book-to-physical comparisons.
- Isolating differences.

Typically, all of these tasks are time-consuming when performed manually.

Reperformance

In many instances, an account balance may represent the result of a computation or an accumulation of computations. Examples of this are the allowance for depreciation and the provision for doubtful accounts. Reperformance of the computation is the principal substantive procedure applied to those account balances. When judgment is the basis of a computation, reperformance of the computation should also include an evaluation of the reasoning behind the judgment.

Cutoff Testing

Cutoff testing consists of examining documentation to determine that transactions were recorded in the proper period. It is usually easier to carry out effective cutoff tests in computer systems, particularly in batch systems. The discussion that follows is limited to cutoff tests of sales and purchases. Cutoff tests should also be applied to cash receipts and disbursements to determine that those transactions have also been recorded in the proper period.

The principal requirements are to identify the last processing run for sales, purchases, and inventory movements in the period being audited. Then, by reference to batches of input around that time, the auditor needs to confirm that data was entered in the correct period and that rejections were dealt with properly. Note that the nominal date of the last processing run may differ from the actual date on which that run occurs, since the files may be held open after the end of the accounting period in order to process outstanding transactions.

Cutoff tests are made even easier when sales or purchases processing is integrated with the related inventory processing. In this case, no cutoff difference between sales and inventory or purchases and inventory is likely to arise, since the updating of accounts receivable or accounts payable and inventories becomes concurrent. In all cases, it remains necessary to test that the sales and purchases documentation reflects actual shipments and receipts on the dates recorded.

Vouching

Vouching is the examination of evidence supporting a transaction or item in order to determine its validity. Vouching includes:

- A review of company procedures for supporting documentation.
- The examination of supporting documentation.
- A review for unusual items.

Vouching is typically used to validate the accounts payable balance and additions to or retirements from the fixed-asset accounts. Computer programs can be used to assist in the selection of items to be vouched. In many cases, the isolation of unusual items for review consists of sifting through extensive selection criteria; the use of audit software can ease this process greatly.

Reconciliation

Reconciliation consists of identifying and accounting for any difference between two amounts that should agree (one of the amounts is usually an account balance). For example, the auditor compares the general ledger balance for accounts receivable with the total of the detailed accounts receivable records by customer, or the book balance for a bank account with the balance shown by the related bank statement. When differences are found, the auditor then performs substantive tests to determine whether adjustments are required to the account balance.

Reconciliations usually are carried out more frequently in computer systems. The individual balances on computer files (e.g., accounts receivable files) are usually reconciled either to an independent control account or to a control record on the file every time the file is updated or reorganized. As a result of these regular reconciliations, the auditor can carry out compliance tests of these reconciliation procedures more easily than in a noncomputerized system. This should reduce the audit effort required for reconciliations during the substantive procedures.

ANALYTICAL PROCEDURES

Analytical procedures are tests of financial information, entailing the study and comparison of relationships among data. They are used:

- To assist the auditor in planning the nature, timing, and extent of other auditing procedures.
- As a substantive test to obtain evidential matter about particular assertions related to account balances or classes of transactions.
- As an overall review of the financial information in the final review stage of the audit.

Statement on Auditing Standards (SAS) No. 56, *Analytical Procedures*, requires the use of analytical procedures in the planning and overall review stages of all audits.

Auditors can use analytical techniques to address audit risk efficiently and to justify reductions in the level of detailed substantive tests. Chapter 2, "The Auditing Profession," discusses audit risk and the risk model as defined by SAS No. 47, *Audit Risk and Materiality in Conducting an Audit*. In terms of that model, the auditor relies on substantive tests—both tests of details and analytical procedures—to reduce overall audit risk to a low level. To meet this low-risk objective, auditors need to select cost-effective procedures that direct attention to the high-risk areas of an audit. Analytical procedures meet this criterion and fall into two categories:

- Inherent risk analytics
- Detection risk analytics

Inherent risk analytics are used early in the audit. They direct the auditor's attention to matters that should be considered to plan the examination. As a planning tool, these analytics identify situations requiring an audit reaction and areas of significant audit risk that may not be detected through conventional techniques such as inquiry and observation. Analytics performed at this stage also direct the auditor's attention to specific accounts that require greater attention than others during the audit. Inherent risk analytics include:

- Analyses of trends, such as fluctuation reviews and time series analyses, which are observations of information made at different times.
- Analyses of ratios, such as gross profit percentage, days' sales outstanding, and days' inventory on hand.
- Analyses of common-size financial statements, which are financial statement accounts expressed as a percentage of some other amount, such as the ratio of certain balance sheet accounts to total assets. These vertical relationships can highlight a change in a particular account that is disproportionate to other related accounts.
- Reasonableness tests, such as extending the number of items sold by average prices to test the reasonableness of sales.

Inherent risk analytics are typically applied to interim financial information. Although this data is unaudited, the results of the analyses are useful for audit planning purposes. (Note that although this discussion relates to external auditors, internal auditors can similarly benefit from use of analytical procedures.)

Detection risk analytics include the techniques previously mentioned and are performed at three stages of an audit:

1. Prior to detailed testing, to highlight areas of audit concern not identified during the planning stage.
2. As a part of substantive testing.
3. At the end of the audit, as an overall review of the reasonableness of the financial statements and to corroborate the results of other procedures performed.

Detection risk analytics are a form of substantive test; as such, their primary purpose is to detect large errors and misstatements in financial statements.

Detection risk analytics encompass identifying, investigating, and corroborating the following:

- Unexpected changes, or expected changes that do not occur, in period-to-period balances; performance indicators (such as key ratios); and trends.
- Differences between actual and planned or budgeted results.
- Unexpected discrepancies in trends or relationships, compared with industry statistics.

In most instances, detection risk analytics performed during the substantive testing stage of the audit provide assurance about specific accounts for specific audit objectives. Sometimes, they provide assurance for audit objectives in a number of areas. For example, a review of common-size financial statements may provide some assurance about the completeness, existence, and accuracy objectives related to many account balances.

To determine the program of substantive tests for an account, the auditor tries to select the most efficient combination of tests that will provide the necessary assurance in meeting the audit objectives for that account. To do this, the auditor first determines the level of assurance required from substantive tests in regard to a particular audit objective, and second, assesses the level of assurance that can be expected from analytical procedures. The auditor then considers which strategy—detailed substantive tests alone, analytics alone, or a combination of the two—is most efficient. In effect, the auditor "trades off" detailed tests and analytics to achieve the most cost-effective way to satisfy the audit objectives.

In many circumstances, a combination of analytics and detailed substantive tests may be most efficient. When the auditor uses this combination to meet a particular audit objective, the level of assurance sought from detailed tests is generally lower than when detailed tests alone are performed. For example, if analytical procedures relating to the cutoff objective for sales and accounts receivable are performed (e.g., a gross profit analysis by product line and detailed sales analyses near year-end), it is usually possible to reduce the extent of detailed testing procedures (e.g., examining shipping documents near year-end) without increasing the risk of not detecting a significant cutoff error.

To illustrate the types of substantive tests—both detailed and analytical—that might be considered and "traded off" for a specific audit objective and account, consider the following example. The audit risk involved is the possibility that slow-moving, potentially obsolete inventory is recorded at values in excess of net realizable values. The audit objective is valuation. Some of the possible substantive tests are listed in the following table.

Analytical Tests	*Detailed Tests*
• Compare inventory quantities with open sales orders, back orders, sales forecasts, or other measures of future requirements. • Compare inventory quantities (e.g., by product group or for individual products) with units shipped or other measure of sales activity during the year. • Develop a three-way analysis of inventory, sales, and purchase activity, and review the relationships and trends for inconsistent or illogical conditions (e.g., increasing sales, increasing inventory, and decreasing purchases). Note: This type of analysis may be useful during the period from an early substantive test date to year-end.	• Investigate the organization's methods of identifying surplus, slow-moving, obsolete, scrapped, or damaged inventory. Evaluate the methods based on observations during the physical count and: —Review, and discuss with management, reports used to identify surplus, slow-moving, scrapped, or damaged inventory. —Discuss with management items in the ending inventory in light of current production requirements, sales orders received, future marketing forecasts, sales records and analyses, production records, and the previous year's inventory lists. Examine and test the accuracy of documentation (including, where appropriate, aged lists of inventory balances, records of movements such as bin cards, etc.) to substantiate the information obtained from management. —Discuss with management all inventory amounts that may not be realizable because of disputes, defective work, or marketing difficulties.

Analytical procedures may be more effective and efficient than detailed substantive tests in achieving certain audit objectives. In some circumstances, they may be the only way to achieve a specific audit objective. For example, analytical procedures are more powerful than tests of details for making valuation judgments, required when financial statement amounts are based on estimates. Common examples of such estimation procedures are the adequacy of bad debt allowances or of warranty reserves.

Analytical procedures may be used, either in combination with detailed substantive tests or alone, as a primary audit procedure for a specific account balance or class of transactions. The auditor may be able to obtain the desired level of assurance about the reasonableness of recorded amounts more efficiently using this strategy than by performing extensive detailed tests. Generally, the auditor performs extensive analytical procedures only when the risk of error in an account is initially assessed as low.

Analytical procedures can be particularly effective in detecting fraud, including collusive fraud. Based on information available from several well-publicized Securities and Exchange Commission (SEC) cases, it has been hypothesized that the application of analytical techniques would have been more likely to detect the material collusive fraud than would the application of standard tests of details. This is because in collusive fraud the underlying documentation often supports the reported numbers. For example, one company official colluded with a supplier to erroneously bill certain period product costs as capital expenditures. This increased current income by deferring a portion of current-period costs to future periods. The cost records supported the erroneous cost-of-sales and inventory pricing figures, but an analysis of the gross profit, or a simple comparison of the year-to-year product costs, would probably have led to further investigation or corroboration of the reported costs.

For analytics to be effective, relevant and reliable information for the specific audit area must be available. For example, the auditor may need to perform some tests to obtain assurance about the reliability of data used in a review, especially when the review provides a major source of audit assurance for a particular account balance or class of transactions. Such tests can include consideration of past audit resullts (tests of controls and substantive tests) and the current control environment testing the controls over the system generating this data, testing specific controls over some of the data, or testing the data directly. In many situations, some or all of this testing may have already been planned in connection with other audit objectives. However, if the auditor determines that the underlying data is unreliable, it is unlikely that analytics will be useful.

The level of assurance that the auditor can derive from analytical review procedures performed as substantive tests is a function of several factors. These factors include:

- The amount of information, both internal and external, that was considered to develop expectations.
- The extent to which the analytical procedures are designed to be performed and evaluated at the individual, detailed segment or account level, rather than on an overall basis.

- The extent of the auditor's follow-up of significant unexpected results (i.e., the consideration of other information and corroboration of explanations).

Comparing the results of analytical tests with expectations—the auditor's bench marks or gauges—is the key to evaluating these results. Without sound expectations, the auditor may be unable to interpret the significance of certain fluctuations or the absence of expected fluctuations properly, or may rely unduly on management's explanations when following up on unexpected results. Expectations should be based on the informed judgment of an auditor who is knowledgeable about the organization's operations and relevant economic conditions, competitors, and industry activity. The auditor should also understand the expected relationships in the organization's data that provide meaningful evidence, and the degree to which current relationships are expected to be consistent with historical relationships.

To develop expectations, the auditor should consider:

- Audit evidence from the current examination, such as results of tests of related accounts, operating statistics, discussions with management, and quarterly review analysis (if applicable).
- External factors (e.g., trends in the economy as a whole and in the industry).
- Changes in accounting methods or classifications.
- Changes in operations (e.g., products, product mix, pricing policies).
- Unusual events that could influence relationships, such as significant transactions and events, related party transactions, and the outcome of contingencies.

The auditor should follow up on all significant unexpected results. Analytical techniques are effective to detect errors or irregularities only if the auditor demonstrates a healthy skepticism while evaluating management's explanations of unexpected results. The auditor should also seek relevant and reliable evidence to support the explanations. All explanations of fluctuations identified through analytical techniques should be tested, corroborated, and subjected to critical analysis. Improper evaluation and failure to corroborate management's explanations have been cited as a cause of several alleged audit failures.

To use analytical techniques properly, the auditor should relate findings to results of other procedures, such as substantive tests of details, evaluations of controls, and inherent risk factors. For example, if an analytical review detects a significant increase in the gross margin of products sold in the current period, and management's explanation is that new equipment and labor efficiencies are responsible, the auditor should determine whether this new equipment is included in schedules of fixed asset additions and should perhaps plan to observe the equipment. The auditor should also ensure that depreciation charges are consistent with company policies and generally accepted accounting principles (GAAP). A review of payroll procedures may provide further evidence—through the existence of fewer or more productive employees—that these gains are real. Inventory pricing tests also may confirm or contradict management's explanations. Direct management intervention in the standard costing system may indicate to the auditor that additional audit procedures are needed.

The level of assurance that the auditor can derive from detection risk analytics performed as substantive tests is a function of the following factors:

- Nature of the analytic procedure performed.
- Number of independent analytics applied and the contribution of each technique toward a specific audit objective.
- Corroboration of analytical results (quantitative and qualitative) with past experience and current-year audit evidence.
- Reliability of underlying data.
- Relevance, consistency, and timeliness of base data used for comparisons.
- Precision of the relationship.
- Level of information analyzed.
- Frequency of measurement.

All evidence-gathering and evaluation processes must be viewed as interactive and dynamic, not as separate, unrelated procedures or conclusions. Even when analytical procedures are performed without the intention of substantially reducing detailed testing, they can still enhance audit effectiveness by directing the auditor's attention to the high-risk areas and corroborating the results of other audit procedures.

A major problem auditors face today is an overload of all kinds of data, including comparative analytical data, such as industry statistics and five-year summaries. Microcomputers are making it easier to organize and systematize data and to analyze different data relationships. Microcomputers can perform complex computations, allowing more complex comparisons of data than were practical or even possible manually; readily locate and print specific data; accumulate, retain, and store large volumes of information;

and provide access to public data bases containing up-to-the-minute industry and organizational information for comparison and analysis purposes.

Auditors are using those abilities of the microcomputer to perform analytical procedures and to report transactions and patterns that deviate from expectations. For example, in a bank, an imbedded audit routine examined the pattern of all deposits and withdrawals in accounts for which plastic cards were used to identify authorized system users. The computer identified and reported a particular unusual pattern of transactions, alerting the internal auditors to a fraud later found to involve bank employees. Auditors are also using computers to obtain specified information needed for testing purposes, to keep track of the results of various audit tests and relate them to each other, and to "keep score" of the amount of assurance drawn from the analyses performed.

EXTENT OF SUBSTANTIVE PROCEDURES

Many substantive tests of details of transactions and account balances involve sampling. If they do, the guidance for determining the level of testing that is presented in Chapter 20, "Reviews and Tests of Controls," is applicable.

In considering sampling risk, tolerable error, and expected error in a sampling application, the auditor should be aware of the following factors:

- The materiality or significance of the items, and their relative risk.
- The nature, number, and size of the items that comprise the particular account balance, or population.
- The extent to which an account balance can be correlated with other accounts and with other information obtained in the course of the audit.
- The extent to which exceptions have previously been identified in the course of applying substantive procedures.
- The degree of reliance that can be placed on the organization's system of internal control based on the results of tests of controls.
- The possibility that someone has taken advantage of control deficiencies (fraud) or that errors have arisen, and their extent.
- The effect of factors and conditions on sample size in performing substantive tests of details, as described in SAS No. 39, *Audit Sampling*, and shown in the following table taken from AU Section 350.47.

Factor	Conditions Leading to Smaller Sample Size	Conditions Leading to Larger Sample Size	Related Factor for Substantive Sample Planning
a. Reliance on internal accounting controls	Greater reliance on internal accounting controls	Lesser reliance on internal accounting controls	Allowable risk of incorrect acceptance
b. Reliance on other substantive tests related to same account balance or class of transactions (including analytical review procedures and other relevant substantive tests)	Substantial reliance to be placed on other relevant substantive tests	Little or no reliance to be placed on other relevant substantive tests	Allowable risk of incorrect acceptance
c. Measure of tolerable error for a specific account	Larger measure of tolerable error	Smaller measure of tolerable error	Tolerable error
d. Expected size and frequency of errors	Smaller errors or lower frequency	Larger errors or higher frequency	Assessment of population characteristics
e. Number of items in population	Virtually no effect on sample size unless population is very small		—

Materiality of Account Balances and Relative Risk

The essence of the materiality concept is that insignificant differences do not matter. In relation to substantive testing, it is a well-accepted practice that items that are not material in the aggregate are generally ignored in the audit process. Thus, the audit effort is related to the significance of the subject matter.

A critical element that must be considered is relative risk. The allocation of audit efforts is also affected by the relative risk of error or misstatement in a particular environment. For example, inventory is likely to present more of a problem than fixed assets in terms of control, valuation, and application of accounting principles, although both accounts may be material. Thus, inventory has a greater relative risk than fixed assets, from an audit standpoint.

The greater the risk and relative materiality of the account balance, the greater the need for extensive substantive procedures.

Account Balance Composition

The extent of substantive procedures performed is also affected by the composition of the account balances, in terms of quantity and value of items and the amount of human judgment required to arrive at the balance. The auditor normally should examine a greater proportion of items in an account balance where judgment is an important consideration, such as inventory valuation of slow-moving items. The use of audit software or computer programs that make the examination of all items possible, and then provide useful account analyses, can be of benefit in these areas.

In a manual environment, there is a tendency to rely on the results of testing of controls and limited substantive testing when an account balance consists of a large number of items with relatively low individual balances. The use of audit software provides the alternative of performing extensive, even 100 percent, substantive testing in preference to testing of controls. When an account balance consists of a small number of items with relatively high individual values, the auditor is likely to subject all (or a substantial portion) of the individual items in the account to direct substantive tests. The use of computer programs in this situation is less advantageous unless the high-value items themselves represent the accumulation of a large number of relatively small individual entries (e.g., in the charges to long-term construction contracts over a period of months or years).

Correlation With Other Accounts and Information

Information obtained from tests that were performed on related accounts (e.g., correlating the interest charge with the related debt after allowing for any variations in the amount outstanding during the period) may reduce the need for extensive substantive procedures. However, other information obtained during the course of the audit may indicate the need for expanded levels of substantive tests. For example, a review of performance indicators may reveal unexplained changes in the ratio of cost of raw materials used to total cost of production. This may indicate an error in cutoff procedures. At this point, the auditor may wish to expand cutoff tests to see if this is the case.

As a result of analytical review procedures, such as comparison of current financial information with information from comparable prior periods, anticipated results, or similar industry averages, the auditor may decide to limit or expand substantive testing. These considerations are made according to the auditor's related experience and professional knowledge.

The auditor should be aware that information relevant to the audit may be available in the form of existing reports generated by the system. In addition, information can be extracted from the system through the use of audit software. Before it is possible to rely on information produced by audit software, an auditor must establish that the data on the file being examined is complete and accurate. It should be remembered that computer programs can examine only the data actually on the file. If that data is inaccurate or incomplete, the results will be also.

Exceptions

When exceptions, such as errors and deviations from established procedures, are found as a result of substantive procedures, the auditor should determine the reason for each type of exception. It is also important to determine the effect of exceptions on the system. This should be done in terms of their implications both for the functioning of the internal control system and for the account balance under examination. The effect on related account balances should also be investigated.

Bear in mind that even a single, seemingly isolated exception can be an indication of a serious weakness in a control procedure. This is particularly true if the breakdown is in a programmed procedure, or if there is a possibly significant misstatement of an account balance, or both. On the other hand, care should be taken to avoid extending substantive procedures because of an exception before its potential significance is ascertained.

All significant exceptions should be investigated, and the auditor should inform management immediately of any significant exceptions noted during substantive testing.

The auditor may need to rely on certain programmed procedures that either form part of the system of internal control or produce additional information at the test date, such as account analyses or exception reports. The auditor must be satisfied that these programmed procedures are functioning properly and that the information produced is complete and accurate. This can be done by testing the programmed procedures as part of the substantive work. Another method is testing the operation of the disciplines for the period until year-end.

The auditor may not wish to do tests of control over the information technology (IT) environment either because they are weak or because it is more efficient to perform extended substantive tests on the programmed procedures. Testing programmed procedures usually involves reperformance of the programmed procedure through the use of audit software or the use of test data. It might also involve examination of the program instructions to confirm that the program functions properly. If this technique is used, it is also necessary for the auditor to follow certain procedures when running the program to ensure that the correct version of the program is used and is run against the correct data file without any unauthorized intervention. The tests should be spread over the period under review, to obtain assurance that the programmed procedures operated properly throughout the period. Tests of programmed procedures often are not straightforward. There is often a lack of visible evidence to indicate exactly how the program has performed its work. Sometimes this visible evidence can be created, so that simple manual tests can be carried out. In other cases, specialized testing techniques are required. A range of testing techniques is available for programmed procedures. (See Chapter 20, "Reviews and Tests of Controls," Appendix A, "*Internal Control Reference Manual—Information Technology Controls*," and Appendix B, "*Internal Control Reference Manual—Application Controls*.")

COMMON TASKS FOR COMPUTER AUDIT SOFTWARE PROGRAMS

There are a growing number of audit software packages available that are capable of performing the kinds of tasks described in the following checklist under each type of application.

1. Accounts Payable:

- ☐ Matching subsequent period payments against earlier period items and balances, and identifying unmatched payments.
- ☐ Identifying old invoices or goods received documentation unmatched on the file.
- ☐ Identifying unusual transactions; for example, large nonstock purchases for particular account codes.
- ☐ Identifying unusual master file data; for example, accounts for inactive suppliers.
- ☐ Identifying accounts not reconciled to suppliers' statements for a significant period of time.

2. Accounts Receivable:

- ☐ Stratifying the balances or transactions into age categories. Often a more detailed analysis than the one prepared by the company is required; analyzing by transaction type may produce useful information regarding payments on account and unmatched adjustments.

- ☐ Identifying balances in excess of credit limits, segregating them into strata by reference to the amount by which the credit limit is exceeded, and computing the amount of excess over credit limits.
- ☐ Identifying accounts with unusual credit limits or no credit limits.
- ☐ Identifying unusual transactions, for example, large sales near year-end or transfers between accounts.
- ☐ Identifying unmatched transactions; for example, payments on account.
- ☐ Identifying unusual master file data; for example, high discount rates.
- ☐ Selecting items for confirmation and printing appropriate confirmation requests. These items can be written to a file and replies can be matched.

3. Work-in-Process:

- ☐ Analyzing the balances into age categories.
- ☐ Identifying items where the full value of work done may not be recoverable. This can be achieved by:
  - Identifying items whose actual costs exceeded authorized or budgeted costs.
  - Identifying items whose costs to date exceed fixed selling prices.
  - Identifying items whose costs are not rechargeable to customers (such as warranty work).
  - Selecting items for comparison of realizable value with total expected cost to complete.
- ☐ Identifying balances that include unusual items; for example, adjustments.
- ☐ Identifying closed work-in-process items not invoiced within a reasonable period of time.
- ☐ Identifying items that have been open for an unreasonable period of time.

4. Fixed Assets:

- ☐ Calculating depreciation and checking the company's figure.
- ☐ Identifying fully depreciated assets and calculating depreciation on them.
- ☐ Identifying unusual depreciation rates.

- ☐ Classifying items according to age categories since last physically inspected.

5. General Ledger:

- ☐ Identifying items that appear unusual in relation to budgets or past periods.

Specialized Applications

Similar tasks can be carried out with respect to applications in specialized businesses, as in audit software tailored to the portfolios in a financial services organization.

TIMING OF SUBSTANTIVE PROCEDURES

When assisting an external auditor in the annual examination of the financial statements, it may be desirable to perform substantive procedures as of a date prior to year-end. This may be done to increase audit effectiveness, detect problem areas early, and satisfy stringent audit report deadlines. However, early substantive procedures are not appropriate in all cases. SAS No. 45, *Omnibus Statement on Auditing Standards—1983*, provides guidance on performing substantive tests prior to the balance sheet date.

When the auditor decides to carry out his substantive procedures on account balances mainly as of the balance sheet date, it still may be desirable to carry out certain substantive work prior to the year-end. Substantive procedures that involve the examination or review of transactions during the year (e.g., purchases and disposals of fixed assets) can be performed prior to the year-end with respect to transactions for part of the year. Transactions for the remainder of the year would then be examined in the course of the substantive work that is carried out as of the balance sheet date. This is particularly relevant when these examinations and reviews are performed by computer programs, since it is usually relatively easy to run the program regularly throughout the period being audited.

SPECIMEN TESTING PROCEDURES

Various kinds of substantive procedures are applied to typical testing situations. The following procedures suggest possible substantive audit procedures for certain applications, particularly when the audit strategy is not to rely on controls. The procedures are designed to assist in:

- Developing substantive audit procedures for when the audit strategy is not to rely on controls.
- Reviewing existing substantive audit programs.

Figures 21-1 and 21-2 present specimen substantive audit procedures. These figures are not intended to be a maximum, minimum, or all-inclusive list of substantive audit procedures. They are provided here as examples of one approach that can be used.

Possible substantive procedures, both manual and computerized, for specified audit situations, including use of audit software, are shown in Figure 21-1 for trade accounts receivable and sales, and in Figure 21-2 for property, plant, and equipment.

If the audit strategy decision is to test and rely on controls, the auditor's objective should be to take this into account in setting the nature and extent of substantive procedures according to management's objectives. The nature of many substantive procedures may not vary greatly whether or not controls are in place, since controls may not address all substantive audit assertions. However, when the controls are relied on:

- The planned extent of the substantive procedures should consider this.
- The timing should be appropriately evaluated giving consideration to early substantiation.

When the auditor does not plan to rely on control tests, procedures such as those described in the figures could be considered. To assist the auditor in locations with significant computer systems, procedures include an indication of where computer audit software can be used efficiently.

Substantive audit procedures should always be tailored to the specific audit objectives. In doing this, the auditor should:

- Select the steps applicable to the audit strategy. Many steps may not be applicable in particular circumstances.
- Modify the steps selected to:
  - —Describe clearly the program steps as tailored for particular circumstances.
  - —Indicate the extent of testing to be performed.
  - —Identify the timing and period to be covered by the tests, including any effects of early validation.
- Add any additional steps necessary to meet the needs of the situation or to achieve the audit strategy or audit objectives.

Whether or not controls are relied on for all, some, or parts of the system processing cycles, the auditor should consider all of the factors in an audit approach when deciding which tests to administer.

FIG. 21-1

Specimen substantive procedures for trade accounts receivable and sales

Substantive Audit Objectives

Obtain audit evidence that

A. Recorded trade accounts receivable exist and represent amounts due to the company at the balance sheet date.

B. Material amounts due to the company at the balance sheet date have been recorded.

C. Trade accounts receivable are carried at net collectible amounts (i.e., the allowances for doubtful accounts, discounts, returns, and similar items are appropriate).

D. Trade accounts receivable pledged as collateral are identified and disclosed.

E. Sales transactions recorded during the period are valid transactions, properly computed and recorded.

Summary of Trade Accounts Receivable

1. Obtain or prepare a comparative summary of year-end trade accounts receivable balances. Verify the mathematical accuracy of the summary and agree totals to the general ledger trial balance and the previous year's working papers. Trace significant reconciling items to supporting documentation.

Analytical Review

Note: Analytical review procedures may be performed during the initial planning stages, during the conduct of the examination, or near the conclusion of the examination, depending on the auditor's objectives. Some of these procedures may be performed in connection with income statement substantive procedures.

2. Review performance indicators relevant to trade accounts receivable and sales; such a review could include some of the following comparisons with budget and/or equivalent ratios or other indicators at periodic accounting dates during the year or at previous year-ends:

- **a.** Average receivables (opening balance plus closing balance divided by 2)
- **b.** Receivables turnover ratio (sales divided by average receivables)
- **c.** Average daily sales (sales divided by 365)
- **d.** Days sales outstanding (average receivables divided by average daily sales)
- **e.** Sales mix (percentage breakdown of sales by product line or other classification)
- **f.** Receivables mix (percentage breakdown of receivables by aging category)
- **g.** Bad-debt ratios (bad-debt allowance dividend by gross receivables; bad-debt expense divided by gross sales)
- **h.** Discount ratios (discounts divided by gross sales)
- **i.** Commission ratios (commmissions divided by gross sales)
- **j.** Interest/finance charge as a percentage of receivables
- **k.** Selling expense as a percentage of sales
- **l.** Advertising as a percentage of sales
- **m.** Account balances for major customers
- **n.** Unmatched cash as a percentage of receivables

Identify and obtain explanations for major fluctuations from expected results and consider their impact on nature, extent, or timing of other audit procedures.

Audit Software: Most of the calculations required above can be economically achieved by manual means, but some of the base figures may not be available in an appropriate format. The sales mix may be obtained through an inventory audit software package, the receivables mix and the unmatched cash by an

(continued)

FIG. 21-1 (*continued*)

accounts receivable audit software package, and account balances for major customers by using generalized audit software, such as AUDITPAK II.

Detailed Trade Accounts Receivable

3. Obtain a detailed list of trade accounts receivable balances aged by customer. Verify the mathematical accuracy and trace totals to the summary obtained in step 1. Determine the propriety of significant reconciling items through inquiry and examination of supporting documentation.
Audit Software: The aging by customer can be reperformed and the mathematical accuracy verified by using an accounts receivable audit software package.

4. For a sample of receivables, trace amounts to subsidiary ledgers (see step 23f for testing of ledgers) or to supporting documentation to determine the reliability of the aging.

Cutoff

Note: In most cases, the cutoff substantive steps for sales can best be carried out in conjunction with the cutoff substantive steps for inventories.

5. Review the cutoff at the time of inventory taking and at year-end (if different):
- **a.** For a sample of sales, determine that the sales invoices are recorded as sales in the proper period by examining the related records of goods shipped and services performed.
- **b.** For a sample of credit (debit) memoranda, determine that the credit (debit) memoranda are recorded in the proper period by examining the related records of returns and claims from customers.
- **c.** Inquire into the processing of returned goods (a large backlog of unprocessed returned goods may be indicative of future credits for which provisions have not been made).
- **d.** Where practicable and where shipping and return documents are prenumbered, account for the numerical sequence of unused shipping and return documents.

Audit Software: An accounts receivable audit software package can be used to determine and report on items incorrectly included in the current period. Additionally, generalized audit software could be used to select items outside the correct period and produce lists of items for confirmation with customers.

6. Where the volume of direct shipments from suppliers to customers is significant, determine that there has been a proper cutoff by confirming shipping information for such sales for a period around year-end directly with the supplier.

7. Investigate significant credit balances to determine cause and consider whether reclassification is necessary.
Audit Software: Either generalized audit software or an accounts receivable audit software package could be used to disclose significant credit balances included in accounts receivable.

8. In conjunction with inventory testing, determine whether sales have been recorded for inventory that is still on the company's premises. Consider any adjustment that may be appropriate.

Direct Confirmation

9. Select customers' accounts for confirmation and the method of confirmation (positive, negative, or a combination). Confirmation requests should be sent under the auditor's control and, where appropriate, itemized statements should be sent to customers to facilitate responses. Second requests should be mailed when responses to positive confirmations have not been received within a reasonable time period.

Audit Software: An accounts receivable audit software package may assist in determining the criteria for selecting accounts for confirmation by using a stratification option to select accounts based on a wide range of criteria, to prepare the confirmation worksheet, and to print the positive and negative confirmation letters.

10. Investigate any discrepancies reported or questions raised by customers and determine whether any adjustments are necessary. Consider whether adjustments required indicate weaknesses in control and whether the scope of the examination should be appropriately revised.

11. For positive confirmations unanswered after second requests or where it is not possible or desirable to confirm a selected account

a. Compare subsequent remittances credited to these accounts with remittance advices or other receipt records to ascertain that payments relate to the account balance (in some cases it may be advisable to examine other related documentation such as sales invoices, etc.).

b. For items not paid since the validation date, examine documentation such as shipping documents, copies of sales invoices, and relevant correspondence supporting the unpaid portion of the account balances.

Audit Software: By using a transaction file subsequent to confirmation date, an accounts receivable audit software package can be used to extract subsequent payments on accounts for which confirmation has been requested.

12. Summarize confirmations and alternative procedure coverage.

Audit Software: An accounts receivable audit software package produces a report and summary of the confirmations.

13. Review the aged trial balance and identify significant old receivables and receivables in dispute based on confirmation replies or other factors and

a. Review subsequent cash collections, examine related remittance advices or other supporting documentation to ascertain that payments relate to the account balance (in some cases it may be advisable to examine other related documentation such as sales invoices, etc.);

b. Determine the adequacy of collateral, if any;

c. Discuss all significant potentially doubtful accounts with management;

d. Review relevant credit file information, such as customer financial data and correspondence.

Audit Software: An accounts receivable audit software package could be used to prepare an aged trial balance of the accounts receivable. Subsequent cash collections for old outstanding balances could be extracted by using generalized audit software.

14. Obtain a summary of the activity in the allowance account during the year and examine authorizations and other documentation supporting significant write-offs. Agree opening balance to prior year's working papers, current year's provision to the income statement, write-offs to the receivables records, and the closing balance to the general ledger trial balance.

15. Determine whether any formulas used are

a. Consistent with past years;

b. Appropriate to the circumstances of the business;

(continued)

FIG. 21-1 (*continued*)

  - **c.** Indicative of actual bad-debt experience or estimated bad-debt experience if the company has not been in business long enough for actual experience to be meaningful.

16. Based on procedures described in steps 13–15, determine whether the allowance for doubtful accounts is adequate.

Other Allowances

17. Consider whether other allowances are required relating to Accounts Receivable or Sales (e.g., trade allowances, rebates, claims, and warranties).

Interest and Service Charges

18. Test to see if interest or service charges on accounts receivable have been properly computed and recorded. (Software is sometimes used.)

Commissions

19. Test the reasonableness of sales commissions (software is sometimes used):
  - **a.** Determine the methods (e.g., percent of sales) and bases (e.g., net sales, net collections) of computing commissions by inquiry, reviews of policy, and/or examination of agreements with salespeople.
  - **b.** Where practicable, perform an analysis of the reasonableness of total commissions as a percent of sales.
  - **c.** Test the propriety of the computation of sales commissions and summarization in the general ledger.

Sale of Consigned Items

20. Where client is consignor, examine the consignment agreement and test the recording of sales and related commissions of consigned items to reports of sales from consignee. In conjunction with the work being performed on the inventory balances, either obtain confirmation directly from the consignee or observe physical count of inventory.

21. Where the company is consignee, examine the consignment agreement, compare consignment reports sent to consignor with accounting records, and test computation of consignee's commission. Obtain direct confirmation from consignor of
  - **a.** Merchandise for which the consignee is responsible as at the balance sheet date, if appropriate;
  - **b.** Amounts owed to consignors for consignment sales; and
  - **c.** Any commissions or compensation due from consignor.

Where significant amounts of consigned inventory are held, observe the physical count of inventory, ascertain that such inventory is not included in the financial statements, and ascertain that the appropriate liability is provided for amounts due consignor.

Sales Commitments

22. Where material losses could arise from unfulfilled sales commitments, assess whether a provision should be made for such potential losses by
  - **a.** Examining open sales commitments (such records, if maintained, are generally presumed not to be under accounting control);
  - **b.** Inquiring of employees who make sales commitments as to any significant unfulfilled commitments at year-end;
  - **c.** Reviewing shipping records and related sales invoices for a period after the balance sheet date for evidence of sales commitments outstanding at the balance sheet date;

   d. Requesting selected major customers to advise of details of any sales commitments outstanding at the balance sheet date when it is considered necessary in the company's circumstances.

   Audit Software: By accessing the open order file, generalized audit software could be used to analyze open commitments and, depending on the company's system, disclose possible potential losses.

Annual Sales, Related Discounts, Returns and Allowances, and Credit Memoranda

23. For a sample of sales (and related discounts, returns and allowances, and credit memoranda) recorded during the period (the sample should include both sales reflected in receivables and collected sales)

   a. Trace to supporting documentation (e.g., sales orders, shipping documents, sales receipts, invoices).

   Audit Software: Can be used to extract a sample of items for comparison with supporting documentation. It could also be used to compare the records in independent transaction files, such as comparison of sales with invoices.

   b. Verify the mathematical accuracy (software can be used).

   c. Determine that sales have been properly authorized or are in compliance with policy.

   d. Compare the prices to authorized catalogs, other official company sources, or approval by an authorized official (software can be used).

   e. Determine that discounts and allowances are in compliance with company policy and/or approved by an authorized official; where authorization is not required or there is no formal policy, ascertain that discounts and allowances are reasonable and/or in line with industry practices, etc.

   f. Trace posting to the accounts receivable subsidiary ledger.

   g. Trace to receipt of cash, if appropriate, by examining the cash receipts book entry, posting to the accounts receivable ledger, the deposit ticket, and entry on the bank statement.

24. For a sample of months during the year, verify the mathematical accuracy of the sales journal and trace the proper posting to the general ledger. (Summarization and posting of the cash receipts book should be performed in connection with the cash accounts.) (Software can be used.)

25. Determine that all sales for a selected period(s) have been posted to the sales journal by accounting for the numerical sequence of invoices and shipping documents. Trace all appropriate information on the shipping documents to the sales invoice and investigate differences. (Software can be used.)

26. Review postings to the general ledger to determine that all material types of transactions have been covered by audit testing. Devise and perform additional procedures, as necessary, to test the completeness, propriety, and validity of transaction types not previously tested, such as:

   a. Sales previously recorded as deferred revenue

   b. Amounts recorded as advances on sales

   c. Sales of scrap

   d. Sales of byproducts

   e. Cash sales

Accounts Receivable Pledge as Collateral

27. Identify assets pledged as collateral for company indebtedness by reviewing debt and lease agreements, confirmation replies, and minutes of directors' meetings; inspecting public records; and inquiring of management.

(continued)

FIG. 21-1 (*continued*)

Early Substantiation

28. If early substantiation of Trade Accounts Receivable is contemplated, additional audit work will be required.

Other Matters

29. If, based on knowledge of the company's business and industry and the results of audit tests, there is a possibility of notes being received in settlement of trade accounts receivable, inquire as to whether such notes have been separately disclosed. Consider whether reclassification is appropriate.

Note: If the existence of such notes is discovered from other audit tests (e.g., confirmation, tests of subsequent cash receipts), decide if the scope of tests should be expanded.

30. Determine if there were any transactions during the year or balances at year-end denominated in foreign currency and whether they have been translated at appropriate rates.

31. Determine that all appropriate matters to be included in the management letter have been noted.

32. Devise and perform any additional steps deemed necessary for this particular client.

Note: At this point, the auditor should consider whether the results of the audit steps performed satisfy the substantive audit objectives for Trade Accounts Receivable and Sales and whether all appropriate comments have been prepared.

FIG. 21-2

Specimen substantive procedures for property, plant, and equipment

Substantive Audit Objectives

A. The cost or other basis of property, plant, and equipment is appropriate and has been consistently applied.

B. Additions to property, plant, and equipment accounts are appropriate.

C. There are no material items charged to expense that should have been capitalized.

D. All retirements of property, plant, and equipment have been appropriately recorded.

E. Property, plant, and equipment recorded in the financial statements exist and are owned or leased under capital leases.

F. Appropriate methods of depreciation have been properly applied to property, plant, and equipment and are consistent with the previous year.

G. Property, plant, and equipment pledged as collateral is identified and disclosed.

Summary of Property, Plant, and Equipment

1. Obtain or prepare a comparative summary of year-end property, plant, and equipment balances. Verify the mathematical accuracy of the summary and agree the totals to the general ledger trial balance and the previous year's working papers. Trace significant reconciling items to supporting documentation. (Software is sometimes used.)

Individual Balances

2. Obtain or prepare a detailed analysis of property, plant, and equipment cost and accumulated depreciation (software is sometimes used) including details of

- **a.** Total amounts, by classification, at the beginning of the year;
- **b.** Purchases, including a description of the assets acquired, and investment tax credit;
- **c.** Assets sold, abandoned, or written off, including a description of the assets, gain or loss on sale, cost, accumulated depreciation, and investment tax credit recapture;
- **d.** Depreciation charges by classification, including the range of useful lives;
- **e.** Other adjustments during the period (e.g., abandonments, fully depreciated assets retired);
- **f.** Total amounts, by classification, at the balance sheet date.

Note: Amounts of minor significance may be grouped.

3. Verify the mathematical accuracy of the analysis, tracing beginning balances and ending balances to the summary obtained in step 1. Trace significant reconciling items to supporting documentation.

Audit Software: Could be used to verify the mathematical accuracy of the detailed property, plant, and equipment records (including selection and recalculation of details of additions, disposals, and depreciation) and compare opening balances to prior period closing balances.

4. Review the analysis for reasonableness, consistency of amounts between years, and any obvious omissions.

Additions

5. Examine suppliers' invoices, title deeds, capital lease agreements, purchase agreements, construction contracts, progress billings, work orders, and other data supporting major additions. (Software can be used.)

(continued)

FIG. 21-2 (*continued*)

6. Obtain or prepare an analysis of repair and maintenance accounts. Examine supporting documentation (e.g., suppliers' invoices) for significant charges to determine whether they should be capitalized. (Software is sometimes used.)
7. Review the minutes of meetings of the board of directors or other authorizing committees for appropriate authorizations for major additions, sales, abandonments, etc.
8. Examine supporting documentation (e.g., bills of sale) for significant sales and trade-ins, and test the computations of accumulated depreciation and the calculation of gain or loss recorded on the sales.
9. Consider the following, which indicate unrecorded retirements or questionable carrying values:
   - **a.** Additions that replace existing property
   - **b.** Major changes to plant layout or product design
   - **c.** Changes in insurance coverage
   - **d.** Idle property, plant, or equipment
   - **e.** Property held for sale
10. Trace significant adjustments made to property, plant, and equipment accounts during the period to supporting documentation.

Existence

11. Review the company's procedures for verifying the existence and ownership of recorded assets and consider the necessity of independently verifying the physical existence of and, if appropriate, the title to property, plant, and equipment, including construction in process. Consider performing physical inspection of major additions during the period under review. (Software is sometimes used.)

Depreciation

12. Determine whether the depreciation practices followed by the company are reasonable in the company's circumstances and consistent with the prior year. These practices may include estimates of useful lives and salvage values, procedures for the depreciation of additions and retirements, and accounting for fully depreciated assets. (Software can be used.)
13. Compare for reasonableness, current and prior year depreciation amounts for each significant category of property, plant, and equipment, obtaining explanations and supporting documentation for any significant fluctuations. Test depreciation calculations to the extent considered necessary. (Software is sometimes used.)

    Audit Software: Could be used to recompute accumulated depreciation and gain or loss on sale. Additionally, it could be used to select significant sales from the detailed fixed assets records.

Recoverability

14. Consider whether adjustments should be made to the carrying value of assets to reflect a permanent diminution in value (step 9).

Leases

15. Examine records of leased assets, lease agreements, and other relevant data for leases capitalized during the period to determine if they were properly capitalized in accordance with Statement of Financial Accounting Standards (SFAS) No. 13 (as amended).

Audit Software: Time-sharing audit software could be used to recalculate capitalization of the leases in accordance with SFAS No. 13 (as amended).

16. Examine support for rentals under operating leases to determine if any leases should be capitalized in accordance with SFAS No. 13 (as amended).

Interest Capitalization

17. Examine supporting documentation for interest capitalized during the period in accordance with SFAS No. 34.

18. Inquire of management as to the existence of any capital projects that require a period of preparation before they are ready for their intended use for which interest has not been capitalized. Examine project authorizations, progress payments, and other supporting data (including notes payable and long-term debt) to determine if interest should be capitalized in accordance with SFAS No. 34.

Property, Plant, and Equipment Pledged as Collateral

19. Identify assets pledged as collateral for company indebtedness by reviewing debt and lease agreements, confirmation replies, and minutes of directors' meetings; inspecting public records; and inquiring of management.

Other Matters

20. Determine whether profit or interdepartmental transfers or intercompany sales of assets is eliminated from property, plant, and equipment accounts.

21. Determine if there were any transactions during the year or balances at year-end denominated in foreign currency and whether they have been translated at appropriate rates.

22. Determine that all appropriate matters to be included in the management letter have been noted.

23. Devise and perform any additional steps deemed necessary for the company.

Note: At this point, the auditor should consider whether the results of the audit steps performed satisfy the substantive audit objectives for Property, Plant, and Equipment and whether all appropriate comments have been prepared.

PART VI

Auditing System Development

CHAPTER **22**

System Development Trends and Practices

SYSTEM DEVELOPMENT LIFE CYCLE

Introduction

The system development life cycle (SDLC) starts with the perceived need for a new system and extends through that system's design, implementation, operation, and maintenance. The term SDLC may be used less now in the high technology world of information systems, but it is still a valuable one for the auditor—emphasizing as it does the long-term view, not just the development and implementation phases.

This chapter describes how systems are developed and procedures an auditor can follow in reviewing them. The chapter starts with the need for a formal methodology, which leads into a discussion of project management and typical system development phases. This information provides background for anyone involved in system development and can serve as a basis for comparison with existing system development practices. The auditing section, which follows, describes documentation to be reviewed and procedures to be followed in auditing system developments. The chapter includes sections on trends that are changing the nature of system development, traditional development methodologies, and some of the new approaches to developing systems.

The Need for a System Development Methodology

Most enterprises, whether in the private or public sector, recognize the increasingly important contribution of information systems to their survival and prosperity. Effective systems are a key factor in containing costs, improving products and services, and thus improving the enterprise's competitive position.

Management is faced with the following problems in relation to computer systems:

- An environment of constant change both in the business environment and in the information processing technology available.
- A need for new systems and changes to be delivered quickly.
- An increasing dependence of the enterprise on information that dictates higher levels of security and control.
- A variety of different approaches to delivering systems—the right approach must be chosen for each project.
- Extravagant vendor claims for many new system development

products and techniques—these new approaches should be exploited while retaining necessary disciplines.

- Lack of confidence in delivery promises (time, budget) and system quality (conformity to user needs, reliability)—historic failures cast doubt on the ability of systems staff to undertake the more demanding and crucial new systems.

As always, the key requirement is to have competent, trained systems personnel working under effective project management. Staff productivity can be enhanced by use of:

- A methodology that specifies the procedures to be followed when developing systems and defines deliverables explicitly.
- Established techniques which improve system quality (e.g., data modeling and prototyping).
- Automated tools to support the methodology and improve programmer productivity.

The methodology should divide the life cycle into phases, each yielding a measurable end product. It should specify:

- The steps to be performed and their sequence.
- Status points and approval procedures.
- Planning and project management procedures.
- The roles and responsibilities of the various parties involved.
- Documentation requirements. It is highly desirable for documentation formats to be standardized.
- Procedures for incorporating security, controls, and audit trails.

In creating methodology, it is desirable to separate the fixed requirements (what has to be done) from the specifics (how tasks are to be done). The latter often require more flexibility (for example, COBOL (Common Business Oriented Language) coding standards may not apply to a fourth-generation language (4GL)). The requirements (what) must always be followed. The standards (how) can be more flexible, although they are still desirable. If necessary, they can be specified and approved for each project.

The use of standards and a defined methodology eases training needs and enhances control. They can help ensure that business needs are satisfied, costs contained, deadlines met, and management requirements for future control and maintainability are satisified.

Consider this example. One company spent a year and a half developing a new billing system without following a set methodology for system development. By the time it was complete, the company had hired a new controller. After reviewing the system, the controller found it produced an insufficient information trail, had no way to balance key reports to input, and had inadequate controls over the data being entered. Since the system was designed without following established procedures, there had been no real analysis of controls and information requirements. The MIS department had created what they thought the old controller requested, but it was not what the organization needed. There was little documentation of the request and no way to be sure of what had happened. The system was scrapped and the project had to be started all over again.

This kind of situation occurs more often than might be expected. However, the problems and frustrations that arise may be avoided if system developers follow proper procedures and document their work.

Any enterprise that wishes and needs to exploit the full potential of information systems is faced with many different types of development projects, such as:

- Creating a network of mainframes, minicomputers, desktop micros, and portable micros.
- Implementing a purchased package.
- Developing and creating an expert system.
- Providing managers and executives with information for decision support.
- Creating a departmental tracking system.
- Replacing an older transaction processing system.

While a single traditional methodology may not be suitable for all these projects, the alternatives—different methodologies for each type of project or no standard methodology—have their obvious disadvantages. Yet, there are few methodologies available that are flexible enough to handle many variations.

SYSTEM DEVELOPMENT TRENDS

Telecommunications

It is not possible to discuss system development without examining the trends in the types of systems being created. One trend in systems involves greater use of communications. Through the application of wider networks, users can gain access to customers, suppliers, and public information systems. Global telecommunications networks are also emerging as yet another way to deliver systems to end users.

Decentralization

Decentralization is a major issue in system development, as well as a major business issue. Although not true for all organizations, many companies are becoming more and more decentralized. Whichever style of organization exists, the fundamental information architecture must match that of the corporate culture. Where businesses are tending to become more decentralized (which is defined here as responsibility given to the divisional or departmental managers who are judged on results), it is natural and necessary to decentralize the information processing that supports those elements of the business.

Data Orientation

The popular press places a lot of emphasis on personal computing and end-user computing (EUC). What is rarely reported is the transition that people are making in system design from a transaction-oriented approach (including the automation of transaction processing) to a data-oriented approach which recognizes that what users really want is wider access to the data for decision support. Users want data so that they can derive information from it. There is also a growing appreciation by corporate management of the fact that the data and related information are themselves valuable assets. This is not to imply that operation-level transaction processing systems are disappearing. It is just that most of those systems have already been built. New systems focus on meeting unfulfilled needs for more information.

This change in orientation is not a revolutionary change, but certainly an evolutionary one. Users are focusing on data all the more. Also, the demand for data storage seems to increase with the technology. As soon as a new technology is released that can store more data, users want to store that much more data. This situation was true in the early days of computing when computer users always seemed to need about 10 percent more memory than they had. This is often true even with the expanded data storage capacities of today.

Flexibility of Systems

The need to provide flexible systems that will support a constant stream of changes is a genuine need that should be noted. Previously, systems were based on the concept that they were built to last. System analysts seemed to believe that once they built a system, it would never need maintenance (i.e., the requirements would never change). In reality, that was never true.

Because the user demand for flexibility is increasing all the time, more functionality is being built into systems to give users greater flexibility. It is no longer assumed that business is not going to change. For example, government regulations regarding a particular type of business may change. Competitive pressure may cause the need for change at very short notice. To accommodate these changes, flexibility must be built into the system. This is particularly true of application packages, discussed subsequently.

Strategic Systems

Today's systems are not just being used for back-office functions. They are used for front-office functions that affect a company's "real" business, such as relationships with customers or the delivery of the product. In some cases, the system itself is the product. In summary, system trends often dictate the future of system development, since they are often inextricably linked.

TRADITIONAL DEVELOPMENT METHODOLOGIES

Traditional system development methodologies are not disappearing. The traditional approach is very useful in projects with many users and high volumes. It is also useful for transaction processing design with clearly defined inputs and outputs. These systems still need to be built. To do so, it is often an appropriate approach to use the more traditional system development methodologies.

Development Pressures

Development pressures are a driving force behind what is happening in the area of system development. There are increasing development costs, mainly because "people costs" are increasing. The software cost is increasing because of the required functionality and complexity of the software. Hardware costs are going down, but for some reason this does not seem to influence the costs of system development.

Until quite recently, there had been no significant productivity gains in system development over the past 20 years. This led to a huge backlog of requests. According to some statistics, the visible backlog of requests averages 14 systems, ranging from two to three years. There is also an "invisible" backlog of systems that the user would like but does not even ask for, due to the small probability of having the system built. Therefore, there is a huge pent-up demand for new systems, only part of which is being satisfied by end-user computing.

The Skills of System Designers

Analysts and programmers need to understand business specialization. Corporate management needs more than "plain vanilla" system analysts. It is looking for analysts who understand its business. To develop effective in-house systems, knowledge and understanding of the business is necessary.

A perceptible erosion is beginning to be seen in the skills of today's experienced data processing professionals. Many senior people came into data processing some time ago. Although they have matured in a technical sense, they may not always have matured in a business sense. Even in the technical area, some professionals may be resistant to the idea of embracing different technologies. These professionals may acquire more skills in their existing technology, but they do not necessarily learn how to integrate new technologies, how to do EUC, or how to create expert systems.

In the purely technical area, there is a shortage of qualified people, such as people with solid experience in communications. Some of the larger banks, insurance companies, and the government have a shortage of technical specialists who can run large operating systems or large telecommunications networks. Smaller companies notice the same gaps, particularly in dealing with newer technologies.

For all of these reasons, there is an obvious need to assess recruitment, motivation, and morale to make sure that shortages in experienced professionals are managed to the greatest extent possible. Appropriate training and development of those already on staff is another part of the solution.

End-User Computing

End-user computing (see Chapter 24, "End-User Computing") techniques have had a significant impact on systems development. The EUC environment affects the development, organization structure, project planning and project management procedures, and the nature of the costs/benefits analysis.

Organizational issues associated with EUC are changing the very character of organizations. When there is a centralized MIS function and something goes wrong, everyone knows who is expected to fix it. With EUC, this is rarely, if ever, the case.

Autonomy is another organizational issue to be addressed. How can a sound corporate plan be developed when everything is being done by the end users?

There is also the possibility of incompatibilities, such as in data exchange and hardware and software. Such incompatibilities must be reconciled, so that an organization can implement a connected system in the future, if necessary.

In addition, if a purchased machine breaks down, a backup unit will be necessary. When there is coordinated equipment purchase, another system can generally be used as a replacement.

Another issue is that vendors are building independent networks, which may not talk to each other. Software from different vendors is incompatible. What is needed is a single-user interface, a number of these so called single-user interfaces. Unfortunately, if each user selects a different one, it can lead to even greater incompatibilities.

NEW APPROACHES TO SYSTEM DEVELOPMENT

Structured Techniques

There are a number of structured techniques used to analyze, design, and program new computerized systems. There are purchased development methodologies that have been used extensively. One technique revolves around team work sessions, which IBM has called Joint Application Development, or JAD. This method places a group of people in a room for a period of time with the sole purpose of creating the basic design for a new system.

Data-oriented design reflects a change in the way people look at systems. Some experts are now suggesting that the data architecture should be created before starting to design the transaction processing system. This means that the first step is to design the data base, which will become the fundamental design and management control. Afterwards, transaction processing systems can be designed to use that data base to satisfy information needs. This approach also allows auditors to plan for security over shared data. Increasingly, security is the responsibility of someone like a data administrator, who has various data-oriented tools to help in that area. This approach often is incorporated into the traditional system development approach.

Prototyping

Prototyping (or heuristic development) is, in actuality, an attempt to create a system through the process of trial and error. This philosophy can be expressed as "let's get something going and see whether it works or not." The emphasis in prototyping is usually on the reports and screens within the system, places where the user can actually see what is going on. It is a method that allows users to see a working model of the proposed system, usually in a short time.

Obviously, prototyping requires faster development tools. One cannot prototype easily with languages like COBOL, for example. However, prototyping can be used with the traditional methodologies such as to help do the feasibility study. It can also be used in whole or in part to satisfy the general system design phase requirements, and perhaps even the detailed system design within the traditional SDLC.

There are two basic approaches to prototyping:

- Build the model first to determine feasibility, or to do the general design. Then go ahead and develop the real system.
- Gradually build the actual system that will operate in production. Use a 4GL that has been determined as appropriate for the system being built.

The problem with the first approach is that there can be considerable pressure to implement the prototype. Most professionals know of instances where the user was shown a working model and then was unable to understand why the system could not go into production the next day. The fact that the system has to be expanded to handle transaction volumes, to handle the terminal network, to institute backup and recovery procedures, as well as provide for auditability and control, is not understood.

Prototyping has proved useful for important applications that are innovative or unique, or not well understood. It can certainly help to improve user involvement and satisfaction with the system. One disadvantage is that prototyping often leads to too many functions, extras that may not be strictly necessary for day-to-day operations. The system may be precisely what the user wants, but perhaps not what the corporation needs, or what senior management wants. Like EUC, prototyping does not always make the best use of system resources. By using 4GLs and some of the newer techniques, the final system can end up being functionally rich but inefficient.

To illustrate problems that may arise with prototyping, consider the situation of New Jersey's motor vehicle system. The system developers decided to build the new system with a 4GL and to prototype it as they went along. Everything went well until the system was put into production use. Although it worked beautifully, it simply could not handle the volume of vehicle registration and license changes for an entire state. It would appear that the system had not been tested adequately at the actual volume of daily transactions.

Another potential risk is that of poor controls over the finished system. By focusing mainly on what the user wants and what the user sees, system developers may miss some of the controls that come out of the traditional system development approach (backup/recovery, security, information trails within the system, and so on).

There is also the issue of change control, both during the development process and afterward. Can there be change control in such a fluid developmental approach as prototyping? Can the system reach the point where it is maintainable? These are only a few of the issues that should be considered when using prototyping.

Computer Aided Software Engineering (CASE)

Automated development aids for design and documentation support, including flowcharts and data flow diagrams, are becoming available on microcomputers. Automated data dictionaries are obviously a great help in the documentation area.

Some project management systems produce Gantt charts, Program Evaluation Review Techniques (PERT) charts, budget-to-actual comparisons, and management summaries. Management of development projects may be improved through the use of this type of product.

The analyst's workbench, also known as the design center, is evolving. This concept integrates different tools, such as a project management system and a documentation system. The workbench may even maintain the links between different components and perform a hierarchical update. (When an update occurs at a lower level, it is automatically reflected higher up in the system.) Vendors are teaming up these analysts' workstations with application generators to allow attempts to generate complete systems directly from design specifications.

Programmer's workbench is a term given to a workstation with a set of tools for programmers. In some cases, the workbench could be a COBOL compiler, access to TSO (Time-Sharing Options), and some test functions. With the advent of 4GL tools, the programmer's workbench is becoming a more meaningful and useful concept.

Testing Facilities

Changes are also taking place in testing. Test data generators have been available for some time. Their use continues to improve the quality of testing. Interactive debuggers and code logic analyzers are being used more often. There is some benefit in using audit software (e.g., comparison software that interrogates program libraries to find out when they were changed, or programs that analyze options within the system or read system tables) as a testing aid.

There are now a few automated "key pushers." With these, the user types in a typical key sequence for an application. The computer remembers the key sequence and repeats it on demand, making it easier to test interactive systems.

In addition, there is increased use of "user interaction" testing. This can take the form of a workshop where the user is videotaped while attempting to follow the instructions on how to use the system. This form of testing helps ensure that the whole system will work, not just the programmed portion. It is particularly valuable for systems designed for untrained or occasional users.

Traditional debugging aids, such as trace facilities and cross-reference listings, have been available for some time. (Trace facilities log each step in a program as it is executed; cross-reference listings show where every occurrence of a data label or procedure label is used.) However, not all of the new generation languages have these facilities. Microcomputer languages and methods of changing purchased software option tables are particularly lacking. The development team may need to purchase additional software or create utilities to make up for the deficiencies.

ADAPTING THE METHODOLOGY TO THE PROJECT

There are substantial variations in the activities required to deliver different types of systems. For example, a large, innovative, custom-built system, on multiple sites using a 4GL, should be developed and implemented using a very different approach from that which is appropriate for a small, routine, single-site system using a package. Selection of the necessary and relevant methodology is a key project management task.

The selection or adaptation of the methodology should not be used as an excuse to skip vital project management tasks or controls. Ideally, the different methodologies should be defined in advance and formally agreed as part of the overall systems procedures. These procedures should define the circumstances in which each methodology should be used. Some of these circumstances are described in the following paragraphs. (Note that the phases of system development referred to throughout this section are from the sample methodology described in Chapter 23, "System Development Methodology and Auditing."

In many cases, System Requirements Analysis needs to be completed before the appropriate methodology for subsequent phases can be determined. However, the initial tasks in System Requirements Analysis are similar for most system development projects and, if Project Planning and Initiation did not determine the methodology to be used, it should become clear by the end of the System Requirements phase.

There are circumstances where a project is split after System Requirements Analysis and progresses from System Specifications or Technical Design onward as several subprojects running in parallel. Thus, more than one methodology may be required for one macro-level project.

Analysis of the characteristics of different types of systems has shown that the critical determining factors should be:

- Definability of requirements (the extent to which system requirements are already defined or capable of definition).
- Project size or scope, taking account of both extent and complexity.
- Status of the user information technology (IT) installation, which either is established already or will be established or significantly upgraded in support of the project.
- Delivery techniques, particularly distinguishing between the use of packages, conventional custom-built methods, and fourth-generation techniques, including prototyping.

The choice of a basic methodology for any project will be determined primarily by those factors and not specifically by the type of application. The specific methodology for any one project will be created by refining the basic methodology in light of the application, user, and technical environment.

Definability of Requirements

Where the application is based on an existing automated or manual system, or where the requirements and benefits can be determined readily by user management, the use of structured analysis techniques is suitable for producing a definitive recommended solution. In System Requirements Analysis, variations can occur in the extent to which a study of the existing physical system is needed in the iterative process of building "top-down" conceptual models based on user management's definition of requirements and on available industry knowledge. Modeling of the current system can be especially valuable where complex mechanisms are to be automated or reautomated.

Data modeling is valuable in systems where decision support or management information issues are more important than operational ones, and in particular where substantial improvements in systems are sought.

Where requirements are not readily definable, or where benefits are speculative, a prototyping approach may be more appropriate. The prototyping concept is used in three ways:

- To help develop the visual and ergonomic aspects of user

interfaces. This technique is now so universal that its use is assumed, and no special impact on the methodology is predicted.

- To help users articulate their requirements, either where the application is not readily definable or where the value of the system only can be assessed by some limited operational use. In these circumstances, a "mock-up" of the system is produced during System Requirements Analysis or possibly System Specification. Once the requirements are defined, and the value can more readily be ascertained, the project continues through one of the basic routes, or is discontinued if the problem proves undefinable or if benefits seem to be inadequate.
- To design the whole system through a series of progressive refinements ("protocycles"), involving iterations through the complete life cycle down to the System Acceptance and Testing phase. A specific decision is then made whether to accept the latest iteration as a satisfactory basis for developing a system. A second decision then needs to be made on whether a further cycle is likely to produce a usable system. The prototype may be discarded, or the code used as the basis for the production system. During the "protocycles" all phases from System Specifications to System Acceptance with testing are used, albeit with many tasks and activities and their associated deliverables being bypassed or combined, particularly in the areas of security, operational facilities, performance, and documentation. Once an adequate prototype has been produced, a final pass through a full version of these phases is required (the appropriate methodology will be determined by other characteristics of the project) to produce a full production system, with all operational and security features.

Project Size or Scope

A project can be classified as "small" if the system shows all the following characteristics:

- Not more than three months' elapsed time.
- Not more than six man-months of IT specialist effort.
- No use of new hardware, system software, or development techniques that are new (either to the user or to the project management team).
- No critical security, safety, or performance requirements.
- Has a single-user patron.
- Is developed and will be run on a single site.

- Does not constitute a new application area.
- Has no connection with any other system.
- Has no immovable implementation date.
- Uses a fully experienced development team.

In this circumstance, phases may be consolidated into "macro-phases," particularly:

- System Requirements Analysis, System Specification, and Product Acquisition.
- Technical Design and Technical Procedure Development.

In other areas, the full structure will normally be used. However, since few projects will satisfy all the criteria listed, projects that fail to qualify as "small" in only one or two characteristics may still be managed as small projects subject to approval by the quality assurance (QA) function.

There is no formal maximum size for a system development project, but experienced project managers will recognize the practical need for some limitation of elapsed time and total resources. Constraint on maximum size is especially important on projects using 4GLs. Project managers may reduce large projects to more manageable units:

- Project Planning and Initiation can split large projects into multiple development projects from System Requirements Analysis onward.
- A single System Requirements Analysis phase can spawn a number of subprojects (from System Specifications through to Transition). These subprojects can progress in parallel, subject to periodic checks on compatibility and to reintegration during the System Acceptance and Testing phase.

It should be noted that these approaches can significantly increase the project management task, and can require temporary interfacing software to be written. Where subprojects are identified, they do not necessarily use the same methodologies. Thus, one subproject can be a package implementation and another may be custom-built.

Status of IT Installation

If the development project requires an IT installation (computer, environment, operations staff, and procedures) to be established, then the amount of work in the Product Evaluation and Product Installation phases becomes more significant. The following points should be borne in mind in these circumstances:

- Any project requiring an installation to be established should be managed by means of a methodology suited to a large or complex project—an obvious exception would be the installation of a microcomputer.
- If a major data center is to be established, then in all normal circumstances the project should be the subject of a specialized project rather than just a system development project. It must involve other specialized services and activities.

Delivery Techniques

Where a system is to be custom-built, most of the activities for a complete system development project are performed. Where an application package is to be used, including office automation systems using, for example, word processing, diary management, or electronic mail products, differences will show as follows:

- System Requirements Analysis usually requires a Product Evaluation exercise to locate and recommend the package. Where a specific operating environment (hardware or system software) is also needed, two interacting Product Evaluation exercises will be required and compatibility between package and technical environment must be achieved in the recommended solution.
- System Specification, Technical Design, and Technical Procedure Development often involve less work than in custom-built systems, except that the way in which the package is used still has to be designed and specified. Packages require parameters to be set, options to be selected, and reports to be customized. These are defined in System Specification and Technical Design and are "coded" in Technical Procedure Development.

4GLs and Similar Tools. When a 4GL or similar delivery tool is to be used, the methodology is influenced by the nature of, and facilities provided by, the development software. The following implications are suggested:

- Code generators will mainly reduce the coding workload in Technical Procedure Development. They also define how Technical Design is undertaken by setting the documentation standards.
- Products offering full software engineering facilities and any

methods offering active data dictionary facilities may affect the way models are produced and documented right back to System Requirements Analysis.

- The use of relational data base management system (DBMS) influences many of the data design and optimization activities.

For the purposes of deciding on a development methodology, a 4GL environment is presumed to exist where all, or the majority, of the following exist:

- Application generator.
- Very high-level code generator or programming language.
- User inquiry language.
- Relational data base.
- Screen painter.
- Integrated data dictionary (active or passive).
- CASE product.
- Analyst workbench.

Maintenance Projects. Maintenance projects often are treated with a special kind of development approach. Only adaptive maintenance projects would normally find a full development methodology appropriate. For this purpose, adaptive maintenance may be defined as the process of modifying an existing computer-based system to accommodate changed business requirements, which involves changes at a relatively low level (i.e., at implementation phase or program code level). Corrective maintenance, the process of modifying a system properly to meet existing business requirements, usually requiring correction of logical or technical faults, rarely involves using a full system development methodology.

Projects that enhance the functionality of a system by adding new subsystems involving the generation of new procedures (rather than the adaptation of existing ones) can be treated as new projects.

Vendor-Supplied Packages. Projects based predominantly on the use of a vendor-supplied applications package are managed by methodology determined by project size and whether the installation is new or established. The following must be borne in mind:

- The activities associated with the selection and installation of an application package will be dealt with through the Product Evaluation and Project Installation phases.
- There are almost invariably some activities in installing a package that are similar to those used in coding custom-built systems, such as the design of custom-built subsystems for data conversion or for adding features (e.g., specialized statistics, interfaces to other systems).
- Installing correct parameters for the package may in itself be a substantial task, involving selective installation of modules, creation of control files, selection of user options with respect to user screens, inquiries, and reports, together with the necessary testing.
- For the purposes of deciding on a methodology, Decision Support Systems (DSS) are treated as being product-based, although the product selection may not be necessary if such systems have already been introduced. As the uses of DSSs often are difficult to define in advance, and their benefits are hard to predict, use of one of the prototyping approaches often will be required in advance of the full installation. A typical approach would be to prototype requirements:
  - Use System Requirements Analysis and Product Evaluation to outline requirements and select a preferred prototyping tool.
  - Use a limited number of activities in Product Installation to acquire and install just enough equipment and software to run an experimental installation from which a full set of requirements are derived. Complete the project by using a methodology suited to the development of a packaged system.
- Office automation systems should be managed by the same methodology as DSSs, since they share the common characteristics of being difficult to predefine and requiring piloting by users. These also require a final pass through to ensure that the system is delivered and installed in good, secure, and documented form.

Quality Assurance

Whichever system development methodology is selected (and selection may be made in Project Planning and Initiation in System Requirements Analysis or modified after completion of protocycles), the selection must be submitted for QA review. This review will be particularly thorough where a methodology other than one of the standard methodologies has been selected, and where a methodology suited to a small project has been selected.

PROJECT MANAGEMENT

Management Requirements for System Development Projects

From a management viewpoint, system development projects are among the most demanding. Factors that contribute to this include the:

- Desire to introduce new systems quickly, at the lowest possible cost.
- Complexity resulting from the number and variety of activities and people (developers and users) likely to be involved.
- Very visible and specific nature of the end product (i.e., a system that works or does not work).
- Obscure and indefinite nature of the starting point for many projects.
- Need to produce not just a working computer system, but to surround it with effective user procedures and trained and receptive users.
- Constraints arising from the need to fit the new system into an inherited combination of hardware, software, and other systems, not all of which can be changed at the same time.
- Requirement at all stages to judge when the work has been completed satisfactorily, achieving the correct balance between superficiality and perfectionism, bearing in mind that mistakes made in the earlier stages may prove extremely expensive at later stages of the project.

This list could be much longer. System development projects are not unique; usually, they are amenable to the same management techniques as other types of projects. In general, they are more complex than other types of projects of a similar size and, of course, some of them are extremely large.

Classification of Management Tasks

The management of system development encompasses project management, user involvement, quality control, and audit. Narrow definitions of those areas follow:

- *Project management* relates to the process of planning the project, setting up the project team, and monitoring, reporting, and controlling progress and deliverables.
- *User involvement* is the process of getting users to take

responsibility for the system—an essential element if the system is to meet their needs. Making sure that users' contributions are effective can be difficult because few of the people involved report directly to the project manager. The project manager must also ensure that management's expectations are met.

- *Quality control* is the process of ensuring that all deliverables are of the required quality and that all work has been carried out accurately and to an appropriate standard.
- *Audit* is a mechanism whereby reviewers, not part of the project team, evaluate whether the project plans, deliverables, and conduct of the project are in accordance with predefined standards and corporate requirements. Sometimes this is known as QA when the reviewers are part of MIS, rather than external auditors or an internal audit department.

Project management and quality control cannot be separated because a task or activity cannot reasonably be considered complete unless it has been carried out to the required quality standards. User involvement is critical. It overlaps with the requirement for good senior management commitment and communication.

It follows that project management, quality control, and user involvement are very closely related. The term "project management" should be understood to include all three.

Audit and/or QA needs to be regarded as a discrete activity because it should be a formal process carried out by people who are not part of the development team.

A meaningful and effective QA review can only take place against a framework of predefined standards and procedures. The review is usually performed by a separate QA group or by EDP audit. Furthermore, someone needs to make sure that the finished system will satisfy the control and security requirements of the organization. This is an important role for the auditor.

Roles and Responsibilities

The roles and responsibilities of the various players in a development project are summarized in Figure 22-1.

The first five roles exist on all system development projects, although on a smaller project they may not be carried out by different people. Clearly, the need for specialist involvement varies among projects, but this depends on the characteristics of the project rather than its size.

It is highly desirable that user department staff be included within the

FIG. 22-1

Project roles and responsibilities

Role	Key Responsibilities
Corporate Management	• Show commitment to project • Assign responsibilities • Approve project at decision points
User Management	• Assume ownership of the system from the outset • Participate in system requirement definition, system testing, user training, system installation • Carry out thorough and timely reviews of specifications and other deliverables
MIS Management	• Provide hardware/software/operations environment for developing, installing, and operating application system • Ensure that the system as developed meets corporate data base administration requirements • Provide technical assistance as required • Participate sufficiently to take over operating support and maintenance role after installation
Project Manager	• Provide overall project direction • Ensure appropriate involvement of other parties • Ensure that all deliverables are of the required quality and that all work has been performed in accordance with the standards • Resolve conflicts and authorize action to overcome difficulties as they arise • Monitor and control costs and timetables
Project Team	• Complete specific work assignments • Involve users throughout the development process • Understand and meet user's requirements • Communicate effectively with users • Observe standards and change control procedures • Report deviations from plan and other problems immediately to project management
Business Sector and/or Applications Specialist	• Provide assistance as agreed, usually with system requirements definition, solution specification, user procedures
Data Administration	• Ensure that the system as developed meets corporate data administration requirements regarding names, definitions, and storage of shared and other data

(*continued*)

FIG. 22-1 (*continued*)

Role	Key Responsibilities
Technical Specialist	• Provide assistance as agreed, usually with: —Selection and implementation of application software —Selection and implementation of system or development software —Specification of and changes to communications network —Data base design
Audit	• Evaluate controls, security, and audit trails being built into the new system • Act as a control consultant to the development team • Plan for future audit requirements
Audit/Quality Assurance	• Perform a preliminary evaluation of the standards and the development methodology to be used • Review the reasonableness of budgets and projections • Monitor compliance with system development standards and procedures • Monitor compliance with other applicable corporate policies • Evaluate the effectiveness of documentation and other deliverables • Review and possibly test the system testing and conversion procedures
Security Officer	• Ensure that system as developed meets corporate security requirements • Participate sufficiently to take over security installation and maintenance for operational system • Provide protection for programs under development and in testing

project team in order to ensure that the system fully reflects user needs and to obtain greater user commitment to the system.

Some aspects of the project may be delegated to outside consultants and contractors. It is essential in each case to specify the tasks and deliverables to be provided by each party, and the dates by which they must be completed.

Project Team Structure

Project team structure may vary considerably depending on the size and nature of each project. It is important that responsibilities are allocated for:

- Liaison with senior management.
- Project management from the business viewpoint, separately for each phase of the project.
- Technical leadership and staff supervision, separately for each phase of the project.
- Ensuring that the users are ready for the system.

While these roles may be combined, they must be recognized separately.

The staff involved in the project fall into the following categories:

- Those involved on a continual basis but part-time—typically the project manager and users, and MIS management.
- Those involved continually and full-time—typically MIS project leaders and specific user and MIS staff.
- Those involved in supporting roles from time to time, including:
  - — QA reviewer.
  - — Internal and external auditors.
  - — Business sector and application specialists.
  - — Data base and capacity planning specialists.
  - — Data administrator.
  - — Network and technical support specialists.
  - — Consultants and vendor personnel.

Traditional approaches to system development are characterized by clear definitions of the roles, and hence the levels of skill and experience, required at each stage in the life cycle. Some of the more modern approaches have a significant impact on this pattern because both technical and business skills are required throughout the project, albeit in varying proportions.

Project Planning (Feasibility Study)

"Project planning" is the term used in this chapter to describe the activities that have to be carried out before approval can be given to begin a development project. It is also known as a feasibility study.

Request for System Design. User departments such as the marketing department, general accounting department, or treasurer's office) are the most frequent source of requests for new systems, but they are not the only source. New application projects are often initiated by MIS to provide greater efficiency or cost-effective use of processing resources. An application in current use may need to be enhanced or modified.

System design requests may be based on a real need, a change in a law, a regulatory requirement, or even a dream or fantasy. However it originates, and whomever it originates with, the request should be in writing to be properly evaluated by the organization. Normally, the MIS department designates one person to receive these requests. Requests can be processed and recorded and, if warranted, prepared for the next phase. It is a good idea to find out how such requests are initiated and tracked in an organization. A common problem is the lack of a set methodology for handling requests. One consequence is a backlog of undocumented requests with the result that some needs go unfulfilled, even when the system is redesigned.

Strategic Plans. Another starting point for projects, particularly major ones, is a strategic system plan. This plan re-examines the information needs of the organization and may create a number of projects for implementation. When a strategic plan is used, much of the work set out in the next section on scoping and evaluating the project will already have been completed.

Scoping and Evaluating the Project. Before a decision can be made to proceed with a development project, its scope and objectives must be defined properly. These can be grouped under two main headings:

- *The project charter* defines project goals and contains an outline proposal for the project. This outline describes the proposed system and the information it will use. Costs, benefits, preliminary schedule, and the impact the system will have on the organization and related systems are major components.
- *The enterprise description* is an important component, especially on larger projects with many people involved. It lays out the users' needs and environment and relates them to those of the organization and external factors. Without an enterprise description there is a greater chance that users' real needs and the overall requirements of the organization will not be satisfied.

The contents of a project charter and an enterprise description are set out in Figure 22-2.

At this stage, consideration must be given to the hardware, system software, and other facilities and resources that will be required to develop, introduce, and operate the proposed system. Matters such as the selection and installation or upgrading of any major component of the technical environment and recruitment or retraining of technical staff may be essential for a successful project. The outline proposal or project charter must identify and emphasize such requirements for facilities and resources. Where appropriate, a separate project should be initiated for them. Hardware, soft-

FIG. 22-2

Major deliverables for project planning and initiation of project charter

PROJECT CHARTER

- Project Goals
  - Business Goals
  - Project Management Goals
- oposed Applications
  - Function Models
  - Data Models
  - Proposed Technology Infrastructure
    - Proposed System Architecture
    - Proposed Hardware
    - Proposed System Software
    - Proposed Application Product Usage
    - Proposed Locations
  - Costs and Benefits
  - Predicted Organizational Impact
  - Preliminary Schedule
  - Preliminary Resource Requirements
  - Terms of Agreements
  - Preliminary Transition Strategy
- Current System Profile
  - Function Models
  - Data Models
  - Events Inventory
  - Deficiencies
  - Performance Characteristics
  - Cost
  - Resources
  - MIS Staff Information
- Current Technology Infrastructure
  - Information System Inventory
    - Information Architecture
    - Hardware
    - System Software
    - Services
    - Age and Reliability
    - Information Technology Investment
    - Application Software
    - Building Environment
    - Security Procedures
  - Information Policies
    - Vendor Selection Policies
    - Security Policies
    - Control Policies
    - Testing Policies
  - Information Technology Constraints
  - Information Technology Performance
    - Development Methods
    - MIS Standards

FIG. 22-2 (*continued*)

PROJECT CHARTER

Project Plan
- Development Methodology Modifications
- Progress Reporting Milestones
- Steering Committee Reviews
- Team Structure
  - Roles and Responsibilities
  - Quality Assurance Participation
  - Audit Participation
- Dependency on Other Resources and Projects

ENTERPRISE DESCRIPTION

Enterprise Information Model
Logical Information System Architecture
Business Objectives and Goals
Critical Success Factors
Business Profile and Trends
Personnel Information
User Information System Policies
Market Description
Business Products and Services
Geography and Location

ware, and personnel requirements for the development phase are particularly time-critical.

Satisfactory facilities must be arranged for system development. Responsibility for the provision of these facilities and any associated costs must be established. If satisfactory facilities for development and testing are not available in-house, they will have to be obtained elsewhere, with due allowance for the costs and extra work involved in transferring the system subsequently to the operational environment. The arrangements for acquiring automated development tools and hardware on which to run them must also be established.

Once these preliminaries have been accomplished, a key project management task is to determine the development methodology used to implement the system. Projects involving new technology may involve selection or creation of a new methodology, or an adaptation of the existing methodology. This issue is discussed in more detail in Chapter 23.

Defining Project Boundaries and Milestones. It is particularly important to define clearly the start and end of the project. The starting point is usually defined in terms of a set of assumptions that have been made, and the end may equate to a given set of deliverables, with the addition of specified post-installation support and maintenance.

Key milestones for the project should also be established. These milestones provide the opportunity for:

- Reassessment of the costs to complete and benefits of the project.
- Recommitment by users.
- Reviewing the project budget and plans.
- Demonstrating progress to users and management.

Go/no go decisions should be built into these milestones. Costs to complete should be compared to the expected benefits. It is sometimes hard, and embarrassing, to kill a project after it has begun. It is necessary, however, to make this decision if external events or difficulties with technology push the cost to complete above the expected benefits. In practice, decisions are not usually as harsh as this, and the decision points allow for reassessment and redirection if external factors change.

Work Breakdown and Estimating. The objective of work breakdown is to identify all activities to be carried out to complete the project, and then subdivide or combine them to arrive at manageable units of work that will take between four and 80 hours to complete. A good development methodology should identify the required activities and the variables that influence their duration. The size of the project will dictate the level of work breakdown needed for project control purposes.

Estimating is a process whereby experience of past projects and analysis of the current project are combined to arrive at a prediction of the time and effort required. The more that is known about the current project, the more reliable the estimate will be. All estimates should include a statement of the assumptions on which they are based. Estimates should be made only by experienced system project personnel. Because of their criticality to the decision-making process, whenever possible they should be checked by:

- Being prepared by two different methods.
- Being prepared independently by two people.

It is probably not feasible, however, to produce a reliable estimate at the beginning of the project cycle for the whole project. At that stage, it is only possible to give:

- A firm estimate for System Requirement Analysis.
- A provisional estimate for System Specification.
- An indicative estimate (which should include a sizeable contingency) for the remaining phases.

The preliminary nature of these estimates makes it essential that revising estimates, together with a review of project viability, be anticipated and built into the project milestones.

Estimating and scheduling are two tasks where only experience helps. However, some of this experience can be captured and institutionalized into the methodology. If all major projects are subject to a post-implementation review, any improvements and experience can be documented into the methodology to service future projects better.

Project Scheduling. Project scheduling is the process of allocating activities (identified in the work breakdown and given estimated times) to members of a project team against a calendar. Considerations for skill levels, project team structure and size, and scheduling and budgeting resources should be included in the development methodology.

Experience has shown that the following points are particularly important:

- The user may have a fixed idea of the required implementation date—if this is unattainable, it should be told to the user up-front. There are very few cases where the implementation date cannot be changed or a phased development adopted, given reasonable notice.
- It is most unwise to plan on the basis that staff will be available 100 percent, considering staff turnover, sickness, training, vacations, commitments to other projects, and the need for emergency maintenance on existing systems.
- Staff productivity will increase if all staff members are given related groups of tasks to work on—this applies particularly to programmers.
- Little will be achieved by piling extra resources into a project at a late stage—this often causes additional slippage.
- Appropriate arrangements (and adequate time allowance) must be made for supervision of staff at all levels—it does not work for supervision to be a spare-time task of a heavily loaded team member.
- Interdependencies should be kept to a minimum so that slippages on one part of the project do not delay everything else.

- Wherever possible, the more junior team members should work on one activity at a time, never more than two.
- Project team members should be rotated so that no one works on the same project for more than one year—a shorter time is appropriate for junior staff.

Before detailed project scheduling is undertaken, it is necessary to consider the possibility of partitioning the system for development or transition purposes. This could occur in the following ways:

- If, after more detailed analysis, the project is found to be more suitable for development as two or more separate projects.
- If it is appropriate to introduce the system functions in stages (phased development).
- If it is appropriate to introduce the complete system progressively in different locations (phased transition).
- If the system is of a distributed nature such that separate elements have to be developed for centralized and local operation.

In any of those circumstances, project planning and scheduling becomes more complex. In particular, project management will need to address the following issues:

- The level to which the entire system should be specified (and the underlying data and process modeling carried out) before partitioning it into separate parallel developments.
- Ensuring that change control and configuration management procedures are good enough to coordinate the parallel developments.
- The need for reintegration testing.
- Possible resequencing of activities—for example, with a phased implementation, user training is better viewed as part of transition rather than as part of user procedure development.

Final decisions about partitioning or phasing may not be possible until the System Requirements Analysis has been completed.

Project Approach. It is highly desirable for the project to be defined formally in a document that describes its scope and the roles of those involved. Experience has shown that users who are prepared to proceed on an informal basis have little understanding of what is involved in implementing a system.

The following guidelines should be followed:

- If the objectives and scope of the system have not been adequately defined, restrict the initial project to the preliminary work necessary to define them.
- If the nature of the proposed system is such that its requirements or the solution cannot easily be predefined, restrict the initial project to the work necessary to establish the requirements and solution. Prototyping can be used as appropriate.

A wide range of issues has to be considered and a considerable amount of planning completed before project planning is complete. Normally, it will be beneficial to include much of the planning material and, particularly, the assumptions that underlie the plans, within the project plan. The advantage is that users will have a more realistic understanding of what the project involves and the importance of their part in it.

Project Start-Up. Once the plan proposal has been approved, work can begin. If pre-project planning has been carried out properly, project start-up will be uncomplicated. The following things should be done:

- Check that all the assumptions made in the project plan are still valid and adjust budgets if appropriate—this will be particularly important if there has been any delay between the submission of the plan and the start of the project.
- Provide liaison with the different departments to:
  - — Agree on a suitable start date.
  - — Brief all project team members.
  - — Arrange initial interviews.
  - — Allocate user staff time as required.
  - — Arrange any necessary training for staff.
  - — Agree on dates for review meetings.
  - — Obtain office facilities, if necessary, including secretarial support, for the team.
  - — Provide computer resources and technical support for developing the system.
  - — Establish staff travel arrangements, if necessary.
  - — Set up project documentation and project administration arrangements.

Work-in-Progress Management

In theory, when planning has been done well, adherence to that plan should result in a high-quality system, produced on time and within budget. In practice, plans are never perfect and unforeseen events occur. Work-in-progress management is a demanding activity, which requires that project management staff be aware of the situation constantly and take early corrective action, involving users and management as appropriate.

The automated project management tools available are of considerable assistance in:

- Validating plans.
- Documenting progress and highlighting variances from plan.
- Preparing revised plans.
- Budgetary control.

However, these tools are no substitute for the knowledge and instincts of an experienced project manager. Furthermore, a project manager would be very unwise to rely solely on paper reports for monitoring progress, and must talk to project staff.

Work-in-progress management includes the following elements:

- Project administration—members of the project team must understand their administrative responsibilities within the project and carry them out conscientiously so that the whole project is administered smoothly.
- Work status reporting and review procedures—effective communications must be in place.
- Budgeting and cost control, which depend on:
  - — Regular assessment of the value of the work completed against the costs to date.
  - — Elimination of factors that delay the work of one or more members of the project team.
- Project control and adherence to project plan—continual follow-up is needed to ensure adherence to the project plan and, where necessary, to adjust resource use, change methods, readjust objectives, and/or replan.
- Software configuration management—strict and formal control of versions of documents and elements of software should be imposed. These should include access restrictions to program code and sensitive data and adequate backup.

- Quality control—an essential project management role is to review all key deliverables personally and get them approved and formally signed off by the user. Structured walk-throughs should be part of the quality plan.

Project management should pay particular attention to the following points where they apply:

- Periodic reassessment of the continued suitability of the chosen methodology or of adaptations of the methodology made for the project.
- Critical review of any prototyping activities in order to:
  - Determine when sufficient prototyping has been carried out.
  - Ensure that prototyping is followed by a "final pass" to add missing elements, controls, and documentation, and to formalize those which are incomplete.
- Coordination of parallel/phased development.

User Communications

Certain formal organizational arrangements should be adopted to facilitate successful exploitation of information technology. These include the importance of having a project "sponsor," the need for informal and formal user involvement, the role of corporate information and project steering committees, and the advantages of standardized communication between these various parties. Historically, many projects have failed because of inadequate contact between MIS and the user departments.

Critical interfaces are those between the project team and:

- Senior management—to keep them informed of progress and secure their approval and commitment.
- User management—to secure their participation in the project and their acceptance of the system.
- User team members—to help them have an effective and satisfying role in the project.
- MIS staff— to ensure that they understand the system, and are motivated to operate it and take over the necessary support roles after implementation.

Recognizing expectations is a key element of the relationship between the team and management. The project director and project manager must ensure that the user understands the need to accept compromise and adopt realistic system objectives. Many projects get completely out of control and break all cost and time constraints because of continual escalation of user requirements and resulting inability to "freeze" the specifications. Project management must constantly focus the user's attention on the true priorities and on what can be achieved in practice.

Personnel Resource Management

The project manager and project leader must motivate project staff to work on the project effectively. Project staff are often of high caliber. Accordingly, they want to understand what they are doing and feel a sense of accomplishment. The following actions should contribute to staff motivation:

- Ensure that all staff understand the overall scope and objectives of the project.
- Hold regular project team review meetings.
- Use structured walk-throughs.
- Invite comments and suggestions concerning the project.

People responsible for controlling projects have a duty to develop the skills, experience, and confidence of those who are working for them. Staff should be given work appropriate to their experience, preferably erring on the side of stretching their skills, but with adequate monitoring.

Staff appraisals should be conducted regularly. More important, praise and/or point out weaknesses to staff immediately, while the circumstances are still fresh in everyone's mind. This approach is far more constructive and effective than retrospective discussions.

Project Conclusion and Turnover

If the project was planned correctly and user involvement has been adequate, the installation of the system and the transfer of support responsibility should proceed smoothly.

It is a specific responsibility of the project director and project manager to satisfy themselves, before allowing a system to be installed, that:

- All stages of testing, including acceptance testing, have been completed properly.
- Adequate user procedures have been prepared and the users are trained to the required level and want to work with the system positively.

- The MIS department is prepared to run the system.
- All required controls and security procedures are in place.

Quality Assurance

QA is an ongoing effort throughout the development cycle and system use. It should include the following activities:

- Formulation of system and programming standards.
- Examination of system design documentation to ensure that it has been prepared in accordance with prescribed standards and that the new system has incorporated adequate functions for effective control.
- Review of program testing, system testing, and parallel or pilot runs to ensure adequacy and compliance with standards.
- Review of data conversion procedures for adequacy and compliance with standards.
- Affirmation that system and programming practice is in accordance with standards.
- Assurance that adequate controls, security procedures, and audit trails are specified and built into the finished application.

QA reviews may be performed by the internal audit department, external auditors, or an independent QA group.

CHAPTER **23**

System Development Methodology and Auditing

A SYSTEM DEVELOPMENT METHODOLOGY

Introduction

Although a wide variety of system development methodologies exist, they all include essentially the same phases during the development life cycle. These phases may (and do) overlap and can be defined with varying degrees of accuracy.

The system development methodology given here is a model of good current practice. It is based on SUMMIT-D, a proprietary method used by Coopers & Lybrand in its worldwide system consulting practice. (An overview of the modules making up SUMMIT-D is shown in Figure 23-1.)

The phases identified and explained in this section are fairly standard and sufficiently generic to apply to most circumstances. Each phase is briefly explained, together with a list of typical tasks and a description of the main product (key deliverable) resulting from that phase.

System Requirements Analysis

Overview. The System Requirements Analysis determines the business or functional requirements to be supported by the proposed system. Initially, no attempt should be made to distinguish between manual and automated components of the system or to dictate how automation might be achieved. Once an adequate definition of the requirements is reached, alternative approaches can be identified and evaluated. Alternatives may include "build or buy" or differing extents to which processes and data should be automated. The impact of alternate solutions in terms of effort, cost, and risks incurred can then be assessed before a solution is recommended. If a solution based on the use of purchased application software products is feasible, the Product Evaluation and Recommendation phase may be initiated to identify and evaluate available products.

Tasks. Typical tasks are:

- Confirm, or prepare, the scope, objectives, and essential background of the project. These would be the project charter and enterprise description described under project planning. The confirmation is particularly important if there has been a significant delay.
- Establish user needs through direct interview and through a study of existing systems. Use of the Team Analysis/Joint Application Design technique is also possible.

FIG. 23-1
System development methodology

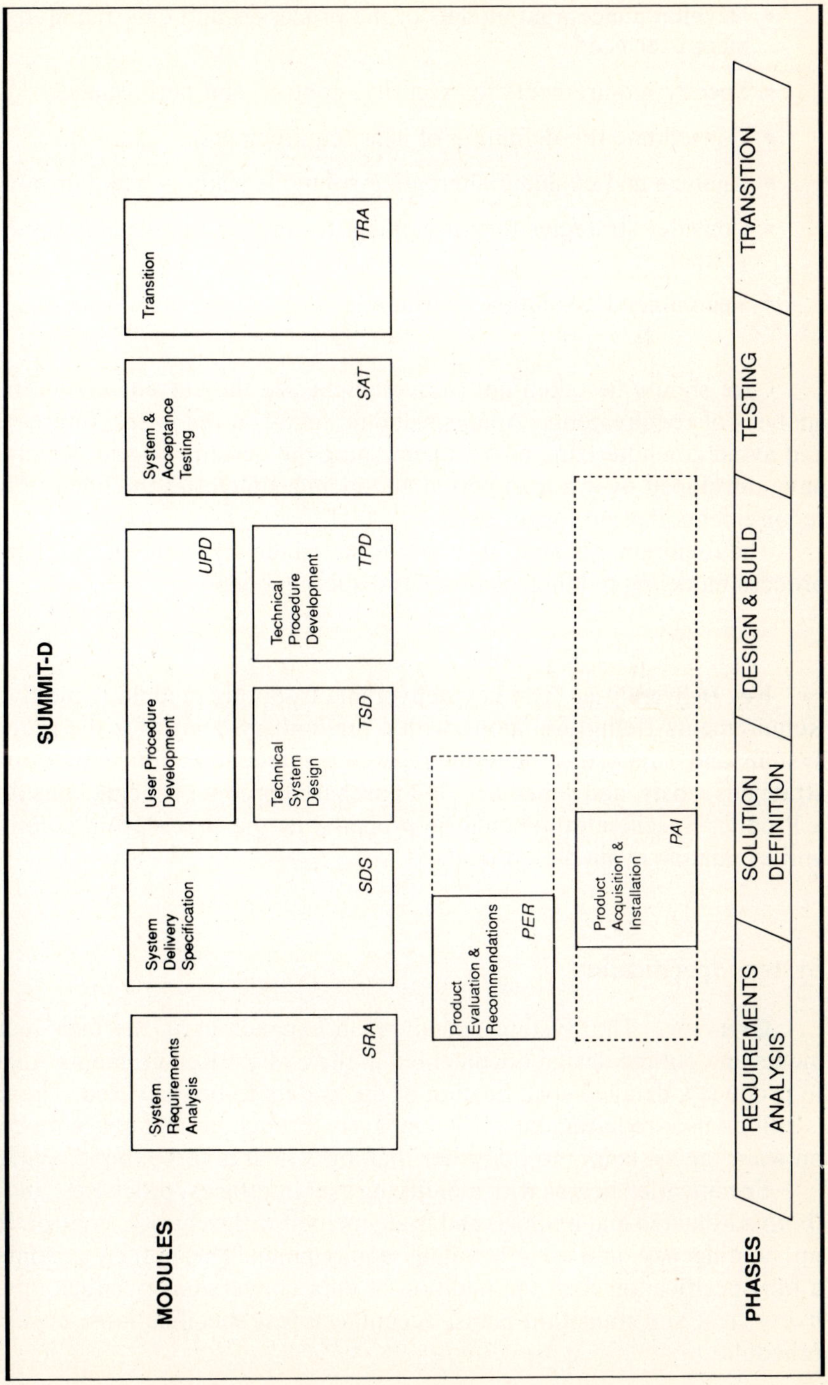

- Develop conceptual models of the processes and data required to meet user needs.
- Specify requirements for security, control, and performance.
- Consolidate the definition of user requirements.
- Analyze and evaluate alternative solutions such as make or buy.
- Consider strategies for developing, testing, and implementing the system.
- Recommend a solution alternative.

Care should be taken not to overemphasize the current system in the analysis of requirements. Analysts should focus on the user's future needs and avoid computerizing or reimplementing the current system, which may have developed over a long period and includes facilities intended to fulfill requirements that no longer exist.

The requirements analysis phase is suited ideally to the use of data and process modeling techniques described subsequently.

Key Deliverables. The key deliverable from this module is the System Requirements Definition, along with a preliminary design for the proposed system and supporting material regarding implementation and transition strategies, costs, and schedules. If a purchased product is being considered, a Product Specification should be prepared as the first step in identifying and evaluating available products.

System Specification

Overview. The System Specification expands upon the user requirements and outline design documented in the System Requirements Analysis to produce a detailed specification of the system to be delivered. The focus is still on user requirements. The emphasis throughout this phase module is on *what* the system is to do rather than on *how* it is to be implemented.

Specification begins with identifying user interfaces, processes, and data (both automated and manual) and is augmented with security, control, backup, contingency, and error handling requirements. This is then expanded to a full specification with the addition of data conversion specifications, delivery, test and transition plans, acceptance test specifications, costs, and schedules.

Tasks. Typical tasks are:

- Define the interfaces between the user and the system, such as screen layouts, screen dialogues, report layouts, and input forms. The emphasis is on user requirements while recognizing any known technical limitations. Prototypes should be used, whether pencil and paper representations or interactive screen-based simulations.
- If necessary, partition the system into functional subsystems consisting of processes and data.
- Define manual and automated processes and how interfaces will work.
- Specify data structures and content.
- Specify error handling, security, control, backup, and contingency procedures.

Key Deliverables. The key deliverable is the System Specification, which becomes the definitive specification for all subsequent design and build activity. This document must be agreed formally with user management, since it is essential that users understand and commit themselves fully to the proposed system.

Key Considerations. The importance of user requirements in this module cannot be overstated; it is crucial that users are committed to provide a sufficient level of input throughout. Without this commitment it is unlikely that the system will ever be genuinely successful.

If prototyping or other tools and techniques are to be used under this module, they need to be installed and fully available before work starts. (See later section entitled "Purchased Products.") If new techniques are to be used, it is essential that staff has had time to familiarize themselves and, if necessary, received training in these techniques.

Technical Design

Overview. The Technical Design describes how the proposed system is to be built, continuing from the System Specification, which describes how the system will "look" to the user. The design is specific to the technical environment in which the system is to operate. It is constrained by the development environment and tools to be used in building the system. The output of this phase drives the subsequent development of software and operational procedures. The level of detail required depends on the development techniques and tools to be used (e.g., programming languages and code generators) and the quality and experience of the development staff.

Tasks. Typical tasks are:

- Establishing the hardware, software, and communications environment within which the system will run.
- Identifying technical constraints imposed by the environment.
- Identifying or preparing the technical standards to be followed for all subsequent design and development.
- Identifying the implementation units (programs or jobs) and specifying the interfaces between them.
- Specifying parameter settings for purchased products.
- Specifying the design of each implementation unit, including hierarchy of modules, user interfaces, and error handling procedures.

Key Deliverables. The key deliverable of this module is the Technical System Design document, which includes:

- Complete definitions of the processes and data bases that comprise the system, ready for subsequent development and implementation.
- Definition of the operational requirements, to support preparation of operations procedures.
- Design and operation procedures for the data conversion system.
- Detailed test plans.

Key Considerations. Very large system delivery projects can be divided into several concurrent and/or overlapping subprojects. The initial phases of Requirements Analysis and Solution Definition should be carried out for the whole project to ensure consistency and successful integration. The concurrent or overlapping subprojects should be confined to the Design and Build, Test, and Transition phases. Hence, Technical System Design could be carried out several times within a single project, each subproject producing its own design specification.

Advances in software engineering and fourth-generation techniques and tools are likely to reduce the emphasis placed on many technical design activities as, increasingly, automated facilities manage the design and development of software.

The technical design should consider future maintenance.

Technical Procedure Development

Overview. This is the program and test activity. It covers the development, unit testing, and integration testing of application software and operational software and procedures. The preparation of the technical environment for development and testing and the training of operations staff are also addressed during this phase.

Tasks. Typical tasks are:

- Review/confirm technical system design, ensuring that the development team is familiar with the technical design and standards to be employed.
- Ensure that adequate facilities are provided to allow development and testing to be carried out effectively.
- Develop and test implementation units.
- Prepare operations procedures for data conversion and installation and production operation of the system.
- Perform integration tests.
- Train operations staff.
- Consolidate all technical documentation.

Key Deliverables. A number of key deliverables are produced during this phase:

- An integrated set of application software ready for system testing.
- Trained operations staff.
- Technical documentation covering all software, procedures, and testing.

Key Considerations. This phase is usually carried out in parallel with the development of user procedures. Communication between the two development processes is essential to ensure that technical procedures and user procedures are consistent, particularly for the user interfaces.

The introduction of fourth-generation and software engineering techniques and tools means that the software development process is becoming increasingly automated, shifting the emphasis away from "traditional" program development and testing. Preparation of operations procedures will continue to be of vital importance to successful system delivery.

All programming should be performed in accordance with programming standards for the specific language being used. Quality assurance procedures should be included to ensure that those standards have been followed. Compliance is essential to ensure smooth maintenance of the future system.

User Procedure Development

Overview. User Procedure Development addresses the preparation of procedures and instructions for system users and training of user staff in those procedures. Procedures for data conversion, transition to the new system, and provision of user resources such as staff, equipment, and consumables are also covered. (Note that EDP and communications operating procedures usually are covered best as part of Technical Procedure Development.)

Tasks. Typical tasks are:

- Prepare user procedures for data conversion, any installation activities to be performed, and production operations.
- Define user resource requirements and initiate procedures to recruit or acquire these resources.
- Prepare user documentation, help screens, and training materials.
- Train user staff.
- Review and rehearse procedures.

Key Deliverables. Key deliverables of this phase are the Approved User Procedures and staff trained in the use of those procedures.

Key Considerations. Work for this module is usually carried out in parallel with Technical Design and Technical Procedure Development. Communication between user procedure developers and staff involved in designing and developing the technical aspects of the system is essential to ensure that technical and user procedures are consistent, particularly for the user interfaces.

It is likely, if not inevitable, that user staff training will not be complete until late in the development process. Indeed, it will continue after implementation of the system. There usually is a need for training of staff new to the system (or parts of it) throughout the life of the system.

It is important that a "core group" of key users be trained fully to take part in system and acceptance testing. All staff who are to use the system immediately following installation (allowing that the system may be introduced gradually, on a department-by-department or similar basis, rather than all at once) should have completed at least basic training programs.

System and Acceptance Testing

Overview. The aim of System and Acceptance Testing is to perform a comprehensive test of the entire system, covering both automated and manual procedures, including data conversion. This test should provide a realistic simulation of the system as it will operate in production. It should include volume tests to assess the performance of the system under realistic peak and average workloads. Pilot and/or parallel runs may be included if required. Formal acceptance should be given by:

- User management, confirming that the system meets their requirements.
- MIS management, accepting the system for future operation and maintenance.
- System auditors, confirming that security and controls are adequate.
- Quality assurance, confirming that the system meets technical standards.

Planning of tests is of paramount importance and begins during the specification and design stages. All parties required to accept the system formally should specify acceptance criteria in advance.

Tasks. Typical tasks are:

- Refine system test plan.
- Create system test environment including test data bases, program libraries, and operating procedures.
- Review version control procedures.
- Perform system test and resolve any problems.
- Prepare acceptance test.
- Prepare production environment for performing acceptance test.
- Perform acceptance test as either pilot runs of the new system or parallel runs with the existing system.
- Accept system.

Key Deliverables. The key deliverable of this phase is the tested, formally accepted, and fully documented new system, ready for installation and production operation.

Key Considerations. System and acceptance tests should cover data conversion as well as the system itself. At least one test cycle should be run on converted "live" data. If pilot and/or parallel runs are to be performed, these will tend to blur the boundary between testing and installation. In the context of parallel running, the old, or existing, system remains the "master" as the new system is run in parallel to check its accuracy.

Transition

Overview. The transition phase deals with the conversion of data and installation of the new system in the production environment. Data conversion includes both automated and manual conversion procedures.

Once installation of new software and procedures is complete, a final formal acceptance of the system is required before the old system is closed down and archived.

Tasks. Typical tasks are:

- Prepare and perform automated data conversion.
- Prepare and perform manual data conversion.
- Get user management to give an acceptance sign-off after the converted data has been checked and any errors corrected.
- Install new procedures.
- Get final acceptance sign-off from management.

Key Deliverables. The key deliverable is the new system, implemented in the production environment with all its software, procedures, data, and documentation.

Key Considerations. Although it is not possible to complete this phase before acceptance testing has been completed, it may be necessary to start the conversion process during an earlier phase. This applies primarily to manual conversion and entry of static data. Dynamic data (e.g., current transactions) usually needs to be converted at the time of installation. Since little data is totally static, it is often necessary to set up interim maintenance procedures to cope with changes occurring between conversion and installation. The need to begin data conversion well in advance of installation is usually due to large volumes of data requiring manual conversion and entry.

It is possible that poor project planning or unforeseen circumstances may delay the implementation date. This can create an environment in which essential controls are bypassed. Any controls or quality assurance steps overridden for important operational considerations should be retrofitted as soon as possible.

Controls Over Conversion

Whenever new systems are ready to be implemented, it is necessary to convert the old master files and suspense files to the new formats, often a data base, so that the system can be put into use. The conversion process, because it is a one-time occurrence and often takes place in a hurry, is susceptible to errors and mistakes. These can have a far-reaching impact, particularly if they occur in converting the master file data. As a result, the conversion process needs to be controlled. In fact, it can be thought of as a mini-application. The normal application control techniques can be applied to ensure the completeness, accuracy, and validity of converted data.

When implementing a new system, the master file data can be loaded for the first time using the future system's normal data input procedures. The new system, of course, should have adequate application controls built into the data change process. Providing that these controls are adequate, the main risk involved is that the controls are being operated by inexperienced people for the first time and in volumes that are higher than normal. Therefore, the entire procedure is more susceptible to errors occurring. The control procedures should be carefully monitored to ensure the correct conversion of the data. When existing systems are changed for new ones, it may also be necessary to load new data. The same considerations apply when the data base change procedures are used.

It may not be practical to convert all the data using the new manual data amendment procedures, whether converting an existing manual or automated system. Account balances and other cumulative transaction data, as well as master file data from existing computer systems, often are converted by computer programs that are written especially for this purpose. These programs may not always be developed and tested with the same care as the new system as a whole. Therefore, there is a particular need to ensure that the conversion process takes place correctly. It is always advisable to test the conversion programs thoroughly. Proper application controls over the conversion process are necessary; they are significant whenever, for any reason, the conversion programs have not been tested. One-for-one checking is a common technique for data entered manually to the new files. It is also commonly applied to data transferred from one file to another, particularly when the data is sensitive and the volume is not too large. At a minimum, when information is transferred from one file to another, control totals should be used for all significant fields. A program should read the existing applications file and establish hash totals for each field on the file. After conversion, these totals should be reconciled independently to similar totals taken from the new file. New data may be added by the conversion programs. The new data should be carefully reviewed and tested. The auditor control technique is to prepare an independent edit program to check the reliability of the wanted data.

Programmed edit checks are valuable control techniques, particularly for controlling the accuracy and the validity of data. Their disadvantage for controlling conversions lies in their complexity and the time necessary to program and test them. However, it is sometimes possible to pass the newly converted data through the edit programs in the new system. This technique should be applied wherever it is feasible. It is not possible to treat all data fields in this way, since the edits in the new system are usually designed to handle input transactions, whereas the conversion process is trying to convert existing master file data and balances. The use of edits is particularly valuable for data that is being collected and used for the first time; data coming from existing manual systems, which tend to be less accurate than well-controlled computer systems; or data that comes from an existing system that is known to be inaccurate in some respects.

Whichever techniques are used, it is always desirable to review the data manually after conversion to ensure that it is valid. This process is similar to the authorization of transactions and should be carried out by someone with sufficient knowledge of the company's operations to be able to notice any substantial errors.

Parallel running may be used to test the operation of the new system, although this is not feasible with most on-line systems. The comparison of the results produced by the new system with the results produced by the old system from the same input may expose some errors on the new master files. The longer the parallel tests are run, the more likely it is that errors on the new file will be picked up. Maintenance controls (over the continued correctness and currency of stored data) may also detect errors on the new file. Although valuable in helping to detect errors, these controls cannot be used as a complete substitute for detailed application controls.

Because of the high risk of error and the potentially significant consequences of those errors, the conversion process is often checked or audited by supervisory personnel, the auditor, a quality assurance group, or a similar function.

Techniques used to check the conversion process include:

- Test checking individual data and records on the new file to the source records.
- The use of audit software or verification programs to look for exceptional or unusual data on the new file.
- The use of audit software or specially developed programs to compare information on the new application files with that on the existing application files, and to report differences.

PURCHASED PRODUCTS

Several different categories of products may be purchased during a system development project, including:

- *Application products* that provide all or part of the application system itself (normally software, but possibly applicable to items of hardware specific to the application such as special-purpose input/output devices).
- *Technology products* that form part of the technical environment necessary either to operate or deliver the required system:
  - —*Operational products* are those that are required to actually run the system in the production environment, such as terminal devices, communications equipment, and data management or security control software.
  - —*Delivery products* are those required during the delivery project itself, such as programming languages, prototyping tools, and workbenches.

The selection and implementation of purchased products should be fully integrated into the development cycle as explained later, in the sections "Product Evaluation" and "Product Installation."

Purchased Applications

The packaged software industry is expected to generate about $25 billion in 1989. This is a huge market, growing rapidly. Contrary to popular belief, some estimate that 70 percent of that market is minicomputer- and mainframe-based, and not at the microcomputer level.

Packaged software is certainly one of the solutions to the application backlog. One of the major trends in software packages today is increased flexibility. At one time, purchased packages came "plain vanilla." Now, when a package is purchased, the buyer gets the equivalent of a packet of flavorings to go with it. Package options allow a mix-and-match approach to package contents, to tailor the system to meet the needs of an organization.

There are also better controls in packages today. This is certainly true for financial accounting packages. However, the controls are also being tied in with the flexibility. In other words, the controls are options within the system. These are better controls, but they can be turned on or off.

Users, too, are demanding compatibility. When users buy a general ledger system and they have DB2 as their data base management system (DBMS), they naturally want a package that is compatible with DB2. They need to maintain compatibility with the growing use of decision support data derived from the transaction processing system—and this can only be done easily if interfaces are compatible.

On a smaller scale, a user may already have a microcomputer spreadsheet package installed. That user will not want to buy a new one in order to obtain a compatible data base. Although an integrated package may be a good idea, what users want is compatibility with their existing products.

There are a number of consequences resulting from this basic trend. When the user community makes a basic buying decision about a particular product, it sets part of the future direction. The trend toward compatibility also suggests that individual users should consider buying what everyone else is buying to be compatible with the community at large.

Especially noticeable in financial accounting packages is the switch from generalized accounting packages to individualized packages with a particular industry focus. Since generalized packages have almost saturated the market, vendors want to increase sales by moving into industry niches. This is a concern to the auditor because the individualized packages will not have as wide a marketplace, and may be rushed to market quickly. The resulting danger could be that these individualized packages will not be as reliable as the generalized packages. It will also require that the auditor learn a large number of special packages.

Application vs. System Software

It is worth distinguishing between application packages and system software. In the past, when an IBM mainframe was purchased, the operating system came with it. No further purchases were necessary. Now an assortment of system software is required, including an operating system, communications software, a DBMS, a tape management system, a security package, a fourth generation language, a scheduler, and numerous other products. There are also a larger number of software vendors and a greater variety of products to choose from. These products are becoming increasingly important as functions and controls move from application software into system software.

Advantages of Packages

Generally, packages are good for systems in common use (e.g., general ledger, payroll). They can reduce the development backlog and implementation cost. With the increasing flexibility being built in, these packages can even take care of some special requirements. For example, McCormack & Dodge's Millennium permits the user to distribute the general ledger system to many subsidiaries or divisions, allowing each one to create its own chart of accounts. Overall, the organization can still benefit from standardization with flexible options allowing decentralized choice.

Potential Risks of Packages

Packages may be more suitable for back-office systems than for strategic systems. A package may not provide a competitive edge, since it does not provide the required level of differentiation.

Packages are easier to select than to implement. Therefore, selecting the package is not the problem—making it work in a business sense is. The organization loses some control over future development. It certainly cannot control the package development directly. The vendor must be trusted to set the appropriate future direction of the package.

Generally, vendors are market-driven. If profits are down, the vendor may not be able to allocate the same resources to user support and software package improvements. This is a cause for concern because in this situation corners often get cut. Will the software be as reliable in the future as it was in the past?

Figure 23-1 is a schematic representation of how product evaluation and installation relate to the other system development phases. Of particular significance is the variation in start and finish points for these activities, depending on the use to which the product will be put.

Product Evaluation

Overview. The purpose of Product Evaluation is to identify, evaluate, and select products and vendors that will be required in the delivery of the proposed system. "Product" in this context refers to an item of hardware or software that can be provided by a third-party supplier.

In the technology product area, this part of the life cycle addresses the selection of hardware and software applicable primarily to the proposed application system. Decisions related to corporate resources such as mainframe computers, communications networks, or DBMS normally should be based on corporate information strategy, rather than the needs of an individual project. This approach to product evaluation may well be suitable for the selection of products to meet corporate requirements, but such decisions are generally considered outside the scope of a system development project.

Product Evaluation is likely to be initiated either during or immediately after the System Requirements Analysis phase for application products; for technology products it may be initiated more flexibly, typically during the System Requirements Analysis, System Specification, or Technical Design phases.

Tasks. Typical tasks are:

- Determine the requirements and constraints for both the application and technology products and identify and rank evaluation criteria. The evaluation criteria may include the following:
  - Cost
  - Availability of support
  - Delivery lead time
  - Ease of use
- Obtain product proposals from vendors. These may be formal proposal documents or, in the case of major reputable vendors, less formal quotations of price, delivery time, and support conditions and terms.
- From the vendor proposals, identify the product or products that most nearly match the defined requirements.
- Recommend the selection of a particular vendor and product and ensure that a detailed specification of the product is available to support further work on the project.

Key Deliverables. The key deliverable of Product Evaluation is a Product Selection (other than in the exceptional case where no product can be found), which usually includes the Product Specification. This forms the key input to the Product Installation phase. However, further details may need to be added to this specification to provide sufficient information to support subsequent stages of the delivery project.

Key Considerations. While the foregoing is structured to address a single product requirement, a typical project may well involve several products. If so, there will be several evaluations, perhaps at different stages of the project. However, when integrating a number of products within an installation, it is often advisable to keep the number of suppliers to a minimum. This will reduce the confusion generated by problems that occur during or after the implementation. Where several products are required, it may be necessary to perform product evaluations in parallel, with the integration of products becoming a key issue in the evaluation process.

In defining the product requirements it is essential to obtain estimates of the likely volumes of data and/or transactions to be handled by the relevant system component, and the required performance (usually stated in terms of response time or run duration). Peak loads should be considered as well as averages.

In the evaluation of supplier proposals, special attention should be paid to costs, particularly in ensuring that all costs have been identified. Cost elements that are sometimes not identified easily include:

- Maintenance (particularly software upgrades when new versions become available).
- Installation support and training.
- Multiple licensing—where software is intended to run on more than one processor (even within the same equipment configuration), there may be multiple license charges.

Product Installation

Overview. Product Installation deals with the acquisition and installation of products supplied by third parties. Products may be hardware, software, or even environmental products such as air conditioning or power supply equipment. They may form part of the application system itself or part of the technical environment required to develop or operate the system. Although this phase is structured to allow for the possibility of acquiring and installing several products at one time, it may also be necessary to repeat parts of the phase several times within the scope of a single project.

Tasks. Typical tasks are:

- Negotiate terms with the vendor and arrange the authorization and placement of purchase orders. If necessary, sign the purchase contract.
- Manage delivery of the product.
- Install environmental, hardware, and software products and perform any necessary integration.
- Perform preliminary installation tuning and acceptance testing.

Key Deliverables. The key deliverables are the installed products and the product installation report, which documents how the product is installed, any problems encountered during installation, and the support procedures for the product.

Key Considerations. Significant delays to projects can be caused by late delivery or faulty installation of products, or even by administrative holdups in placing purchase orders. The actual activities of acquisition and installation often are outside the direct control of the project team. Care should be taken when planning the project that adequate time is allowed for these activities and that contingency plans are included to allow for possible delays. Project managers should try to ensure that these activities are carried out as effectively as possible.

SYSTEM DEVELOPMENT AUDITING[1]

Introduction

As computer systems and applications evolve, it becomes more important for organizations to define standards to control system development. Auditors need information to aid in the review and audit of an organization's system development activity. The auditor should review the methodology used by an organization to monitor and control the system development function. The results of this review enable the internal auditor to determine, at a global level, whether it is appropriate to rely on the system development activity. If so, the auditor can test the development activity of selected applications. If not, all applications developed under the inadequate system development methodology can be considered at risk, since the controls over developing those systems are insufficient. Therefore, the application may be developed inappropriately.

A wide variety of system development methodologies are in use: packaged, internally developed, and a combination of both. The information in this section is generic and should be useful in most circumstances. The review guidelines are structured around standard system development stages to facilitate referencing. Strict adherence to the sequence of events is not advocated. Rather, an overall concept of the stages can be developed and applied to particular circumstances. Auditors should also understand that because some overlap between phases often occurs, they must assess the impact of such concurrent efforts.

---

[1] Extracted and adapted from "System Development Audit Review Guide," © 1986 by Coopers & Lybrand (U.S.A.), published by the Institute of Internal Auditors.

By testing the controls over development of applications under whatever system development methodology is actually employed, the auditor is able to:

- Determine whether reliance can be placed on the system development process and its controls and, if so, possibly reduce the testing of programmed procedures conducted on applications after implementation.
- Ensure that user needs and management objectives are met by the application.
- Confirm that appropriate controls and management trails are incorporated into the design of the application.
- Identify potential problem areas in a timely manner.
- Gain a detailed understanding of the application, and thereby help develop an audit strategy for future review of that application.

Decisions about whether this audit approach is feasible depend in part on an assessment of the adequacy of the methodology, as indicated by the preliminary review, in addition to other factors.

The sequence of events that can be followed includes:

- Conduct a preliminary review of the system development methodology in place to assess how well it is structured, controlled, and documented.
- Based on that assessment, determine whether it is likely that reliance can be placed on those controls.
- Test compliance with the methodology by selecting applications for review on the basis of associated risk and, using the review guidelines provided, verify that controls are operating.
- After testing, determine whether reliance on controls is appropriate and, if so, whether it is possible to reduce the level of audit review work required on the newly developed system.

Where this approach to system development is not appropriate, alternate approaches available to the auditor include:

- Performing a preimplementation review on an application basis, assessing the system controls at some point prior to implementation.
- Placing reliance on program security controls and performing detailed tests on the programmed procedures, preferably before implementation.

- Where no reliance can be placed on program security controls, performing substantive tests on the information generated by the system.

Preliminary Review of the System Development Methodology

The preliminary review of the system development methodology in use should be conducted once. It should be updated periodically for changes as required. If an organization maintains a variety of system development methodologies across application areas, it is necessary to identify how each is used and to complete the preliminary review for each major methodology.

The methodology review is designed to be relatively brief. By its completion, the auditor should be able to:

- Establish whether the organization is using a controlled and structured approach to monitoring the system development activity.
- Assess the usefulness of the methodology from an audit and control viewpoint.
- Determine at a global level whether it appears to be feasible to adopt an approach to the system development activity that relies on controls.

The following outline shows some of the procedures and questions involved in a preliminary review.

General. Obtain access to a copy of the system development methodology used by the organization to monitor the development of new applications or systems. Determine by inquiry whether steps are mandatory or advisory in nature. Determine whether any prior evaluations have been performed on the methodology; if so, review them for background information.

Through observation and inquiry of relevant personnel, and review of available evidence, determine whether:

- The methodology, as documented, is up-to-date, developers are trained in its use, and systems are being designed in compliance with it.
- There are any concerns expressed within the organization about the methodology as it exists.
- Deviations from the formal methodology are permitted, and if so:

— Are the reasons for deviations adequately documented and alternatives identified?
— Are the deviations formally approved?

Note that if the frequency of deviations from the methodology is unusually high, the auditor should reassess the rationale for, or the benefits derived from, evaluating system development activities.

Structure. By inquiry and review of documentation, evaluate the effectiveness of the system development methodology, as follows:

- Is it formually structured into phases and modules that each yield a measurable end product and cover the following areas (or their equivalent):
  — Feasibility (including cost/benefit analysis)?
  — System requirements analysis (including functional specifications)?
  — Product evaluation and recommendation?
  — System specification (including general design)?
  — Technical design?
  — Product acquisition and installation?
  — Technical procedure development?
  — User procedure development?
  — System acceptance and testing?
  — Transition (operations and maintenance)?
- Are there major status points at each designated phase that require formal documentation to:
  — Evidence a review and approval function conducted by officials from user, data processing, and quality assurance departments (where appropriate)?
  — Indicate that a stage has been successfully completed?
  — Enable an ongoing evaluation of project status for costs and meeting the established schedules?
  — Reach a decision to continue with the project or terminate it?
- Is emphasis placed on the importance of incorporating security and controls into systems being developed, thus ensuring that they exist and are consistent with management objectives?
- Are planning requirements for subsequent phases clearly identified?

- Does the methodology incorporate controlling changes in requirements that may occur over the life of the project?

Participation. Has a data processing steering committee been established to supervise the system development process, assign priorities to projects, and resolve problems as they arise? Does it include senior officials from the following departments:

- Corporate management (responsible for business strategy and objectives)?
- Users?
- Data processing?
- Internal audit?
- Quality assurance?

Does the system development methodology formally recognize participation of the following groups in the development process:

- Users?
- Data processing?
- Quality assurance?
- Internal audit?

Have responsibilities been formally established in each designated phase for those participant groups?

Are the roles and responsibilities of the members of the data processing project team or its equivalent clearly defined (system analyst, system designer, programmer, technician, data analyst, data base administrator)?

To ensure that the needs of users and the organization are met at each phase, does the methodology provide sufficient opportunities for:

- User involvement?
- Communication among users, system developers, and auditors?

Do well-defined, written standards exist to facilitate adequate documentation of:

- An understanding of the objectives of the system and concepts employed?
- Information necessary for all personnel responsible for maintaining, enhancing, and running the system?

- A basis for training new personnel?
- The structure of security and controls in the system?
- Information required by computer operations personnel to run the system?

Are requirements for program, user, system, and operations documentation for each phase adequate and clearly identified?

Do well-defined, written standards exist for programming, including:

- The use of conventions regarding syntax, format, logic, discipline, and naming conventions?
- Incorporation of comments in source code to document the logic and structure of programs?

Scope. Has the methodology incorporated considerations for the following:

- Data base environments?
- Telecommunications?
- Networking?
- Distributed processing?
- End-user computing?
- Prototyping?
- Packaged software selection and implementation?

Audit Documentation and Planning. Prepare audit workpapers to evidence review work performed.

Formally document an assessment of how well the methodology is structured, controlled, and documented and of whether it is likely that:

- Reliance can be placed on the controls in operation and a compliance approach adopted.
- Reliance cannot be placed on the controls in operation.

Where an approach based on controls is adopted, select applications for review on the basis of financial significance and associated risk, and test compliance with that methodology.

Where reliance cannot be placed on the methodology, is it possible to:

- Conduct a preimplementation review?
- Rely on program security controls and perform substantive tests of implemented programmed procedures?
- Not rely on program security controls and perform substantive testing of financial information generated by new system?
- Develop a suitable combination of the preceding items to achieve defined objectives?

System Development Review Guidelines

The system development review guidelines consist of detailed questions and audit procedures that can be completed at various stages of an application's development. To facilitate referencing, these guidelines are structured around the same system development phases previously discussed. The request for system design is not included as a phase, since it is relatively easy to determine whether appropriate methods exist within the organization to initiate and approve such requests.

A wide variety of system development methodologies exist that may not adhere strictly to the sequence of events assumed in the previous discussion. Accordingly, it may be necessary to complete questions in the various sections at alternate stages in the development process. Regardless of the system development methodology employed, however, these audit review guidelines apply to most situations. As indicated previously, any overlap between phases should be considered as well.

The guidelines assume the use and production of audit documentation normally employed by auditors. The documentation produced should be sufficient to develop an audit strategy and, in some cases, can replace what would normally be developed during postimplementation system work.

Depending on management requirements, it is recommended that reports be produced and forwarded to management at the completion of each phase of the review (however defined under the methodology employed).

Documentation Guidelines

The following are listings of suggested documentation to be collected, reviewed, and/or completed during the various phases of the review. Although a detailed program for each phase is not included here (since one was described previously), the documentation requirements listing does provide an overview of the content of each stage.

1. *Project planning*
    - Project goals

- Outline proposal:
  - Hardware
  - Software
  - Costs and benefits
  - Preliminary schedule
- Current system profile:
  - Deficiencies
- Policies and standards:
  - Information policies and procedures
  - Control and security policies
  - External regulations and laws
- Project plan:
  - Development methodology
  - Milestones
  - Reviews and approvals
  - Team composition

2. *Product evaluation and recommendation*
   - Application and technology product requirements:
     - Product definition
     - Product constraints
     - Evaluation criteria
     - Product requirements
   - Evaluation of vendor proposals:
     - Potential vendors and products list
     - Vendor short list
     - Vendor proposals
     - Product evaluation
   - Recommendations:
     - Product/vendor recommendation
     - Product specifications

3. *Product acquisition and installation*
   - Product specification
   - Authorized purchase orders
   - Hardware installation report
   - Software installation report

4. *User procedure development*
   - User conversion and installation procedures
   - User resource requirements
   - User documentation/procedure manuals, including:

- — Definitions of input fields and user naming conventions, samples of input documents, and procedures for their preparation and submission.
- — Description and samples of reports produced; procedures governing their use, security, review, disposition, and retention (including timing and frequency of distribution).
- — Procedures to be followed to log on/log off the system, and descriptions of screens, menus, and commands to be used.
- — Control techniques to be exercised, including cutoff requirements, reconciliation procedures, error correction, and resubmission.
- — Responsibilities and delegation of duties (such as for converting data to machine-readable form or for resolving errors).
- — General description of the system and programming logic, including critical calculations performed.
- — Graphic representation of the system structure and of the sequence of activities involving both the system and manual operations.
- — Information about the assignment of job priorities and probable turnaround times (for batch-processed transactions).

- User training material

5. *System acceptance and testing*
   - System test design specifications
   - System test case specifications
   - System test documentation
   - Acceptance test plan
   - Version control procedures
   - Production system documentation
   - Test results documentation
   - Error reports
   - Acceptance test documentation

6. *Transition*
   - Conversion plan and actual results
   - System test documentation:
     - — Data file reconciliations
     - — Master file test-checks
     - — Error/exception reports
   - System acceptance documentation
   - Converted data documentation:
     - — Manual

   — Automated
- Consolidated production documentation

These documentation requirements provide an idea of the information that should be obtained and the questions that need to be asked to produce such documentation at each phase of the system development audit. Obviously, the needs of each audit, the resources available to devote to the various phases, and the approach developed are determined in relation to the particular situation.

Design Review Guidelines

One concern that may be critical to an organization is that the software and the system do what management and the users need them to do. Although some auditors do not become involved in evaluating the design of the system itself (as opposed to the design of the controls within the system), many auditors, particularly internal auditors, do. In those situations, the following guidelines can be employed.

1. *Input to the system*

   Examine proposed input forms/screen designs to ensure that:
   - The omission of data is inhibited (e.g., by the use of preformatted screens, forced input, or default responses).
   - The use of the wrong form/screen is inhibited.
   - Adequate authorization is provided where appropriate (e.g., on the source document itself through the matching of fields entered to preauthorized data held on a matching file).
   - The transaction has appropriate identification for subsequent follow-up, where required.
   - The design permits ease of completion (e.g., data sequence is consistent with source data).
   - Data conversion is facilitated (e.g., preprinting or precoding of appropriate common fields, or protected fields).

   To facilitate the early identification and correction of errors, do screen designs provide for both error notification and error correction?

   Has a suitable combination of physical security of terminals and logical security and access control implemented via system software been designed to help enforce application controls and ensure that only authorized transactions can be entered in the system (e.g., operator authority checks, terminal timeouts)?

   Have the following been given consideration for on-line entry applications:

- Safeguards to prevent loss or inaccuracy of data as a result of transmission errors (e.g., answerback, dual transmission)?
- Access controls (terminal IDs, passwords)?
- Controls to cover situations when communication lines to the host computer are down (to ensure that all transactions are subsequently entered)?
- Security (e.g., logging of screen transmissions)?
- Provision to cancel transactions?
- Security code display suppression?

2. *Processing considerations*

Has the effect (if any) of statutory or legal restrictions, SEC requirements, and generally accepted accounting principles (GAAP) been incorporated into the design where necessary?

Has the design incorporated (where necessary) considerations for the interface between the proposed system and existing system? Identify the extent of the interface.

If an interface with an existing system has previously been identified:

- Does the design appear to be complete?
- Is there an adequate management trail between systems?
- Have adequate control procedures been designed to ensure that information transferred between systems is both complete and accurate?

Determine by inquiry and examination of design documentation whether each transaction master record and report has a unique ID and therefore can be subsequently traced through all stages of processing.

Using information gained in response to the previous item, can specific items of data be traced backward and forward through the processing cycle?

Review the detailed design of management trails to determine whether the following items are included, so that the actual sequence of events can be reconstructed:

- The event causing the entry.
- Date and time of occurrence.
- Application program concerned.
- Transaction sequence number.
- User and terminal involved.
- New value and old value.
- Name of the data object concerned.

Is the design of the management trail such that:

- It is transparent to the process and to the people using the process being audited?
- Where recording of events can be selectively or dynamically started or stopped, this action is recorded elsewhere?

3. *Output from the system*

   Review the proposed output reports and screens:

   - Do they appear complete?
   - Is the right information grouped together on screens?
   - Are the content and format of reports adequate for management purposes (e.g., page numbering, understandability)?
   - Is an audit trail provided?
   - Have the output requirements of users been met (e.g., by categorization or summarization)?
   - From a control perspective, is there sufficient information to evaluate the performance of application controls that ensure the completeness and accuracy of data, processing, and authorization (e.g., the reconciliation of control totals)?

   Have provisions been made for the authorization of users who are to receive reports produced by the system?

   Does the design of output leave no doubt about its contents, periods, origination, destination, and level of confidentiality?

   Have the retention period and storage requirements for reports and files been considered?

4. *Telecommunications considerations*

   Through inquiry of relevant personnel, identify the major components of the telecommunications system to be used, including:

   - Teleprocessing monitor (e.g., CICS or IMS/DC).
   - Transmission path (e.g., wire, cable, microwave, satellite, coaxial cable, fiber optics).
   - Terminals (e.g., dumb, smart, intelligent, storage).
   - Communications controller.

   Has adequate consideration been given to the physical security of telecommunications lines and devices (e.g., modems, terminals, controllers)?

   Does the design of the system prevent abnormal and conflicting conditions, such as a user being able to sign on twice?

   Where dial-up access is used, determine whether:

   - Dial-up modem numbers for authorized personnel are confidential.
   - Procedures have been documented for the changing of modem phone numbers at regular intervals.

- Procedures have been established for the periodic inspection of communications for illegal devices.
- Appropriate dial-up transmission controls are in place (e.g., automatic call-back).

Have appropriate controls, such as the following, been incorporated into the design of the system to prevent transmission errors, losses, delays, or duplication of data:

- Communications line routing?
- Line conditioning?
- Automatic store and forward?
- Automatic dial backup?
- Modem loop-back switches?
- Forward error correction?
- Validity check?
- Echo checking?
- Message intercept function?
- Packet switch networks (where applicable)?

Review the telecommunications software in use to determine whether it provides for the following:

- Encryption of critical data.
- The logging of message transmission information, such as:
  - —Terminal ID number.
  - —Sequence number (of transmission).
  - —Date.
  - —Time.
  - —Transaction type (to what system).
  - —Screen number.
- Backout and restart.

Where encryption techniques are to be employed for the storage and transmission of critical data, determine whether:

- Encryption devices, keys, and algorithms will be protected from unauthorized access.
- Encryption software is secure.
- Keys are adequately controlled.

Review proposed backup procedures to determine whether they are adequate (including backup modems, power sources, lines, and so forth).

5. *Data base considerations*

Identify the type of proposed (or existing) data base environment (where applicable) by obtaining access to descriptions of the following:

- DBMS (e.g., IMS, IDMS).
- Data dictionary/directory or its equivalent if in use or, if not, the method proposed to store and control data definitions.
- Teleprocessing monitor.
- Proposed conceptual views of the data base (defining the logical data structure and physical storage).
- Any third-party products being used (e.g., monitoring tools and utilities).
- The structure of the data base (hierarchical, network, relational).

Through inquiry of relevant data processing personnel, determine which applications use (or intend to use) the data base.

Review evidence to verify that responsible officials have determined what information is to be maintained on the data base.

For the DBMS software identified previously, determine through inquiry of appropriate data processing personnel whether features exist to:

- Prevent concurrent updates of the same data element.
- Resolve data access "deadlocks" (including a description of how this is achieved and the method used to resolve problems).
- Ensure that events are executable only in a predetermined sequence.

Is the data dictionary active (i.e., integrated into the DBMS operation so that it is possible to gain access to DBMS-controlled data only through the data dictionary) or passive (not required to gain access and, therefore, used only as a standard documentation tool)? If passive, is it kept current?

By review of available evidence and discussion with appropriate personnel, verify that the data base administrator has been involved at this stage to ensure specifically that:

- The proposed application can be integrated into the existing data base structure (or, if not appropriate, that modifications to either are feasible) and is in line with data base capabilities.
- Application processing will preserve the consistency, reliability, and integrity of the data base.

Where a new data base environment is being developed, determine whether:

- Appropriate user responsibilities have been defined to provide data integrity.
- All parties potentially affected by the proposed data base have been consulted about its general design.
- Generally accepted rules regarding common formats and conventions have been established to facilitate data sharing and reduce data redundancies.

Has the data base been structured to permit flexibility and to accommodate the following:

- Change (such as modularity to reduce the need for costly reorganization)?
- Increases in the volume of data being processed?
- Satisfaction of end-user needs (by multiple views of the data base)?

Where the new application requires significant changes to be made to the existing data base, review evidence to verify that these have been approved by a responsible official.

Where programs are being designed to update, modify, or delete data from a data base, ensure that special consideration has been given to the following:

- Edit and validation controls.
- DBMS return code processing and other error procedures.

Have procedures been designed to ensure that all users will be notified immediately when inaccurate or incomplete data conditions are identified?

In relation to data base security:

- Have all potential data base users been identified?
- Have user profiles been designed appropriately, defining access rights to data and/or resources?

Obtain a copy of the proposed data dictionary (or its equivalent) and identify data elements of audit significance. Does it include, at a minimum, the following:

- Data element name?
- Narrative definition?
- Aliases (if applicable)?
- Format (e.g., signed, alphabetic, numeric, size)?
- Source?
- Destination?
- Individual responsible for correctness?
- Individual responsible for authorizing access?
- Relationship to other data elements?
- Programs that access the element and type of access (inquiry, update)?
- Data validation rules?
- Reports on which the element appears?

For the application under review, verify that:

- Individuals assigned responsibility for data elements have authorized the use of those elements by the application.

- Unique logical views exist for each program within the application.
- The design incorporates appropriate methods to ensure correct cutoff processing of key financial transactions at the close of significant accounting periods.
- Controls are appropriate to ensure the correct sequencing of updates to the data base where out-of-sequence processing will have a significant effect on the financial statements.

Is each logical view identified previously designed to:

- Permit the application to access only the data elements and functions necessary to perform specified tasks?
- Specify the type of access permitted (e.g., to read, to write)?

Auditing systems under development is an area of interest and concern to both internal and external EDP auditors. While the aspects to be considered vary according to the situation, many elements of the review remain the same. This section has presented some of those elements to offer a better understanding of the process.

CHAPTER **24**

End-User Computing

OVERVIEW

Constant technological change makes systems easier to use. As a result, end-user computing (EUC) is growing steadily as users employ local computing power. With the backlog of projects awaiting traditional development within management information system (MIS) departments and users' desires for direct control, EUC is also spreading rapidly. There are various types of EUC activities.

Small computers are bringing in-house computer processing ability to small and medium-size businesses and to individual departments in larger organizations that, in the past, relied on manual methods. The potential for improved efficiency, quality, and timeliness of information is an important computer advantage. Additionally, small computers help:

- Satisfy the increasing need to analyze data, produce reports, and respond to queries.
- Meet changing requirements, including information needs and temporary, "throw-away" systems created to respond to "one-time-only" situations.
- Reduce user/MIS conflicts, while providing users with more direct operational control.
- Shorten the development cycle.
- Reduce the load on central MIS, possibly reducing the request backlog.
- Match a decentralized corporate style.
- Respond to unique needs of individuals, or departments with few users and low volumes that normally are too small for traditional system development.

The change from manual to automated processing can be problematic when users have little or no understanding of how to choose, design, or control computers and computer systems in operation, or to assess software packages. In smaller businesses where manual control systems traditionally have been weak, there may be too few staff members to allow controls such as division of duties to be set up over a small computer system, even when the need for control is known and understood.

It is helpful to consider controls and risks from two perspectives—company or departmental management and user.

MANAGEMENT RISKS AND ISSUES

Organizational experience may not apply to new technologies and changing environments. Adhering to familiar methods without recognizing the need for change to cope with EUC systems can pose the risk of management's inadvertent reliance on inappropriate data. Since the output from microcomputers often resembles that of traditional, controlled systems, this can be a real problem.

Data integrity and correctness of processing results are major concerns, among many issues that can have an impact on the organization. The attitude toward EUC and related acquisitions can have a profound influence on corporate goals. Some issues of concern follow.

Strategic Issues

With the high cost of EDP systems and their strategic business advantage when developed appropriately, a sound corporate information architecture is vital to good organizational planning. In some businesses, it is critical to success.

To ensure compliance with overall corporate guidelines, it is important to have a plan that encompasses microcomputer and other EUC considerations. Planning for corporate information-sharing and the creation and use of departmental data is also critical. Corporate management should require that local management designate someone to ensure that local systems meet corporate needs. To accomplish this, the following should be considered:

- The long-term impact of purchasing decisions.
- The operating needs of individual units in relation to the overall plan.
- Whether strategic and long-term goals are being met.
- Whether key management decisions will be based on this system's information, or models produced by the system.
- Provision for adequate controls over sharing of department data.
- Corporate use of the systems.
- Possible duplication of another system already available in the organization.

Organizational Issues

The dispersed nature of EUC limits the effectiveness of many traditional controls. Often, MIS is not involved in the decision-making and approval process. Problems arise regarding enforcement of standards, management assurance that its intentions are executed; and excessive user autonomy.

Uninformed supervision and lack of direction in user departments may exacerbate problems, caused by:

- No EDP/MIS management experience.
- Poor appreciation of the risks.
- Short experience with end-user computing.
- No common body of knowledge of risks and required controls.
- Executive "computerphobia."
- Overenthusiastic users tackling inappropriate tasks.
- Desire for technology without a business need.
- Inappropriate delegation of decisions.

Erosion of corporate data base integrity becomes an issue if users maintain local data bases that feed it. When data from local data bases updates a central data base, or local users share their data base, the data itself may not be controlled properly.

Often, new users responsible for maintaining EUC systems and data have little appreciation of the need for controls. Fragmentation of systems raises questions of responsibility and data ownership—For example, who coordinates between the users of a shared system? Who fixes user-created problems?

Control Issues

Poor controls can result in bad data, erroneous software logic, use of improper assumptions or models, inadvertent reliance on inaccurate or incorrect data, inadequate exception and error handling, inconsistent data, and incomplete information trails.

Inconsistent Data. Inconsistent data is data created in different ways or with different assumptions which is subsequently used as if it were the same. It can result in inconsistent cutoffs, meaningless comparisons of data, and difficult or meaningless consolidations of data. This raises the question: How reliable is data interchange between departments?

Incomplete Information Trails. Incomplete information trails can result in the inability to exercise "after the event" controls (which are perhaps the most common and effective for EUC) and can inhibit the proper investigation of problems.

Poor System Change Controls. Poor system change controls, before and after development, raise other control issues. Frequently, the result is errors in the system and possible questions of which version of software is correct. When system changes are not tested and documented properly, repairing damage and fixing problems can become formidable tasks.

Poor Documentation. If high-quality documentation is not created or maintained, risk increases. Whenever a key person who knows the system leaves the firm, or changes departments, system changes may be difficult, expensive, or impossible to make. Such systems may rely too heavily on one person's ability to maintain the system "in their head." Obviously, systems are not maintainable without good documentation.

Poor Security. Poor security arises when users not accustomed to standard MIS controls fail to recognize the need for appropriate security measures. Without logical and physical controls over access, unauthorized updating of corporate data bases, misuse or destruction of data, and/or loss of confidentiality can result. Many privacy restrictions are based on federal rulings. Therefore, leaving data files open to "browsing" can have a more severe impact than users might expect.

Inadequate Backup and Recovery Procedures. Inadequate backup and recovery procedures can lead to data being unavailable, or the inability to recreate a system and/or its data. Often, new users are hard to convince of the need to back up data until they have the experience of losing hours, or weeks, worth of work. Whatever the need, if backups do not exist, the costs of recreating the data can be high.

Software Piracy. Software piracy is a risk. Users may not understand that copying certain software is illegal. Negative organizational exposure can result from the adverse publicity resulting from legal actions by vendors. Users should be well-informed about the consequences of such actions, and acknowledge that understanding in writing.

Practical, cost-effective control solutions may seem hard to find. However, overly rigid control solutions may be worse than the original problems. Compliance with corporate and external standards cannot be achieved without user cooperation. Frequently, when aware of the legal exposures and control risks, users are more amenable to controls. When controls are imposed without education and understanding, users may feel there is an attempt to stifle creativity and suppress their use of EUC in general.

Technology Issues

The most important issue may be compatibility. Users often acquire systems for their own use without adequate consideration of issues. Potential ramifications include:

- Incompatible systems and/or data structures.
- Networks not able to talk to each other.
- Mainframes, minicomputers, and microcomputers unable to use the same software.
- Software from different vendors may make data transfer difficult or impossible, increasing user relearning time and complicating maintenance and support.

Often, practical solutions to such issues are not found in the very latest technology. Even user-friendly software still requires learning and skill for effective use. Such user-friendly solutions may require intensive use of hardware and other resources, overloading MIS and increasing hardware costs. Untrained users may expend misdirected energy learning as they go. Enthusiasm for technology without a business need often leads to inappropriate choices.

Uninformed users face risks from software obtained without going through official channels. Examples include untested software downloaded from bulletin boards. Some of this software is dangerous, as it can include viruses and other hidden instructions that can damage the system or compromise security.

Cost Issues

When new users become almost obsessed with computing, inefficient use of time becomes a cost issue. Too much time is spent developing systems and too little addressing the original business need. As these enthusiasts head in the wrong direction, they can waste much of an organization's time and money.

Users may select inappropriate methods for a particular task. An example is trying to create a complex transaction-based accounting system using a spreadsheet, when even opting to build, instead of buying, an accounting package is a mistake.

Other cost and efficiency issues include:

- Duplication of efforts and/or data.
- Functionally rich, but uneconomic solutions.

- Increased user training and support costs.
- Difficulty in estimating the actual hardware, software, and personnel costs.
- Unknown total MIS costs when managers include computers and software in department budgets, without following standard MIS channels.
- Loss of discounts and other benefits of volume purchases.
- Hidden costs of users' time for do-it-yourself learning, mistakes, and retries.
- Difficulty allocating centralized support costs.

The less rigid or nonexistent cost/benefit evaluation can present a problem. Different criteria may be used to create estimates, and the risk of inappropriate choices and unnecessary purchases increases. It is even worse when there is no cost/benefit analysis at all. Once the system is in use and real needs become known, the hardware and software might be wrong for the environment. As needs change, entire systems may need to be replaced.

MANAGEMENT CONTROL OF MICROCOMPUTERS

Most of the following recommendations are appropriate to the more formal environments typical of large organizations. In smaller organizations, a subset should be used, along with direct staff supervision.

Education

Education may be the single most effective control mechanism. Experience shows that after initial training, update sessions and user groups are good ways of maintaining awareness.

Training programs should orient users to risks and demonstrate that controls fulfill an obvious, agreed-upon need. Users who have experienced the effects of poor controls may help others understand the need for control. Management should be trained in long-term organizational needs.

To develop effective programs, a plan containing a strategic information architecture, as well as the responsibility for coordinating information resource management, should be established. Someone should monitor changing technology, set long- and short-term EUC goals, plus review plans and current practices, and assess ongoing risks and exposures of EUC, including:

- What types of applications are in use?
- How sensitive are those applications?
- Wha are the main risks associated with each type?
- How will risks change in the future?

Guidelines and Policies

There should be clear organizational standards for hardware and software acquisition, to ensure compatibility in:

- Communications.
- Data sharing.
- Transferring data between computers.

Clear standards, guidelines, and policies help:

- Prevent software piracy.
- Develop methods of making cost-based decisions and establish charging guidelines.
- Define responsibilities and accountability for:
  - — Data ownership.
  - — System integrity.
  - — Support.
  - — Standards and monitoring.

Guidelines should assist users in developing appropriate controls, backup procedures and contingency plans, application development (including user-developed reports and spreadsheets), security, confidentiality, and privacy. Potential risks should be evaluated, and users trained in applying preventive controls.

Guidelines and policies must be concise. Voluminous guidelines tend to be ignored and become outdated. Simple control techniques are automatic or easy to use. Users often resist attempts to control their work. Therefore, overly restrictive control procedures may be ignored.

Once established, guidelines and policies should be communicated and awareness training conducted. Users who understand how poor controls can affect their work will follow procedures, as shown by the fact that they will almost always do so after personal work was lost due to a system problem, with no backup. Good training can create this awareness without the bad experience.

The use of EUC can be assimilated into the organization by:

- Including planning and budgeting in the normal budget process.
- Tracking expenditures.
- Expanding traditional SDLC to include EUC systems considerations.
- Monitoring compliance and effectiveness by emphasizing the importance of an operating manager's supervision, as well as internal audit's role (or an alternate quality review process).

Classifying Systems

An organization should classify systems and customize control requirements for each level of risk, while realizing that critical applications may not be suitable for EUC. Possibilities include classifying:

- Systems by risk.
- Systems by organizational impact.
- Systems by key output.
- Each end-user computer by critical application.

It is also important to distinguish between centrally controlled and end-user computing reports. This can be done by printing those reports on different-colored paper and/or labeling centrally controlled reports as "controlled."

Classifying Systems by Risk. Confidentiality of corporate information requires tight security. Therefore, it is important to evaluate what EUC systems are being used to do. Privacy requirements of personal data require tight security, including provisions for the individual's right to review.

Key business functions being performed by end-users (such as customer service) usually require formal control procedures for:

- Accuracy, completeness, and validity of data.
- Reliable processing.
- Regular backup and recovery.
- Disaster recovery.

Classifying Systems by Organizational Impact. External reporting usually requires formal control procedures, including:

- Accuracy and reliability of results.
- Mandated requirements (regulatory and external audit).
- Fraud protection.
- Risk of embarrassment and adverse publicity.
- Internal audits or other independent reviews.

Organizational and/or corporate-wide systems must reconcile multiple users and departments. These systems may not be appropriate for end-user developments. Their characteristics include:

- Highly integrated
- Complex
- Long-term
- High volume

Generally, such systems are not susceptible to personal supervisory controls and require formal control procedures. They are best developed by professionals.

Departmental systems have a medium-scale impact on the organization. Characteristics include:

- Meeting a functional need.
- Usually having medium-term as opposed to long-term impact.
- Possible interfacing with corporate systems.

Those systems can be controlled by personal supervision within a department or other departments, although they require some level of formal controls. In addition, they can be developed or purchased by either professionals or users. Departmental systems are most likely to be misused within EUC. The role and responsibility of the department head are critical to avoiding such misuse.

Individual systems have the lowest potential organizational impact. Characteristics include:

- Diversity
- Simplicity
- Short-term impact
- Low volume

They are susceptible to personal control by their users and often are user-developed or purchased. Some could become departmental systems. Minimal formal controls are needed unless they become a formal departmental or organizational system.

Classifying Systems by Key Output. One way to classify systems is through how their reports and other output are used. For example, consider the output of three systems: (1) purchase orders, (2) checks in payment of purchases, and (3) a report comparing money spent to budget. Those who really know an organization probably are able to evaluate criticality by looking at such output.

Classifying Each System by Critical Application. Another evaluation process (similar to classifying a system by its output) is to look at each system's processing abilities. The organizational impact that could result from major weaknesses in security and access to the system and its programs should be assessed.

CREATING AN EFFECTIVE INFORMATION CENTER

An effective information center (IC), or development center, serves as an internal corporate resource for support of EUC techniques, helping users achieve their goals quickly and reliably. Alternate methods of achieving a support structure may be used, depending on organizational skills and resource availability.

An effective information center includes:

- Training.
- Advice and consulting (including a hot-line or help desk for troubleshooting and application development consulting).
- Recommendations on procedures (control guidance).
- Standards for information-sharing.
- Central data management (if creating input to a mainframe data base).
- Hardware and software recommendations (including purchasing assistance, contract negotiation, and hardware and software tryouts).
- Installation assistance.
- Arranging for backup equipment and loaners.

- Assistance with furniture and office layouts.
- Supplies (paper, diskettes, ribbons, etc.).
- Repairs and maintenance.
- A users' club (including solution-sharing and newsletters).

In addition, an effective IC increases the knowledge and effectiveness of its users, thereby reducing costly mistakes. It helps to reduce duplication of effort, inefficiencies, and compatibility problems, as well as encouraging compliance with key controls and applicable legal requirements.

Further advantages include providing information to executive management on progress, problems, and planning. An effective IC makes for a higher level of vendor support. Generally, this includes easier access to the vendor, who is more responsive to known, larger clients. With all purchases coordinated centrally, the IC can magnify vendor support.

An effective IC is most important in the early years of EUC. After that, use declines, as does the IC's ability to influence direction. An alternative for small businesses may be to join a local user group.

SECURITY

Security is a major issue, since uninformed users rarely understand risks. Protection is needed for confidentiality of proprietary, personal, or otherwise sensitive data. However, the system cannot be slowed or degraded to the point where users feel frustrated by processing delays. Giving people the access to systems and data while maintaining full data integrity and accuracy can make it hard to provide adequate security.

Protection is needed against people both inside and outside the organization. As local data volumes and dependence on computing grow, so does the need for security. Protection costs money, takes time, and may restrict the free flow of information and slow productivity. Protection can create bottlenecks in times of crisis. For example, if everyone is working late on a major proposal and the computer is locked, key data may be unavailable. Practical, cost-effective security must be in use, automatic, and nonintrusive.

Security is an organizational concern, not an individual problem. There should be appropriate guidelines; it is important that everyone in the organization think about security. For example:

- Unusual activity should be challenged.
- Corporate security functions should be used and procedures followed.

- A designated security administrator should maintain a record of all security schemes and passwords, identify sensitive areas, and recommend appropriate, cost-effective, and preventive measures periodically.
- Employees should not be permitted to use unnecessary or unauthorized security, particularly since it may hide their own illicit activity.
- Senior management should set a good example.

Other security precautions include the need to:

- Restrict access to the office and not let visitors enter without identification or supervision.
- Lock up machines or keyboards.
- Use a password system.
- Protect key files with a simple file encryption system. (Some software packages include encryption for sensitive data.)
- Hide or remove dangerous utilities like FORMAT (which can completely wipe out a hard or floppy disk).
- Keep at least one copy of keys, as well as of protection schemes, secured in a safe place.
- Protect passwords. Do not store them in an easily accessible place or code them into communications software sign-on sequences where anyone can use them.

Another security consideration is unknown copies of sensitive data. The typical delete utility does not erase data; it just erases the pointer to the file. The data can still be read by someone with advanced computer skills or a copy of a utility package that recovers deleted files.

Special utilities are available to erase data from a disk completely. Another technique is to delete the file by copying a bigger, nonsensitive file into the file (thereby overwriting the sensitive data) and then deleting the file. However, the best technique is not to store sensitive data on a hard disk.

Other possibilities for unknown copies of sensitive data include:

- A print buffer.
- Software that creates unnoticed temporary copies of files (for example, some word processing programs create backup copies automatically that remain until deleted).

- Paper copies, including trash, test results, program documentation, and paper filing.

Generally, outsiders are less of a problem than insiders. Dismissed employees are a concern during the period before they actually leave. After they leave, questions might still arise, since they know the office layout and procedures—do they have keys? Do they know the passwords?

Security can be penetrated in many ways. If data is worth enough, sophisticated techniques are available to obtain it: transmission lines can be tapped; electromagnetic signals from screens and cables can be read remotely; and eavesdropping bugs can be installed in keyboards, screens, and telephones. Although unlikely in the average situation, these are all possibilities.

There is no stereotypical computer criminal. People tend to trust those they know, or those most like themselves. If anything, the computer abuser does not appear to be a criminal, and may be the individual least suspected.

To provide proper security protection, first classify the data as sensitive or nonsensitive. Shared data and systems are more difficult to protect than stand-alone PCs. Dial-up and other remote access systems pose their own risks (mainly because of difficulties in identifying the user properly).

Threats against security include:

- Lack of organizational awareness or concern for risks.
- Mistakes (including errors, omissions, carelessness, mislabeling, and forgetting). Unintentional error is still the major computer problem, not intentional sabotage.
- Incompetent or inexperienced employees.
- Well-intentioned, but misguided, "system fixers."
- Busybodies, mischief-makers, disgruntled employees, overambitious employees, hackers, thieves who steal equipment or software, saboteurs, and corporate spies who steal or copy confidential data.

Other possible threats to an organization include:

- Bad publicity that exposes vulnerability; this has serious ramifications when an entity depends on its good image.
- Equipment failures and system breakdowns can put an organization out of business.
- Additions of new features to enhance the system may cause the old ones to fail.
- Minor catastrophes, including power failures, power surges, pollution, food and drinks, static electricity, physical damage, overwriting or deleting files, magnetic media, and pressing the

wrong key. These can be avoided by simple practices such as having an understanding of risks and selection of reliable hardware and software.

- Major catastrophes, including fire, floods, earthquakes, war, and terrorist activity.

Control strategies are designed to:

- Prevent threats from occurring.
- Detect problems quickly.
- Correct problems or recover from them efficiently.
- Review the risks and adequacy of the protection periodically.

USER CONTROLS AND RISKS

Users should follow departmental guidelines to control their systems appropriately. Important aspects of user awareness include controlling development, maintenance, security, and backups. Broad security guidelines were noted previously. Some specific security and backup and recovery procedures for users follow.

Security Procedures

Simple security precautions are often enough. Some of these include the need to:

- Take sensitive data off the hard disk and lock it away.
- Avoid readily understandable labels on diskettes containing sensitive data.
- Take good care of diskettes, file away properly, and index and label them clearly.
- Use write-protect tabs to prevent accidental erasure. Also, use other software locks designed for the same purpose (such as the protect feature in spreadsheets).
- Use code words for confidential files, both in the computer and file cabinets.
- Take a periodic inventory of hardware and software.
- Lock rooms containing valuable equipment.
- Do a periodic self-audit.

Backup and Recovery Procedures

Until data is lost, users often ignore the precaution of backing up their information. Obviously, it is better to take precautions before an accident. Some tips are to:

- Keep at least two backup copies of important programs and data in separate places.
- Make sure data can be recovered easily from backups.
- Test the recovery procedures from time to time or as part of regular procedures (for example, keep all data on diskettes and load data alternately from the two backup copies each morning).
- Have at least two of each piece of important equipment.
- Ensure that backup machines are configured properly (particularly memory and boards).

Ideally, everyone in the department should use the same software. At least two people should be trained in each hardware and software product.

SPREADSHEETS

Spreadsheets have become almost a business necessity. Many people consider them the impetus behind the proliferation of microcomputers in the 1980s. Still, many spreadsheets have little or no controls. Where controls do exist, they may be performed unevenly or they may not be appropriate to the application's significance. The level of control should depend on the risk. This section on spreadsheets gives a specific example of a microcomputer application that can help understanding of control over other applications, and it discusses how to assess the risks and provide appropriate controls.

Spreadsheet Use

Spreadsheet use involves the following concerns:

- Identify spreadsheet uses.
  - — Outside the company (customers, vendor bids, regulatory compliance, etc.).
  - — Outside the department (management, internal reporting, etc.).
- Is the data confidential?

- Who will use the spreadsheet?
- Is a spreadsheet the right software tool?

Input Controls

A critical area overlooked frequently in spreadsheets is control of the completeness and accuracy of the data entered. An effective control is to use control totals to check the numeric input of values. Data may already have a control total developed as part of an earlier processing cycle. If there is no total, it may be worth creating a total with a calculator. Input the control total and have the spreadsheet print a computed total next to it. (Having the spreadsheet compute a total that is manually checked to the control total is a less effective method.) Comparing the control total ensures that all of the data is in the spreadsheet before it is manipulated or otherwise changed in processing (usually through application of formulas).

If control totals are not used, each figure must be checked carefully to its original source document using sight verification. In mainframe controls, this is called a one-for-one check. If there is a lot of data, it is tedious and error-prone. In checking, do not omit any important figures. Such checking is best done by a second person.

After input, make sure labels are aligned properly with the corresponding data. Mistyped descriptions can cause problems. Check each description to its original source and ensure that every descriptor is entered.

Controlling Changes

Spreadsheets tend to grow quickly and sometimes wildly, often with no record of changes. What was correct when entered originally can become incorrect. Good documentation and design can prevent some of these problems.

When a spreadsheet is changed, errors can occur due to lack of knowledge of its structure. For sensitive applications, policy should forbid the use of other people's spreadsheets without extra precautions (e.g., additional independent testing). Spreadsheets created by others may be inappropriate for a task, even if they appear suitable.

Protect every cell except those that will need to be changed in the future. Unprotected cells then become the data input area, just like the fields in an input screen for a mainframe application. (They can be unprotected with a global unprotect when absolutely necessary.)

Labeling Spreadsheets

The ability to identify a spreadsheet and its corresponding disks is vital. Every spreadsheet should be named and dated. The name should reflect the version number. When a new version is created, it should be clearly shown by a corresponding change in name or number. Reports should be dated and labeled with the specific spreadsheet name.

Designing Spreadsheets

Design the spreadsheet and document the layout so others can understand it. A simple, diagonal structure avoids changing unwanted parts, for example:

- Labels
- Documentation
- Reference area
    - Macros
        - Input area
            - Calculation area
- Output area (display and print)

Areas of the Spreadsheet

Reference Area. The reference area should include the DOS file name and version number of the spreadsheet. In addition, it should include the name and version of any templates being used, the creation date and time the date of last change, its purpose, the author, and a list of available macros.

The reference area can also be used to list the locations of areas in the spreadsheet. It is good practice to include important assumptions, the calculations and formulas, the purpose of the spreadsheet, and its limitations.

Macro Area. In many products, the macros are in the spreadsheet. In this case, the area should contain all the macros in logical sequence, with narratives about their purpose, and the purpose of each individual step within the macro. Naming conventions and a list of all the names should be developed. When possible, the macros should be in a menu. Macros can be created for common routines such as saving a file, recalculating, and printing and/or displaying areas of the spreadsheet.

Input Area. The amount of input varies with the purpose of the spreadsheet. The input area should be designed like an input form. It can include the descriptions of required entries, which can be controlled with a macro.

Using macros with input can provide security by regulating where data can be entered, changed, and seen. Cells requiring input should be the only cells not protected.

Calculation Area. The calculation area contains most of the calculations and formulas. An extremely long formula should not be contained in one cell; it is more efficient to break it down into logical pieces and put the contents into several cells. If possible, do not embed constants in a formula, since those constants may change. Rather, put each constant in a unique cell. Narrative in the next cell can describe the formula's purpose and underlying assumption.

Display Area. The display area should contain a summary of the spreadsheet's major aspects and be limited to one screen (whenever possible). Included, for example, may be control totals over the input and the final results.

Print Area. The print area should be designed as a report and contain reference to the spreadsheet and template, the version, the date, and other information to identify the file. Usually, the print area and the display area are identical.

Test Data Area. This area contains test data designed to produce easy-to-check results. Alternately, the test data may be contained in a separate spreadsheet and may be invoked by consolidating the two.

Using Multiple Spreadsheets

When designing a spreadsheet, it is important to consider how many would suit the application best. For example, budgets for a company, its divisions and departments, should have a spreadsheet for each department, using consolidation to calculate at a division level. Then division-level spreadsheets can be consolidated to company-level. It is important to ensure that all underlying formulas are the same. (Instead of multiple spreadsheets, people often use enormous spreadsheets that take a lot of time to calculate and contain too many formulas and repetitions.) Many spreadsheet packages allow design of macros (or their equivalent) to automate the consolidation process. Multi-dimensional spreadsheets also make the linking process easier.

Errors

Spreadsheets should be rechecked whenever a significant change is made. They can look perfect and still contain errors, the most common of which are in formulas. The error that occurs most often is adding incorrect ranges. Typically, problems with ranges happen when the wrong reference is entered or when rows or columns are added after the formulas have been entered. In particular, complex spreadsheets, with many subtotals and grand totals, are prone to error.

A second common formula error is using incorrect cells in formulas. One great advantage of spreadsheets is the ease with which their part and formulas can be copied. However, once copied, the references may need to be changed or the formulas will point to the wrong cell. All the formulas and underlying assumptions must be documented, preferably within the worksheet or in the associated documentation.

Saving spreadsheets before a calculation is done, checking the result of that calculation, and saving afterward can be helpful. A spreadsheet may have to be calculated more than once for an accurate result. In some products, it is possible to set the number of iterations needed for "one calculation." Priority indicates which columns or rows to calculate first. However, most products have a "natural calculation priority" that decides automatically which order to calculate cells for an accurate result.

When there are circular references, loops should be considered (i.e., the calculation of a cell is dependent on the calculation of another). The loops may be indicated by the spreadsheet program itself; if not, they can be difficult to find.

A graph may be an important part of a spreadsheet. If it is saved independently, it must be redrawn and resaved whenever the spreadsheet is changed to remain accurate.

Another common error occurs when the input area is not well designed and the user must move around to different cells to input data. Too much movement is confusing and leads to errors. When the input area is designed like a conventional input form, this problem is minimized.

Another problem is that of rounding. Incorrect or inconsistent techniques can have negative effects on result accuracy.

Perhaps one of the most serious errors is the failure to state the limitations of the spreadsheet when defining its formulas and purpose. Without knowing any limitations, management may use the results to make an inappropriate decision in relation to the spreadsheet's underlying purpose.

Testing

Testing a spreadsheet before using its results is an essential control feature. One technique is to have a test data area. Running the tests using a macro is a good idea. This may include printing results, formulas, and the test data itself. A macro can also help check test results. A hard copy of the output should be retained to identify errors uncovered.

Many common errors can be detected using packages designed specifically to evaluate spreadsheets. These packages test for circular references, unused cells (not referenced by any formula), formulas that reference labels, and many other common errors. They also provide the ability to "map" the spreadsheet, identifying features such as overlapping ranges, cells referenced by a formula, formulas referencing a cell, cells that are copies of other cells, cell type (macro, formula, label, blank), named ranges, and many other characteristics. Such packages are quite useful to anyone who relies on the integrity of a worksheet.

Spreadsheet Implementation Work Program

This work program helps decide whether a spreadsheet is right for the business purpose. First, consider whether a spreadsheet is the right tool for the job. Has anyone already done something similar? Would another package be more suitable? Will it create special hardware, software, or storage requirements?

Approval must be obtained for the project. Follow all departmental or organizational procedures and start completing the required documentation. Design the spreadsheet by mapping and documenting its layout. Decide which input controls will be used and how formulas will be controlled. Key in the spreadsheet and debug by evaluating reasonableness of results, printing out and checking all formulas, reconciling and reviewing tests with independent people, and modifying as required.

Execute the final live run. Review reports for reasonableness and reconcile all controls. Repeat the debugging procedures for any changes. Also create disk backup copies of the final spreadsheet, complete the documentation, and get final approval.

It is important to label and file the:

- Completed spreadsheet documentation form.
- File copy of the final printout.
- Map of the spreadsheet layout.
- Formula printout.
- Test results.
- Operating instructions for the future.

- Project memo or report (if applicable).
- Main disk and backup copies.

Spreadsheet Change Work Program

This program is designed to define the purpose of a change and to get it approved according to departmental or organizational procedures.

Copy the original disk and documentation and file them safely. Change the documentation and rename the file for the new version. Change the name or version number within the spreadsheet and documentation.

Modify the spreadsheet and debug by evaluating reasonableness of results, printing out and checking all formulas, reconciling and reviewing tests with independent persons, and modifying the spreadsheet as required. Repeat the implementation steps, changing operating instructions, if necessary.

Execute the final live run. Review reports for reasonableness and reconcile all controls. Repeat the procedure for additional changes and create disk backup copies of the final revised spreadsheet. Finish revising the documentation and get final approval.

It is very important to label and file the:

- Revised spreadsheet documentation form.
- Revised file copy of the final printout.
- Current map of the spreadsheet layout.
- Current formula printout.
- New test results.
- Current operating instructions for the future.
- Project memo or report (if applicable).
- Main disk and backup copies.

Operations

Operations include backup and recovery procedures, security, physical security, environment, cleanup, and departmental and organizational standards. Operations should include:

- Backing up the worksheet to a disk at least every 20 minutes.
- Keeping at least two disk copies of the model. Having a backup of the previous version is good protection. If a hard disk is used,

keep at least one copy on diskette and back up the hard disk regularly.

- Knowing where there is an alternate machine with enough memory to run the spreadsheet. Does it require any special features (e.g., a plotter for printing graphs)? Is another backup copy of the software available?

For confidential data, be sure to:

- Remove the data from the hard disk and lock up the diskettes.
- Dispose of the printouts properly (e.g., shredding).
- Consider password protecting the machine.
- Consider encrypting the file.

THE AUDITOR'S ROLE IN EUC

Today's auditor provides many different services to an organization and deals with a variety of issues. Therefore, it is important for the auditor to understand the impact of EUC on the organization and to plan appropriately.

Developing a self-assessment format for departments to evaluate which applications are sensitive or critical enough to require audit attention helps both auditors and users. Auditors can also act as control consultants to management, MIS, user groups, key users, and ICs. For example, when policies and procedures are inadequate, or do not exist, the auditor can assist in their development.

Categories of Risk

At a minimum, the auditor should evaluate EUC in the following risk areas:

- Software and data integrity.
- Backup and contingency planning.
- Auditability.
- Multi-user microcomputers.
- Communications equipment.

Related issues that increase or decrease risk include:

- Lack of strategic plan.
  - — Misuse of corporate resources.
  - — Failure to reach corporate goals.

- — Technological mismatches.
- — No connectivity inter/intra department.
- — Out-of-step with technology.
- — Hard transitions to new technology.
- — Overall lack of direction.

- Lack of organizational structure.
  - — Inefficient use of resources.
  - — Inadequate supervision.
  - — Conflicting directions.
  - — No central authority.
  - — No acquisition standards.
- Lack of departmental compliance with procedures.
  - — Uninformed supervision.
  - — Inappropriate approval (no centralized authority).
  - — Lack of accountability.
  - — Failure to maintain the system.

Inadvertent Reliance

A major audit concern in EUC systems is the risk of inadvertent reliance on bad data. Since these systems have become widespread, users often base decisions on their output. Examples of inadvertent reliance include:

- Failing to check output before using it in the decision-making process.
- Not realizing changes were made to the system after the last check.
- Missing hidden computations that cannot be checked easily, where errors may go unnoticed.
- Missing hidden assumptions.
- Erroneously using output because it is neat and appears to be correct computer output.
- Assuming consistency between different forms of data or consolidating what should not logically be consolidated.

Performing Audits

Normally, auditors look at those applications where EUC has replaced central processing. However, in some organizations, the use of microcomputers has grown so spectacularly that management has requested specific audits. In either case, it is important to establish an overall audit plan. Individual objectives should be stated clearly. The self-assessment concept mentioned earlier can help determine which departmental systems are critical and need audit attention.

To assess the environment:

- Evaluate administration.
- Identify, analyze, and assess policies and procedures (for example, over acquisition of hardware and software, or changes to an application).
- Review guidelines established to help users.
- Perform organizational and compliance reviews.
- Review user areas for evidence of adequate training and support.
- Cover EUC as a part of regular audits.

For audit-specific applications:

- Monitor compliance with guidelines and policies.
- Ascertain significant/sensitive applications.
- Test the reliability of controls.
- Identify major control deficiencies and inefficiencies.
- Emphasize checking key information produced by micro applications (due to higher risks).

Audit Procedures

It is rarely efficient to perform an in-depth evaluation of every computer in use. Yet, there must be some assurance that critical applications are controlled adequately. Increased risks and lessened ability to look at particular systems often make it necessary to test reports and check the following four aspects:

- Input or extraction (copying), including the derivation of data. For example, in a report, what does a "sale" mean? Orders? Invoices? Shipments? Shipments less returns?
- The appropriateness of assumptions.
- How those assumptions are coded (formulas and selection logic).
- Output and how it can be used to check the previous aspects.

If the user downloads data from a mainframe and processes it further via an EUC application, it is important to:

- Verify that the extracted data is correct. Possible errors include:
  - — Wrong files.
  - — The selection logic is wrong.
  - — Misunderstandings about how the data was created.
- Check the assumptions used. Possible errors include:
  - — Incorrect accounting procedures.
  - — Overoptimistic business judgments (e.g., value or future marketability of high-tech consumer goods).
- Check the coding for assumptions. Common errors occur, such as coding GREATER THAN with the symbol "<."

An example of how auditors can check a spreadsheet is demonstrated by the steps used to compute a provision for accrued liabilities:

- Check that the data input is correct (checked in detail to the original or has control totals).
- Check that the calculations are correct. They could be more complex or overly complex (uses the system date, compared to the transaction date, compared to the computed accrual). Could go wrong if the spreadsheet is rerun with the same figures one month later.

Audit Tools

Audit tools include the following:

- Spreadsheet auditing packages make the formulas coded in spreadsheets clearer.
- Usually, all formulas can be displayed with certain commands.
- Packages often have easy-to-use report writers and inquiry facilities.

Remember that these audit tools may need a specialist who knows the software well, especially to check coded instructions.

Providing Management Guidance

It is helpful to organizations when auditors can talk to management in nontechnical terms. Translation from EDP jargon into business terminology allows the auditors to describe technically complex subjects and helps management both understand and appreciate the risks. The organization, as a whole, can benefit from an improved control environment and better communications.

CHAPTER **25**

Implementation Reviews

INTRODUCTION

One of the primary reasons for implementing a computerized information system is to enhance the efficiency, integrity, and use of an organization's data. Many technically sound systems may not function as anticipated and, in fact, may fail to meet desired objectives due to inadequate controls. If proper controls are not incorporated into the initial system design, significant costs and additional losses may be incurred later. Data and system auditability are essential to system control. Implementation reviews monitor, review, and audit information systems at vital points in system development and implementation. This can ensure that controls protect programs, information, and system resources from unplanned or unauthorized modifications.

Implementation reviews include testing techniques employed by auditors to identify, review, and evaluate internal controls in an organization's computer-based system before and during operation. Among the types of implementation review are the following:

- *Pre-implementation review.* An independent review and assessment of the internal controls and auditability of a proposed information system. This may also include review and assessment of the project implementation controls.
- *Post-implementation review.* Identification, review, and evaluation of the internal controls in an information system after operation begins.
- *Third-party review.* An examination and assessment of the general and application controls of a service bureau's EDP environment.
- *Software evaluation.* An examination of software packages in order to determine the quality of controls, audit or information trails, documentation, and, when applicable, the ability to support generally accepted accounting principles (GAAP) and generally accepted auditing standards (GAAS).

A complete implementation review evaluates the system according to an established set of control objectives that can be modified, if necessary, for a particular environment. Thus, discrepancies between existing controls and the control objectives can be identified, taking the costs and benefits into consideration. If certain controls are absent or need improvement, EDP auditors can offer specific recommendations. A review should incorporate four phases:

1. *Planning.* This determines the scope of the audit and tailors the control objectives and checklists to the particular environment.

2. *Fact-gathering.* Existing system documentation, reports, and procedures are reviewed and personnel are interviewed.
3. *Analysis.* Existing controls are compared with predefined control objective, differences are identified, and findings are reviewed with staff.
4. *Reporting.* A written evaluation is made of the major manual and automated control procedures, along with the findings and recommendations of the reviewers.

PRE-IMPLEMENTATION REVIEW

A pre-implementation review is the examination of a proposed computer system or set of programs performed by auditors during the system development phase to determine the extent of control over and the auditability of the proposed system. Management requests for pre-implementation reviews are increasing as organizations recognize the need to provide adequate controls over their computer environments. Frequently, this review uncovers potential inefficiencies in an organization's data processing operation or physical security risks.

The primary purpose of a pre-implementation review is to provide an independent evaluation of the controls designed into the system. The computer system stores data that represents an organization's customer or client, and management information and financial records, two of its most valuable assets; therefore, it is critical to ensure that there are adequate controls in place during implementation and when the system goes "live." The point is not to critique the basic design of the system, nor the selection of computer equipment, nor the methodologies employed by those responsible for its implementation. Rather, the auditor is interested in the system's ability to function properly with adequate controls.

If proper controls are not built in during initial system design, significant costs and additional losses can be incurred later. This applies to packaged software as well as software developed internally within the organization. The auditor may also review a system to ensure that it complies with management's standards for development, design, and processing. It is important to monitor or audit system design to ensure its adequacy and to evaluate its processing results.

In addition to evaluating the designed controls, a pre-implementation review includes evaluation of the following:

- The adequacy of testing.
- Defined user responsibility.

- The planned conversion procedures.
- The adequacy of audit or information trails.
- The recovery capability, that is, in the event that the new system fails, can the old system be put back into operation, or is there an appropriate manual system that can be used?

Often, the auditor is requested, as part of the pre-implementation review, to review and assess the project implementation control procedures. This review determines whether the implementation control procedures provide the tools for properly planning and using resources in the implementation effort. Without such control procedures, the organization may face major losses through improper use of resources, delayed implementation of systems, or use of systems which, although properly controlled, do not satisfy the purposes for which they were designed.

When a pre-implementation review is complete, the auditor issues a detailed report outlining the scope of the review and the auditor's findings and recommendations to correct any weaknesses. The auditor may also issue interim reports during the implementation, noting weaknesses and recommendations for proper, timely correction.

The system development phase is the best time to determine whether proper controls are in place to ensure that system data will be entered and processed completely and accurately, in accordance with management's intentions. The advantages of reviewing a new or modified system before using it in daily production are:

- Corrective action can be taken before the system is implemented if significant weaknesses are found. This avoids the problem of uncovering weaknesses during the annual review, which might affect the degree of reliance that can be placed on controls adversely.
- The user gets an objective review of the planned system.
- An EDP auditor can suggest conversion procedures and planning that will result in a controlled implementation.

A pre-implementation review may include evaluation of the following:

- Compliance with system development standards.
- The system of a test site or during parallel processing.
- Reporting and input features to ensure the adequacy of controls over completeness, accuracy, and authorization.
- System design to ensure that reports provide an adequate audit or information trail.

- Adequacy of user, programmer, and operations documentation.
- Design and implementation of appropriate control procedures.
- Adequacy of control over access to information for authorized personnel who can manipulate the data.
- Whether design includes controls for all major transaction types.
- Whether user responsibilities are clearly defined.
- Whether files created in other systems that will interface with this system meet the control requirements of both systems.
- The plan for ensuring accurate conversion of data as the system becomes operational.
- Error resolution procedures, to ensure that errors are corrected and reviewed.
- Provisions made to train user and data processing personnel.
- Business continuity procedures, including system backup and recovery.
- Adequacy of the evaluation of organizational impact of the new system.
- Adequacy of personnel staffing, implementation planning and monitoring, definition of implementation deliverables, and quality assurance.

Pre-implementation reviews involve a close working relationship among all members of the internal audit staff, including EDP audit professionals. In this way, auditors can gain on-the-job knowledge in evaluating automated controls.

Work Plan

Following are some steps for the auditor in performing a complete pre-implementation review:

1. **Review Planning:**

☐ Plan the review, including determining system-specific scope and objectives, number of hours required, length and location of the review, and structure of the review team.

☐ Determine and complete any required training for members of the review team.

☐ Explain to system operations personnel and users the nature, scope, and extent of upcoming review.

2. Pre-Implementation Questionnaire:

☐ The EDP auditor conducting the review should formulate and complete a pre-implementation questionnaire, such as an internal control questionnaire (see Chapter 19, "The Control Risk Assessment Process") identifying and obtaining information about any potential control weaknesses, conversion procedures, and user acceptance procedures.

☐ Complete a testing documentation, focusing on the conversion and user acceptance testing procedures.

☐ Draft an interim review memo, identifying weaknesses or concerns for management.

☐ Organize, number, and index working papers that relate to the proposed system, including conversion and user acceptance.

☐ The EDP auditor should review working papers and interim memos.

☐ Prepare and clear review notes.

3. System Controls:

☐ EDP auditors should gain an understanding of the system under development. Activities include appropriate meetings with the management of EDP and user departments, interviewing users, and studying the project documentation.

☐ Record understanding of procedures by using standard flowcharting techniques (see Chapter 17, "How to Document Systems: Using Flowcharts"), including supporting narratives and exhibits.

☐ Identify key and significant:

- Transactions.
- Data files—transaction, master, standing or reference data.
- Data fields.
- Programmed procedures.

☐ Identify control procedures ensuring the proper processing of transactions through the system. These control procedures must ensure that:

- All transactions are valid and accurate when created.

- All valid transactions, and only those transactions, are accurately input to the system.
- Transactions are created and processed on a timely basis.
- Appropriate transaction data is completely and accurately updated to the master files.
- Programmed procedures operate properly and continue to function properly through time.
- Correct programs are executed at the correct time.
- Correct versions of transaction, master, and standing data files are used.
- Files are properly protected against unauthorized access and/or change.
- Files are protected from physical damage or loss.

☐ Confirm that the recorded understanding of the system is complete and accurate.

☐ Evaluate the controls that have been developed for the system.

☐ Draft an interim audit memo describing weaknesses or concerns relating to the review of the proposed system of controls.

☐ Follow up on review comments about deficiencies until resolved.

☐ Organize, number, and index separate working papers; prepare review notes.

☐ Discuss any remaining control issues with the management of EDP and user departments.

☐ Draft and review audit report before its final issuance.

4. Implementation Controls:

☐ Gain an understanding of the implementation project, including management objectives, staffing, and control procedures. Activities include meetings with senior management, the project manager, and project staff; review of scheduling and control documentation; and study of the implementation plan.

☐ Evaluate control procedures in place to ensure that procedures:

- Assign responsibility to management, users, and data processing, as appropriate.
- Accurately reflect the planned and actual use of resources on both a cost and time basis.
- Include project status monitoring and reporting.

- Include measurable criteria for deliverables.
- Include methods for incorporating changes to schedules, deliverables, and tasks.

☐ Periodically evaluate the control procedures.

☐ Draft interim audit memos describing weaknesses or concerns, relating the implementation controls to system development.

☐ Follow up on review comments about deficiencies until resolved.

☐ Organize, number, and index separate working papers; prepare review notes.

☐ Discuss any remaining control issues with senior management.

☐ Draft and review the audit report before its final release.

5. Review Requirements:

☐ EDP auditors should define computer-assisted procedures that are required for effective and efficient ongoing reviews of the implemented system.

☐ EDP auditors can develop a program for testing the system subsequent to implementation, maximizing the use of computer-assisted audit techniques and software.

☐ EDP auditors can help develop and document detailed program specifications for audit software required to support those tests.

☐ Have the test plan and specifications reviewed by management.

☐ EDP auditors should develop, test, and document audit software.

☐ Review test results; draft detailed working papers for entire review.

6. Conduct Detailed Presentation of New System for Internal Auditors and System Personnel; Coordinate Training Session.

7. Plan Post-Audit Evaluation.

Pre-Implementation Review of a Payroll/Personnel System

This section provides a brief sample of the contents of a pre-implementation review report regarding a planned payroll/personnel system, including the objectives as well as a summary of findings and recommendations. Of course, these assessments would be documented in detail in the audit report.

The objective of this pre-implementation review was to assess the adequacy of controls over the payroll/personnel system. The general work plan and specific findings and recommendations for the payroll/personnel system are given here to provide an example of this type of review.

The planned approach included a detailed review of all existing systems documentation:

- Flowcharts
- File layouts
- Transactions
- Output

The EDP auditor interviewed key individuals in data processing, payroll, and personnel departments to obtain an understanding of the system. The auditor documented the understanding in the form of process flowcharts and narrative descriptions. This understanding was confirmed with the appropriate user personnel prior to assessing identified controls. (Audit procedures for a payroll system are discussed in Chapter 10, ‘‘Disbursement Systems.’’)

With this detailed knowledge of the system, the EDP auditor developed a set of control objectives in order to review the quality of control provided by the proposed systems. These control objectives were based on the typical controls as identified using an internal control questionnaire on which the auditor relied in the course of audit work.

The EDP auditor compared the control objectives with the actual or planned methods and facilities and formulated assessments. In addition, where appropriate, the auditors made recommendations about how various controls could be strengthened and how the system could be enhanced to provide additional reporting capabilities for management purposes.

These recommendations and assessments were then reviewed informally with the payroll, personnel, and MIS departments prior to formal release of the report. Once formalized, these assessments and recommendations appeared in a detailed report.

Summary of Findings and Recommendations

In the review of the payroll/personnel system described here, the following recommendations were made:

1. Data Entry:

☐ Hourly payroll:
  - Establish a manual batch control log book.

- Create an exception report of unreasonable overtime hours entered.
- Alter data entry procedures to provide system messages on a terminal when a batch is out of balance.

☐ Administrative payroll:

- The methods currently planned should be adopted (this was in relation to the changes in the particular system for processing administrative payroll as compared to processing hourly payroll).

2. Master Files:

☐ Hourly payroll:

- Clarify error messages reported on the edit report.
- Check one-for-one change transactions entered against the file maintenance report.
- Utilize the batch control log book to control update.
- Implement the planned payroll user manual.

☐ Administrative payroll:

- Implement the planned procedures; document them in the user manual currently under preparation.

3. Report Preparation/Reconciliation:

☐ Hourly payroll:

- Design a report distribution form.
- Specify report retention periods.
- Conduct a supervisory review of reports.

☐ Administrative payroll:

- Implement planned controls.

4. Computer File Access, Security, and Recovery:

☐ Lock the computer room when unattended.

☐ Change passwords periodically.

☐ Change the safe combination periodically.

☐ Review the system history log periodically.

☐ Review user capabilities periodically.

☐ Implement a source code change log.

☐ Consider moving backup diskettes to an off-site location.

☐ Develop a contingency plan.

☐ Review alternate compatible hardware installations for backup purposes.

5. System Implementation:

☐ Establish control totals for file conversion.

☐ Check data, using one-for-one technique, entered to computer during user training programs.

☐ Run the automated and manual hourly payroll systems in parallel for a test period.

Pre-Implementation Review of a Financial System

At the request of the management of a major corporation, an external accounting firm conducted a pre-implementation review of three major systems that were being automated. The systems were the insurance processing system, the financial general ledger system, and the voucher payable system. The review is presented here to provide an example of such a review.

Like the pre-implementation review in the previous section (payroll/personnel), the financial systems pre-implementation review is designed to assess the adequacy of controls in the systems. The pre-implementation review generates several reports that are to be included in the audit team's final report to management:

- The system descriptions
- Overview flowcharts
- Computer control matrices

Alternate approaches to satisfying internal control objectives may be discovered and also should be presented in the report to management. Ways to ensure continuing proper operation of the systems should be included in the report. For example, the audit procedures that could be computerized are illustrated in Figure 25-1.

IMPLEMENTATION REVIEW

Since so many systems do other things than process financial data and transactions, all different types of computerized systems are reviewed. As an example, this section presents a review of a kind of system that is frequently

FIG. 25-1

Audit procedures from a pre-implementation review of financial systems

Audit Concern	Audit Procedures	Manual	Computer
	INSURANCE TRANSACTIONS		
Insurance transactions processed are documented and authorized.	Test accuracy and completeness of input by referring to supporting documentation, and review supervisory controls over such input.	X	
Programmed procedures used to edit and validate incoming insurance transactions are operating in accordance with management's understanding.	Reperform significant edit, validation, and authorization procedures through the use of test data.		X
Rejects and corrections are resubmitted completely, accurately, and on a timely basis.	Review procedures and controls over resubmitting rejected insurance transactions.	X	
Programmed procedures used to generate voucher payable transfer entries are operating in accordance with management's understanding.	Reperform generation of voucher payable transfer file using daily insurance transactions.		X
Programmed procedures used to generate journal entries to the general ledger system are operating in accordance with management's understanding.	Reperform generation of general ledger journal entries using insurance transactions.		X
	Reconcile journal distribution back to source documents.	X	
	VOUCHER TRANSACTIONS		
Voucher input transactions processed are documented and authorized.	Test accuracy and completeness of input by referring to supporting documentation, and review supervisory controls over such input.	X	
Programmed procedures used to edit and validate incoming voucher transactions are operating in accordance with management's understanding.	Reperform significant edit, validation, and authorization procedures through the use of test data.		X

Audit Concern	Audit Procedures	Manual	Computer
Rejects and corrections are resubmitted completely, accurately, and on a timely basis.	Review procedures and controls over resubmitting rejected voucher transactions.	X	
Programmed procedures used to generate journal entries to the general ledger system are operating in accordance with management's understanding.	Reperform generation of general ledger journal entries using voucher transactions.		X
	Reconcile journal distribution back to source documents.	X	

of particular concern to local or state governments—a computerized election system.

Computerized Election System Evaluation

A system review can help minimize problems that can undermine the reliability and credibility of a computerized election system that counts votes. The objectives of the review are to identify and correct weaknesses that may exist. This type of review encompasses performance of a quality review of the computerized election system and provision of complete recommendations for improvement.

The following items are reviewed and tested:

- Accuracy of ballot processing.
- Reliability of the system.
- Ability of the system to detect and report on errors.
- Software and hardware disaster recovery procedures.
- Security of the data center, programs, and ballots data files, once they are transcribed to machine-readable media.

Benefits of this evaluation include increased reliability of the computerized vote counting procedures, reducing:

- Public skepticism about computers.
- Challenges by candidates regarding vote tabulation accuracy.

- Concerns regarding the county data processing staff's qualifications and experience.
- Occasional delays and breakdowns in computer vote counting, by evaluating contingency procedures.

The objectives of an evaluation of this nature are to give reasonable assurance that:

- The computerized election system is properly controlled.
- The computerized election system can accurately count the vote and resist unauthorized manipulation.
- The system's basic design complies with the established requirements (including, after consultation with attorneys, local election laws). In cases of noncompliance, the review should indicate changes needed.

To accomplish these objectives, a review and test of a computerized election system—as would a review of most systems—should focus on several characteristics:

- Accuracy
- Reliability
- Error detection
- Disaster recovery
- Security

The review and test include:

- Meeting with election officials and data processing management to discuss and coordinate testing and processing requirements.
- Reviewing program code, flowcharts, and documentation to become familiar with the system's logic and operating characteristics.
- Reviewing operating instructions, including recovery procedures.
- Reviewing processing controls.
- Developing computer audit software to test the computerized election system program procedures.
- Observing and verifying logic and accuracy tests on election system equipment.

- Evaluating source programs and election program parameter requirements.
- Using test ballots to conduct tests of key programs and the system as a whole.
- Evaluating hardware facilities and determining whether contingency and backup arrangements have been made for these facilities.

A report evaluating the computerized election system is prepared as a result of the preceding process. It should note weaknesses and recommend a corrective action plan.

POST-IMPLEMENTATION REVIEW

A post-implementation review is similar in nature to a pre-implementation review, the basic difference being that the system is already in use. It employs the skills of EDP auditors and automated testing techniques to identify, review, and evaluate the internal controls in a company's computer-based system once it is operational.

This type of review generally arises from management's desire to receive a special report, or a more in-depth review, of one or more of their applications outside of the normal audit review. This type of review may be performed in conjunction with a company's internal auditors or as an on-the-job training exercise for the staff.

Post-Implementation Review of a Tracking System

Whether it processes dollars or information, a computerized system should have controls over completeness, accuracy, maintenance, and authorization. Consider the effect of a computerized system that detains prisoners even after the courts have released them. This was a real concern of jail officials in a certain county after several complaints were filed against those officials by prisoners. The resulting adverse publicity, as well as the complaints themselves, led the county's board of commissioners to focus on two main issues:

1. Were prisoners held in jail after being ordered released by the courts?
2. Were there serious problems with the county's computerized prisoner tracking system?

To help address these concerns, the commissioners contacted a major accounting firm. It was decided that a physical inventory of prisoners would be taken to find out if, in fact, prisoners who should have been released were being detained.

To determine if there were any problems with the county's computerized prisoner tracking system, an EDP auditor was called in to perform a review of the system. The objective of the review was to identify and evaluate the manual and automated controls and recommend improvements to the existing system of controls. The EDP auditor was assisted by a criminal justice specialist from the firm's management consulting services staff.

The county's automated tracking system is still one of the most sophisticated systems in use in the United States today. It was implemented with the opening of a new county jail and was designed to record on-line all information pertaining to an individual, from the moment of entry into the criminal justice system until final release or transfer out of the facility.

This on-line, real-time data base system runs on two large-scale mainframes. All data entry is done remotely through terminals located in the detention area, the courts, and several police precincts throughout the city.

Evaluating System Controls. To identify and evaluate the system controls, the EDP auditor:

- Gained an understanding of the system.
- Reviewed computer operations, system design, and change procedures.
- Reviewed data file control, disaster recovery, and contingency planning.

These reviews were conducted by interviewing key personnel, observing procedures, and reviewing documentation. In addition, transactions were submitted through the system to a test data base to confirm the understanding of system processing. A written report of findings and recommendations was provided to the commissioners.

A Better Audit or Information Trail. In addition to accounting for all prisoners who were physically in jail at the time of the inventory, there were several recommendations to improve the security and auditability of the system. Satisfactory application controls were found to be in place. However, in order to provide a better trail of transaction processing and to increase security over transaction input, the EDP auditor recommended that additional security codes be required for transaction input.

Virtually all transactions entered into the system are based on hard copy documents from law enforcement or the courts. To ensure that the computerized data base stays current with the paper flow, a complete set of exception reports was recommended. Jail and court personnel could then control the input of information by monitoring these reports.

The report also recommended that the county develop and test a contingency plan to be put into effect should computer operations be disrupted for a significant period of time. Other recommendations concerned the review of attempted access violations and manual procedures to ensure the integrity of the data base.

The review pointed out several ways that the criminal justice system could improve the quality and timeliness of its information. As a result of the review, the county gained assurance that its automated tracking system operates in a controlled manner. Still, a computer system is only as useful and current as the data it processes.

THIRD-PARTY REVIEW: SERVICE BUREAUS

Many businesses find computer service bureaus an efficient and economical alternative to a large in-house computer. However, while realizing savings in time and money, the user may suffer a loss of control. While it is obviously impractical to have group after group of outsiders—users and their representatives—observe the service bureau operations on site, users want to be reassured that the service bureau has adequate internal controls.

How can the user be reasonably assured that the service bureau is processing data correctly and that the service bureau's controls address concerns that:

- Applications systems and programs are developed, implemented, and maintained in accordance with management's intentions (or understanding)?
- Processing results are complete and accurate?
- Data is kept secure and confidential?
- Service can be maintained in the event of a disaster, such as system failure or fire?

In the past, management may have been able to maintain control over data processed at the service bureau by using extensive manual control procedures, but, as systems become more complex, this may not be possible. An organization can have its external auditors review the service bureau, but this would be costly and may not produce the desired results because of constraints at the service bureau. Such constraints might include the service bureau's unwillingness to provide complete access to their data center, system, and information at any time.

An effective solution to this problem is the third-party review, an objective appraisal of service bureau control policies and procedures by independent auditors or independent accountants. This review, performed in accordance with the auditing standards set forth in the guide published by the American Institute of Certified Public Accountants (AICPA), *Audits of Service-Center-Produced Records* (REVISED 1987), Office of the Comptroller of the Currency Banking Circulars and in Federal Home Loan Bank Board bulletins, may incorporate both application and general data processing control concerns.

Findings and recommendations are discussed in a detailed report, which can be used by management to make decisions about the reliability of the service bureau's internal controls comptroller and by other auditors in their examinations. The ability to provide this type of documented evidence of the reliability of internal controls is often used as a major selling point by the service bureaus themselves once they have received a favorable review.

Reports cover matters such as:

- *The computer environment and general controls*. These include the service bureau's plan of organization, procedures for new system development, application programs and operating system maintenance, access to data files and program libraries, standardized procedures in computer operations, whether those procedures are actually followed, and physical security and contingency planning. They may also address the adequacy of new applications through the development life cycle, focusing on the definition of the system, feasibility study, general design and detailed specifications, program development and testing, system testing, and conversion and documentation.
- *Application controls*. These include controls over the system's input, processing, and output, with emphasis on existence of controls that provide for completeness and accuracy of input and update, proper authorization of data, and proper maintenance of data on the computer files.

Normally, the report describes the control objectives and related controls that are in place at the service bureau and gives an overview of procedures used to confirm that controls are functioning properly. It also reports weaknesses and provides recommendations.

A report on the extent and effectiveness of the service bureau's internal and operational controls is the primary benefit that both service bureaus and users obtain from a third-party review. However, a number of additional benefits accrue to service bureau management, including:

- Ongoing discussions concerning the bureau's data processing systems and operations.
- Identification of operational problems and opportunities.
- Suggestions for enhanced marketability of the bureau's services.

Work Plan

Following is a specimen work plan for a third-party review of a service bureau.

1. Organizational Review:

- ☐ Obtain and review service center organization chart.
- ☐ Examine contracts with customers:
  - Review for consistency.
  - Review for completeness.
- ☐ Examine coverage defined in insurance policies:
  - Blanket bond.
  - Building and contents insurance.
  - Emergency flood insurance.
  - Data processing equipment insurance.
  - Errors and omissions insurance.
  - Lost data insurance.
  - Business interruption insurance.
  - Other types of coverage that may exist.
- ☐ Identify applications processed.
- ☐ Obtain list of all hardware.
- ☐ Obtain list of all software.
- ☐ Review physical and data security.
- ☐ Complete service bureau review questionnaire—background.
- ☐ Obtain and record an understanding of service bureau's general controls.
- ☐ Confirm understanding.
- ☐ Complete service bureau review questionnaire—general controls.

- ☐ Test the general controls, as required.
- ☐ Test application controls, as required.
- ☐ Discuss control weaknesses or deficiencies noted with appropriate user management personnel.
- ☐ Draft comments to be included in the report.

2. **Application Review.** Identify applications to be reviewed and for each application:

- ☐ Obtain an understanding by interviewing service organization personnel, examining application documentation, and observing processing procedures.
- ☐ Document understanding in flowchart or narrative form.
- ☐ Identify significant control procedures over the following:
    - Completeness of input.
    - Completeness of update.
    - Accuracy of input.
    - Accuracy of update.
    - Authorization of transactions.
    - Maintenance of data on files.
- ☐ Identify significant procedures being performed by the computer:
    - Classification of data.
    - Summarization of data.
    - Arithmetic functions, calculations, and so forth.
    - Reporting of data.
- ☐ Confirm the accuracy, correctness, and operation of the controls and procedures documented as being in effect.
- ☐ Identify control weaknesses or other deficiencies noted as a result of the application review.
- ☐ Draft comments to be discussed with service bureau management.
- ☐ Draft final report to user management or third-party report to the service bureau, as appropriate.

Service Bureau Review Questionnaire

The following questionnaire provides an example of information to gather that can be used to review a service bureau.

SECTION A—BACKGROUND

1. Name of the data processing organization ______________________
2. Address ______________________
3. D&B or other report on financial condition ______________________

____

4. Describe major computer equipment:

   Hardware

   Mainframes ______________________

   Storage capacity ______________________

   Peripheral devices ______________________

   ____

   ____

   ____

   Software (include version number as well as name)

   Operating system ______________________

   Data base management system (DBMS) ______________________

   Telecommunications software ______________________

   Library software ______________________

   Job accounting software ______________________

   Application software ______________________

   Utilities ______________________

   ____

5. List of applications being processed:

   Name ______________________

   Program language ______________________

   Processing mode (e.g., batch, on-line, data capture, real-time, etc.) ______

   ____

   Documentation available:

   System

   Narrative ______________________

   Flowcharts ______________________

   Programs ______________________

Narrative ______________________________

Listing ______________________________

Record layouts ______________________________

Report layouts ______________________________

Control procedures ______________________________

Operation run books ______________________________

Job control language (JCL) listings ______________________________

6. Review of service bureau contracts:

☐ Identify term, renewal options, and cancellation provisions.

☐ Identify cost of the following:

- System design ______________
- Programming ______________
- Preparation of data ______________
- Computer time ______________
- Special reports ______________
- Materials ______________
- Transaction processing ______________
- Pick-up and delivery ______________
- Storage ______________
- Special reports ______________
- Processing not at normal times ______________
- Conversion of data ______________

☐ Identify form and frequency of billing. ______________________________

☐ Identify user's responsibility regarding:

- Data preparation ______________
- Input control ______________
- Master file changes ______________
- Batching of source documents ______________
- Balancing procedures ______________
- Coding ______________

☐ Identify procedures for conversion/deconversion of data and parallel processing. ______

☐ Identify party owning data files, programs, and documentation.

☐ Identify the service bureau's responsibility for:

- Output or report preparation ______
- Schedules for above ______
- Control of processing ______

☐ Identify responsibilities and liabilities for:

- Errors and irregularities ______
- Computer rerun charges ______

☐ Does contract permit visit by the user's external auditors and regulatory agency representatives? ☐ Yes ☐ No

☐ Is a consulting fee involved? ☐ Yes ☐ No

7. Name and title of the person in the user organization responsible for liaison with the service bureau. ______

8. Name and title of the person at the service center responsible for client contact. ______

9. Security of data:

   ☐ Do the service bureau contract and procedures preclude the unauthorized disclosure of any user data? ☐ Yes ☐ No

   ☐ What procedures are in effect for error recovery, backup, and disaster recovery? ______

   ☐ How are the user's program and data files protected and secured?

SECTION B—General Controls

(Only summary-level questions are included here; a supplemental report would contain details.)

1. Is there an adequate separation of responsibilities within the data processing function? ☐ Yes ☐ No

2. Are there adequate controls over computer operations?

   ☐ Yes ☐ No

3. Is there adequate supervision of computer operations?

   ☐ Yes ☐ No

4. Are there adequate controls over systems maintenance.

   ☐ For application program modifications? ☐ Yes ☐ No

☐ For operating system modifications? ☐ Yes ☐ No

5. Is there adequate supervision of systems maintenance:

   ☐ For application program modifications? ☐ Yes ☐ No

   ☐ For operating system modifications? ☐ Yes ☐ No

6. Are there adequate controls over access to data files?

   ☐ Yes ☐ No

Detailed questions on general controls, such as those found in an internal control questionnaire, should be used to provide adequate information about the general controls.

SECTION C—APPLICATION CONTROLS
(Only summary-level questions are included here; supplemental report, if any, contains details.)

For each significant transaction processed by the application, identify the control technique or procedure that satisfies the specific control objective.

Controls Over	*Transaction I.D.*		
Completeness of input	________	________	________
Accuracy of input	________	________	________
Completeness of update	________	________	________
Accuracy of update	________	________	________
Authorization	________	________	________
Maintenance	________	________	________

Figure 25-2 is an example of an executive summary for a report on a third-party review of an organization's banking applications and data centers, conducted by an independent auditor. It illustrates the scope of the review and the types of comments and recommendations resulting from the work done.

Report

Figure 25-3 is a third-party review report of four data centers. It illustrates some of the procedures assessed in a data center review.

FIG. 25-2

Specimen executive summary on a third-party review of applications and data centers

CLIENT USER GROUP
EXECUTIVE SUMMARY

On behalf of the client's user group, we have completed a third-party auditor's review of the client's applications and data centers. The objectives of the review were to:

- Provide management assurance about the design and operations of the systems of internal control, in conformity with professional standards and regulatory requirements.
- Provide the user group members with an appraisal of new developments affecting their EDP support systems and provide the group with practical recommendations to maximize the benefits of the new developments.

Major Findings and Recommendations

Our detailed findings and recommendations are combined in a separate section of this report following the Executive Summary.

This year, we reviewed the client's commercial loan system. This system supports basic loan accounting requirements and operates with a high degree of reliability. Significant manual efforts are required to process and control loan activity. Such efforts are particularly cumbersome in processing multilevel loans and loan participations. The degree of manual effort should be considered when establishing loan products and determining staff support requirements. The client is evaluating other commercial loan systems to address some of the noted weaknesses.

As each user group addresses its respective EDP system requirements in an era of continued deregulation — permitting greater product diversification and the introduction of new product and service lines — we suggest that the user group, as a whole, increase its liaison with the client in setting system development priorities. Failure to organize and present system priorities may result in delays in obtaining the necessary EDP support systems to meet competitive challenges.

Significant Organizational Changes

The client was acquired by a major corporation for a purchase price of approximately 10 times its net book value. The acquisition has not changed the client's management. The Chairman of the Board and President have retained their positions.

As a wholly owned subsidiary, the client will provide all data processing services to its parent company. To accommodate the additional processing requirements, several new data centers will be constructed to complement the expanding geographic network of the client's major data centers.

A major data center campus is being constructed that will facilitate certain processing for the parent company and may assume some processing currently performed at other data processing centers.

One of the client's information processing centers has been reorganized to accommodate centralized management of satellite data centers. Under this concept, certain data center management functions, such as scheduling, production control, and resource management, are centralized. Eventually, centralized, remote management techniques will be employed at all of the client's major data centers.

Certain insurance plans and employee benefit plans are being consolidated with the parent company to expand coverages cost-effectively.

(*continued*)

FIG. 25-2 (*continued*)

Major System Enhancements

NOW account line of credit features were extended to permit greater flexibility in differentiating the line of credit product. In addition, system support for an equity line of credit attached to a passbook savings account was introduced in response to consumer demand and other competitive product offerings.

Modifications to the installment loan system enhance management's ability to control profitability over loan portfolios. These changes provide greater flexibility in establishing a method to automatically control accident and health insurance policies covering installment loans as well as controls over account number assignments.

Enhancements in the mortgage loan system improve escrow analysis capabilities and ensure timely review and adjustment for changes in related property taxes and insurance premiums.

To accommodate growth, the number of teller terminals supported by the system was substantially increased.

Security controls over savings, loans, and general ledger transactions were enhanced through extended security features.

Future Developments

Two major system enhancements are expected to be available later this year.

Continuous on-line support for automatic teller machines will increase customer servicing flexibility and ensure that the latest balance information is available. The network would be interrupted only for maintenance and a brief daily period for file refreshing.

An investor servicing system is being developed that will significantly enhance current capabilities. Automated support will include:

- Loan portfolio analysis and packaging of loans for sale
- Management reporting of loan spreads and margin calculations
- Enhanced investor servicing and accounting

Scope of Review

Our review procedures comply with AICPA professional standards for third-party reviews and with applicable regulatory agency standards, including AICPA Statement on Auditing Standards No. 44, the AICPA audit guide, "Audits of Service Center Produced Records," and Federal Home Loan Bank Board Bulletin PA-7-1a.

The review included on-site visits to each of the client's locations providing support services.

The objective of a third-party auditor's review is to provide a description of the computer-based systems and general controls in enough detail to permit users of the report to evaluate the overall system of internal controls of each computer-based application — including manual procedures exercised by the user, procedures exercised by the client at the data centers, and programmed procedures incorporated in the computer-based systems. With this objective, our review work included necessary steps to gain an understanding of the computer-based portions of the systems and general controls, perform sufficient tests to form an opinion as to whether the computer-based applications and general control procedures provide a basis for a strong control environment, and determine the degree of compliance with the prescribed procedures throughout the review period.

Test procedures are described in detail in the report. In general, they included observations during the time of our review, inquiry of personnel, examination of evidence at the sites, reperformance of manual procedures performed by personnel, reperformance of computer programmed procedures through the use of test data, and reperformance of programmed procedures through use of our internally developed audit software. In addition, certain tests of the installment loan and security systems were performed at members' sites.

Our testing, performed during the period, was limited to specific procedures and controls at the client's locations and, as such, did not assess the adequacy of controls exercised at the member associations. Our report is organized to enable evaluation of the manual user controls that can be applied at the associations, given the design and nature of procedures performed by the client. Our compliance tests were designed to ascertain whether programmed procedures included in the computer-based applications and data center general control procedures functioned as described herein and whether a sufficient degree of compliance existed to express an opinion on the overall adequacy of the system of internal control designed to achieve the specified control objectives.

SOFTWARE EVALUATION REVIEW

With more and more businesses turning to packaged software as an economical alternative to in-house system development, vendors are scrambling to meet the seemingly endless demand for various types of financial applications software. In the 1980s, packaged software is the segment of the computer services industry that is growing most rapidly; this market has increased at an amazing rate.

Assessing Controls

Software packages are receiving close scrutiny as buyers seek to maximize an often sizable investment in software, especially since no mandatory standards for software development controls have been issued. (Development controls are procedures for developing, testing, and modifying software. They have a significant impact on the reliability of information generated by the software.)

Vendors' quality assurance programs usually deal with the proper operation of the software. Buyers are concerned initially about ease of installation, training, and accurate and efficient operation. Businesses that use

(*Text continues on page 25-34*)

FIG. 25-3

Specimen third-party data center review report

DATA CENTER 1

Organization

Data Center 1 (DC1) is a data processing service corporation that employs a president, a director of marketing, and a secretary. DC1 is managed and operated by the company under a facilities management agreement. The company has 36 employees at DC1 in accounting, operations, systems, customer service, operations support, and new accounts. DC1 operates as a communications link between 14 users and another of the company's data centers, DC3. On-line and batch processing is performed at DC3, with the output reports transmitted to DC1 for high-speed printing and report distribution. Computer hardware located at DC1 is owned or leased by DC1 and the company.

Physical Security

The computer center and employees are located on the third floor. There are three DC1 locations on the third floor, each of which is accessible through a public corridor:

- Administrative offices
- Training room and system engineering offices
- Computer center

A receptionist is stationed in the administrative offices during normal business hours. These offices are locked after normal business hours and during weekends and holidays.

The computer room is located at the end of the corridor, and access to the room is controlled by a combination lock and an operator release button from inside the room. A second door, located in the rear of the computer room, connects it with the system engineering offices and training room. This door is normally locked and is used only as an emergency exit. A sign above the door indicates that an alarm will sound when the door is opened. The programming area is also accessible from the public corridor and is located directly in front of the elevators. This entrance is secured with a simplex combination lock and remains closed at all times.

Six hand-held fire extinguishers are installed in the computer room, which is also equipped with ceiling and floor smoke/heat detectors. Five other hand-held extinguishers are installed throughout the remaining office areas.

System Implementation

Each user file must be converted to the proper format through the use of conversion programs that are written under the supervision of the account representative. This is the primary type of implementation that occurs at DC1, since system maintenance is generally performed by another data center, DC4.

Program Modification

Program change requests can be initiated by completing a service request. These sequentially numbered forms are sent to DC1 for assignment of a customer service representative to research and resolve the request.

The service request is logged and categorized as research, maintenance, or enhancement. As needed, a system maintenance request is completed, assigned priority by customer service, and sent to the programming area with the service request and any other related documentation. The system engineering manager reviews all service maintenance requests and assigns a programmer to the project.

The programmer copies the required module to a test library and the changes are made. Testing is performed using test data files. On completion of the testing, the test results are sent to the requestor for review. Customer acceptance of program changes is not documented. For major changes, associations are kept informed through letters and memoranda.

Internally generated system maintenance requests are created for problems that hinder production. Each one must be approved by the system engineering manager and logged with a unique sequential number.

Program modifications are first approved for implementation by the system engineering manager, who uses a source compare utility to identify program code changes. The approved program and the utility program printout are then forwarded to central support, where the program is reviewed and authorized for placement into production. New and modified programs are placed into production weekly.

Urgent modifications (those necessary to provide for completion of an abnormally terminated production job or those that must be implemented before the next run) are handled by the use of override libraries. Account representatives are authorized to effect JCL overrides. Use of these overrides enables substitution of regular production programs.

Control of Computer Operations

Computer operations is responsible for scheduling the receipt of external transaction data, the transmission of data between DC1 and DC3, the reconciliation of transmission record counts, and report distribution. The schedule of production jobs is determined by a master scheduler at DC3. External transactions are received at DC1 on magnetic tape. Record counts for each user are recorded on the external label of the magnetic tape. Each tape is processed by computer operations, which prints a listing of record transmission totals. Record counts are reconciled between totals transmitted to DC3, totals verified as received at DC3, and the total on the external label. Transmission listings are sent with other output reports to the user. A transmission log is completed by the operator, with the production job name, time of transmission, and comments.

The operators record problems and abnormal terminations on various logs. The problem log contains hardware or transmission problems that occur. The trouble log is generated for transmission problems affecting specific branches. It is used for correspondence with, and to record the actions taken by, the phone company to resolve the problem. An entry in the trouble log also appears on the problem log. The service/maintenance log describes hardware and equipment problems and the resulting maintenance and repairs. Logs are initialed by the operations manager daily, when reviewed.

Data control is responsible for the completion of the daily report inventory and report distribution for each user. The three-part inventory form contains daily reports, generalized reports, delinquency notices, statements, and other reports distributed. Two parts of the form are sent to the customer with the reports, and the third copy is filed at DC1 with the returned signed copy. All reports printed at

(*continued*)

FIG. 25-3 (*continued*)

DC1 are reviewed by quality control to ensure that the print positions and ribbon texture are correct, the check date is proper, and each association has a separation banner page.

The company employs two drivers who are responsible for delivering all reports to the local associations. Reports sent to the other areas are delivered on a public bus and picked up by a carrier at the destination. This procedure has been used for some time because of its cost-effectiveness and proven reliability.

Data File Access

Access to production files and programs and other user data is restricted by the access controller system resident at DC3.

Telecommunications

Terminals at association branches are connected through a modem to a port at DC1. The data speed of the terminals is 2400 baud. The ports are connected to another modem at DC1 that transmits the data to DC3 at 9600 baud. DC1 has 19 circuits, two of which are direct lines to DC3.

The trend over the last several years has been to install more direct lines between customer sites and DC3. This practice eliminates the need to install modem links between the association, DC1, and DC3. As the company's network is expanded and as staffed concentrator communication centers are established, it may be more cost-effective to consolidate transmission through local networks to the respective information processing center. Such communication centers may allow for better control over communications costs, line servicing, and trouble shooting and may enhance line recovering ability in the future.

Backup and Recovery

Data files and program modules are backed up on a regular basis at DC3. The exact files to be saved are determined by the system engineers. External transmissions are kept for recovery purposes at DC1 for five days. The programs to process the external transactions prior to transmission are backed up periodically onto tape and stored in the computer room.

Contingency and Disaster Recovery

A Disaster Recovery Procedure Manual has been developed to outline the procedures to be used in case of an emergency. The alternate site for communications is located 10 blocks west of DC1 at a customer site. DC3 is the alternate printing site. Included in the manual is a list of the circuit numbers, line numbers, ports, and vendors; however, it would take three weeks to set up the lines and circuits. Some customers use dial backup to communicate directly with DC3 in the event of a disaster. DC1 is currently developing configurations that include concentrators with several lines.

Contracts

DC1 has two types of contracts: a contract with each user and one with the company to operate a facilities management agreement. The contract with the user details services to be provided, features of the system, system reports, and charges. The contract with the company specifies that upon mutual termination of the contract, the company must supply DC1 with a current version of the programs, operating system, and data.

DATA CENTER 4

Organization and Location

DC4 is located in a custom-built building which provides a sound basis for good physical security. Access is restricted to properly authorized data center personnel, and unauthorized entry is prevented around the clock on all days of the week.

The data center is maintained in a clean and disciplined manner with reasonable precautions taken to avoid, prevent, or immediately detect any breach in physical security or breakdown in physical conditions.

The organizational structure provides for a division of duties. There are no systems and programming staff at the data center. Instead, these departments are located in separate buildings some distance away from the center, and systems and programming staff are not authorized to enter the data center. Duties are also segregated among data center staff. Scheduling, network control, tape handling, tape library control, and microfiche production are all done by separate teams of employees. Printing is not performed at the data center, but at a separate print center. Any reports needed on paper rather than on microfilm are produced at the print center.

In February 19YY, the company's audit personnel performed a control review of DC4. In addition to performing their regular annual audit procedures, they verified corrective actions taken in response to minor comments by the Federal Reserve Systems Auditors. Areas covered in their review included: physical security, accountable forms control, emergency procedures/disaster recovery, data media library procedures, JCL overrides, scheduling, data preparation and input/output control, teleprocessing network, and on-line system controls.

Physical Security

Physical security in and around DC4 is strong. The main entrance is protected by a badge reader that also requires a four-digit access code. This system provides two levels of security: (1) building access and (2) access to the data center area. During working hours, a receptionist is present at the main entrance. The main entrance is the only windowed area and the windows are of bullet-proof glass.

Visitors are required to sign a log when entering the building. Visitors are the responsibility of their host while in the building and must be escorted while in the data center areas.

The building is equipped with interior and exterior closed circuit television cameras that provide building surveillance. The security monitors are located in the network monitoring area of the computer room, which is manned 24 hours a

(continued)

FIG. 25-3 (*continued*)

day. Security guards make periodic rounds and record their checks on a key/lock station system. Day shift guards are the company's employees. At night and on weekends, a guard service is used that provides fidelity bonded personnel.

The data center power supply is backed up by an Uninterruptable Power Supply (UPS) system, which is located in a locked room within the computer facility. A limited distribution key is required to enter the room. The UPS room is monitored by a closed circuit television camera and protected from fire by a full flood system. The temperature and humidity are recorded and monitored. There is on-line monitoring of current drain as well as monitors for power and voltage. There is also a battery backup room that is adjacent to but separate from the UPS room. This is also accessible by a master key and is equipped with an eye wash for personnel safety. The room is equipped with instrumentation to monitor hydrogen levels and ventilation fans are installed to minimize the threat of explosion.

Access to the data center area is by badge and combination code. The data center is in use at all times and is therefore never unattended. The entire data center area is built on a raised floor and uses approximately three-quarters of the available first floor footage. Operations support personnel, including tape librarians, network monitoring technicians, scheduling clerks, and system engineers, work within the restricted data center area.

Fire Protection

Smoke/heat detectors are located above and below the data center raised floor and are connected to an annunciator panel in the communications network monitoring area. Numerous hand-held fire extinguishers are conveniently mounted and marked throughout the data center area. Smoking is not prohibited in the data center, except for the console area. The local fire department and the fire insurance company inspect the data center on a regular basis. The tape library, which is located in the data center, has a dry pipe sprinkler system plus hand-held halon extinguishers.

System Access Controls

The prevention of unauthorized amendments to live production programs and the control over access to computer resources depend principally on a proprietary software package that was developed and is maintained by the company's software systems and programming group. The intentions behind it are:

- To prevent any user from accessing any programs or data belonging to any area other than its own.
- To prevent the members of any systems and programming group from accessing any programs or data belonging to any user other than the one for which they are responsible.
- To prevent anyone other than the production scheduling staff at the data center from making amendments to the live production programs for any user.

The software package is linked to the operating system and is continually active. Whenever any job attempts to use any program to read or write any data, the package first demands that the necessary job identifications and password be checked against a table showing whether that job is appropriately authorized. The table of job identifications and passwords is available only to the data center security controller and his staff and to the internal auditors.

The table for each user must be set up initially to provide at least a recommended minimum of security, by allowing certain user ID's to do more or less depending on whether they relate to the systems and programming group or to the user. For example, the user cannot access the production programs, whereas the system engineers are able to obtain copies of their programs in order to prepare amendments and to test them. The security controller ensures that each user area has at least this degree of security at the center.

The access control system cannot distinguish between different members of user personnel, systems and programming staff, or production scheduling, but it can be used to keep these three areas apart and to limit what they are able to do.

The access control package produces some exception reports, showing attempts at invalid access, but these reports can be lengthy and are quite difficult to read. They are not used to investigate the reasons for failure.

After the table has been set up initially for a new user and approved by the security controller, it usually remains unchanged. It does not discriminate among individuals in each group, so there is no need to alter the table when people leave.

Control Over Computer Operations

An automated operations scheduling system, production management information system, and master scheduler are installed and in use at DC4. Because the automated scheduling system has only recently been installed at DC4, the schedulers continue to use a hardcopy flowchart of jobs as they are completed. This is a double check for the schedulers as it makes them aware of the logical job flow as well as ensures them that the proper job is being initiated by the system.

Overrides are initiated by the system engineers and automatically inserted into the execution JCL by the system for the designated length of time. The production control personnel are responsible for reviewing the overrides from an operational perspective.

Any abnormal terminations are logged by the operators and subsequently reported in the daily morning report problem logs. The problems logged could be a result of hardware, system software, teleprocessing, or application programs. A report is also available to examine, in detail, each job scheduled, times scheduled, actual time processed, variances, and terminations. This is used to review both normal and abnormal situations encountered during the production cycle.

Data Library Backup Procedures

A tape library system is also used at DC4 to control the movement and use of magnetic tapes. This system monitors the location of all tapes, the contents of each tape, and the control of foreign tapes in the library. It produces a series of reports for management review that include volume serial number and data set name, volume sequence, creating job name, and other pertinent information.

Tape files are copied periodically and rotated between the data center and the disaster recovery area. Data files that require the backup of generations to be sent to the disaster recovery area are recorded in several tape library system

(continued)

FIG. 25-3 (*continued*)

reports. The reports highlight tapes sent and returned as specified by the system engineer. The tape librarians review these reports daily to match the tapes to the list and verify that the tapes are in the proper location.

The direct access devices are fixed. Disk storage data management is monitored through the use of a software package.

System Software Controls

The company's corporate software group developed and maintains most of the significant system software. The operating system software is supplied by IBM.

There are also several powerful system utility programs, as is normal in an installation of this size, but such utility programs could be misused either deliberately or in error. To prevent the unauthorized use of utilities, these programs have been set up on a separate system "library" of programs on a disk, and they cannot be accessed and used without the correct identification and password.

Disaster Recovery

Reasonable and practical arrangements have been made for resuming normal processing after any large-scale disaster. A responsible official from the data center is in charge of keeping the disaster recovery plan up-to-date and ensuring that all data center staff are aware of exactly what they are expected to do in the event of an emergency. Drills are held from time to time. The internal auditors review the disaster recovery plans and arrangements as part of their annual data center work.

a computer to process vital information, however, should consider another major issue: whether management can depend on the information that the software generates.

When businesses kept their financial records by hand, management—and auditors—could check "visible" evidence such as ledgers and invoices. But now, with financial records kept on tapes and disks, how does the user know that the information stored in these "invisible" records has been processed in accordance with management's intentions? How does the user know that the package that processes the information is auditable? In the process of acquiring financial applications software, businesses often overlook these questions. And yet, controls over the processing of financial data are critical.

Both users and vendors may be risking exposure to errors and misstatements if financial applications software is developed without an awareness of:

- Generally accepted accounting principles (GAAP).
- Generally accepted auditing standards (GAAS).

- The need for an independent review of control procedures and audit or information trails embodied in a package.

Is there a way of ensuring that a software package encompasses controls that facilitate the proper processing of information? A software evaluation, performed by external EDP auditors and accompanied by a report attesting to the package's documentation and internal processing controls, can go a long way toward diminishing the uncertainty of potential users.

Software Evaluation Review of Financial Applications

In a software evaluation, the auditor reviews the controls and accounting procedures in a package. Tests are performed to ascertain how well these controls and accounting procedures actually function.

Reports about the package resulting from this type of review should answer the following questions. Does the package:

- Provide adequate documentation to allow its intended users to understand the package?
- Provide internal processing controls, reports, and/or data files that are adequate to permit the performance of audits in accordance with GAAS?
- Process accounting information using procedures that produce reports that enable users to prepare financial statements in conformity with GAAP?

Limitations of Software Evaluation

When considering a software evalution review, it is important to know its limitations. These include the following:

- A review normally relates only to the specific release level of the software reviewed. It does not extend to the installation or customization of the software package.
- As a normal part of a review, the reviewers do not accept responsibility for testing the functioning of the operating systems per se, even when the package is tested using the vendor-specified operating system.
- A software evaluation also does not involve the evaluation of the functional adequacy (such as whether a general ledger package provides enough subaccounts) or performance specifications (such as response time) of a package.
- Reviewers generally do not endorse the software product, they only evaluate it.

Therefore, an evaluation does not cover the following:

- The potential effectiveness of the system.
- The suitability of the system for a specific user environment.
- The relative efficiency or reliability of the system or its underlying hardware and software.
- The ease with which the system can be installed.
- The capabilities of vendor personnel.

Stages of a Software Evaluation Review

The following list outlines the individual stages to complete a software evaluation review:

1. Environment factors.
2. Development controls.
3. Application design and controls.
4. Detailed application documentation.
5. Technical design.
6. Application test plan.
7. Testing.
8. Evaluation.
9. Report.

The possible steps involved in each phase of the review are discussed in the following sections.

Review of Environmental Factors. This stage assesses whether the vendor environment—its policies, procedures, and personnel—is conducive to developing reliable software products, encompassing the following:

- Project management plan (product development).
- Development and testing standards.
- Documentation and documentation standards.
- Automated testing support tools.
- Software change/release control procedures.

- Test plan and test document.
- Competence of vendor personnel.

This stage also includes tasks relating to reviewing, testing, and evaluating a software package in light of the standards, procedures, and controls in the vendor environment.

Review of Development Controls. Reviews procedures for developing, testing, and making changes in the package:

- Identifying how the development controls were applied to the package.
- Considering whether it is more efficient to rely on and test the development controls than to apply extensive procedures in testing the application.
- Evaluating the development controls if it is decided that reliance will be placed on them in establishing the scope of the application testing.
- Testing whether the development controls to be relied on were operating during the period of reliance (such as the period during which the package was developed).

Review of Application Design and Controls. Activities involved in this task include:

- Verifying that implementation documentation adequately supports the applications.
- Verifying that internal processing controls and reports and/or data files:
  - — Are described in the documentation of the package.
  - — Are adequate to permit the performance of audits thereof in accordance with GAAS.
- Verifying that procedures in the package for processing accounting information produce reports that enable users to prepare financial statements in conformity with GAAP.

Review of Detailed Application Documentation. Elements of documentation to be reviewed include:

- All documentation that will be delivered to the customer with the software product.

- System and program documentation, including system and program documentation delivered to the customer and proprietary documentation held by the vendor.

This documentation review should:

- Assure that the documentation is adequate to allow its intended users to understand the package.
- Assure that the documentation is adequate for the vendor to maintain the package.

Review of Technical Design. This procedure should determine:

- The hardware, components, and features relied on by the application.
- The system software, releases, and version relied on by the application.
- Whether the system software has been modified.

Development of Application Test Plan. The purpose of this procedure is to determine the extent of application testing that is necessary. Emphasis is placed on controls, balancing procedures, and exception conditions. Test conditions include those relating to the accuracy and completeness of processing and to conformance with GAAP or another comprehensive basis of accounting, such as those prescribed by government regulations.

Testing. All tests are performed according to the application test plan and, where applicable, using the operating system software needed to operate the package.

Evaluation. The results of the preceding procedures are evaluated to determine whether the software package meets the specified objectives of the evaluation.

Report. A report on software evaluation is prepared. It should:

- Identify the software package reviewed.
- Direct potential users to consider the internal controls included in the entire system of which the package is a part.

- Direct users to compare their particular requirements with the package documentation and the report.
- Describe the factors included in the review.
- Describe the factors excluded from the review.
- Describe the inherent limitations of a software evaluation (such as test limitations, human error, or subversive intent).
- State that the report is neither a warranty nor an expression of an opinion on a specific user's system of internal accounting control.
- Describe the conclusions.
- Include a restriction on the use of the report.
- Specify the date the review was completed and the version of the software reviewed.

PART VII

Auditing Advanced Systems

CHAPTER **26**

Testing Techniques for Computer-Based Systems

TESTING COMPUTER-BASED SYSTEMS

Due to the nature of computer system processing, the auditor cannot always carry out tests using conventional methods. As a result, a number of specific testing methods for computer-based systems have been developed. The basic techniques available to the auditor for testing computer-based systems and the circumstances in which they are commonly used are described in this chapter. Those techniques are often called Computer-Assisted Audit Techniques, or CAATs. (See Appendix C for three case studies which describe real-life applications of CAATs at three organizations.)

What Data Is Available?

Modern decision-support systems contain much more data than traditional accounting systems. With proper design, large quantities of relevant data can be stored on computer media. Modern systems are designed to maintain the organization's data in forms that can satisfy most management demands, even those unanticipated when the system is designed. Data stored that is relevant to management and to the auditor includes the following:

- Accounting data.
- Historical results.
- Statistical information.
- Computer programs.
- Operational data (e.g., computer operating logs).

This data is not stored indefinitely. As soon as its usefulness has expired, data stored on computer media is regularly destroyed. The auditor may have to make a special request to ensure that the relevant data is retained for audit examination.

What Methods of Testing Are Available?

Special testing techniques are available to auditors of computer-based systems. In many instances, these tests, performed using software tools, are the only efficient and effective way to evaluate computer-based systems. Audit tests fall into two general categories: (1) tests of controls, and (2) substantive procedures. To perform these tests, the auditor chooses a strategy and specific testing methods. In computer-based systems, the strategy usually includes software tools.

The auditor can test the accuracy of data processing results and the adequacy of controls over that processing using manual tests, including checking and simulation, and/or EDP testing methods, including program code analysis, parallel simulation, and test data and Integrated Test Facility.

MANUAL TESTING

Many of the tests for computer-based systems are the same as those used to test manual systems, although the documents that are examined may be different. Customary manual audit testing techniques can be used whenever:

- Adequate evidence is readily available.
- Information is presented in normal accounting terms.
- Volumes of data are not too large to carry out the test.

Accordingly, many transaction review techniques, compliance tests, and substantive procedures do not change significantly in a computer-based system.

Some manual audit tests require special EDP skills. For instance, general controls and program coding are usually described in data processing terminology. Review may require the assistance of a specialist, both to understand the evidence examined and to test the relevant processing functions. In those cases, some form of software can normally be used. Audit software is discussed later in this chapter.

Manual Checking

Manual checks that can be used to perform tests of controls generally include the following:

- *Examination*—For example, examining reports indicating that the numerical sequence of prenumbered documents is checked periodically and missing numbers are investigated by someone who does not normally work with these documents, or examination of program amendment forms to see that they have been approved by the appropriate people.
- *Reperformance*—For example, selecting items from the report of missing numbers and verifying that the correct follow-up action has been taken; selecting approved program amendment forms and confirming that the amendment forms and amendments have been adequately designed, tested, and documented.
- *Observation*—For example, attending physical inventories; observing the physical restrictions on access to the computer room.

User controls and many of the general controls can be tested in conventional ways. Therefore, they present no major change in procedures for the auditor.

Similarly, substantive procedures, although likely to be carried out on computer printouts instead of on traditional lists of balances, can be performed by conventional manual tests in some instances.

Limitations on Manual Checking. The auditor should also test certain programmed procedures. These are checked as part of tests of controls on implementation controls or as substantive procedures to provide assurance that a particular programmed procedure is operating. Some evidence that the programmed procedure is functioning usually is available, but steps taken to produce those results by computer processing are rarely printed out in detail. In the absence of such a printout, the auditor cannot test the operation of programmed procedures by conventional means. There are two ways this difficulty can arise:

1. Totals and analyses are often printed out without supporting details, making it impossible for the auditor to check the method used to arrive at that total or analysis.
2. When exception reports and rejection listings are produced, it is often impossible to establish that all items that should have been reported or rejected have been. By examining the reports or

listings themselves, the auditor only sees the ones that were reported. Another method of testing, obviously, is called for.

In both cases, there is a lack of visible evidence showing how the programmed procedure operates within the computer, since only the results of its operations are seen.

Manual Simulation Techniques

Manual tests can also be carried out when full visible evidence is not readily provided by the system, but can be re-created by special means. Methods for achieving this re-creation of evidence are known collectively as "manual simulation." They include:

- Reassembling processed data so that it is in the same condition as it was when the programmed procedure was first applied. For example, reassembling batches of sales invoices to test the batch totals that were posted to the sales ledger control account.
- Working on current data before it is sent for processing by the computer. For example, checking the additions of batches before they are sent for conversion in order to test how a total, used to control subsequent processing, was reached.
- Selecting a small number of items from those submitted for processing and processing them in a separate run. For example, splitting a batch into two batches, one large and one small, and then processing the small batch separately to see whether the computer-produced totals agree with precalculated results.
- Simulating a condition that will produce a report if the programmed procedure is working properly. For example, altering a batch total to an incorrect figure so that the batch is rejected or withholding a document so that it is reported as missing. This approach requires careful planning, execution, and the agreement of a responsible user-department official.
- Requesting a special printout of items processed. For example, a listing of sales invoices included in a sales total produced by the computer.

When visible evidence of the operation of a programmed procedure neither exists nor can be created, and the appropriate condition cannot be simulated, it may not be possible to carry out some kinds of manual tests.

EDP TESTING TECHNIQUES

Program Code Analysis

Program code analysis is used by an auditor to confirm the existence of programmed procedures in a program or series of programs. The programmed procedures to be confirmed are identified in an internal control questionnaire or similar document. The technique may also be used by the auditor to obtain or confirm an understanding of the programs, or parts of programs, in the system.

For this technique to be effective, the auditor must either examine the code in object form (the machine language the computer uses internally), which is probably not practical, or confirm that the code examined in source statement form (the language programmers use) relates to the instructions in the executable programs (the programs in form the computer can run).

This confirmation usually can be obtained from the tests carried out on program security controls and computer operation controls. In more advanced installations, where the auditor is most likely to use program code analysis, system software may ensure that the source and executable programs are the same. The auditor can often rely on tests of these procedures. As an alternative, the auditor may be able to make special use of testing software. (Testing software is discussed more fully in the later section "Comparison Programs.") This software can check a newly compiled version (the version of source program after conversion into machine code) of the source program in question against the executable program in use.

Program code analysis usually consists of three steps:

1. *Identifying the programs to be examined.* This can be done by referring to the company's system documentation, which may include block diagrams of programs and detailed specifications of individual programs.
2. *Selecting the form of code to be examined.* The auditor normally decides to examine the source statement program. This requires:
   - A knowledge of the source (or high-level programming) language used, such as COBOL (Common Business Oriented Language) in many environments.
   - Care in selecting the version of the source statement program to be examined. It is usually preferable to compile the authorized source for the production program and check the compiled results against the production version that is actually in use. The software also may provide options such as cross-referenced data names and verb listings.

3. *Analyzing the selected code*. Understanding the logic of programs written by someone else can be difficult. It is usually easier when the auditor is in an installation which follows standards for programming and program documentation. In any case, it is important to adopt a systematic approach to reviewing the code. Starting with the first program statement and following the code through line by line to the last statement is unlikely to be an efficient or effective way to proceed. The following approach is more practical:
   - Obtain an understanding of the data and files used by the programs being analyzed.
   - Analyze the logic of the relevant lines of code.
   - Ensure that the relevant lines of code analyzed are not bypassed or distorted by another part of the program or by an entirely different program.

To analyze the code, an auditor may use audit software packages to provide additional documentation and comparison programs to uncover changes made in programs during the period under investigation. Comparison programs are, therefore, particularly useful in subsequent years' audits.

Parallel Simulation

Parallel simulation tests the proper functioning of programmed procedures and the accuracy of the financial data processed. The method consists of taking real data that is being run through production programs and processing it through programs developed by the auditor. For this method to work, the test programs must perform some, but not necessarily all, of the same functions as the production programs being simulated.

Parallel simulation can check the following:

- Input validation procedures.
- Data updating logic.
- Processing logic and controls.

In parallel simulation, all transactions chosen for the test are checked. Checking can take place at any time; the programs can be run whenever computer time is available.

The method of parallel simulation employed depends on the software tools selected. These can consist of generalized audit software, industry-oriented audit software, application audit software, or custom audit software developed for special circumstances.

To perform parallel simulation, all data and files processed by the auditor's programs must be exactly the same as those required to run the production programs. Additionally, reports should be generated for the same periods of time. Any and all documentation that refers to controls, or to reconciliations conducted, should be retained.

The parallel simulation programs used are usually less complex than the regular production programs they are simulating. Certain discrepancies can occur as a result of this difference. Rather than trying to amend the test program to conform exactly to the processing requirements of the production program, it may be far more cost-effective to reconcile the discrepancies manually. Most likely, the auditor will choose to use a program and compare the test processing results to detect any differences or discrepancies.

In all cases, exceptions and unexplained discrepancies should be documented fully. The auditor should then recommend corrective measures, if necessary.

Parallel simulation can be repeated using the same testing programs, provided the production programs have not changed in ways that have audit significance. To verify whether authorized programming changes have been made, the auditor should check the program change log and then test it by comparing the current version of the source program to a controlled version of this program. Unauthorized or unrecorded changes would probably show up as differences in the results between the simulation and the production run. Hence, the importance of following up on discrepancies.

Test Data and Integrated Test Facility

Test data is one method used as an EDP audit technique to test processing and controls in application systems. In parallel simulation, test programs process real data; in the test data method, real programs process test data. The output of this processing is then compared to predefined results.

Audit test data should not be confused with the comprehensive test data prepared by the organization's data processing staff to test the operation of new programs. Audit test data is restricted to testing only the particular programmed procedures for which the auditor wishes to assess control risk. It is designed to be as representative as possible of the actual data processed by the company. However, when it has been decided that audit test data will be used to test particular procedures, it is often efficient to include tests on other procedures that would otherwise be done manually.

Test data is used to check the following:

- Input validation routines, error detection, and transaction data control procedures integral to the programs.

- Processing logic and controls on master file data.
- Standard calculations, such as interest, taxes, or gross pay.
- Program modifications.
- Manual procedures in use.

The test data method is applicable for the following:

- Acceptance testing of a new system or a system modification.
- Compliance testing of a system already in use.

Therefore, the test data method can be applied to program processing verification and evaluation. It is not a way to check completeness or accuracy of input and update of data or master files.

There are two methods of running test data:

1. Test data can be processed using the organization's operational programs, separately from the actual data, using copies of master files or dummy files specially designed and set up for the purpose.
2. Test data can be included with the organization's data for regular processing, with approval from a responsible department official.

A second testing method is called an Integrated Test Facility (ITF). (See Figure 26-1.) When specific records on the master files are reserved or created for this purpose and consistently processed for testing at regularly established milestones, the ITF is also referred to as the Base Case System Evaluation.

Test data can be created in three ways:

1. The simplest, although the most time-consuming, is to complete actual input forms in such a way that each condition specified in the test plan will be tested. This would include creation of master records, followed by running the transactions to test processing and controls.
2. A related method is to copy existing master file records onto a test master and then, as in the first method, to run transactions. When this is done, the auditor should be sure that each possible condition as described by the test plan is covered in the processing of master file records.
3. Auditors also make limited use of special computer programs called test data generators. A test data generator assists in preparing test data sets. Although cost often becomes a consideration when deciding whether to use test data generators, their advantages include (a) reduction of clerical effort and

FIG. 26-1

The relationship of an Integrated Test Facility to generated production program output

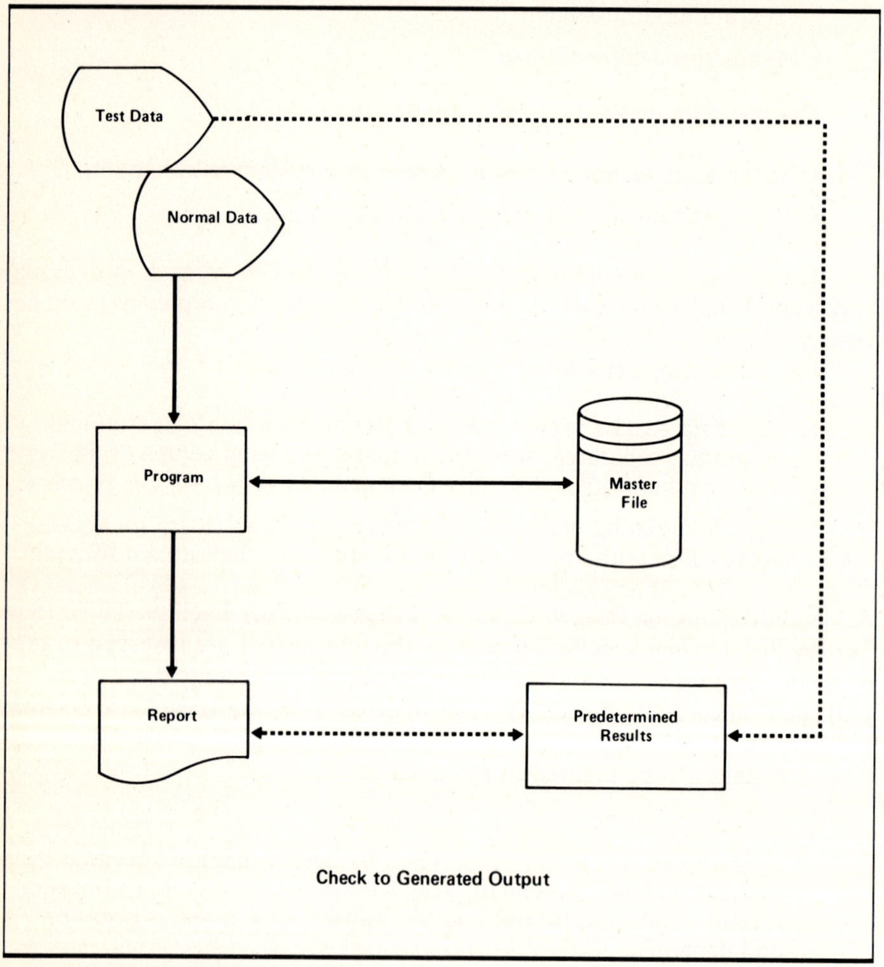

(b) increased thoroughness in testing input validation routines, error detection procedures, and calculations.

Test data transactions should be run on executable programs as they exist in the production library. The auditor should receive output that was either observed being run or was handled in a manner that prevents tampering. Care should be taken that production files are not affected by the presence of test data. The output should then be compared to the expected results. Differences should be analyzed; in those cases, the test should be rerun to verify the results. Where differences in procedures do exist, they should be documented, researched, and reported.

Test Data (Application Development)

In some cases, auditors design test data to test important programs independently before an application goes into production. This testing helps assure that critical programs are functioning properly. It may sometimes reveal significant deficiencies and help avoid operational problems.

This technique usually does not require auditors to have a high level of data processing skill. However, designing test data can be time-consuming, and an in-depth knowledge about the operations of the application is required. It may be difficult to test all paths through a large program.

AUDIT SOFTWARE TOOLS

Introduction

Auditors have been using computers as part of the audit process for many years. The use of computerized techniques affords access to the large amounts of data stored in EDP systems. The audit software available can be particularly effective in accessing this information.

When complex, integrated computer systems are involved, the use of audit software tools is not only audit-efficient; it is often a necessary ingredient of an effective audit. Audit software is not, however, a panacea for computer audit problems. This is an important technique, yet it is only one of many an auditor must master to audit complex business systems successfully.

What Is Audit Software?

Audit software is a special program or set of programs that can audit data stored on computer media. Audit software has functions similar to query facilities, report writers, utilities, computer languages, and other data processing software techniques. Indeed, the auditor may well use these standard data processing techniques to assist with the audit if they are more efficient. In many cases, audit software is more suitable.

Following are the principal features of audit software:

- Complete files can be read speedily and accurately, resulting in:
  - Examination of all data on file rather than a small sample.
  - The ability to obtain information that would not be available otherwise.
  - The ability to specify and identify data that meets a particular condition, such as all customer balances that are more than double their credit limits.
  - The ability to quantify the extent of unusual or erroneous data on the file, such as the total number of customers with credit totals that exceed their limits and the total of the balances involved.
- Conventional audit time can be devoted to an examination of items identified as needing audit attention.
- The software can be made flexible by using parameters that can be altered each time the program is run.
- Once audit software is set up, subsequent running costs are reasonable and overall time savings are often considerable. The same program is used for each audit until there is a major change in the system.
- To run the program, computer resources must be obtained. These should be planned in advance, as should the procedures for capture and retention of the data to be examined.

See Figure 26-2 for typical audit software functions.

Audit Objectives

A critical part of using audit software effectively is to translate audit objectives accurately into actual computer processing functions.

To set the audit objectives, the auditor should have a knowledge of fundamental EDP concepts. An auditor whose knowledge of EDP is more comprehensive can also prepare and execute the software. Otherwise, the broad computer functions can be discussed with an EDP audit specialist or a data processing technician. The specialist or technician can then develop the automated application specifications and prepare the computer programs. The degree of technical ability needed depends on the technique used. In general, the more flexible the software is, the more the auditor needs to know to use it.

For example, a typical audit objective might be to determine that the general ledger control account balance agrees with the total of the individual account balances included in the subsidiary records. The corresponding computer function would be to total the amount in the dollar balance field

FIG. 26-2

Audit software functions

- **Computations -** Accounting computations such as addition, subtraction, multiplication, division and percentage calculation. Complex calculations may involve complex formula with the use of exponentiation.
- **Data extraction and reformatting —** Extract and print data in a format required by the auditor, e.g., printing confirmation letters.
- **Data analysis —** Analyze data within the same record to identify certain information for audit follow-up purposes, e.g., negative stocks and long outstanding debtors.
- **Simple sample selection —** Simple selection basis such as HIGH-LOW method.
- **Statistical sampling —** Sample selection procedure based on different sampling algorithms, e.g., every *n*th item starting from *x* item, dollar unit sampling, sampling that provides a predetermined confidence limit, or true random sampling that utilizes a random number table or random number generator.
- **Summarization —** Accumulate one or several levels of totals for a specified field.
- **File stratification —** Determine the distribution of a file's records (value and number of records) into specified categories.
- **Sort —** Resequence the records in a way that the auditor requires.
- **Field comparison —** Compare two fields between records to determine whether inconsistencies or logical errors exist.
- **File matching —** Compare related records between two files to determine whether inconsistencies or logical errors exist.
- **Reperformance —** Duplicate production processing for audit purposes.
- **File creation —** Build a file for use in later processing.
- **File updating —** Create and recalculate files containing information that can be updated.
- **Statistical analysis —** Operational research techniques used to generate histograms, bar graphs, pie charts, trend charts, linear programming and trend line, correlation and regression analyses.
- **Downloading —** Downloading of corporate data from a mainframe or a minicomputer to a microcomputer where the data is further analyzed and processed.

FIG. 26-3

How audit objectives can be translated into basic computer functions which can in turn be translated into computer programs that perform those functions

Audit Objectives	Computer Function
1. Determine that the total of the balances of individual customer accounts agrees with the general ledger account balance.	**1.** Add the balance due amount for each record on the balance forward file and print total.
2. a. Request confirmation of amounts due from customers on a given basis of selection.	**2. a.** Compare balance, customer name, or other relevant information on each record with established selection criteria and select those records that meet or exceed the criteria; print confirmation requests.
b. Test the aging calculations by selecting individual customer accounts on a given basis and check the aging of unpaid amounts by tracing to source documents.	**b.** Compare selection criteria with relevant information on each record and select those records that meet or exceed the criteria. For each of the accounts selected, print the customer number and the invoice number and amount for items comprising each aging category for manual comparison to source documents.

of each record included in the file or data base and to print the total. To prepare for the computer specialist to do this, the auditor would:

- Indicate the location of the relevant fields on the records in the file.
- Direct that the amounts in those fields are to be added.
- Specify the format of the report on which the totals are to be printed.

Although the previous example is simple, it demonstrates the basic, step-by-step thought process that is required. By following the same process, even complex audit objectives can be translated into specific computer functions. Figure 26-3 illustrates how some of the compound audit objectives relating to accounts receivable processing may be translated into basic computer functions and thus converted to a computer program.

For purposes of illustration, assume that EDP maintains a file containing each customer's balance-forward information. Typically, this file would include customer name, number, balance due, and the totals of the aging categories within which the amounts comprising the balance fall. In addition, a supporting transaction file is maintained, which shows customer number, invoice number, and amount of all items uncollected at the end of the month. To meet some of the audit objectives, the auditor would follow the procedures shown in Figure 26-3. The relationship between various types of audit software and audit objectives is shown in Figure 26-4.

Planning Considerations

Aside from knowing the exact audit objectives that audit software and its use are to achieve, few other implementation functions are as important as planning the scope of audit procedures. An overview of scoping procedures includes the following steps:

- Gathering all necessary data on:
  - —The EDP environment in which the software will be executed.
  - —The exact results expected.
  - —The timing and performance of audit support.
- Evaluating and estimating ability to accumulate and evaluate data within specific guidelines:
  - —Scoping of the program and gathering information.
  - —Evaluating and estimating time required.
  - —Learning from other auditors.
  - —Coordination of efforts.
  - —Participation of appropriate personnel.
- Program development, including the following:
  - —Detailed program specifications.
  - —Program coding.
  - —JCL (Job Control Language) development and coding.
  - —Obtaining an executable load module—compiling and linkediting.
  - —Program testing.
  - —Program processing.
  - —Output results reconciliation.
  - —Turnover of output for use.
  - —Program documentation.
  - —Completion report.

FIG. 26-4

Audit software related to audit objectives

Micro-Based Audit Software	System Utilities and Service Aids	Query Functions and Report Writers	Embedded Code	Custom Audit Software	Application Specific	Generalized Audit Software	AUDIT SOFTWARE CLASSIFICATION / AUDIT SOFTWARE FUNCTIONS / AUDIT OBJECTIVES	Completeness of Input	Accuracy of Input	Validity (Existence)	Completeness of Update	Accuracy of Update	Maintenance of Data	Appropriateness of Program Procedures	Analytical Review
★		★	○	○	★	★	Computations: Simple		★			★	○		★
★		○		★	○	○	Computations: Complex								
○	★	★	★	★	○	★	Data Extraction and Reformatting	★	★	★	★	★	★		
★		★	○	★	★	★	Data Analysis		★			★	○		
○	○	★	★	★	★	★	Simple Sample Selection	★	★	★	★	★	★		
★			★	○	★	★	Statistical Sampling	★	★	★	★	★	★		
★		★	○	★	★	★	Summarization	★	★		★	★	★		★
○		○	○	○	★	★	File Stratification								★
○	★	○		○	★	★	Sort	★			★		○		
★	○	★	★	★	★	★	Field Comparison		★	★		★	○		
○	★	★	★	○	★	★	File Matching: 2 Files	★	★	★	★	★	★		
○		○	○	★	○	○	File Matching: > 2 Files								
★		○		○	★	★	Reperformance: Simple	○	○	○	★	★		★	
○				★	○	○	Reperformance: Complex								
★	★	○	★	★	★	★	File Creation	○	○	○	★	★	★		
★	○	○	★	★	★	★	File Updating	○	○		★	★	★		
★		○		○	★	★	Statistical Analysis								★
★	★	○		○			Downloading								★

Micro-Based Audit Software	System Utilities and Service Aids	Query Functions and Report Writers	Embedded Code	Custom Audit Software	Application Specific	Generalized Audit Software	*ENVIRONMENTS:*
	★	★	○	★	★	★	*MAINFRAME*
	★	★	○	★	○	★	*MINICOMPUTER*
★	★	○		★	○	○	*MICROCOMPUTER*

★ TYPICAL USE

○ POSSIBLE USE

Complicating considerations include:

- Limited or nonexistent on-site support.
- Limited or nonexistent organizational support.
- Incompatible hardware.
- Limited computer time available.
- Nonstandard data structure or data access.

- External sort(s) required.
- Large data volume input file(s).
- Extremely slow input/output (I/O) devices.
- Complicated or extensive output reconciliation procedures required.

When establishing budgets, many factors have to be considered. Some of the more important are:

- Situation-related factors:
  - — Hardware type.
  - — Generalized audit software type.
  - — Extent of documentation.
  - — Availability of technical support on site.
  - — Amount of computer time available.
  - — Program coding requirements and support.

Audit software development and processing can be divided into three distinct categories:

1. To develop programs:
   - Develop detailed program specifications.
   - Code the source program.
   - Develop JCL.
   - Prepare source program and JCL.
   - Obtain an executable program—compile and linkedit.
   - Test the executable program.
   - Reconcile the test results.
2. To process the tested programs:
   - Confirm access to the computer.
   - Confirm the availability of required input data files.
   - Confirm that the proper version of the reconciliation report is the one on hand.
   - Keep a written record of any processing problems encountered.
3. To complete reconciliation of the audit software reports:
   - Reconcile all key items, noting any discrepancies.
   - Establish any discrepancies that could affect the audit (such as those that would require an adjustment to the financial statements).

- Determine if audit software must be revised to obtain reconcilable results.

Implementation Considerations

The success of using audit software is attributable to effective implementation. No system, however appropriate its abilities, will meet auditor or organization needs without careful selection, preparation, and implementation strategies. The following list provides a summary outline of considerations for the successful integration of audit software.

To be successful, audit software should:

- Be properly executed.
- Meet all of its intended audit objectives.
- Be completed within the approved budget.

The skills required to implement audit software effectively are:

- Training in selected audit software.
- Skills in programming language (frequently COBOL).
- Strong knowledge of JCL.
- Ability to translate audit objectives into software procedures.
- Ability to function with user staff and data processing personnel.

Audit software solutions are dictated by the following data processing environment considerations:

- Available computer hardware.
- Available generalized audit software.
- The automated system being tested.
- The abilities of the available data processing personnel.
- Computer operations schedule.

To implement audit software within an audit plan, time must be allocated for the following:

- Specific audit test factors:
  - — Test file availability.
  - — Input file sizes.

— File access methods.
— Difficulty of calculation methodology.
— Existence and retention of all required files.
— Defined reconciliation report or information.

In summary, when using audit software the auditor should:

- Plan what is to be done before beginning.
- Understand the environment in which the auditor will be operating.
- Develop a clear-cut strategy.
- Pay attention to details and follow the plan.
- Reconcile all results and investigate discrepancies.
- Write appropriate documentation, letters, and reports.

The various audit software tools available are discussed in the following sections. Widely used tools are described in Figure 26-5.

GENERALIZED AUDIT SOFTWARE

The examples of audit software tools discussed subsequently are representative of the ones currently available. With the staggering pace of technological EDP developments, auditors should always be prepared to learn new techniques and keep abreast of current audit developments.

The auditor who knows how to use standard data processing techniques, such as languages or utilities, may be able to use those techniques to satisfy some audit requirements. However, when an audit department is using software extensively, it is best to choose software aids specifically suited to the environment.

Generalized audit software exists because, in the normal course of events, many different audits require similar audit tasks (e.g., adding files, formatting reports) and this software can be adapted easily to carry out these tasks in different computer environments. This software can be adapted quickly to the specific goals of an audit. Generalized software is usually more cost-effective than custom software, which is written specifically for a job.

FIG. 26-5

Software tools for accessing and processing client application data

Tool	Use; Frequency	Advantages	Disadvantages	Concerns
Generalized audit software packages	Footing, identifying exceptions, selecting and analyzing data; most common.	Easy to use. Limited programming skills required. Relatively short development time. Often self-documenting. Reduces reliance on EDP staff.	Less flexible than customized software and utilities. Limitations on number and structure of files accessed. Operationally inefficient. Usually limited to testing data files.	Must be purchased and installed. Training is required.
Application audit software packages	Applications with common audit objectives, such as accounts receivable, accounts payable, general ledger, payroll, and inventory; less common than generalized audit software.	Predefined functions can save audit time and costs in developing software. Efficient for testing many locations with the same system.	Predefined objectives may not be relevant.	File conversion into compatible format is normally required.
Customized audit software	Performing specialized functions not provided by a generalized audit software package; common.	Efficient processing. Flexibility. Can handle more complex logic and calculations.	Requires knowledge of computer language and greater technical skills. More expensive, longer development time.	Some languages are easy to use and can be efficient if used frequently.

Embedded audit data collection	In telephone, banking, insurance, and similar industries where, because of the size of files, it is not practical to use other techniques; rare. May be used more in the future, e.g., in capturing transactions in a transaction processing system or in monitoring performance of branches or retail stores to identify high-risk locations.	Continuous monitoring.	Auditor needs to be involved in system design; requires highly technical skills. High cost of development and maintenance. May have to retain large volumes of data.	Technique must be built into application programs.
Query functions and report writers	On installations that have purchased such software; becoming common.	Usually easy to use.	Unique to particular environments; therefore, auditor must learn each time. Usually limited to information retrieval.	May be available on system; therefore, no additional purchase or installation costs are involved.
System utility software and service aids	Setting up audit software, e.g., copying or sorting files; common.	Powerful. Easy to use.	Unique to the environment so auditor must learn each time, often requires technical knowledge. May produce little or no audit trail. Reports may be difficult to read.	No purchase or installation costs involved. Technical manuals sometimes difficult to understand. Can damage system and files.

(*continued*)

FIG. 26-5 *(continued)*

Tool	Use; Frequency	Advantages	Disadvantages	Concerns
Microcomputer-based audit software	Automating audit workpapers and analytical procedures; common.	Easy to use. Inexpensive. Can be used to download data from mainframes.	Limited storage available in microcomputers. Not all auditors have micros.	Should take into account maintenance and support fees when purchasing such packages.
Time-sharing programs	For analytical reviews such as balance sheet analysis, operating analysis and financial analysis; use declining rapidly.	An efficient way of making use of audit software. Quick turnaround.	May not be able to obtain all required programs from one vendor.	Should not let confidential data be present in a time-sharing system. Should test the programs before relying on the output.
Public data bases and bulletin boards	Sharing information with others, obtaining difficult to get but public data (e.g., economic trends); becoming more frequent.	Current information on industry and peers.	Difficult to integrate data with other automated data.	Data may not be reliable. Needs a modem and a micro. Needs subscription and frequent use to be cost-effective.

The auditor uses generalized audit software to examine the information held on computer files and to:

- Carry out audit tests, such as verification of calculations and totals or analyses produced. An example would be the evaluation and summation of aged inventory balances.
- Create and print additional analyses of data for audit purposes, such as the calculation of total inventory holdings in excess of current demand or total receivables that exceed credit limits.
- Examine the state of the data held on the file in order to:
  - — Provide totals of unusual items, such as customers without any credit limit or inventory issues with invalid dates.
  - — Select and print data from the file for subsequent examination, either as a sample of normal data or because it falls within the auditor's definition of unusual, such as customer credit balances over $X or unusual discount terms.

Generalized audit software is specifically designed for audit use. It should make it easy for the auditor to translate audit objectives into program code. A package can perform varied data processing functions: reading data from computer files; selecting all or only certain records for processing; performing auditor-specified computations; sampling, sorting, and summarizing data; and printing reports in the form requested by the auditor. It may offer the auditor the following abilities:

- Read and analyze information stored in a data file or match and analyze information stored in two separate but logically related files.
- Select items for review, stratify selected items or complete files, and analyze the resulting information.
- Apply interval sampling methods, beginning the analysis at any random start point and continuing the selection at fixed intervals.
- Summarize data files and analyze the data.
- Subtotal and develop column totals or column averages for different logical levels (e.g., payroll by department, plant, and division).
- Develop statistics on any number of data elements in the file and calculate percentages for selected items in relation to the total population and control totals showing positive, negative, and zero constituents as well as net values.
- Assist substantive testing by sampling the data file and generating reports.

- Perform any number of mathematical calculations on an entire file or selected records.
- Format reports with descriptive headings, automatic horizontal columns, and page numbers.
- Produce multiple reports and machine-readable output files.
- Reports designed by the auditor, such as:
  — Accounts with balances over credit limit.
  — Confirmation control.
  — Selected representative accounts.
  — Statistics for specific data.
  — Wrap-up report showing file statistics.

Comparison Programs

Comparison programs are used to compare the source or executable versions of operational programs with controlled copies that have been investigated previously and held by the auditor. They provide listings that set out the contents of the programs being compared and the differences (if any) between them. This technique is useful in identifying changes, or to confirm a lack of changes, in programs. Each change identified is investigated manually to determine its nature and authenticity.

The software can confirm that source programs are logically identical to their executable form. This is useful not only for the programs and software developed in-house, but also for testing vendor-supplied modules used in production. If these tests are performed on vendor software, the auditor should determine that the user has not customized the software with the vendor's permission or made maintenance updates as prescribed by the vendor.

In addition, source code comparison programs can compare other types of computer media containing data files and JCL to determine if changes have been made. However, comparison programs would not detect a change that was made at a particular point in time if, in the interim, the programs and/or data files were changed back to their original state. This software does not explain the reasons for differences. Therefore, the auditor must have a high level of technical skill to interpret results and understand the concepts involved. The software also does not evaluate the correctness of the code logic.

Program Tracing and Mapping

Software is available that monitors the execution of a program and produces a report showing the number of times each line of source code was executed during processing. This report can be useful when performing code analysis, since it indicates lines of code that are not executed. All unexecuted code should be investigated. It may exist for occasional, annual, or other periodic authorized runs. On the other hand, the investigation may make the auditor aware of code that is fraudulent, redundant, or erroneous.

Flowcharting Programs

Flowcharting programs create flowcharts as they document and analyze a program's procedures. The flowcharts produced by such programs are often too voluminous to be helpful in an audit. Also, if the program is not well-structured, the flowchart produced will be difficult to follow. However, the verb listings and cross-referenced data name listings generated may be helpful. They are often used to assist in program code analysis. JCL flowchart programs can assist in understanding and confirming system flows.

APPLICATION AUDIT SOFTWARE

The increased use of purchased software packages has shown that data processing functions can be largely standardized to meet the needs of different organizations. Audit software tasks for common applications such as accounts receivable, accounts payable, general ledger, payroll, and inventory can be similarly standardized.

Application audit software is developed to achieve common audit objectives. Those functions are then precoded into the package and its associated documentation. The auditor saves time and effort, since audit functions are predefined. As an example, for accounts receivable: age analyze the ledger, select items for audit testing, produce confirmation letters, and match subsequent cash received. Of course, it may be necessary to alter the functions somewhat, depending on the particular audit concerns, but this flexibility is built into the software. To run the software, the auditor converts the data files into a format compatible with the package, determines the appropriate parameters, and then executes the software.

INDUSTRY-RELATED AUDIT SOFTWARE

Some audit tests are specific to particular industries. Among these are the insurance, health care, and financial services industries. Tests are also designed for applications within those industries, such as investment portfolio accounting. Because of the intricacy, and resulting cost, of designing the kinds of programs that are necessary to achieve common audit objectives, firms have produced standard software packages and routines to meet those special needs.

CUSTOM AUDIT SOFTWARE

In some circumstances, prepackaged audit software is unsuitable, usually because system constraints make it difficult or impossible to use. To use audit software in such a location, EDP audit specialists and computer programmers can write programs to order. These are sometimes referred to as "one-off" programs. However, the expense involved in designing and writing a program to meet particularly complex goals may be prohibitive.

Although prepackaged software is useful in the majority of file interrogation audit applications, normally the auditor must be able to develop software for special circumstances that may exceed the capabilities of the prepackaged software. This may be necessary because the package is not available for the particular computer, the output required is very specialized, or the computations and data handling are particularly intricate.

SYSTEM SOFTWARE AND SERVICE AIDS

The auditor should know how to use various system utilities and service aids provided by computer manufacturers and software vendors. These software tools are used in running the system. They can be very useful to the auditor for examining processing activity, developing data interrogation audit systems, and testing programs and operational procedures.

For example, under IBM OS, the utility IEBGENER can be used to copy and reblock sequential files. OS/DITTO can be used to extract particular records from one file, thus creating a subset file for audit examination.

Audit uses of utility software and service aids may include:

- Copying data.
- Transferring all or selected data from one file to another.
- Copying data while changing the media (e.g., copying a disk file to tape).
- Printing all or part of a file.
- Printing a file label, index, or table indicating the nature of file, its internal structure, and the data relationships.

- Creating or erasing files.
- Inserting, deleting, or changing records within a file.
- Sorting records into a new sequence.
- Merging records from two files.
- Printing individual records within a file.
- Processing and listing selected data from a file.
- Compiling or linking programs created by the auditor.
- Changing the name of a program, file, terminal, user, or password.
- Communicating with a computer from a terminal or another computer.
- Reformatting the backup copy of a file.

The auditor must often use such utilities in setting up and executing computerized audit procedures. Utilities can substitute for procedures that would otherwise be performed by generalized audit software or specially written programs. The utilities user manuals describe their abilities and uses.

Utilities provide the auditor with many powerful, easy-to-use functions. A disadvantage is that they are usually specific to a particular computer and operating system, which means that the auditor must learn new utilities for each different computer and system that is audited.

Library Software

Packaged library software provides security over libraries containing programs, JCL, and other files. Such packages produce reports that can serve several audit purposes. The most common audit use of those reports is in gaining an understanding of the system.

Examples of information that the auditor might obtain are the programs that are run and the sequence of their execution, the data files accessed, file descriptions, and record descriptions. Library software packages also produce reports of changes made to programs, which the auditor can use when testing program change control procedures. Following are examples of reports generated by software that analyzes load libraries in an MVS environment:

- *Messages and Information Report*—Specifies inconsistencies in information regarding the user's load modules.
- *Serial Partitioned Data Set (PDS) List Report*—Lists all load modules, with more recent data listed first.

- *Compile/Linkedit Report*—Lists the program name, compiler name, date of compile, and the linkedit date. This information helps the auditor to trace all changes and implementations for the examination period.
- *ZAP Report*—Lists ZAPs or SuperZAPs. ZAPs are service aids or utilities that can change an object program or an executable program. ZAPs can change programs or data files directly, thereby bypassing controls over programs or data file changes. The report indicates the control section, the linkedit date, the ZAP date, and the area where the ZAP occurred. It can be used to trace changes to proper documentation.
- *Change Report*—Compares two examination periods and lists changed programs, new programs, and programs no longer used. When used in conjunction with source program comparison software (which detects what was changed within the program), it allows the auditor to assess the control risk over changes to programmed procedures.

Query Functions and Report Writers

When they are available, standard inquiry (or interrogation) programs can be an economical audit tool. Relatively easy-to-use interrogation methods exist for many smaller computers, and are often built into larger DBMSs (data base management systems). One of the disadvantages of using inquiry programs is that they are often unique to a particular data base or application. This may mean that the auditor has to learn to use each different data base or application's functions. There is often no need to define files, since the data access function is usually integrated with the package; thus, some time is saved.

ANALYSIS OF SYSTEM FUNCTIONS

System Log Analysis

Many installations automatically produce a log of all computer activity, such as IBM's SMF (System Management Facility) log for the OS system. Programs have been developed that analyze the systems log to report specific defined items. Using this software, the auditor can carry out tests to ensure that:

- Only approved programs access sensitive data.

- Utilities or service aids that can alter data files and program libraries are used only for authorized purposes.
- Approved programs are run only when scheduled, and conversely, unauthorized runs do not take place.
- The correct data file generation is accessed for production purposes.
- Data files reported to be password-protected actually are protected.

In addition, there are software packages that provide facilities to log and report all incidences of terminal logon/logoff, hardware malfunctions, system start-up/shut-down, and job start or stop.

Operating System Analysis

Setting up and implementing the operating system requires that parameters are defined to the operating system, as shown by the following example. (Although examples given are in relation to IBM systems, the same concepts apply in other environments.) Software packages such as the PARMLIB Analyzer and CA-EXAMINE are available to aid in the analysis of parameters to determine whether integrity of the system has been compromised due to inadequate considerations in their definition. Integrity of the system may be compromised if the parameters are not properly defined to the operating system, as shown by the following examples, under an IBM OS environment:

- *Operations Controls*
  —Operator intervention is not adequately prevented at initial program load (IPL).
  —Important logging facilities under SMF are not activated.
- *Program Security Controls.* PARMLIB can be used to facilitate temporary unauthorized overrides or modifications.
- *Data File Security.* PARMLIB can be used to allow programs to circumvent standard software protection.

Analyzers are particularly useful in an installation that relies heavily on PARMLIB, has made many customized additions to it, and believes in reducing operator intervention at IPL to an absolute minimum. At the other extreme, however, where an installation has made few or no additions to the standard IBM default PARMLIB members and allows considerable operator intervention at IPL, such analyzers will be of little use. The software will not be able to report on the commands actually issued at IPL, since they are largely manual and therefore not recorded on PARMLIB.

Data Base Analysis

A DBMS, if properly administered, can enhance controls over data and programs. Software aids can help the auditor understand the data base structure. Information Management System/Virtual Storage (IMS/VS) is an IBM product designed to organize and maintain a large centralized information file for on-line and batch data processing applications.

In this type of system, the auditor's ability to assess the adequacy of data base security may be important. IMS analysis software is available. It can read the control program load library and program specification block (PSB) library to extract information describing the teleprocessing network. The network is described in terms of the transactions that can be entered, the programs that process the transactions, and the data base(s) that can be accessed.

Using the reports generated, the auditor can test the validity of the DBA's (data base administrator's) documentation to determine whether standards are being followed and necessary security features are in place.

In addition, the DBMS library can be examined to extract information from the IMS communication security tables. This can help identify resources (such as terminals, transactions, and data elements) that are supposed to be secured.

The reports generated by the data base analyzers can help the auditor determine whether the controls that are documented are actually in place. They can furnish data to answer questions such as:

- What does the data base structure look like?
- How many data bases are there?
- Who can access the data? What information is available to them?
- What is the interaction between the data bases?
- Which terminals can be used to enter certain types of transactions?
- Which on-line transactions can access certain data bases?

This information makes it easier to check on whether data base security is actually implemented as documented.

Access Control Analysis

Access controls over critical data sets/bases and programs can be established using a combination of security software packages, such as RACF, ACF2, and TOP SECRET, and security facilities included in certain communications systems and DBMSs, such as Customer Information Control System (CICS) and IMS/DB.

Audit software packages, such as the CICS and IMS Analyzers, analyze the entries in the system tables of the respective packages. They provide the auditor with information that can be used to help ensure that effective use was made of the packages' security functions. Information produced, useful to the auditor, includes:

- Protected or unprotected data sets/bases.
- Authorized operators and the resources (program data sets/bases) they can access, and in some cases, when they can do so.
- Activities to be recorded in journal log.
- For communication systems, characteristics of terminals connected to the network.

OTHER AUDIT TECHNIQUES

Embedded Code

Special audit subroutines can be embedded into production systems. These routines periodically or continuously monitor all transactions and report those that pass or fail tests established in the embedded code. This technique is sometimes referred to as a System Control Audit Review File (SCARF). The subroutines can make random sampling selections of transactions, a technique known as Sample Audit Review File (SARF). "Snapshot" is a variation in which an image of the transaction is taken at important control points in the processing.

To ensure that these subroutines are properly integrated into the programs, the auditor must be involved in system design. Embedded audit data collection is used mostly in banking, insurance, and telephone and other utility company audits, where it is the most practical method of auditing due to large file sizes.

Automated Internal Control Questionnaires

Automated internal control questionnaires are micro-based packages that are used to generate questionnaires that help evaluate internal controls; thus, they apply to both general, or information technology (IT), controls and application controls. Control evaluation ability may also be included. If so, it is usually combined with facilities to design compliance tests (sometimes substantive tests) and report control weaknesses. Recent developments in this area include expert systems used for identifying the strengths and weaknesses in accounting information systems.

Microcomputer-Based Audit Software

Portable computers and microcomputer-based audit software are widely used in today's auditing profession. Commonly used micro-based audit software includes electronic spreadsheets, electronic mail, downloading software, and hard-coded automated workpaper programs. These packages link individual workpapers through commands that perform functions such as posting adjustments to a trial balance, summarizing trial balances into financial statements, and consolidating and performing analytical procedures, such as ratio analyses.

There are also packages that assist in audit planning, doing functions such as risk assessment, and budget and performance evaluation. Recent developments include knowledge-based expert systems. These assist in audit work, such as assessing the adequacy of allowances for bad debts and selecting the most appropriate audit software tool. (See Figure 26-6.) Generic microcomputer programs can also be used, as shown in Figure 26-7.

USING CAATS IN TYPICAL AUDIT ASSIGNMENTS

Application Program Review

The purpose of an application program review is to determine whether adequate control procedures have been built into the application programs to ensure that the input and update of data is complete, accurate, and valid (e.g., matching of a vendor invoice to a vendor master). The auditor reviews the documentation, testing plan, and so forth to evaluate the controls designed into the application. To satisfy that the controls are functioning in accordance with the documentation and representations, the auditor might use test decks. Test decks are designed to test the programmed procedures in the system. They may be of the auditor's own origin or, after review, the test data of the programmers or the quality assurance department.

Security Review

The purpose of a security review is to ensure the effective use of security facilities. To test the security system, auditors may use facilities available

FIG. 26-6

Microcomputer-based audit tools for audit management

Audit Tool	Audit Planning	Controlling the Audit	Audit Documentation	Audit Reporting
Automated Working Paper System	Perform ratio analysis to help identify unusual fluctuations.	Debit and credit balancing checks. Keeping track of late adjustment, scoresheet items, etc.	Lead schedules, trial balance, financial statements.	
Risk Management Systems	Evaluate the risk factors associated with each application to help determine urgency of audit efforts.			Report risks compared to audit coverage.
Audit Sampling	Help determine the sample size for carrying out substantive testing.	Selecting test items.		
Project Control Systems	Scheduling audits.	Assist in assigning staff and controlling audit assignments.		Summarizing audit results.
Automated Internal Control Questionnaire		Automated audit programs.	Automated control evaluation questionnaires.	Generate management letters based on results of evaluation.
Audit Expert Systems: Expert systems Tax accrual Bad debts provision CICS RACF MVS Physical Security Internal Control Review	Advise on which audit software tool to be used for a particular audit engagement.	Advise on which audit steps to perform.		

FIG. 26-7
Using generic microcomputer products in an audit

Product	Audit Planning	Controlling the Audit	Audit Analysis	Audit Documentation	Audit Reporting
Flowcharting aids				X	
Spreadsheets	X	X	X	X	
Data base	X		X	X	X
Word processor	X			X	X
Graphics	X		X	X	X
Communications		X	X		

in the system, such as the ACF2 report writer, or use software, such as an ACF2 Analyzer, which uses the data in the ACF2 rules to audit the access controls.

When security is implemented without using a security package such as ACF2 or RACF, but using the facilities of the communications system such as CICS, the auditor may use the output from CICS SysGen or software which reports on the access controls provided by CICS. Similarly, for an installation using the security facilities provided by a DBMS, such as IMS, the auditor can use CAATs which report on the security facilities and access controls provided.

Operating System Review

Generally, the auditor is concerned with the operating system facilities that provide access controls, system resources controls, and recoverability. To review controls provided by the operating system, the auditor would examine the various options that can be elected when the user generates the system. To evaluate the use of these options, the auditor can use software to interrogate the operating system to see whether the elected options are still in place.

Data Base Review

This type of review is performed by the auditor to ensure that proper controls are established over the contents of and access to the data base. Since the data base is used by application software, the auditor will want to determine whether users accessing the application software and related logical data base are authorized, and that they take only appropriate actions. When an active data dictionary is present, such as in IDMS (Cullinet Software, Inc.'s DBMS), auditors can aid the evaluation by using the dictionary facilities to indicate relationships. The objectives in this type of review are to evaluate the completeness, accuracy, and existence of data base contents. The auditor should work closely with the DBA to determine that the control standards are documented and are actually in place.

General or IT Controls. As seen in the preceding sections, CAATs are used to review IT controls. This is shown in Figures 26-8 and 26-9.

CURRENT STATUS AND FUTURE POSSIBILITIES FOR CAATS

As currently used, each CAAT has its particular strengths and weaknesses. Their abilities are often tempered by limitations. It is interesting to look at what existing CAATs have and have not achieved from a technical perspective. From that perspective, possible future needs can be considered.

Perhaps one of the most obvious limitations is the need for software to help evaluate controls over minicomputers and microcomputers. Available software packages are predominantly mainframe-oriented, reflecting the generally greater emphasis put on controls by mainframe users. This is partially due to the complex hardware and software surrounding a mainframe environment. More important, however, is that most mainframe users belong to high-risk industries, such as insurance and financial institutions, which call for additional security and concerns.

With the staggering pace of change in information technology, new and more powerful micros and minis (in terms of both real memory and data storage) are constantly being put on the market. The distinctions based on the power and most appropriate use of micros, minis, and mainframes have become increasingly hard to make. More and more application systems are being designed for minicomputers, even for the large-scale applications used in banking, insurance, and government.

The increasingly important role that minis and micros play in the business world has clear implications. The demand for CAATs in general, and

FIG. 26-8

Techniques for testing general controls

Tool	Use; Frequency	Advantages	Disadvantages	Concerns
Data base analysis	To test data file security general controls; common.	Efficient testing technique.	Highly technical skills required.	Limited available audit software. Can use vendor software for some data base management systems.
Operating system analysis	Evaluate operating system security; reasonably common.	Efficient testing technique.	Highly technical skills required.	Will be of little use if few or no additions to the standard default parameters and installation allows considerable operator intervention at initial program load.
Access control analysis	Evaluate access controls; reasonably common.	Efficient testing technique.	Can cover on-line transactions which can define, allocate and deallocate resources dynamically.	Security function does not protect resources against unauthorized access by authorized users.
System log analysis	To test data file and program security general controls; common.	Data produced as part of normal computer operations.	Highly technical skills required. High volume of output.	Specialized software or vendor software is often available. Depends on logging being turned on.
System utilities and service aids	Setting up audit software; common.	Powerful. Easy to use.	Unique to the environment so that auditor must learn each time. May produce little or no audit trail. Report may be difficult to read.	No purchase or installation cost involved.
Automated internal control questionnaires	Evaluation of control procedures; becoming more common.	With integrated compliance test design and reporting facilities.	Long set-up time.	Usefulness largely depends on the adequacy of the design of questionnaires and compliance test.

FIG. 26-9

General controls computer-assisted audit techniques matrix with practical examples

Technique	Implementation and Maintenance	Program Security
Comparison Programs	Used during system change-over to verify program conversion	Compare the following types of Source Programs, Object Programs, Load Modules
Library Analysis		Produce information regarding Programs (e.g. retrieve compile and link-edit information from a load library)
Program Tracing and Mapping	Can be used in conjunction with Program Code Analysis during system development to confirm an understanding of critical programs	Produce information of executed and unexecuted program instructions
Program Code Analysis	To confirm correctness of key program functions	Identify unauthorized code
Flowcharting Programs		(From source code) Assist in program code analysis by documenting and analyzing the flow of program logic
Test Data (System Development)	To independently test programs and systems	Base case test data to detect changes
Data Base Analysis	Test the performance of the data base administrator Verify Data Base Design	Produce information about the online transactions which can access the data base
Operating System Analysis		Software options vary between Examine the relevant parameters to determine the extent of temporary unauthorized overrides allowed
Access Control Analysis		Produce information about programs and their level of protection
System Log Analysis		Log and report the following to Programs executed
System Utilities and Service Aids	Assist auditors generally in extracting data, examining	
Automated Internal Control Questionnaires	Assist in evaluating general controls and designing	

(continued)

FIG. 26-9 *(continued)*

A = Mainframe
B = Minicomputer
C = Microcomputer

Data File Security	Computer Operations	System Software	A	B	C
magnetic media to ensure that no unauthorized changes have been made to them:					
Data Files	JCL	Vendor-supplied System Software	*	o	o
security over libraries or selective subsets of libraries containing:					
Data Files (e.g. report scratched data files)	JCL and Procedure Libraries (e.g. programs in use and data sets accessed)	Programs (e.g. retireve ZAPs / SUPERZAPS usage from a load library)	*	o	o
			*	o	*
			*	o	*
	(From procedure library/JCL) Assist in understanding and confirming system flows		*	o	o
			*	*	*
Produce information about the data base structure and any access restriction	Produce information about master terminal operator commands		*	o	o
computer manufacturers and models. Examples of operating system analysis are:					
Identify those privileged programs which can bypass access protection	Examine the relevant parameters to determine the extent of operator intervention during IPL	Examine the options selected to obtain an understanding of the operating system	*	o	
Produce information about protected and unprotected data sets/bases	Produce information about the characteristics of terminal connected to the network (e.g. master terminal,supervisory terminal)		*	o	o
ensure no unauthorized access to programs, data files, and utilities and service aids:					
Scratched or renamed data files	Job executed and abended	Usage of selected utilities	*	o	
processing activity, developing data interrogation audit systems, and testing programs and operational procedures			*	*	o
test for testing compliance of control procedures					*

audit software in particular, by non-mainframe users is undoubtedly increasing.

An Integrated CAAT Solution?

Available software packages to evaluate system use are generally limited in scope. They address a particular system software product (e.g., MVS, IMS, DC, CICS) or a particular general control area (implementation, program file security, data file security, computer operations, and system software controls) in isolation. In actual computer production runs, these various software products execute interactively, often affecting more than one area of IT controls.

To carry out a general control review effectively, the auditor must understand the implications of the interaction among system software products, and identify any loopholes that may exist. CAATs, such as automated internal control questionnaires, or integrated software that can address multiple system software products or general control areas are under development. However, few such products are available currently.

Moreover, most general control software packages do nothing more than produce raw information for the auditor. Much technical skill is required to analyze the information thus obtained to arrive at sensible audit comments. Software to summarize and/or analyze the information would be helpful.

Audit as It Happens

Since most software packages run in batch mode, the auditor can only assess the control environment at a particular point in time in the past. Given the increasing pace of business transactions, along with the increasing ability of system software to change processing and control environments dynamically, the auditor must carry out audit tests on a more timely basis to ensure that internal controls are in place. Software packages to help assess controls interactively in a dynamic environment are rarely available.

Audit Management Functions

Many microcomputer-based audit management packages are available. They help prepare audit documentation, and carry out some audit procedures, such as analytical review techniques. Certain packages also perform audit planning functions, such as assessing the risk factors associated with various applications to help determine the priority and extent of audit tests to be applied. A few microcomputer-based audit expert systems are becoming available, such as those for assessing bad debt provision or selecting audit software tools.

Potential microcomputer applications, using expert system and artificial intelligence (AI) technologies in audit management functions, provide future avenues of exploration. For example, there are packages under development that will deal with the following audit planning functions:

- Audit risk analysis, with quantification.
- Internal control evaluation.
- Audit program generation, with evidential rank ordering.
- Comment letter generation, based on internal control findings.
- Budgeting.
- Scheduling and performance monitoring.

After all, "a paperless audit" will include the potential application of AI and microcomputer technologies to auditing in the future.

Software is a key to the future of EDP auditing (and probably all auditing, for that matter). It is becoming easy to envision an "analytics-based" audit in the near future, where audit software will automatically track a set of financials and compare those financial statements to industry averages and five-year smoothed data. Subsequently, software will perform ratio analysis and regression analysis, perform risk analysis, generate and allocate materiality, determine sample sizes, and draft audit programs based on the previous soundings. Further, the software, via artificial intelligence could prompt the auditor through the internal control evaluation process and generate a subsequent comment letter. Finally, software would assist in the audit report drafting process and check for generally accepted accounting principles (GAAP) and Securities and Exchange Commission (SEC) disclosure requirements. Many of these steps are already being performed by computers. The difference in the future will be the automation and integration of these steps, probably through AI technology.

Expert Systems

Super-microcomputers allow the development and use of expert or decision support systems. Systems to assist in decision-making by bringing users the knowledge of experts in the field will no doubt proliferate in the future.

Areas where such systems will be invaluable to the auditor include audit management, as discussed previously, and CAATs used in risk evaluation, such as analysis of a security system. Having identified the risk areas, other systems—or part of one large system—will help the auditor, selecting or bridging to the appropriate CAATs to be performed.

Distributed Processing

Potential processing ability is increasing at local sites, frequently using microcomputers and minicomputers. Local nodes process data and summarize results, often for transmission or uploading to a central computer. Therefore, nodes have many of the control problems and control requirements associated with communications to and from a host computer.

While some access control software currently exists in the minicomputer and super-microcomputer environments, more often access controls are embedded in the applications. CAATs to evaluate these controls should be designed and implemented on a more widespread basis.

On-Line Real-Time Environments

Increasing power of even the smallest computers, as well as that of the large mainframes, allows for implementation of more on-line real-time systems. This is commensurate with the increasing demand by business for systems to meet competitive demands.

Many application area CAATs are directed toward batch systems. To audit on-line real-time systems effectively, new techniques will have to be developed. Increased use of techniques such as embedded audit code, transaction trapping, and audit test files will probably occur.

Telecommunications

In telecommunications, facilities provided by audit software include logging and reporting of access violations, analysis of access rights by individual operators, and analysis of the physical and logical network. Few facilities, however, are available for auditing the completeness and accuracy of data transmission.

Networks tying processing abilities of the organization, its suppliers, its vendors, and its customers may increase rapidly in the future. A current example is that a major supplier of hospital supplies placed terminals for input of orders into the hospitals, thereby increasing orders reviewed. Network security for transmission and receiving of data will become an area of increasing concern to auditors. Auditors will have to become familiar with network architecture, and design CAATs to test controls over the network effectively.

Downloading

Most software used to help evaluate system controls is far from user-friendly. Knowledge of JCL, on-line facilities, and sometimes programming languages is required for the auditor to use these packages. Aside from adding user-friendliness to this software, downloading technology seems to provide one answer to such centralized EDP impediments. Since the programs and operating procedures for microcomputers are much simpler, downloading data to micros is a good current solution. Coupled with the fact that many organizations have started charging auditors for computer time used, downloading will no doubt become increasingly important in the future to audit minicomputers and mainframes.

Microcomputers

The explosive growth of desktop computing power will continue in the foreseeable future. Increasingly, financial decisions will be made relying on data that is microcomputer-based or downloaded from mainframes and manipulated on micros. Local area networks will become increasingly common.

In addition to concerns about security and backup, additional application control techniques may be needed to ensure appropriate processing and audit trails. Certain CAATs are now available for limited purposes, such as spreadsheet analysis programs, but these should be expanded. Problems such as template protection and reverse engineering of software via powerful new utilities must also be considered.

Application Packages

Many improvements in audit effectiveness and efficiency have already been achieved in the application area. Companies are installing packaged software for both operations and accounting systems. These packages may be installed as is or modified by the company (or vendor), often using options built into the package. Many packages have query and/or report facilities built in, from which CAATs can be implemented.

Because of the availability of software such as nonprocedural languages, and those easy-to-use query packages and report writers, an increased use of such CAATs in the future is probably inevitable. As the marriage of query functions to application software becomes even more common in application systems, auditors will use these functions to assist in the audit.

Data Bases

Increasing use and flexibility of internal data bases that now allow dynamic redefinition, plus the availability of public data bases used to obtain more data for comparative purposes, allow the auditor to develop new CAATs that use analytics. Selected data from data bases may also be downloaded for use with the auditor's microcomputer-based analytical software. The analytical software is likely to be coupled with graphics software to depict results of the analytics more clearly.

System Design

System design methodologies are changing rapidly. Fourth-generation languages (4GLs), coupled with prototyping, are beginning to allow users to design their own systems.

Auditors must become familiar with these new design techniques and related software. Such software normally has the ability to flowchart the system; other abilities may allow auditors to design CAATs to test the controls built into the system.

CHAPTER **27**

System Software

SECURITY AND CONTROL ISSUES

Computer security involves many issues, including:

- Confidentiality
- Integrity
- Availability

Most security controls currently available were designed to support data confidentiality; fewer controls support data integrity specifically, and special availability controls are found rarely in security functions. However, many of the confidentiality controls support the other two elements at the same time. System software is a critical element in that support.

The importance of these issues, in relation to the effectiveness of overall computer security, depends on the functional requirements the environment places on an installation. For example, computer security requirements for the military differ from an educational institution's needs, which, in turn, differ from those for a large banking concern.

Regardless of the environment, implementing effective security in sophisticated computer systems can be a challenge. Maintaining the desired level of security requires constant monitoring, as well as periodic reviews. This chapter discusses the security and information technology (IT), or general, controls over IBM's Multiple Virtual Storage (MVS) operating systems and its subsystems, to provide an example of such controls over system software.

Authorization Techniques

As computer systems become more complex, control techniques that once were effective fail to address developing security requirements adequately. As a result, control techniques have evolved over time to meet the demands of a changing technological environment. Historically, different philosophies have been used as a basis for various levels of security.

Job-to-Data Authorization. This approach was used frequently in system environments where batch jobs were the only processing methods available. Since on-line access was not available, this approach, combined with physical controls over job submission, provided adequate security.

Terminal-to-Data Authorization. When data processing systems were less sophisticated, one control over on-line access was to restrict user access to terminals physically. This may still be an effective technique for environments where physical security is highly effective or individual accountability is not needed.

User-to-Data Authorization. A truly effective security design must enforce personal accountability. Access to data should be granted only after the user has been identified. Popular access control software packages (e.g., CA-ACF2, RACF, CA-TOP SECRET) use this philosophy as the basis for their design. User identification and authentication and access authorization checking are performed independent of the access environment for on-line or batch processing.

Additional Constraints for Data Access. Often, additional controls are implemented to complement the basic user-to-data authorization scheme. These controls include requirements for job submission, conditions that specify data set accessibility through predefined and controlled programs, transactions, and so on. Often, additional constraints are designed for integrity rather than confidentiality reasons.

MVS SYSTEM PERSPECTIVE

Layered Architecture

Figure 27-1 simplifies the layers that compose the MVS architecture. The top layer consists of two components—JES (job entry subsystem) and

FIG. 27-1
Layered architecture of MVS

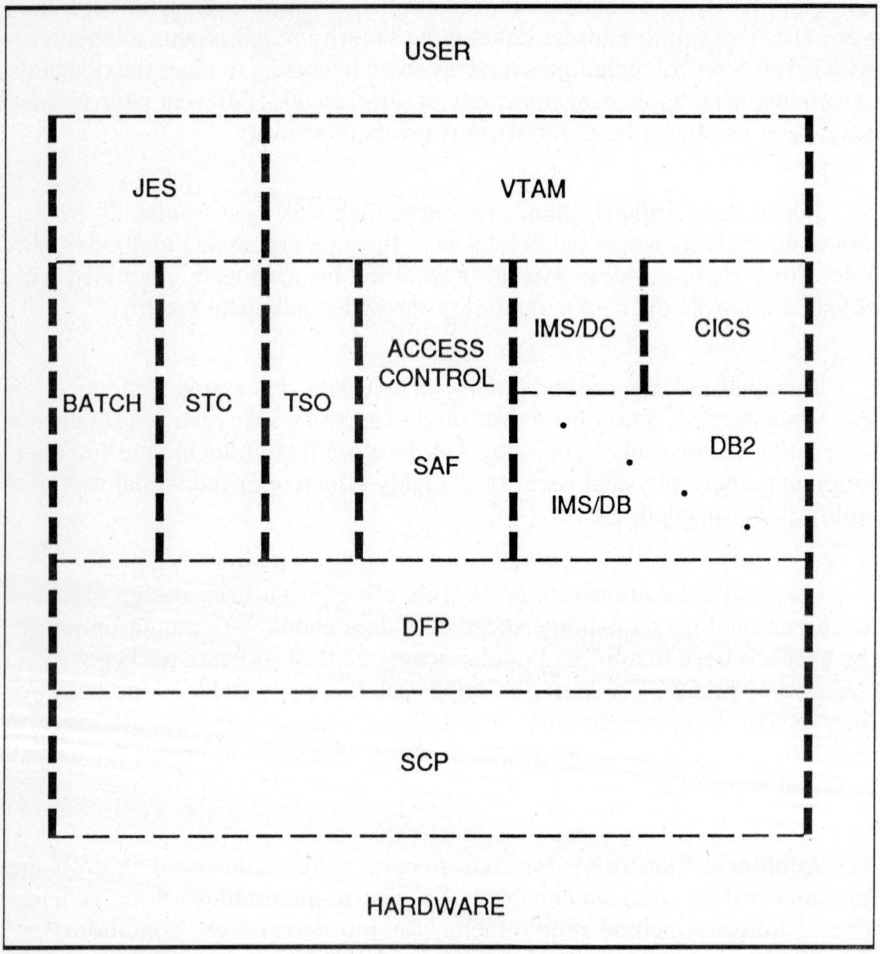

VTAM (virtual telecommunications access method)—that provide the user interface in MVS. The two bottom layers—SCP and DFP (system control program and data facility product)—are the MVS hardware interfaces. The functions appearing between the top and bottom layers represent, with the exception of central access control function, the different application environments available under MVS. The access control function in this illustration is the central point of MVS security control with which all other components can communicate. The following sections describe the layers and elements in more detail.

System Control Program. SCP is the collective term for fundamental MVS functions that interface with processor hardware. It includes the MVS Nucleus, the Input/Output Supervisor (IOS), error recovery routines, real and virtual storage managers, and similar basic operating system functions. The most important function related to security controls is the System Management Facility (SMF), the general MVS logging facility.

Data Facility Product. The DFP is the interface between MVS and input/output (I/O) devices. It contains access methods and storage management functions. The Virtual Storage Access Method (VSAM), the Queued Sequential Access Method (QSAM), and the Basic Partitioned Access Method (BPAM) are examples of access methods. Functions such as ALLOCATE, RENAME, and SCRATCH are examples of storage management functions. In MVS/ESA, the System Management Storage (SMS) function has become part of DFP.

DFP contains many control points at which the access control software (e.g., RACF) is invoked (ALWAYS CALL) to check a user's authorization to a file. Examples of such control points are OPEN, End of Volume (EOV), SCRATCH, and RENAME.

Job Entry Subsystem. The job entry subsystem (JES2 or JES3) and related initiator functions manage batch jobs submitted for execution under MVS. The user's job control language (JCL) statements are handled, jobs are queued for execution, and direct job input as well as printed output is "spooled." JES also supports started tasks (STCs).

This environment contains control points that manage the user identification (userid), the group identification (groupid), and the password information of a job. These control points invoke the central security function to check and process such information.

Virtual Telecommunications Access Method. VTAM is the interface most generally installed into MVS for terminal access. It manages lines and terminals and connects them with the on-line application environments under MVS.

VTAM does not interface with the central security function directly. These interfaces exist in the "VTAM Applications," such as TSO (Time-Sharing Option), IMS (Information Management System), and CICS (Customer Information Control System). (Note, however, that advanced methods to secure networks use security controls in special network management products at the VTAM level.)

Central Point of Security Control

The MVS architecture provides a central point of security control. It consists of two elements, the System Authorization Facility (SAF), which contains a "Router" function, and the access control facility, which is the intrinsic decision mechanism.

System Authorization Facility. All MVS system and subsystem functions requiring security services can call SAF, the central security control point in MVS, and request security services and decisions. SAF has a router function that relays, based on table entries, requests to the appropriate security system. The standard table definitions provided by IBM route all requests to IBM's Resource Access Control Facility (RACF).

Access Control Facility. RACF is IBM's MVS access control software. Other products offering equivalent functions are CA-ACF2 and CA-TOP SECRET. In general, the access control facility performs user authentication, user authorization to resources, and security-related logging. It also manages security data bases containing installation-supplied information about system users, system resources, and access rules.

Application Environments

Two general application environments exist under MVS: the standard MVS environments for batch, time sharing (TSO), and STCs, and the data base/data communications (DB/DC) subsystem environments.

Batch, TSO, and started task environments are part of MVS and offer MVS functions. They are described in the later section "Unconstrained Environments."

DB/DC environments are implemented through separate products, such as IMS and CICS, that may run as subsystems under MVS. Usually, they limit the capabilities of a user or program. DB/DC systems are described in the later section "Constrained Environments."

MVS APPLICATION ENVIRONMENTS

From a security standpoint, the work performed in most MVS installations can be divided into two distinct categories: a constrained environment and a basically unconstrained environment.

Constrained Environment

A constrained environment includes subsystems that use advanced transaction processing capabilities (CICS), and data base management systems (such as IMS, IDMS, DB2). Typically, major on-line applications with many terminals are implemented in this environment. Such applications, as an example, predefine data elements a user will be able to access and the types of transactions a user can initiate. In general, the following links can be established to provide security:

- User-to-transaction
- Transaction-to-data
- User-to-programs
- User-to-data

Basic integrity features (such as logging, backout, and recovery) are built into those data base management subsystems. Application programs (executing as transactions) under a DB/DC subsystem usually must follow certain rules and conventions. Typically, they are not allowed to use I/O or system functions other than those provided by the subsystem. Therefore, application processing using these techniques can be said to occur in a "constrained environment."

In addition to the aforementioned data integrity features, security controls usually are built into the DB/DC systems. These controls can be "internal" to the DB/DC subsystem or implemented as "external security" in conjunction with MVS access control. (The controls in this environment are addressed in the later section "MVS Access Path—DB/DC Environments.")

Unconstrained Environment

The second category of work performed under MVS is the activities of system developers, programmers, and others who generally use MVS TSO and batch facilities rather than transaction subsystems. Typically, these facilities do not contain automatic integrity features (i.e., logging, backup, and recovery), but do offer full MVS capabilities, including all access methods, system services, commands, macros, and so on. This environment can be regarded as virtually unconstrained.

If an access control package is used with MVS, the resulting system environment still tends to be relatively unconstrained if only the user-to-data authorization controls are used. However, additional features available in most access control packages can be used to establish a better controlled and more constrained environment. (The controls that can apply are discussed in the later section "MVS Access Path—Batch, TSO, and Started Tasks.")

MVS ACCESS PATH—DB/DC ENVIRONMENTS

The MVS access path for the DB/DC environment provides a conceptual framework for understanding the relationship of the various components for a given system configuration. This understanding can be used to determine the levels of security implemented by an installation. However, since the access path represents only a high-level view, care must be exercised when using the figures. The system interfaces depicted can be substantially more complex than they appear.

User View

For the general user community, system components and security mechanisms are essentially transparent. This is especially true in advanced transaction-based systems, where the user indicates what the user would like performed (task orientation) without having to tell the system how to do it (function orientation).

Most users are aware of security controls for signing on to a computer because they have to go through an identification and authentication dialogue. However, after their session is started, they usually are unaware of the security layers controlling transaction execution and data access.

Sign-On. Systems with a need for accountability require users to sign on or logon by supplying their individual userid and passing an authentication process. The most common authentication technique uses a secret password along with a public userid. The basic security of a system is determined by the strength of its password scheme. Although passwords generally are regarded as the most vulnerable element of information security, the installation can choose between extremely weak and relatively strong password schemes. Therefore, the audit will focus on the individual password scheme for user authentication.

A user signing on to a computer through dial-up may first have to deal with a layer of security external to the MVS system at the network level. A variety of devices can be used to request additional security codes and then dial back instead of directly passing incoming calls to the target system.

Recently developed and stronger authentication techniques include biometric devices that determine physical characteristics of the user, such as voice, fingerprints, or signature dynamics, and smart cards/tokens that generate one-time passwords. These techniques, often used in addition to the traditional password checking, are called secondary authentication techniques.

Data Access. After initial authentication at session start, the authorized user generally is not aware of system layers and security controls involved in transaction processing. As long as no rules are violated, the user's perception of the system is similar to the user view depicted in Figure 27-2. Note that although users know that data bases or files exist, they may not realize the steps the computer goes through to accept transactions and respond to user requests.

In a traditional batch installation, restricting access to a computer room provides good security over programs and data. With the advent of on-line systems, users have the ability to access data from terminals without physical access to the data center.

Controls to provide adequate security are built into the various software layers found in contemporary computer environments. Since various issues exist at each level, different control techniques are used to implement security and control. Correspondingly, the auditor will find it necessary to use different tools and techniques to review the effectiveness of the security controls.

Telecommunications Software

Various system components enable users to access data. A primary component is the telecommunications software, usually the VTAM. (See Figure 27-3.) Controls at the VTAM level make it possible to restrict terminals to specific applications. However, VTAM cannot restrict individual users to specific terminals or applications. (VTAM definitions can also control the use of encryption.)

Control Issues. Unauthorized modifications of VTAM definitions can change the authorization of terminals to application subsystems or can change or remove requirements for encrypted transmissions.

Optional network management applications can contain individual sets of internal or external controls to authorize users and groups to applications. These controls, if not designed and protected properly, are vulnerable to attacks. In addition, secondary authentication controls can be implemented in a network management application to complement or replace the standard authentication schemes.

FIG. 27-2
The user view

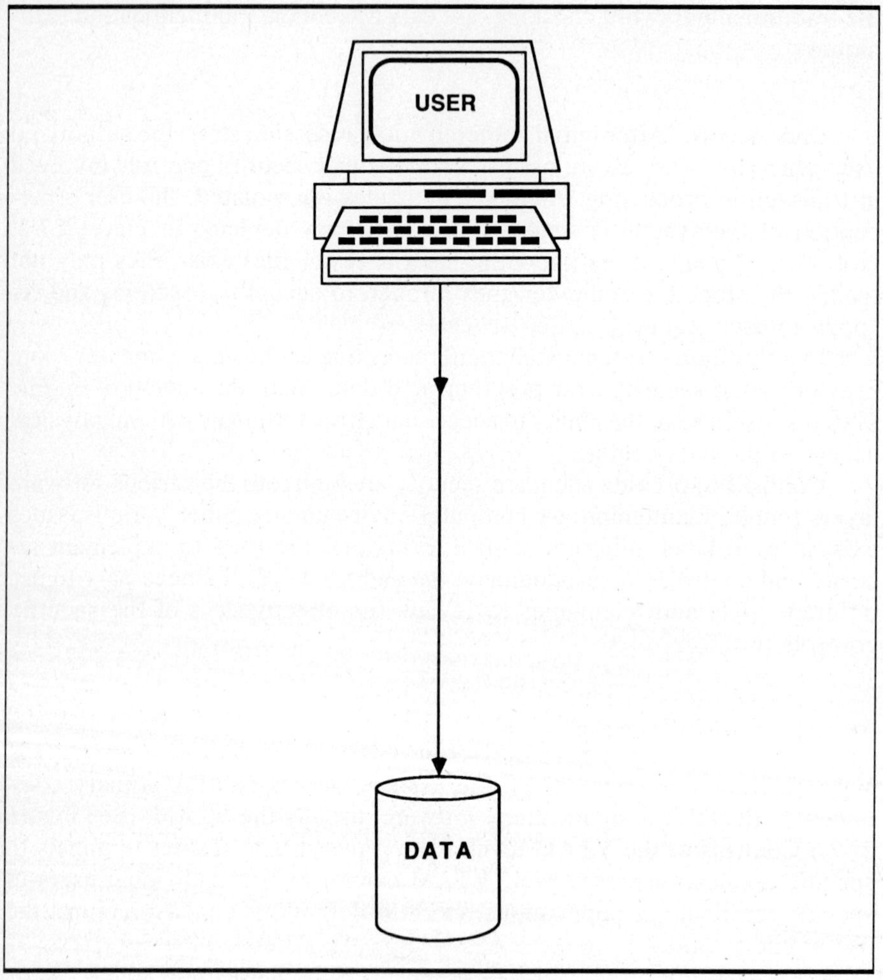

Control Techniques. VTAM controls are, in principle, internal to the product. However, some redundant external controls can complement VTAM definitions. If network management products are present, they may have their own internal security or may interface with external security.

- *Internal security controls*—VTAM knows all terminals and "applications" by name. The term application, as used here, refers to major transaction processing systems (such as CICS and IMS).

FIG. 27-3
Telecommunications software

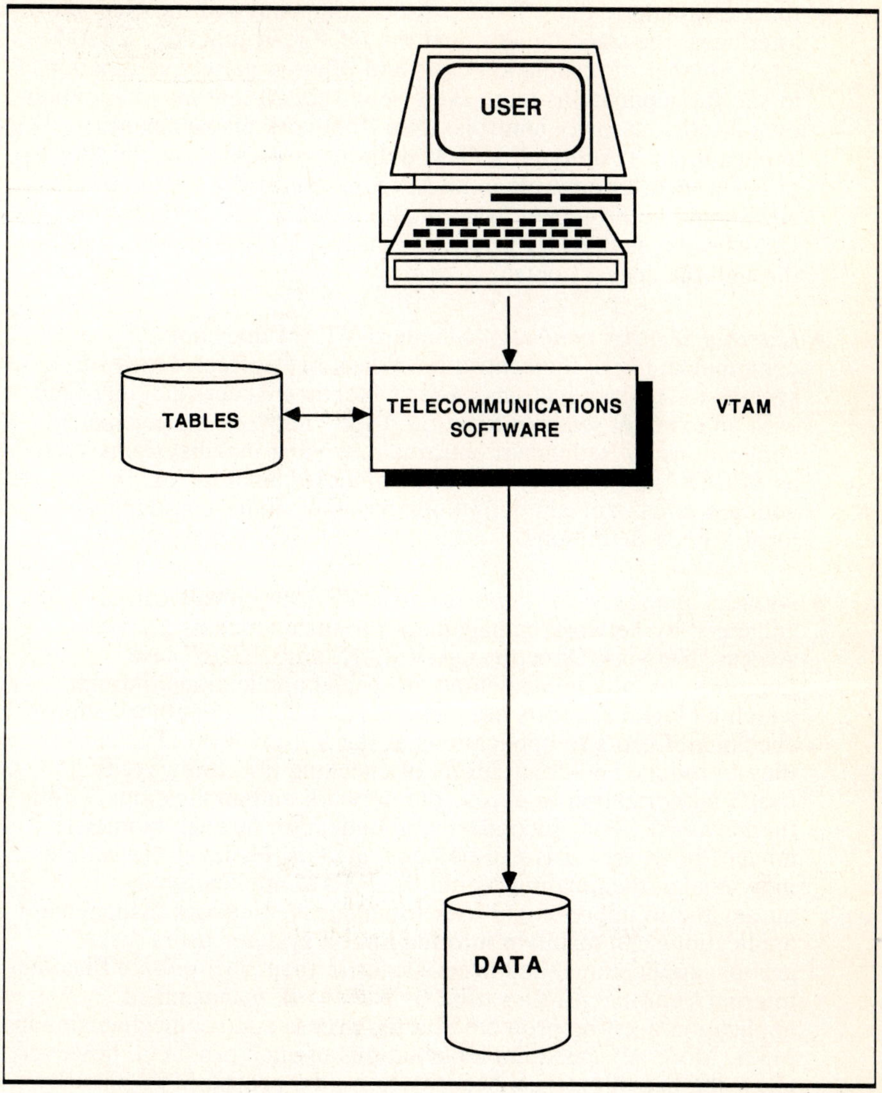

Unless specifically defined, a terminal cannot access these applications. VTAM does not have the notion of users. Restricted functions include the VTAM console command and the Netview interfaces, the trace facility, and the NCP load function. VTAM has a number of installation exits and offers a variety of functions in special applications (e.g., Newview/Access) that may have their own internal security controls. (See "network management applications.") Although VTAM definitions usually are not the primary security controls in an MVS system, they are important and should be protected from unauthorized access and change. Usually, this is done by protecting critical VTAM files and tables through the access control system.

- *External security controls*—Standard VTAM does not communicate with the central MVS security system. However, special VTAM applications such as Netview/Access can interface with an external security function. (See "network management applications.") Redundant controls may exist in subsystems such as IMS/DC and CICS that also maintain terminal tables. In addition, cross-domain definitions on other nodes can duplicate local VTAM definitions.

- *Network management applications*—VTAM controls can be enhanced by network management products (such as Netview/Access, Network Director, CA-VMAN, and NCI). These functions, usually implemented as special applications through which all logon requests are routed, often perform authorization checking of users to applications at the VTAM level. Typically, they introduce additional levels of checking (i.e., they verify a user's authorization to access the network and applications within the network). Also, secondary authentication through biometric devices or smart cards can be performed at this level. Sometimes individual authentication within the VTAM application is automated to improve end-user friendliness. Network management applications can maintain information on systems users, user groups, applications, and access rules in their own private files for internal security. All files used by a network management application must be protected by the access control mechanisms in MVS. More advanced implementations of such products, however, allow the use of external security (e.g., the central MVS security mechanism such as RACF).

- *Security logging and journaling*—VTAM does not create or write any audit trails. Usually, network management products generate an audit trail of some kind if they use internal security. For external security, the logging function of the access control package creates the audit trail.

Audit Tools and Techniques. VTAM controls can be reviewed through system browse and list functions or using specialized tools like Coopers & Lybrand's VTAM Analyzer.

The audit of internal security in network management applications can require administration and audit functions within the applications. If they use external security, the review of those controls is part of the access control review, using its tools and facilities.

Transaction Processing Software

The next level of active software is transaction processing (TP). (See Figure 27-4.) Two common examples of TP monitors are CICS and IMS/DC. TP monitors provide advanced TP capabilities for a large number of concurrent users by handling incoming requests and routing them to the appropriate application programs. Typically, TP software queues incoming and outgoing messages.

Control Issues. Control issues are user identification and authentication and user access to transactions, programs, and so on. In particular, the protection of privileged transactions, operator console commands, and maintenance or debugging tools are critical controls.

Often terminal tables (that may be redundant with VTAM definitions) are maintained at this level. The integrity of these tables is another control issue.

Control Techniques. Generally, two different security control functions are available at the TP level. One is at session start when the user's identity is established through a sign-on procedure. Such procedures require the presentation of valid userids and proper passwords for a successful session establishment.

The other security function checks the user's authorization to specific transactions and (optionally) programs during an on-line session. These checks use pre-established access rules. Sometimes, a combination of both functions can be found (e.g., the IMS reverification function that requires re-entering of the sign-on password for critical transactions).

These security controls can be implemented as part of the TP monitor as internal security or, in combination with an access control package, as external security. Internal security can be based on facilities provided as part of the TP monitor or can be implemented through special third-party packages (e.g., OMNIGUARD for CICS). Often, installations with an access control package and different transaction-oriented applications prefer the external security approach because it avoids redundancy and maintains all major security controls in one place.

FIG. 27-4
Transaction processing software

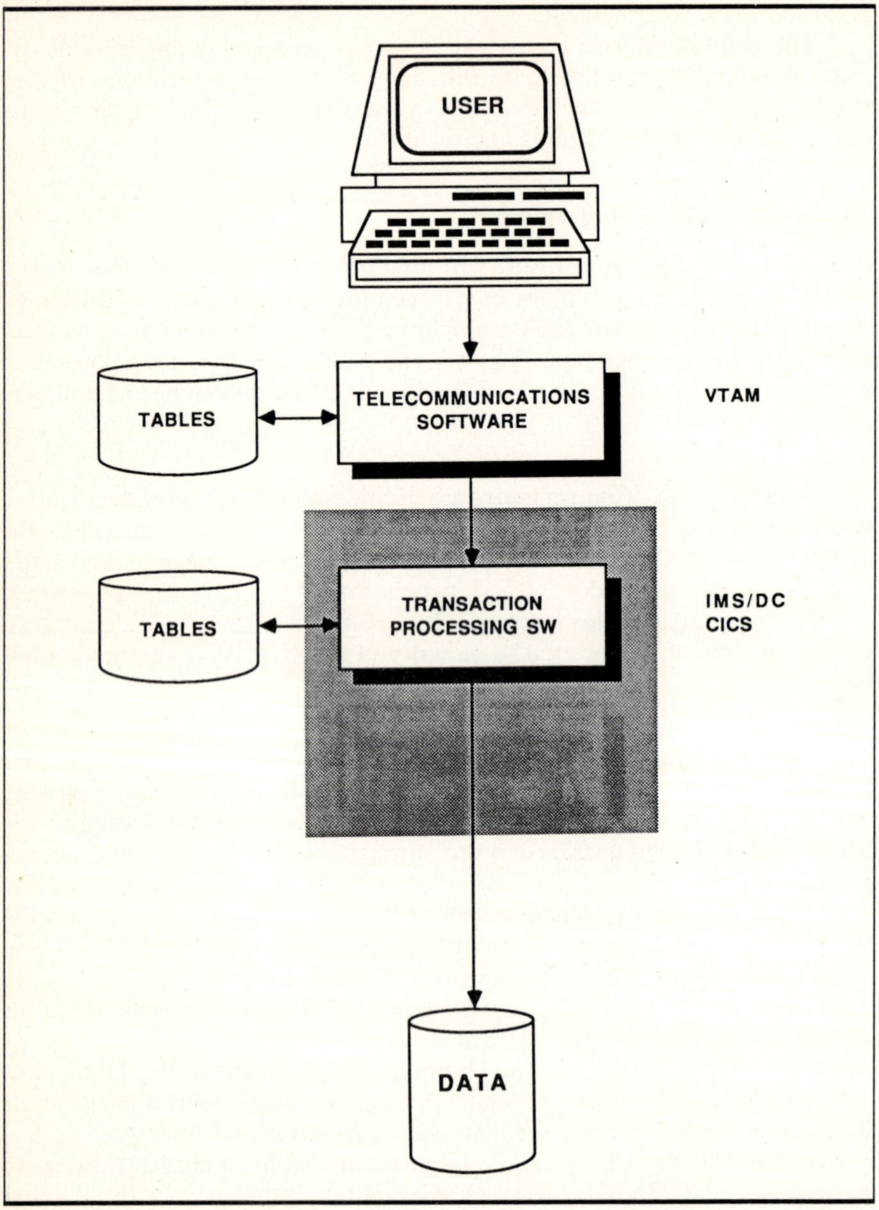

- *Internal security controls*—Internal security controls are based on macros, or tables (e.g., in the TP monitor product or in add-on packages). These files and tables should be protected against unauthorized access at all times. All files must be protected by access control software. When the tables reside in the same MVS address space where user transactions are executed (e.g., CICS), effective protection can be difficult.
- *External security controls*—An access control package that interfaces with the TP monitor is needed for external security. All major TP monitors provide interfaces to the major MVS access control packages (i.e., CA-ACF2, RACF, and CA-TOP SECRET).
- *Security logging and journaling*—Usually, important TP monitor events are logged together with data base events by their related DB/DC system. Depending on the DB/DC system, audit trails can be written to their internal log or journaling files, or, optionally, to SMF. Security logging can occur through the access control package for external security or through special log files for internal security.

Audit Tools and Techniques. The controls review technique at this level depends on the type of security. For internal security, it can be related strictly to the TP monitor or be based on an add-on internal security package that requires use of provided product tools. For external security, most relevant information is found in the access control package and the software's audit functions should be used.

Monitoring security events requires an analysis of the logging functions and can involve the merging of information from several log and journaling files to obtain a complete picture.

Application Programs

Common application programs are accounts receivable, general ledger, and payroll. (Figure 27-5 illustrates their position in the access path.) Applications can be developed with a number of languages, including COBOL (Common Business Oriented Language), PL/1 (Programming Language/1), and Assembler. Security controls implemented at this level are often application-specific (edit checking, range and reasonableness tests). For example, a payroll application will verify if the user is allowed to authorize transactions greater than a certain dollar amount.

Applications can be installation-written or packages obtained from third-party vendors. Many vendor products have built-in application security controls.

FIG. 27-5
Application programs

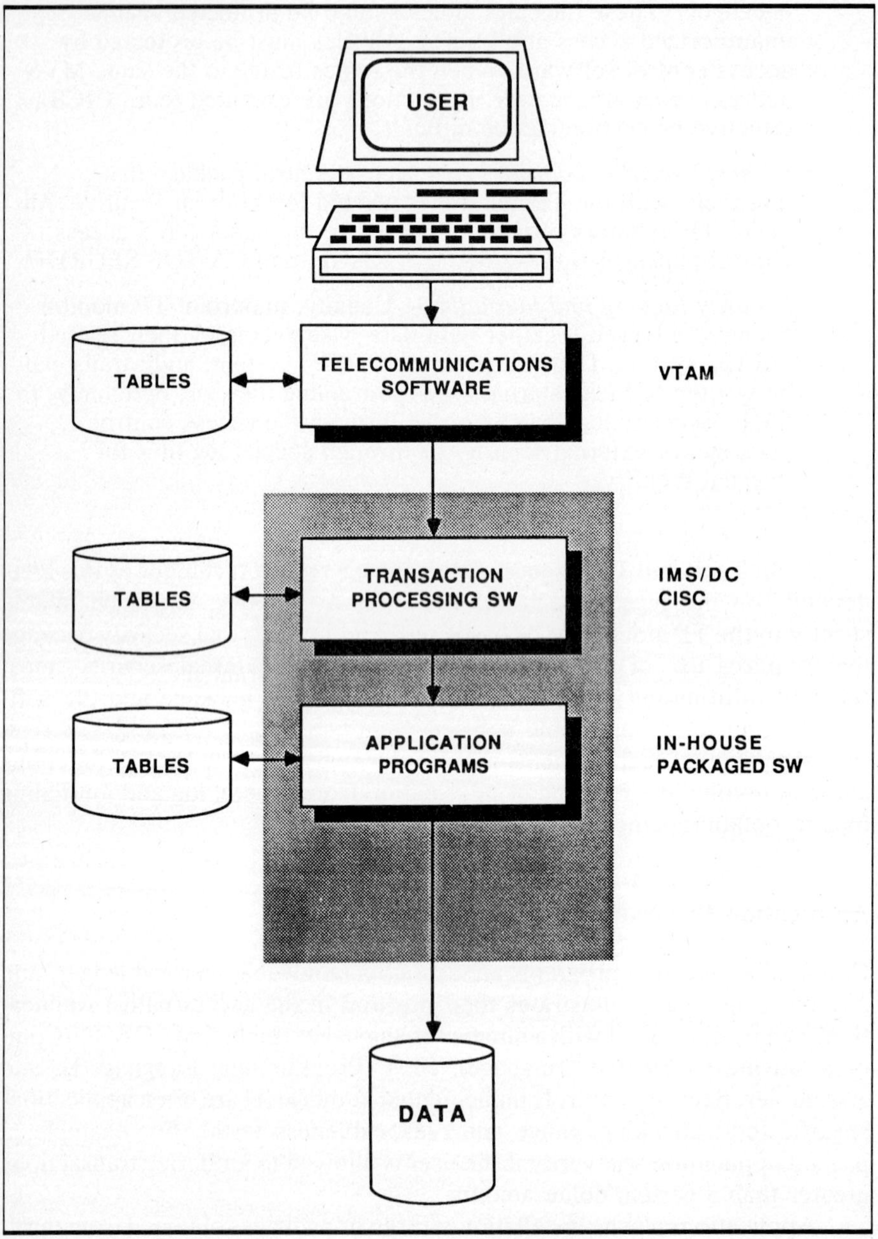

Control Issues. The most important control issues are code integrity, change control, and the protection of security files and tables.

Control Techniques. Application programs can have internal security controls or interface with the central MVS access control (i.e., use external security).

- *Internal security controls*—Internal security controls can be hard-coded decision mechanisms or, if more sophisticated, table- or file-oriented. In any case, they can be vulnerable if table and file protection are insufficient and they lack code integrity. Note that security code must follow strict guidelines to avoid exposure.
- *External security controls*—External security controls in the form of calls to the MVS access control packages are preferable. Generally, they are less vulnerable to attacks and are easier to maintain.
- *Security logging and journaling*—Internal security has its own audit trails, while external security uses the logging functions of the access control package. Applications can write log records to SMF; however, they must be authorized in MVS, raising additional integrity issues.

Audit Tools and Techniques. The review of internal security involves the use of tools and techniques available in the security functions. For external security, the pertinent information can be found in the access control environment. For locally developed applications, a code review may be performed to analyze the integrity of the security function.

Data Base Management Systems

Data base management systems (DBMS) provide access methods that can be used to reduce data redundancy, decrease access time, and provide basic security over sensitive data elements. (See Figure 27-6.) Sophisticated DBMSs include active data dictionaries that can be used to implement security at the following levels:

- User/data base
- Program/data base
- Transaction/data base
- Program/field
- User/field

FIG. 27-6
Data base management system

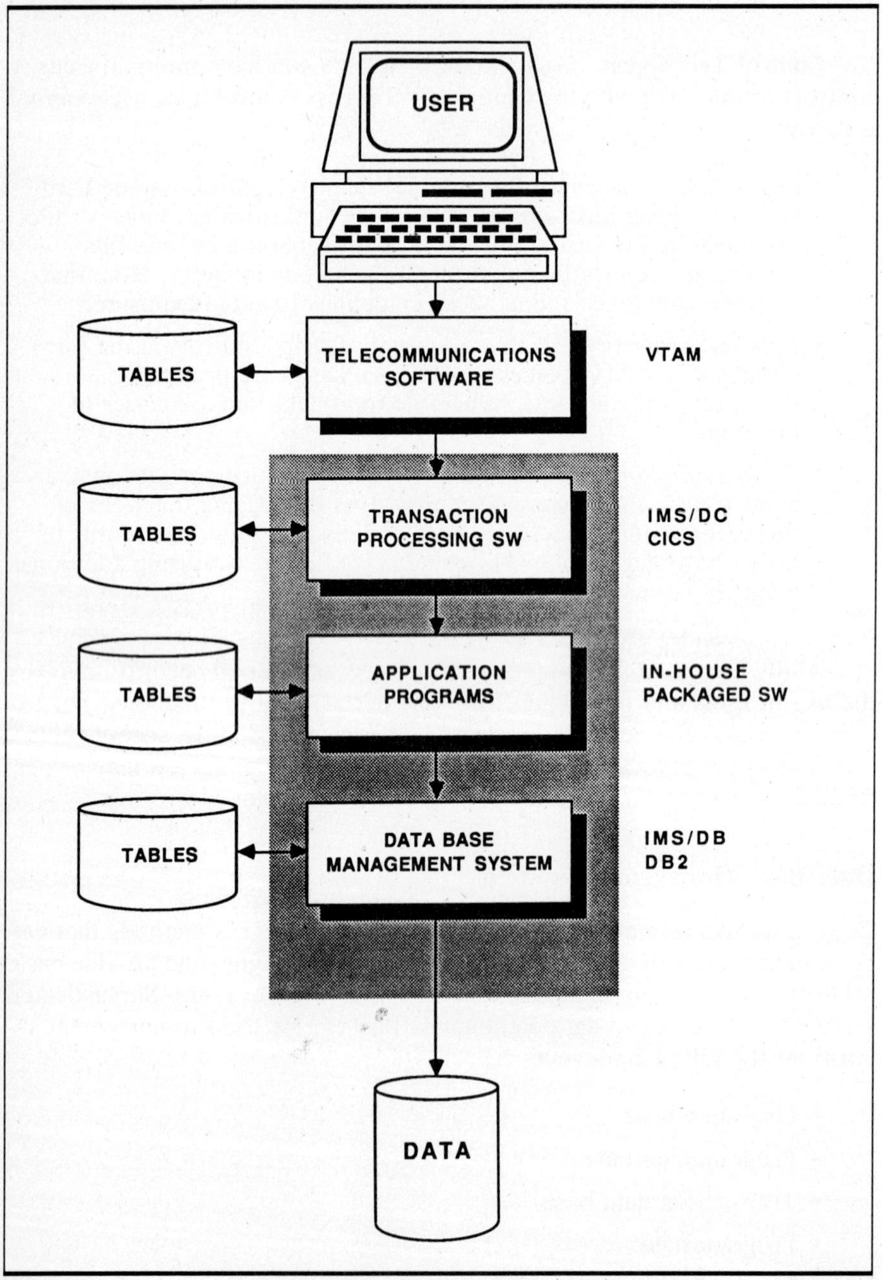

Security can be implemented with various access authorities to data (e.g., read, write, update, delete).

DBMSs also include backup and recovery capabilities, logging, and methods for enforcing data integrity. Effectiveness can vary greatly by DBMS.

Control Issues. A major issue in DBMSs is control over user access to data at the proper level of granularity. Frequently, access authorization is granted to larger units of information than are needed and intended for a particular user and application. Reasons can be the lack of functionality in the DBMS or inadequate administration and protection. Other control issues are related to the proper control of administration privileges.

Control Techniques. DBMSs can have internal security mechanisms or can interface with the MVS access control package. Sometimes, a combination of both approaches is used if the interface with the access control system does not cover all required security functions.

- *Internal security controls*—A number of controls internal to the DBMS are vital to security. These features isolate data elements to the desired level of granularity (e.g., views, segments). In addition, internal security controls to manage users, groups, and access rules may exist and use table, files, and so on.
- *External security controls*—External security controls interface with the central MVS access control software and rely on that function for the maintenance and administration of user/group information and access rules.
- *Security logging and journaling*—DBMSs can maintain their own sophisticated logging and journaling facilities to support data integrity and recovery. Usually, security-related events are included in these log records as well.

When external security is used, the audit trail can be split between different log files, one part existing in the DBMS log and another being recorded by the access control system.

Audit Tools and Techniques. A review of internal security controls requires use of product-specific tools and techniques. External security is reviewed through the facilities in the access control package. To monitor security events, it may be necessary to select and merge information from different log environments.

File Access Methods

File access methods, as shown in Figure 27-7, are the interfaces between programs and data. Generally, they are part of the operating system software. (Some DBMSs have their own access methods that usually are based on lower level operating system access methods.)

The access methods and other DFP functions contain the basic access control interface in MVS. A user's authorization to access a data set is checked at OPEN time. For single-user address spaces, these checks test whether a user is authorized to access a data set at a certain level, such as WRITE/UPDATE, READ, or EXECUTE. For DBMS and other multi-user address spaces, these checks verify the authorization of a certain DBMS, rather than an individual user, to a set of data bases (e.g., production system to production data bases versus test system to test data bases).

Control Issues. The most important issues at this level are outside the control of the installation. They concern whether the invocation of access control is complete and covers all security-related functions. Responsibility for the controls is with the software vendors (e.g., IBM is responsible for standard access methods and access control software using the standard SAF security interface).

Control Techniques. External security controls are most common at this level, although some internal security features are available.

- *Internal security controls*—Prior to the advent of separate access control packages, data management developed its own password-based internal security controls. OS password protection is available for non-VSAM files, and VSAM password protection can be used with VSAM. Generally, OS password is regarded as inadequate in comparison with RACF or equivalent products. The VSAM password scheme also has severe limitations. Both techniques should be replaced by external security through the standard MVS access control package.
- *External security controls*—External security controls are the generally accepted control technique for file access methods. Data management makes calls to the access control environment at various processing stages (e.g., OPEN, EOV, SCRATCH, and RENAME). In data management these controls are transparent to the installation and the auditor. The definitions in the access control package determine what level of protection (e.g., READ, WRITE) will be established at what level of granularity (e.g., VOLUME, DATASET, CONTROL INTERVAL).

FIG. 27-7
File access methods

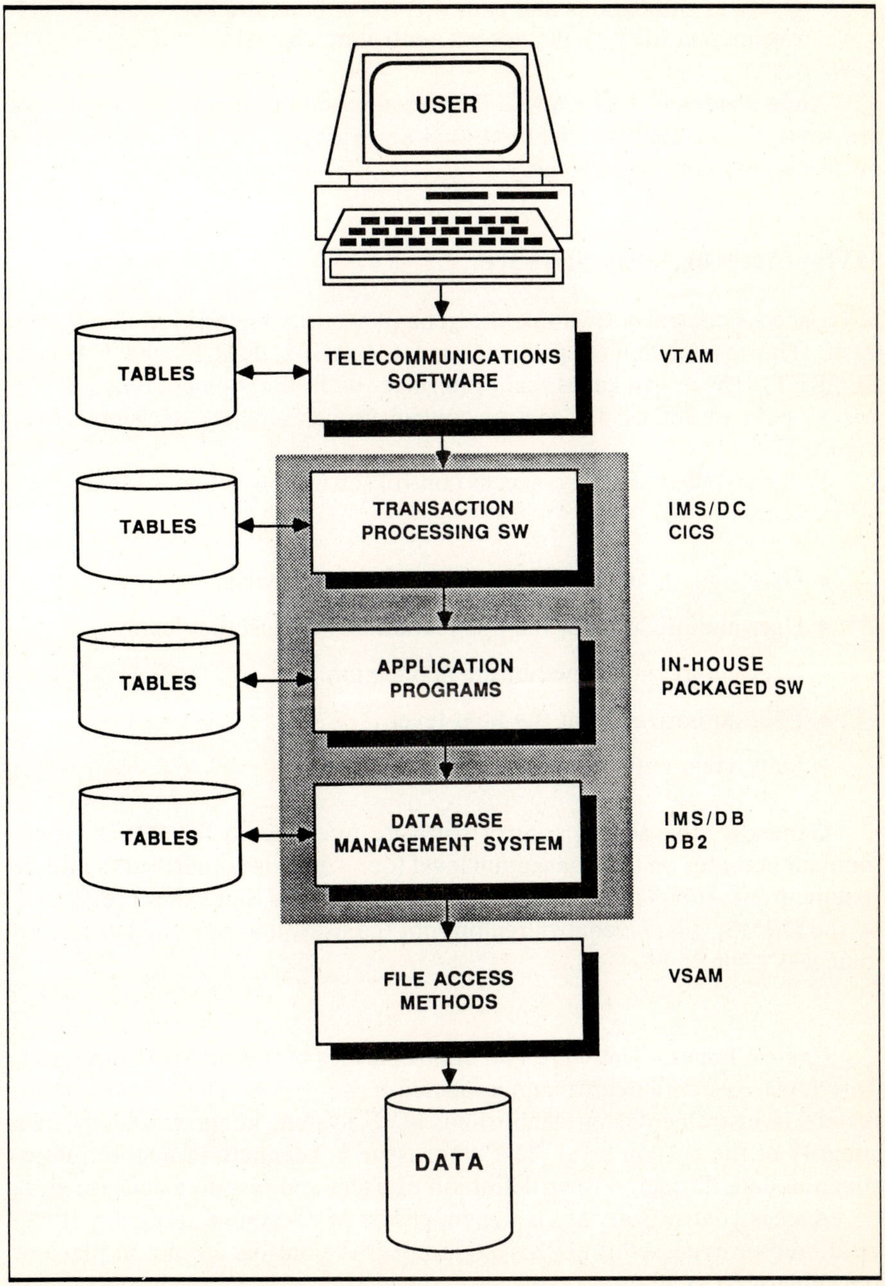

- *Security logging and journaling*—Data management writes a variety of log records to SMF. Those records also contain user and group identifications and can, therefore, be related to security events recorded by the access control mechanism.

Audit Tools and Techniques. Password-based internal security controls are reviewed manually. When external security is used, the audit focuses on the access control package.

MVS—Access Control Software

MVS access control software is the general security installed at the system level. The most common packages are CA-ACF2, RACF, and CA-TOP SECRET. These packages can interface with the components of the access path to act as the central control for all security decisions. (See Figure 27-8.)

When installed properly, access control software is active at these levels of the access path:

- User sign-on at the network and subsystem levels.
- User authorization at the application and transaction levels.
- User authorization within the application.
- User authorization at the field level.
- Subsystem authorization at the file level.

Generally, the access control software interface to the DB/DC environment operates on the transaction level (i.e., a user is authorized to initiate specific transactions rather than access specific files). Since files are opened by the DBMS, it is the control region, not the user, that must be authorized to access a file.

Control Issues. There are two control issues at the access control software level: system integrity and application protection. The access control system is instrumental in establishing MVS system integrity and its own integrity at the system level. The other issue is adequate protection of application data through proper definition of users and resource access rules.

Access control software is dependent on MVS system integrity. It can be altered or bypassed if MVS system integrity controls are not in place or are vulnerable to attacks.

FIG. 27-8

Access control software

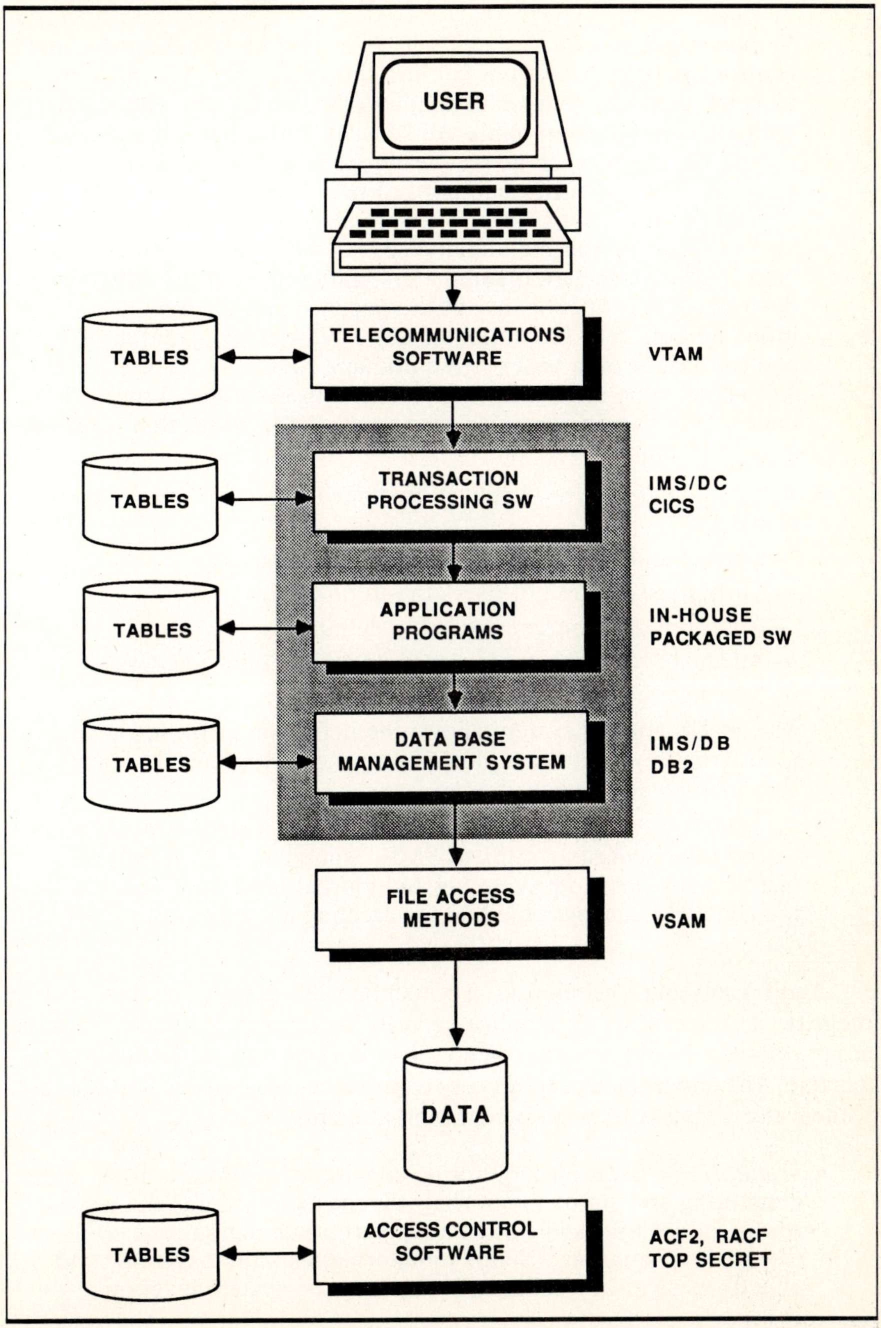

Control Techniques. The control techniques used can be system-oriented or designed to control the use of application data and resources.

- *System controls*—The user privileges necessary to administer and control the security system fall into this category. They must be assigned carefully to a small number of trusted users with separation of duties in mind. All security software contains some critical functions, such as recovery features, that should be guarded tightly against unauthorized use. Modifications and extensions to access control software also can have an impact on system integrity and the effectiveness of all access controls. A variety of customization parameters and options in the software determines the functionality of the package and the extent of protection offered. Protection of key MVS data sets and access control files or data bases is the primary control for establishing and maintaining system integrity. The considerations discussed under "application controls" also apply to the protection of these system resources.
- *Application controls*—Application controls consist of these basic elements:
  - —Correct and complete definition of system users.
  - —Correct association of users to job functions/groups.
  - —Appropriate resource ownership definitions.
  - —Adequate resource access rules, including public access.
  - —Adequate administration structure.

  The access control system allows the definition of these elements at different levels, from a global and generic approach to a very fine and detailed design.
- *Security logging and journaling*—All access control systems can record their security events to SMF. Some have the option of directing log data to private log and journal files. SMF logging is the generally accepted method for creating an audit trail.

Audit Tools and Techniques. To maintain the desired level of system integrity, it is necessary to monitor security on an ongoing basis. Periodic audits complement the system-oriented monitoring from an application perspective. The importance of the access controls can also justify real-life tests of their effectiveness through penetration attempts.

- *Monitoring*—Security monitoring consists of two basic tasks: event monitoring and status monitoring. Event monitoring is the regular review of security audit trails and appropriate action for exceptional situations. Status monitoring tests the existence and effectiveness of key security controls at the system level on a regular basis. Tools like the RACF DSMON utility are designed to monitor the security status.

- *Auditing*—Periodic audits of the security system review the contents of the security data bases, primarily from an application point of view. Generally, they include the review and verification of user and resource definitions and access rules. They also address system-level controls in the absence of regular security monitoring.
- *Penetration attempts*—Another way of testing security controls and identifying actual, as opposed to potential, exposures is to perform penetration attempts. Usually, they are part of penetration studies that address MVS integrity and other controls.

MVS—Control Program

As shown in Figure 27-9, all elements of the system software environment and the application programs run under the control of the MVS operating system. Without appropriate controls at this level, controls in the previously described system software elements may be ineffective. If properly maintained by the installation, MVS provides system integrity by ensuring that unauthorized programs cannot bypass store or fetch protection, OS-password checking, or security software checking, nor obtain control in an authorized state.

Control Issues. The most important control issue at this level is IT control effectiveness. If IT controls are ineffective, programs and users potentially can bypass MVS controls and resource access controls (e.g., RACF), including the alteration or suppression of audit trails.

Control Techniques. An MVS installation must maintain a number of controls to achieve an acceptable level of system integrity. Those controls fall into the following categories:

- *Privileges*—System privileges are assigned through the MVS Authorized Program Facility (APF) and the Program Property Table (PPT). For TSO, additional authorization tables are used. These functions must be used and protected carefully.
- *Restricted functions*—Restricted MVS functions include the MVS console function (operator consoles and equivalent software functions), critical utility programs and commands, and so on. These functions must be protected and assigned to only a few trusted users.

FIG. 27-9
MVS control program

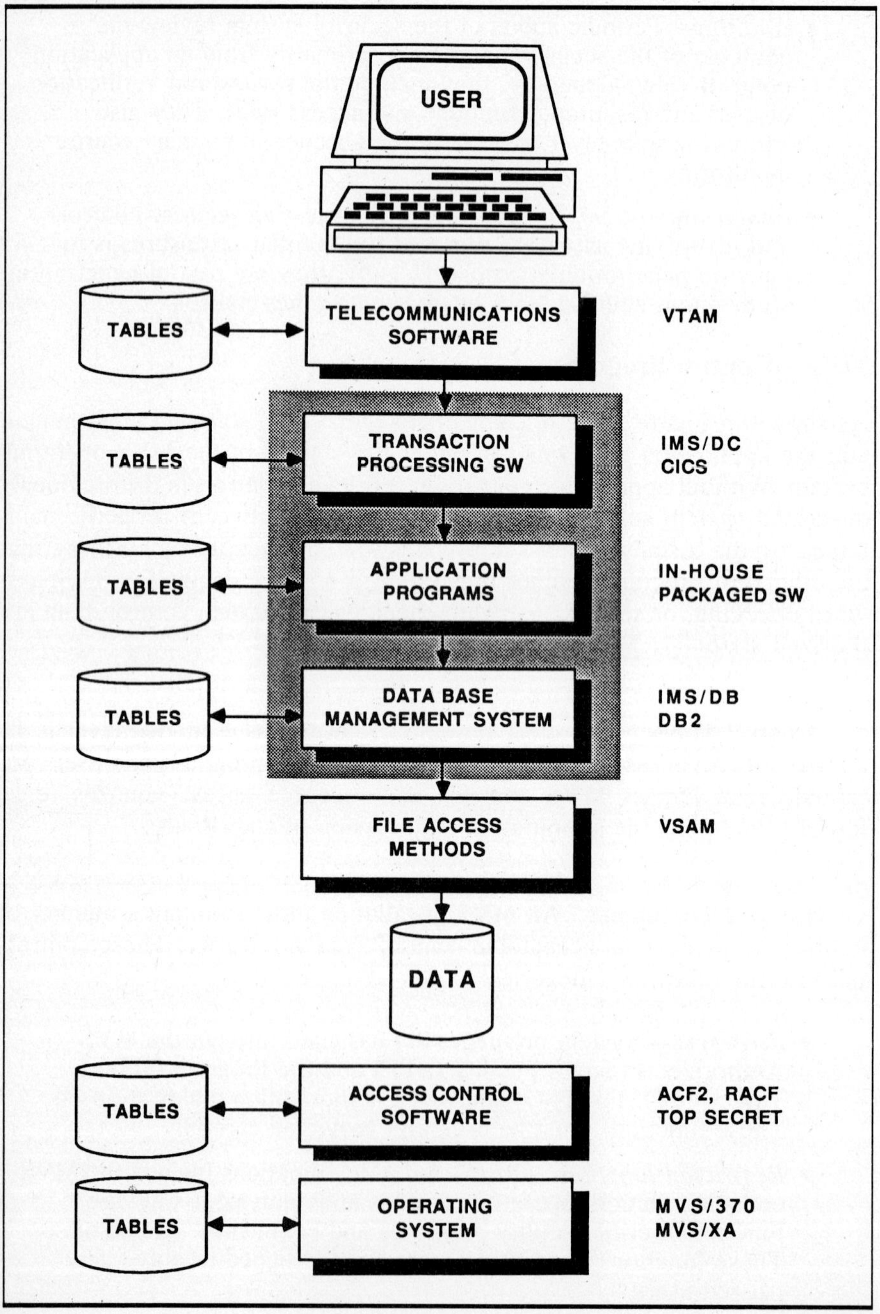

- *Extension/modifications*—MVS can be extended and modified in many ways. Typical techniques include:
  - Installation exits and appendages.
  - User supervisor call (SVC) routines.
  - Installation-supplied subsystems.
  - Code modifications (via MLPA/FLPA).

  These facilities are used to add installation-written code, as well as vendor-supplied system or application packages.
- *Customization*—These controls often include the proper start-up of the access control package and the selection of adequate SMF logging options.
- *Resource protection*—The preceding controls are enforceable only if access to MVS system libraries, tables, and so forth is controlled properly. As much as access control software is dependent on MVS system integrity, MVS itself is dependent on file protection through the access control system.
- *Security logging and journaling*—MVS does not log security events directly. It provides SMF as a vehicle for logging to its subsystems. As described previously, subsystems such as DFP and RACF use SMF to create their audit trails.

Audit Tools and Techniques. A manual review of MVS requires an understanding of MVS internals. However, a review can be effective without a system programmer's level of skill, if the right tools are used.

Information can be retrieved, in principal, from two sources: control blocks in main storage and definitions in MVS files. The control block information is preferable because it reflects the actual control, while information from disk may not. Programs such as CA-Examine are effective in retrieving control information from MVS systems. Experience shows that MVS IT controls tend to degrade over time. Therefore, it is essential that they be monitored on a regular basis, and that in-depth reviews are performed periodically.

In addition to the traditional audit and review techniques that can be used to identify potential exposures, penetration studies can demonstrate how exposures can actually be abused to bypass controls.

MVS ACCESS PATH—BATCH, TSO, AND STARTED TASKS

MVS allows the execution of programs in three different environments. In addition, data access can be achieved through different tools and techniques.

Figure 27-10 illustrates, from a system perspective, the three execution environments discussed here.

Limitations and controls can be implemented to confine a user to a certain execution environment and a specific access technique.

Execution Environments

Batch jobs, time-sharing sessions, and started procedures are the three standard ways to perform work in MVS. These environments are described in the following sections.

Batch. Batch is the traditional environment in which jobs are executed in the background. Batch jobs are independent units of work executing in their own MVS address space. They can contain multiple steps that are executed in sequence. Batch jobs are used primarily for production work, often complementary to on-line production systems.

Batch jobs can enter the system via various sources:

- Card readers (local and remote).
- Internal reader.
- TSO submit command.

In some installations, production jobs are submitted to the system via specialized scheduling software (e.g., UCC-7), while test jobs generally enter via the TSO submit command. Local card readers are becoming more rare, although they can still be found in some installations.

Time Sharing Option. The MVS Time Sharing Option (TSO) allows the interactive execution of commands and programs in the foreground. TSO sessions are established by issuing a "LOGON" command on a terminal. For each session, a separate MVS address space is created. Although theoretically all batch programs can be executed interactively, typical TSO users work with menu-oriented time-sharing facilities, such as ISPF, that contain convenient edit, browse, and other utility functions, together with compilers that allow interactive program execution and test. TSO is an ideal environment for users to explore potential system control weaknesses.

Started Tasks. These programs are initiated by the START command on a console and, generally, are associated with the activities of an operator. Typically, subsystems (including some security systems) or system utilities (such as volume dump/restore) run as started tasks, but any program can

FIG. 27-10
Batch, TSO, and started task system perspective

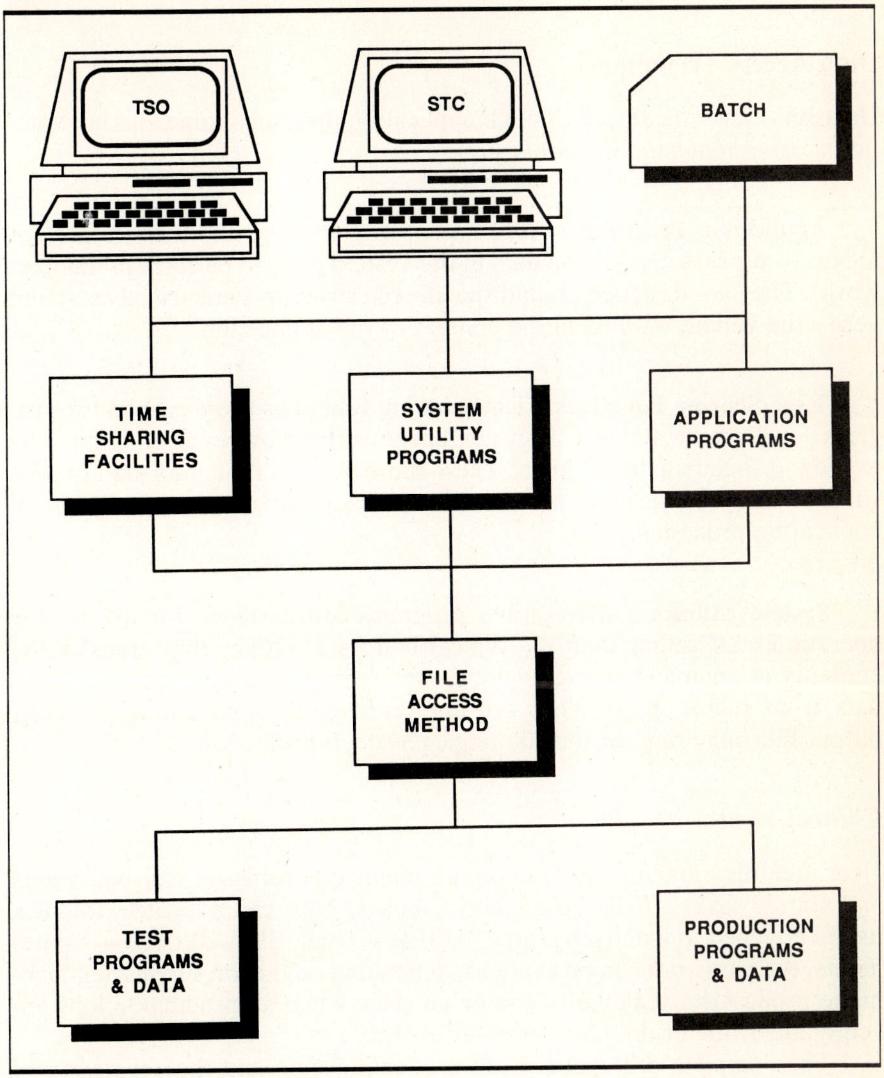

be initiated as a started task, provided a corresponding procedure has been set up.

Data Access Techniques

Data sets can be accessed through application programs, time-sharing functions, or system-supplied utility programs.

Application Programs. Application programs are the most important means to process application data in the system (i.e., to perform production work). They are designed around specific file structures and usually test and verify the validity of data in the context of the application.

Time-Sharing Functions. Time-sharing functions are designed for program development and test. They contain powerful browse and edit functions to view or manipulate test data. These more general functions are not sensitive to applications and, therefore, have no validity checking, as found in application programs.

System Utilities. Many utility programs are designed for use by the operation staff rather than the typical end user. Often, they transfer the contents of complete storage volumes to create backup copies (or restore data from such copies). They are not sensitive to applications and their output files may require specific (e.g., physical) protection.

Control Issues

User identification and verification are major control issues for batch jobs and started tasks. If the installation chooses, both can execute without a userid attached. If batch jobs carry "USER = " and "PASSWORD = " statements, the password can be exposed, depending on the job submission technique used. Also, granularity can be an issue when all production jobs execute under one or only a few powerful IDs.

The complete protection of all production data and the separation of production and test is another general control issue. Ideally, production data cannot be accessed by programmers and test programs cannot be used in production runs.

Application integrity is also an issue in the unconstrained MVS system (i.e., outside DB/DC environments). Application integrity can be exposed if programs other than the appropriate application programs can access and change application data (e.g., time-sharing editors).

Other controls, such as the limitation of production work to the batch environment or the confinement of jobs submitted through remote job entry (RJE) to a closed environment, can be useful and necessary restrictions in a given situation.

Control Techniques

The major MVS access control packages offer a variety of functions to control and constrain the standard MVS environment. The requirement to execute under a valid userid can be forced to batch as well as started tasks (STCs). Potential password exposures in batch jobs can be eliminated through a propagation process in the Job Entry Subsystem (JES). STCs have IDs allocated in the access control product.

Most access control systems support the restriction of userids to certain paths into the system (e.g., batch, TSO, or STC). One of the most powerful controls in all MVS access control systems is the function to restrict access to a data set through predefined programs. This facility, often called data pathing or conditional access, allows the exclusion of programs other than the intrinsic application programs from accessing or changing data.

Effective protection of sensitive data and separation of production and test are possible only through default protection. All access control packages offer this protection mode as an installation option. The name of this function differs among packages (e.g., Fail-Mode, Abort-Mode, Protect-All).

Logging/Journaling

Since all of the controls discussed above are found in access control packages, audit trails are provided through those systems.

Audit Tools and Techniques

The audit and review are part of the access control package review.

Access Path—Examples: Controlled Access

For controlled processing in the unconstrained environment, access control software can be used to restrict access to programs, data, and other resources. Typical examples of how these controls can be implemented in an MVS environment are described in the following sections.

Controlled Batch Production Environment. To protect production data from unauthorized changes, access by any means other than approved ap-

FIG. 27-11

Controlled batch production environment

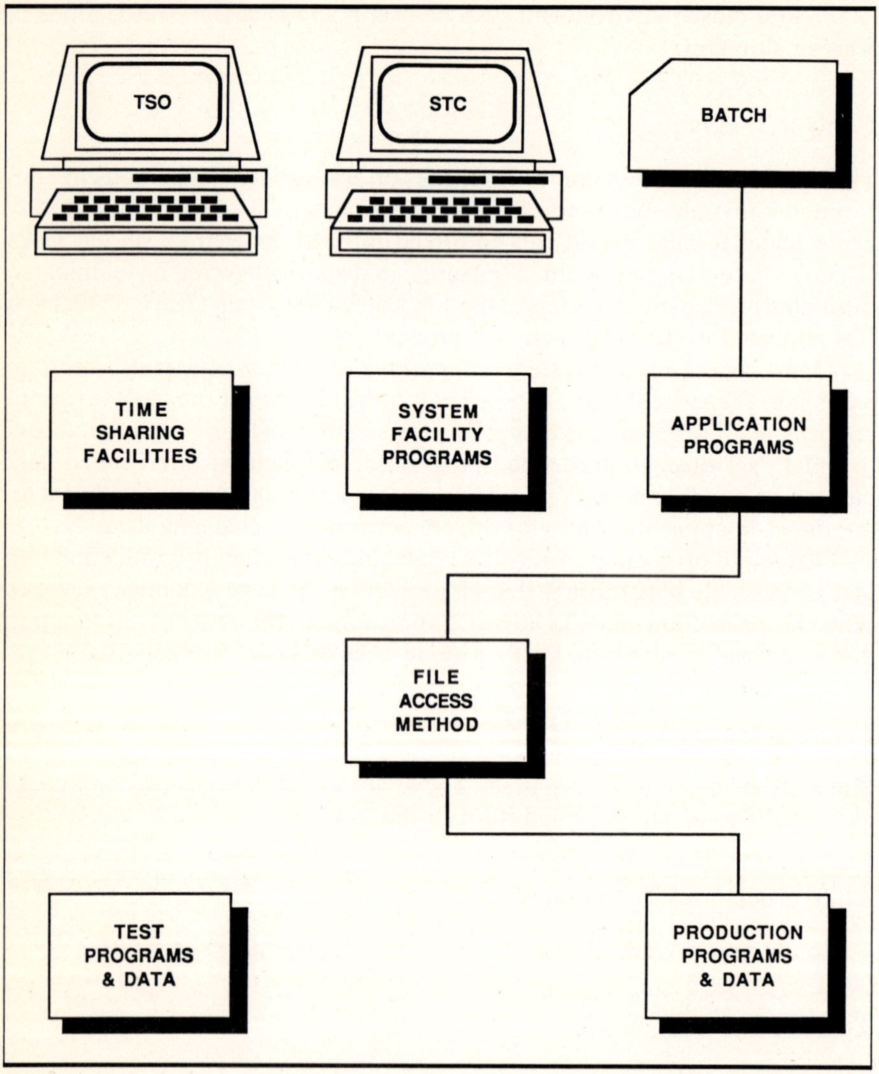

plication programs should not be allowed. Batch jobs should not be submitted without userids. In addition, password use should be controlled.

Security available through access control software includes the ability to specify which programs can access production data (program pathing), the ability to identify which terminals can submit production jobs (source control), and the use of restricted logons (when passwords are not required). Production IDs are not authorized for TSO and STC. Figure 27-11 illustrates a controlled batch production environment.

Controlled TSO Test Environment. Access control software can be used to achieve an appropriate separation between test and production systems at various levels:

- On the file level (separate test and production files and libraries).
- On the program level (library and change management controls).
- Through program pathing for production files.

As illustrated in Figure 27-12, programmers and system developers have an array of tools available to them for use in application development (e.g., time-sharing facilities and system utilities). As a result, if the test environment is not controlled properly, programmers have the potential to compromise the production environment. Specifications within MVS (that restrict the ability to submit commands through JES) and the use of access control software (that provides protection for sensitive utilities and allows for program pathing) can help prevent unauthorized access to production data.

Controlled Maintenance Through Started Tasks. The objective in controlling system maintenance activities is similar in nature to that in controlling the test environment—protect production data. (See Figure 27-13). Like all jobs, started tasks should run under unique userids, and the use of maintenance programs requiring special privileges should be restricted. The additional restriction in this example is that maintenance activities must be performed through started tasks.

FIG. 27-12
Controlled TSO test environment

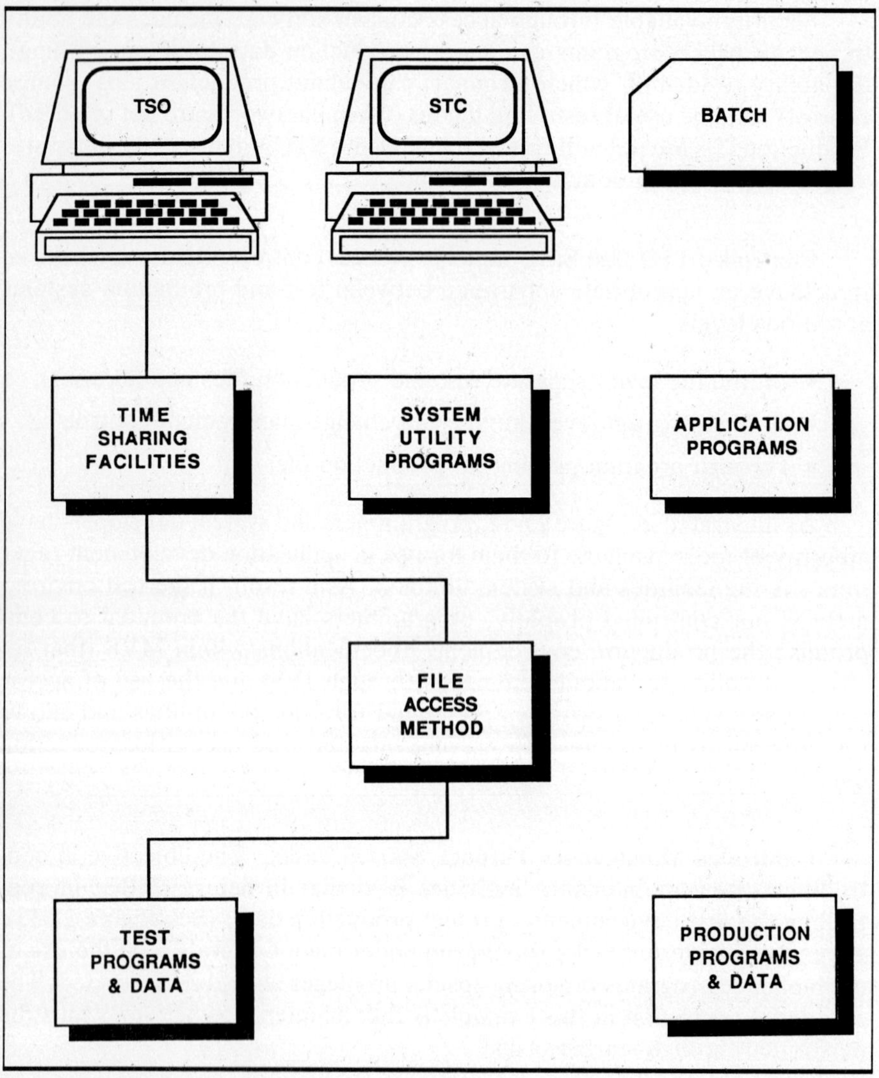

FIG. 27-13

Controlled maintenance through started tasks

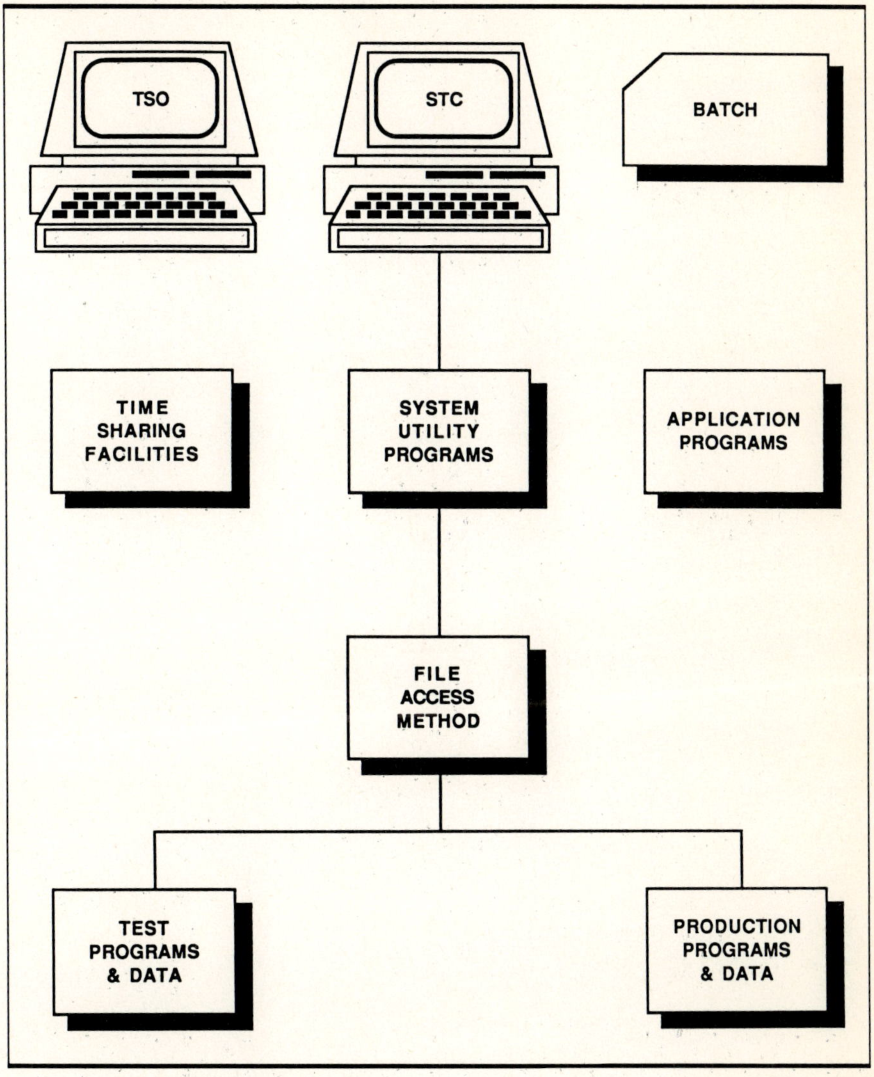

CHAPTER 28

Data Base

DATA BASE CONCEPTS

The data base is a collection of structured data elements with a particular organization; this physical structure is the way data is stored by the data base management system (DBMS). A data base is a collection of logically similar records; those records contain data elements, which are collected and stored in the data base. In a data base, elements for an application are defined as needed, giving more flexibility than the standard file structure. Access to the data base can be made according to the data base structure and is controlled by the DBMS.

The data base system is composed of three components: (1) the data, (2) the schema that describes the arrangement of the data, and (3) the programs that perform operations on the data. A structural component of the schema (a view of the entire data base) (see Figure 28-1) is the subschema; each subschema describes the data base as seen and accessed by one particular user or application. Usually, there are indices, used somewhat like an index in a book, maintained by the system to locate requested information more quickly.

Each request for data made by an application program must be analyzed by the DBMS program. The request is stated in terms of the logical name of the data (used in the application). It is converted by the DBMS into a set of physical file addresses, so that the physical data can be retrieved and transmitted by the DBMS to the application program.

Data Independence

Prior to the development of data bases, data files were designed for, and viewed as belonging to, one or more closely related application programs. The data was stored in the logical and physical relationship required by the application. (See Figure 28-2.) When new applications were developed, it was more practical to create new data files containing the specific data and format requirements. This made it possible to avoid program amendments in existing applications, since generally any change in data structure required a program amendment. Data could only be obtained from existing files in inflexible formats, unless extraction and reformatting programs were written. This data-dependent style of processing resulted in program maintenance problems, piecemeal development efforts, and duplication of data.

FIG. 28-1
Four viewpoints of the schema

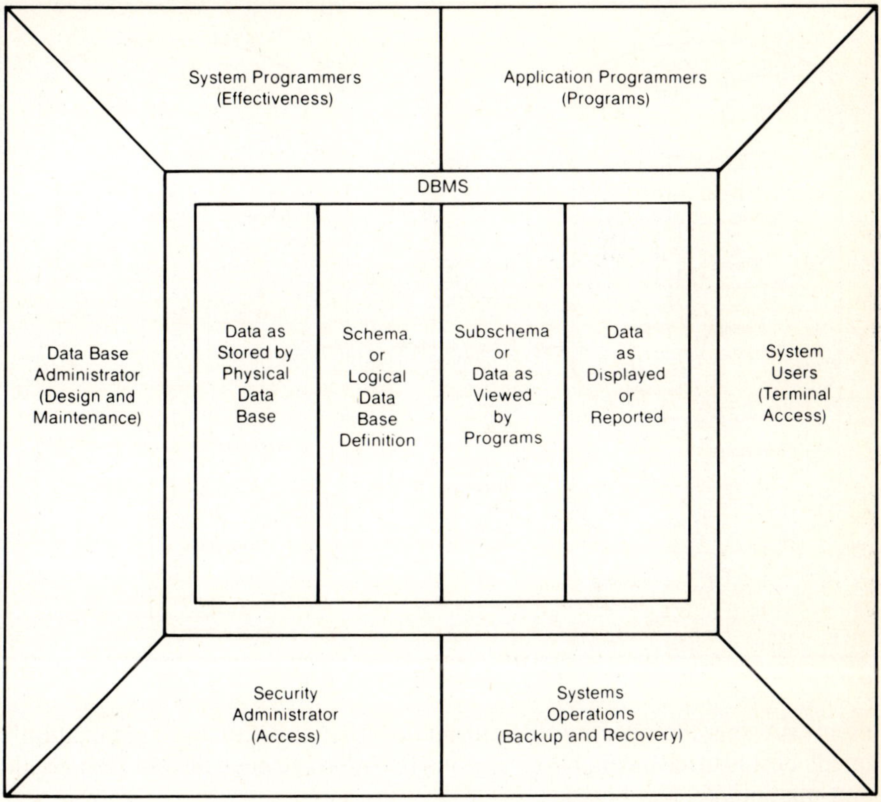

The data base concept separates the data requirements from the application requirements. Both requirements are evolving processes that are not necessarily compatible. A data base provides for the integration and sharing of common data among different programs. (See Figure 28-3.) In a data base approach, the data elements (fields and segments) are stored with little or no redundancy, and the physical (or real) file structures may bear little resemblance to the logical records and files being processed by application programs. From a data processing point of view, a data base is a means of gaining flexibility by creating independent data and application programs.

Data Base Management Systems

The data that an organization generates, manipulates, and stores for the continuing operation of the organization is one of its most important tangible

FIG. 28-2

Before the data base, data was stored logically by application requirements; creating a data base satisfies data requirements

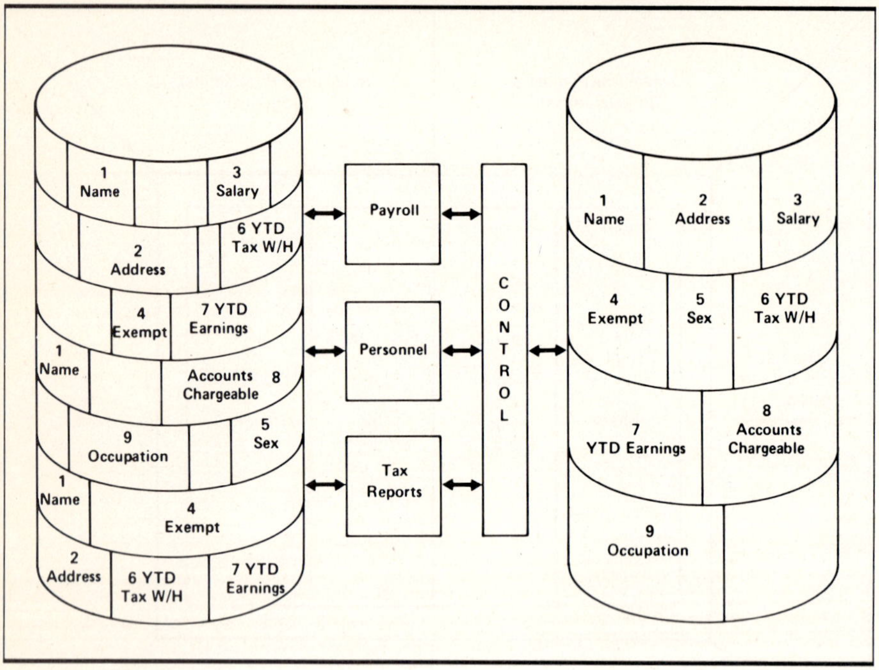

assets. A shared collection of information that satisfies the organization's needs best is often a data base. Various DBMS have been developed to build and manipulate data bases.

The DBMS translates data requirements of application programs and executes data management functions (store, update, delete, retrieve) on behalf of those programs.

When an application program using a DBMS requests data, the DBMS looks up the description of the data. This description is defined when the data base is implemented. If there is an index, the DBMS uses it to find the data. The DBMS also determines whether the program has permission to access or update the data, information that is defined when the data base is constructed.

If the application program is used to update a record, additional instructions from the application program return the modified data to storage.

Role of the Data Base Administrator

The data base administrator (DBA) is the manager of the data base. (See Figure 28-4.) One responsibility of the DBA is security and information

FIG. 28-3
Relationship between data bases within the data base organization (courtesy of International Business Machines Corporation)

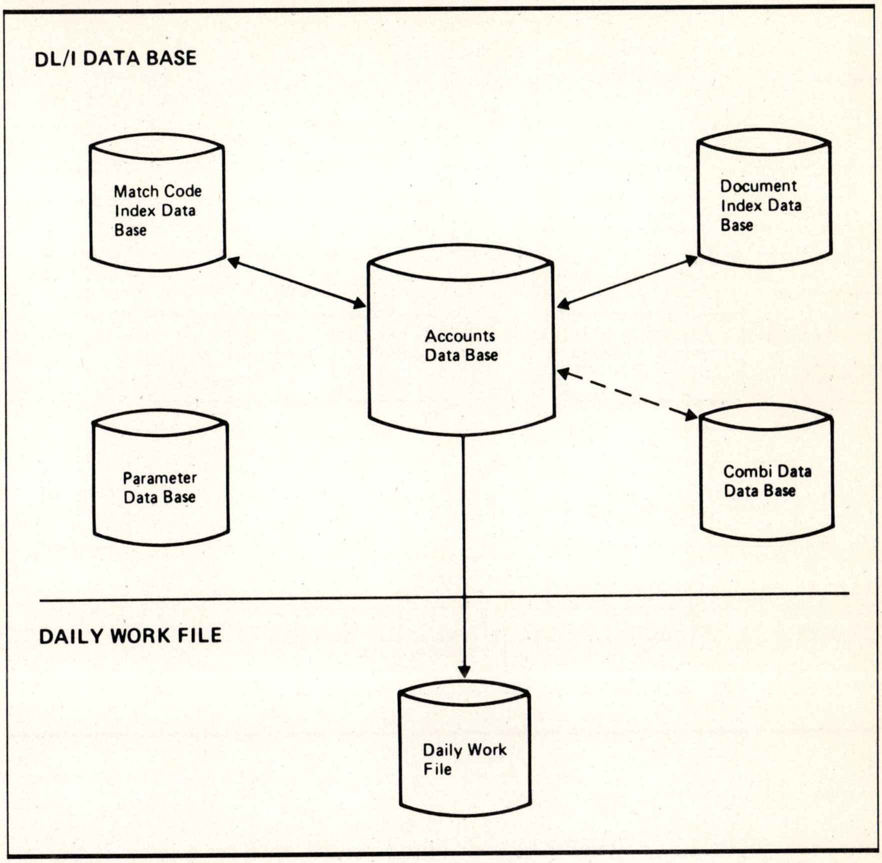

classification—not everyone has access to all the information. This duty may be shared with a data security administrator in a large data base environment. (In fact, the access to information is the primary audit concern.)

The DBA is responsible for the data base design, definition, and maintenance. Other functions include setting policies and procedures for backup and recovery, determining appropriate access permissions for applications programs and users, and resolving any conflicts among users of the data.

Data Organization

A data base system can be described as being information-oriented, then user-oriented or data-oriented. Information-oriented data is meaningful to

FIG. 28-4
Functions of a data base administrator

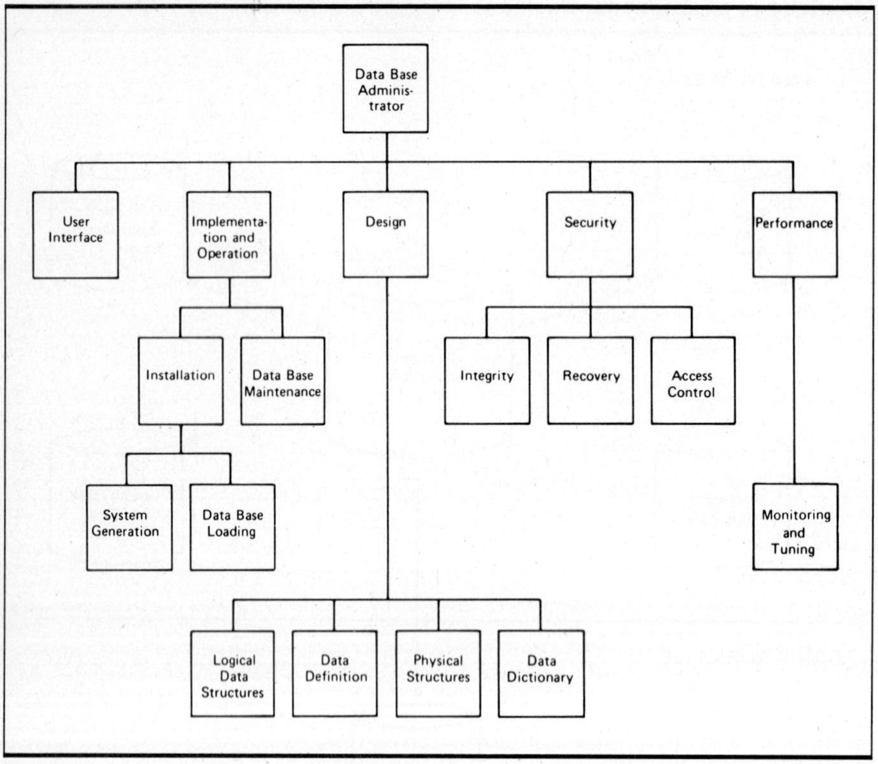

the organization as a whole; user-oriented relates to how a user of the information wishes to manipulate or retrieve the information; and data-oriented means storing the data only once and being able to access and retrieve it easily.

The data in a data base is stored in fields that represent units of information (e.g., the number "4891100" is seven digits, which, taken as a whole, could be the telephone number 489-1100 or an invoice amount of $48,911.00). Interpretation of the data depends on the user and the computer application program processing the data.

Perhaps the easiest way to describe the data base concepts as implemented is to describe how a hospital may create, manipulate, retrieve, and store data. Figure 28-5 illustrates the concept of data in a hospital environment.

The patient information shown can be used to identify patients for bill-

FIG. 28-5

Data base concepts illustrated using a hospital's data requirements

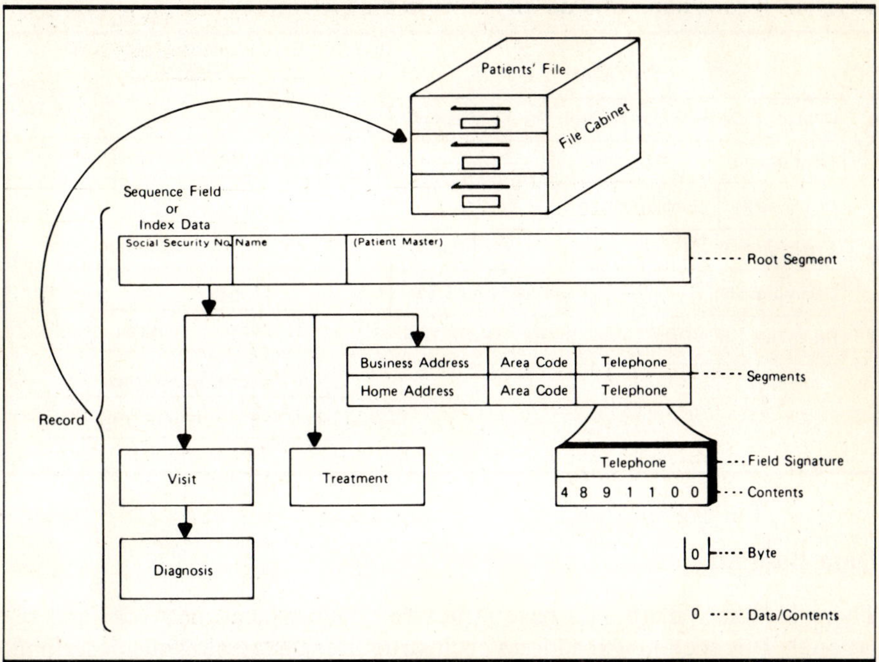

ing, treatment, insurance reporting, and such, each of which is an application system in the data base. One application program in the billing system is the invoicing of patients for treatment received. In this case, the invoice is triggered by treatment, which may have been triggered by an appointment register. All of these activities represent different data base applications. The receptionist making appointments in a doctor's office does not need access to the patient's entire file, only to the information necessary to make the appointment. When the receptionist enters the the appointment in the appointment register, it may be done via a terminal that allows only appointment transactions to be entered. This transaction simultaneously causes the scheduling of a doctor and an examination room for the day and time of the appointment.

Figure 28-6 presents the data elements (fields) in a physical relationship that describe their location as stored on disk versus the logical relationship. This is a very simple description of a system, but it suggests how important it is to have a DBA design the logical relationships of data, control the access to the data via terminals, and determine how the data is to be maintained.

FIG. 28-6

Data structure based on the logical relationship of data versus the physical organization of data elements in their hierarchy

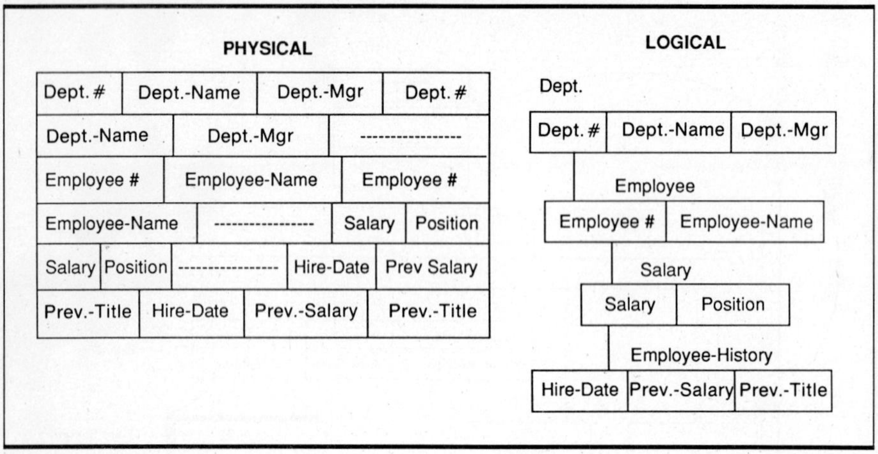

Data Base Structure

There are three main data base structures: hierarchical, network, and relational. This section will address each structure in general, while describing a popular DBMS for each.

Hierarchical. In a hierarchical data base, data is organized in a tree structure. (See Figure 28-7.) IBM's IMS (Information Management System) uses hierarchical architecture and concepts. The uppermost data element in the hierarchy is called the root. The root is linked to data elements or nodes on a lower level, each called a child. The higher level node to which the child is linked is called a parent.

A hierarchical structure only has one root. Each parent can have numerous children, but a child can have only one parent. Subordinate segments are retrieved through the parent segment. Reverse pointers are not allowed. Pointers can be set only for nodes on a lower level; they cannot be set to a node on a higher level.

Network. The network structure is more flexible, yet more complex, than the hierarchical structure. Data records are related through logical entities called sets. (See Figure 28-8.) Within a network, any data element can be connected to any item.

Unlike IMS, a data element called a member (the equivalent of a child

FIG. 28-7

Organization of a hierarchical data base

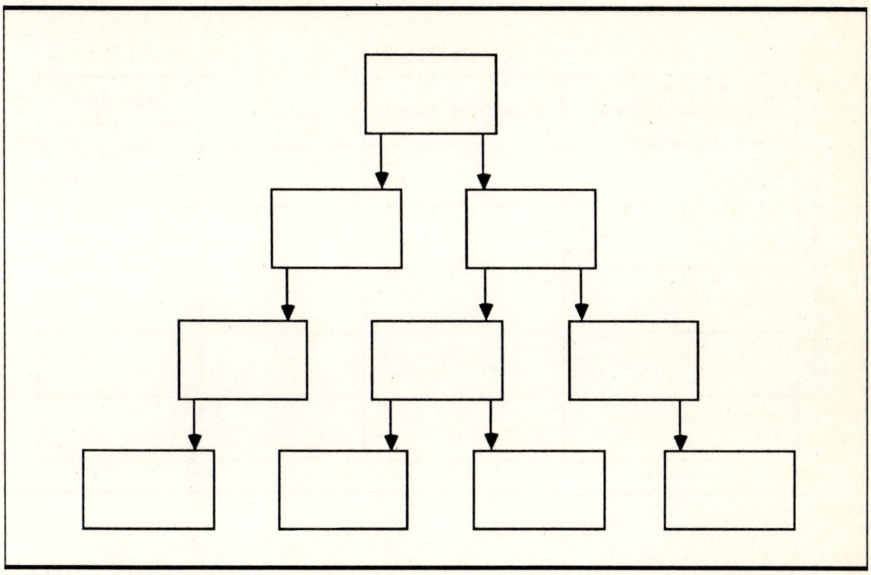

FIG. 28-8

Organization of a network data base

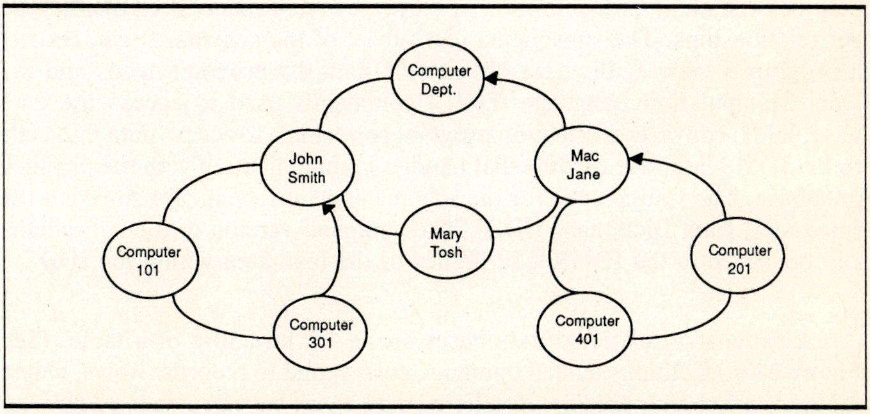

FIG. 28-9

Table-like layout of a relational data base

Rows (Tuples)

Columns (Domains)

Customer Number	Customer Name	Balance	Last Date of Payment

in IMS) can have more than one owner (parent). Because networks allow reverse pointers, an item can be both an owner and a member of the same set of data. Members are grouped together to form records, and records are linked together to form a set. A set can have only one owner record but several member records.

A popular network data base is Cullinet's IDMS (Integrated Database Management System). IDMS uses the Data Definition Language (DDL) and the Data Dictionary Definition Language (DDDL) to define the schema and the subschema of the data base. These languages follow the CODASYL standards. A schema is a conceptual description of the entire data base. It includes the name and definition of all files, areas, records, elements, and set relationships. The subschema is a subset of the schema. It can restrict a program's view of the data base to the data the program needs and the Data Manipulation Language (DML) commands used to access the data base. DML converts application program commands to access data into calls to the IDMS interface module that handles communication with the physical data base. The source code for the schema and subschema are stored in the Integrated Data Dictionary (IDD). The compiled version of the subschema can be stored in the IDMS load library or the load area within the IDD.

Relational. Relational data bases are in the structure of a table. (See Figure 28-9.) Columns, called domains, correspond to records. Rows, called tuples, correspond to fields. Relational data bases have grown in popularity over the last few years because they are easier to set up and maintain than other DBMS. Relationships are defined at the data value level so that physical pointers do not have to be set up. As a result, application programs are more independent of the data structure. Adding or deleting a field from the data base does not require the program to be recompiled. In addition, relational data bases are more flexible in supporting user requests for data because files are loaded into the DBMS. Application programmers define how their applications view the data. The user need not be concerned with the access path or the pointers used to retrieve the data.

IBM's DB2 and most PC data base software (e.g., Paradox, dBASE IV) use relational architecture and concepts. The Structured Query Language (SQL) data definition statements are used to define the tables and retrieve information in DB2. Similar statements are used in the PC DBMS; these consist of table operators such as join, project, and select.

Data Manipulation Language

The DML interfaces between the application program and the DBMS to perform a function (e.g., open a file, insert a record). IMS uses DL/I commands to manipulate data. IDMS and other networks usually use the CODASYL DML standards.

Data Dictionary

The data dictionary (DD) describes various attributes of the data elements. In some DMBS, it also contains information about the physical location of the data. It may include the data name, the segment on which it occurs, and the programs using the field. A DD can be used to ensure that data is defined uniformly. It also supplies the application programmer and the user with information as to what data is available and in which data base it is located. DDs are classified as passive or active. Active DDs are updated automatically whenever there is a change in the DBMS. A passive DD is not integrated with the DBMS and must be maintained separately. IMS has a passive DD, IDMS has an active integrated DD, DB2 has the DB2 Catalog that performs some active DD functions.

DATA BASE PRODUCTS: FUNCTIONS AND SECURITY

IMS

IMS uses Program Specification Blocks (PSB), Program Control Blocks (PCB), and the Data Base Dictionary (DBD) to define the data base structure.

FIG. 28-10

Two views of the data base through the PSBs and PCBs (courtesy of International Business Machines Corporation)

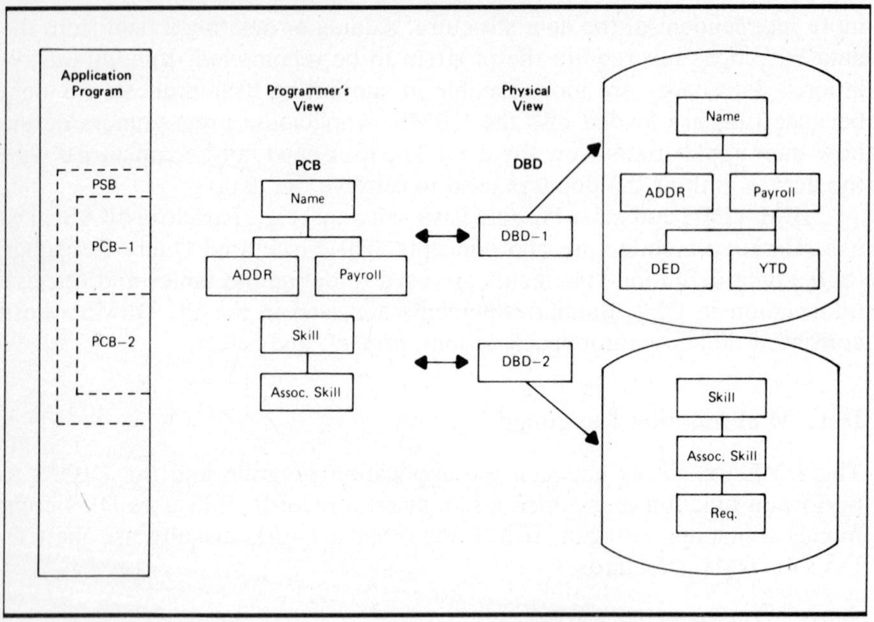

The DBD describes the physical structure of the data base. It contains the name and the length of the segment, and the relationship among the segments. The PCB defines which segments of the DBD the program can view, the relationship between the segments, and the processing codes they can use (e.g., retrieve, delete, insert). The processing options associated with an application program are described in the PROCOPT parameter on the PCB. The PSB is composed of one or more PCBs that define how the application program can view the data. Typically, a DBA establishes naming convention standards so that the PSBs are readily identifiable to the application program and to the data base. (See Figure 28-10 for an example of a layout of a DBD, PCB, and PSB.)

IMS has the capability to describe logical data bases (i.e., that use the data for a specific application) that may be composed of already defined physical data bases. Logical data bases do not have a separate existence. Instead, segments that compose the local data bases are defined, as required, from the underlying physical data base that connects two or more physical data bases in a DBD. They are passed to the application program on request after the DBMS has determined that the defined program can access the data elements requested. Conversely, logical data base segments are accepted from the application program and inserted, replaced, or deleted as appropriate.

To optimize processing, an indexed data base can allow alternate keys to access data elements. In the earlier example of the hospital environment the patient's name relates to the patient's files and can be used as a key to accessing that data. The receptionist making appointments can enter the patient's name and the insurance clerk can enter the patient's social security number; both gain access to the same set of patient information. The index also allows access using a key other than the one used to store the data.

On-line capabilities for IMS are provided through the Data Communication (DC) feature, which allows users on-line execution of the IMS system with user access via terminals. Two or more IMS systems can transmit transactions to each other through the capabilities of the Multiple Systems Coupling (MSC) feature.

The transaction-processing facilities of IMS/VS permit the messages entered via terminals to be processed by application programs. Application programs may communicate via transactions that are messages. There are two general categories of transactions:

1. DC transactions processed by the DC feature
2. Fast Path (FP) transactions processed by the FP feature

The primary difference between these two features, from an audit viewpoint, is that FP transactions can originate only from terminals, whereas non-FP transactions can originate from a terminal or from an application program.

When an application program is scheduled for execution, IMS/VS must first have available the DBD and the PSB control blocks previously created by the DBDGEN and PSBGEN procedures. These control blocks are merged and expanded into an IMS/VS internal format called application control blocks (ACB). The ACBs must be created before the on-line system is started in a process called ACBGEN.

The DC feature provides two types of transaction processing: (1) message processing programs (MPP), and (2) batch message processing (BMP). A batch program may use an ACB or a PSB; DC must have an ACB.

IMS restricts access to data through a combination of terminal, password, transaction command, and user identification (ID) security. Terminals are classified as physical, logical, and master, as follows:

- Physical terminals are the hardware devices as defined in the OS/VS SYSGEN via data definition statements in the IMS start-up. Physical terminals are defined in OS/VS SYSGEN so that IMS knows they exist. Without such definition they cannot interact with the system. They are protected by restricting access.

- Logical terminals are the names related or assigned to a physical terminal so that IMS/VS can construct and transmit messages. One physical terminal can have one or more logical terminals associated with it. Logical terminals exist so that if one particular physical terminal breaks down, another physical terminal can be substituted to receive data that might be queued for processing. Logical terminal security is established by defining which transactions and commands can be entered via the logical terminal.
- The master terminal is a logical terminal that acts as the operational hub of IMS/VS. This terminal has complete control over IMS/VS communication facilities, message scheduling, and data base operations. Note that because the master terminal is a logical terminal, it can be reassigned dynamically to another physical terminal. The operating system console can be used as an alternative master terminal. Often, the master terminal is named CTRL and the operating system console is named WTOR. However, they may be assigned any name (of one to eight alphanumeric characters) that relates to the physical devices defined during the OS/VS SYSGEN. Obviously, the master terminal requires the greatest security protection because it is capable of entering all commands.

Passwords provide another level of security that identifies a user, thereby enabling him to access the data. The problem with passwords is that they must be controlled (e.g., through frequent changes) and users must be educated to ensure that the passwords remain secret. Passwords can be used to limit or restrict access to physical terminals, logical terminals, transactions, commands, and data bases. Passwords do not accomplish their purpose if they are posted on the physical terminal for easy reference.

Command security determines which users are permitted to issue IMS/VS commands. The command language is designed to provide for interrogating or altering the processing functions. Figure 28-11 indicates the need to audit the commands associated with logical terminals. The organization's commands to the data base are identified by a unique name (from one to eight alphanumeric characters in length). Functions are defined by the user and can be named appropriately according to naming conventions. The commands are predetermined by IMS/VS. If terminal security is not defined to the system, then the default allows all IMS/VS commands to be entered from any terminal. Furthermore, the default allows transactions to be entered from any terminal.

The final mechanism for security within IMS/VS is the user ID verification, which defines which physical terminals require sign-on processing.

FIG. 28-11
IMS/VS terminal commands

IMS/VS COMMANDS	MASTER TERMINAL	REMOTE TERMINAL	ELIGIBLE AS TRANSACTION	AUDIT CONCERN	DESCRIPTION
ASSIGN	X		X	*	This command alters the relationships between various IMS/VS system resources and resets certain values specified during IMS/VS system definition. The relationships that can be changed that cause audit concern are: The logical terminals can be assigned to a non-switched physical terminal for output and input purposes. Consequently, logical terminals can be moved from one physical terminal to another physical terminal.
BROADCAST	X	X	X		A command used to send a message to terminals in one or more IMS/VS systems.
CANCEL		X			Cancels all segments of an input message. Usually used to correct input errors.
CHANGE	X		X	*	Changes one password to another password. Password protection is subject to breakdown if non-authorized terminal users have access to this command.
CHECKPOINT	X		X		Records control and status information on the system log tape and restart data set.
CLSDST	X		X		Causes IMS/VS to disconnect a VTAM terminal.
COMPT	X		X	*	Sets a particular terminal component to an operable (ready) or inoperable (not ready) state. Output messages queued for a particular component will not be sent unless the component is operable. A terminal could be turned off, thereby eliminating control messages.
DBDUMP	X		X	*	Is used to stop the scheduling of transactions that can update IMS/VS data bases. Impacts the updating of data bases, so should only be entered by authorized terminals.
DBRECOVERY	X		X	*	Used to stop the scheduling of transactions that update or read IMS/VS data bases. Impacts the data bases so should only be entered by authorized terminals.

Sign-on processing is accomplished through the use of the SIGN command, which requires entering up to eight characters of user ID and user data. Thus, the SIGN ON/OFF command is designed to safeguard physical terminals.

The application programs that process transactions are called transaction processing programs. On-line transactions are processed by message processing programs. BMP programs generate transactions to access on-line data bases. A transaction entered at a terminal may result in more than one message being processed. An example is a transaction that permits information to be entered for updating a data base. The transaction is edited on-line and, when all processing is complete, a message is generated for later batch message program processing. This means that once a batch of transactions is processed, the master file will actually be updated.

IDMS/R

Cullinet's Integrated Database Management System/Relational (IDMS/R) combines relational and network capabilities and provides for ad hoc end-user requests and small applications (like a relational data base) and, for high-volume applications, the power of a network structure. All functions are integrated into one DBMS with a central location that maintains all data and performs access, input/output (I/O), and space management functions.

IDMS/R features enable MIS end-users to create applications of various sizes. All data is shared, eliminating duplication. Several forms of internal security are provided as well. The Automatic System Facility (ASF) generates the structure for the development of applications. This includes data definitions, screen formats, processing logic, and documentation, as necessary.

MIS staff can use ASF to reduce development time and create relational production applications for regularly scheduled processing and ad hoc queries. In addition, private applications can be developed with IDMS/R, helping end-users to meet their independent information management demands. On-line capability enables users to bypass backlogs that often exist in a central MIS department.

IDMS/R can be used to create prototype network data base applications. Its combination of relational and network capabilities allows migration from relational to network structure by redefining data records.

IDMS restricts access to terminals, programs, tasks (transactions), users, and systems. It defines each in the IDD and assigns them security codes. The user requesting access must have a matching security code to obtain access through the resource. IDMS allows up to 255 security codes.

IDMS also controls security through the USER statement, the authorization set on the OPTIONS statement, the PROGRAM REGISTRATION statement, and the subschemas defined to the users.

Users are defined in the IDD either by a SYSGEN USER statement or a DDDL ADD USER statement. Encrypted passwords are assigned in the user entity definition. User standards also can contain clauses that restrict or allow access. The following are examples of possible clauses:

- *INCLUDE AUTHORITY FOR UPDATE PASSWORD*—Allows the user to modify another user's password.
- *INCLUDE AUTHORITY FOR UPDATE USER/IDD*—Allows the user to modify or set up a user statement.
- *AUTHORITY IS ALL*—Allows the user all types of authority.

The SECURITY FOR clause is a system option. When SECURITY FOR entity IS ON, a user must have authorization in its user definition to access the secure entity type definition in the dictionary. It can restrict access to systems, subsystems, terminals, and other resources (i.e., IDD, DC, ASF). For example, if the IDMS security is not on, any user can access the SCHEMA or SUBSCHEMA compiler. If it is turned on, only users with AUTHORITY FOR UPDATE IDMS can access the compiler.

The following description of this aspect of IDMS is taken from the manual:

> - AUTHORIZATION IS ON/*OFF*—When ON, the DML processor will only accept to process program[s] whose name[s] have been formerly catalogued as entity type occurrence in the IDD. This clause can be overridden on an individual basis in the subschema definition.
> - INDIVIDUAL PASSWORD SECURITY OVERRIDE IS ON/*OFF*—When ON users will be allowed to modify their own passwords.
> - REGISTRATION OVERRIDE—When specified, entity occurrence security as defined in the next subsection is turned off for the DDDL session. To issue this clause, the user must be assigned "AUTHORITY FOR UPDATE IS ALL."

A major restriction of access in IDMS/R DB is to define restrictive subschemas associated with the specific program needs. Four conditions are needed in order for this security to be effective:

- The default OPTION for DICTIONARY of the AUTHORIZATION clause must be turned to ON. Thus only programs associated in their IDD definition to the subschema will be allowed to access the subschema through the DML preprocessor. This restriction only applies to the DML processor.

- SECURITY FOR IDD must be ON in the general OPTIONs (see above) in order to require IDD authority to modify program definitions.
- SECURITY FOR IDMS must be ON in the general OPTIONs (see above) in order to require IDMS authority to modify subschema definitions.
- The number of users with IDD and IDMS authority should be highly restricted in order to protect program and subschema definitions.

It should be clearly understood at this stage that program security enforced through AUTHORIZATION specification is not absolute. It is possible to create an executable version of a program without using the DML preprocessor. In order to do it, one should only be able to code directly the statements coded automatically by the DML processor (i.e., IDMS controls blocks and DML calling sequence).

All the default options in effect for the dictionary can be obtained by the command "DISPLAY OPTIONS FOR DICTIONARY" after having signed on to the dictionary.

. . . Program registration . . . deals with the use of the executable version of a program on-line or in a batch mode.

The program registration option is specified during sysgen. . . . This option is stored in the nucleus and can not be changed dynamically. If program registration is enforced, programs will have to be registered with a subschema during the sysgen. . . .

Note: There is a major exposure in an IDMS Central Version with the use of batch programs.

It is possible to directly access data base areas without any kind of checking being performed at the IDMS Central Version level. In order to do this you only need to create a COBOL program. If AUTHORIZATION IS ON, you will only need to code in all the relevant calls to the data base. If program registration is enforced, you can use an existing program name already registered with the subschemas you want to access.

Such a program will not only be able to access a data base area but also the data dictionary areas by specifying the relevant subschemas names. These names are standard and are most of the time IDMSNWKX, IDMSNWKS, IDMSNWKA, and IDMSRSSA. A program that will always be registered with these subschemas is for instance the DDDL compiler IDMSDDDL. Using such a name, the user defined batch program could for instance modify a USER-047 record, i.e., a user definition. The layout of these records can be found in IDMS/R Network Reference Manual.

The only way to secure such a type of violation is by protecting the areas of the dictionary. This can be done by having the sensitive data base areas default to retrieval mode at startup time by way of the IDMSAREA statement at SYSGEN time. These areas are only to be "varied on-line in update mode" by the DBA during scheduled updates to the data base areas. Although this does not eliminate the exposure, the window of vulnerability is narrowed. This solution is only applicable to the dictionary and cannot be used to secure data areas.

Data areas can be secured using external security packages.

DB2

IBM's DATABASE 2 (DB2) is a relational structure with a data manipulation language, SQL, that retrieves and manipulates physical data organized within tables.

The user creates and defines tables with the SQL DD. SQL is used to invoke all table operations as well (e.g., selection, deletion, update, summation). The language can be embedded in an application program, or it can be interactive from an on-line terminal.

The Query Management Facility (QMF) is DB2's on-line query system and interactive report writer. It allows users to perform calculations, modify, and manipulate accessible data.

DB2 security is provided on a column/row level and on a table level. Protection and authorization are provided through two features: views and GRANT/REVOKE statements. Data backup and recovery procedures help to ensure data consistency and integrity. The DB2 DBA can recover data at various levels in the data base. The DBMS provides an option to partition table spaces into smaller units to facilitate recovery. Each partition can then be restored and reorganized independently.

DB2 controls access to data through views and the GRANT/REVOKE privileges contained on various tables in the DB2 Catalog. The strength of these controls are dependent on the DB2 system options and exits in place.

DB2 interfaces with CICS, IMS/DC, RACF, or other security packages to determine if a user should be given access to DB2. Generally, if DB2 does not recognize the user ID, it assigns the default ID IMBUSER. In addition, in DB2, more than one user can have the same user ID. This greatly limits accountability.

Views are not actual tables, but rather, a subset of real tables. Their data is extracted when they are accessed. Views can limit user or program access to data. They are created using the SQL CREATE command. For each view or table created, a record containing its information is stored in SYSTABLES of the DB2 Catalog. SYSTABAUTH is updated with information pertaining to the creator of the views and tables. Other authorization tables can also be set up to assign who has access to the views and tables, the type of access they have (e.g., read, update), and which programs can use which tables or views.

The security administrator can specify which commands a user is allowed to use. To ease maintenance, these commands are grouped into five privilege levels. The user is then assigned a level.

A user's access can be controlled by either granting them a privilege or by selecting commands that they can use. DB2 allows five privilege options.

- SYSADM—Allows the users access to everything in the DB2 system; they can grant and revoke privileges to users and have access to almost all the DB2 system files.
- DBADM—Allows users complete control over their assigned data bases.
- DBCTRL—Allows users to run utilities to maintain data bases, but they do not have the authority to change data in the table.
- DBMAINT—Allows users similar access as with DBCTRL; however, they are more limited in the utilities they can run.
- SYSOPR—Allows users to issue DB2 commands, but they do not have access to the data bases.

DISTRIBUTED DATA BASE SYSTEMS

In a centralized system, the data files, programs, and directories reside in the same processing system. In a distributed system, the programs, directories, and files associated with a particular request are spread among different processors. (See Figure 28-12.) It is this separation that creates the unique audit and other problems associated with distributed data base systems (DDBs).

A DDB exists when an information network has two or more computers, each of which has permanent files attached. The set of permanent files forms the DDB.

DDBs provide certain potential advantages not offered by centralized data bases. The DDB allows files to be located at the point of need in a geographically dispersed organization and thus offers the potential for reduced communications costs and reduced response time.

The designer of a DDB system is faced with several design factors that do not exist in a centralized data base system. These factors must be considered carefully if performance is to be satisfactory to the system's users. The designer must decide how to split the files, how to split the directories, where to locate the programs, and how to design the communications network to support the message flow between nodes or parts of the system created by splitting the components of the data base. (See Figure 28-13.)

FIG. 28-12
Overview of how the DDB spreads processing from the central data base to separate local processing units

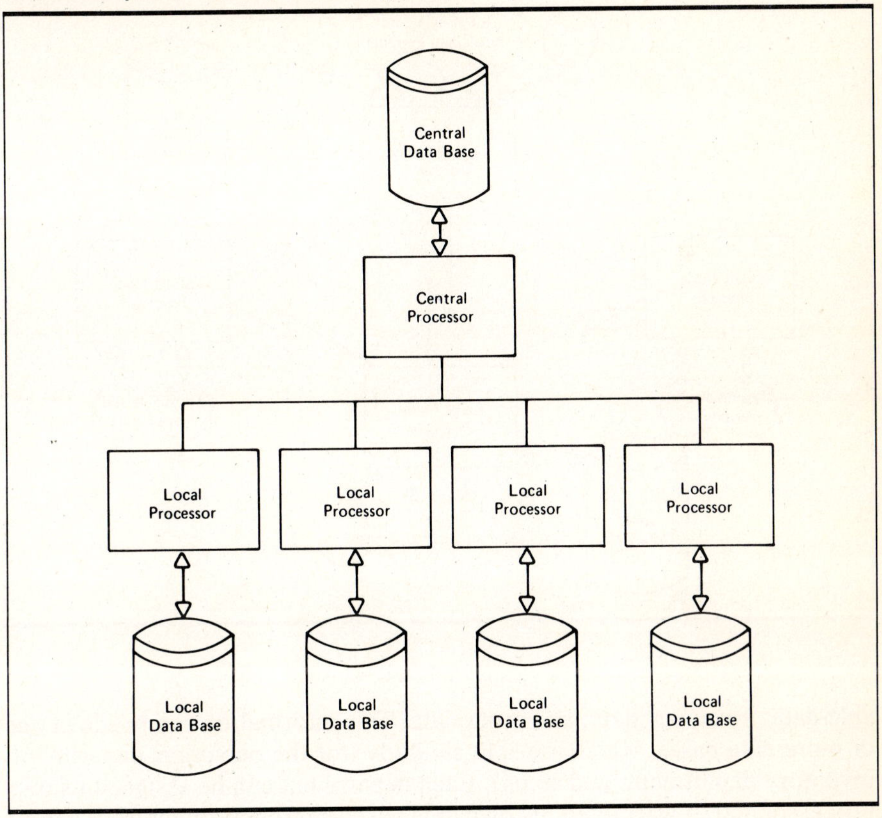

File Splitting

The typical DDB system splits its files according to geography or function. For example, an organization may be distributed geographically, with each branch serving a reasonably unique set of customers. It would be logical to place all records and files relevant to that segment of the customer base at the local branch. The branch computer would process all requests pertaining to its data base without requiring any assistance from other processors. If a customer account requires data that is stored elsewhere, the local processor can issue a request to the appropriate branch processor to retrieve the desired record. (See Figure 28-14.)

Another way to split a data base is by function. A typical business operation may have personnel data, accounts receivable data, accounts pay-

FIG. 28-13
Distributed processing in a loop network structure

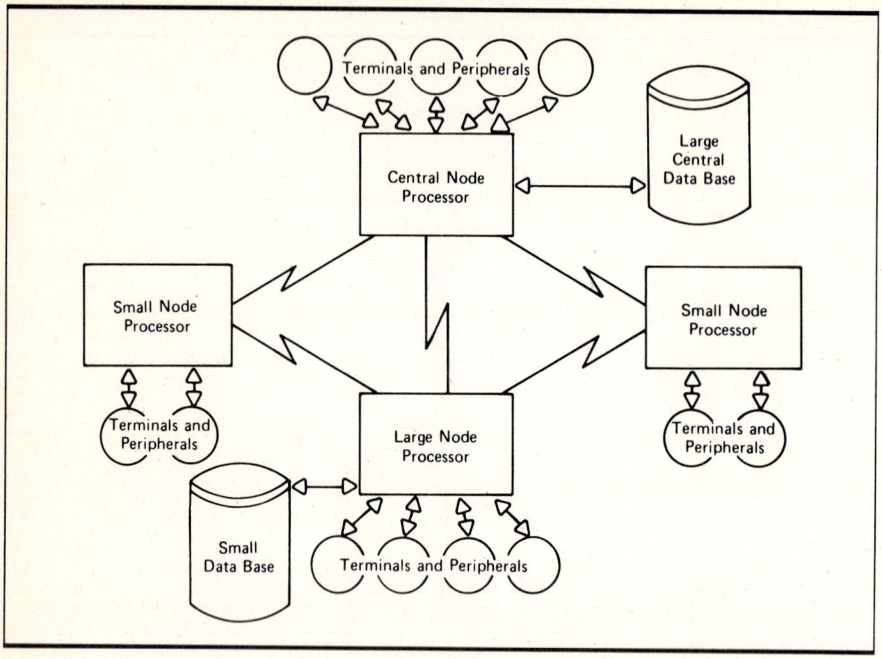

able data, inventory data, and order data. This information can reside in one or more data bases, which are split similarly (for the personnel department, inventory department, and so on). Each department can be assigned its own processor and, if warranted, its own data base. Interdepartment transactions are handled via intercomputer communications. (See Figure 28-15.)

Directory Location

Directory location techniques can be divided into three major categories:

1. *Centralized.* The directories in the entire data base are located at one processing location or node. Subdirectories associated with local data bases may or may not be located at the local nodes.
2. *Distributed/Total.* A copy of the entire directory is located at each node.
3. *Local.* A copy of that portion of the directory pertaining to the local node is located only at that node.

FIG. 28-14

Distributed processing with a limited sharing of local data bases

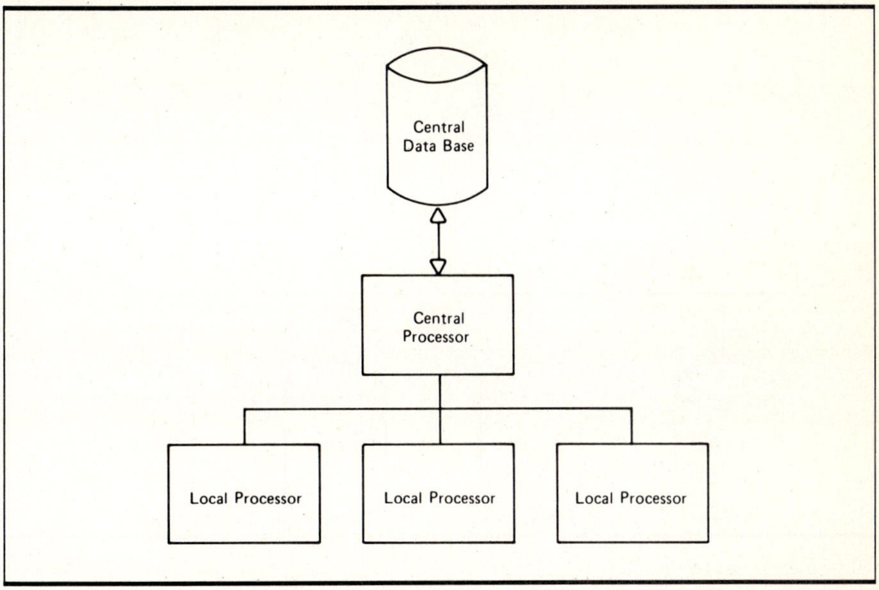

The selection of the appropriate technique depends on various tradeoffs between the costs of storage, processing, communication, the time required to respond to a data request, and the need to keep all data current.

Program Distribution

There are situations in which a program must operate on an entire file, rather than on a small set of records. It is desirable to locate these programs at the nodes where their supporting files reside. This can be done where there is ample storage at each node for the programs. In many systems, the data base is large relative to total program size, so that room is readily available for program storage on the physical devices that store the data. However, if storage space is at a premium, it may not always be possible to associate programs with files.

If programs are to be moved, the question becomes how and where to store the programs and how to control their movement. The programs can be centralized at a master node and dispatched as needed to requesting nodes. Copies of heavily used programs can be stored at local nodes to reduce the program data flow. Alternately, the programs could be distributed locally according to use, with no central node. This would reduce the overall

FIG. 28-15
A fully distributed system

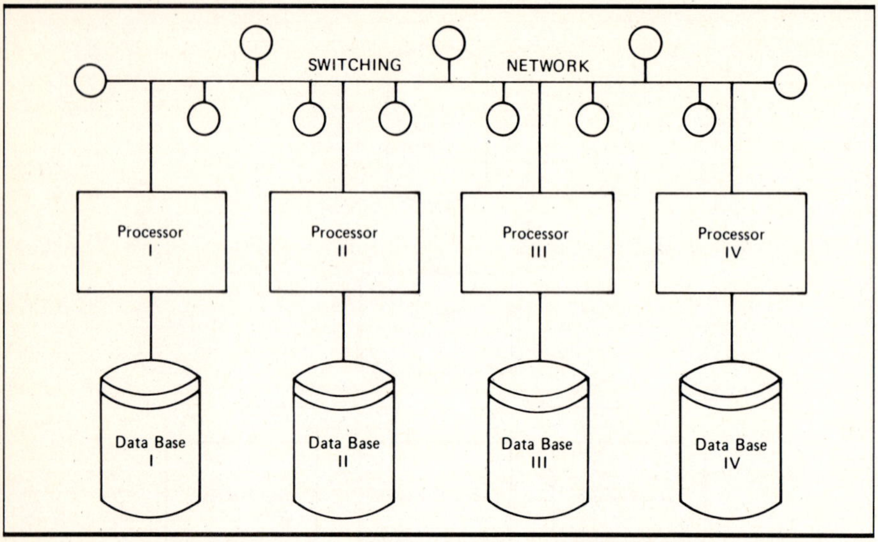

amount of program storage. However, each node would then need a directory of program locations so that nonlocal programs could be requested. It may be possible for the directory to be located at one or several nodes through which all program requests would be directed.

Communications

The DDB system closely relates data base software with communications. The network characteristics must be designed to support the data transfers necessitated by the distributed data base.

File Consistency

Problems of data consistency arise when an application updates files at more than one node and when files at one node are updated by more than one application. Although these problems exist in conventional centralized data base systems, they are potentially more critical in a remote system because of update time delays.

A simple way to avoid inconsistencies is to lock out a record from further use while it is being updated. This can be done by the DDB in the node receiving the request. However, to avoid unnecessary lockouts, the requestor should inform the node whether an update is to be performed. If the file action is read-only, there is no need for the file to be locked out.

Another approach is to allow files to be updated only by processes located at the node where the file resides. The update request is then transmitted from the processing node to the resident file node. The update is carried out at the resident file node. The record has to be locked out only for the duration of the update.

Deadlock

A deadlock occurs if two or more processes bid for the same resources in a mutually exclusive manner. Consider the following: Process *A* starts and seizes and locks out File A while Process *B* starts and seizes and locks out File B. Process *A* then requests File B while Process *B* requests File A. Both files are locked out. Hence, neither process can complete and release its file, causing an indefinite impasse. Most DBMSs provide facilities to identify this situation and control it.

Error Recovery/Reliability

The DBMS DDB systems must provide a mechanism for recovery of lost files and for operation while certain nodes are unavailable. The responsibility for recovery could be left to each node. Local data base and directory updates could be logged. In case of a file failure, the start-of-day file is reloaded and the day's activities restored by processing the log tape. The failed node is unavailable until the restoration is complete. A way to inform the other nodes of the failed node's condition must be developed, so that processes do not stop while awaiting responses. For example, this mechanism can be a time-out function (that ends a request after a certain period of nonprocessing time) associated with each request, or an explicit message sent from a monitoring node indicating the unavailability of the failed node.

Files that are crucial to system operation must be duplicated to ensure continuous availability. This can be accomplished by placing redundant physical files and processors at the critical node. Another approach is to place copies of critical files at more than one node, which in turn brings up the problem of keeping these files consistent. A third approach is to log the file updates to a neighboring node, so that if the original node fails, the file can be reconstructed at the neighboring node. The other nodes in the network will then be informed of the change in location of the critical file.

Application Areas

The general characteristics of applications suitable for DDB systems include a clear, logical split of data needs according to either a functional or a geographical basis; a low (less than 20 percent) probability that a user at one node will need data from another node on any particular transaction; a low probability of file transfer or, stated another way, a low volume of data transferred per request; and a dedicated application that can be built around relatively homogeneous systems.

The following is a list of some application areas in which DDBs have been used successfully:

- *Retail point-of-sale.* Each store is a node with terminals, a local processor, and a store-wide data base. The nodes communicate with a central system-wide data base.
- *Large banks.* In one type of system, each branch has its own customer data base, which contains partial files. Detailed history files are stored in a central data base.
- *Airlines reservation systems.* These tend to be heterogeneous. Each airline has its own reservations data base but can access each other's airlines' data bases through well-structured message requests and data transfer formats.
- *Distribution systems.* A manufacturing organization has installed a computer at each major distribution center. Each node has its own customer file and inventory file. A central node retains a complete inventory file for the entire system.

AUDIT APPROACH IN A DATA BASE ENVIRONMENT

The existence of a data base environment does not affect basic control considerations. However, it will affect the audit procedures for gaining an understanding of the system, identifying controls, and designing tests.

Obtaining and Confirming an Understanding

The auditor obtains an understanding of the accounting system through discussions with personnel and through observation and review of existing procedures and policy manuals. The auditor must identify the data elements of accounting significance and determine their relationship within the accounting structure. The auditor should clearly recognize the logical relationships between financially significant data elements, programs, and transaction types. The DBA should be able to supply this information from the DD.

Documentation can include narratives, flowcharts, and listings. The data base documentation to be audited should show the following clearly:

- The elements of each data base (fields, keys, segments), or the schema.
- The transactions affecting those data elements.
- The logical view of the data bases, or the subschema used by those programs.
- The programs processing those transactions.
- The terminal and/or users entitled to enter those transactions or commands.

The auditor should document the relationships for only those data elements that have accounting significance. This documentation is necessary for the auditor to understand the processing flow. In an audit of the system itself, the EDP auditor may need a broader understanding, since the audit will be concerned with the system and not just the elements of accounting significance.

Information Technology Controls in a Data Base Environment

Because information technology (IT) or general controls are concerned with preventing unauthorized access and changes to data stored on computer media, they have been affected by advances in data base technology. The concept of data shared by many users is essential to understanding a DBMS. The fact that data elements can be assessed by many users makes it necessary to control access to specific data elements. In a data base, the application programs no longer access data or perform data management functions directly; rather, the DBMS acts as an interface to all the programs accessing the data base. This access mechanism is the technique whereby data independence, sharing, and manipulation are controlled.

- *Data independence.* The organization's data is integrated and available to all application programs using the data base. This alters the traditional relationship between application programs and data, where specific data files were created for each program.
- *Data sharing.* The organization's data elements are no longer application-owned. Individual data elements may be used by many applications, and the users and providers of data may be different. For example, certain users may only retrieve data elements, while others may have the authority to add, delete, or modify the data elements. Finally, certain users may have no reason to access the data element because it is not relevant to their tasks.
- *Data manipulation.* The processing requirements (read, update,

insert, delete) of the programs are carried out by data manipulation routines that are a part of the DBMS.

Establishing who can access data elements and who can perform manipulation (add, change, and delete) functions is an important audit consideration. The relationship between functions, transactions, programs, and data may not be as easily established as in the case of traditional file systems. The use of a DBMS makes the task of gaining and confirming an understanding of the internal control system more complex.

Organizational Change

Establishing a DBMS means that an organization must change to cope with the system's many technical complexities and must control coordination of the activities and communications between the many applications and departments that share the data base resources. These functions are usually undertaken by a DBA and a data security administrator. The DBA plans and manages the overall needs for data resources and may handle discipline and set standards for the data bases. The security administrator is usually responsible for determining and monitoring the controls over access to the data.

The DBA is an important factor in the auditor's review and evaluation of controls. The auditor obtains much of the understanding about how the data base is used and which controls are employed from talking to the DBA and reviewing activities. Confirmation of that understanding is accomplished by using software and techniques that relate to the system.

The DBA and the security administrator may not exist in an organization; individuals should be assigned the functions they would normally perform. The absence of coordinated structure to fulfill these responsibilities may constitute a control weakness in itself.

The DBA uses tools to assist in carrying out his responsibilities, and some of these tools can also be used by the auditor. The most important and useful tool for the auditor may be the data dictionary. It organizes and maintains information concerning the relationships, attributes, and definitions of the data elements within the data bases. There are two types—integrated and non-integrated. The IMS DD is non-integrated and it may or may not reflect the actual data base.

Batch Processing vs. On-Line Processing

Batch processing is the processing of transactions at given time intervals or after a certain number of transactions have been accumulated. A data base provides facilities for running batch applications. It is possible to extend the data base with a data communications feature to develop on-line applications (i.e., applications that support access to the data base from a remote terminal). Such an application may use the same facilities as a batch application to actually access the data base. The IMS/DC data communications feature provides the facilities required for the terminal to access the application, not the data base.

Many environments have both batch and on-line applications. The on-line applications are often data base inquiry or on-line data capture. Updating or maintenance is often handled as a batch application, since it is easier to control batch processing. Since one of the reasons for a DBMS is to have timely, current data, on-line updating is used in systems that require it, such as airline reservations or credit approval systems.

The audit concerns in an on-line environment are an extension of those in a batch data base environment. The introduction of on-line processing means that security must include adequate controls over access to the on-line teleprocessing (TP) network. (See Chapter 7, "Telecommunications Networks and Systems.") In a data base environment, access is often controlled by user passwords, transaction passwords, and terminal commands, managed by a data security administrator.

Control Over Access

The implementation objectives of DBMS—to eliminate redundant data and integrate the data of many users into a common pool—make it necessary to establish controls over who may access which elements of data. For example, an accounts receivable system can share a customer data base with a customer service system. The customer's accounts are updated with invoices and payments entered by the accounts receivable department and transactions that result when returned merchandise is entered by the customer service department. The control over access for this example means that only these two departments may adjust the customer's balances. The sales department also has access to the data base. Although they may write sales orders, they cannot enter payments or invoices. The audit concern is that proper controls have been implemented to ensure that the sales department does not have access to information reflecting accounts receivable or have the ability to enter unauthorized transactions.

An important aspect of auditing a data base is identifying authorized users and their EDP capabilities. The audit concern for controlling access to data residing in a data base system can be further divided into the following:

- Data element access
- Password systems
- Terminal security

Data Element Access. Authorized programs should access only those data elements required to execute their processing tasks. The control objective for this concern is that the data base description should be adequate to minimize unnecessary access. The data base is designed to aid in providing the appropriate control over access to pertinent data elements. The design of data base structures and the translation of user requirements for data access to a data base are complicated tasks. Therefore, the auditor is likely to encounter data bases that do not have the appropriate access controls. For example, in IMS, a PSB may access all the data requested for all the programs in an application system, or the same PSB may be used for more than one program in a batch environment.

Controlling access to data during normal production is a major concern, but control over access during testing of application programs and systems is just as important. Testing should be done using a test data base to ensure that production data is not distorted and that sensitive data is not vulnerable to exposure. Therefore, the auditor should determine that test data bases, not production data bases, are used during applications development.

Password Systems. Unauthorized access can be prevented by passwords. The control requirement for this concern is whether the password system is adequate to prevent unauthorized access.

Password security is provided in the on-line environment at two levels:

1. *Sign-on verification security*—Identifies a particular user as being present at the physical terminal.
2. *Transaction entry and command functions*—When a transaction is defined as requiring a password, the system should not allow the user to execute the transaction unless the password is specified with the transaction code.

Command functions can be protected against unauthorized use in three ways:

1. Permit the command verb to be entered only from certain logical terminals.
2. Require that a password be entered with the command verb.
3. Use a combination of both.

If a data base has been implemented without defining passwords, then no passwords are required to access the data. The control is nonexistent. When passwords have been implemented, the auditor should ensure that they are controlled on an ongoing basis, such as maintaining accurate, secured records of users and their permissions, and promptly removing employees from the system when they leave or transfer.

Terminal Security. The control requirement for terminal security is that it be adequate to prevent unauthorized access. The security of the physical location of the terminal and of the physical/logical terminal link are both important, as is security over the telecommunications network. One physical terminal may have more than one logical terminal associated with it. Terminal security restricts the entry of transactions and commands to specified terminals. When a terminal security feature is not used, all terminals may enter all transactions and commands, thereby negating the control.

The effectiveness of the controls over access is determined by how the environment is implemented and what standards are enforced to maintain the established controls. The impact of DBMS on general controls varies depending on the data base functions, the complexity and extent of data base usage, the use of telecommunications, and to what extent source/user and application program procedures ensure the reliability of data.

Audit Testing

The two major concerns in the audit of a data base are security and integrity. Security concerns relate to protecting the data base from unauthorized access. Integrity concerns relate to protecting the data base from accidental or erroneous destruction of data by authorized users.

The extent of data file security should be based on data sensitivity, characteristics of the related assets, and the effectiveness of other internal controls.

As part of the security review of the data base the auditor should obtain assurance that:

- Users can only access data that they are authorized to access or need to perform their jobs. Usually, this is controlled through logon IDs, passwords, and an external security package.
- Transactions processed by a program can access only the elements they need. Usually, this is controlled by the schema or subschema.

As part of the integrity review, the auditor should obtain a complete understanding of:

- How the DBMS handles concurrent updates. Does the DBMS lock the data before allowing an update function? Is there a logical order for handling requests?
- How the DBMS is maintained. What are the procedures for implementing a fix or enhancement? How are the changes tested?
- The functions performed by the DBA. Do they include procedures for logging and recovering data and periodic testing of internal pointers?
- Programming standards to ensure that the application programs test the return codes from the DBMS correctly.

The auditor should test controls over maintenance of the DBMS and data access. Testing related to the DBMS should be designed to ensure that the DBA's responsibilities are performed and supervised effectively. The auditor should also reperform certain procedures to ensure that the exercise of control is evident. Data base definitions and logical relationships existing in the system must remain in accordance with established standards and data dictionary representation.

Various audit software programs exist or can be developed to help the auditor review the validity of the DBA's documentation and determine that the control standards operate properly. Reports on the following can be generated:

- Transactions that access a segment or data element.
- Users with access to the transaction.
- Terminals that can issue a transaction.
- Transactions a password can authorize.
- Users with direct access to the data base or specific segments.

SPECIMEN AUDIT PROGRAM

This section describes an audit program for gaining and confirming an understanding of a data base environment.

1. Identify data elements that have audit significance.
2. Interview the DBA or security administrator to obtain the following information about security:
   - The records/segments where the financially significant data is located.
   - The transactions that update the data.
   - The users who have access to the identified transactions.

- The terminals from which these transactions can be executed.
- The users who have direct access to the segments and the type of access they have (i.e., read, update).

3. Using inquiry, observation, or examination, test that the controls described by the DBA are effective. This can be accomplished by inquiry of technical support services, querying the data dictionary, or processing software against the data dictionary to obtain corroborating evidence. (Note that the IMS data dictionary is not an integrated dictionary and may not reflect the actual data base environment. For IMS, a better approach would be to review the PSBs, PCBs, and the DBD that affect the data being reviewed.)
4. Inquire if a security package (e.g., RACF) is being used to protect the data base. If so, review the implementation of the software.
   - Are transactions protected?
   - Is security established on a file level or data element level?
   - Which users have access and what type of access do they have?
5. Review the system options used to implement the DBMS to ensure that all the appropriate security features are in effect. For example:
   - In IDMS, are the Program Authorization and User Authorization options switched to ON?
   - In DB2, has the default ID that gets assigned to all users who are not recognized by the DBMS been deleted?
6. Review the maintenance controls for the DBMS.
   - What procedures are in place to ensure that all modifications and fixes to the DBMS are appropriate and function as expected?
   - How does the DBA ensure the integrity of the data?
     — What logging facilities are in place so that the DBA can recover without loss or corruption of data?
     — Does the DBA verify the integrity of the internal pointers periodically?
7. Analyze the results of testing and reach an overall conclusion as to controls.
8. Prepare a letter to management where appropriate.

PART VIII

Information Security

CHAPTER **29**

Computer Abuse

INTRODUCTION

Computers solve problems. However, for many people computers are not merely problem-solvers. The computer itself becomes a problem or puzzle that challenges users to control or develop it.

Early computers were severely limited in memory and speed; programmers responded with compact code. Successive computer generations confronted the limitations and annoyances of hardware and software. Some of these were addressed by new ideas and improvements. Cumbersome machine language was supplemented with assembler, and then higher-level languages; keypunch gave way to on-screen terminal entry; and operating systems evolved from proprietary, incompatible systems to virtual machine architectures that simulate the programmer's preferred working environment.

In the 1950s and early 1960s, there were few computers. Most were owned by the government and the largest organizations. Because computers were a precious, limited resource, access to them was tightly controlled and could be physically protected. Controls were viewed by system programmers as additional problems to be solved in the quest to dominate the machine.

The urge to overcome problems and controls became known as the "hacker ethic." Unfortunately, the hacker ethic continues today as an underground movement among programmers. Hacking is any unauthorized attempt to access a computer system. Often, hackers attempt to breach computer security for the challenge of doing so. Usually, they do not take advantage of that access for illicit purposes. Despite such presumably innocent motivation, hackers may be charged with the crime of computer trespass in several states.

A far more serious development of the hacker ethic is destructive programming, known as "computer virus," "Trojan horse," or "trap-door code." In this case, the programmer makes unauthorized and malicious changes to the computer operating system code. These changes may be passed from machine to machine or across operating environments through inadequately controlled communications networks or inadequately controlled software acquisition procedures. Some changes may seem innocuous, such as the 1987 IBM Christmas message virus, which sent an unauthorized greeting throughout IBM's internal V-NET network. Others may qualify as practical jokes; there is a rumored "war" going on on the West Coast between IBM PC users and MacIntosh devotees, where each side loads software with viruses to attack the "enemy" machines. Such programmers alter code for senseless destruction. In 1988, a virus, allegedly created by a graduate student, swept rapidly through the nation's major computer research installations, destroying data and seriously compromising government and industrial security. Regardless of the programmer's motivation, creating and propagating computer viruses may be a criminal offense under both federal and state law.

This chapter examines the full range of computer abuse and issues of privacy and copyright. The criminal law may merit close inspection. Some computer crimes, such as fraudulent diversion of funds made possible by weak system controls, may be committed by less sophisticated employees. For other systems more skilled employees may have to bypass good security intentionally to commit a crime.

Whether it is a deliberate fraud, a "browsing" hack, or a malicious attack, such activities compromise system security and controls over the computer. They should not be considered simple mischief or harmless pranks. They may become a major concern of the EDP auditor and, potentially, law enforcement authorities as well.

COMPUTER ABUSE AND CRIME

Computer abuse is not only one of the most recent developments in white-collar crime, it is also one of the most controversial. Criminologists even have difficulty defining their terms. The U.S. Department of Justice's *Computer Crime: Criminal Justice Resource Manual* (1979) defines computer crime as

> any illegal act for which knowledge of computer technology is essential for successful prosecution. . . . [C]omputer crime includes crimes and alleged crimes [that] may involve computers not only actively but also passively when usable evidence of the acts resides in computer stored form.

The textbook *Computer Crime* (1978) restricts the term crime to use of the computer "to perpetrate acts of deceit, concealment, and guile that have as their objective the obtaining of property, money, services, and political and business advantages."

Donn B. Parker, a criminologist at SRI International, provides a working definition and distinction between computer abuse and crime. To Parker, computer crime is "any illegal act for which knowledge of computer technology is essential for successful perpetration." Computer abuse, in contrast, involves "any intentional act involving a computer where one or more perpetrators made or could have made a gain and one or more victims suffered or could have suffered a loss."

These disagreements on definitions are not merely academic exercises. Lack of clear definitions has led to errors in reporting the extent of the problem, in determining whether there is a need for special legislation, and, indeed, whether computer crime is distinguishable (or should be distinguished) from other crimes. Some of those issues are discussed in the following sections.

Extent of Computer Abuse

Instances of computer abuse were first documented in the 1950s and first prosecuted in the 1960s. Since those early days the problems and prosecutions have grown as rapidly as computer technology itself.

Collecting data on computer abuse is difficult, partly because such abuse often goes unreported. Reasons for the lack of reporting include:

- Resulting adverse publicity that might hurt a company's business.
- Difficulties in prosecution that make convictions for such crimes somewhat unlikely, even when they are reported.
- If the crime is reported but prosecution is subsequently declined, there is a strong possibility that the alleged perpetrator will sue for defamation or wrongful termination.
- Widespread publicity increases the possibility that someone may attempt to mimic the abuse, especially when computer security cannot be strengthened cost-effectively or in a manner that secures the entire system.

Estimates of the percentages of computer abuse detected and of the numbers reported to law enforcement agencies also vary considerably. In an American Bar Association (ABA) survey of major American corporations conducted in 1984, only 16 percent of respondents stated that all such incidents were reported. Five percent said that most incidents were reported; 20 percent stated that none were.

Government appears to be more aggressive than business in prosecuting computer abuse. The Department of Health and Human Services conducted two studies on such abuses in government agencies: "Computer-Related Fraud and Abuse in Government Agencies" and the follow-up "Computer-Related Fraud in Government Agencies: Perpetrator Interviews." Appendix D, "Interviews With Perpetrators of Computer Fraud," presents an overview of the first study and excerpts from the interviews held in the second study.

Statistics on losses from computer crimes have shown an increase over the years. In the ABA corporate survey mentioned previously, the "known and verifiable loss" estimation of 72 respondents who had this information exceeded $145 million. The most recent reliable survey, conducted by Reimer for the *Insurance Counsel Journal* in 1986, estimated the annual losses at $100 million to $300 million. Whatever the precise figures, the amount of money involved in computer-related crime is staggering.

Categories

Specific computer crimes are examined in the later sections "State Crimes" and "Federal Crimes." Some common methods of computer-related abuse listed in the U.S. Department of Justice's *Computer Crime* manual include:

- *Data diddling.* Possibly the most widespread abuse, it involves changing data before or during input to the system.
- *Trojan horse.* This consists of writing unauthorized, hidden instructions into a computer program so that the computer performs these functions in addition to its regular functions. This is also known as a computer virus.
- *Rounding down.* This method involves siphoning small, almost undetectable, amounts of money from a number of larger transactions, so that the quantity taken is not readily apparent. Rounding down is used to round fractional remainders down to the nearest whole, placing those tiny fractions into an unauthorized account. Performed repeatedly on numerous transactions, the fractions can grow into considerable sums of money. Although this technique is among the great scare stories of computer fraud, by the end of 1988 there were no successful prosecutions of it. In fact, Taber, in a 1980 article in the *Computer Law Journal*, offered a mathematical proof attempting to show that theft of significant amounts of money using this method was improbable.
- *Superzapping.* This technique consists of using a ZAP utility program (see Glossary), which can modify programs, bypassing controls, to change programs or data stored in the computer. ZAP programs have legitimate uses, but they can easily be misused because their use leaves few or no traces. Computer installations should have severe restrictions on access to ZAP and SUPERZAP utilities.
- *Trap doors.* Trap doors are breaks in program code that make it possible to insert additional instructions and intermediate output capabilities. These are sometimes called "user exits." Useful tools for programmers attempting to debug a program, they also make it possible to insert unauthorized program procedures.
- *Logic bombs.* These are unauthorized programs that trigger a computer action based on a certain prespecified condition. For example, one employee inserted a logic bomb in his company's personnel file to erase the whole personnel data base when the employee's name was deleted.
- *Scavenging.* Scavenging is searching for leftover information after an authorized job has been executed.
- *Data leakage.* This is removal of data from a computer or a computer facility, taking printouts or other seemingly innocuous data, such as scratched tapes scheduled for reuse but then rerouted improperly to take the data they still contain.
- *Piggybacking and impersonation.* Both of these methods are used physically as well as electronically. Piggybacking is a way to gain

access to controlled areas, such as by walking in behind an authorized entrant. It also refers to intercepting messages to add to or alter them, or to a hidden terminal attached to a line that is used to access the system when it is not otherwise in operation. Impersonation occurs when one person assumes the identity of another, either for physical access or for electronic access such as by using another's password.

- *Wiretapping*. Much like wiretapping telephone lines to listen to conversations, this involves tapping into data transmission lines to collect information.
- *Simulation and modeling*. Simulating is copying a computer process to learn it, in this case in order to alter it. The abuse occurs in the intent to alter the original program. Modeling is a type of planning using a computer program, here, with the intention of planning a crime.

The preceding are techniques for manipulating data, programs, or computers. They may or may not necessarily be criminal acts, depending on the specific state or federal legislation.

Mental State Required for Computer Crime

A crime has two parts, physical and mental. The physical part is the act or omission that the law forbids. The mental element, or *mens rea*, refers to the state of mind of the criminal. The prosecution must prove both elements beyond a reasonable doubt. Criminal intent is one of the more complicated areas of modern criminal law, and this discussion only highlights a few of the important points.

Almost all computer crime statutes require a particular kind of mental state. According to the Model Penal Code, these mental states include:

- *Intentional*—Crimes that require the intention (or purpose) to commit the act (or omission) or to cause the forbidden result.
- *Knowing*—Crimes requiring knowledge of the nature of the act or omission or the foreseeable results of the act.
- *Reckless*—Crimes where the actor does not intentionally or knowingly commit a wrong, but must in his own mind understand the risk that his conduct involves.
- *Negligent*—Crimes where the actor does not intentionally or knowingly cause harm nor does he realize the risk, but nevertheless creates an unreasonable risk.

Crimes usually require that the alleged criminal have one of these four mental states. In non-Model Penal Code states, other terms such as "willful" and "malicious" may describe the forbidden mental state. However, in some crimes, no particular mental state need be proved by the prosecution; in these "strict liability crimes," the law will imply a criminal mental state whenever the act is done.

An example may help to clarify these principles. The New York statute on computer trespasses (NYPL, § 156.10) reads as follows:

> A person who knowingly uses (or causes others to use) a computer or computer service without authorization and does so with intent to commit (or attempt) or further the commission of any felony shall be charged with computer trespass.

In this example, several acts and several mental states must be shown before the crime of computer trespass occurs. Somebody has to use a computer or computer service without permission, and this action must be a prerequisite to committing a felony (the latter felony does not have to be committed; it can be attempted or furthered). In addition, two mental states are necessary. The perpetrator must "know" that he is using the computer without authorization, and he must be using the computer with the intention or purpose of committing a felony. Both mental states must be proven by the prosecution, or this crime has not been committed. Even if a person used another's computer by accident, and discovered financial information that he later used for embezzlement, that person has not committed the New York crime of computer trespass (although he could be charged with embezzlement).

STATE CRIMES

By the end of 1988, at least 46 states and the District of Columbia had enacted statutes dealing specifically with computer crime. Thirty-nine of the states had new comprehensive computer crime statutes, covering a full range of transgressions in addition to simple trespass. Three states had extended their current penal laws to cover computer-related offenses, and four states had added unauthorized access provisions to existing statues. Most of the statutes proscribe as computer crime a core set of activities such as accessing, altering, damaging, or destroying a computer with the intent to devise or execute any scheme or artifice to defraud or deceive.

Two criminal acts are common to most of the statutes. The first is computer fraud, which is expressly proscribed in 28 states. Although the language varies to some degree, the computer fraud provisions typically apply to accessing any aspect of the computer system, including computer equipment, computer programs, and data.

The second type of computer crime is computer trespass. Under this type of provision, a person who "directly or indirectly accesses, alters, destroys, or attempts to damage or destroy any computer" has committed a computer crime. Of the state computer crime statutes, 27 expressly proscribe this activity, with some variation among the provisions of the various statutes.

Using a Computer to Steal Assets or Embezzle Funds

Theft and embezzlement are crimes in all 50 states and the District of Columbia. Accountants, auditors, and managers consider these serious crimes, in part because they can be so difficult to detect and in part because it is possible to steal huge amounts of money. The widespread use of electronic funds transfer (EFT) systems illustrates one aspect of this category of computer-related crime. EFT crime occurs in both corporate and consumer EFT systems, including cash management services, automated clearinghouses, point-of-sale terminals, telephone banking services, and automated teller machines (ATMs).

Often, this type of computer crime involves stealing assets (tangible or intangible) through use of a computer, as the following prosecuted case illustrates. A computer expert was called in by a major league baseball team to design a computer system to print and issue tickets for games. Once the system was installed, the expert used his knowledge of the process to print more than 1,000 tickets without authorization. This crime went unnoticed until the beginning of the next baseball season, when officials compared the accounts with the tickets purchased. They discovered that three accounts belonged to nonexistent companies, and ultimately traced them back to the computer expert. The expert had sold the tickets for $15,000. He was fined, put on probation, and ordered to make restitution to the baseball team.

Using a Computer to Commit Fraud

Twenty-eight states with computer crime statutes explicitly prohibit the use of computers to defraud. This is a broad category of computer crime in which records or data are manipulated for illegal gains or similar purposes.

Manipulation to commit fraud can be illustrated by the following example. Several members of a midwestern family pleaded guilty to conspiracy to commit mail fraud after an internal audit showed that an insurance company's computers had been used to issue false benefit checks. Two members of the family who worked for the insurance company's customer claims division and had clearance to process claims with the company computer were charged, as were one employee's sons. The two family members had authorized payments to themselves and their children; after receiving checks, they deleted the transactions from the files. Four years after the scheme began and both people had left the company, an internal audit revealed that there were no claims to justify numerous expenditures. By the time authorities caught up with the family, one member was working for another insurance company and was already involved in a similar scheme at the new location.

Another example occurred on the West Coast, where two county welfare employees gained over $500,000. They approached welfare recipients and offered them kickbacks for cooperation. Then, they would reactivate dormant files, substituting the name of a friend who had the same surname, but a different first name, as the former recipient. To complete the process, they forged authorizations of the transactions. When a check came with the slightly altered name, the former recipient would notify the pair, who in turn would notify the friend or relative whose name was on the check. Armed with proper identification, the friend or relative would claim the check at the bureau, and everyone involved would divide the proceeds. An alert coworker unearthed the scheme when he questioned various omissions on an input document. He asked the person who allegedly authorized payment and discovered that the document had been forged. They notified superiors, who began an investigation that uncovered the scheme.

Computer Trespass and Tampering

A majority of states restrict unauthorized access to computers. A few of the computer crime statutes forbid tampering with computers and related materials in specific contexts. Four states address the problem of access to computerized credit information. Another, more specific computer tampering provision is aimed at trade secrets; five states have computer crime statutes that forbid the unlawful taking of trade secrets stored in electronic form. Although provisions are different in nature, they all identify the special need to keep trade secrets confidential and protect them from further dissemination.

Still another form of computer tampering acknowledged in many of the statutes involves accessing a computer without causing any injury. In at least 24 states and the District of Columbia, unauthorized access to a computer without injury is a crime. In many of these provisions, "access" is included in the enumerated activities constituting computer tampering. In other statutes, the act of access violates the rights of computer users because it is an intrusion on their possession and privacy. Finally, a computer offense proscribed in several tampering statutes involves the disruption of computer services. These statutes contain a provision outlawing both the disruption and the degradation of computer services as they would affect an authorized user.

Destruction, Interception, or Alteration of Data or Software

Twenty-six states forbid the destruction, interception, or alteration of data or software. A case of interception of data occurred when an economist for a major brokerage house was accused of tapping into his former employer's computer. He did this because he wanted to obtain confidential information on money supply trends that he hoped would give him an edge in his new job. The accused worker's former supervisor became suspicious when she received an automatic printout of all of the data that had been requested. She then realized that one of the access codes used belonged to this former employee. Authorities traced subsequent outside calls to the computer and eventually arrested the former employee, who faced up to five years in prison and a $1,000 fine.

Theft of Hardware, Software, or Data

The theft of hardware, software, or data is not as obvious a crime as it may appear. Theft of computer hardware is, of course, forbidden in all states under the general theft laws. When a portable or desktop computer disappears, it is usually safe to assume that someone stole it. However, when a copy of a software program is made—with the original left in place, intact—how easily can that be traced? Or, when traced, how can it be prosecuted?

Now that computer programs are protected by the Copyright Act, copyright protection may ease some aspects of this situation. Yet, unauthorized copying is still extremely difficult to detect. When data itself is stolen—in the form of a diskette, for example—the only crime that can be prosecuted in two states is the theft of the diskette. This is hard to reconcile with the actual monetary losses incurred when the data is irreplaceable. Even when the data can be recaptured, it might involve days or weeks of work.

An example of theft of output/data is illustrated by a case where a computer executive obtained classified information about U.S. energy sources and resources via a remote terminal and a telephone. The employee, from a large company that provided computer services, was convicted of fraud.

Other State Computer Crimes

In addition to these general crimes, some states have special statutes governing computer matters. In 10 states, it is an offense to deny or interrupt computer services, three states forbid the public disclosure of passwords, and North Carolina has a specific prohibition against the use of computers in extortion.

Penalties

The penalties provided for in the computer crime statutes vary greatly among states. Both the penalties themselves and the manner in which they are delineated differ. There are three distinct patterns, as follows:

1. A general penalty provision setting one maximum penalty for all offenses under the statute.
2. Several penalty provisions that address each offense individually.
3. Either 1 or 2 above, with the penalty provision based on the value of the damage.

Several states use a single maximum penalty scheme. These statutes set out a general sentence and/or fine for the courts to administer, without detailing specific guidelines as to how to apply it. In other words, the individual court has significant discretion in determining the harshness of the perpetrator's sentence. The effect of this may be great discrepancy from court to court within one state in administering the computer crime statute. In some states, the penalties are based on the value of the property damaged.

The majority of the computer crime statutes provide different penalties for each type of offense. Thus, the particular offense determines the maximum penalty. Again, some of these states further distinguish their penalties based on the value of the property damaged. In most states, computer fraud is a felony. The penalties for computer trespass are even more varied than those for computer fraud. Some states punish computer trespass as a misdemeanor and some as a felony. The obvious result of these assorted penalty schemes is great variation among the states in the punishment of computer crime.

Unclear Definitions

A fundamental weakness of many state computer crime statutes is their failure to define simply and clearly the elements of the crimes so that enforcement officials can easily apply the definitions. It is theoretically possible in Colorado, for example, to commit computer fraud by using a television, radio, or videotape recorder without authorization, since the definition of "computer" in that state's computer crime law includes "any electronic device performing memory functions in the manipulation of electronic or magnetic impulses." Nevada has adopted much the same language, but has made the foregoing definition more clear by explicitly excluding devices "such as a radio or television transmitter or receiver, television camera, video tape recorder, sound recorder, phonograph or similar device." But in so doing, Nevada also adds complexity to its statute by requiring that law enforcers determine that such noncomputing devices are "used for reproducing information in oral or visual form without changing the nature or content of the information unless such a device is connected to and used by a computer." Because of the broadness of this qualification, for example, those who edit commercials out of a television broadcast by means of an employer's videocassette recorder might be deemed to be committing computer fraud.

Another example of unclear definitions is Arizona's inclusion of the term "approach" as one kind of access to a computer system that, if unauthorized, would be a crime under the law. If construed literally, any unauthorized physical proximity to a computer by an individual would constitute a felony. Unclear terms such as these are difficult to apply. Individuals who enforce the statutes are most often not computer experts, nor are the judges and juries who hear the evidence.

Lack of a Simple Trespass Violation

Some authorities have suggested that truly effective computer crime legislation would include criminal penalties for the full range of acts incident to gaining unauthorized access to computer systems and data bases. Most state computer crime laws address the need for sanctions against those who cause injury or the disruption of computer systems and services by their intrusions, However, the security and integrity of computer programs and data can also be compromised by the unauthorized access itself, apart from any damage that might result.

Intrusion on computer systems and data bases has been likened to criminal trespass, which is an offense that traditionally has not required either the element of injury or an intent by the trespasser to cause injury to another's property. However, many states have enacted computer crime laws that require some damage, or at least an intent to cause some loss, before the activity in question becomes criminal. The crimes of computer invasion of privacy and personal trespass by computer also require similar intent. In one state, however, an individual can be convicted of computer crime merely for using a computer without authorization.

If computer crime legislation is adopted, in part, to deter acts of which society strenuously disapproves, it can be argued that the definition of a crime should not hinge merely on whether injury results or is intended, but rather on whether unauthorized access in itself should be punishable behavior. Making intrusion only, without monetary loss or invasion of privacy, a crime might deter far more serious acts of computer crime. The failure of many state statutes to do this is seen by some as a serious deficiency in state legislation.

Lack of Consistency From State to State

As in most criminal statutes, computer crime legislation usually includes a recitation of specific offenses, a definition of terms for the various elements of the offenses, and a list of penalties to which commission of the enumerated crimes subjects the perpetrator. While it is not unusual for any of these items to vary from state to state, computer crime statutes are particularly inconsistent among jurisdictions. This may be related to the exceedingly technological nature of the acts and the comparatively recent acceptance of intrusion as a crime.

The lack of consistency among jurisdictions is particularly troublesome because computer crime is frequently an interstate crime. Apart from the complex jurisdictional issues that computer crime engenders when it is facilitated by telecommunications media, significant variations from statute to statute discourage unified and consistent law enforcement and provide mixed messages to perpetrators. In 1983, for example, the "414 Gang" in Milwaukee accessed computers in Wisconsin, New Mexico, and New York. At the time, New York had no computer crime law; Wisconsin and New Mexico did, but the provisions were different even though the acts committed were identical.

To complicate matters further, there are numerous inconsistencies in the definitions of important terms and penalties included in the computer laws of different states. Such definitions might be more successful if they were less technology-dependent. In the years since the first computer crime bill was passed, computer technology has advanced rapidly and will continue to do so. Any efforts to anticipate every possible mode of data processing must inevitably be frustrated by innovation and change. Moreover, it is becoming clear that the focus of computer crime statutes should shift toward the deterrence of acts that cause damage or disruption to the data and programs stored in computers or computerized data bases rather than to the equipment or media on which that information resides.

Jurisdiction

One of the greatest weaknesses in efforts to deter and prosecute computer criminals through the enactment of state legislation involves the numerous instances of interstate intrusion. In recent years, the merger of data processing services with telecommunications has meant that individuals can use the telephone to obtain access to computers and data in other states as easily as in their own. When that occurs, questions often arise with regard to which state has jurisdiction over the crime.

Jurisdiction over an offense resides solely in the courts of the state where the crime is committed, and its laws govern. A crime is deemed "committed" in any state where an essential part of the crime occurs. The law also recognizes that the victim state may have jurisdiction over an offense in situations where a person, while in another state, sets in motion a force that operates to affect the victim state. In addition, the state in which the person was located at the time of the crime's commission may also have jurisdiction over the offense in certain circumstances.

This possible dual jurisdiction of the courts over the subject matter of an offense is particularly troublesome in the context of computer crime. It is conceivable that someone accused of an interstate computer offense may be charged under the law of the state where the intrusion took place, under the law of the state where the telephone call was placed, or both.

As mentioned previously, both the penalties and the types of offenses charged under the various state computer crime statutes differ substantially. A number of states have not yet enacted computer crime statutes and therefore could prosecute only under traditional theft or malicious mischief laws, which may not be appropriate to computer offenses committed. The uneven results of such varied ways in which an interstate computer offense could be handled are evident. For instance, an individual located in Connecticut who recklessly disrupted computer services valued at more than $10,000 in Minnesota would be guilty of no computer crime under Minnesota law, since Minnesota law requires that the act be intentional, but would be guilty of a felony under Connecticut law, with a maximum jail sentence of 20 years.

The competency of a court to hear an interstate computer crime case is further complicated by the issue of jurisdiction over the person. The state where an accused person is located automatically has jurisdiction over the person. However, if the accused resides outside the state where the intrusion takes place and that state wants to prosecute the case, it must gain jurisdiction over the accused by one of four alternate methods: extradition proceedings; voluntary submission of the accused to the jurisdiction of the victim state; sufficient contacts with the state for the accused to be subject to service of process; or voluntary surrender of the accused by the governor of his state to the state that wants to prosecute.

Because of the complex jurisdictional issues surrounding instances of unauthorized intrusion into computer systems and data bases located across state boundaries, state officials may be unable to prosecute computer criminals. Intruders can use the jurisdictional complications to shield themselves from criminal prosecution. Moreover, when state officials decide to attempt prosecution, their efforts may be frustrated because of the complexities of gaining jurisdiction over both the offense and the person. These difficulties deter the vigorous prosecution of interstate computer crime.

Current Trends in State Legislation

As states become increasingly aware of the need for strong, easily applied legislation, better statutes are being drafted and old ones are being amended. These issues are addressed in the following paragraphs: the need for reduced thresholds of criminal intent; legislation making simple trespass by computer (without damage) a crime; and legislation focusing specifically on the jurisdictional issues already discussed.

Reduced Threshold of Criminal Intent. Under the laws of many states, unauthorized access to a computer system is a crime only if the intrusion was accompanied by a malicious intent. An exception to that principle is California's computer crime statute, which makes any intentional and knowingly unauthorized, but nonmalicious, computer access punishable. The amendment further provides that a computer owner may recover attorney fees in a civil action for damages caused by unlawful computer access. The California statute is typical of current efforts to deter and prosecute acts of intrusion that may be committed without the degree of intent formerly required in many jurisdictions.

Simple Trespass. Many commentators have argued that simple, intentional access that does not cause injury should not be subject to penal justice. Others, however, have noted the undesirable results when intruders become aware that a state has no recourse to discourage such access into computer systems. The California statute described previously expands the range of penalties, depending on the extent of damage suffered. Even if no direct injury was suffered and no damage caused, a first-time perpetrator of unauthorized access has committed an infraction simply by entering another's computer system, network, or program. Subsequent offenses are misdemeanors and subject to a fine of $250. This amendment makes it much easier to prosecute—and it is hoped deter—those who would access computer systems without causing substantial injury or disruption.

The New York Model

In 1986, New York passed a comprehensive statute on computer crime that revised the current law and created new sections for uniquely computer-related abuses. According to the *1986 Annual Survey of American Law*, the New York law clarly defined "computer," "computer program," "computer data," "computer service," "use [of a] computer or computer service without authorization," and "computer material."

The New York statute forbids the unauthorized use of a computer if it is equipped with a security system. It bans unauthorized copying of computer data or programs valued over $250 or copies made with the intent to commit any felony. The statutes amend the existing laws of theft, theft of services, fraud, and forgery to make them consistent with computer technology.

Although there have been complaints that the New York law is too specific, it is probably the nation's clearest and most comprehensive effort to restrict computer abuse.

Civil Liability

In addition to criminal sanctions, seven states now allow the victims of computer crime to bring civil actions. The civil alternative can be very attractive on two grounds:

1. A civil action can provide direct compensation to the victim, while sheltering the victim from the undesirable publicity of a criminal trial.
2. The burden of proof in a civil action is "preponderance of the evidence," rather than the "beyond a reasonable doubt" standard in criminal law. Consequently, more abusers should be found liable under this procedure, and the deterrent value of litigation will be enhanced.

As with the criminal law, however, there is great diversity in the actions and remedies available among the states. Wisconsin only allows a suit to enjoin the disclosure of information that might help someone gain unauthorized access to a computer system. California, Illinois, and Virginia require that civil actions must be preceded by criminal convictions. Connecticut, Delaware, and New Jersey also base their civil actions on the criminal statutes, but do not require a previous conviction for bringing the lawsuit.

Direction for the Future

The disastrous implications of a rapid proliferation of criminal activities involving computers, the demonstrated lack of uniformity among states with respect to computer crime legislation, and the interstate nature of computer crime all argue strongly for a need to formulate and pursue a coordinated effort to deter and vigorously prosecute computer crime. This effort might include the development of model computer crime legislation that states could adopt much as they have adopted other uniform laws. A more concerted attempt to report and gather useful information about computer crime and computer crime legislation that could be shared by states would also be helpful.

FEDERAL CRIMES

On October 12, 1984, Congress added Section 1029, "Fraud and Related Activity in Connection With Access Devices," and Section 1030, "Fraud and Related Activity in Connection With Computers," to Title 18 of the United States Code. Section 1030 proscribes accessing a computer without authorization or exceeding the bounds of a lawful access to (1) use that opportunity to obtain restricted information with the intention or reason to believe that such information is to be used to the injury of the United States or to the advantage of any foreign nation; or (2) thereby obtain information contained in a financial record of a financial institution or contained in a file of a consumer reporting agency on a consumer; or (3) knowingly use, modify, destroy, or disclose information in or prevent authorized use of such computer if it is operated for or on behalf of the U.S. government and such conduct affects such operations.

Punishment for these crimes is a fine or imprisonment, with graduated penalties. Attempts to commit these crimes are also punishable by fine or imprisonment. However, unauthorized access simply for use of the computer is not a crime. In addition to other agencies, the U.S. Secret Service is empowered to investigate offenses under Section 1030.

Section 1029 makes it a crime to knowingly and with the intent to defraud do or attempt to do the following: produce, use, or traffic in a counterfeit access device; traffic in or use such a device during any one-year period and thereby obtain anything of value aggregating $1,000 or more during that period, possess 15 or more devices that are counterfeit or unauthorized access devices; or produce, use, have control or custody of, or possess device-making equipment. If the offense affects interstate commerce, there are graduated penalties, including those for conspiracy to commit the offense.

The Secret Service, in addition to other authorized agencies, is empowered to investigate offenses under Section 1029. The section does not prohibit any lawful authorized investigative, protective, or intelligence activity of a federal, state, or local agency or any activity authorized under the Organized Crime Control Act of 1970.

The Computer Fraud and Abuse Act was amended in 1986. The most important change was the addition of a subsection that makes it an offense to traffic in passwords or other data used to gain access to computers, if such computers are used by the government or are involved in interstate or foreign commerce. The amendments also changed some fines and terms of imprisonment, and made an attempt to commit any of the offenses proscribed in the act punishable to the same extent as the offense itself.

Although the Computer Fraud and Abuse Act has been in effect for almost five years, as of the end of 1988 there have been no successful prosecutions. Among the possible reasons cited for the lack of federal prosecutions are the following:

- The Computer Fraud and Abuse Act may be too difficult to prosecute.
- It may be easier and more efficient to prosecute under existing state statutes, or under "generic" rather than "computer-specific" statutes.
- Unauthorized access to computers may be less of a problem than anticipated.

Other Federal Computer Crime Legislation

In addition to the Access Devices and Computers Act, Congress passed the Small Business Computer Crime Prevention Act. The principal thrust of that statute is to encourage the formation of a task force to study the impact of computer crime on small businesses and to disseminate to small businesses information about managerial approaches to deter computer crime.

A much earlier statute, Section 1343 of Title 18 of the United States Code, makes it a crime to use the interstate telephone system for the purpose of executing or attempting to execute a fraud or a scheme to obtain money or property under false pretenses. The courts have been very liberal in defining the terms "fraud" and "property." The purpose of this statute is to give federal jurisdiction to many types of crimes otherwise prosecutable only by the states. The statute has the advantage of making prosecutions of computer crime more feasible in instances where state laws are inadequate or where state officials decline to prosecute. In addition, 40 other sections of Title 18 of the United States Code may be used to prosecute computer crimes ranging from mail fraud to infringement of copyrights.

These legislative efforts represent an important first step toward addressing the problem of unauthorized access to computer systems on a federal level. Computer crime cannot be sufficiently controlled by the states alone. As one of the most prominent victims of computer crime, the federal government has a substantial interest in its deterrence and prosecution. With proper legislative guidance, the Department of Justice and other federal law enforcement agencies could become partners with the states in the formulation of coherent, consistent policies with regard to computer crime.

Privacy and Confidentiality

Privacy and confidentiality are related to abuse of computerized information. Privacy is an individual's right to limit the recording and dissemination of personal information. Since much of this information is now kept on computer, abuse can occur when such records are accessed on an unauthorized basis.

Confidentiality is the right to limit access to sensitive data. This confidential information is the kind of material that, if revealed about an organization, might diminish that company's competitive edge in the marketplace or lead to a rival company's gaining an advantage. Examples of such confidential information are customer, supplier, shareholder, and personnel data; development, sales, and marketing strategies; security measures; research findings and other proprietary information.

The balance between the issues of privacy and confidentiality is of concern to organizations, government, associations, and private individuals. Formal protection, and legislation to protect all concerned, including a comprehensive definition, has been sought.

During the 1970s, efforts were made to collect guidelines protecting individual and organizational rights to privacy, based on generally accepted principles and existing laws under "fair information practices" rules, and directed toward:

- Limiting the kinds of data that business or government organizations may maintain on individuals.
- Limiting access to that data.
- Limiting the length of time certain data may be maintained (such as criminal and/or credit histories).
- Allowing individuals to know who maintains data about them.
- Allowing individuals to review and change data gathered and maintained about themselves.

As a result, organizations that gather and maintain data, especially those with extensive EDP facilities, should:

- Maintain the validity of data.
- Control access to the data.
- Monitor accesses to the data.

Privacy protection is similarly a concern, relating to credit reporting agencies, employment and insurance investigations, law enforcement agencies, education and medical records, and computer and program design.

Limiting Access to Data. Traditionally, access to data was restricted by retaining confidential data and records in user departments under suitable physical security arrangements. The proliferation of computerized systems concentrated data in the MIS department, resulting in growing concerns about security arrangements for computer operations, data files, and distribution of reports. When data can be accessed on-line from a terminal outside the MIS department, controls are needed to ensure that terminal use is restricted to authorized users and that access to data is restricted outside of authorized functions.

Controls in use for restriction of access to computers and data include physical security, software checks, such as passwords, terminals dedicated only to certain processing functions, automatic disconnect of terminals unused for a given time or after a specified number of unsuccessful password entries for attempted access, and controls over the master terminal that controls other terminals and the passwords used.

The problems in controlling access to data have been complicated by the phenomenal growth of microcomputer use by general office personnel. Controls and standards for these new uses rarely exist, since organizations are just becoming aware of the need to control and audit microcomputer use. Other issues over growing use are the data gathered and how it is used, how such recordkeeping may affect compliance with legislation, and controlling and protecting messaging systems.

A survey conducted by a computer industry publication found that as computers move out of a strictly MIS environment, their new users inadvertently circumvent controls, ignore procedures, or violate standards of privacy because they do not know the principles involved. Microcomputer users may handle very sensitive data, since they frequently work with whole documents, not unassembled data as in an MIS department.

The information contained in personnel files is a particular case in point. This data can be obtained all too easily by unauthorized people in many organizations. Management should act to rectify such control deficiencies, auditing operations to see how data is handled and accessed. Standards applicable to all employees should be developed and enforced, and the personnel educated. Many companies have designated a compliance manager, whose duties include monitoring activities and keeping up-to-date on trends and legislation to help ensure that corporate policy conforms with evolving control standards.

Transborder Data Flow. The transmission of data across national borders is generally referred to as transborder data flow (TBDF). The term encompasses a wide range of issues relating to the international flow of information. These issues revolve primarily around restrictions imposed by governments on information flow among countries through computers. The issues surrounding TBDF are a serious concern for U.S. multinational corporations, which depend on the unrestricted exchange of information among their affiliates worldwide.

Information restrictions first appeared in Europe during the 1970s. In 1980, the Organization for Economic Cooperation and Development (OECD), an international organization of industrial countries, drew up guidelines intended to encourage voluntary compliance with privacy laws and the establishment, on a voluntary basis, of safeguards to prevent the abuse or disclosure of personal data. The U.S. government is not a signatory but supports the guidelines. Since the OECD guidelines were developed, the problems raised by TBDF have become more complicated, largely because of the merging of computer and telecommunications technology. The issues have expanded beyond the transfer of data to the transfer of information resources such as computer power, software, hardware, data bases, and both skilled and nonskilled labor.

Countries are concerned about a number of issues in connection with TBDF, including protection of personal privacy, preserving employment opportunities for their citizens and furthering their economic development, trade barriers, and preserving cultural and national identities. Although the U.S. government has recently been promoting a deregulation policy, many other countries have taken steps toward increased regulation. The interests of those countries are focused on financial and national security, as well as on the creation of jobs for their own citizens. Because information technology (IT) is viewed by both developed and developing countries as the avenue to modernization, economic growth, and employment opportunity, information industries are often the subject of nationalism and protectionism.

In their attempts to resolve the various TBDF issues, foreign governments are taking different courses, many of which involve intervention in the processing, transmission, storage, and use of information. This intervention has important repercussions for U.S. multinational corporations, whose operations abroad are affected by the laws and regulations of the overseas countries in which they transact business. Many developed countries have enacted legislation that may inhibit U.S. multinationals from applying technology and may interfere with legitimate business data flow. In developing countries, many of which are wary of becoming dependent on information and information technology, regulations such as import restrictions and hiring quotas may be particularly onerous.

A first step that multinationals might take domestically to deal with these obstacles might be to adopt the OECD privacy guidelines (close to 200 U.S. companies have agreed to abide by them). An EDP audit of a company's administrative, operational, documentation, and security controls to provide assurance that the company is in compliance with the privacy standards might be helpful in minimizing the risk of loss from overseas operations.

Some other actions that multinationals may find helpful in dealing with the uncertainities of international business include:

- Monitoring foreign regulatory developments in countries where they have significant operations.
- Employing local consultants who are familiar with operations and have experience dealing with local regulatory agencies.
- Arranging with overseas affiliates to report on local conditions relevant to the corporation.
- Maintaining contacts with local trade associations and government officials.
- Supporting national and international trade and business associations involved in telecommunications and information issues.
- Encouraging the executive branch and Congress to establish policies and laws to advance U.S. business interests.

Legal Protection. Protection of privacy and confidentiality is a concern of individuals and a growing concern of business and government. Usually, privacy and confidentiality statutes are not computer-specific; much of the legislation in this area has been enacted recently and regards the general protection of information. Such statutes impose penalties for unlawful access or disclosure of information to safeguard confidential information. Some enable law enforcement groups to access confidential information following certain requirements.

Statutes Relating to Access or Disclosure of Information. The 1974 Privacy Act makes it illegal to gather, maintain, use, and disseminate information held in federal computer systems. Since the government's computers have been estimated to store 4 billion records on individuals, the Privacy Act was important legislation. The Espionage Act makes it illegal to obtain information for use against the United States (relating to espionage per se, not industrial espionage).

Other provisions sometimes used against computer abusers are the Soliciting Federal Tax Information provision of the Tax Code; the Fair Credit Reporting Act, which imposes penalties for those who obtain information from credit agencies under false pretenses; and the Electronic Funds Transfer Act, which makes it a crime to use fictitious, altered, lost, stolen, or fraudulently obtained debit instruments. There are other statutes that apply to privacy of federal, state, and industry information.

Several statutes also cover unlawful disclosure of information, including the Privacy Act, the Espionage Act, and the Fair Credit Reporting Act. Other relevant statutes are the Trade Secrets Act, which makes it illegal for federal employees to release such information; the Disclosing Federal Tax Return Information provision; the Redisclosure of Privileged Information provision; and the Disclosure of Prepared Income Tax Data provision.

Copyright Protection

Computer programs and computer data were not clearly protected under copyright law until the adoption of the Copyright Act of 1976, as amended by the Computer Software Copyright Act of 1980. Computer programs are now protected whether in source code (the human-readable code in which the programmer initially writes the program) or in object code (machine-readable code). The courts have also extended copyright protection to different types of programs, ranging from applications such as spreadsheets or word processors to operating systems. Text or graphic displays caused to appear on a monitor or printout may also be copyright-protected as audiovisual, graphic, or literary works.

What applies to computer programs applies equally to files, text, and data bases held on computer-based media such as floppy disks, cassette tapes, or the circuitry of a ROM (read-only memory) chip. There is no question that the integrity of text, data bases, and other writing in computers is protected under the copyright law.

The Copyright Act provides copyright owners with exclusive rights and weapons against the misuse of their proprietary programs, files, and data bases. These include the right to reproduce the copyrighted work in copies; to prepare derivative works substantially based on the copyrighted work; to distribute copies by public sale, rental, lease, or lending; to perform the copyrighted work in public; and to display the copyrighted work. Anyone who violates any of these exclusive rights of a copyright owner is an infringer of the copyright.

For example, copying a computer program from one floppy disk onto another without authorization is an infringement of the copyright owner's exclusive right to make copies (there is a limited right of purchasers of software to make backup copies of the software program for archival purposes). Modifying a computer program or data base by deleting, adding, or otherwise altering the sequence of instructions or information may be considered the preparation of a "derivative" work in violation of the copyright holder's exclusive license to create derivative works. Distributing stolen or otherwise unauthorized copies to third parties by any means, including downloading through the telephone lines, is a violation of a copyright owner's right to public distribution of his work. Finally, the unauthorized display of the program, data base, or part thereof in a public place may be considered a violation of the copyright owner's exclusive right to perform or display the work in public.

Most forms of computer abuse, as previously noted, are difficult to prove in court. The copyright owner, however, has the advantage of a number of presumptions that make it easier to prove copyright infringement. Proof of copyright infringement depends on proof of both copyright ownership and copying. If the copyright owner registers the computer program or data base within five years after first publication of the work, the certificate of registration is taken as presumptive proof of the validity of the copyright and of the facts stated on the certificate. Thus, the copyright owner does not have the initial burden of proving ownership of the copyright in the work and that the copyright is valid. Since early registration establishes copyright ownership, most cases depend on the ability to provide proof of copying, which can be proved by direct evidence such as unauthorized printouts or copies on floppy disks or other magnetic media.

When an infringer alters a program or data base or otherwise creates a "derivative work," infringement can be proved by showing substantial similarity between the original and the unauthorized derivative work. Although most computer copyright cases have involved copying in which 85 to 100 percent of the defendant's code was identical to the plaintiff's, infringement may be found where, for example, only 25 percent of the code is identical and there is other evidence of similarities. In one recent case, the court found infringement based on the translation of a program from one computer language to another. Even though the translation was not literal, because of the different abilities and strengths of the two languages, the translation infringed the original by copying "the manner in which the information flows from one function to another in the program."

The use of copyright law in battling computer crime has been largely overlooked. However, a recent computer crime census survey by the National Center for Computer Crime Data showed that of the five major types of computer crime—theft of money, taking programs and data, alteration of data for gain, damage to programs or data, and theft of services—three are candidates for civil and criminal prosecution under the Copyright Act. In many businesses, the computer programs and data bases are valuable business assets. The theft, alteration, or use of those assets in competition with their rightful owner can cause serious damage to the business. However, many businesses hesitate to pursue employees or third parties who penetrate their computer systems under embezzlement, theft, or computer crime statutes for fear that the publicity may signal a basic weakness in their security. No such message is likely to be conveyed by a civil suit based on copyright infringement.

AUDIT IMPLICATIONS

The growing use of on-line facilities and data bases has affected the ease of access to information. These environments, if uncontrolled, may allow unauthorized access to data, procedures, and possibly permit learning how to circumvent the controls over the environment. Susceptibility to unauthorized access of sensitive records, such as salary information, may be greatly increased. As part of auditing such systems, the internal or EDP auditor frequently recommends additional or improved controls.

Included in audit assessments may be the sharing of data by different organizations, a possible infringement of individual privacy or confidentiality. As a result, it is important to ensure that adequate controls are in place or are implemented over data transfer and the sharing of data.

As an auditor tests the continued existence of controls, they may also affect the auditor's procedures. For example, when strict confidentiality controls are in place it may actually become more difficult to obtain the data and other information needed for the audit. Naturally, the auditor also checks controls over access to data. Audit tests to ensure the security of the files, data elements, and systems operations as a whole are discussed in Part IV, "Control Concepts" (Chapters 13–15), and in Part VII, "Auditing Advanced Systems" (Chapters 26–28).

Another of the auditor's responsibilities is to ensure that controls comply with applicable federal, state, and local regulations. Therefore, the auditor needs to be well-versed in such rulings and interpretations to relate this information to the computer system under audit.

Auditor's Role

An EDP auditor's primary task is not to go into an area to try to uncover computer abuse or crime. Instead, an auditor can focus on performing audits of systems throughout the year, suggesting ways to improve controls, watching the behavior of MIS personnel, noting changes in established patterns, conducting periodic surprise audits, and broadening the scope of audit support to include review of implementation of applications and user and supervisory controls. Of course, management must sanction such procedures. High visibility of the EDP auditor may be an effective deterrent to computer abuse in itself.

Computer abuse may be discovered during the regular course of an audit. When fraud or other computer crime is uncovered, an EDP auditor can help with the investigation and subsequently provide litigation support for prosecution. An audit committee may also request an investigation when computer crime or fraud is suspected. Proceeding on such assignments requires a high degree of tact, knowledge, and discretion.

One of the auditor's first tasks might be to determine whether the situation was a one-time occurrence or part of an ongoing process. Where the abuse is part of an ongoing scheme, obviously the auditor has to try to find out when it started. Once the full extent of the problem is uncovered, if that is possible, the auditor reports his findings to management. Management can then decide how it wants the situation to be handled. That decision can include attempting to recover lost money, goods, or services; bringing the incident to the attention of legal authorities; and recommending improved controls to avoid having the situation, or a similar one, recur.

Performing a regular or an investigatory audit, the auditor is naturally aware that auditing procedures followed are subject to outside scrutiny, such as from the Securities and Exchange Commission. This has been particularly true since the 1970s, when landmark court cases established that an auditor may be liable for prosecution if an unreported situation that materially affects a company's financial records has not been discovered and properly reported. Obviously, one way to preclude unanswerable questions is for an auditor to carefully document audit strategy, each procedure performed during an audit, and principles applied.

Preventing Computer Abuse

Without established organizational procedures and detection/reporting systems, the problems of detecting and prosecuting computer crime and abuse will continue to plague owners and users of computer systems. Management's growing concerns in the area have led many to realize how important it is for an organization to protect its systems so that opportunities for abuse are lessened. To help develop workable plans, the following list asks some essential questions about computer abuse prevention:

- Does the organization have a contingency plan to put into effect once computer abuse is suspected?

- If confirmed abuse occurs in the organization, would notification of the proper officials be timely?
- Does the organization have insurance coverage commensurate with the increased risks due to modern computer technology?

If computer abuse is suspected:

- Does the organization know its responsibilities to its insurance carrier, and vice versa?
- Is the organization aware of responsibilities to investors, stockholders, and reporting agencies?
- Has the organization ever had a complete diagnostic security study conducted?
- Has the organization had a review of computer integrity controls within the last year? Were all recommendations and directives implemented?
- Is there assurance that the organization's internal audit program is comprehensive?
- Do relevant personnel know the legal limitations regarding questioning individuals, discharging employees, or discussing suspected events with third parties?
- Has the organization embraced an overall corporate security plan or philosophy?

CHAPTER **30**

Security Reviews

RISKS IN TODAY'S SYSTEMS

Today's computer systems hold ever-larger quantities of valuable data. Access to these systems—from increasing numbers of terminals—is a growing concern. Although risks from hackers have received widespread publicity, there is usually a far greater risk from insiders, who have the knowledge and ability to abuse the system.

Computer knowledge is no longer restricted to a select few. More systems use software packages with manuals that make the package easier to use, but also make knowledge of how to abuse it more readily available. In general, it can be said that the easier a system is to use, the more it is at risk. (See Figure 30-1 for typical computer system threats.)

There has been a marked increase in the risks business information systems face. Studies show many examples of business losses via computer systems through both theft and error. There have been cases of terrorism, extortion, industrial espionage, and bribery, with resulting public embarrassment to the organizations involved.

Management has recognized the growing need for security to protect systems from unauthorized change, disclosure, destruction of data and programs, and misuse of system resources. As a result, increasing attention is being paid to access controls, a key to both the prevention and detection of such abuse.

Modern Access Controls

Access controls need to fulfill two important requirements: (1) stopping unauthorized users from accessing the system, and (2) enforcing an appropriate division of duties among those permitted to use the system, so that one person cannot both commit an unauthorized act and hide it from detection. Because a typical system has many users, and they are often connected via communication lines, physical security is rarely sufficient to protect information resources. More complex controls, usually based on passwords and security software, are needed.

FIG. 30-1
Computer system threats

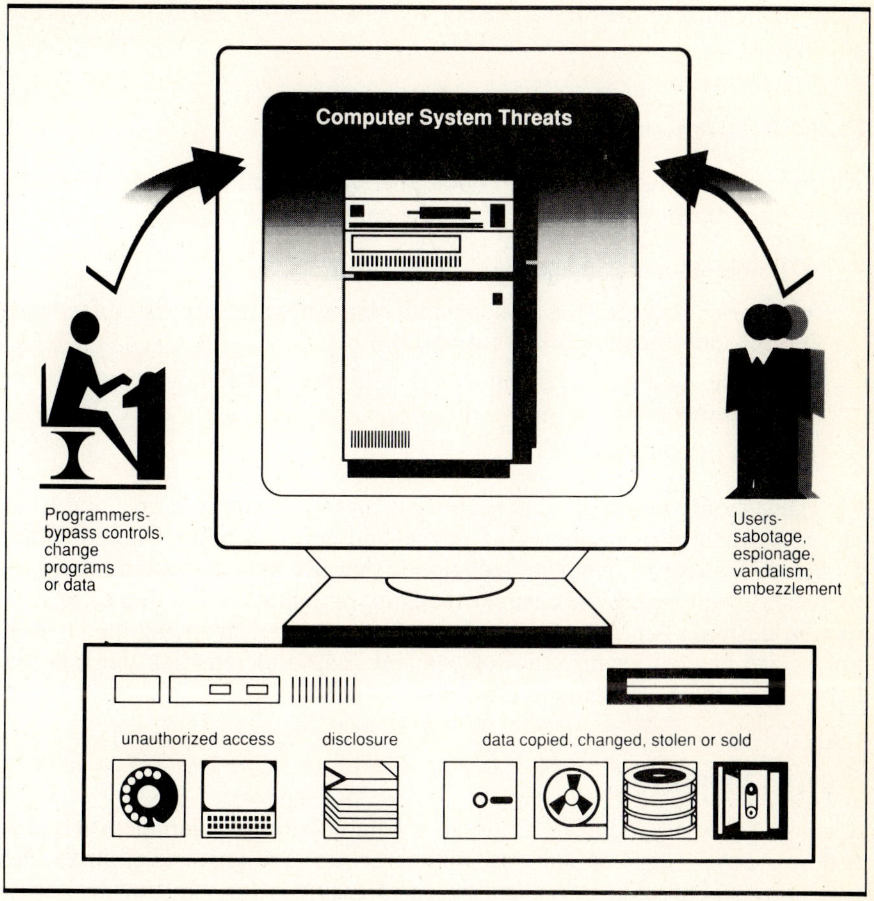

This section describes some of the procedures and techniques that can be used to meet security requirements. It does not cover physical controls, operating system controls, or contingency planning. Some control techniques depend on the functions within the access control software or hardware in use. When necessary, additional features can be added to purchased systems. The most common weaknesses in the effective use of security systems are poorly designed or implemented administrative procedures, inadequate security awareness among users, and incomplete use of protections available within system software.

Basic application controls over the completeness, accuracy, and authorization of data are always important. Security controls complement these by helping in their enforcement and ensuring that normal controls are not bypassed.

Cost-Effectiveness of Security Controls

All controls involve a cost. Of course, the cost/benefit relationship should be evaluated. The major costs of access controls are:

- Potential costs of software and hardware.
- Salaries and fees for those maintaining software, access tables, and user identification codes (user IDs).
- Salaries and fees to monitor user activities and follow up on violations.
- Loss of convenience.

This should not imply that security is merely a matter of cost and trouble; it can help provide increased profits and peace of mind. There is often a choice. Instead of choosing techniques that are expensive and intrusive, there may well be easier, cheaper methods of achieving the degree of protection desired. A practical security system involves balancing the level of protection needed against ease of use and cost, and selecting the least intrusive and most cost-effective techniques.

Security Controls

Security is usually achieved through a combination of administrative procedures, access control, software and hardware, and physical controls. No two organizations have identical needs or facilities for implementing their requirements. Each organization faces different risks of varying probability and criticality. Each organization should relate its unique exposures and risks to the procedures and techniques available.

Management's attitude toward security should encourage active support and continued review and update to maintain its effectiveness. As information processes and business change, so do access control requirements.

SECURITY ENVIRONMENT

A variety of factors contribute to the security environment. Each needs consideration to evaluate the whole.

Security Awareness

Security awareness is a key to successful implementation of security policy. All people within the organization should understand the security procedures to be followed. This awareness can be developed through user education.

Management Commitment. Management support is an important prerequisite for successful security implementation, requiring involvement and support of all levels. Organizations must train management to understand and evaluate security risks. Particularly, top management should demonstrate its commitment.

Corporate Security Policy. Corporate management should encourage the development and enforcement of a written security policy. Policies should be established and documented to indicate the importance and level of security for each component of the environment. Corporate requirements may be defined in general policy statements and should contain the following:

- The responsibilities of the data security administrators and users for the security of all operations and assets entrusted to their care.
- The minimum standards for security and procedures to be followed.
- A framework for conducting internal investigations, when it appears that security has been compromised.

This policy should provide the definition of security in place at a general level. Specific security procedures over the computer system are then defined on the detailed level, to meet corporate objectives.

Corporate Awareness Program. Employees should understand that corporate information and the systems that provide it are extremely valuable assets. Users should be made aware of their responsibilities. For example, they should report unauthorized uses of their IDs and suspected security violations. A security awareness program may consist of:

- Assigning responsibilities to users:
  - —To keep user IDs, passwords, and all accounts used to access data processing resources and facilities confidential.
  - —To notify a responsible person (e.g., the data security officer) of each suspected system abuse.
  - —To support all security policies actively.

- A nondisclosure statement that is signed by new users and users granted new access authorizations. An annual renewal of signed statements serves as a reminder.
- Periodic security assessments performed by internal auditors or the quality assurance group to monitor the effectiveness of security procedures and controls in operation. This function may include:
  - — Evaluating security policies set by security administration.
  - — Auditing access to critical system and application resources.
  - — Periodic monitoring of user activity.
  - — Monitoring adherence to policy by all users.
  - — Advertising the existence of data security controls so that users know their activity is recorded and might be reviewed.
  - — Notifying employees to expect both supervisory checks and surprise periodic audits.
  - — Taking disciplinary actions for violations.

Consideration should be given to the general distribution of results of audits performed. Such publication of security breakdowns can serve to reinforce security policy.

Automated records of security violation attempts can be maintained. When they can be attributed to individuals, some companies place these activities into employee files. Employee performance could be evaluated, in part, according to adherence to security policies. After a certain number of events, the employee is counseled and eventually may be terminated.

In any event, a computer use policy should be established and communicated, so that users are aware of adverse consequences from unauthorized activities. Presently, many organizations do not prosecute employees for computer abuse or fraud, fearing public embarrassment and possible repetition of such cases, since publicity may make system weaknesses known. For example, banks fear such publicity due to the possibility of runs and encouragement of further abuse.

Businesses, however, are now recognizing the lack of deterrence that results from not prosecuting perpetrators of abuse and fraud. An increasing number of companies have become more willing to prosecute to deter such behavior.

Data Security Administrator

Part of the response to security concerns is appointing a data security administrator (DSA). If an organization is small to medium-size, it may not be necessary to have someone handling this responsibility on a full-time basis. This role is important, however, and the position should be considered one of high responsibility. The DSA should not be involved in programming applications, operating the computer, and so forth. In addition, he should not report to data processing management, but to a senior manager outside of MIS.

The DSA's role is to act on behalf of the owners of the application and system files. The DSA should be responsible for the implementation, modification, monitoring, and enforcement of the access control strategy.

There may be several DSAs, each serving a different aspect of the security administration function. For example, an installation may have one DSA responsible for maintaining user IDs and passwords, another who maintains access rules to files and other resources, and a third who investigates and reports violations.

Centralized vs. Decentralized Security

Centralized security provides concentrated control over changes to many applications and units. It requires a well-defined and formalized management authorization process. Centralized administration may add strength in enforcing security, but gaining access to needed resources may take longer. Such delays in the authorization process may have an adverse operational impact, or may drive well-intentioned individuals to attempt to bypass or subvert controls.

Some installations choose to decentralize security administration. The usefulness of decentralization depends on the organization's needs. Decentralized security distributes the security maintenance effort so that the function is not a burden on any one area. One way is to make those with specific knowledge of the application or system software being protected responsible for that software. This may provide better maintenance than is possible at the central level, since it is difficult for a centralized unit to know the value and risk associated with every resource. On the other hand, uniformity of protection normally results from centralized security, while there may be gaps due to imperfect coordination between units in decentralized security.

Inefficient or ineffective administration is the biggest practical block to effective access controls. Many systems have more security potential than administrators use effectively. Purchasing additional security software and devices is rarely all that is needed. Without adequate procedures for assigning and maintaining access controls, even the best security system items are not successful.

INFORMATION SECURITY EXPOSURES

All organizations face possible information security exposures. The potential seriousness of a breach in security can be evaluated according to the function of the organization's business, dependence on the information, and sensitivity to the potential loss.

Risks can be classified into five categories. The events in these categories can occur either accidentally or deliberately, and are:

1. *Information disclosure.* Unauthorized disclosure can affect an organization's profitability, impair customer relations, be used for personal gain or for malicious purposes.
2. *Corruption of data or programs.* Modified or altered documents, computer programs, data files, transactions, or reports can result in misstated assets, erroneous management planning and control data, or be used to conceal possible fraud or defalcation.
3. *Destruction of physical assets or information.* Business can be seriously interrupted or indefinitely curtailed depending on the degree of information or processing dependency, the target, and extent of destruction.
4. *Interruption of service.* Interruption of processing schedules can impair or curtail basic service and product delivery.
5. *Removal of physical assets or information.* Unauthorized or accidental removal of hardware components or storage media can seriously disrupt an organization's ability to continue normal business operations.

Security safeguards should be tailored to meet each organization's specific needs. They are effective to the extent that the costs of implementing safeguards are properly balanced against the potential losses.

SECURITY BREACH CAUSES

Other than natural hazards, the integrity of any security system is ultimately vested in personnel, and depends on the integrity of individuals.

Generally, data processing is exposed to physical disaster, fraud, vandalism, mischief, and human error. During a security review, each area of data processing is evaluated to determine what security measures are being used to prevent, detect, and control the potential for abuse, and to identify areas where additional control mechanisms should be employed.

Physical Disaster

Disaster-causing events occur in many different ways. The end result could be a discontinuance of business. Recovery time varies depending on the cause of the disturbance; in some cases, the damage is irreparable. Disaster-causing events can be intentional (e.g., bombings, fires), natural hazards (e.g., hurricanes, tornadoes, floods, and earthquakes), or acts of negligence (e.g., dropping a disk pack).

The primary concern is to determine what and how data and assets should be protected or duplicated to ensure that the business can recover. The type of protection required depends on the nature of the business and, because even similar businesses do not operate identically, the unique protection methods available for that environment.

Analysis of probable occurrence is done by examining disaster vulnerabilities. Cost-effectiveness is then determined after rating alternate protection techniques. For example, a fire suppression system may not be cost-justified for a small retail establishment with a computer operator in attendance during all processing, but a system of fire extinguishers and smoke alarms could be a sufficient substitute.

Fraud

When system designers initially developed automated systems, few realized the potential for criminal abuse by embezzlement, fraud, or theft of organizational assets. Protection or detection techniques were generally not included in early systems. The complexity of new systems has made defalcation even more difficult to detect. Data previously maintained within different departments has been compressed and centralized for faster and easier use. Often, organizations were restructured and manual document processing procedures, which allowed many people to observe how data was being handled, were replaced by automated processing without accompanying security measures.

Automated processing systems were designed to require fewer people with more authority to handle transactions at a faster rate. In fact, fewer people were familiar with the new processes and not many questioned their use. Even fewer understood that data could be entered or processed fraudulently. As a result, authorized individuals who wished to do so had a vehicle for perpetrating crime through unauthorized use of the computer. There were fewer methods of detecting fraud by those select individuals who had access to vast amounts of information.

Elaborate schemes can be developed to defraud an organization for personal gain. Computer-related crimes over the past decade substantiate this. Such crimes may occur because security controls are either missing or lax, and personnel have enough knowledge of the system to use it for their own advantage. When weak controls are in place, they can be circumvented. Very few systems have sufficient controls to detect fraud as it is occurring.

Typically, the crime is detected only after it has been committed, and it is usually detected because the perpetrator makes a mistake, or an inconsistency is accidentally discovered. (See Chapter 29, "Computer Abuse.")

Many systems do not have adequate audit trails to indicate how a transaction has been processed and which personnel were involved. Methods commonly used in manual systems, such as journals, ledgers, receipts, and other documents, are now automated. Reports are printed, but source documents used to create these reports are often destroyed. Those with access authority may be able to manipulate data for fraudulent purposes by falsifying transactions and records.

To reduce the opportunities and instances of fraud, adequate controls with prescribed audit checkpoints should exist. The complete processing of a transaction must be traceable from creation to disposition. Cross-checking involving more than one individual should exist, but may serve only as a deterrent rather than an absolute means of fraud prevention.

Vandalism

Vandalism takes many forms. It can be planned or spontaneous and can arise from external or internal sources. For example, children can use windows as targets for rocks or a disgruntled employee may destroy data. Neither of these events is predictable.

Vandalism has long been a method used by disgruntled employees seeking revenge against an employer they believe to be unjust. Such employees are tempted to destroy resources needed by the employer, such as computer hardware or programs and essential data. Destruction is usually camouflaged and not detected until much later; often it is untraceable. Unprotected storage media, such as tapes, are prime targets; if backup copies do not exist at some secure location, it may be virtually impossible to recreate the contents of the tapes. Program modification is another method of revenge. Modifying a program by introducing destruct instructions or illogical processing instructions can cause a system to fail or to create invalid data.

Mischief

Mischievous acts, unlike vandalism, are usually nondestructive. Although those involved usually do not realize it, the disruption caused is often serious. The acts are generally pranks, such as hiding or purposely misplacing media.

Human Error

The greatest ongoing cause of disruption within an EDP installation is human error. For example, computer operators may accidentally damage equipment and storage media; incorrectly coded programs may be entered into production without adequate testing or quality control; or sensitive information may be publicly disclosed through inappropriate procedures.

Human error cannot be completely eliminated, but the security and control techniques used to reduce the risk of other exposures also reduce the frequency of errors.

CONTROL MEASURES

Control measures to protect assets are designed according to the asset type, location, and value. Careful analysis of the environment is required to determine the degree of protection necessary to ensure a secure facility. There are a variety of controls and protection methods available. Usually, a combination of control mechanisms is employed to provide an effective level of security.

Access Control

Normally, there are two types of access control systems: physical controls and logical controls. Physical systems control access to specific areas, whereas logical systems control access to the computer systems and the information stored in them. Both are intended to restrict the use of the computer's resources to authorized people.

Physical Access Control

A variety of physical access control systems are used to regulate an individual's movement within a complex or structure. In some instances, security requirements demand concurrent use of several methods for restricting access to an area. Access systems, other than guards, are categorized as:

- Mechanical
- Electronic
- Electromechanical
- Digital
- Computerized

Mechanical

Mechanical controls are padlocks, combination locks, key locks, and deadbolts, and are used either individually or jointly to secure an area. These are usually the least expensive security controls but provide no trace of an individual's movement within the building. As a result, the level of security is low because duplicate keys can be made for key locks and combinations can be discovered.

Electronic

Electronic devices usually consist of an electronic control box used with a plastic card, which acts as a key. A special code is stored on the card, and if the code matches the one required, it activates the electronic component which, in turn, operates the mechanical device that unlocks the door. Cards are read either optically or electronically when inserted. Decoders read the encoded geometry or unique code and, if it is correct, allow access. Silent or audible alarms can be installed that will alert security personnel to unauthorized access attempts. These devices are not easily manipulated and are virtually tamper-proof because they cannot be readily duplicated or deciphered. However, if a card is lost and goes unreported, unauthorized individuals could find and use the card to gain access. If an effective reporting procedure for lost cards is implemented, new cards can be prepared with new codes, rendering the lost card useless and maintaining the facility's security.

Electromechanical

Electromechanical devices require some manual effort. They are usually pushbutton or rotary combination devices that work independently with an electronic card reader to activate and open the lock. This system is more secure than the electronic system, since only having either the code or the card is not enough to gain entry.

Digital

Digital devices allow the user to set any combination, thus providing an easy means of changing the combination on a regular basis to reduce the potential for unauthorized use. However, there is no assurance that entry of the number code will not be observed by a bystander. Authorized users should be made aware of this risk and exercise proper care when using the number code.

Computerized

Computerized systems provide the most automatic, advantageous, and sophisticated means of controlling access to a facility. They offer the most complete method for capturing entry and exit data and for tracing an individual's movement within a facility. By continually monitoring an access path, they ensure that only properly identified and authorized individuals are permitted to enter or leave.

Computerized systems can be equipped to sound alarms when an unauthorized access is attempted or the environment changes, such as changes in temperature, humidity, or air flow. In addition, these systems can record data for employee attendance, payroll hours, current employee location, time reports by entry and exit, as well as operational control reports.

Computer Room

The computer room contains the EDP equipment required for running the computer programs. An installation should have security measures and procedures that control all access and observe movement throughout the facility. These can be automated, using access control and television systems that:

- Verify the identity of the person requesting entry.
- Log all requests for access.
- Alert security to unauthorized access attempts.
- Identify movement in areas at restricted hours.
- Detect unauthorized removal of items.

Some systems are also designed to trap violators, either by locking or sealing off the area involved. The violator's movement can be observed through television cameras to determine the proper action to be taken.

Terminal Room

All terminals should be protected against damage or misuse by having separate areas, either independent rooms or sections of rooms that control access. This eliminates the possibility that sensitive data will be observed when it is entered or requested. Each room or section should be arranged by specific business function, such as credit authorization, order processing, and customer service.

The use of terminals should be regulated by system authorization controls that verify the identity of the user before permitting access. In addition, terminals can be equipped with mechanical locks.

Data Communication Facilities

Safeguarding and controlling access to the location where communication lines terminate can be difficult where more than one tenant resides in a building. Generally, the location of communication line entry is under the physical control of building management. It is, therefore, important that the property manager understands the need to protect these facilities from damage and provide for their security. Tenants might assume responsibility for providing a fair share of the cost of securing the area. Common carrier facilities are beyond the user's physical control. The carrier's responsibility to provide protection from penetration may not be specified.

Communication lines should not terminate on a hallway wall where access is unrestricted. A separate room or area with access control should be used. In many instances the communication facilities should be combined with the computer room's communication area, which houses the modems, line-switching facilities, line test equipment, and modem racks.

Movement Detection

Intrusion detectors and closed-circuit television cameras and monitors are the foundation of most systems that observe and detect movement (e.g., the electronic eyes or infra alarms). Electronic eyes are photoelectric devices, which detect movement and sound an alarm. Infra alarms are sensing devices that measure the change in thermal radiation within the environment. When an intruder is present, heat emitted from the moving body generates a change in the thermal radiation and triggers an alarm.

Closed-circuit television is used wherever constant surveillance is required. It provides continual coverage of remote locations and deters potential intruders who would be wary of entering an area under surveillance.

Fire Protection

Fire-suppression and alarm systems are essential if areas with valuable contents, important equipment, or vital functions are to be protected. They are designed to detect and suppress fire within the first few seconds and reduce the need for manual fire-fighting techniques, which may prove unsatisfactory or too late in arriving.

Fire-suppression systems can also provide a variety of significant support functions automatically, such as opening fire exits and smoke doors, controlling elevators and shutting off equipment fans, in addition to warning the fire department through a municipal communication link. Fire control systems usually use Halon 1301 as the fire-extinguishing agent.

Where sophisticated and costly suppression systems are inappropriate, water sprinkler systems, self-contained smoke alarms, and fire extinguishers should be used.

Power Sources

Power is terminated at breaker junction boxes that usually are not on the tenant's site. (These boxes may be located in the basement or elsewhere in the building.) They, too, should be protected against tampering, since power disruptions can curtail use of the facility. Power interruption systems and generators may be used to power the equipment and building so that operations can be sustained for a short time.

Duplicating Facilities

Most organizations have duplicating facilities. They may consist of copying machines, computer equipment, photography equipment, output microfiche equipment, or other devices capable of duplicating information. Access to, and use of, this equipment should be controlled, especially when confidential documents are nearby.

COMPUTER OPERATIONS CONTROLS

The information technology (IT) controls over computer operations can have an effect on security. These procedures can contribute to, or detract from, overall security. For example, operators may start the system without activating the access control software (such as ACF2, RACF, or TOP SECRET; see Chapter 32, "Access Control Software") if they are permitted to do so. Operator intervention should be as limited as possible, and operators should be able to perform only the specific tasks required to do their jobs. Additionally, all operator activity should be recorded on a log and supervised to ensure that it is appropriate.

Source Document Control

Source documents are the original documents used to record information required by the organization. Their movement among departments that need to use them should be safeguarded. Central or locally controlled storage areas should be available, and document storing, handling, and retaining procedures should be implemented.

Data Entry

Data entry systems vary from full on-line terminal systems performing key-to-tape or key-to-disk operations to off-line key-entry diskette recorders and/or keypunches. Whatever the mode of operation, the equipment involved should be protected in a controlled, secured area. Documents received should be safeguarded, and all sensitive data should be secured in locked cabinets.

Input/Output Control

Input/output (I/O) control functions include source document receipt and logging, batch control posting, job scheduling, job set-up, and output logging and distribution. Because information received or distributed is sometimes sensitive and confidential, precautions should be taken to ensure that all data handled is safe from modification, loss, or theft. Only authorized employees should handle the documents.

I/O control should be in a separate area that is accessible only by authorized employees. Procedures should be established that describe job submission and output distribution methods.

Report Distribution

For data security, the major exposures are unauthorized changes to data sets. However, confidentiality can also be a security risk. Controls over the printing and distribution of reports containing sensitive information should be implemented. Passwords and access paths can be discovered from reports and other manual records. Obviously, such records should be locked away securely. Sensitive reports should be printed under controlled conditions. Procedures and equipment can be installed to protect against loss or mishandling of important reports.

Programs

The programs that comprise the system are assets. They define the technology and methodology required for processing essential business functions. Program safeguards include control and authorization of access, use, and modification. Safeguards from destruction include keeping backup copies at a secured site that are retrievable when necessary and updated regularly so that the most current version is available.

Data Files

Securing data files against unauthorized changes or use is essential. Backup copies of data files should be stored at a secured site. Procedures should describe replacement frequency, retention cycles, and methods to be used if recovery becomes necessary.

Documentation Control

Implemented systems and their operational features must be documented and protected. In addition to being required for maintenance or system modifications, the documentation is also needed for recovery purposes.

To provide a satisfactory level of control, documentation may be classified by sensitivity, such as restricted confidential, confidential, and unclassified or public, as may be the case with vendor manuals. Retention cycles should be prepared for all documentation, reports, and data, and procedures should be established in accordance with applicable laws, rules, and regulations to control access/return and disposal.

Installations usually maintain protected documentation libraries, which are housed in special cabinets with access controlled by a librarian. Normally, documentation is also stored off-site to ensure that backup copies of critical documents are available if the library copy is destroyed.

Distribution of confidential or sensitive reports/output requires a special data control area with strict procedures to limit distribution to the proper individuals. Similar control is essential for destroying unnecessary or outdated reports. Special equipment, such as paper shredders and compacters, is used to ensure total destruction.

Logical Access Control

On-line information includes both data and software. Modern EDP technology has been made easier to use, but also easier to destroy. To protect information from deliberate or accidental destruction and unauthorized use, logical access methods are implemented.

Effective logical access methods restrict the EDP resources each user may access and how they can access them. These controls are implemented within computer hardware and software and generally consist of passwords, user IDs, and logical mapping between physical devices and data files.

The use of a communication network and public carriers further complicates the access issues. Communication networks may be secured against penetration by foreign terminals and wiretapping by using identifiers and encryption methods. When identifiers are used, each connected terminal "signs on" with an identity code. Identifiers can be passwords with additional unique codes that identify each terminal and user. When a disruption in communications is detected, the terminal is required to identify itself again. This prohibits substitute terminals from switching into the network. (This is discussed in detail in Chapter 31, "Logical Access Controls.")

Data encryption is used to prevent data theft by wiretapping. Installing hardware scrambling devices at both ends of the communications line, or implementing a complex data coding algorithm within the computer program, makes the transmitted data unintelligible to the wiretapper.

Legal Obligations and Insurance

Organizations must be aware of any privacy legislation that has been enacted, or that is being considered, that sets out the measures a business must follow to prevent the disclosure of sensitive data about its employees or customers. (See Chapter 29.) Legislation of this kind usually refers to information on credit, mailing lists, employment, medical care, and other personal information. Security procedures and policies must protect this data from improper disclosure and use.

Improper disclosure of data or technology can also affect a business's position in the marketplace. A business uses contracts, insurance policies, copyrights, patents, licenses, and other agreements to establish protection and ensure that it will have legal recourse against any unwarranted disclosure. Normally, legal action can be taken only if the organization has exercised due care in protecting its interests.

Insurance can be purchased to cover loss related to MIS activities; however, the coverage must be specific and comprehensive. Most policies only cover the replacement of physical equipment, unless specific riders or additional insurance is obtained to cover such things as:

- Valuable records.
- Program and data reconstruction.
- Extra expense.
- Business interruption.
- Employee infidelity.

Audit Controls

Information is protected against unauthorized penetration by installing a control system capable of identifying and logging attempts at unauthorized use and notifying security for immediate investigation.

Users can gain access to computerized information from terminals only through established recognition and authorization procedures. Attempts to gain access by entering invalid codes or passwords are logged and either the terminal is disconnected or the keyboard is locked to prevent entry until the violation is resolved. Jobs submitted for execution are monitored, so that any unauthorized attempt to access files is detected and logged and the offending job is canceled. Performance measurement logs and accounting information are also used to detect problems that can invalidate the computerized results or data files. Any significant changes that the DSA or the auditor detects in the performance of the operating environment can alert management that unauthorized access attempts may have been made.

Logs and procedures, whether automatic or manual, provide an audit or information trail of all transactions inside and outside the MIS facility. They identify all data movement, security violations, errors, and changes that have occurred. Internally implemented program controls complement external controls, detect and account for input errors, maintain intermediate results and file control balances, and reconcile controls to results. Circumvention of controls, security procedures, logs, and audit trails should not be permitted.

Personnel

Usually, competence is the primary characteristic used to judge candidates for employment. Honesty and loyalty are sometimes overlooked, although these attributes are equally important. The damage done by a dishonest or disloyal employee is potentially more devastating than damage from external sources or incompetent staff. Careful hiring practices should be followed to provide reasonable assurance of employee integrity.

Employees should be given job descriptions that include a full outline of their responsibilities with respect to security issues. The consequences of failure to follow security policies should be communicated clearly. To ensure that there is no misunderstanding of these matters, particularly when employees hold senior positions, specific requirements or limitations should be stated in an employment contract.

If for any reason, employees involved in MIS activities require termination, they should be removed from their responsibilities immediately and escorted from the premises. Procedures should include immediate notification of building security and appropriate changes in password and access systems.

Rules and Regulations

Any security program must be based on rules and regulations that employees are expected to observe. Those rules are derived from policies and guidelines set forth by management and should include all facets of the employer/employee relationship. Rules and regulations most important to an MIS facility deal with control and access to the computer and related resources and disaster-related activities. They include which personnel are permitted in certain areas, "need-to-know" criteria, distribution and destruction of sensitive reports, program submission procedures, and other security measures within the installation, such as emergency evacuation of the premises.

Procedures should exist to describe the proper interface with temporary personnel, delivery people, repairmen, and vendors who may come on-site.

Emergencies

The more secure the system, the less flexible it will be in responding to unusual circumstances, which may make it necessary to bypass some of the security protections. A policy for dealing with emergencies should be prepared. Activities during the emergency should be logged carefully. Once the emergency is over, security protections should be reinstated immediately. The impact of the activities during the emergency should be assessed and authorized retrospectively, and appropriate corrective action should be taken.

Emergencies during the day can be corrected by a responsible technical support person with a user ID with special privileges. If a problem occurs outside of normal working hours, the off-shifts may need a special user ID. It should be kept in a controlled, sealed envelope under procedural controls maintained by the off-shift supervisor and the DSA.

Unauthorized users may deliberately cause the entire system or the access control system to crash. The installation may have to remove the controls for a certain time, during which users may gain access without detection.

Adequate backup/recovery procedures for security files are necessary to facilitate a prompt resumption of access controls when necessary. An automatic backup procedure should be set for all security files. A recovery procedure should be available that allows for quick recovery of the necessary security files. This procedure should be tested periodically and all parties involved should be educated.

As mentioned earlier, system programmers may be able to bypass security controls, as may the manufacturer's system maintenance engineers. They can breach security by discovering passwords and entry methods, by substituting hardware components, or by disabling the control mechanisms. They can also use powerful diagnostic tools that grant unlimited access to the system. All sensitive data should be removed, if possible, before diagnostic routines are allowed to run. The diagnostic aids should be removed after use or kept secure.

SECURITY REVIEWS

Objectives of the Security Review

When MIS systems are used to conduct an organization's business, management is responsible for ensuring that those systems are controlled and used effectively. The EDP auditor is responsible for ensuring that management knows what needs to be done.

The security review is designed to provide management with an independent assessment of the controls over and security structure of current MIS systems.

A security review should address four major issues:

1. Ability to deliver uninterrupted service.
2. Quality and timeliness of information processed and produced.
3. Impact of, and the ability to make timely recovery from, disruptive events.
4. Preservation of confidentiality of information.

The review is designed to achieve the following objectives:

- Provide management with an assessment of their current position as it relates to the security and control exercised over their computer system.
- Identify for management the potential exposures that result from deficiencies in current control or operating practices.
- Provide management with practical recommendations for improvement (for example, it might be good security to implement data encryption, but the costs of doing so, for example in a satellite network, might be prohibitive).
- Provide management with a plan to correct identified deficiencies

and the associated costs for the implementation of recommendations.

To achieve these objectives, the following areas require detailed examination and evaluation:

- The MIS environment, including the arrangement of physical facilities, access to equipment and storage media, and physical security devices installed (fire detection, suppression systems, etc.).
- The computer department operations including procedures, documentation, and controls used in:
  - —Operating and maintaining equipment.
  - —Developing and modifying programs.
  - —Security data files and program libraries.
  - —Backup and recovery of programs and data files.
- The administrative practices such as policies and procedures that govern personnel matters, insurance protection, and the interaction between system users, the EDP resources, and support services personnel.

The information gathered throughout the examination and evaluation should be in sufficient detail to assess accurately the areas of exposure and their potential impact on the operation. This assessment should identify for management those areas in the operation where improvement should be considered, and recommend strategies for correcting those deficiencies.

Scope of a Security Review

A security review is normally undertaken as a result of management recognition that security needs to be improved, or to evaluate existing security to determine if it is sufficient. In both situations, it is critical to determine the extent of examination required. Development of a security-scoping information sheet or similar document assists in gathering information and determining the areas of concern to management. In the future, security reviews may be performed on a somewhat continuous basis.

The areas to be reviewed should be selected and presented to management for agreement. Once all of the people concerned have agreed which areas are to be included in the review, detailed work plans should be prepared, and appropriate MIS and other audit staff assigned.

Security reviews are frequently performed by third-party reviewers to provide the objectivity of an independent evaluation.

SECURITY REVIEW APPROACH

The security review can be conducted in a series of discrete phases. The work in each phase depends on the accuracy of the findings from the previous phase. Therefore, it is essential that the findings for each phase be confirmed before beginning the next phase. This verification process includes meetings with appropriate line management, MIS staff, and audit staff. These meetings also allow management to keep abreast of review progress.

The four phases of the review are:

Phase I—Review and Evaluation of Current Operations

Phase II—Exposure Assessment

Phase III—Preparation of Recommendations

Phase IV—Implementation Plan

Each of these phases is outlined below, together with a description of the tasks to be performed.

Phase I—Review and Evaluation of Current Operations

The first phase is designed to review, document, and evaluate current MIS operations to determine the strengths and weaknesses of the existing security and control structure within the organization.

To gather the information necessary for the evaluation process, the following tasks are performed by the EDP auditor and other audit staff members:

- Inspecting sites.
- Conducting interviews.
- Completing detailed control questionnaires.
- Observing operations.
- Examining previous audit reports.
- Examining available system documentation.
- Examining relevant correspondence, insurance policies, and contracts.
- Examining computer access controls and listings, such as use of security software or access reports based on system logs. (See Figure 30-2 for a checklist that is used to review access controls.)

FIG. 30-2

Partial security review checklist: communications security—access protection (RCW = Record of Control Weaknesses; CC = Compensating Controls)

Access Protection	Workpaper Reference	Yes	No	RCW	CC
Access Security					
Communications Network					
1. Are terminals equipped with physical key locks?	....	☐	☐	....	....
2. Are terminals identified and verified by software?	....	☐	☐	....	....
3. Are operators required to supply a user identification?	....	☐	☐	....	....
4. Are user identification and terminal identification cross-referenced?	....	☐	☐	....	....
5. Are user identification and time cross-referenced?	....	☐	☐	....	....
6. Are passwords required for:					
a. System access?	....	☐	☐	....	....
b. Program access?	....	☐	☐	....	....
c. File access?	....	☐	☐	....	....
d. Data field access?	....	☐	☐	....	....
7. Are passwords required to be at least five characters in length?	....	☐	☐	....	....

Current security procedures, policies, and practices should be evaluated to determine their completeness, intent, and effectiveness.

For each area selected for review, the auditor needs to identify the controls in place, assess their effectiveness, and identify where additional control mechanisms should be employed. Work plans and checklists should be used to guide the review process.

This phase is critical to the overall success of the project, since it establishes the current security structure and related exposures, and leads to the development of recommendations.

Phase II—Exposure Assessment

Risk can be defined as the possibility of loss or injury. Exposure is the deprivation of protection, shelter, or care provided to an asset that may have the effect of increasing risk. Phase II identifies the risks to which the organization is exposed as a result of the specific weaknesses identified in Phase I. Risks can include both loss of assets and public embarrassment to an organization. For example, if confidential business information is revealed, the consequences could include stockholders' loss of confidence in management.

There are five major risk classifications that can affect information processing and place the assets of the organization in jeopardy. These risks can arise either accidentally or deliberately (accidents may be an act of God, such as a fire; deliberate events may be someone taking advantage of a weak control over system access) and are as follows:

1. Destruction of physical assets or information.
2. Disclosure of confidential information.
3. Removal of physical assets or information.
4. Corruption of data or programs.
5. Interruption of service.

A weakness may expose an asset to one or more of these risks. The impact of any event can be determined using two factors: (1) the frequency of occurrence and (2) the amount of the potential loss. These two factors are considered to ascertain the priorities for addressing any identified weaknesses. It is important to note that the loss of an asset cannot be determined by replacement value alone. Consideration must also be given to additional loss that may result if the asset is no longer available. For example, accidental damage to a disk would not only result in the loss of the physical component, but also the loss of the information on the disk and system disruption until the information is restored.

At the completion of Phase II, exposures will have been identified and ranked in a practical, logical manner consistent with the company's business environment. The auditor should discuss the assessment of dangers resulting from exposures in the organization's current procedures with management before proceeding to Phase III.

Phase III—Preparation of Recommendations

Recommendations can be prepared based on the assessment of exposures. Those recommendations should include procedures that should be implemented to mitigate the exposure and its potential impact on the organization. In many situations, more than one solution may be available, in which case the alternatives should be presented for consideration.

Although the specific recommendations vary from one situation to the next, normally they fall within the following broad categories:

- Additional hardware and software requirements.
- Software modifications.
- Manual controls.
- Writing of procedures and guidelines.
- Contractual agreements.
- Preventive maintenance.
- Management review.

On completion of Phase III, the auditors should discuss the recommendations with management to ensure that the solutions presented are the most practical for the organization.

Phase IV—Implementation Plan

Phase IV work results in a plan for implementation of the recommendations developed in Phase III. The sequence and timing of implementation depends on:

- Urgency for improvement.
- Availability of company personnel with the appropriate skills to implement improvements; alternately, using an independent organization to assist with the implementation.
- Availability of software tools and other products in the market to quickly address the issues.
- The organization's future development plans.

For example, some high-priority recommendations may not be implemented first because they can logically be incorporated into future system development activities and will thereby be implemented on a more cost-effective basis.

The implementation plan consists of identifying the sequence and timing of activities, the nature and extent of the resources required, and the estimated costs of implementation. In addition, those recommendations that are independent of others are identified. These can then be implemented concurrently with other recommendations, delayed, or brought forward, as need dictates.

The auditors should review the implementation plan in detail with management to ensure that the plan is clear and the timing of events is agreeable.

Staffing Requirements

A security review should be staffed with experienced EDP auditors, other senior personnel with a background in security and exposure analysis, and information technology specialists. Since it is not always easy to find internal personnel with enough technical depth and breadth to conduct a review of all areas, the use of an external group of qualified people should be considered. Some areas require specialized technical skills. For example, system software integrity evaluation requires extensive experience in the use and design of operating systems.

DISASTER RECOVERY AND CONTINGENCY PLANNING

A security review describes the security deficiencies and potential problems that may result. Some events that can disrupt MIS activities are not security breaches but are unlikely operational events that merit contingency planning. Contingency planning is frequently a forgotten function, but is perhaps one of the most important in running an MIS facility. Many businesses are so highly dependent on their computers that contingency plans exist to ensure that business operations will continue in the event computer service is disrupted. Equal care and planning must be expended to ensure that adequate security measures and controls are maintained both during and following a disruption. These plans are often reviewed as part of an operational audit.

The best way to ensure a rapid recovery from either short interruptions or a catastrophe is to have a written plan. The vague ideas of a few people do not constitute a viable recovery plan. When they are not available or cannot remember the details of a complex system, an undocumented plan is ineffective. Figures 30-3, 30-4, and 30-5 show sample checklists used to evaluate and review a contingency plan.

For a business to continue operating following a disaster, a recovery manual should be prepared to:

- Identify the critical applications.
- Provide a step-by-step plan defining the responsibilities of each organizational unit.
- Identify locations where EDP operations may continue.
- Specify the security controls needed during recovery.

Some organizations are large enough to have both decentralized EDP facilities and centralized EDP activities. If such an organization plans to maintain continuity of processing by switching from one site to another in

FIG. 30-3

Partial security review checklist: contingency planning—plan status (RCW = Record of Control Weaknesses; CC = Compensating Controls)

Plan Status	Workpaper Reference	Yes	No	RCW	CC
1. Is a contingency or disaster recovery plan written?	....	☐	☐	....	....
2. Has plan been updated in the last 6 months?	....	☐	☐	....	....
3. Have all current systems been evaluated?	....	☐	☐	....	....
4. Has plan been distributed to all concerned staff?	....	☐	☐	....	....
5. Has plan been approved and resources budgeted?	....	☐	☐	....	....
6. Are recovery staff identified?	....	☐	☐	....	....
7. Are staff familiar with their responsibilities?	....	☐	☐	....	....
8. Are potential disasters identified?	....	☐	☐	....	....
9. Are potential disasters not covered under the plan identified?	....	☐	☐	....	....

a disaster situation, it must be supported by a detailed recovery plan. Procedures must be established to communicate hardware and software changes at one location to all other sites that are relying on that one for recovery, while ensuring that appropriate levels of security over the systems exist.

PHYSICAL LAYOUT AND INFORMATION HANDLING

Auditors also evaluate the physical layout of all equipment used by the business for data processing in a security review. Figure 30-6 shows a sample set of questions used to evaluate physical security during a review.

AUDIT POINTS TO CONSIDER

Good system confidentiality practices may actually become a problem for the auditor. The system may be too secure to obtain audit evidence, and

FIG. 30-4

Partial security review checklist: contingency planning—plan requirements (RCW = Record of Control Weaknesses; CC = Compensating Controls)

Plan Requirements	Workpaper Reference	Yes	No	RCW	CC
1. Have all functions of data processing been considered in contingency planning?	....	☐	☐	....	....
2. Has a checklist of requirements and supplies been compiled?	....	☐	☐	....	....
3. Have business functions not covered been identified?	....	☐	☐	....	....
4. Have meeting places been identified?	....	☐	☐	....	....
5. Have necessary supplier contacts been established?	....	☐	☐	....	....
6. Are non-EDP departments aware of their individual requirements?	....	☐	☐	....	....
7. Do non-EDP departments have their own action plans?	....	☐	☐	....	....
8. Is alternative processing required?	....	☐	☐	....	....

the organization may feel that it is not desirable for the auditor to know certain details. From the auditor's perspective, audit workpapers should always be kept extremely confidential. In the course of conducting an audit of a system and creating workpapers, the very ability to obtain evidence may be a weakness, since it may indicate that the information is available too readily. These potentially conflicting concerns must be balanced. Some of the factors an auditor can consider are listed below.

1. *Common Audit Testing Techniques.*
   - Inquiry of:
     - — Security administrator.
     - — Users.
     - — System programmers.
   - Observation of:
     - — Data entry procedures.
     - — Update procedures.

FIG. 30-5

Partial security review checklist: contingency planning—plan implementation (RCW = Record of Control Weaknesses; CC = Compensating Controls)

Plan Implementation	Workpaper Reference	Yes	No	RCW	CC
1. Has contingency plan been fully implemented?	....	☐	☐	....	....
2. Have the following areas been checked for availability, compatibility, and readiness:					
a. EDP equipment and facilities?	....	☐	☐	....	....
b. System and data base management software?	....	☐	☐	....	....
c. Special software and utilities?	....	☐	☐	....	....
d. Communication services?	....	☐	☐	....	....
e. Programs and files?	....	☐	☐	....	....
f. Procedures?	....	☐	☐	....	....
3. Is there a test cycle for the plan?	....	☐	☐	....	....
4. Has the plan been tested?	....	☐	☐	....	....
5. Has a procedure for updating the plan been identified?	....	☐	☐	....	....

- Documentation review, including:
  - — Policy and procedure manuals.
  - — Record of assignment of duties.
  - — Issue logs.
  - — Problem logs.
  - — Written authorizations.
  - — Change requests.
- Use of audit software to examine:
  - — Privilege tables.
  - — Access control files.
  - — Change logs.
  - — Activity logs.
- Surprise testing
- Electronic observation of system activity, such as:
  - — Transaction trapping.

FIG. 30-6

Partial security review checklist: physical security, internal—access protection (RCW = Record of Control Weaknesses; CC = Compensating Controls)

Access Protection	Workpaper Reference	Yes	No	RCW	CC
1. Is prior approval of off-hour entry by employees required?	....	☐	☐	....	....
2. Are programmers prohibited from all processing areas?	....	☐	☐	....	....
3. Are movement detection devices used during unstaffed hours?	....	☐	☐	....	....
4. Is video surveillance used?	....	☐	☐	....	....
5. Are locks and combinations changed regularly?	....	☐	☐	....	....
6. Is employee entry/exit controlled and logged?	....	☐	☐	....	....
7. Are electronic access control devices equipped with backup power supply?	....	☐	☐	....	....
8. Are all external windows in the data center reinforced and barred?	....	☐	☐	....	....
9. Do employee identification badges bear a photograph of the owner?	....	☐	☐	....	....
10. Are badges used to identify areas of access?	....	☐	☐	....	....

— Comparing before and after images.

- Penetration testing—attempting to circumvent security

2. *Small Systems.* Simple security requirements in response to relatively low risk are suitable for small systems (such as a departmental microcomputer or a small minicomputer). Some questions that can be asked to assess such simple security requirements follow:
   - What data is stored on the system?
   - Who uses the system?
   - What are the risks?
   - Is there a password system in place? Is it used?
   - Who is responsible for password administration?

- What passwords, confidential procedures, or resource names are used?
- How are passwords kept confidential?
- What other physical restrictions or security measures are used?
- Is level of protection afforded commensurate with the risk?

3. *Higher-Security Systems*. Complex security requirements in response to relatively high risk are suitable for systems needing high security (such as a mainframe computer with dial-up access). Some of the questions to ask in such environments follow:
   - Security administration (overview level):
     - —Is there an EDP steering committee with senior management involvement?
     - —Have members of senior management had EDP awareness training?
     - —Do data processing personnel have any responsibilities outside of the computer department?
   - Is there a formal security policy that covers:
     - —The role of the security officer?
     - —Determination of security requirements and protection levels?
     - —Assignment of responsibilities and access privileges?
     - —Selection of security software and security devices?
     - —Periodic security evaluations?
   - Has the security policy been communicated to users?
   - Is there a written security administration manual that covers:
     - —Responsibilities and duties of the DSA?
     - —Responsibilities and duties of users?
     - —Documentation of data security classifications?
     - —Documentation of expected standards of protection?
     - —Documentation of responsibility assignments and access privileges?
     - —Documentation of procedures for conducting investigations into suspected offenses?
   - Is there a security awareness program?
     - —Are new employees given a security briefing?
     - —Are users required to acknowledge their security responsibilities?
     - —Are they given appropriate instructions?
     - —Do they receive regular reminders?
   - Are the security procedures regularly reviewed?
     - —Does the internal audit mandate extend to EDP security?

  - Are there scheduled reviews of security?
  - Is it possible to obtain a copy of the last review?
  - Does the review cover all of the aspects listed above?
  - What were the conclusions of the review?
- What physical access restrictions are in force?
- What password or access control software is in use?
  - What features are available?
  - What features are used?
- Is there a written password administration manual that covers:
  - Responsibilities and duties of the password administrator?
  - Password composition or format?
  - Password generation procedures?
  - Procedures for adding new system users?
  - Issue and distribution of passwords to users?
  - Maximum password lifetimes?
  - Procedures for changing passwords?
  - Procedures for deleting terminated or transferred users?
- What other security devices are used (e.g., card keys, terminal locks, encryption devices)?
- How are passwords selected?
  - Are passwords created using a random method?
  - What ensures that users do not choose easily guessed passwords?
  - What is the total number of possible passwords?
- For users:
  - Must all requests for new passwords or access privileges be approved?
  - Can request procedures be bypassed in an emergency?
  - Are requests rejected if not appropriately approved?
  - Are all users assigned a unique identification code?
  - Are there procedures for requesting emergency changes?
  - Is the distribution of passwords and IDs kept confidential?
  - Does the administrator positively confirm receipt of passwords?
- What are the procedures for changing passwords?
  - How frequently must passwords be changed?
  - How is the regular changing of passwords enforced?
  - How is the re-use of old passwords prevented?
  - What ensures that passwords and IDs are removed immediately upon a user's termination or transfer?

- What are the procedures for logging on to the system?
  - Is the logon procedure kept confidential?
  - Have the logon keywords been changed (e.g., logon, CICS)?
  - Is the entry of passwords masked on both CRTs and printers?
  - Does the system inform the user when he last logged in?
  - What ensures that users check this information and report violations?
  - Does the system detect repeated logon attempts?
  - What action is taken as a result?
- How are stored passwords kept confidential?
  - Who, aside from each user, would know a password?
  - Are passwords stored on the system inaccessible?
  - Are they encrypted?
  - Can encrypted passwords be decrypted?
  - Are hard copy listings of passwords, IDs, and privileges kept secret?
  - Have all standard manufacturer-supplied IDs and passwords been changed?
- Network security:
  - Has a network configuration map been prepared?
  - Are terminals controlled to prevent unauthorized access (e.g., keys or plastic cards)?
  - What is the time period before inactive terminals are timed out automatically?
  - Is dial-up access permitted?
  - Is a call-back device in use to prevent unauthorized dial-up access?
  - Are password transmissions between terminal and host secured?
  - Are transmissions encrypted?
- Security file protection:
  - Are all versions of the access authorization tables protected?
  - How are changes to authorizations restricted?

- Do access authorizations enforce separation of duties?
  - Are end users restricted to access only their production files?
  - Are application programmers prevented access to production files?
  - Are system programmers restricted from accessing data files?
  - Is the activity of the security administration group reviewed?
  - Is the use of utilities restricted?

- Are proper records kept of the following:
  - Dates passwords and IDs were issued?
  - Access privileges granted?
  - Security violations?
  - Use of sensitive data?
  - Use of sensitive programs?
- Computer operations security:
  - Are there written operator instructions?
  - Are operators prevented from amending JCL?
  - Do the operators keep manual shift logs?
  - Is all activity recorded on the console log?
  - Are operators supervised at all times?
  - Is there an emergency situation procedure?

CHAPTER **31**

Logical Access Controls

LOGICAL ACCESS CONTROLS

Today's systems allow employment of a wide range of controls. As these modern systems provide many control opportunities, they rely more and more on software. Software can direct users to only the functions they should perform, or protect valuable data from prying eyes. Such software-provided controls are called logical access controls (in contrast with the physical security controls that were prevalent in the past).

When reviewing logical access control requirements, it is important to remember that while the goal is to leave valuable assets exposed, it is also possible to overcontrol. To avoid either extreme, it is best to develop a program to evaluate requirements based on sensitivity, risk, and potential exposure. This helps ensure that an organization's logical access controls meet its real needs.

Access Control Requirements

Access control requirements depend on security risks, which vary in probability and criticality for each resource. To define requirements, sensitive data must first be identified and then classified as to the type of protection it needs.

Identifying Resources. To ensure that all resources are identified, an inventory should be performed. The inventory can be done in two stages: (1) An inventory of all computer hardware (terminals, disk and tape drives, etc.), and (2) an inventory of data files, programs, and transaction types (such as IMS (Information Management System) or CICS (Customer Information Control System) transactions. Each resource or set of resources should be defined as to type and purpose. Figure 31-1 shows an example of a resource inventory. This background information is used to determine whether, and to what extent, a particular resource requires protection.

FIG. 31-1
Specimen resource inventory

Data Set	Type	Storage (vol)	Description
Payroll.master	data	Disk (disk01)	Payroll master file
Payroll.source	source	Disk (disk03)	Payroll source library
Payroll.load	load	Disk (disk02)	Payroll load library
Payroll.jcl	JCL	Disk (disk03)	JCL production library
Payroll.trans	data	Tape (873021)	Payroll transactions
Transaction	**Type**	**Description**	
Payup	Update	Payroll master file update transaction	
Payenq	Read	Payroll master file read transaction	
Terminal	**Type**	**Description**	
Master	Console	Master console	
Tp0001	User	Payroll department terminal	

DATA CLASSIFICATION

With the growing number of automated applications, the computer has become an essential management tool. Decisions are made based on the information contained within the data processing environment. This information is an important corporate asset that should be protected relative to its sensitivity and importance to the organization. It may take the form of data files, transaction types (such as IMC or CICS), or output reports.

Access control or security software is often used to ensure that information is protected. The decisions as to what to protect and to what degree are important to provide effective control and minimize the costs of protection. By assigning security classifications to information, the decisions regarding protection criteria are made more effectively and efficiently. A structured approach to the classification of data will result in the implementation of access controls consistent with the intent of management.

Assigning Security Classifications to Key Data. Information assets should be classified according to their sensitivity and importance to the organization. Classification may reduce costs by avoiding overprotection of data. To classify data, the owner should consider the consequence of its disclosure, modification, or destruction.

Data can be classified by level, such as:

- Confidential, restricted, internal use, unclassified.
- External reporting, corporate internal use, departmental use, individual use.
- High, medium, low.
- Annotating each data item with specific exposure consequences.

The most cost-effective method that deals with all identified risks should be used. Some risks may be accepted when their prevention is more costly than their consequences. The protection chosen should be documented and approved by the appropriate level of management.

Assessment Criteria

Historically, the importance of information has been determined by the potential loss to the corporation if the data is lost or destroyed. While it is important to ensure that information is available in the event of a disaster, access controls should be based on a need and right to know the information. In evaluating the sensitivity of data, the effect of disclosure and unauthorized modification should be considered. For example, the salaries of chief executives may not be needed for contingency planning purposes, and the disclosure of this information could have an adverse effect both within and outside the corporation. The following attributes of the data should be evaluated in order to assign classification categories:

- *Financial Significance of the Data.* Would unauthorized modification of the information have a material effect on the preparation or presentation of the company's financial statements? Could the disclosure of the information have an effect on the competitive advantage of the corporation? Does the data lend itself to fraudulent activities (i.e., would this be the type of information that would be changed in order to commit fraud)?
- *Indirect Value to the Corporation.* Is the information, because of special interest and sensitivity, more apt to be disclosed? If disclosed, would it adversely affect or result in embarrassment to the corporation?
- *Confidentiality and Privacy Requirements.* Is disclosure of the information protected by regulatory or privacy legislation? Should access to the data be protected for legal or ethical reasons?

Responsibilities

To ensure that the proper level of protection is applied to information, it is essential that the appropriate personnel determine the proper classification category. Following is a description of the responsibilities of the key personnel within the classification process:

- *Data Owner*—The data owner is responsible for the information as it is maintained on the computer. Data owners have the most knowledge about the importance and sensitivity of the information. It is the data owners who should ultimately decide what level of protection should be applied to their data.
- *Data User*—The data user may be, and often is, the same person as the data owner. However, the data user may be a member of a separate department within the corporation. The data users access the information to satisfy the needs of their own function. The data users may contribute to the classification process by exemplifying the importance of the information as it pertains to their needs.
- *Data Custodian*—The data custodian is responsible for the safeguarding of information after the decision as to protection criteria has been determined by the data owner. The data custodian will usually have little knowledge concerning the sensitivity of the information.
- *Data Security Officer*—The data security officer advises the data owners of the options that are available to protect their information. The data security officer will also assist the data owners in determining appropriate classification categories for the data. The data security officer also documents and maintains the decisions reached by the data owner.
- *Auditor*—The auditor's role is to ensure that a consistent approach is used in evaluating the sensitivity of information. Because the auditors are exposed to many different departments throughout the organization, they are better able to judge if the data owners are overclassifying or underclassifying their information in relation to other departments. The auditor's role is to advise the data owners of their responsibilities, but they should not make the decision as to protection criteria.

Classification Categories

Information may be grouped by sensitivity level into classification categories. Each category would have different access control guidelines based on protection criteria established by management for each classification level.

Following is a definition of each classification category and an example of the type of information normally assigned to them:

- *Confidential-Restricted.* This category contains information that is highly private or sensitive. This information should be closely controlled from creation to destruction. Typical examples include salary information and strategic business plans.
- *Confidential.* This category contains private and sensitive information. This category would normally not have a financial impact on the corporation or deal with strategic business planning. It is usually sensitive to an individual or would cause embarrassment to the company if disclosed. Typical examples might be personnel history or customer names, addresses, and social security numbers.
- *Internal Use Only.* This category contains information that is not sensitive or private. The information in this category represents data that is used internally within the corporation. Discretion should be exercised to protect this data from loss, misuse, or improper disclosure, but not to the same degree as the first two categories. Typical examples include fixed-asset transactions and accounts payable edit criteria.
- *General.* This category contains information that is widely known and may be available from sources outside the corporation. A minimal amount of protective measures are normally applied to this information. Examples include stock prices or Dun & Bradstreet market information.
- *Backup.* This category contains information that is used for restart and recovery purposes only. Access to this type of information should be closely controlled in order to maintain its integrity. Examples include backup files and data base logging files.

Classification Approach

As mentioned, the classification approach may be used for any type of information. The approach may be used for computer files, transactions, source documents, or even output reports. The first step is to determine what type of information is to be assessed as to sensitivity.

The next step is to identify the data owners, data custodians, and any other personnel who will be involved in the classification methodology. These personnel should be contacted with enough lead time so that they may be able to support the classification process with the attention it deserves. A meeting of all the key players should be scheduled so that the classification methodology and expected results may be explained to the data owners.

A list of information to be classified should be assembled and provided to the data owners. The data owners should then use the questionnaire shown in Figure 31-2 as a tool in assessing the information. The data owners may wish to consult with data users and systems and programming personnel in order to gain a better understanding of the information. Once the data owners have completed the questionnaire, they should forward it to the data security officer.

Upon receipt of the questionnaire, the data security officer will schedule a meeting with the data owner, data custodian, programming support, and the auditor. The purpose of this meeting is to substantiate the responses to the questionnaire as prepared by the data owner. Within this meeting, the data security and audit representatives should play a "devil's advocate" role. There is usually a tendency for data owners to overclassify the information for which they are responsible. The data security officer and auditor should attempt to lessen the amount of information that must be classified, if possible.

The responses to the questionnaire are recorded on a summary form, as shown in Figure 31-3. The highest resulting classification category rating will be the rating for the information. The data security officer advises the data owner on the guidelines for protection criteria as they relate to the classification category. A matrix, similar to the one shown in Figure 31-4, may be used to highlight these guidelines. With this information in mind, the data owner may decide to raise or lower the classification rating. Reasons should be adequately documented.

The resulting classification ratings and sensitivity issues are recorded on a classification matrix, as shown in Figure 31-5. The data owner should sign this matrix, indicating his approval of the results. The data security officer will use this document in defining access rules to the information. A copy of this matrix should be maintained in their files to substantiate rule definitions.

Maintenance

It is important to note that the classification methodology should not be performed once and then forgotten. Information needs change for a variety of reasons (e.g., new laws and regulations, business planning needs, market fluctuations, etc.). Therefore, a structured mechanism is required to ensure that the classification ratings remain current and correct.

On a periodic basis, the data security officer should distribute a copy of the classification matrix to the data owners. The data owners should

FIG. 31-2
Data classification questionnaire

DATA IDENTIFICATION: ______________________

PREPARED BY: ______________________

DATE: ______________________

Financial Significance of the Data

1. *Material Effect on Financial Statements*
   This information is of a financial nature that supports the preparation of the corporation's financial statements. In terms of the accuracy and integrity of the financial statements, the destruction or modification of this information would be of:
   3 — major financial significance
   2 — moderate financial significance
   1 — minor financial significance
   0 — no significance

2. *Competitive Advantage*
   This information provides the corporation with an advantage over its competition, or if improperly disclosed or misrepresented, would result in the corporation's competition gaining a market advantage. The disclosure of this information would constitute a potential:
   3 — major exposure
   2 — moderate exposure
   1 — minor exposure
   0 — no exposure

3. *Exposure to Fraud*
   This information, due to the nature of the application(s) it supports, may be susceptible to fraudulent activities. This information:
   2 — could be easily manipulated without detection
   1 — could be manipulated with a moderate level of effort without detection
   0 — could be manipulated only through a significant level of effort without detection

   and involves:
   2 — large dollar values or controls the disbursement of funds
   1 — medium dollar values
   0 — small dollar values

Indirect Value to the Corporation

4. *Unusual Interest*
   This information, due to its content and nature, may be of unusual interest to employees and may therefore be more susceptible to unauthorized access and potential disclosure. This information is of:
   2 — exceptional interest to employees
   1 — moderate interest to employees
   0 — no special interest to employees

5. *Effect of Disclosure*

   This information, due to its content and nature, would have an adverse effect on employee morale, loss of productivity, or embarrassment to the corporation or individual to whom it pertains if improperly disclosed. The adverse effects of the disclosure of this information would be:

   2 — substantial
   1 — moderate
   0 — immaterial

Confidentiality and Privacy Requirements

6. *Privacy Considerations*

   This information is currently sensitive in nature to an individual or entity. This information is of:

   3 — a very sensitive nature to the individual or entity
   2 — a moderately sensitive nature to the individual or entity
   1 — a minimally sensitive nature to the individual or entity
   0 — a nonsensitive nature

7. *Regulatory Requirements*

   The disclosure of this information is protected by regulation or is a prime candidate for regulatory protection. This information, if disclosed, could result in legal penalties against the corporation.

   1 — Yes
   0 — No

reassess the sensitivity issues and classification ratings as they pertain to the information classified. If changes are required, another meeting should be scheduled to substantiate the changes.

The classification methodology should also be incorporated within the System Development Life Cycle (SDLC) program in use by the corporation. The sensitivity of information should be assessed before it is created and distributed. As new programs and procedures are developed, the access needs for information may change. The SDLC methodology should address this issue.

Security Recommendations

Effective security is only accomplished through the implementation of several procedures, both manual and computerized. Following is a list of access control guidelines as they relate to classification categories. This list is not

FIG. 31-3
Data classification summary

DATA IDENTIFICATION
PREPARED BY:
DATE:

Attribute	Question	Score	Factors	Rating
	Material effect on financial statements		3 — Confidential-Restricted 2 — Confidential 1 — Internal Use only 0 — General	
Financial significance of the data	Competitive advantage		3 — Confidential-Restricted 2 — Confidential 1 — Internal Use only 0 — General	
	Exposure to fraud (total score)		4 — Confidential-Restricted 2/3 — Confidential 1 — Internal Use Only 0 — General	
Indirect value to the corporation	Unusual interest plus effect of disclosure Total score		4 — Confidential-Restricted 3 — Confidential 2 — Internal Use Only 2 — General	
	Privacy considerations plus regulatory requirements Total score		4 — Confidential-Restricted 3 — Confidential 2 — Internal Use Only 2 — General	

FIG. 31-4
Protection guidelines

OVERALL CLASSIFICATION RATING:

Access Rule / **Classification Rating**	**Confidential — Restricted**	**Confidential**	**Internal Use Only**	**General**	**Backup**
Log all accesses	Yes	Yes, unless Data Owner says No	No, unless Data Owner says Yes	No, unless Data Owner says Yes	Yes
Identify personnel with access	Yes	Yes	Yes	Yes	Yes
Time-of-day restrictions	Yes	Yes	No	No	No
Date restrictions	Yes	Yes	Yes	No	No
Specify physical device restrictions	Yes	Yes	No	No	Yes
Specify program restrictions	Yes	Yes	No	No	Yes
Specify library restrictions	Yes	No	No	No	Yes

FIG. 31-5

Data classification access rules

Data Identification	Description	Classification	Access Rules

.... Data Owner

.... Date

meant to be all-inclusive, but to provide a basis for establishing detailed access controls.

- Confidential-Restricted.
  - — Each access permission should be logged.
  - — Program pathing should be implemented. That is, only specified programs from authorized libraries may access the information.

  - The dates and/or time of day that the information may be accessed should be specified.
  - The physical devices that may be used to access the information should be identified.
- Confidential.
  - Access permissions should be logged unless the data owners specifically request that accesses are not logged.
  - The dates and/or time of day that the information may be accessed should be specified.
  - The physical devices that may be used to access the information should be identified.
- Internal Use Only.
  - Accesses need not be logged unless the data owners request a report of logged accesses.
  - Each individual with access should be identified.
- General: Care should be exercised over all information that is physically transported outside the company's premises.
- Backup.
  - Each access permission should be logged.
  - Each individual with access should be identified.
  - Access should be restricted to physical devices that are under close control.
  - Program pathing should be implemented (see Confidential-Restricted).

Grouping Key Data Using Consistent Naming Conventions. Using a standard naming convention helps administrators implement security, since it allows prefixing or patterning to define resources. Rather than having to define each individual resource, resources can be grouped together by prefix or pattern, based on security classification.

Assigning Ownership and Responsibilities. The security scheme should grant authority to access data on a need-to-know basis. One way to do this is to determine the data owners and give them responsibility for identifying the access rules for their resources. The owners can be held responsible for compliance with corporate policy.

Determining Access Paths to Key Data. Access to data may travel through one or more computer networks. Even within a particular network, the access, and therefore the access restrictions, may involve several software components. It is important to understand the nature of each component and how it could be used to enforce restrictions or to bypass them. The overall nature of security at a given installation will be determined by the combination of software components available and how they have been implemented. (See Chapter 26, "Testing Techniques for Computer-Based Systems," for a more detailed explanation of this area.)

Restricting Software That Bypasses Access Controls. Powerful terminal commands and utility programs are available to the technical support, programming, and operations staff. Such tools can read, change, and delete data and files, bypassing the usual access controls. These service aids can compromise security by circumventing controls established within the computer network. The availability of these tools should be limited, and their use tightly controlled and closely monitored.

ACCESS AUTHORIZATIONS

Access authorizations should control access to the resources. The people who may create data access exposures are:

- Unauthorized employees.
- Authorized users.
  - End users.
  - MIS programmers.
  - EDP auditors.
  - Security group.
- Contract or temporary personnel.
- Remote users outside the organization.
- Former employees.
- Hardware and software vendors.
- Consultants.

All of those people may have access to systems that is unwarranted and may be abused. (Depending on the transaction attempted by a user, the system may allow processing to continue or deny the request.)

Access Rule Tables

An access rule or permission table defines which system resources (programs, functions, transactions, menus, data, and so on) a user is authorized

FIG. 31-6
Specimen access authorization table

DATA SET	PAYROLL	SALE
User ID	Type of Access	Type of Access
JOHNID	READ(Allowed)	NONE
CAROLID	UPDATE (Allowed and Logged)	NONE
DAVEID	ALL	NONE
JANEID	NONE	READ(Allowed) UPDATE (Allowed and Logged)

to execute or access. Different access privileges to each user (e.g., read, write, execute a program, reorganize, set security privileges) may be specified for each resource. An example of an access rule table is shown in Figure 31-6. A complementary rule table is often associated with each significant resource. Each resource requested by a user is first checked to those tables. Access is allowed if the information given matches the tables.

Implementation Strategies

Many strategies can be used for the initial implementation of access controls. No one method is best; a combination is often used. Resource inventory, data classification, risk analysis, and need-to-know can be employed. Critical factors in protecting data include the cost of protection, value of data, risk evaluation, and convenience of access. Human factors must also be considered. Users may require considerable adjustment to work in a newly controlled environment. It will take time before all resources requiring protection are defined and controlled.

One way to implement access controls is application by application. A minimum level of control for each application's data can be established in a short time. Once this general security structure is in place, the process can be repeated until the maximum desired level of control is reached. This approach allows for human factors, changes in the organization, technology, and incremental program development.

Division of Duties

Access controls lock out unauthorized users and enforce a division of duties among those permitted to use the system. Obviously, this can be done only in organizations with defined individual accounability and division of responsibilities. First, the organization must define which data and functions may be accessed by which users. For example, the data processing personnel should not have any responsibilities outside of MIS; at the application level, the cash clerk should not have incompatible responsibilities such as bank reconciliations or cash adjustments. Such a defined division of duties can then be enforced by reference to an access rule table built into the access control system, as previously discussed.

A definition that is too strict can severely inhibit productivity and may lead to a reaction against any level of controls. A definition that is not strict enough may enhance productivity, but leave important data resources unprotected.

Classes of Users

Different types of users need different levels of access. Restrictions can be enforced on a need-to-know basis. Figure 31-7 shows a table of access restriction to types of data sets for each class of user.

End Users. Typically, end users are the largest class of users. They usually know the most about how the system is used and have the most ready access to physical assets and data. Their access privileges should usually be the most restricted. They should not have access to programming and system functions. This is difficult to achieve when there is end-user computing (using fourth-generation languages or utilities). Segregation between departments should be enforced, together with an appropriate separation within departments.

Application Programmers. There are typically fewer application programmers than users. Programmers require use of more powerful system functions than do end users; programmers need access to programming and testing aids. Their activities should be restricted to test programs and files, with access only to those programs and files needed for a given assignment; they should not be granted access to production files. In the event that a

FIG. 31-7

Division of duties—resource access authorizations

RESOURCE \ USER		Application Users	Application Programmers	System Programmers	Computer Operation
Application Data	Prod.	YES (1)	NO	NO	NO
	Test	NO	YES (1)	NO	NO
Application Program Libraries	Prod.	NO	YES (1)	NO	NO
	Test	NO	YES (1)	NO	NO
Job Libraries	Prod.	NO	NO	RESTRICTED (3)	RESTRICTED (4)
	Test	NO	YES (1)	RESTRICTED (3)	YES (1)
Utilities		NO	RESTRICTED (2)	YES (1)	NO
System Libraries		NO	NO	YES (1)	NO

(1) Access allowed but restricted on a need to know basis

(2) Use of sensitive utilities should be logged

(3) All access is logged

(4) Execute only for operators and update logged for job scheduling

programmer is allowed access to a production file, its use should be logged and closely monitored. Programmers should not have user department responsibilities. The use of particularly powerful utilities should be restricted and monitored. Programmers should not need access to the system or application libraries, which would provide the means of bypassing controls.

System Programmers. System programmers may be a special concern. The nature of today's systems places some operating system functions outside the control of access security software. The technical support personnel who maintain the hardware and system software must have a special level of trust. Their activities must be restricted to the extent practical, and their work must be supervised. System programmers should be instructed to maintain logs of their work; many of these records can be kept automatically by the systems. They should be forbidden to access application data and programs except for necessary troubleshooting activities. They should have access only to system libraries of the particular software that they maintain.

For example, in a typical IBM environment, the CICS technical support engineer should not have access to the RACF (Resource Access Control Facility) system libraries. Most activities can, and should, be restricted by the access control software. The use of powerful utilities should be restricted according to job function.

Security Administrators. Security administrators (SAs), because of their powers, must be trusted individuals. Nevertheless, they should be required to document their work to allow review and checking. It is important that the SA is not allowed to act unless appropriately authorized by the owner of the data, based on a written request. Since the SA acts as an agent on behalf of others, unilateral decisions should be strictly forbidden. An adequate division of responsibility over the SA's assigned functions is also desirable: no application responsibilities, no programming duties, and restricted access to application descriptions, data, and programs. Some access control software provides techniques for enforcing some of these restrictions: Users may select passwords that are stored on the system in encrypted form unknown to the SA; the system may provide for multiple levels of security, each with its own SA.

In theory, the SA should be the only person to use the access control administration mechanisms. In practice, due to the technical nature of many access control techniques, the SA often has to rely on system support personnel to some extent.

Data Definition

To extend protection techniques beyond the file or data set level, each field or data element of all affected record types can be examined. Individual fields or data elements need separate access authorization rules only when their protection requirements differ from other fields on the file. For example, a personnel file may contain personnel records available to all users of the personnel department, but the salary field need be accessed only by the payroll program.

System Storage of Access Authorization Tables

Since the authorization table is the master key to controlling the processes and transactions, its security is critical. Changes to tables are initiated on the basis of written requests by the security administration group and should be logged. Where access authorization tables are established in source form and then compiled (e.g., CICS, ACF2 (Access Control Facility 2) rules), both the source and the executable form should be protected.

Backup files should also be protected from unauthorized access, since they could be read by users outside the security group and could be used to gain unauthorized access to the system. A user could also modify the access authorization tables stored on the backup files, cause a system failure so that the (modified) backup is loaded, and then, using the modified tables, gain unauthorized access.

Logging and Recording—Audit Trails

The original design objective of logging and recording software, such as SMF (System Management Facility) in an IBM environment, was to gather information to analyze the system configuration, workload, and job scheduling procedures. Logs are also used to charge users for the resources they use. Security features have been added, and this logging is becoming a useful factor in designing a successful security program.

Billing. A billing system collects system information installations needed to account for system use and to analyze performance. An installation uses the recorded data to measure its processing performance and charge users for processing time and resource use. Such billing systems can also allow users to confirm and monitor the use of resources and identify unexpected uses of the system, as well as lock out unauthorized users attempting to use nonexistent charge codes.

Attempted Violations. A secure system must be able to identify all attempted violations, accidental or malicious. Any mismatch of user or password or any unauthorized request to access data should be recorded in a log.

Details of all violations should be provided to appropriate security officers. A branch security officer, for example, should see a listing of all violations within the branch. A data file owner should be aware of all unauthorized attempts to read or change records in the file. The list of violations should be distributed as often as necessary (e.g., weekly or daily), depending on the sensitivity of the data, the size of the system, and the level of activity. If local SAs are advised as soon as possible after a violation, the unauthorized user may be identified before extensive damage occurs.

The violation log should be analyzed by the system SA to detect unusual activity. Most violations are the accidental result of honest, perhaps careless, mistakes by terminal users. They may also indicate that someone is tampering with the system, possibly exploring methods to gain access. Reviews of violations also inhibit abuse by users, since they know they are being monitored.

Changes to the Security Files. All changes to the security files, including those involving user identifications (user IDs), passwords, user privileges, and access rule tables, should be logged. However, neither passwords nor authorizations should appear together on the audit log. The log should indicate only the identity of the person making the change, the type of change, and the people whose authorizations are being changed. The detail log of all changes to security tables should be reviewed daily to note and follow up on unauthorized changes.

Tracing Facility. It may be useful to record the activity of a specific user or the access to a specific resource either on a random basis or when there is cause for suspicion. It also may be useful to maintain statistical data on the use and type of access of specified files. A detailed examination would occur only when activity reached unexpected levels.

The logging and reporting procedures should be reviewed to ensure that opportunities to bypass security routines are reduced and that those routines cannot be disabled. The system logs should be protected from unauthorized reading and change.

PASSWORD SYSTEMS

Despite criticism from those searching for perfect security, user IDs and associated passwords are a proven, practical method to lower the risk of unauthorized activity. No system, with the possible exception of those using secret and expensive defense technologies, can ever provide perfect security. Properly administered password systems can achieve cost-effective risk reduction to the protection levels commonly needed in most businesses.

Passwords can be classified into two types, those associated with individuals and those associated with particular system resources, called user passwords and resource passwords, respectively.

User Passwords

User IDs identify users signing on to the system. They commonly establish accountability and are sometimes used for billing purposes. They can also be used to restrict access. The control system checks each identity to a table of authorized access privileges. Confidential personal passwords are used to authenticate these claimed identities—that is, to help ensure that the person using the ID has the authority to use it. Once the user enters the user

ID, the system asks for the password. The system validates the password entered to ensure that the correct password has been entered for the particular user ID.

User passwords are assigned with a user ID and should be kept confidential. When the user ID is kept confidential as well, security is improved because of the difficulty of discovering both.

User IDs are sometimes used without a separate password. Such systems are easier for users who remember and enter only one item. To achieve a reasonable level of security, such user IDs must be kept confidential. Confidential user IDs are often called "passwords" although they could be described more accurately as "password IDs." User IDs alone offer lower protection than a user ID and password combination because there is only one factor for an unauthorized user to discover, and this may be fairly easy to do. Also, a user ID has to be known to the password administrator and is usually stored on the system in an unencrypted form. The confidential ID is thus potentially accessible to the systems programmer as well as the password administrator. In high security systems with this combination, the user ID is known to the password administrator and stored on the system in readable form. The personal password can be stored in an encrypted form, so that only the owner of the user ID knows it.

For greater security, unique user IDs and passwords should be assigned to each user, rather than assigned in common to a group of users, as is the case with access passwords. Unique user IDs and passwords improve confidentiality, limit the effect when someone leaves or transfers, establish accountability, and record individual activities.

A user password system can be set up with the default either unprotected or protected. If the default is protected, no one has access to data or system resources unless specific privileges have been granted and enabled on the system. Greater security is achieved since specific administrative action has to be taken before any user is allocated an access privilege. If the default is unprotected, access restrictions are applied only to those system resources for which security has been turned on. In some systems, anything not specifically protected is unprotected.

Small Systems

In principle, the requirements for small systems, such as microcomputers, are the same as those for more sophisticated systems. However, the nature of exposure is often more limited, and consequently the security requirements are lower. There may be practical limitations on how security can be implemented, as well.

Renaming Sensitive Functions

In small systems, access restrictions are often implemented by renaming sensitive functions, files, or programs with secret names. For example, a data change utility may be renamed with a new name known only to the technical support personnel. In fact, any confidential access method, such as a confidential phone number and sign-on sequence, acts in part as an access password and improves security. Many systems with user passwords also use resource passwords or transaction codes to provide additional security protection for key resources.

User Resistance

A major cost of access restrictions is loss of convenience. Often, the greater the protection against unauthorized activity, the more difficult a system is to use.

Users may resist remembering passwords and the delays caused by entering them. Procedures for changing passwords or obtaining a replacement when forgotten may be even more onerous. Access restrictions may adversely affect the ability to get the job done, particularly in an emergency. Working outside of normal hours, getting temporary assistance from another department, coping with changing circumstances, or recovering from an emergency may all be more difficult. There may be times when the password administrator or the only employee with the password is unavailable. When the procedures seem intrusive, users and management may need to be convinced of the need for security.

Password System Threats

Security systems are subject to various threats. Passwords are susceptible to disclosure whenever they are stored or transmitted. Untrained users may write their passwords on manuals or tape them to terminals. Passwords may be discovered if they are printed on reports or other manual records, when password files stored on the system are read, or when transmitted to or from a terminal to the mainframe.

Passwords can also be guessed. Users and non-users may deliberately attempt to discover user IDs and passwords for which they are not authorized. The probability of a password being discovered depends on the:

- Number of failed attempts to log on allowed by the system.
- Sign-on procedure.
- Interval of password changes.
- Way passwords are created.

Depending on the access and operating system controls, opportunities may allow a skilled user, such as a system programmer or an application programmer, to bypass the security system.

PASSWORD AND SIGN-ON ADMINISTRATION

Selecting Software and Hardware

Access control software products such as ACF2, RACF, and TOP SECRET, discussed in Chapter 32, "Access Control Software," provide an installation with the ability to:

- Implement user ID and password controls.
- Limit user access to information and system resources.
- Monitor user activity.
- Report on security violations for follow-up.

They are valuable tools that, if implemented adequately, can help reduce exposure. These products have features that can provide some of the controls described in this section, and can be customized to integrate further controls.

When implementing an access control software product, security administration should ensure that:

- All applicable security options are active.
- Adequate reports on user activity and security violations are produced.
- Subsequent changes made to the options, user IDs, and rules are appropriate and supervised.

Installing access control software does not provide protection in itself. It must be properly implemented to be effective and requires a number of administrative procedures. Access control software products should be viewed as management tools and not just as security packages. Their ability to enforce management policies and standards is not normally thought of as a security issue. For example, access control software is an ideal tool to enforce naming conventions systematically. It provides resource control and reporting tools that do more than just protect resources.

Authentication Devices

Passwords are the most widely used authentication devices because they are the most economical. However, there are other ways to verify the identity of a user. Normally, this verification relies on a combination of the following:

- Something that only one user knows, such as a keyword or password.
- Something that only one person has, such as a key or card.
- Some unique physical characteristic, such as a fingerprint or hand geometry.
- Some unique but reproducible behavior, such as the way a person speaks.

Organizations with large user populations and sensitive resources use a key or magnetically encoded card in addition to a password. Keys are appropriate where a user is assigned the exclusive use of a terminal for a fixed and regular period of time. Magnetically encoded cards are appropriate where multiple users share terminals.

Those devices provide a degree of control not possible with exclusive reliance on passwords or security codes. Since the user must have a key or badge to operate the system, a loss is bound to be recognized and reported. In addition, when a security code is combined with a machine-readable badge, the badge is of little value to anyone who takes or finds it.

Secondary Authentication

All security systems have a built-in user authentication function. This primary authentication is commonly implemented by verifying a user ID through password checking. Secondary authentication is the term used for user authentication through external devices and procedures, in addition to, or in place of, the primary authentication. A variety of secondary authentication devices have been developed in recent years in response to the need for stronger authentication methods, mostly for on-line access.

Secondary authentication devices can solve two recognized problems:

1. Weaknesses in existing password schemes.
2. Exposures from the use of dial-up facilities.

Built-in password schemes have two problems in common:

1. Simple passwords are memorized by the legitimate user, but may be easily guessed by an attacker.
2. Sophisticated password rules minimize the risk of password guessing, but these passwords are often exposed because the legitimate user writes them down.

In essence, dial-up ports allow every person with a terminal and a modem to dial in to the computer facility in which they are installed. Only an effective user authentication mechanism will prevent unauthorized individuals from accessing such systems. The potential exposure is higher in this environment than in a closed network; therefore, a variety of additional mechanisms, such as call-back units, are used to provide additional security. There are concerns that such devices are expensive, may create usability problems, and offer only limited additional security. In a number of applications, they are not feasible. Secondary authentication is one good alternative.

Secondary Authentication Devices. Secondary authentication devices usually fall into two categories:

1. Biometric devices.
2. Devices that generate "one-time passwords."

Biometric devices measure and recognize unique features and properties of an individual's body; associated software algorithms evaluate the measurement against predefined profiles and approve or disapprove access attempts based on the evaluation. Typical devices in this category are signature verification and voice recognition units. These devices are usually installed on or near computer terminals.

One-time password schemes usually involve hand-held devices (smart tokens) similar to credit cards or pocket calculators that are carried by individual users. There is corresponding software (and sometimes hardware) on the host system. These systems use a cryptographic algorithm and a secret cryptographic key to generate a one-time password for each user. This process may be based on timer values (synchronized timers in the token and at the host) or challenge numbers (which are randomly generated by the host system and displayed at the terminal). The advantage of this approach is that the password:

- Can be made very complex, since the user does not have to memorize it.

- Can only be used once and, if compromised, does not cause a security exposure.
- Cannot be generated without the authentication device, which often can be activated only through another secret code.

Prototypes of secondary authentication devices are demonstrated often. Biometric devices will be used in normal computer applications as soon as the remaining problems of fine-tuning the evaluation algorithms have been solved. "Smart tokens," which generate one-time passwords, will be popular because of their attractive price once software support is available in all major access control packages.

Usability Considerations. Current access control implementations have another problem in common that is related to the fact that different applications (on the same or on different systems) may require different authentications. A given user may have to go through a new authentication process whenever switching to another application, and may have to use a different user ID and a different password for each application the user is authorized to use. This may be acceptable or even desirable in some situations. In general, however, it should be possible to assign only one ID to a user and have each user go through the authentication process only once.

User Profile

To provide individual accountability, it is important, whenever possible, to assign a unique ID to each user. All members of a department should not share the same user ID. A user who can be held individually accountable for actions is less likely to disrupt or compromise operations. Separate user IDs are recommended even if all users in a group have the same access authorization to the resource or data. The objectives of individual accountability are:

- To provide an audit trail of user activities.
- To determine who accessed what resource and for what purpose.
- To establish the illicit use of a user ID.
- To avoid the need to change the password of an entire group when a member of the group leaves.

Access privileges and restrictions can be assigned to an ID. These attributes determine various privileges and restrictions a user has within a system. Such privileges can include the following:

- Ability to change the system options.
- Ability to change user ID attributes.
- Ability to change access authorization.
- Ability to read all files.
- Ability to bypass password controls.
- Ability to use tape bypass label processing.
- Ability to audit the system.

Password Generation or Selection

A password selection procedure must be specified by the organization. Passwords may be selected by users, the SA, or an automated password generator. It is important to determine their length, composition, and method of selection. Passwords should be difficult to guess, but easy to remember. Some systems set a minimum length, prohibit the use of repeated characters, and specify other requirements. Machine-generated passwords are more random and more likely to comply with predetermined specifications, but are usually more difficult to remember. Figure 31-8 describes the significant characteristics of passwords.

Memorizing Passwords. Passwords should be easy to memorize, and they should never be written down. Words or phrases are easier to remember than randomly chosen characters, more convenient to use, and more secure. They reduce the frequency with which forgotten passwords must be replaced and the attendant risks.

If a user forgets the password and the system is such that the SA does not know it, the procedures should be the same as for the initial issuance of passwords. The SA must positively identify the user and reset an initial password to override the forgotten one. Such emergency procedures should be documented appropriately.

Issuing Initial Passwords. The SA often creates a temporary password for a new system user. It is recommended that this initial password be used only for the first access. Many systems require that the user replace the original password with one that only the user knows. (This can be done by setting the initial password as an "expired password.") User-selected passwords may be checked by an automated password system to ensure that they meet the format criteria.

FIG. 31-8

Characteristics of passwords

Format

The ideal password is easy to remember, simple to enter, and impossible to guess. In reality, these contradictory requirements are fulfilled as nearly as possible by balancing practicality against security needs.

Difficult to Guess

To be difficult to guess, passwords should be long and complicated, selected or generated from a very large set of possible passwords. The minimum recommended set size is 10,000, although a set of 1 million or more would be much more secure. The potential set size depends on the password's format: its composition and length.

Composition

Composition is the set of characters that may be used to create a valid password. Although this can include any allowable characters, for compatibility purposes the 95-character subset of the American Standard Code for Information Interchange (ASCII) is the recommended set from which the security administrator selects the characters to be used. For the greatest security, the composition should consist of as many characters as is practical, if possible the whole 95. (In some systems, this cannot be done, since special characters have a system meaning and cannot be used.)

The characters usable in a password depend, in part, on the device from which the password is entered. They also depend on how and where the password is stored and how the system compares the stored password with the entered password.

The minimum recommended character set is the digits 0 through 9. This small set should be used only when the input device is a 10-digit key pad (e.g., a telephone or automated teller machine). A small character set reduces the size of the set of possible passwords significantly.

Many password systems use just the 26 letters of the alphabet. In such systems, however, there is a tendency to select a person's name, initials, nickname, relative, address, department, or some other easily guessed word. Using a mixture of letters, digits, and special characters reduces the chances of a password being compromised. Unfortunately, it also reduces the chances of its being remembered.

Length

Longer passwords are more secure, but they take longer to enter and there is greater chance for error. Generally, they are more difficult to remember, particularly when the password consists of numbers or random characters.

The minimum recommended length is four characters. Ideally, the acceptable length should include a range, such as five to eight characters. Use of a range does not increase the size of the set of possible passwords significantly from when only one length is permitted, but it is a good idea because it makes the password format more difficult to guess. A range is also recommended for user-selected passwords, due to the greater flexibility and ease of use in selecting a memorable password.

Selection

For greatest security, passwords should be selected at random from the acceptable set. The random number generators used for statistical purposes may not be acceptable: Frequently, the sequence of random numbers generated is predictable.

The Data Encryption Standard (DES) algorithm, together with a nondeterministic parameter, such as the least significant bits of a high resolution computer system clock, may be used. The results of the random generation can then be combined with the password format rules to obtain an acceptable password. Random passwords are not particularly easy to remember.

The security administrator often creates a password for a new user of a system, to be used for the initial access. The system may then require that the user replace this password with one that only the user knows. If possible, passwords that the user selects should be checked by an automated password system to ensure they meet the format criteria for acceptable passwords.

Passphrases

A passphrase is a group of words or character strings used as a password. It can take a number of forms:

- A meaningful sequence of words, such as a sentence or phrase (e.g., MANNERS MAKETH MAN)
- Two or more words, each chosen at random from a dictionary of acceptable words (e.g., SMOG SOCCER)
- One of the above with the addition of digits and special characters between the words or to substitute for particular letters (e.g., MANNERS?MAKETH?MAN, MOGOCCER7)

A passphrase has the advantage that it is generally easier to remember than a random character string. The number of possibilities for understandable passphrases is considerably smaller than for a random sequence of characters of the same length. Although long passphrases can be easy to remember, they do take more time to enter.

For compact storage on the system, a passphrase may be converted into a virtual password by transformation, such as a hashing or a cryptographic function. An added advantage is that the passphrase is not stored in readable text on the system. These functions should compute a value using the entire passphrase as input in such a way that any change in the passphrase results in a different computed virtual password. The value of the virtual password computed is often 64 bits, as specified in the DES. This allows all password systems to allocate a maximum of 64 bits for each stored password; therefore it allows up to two COMPUTE VALUE possibilities. Such a passphrase thus provides the benefits of being easily remembered with a small additional time to enter the longer passphrase, plus the processing time to compute the virtual password.

Pronounceable Passwords

Password-generating algorithms that produce a random but pronounceable character strings (e.g., SWONGA) are available. As with passphrases, the number of pronounceable character strings is smaller than the set of completely random strings of the same length. To achieve the level of security required may require a longer pronounceable password, which becomes more difficult to remember and enter. Pronounceable passwords are most convenient for medium-level security requirements where it is not desirable for the users to select passwords.

The following controls should also be considered when issuing initial passwords:

1. *Initial passwords should follow full password configuration requirements.* To avoid initial passwords being guessed by unauthorized users, they should not be based on user ID, department, function, or other defaults. A record should be kept when a new initial password is issued.
2. *Confidentiality of password distribution should be ensured.* If the initial password is generated by the password system or selected by the SA, it must be communicated to the user. The SA must ensure that the user is authorized and that no one other than the assigned user receives the password. The most secure procedure is for the user to be present during password generation, and to be cautioned against writing it down. If the password must be transmitted in writing, it should be in a sealed envelope. To ensure receipt, the user should return acknowledgment within a specified time. The printed password should be destroyed after memorization.
3. *The need to change initial passwords and IDs.* Software usually comes from the vendor with standard user IDs and passwords (such as MASTER, SYSTEM, USER, TEST, PASSWORD). These passwords may be documented in the manuals and should be changed before the software is placed in production. Some systems do not permit changing certain standard IDs or passwords. Purchasers may want to encourage vendors to allow such changes and, in the meantime, to install appropriate alternate restrictions.

Changing Passwords

The password system should have the ability to replace the password quickly, initiated either by the user or the SA. Passwords should be changed often enough so that there is an acceptably low probability of guessing them. An interval of three months or less is desirable; some high security operations change passwords every two weeks. The interval depends on the risks associated with compromise. The change interval can be different for each user and should be shorter for users with more power (such as the SA and system programmers). It is a good idea to choose a period that seems adequate and then reduce it, if necessary. The interval can also depend on the number of users of the system. Some systems have automated features that enforce predefined change intervals, usually via expired passwords. When the user logs on, a message states that the password has expired and must be changed.

A password should be disabled as soon as its user leaves. The SA should be notified promptly when people leave; their user IDs and passwords must be revoked immediately. Some sophisticated systems include a weekly or monthly matching of the user ID file against the payroll file to ensure that all deletions have been made. When an employee who leaves has shared a password with a group of other employees, the group password should be changed immediately. Passwords should also be changed whenever a breach of confidentiality is known or suspected.

Change Procedure. Only the user or SA should be able to change passwords. Users should be able to change their passwords voluntarily. The new password should follow full password configuration requirements. If users can change their own passwords, the system should provide change instructions; to change generally requires the user to supply the old password.

The use of previous passwords should be prohibited. In some systems a history file of former passwords is maintained. When a user changes a password, he may not use the previous ones on file. Users may bypass this by changing passwords frequently enough to use up the password storage ability, which is usually limited. To prevent this, some systems define a minimum number of days that a newly changed password must remain active before the user may change it. This can keep users from changing their passwords to temporary ones and then immediately changing back to the old favorite. The replacement should be logged to record the date and time of the change, but the old and new passwords should not be recorded.

Sign-On Sequence and Entry of Passwords

Passwords are susceptible to disclosure whenever they are entered on the terminal during the sign-on sequence.

Ease-of-Use Sign-On Requirements May Contradict Security Requirements. Some installations provide a very user-friendly sign-on sequence to encourage employees to use the system. Such procedures may consist of:

- Clear instructions displayed on screen.
- Short passwords displayed on screen to speed their entry and reduce the number of errors.
- Terminals that prompt users with meaningful error messages.
- Passwords built into the microcomputer's automatic sign-on procedures.

Such systems are user-friendly, but may not meet security requirements.

Sign-On Sequence. All access to the system should require the user to enter the full sign-on sequence. For example, if it requires a person to enter a user ID and a password, there should be no way to bypass the sequence by entering a specific command.

The sign-on sequence could be modified from the normal procedures provided. For example, often-used keywords, such as LOGON or the software name (e.g., CICS), should be changed to a secret name, providing an additional level of control. Obviously, the sign-on sequence, including phone numbers for dial-up access, should be kept confidential. Users should be encouraged to check that no one is watching their key strokes as they enter passwords.

The terminal should give no response at all until successful sign-on is complete. Users should not be prompted at logon or given any clues to the correct procedure until after the entire logon has been completed successfully. HELP commands and files should not start until a user has been validated. The screen should not display the following information:

- Sign-on instructions and password format.
- Company name, hardware type, or operating environment.
- Help responses to invalid attempts (e.g., not distinguish between invalid passwords and invalid IDs).

To reduce the risk of disclosure, it is recommended that echo (display) of passwords typed into a terminal be suppressed. If the system cannot prevent a password from being echoed, an overprint mask should be printed before the password is typed. The masking characters should be longer than the actual password length. No printed copy of the password should exist after password entry.

On successful logon, the user may be notified of: the date and time of last logon, the location of the user at last logon, and any unsuccessful logon attempts. This information allows users to determine if someone else is using or attempting to use this user ID Any unexpected information should be reported to the SA. (Many systems do not provide this information, however.)

Deliberate Attempts to Discover Passwords. The sign-on sequence should detect attempts to discover user IDs and passwords. Many passwords can be broken by guessing or using a personal computer programmed for repeated attempts. Discovery of a user ID and its related password may be prevented by using the following techniques:

1. *User IDs*—Repeated attempts to logon can be blocked by slowing down the rate at which they can be made. The first few logon attempts can be fast and then reduced to about 10 to 60 seconds per attempt. After a defined number of attempts, perhaps five, the system should provide immediate real-time notification to the SA or system operator. After additional repeated attempts, perhaps 15, the terminal or port should be deactivated and require a restart procedure to be initiated. This protection should prevent an automated, high-speed, trial-and-error attack on the user IDs.
2. *Passwords*—Users should be allowed more than one attempt to enter a password correctly, to allow for inadvertent errors. However, there should be a maximum number for each user; three to five attempts are adequate for typical security systems. After five attempts in a single day, the password system should deny access to the user ID and require a reset procedure. This should prevent an unauthorized user who has identified a user ID from accessing the system. Similar control can be achieved by measuring user response time to ensure that the request is entered by a user, not a computer.

When other password systems are used, such as access passwords, similar protection can be achieved by closing down the port or the access path. The maximum number of incorrect user IDs or password entries depends on their sensitivity. Some installations set the parameters high to prevent user dissatisfaction, while other organizations set the parameters low to prevent security compromises.

Only the SA should be able to restore a line or a user ID. Audit trails identifying access attempts should be recorded and reviewed daily. Unattended terminals should be deactivated to limit the time an activated device may remain unused. After the time limit (perhaps 15 minutes) expires, use requires a new logon. This should deter unauthorized use of unattended terminals.

Transmission From Terminal to Mainframe

Line Taps. Communications from a terminal to a mainframe can be wiretapped fairly easily with the right equipment, knowledge, and access to the line. This is especially true for signals on telephone lines, although nearly all communications lines are at risk. Line monitoring equipment can be used to read transmissions. This is common in large installations, using devices that can be purchased for a few thousand dollars. The whole transmission, including the password, can be read in this way. It may also be modified before retransmission. Protection can be achieved by restricting physical access to the line or by encryption of the transmission.

Penetration. In some cases, someone with high-level skills can write a program that simulates normal screen display. This program can then capture the sign-on entry from what appears to be a normal screen layout.

Many terminals, communication lines, and other hardware emit signals that can be monitored. The difficulty of doing so increases with the distance, the degree of shielding, and the number of devices emitting similar radiation. One solution is to use equipment that complies with requirements, such as those on the National Security Administration (NSA) approved list. The NSA prohibits publication of specific risks and methods of penetration, for obvious reasons.

Logging on to a Second Machine. When a network is composed of more than one host machine, logon to a second machine should be authenticated. This can be done through an identification method called Trusted Identification Forwarding. The sending host transmits the user authentication to the receiving host, which verifies that the user is validated for access to its system. This control is transparent to the user. The same type of control can be achieved by a second logon procedure for the second host.

Storage on the System

Files containing passwords have to be secured from unauthorized reading or modification, although passwords must be available for checking when the user signs on. Passwords are stored in files on the system at identifiable physical addresses and are called into main memory when required. These data files are among the most sensitive in the entire computer system and must be protected. No user ID should have read or write access to these files. Only the logon program should have read access; update should be allowed only to the authorized program that changes passwords.

Although these files may be subject to a high level of access control, it may be possible for system programmers and application programmers to bypass the access controls. To prevent passwords from being read, they should be stored in encrypted form on files and in main memory, and should be one-way encrypted so that the original password cannot be decrypted. In this case, when a user logs on to the system, the password is encrypted and compared with the stored encrypted password; the memory containing the clear text password should be erased immediately. The user ID and other identifier could be encrypted in the same way. If the system uses a two-way encryption, the key that can be used to decrypt must be kept secure.

JCL (job control language) or other standard command files used to initiate jobs should not be stored on the system with passwords precoded in. (Many microcomputer communication packages can store passwords in an automated sign-on sequence. It is usually impossible to disable it, but users should be instructed not to use it.) If passwords must be in the JCL in procedure libraries, users should blank the password after use and reinput it if necessary. Procedures libraries that contain passwords should be protected from unauthorized access.

All versions of the security files should be protected. Where access authorization tables are set up in source form and then compiled (e.g., CICS), both the source and the executable form should be protected. If the backup version of the security files is not protected, a user could read the passwords to gain unauthorized access to the system. All bypass opportunities should be identified and tightly controlled.

Bypasses

Utilities. Usually the access control software or the operating system provides utilities that can read passwords or access control tables. The use of these utilities should be restricted as much as possible, and logged. The use of dump memory functions should also be restricted. In some security systems, these utilities are surprisingly easy to use.

Turning Off Security Bits. Operating systems can provide opportunities to compromise system security. For example, under IBM's MVS operating system, when a file is password-protected (by OS), the security bit is set on the VTOC (Volume Table of Contents) of the disk on which the file resides. However, this security bit may be turned off using a ZAP utility. This problem has been addressed by IBM in RACF 1.7, but similar bypass opportunities may exist in other systems and should be restricted.

Trojan Horse. Trojan horses are programs that seem to be, or actually are, useful, but that contain extra code that compromises security. They can be used to penetrate controlled systems. They may make it possible for a user with low-level access authority to bypass some controls.

Periodic Revalidation of User IDs

User ID profiles should be revalidated periodically to ensure that invalid users have been removed. Information such as function, address, and phone number can be revalidated by sending confirmations to users, who approve the information and send it to the SA. User IDs for which the confirmation is not returned within a specified time should be suspended from the system. Information can be matched with files in the personnel department. Special privileges should be reviewed periodically to ensure that users have not been granted unnecessary attributes.

CHAPTER **32**

Access Control Software

ACF2

ACF2 is a logical access control facility designed to restrict and monitor access to computer resources in the IBM OS/VS, OS/MVS, and VM operating systems. All data defined to ACF2 is protected by default. The software controls access to the system and data files, logs events to IBM's System Management Facility (SMF), and provides management with information for validating the appropriateness of access and following up on unauthorized access attempts.

In addition to restricting and monitoring access, ACF2 supports individual accountability. In a well-controlled EDP environment, authorized users are assigned unique logonids (user IDs) to access the system. Each logonid has a password associated with it for verification. Security limitations and authorizations are based on information contained in each logonid record, combined with access rules stored in the ACF2 control data base.

Access to data sets and system resources, such as CICS (Customer Information Control System) and IMS (Information Management System) transactions, is controlled by rules that govern whether access is allowed, allowed and logged, or prevented and logged. If no rule is defined, access is denied. All failed data set access attempts are logged by ACF2 in the system's SMF files.

Program and data file security procedures are examined in an ACF2 environment through review and evaluation of:

- The overall access control environment.
- The appropriateness of logonid records.
- The appropriateness of data file access rules.
- The appropriateness of resource access rules.
- Administrative procedures that ensure the continued and proper operation of access control procedures.

Figure 32-1 illustrates the processing flow of ACF2.

The ACF2 Control Environment

ACF2 Field Definition Record (ACFFDR) and Global System Option (GSO) records are used by each installation to customize its control environment, thereby satisfying individual requirements. ACFFDR is a set of macro instructions that are needed to initialize the ACF2 subsystem; GSO records are maintained using an on-line facility that permits selection of operational and performance-related options.

The ACFFDR is a module generated from a series of ACF2 macros that

FIG. 32-1
ACF2 processing flow

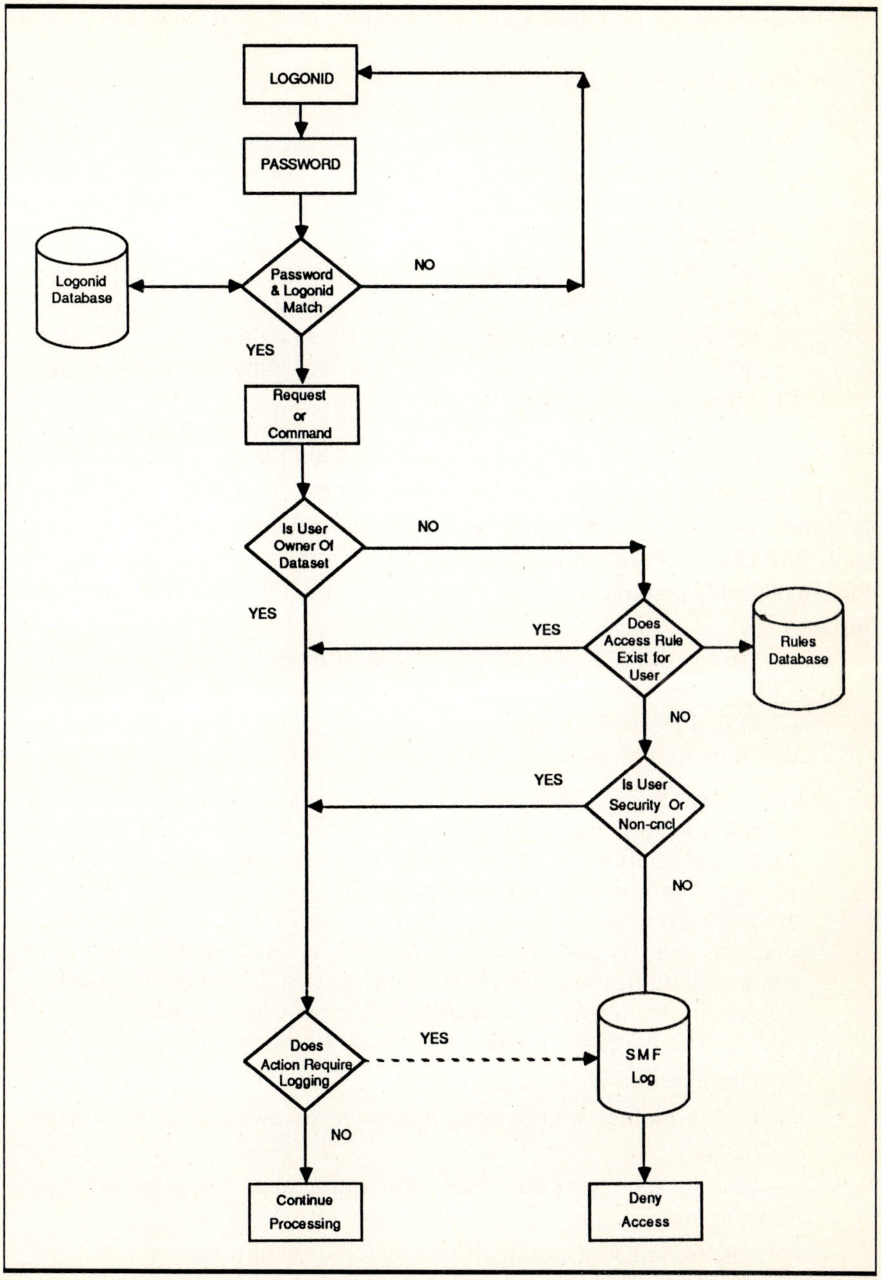

define the fields contained in the logonid record and specify initialization options of the system.

Key macros of potential audit significance are:

- *@CFDE (Create Field Definition Entry).* Collectively, these entries define the record layout of the logonid record; individually, each entry defines one field on the record and the privilege class granted authority to alter the content of the field. The auditor should evaluate the appropriateness of the privilege class granted to users for each significant field.
- *@SMF.* This macro specifies the default SMF record number to be used for ACF2 SMF recording. These records are processed by ACF2 report generators. Since all ACF2 audit trails are journaled to SMF, the auditor should review the recording procedures and the integrity of the SMF files.

GSO records define most ACF2 system-wide options. Using the ACF2-provided on-line facility, the system administrator can modify the setting of an option at any time and can request the console operator to dynamically apply the change. Since those options determine how ACF2 operates, the auditor should examine them to determine whether they have any audit impact.

Key options in the GSO records of potential audit significance are:

- *GSO BLPPGM Record*—Used to identify programs authorized to use tape bypass label processing.
- *GSO EXITS Record*—An ACF2 facility that allows an installation to insert local code into the normal processing flow. There are 17 local exit locations in the standard ACF2 package that can be activated through the EXITS option. If user exits are activated, special care must be taken to review them. While exits may perform valid system checks or provide accounting information to the installation, they can also circumvent ACF2 security. Weak control in this area can compromise the security afforded by ACF2. The auditor should review exits to ensure that:
  - —The function of the exit is valid.
  - —The assembler source code has been reviewed by a responsible official.
  - —The storage locations of the exit source and object modules are protected.
  - —Amendments to exits can take place only in a secure environment.

- *GSO LOGPGM Record*—Identifies programs that have unrestricted access to data sets and require an audit trail to enable use to be monitored. The auditor should inquire about the reasons for including programs in this macro and, more important, whether there are any other sensitive programs that should be included and whether the use of these programs is reviewed and approved by a responsible official. AMASZAP and IMASZAP (SuperZAP) are specified as logged programs by the ACF2 default option. However, the auditor should ensure that the data sets containing these programs are adequately protected; if they are not, it may be possible to copy, rename, and make unauthorized use of these programs.
- *GSO MAINT Record*—Specifies a maintenance environment to ACF2. When a specified program, resident in a specified library, is executed by a specified logonid, ACF2 rules validation is bypassed. This is normally used for disk maintenance programs; it avoids rule access overhead and the great number of SMF records created by these highly active programs. Since these combinations of logonids, programs, and libraries are authorized without checking rules and logging records, the auditor should ensure that the programs identified do in fact perform only valid maintenance functions.
- *GSO OPTS Record*—Specifies many of the ACF2 options, and thus is one of the more important records for audit purposes. The more significant options follow:
  - —*BLPLOG*—Specifies whether tape bypass label access should produce an ACF2 logging record.
  - —*CHANGE*—Specifies whether the %CHANGE authorization in the access rules is to be active. If YES is specified, additional review of the %CHANGE entry in the rule sets must be done.
  - —*DFTLID*—Assigns a default logonid to jobs entering the system that do not have an ACF2 logonid specified in the JCL (job control language). Since any job entering a system without the logonid specified would be flushed, it is important to create a default ID, especially during implementation. Once the ACF2 environment is stable and all jobs have logonids, an installation may eliminate the default logonid. The auditor should review how jobs with the default logonid are monitored.
  - —*INFOLIST (SECURITY, AUDIT/authority list)*—Defines the logonid authority required to list GSO records, entry lists, shift/zone records, and scope lists.
  - —*MAXVIO*—Specifies the maximum number of security violations allowed in a single job or TSO session before ACF2 will terminate the entire job or session.

— *MODE*—Defines the action ACF2 should take as it relates to data set access. The five modes are QUIET, LOG, WARN, ABORT, and RULE. Unless an installation is in the process of implementing ACF2, this should always be ABORT.

— *STC*—Specifies whether ACF2 is to monitor data set accesses by started tasks. This should be YES; otherwise, started tasks will be allowed to access any file without regard to ACF2 rule or security specifications.

— *TAPEDSN*—Specifies whether ACF2 is to protect tapes on volumes at a data set level. The default of NO would provide no ACF2 protection for these tape volumes.

— *UADS*—Specifies whether the TSO User Attribute Data Set (UADS) should continue to be used for account and procedure information. Since UADS often duplicates ACF2 data and makes maintenance more cumbersome, it is a better control to bypass UADS.

- *GSO PPGM Record*—Defines the set of APF (authorized program facility)-authorized programs that bypass system integrity features of the operating system and therefore bypass the security systems. These programs can be executed only by users whose logonid record has an unlimited scope (security officer) or is noncancellable (NON-CNCL). ACF2 has supplied this macro with defaults of three program patterns: IBM's IEHD and DRWD and Innovation's Fast Dump Restore (FDR). Thus, all programs starting with these three patterns are authorized to bypass security. The auditor should review which programs are included and should ascertain that all backup programs are included and that no unauthorized programs are included.

— *GSO PSWD Record*—Defines the various user password options and controls.

— *ENCRYPT*—Specifies which password encryption algorithm ACF2 uses for encrypting user passwords.

— *MAXTRY*—Defines the maximum number of attempts that the TSO logon validation routine will allow before the line is disconnected. This number should be less than 10.

— *MINPSWD*—Sets minimum number of characters for a new password. This number should be at least 6.

— *PASSLMT*—Sets a maximum number of invalid password attempts allowed in a single day. After that number has been reached, ACF2 will deny all accesses to the system by the logonid. This number should be less than 10.

— *PSWDALT*—Is set to YES if users may change their own password at system entry time.

— *PSWDJES*—Specifies whether invalid passwords entered through batch jobs should be counted towards the invalid password limit in a single day (i.e., update the PSWD-VIO count in the logonid record).

Controlling Access to the Computer System

Authorization of system access may be controlled in four ways: (1) logonid records; (2) entry control settings (i.e., specific terminals authorized for specific logonids); (3) shift settings (i.e., access is permitted only at certain predefined times); and (4) submission paths (i.e., specific tasks must be initiated from a predefined authorized library and calling program).

All users are validated on entry to the system by ACF2. This validation takes place during TSO logon, JES2 JCL conversion processing, JES3 input services processing, or similar on-line system logon. Optionally, this validation can control CICS, IMS, or IDMS sign-on. ACF2 facilities provide for a common user identification for all environments. System users need to be defined only once, regardless of the combination of subsystems they are authorized to use (e.g., TSO, IMS, batch). Validation consists of matching a user-supplied logonid and password with the appropriate logonid record and password stored in the ACF2 logonid data base.

Logonid Record. Each system user should be identified to ACF2 by a unique logonid that defines the user's privileges (such as the ability to use CICS or TSO), the user's system history (such as the number of security violations to date), the user's TSO attributes, and other ACF2 system-related information.

User Identification String. ACF2 uses a "pseudo field" called the User Identification (UID) string. It allows the installation to add pertinent information such as department, job responsibility, employee ID number, or other data necessary for monitoring and defining system access.

The UID string is used to identify individual users or groups of users in writing rules for access to data and resources. The UID string, which is typically a character string longer than the logonid, is not used to log on to the system. The UID string shown in Figure 32-2 consists of four installation-defined fields plus the user's logonid. The advantage of the UID string is that it can be used to define subsets of users in ways that the logonid cannot.

Attributes. Attributes are assigned to individual logonids to control the users' abilities. A number of sensitive attributes carry special power and

FIG. 32-2
Specimen user identification (UID) string

```
                          NA0644CLTPTH
                          •••  •  •
New York ________________ •••  •  •
Audit ____________________ ••  •  •
06 (department) ___________ •  •  •
44 (function code) ___________ •  •
CLTPTH (logonid) _________________ •
```

should not be assigned indiscriminately. No logonid should have all attributes, and SECURITY, ACCOUNT, and AUDIT attributes should be mutually exclusive.

Users whose logonids have the following attributes should be identified:

- *SECURITY*—The SECURITY privilege identifies a user as a security officer with the authority to insert, change, list, and delete access rules. Simply by adding rules, anyone with this attribute can access all data without a violation report. However, any access granted by the SECURITY privilege can be restricted through a scope limitation.
- *ACCOUNT*—The ACCOUNT privilege provides the ability to add, delete, or change logonid records within the limits defined by the user's scope. ACCOUNT managers may be given this authority in order to establish, maintain, and/or delete logonid records for their own departments.
- *AUDIT*—The AUDIT privilege allows a user to list logonid records, data file rules, generalized resource rules, entry records, shift/zone records, scope lists, and GSO records.

Other Fields. Several other fields of the logonid record grant special privileges and have major effects on ACF2 validaton procedures. Examples of those fields are:

- *CANCEL, SUSPEND, MONITOR, PSWD-EXP, TRACE, and TSO-TRC*—Used to temporarily or permanently remove a user's privilege to access the system and to produce special audit trails and/or reports of activities.
- *MAINT*—Allows a user any type of access to a data set without logging if executing a specific program from a specific library. Otherwise, the access is subject to normal ACF2 validation.

- *MAXDAYS*—Identifies the maximum number of days allowed between password changes before ACF2 "expires" the password and forces a change. This value can be different for each user and should be a smaller number for those users with more powers (such as security administrator) to help prevent passwords from being discovered.
- *MINDAYS*—Defines the minimum number of days that a newly changed password must remain active before the user may change it. One use may be to keep users from changing their password and then changing back to the old one immediately.
- *NON-CNCL*—Allows a user or batch job any type of access to a data set or resource, despite any access violations.
- *PROGRAM*—Specifies the APF-authorized program that must be used to submit jobs for this logonid. Proper use of this "program-pathing" facility also requires that this logonid be defined with the RESTRICT and SUBAUTH attributes.
- *PSWD-DAT, PSWD-VIO, SEC-VIO, SHIFT, ZONE*—Include information on the violations incurred by the user, allowable access time periods, and time zone definitions.
- *RESTRICT*—Specifies a restricted logonid for production use. This logonid does not require a password for user verification. Jobs submitted under this logonid are logged.
- *SCPLIST*—Specifies the name of the scope record that restricts accesses for the user.
- *SOURCE, CICS, IDMS, IMS, JOB, TSO*—Identify subsystems from which the user can execute jobs or enter the system.
- *TAPE-BLP*—Indicates that the user may use full Bypass Label Processing (BLP) when accessing tape data sets. When the user has the TAPE-BLP privilege and is accessing tape through BLP, ACF2 allows the access. Because the user can possibly bypass data set validation and read any tape, this privilege should be tightly controlled.
- *TAPE-LBL*—Indicates that the user has Limited Bypass Label (LBL) Processing authority when using tapes. When A BLP access request is made under this privilege, ACF2 validates the actual volume serial number written on the tape label (if available) and validates any data set name (DSN) specified in the JCL.

Entry Control Setting. If desired by management, logonid access can be restricted to certain logical input devices. Entry control settings are used by CICS and IMS to control the source of transaction processing.

SCOPE Record. A SCOPE record can restrict the access granted to a user by any logonid attribute. A SCOPE record becomes effective for a given user when it is specified in that user's logonid record (in the SCPLIST field). The SCOPE facility is especially useful to restrict access granted to a security or account administrator.

SHIFT/ZONE Record. A SHIFT record can be used to define the specific days, dates, and/or times of day at which accesses can be made. A ZONE record specifies a time-zone adjustment value, which is used when SHIFT records are processed.

Submission Paths. Certain production jobs are critical, either because of the sensitivity of data being processed or the impact of the processing. ACF2 makes it possible to limit the submission path of such jobs. For example, a production job may be executed only from a restricted library.

Data Set Access Control

The principle of data set access control is that all data sets are owned by a user and, by default, are protected against use by everyone except the owner. For other users to gain access to these data sets, it is necessary to establish a set of rules that associates a logonid with permitted access levels.

Rules for Access. Each logonid is prefixed by an "owner data set prefix." ACF2 uses this prefix to determine whether access to a data set is allowed. Initially, ACF2 compares this prefix with the high-level index (the characters in the data set name before the first period) of the data set being accessed. If a match occurs, access is automatically allowed. If the prefix and the high-level index do not match (which indicates that user does not own the data set), a search of the rules for that data set takes place to determine which access privileges apply to the UID prefix.

The protection levels that may be defined are READ, WRITE, ALLOCATE (which includes allocation, catalog, scratch, and rename functions), and EXECUTE. The allocated privilege is then processed in one of three ways:

- Allow the request (A).
- Allow the request but write request details to SMF (L).

- Prevent the request and write request details to SMF (P or default).

These rules may be enhanced by checking entry devices, time of day, or program pathing. Only the access level specified in the rule may be used.

Data Set Access Rule Structure. Examples of data set access rules:

Data Set Access Rule	*Description*
$KEY (SYS1) %CHANGE CL1234 CL5678	This rule set applies to SYS1 library. UIDs CL1234 and CL5678 can store, change, or delete this rule set.
PARMLIB READ (P)	Prevents users from reading SYS1. PARMLIB.
PARMLIB UID(CL) SHIFT(NORMAL) (READ) (A) WRITE (L)	During normal hours, users with UIDs beginning with "CL" can read without logging or write to SYS1.PARMLIB with logging.

The auditor should identify key application and system files whose security is important and review the corresponding access rules to ensure that access to such files is adequately controlled.

Generalized Resource Rule Sets. In addition to protecting the system and data set access, ACF2 may be set up to protect other logical resources. Examples of logical resources are account numbers, TSO procedure names, and CICS transaction names.

Resources are grouped logically by TYPE (e.g., TAC = TSO account resource rule sets, CKC = CICS transaction resource rule sets), and each resource is assigned a unique name. Rules are then set up.

Examples of generalized resource rules:

Generalized Resource Rule	*Description*
$KEY (PREDIT) TYPE (CKC)	This rule set applies to the CICS PREDIT transaction.
%CHANGE PRSPRV1234	Only the supervisor of payroll (PRSPRV1234) may change the rule.

Generalized Resource Rule	*Description*
PREDIT UID(PR) ALLOW	Allows payroll department staff (UID string starts with "PR") to use PREDIT transaction.

ACF2 Reports

ACF2 produces various reports that assist in monitoring access controls and facilitate follow-up procedures for security violations. A brief description of the reports provided by ACF2 follows. Note that even when the installation does not produce these reports, they can still be executed for audit purposes.

- ACFRPTDS—Data Set/Program Event Log.
- ACFRPTEL—Information Storage Update Log. The ACFRPTEL report provides a listing of all changes to the Information Storage Facility data base, including entry lists, resource rule sets, SCOPE lists, and Shift or Zone records.
- ACFRPTJL—Restricted Logonid Job Log.
- ACFRPTLL—Logonid Modification Record.
- ACFRPTNV—The Environment Report. The ACFRPTNV report generator produces loggings of each START (S ACF2), STOP, or PURGE (P ACF2) operator command issued. This report generator also produces logging of system initial program loads (IPLs) and possible losses of SMF data.
- ACFRPTPW—Invalid Password/Authority Log.
- ACFRPTRL—Rule/ID Modification Log. This log lists all updates to the access rule data base.
- ACFRPTRX—Logonid Access Report. This utility reports all data set access rules or generalized resources rules that apply to a specific logonid or UID string.
- ACFRPTSL—Selected Logonid List. This utility provides a listing of all logonid records that match the set of selection criteria specified in the JCL parameters.
- ACFRPTXR—Cross Reference Report. This utility, which is the most useful to the auditor, determines which users have access to a specified data set or generalized resources, based on standard ACF2 security controls.

The auditor should ensure that required reports are produced on a regular basis and that the security administration group follows up the violations and changes adequately.

RACF

The Resource Access Control Facility (RACF) is an access control system developed by IBM for use on its mainframes running under the MVS and VM operating systems. It was first released in the early 1970s.

The security needs of companies vary widely. In some companies, "good" security over the payroll and personnel master files is adequate, while in other companies, due to trade secrets and so forth, security must be very strict. RACF was designed to accommodate various situations. To be RACF-protected, every resource must have a RACF user as an owner. Typically, the owner of a protected resource is the individual user or group of users (i.e., department) responsible for the resource. For example, the owner of the payroll master file will most likely be the payroll/personnel department. A resource owner can exercise absolute power over an owned resource. Therefore, it would be inappropriate for someone in data processing to be the owner of production data sets. It is possible for an owner to have no access to the resource.

An access control system is of little value to an organization if accountability and auditability of resource access is not complete. RACF provides a complete loggging and reporting facility to meet this need. When RACF is appropriately implemented, it is difficult to circumvent.

A security system is only as reliable as the operating system of the host computer, the security profiles, the options implemented when the system was installed, and the monitoring function subsequent to installation. It is these areas that may be of concern to auditors. The best software provides no security if it is not appropriate for a particular site. Auditors may need an understanding of the functions and selected options of RACF.

Operation of RACF

RACF allows the installation to control access to the computer system by controlling:

- *Groups*—A group of similar users.
- *Users*—Those who can use the system.
- *Resources*—Programs, data, and terminals.
- *Access authorities*—How each user can access the resources.

An overview of the RACF access model is presented in Figure 32-3.

A data security administrator creates records called "profiles" that are referenced by RACF to determine who can use which resource. These profiles are maintained in the RACF data set. RACF uses these profiles to

FIG. 32-3

Overview of the RACF access model

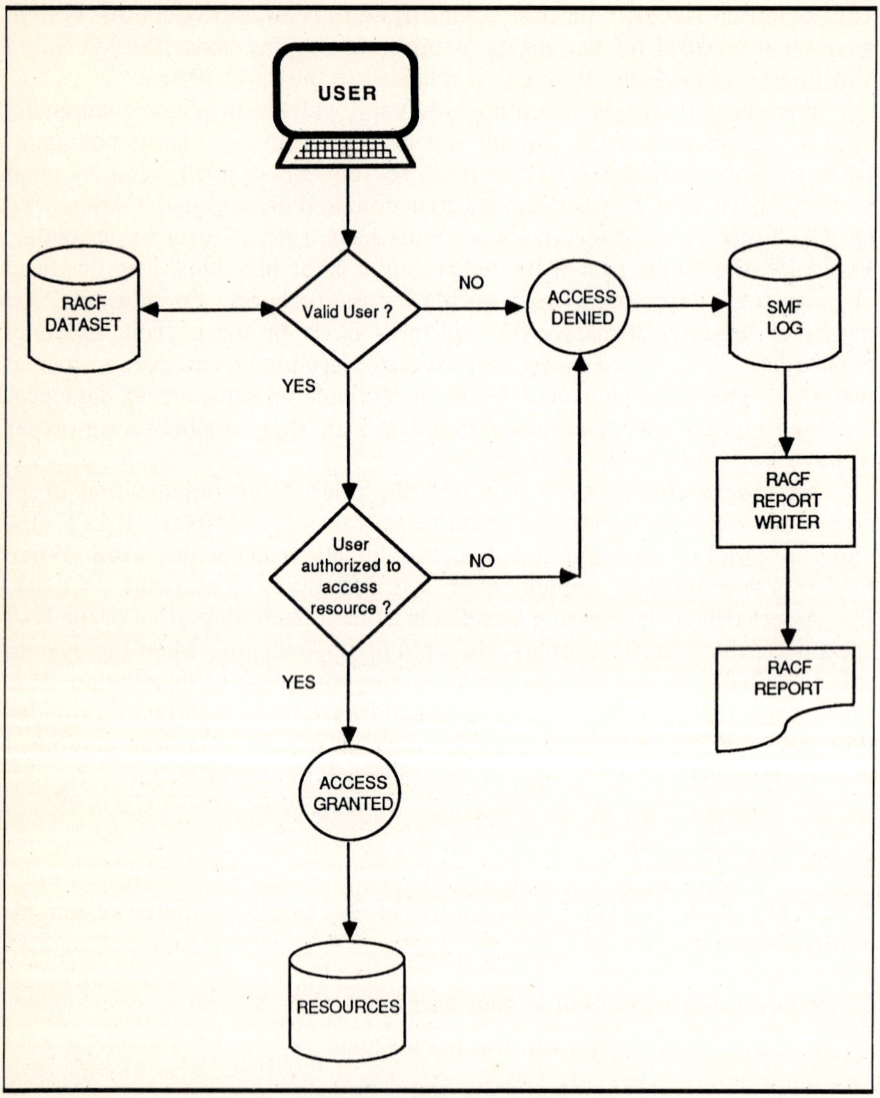

identify the user during logon and to grant or deny authority when a user wishes to access a resource or update the RACF data set. Resources defined to RACF are referred to as RACF-protected resources. Resources not defined to RACF are not protected by RACF, which does not issue a warning that such resources are not protected.

Whether access to a particular resource is allowed depends on the RACF profile for both the accessing user and the resource to which access is requested. If either the user profile or the resource profile indicates that access is not to be allowed, access will not be allowed. The quality of protection afforded by RACF depends directly on the quality of the security profiles established by the installation.

RACF provides for accountability of the use of RACF-protected resources through its logging and reporting features. RACF writes records to SMF files for authorized and unauthorized accesses to the system and RACF-protected resources. Also, SMF logging can occur when the RACF profiles are changed. RACF has a parameter-driven report writer (RACFRW) that allows the security administrator or auditor to extract selected data from SMF logs to produce reports on system and resource use and violations.

Organizational Considerations

Effective implementation of RACF requires three functions for proper execution and monitoring. These organizational functions are:

1. *Security administrator*. The security administrator controls the day-to-day functioning of RACF, including addition, modification, and deletion of RACF security profiles. The security administrator has the ability to issue any RACF command.
2. *System software specialist*. The system software specialist is responsible for the technical maintenance of RACF, including performance tuning of RACF through placement of the RACF data set, coding and implementation of the RACF installation exits, and placement of certain RACF-protected resources.
3. *Auditor*. The RACF auditor is responsible for monitoring accesses to sensitive protected resources and the activity of certain users, such as the security administrator and system software specialist. The auditor also can log and report resource accesses and user activity and violations.

RACF can support centralized or decentralized security organizations. A centralized security organization is usually composed of a single security administrator, two or three backup security administrators, two or three system software specialists, and auditors. Their responsibility includes all users and protected resources. In contrast, a decentralized security organization is characterized by delegation of some security administration duties to the group level. A group is a collection of users with common responsibilities and access needs. Group security administrators take on the day-to-day duties of security administration for group resources. In addition, there may be a need for a group system software specialist and a group auditor. Their responsibility is restricted to the group.

Control Over Access

A computerized access control system should adequately control access to the resources defined to it. RACF controls access to defined resources using a resource profile, which defines both general and specific rules governing access to that resource. The user or group profile and resource profile determine whether access is to be allowed to the resource. RACF can also perform logging and statistics-gathering for later reporting.

Merely controlling access to the system is not sufficient to provide an adequate level of control. The following aspects must be considered in conjunction with limiting access:

- *Individual accountability*. A security system must be able to positively associate a job or transaction with the person (or department for a production job) initiating the activity. RACF provides for a unique identifier (user ID) for all users that access the system. This enables attempted and unauthorized access to be tracked to a particular individual so that appropriate follow-up action may be taken.
- *Auditability*. Regular audit trails and reports of who accessed which resource should be produced. Specific reports regarding maintenance of the security system can be produced using the RACF report writer. In addition, the RACF report writer can be used to report both successful and unsuccessful resource access attempts. Exactly what data is available to be reported is a function of the options specified when RACF was installed. Unless the appropriate logging and statistic-gathering options are active, the information needed for an adequate audit trail will not be available. These logging and statistics options can be activated at any time without re-installing RACF.

Installation-Defined Options

RACF allows the installation to specify certain processing options that apply to all RACF operations. Since these options determine how RACF operates, the auditor may want to examine them to determine any audit impact. The RACF security administrator is responsible for maintaining this environment and documenting any changes to it. To obtain information about the RACF environment, it is useful to print the "SETROPTS LIST" report, which can be obtained by entering the RACF command SETROPTS LIST. The installation-defined options include:

- Definitions of the types of resources that can be protected by RACF (i.e., disk (DASD) data sets, tape volumes, IMS transactions).
- Option to log RACF events.
- User ID and password rules governing password syntax, mandatory password change criteria, and optional revoking of passwords.
- A global access checking feature that can be used to increase efficiency.
- An option to allow or deny universal access to terminals.
- An opinion to allow automatic protection of any data set created by a user.

Installation Exits

Installation exits provide the means to customize RACF to suit a particular operating environment. An installation exit is a point in processing where the normal program processing may be exited and installation-specific and installation-written "own code" processing performed. Usually, control returns to the RACF calling program. While the points in processing where an exit may be given control are fixed by IBM, the processing performed is up to the installation. Since the RACF installation exits execute as an integral part of RACF, they can be used to provide additional security checks or to bypass RACF security checking entirely.

The auditor concerned with RACF should pay special attention to the appropriateness of active RACF installation exits and ensure that:

- The function of the exit is valid.
- The assembler source code has been tested and reviewed by a responsible official.
- The libraries in which the exit source and object modules reside are protected.
- Amendments to exits can only take place in a controlled manner.

While installation exits may perform valid system checks or provide accounting information to the installation, they can also be used to circumvent RACF security. Weak control in this area can seriously degrade the security afforded by RACF.

RACF Access Controls

RACF uses the concepts of authorized users and protected resources to control access to the computer system, data files, tables, and libraries. Users are defined in RACF by user profiles. Group profiles and connect profiles are additional types of user profiles that can be associated with one or more users that make up a group.

Resources are separated into two categories for definition purposes—disk data set and other system resources:

- Disk data sets consist of all data files, program libraries, and system libraries residing on disk volumes. Disk data sets are defined to RACF using data set profiles.
- Other system resources consist of disk volumes, tape volumes, terminals, CICS transactions, IMS transactions, and so forth. Other system resources are defined to RACF using resource profiles.

Based on the collective contents of the user profiles, data set profiles, and resource profiles, RACF can be configured to grant or deny access requested by a user to a system resource. RACF can also restrict certain users to certain terminals.

Defining RACF Users

All users requesting access to RACF-protected resources must be positively identified and verified by RACF; therefore, all users must be defined to RACF by a user profile. Each user profile is owned by another RACF user profile. The owner can modify and delete his own user profiles and can also disable user IDs. RACF users may be assigned certain user attributes that confer special abilities within RACF. The user attributes, which are contained on the user profile, should be assigned to enhance separation of duties. User attributes are described in the following table.

Attribute	*Description*
NONE	Defines the user as having no special authority to override the access level specified in the resource profiles. This means that unless permission for access to a protected resource is explicitly or implicitly given by definition in the resource profile, the user is not able to access that resource.
AUDITOR	Grants authority to request logging to the SMF file as follows: • Log all uses of certain RACF commands that can change RACF security. • Log all accesses or selected accesses to specified data sets. • Log RACF commands issued by selected users. The AUDITOR attribute gives the user the authority to monitor successful and/or unsuccessful attempts and to list the RACF data set and/or RACF-protected resources by using the RLIST, LISTDSD, and LISTUSER commands. The auditor can also change the AUDIT/NOAUDIT parameter.
OPERATIONS	Allows a user to copy, rename, catalog, reorganize, and scratch data sets that are protected by RACF.
SPECIAL	Allows a user to issue all RACF commands. This gives the user full control over all RACF profiles in the RACF data set. This attribute should be limited to RACF security administrators, whose activities should be monitored by the RACF auditor.
GRPACC	Automatically authorizes all users in the group of a user with GRPACC authority to have UPDATE access authority to any group data sets that user defines to RACF. This authority is a control concern, since a user with GRPACC authority could allow unauthorized groups of users to update data sets.
REVOKE	Prevents a user from logging on to the system even though the user profile is still defined. This can provide control by disabling a user ID for a user who has left the installation. However, if a user is the owner of resources, the user profile cannot be deleted until the resources are assigned to another owner.

FIG. 32-4
Specimen RACF user profile

```
LISTUSER   IBMUSER

USER = IBMUSER     NAME = I.B.GOOD              OWNER = IBMUSER          CREATED - 79.151
 DEFAULT - GROUP = SYS1
 ATTRIBUTES = SPECIAL OPERATIONS REVOKED
 LAST - ACCESS = 83.334/08:32:06
 CLASS AUTHORIZATIONS = NONE
 INSTALLATION - DATA - D1CBKD              IBM SPECIAL USER ID
 NO-MODEL-NAME
  GROUP = SYS1        AUTH = CREATE        CONNECT-OWNER = IBMUSER     CONNECT-DATE = 79.151
   CONNECTS=          17 UACC=READ           LAST-CONNECT = 79.173/08:32:06
   CONNECT ATTRIBUTES = NONE
  GROUP = VSAMDSET  AUTH = CREAT         CONNECT - OWNER = IBMUSER   CONNECT-DATE = 79.151
   CONNECTS=             00 UACC=READ      LAST - CONNECT = UNKNOWN
   CONNECT ATTRIBUTES = NONE
  GROUP - SYSCTLG     AUTH = CREATE        CONNECT - OWNER = IBMUSER   CONNECT-DATE = 79.151
   CONNECTS =            00    UACC=READ     LAST - CONNECT = UNKNOWN
   CONNECT ATTRIBUTES = NONE
```

Attribute	*Description*
ADSP	Stands for "Automatic Data Set Protection." All permanent data sets created by this user are protected by RACF. This is accomplished by creating a data set profile in the RACF data set with a universal access of "NONE."
CLAUTH	Allows a user to define profiles in one or more of the RACF resource classes. This capability is known as "class authorization" and is useful when certain users are responsible for maintaining RACF profiles in a restricted number of resource classes. For example, data resource management personnel frequently need to be able to manipulate RACF disk and tape volume profiles. These users would be assigned class authorization to the DASDVOL and TAPEVOL classes, rather than the SPECIAL user attribute.

When reviewing user profiles, the auditor should ensure that the assignment of user attributes and class authorizations is reasonable and proper. Figure 32-4 illustrates a user profile.

RACF User Groups

Each RACF user is a member of at least one RACF group. RACF group IDs may be listed as user profile owners and entered in resource profile user access lists instead of user IDs. Users belonging to the group automatically have access to all resources for which the group ID is listed in the resource profile user access list. Users may belong to more than one group, thereby expanding their scope of potential access ability. However, a user may be an active member of only one group during a given session. A user who is an active member of the group is considered "connected to" the group. At system access (LOGON) time, a determination is made as to which group the user will be connected to for that logon session. If the user does not specify a group, he will be connected to a default group, or to the group specified at system access time, if the user is a member of the specified group.

The concept of grouping allows resource profiles to be "owned" by the group in a logical manner. For example, the payroll data set profiles can be "owned" (and therefore controlled) by the payroll department.

Data Set Access Control

All RACF-protected disk data sets are members of the DATASET resource class and are protected by "data set profiles." The data set profile contains an access list that defines user profiles or group profiles that are allowed to access the data set and specifies the level of access granted to each.

Data set protection may be defined in the data set profile by universal access authority (UACC), entry in access list, or both. Universal access authority is a specific level of access that is to be allowed to all users. This level of access is stored permanently in the resource profile.

More specific protection can be implemented by making entries in the data set's profile access list. Under this scheme, an entry is made in the data set profile access list for each specific user or group with the allowed level of access. In most cases, the universal access authority provides an adequate level of access for most users, and the access list contains only a few entries.

It should be noted that an entry in the data set profile access list overrides the universal access authority for that data set. For example, if a user requests UPDATE access to a data set that has a universal access authority of UPDATE, but an entry in that data set profile access list specifies that the requesting user has a lesser level of access (NONE or READ), the requested access will be denied. In the absence of an entry in the data set profile access list for the requesting user or group, the universal access authority specifies the allowed level of access. Figure 32-5 is an example of a data set profile.

Other System Resources—Access Control

RACF provides access control for resources other than data sets. These resources are known as system resources and may include disk (DASD)

FIG. 32-5
Specimen RACF data set profile

```
LISTDSD DATASET('SYS1.VTAMLIB') ALL

INFORMATION FOR DATASET SYS1.VTAMLIB

LEVEL   OWNER     UNIVERSAL ACCESS    WARNING
-----   -----     ----------------    -------
 00     L322SUP        UPDATE            NO

AUDITING
--------
FAILURES (READ)

YOUR ACCESS        CREATION GROUP    DATASET TYPE
-----------        --------------    ------------
 NONE GIVEN             L322            NON-VSAM

GLOBALAUDIT
-----------
   NONE

VOLUMES ON WHICH DATASET RESIDES     UNIT
--------------------------------     ----
              OLDRES                 3380

NO INSTALLATION DATA

CREATION DATE        LAST REFERENCE DATE      LAST CHANGE DATE
-------------        -------------------      ----------------
(DAY)  (YEAR)           (DAY)  (YEAR)            (DAY)  (YEAR)
 107     85              107     85               107     85

ALTER COUNT      CONTROL COUNT      UPDATE COUNT   READ COUNT
-----------      -------------      ------------   ----------
   00000             00000              00000          00000

USER           ACCESS           ACCESS COUNT
----           ------           ------------
L322           ALTER               00000
L321           UPDATE              00000
```

volumes, tape volumes, VTAM or TCAM terminals, and IMS or CICS transactions. Each system resource profile is similar to the data set profile in that a universal access authority may be specified and entries may be made to the resource profile access list. Access controls over system resources are described as follows:

- *DASD volume access controls*—RACF-protected disk volumes are members of the DASDVOL class. Disk volume protection restricts access to the disk volume VTOC (volume table of contents) and other operations performed on a disk volume-wide basis. These activities include initializing the volume or performing a dump to tape.

- *Tape volume access controls*—Many installations keep the majority of their protection data files on tape. RACF can be configured to protect a tape volume. When system-wide tape volume protection is active, RACF performs authorization checking every time a tape volume with a standard IBM or ANSI tape label is accessed, whether or not the tape volume is defined to RACF. There are two significant audit concerns about the quality of RACF protection of tape volumes. First, bypass label processing will bypass RACF protection of the tape volume because the volume serial number is contained in the tape volume label. Second, RACF protects only the tape volume, so that data set level protection is not available on tape. With RACF Release 1.7, files on tape can be protected at the data set level.
- *Terminal access controls*—All VTAM or TCAM terminals are candidates for RACF protection. Terminals can be defined to RACF and accessibility checked at system access time. The RACF profile for terminals can specify a universal access authority and access list for the terminal. This level of protection is valuable when the installation desires to restrict the use of certain terminals to certain users or groups.

Logging RACF Events

RACF events can be logged to the SMF log, provided that SMF record types 80 and 81 are included in the SMFPRM member in SYS1.PARMLIB. All logging by RACF is optional and can be changed by users with authority to do so. The auditor should review the logging options before RACF testing using the RACF Report Writer, since the integrity of the tests depends on the appropriateness of the logging features.

Resource Access Logging

Owners of resources and users with authority to change resource profiles can specify that certain types of access (READ, UPDATE, CONTROL, or ALTER) be logged. The logging options are set in the AUDITING operand on the resource profile.

Any user with the AUDITOR attribute can also set logging options for resources. The options set by the user auditor may be different from those contained in the AUDITING operand. These AUDITOR logging options are contained in the GLOBALAUDIT operand. The user auditor may desire to log accesses to a specific resource as a source of data for audit testing.

Logging Activities of Users

Any user with the AUDITOR attribute can specify the RACE events of a specific user to be logged. The events that are logged include all accesses to resources and all uses of RACF commands except SEARCH, LISTDSD, LISTGRP, LISTUSER, and RLIST. The auditor can monitor the activity of users with RACF control abilities, such as the data security administrator. Because of the volume of data logged, however, consideration should be given to the duration of the logging.

In addition to the ability to audit activities of specified users, there is a system-wide RACF resource option that allows logging of all uses of RACF commands (except SEARCH, LISTDSD, LISTGRP, LISTUSER, and RLIST) for all users.

Logging IMS and CICS Transactions

Since RACF bypasses logging for IMS and CICS transactions, the installation should use the logging features of IMS and CICS to monitor IMS and CICS access violations.

TOP SECRET

TOP SECRET is a security software product designed specifically for MVS/370 and MVS/XA environments. Its primary function is to validate all requests to access various resources under the control of MVS.

In its full operational mode (FAIL), TOP SECRET provides protection by default. This default protection applies to all methods of accessing the system and all data sets resident on disk.

Default protection is effected through the concept of ownership. There can be only one owner of a resource. The owner has total access; non-owners must be granted permission to access the resource. TOP SECRET examines each user's security record to determine whether permission has been granted to access the resource. Any unauthorized access is denied, and the event is logged. Depending on the logging parameters, the violation is written to the SMF and/or the audit/tracking file.

Facilities

TOP SECRET controls access to all facilities in MVS, including BATCH, TSO, CICS, and IMS. Each user of the system must be given explicit authority to use these facilities. Because control has been placed at the facility level, undefined users have been effectively cut off from using the system.

Resources

TOP SECRET can protect various types of resources, including data sets, programs, volumes, and terminals. All resources other than data sets resident on disk are protected by exception. Access authority levels vary with the individual resource. Access levels for a data set include NONE, READ, WRITE, UPDATE, FETCH, CREATE, SCRATCH, CONTROL, and ALL. In addition to this permission, users are permitted or denied access via specific terminals. Common restrictions for all resources also include days of the week, time of day, and expiration date details. File access can be restricted to specific programs coming from designated libraries. The auditor should identify all files of audit significance and ensure that access authority levels granted are adequate.

Modes of Operation

TOP SECRET has four modes of operation. These modes are provided to allow the gradual implementation of the product. The following conditions exist in the various modes:

1. DORMANT—TOP SECRET is active; however, no security checking takes place.
2. WARN—TOP SECRET performs all security checks, issues violation messages to the user, and logs all violations. It does not, however, prevent the user from accessing a resource.
3. IMPLEMENT (IMPL)—TOP SECRET functions as if in FAIL mode for all users that have been defined to the system and as if in mode for all undefined users.
4. FAIL—All users must be defined and all resources are protected.

Unless an installation is in the process of implementing TOP SECRET, the mode should alway be FAIL.

Control Options

TOP SECRET allows the installation to specify certain processing options to apply to all TOP SECRET operations. Since these options determine how TOP SECRET operates, when appropriate, the auditor should examine them to determine any audit impact. The following table lists those options with potentially significant audit implications. The default option is in italics.

Option	*Audit Implications*
ADSP(*YES*/NO)	Automatic Data Set Protection. Causes the RACF bit to be set on all new data sets.
DEFDSN PROT(YES/*NO*)	Determines whether undefined data sets will be protected in WARN and IMPL modes.
BYPASS(jobname/ EVERYJOB)	Allows selected or all job/users to bypass security.
DOWN(NN)	Determines how job initiation will be handled when the TOP SECRET address space is not active.
LOG	Specifies the type of logging that will occur, such as violations, access to resources, or audited events. Also determines whether these events will be recorded on the audit/tracking file, SMF, or both.
ACTIVITY	Requests logging of all activity for all facilities.
VIOL	Requests logging of all violations for all facilities.
ACCESS	Requests logging of resource access and use in all facilities.
SMF	Requests SMF recording of selected events.
INIT	Requests logging of all job/session initiations and terminations.
AUDIT	Requests use of the audit/tracking file.
ALL	Selects all LOG options for all facilities.
NONE	Deactivates all logging, except for violations and audited events in FAIL mode.

Option	*Audit Implications*
MODE(DORMANT/ WARN/IMPL/*FAIL*)	Sets the mode of the entire installation.
NEWPW(MIN = 4, MINDAYS = 1, NR,ID,RS,WARN = 3)	This establishes the rules that will be applied when a user creates a new password. Typically, the option will establish the minimum length (MIN = 4) and that no repeat characters can be used (NR).
PTHRESH(NN)	Determines the number of times a password may be entered incorrectly before the accessor ID (ACID) is suspended.
TAPE(ON/*OFF*/DSN/DEF)	Determines the type of tape protection to be in effect.
ON	Protection for all tapes.
DSN	Security at the data set level.
DEF	Protection only for tapes defined to TOP SECRET.
OFF	Should be used when using external tape management system (TMS or TLMS) to avoid redundant tape security checks.
PROMPT(YES/*NO*)	Forces the user to wait for a prompt before specifying his password, INTSO.
VTHRESH(n,act)	Sets the number of times an on-line user can attempt to access a resource to which he does not have permission before some action is taken. The action will typically cancel the on-line session or notify the security administrator.
FAC	Sets control options for each facility.
MODE	Selects the mode for the facility.
LOG	Selects log options for the facility.
AUDIT	Audits all user activity within the facility.

Accessor IDs

There are four types of accessor IDs (ACIDs) within TOP SECRET. Figure 32-6 illustrates the structure of the TOP SECRET data base and the scope of authority for each type of ACID.

FIG. 32-6
Structure of TOP SECRET data base and scope of authority for each type of accessor ID

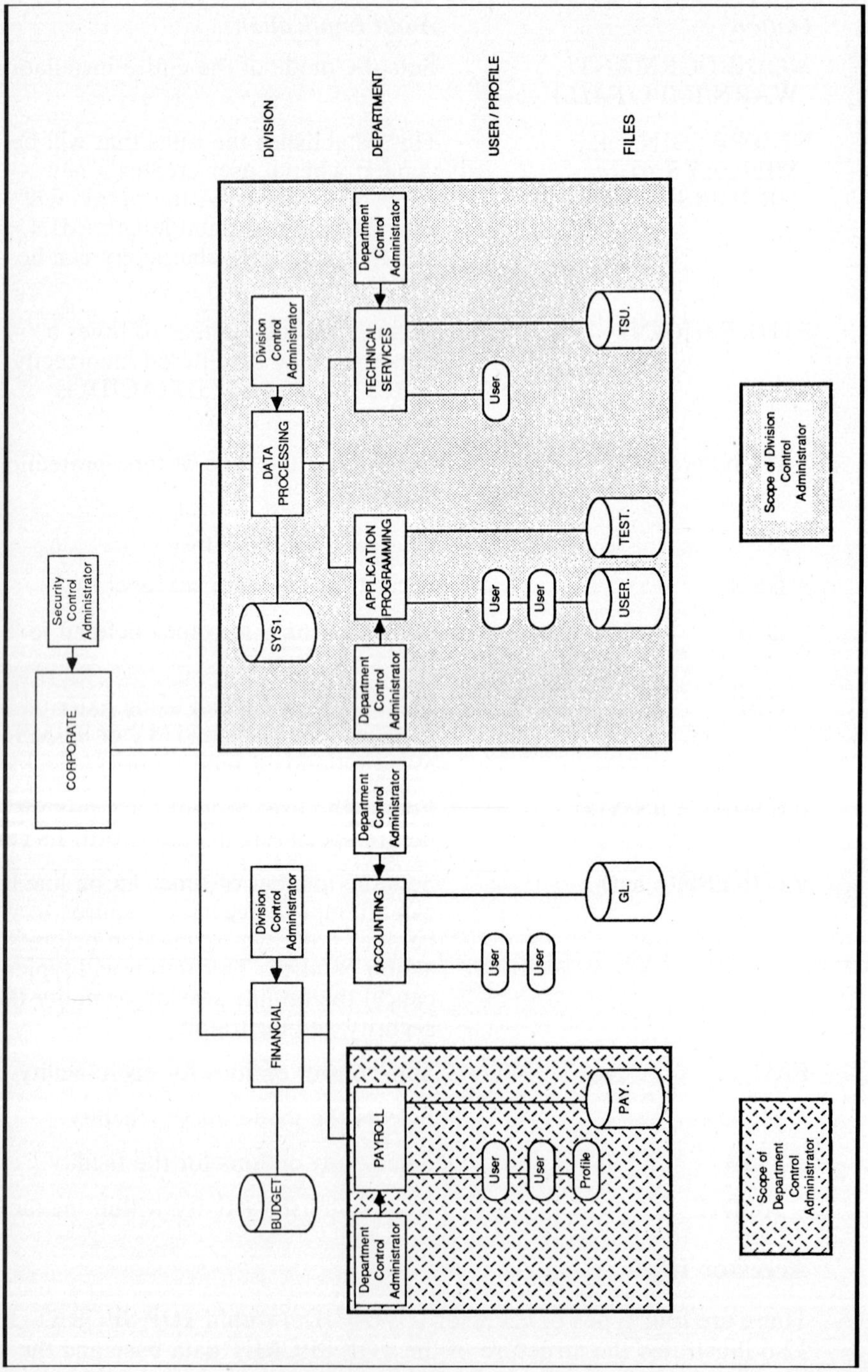

1. *User ACIDs*. Each user of the system must be assigned an ACID. Each ACID has a password that must be entered in conjunction with the ACID in order for the user to sign on to the system. Each ACID has a unique user record associated with it that contains all the permissions and authorities granted to that user.
2. *Profile ACIDs*. Profile ACIDs are similar to user ACIDs in that they contain permissions and access levels to resources. The primary differences are that profile ACIDs do not have a password and cannot sign on to or perform work on the system. Their sole purpose is to provide a place in the security data base where common accesses to resources can be held. These ACIDs are subsequently associated with user ACIDs.
3. *Department/division ACIDs*. The purpose of department/division ACIDs is to provide a basis for the structure of the security data base and a place to define the ownership of resources.
4. *Administrator ACIDs*. Security administrator ACIDs have the ability to modify the security data base. There are four types of administrator ACIDs, each of which has a different scope of authority over the security data base.
   - *MSCA (Master Security Control Administrator)*. The MSCA has total control over the entire security data base. The MSCA can perform all the functions of TOP SECRET. This ability is granted by default.
   - *SCA (Security Control Administrator)*. The SCA's scope of authority is also over the entire security data base. However, the SCA must be granted the authority to perform TOP SECRET functions by the MSCA.
   - *VCA (Divisional Control Administrator)*. The VCA's scope of authority is over the division with which it has been associated. It cannot effect any changes or grant access to resources owned by other divisions or by departments not associate with its division.
   - *DCA (Departmental Control Administrator)*. This administrator has authority over only the department with which it has been associated. It cannot effect changes over any other department within the security data base.

ALL Security Record

The ALL Security Record is essentially a profile containing access rules common to all users.

User Attributes

TOP SECRET has a number of attributes that can be assigned to individual ACIDs. These attributes may allow the individual to circumvent security. When necessary, the auditor should identify users whose ACIDs have the following attributes and ensure that such privileges have been granted appropriately.

Attribute	*Description*
MODE	Each individual ACID may have its own mode (e.g., WARN, DORMANT, FAIL).
NOADSP	This will override the ADSP control option.
NODSNCHK	This allows the user to bypass all security checking for data sets.
NOSUBCHK	This allows a user to submit jobs using an ACID other than his own.
NOVOLCHK	This allows a user to access any volume.
CONSOLE	This parameter allows the ACID to enter TOP SECRET control options through the OS MODIFY command.

Password Controls

To sign on to the system, a user must supply his ACID and a password. By default, passwords expire every 30 days. Users may change passwords voluntarily at any time within the default period. Once changed, a password may not be changed again until the following day. TOP SECRET maintains a history of the user's previous three passwords. When a user changes his password, the previous three passwords may not be used. These two features deter a user from continuously using a favorite password.

TOP SECRET counts the number of times a password is entered incorrectly. Entering the password incorrectly a specified number of times cause the user's account to be suspended. Once an account has been suspended, only an administrator can release the suspension.

TOP SECRET Data Sets

TOP SECRET uses five primary data sets:

1. *The security data base*—Contains all the accesses to facilities and resources under its control.

2. *Parameter file*—Contains global control options.
3. *The audit-tracking file*—An optional on-line file to record all violations that occur while TOP SECRET is active.
4. *The recovery file*—Contains all changes that have been made to the security data base.
5. *The backup file*—Used to hold a copy of the security data base.

Installation Exits

TOP SECRET can be customized through the use of installation exits. An installation exit is a point in processing where the normal program processing may be exited and installation-specific processing performed. When required, the auditor should review such exits to ensure that they are not written to bypass the normal security checking.

Auditing Resources/ACIDs

When the name of a resource field is placed in the AUDIT record, all accesses to the resource cause a record to be written to the audit/tracking and/or SMF file. If the AUDIT attribute is added to an ACID, any activity by that ACID will cause a record to be written.

Reporting Abilities

TOP SECRET has a number of reporting abilities that can be used to assist the auditor in performing an audit of the security environment.

Report	*Description*
TSSAUDIT	A batch program that can be used by the auditor to list changes made to the security file, special privileges issued to ACIDs, and information about authorized program facility (APF) libraries, SVCs, or Program Properties Table (PPT).
TSSUTIL	Used by the auditor to monitor activity on files or ACIDs that are of significant audit concern. This provides a means of generating regular reports to evaluate the security events on critical data sets, ACIDs, or resources.
TSSTRACK	The on-line version of TSSUTIL. It allows the auditor to view events as they are being logged.

Report	*Description*
TSS LIST	Produces an on-line display of the contents of the security data base. This facility enables the auditor to determine whether adequate security exists within the installation.
ACID	Displays a specific ACID (e.g., resources, attached profiles).
ACIDS	Displays all the ACIDs on the security data base.
ALL	Displays the ALL security record.
AUDIT	Displays the AUDIT record.
TSS WHOHAS/TSS WHOOWNS	Two functions; allow the auditor to display the individual who has been designated as the owner of a resource and the individuals who have been given permission to access it. By using this utility, the auditor can immediately determine the extent of security over sensitive files and resources.

APPENDIX **A**

Internal Control Reference Manual—Information Technology Controls

INTRODUCTION

The *Internal Control Reference Manual* (ICRM) was developed by Coopers & Lybrand to assist the auditor in reviewing general, or information technology (IT), controls. The relevant section of the Control Assessment and Record of Tests (CART) normally is completed by an EDP auditor. It can be reviewed using the ICRM, which is also helpful in completing the Record of Control Weaknesses (RCW).

The ICRM is presented here in an edited format to show how general control questions can be addressed. (Appendix B is the "*Internal Control Reference Manual—Application Controls*.") The material discussed in this appendix can be summarized as follows:

- The nature of general controls.
- Appropriateness of evaluation of control procedures.
- Evaluation of answers that indicate lack of control.
- Organization of the ICRM.

THE NATURE OF GENERAL CONTROLS

Two important features of computer systems are:

1. The inclusion of procedures relating to internal control and accounting in computer programs and, as a result, their concentration in the computer department. These procedures are referred to as "programmed procedures."
2. The maintenance of data in the form of computer files in the data processing department that can normally be read only by the computer.

Therefore, the auditor is concerned with the consistent and proper operation of the programmed procedures and the protection of data stored on files.

Controls Over Programmed Procedures

Computer systems use computer programs that incorporate precise instructions for processing. The programmed procedures are of concern to the auditor when they relate to:

- Procedures that would be considered control functions if they were carried out manually; for example, a programmed sequence check and preparation of a list of missing numbers.
- Accounting procedures that ordinarily would be subjected to checking in a noncomputer system; for example, the calculation and preparation of sales invoices or the automatic generation of insurance premium renewals.

Usually, the effective and consistent operation of programmed procedures can be assured by controlling the design, implementation, security, and use of the programmed procedures within MIS. The same assurance might, of course, be achieved by checking the results of processing in the user department. However, the latter method is generally less efficient because of the large volume of data that would have to be checked; indeed this method can be carried out only when the results of each processing step are reported, as they are in the simplest computer systems.

Controls Over Data Files

Information of several types is stored on computer files. The information of particular concern to the auditor includes the following:

- *Transaction data*—Representing individual transactions and the cumulative effect of these transactions (such as the invoice number, invoice date and amount, and the total amount due).
- *Master file data*—Permanent or semi-permanent reference information applicable to many transactions (also called standing data, this includes information such as sales prices, customer name, and account number).
- *Programs*—Programs can serve many purposes and are normally stored in several different forms (such as in a source statement form written by the programmer and in object form as executable programs).

Information stored on computer files normally can be read only through the use of programs designed to print out the contents of a file. The information stored on a file might therefore be changed without visible evidence of the change. The files are normally kept in the custody of computer operations, which is also responsible for their correct use.

Application controls are designed to ensure that authorized data is completely and accurately processed, and that the stored data continues to remain correct. However, unless the results of processing are checked in detail, some reliance must be placed on the security controls within the MIS department to ensure that unauthorized changes are not made to data files.

General Controls

The controls over the design, implementation, security, and use of computer programs and the security of data files are known as general, or IT, controls. Those controls, performed mainly within MIS, are a combination of manual controls and system software. Like other controls, they consist of basic controls and disciplines over basic controls. Generally, they are performed manually by department personnel. When effective general controls exist:

- Appropriate procedures are included in the programs, both when the system originally becomes operational and when changes are made subsequently. These are defined as "implementation controls."
- Unauthorized changes cannot be made to computer programs. These are defined as "program security controls."
- Procedures in computer programs are applied consistently. These are defined as "computer operations controls."
- Unauthorized changes cannot be made to data files. These are defined as "data file security controls."
- System software is properly selected and implemented, and unauthorized changes cannot be made. These are defined as "system software controls."

System Software

System software is a variety of programs that are not specific to any particular application, but may be used in the design, processing, and control of all applications. It includes operating systems, librarian packages, security packages, data base management systems, and communications software. For example, programs may be protected against unauthorized change by program library software; use of the correct files can be assured by software label checks; and the proper processing of jobs depends on procedures included in the operating system and related software. Just as application controls may depend on the consistent and proper operation of application programs, many general controls may depend on the consistent and proper operation of system software. Controls over system software do not affect the application programs and data directly, but rather affect the auditor's ability to rely on the other general controls.

Materiality of Programmed Procedures and Data Files

As part of the review of each application control objective, the auditor should identify significant programmed procedures and data elements. General controls are important insofar as they control the integrity of these programs and data. The auditor should consider at all times the materiality of the programs and data in relation to the control objectives involved.

User-Controlled Systems

The effective operation of manual application controls can provide assurance as to the consistent and proper operation of programmed procedures or protection of data files. For example, if a computer-produced listing of missing prenumbered documents includes the numbers of all documents that should have been processed, together with an indication of those documents that are missing, and the manual application controls include an investigation of missing numbers and a review to determine that all documents sent for processing appear on the listing, then no reliance need be placed on the general controls. This option is usually limited to very simple computer systems.

In simple computer systems, detailed printed reports are available at each stage of processing. All output is directly identifiable with corresponding input. Calculations, summarizations, and categorizations are printed out with supporting detailed information. Exception and rejection reports show accepted and unaccepted items. Master file data is printed out each time it is used. Accordingly, an individual can reperform the processing functions carried out by the computer and can check that data stored on computer files is correct (for example, by performing a one-for-one check of output to input or by manually reperforming calculations). Control over the consistent and proper operation of the programmed procedures therefore can be exercised manually.

If manual application controls are to be relied on rather than general controls, the following elements must be present:

- The manual checking of output must actually be carried out; it is not enough to have the information available for checking.
- The actual checking must cover all significant programmed procedures and data.
- The output that is checked must be produced at an appropriate stage of processing. For example, an edit report cannot be used to check that the update took place properly.
- The manual application controls must be designed to detect significant errors and irregularities that might occur through unauthorized changes in programs, data files, software, or operating procedures.

Most computer systems are not user-controlled but rely on a suitable combination of user controls and general controls. While the consequences of weak user controls are fairly obvious, the consequences of weak general controls are less so. Therefore, there may be a tendency to dismiss such weaknesses without considering their impact. A weakness in general controls can affect all programmed procedures and data files that are not user-controlled. As the general controls are common to all applications, a weakness can have a significant impact on the overall audit plan by affecting many applications.

TECHNICAL COMPUTER KNOWLEDGE REQUIRED

The auditor needs a knowledge of the techniques of computer system development and computer operations in order to understand and audit general controls, just as a knowledge of accounting and manual accounting procedures is necessary to audit manual systems. While auditors cannot be expected to have the technical knowledge and experience required of an EDP auditor or IT audit specialist, those members of the audit team involved in the planning and audit decisions must have an understanding of the audit implications of EDP controls and should be able to recognize the need for technical assistance.

APPROPRIATENESS OF EVALUATION OF CONTROL PROCEDURES

As with other portions of the CART, the auditor completes the general controls section after recording and confirming an understanding of the system.

For general controls, this understanding frequently is recorded following a data processing interview guide, or using a narrative, rather than flowcharts. The confirmation process does not involve a transaction review, as in a manual system, since accounting transactions are not usually involved. Instead, similar review procedures are followed to confirm the understanding of MIS department procedures.

Before evaluating general controls, the auditor should consider whether:

- The programmed procedures and data files involved are material in terms of the control objectives involved.
- The computer systems can be user-controlled and, if so, whether the company relies on user department checks of the system output, general controls, or both.
- Extended substantive testing of the programmed procedures, the data stored on computer files, and/or the final results of processing would be more efficient than evaluating the general and application control procedures, performing tests of controls, and maintaining normal levels of substantive procedures.
- Questions related specifically to the company's particular data processing methods are needed in addition to those in the CART.

These determinations must be made for all applications covered by the general controls.

Efficiency of Extended Substantive Procedures

In some cases, it may be more efficient for the auditor to apply extended substantive procedures, rather than to evaluate the control procedures, perform the necessary tests of controls, and carry out normal levels of substantive tests. The factors to be taken into account (usually by external auditors) are:

- The extent to which there appear to be weaknesses in the general controls or the application controls.
- The nature and significance of the programmed procedures and the data stored on computer files.
- The number of significant programmed procedures and data elements involved.
- The volume of data that needs to be substantiated. This may not be a problem when audit software can be used to assist in the substantiation procedures.
- The extent to which important data, which might be used for audit

purposes, has been destroyed because the company's normal retention period has expired.

- The relative effectiveness, efficiency, and coverage of substantive procedures, including the use of audit software and other computer-assisted audit techniques.
- The possibility of carrying out substantive tests on programmed procedures to ensure that any breakdown in controls has not had an adverse effect on programs and data. The effect of using audit software in this area should be considered.
- The extent to which audit software and other tests can be, or have to be, set up or carried out before year-end.
- The extent to which it is more difficult to perform substantive tests to ensure the completeness of the accounting records as opposed to relying on, and testing, the application controls over completeness.

Supplementary Considerations

An organization may employ unusual or advanced data processing methods. In this case, the auditor may find it appropriate to devise additional questions to supplement the standard questions. The format and style of the questions should be similar to the standard questions and should be drafted by someone with experience in the particular processing methods involved.

Evaluation of "No Control" Answers

The auditor should consider carefully the audit response to a "no control" answer in the CART. It may be helpful to follow these steps:

- Determine whether the effect of the answer is inconsequential.
- If the effect is not inconsequential, determine whether the organization is willing to correct the weakness.
- If the organization will not correct the weakness, consider whether the weakness could give rise to a material error in the financial statements (an external auditor's concern).
- Consider, based on knowledge of the system as a whole, whether other control procedures reduce or eliminate the significance of the answer.
- If the significance is not reduced or eliminated, decide what specific substantive procedures will allow the auditor to determine whether or not the financial statements are materially in error.

Inconsequential Weaknesses

In some cases, the effect of answers that indicate lack of control to the questions in the general controls section of the CART may be so minor that no errors in the programs or data files are likely to occur as a result. For example, this can occur in relation to weaknesses in the system software controls when the system software in use is relatively unsophisticated and the weaknesses are not that widespread. In this circumstance, the auditor may conclude that the most likely result is a failure of the computer system to function at all, rather than for it to produce results containing undetectable errors. The circumstances should be explained on the questionnaire in the space provided. The assessment of the adequacy of the general controls would then disregard such answers.

Corrected Weaknesses

If the auditor concludes that the effect is not inconsequential, the possibility of corrective action should be discussed with the organization. If the organization is willing to correct the control weakness, the auditor may be able to reduce the overall audit time by delaying tests of controls until the corrective action has been taken. For example, if the organization has not properly retested the unchanged portions of modified systems but agrees to carry out the testing before the end of the year (to include assurance that any errors discovered have not distorted previous processing results), the auditor can delay testing in this area until the control has been installed.

Possibility of Significant Errors or Irregularities

If the organization does not take corrective action, the auditor should consider carefully whether significant error can arise. For this purpose, the word "error" refers to unintentional mistakes made in processing. It includes mathematical or clerical mistakes in, and omissions from, the underlying records and data. The word error does not refer to mistakes in financial statements arising from misappropriations of assets related to internal control weaknesses. The word error also does not refer to intentional distortions of financial statements, such as deliberate misrepresentations by management or misappropriation of assets arising from circumvention of the company's system of internal control. The latter kinds of misstatements are referred to as "irregularities."

Thus, errors arise because of the absence of, or weaknesses in, internal control procedures, while irregularities arise from a circumvention or overriding of the system of internal control. Accordingly, the auditor's evaluation of internal control and reperformance of tests of controls may help to reveal errors that may be present. Substantive procedures, including those procedures carried out on programmed procedures and other data available within the EDP function, are more likely to identify irregularities that may have occurred.

To determine whether or not material error can arise, the auditor must first consider the effect of the weakness on the programmed procedures or data elements at risk. These are the same programmed procedures and data identified in each application control objective as not being checked in detail by the user.

Weaknesses in the different areas of general controls have different effects on the programmed procedures and data as follows:

- Weaknesses in the implementation controls may cause new systems or systems that have been modified to function incorrectly. Often, such errors are imbedded in the system, and erroneous processing will continue until the error is identified and corrected.

- Weaknesses in the program security controls generally mean that unauthorized changes can be made to the system, so that changes can be made that are not subject to the normal implementation controls just discussed. Since the organization may not be sure which systems have been changed and which have not, opportunities for misappropriation of assets are increased.

- Weaknesses in the computer operations controls generally mean that random errors may occur in the system. While some errors, such as those in master file data, may have a lasting effect, the main effect of these weaknesses is similar to that of weaknesses in a noncomputer system: Most processing is correct but occasionally it is not. This contrasts with the continuous errors arising from implementation control weaknesses, as discussed previously.

- Weaknesses in the data file security controls generally mean that unauthorized changes can be made to stored data. The time taken to discover these unauthorized changes depends largely on the structure of the application controls. Some errors in transaction data may be discovered fairly quickly through the operation of control accounts or through the mailing of statements. If the system is a payment one, however, the error may never be picked up (for example, incorrect overpayment of pensions or suppliers). Errors in master file data usually take longer to detect. Weaknesses in data file security controls combined with weaknesses in program security controls provide a particular opportunity for undetectable misappropriation of assets. Weaknesses in data file security controls coupled with weaknesses in the application controls over the continuity of the data increase the chances of undetected errors occurring.

- Weaknesses in system software controls do not have a direct effect on the applications. Such weaknesses may mean, however, that system software that is relied on for the proper functioning of the controls described previously is not appropriate. As a result, one or more of those control areas may be weak.

Having identified the general control weaknesses as well as the programmed procedures and data elements at risk, the auditor should then determine whether or not significant errors or irregularities could arise. These factors, among others, should be considered for each programmed procedure or data element at risk:

- The approximate volume or number of transactions that pass (or should pass) through a programmed procedure or data file. The auditor can use a number of techniques to make a reasonable estimate of volume. Examples might include inquiries of knowledgeable organization personnel, review of statistical records maintained by personnel operating the system, review of usage of serially numbered documents, use of audit software, or review of record counts printed on reports.
- The estimated monetary value of the transactions that pass (or should pass) through the programmed procedure or data file and the approximate range of individual transactions. The auditor can use a number of techniques to make a reasonable estimate of the monetary value, such as inquiries of knowledgeable organization personnel, review of records maintained by personnel operating the system, review of the organization's internal financial operating statements, use of audit software, or review of report totals.
- The effect of errors on management information.
- Whether the organization applies special control procedures to certain kinds of transactions. An example might be the review of exception reports of transactions that have a relatively high monetary value or fail to conform with established norms. In this case, however, the auditor will be concerned with the correctness of the exception reporting programs.
- The specific effect that a program or data error would have on the financial statements. Ordinarily, the materiality threshold is lower for items such as net income, working capital, and restrictions on retained earnings than it is for items that affect only classification in financial statements. For example, a control weakness that can lead to an overstatement of inventory is more likely to be material if the offsetting erroneous credit is to income than if it is to

accounts payable. Errors in master file data are likely to have a greater cumulative effect than errors in transaction data.

The external auditor should consider these factors, among others, in answering the RCW question, "Could material error arise?" If the auditor's judgment is that there is only a remote possibility that a material error could arise, the auditor should answer the question "no."

Other Controls

If the auditor concludes that significant error can arise from a control weakness, consideration should be given to whether other controls can be relied on to ensure that material errors do not, in fact, arise.

Modification of the Substantive Procedures

If an external auditor concludes that material error can arise, it is necessary to modify the substantive procedures to determine whether the financial statements are materially misstated as a result of the control weakness. The auditor should ensure that the modification is relevant to the specific control weakness.

Ordinarily, the auditor performs the procedures related to balance sheet accounts as of the year-end date. The extent, if any, to which substantive procedures should be applied to transactions, data files, or programs processed during the year depends on the need to see whether material losses have occurred as a result of the control weakness. Those losses need to be disclosed in the financial statements or as a service to the organization. In some cases, the results of the auditor's review of relevant performance indicators may be of some assistance in determining the required extent of substantive procedures on transactions processed during the year.

As mentioned subsequently, the ICRM includes a discussion of the effect of a "no control" answer on the audit procedures. In practice, the auditor should consider all the relevant answers before finalizing the substantive procedures. Whether the organization has other controls that would mitigate the audit significance of the control weakness should be considered.

Organization of the ICRM for General Controls

The ICRM for general controls in computer systems is organized under headings that correspond to the different types of general controls. The explanation of the questions within the control objectives is structured as follows:

- *Group*—A heading describes the type of controls considered.
- *Purpose*—Appears immediately following the question and explains the purpose of the control procedures covered by the question.
- *What constitutes adequate control procedures?*—Sets forth in general terms the procedures usually necessary to ensure adequate internal controls. The procedures described assume a familiarity with computer processing, EDP department procedures, and system software, but do not deal with procedures specific to particular processing environments or sytems.
- *Possible errors and audit effect*—Describes the usual effect of answers that indicate lack of control on the application systems or other general controls and on the audit procedures. This section describes the general effect when two or more of the questions are answered in the negative. The information is set out in three parts, as follows:
  - *Possible errors in application systems*—Explains the types of errors that could be present in the application systems or other general controls as a result of the control weakness described. The actual errors can be determined only by analyzing the systems.
  - *Example*—Illustrates some of the errors that may be present as a result of the control weakness.
  - *Effect on audit procedures*—Describes the changes that usually would be made in audit procedures as a result of the control weakness. This assumes that if the control were present, the audit procedures would have been based on reliance on that control. That is, tests of controls would have been emphasized and substantive tests restricted to the extent possible. In this context, substantive tests include direct tests of programs and data carried out separately from the tests of control procedures.

Other points to keep in mind while using this section include the following:

- The paragraph on the effect on audit procedures often refers to audit software and other computer audit testing techniques. It is assumed that the reader is familiar with these techniques and with the circumstances in which they can be used. The actual tests applied are usually a suitable combination of the audit procedures suggested. This depends on many factors, such as the nature and number of application programs and data files at risk; the applicability, effectiveness, and efficiency of the technique in the actual environment involved; and the compounding effect of other weaknesses. References to audit software include generalized audit software packages, specially written programs, retrieval software, or any other method of achieving the same purpose (such as utility programs or a report generator program).

- The auditor should consider whether the procedures set out under the heading "Effect on Audit Procedures" can be performed by organization personnel, subject to review and testing of results.
- The effects on audit procedures are discussed only in general terms. The auditor, in fact, performs specific audit procedures determined by the nature of the programmed procedures and data elements at risk. References to the use of audit software and other techniques do not imply that use of the technique in isolation is a sufficient test. For example, audit software must be properly set up and applied to the correct data; the resulting reports must then be reviewed and tested by the auditor as required to complete the test.

IMPLEMENTATION CONTROLS—APPLICATION SYSTEMS DEVELOPMENT

PURPOSE:

To determine whether new application systems are suitably designed, authorized, and tested.

ADEQUATE CONTROL PROCEDURES:

All new systems descriptions, as revised during the design stages, are written down in appropriate detail and used as a basis for recording the mutual understanding and approval of both the user organization and the EDP systems design and programming staff.

Comprehensive program and system testing is carried out or checked by EDP personnel, independent of the programmers who wrote the programs being tested, to confirm the compliance of the system in accordance with the approved system specifications.

POSSIBLE ERRORS. If system specifications are not prepared, not approved, or not properly tested, new applications may not function in accordance with management's intentions.

EXAMPLES. Programmed pricing or costing is performed accurately and consistently but contrary to company policy regarding rate classifications and discounts.

Due to a misunderstanding, the total inventory figure includes goods in transit which have already been sold to customers and therefore are included in accounts receivable.

EFFECT ON AUDIT PROCEDURES. If no system descriptions exist, the auditor should obtain oral representations of significant programmed procedures. The auditor reviews oral representations or system specifications to ensure that the applications appear to conform with generally accepted accounting principles (GAAP) and the organization's requirements. If necessary, the auditor discusses the procedures with users and supervisory staff to ensure that the programmed procedures are appropriate.

To conform oral representations or to check on unapproved or untested systems specifications, the auditor should consider:

- Checking specifications or oral representations to source code, then independently confirming that the source code is actually in use (for example, by recompiling the source and carrying out an audit software program comparison). (See the section titled "Program Security Controls.")
- Reprocessing data manually or with audit software and comparing the audit result with the organization's result.
- Using test data or an Integrated Test Facility (ITF).
- Using audit software to analyze processed data for unusual or unlikely results.

IMPLEMENTATION CONTROLS—APPLICATION SYSTEMS MAINTENANCE

PURPOSE:

To determine whether program modifications are authorized, and are implemented completely and accurately.

ADEQUATE CONTROL PROCEDURES:

- Modifications are recorded and approved.
- All programs and systems are adequately documented so that when changes have to be made they can be made accurately.
- Changed program procedures are tested, together with the effects of the modification on unchanged parts of the system.
- Program modifications are controlled for completeness and implementation.

POSSIBLE ERRORS. If program modifications are not documented, not approved, or not properly tested, the possible errors and the effect on audit procedures are the same for changed systems as for new systems, described in the previous section. The auditor should also consider the use of program comparison software to check the accuracy of changes made. (See the later section titled "Program Security Controls.")

If program modifications are not controlled for completeness, the organization may not know which systems have been changed, and critical changes or changes due on a certain date may become overdue.

EXAMPLE. Legislation required changes to a payroll system in relation to withholding and payroll taxes. Because the change was not made, the company has an undisclosed liability for back taxes and penalties.

EFFECT ON AUDIT PROCEDURES. By reviewing documentation and by discussions with users and data processing staff, the auditor should determine changes that should have been made and confirm that these changes have been made.

The auditor should consider using program comparison software or other techniques to identify unchanged programs that should have been changed.

IMPLEMENTATION CONTROLS—APPLICATION SYSTEMS FINAL ACCEPTANCE

PURPOSE:

To determine whether the necessary supervisory reviews have been performed before new and changed systems are accepted into production. The review helps to ensure adherence to standards of documentation, testing, and approval.

ADEQUATE CONTROL PROCEDURES:

Adequate procedures deal with controls for supervisory review and approval.

POSSIBLE ERRORS. If final reviews by responsible officials in user departments and the data processing functions are not carried out, refer to application system development and maintenance for procedures to follow. In the absence of a supervisory control, these procedures may not be performed. Accordingly, the possible errors are the same as when the control procedures do not exist.

EXAMPLE. The personnel performing the procedures observe that their work is not reviewed by anyone and they start to omit some of the important control steps.

EFFECT ON AUDIT PROCEDURES. To determine whether the related basic and division of duties controls have continued to operate properly, the auditor should perform the supervisory review for selected periods during the year. (Refer to the common control procedure for "Supervision.")

IMPLEMENTATION CONTROLS—CATALOGING

PURPOSE:

To determine whether procedures are adequate to ensure that only authorized and tested programs are properly taken into production.

ADEQUATE CONTROL PROCEDURES:

- An appropriate combination of manual and software procedures ensures that programs are properly tested and authorized prior to being taken into production.
- Procedures are adequate to ensure that no unauthorized changes can be made to programs after final testing and authorization but prior to their being taken into production.
- All forms of a program (such as source listing, source library, object program, executable program) are checked as being accurate and derived from the same source.

POSSIBLE ERRORS. If unauthorized or untested programs can be taken into production, the possible errors and effects on audit procedures are the same as those described under "Application Systems Development" and "Program Security Controls." Refer to tests indicated there.

If all forms of a program are not the same—specifically, if source versions differ from executable forms—subsequent modification and recompilation of the source version will introduce any deficiencies present in the source program into the executable program.

EXAMPLE. A utility program has been used to modify an object program without altering the source library program, which, as a consequence, is out of date. A subsequent modification is required and achieved by amending and recompiling the source library program. However, this produces an executable program that lacks the modification originally introduced using the utility, and consequently the processing using the program is incorrect.

EFFECT ON AUDIT PROCEDURES. The auditor should consider using program comparison software to ensure that source and executable forms of programs are the same. If there is a possibility that an error has already been introduced (as in the preceding example), the following procedures can help identify it:

- Reprocessing actual data using audit software, and comparing the results with those obtained using the organization's program.
- Using test data or ITF to test the correctness of the important programmed procedures, taking care to ensure that the program tested is the one actually in use.
- Using linkage analysis software to determine potential mismatches due to the use of utility programs. (See Chapter 26, "Testing Techniques for Computer-Based Systems.")

IMPLEMENTATION CONTROLS—SUPERVISION OF CATALOGING

PURPOSE:

To determine whether cataloging procedures are reviewed, thereby ensuring that the basic and disciplinary controls have continued to operate.

ADEQUATE CONTROL PROCEDURES:

These questions deal with the controls for supervisory review and approval.

POSSIBLE ERRORS. If the supervisory control is absent, refer to "Implementation Controls—Cataloging." In the absence of a supervisory control, these procedures may not be performed. Accordingly, the possible errors are the same as when these control procedures are not performed.

EXAMPLE. The people performing the cataloging procedures observe that their work is not reviewed by anyone and they start to omit some of the important control steps.

EFFECT ON AUDIT PROCEDURES. To determine whether the related basic division of duties and custodial controls have continued to operate properly, the auditor should perform the supervisory review for selected periods during the year. Refer to the common control procedure for "Supervision."

PROGRAM SECURITY CONTROLS

PURPOSE:

To determine whether all changes to production programs are authorized.

ADEQUATE CONTROL PROCEDURES:

- Access to originals or copies of production program and system documentation is restricted, on a need-to-know basis, to computer programmers and systems analysts, librarians, custodians, EDP officials, and auditors and "user" organization officials.
- All changes to programs loaded or resident on the computer system are authorized either before or after the change takes place.
- Access to backup copies and other copies of programs stored on computer media is restricted to authorized users.
- Unsupervised access to the computer room and libraries is properly restricted.

POSSIBLE ERRORS. If changes can be made to production programs, bypassing the normal controls over program modifications, then:

- Unauthorized or incorrectly made changes may cause the programs to cease functioning in accordance with management's intentions.
- Users may not be aware of changes made; as a result user procedures on the output may no longer be appropriate.
- Opportunities for the misappropriation of assets through changes to programs are increased.

EXAMPLES.

- A programmer believes a program can be made more efficient and makes a change. Because the change is not tested, the program now produces incorrect results.
- A change is made to the inventory system to show "inventory in transit" as a separate figure. However, the control account procedures are not changed and the company's inventory figure in the general ledger is understated by the amount of goods in transit.
- A change is made to a payments system to make fictitious payments. The control total balancing programs are also adjusted to disguise the difference.

EFFECT ON AUDIT PROCEDURES. The auditor should consider:

- Using program comparison software or other techniques to identify changed programs and ensure that the changes made were properly documented, approved, and tested.
- Reviewing the source code for unusual or inappropriate code, then independently confirming that the source code is actually in use. For example, an auditor might recompile the source code and

reprocess actual data using the recompiled programs to ensure that the result is the same as the organization's result.

- Reprocessing actual data manually or with audit software, and comparing the audit result with the organization's result.
- Using test data or ITF to test the correctness of the programs. If the user retains test data and results, consider reprocessing this test data to ensure that the programs are still functioning properly. Precautions must be taken to ensure that the programs tested are those in use.
- Reviewing records of processing activities for evidence of unauthorized changes to production libraries, such as the use of an SMF (IBM's System Management Facility) analyzer audit software program.
- Taking inventories of documentation and backup copies of program files to identify any unauthorized withdrawals.
- Using audit software to analyze processed data for unusual or unlikely results. Software can also assist in ensuring that control accounts are made up of individual items by footing the file and printing a selection of detailed records.

Note that most of the preceding techniques do not always detect deliberate irregularities when the evidence of changes has been removed (such as a program that is changed and then changed back). The auditor should therefore consider performing tests on a surprise basis.

PROGRAM SECURITY CONTROLS—SUPERVISION

PURPOSE:

To determine whether the procedures that control the security of programs are reviewed. This review helps to ensure that the basic controls continue to operate.

ADEQUATE CONTROL PROCEDURES:

These questions deal with the controls for supervisory review and approval.

POSSIBLE ERRORS. If the supervisory control is absent, these procedures may not be performed. Accordingly, the possible errors are the same as when these control procedures are not performed.

EXAMPLE. The people performing the procedures observe that their work is not reviewed by anyone and they start to omit some of the important control steps.

EFFECT ON AUDIT PROCEDURES. To determine whether the related basic division of duties and custodial controls have continued to operate properly, the auditor should perform the supervisory review for selected periods during the year. (Refer to the common control procedure for "Supervision.")

COMPUTER OPERATIONS CONTROLS—JOB SET-UP

PURPOSE:

To determine whether jobs are set up in accordance with authorized instructions.

ADEQUATE CONTROL PROCEDURES:

There should be authorized standing instructions for each production job. All variations to parameters and departures from the instructions should be checked and authorized.

POSSIBLE ERRORS. If jobs are not set up in accordance with authorized procedures, the results of processing may be incorrect. The incorrect results could occur at any time.

EXAMPLE. The cycle billing calendar requires two cycles to be run on a particular day. Because the calendar was not referred to, or checked, the job was set up to bill only one cycle. Statements for the other cycle were not sent and amounts due were not shown as past due.

EFFECT ON AUDIT PROCEDURES. The auditor should determine for each production job what could go wrong and whether or not the error would be detected. The audit procedures used depend on the type of error discovered. The auditor should consider:

- Using audit software to analyze files (particularly cumulative transaction files and master file or standing data) for unusual or erroneous conditions.
- Using audit software to reprocess user data and compare results to user's results.
- Spreading substantive tests throughout the year to search for the effects of inconsistent processing.
- Extending cutoff tests.
- Searching for significant errors, particularly in payment systems and other systems where people might also have some access to assets, by:

—Use of audit software to search for erroneous or exceptional transactions.
—Surprise visit to interrogate files and compare programs.
—Surprise manual audit of assets at risk, such as surprise securities count.

- Carrying out extended tests on account balances. Consider use of audit software, as indicated previously.

COMPUTER OPERATIONS CONTROLS—SUPERVISION OF JOB SET-UP

PURPOSE:

To determine whether job set-up procedures are reviewed, thereby ensuring that the basic and disciplinary controls have continued to operate.

ADEQUATE CONTROL PROCEDURES:

This question deals with the controls for supervisory review and approval.

POSSIBLE ERRORS. If the supervisory control is absent, refer to questions under "Job Set-Up." In the absence of a supervisory control, these procedures may not be performed. Accordingly, the possible errors are the same as when these control procedures are not performed.

EXAMPLE. The people performing the procedures observe that their work is not reviewed by anyone and they start to omit some of the important control steps.

EFFECT ON AUDIT PROCEDURES. To determine whether the related basic division of duties and custodial controls have continued to operate properly, the auditor should perform the supervisory review for selected periods during the year. Refer to the common control procedure for "Supervision."

COMPUTER OPERATIONS CONTROLS—OPERATOR ACTIONS

PURPOSE:

To determine whether the activities of operating the computer system are performed properly.

ADEQUATE CONTROL PROCEDURES:

- Up-to-date operating instructions exist.
- The activities of operators are supervised. Unusual situations and resulting operator actions are reviewed and approved.

POSSIBLE ERRORS. If up-to-date operating instructions do not exist, required operating procedures may not be followed.

EXAMPLE. An external person telephoned the operator to say he had forgotten the password. Because there were no instructions stating that passwords were not to be given out, the operator gave this person the password. As a result the person was able to fraudulently read and amend data through a telephone connection in the system.

EFFECT ON AUDIT PROCEDURES. Refer to the procedures set out under "Job Set-Up."

POSSIBLE ERRORS. If operator actions are not supervised, unusual situations are not investigated, and recoveries from system failures not controlled, unauthorized or incorrect operator actions may remain undetected.

EXAMPLE. As a result of a disk head crash, the file containing the inventory costs was destroyed. The operator mistakenly loaded the previous year's costs file from backup data. Through lack of supervision, no entry was recorded in the problem log and thus no check was performed to ensure that the correct action was taken. Inventory was understated.

EFFECT ON AUDIT PROCEDURES. Refer to procedures set out under "Job Set-Up."

DATA FILE SECURITY CONTROLS

PURPOSE:

To determine whether data files are protected against unauthorized change or access.

ADEQUATE CONTROL PROCEDURES:

If user controls are adequate to detect unauthorized use of data files, general controls need not be relied on in this respect. However, it is unlikely that this will be so, except in the simplest computer systems. In any case, general controls may still be important for operational reasons.

- A comprehensive security plan is in existence to identify all access paths into the system and to restrict access to resources and data on a need-to-know basis.

- Access to all documentation that provides details of file layouts or contents is restricted to authorized staff. In particular, computer operations personnel are not allowed access to this type of information.
- Physical security of files not in use (including backup copies) ensures that these are only issued for authorized processing.
- All access to loaded or resident data files is authorized either before or after it occurs.

POSSIBLE ERRORS. If unauthorized changes or access to data files can occur, opportunities will exist for the fraudulent or mischievous manipulation of data and misappropriation of assets.

The concentration of data in the EDP department means that changes can be made to all types of data records including individual transaction details, control data, and master file data. If controls over program file security are also weak, the possibilities for undetected manipulation of both data and processing are essentially limitless.

Changes to data may be used to cover up errors in processing arising from inadequate program procedures.

EXAMPLES.

- Fictious employee data is written to the payroll master file. Payments are made automatically each period to the bank account so indicated.
- Fictitious suppler records are written to the accounts payable master file. Fictitious invoices are then written to the accounts payable detail file; checks are generated automatically each month for these items and sent to the address indicated in the master file data. Program procedures are amended to ensure that the fictitious information is never printed out or included in control totals, except in the case of checks, which are included in the detail check listing used for bank reconciliation procedures.
- Programmed reconciliation of file totals to a separate control file is relied on to ensure completeness and accuracy of update. The program has not been completely debugged and occasionally differences arise. Control records are amended to force a balance, and the user is not aware that the reconciliation is in error.

EFFECT ON AUDIT PROCEDURES. Detailed audit procedures depend on the application controls over data files and the auditor's assessment of the likelihood that material error could arise. The auditor should consider:

- Using audit software to analyze files (particularly cumulative transaction files) for unusual or erroneous conditions.
- Using audit software to reprocess user data and compare the audit results to the user results. This may indicate whether fictitious transactions have been inserted and then deleted from the history files.
- Spreading substantive tests throughout the year to search for unauthorized transactions.
- Searching particularly sensitive systems (such as payment systems and those involving liquid assets) for unauthorized processing. Methods might include:
  - —Use of audit software to search for errors or to assist in carrying out extended substantiation of account balances.
  - —Surprise interrogations of data files.
  - —Manual audits of assets at risk.
- Reviewing records of processing activities for evidence of unauthorized changes or access to data files, such as the use of SMF analyzer audit software.
- It should be noted that, depending on the extent of the weakness, deliberate irregularities could have occurred and all evidence removed subsequently. Carrying out tests on a surprise basis should be considered in an attempt to identify such situations.

DATA FILE SECURITY CONTROLS—SUPERVISION

PURPOSE:

To determine whether the procedures that control the security of data files are reviewed, thereby assuring that the basic controls continue to operate.

ADEQUATE CONTROL PROCEDURES:

These questions deal with the controls for supervisory review and approval.

POSSIBLE ERRORS. If the supervisory control is absent, refer to questions about data file security controls. In the absence of a supervisory control, these procedures may not be performed. Accordingly, the possible errors are the same as when these control procedures are not performed.

EXAMPLE. The people performing the procedures observe that their work is not reviewed by anyone and they start to omit some of the important control steps.

EFFECT ON AUDIT PROCEDURES. To determine whether the related basic division of duties and custodial controls have continued to operate properly, the auditor should perform the supervisory review for selected periods during the year. Refer to the common control procedure for ''Supervision'' for guidance on procedures to follow.

SYSTEM SOFTWARE CONTROLS

PURPOSE:

To ensure that system software that is relied on for the purpose of the general controls is appropriate.

ADEQUATE CONTROL PROCEDURES:

- The system software is appropriate to control the functions desired by the organization.
- The controls over system software are adequate to ensure that the software is properly implemented and kept secure.
- All appropriate action is taken with respect to system software output.

Just as application controls may depend on the proper functioning of programmed procedures, so general controls may depend on the proper functioning of system software. The relationship between the controls over system software and the rest of general controls is similar to the relationship between general controls and application controls.

POSSIBLE ERRORS. If system software procedures are not appropriate for the purposes intended or controls over system software are weak, the relevant portion of the general controls may be ineffective. Refer to the section of the general controls involved.

EXAMPLE. Management authorized the purchase of a well-known program library maintenance software product to control changes to production libraries. In order to enable the system to work more efficiently and to increase flexibility, the software programmer who installed the product did not also install its security features.

EFFECT ON AUDIT PROCEDURES. Refer to the section of the general controls involved.

POSSIBLE ERRORS. If system software output is not properly reviewed and acted on, the general control that depends on the action will be ineffective.

EXAMPLE. All changes to system-resident production program libraries are reported. However, the report is sent to the programmer who makes the change and not to an independent reviewer.

EFFECT ON AUDIT PROCEDURES. To determine if the review would have disclosed problems, the auditor should reperform the review spreading the tests throughout the year. Also, refer to the section of the general controls involved.

SYSTEM SOFTWARE CONTROLS—IMPLEMENTATION

PURPOSE:

To determine whether new system software and software changes are properly designed, authorized, tested, and implemented, and whether security of system software is adequate.

ADEQUATE CONTROL PROCEDURES:

- Specifications for new system software and software changes are recorded and approved.
- Changes to system software are controlled for completeness.
- System software designed or modified by the company is adequately tested.
- System software programmers are supervised.
- The security of the software is protected.

POSSIBLE ERRORS. If controls over system software are inadequate, the general controls that depend on the system software may not function correctly. Refer to the section of the general controls involved.

EXAMPLE. Management authorized the development of comprehensive software to protect its data files. However, management claimed that system software programmers were too difficult to control. The new software was designed, written, and installed to provide password protection to all data files. Because the work was not documented and supervised, no one noticed that the password file, all program files, and all system software files (including the protecting software itself) were not controlled. In addition, the data bases, which remained open all day, were unprotected.

EFFECT ON AUDIT PROCEDURES. The detailed audit procedures often depend on the general controls at risk. However, the auditor may be able to examine records of system software implemented to ensure that the proper procedures have been adopted. Some systems provide internal records of system software change activity which can be examined by the auditor. Refer also to the relevant section for the general controls at risk.

SYSTEM SOFTWARE CONTROLS—IMPLEMENTATION: NEW VENDOR-SUPPLIED SYSTEM SOFTWARE

PURPOSE:

To determine whether all new vendor-supplied system software is approved by both users and the people responsible for the system software function.

ADEQUATE CONTROL PROCEDURES:

Note that the controls over approval of new system software are essentially the same as those for application programs. Specific points relating to system software follow:

- Vendor-supplied specifications and literature, covering both the basic software package and any available options, are reviewed and approved by both those responsible for the system software function and the users of the new system software.
- Control will be adequate provided:
  - —The people responsible for approving the software are sufficiently knowledgeable to determine whether the proposed software will meet the organization's needs.
  - —The review covers both the basic software package and any options that may be available.
  - —Consideration is given to the technical implications and requirements of the new software, and the impact of the software on existing systems and operating procedures.

For example, all vendor-supplied system software is subject to review and approval by a joint committee that includes members of both the system software support group and the applications programming group. The proposal to implement a particular software package is in writing and includes details of options that are to be included and a summary of the impact of the new software on existing system software, application programs, and operating procedures. The various group managers are responsible for finally approving the new software in writing.

POSSIBLE ERRORS. If system software procedures are not appropriate for their intended purposes, the general controls that depend on the operation of the system software may be ineffective. Refer to the section of the general controls involved.

EXAMPLE. Management purchased a well-known program library maintenance software product to control changes to production libraries. To make the system work more efficiently and to increase its flexibility, the software programmer who installed the product did not install its security features. This was not identified because there was no procedure for specifically authorizing the options to be implemented with respect to purchased system software.

EFFECT ON AUDIT PROCEDURES. The detailed audit procedures often depend on the general controls at risk. Refer to the relevant section for the general controls at risk.

SYSTEM SOFTWARE CONTROLS—IMPLEMENTATION: REVIEW OF NEW SYSTEM SOFTWARE

PURPOSE:

To determine whether new system software operates correctly and is appropriate to the needs of the system. Are review or testing procedures adequate to ensure that system software procedures operate as intended, and the correct implementation of all approved options?

ADEQUATE CONTROL PROCEDURES

Note that procedures for testing system software are essentialy the same as those for testing new application systems and amendments thereto. Additional factors to be considered with respect to testing system software include:

- System software is purchased from an outside manufacturer or software vendor. Reviews should be carried out to ensure that:
  - — All approved options are properly selected.
  - — The software interfaces properly with existing system software and application programs.

However, it is not normally necessary to carry out detailed tests to ensure that the software operates as specified. For example, all system software obtained from outside sources is tested using live data and established application programs that are known to produce reliable results. Reports generated by the system are examined to ensure that the software appears to operate correctly and processing results are compared with those obtained using the existing software, insofar as this is practical.

- New system software interfaces directly with existing application programs.

It is important to test the system software using proven application programs so that any discrepancies that may occur can be identified as resulting from the system software rather than the application program. This is particularly true if the new system software necessitates changes to application programs to achieve compatibility.

For example, an organization introduced a data base system. To ensure that the basic functions operated correctly, the system was tested using the organization's existing application programs, which were known to be correct, even though full implementation would eventually include substantial amendments to the application programs themselves.

- If system software is not specifically related to running application programs, the proper functioning of the software and the inclusion of the appropriate options may be confirmed by a review of the system-generated output, rather than by detailed testing procedures.

For example, the correct functioning of software that produces reports of operator actions and file set-up can be tested by reviewing the report generated and comparing its detailed content with known operator actions and files loaded on the system.

POSSIBLE ERRORS. If new system software is not properly reviewed or tested, it may not function as intended. Consequently, the general controls that depend on the operation of the system software may not be adequate. Refer to the section on the general controls involved for further guidance.

EFFECT ON AUDIT PROCEDURES. The detailed audit procedures often depend on the general controls at risk. Refer to the relevant sections for the general controls at risk.

SYSTEM SOFTWARE CONTROLS—IMPLEMENTATION: DOCUMENTATION

PURPOSE:

- To determine whether a permanent record exists of system software options actually implemented. This record is the basis of the final approval of options implemented.
- To determine whether instructions for setting up and running the system software and for making use of the software procedures are

prepared before new system software is finally taken into production. If instructions are not available, incorrect action by people running or making use of the software may adversely affect the operation of the system software procedures. Is the following documentation prepared prior to final acceptance of the system software: (a) descriptions of the options actually in use; (b) instructions for using and operating the software?

ADEQUATE CONTROL PROCEDURES:

Note that the requirement for adequate instructions is substantially the same as that discussed in relation to application programs. Specific control considerations relevant to purchased system software include:

- Instructions for using and operating the system software should be supplied by the software vendor and reviewed by appropriate EDP personnel.

Control will be adequate provided the organization reviews the instructions to ensure that they describe the procedures necessary to correctly operate the software properly. This review should be performed by people technically competent to assess the adequacy of the instructions.

For example, all instructions supplied by software vendors are reviewed by the software support group and by the programming and operations managers, who ensure that the material adequately describes the use and operation of the software.

- Written documentation should be prepared describing the software options actually implemented.

The basis for proper supervisory control is established, since, in a situation where software may function in different ways depending on the options selected, it is necessary to confirm that the actual options selected were those originally authorized.

For example, the organization's standards require, for all new system software, that the software support group provide documentation of which options, if any, were selected and implemented.

POSSIBLE ERRORS. If the actual options selected are not documented, it may not be possible to confirm that the system software functions in accordance with management's intentions. The selection of different options within the software package can radically affect the function and operation of the package. If important options are not implemented, the general controls that depend on those options may not function.

EXAMPLE. Several software products that are designed primarily as library maintenance packages may also provide file security if certain options are selected. If management intends the package to be used for security purposes, the relevant options should be selected and implemented.

EFFECT ON AUDIT PROCEDURES. The detailed audit procedures often depend on the particular general controls at risk. However, the auditor may be able to carry out the following alternate procedures to confirm the options implemented directly:

- Examining systems documentation to determine the available options.
- Obtaining oral representations of the options selected and, if possible, determining that the selection was in accordance with management's intentions.
- Performing selected tests to confirm the options actually implemented, such as using test data or ITF, or using audit software to access system software files and print information relating to options.

Refer also to the relevant sections for the general controls at risk.

SYSTEM SOFTWARE CONTROLS—IMPLEMENTATION: SUPERVISION

PURPOSE:

To determine whether supervisory reviews are performed of the appropriateness and results of reviews of new system software, the appropriateness of the related documentation of options selected and instructions for operating and using the software, and the implementation date. As part of the final accepance procedures, does a responsible official review and approve: (a) the appropriateness and results of the review or testing procedures; (b) the appropriateness of the documentation; (c) the appropriateness of the instructions for using and operating the software; (d) the date of implementation?

ADEQUATE CONTROL PROCEDURES:

This question deals with the controls for supervisory review and approval. The specific points to be considered are essentially the same as those discussed for application systems. It should be noted, however, that in this case the user department will be another section of the computer department, commonly either the applications programming function or operations staff.

POSSIBLE ERRORS. If final reviews by a responsible official are not performed, the related basic control procedures may not be performed. Accordingly, the possible errors are the same as those described under "Review of New System Software" and "Documentation."

EXAMPLE. The people performing the new system software and related documentation procedures observe that their work is not reviewed by anyone and they start to omit some important control steps.

EFFECT ON AUDIT PROCEDURES. To determine whether the related basic controls have continued to operate properly, the auditor should perform the supervisory review for selected periods during the year. Refer to the common control procedure for supervisory review and approval for guidance as to the procedures to follow.

SYSTEM SOFTWARE CONTROLS—IMPLEMENTATION: DOCUMENTATION OF MODIFICATIONS

PURPOSE:

To determine whether written evidence exists of all changes, including immediate modifications, to system software. Are all system software changes, including immediate modifications, supported by appropriate documentation?

ADEQUATE CONTROL PROCEDURES:

- The company's standards require that all changes to system software be documented in writing.

The basis for adequate control is established, since a permanent record of the change exists and can be approved by a responsible official.

For example, the technical support group is required to complete a standard change form whenever amendments are made to system software.

- System software change forms are controlled in such a way that it can subsequently be established that they are all accounted for.

It is possible to ensure that all changes are submitted to an appropriate responsible official for final approval. (See detailed discussion of controls over completeness of processing.)

For example, all software change forms are prenumbered. Once completed, they are forwarded to the technical support manager for review and approval. The manager, as part of the review, ensures that all change forms are received.

- Procedures exist whereby immediate modifications are identified and reported and retrospective documentation and approval procedures are applied.

Control will be adequate provided the procedures, whether manual or based on computer reports of system software changes, are adequate to identify and report all immediate modifications.

For example, all immediate modifications to system software are identified by computer operations staff and recorded in the problem log. A copy of this log is forwarded to the technical support manager, who is responsible for ensuring that the modification is properly documented, tested, and approved. This is evidenced by the manager's signature on the copy of the problem log, which is cross-referenced to the software change documentation.

POSSIBLE ERRORS. If changes to system software, including immediate modifications, are not properly documented, their appropriateness cannot be reviewed. Consequently, system software may not function in accordance with management's intentions and general controls that depend on the system software may not operate.

EXAMPLE. Management does not require that all changes to system software be documented. Technical support personnel changed certain software procedures for the purpose of increasing system throughput and efficiency. However, they bypassed certain security procedures intended to prevent unauthorized access to sensitive data files. This problem was not identified because of the lack of proper documentation of changes.

EFFECT ON AUDIT PROCEDURES. The detailed audit procedures often depend on the general controls at risk. The auditor should refer to the relevant sections for the general controls at risk.

POSSIBLE ERRORS. If changes to system software are not controlled for completeness, management may not know which systems have been changed. In addition, critical changes, or changes due on a certain date, may not be made.

EXAMPLE. A complete record of manufacturer's changes applied to the operating system was not maintained. Consequently, when further changes were issued that depended on the previous implementation of earlier changes, management did not have the information to apply the further changes correctly.

EFFECT ON AUDIT PROCEDURES. To obtain assurance as to completeness of changes, the auditor should review documentation, discuss with data processing staff the changes that should have been made, and confirm that those changes were made. If there are no critical changes outstanding, the auditor may conclude that the lack of a completeness control has only an operational effect and does not place the functioning of other general controls at risk.

SYSTEM SOFTWARE CONTROLS—IMPLEMENTATION: REVIEW OF MODIFICATIONS

PURPOSE:

To determine whether the organization's procedures ensure that amended system software procedures operate in accordance with management's intentions and do not adversely affect processing by unchanged system software. Are system software changes, including immediate modifications, adequately tested or reviewed to ensure that (a) implemented procedures operate as intended; (b) the changed procedures do not affect the operation of unchanged system software procedures adversely?

Unlike application programs, system software is not usually formally transferred from test to production status. In the event that such a transfer does take place, the auditor should answer questions relating to testing for system software as well as for application programs.

ADEQUATE CONTROL PROCEDURES:

Note that procedures for testing changes to system software are essentially the same as those for testing new software. Additional comments regarding testing of changes include:

- Tests or reviews of changes are designed to confirm the proper operation of both the changed and unchanged system software procedures.

Control will be adequate to ensure that the changed procedures properly interface with unchanged system software and therefore that the overall processing continues to be in accordance with management's intentions.

For example, software changes are reviewed by technical support staff for their possible effects on other, unchanged parts of the system. If appropriate, tests or reviews are extended to ensure that the overall system still operates properly.

POSSIBLE ERRORS. If system software modifications are not properly reviewed or tested, the possible errors and effect on audit procedures are the same for changed system software as for new system software, as discussed under "Review of New System Software."

SYSTEM SOFTWARE CONTROLS—IMPLEMENTATION: SUPERVISION OF MODIFICATIONS

PURPOSE:

To determine whether supervisory reviews are performed of the appropriateness of changes and the appropriateness and results of reviews of changes. As part of the final acceptance procedures, does a responsible official review and approve: (a) the appropriateness of the documented change; (b) the appropriateness and results of the review or testing procedures?

ADEQUATE CONTROL PROCEDURES:

These procedures are the same as those generally applicable to controls for supervisory review and approval.

POSSIBLE ERRORS. In the absence of a supervisory control, the related basic control procedures may not be performed. Accordingly, the possible errors are the same as those described under "Documentation of Modifications" and "Review of Modifications."

EXAMPLE. The people performing the procedures observe that their work is not reviewed by anyone and they start to omit some important control steps.

EFFECT ON AUDIT PROCEDURES. To determine whether the related basic controls have continued to operate properly, the auditor should perform the supervisory review for selected periods during the year. Refer to the common control procedures for supervisory review and approval for guidance about the procedures to follow.

SYSTEM SOFTWARE CONTROLS—SECURITY

PURPOSE:

To determine whether there are adequate procedures to prevent unauthorized changes or access to system software when it is temporarily or permanently loaded on the computer system and when it is not in use.

ADEQUATE CONTROL PROCEDURES:

The procedures for preventing unauthorized changes to system software are essentially the same as those for production programs. Refer to the earlier section entitled "Program Security Controls" for a discussion of adequate control procedures.

POSSIBLE ERRORS. If unauthorized changes can be made to system software, system software procedures may not operate in accordance with management's intentions and general controls that depend on those procedures may not function. The auditor should refer to the section dealing with the relevant general controls at risk.

EXAMPLE. Management implemented a program file security software package that offered protection against unauthorized changes to programs through the use of passwords. Unknown to management, however, the software was amended to permit programmers unmonitored access to certain files on which sensitive financial programs were held. Although the data processing manager reviewed software-based reports regularly for evidence of unauthorized access to programs, the control was meaningless because the software protection was no longer functioning as intended.

EFFECT ON AUDIT PROCEDURES. Certain systems provide internal records of system software change activity, which the auditor may examine. In the absence of this type of information, the detailed audit procedures often depend on the particular controls at risk. For further guidance on procedures to follow, refer to the relevant sections for those controls.

SYSTEM SOFTWARE CONTROLS—SECURITY: SUPERVISION

PURPOSE:

To determine whether supervisory reviews are performed of the controls for preventing unauthorized changes or access to system software. Are the procedures reviewed and approved by a responsible official?

ADEQUATE CONTROL PROCEDURES:

These procedures are the same as those generally applicable to controls for supervisory review and approval.

POSSIBLE ERRORS. If supervisory control is absent, the related basic control procedures may not be performed. Accordingly, the possible errors are the same as those described under "Security."

EXAMPLE. The people performing the procedures observe that their work is not reviewed by anyone and they start to omit some important control steps.

EFFECT ON AUDIT PROCEDURES. To determine whether the related basic division of duties and custodial controls have continued to operate properly, the auditor should perform the supervisory review for selected periods during the year. Refer to the common control procedures for supervisory review and approval for guidance as to the procedures to follow.

APPENDIX **B**

Internal Control Reference Manual— Application Controls

INTRODUCTION

The *Internal Control Reference Manual* (ICRM) for computer systems was designed by Coopers & Lybrand to assist the auditor in evaluating internal control in computer-based systems. The evaluation of internal control is based on consideration of control objectives in the Control Assessment and Record of Tests (CART) and may be achieved either by completing the CART or by using the Control Matrix. The material discussed can be summarized as follows:

- Internal control in computer systems.
- Structure of control in computer systems.
- Organization of the ICRM for computer systems.

Reference should also be made to Appendix A, "*Internal Control Reference Manual—Information Technology Controls.*" The following points are relevant to both manual and computer systems:

- Appropriateness of evaluation of control procedures.
- Evaluation of answers that indicate there is no, or inadequate, control.

INTERNAL CONTROL IN COMPUTER SYSTEMS

The definition and related basic concepts of control are expressed in terms of control objectives independent of the method used to process data. Consequently, they apply equally to manual or computer-based data processing systems. However, the nature of computer processing creates significant changes in methods of processing and controlling data. The availability of different control techniques therefore results in changes in the manner of applying and evaluating control in computer systems. The extent of change depends on the scope of computer processing. The principal features of control in computer systems are:

- Many accounting and control procedures that had previously been carried out manually are replaced by steps in the computer programs. These steps are called "programmed procedures." Manual follow-up is still necessary.
- Data is held on computer files as well as in manual records. This may affect the way controls are applied to prevent unauthorized changes to data. In particular, consideration should be given to controls in the EDP department that are designed to prevent unauthorized access to data files. These controls may be particularly important when reliance on programmed procedures results in reduced checking of the output from processing. Therefore, the need for controls over the continued correctness of data on computer files is increased.

Programmed Procedures

Programmed procedures are precise processing instructions embedded in the computer programs. Good control requires that these instructions are correct and function consistently. Then, the organization and the control designer/reviewer can place reliance on the programmed procedures in their contribution to an adequate system of internal control. Usually, the effective operation of programmed procedures is achieved by controlling the design, implementation, security, and use of computer programs. Although the same assurance might be obtained by checking the results of processing, this method is usually less efficient due to the volume of data that would have to be reported and checked.

Programmed procedures are of concern when they relate to:

- Procedures identified as control functions when carried out manually, such as a programmed sequence check that produces a list of missing or duplicate numbers.
- Procedures of an accounting nature that would be subject to checking in a noncomputer system, such as the automatic generation of insurance premium renewals.

In many cases, programmed procedures are an important part of the control procedures. The appropriateness of the programmed procedures is therefore relevant to the adequacy of a particular control technique. For this reason, comments on adequacy of control should include, where applicable, a note of what would be an acceptable programmed procedure.

General Controls

The controls over the design, implementation, security, and use of computer programs, and the security of data files, are referred to as general, or information technology (IT), controls. These controls usually apply equally to all applications, operate within the MIS department, and are a combination of manual and software procedures. System software is computer programs of a general nature that often supports general controls. It includes operating systems, compilers, librarian and utility programs, and data base management systems. General controls should also ensure the correct implementation and security of system software. Adequacy of general controls is discussed in Chapter 15, "Application Controls—II," and in Appendix A.

User Controls

User controls refer to those manual controls carried out by a user department on the data being processed. Here, a user is defined as a person, other than those in systems development, systems maintenance, and computer operations, who is involved with computer processing. Users are those who prepare input, take action on output, or otherwise use the system for business functions. User controls often depend on programmed control procedures, such as when users follow up on exception reports.

STRUCTURE OF CONTROL IN COMPUTER SYSTEMS

Overall control of computer systems is achieved by a suitable combination of application controls and general controls.

Application Controls

Application controls are the specific controls over each separate computer system which should ensure that only authorized data is completely and accurately processed. They consist of a combination of programmed procedures and user controls and are the subject of this appendix.

Application controls, as they relate to a computer system, may be considered under the following headings:

- *Completeness of input and update.* All transactions must reach the computer and subsequently be recorded on the computer files, once and once only.
- *Accuracy of input and update.* Data reaches the computer accurately and is recorded correctly on the computer files.
- *Validity (authorization).* Data is authorized or otherwise checked as to the appropriateness of the transaction.
- *Maintenance (continuity).* Data on computer files continues to remain correct and current.

If adequate overall control of a computer system is to be achieved, the combination of user controls and programmed procedures must ensure that all these aspects of control are satisfactory.

The control structure adopted for each application should take the whole sequence of processing—from the time transactions occur to the time the relevant output is used—into account. A wide variety of control techniques may be applied to ensure that the overall system of control is effective. Consideration should be given to the fact that an apparent control weakness at one point can often be compensated for by the operation of a strong control at another stage of processing. For instance, certain types of controls over the maintenance of master file data, such as a manual check of all items reported on a full printout of the file, may compensate for weaknesses in the areas of input and update. In this case, the maintenance controls become the controls over input and update.

Since different controls are likely to be applied to the different stages of processing, it is necessary to be satisfied that there is no break in the control sequence and that overall control is achieved. When considering the effectiveness of a series of controls, it is important to identify two stages in the exercise of a control technique:

1. The stage of processing at which control is established, such as recording transactions on sequentially prenumbered documents.
2. The stage of processing at which the control operates, such as identification and reporting of missing and duplicate numbers for investigation.

To achieve an unbroken line of control, each control technique in a sequence of controls must establish control at or before the stage at which the previous control operates. For example, if completeness of input is ensured by a computer sequence check of sequentially prenumbered documents, and completeness of update by run-to-run control totals, then a total of accepted items must be accumulated during or before the run in which the sequence check operates and must subsequently be agreed to the total of items updated to the master file. This ensures that transactions are not lost between input and update stages. Assessing the series of different controls and associated possibilities for uncontrolled gaps are particularly important when evaluating controls over the completeness of transaction processing.

Standards of Control

Establishing an adequate overall control system may involve a variety of control techniques. The decision whether to control or not includes consideration of the cost/benefit relationship of the control. Two factors that can be expected to influence the decision are:

1. Different control techniques have different levels of complexity, efficiency, and expense.
2. Different transaction and data types require different standards of accuracy and checking: The strength of control required depends on the ultimate use of the data, the existence of compensating controls during later stages of processing, and the effect of errors on the financial statements.

Common standards of control are:

- Master file data usually requires a higher standard of control than transaction data. In general, an individual error in transaction data affects only that one transaction, whereas an error in master file data, which may be used each time the file is processed, may affect many or even all transactions processed.
- Programmed procedures require the highest standard of control, since a program error will affect all data processed each time the program is run.
- Different data fields within a transaction or record may also vary in the standard of control required. Financial data is usually significant, but the level of control necessary for reference data (such as codes, indicators, and dates) depends on the ultimate use of that data.
- Transactions that deal with liquid assets (such as cash, payroll, accounts payable, credits, or receivables) may require a higher standard of control.
- Data processed manually generally requires more checking for accuracy and completeness due to users' inconsistent

performances. Data processed by programmed procedures generally requires greater manual scrutiny for unusual situations or errors that may not have been foreseen when the system was designed and therefore are treated incorrectly by the programs.

Principal Controls

In many situations, several control techniques that satisfy the same control objective are in use. This happens due to the operational requirements of computer systems. Errors must be continually monitored and controlled so that subsequent computer processing is not repeated or corrected inefficiently. Principal control techniques are those that:

- Give more conclusive evidence of control. For example, a cumulative report of missing sequence numbers, with evidence of the taking of appropriate corrective action, provides more conclusive evidence of completeness than the manual reconciliation of batch totals.
- Are stronger alternatives. For example, a one-for-one check usually provides greater certainty as to the accuracy of input than does an edit check that the data is within a range. The strength of a control depends both on the effectiveness of the clerical action and on the function of the appropriate programmed procedures.
- Cover several areas of control. For example, a control account that covers completeness of input and update, accurate input and update of the dollar total, and maintenance of the dollar total is more efficient to test than a combination of alternate controls.
- Provide evidence as to the consistent and proper operation of programmed procedures.
- Detect the error earlier in the processing cycle.
- Automatic the control process.

ORGANIZATION OF THE ICRM

The ICRM for computer systems consists of two parts. The common application control procedures have been edited for inclusion in this appendix. Considerations relating to general controls are presented in Appendix A.

Common Control Procedures

As discussed previously, it is convenient to classify controls in computer systems according to the particular aspect of processing that they cover, such as input, update, maintenance, validity, and so forth. Superimposed on this categorization of controls are the particular techniques that can be used to achieve control.

This discussion of common control procedures is structured to relate to computer control objectives. The adequacy of individual control techniques is discussed within each aspect of control. Consequently, certain control techniques appear under more than one heading. For example, the use of batch totals is included under completeness of input and update, accuracy of input and update, and maintenance of data files.

Disciplines over user controls—the specific requirements for supervisory controls, custodial controls, and a proper segregation of duties—are not considered in detail in the ICRM.

STANDARD CONTROL OBJECTIVES BY APPLICATION CYCLE

Some of the common control objectives for widely used applications are discussed in the following sections.

Payment Cycle

Orders. Purchases should be initiated only on the basis of appropriate authorization. Records of commitments should be maintained as a basis for:

- Determining that transactions are executed in accordance with authorization.
- Establishing the amount of any provision required for losses arising from unfulfilled commitments.

Receipts. Control should be established over goods and services received as a basis for:

- Determining and recording the liability for goods and services received but not entered as accounts payable.
- Where required, posting the items to detailed inventory records.

Returns. Control should be established over goods returned to, and claims on, suppliers as a basis for:

- Obtaining credit for all such items.
- Where required, posting the items to detailed inventory records.

Approval. Invoices and related documentation should be properly checked and approved as being valid before being entered as accounts payable.

Posting. All valid accounts payable transactions, and only those transactions, should be accurately recorded as accounts payable.

Petty Cash. Reimbursements of imprest and similar funds (such as postage and other franking meters) should be made only for valid transactions.

Checks. Disbursements from bank accounts should be made only for valid transactions.

Raw Materials. Accurate detailed records should be maintained of materials and supplies inventories.

Fixed Asset Approval. Additions to and disposals of property, plant, and equipment should be properly authorized.

Fixed Asset Depreciation. Accurate records should be maintained of the cost and accumulated depreciation of property, plant, and equipment.

Account Distribution. General ledger entries arising from the payment cycle should be accurately determined.

Payroll. Payments with respect to wages and salaries should be:

- Made only to company employees at authorized rates of pay.
- Where required, in accordance with records of work performed.
- Accurately calculated.

Deductions. Payroll deductions should be correctly accounted for and paid to the third parties to whom they are due.

Production Cycle

Approval. Control should be established over:

- Issues from inventories of materials and supplies to production and returns.
- Charges to production for labor and overheads.
- Transfers from production to inventories of parts and finished products, as a basis, when required, for making the entries in the inventory records.

This control objective does not cover the controls over the receipt of materials and supplies from suppliers that are put directly into production or the shipment of finished products directly from production to customers. These are included within the scope of other control objectives.

Posting. Accurate inventory records should be maintained for work in progress.

Account Distribution. General ledger entries arising from the production cycle should be determined accurately. This control objective does not cover the general ledger entries for the receipt of raw materials and supplies that are put directly into production and the shipment to customers of finished products directly from production, which are included within the scope of other control objectives.

Revenue Cycle

Orders. Records should be maintained of unfulfilled sales commitments, as a basis for determining any provisions required for losses that may arise.

Shipments. Control should be established over goods shipped and services performed as a basis for:

- Making charges to customers for all such sales.
- Determining the amount of the related revenues that have not been entered as accounts receivable.

- Making the related entries in the detailed inventory records, when required.

This control objective is not intended to cover sales in retail and similar businesses, where the invoices or similar documents are issued to customers at the same time the goods are supplied or returned.

Cash Sales. Control should be established over cash sales of goods and services as a basis for:

- Accounting for all such sales.
- When required, making the related entries in the detailed inventory records.

For this purpose, "cash sales" should be regarded as including credit sales made under similar conditions, such as when the customer receives the goods or services on the vendor's premises and the sales invoice or similar document is issued to the customer simultaneously.

Returns. Control should be established over goods returned by and claims received from customers as a basis for:

- Determining and recording the liability for goods returned and claims received but not entered in the accounts receivable records.
- When required, making the related entries in the detailed inventory records.

Approval and Pricing. All charges and credits should be appropriately checked as being valid before being entered in the accounts receivable records.

Posting. All valid accounts receivable transactions, and only those transactions, should be accurately recorded as accounts receivable.

Cash Receipts. Control should be established over all cash and checks received, and they should be deposited promptly in the organization's bank accounts.

Finished Goods. Accurate, detailed records should be maintained of finished products.

- Normally, the procedure should cover inventories of finished products that have been manufactured by the company and are held in stock (either on the company's premises or in the hands of third parties). In some cases, it may also be appropriate to cover certain of the inventory categories covered by other controls, as when these are accounted for by the company as part of finished products, rather than materials and supplies inventories.
- If the inventories of finished products are recorded in the same records, and are subject to the same controls, as those for materials and supplies covered under other control objectives, there is no need to complete a separate questionnaire.

The inventory categories covered by the answers to CART questions should be stated.

Account Distribution. General ledger entries arising from the revenue cycle should be determined accurately.

Time Cycle

Financial Reports. All financial reports (both internal and external) should be prepared accurately and submitted on a consistent and timely basis.

Inventory. Adequate procedures should be followed to confirm the physical existence of inventories recorded in the general ledger. When the physical existence of inventories is determined other than on a continuous basis, the tests of controls, as described in CART questions, normally are carried out as part of the substantive tests.

Inventory Costing. Costs attributable to inventories should be determined accurately.

Inventory Provisions. Adequate steps should be taken to identify all inventories for which provisions may be required.

Fixed Asset Counts. Adequate steps should be taken to confirm the physical existence of and, when appropriate, the titles to property, plant, and equipment.

Bad Debts. All doubtful accounts receivable should be identified, either individually or by category, as a basis for determining any provisions required for such accounts.

Bank Reconciliation. Adequate steps should be taken to confirm the accuracy of the bank balance shown in the general ledger.

Investments. Investments should be adequately safeguarded and accurately accounted for in a company that does not have sufficient volume of trading in, or holdings of, securities to justify more detailed procedures for control over security transactions.

Accurate records should be maintained for outstanding capital stock and debt obligations. Transactions relating to these should be considered under adequate accounting control, including appropriate segregation of duties.

General Ledger

All valid general ledger entries, and only those entries, should be accurately recorded in the general ledger.

ADEQUACY OF CONTROLS OVER COMPLETENESS OF INPUT AND UPDATE

Obviously, it is important that all transactions are recorded, input, and updated to the correct master file. This requirement is referred to as completeness of input and update. It should not be confused with accuracy of input and update. The reason for the distinction is that different techniques are often used to control completeness and accuracy. Completeness means simply that all the transactions were processed, whereas accuracy is concerned with information in the data fields making up each transaction.

Adequacy of control is discussed here. However, similar control procedures may apply to different cycles and different control objectives.

Various techniques are available to establish completeness of input and update. For convenience, they can be considered under the following headings:

- One-for-one checking.
- Agreement of manually established batch totals.

- Computer sequence check of serially numbered documents.
- Computer matching with a file of previous accepted data.
- Run-to-run controls.
- Rejections.
- Reliance on controls over another application.

Each of these techniques is discussed in detail in the following sections.

Some controls over completeness of input can also ensure completeness of update. To ensure completeness of update in this situation, the input control must be exercised at or after the update process. For example, input controls involving the checking of reports may ensure completeness of update, provided the output report is produced at, or after, update. If separate controls are used to achieve completeness of input and update, the update control must be established at the time, or before, the input control is exercised. Otherwise, there will be a break in the control sequence and overall control will not be adequate.

ONE-FOR-ONE CHECKING

SITUATION 1:

The user department retains copies of all documents submitted for processing and checks these off individually against a report of transactions processed.

IMPACT ON ADEQUACY OF CONTROL. The extent of control achieved depends on the stage of processing at which the information on the report is gathered. If this is done during the input stage, control will be adequate to ensure that data is input completely. If the report shows data actually updated onto the master file at the time of update, control over completeness of both input and update will be assured.

EXAMPLE. Amendments to payroll master file data are prepared by the personnel office staff, who retain a copy of all documents submitted for processing. A report is received that shows data updated onto the payroll master file. This is checked on a one-for-one basis with the document copies retained in the personnel office.

SITUATION 2:

The user department agrees details on a report, produced during either input or update, to input documents returned from data processing.

IMPACT ON ADEQUACY OF CONTROL. Control is not adequate unless there are additional procedures to ensure that all documents are returned from the MIS department. Adequate procedures would include a document count over data sent for processing or a manual sequence check over documents submitted for processing.

EXAMPLE. In the example for Situation 1, the personnel office does not retain copies of documents submitted for processing. Instead, all documents are serially prenumbered and the personnel office maintains a control list of the numbers of the documents submitted. Checking this list against the document reference number recorded on the update report ensures that all documents are updated to the master file.

SITUATION 3:

A one-for-one check of a computer report is considered an adequate control over completeness of update.

IMPACT ON ADEQUACY OF CONTROL. The programmed procedures must ensure that the information reported reflects data actually written to the master file and not just that accepted by the system.

EXAMPLE. In this example, the report identifies not only data written to the master file but also the old data overwritten. This provides some assurance that the report is not produced at the data acceptance stage.

SITUATION 4:

User procedures relating to a one-for-one check are considered adequate.

IMPACT ON ADEQUACY OF CONTROL. The procedures should include procedures to ensure that a copy is retained of all documents and that the file of unprocessed documents is controlled for completeness; a regular review of retained source documents or missing documents (see preceding examples) to ensure that all transactions are processed; and an investigation of all differences disclosed by the checking procedure.

EXAMPLE. In the Situation 1 example, the personnel office notes on the update report any differences identified and the follow-up action taken. Once the report has been cleared, it is filed together with the appropriate source documents. The file of source documents is reviewed each week for any items not yet processed.

SITUATION 5:

The one-for-one check is only adequate to ensure completeness of input (because of the stage of processing at which the report is produced).

IMPACT ON ADEQUACY OF CONTROL. A separate control is required to ensure the completeness of update. If this involves the use of control totals, a total of accepted items must be generated by the computer during the run in which the report is produced.

EXAMPLE. Amendments to rate of pay are input to the computer, and retained copies of source documents are agreed to the input validation report, which lists all accepted amendments. During the input validation run, a hash total is produced of all rates of pay and this is agreed (by the user) to a similar total accumulated and reported during update of the master file.

BATCH TOTALS

SITUATION 1:

To ensure that all documents are included in a batch, sequentially prenumbered documents are used. In this case, the following conditions are met: Physical control is maintained over unissued documents, documents are issued in numerical order, and all series are controlled.

IMPACT ON ADEQUACY OF CONTROL. Control is adequate if periodically (at least monthly) the organization identifies missing documents by using a complete list of document numbers against which an appropriate cross-reference is made at the time batch totals are established. Voided documents should be so indicated on the list and retained intact by the organization. Another method is to use a numerical file of document copies on which appropriate cross-references are made at the time batch totals are established. Once missing numbers have been identified, they should be properly investigated and adjustments made as needed.

EXAMPLE. Sequence numbers are indicated on a list of sales invoice numbers at the time the invoices are batched and totals established. Copies of receiving reports are filed numerically and the relevant batch number is noted on each document.

SITUATION 2:

As in Situation 1, but documents are numbered as they are prepared (internal documents) or received (external documents).

IMPACT ON ADEQUACY OF CONTROL. Control may be exercised as in Situation 1, but it is not as strong as when documents are prenumbered. Control may be adequate, however, if there are additional procedures to ensure that all documents are numbered immediately upon preparation or receipt; the documents are numbered sequentially; there are no duplicate or missing numbers; and the documents are only prepared/received in authorized locations.

EXAMPLE. Shipping advices are numbered sequentially when goods are transferred from the finished inventory warehouse. The shipping supervisor ensures that a shipping advice accompanies all goods shipped and that the numbers are sequential.

SITUATION 3:

Documents are numbered some time after they are prepared or received.

IMPACT ON ADEQUACY OF CONTROL. Control is not adequate because documents may be lost or misplaced between the time of preparation or receipt and numbering. This may be compensated for by other controls.

EXAMPLE. Purchase invoices are not numbered until after matching with receiving reports. However, each month all recorded accounts payable balances are reconciled with supplier's statements.

SITUATION 4:

Documents are entered in a register immediately upon preparation or receipt.

IMPACTION ON ADEQUACY OF CONTROL. Control is adequate if the appropriate cross-reference is indicated in the register when batch totals are established. In addition, procedures are required to ensure that the register is complete (no pages are missing) and unauthorized alterations cannot be made.

EXAMPLE. All purchase invoices are entered in a register when received in the mail office. The register is a loose-leaf book, but all pages are prenumbered and all entries are in ink. When invoices have been batched, the batch number is entered in the register. Any amendments must be initialled by the accounts payable supervisor.

SITUATION 5:

A numerical control list, register, or file is merely marked off when the document is batched; an actual cross-reference is not given.

IMPACT ON ADEQUACY OF CONTROL. Control is less effective because the control documents do not demonstrate that an item has actually been batched. The effectiveness of a supervisory review procedure is reduced because the supervisor cannot see that a valid batch has been prepared.

EXAMPLE. A check mark rather than a batch number is placed against the sales invoice number when that invoice is batched. A check mark can be made even if the invoice is not processed.

SITUATION 6:

No numerical control or register exists, but the organization maintains a file of documents not yet batched.

IMPACT ON ADEQUACY OF CONTROL. The file, by itself, is not an adequate control, since documents may be improperly added or removed without detection or may never be filed at all.

EXAMPLE. Shipping advices are removed to suppress production of an invoice.

SITUATION 7:

The cross-references referred to in any of the preceding controls are made before actual batch totals have been established.

IMPACT ON ADEQUACY OF CONTROL. Control is not adequate because documents may be lost or mislaid between the time of making the cross-reference and establishment of control totals. Control may be adequate if, for example, all batches must contain a fixed number of documents and this is checked at the time the batch totals are established.

EXAMPLE. Purchase invoices are batched each time a convenient number of documents has accumulated. At this stage a prenumbered batch header is attached and the batch number is entered in the invoice register. Value batch totals are not established until the end of each day.

SITUATION 8:

To ensure that all batches are submitted for processing, batch headers are prenumbered and the conditions specified in Situation 1 are met.

IMPACT ON ADEQUACY OF CONTROL. Control is adequate if the company periodically (such as daily) identifies missing batches not returned from EDP by one of the methods specified in Situation 1. Alternately, control may be exercised by a computer sequence check on batch numbers. Although such a procedure is unusual, control is adequate provided requirements similar to those specified subsequently for a sequence check on transaction documents are met.

EXAMPLE. Batch headers are prenumbered and a control list is maintained of all numbers used. As batches are returned from EDP, the date of return is noted on the control list.

The batch number is input to the computer and, by reference to a table of permitted and used numbers, the input validation program identifies duplicate and missing batch numbers. These are reported separately at the end of each input run for investigation by the user department.

SITUATION 9:

Batch headers are numbered when prepared.

IMPACT ON ADEQUACY OF CONTROL. Control is adequate provided there are procedures to ensure that all batches are numbered, the numbers are sequential, and batch headers are only prepared in authorized locations. Frequently, these requirements are achieved by use of a register in which details of each batch are recorded. The register itself should be controlled as described in Situation 4.

EXAMPLE. A permanent bound batch register is maintained. As each batch is prepared, reference is made to the register to obtain the next number in sequence, and the batch details are recorded in the register. This includes batch number, batch total, and date returned from EDP.

SITUATION 10:

All batches are recorded in a register when they are prepared.

IMPACT ON ADEQUACY OF CONTROL. It is unlikely that entry in the register will not be accompanied by allocation of a batch number. The control is then identical to that in Situation 9.

SITUATION 11:

For agreement of totals, manually established batch totals are recorded in a register before batches are submitted for processing.

IMPACT ON ADEQUACY OF CONTROL. Control is adequate if these totals are agreed subsequently to batch totals based on the same variable as used manually, but accumulated and reported by the computer. It is probable that the computer totals will be produced early during input validation and, therefore, that control will only be effective over completeness of input. Additional run-to-run controls (discussed subsequently) will be required to ensure completeness of update.

EXAMPLE. Batch totals over quantities of goods shipped are entered in a register. The input validation program accumulates and reports quantity batch totals that are agreed each day to those entered in the register. The check is evidenced by recording the computer total in the register.

SITUATION 12:

Manually established batch totals are accumulated and posted to a manual control account.

IMPACT ON ADEQUACY OF CONTROL. Control over completeness of both input and update is adequate if periodically the organization agrees the balance on the manual control account to that reported for the computer master file.

EXAMPLE. Dollar batch totals are calculated manually for all transaction types input to the accounts receivable file. Each day these totals are accumulated and posted to a manual control account that is agreed at the end of each week to the balance reported for the accounts receivable file.

SITUATION 13:

Batch totals are recorded on a batch header slip and entered into the computer, which accumulates the total of the details in the batch independently and compares it with the manual total input from the header slip.

IMPACT ON ADEQUACY OF CONTROL. Control over completeness of input is adequate provided there are procedures to ensure that all batches are input to the computer, such as by use of a register, and programmed procedures result in all out-of-balance batches being reported. This is likely to involve reliance on general controls, unless all batches input are reported for manual review; there is adequate evidence that the computer agreement of batch totals was satisfactory. Additional run-to-run controls (discussed subsequently) are required to ensure that update is satisfactory.

EXAMPLE. Batch totals are recorded on a prenumbered header slip and all batch numbers are entered in a register before batches are sent to EDP. The computer input validation procedures provide that a batch total is accumulated for each batch and compared to the manual total input. All out-of-balance batches are rejected and reported. Both manual and computer totals are reported to facilitate investigation; all accepted batches are separately listed at the end of the validation report. The user ensures that all batch numbers in the register are reported either as out of balance or accepted.

SITUATION 14:

Batch totaling is employed as an effective control over completeness.

IMPACT ON ADEQUACY OF CONTROL. The total used must be capable of demonstrating that all transactions have been processed (e.g., a document count over multiline documents does not ensure that all transactions are processed). Provided this requirement is met, the total may be established over any field that is meaningful within the context of the particular application.

EXAMPLES. Acceptable batch totals include gross dollar values on purchase invoices, hash totals over selling prices for amendments to sales master file data, or total of hours worked for employees' time records.

SITUATION 15:

Any of the reconciliation procedures discussed previously disclose differences.

IMPACT ON ADEQUACY OF CONTROL. Control is adequate provided there are procedures for investigation and correction of all differences by the user.

SITUATION 16:

Input and/or update procedures can result in rejection of data from the system.

IMPACT ON ADEQUACY OF CONTROL. Batch totals provide adequate control if there are procedures to adjust any manually established totals for rejected items and to ensure that rejected data is corrected and later reinput. (See later section "Rejections.")

COMPUTER SEQUENCE CHECK

SITUATION 1:

All transactions are recorded on serially prenumbered documents.

IMPACT ON ADEQUACY OF CONTROL. Control is satisfactory provided the issue of documents is controlled so that the numbers of all documents in issue are known.

EXAMPLE. Details of goods received are recorded on serially prenumbered forms. Unissued pads of forms are held by the purchasing department, which issues them to the receiving areas on request. A register is maintained which records the number series of all pads of documents and the date of their issue to receiving areas. A documents-issued report is sent to the EDP department daily.

SITUATION 2:

Transactions are recorded on forms that are numbered at the time or after they are completed.

IMPACT ON ADEQUACY OF CONTROL. It may be possible to establish adequate control if there are additional procedures to ensure that all documents are numbered, a proper number sequence is generated, and there are no missing or duplicate numbers. Control is not as strong as when prenumbered documents are used.

EXAMPLE. Shipping advices are numbered sequentially when goods are transferred from the finished inventory warehouse. The shipping supervisor ensures that a shipping advice accompanies all goods shipped and that the numbers are sequential.

SITUATION 3:

Programmed procedures are considered adequate.

IMPACT ON ADEQUACY OF CONTROL. The following factors must be considered: The sequence check must be logically sound. In this context, procedures are required to deal with more than one sequence of numbers running concurrently, changes or breaks in sequence, identification of missing numbers until the document is processed or the number is voided, and identification and rejection from further processing of duplicate numbers. All exceptions identified should be reported regularly in sufficient detail to permit proper investigation and follow-up by the user. General controls must ensure the continued and proper operation of the programmed procedures.

EXAMPLE. In Situation 1, the documents-issued report is used to set the issued-numbers parameters for use by the sequence check program. The document number of all goods received forms is first compared with an index file that records all numbers previously accepted by the system. This step identifies duplicate numbers and rejects them from further processing. Accepted numbers are written to the index file, which is then compared with the issued-numbers parameters to identify any missing numbers. Any numbers falling outside the parameters are also identified and rejected from further processing. Rejections are reported immediately and all other exceptions are reported on a cumulative basis at the end of each week.

SITUATION 4:

Exception reports are not cumulative and data can be rejected by the system.

IMPACT ON ADEQUACY OF CONTROL. Additional user procedures are required to ensure that all rejections are investigated and reentered. (See later section "Rejections.")

EXAMPLE. In the preceding example, housekeeping procedures on the index file mean that once a number sequence has been in issue for three months, it is cleared from the file and the issued-numbers parameters are adjusted accordingly. This means that missing-numbers reports are cumulative only for number sequences issued within the last three months. However, any documents submitted that fall outside the current parameters are rejected and reported, and therefore must be investigated by the user department.

SITUATION 5:

User procedures described previously are considered adequate.

IMPACT ON ADEQUACY OF CONTROL. The following conditions should be met: The user must understand the nature of the programmed procedures on which the exception report is based and the extent to which general controls are relied on to ensure the continued and proper operation of the programmed procedures. All reports must be properly reviewed in a timely manner. All exceptions must be investigated and appropriate action taken.

EXAMPLE. In the preceding example, the user (purchasing department) approved the sequence check at the system implementation stage and has been provided with a manual describing the way in which exceptions will be identified and reported. Each week rejections are investigated and re-input; missing numbers are queried with the goods receiving area. The user ensures that all number sequences issued are accounted for completely within three months of their issue.

SITUATION 6:

A sequence check is relied on to ensure completeness of input.

IMPACT ON ADEQUACY OF CONTROL. A separate control is required over completeness of update. It is likely that this will involve the use of run-to-run totals (discussed subsequently). In this situation, a total of accepted items must be produced at the time of, or before, the point at which the sequence check operates.

EXAMPLE. In the previous example, as each accepted number is written to the index file, the quantity of goods received for that transaction is added to an accumulator to produce a total for all accepted items. This total is reported at the end of the input validation report.

COMPUTER MATCHING

SITUATION 1:

Matching is acceptable as a control over completeness of input.

IMPACT ON ADEQUACY OF CONTROL. The relationship between input data and the reference data used in the matching process must be such that an input transaction is expected for each element of reference data. If this is not the case, a report of unmatched reference data cannot be used to ensure that all transactions are entered.

EXAMPLE. An employee master file is maintained and payroll transaction data is matched against the file. Transaction types processed include time records for each production worker (paid at an hourly rate) and overtime records for salaried staff. Matching can be used to ensure completeness of production time records, since a time record is expected for all production employees, who are identified separately on the employee master file. Since, however, not all salaried staff may work overtime during any one period, matching cannot be used to ensure that all overtime records are entered.

SITUATION 2:

Transaction data input is matched with a file of master file data or previously processed transaction data.

IMPACT ON ADEQUACY OF CONTROL. The matching procedures ensure completeness of input only if there are adequate controls over the file holding the master file reference data. Those controls must provide assurance that all reference data held on file is validated, the master file reference file is correctly maintained, and all amendments to the reference data are appropriately authorized. (The procedures necessary to achieve adequate control over validity of data and maintenance of data are discussed in subsequent sections of this appendix.)

EXAMPLE. Completeness of input of purchase invoices is achieved by matching against a file of goods received. All entries to this file are properly controlled for validity and for completeness and accuracy of input and update. Maintenance of the file is controlled by use of a total over the quantity field, which is agreed to a manual control account. Any adjustments to the file are printed separately for authorization by the purchasing supervisor.

SITUATION 3:

Programmed procedures are considered adequate.

IMPACT ON ADEQUACY OF CONTROL. The following condition should be met: The data fields matched must ensure that mismatches will be properly identified and reported. This usually involves matching on more than one field to ensure that an erroneous match is not possible, and it is particularly important if matching is also used to ensure accuracy of input. (See later section, "Adequacy of Controls Over Accuracy of Input and Update.")

EXAMPLE A. In the example in Situation 1, purchase invoices are matched with goods received on the following fields: goods received number, product code, supplier code, and quantity.

IMPACT ON ADEQUACY OF CONTROL. The matched records must be indicated appropriately on the reference file to permit production of a report of unmatched items.

EXAMPLE B. Any "matched" goods received record is deleted from the file; consequently, only unmatched items are held on file.

IMPACT ON ADEQUACY OF CONTROL. Reports must be produced at regular intervals, listing outstanding items for user investigation. It may be appropriate to list only long-outstanding items if there is a time lag associated with processing of master file reference data and processing of transactions.

EXAMPLE C. The company expects to receive suppliers' invoices within two weeks of receiving goods. Consequently, the report of "unmatched" goods received does not list any items where the goods were received within the two weeks prior to the date of the report.

SITUATION 4:

User procedures relating to Situations 1, 2, and 3 are considered adequate.

IMPACT ON ADEQUACY OF CONTROL. The user should understand the principal programmed procedures on which the matching control relies and the fact that the continued and proper operation of these programmed procedures is ensured by general controls, and investigate and correct, as appropriate, all mismatches and reports of long-outstanding items.

EXAMPLE. In the example in Situation 1, the purchase accounts department is responsible for following up all mismatches and unmatched goods received reports.

SITUATION 5:

Matching is used to ensure completeness of input.

IMPACT ON ADEQUACY OF CONTROL. A separate control is required to provide assurance that all data is updated to the computer file. Usually, this is achieved by use of run-to-run controls (discussed subsequently). In order to be satisfied that there is no gap in control between the input and update stages, a total of accepted items should be generated during the run in which the matching control operates.

EXAMPLE. In the previous example, during the run in which purchase invoices are matched with the goods received file, whenever a match is achieved, the gross dollar value of the invoice is accumulated to produce a total of accepted items, which is reported at the end of the input run. This total is reconciled to the update report.

RUN-TO-RUN CONTROLS

SITUATION 1:

This type of control can be used only to ensure completeness of update. An additional control is required to ensure completeness of input.

IMPACT ON ADEQUACY OF CONTROL. The total of accepted data must be established during the run in which the input control operates. A total established in this way automatically includes all data accepted into the application and ensures that there is no break in control between input and update stages.

EXAMPLE. During a computer sequence check of serially numbered documents, the reference number of each accepted transaction is written to an index file. At the same time, the quantity field for that transaction is added to an accumulator to produce a quantity total for all accepted transactions. This total is recorded at the end of the input validation report and is subsequently agreed to a total of updated transactions.

SITUATION 2:

The total of accepted items is agreed manually to the total of items actually updated onto the master file.

IMPACT ON ADEQUACY OF CONTROL. Control is adequate provided there are procedures to investigate any differences disclosed by the reconciliation and to take appropriate follow-up action. Reconciliation procedures may have to take account of summarization of totals, when input runs occur more than once during a day, but a single update (often overnight) is carried out. Rejection of data between input and update stages must be considered. This is more likely in a batch processing situation than in on-line/real-time systems, since the increased availability of master file reference data associated with on-line entry facilitates validation of data at the input stage. This usually eliminates the need for pre-update validation of data.

EXAMPLE. A company operates out of several locations, each of which has its own computer processing facilities. Inventory movements are entered at each location and updated to detailed inventory master files maintained (by quantity only) at each site. In addition, all accepted input is transmitted to the head office (via terminals at each site) where it is consolidated, evaluated, and updated to the company's financial inventory records. The head office receives input control totals from each site. These totals are summarized to produce a grand total of all accepted input data; adjusted to take account of rejections, which may occur if financial information is not available for a particular inventory; and reconciled with the total of inventory movements reported as updated to the financial inventory records. The reconciliation is carried out by head office staff, who also ensure that all rejections are investigated and reentered.

SITUATION 3:

The total of accepted items is reconciled by the computer with the total of items updated onto the master file.

IMPACT ON ADEQUACY OF CONTROL. Control is adequate provided that programmed procedures take account, as appropriate, of summarization of totals, changes in totals, and rejections. Adequate evidence of the result of the reconciliation is reported and any differences are reported in sufficient detail to permit user investigation. The user department confirms that the reconciliation was satisfactory, investigates and acts on any differences reported, and ensures that all rejections are entered. General controls are sufficient to ensure the continued and proper operation of programmed procedures.

EXAMPLE. Details of shipments are entered to a sales accounting system; they are then evaluated and updated to the accounts receivable file. Control over completeness of input is assured by a computer sequence check and, during the sequence check run, a total over the quantity field is established for all accepted data. As each accepted item is evaluated, the computer accumulates totals over the quantity field and the value field, and at the end of the evaluation run, it agrees the total quantity evaluated to the total of accepted items. Evaluated shipments are then updated to the accounts receivable file, and the computer agrees the total value updated to the previous total. All totals are reported and the differences are evaluated and specified to assist in user follow-up procedures.

SITUATION 4:

Run-to-run controls are used to ensure the completeness of update in an on-line system.

IMPACT ON ADEQUACY OF CONTROL. Although the concept of a single program run total is no longer valid in an on-line system, it is still possible to accumulate totals at various stages in processing. The totals can then be reconciled to ensure that data is not lost during processing. For example, programmed procedures are designed to ensure that during any fixed time period, separate totals are accumulated for all accepted transactions and all transactions updated to the master files. Provided these requirements are met, the totals can be reconciled subsequently (see preceding situations), thereby ensuring that accepted data is completely updated onto the computer files.

EXAMPLE. In the system described previously, details of shipments are entered via on-line terminals situated in the shipping area. Data is validated on entry and, if accepted, immediately written to a transaction file, evaluated, and updated onto the accounts receivable file. Throughout the day, the following separate totals are accumulated for all transactions: the quantity field of all accepted items, quantity fields of all updated items, and the value fields of all updated items. These totals are subsequently reconciled in the way described previously.

SITUATION 5:

Run-to-run controls are used to ensure completeness of update in a data base system.

IMPACT ON ADEQUACY OF CONTROL. The totals used may only be item counts over data elements accepted and updated. In this case, system software is relied on to ensure that all necessary linkages are set up to establish the logical relationships between individual items of data. The function of systems software procedures should be ensured by appropriate general controls. Periodically, the completeness of the linkages should be tested by reconciling the various logical groupings with independent control accounts.

EXAMPLE. A company has a fully integrated, computerized accounting system that covers all accounting functions. Data is organized as a data base, and various control techniques are used to ensure that all items of data are written to the data base. In order to confirm the completeness of the logical linkages within the data base, each month value totals for each logical unit—accounts receivable, accounts payable, inventory—are reported and reconciled with control totals established independently by users using transaction reports produced during normal day-to-day processing.

REJECTIONS

SITUATION 1:

Data is rejected by the system at input and/or update stages and written to a suspense file.

IMPACT ON ADEQUACY OF CONTROL. Control is adequate if the following requirements are met: Programmed procedures are appropriate to ensure that all rejected items are written to the suspense file completely and accurately; the suspense file is subject to proper maintenance controls (discussed subsequently); programmed procedures are adequate to ensure that re-input of rejected data is identified by the system; data found to be correct is matched with the suspense file and the appropriate record deleted from the suspense file; records still on the suspense file are reported regularly and the reports are investigated by the user. Corrective action taken should be noted on the report to facilitate a supervisory review of follow-up procedures. The function of appropriate programmed procedures is assured by adequate general controls.

EXAMPLE. Batch totals are entered in a register and the documents are entered to the sales invoicing system. Documents with invalid customer or inventory codes are rejected by the input validation program and written to a suspense file. The suspense file is controlled via totals over the quantity field. After each update, a report is produced showing totals for balance brought forward, additions, deletions, and balance carried forward. All rejections are listed as they arise, and the suspense file is then printed in full at the end of each week. The following procedures ensure that rejections are dealt with properly: Totals of rejected items are noted in the batch register during reconciliation of batch totals and are also posted to a manual suspense control account; rejections are investigated and corrected, and re-inputs are rebatched, these batch numbers being prefixed with an "R." Reentered totals are posted to the suspense control account. If reentered data is correct, it is matched with the suspense file and the relevant suspense record is deleted; at the end of each week, the manual suspense balance is reconciled to that reported for the computer file, and the suspense listing is reviewed to ensure that there is no undue build-up of rejections.

SITUATION 2:

Data is rejected by the system at input and/or update stages but no suspense file is maintained.

IMPACT ON ADEQUACY OF CONTROL. Control is adequate if there are appropriate programmed and user procedures to ensure that all rejections are reported and investigated promptly, and that the appropriate corrective action is taken. The actual procedures depend in part on the input control used. When batch or control totals are used, a manual control total over rejections not yet resubmitted may be used.

EXAMPLE A. The example in Situation 1 demonstrates use of a manual control account. Control is not as good as in that example because there is no suspense file or related reports.

IMPACT ON ADEQUACY OF CONTROL. When other input control techniques are used (such as matching or sequence check), it is likely that the associated exception reports will be cumulative. Therefore, a regular review of those reports to identify and investigate old items should ensure that all rejections are reentered eventually. If reports are not cumulative, manual procedures that ensure that all items on all reports have been cleared properly, plus an appropriate level of supervision, may be the only assurance that all rejections are dealt with properly.

EXAMPLE B. Data is rejected as in the example in Situation 1. However, the input control is a cumulative sequence check that produces regular reports of shipping advices not yet accepted by the system. Investigation of those reports on a regular basis ensures that all transactions eventually are accepted into the invoicing system.

IMPACT ON ADEQUACY OF CONTROL. In on-line systems, rejections are most likely to occur at the time of original input of data. Usually, corrections are made immediately. If checking reports, computer sequence check, or computer matching is used as a control over completeness of input, rejections probably are controlled as described previously. If these techniques are not used, pre-input or session control totals should be established manually. By reconciliation with accepted data totals, these are used to ensure that rejections are reentered.

EXAMPLE C. A company ships goods to its customers based on shipping advices that are output from the sales order processing system. A file is maintained of sales orders not yet shipped. Controls over the maintenance of this file are considered adequate. When goods are shipped, a copy of the shipping advice is reentered via on-line terminals in the shipping department and matched against the outstanding order file. Accepted shipping advices are valued, a sales invoice is produced, and the transaction is updated on the accounts receivable file. Any rejections are investigated and corrected in the shipping department and re-input. Each week an exception report of unshipped orders over one month old is produced. Proper investigation of this report ensures that all orders are completed and, therefore, that all shipments are entered to the invoicing system.

SITUATION 3:

Data is not actually rejected by the system. Unusual situations are reported and processing continues.

IMPACT ON ADEQUACY OF CONTROL. Control is adequate if there are procedures to ensure that all unusual situations are identified (by programmed procedure) and reported, all reports are investigated promptly, and all necessary adjustments are made. It is particularly important that reports are investigated and adjustments made promptly, since, when the "unusual situation" is actually an error, the company's accounting records will be inaccurate until the adjustment is made. Similarly, the function of proper programmed procedures is essential to ensure that all possible error situations are identified.

EXAMPLE. Customer remittance advices are entered to the accounts receivable file, which is organized on an open-item basis. If the remittance cannot be matched accurately against an outstanding transaction, it is updated as a new unmatched item and coded as "unmatched cash." A cumulative report of all such items on the accounts receivable file is produced each week to permit manual matching. The accounts receivable supervisor reviews this report at the end of each month to ensure that all cash is matched and that therefore an accurate age analysis of outstanding accounts will be produced.

RELIANCE ON CONTROLS OVER ANOTHER APPLICATION

SITUATION:

Data input to one application system is updated to a different system.

IMPACT ON ADEQUACY OF CONTROL. Control over completeness of update of data to the second system is adequate if control over entry of data to the initial system is satisfactory and programmed procedures are adequate to identify and extract all accepted data required for update to the second system. In particular, a total of data so identified should be accumulated during the extraction process. Adequate run-to-run controls are needed to ensure that all data extracted is actually updated to the relevant computer files and the function of proper programmed procedures is assured.

EXAMPLE. A company has computerized all of its inventory systems. All inventory movements (including scrappings, interstore transfers, perpetual inventory) are input via terminals in the various inventory locations to an integrated data collection (IDC) system. Completeness of input is ensured by computer sequence checks. Data is then extracted for update to the various inventory and production control systems. Item counts and quantity totals are accumulated during the extraction procedures. These are reported and reconciled, by an inventory control section, with the totals updated to the appropriate inventory systems.

ADEQUACY OF CONTROLS OVER ACCURACY OF INPUT AND UPDATE

It is important that transaction data be entered and updated accurately. For those purposes, input includes initial recording, transcription from source data to input documents, or the conversion of the data on documents into machine-readable form.

Adequacy of control is discussed here. However, similar control procedures may apply to different cycles and different control objectives.

Accuracy of input and update is concerned with individual data fields, as opposed to transactions. It can be achieved only if all significant data fields are controlled adequately. Consequently, it is necessary to identify those data fields that must be controlled and the level or standard of control that is required. Two other factors that must be considered are:

1. It may not be practical to establish a high standard of control over all important data fields.

2. Different control techniques may be applied to different data fields within the same transaction.

In general, all value and quantity fields are financially significant and should be subject to adequate control procedures. Certain reference data fields may also be important. Examples of these are:

- *Reference numbers*. These include account numbers, general ledger codes, and inventory codes. The latter are important, for example, in ensuring that inventory is priced correctly.
- *Dates*. There are many instances where dates are of accounting significance. For example, dates may be used either to analyze data, as in aging of accounts receivable or inventory balances, or to initiate accounting procedures, such as due date of installment repayments.
- *Indicators*. These also may be of accounting significance. For example, in payroll systems, the distinction between new hires and terminations may be made by use of different indicators. Credit control procedures within an accounts receivable system also may rely heavily on the use of indicators. Failure to input and update these indicators accurately may result in a breakdown of control procedures and a loss of revenue to the company.

In order to achieve control over accuracy of update, procedures must ensure that:

- The correct amount is updated to the correct account.
- The correct generation of the master file is updated.

Although user controls may be of some assistance in these areas, considerble reliance will be placed on programmed procedures, particularly to ensure that data is updated to the correct account.

There are a wide variety of techniques available to establish accuracy of input and update. They are designed to ensure that:

- There are adequate controls over data fields of accounting significance.
- There are adequate procedures to identify and investigate any differences.
- The programmed procedures are adequate to ensure that the correct account will be updated.

The following techniques can be used to achieve control over accuracy of input and update:

- Extension of the controls used to achieve completeness of input and update.
- Programmed edit checks.
- Review of output.
- Use of prerecorded input.
- Verification of data conversion.

These techniques are discussed in more detail in following sections.

In practice, the auditor is likely to be confronted with a combination of techniques. It is important to identify the principal controls on which to place reliance. In general, controls should be selected in the order just listed. As is discussed subsequently in more detail, verification of data conversion is not considered an adequate control for audit purposes.

EXTENSION OF CONTROLS OVER COMPLETENESS OF INPUT AND UPDATE

SITUATION 1:

Batch totals are used to control completeness of input via manual or computer agreement of pre-established totals.

IMPACT ON ADEQUACY OF CONTROL. Control over accuracy of input is adequate only with respect to the particular data field used to establish totals. Also note that the use of batch totals does not guard against compensating errors in one or more individual items. Additional procedures are required to ensure that all entries are updated accurately to the correct computer files. The use of computer agreement of pre-established totals entered on a batch header does not provide any security protection over unauthorized change because it allows anyone who has access to the batch access to both the data (the transactions) and the control (the batch header).

EXAMPLE. Employees' time cards are entered into the payroll system. Batch totals are established over hours worked. These are agreed manually to similar batch totals accumulated and reported by the computer as part of the input validation system.

SITUATION 2:

Batch totals are posted to a manual control account that is reconciled periodically with the balance on the master file.

IMPACT ON ADEQUACY OF CONTROL. Controls are adequate to ensure that the particular field totaled is updated in total, accurately, to the correct generation of the master file. Additional controls are required to provide assurance that the correct individual account is updated accurately. This may be achieved by user controls, such as periodic reconciliation of accounts payable balances with suppliers' statements. However, in the absence of adequate user procedures, reliance is placed on programmed procedures, and therefore on general controls, to ensure that individual accounts are updated accurately.

EXAMPLE. All transactions types entered into the accounts receivable system are batched and totals are established over gross dollar values. Those totals are posted to a manual control account that is reconciled each month with the total balance reported for the accounts receivable file. There are no specific user controls to ensure that individual accounts receivables balances are stated accurately, but the general controls are adequate.

SITUATION 3:

A one-for-one check is carried out, using retained copies of source documents.

IMPACT ON ADEQUACY OF CONTROL. Control is adequate to ensure accuracy either of input or both input and update, depending on the stage at which the output report is produced. (See earlier section "Adequacy of Controls Over Completeness of Input and Update.") This control is particularly effective, since it can cover all data fields of significance. It is, however, time-consuming and therefore relatively costly. It is usually encountered only when low volumes of financially sensitive data are being processed.

EXAMPLE. Following the example in Situation 1, the personnel department agrees all data fields on the source documents to the details reported on the report.

SITUATION 4:

A one-for-one check is carried out, using documents returned from data processing.

IMPACT ON ADEQUACY OF CONTROL. Control over accuracy of input and update is not adequate, since unauthorized amendments to data can be made while the documents are outside the user department's control.

EXAMPLE. In the payroll example of completeness controls, there is no control to ensure that data recorded on source documents (such as rates of pay) cannot be amended in an unauthorized manner while outside the control of the personnel department.

SITUATION 5:

Run-to-run totals are used to ensure completeness of update.

IMPACT ON ADEQUACY OF CONTROL. The control is also adequate to ensure that, for the particular field totaled, the computer file is accurately updated in total. This type of control does not, however, guard against compensating errors involving more than one individual account; neither can it ensure that the correct individual account has been updated.

EXAMPLE. Details of good shipped are entered into a sales accounting system for evaluation and update to the accounts receivable file. Run-to-run totals are accumulated at each stage of processing, including data acceptance. The totals, which are reported, are as follows:

- During data acceptance, a total over the quantity field.
- During evaluation, totals over both the quantity and the value fields.
- During update, a total over the value field.

The user department reconciles all totals and investigates differences, thereby ensuring that the accounts receivable file is accurately updated in total.

SITUATION 6:

Computer matching is used to ensure that data is entered completely.

IMPACT ON ADEQUACY OF CONTROL. Control is adequate to ensure that, with respect to those data fields matched, data is also entered accurately. The effectiveness of this control is determined by:

- The availability of reference data to use in the match. For this reason, matching as a control over accuracy of input is most commonly used in on-line systems.
- The extent to which the reference data can be relied on. Controls should exist to ensure that only valid, authorized data is used in the matching process.
- The function of appropriate programmed procedures that are relied on to ensure that:
  - — Only matched data is accepted.
  - — All mismatches are reported.
- In on-line systems, the facility may exist to override a mismatch. If this is possible, programmed procedures should be appropriate to ensure that all such situations are reported.

- The diligence of the user department in investigating and following up all mismatches (and overrides, as just described for on-line systems).

EXAMPLE. Purchase invoices are entered into a purchase accounting system and, during input validation procedures, certain fields are matched with data held on a goods received suspense file. The following fields are matched:

- Supplier code
- Product code
- Quantity received
- Purchase price

All mismatches are rejected and investigated by the accounts payable staff.

SITUATION 7:

A transaction log is produced during processing of data in an on-line, real-time system.

IMPACT ON ADEQUACY OF CONTROL. It may be possible to ensure accuracy of update by using special programs and the transaction log to reperform processing and compare the results (on an item-by-item basis) with the original results of processing. In a large, complex computer installation where it is impractical, or even impossible, to rely on user procedures to ensure accuracy of processing, this method may be effective. However, controls of this nature rely heavily on programmed procedures, and therefore on the adequacy of general controls, for their effectiveness.

EXAMPLE. A company operates an on-line, computerized accounting system. Once accepted, all data is captured on a transaction log. At the end of each day's processing, security dumps are taken of all data files. Overnight, a set of programs reperforms the day's processing using the current day's transaction log and the file dumps from the previous evening. The results are then compared, on an item-by-item basis, with the original results of processing as shown in the most recent file dumps. All differences are reported and then investigated by a central data control section.

PROGRAMMED EDIT CHECKS

SITUATION 1:

Edit checks are considered adequate to ensure accuracy of input.

IMPACT ON ADEQUACY OF CONTROL. Edit checks are programmed procedures that usually result in the production of exception reports. If user controls do not ensure the function of the appropriate programmed procedures, the adequacy of general controls must be established.

- The effectiveness of edit checks in ensuring accuracy of data is determined by:
  - — The extent to which possible error conditions were identified at the time the system was designed.
  - — The skill of system designers, system analysts, and programmers in incorporating checking procedures capable of identifying and reporting the error conditions expected to occur.
- In many cases, edit checks cannot provide conclusive proof that only accurate data is accepted; however, a suitable combination of edit checks may help considerably in reducing the likelihood of error.
- In on-line systems, it may be possible to override edit checks. If so, the system should ensure that all instances of override are reported suitably for investigation.

EXAMPLE. Input validation programs often incorporate edit checks on data input to the system. Any data failing these checks is rejected and reported as an exception, but accepted data is not reported. Consequently, user procedures cannot ensure the function of the validation programs.

A company has set up a product coding structure that allows any number in the range 01 to 99 as a valid code. A programmed edit check can ensure that the code is valid (by checking whether it is in the range 01 to 99), but cannot ensure that no errors of transposition have occurred, since any valid code transposes to another valid code. Protecting reference codes from such error usually is achieved by use of techniques such as check digits and alphanumeric combinations.

SITUATION 2:

Edit checks are identified as controls over accuracy.

IMPACT ON ADEQUACY OF CONTROL. The edit checks are likely to be from one of the following categories:

- *Format check.* Ensures that data is in the correct format.
- *Reasonableness check.* Compares the data with predetermined parameters that indicate expected values of the data.
- *Dependency check.* Presumes that there is a logical relationship between two or more data fields.

- *Existence check.* The standard validity check; compares reference data with a table or master file of permitted data.
- *Double matching check.* This method requires that the input include both new data and the old data to be overwritten. By matching input against data already on file, some assurance is obtained that the correct account is updated.
- *Document reconciliation.* This technique, which is common in on-line systems that permit individual entry of transactions, involves checking the mathematical accuracy of numeric data prior to entry. A hash total is established of all, or all important, numeric data fields on the document. The hash total is entered, with the transaction data; the program totals the numeric fields and compares the result with the hash total. Transactions that do not balance are rejected.

EXAMPLES. The following examples are in the same sequence as the preceding categories.

- Data field is checked as numeric.
- Quantities of goods shipped are checked as being within an average range. The average is determined by the sales department, based on sales over the past year.
- All employees coded as "production" should have an hourly rate of pay, whereas all "staff" should have an annual salary.
- All inventory product codes are checked against the product code master file to ensure that only valid codes are used. The codes should be set up to identify transposition errors. (See the example in Situation 1.)
- Adjustments to payroll master file data require that both old and new salaries are entered. Thd old salary is matched against that recorded on the master file for the particular employee.
- Multiline sales orders are entered into an on-line system. A hash total is calculated manually including all product codes, quantities, account numbers, and date. The hash total is also entered and compared by the computer program with a similar total that it computes from the data entered. Any out-of-balance orders are rejected.

SITUATION 3:

User procedures associated with programmed edit checks are to be considered satisfactory.

IMPACT ON ADEQUACY OF CONTROL. The procedures must comply with the following requirements:

- The user must fully understand:
  - The nature of both the programmed procedures involved and the exception reports produced.
  - The fact that general controls are being relied on to ensure the continued and proper operation of the programmed procedures.
- All exceptions must be promptly investigated and corrected.

EXAMPLE. The user department approves all edit checks at the time of system design and implementation. Investigation of exceptions and follow-up action is noted on the exception report for review by a responsible official.

SITUATION 4:

Edit checks rely on reference data or parameters.

IMPACT ON ADEQUACY OF CONTROL. Control is adequate only if there are procedures to ensure that all reference data and parameters are authorized and maintained properly. The reference data may be held in program tables or in master files.

EXAMPLE. All files of reference data should be properly maintained (see later section "Adequacy of Controls Over Maintenance of Data") and amendments should be properly authorized (see later section "Adequacy of Controls Over Validity of Data"). Parameters used in validation procedures should be printed on the validation report and checked by the user department.

REVIEW OF OUTPUT

SITUATION:

User review of output is used to ensure accuracy of processing.

IMPACT ON ADEQUACY OF CONTROL. It is unlikely that the review by itself will be adequate to achieve control unless it is actualiy a one-for-one check. (See earlier section "One-for-One Checking.") However, if the review is of selected output only—the selection being made by appropriate edit checks—the combined edit/review procedures may provide reasonable assurance that only accurate data has been processed.

EXAMPLE. A company expects that 90 percent of all credit given to customers will be for less than $3,000. All credit notes of a value greater than or equal to $3,000 are reported. A responsible official reviews the list to ensure that all such items are valid and correct.

PRERECORDED INPUT

SITUATION 1:

Data to be entered is prerecorded on the input document.

IMPACT ON ADEQUACY OF CONTROL. Control over accuracy of initial recording of prerecorded fields is adequate provided there are procedures to ensure the data so recorded is correct. This situation may be associated with a turn-around document, where information is output by the computer and subsequently used as input during a later stage of processing. Procedures must ensure that if correct data values are different from those prerecorded, the correct value is recorded and entered in place of the prerecorded value. Separate controls are required to ensure the accuracy of input of altered data.

EXAMPLE. If data is rejected from processing, it is written to a suspense file and reported on an error correction turn-around document. The fields causing the error condition are asterisked. The user investigates and corrects those fields and resubmits the error correction form. A one-for-one check is used to ensure accuracy of input of the amended data.

SITUATION 2:

Turn-around documents are used to make amendments to master file data.

IMPACT ON ADEQUACY OF CONTROL. Control is adequate provided the user ensures that the correct input form is used by checking the relevant reference data.

EXAMPLE. Personnel history cards are printed by the computer. When a personnel change is necessary, the card is retrieved from the file, the name checked to ensure that the correct card was pulled, and changes indicated by amending the appropriate fields. (Output is checked one-for-one for changed fields.)

SITUATION 3:

Prerecorded data is in one of the following machine-readable forms:

- Optical character recognition (OCR).
- Optical mark recognition (OMR).
- Magnetic ink character recognition (MICR).
- Punched card.
- Bar code.
- Magnetic stripe.

IMPACT ON ADEQUACY OF CONTROL. Control over both initial recording and conversion to machine-readable form is adequate provided that:

- The edit check used is appropriate to identify, report, and reject any incorrect input form from further processing.
- General controls are adequate to ensure the function of proper programmed procedures.
- User procedures include investigation, correction, and reentry of rejected data. If documents are damaged so that the particular input technique can no longer be used, alternate procedures and controls are necessary to ensure that such data is entered accurately.

EXAMPLE. Remittance advices are sent to customers. The customer number and amount outstanding are recorded using OCR characters on a returnable remittance advice. The company need only key the amount paid if it differs from the amount due.

INTERACTIVE FEEDBACK CHECK

SITUATION:

Reference data is entered via terminal. The system replies with descriptive information that can be used to check the data entered.

IMPACT ON ADEQUACY OF CONTROL. Control is adequate if the feedback data actually is used to check the accuracy of the input.

EXAMPLE. A sales clerk takes orders over the telephone. The customer number, product number, and quantity ordered are entered via terminal. The customer's name, product name, quantity, price, and dollar value appear on the terminal screen. The clerk verifies the customer's name, product name, quantity, price, and dollar value with the customer before releasing the order to the system.

VERIFICATION OF DATA CONVERSION

SITUATION:

Verification of data conversion is the only control over accuracy of input.

IMPACT ON ADEQUACY OF CONTROL. It may be possible to rely on key verification to ensure that data is converted accurately to machine-readable form. Programmed procedures must be adequate to ensure that all data is processed accurately. This is a very weak control; it should not be relied on to control financially sensitive data.

EXAMPLE. Certain customer master file data (such as delivery address) is not financially significant, and therefore is not controlled for accuracy of input and update except by key verification and reliance on programmed procedures.

CORRECT GENERATION OF FILE

SITUATION 1:

Either batch totals or totals of accepted items are posted to a manual control account that is agreed periodically to the balance reported for the computer master file.

IMPACT ON ADEQUACY OF CONTROL. Control is adequate to ensure that the correct generation of the master file is updated. If this was not the case, manual and computer control totals would disagree. Any differences should be investigated and acted upon by the user responsible for maintaining the control account.

EXAMPLE. The following totals are posted to a manual accounts receivable control account in the general ledger:

- Invoice values, as reported by the computer during the evaluation of goods shipped records.
- Customer remittances, as recorded in the cash book.
- Adjustments, write-offs, and such, as recorded in a batch register.
- Credit note values, as accumulated by the computer during input validation procedures.

At each month-end, the accounts supervisor reconciles the balance in the general ledger with that reported for the computer accounts receivable file.

SITUATION 2:

A manual control account is not maintained.

IMPACT ON ADEQUACY OF CONTROL. Control may be adequate to ensure that the correct generation of file is updated if either:

- A user department ensures that the brought-forward total agrees with that carried forward after the last update.

- Computer operations controls are adequate to ensure that the correct file is used.

EXAMPLE. Each time the accounts payable file is updated, a movements report is produced showing the following:

- Balance brought forward.
- Movements by transaction type.
- Balance carried forward.

The accounts payable supervisor ensures that the balance brought forward is the same as that previously carried forward.

UPDATING CORRECT ACCOUNT

SITUATION:

Programmed procedures relating to update of individual accounts are considered appropriate.

IMPACT ON ADEQUACY OF CONTROL. Programmed procedures must ensure that if it is not possible to update the incorrect account (for example, because there is no corresponding master record on file), all relevant data will be reported and either rejected or written to a suspense account, as considered appropriate. User procedures must provide that all reports are investigated and the necessary adjustments made. (See earlier section "Rejections.") Since it is unlikely that user procedures will be adequate to ensure the continued and proper operation of the programmed update procedures, general controls should be adequate to provide assurance in this area.

EXAMPLE. Accepted inventory movements are updated to the financial inventory file, which reports inventory valued at a moving average price. The calculation of the average price requires that negative stock balances do not exist. Consequently, if outward movement would result in a negative inventory balance, it is not updated to the inventory master file but is posted to a suspense account until there is adequate inventory to cover the movement. Any movements of inventory for which a financial master record is not available are also reported and written to the suspense file. The suspense file is printed out in full after each update to permit user investigation.

ADEQUACY OF CONTROLS OVER VALIDITY OF DATA

An organization's procedures for ensuring that transactions are valid and are being executed in accordance with management's intentions are an important part of its internal control. Adequacy of control is discussed here. However, similar control procedures may apply to different cycles and different control objectives.

Computer systems rely on a highly structured environment for their effectiveness. The specific definition of standard procedures associated with such an environment usually results in increased requirements for authorization. For example, in addition to authorization of individual transactions, it may be necessary to authorize control reconciliations, treatment of rejections, overrides of normal procedures, and master file data amendments.

The procedures which ensure that only valid data is processed usually take one of two forms:

1. Transactions are subject to a manual check and/or authorization by a responsible, supervisory official.
2. Transactions are checked by programmed procedures that examine the data by reference to criteria set by management.

The term ''validity,'' as used in this context, refers to the authorization of data. It should not be confused with the term ''validation,'' as applied to the edit programs. The latter refers to an existence check against a table or file of valid numbers. (See the discussion of existence checks in earlier section ''Programmed Edit Checks,'' Situation 2.)

One of the important aspects of authorizing data in computer systems is the timing of authorization. This refers to the fact that frequently data is authorized at the time it is first introduced into the system, rather than at the time the data is used. This is particularly true of master file data, but also occurs with transaction data. For authorization to be effective and to ensure that only authorized data is processed, it is necessary to structure procedures so that authorization is either:

- Carried out or rechecked after control has been established over completeness and accuracy of input and update.
- Carried out or rechecked after processing is complete.

The adequacy of control procedures is discussed in more detail in the following sections.

TIMING OF AUTHORIZATION

SITUATION 1:

Authorization is carried out or rechecked on documents after control has been established over completeness and accuracy.

IMPACT ON ADEQUACY OF CONTROL. Provided that the completeness and accuracy controls are satisfactory, control over authorization is adequate to ensure that:

- Only authorized documents are processed.
- Only authorized amounts are processed.

EXAMPLE. Purchase invoices are posted to an accounts payable master file and check payments are generated automatically for all invoices on file. It is therefore important to ensure that all invoices on file have been properly authorized for payment. Control over completeness and accuracy of input and update of invoices is achieved by use of batch totals that are posted to a manual control account. All user procedures are considered satisfactory. Batched invoices are passed to the accounts payable supervisor after batch totals have been established and recorded on a header slip. The supervisor test-checks the batch totals, authorizes all invoices in the batch, and notes the batch total in a register. At the end of each day, the supervisor totals the register, thereby accumulating a figure of authorized purchase invoices for posting to the manual control account. Checking the agreement of manual and computer control accounts ensures that only authorized data is processed.

SITUATION 2:

Authorization is carried out or rechecked on reports after processing.

IMPACT ON ADEQUACY OF CONTROL. Control is adequate to ensure that only authorized data is processed, provided that the organization is satisfied that all processed data is, in fact, reported. This can usually be ensured by appropriate programmed procedures and adequate general controls.

EXAMPLE. A company awards salary increases every six months. After the amendments have been processed, a full report of the employee master file is produced. Each person's salary is authorized by the personnel director. The completeness of the list is ensured by checking entries against a master list maintained by the personnel office.

SITUATION 3:

Data is authorized at the time a document is prepared.

IMPACT ON ADEQUACY OF CONTROL. The presence of an authorizing signature is not, in itself, adequate to ensure that only authorized data is processed. For authorization to be effective, it must be controlled in one of the ways described in Situations 1 and 2.

EXAMPLE. Selling price increases are authorized by the sales director.

A copy of the relevant memo is sent to the sales department that is responsible for updating the sales price file. The sales director does not check subsequently that only amendments authorized personally are updated to the sales price file.

SITUATION 4:

Rejections occur.

IMPACT ON ADEQUACY OF CONTROL. It is necessary to ensure that unauthorized data cannot be introduced during correction and reentry of errors. This might be achieved in one of the following ways:

- Ensuring that any adjustments to previously authorized control totals are themselves subjected to authorization.
- Ensuring that all data reentered is controlled for authorization in one of the ways described in Situations 1 and 2 for original data.

EXAMPLES. In the example in Situation 1, insertion of unauthorized data would be identified during agreement of the control accounts.

In the example in Situation 2, if the master file report is not produced until all data has been accepted, the post-processing authorization is effective over both original and reentered data.

PROGRAMMED VALIDITY CHECKS

SITUATION:

The validity of data is checked by the computer.

IMPACT ON ADEQUACY OF CONTROL. Control is adequate if the following requirements are met:

- Programmed procedures can be relied on to ensure that all exceptions are reported in sufficient detail to permit adequate user investigation.
- All reference data items, or parameters, used by the validation procedures are themselves subject to adequate controls with respect to maintenance of data and authorization of amendments.
- All reference data items, or parameters, are set at levels that result in the production of meaningful exception reports.
- Any facility to override the validation procedures is subject to appropriate approval procedures.
- All exception reports are investigated and acted on by user

departments in a timely manner. To do this effectively, the user must understand the programmed procedures on which the reports are based.

EXAMPLES. The following examples are arranged in the same sequence as the requirements.

- General controls are adequate to ensure the functioning of proper programmed procedures.
- Credit limits used in validation of incoming sales orders are controlled satisfactorily for authorization and maintenance. (See relevant sections of this appendix.)
- All credit memos over $1,000 are printed for manual authorization, but this results in 40 percent of all credits being printed. Clearly, the $1,000 limit is too low to produce a useful report.
- A separate validation report lists any instances of override and is distributed directly to the person responsible for approving those events.
- Exception reports are distributed directly to those responsible for investigating and authorizing the exception conditions.

ADEQUACY OF CONTROLS OVER MAINTENANCE OF DATA

An organization's procedures for ensuring that data is maintained correctly on computer files are an important part of its internal control. Adequacy of control is discussed here. However, similar control procedures may apply to different cycles and different control objectives.

The term "maintenance" is used in this context to describe those procedures intended to ensure the following:

- *Data remains correct.* It must be valid, accurate, and complete as input and updated to the file, until such time as it is deleted during authorized processing.
- *Data remains current.* All data requiring amendment is identified and appropriate action taken.

In manual systems, all data is visible. As such, it is subject to scrutiny during normal day-to-day processing. Usually, this ensures that the data remains reliable. In computer systems, data stored on magnetic media may be changed erroneously without visible evidence of the change. Consequently, maintenance controls are required to ensure that stored data is not altered, except in accordance with management's intentions.

The requirement to ensure that data remains correct applies to both transaction data and master file data. In theory, the fact that errors in master file data will be more far-reaching in effect than errors in transaction data means that master file data should be subject to a higher standard of control. However, in practice it is often found that:

- Maintenance of transaction data is more secure than that of master file data.
- Maintenance controls are only adequate for particularly significant data fields, such as value fields. Maintenance of fields of lesser accounting significance are often dependent on the existence of adequate data file security controls. (See the discussions of general controls in Chapter 15, "Application Controls—II," and in Appendix A.)

The term "maintenance" (also referred to as "continuity") as used here should not be confused with the term "maintenance" as applied to computer files. The latter refers to procedures used to amend data stored on files.

CORRECTNESS OF DATA

SITUATION 1:

Batch totals are posted to a manual control account that is agreed periodically to the balance reported for the computer master file.

IMPACT ON ADEQUACY OF CONTROL. Control is adequate to ensure that the particular data field used to generate the totals is maintained properly. It does not, however, identify compensating errors within one or more individual records on the file. This control technique is most commonly applied to transaction data held on master files. Usually the relevant value field is totaled. It also may be used to control master file reference data (by producing a hash total of the relevant field). However, since master file data normally requires more stringent control than transaction data (bearing in mind the problem of compensating errors inherent in the use of control totals), it is preferable to use a stronger maintenance control over master file data.

EXAMPLE. All transaction types entered into the accounts receivable system are batched and totals established over gross dollar values. Those totals are posted to a manual control account that is reconciled each month with the total balance reported for the accounts receivable file. There are no specific user controls to ensure that individual accounts receivable balances are accurately stated.

SITUATION 2:

Computer-produced control totals (of accepted data) are posted to a manual control account that is agreed periodically to the balance reported for the computer master file.

IMPACT ON ADEQUACY OF CONTROL. Control over maintenance of data is adequate to the same extent as in Situation 1.

EXAMPLE. Control totals of accepted data are produced for all entries to an inventory master file. Those totals are posted to a manual control account that is reconciled regularly to the reported inventory master file balance.

SITUATION 3:

A control account is used to ensure that data is maintained correctly.

IMPACT ON ADEQUACY OF CONTROL. The frequency of the reconciliation procedures should be sufficient to ensure that errors cannot accumulate to an extent that it is difficult to investigate and correct them. Within this basic requirement, it is likely that the frequency of reconciliation procedures will be affected by the method of processing used. For example, if the file is accessed sequentially, it is convenient to produce a total after each update. However, if the file is accessed directly, a special run is required to produce a total. Therefore, it is unlikely that this will be done after each update.

EXAMPLE. A company has an inventory recording system. The master file is held on disk and is on-line to several terminals in the major inventory locations. Each week, this direct access file is sorted to produce a sequential file used in the production statistics system. At the same time, a file total is accumulated. This is then reconciled to a manual control account, prepared each day from inventory movement totals.

SITUATION 4:

The computer reconciles the total of items on the master file with a control record on the same file.

IMPACT ON ADEQUACY OF CONTROL. Control is adequate if there are procedures to ensure that:

- Programmed procedures are adequate and can be relied on to identify and report any differences arising.

- The total brought forward prior to update is agreed manually to that carried forward after the last update.
- Controls over data file security are adequate to ensure that the correct file is used.

The latter two requirements mean that this control is not usually as strong as when a manual control account is used. The user must also ensure that either the reconciliation is reported as satisfactory or any differences reported are investigated and corrected.

EXAMPLE. An open-item accounts receivable file is updated twice a week from transaction files accumulated during the intervening period. After each update, the total of individual items on the file is reconciled with a header record that contains a control total for the file. The control total is itself updated directly from the transaction files. The movement report, produced after each update, records brought forward and carried forward totals, movements updated, and the results of the reconciliation procedure. This report is reviewed by the accounts receivable supervisor who ensures that:

- The total brought forward agrees with that carried forward on the previous report.
- The reconciliation is reported as satisfactory or any differences reported are investigated.

SITUATION 5:

The computer reconciles the total of items on the file with the total on a separate control file.

IMPACT ON ADEQUACY OF CONTROL. Control is adequate provided the requirements specified previously are met. This control is usually stronger than using a control record because:

- It requires use of an independent set of programs, whereas the control record reconciliation is usually part of the update program.
- It can provide a check on the results of processing by many programs. Since, however, the effectiveness of the control is very dependent on the appropriate functioning of programmed procedures, strong general controls are necessary.

EXAMPLE. A large corporation has a multilevel divisional and departmental structure. It has developed a general ledger system that accumulates data from all of the various organizational levels, either by direct interface with their other accounting systems or by entry of journal vouchers. Output includes trial balances and financial statements at departmental, divisional, and corporate levels, and also management accounts at departmental and divisional levels. Before any update of the general ledger files can occur, all accepted data is written to a control file. The control file movement total is reconciled with the various accepted data totals. After each update of the general ledger files, a separate set of programs reconciles the control file with the general ledger files and produces a variety of reconciliation reports. These are reviewed by the user to ensure that both update and maintenance of the files are satisfactory.

SITUATION 6:

Neither manual nor computer control accounts are used.

IMPACT ON ADEQUACY OF CONTROL. Control over maintenance of data can be achieved by obtaining a full printout of the file and checking each item with source data manually. The work load can be spread by having the file printed out on a cyclical basis. In any case, the frequency of checking should take both the volume of data and its financial sensitivity into account. This is an effective but costly control procedure. As such, it is usually used only for low volumes of financially sensitive data.

EXAMPLE. A carpet manufacturer produces several different ranges of carpet in a variety of designs and colors. Selling prices reflect the quality and range of carpet. Consequently, there are relatively few standard selling prices. Volumes of turnover, however, are high. As a result, errors in selling prices would have far-reaching effects. Therefore, the selling price file is printed in full each month and a one-for-one check is carried out to ensure that prices remain correct.

SITUATION 7:

There are no application controls over the maintenance of data.

IMPACT ON ADEQUACY OF CONTROL. It may be possible to rely on strong general controls in the area of data file security to ensure that data is maintained properly.

CURRENCY OF DATA

SITUATION 1:

Data held on file is printed on a cyclical basis for review by the user department.

IMPACT ON ADEQUACY OF CONTROL. Control is adequate provided that:

- All data on file is printed within an appropriate time span.
- The user reviews the data and ensures that all necessary amendments are made.

EXAMPLE. A company has an order processing accounts receivable system. Initial order entry includes validation against credit limits. To ensure that credit limits are set at reasonable levels, the customer file on which they are recorded is printed on a cyclical basis. Each month, 100 accounts are printed for checking. The accounts are selected for printing in order of account number. As well as reviewing the credit limits, the credit controller checks the accounts against a master list to ensure that all accounts are covered during a six-month period.

SITUATION 2:

The computer produces exception reports of data that has remained unchanged for a certain period of time.

IMPACT ON ADEQUACY OF CONTROL. Control is adequate if the following requirements are met:

- General controls are adequate to ensure the appropriate functioning of programmed procedures.
- Programmed procedures are appropriate to ensure that all exceptions will be identified and reported (such as interrogating each record and comparing the relevant data with predetemined limits or parameters).
- Parameters or limits used in the programmed procedures are set at reasonable levels and in accordance with management's intentions.
- All exceptions are investigated by the user and amendments are made as necessary.

EXAMPLE. During a period of inflation, a company expects the cost of purchased inventories to increase at least once a year. Provided that the appropriate data is maintained on file, it can be reviewed by the computer. Any items where the cost has not changed in the last year can be reported for manual investigation.

The aging of inventory and accounts receivable balances to identify old items is another example of this type of review.

APPENDIX **C**

Computer Assisted Audit Techniques: Case Studies

INTRODUCTION

In 1987, the EDP Auditors Foundation (EDPAF) commissioned a study by Coopers & Lybrand to learn more about computer-assisted audit techniques (CAATs) and how they are actually used in today's internal audit environments. The research was aimed at identifying:

- CAATs that are available currently.
- How to achieve audit objectives using CAATs.
- Typical computer environments in which CAATs are being used.
- Functional areas to which CAATs can be applied.

Three case studies were conducted and are presented in this Appendix. Manville Corporation, Manufacturers Hanover Corporation, and Johnson & Johnson cooperated in the effort to provide a view of "real-life" use of CAATs.

The three case studies included issues pertaining to implementation and use of CAATs particular to the organizations studied. The report sections on techniques in general cover what was in use at the time of the study. Other CAAT-related issues, such as how to select an appropriate CAAT, how to control implementation, and the training required, were beyond the scope of the research.

CASE STUDY: MANVILLE

Company Description

Manville Corporation was incorporated in Delaware in 1981 to continue businesses begun by the predecessors of Johns-Manville Corporation in 1858. Manville employs approximately 21,000 people worldwide, and operates 62 facilities, over 700,000 acres of timberland, and six mines in the United States and eight other countries. Their significant asset base underlies three distinct groups of businesses: the Fiber Glass Products Group, the Forest Products Group, and the Specialty Products Group.

The Fiber Glass Products Group, which is Manville's largest group, produces both insulation fiber and continuous strand fiber glass filament. End products manufactured from Manville's technologically advanced production techniques include a wide range of thermal and acoustical insulations, fiber glass specialty and roofing mats, and glass fibers and reinforcements, for use by a variety of industries.

Manville's Forest Products Group consists of vertically integrated operations from timber plantations to lumber, plywood, paper, and packaging products. Pulp plants use the wood chips from the lumber and plywood operations to produce coated and uncoated paperboard, corrugating medium, and kraft paper. Paperboard and paper are used to produce beverage carriers, folding cartons, paper bags, and, in Brazil, corrugated containers.

The Specialty Products Group manufactures and sells a wide variety of lighting fixtures, roofing materials, filtration material, and industrial insulations and products. They also mine and process diatomite and perlite. These minerals are used in some of Manville's manufacturing businesses and are sold to other industrial users.

Manville operates three data centers in the United States to support its business data processing needs. The largest center is at the company's world headquarters in Denver, Colorado. The world headquarters' data processing facilities also include three distributed computer configurations.

The Internal Audit Department

Internal audit is an independent appraisal function established by the Manville Corporation Board of Directors. Internal audit's mandate is to examine and evaluate the company's activities to promote efficient and effective internal controls, and to assure optimum care and use of corporate assets. The objective of internal audit is to help both the Audit Committee of the Board of Directors and the full board, as well as all management levels, to discharge their duties and responsibilities effectively, by providing analyses, appraisals, recommendations, counsel, and other information.

The General Auditor supervises the Internal Audit Department and, for administrative purposes, reports to the Executive Vice-President of Finance and Administration. Functionally, however, he reports directly to Manville's Audit Committee. The General Auditor and his staff, to the extent authorized by him, have full and free access to the records, property, and personnel of all Manville departments, subsidiaries, and affiliates. Auditing activity is restricted only where the Audit Committee or Chairman of the Board assigns this responsibility to others in writing, and the General Auditor must obtain the approval of the Chairman of the Board before eliminating any scheduled audit at the request of any manager.

There are currently 31 professional internal audit personnel, and all are resident in Denver, Colorado. The average staff member has over 12 years of Manville experience and almost five years of audit experience. Eight internal auditors are certified public accountants (CPAs), two are also Certified Internal Auditors (CIAs). There are three Certified Information Systems Auditors (CISAs) on the staff.

The Department's Audit Objectives

The overall objective of the Internal Audit Department encompasses the examination and evaluation of the adequacy and effectiveness of Manville's system of internal control and the quality of performance in carrying out assigned responsibility. The internal auditors give special attention to:

1. Requirements for authorizing transactions and financial commitments.
2. Reliability and integrity of financial and operating information.
3. Systems established to ensure compliance with policies, plans, procedures, laws, and regulations.
4. Means of safeguarding assets, including the company's important documents and records.

Specific internal audit objectives outlined in their current year's plan include continued strong emphasis on the evaluation and testing of control systems, particularly those related to authorization and accounting for transactions and safeguarding of assets. Audit efforts are directed toward ensuring continued corporate compliance with the provisions of the Foreign Corrupt Practices Act of 1977.

The department expends major amounts of resources in auditing Manville's information systems to ensure their integrity. Financial auditors are teamed with EDP audit personnel to maximize the efficiency of these reviews of information systems. They review significant financial reporting areas to evaluate the internal controls, the accuracy of recorded balances, and the effectiveness of transaction processing.

Additional specific objectives include the continued use and further development of advanced CAATs to reperform key system processes, identify key production program changes, test data file accuracy, create special listings of accounting transactions, analyze accounting records, and select random samples for use in audit tests.

Advanced CAATs at Manville

Although Manville's internal EDP auditors have developed hundreds of audit software programs over the past 12 years to satisfy specific audit requirements, the spread of sophisticated and complex application systems forced them to consider alternative CAATs. Internal audit management realized that the productivity of the EDP internal auditors had to increase. Internal audit management's objective was to provide Manville management with timely and accurate assessments of transaction processing and the degree of compliance with company policies and procedures. Therefore, internal audit management sought methods to review significant transactions frequently and analyze summary financial information to highlight trends.

One method internal audit management considered was to imbed audit procedures within an application's production program code. This CAAT would subject transactions to immediate review and test them for reasonableness and compliance with company policies. It would have also given auditors the ability to randomly select transactions for subsequent review.

A variation of the above was also considered. Instead of embedding audit code into production programs, internal audit considered the use of an Integrated Test Facility (ITF), also known as a "mini-company" technique. Artificial departments would have been created to accept transactions, and output reports would have been analyzed to determine whether or not proper data processing had occurred.

A major weakness in both of the above techniques, however, is that they would have required a special program code in the application systems. Such additional programming would have added to the complexity of the systems and caused additional work for the Information Services Department in the maintenance of the program code. Another significant problem with these techniques is that internal auditors would have been forced to rely on personnel in the Information Services Department, and the auditors would have lost some of their independence.

After considering these alternatives, among others, Manville's internal EDP auditors began the development of other advanced CAATs that they believed would meet their objectives in a cost-effective manner. These techniques include the Audit Database Facility, Continuous Auditing Procedures, and Automated Program Change Control Techniques.

Audit Database Facility. The Audit Database Facility was developed as a productivity tool for audit personnel using Statistical Analysis System (SAS), a powerful programming language marketed by the SAS Institute. The facility was designed to eliminate the need for detailed knowledge of operating system job control language (O/S JCL), SAS, and time-sharing option (TSO) commands and to provide a library of audit knowledge.

The basic component of the Audit Database Facility is a TSO command language processor that creates a working environment for the user. This basic component is called the Base System. It copies required files, issues necessary commands to the operating system to connect users to their files and work areas, and provides basic input, output, and support facilities through the use of SAS macros. The Base System is self-documenting so that the audit steps can be accurately reperformed at a later time.

The Base System provides the user with all necessary information on-line. It has multiple how-to-use help commands. Each data base has an on-line description of each file, and a bulletin board is available for the user to leave messages.

Easy maintenance was another design criteria. The various support files that provide services (e.g., help, directories, report printing) are simple structure files that are easily maintained through the basic TSO editor.

One of the most frequently used features of the Audit Database Facility is the Menue (sic) System. It was designed to allow less sophisticated computer users, such as Manville's financial auditors, to review and manipulate data interactively and create reports from standard SAS data sets supplied by the EDP internal auditors. Those same users also have the ability to access corporate production data independently and to create their own data bases with no knowledge of SAS or TSO. The Menue System provides the use of menu-driven prompts and other "friendly" options. The standard SAS data bases supplied to users are prepared each weekend by the internal EDP audit staff, based on the following week's audit schedule. For example, if the week's schedule includes a visit to a fiber glass plant in Defiance, Ohio, the following data bases specific to Defiance would be prepared and waiting for the financial auditors on Monday morning:

1. A current month's trial balance.
2. Two years of general ledger data.
3. Two years of accounts payable and other disbursement data.
4. Two years of costed sales data.

Functions that can be performed on the data bases using the Menue System include the following, which are the menu choices:

1. Sorting based on parameters provided by system prompts.
2. Reviewing or "browsing" through the data.
3. Selection of data fields for printing.
4. Summarization of data fields.
5. Selection of data based on value.
6. Totaling of data fields.
7. Calculation and arithmetic functions on data fields.
8. Multiple combinations of the above functions.
9. Report printing.

The resulting files created by one or more of the above functions can be reviewed by the user on-line prior to printing. The files can also be used for additional processing against other data bases or files created by the user.

In addition to the Base System, the Audit Database Facility provides three specialized facilities for the sophisticated SAS user. These include automated workpapers, automated quantitative analysis, and automated qualitative analysis.

1. *Automated workpapers* uses the SAS word processor FSLETTER to provide a department word processing data base as well as user-supplied data bases. Workpapers are created and reviewed on-line and then archived for future retrieval. The Audit Database Facility log function can also import data into this automated workpaper facility to provide a permanent record of audit software logic employed.
2. *Automated quantitative analysis* provides certain standard statistical profiles on audit data, such as minimum, maximum, mean, and mode statistics, as well as "a" and "b" factors for linear regression analyses.
3. *Automated qualitative analysis* provides the user with an "expert" system that was developed by Manville. Questions are supplied by an SAS macro, and responses are stored in another SAS data base. Once all questions have been answered, an analysis program is executed, which ultimately provides the user with an opinion on the subjects being audited.

Continuous Auditing. Manville's continuous audit system consists of TSO CLISTs, TSO files, and programs written in SAS. The CLISTs determine the specific SAS programs that should be submitted to the IBM 3084's background processor and which production data files should be processed. The SAS programs read in the appropriate data files and subject them to various tests, select records, produce reports, and transmit messages to various terminals.

CLISTs determine which SAS programs to execute in one of two ways. The first method is based on comparison of the generated data set name. If the generated data set name of a "standard" file to be reviewed is different from the name last reviewed, SAS programs are executed against the new version of the file. The second method is based on the date of the last SAS job stream execution. If the specified period of time has elapsed since particular files have been subjected to continuous audit review, SAS programs are automatically executed. These automated job stream executions are controlled by master audit files maintained by a CLIST. These master files also provide internal audit with a history of production data files reviewed.

Once the CLIST has determined what specific set of SAS programs should be executed, the CLIST prepares the appropriate execution JCL and other necessary technical information. The completed job stream is then submitted to the background processor.

The continuous audit job streams currently perform audits in six principal areas:

1. Accounts payable data.
2. Billing data.
3. General ledger data.
4. Production data file accesses.
5. Production program changes.
6. Production program failures.

A random sample of daily accounts payable transactions is selected and saved in a separate data set for subsequent audit procedures. All transactions that meet specified criteria, such as dollar amount and account codes, are also selected, saved in a data set, and printed for vouching purposes. Statistical information is also accumulated and saved for future use in data modeling.

Billing and general ledger transactions are tested in a similar manner for specific criteria. Selected transactions are also saved and printed for manual follow-up.

IBM's System Management Facility (SMF) files produced by the MVS operating system are tested by another SAS job stream for specific file access types. SMF records reflecting these file access types are monitored for evidence of potential nonproduction updates to Corporate Accounting, Salary Payroll, and Accounts Payable master files.

The fifth SAS job stream submitted through the continuous audit process interrogates the production program load module library, PRODLIB. The purpose of this process is to detect which production programs have changed. This is the first step of Manville's program change control CAAT, which is discussed in detail in the next section, "Program Change Control."

The final SAS job stream processes SMF data to check for abend codes that indicate production program failures. Reports are produced that highlight developing trends, and they are given to the Information Services Department for follow-up purposes.

Once the various software components described above have completed processing, reports are printed of the selected records, copies of the records are stored on disk files, messages are transmitted to appropriate terminals indicating the number of records selected, and control files are updated. The output reports are distributed to members of the internal EDP audit staff, and the appropriate manual audit procedures are performed.

Program Change Control. The three major files that contain targets of automated program change control are:

1. PANVALET, the source code.
2. PRODLIB, the executable load module code.
3. PROCLIB, the JCL and job execution parameters.

Internal audit's strategy was to identify changes to either PRODLIB or PROCLIB and then compare those changes to the source code in PANVALET and other supporting authorizing documentation.

PRODLIB is a standard, load module format PDS (partitioned data set) which contains an internal directory along with the individual members (production program executable load modules). The internal directory contains a field associated with each PDS member name that indicates the size of the member. Manville's internal EDP auditors wrote SAS programs to read the member names and sizes and store that data in a SAS data base. Each day, a similar data base is created and compared to the previous day's version, and the name, size, and date of each new, deleted, or changed program is placed into another SAS data base. The entire executable load module for a changed program is also copied automatically into an internal audit library, and the associated source code for that program is later copied from PANVALET. These copies are used for subsequent auditing procedures.

Manville's Information Services Department maintains an on-line file of Change Control Requests (CCRs) to track authorization of production program changes. Audit processes this file against the SAS data base of changed programs, and CCR numbers that match within a specified time period are posted against changed programs. A weekly report is then produced of production programs that have been changed with no authorizing CCR, and this report is distributed to data processing and audit management for follow-up. This process also identifies program changes that will be subjected to further advanced CAATs.

Although PROCLIB is also a PDS, its format does not lend itself to change testing like PRODLIB. To detect changes in PROCLIB, therefore, a daily "hash total" is computed for each PDS member, and it is then compared to that member's hash total on the following day. Any JCL changes to a member will produce a new hash total. If a difference is detected, the member's name and date of change is posted to a SAS data base, and a copy of the new member is placed in an audit library. Reports are produced to facilitate audit follow-up to verify these JCL changes for proper authorization.

The libraries of changed source code from PANVALET and changed JCL are then periodically compared to reference copies maintained by internal audit. Coopers & Lybrand's Source Compare program is used to highlight the changes. When deemed appropriate, those changes are vouched to authorizing documents. These same audit libraries of changed programs and reference copies are used to verify the relationship between program source and executable code. Coopers & Lybrand's Object Compare program is used in this process, to ensure that a program's source code matches its executable load module code.

Processing Concerns and Techniques

The processing techniques for all of the above CAATs involve the execution of batch job streams initiated by members of the internal EDP audit staff. The SAS data bases that support the Audit Database Facility are created based on a review of the upcoming week's audit schedule. These data bases are created over the weekend to be ready by Monday morning.

The continuous auditing process is also initiated by a batch job stream. It is submitted for execution early each day, to allow time for normal audit staff follow-up activity. The batch job stream for Program Change Control is submitted after the continuous audit job stream, since PRODLIB must first be interrogated. The resulting data base is then used for further testing in the Program Change Control process.

This dependence on manual job stream submission is a processing concern to Manville's audit management. They are pursuing techniques to automate this process more completely, as well as continuing to refine the entire mechanized approaches discussed above.

Security and Control Concerns

Since Manville's Internal Audit Department places so much reliance on their CAATs for detecting unauthorized production program changes, they have developed audit tools using IBM's AMBLIST utility to determine independently whether production load modules have been changed. These tools, however, consume a great deal of computing resources. It is not unusual to take five hours to review the PRODLIB completely, so they are only used periodically as a cross-check to ensure that the normal audit procedures are functioning properly.

To maintain security over their advanced CAATs, internal audit retains full control over all of its audit software programs and data. Separate catalogs are set aside for programs and data, and all catalogs are fully protected by ACF2, a sophisticated system software security package.

Internal audit also runs independent SAS programs against the SMF files to check against unauthorized attempts to access either its programs or data files. The Manville Information Services Department performs no programming maintenance or data processing duties for internal audit.

CAATs at Manville: A Summary

In 1982, Manville had five full-time EDP auditors performing computer audit tasks, primarily associated with reviews of data centers and their systems of general controls. Through the use of the CAATs described above, as well as other techniques currently employed, only two full-time EDP auditors are now used in that capacity. The other three members of the EDP staff are now performing "integrated audits" with their financial audit counterparts, and Manville's audit coverage has expanded greatly.

The financial auditors now have ready access to corporate data prior to starting an audit, rather than waiting for the audit software to produce results several weeks after audits had begun.

Reviews of program changes and data file accesses are now accomplished in a fraction of the time required previously, and the universe of data that is audited has been substantially increased. The standard computer routines now used are also much easier to understand and maintain. Auditor attention is now more focused on areas of greater risk, and rapid auditor reaction to unusual events is possible.

Some of the problems and disadvantages of the above techniques include the audit staff's resistance to change. A great deal of experimenting and research was required, and this required heavy use of computing resources. Auditee reaction was initially negative, due to the speed of inquiries by auditors following the input of unusual transactions, although they are now getting used to the situation.

A key advantage of these techniques is the independence the financial auditors now feel from the internal EDP auditors. They are now capable of using these tools themselves to produce meaningful audit reports for their special purposes. All members of the internal audit staff, including the EDP auditors, have improved their technical skills. This has produced a positive and rewarding atmosphere in which to work.

Future Advanced CAATs

Manville plans to expand the "standard report" features of the Audit Database Facility in the near future. The company also plans to expand the capabilities of the automated qualitative analysis (expert) system and add graphics and analytics sections to the facility.

More job streams in the continuous auditing process are planned. Profiling of data and early detection tests are also planned for the future. Direct access to the corporate data bases is yet another area for improvement.

Finally, a closer connectivity between the mainframe and microcomputers is being studied. The internal auditors would like their CAATs employed on the mainframe to be closely tied to their audit procedures being conducted on microcomputers. Mainframe audit procedures and results would be downloaded to microcomputers to facilitate the creation and maintenance of workpapers. Computer-generated internal control questionnaires would be produced from expert systems, and predictive tests would be performed based on data models to help pinpoint high-risk areas in need of audit.

CASE STUDY: MANUFACTURERS HANOVER

Company Description

Manufacturers Hanover Corporation is a large international money center bank, with its headquarters in New York. The corporation is organized into five strategic business sectors, corresponding to its five major customer groups. They reflect the corporation's evolution into a diversified financial services organization. This structure naturally requires considerable decentralization of management.

Led by a Sector Executive Vice President, each sector is managed as a stand-alone business group. The sectors, the principal customer groups they serve, and their products are:

1. *Asset Based Financing*—Secured lending to national middle market customers, major equipment financing worldwide, and commercial real estate.
2. *Banking and International*—Local currency and cross-border lending, specialized investment banking products, operating services to corporate and government accounts worldwide, and correspondent banking.
3. *Corporate Banking*—Innovative and traditional banking services, including credit, trust, securities, and transaction/information products; servicing corporations and individuals in the United States and Canada.

4. *Investment Banking*—Wide range of investment banking services, delivered on a global basis, including the origination, trading, and distribution of securities, foreign exchange, and other financial instruments; merger and acquisition financing; venture capital investments; fee-based advisory products, including investment management and specialized corporate services.
5. *Retail Banking*—Deposit services, loans, leases, and credit cards to consumers and small businesses nationwide.

Sector results are monitored by a management information system, which is continuously refined to improve its measurement of organizational profitability. This system includes balances recorded on the books of the sectors, as well as allocations of corporate-level balances not specifically identified in the corporation's core accounting systems. Allocations are not made to sectors for items reflecting corporate-level decisions, which, if allocated, might detract from a complete understanding of how the sectors actually performed.

Manufacturers Hanover Corporation has five major data centers in the United States. It also has its own extensive worldwide communications network. This private network links the bank's disparate offices, creating a timely reliable pool of global information. It reflects the fact that Manufacturers can be considered a truly global electronic bank.

In addition to the major data centers, there are 25 smaller data centers, supporting areas such as Wire Transfer, Check Processing, and Real Estate and Mortgage. Another large data center is located in London, as well as others in smaller cities containing European, Asian, and South American branches. Recently, the trend is moving away from these large mainframe environments to minicomputer- and microcomputer-based systems.

The Internal Audit Department

The audit department is responsible for auditing all entities of Manufacturers Hanover worldwide. The General Auditor reports directly to the Audit Committee on the scope and results of audit coverage. Only outside directors of the board can sit on the Audit Committee.

The main internal audit office is in New York City, with regional offices in London, Singapore, Los Angeles, and Atlanta. The department is composed of six divisions, each led by a Division Executive who reports directly to the General Auditor. The department consists of 313 individuals; 41 percent of the professional staff are certified (CPA, CIA, CBA, CISA, and CMA). The department requires that individuals hold at least one of those five certifications in order to attain the level of Audit Manager.

The five line divisions of the department are responsible for conducting audits of the business entities assigned to them. One of those divisions is also responsible for computer audit assistance (called CATS at Manufacturers). The CATS group is responsible for conducting all data center audits and assisting the business auditors (formerly called financial auditors) in their application review and system development life cycle reviews.

The Professoinal Practices Division (PPD) is responsible for establishing policies that are followed universally in the department. In addition, the department has adopted the Institute of Internal Auditors (IIA) and Bank Administration Institute (BAI) standards. The PPD also is responsible for ensuring consistency through Quality Assurance Reviews.

A microcomputer-based risk analysis model is used to plan the overall audit coverage. It helps ensure that high-risk areas are being covered. Results of the audit planning process are communicated to the Audit Committee at the beginning of the audit year and a reassessment of the plan is made at midyear. Any significant changes to the original plan are communicated to the Audit Committee.

Results of audit examinations are formally communicated in reports. A Level I report is issued to the area's Executive Management, with a copy to the Sector Executive Vice President. This report gives an opinion on the adequacy, efficiency, and effectiveness of the system of internal control. It highlights major conditions requiring corrective action. A Level II report is issued to local management and contains items that are not as significant as those in Level I, but still need corrective action. At each month end, a summary of the major findings is issued to the Audit Committee. In addition, the General Auditor meets with the Audit Committee eight times a year.

The Department's Audit Objectives

The audit objectives are summed up in the Manufacturers Hanover Corporation Audit Department Charter, which reads as follows:

> The internal auditing function is a continuous independent management control and appraisal activity involving the review of manual and automated accounting and financial operations. The objectives are to determine whether:
>
> - Assets are properly used, accounted for, and adequately safeguarded.
> - Adequate accounting and administrative controls exist and are functioning properly.
> - Plans, policies and procedures are in existence and are carried out in accordance with management's intentions, applicable laws, regulations and sound fiduciary principles.

- Any material weaknesses in controls have been reported to the proper levels of authority and corrective action has been taken.

The department's primary activity is to report on systems of internal control in place throughout the organization. This includes obtaining an understanding of the systems being examined, evaluating their adequacy, and testing the degree of compliance with key controls in the systems.

The department performs periodic examinations of key operating areas. It is available to support corporate management in other capacities, such as:

- Participating in the systems development life cycle of major automated systems to help ensure that they include adequate and efficient controls.
- Performing limited examinations of potential acquisitions.
- Performing reviews to determine compliance with a specific law or regulation.
- Providing assistance in developing new policies or regulations that affect the Corporation.
- Reviewing matters relating to possible violations of the Corporate Code of Conduct.
- Reviewing controls and other related aspects of new products.
- Performing special investigations of embezzlements, defalcations, kites and other fraudulent activities.

The department recognizes that Corporate management may occasionally avail itself of the expertise and experience of audit staff. In such cases, the department will be cooperative to the extent that staff members do not become involved in projects that constitute a real or an apparent conflict of interest.

The department has committed itself to keep pace with technology. A major goal is to move forward with the corporation as it introduces new products and services, and their supporting management information systems. This is accomplished by an effective assessment of inherent risks related to new products and lines of business, as well as control risks related to the new policies and procedures implemented to introduce these services.

The department is taking on increased responsibility as a business consultant and adviser, apprising management of audit concerns within a practical business context. This increased role, accompanied by the corporation's growth in new areas of business, has increased the emphasis on cost performance and efficiency of the department. This also drives the automation of the department itself, as evidenced by the increased use of audit software and automated risk analysis tools, and increased use of microcomputers for flowcharting, reporting, project tracking, and various word processing applications, which all contribute toward this goal.

There is also an increased audit emphasis on access and security concerns. Related to logical and physical access to data centers and communication networks, this emphasis reflects the need for good controls to prevent unauthorized access and possible disruption of business-related processing.

Advanced CAATs at Manufacturers Hanover

The department employs an integrated approach to its audits of computer-based systems. This approach links the results of general control reviews of data centers with application reviews of business functions. Audits of business functions are also integrated: Programmed procedures and manual procedures are evaluated jointly to express an opinion on the adequacy, effectiveness, and efficiency of controls. These audits are staffed with both business and CATS audit personnel.

This approach is beneficial. It has:

- Increased interaction between the business and CATS audit groups.
- Increased audit effectiveness and efficiency.
- Provided management with an overall assessment of risks and exposures.
- Increased the use of automated testing techniques.
- Increased the overall computer literacy of the department.

CAATs used by Manufacturers Hanover include the use of specialized and generalized audit software, utility programs, program comparison, and test data. They are used on audits of data centers and integrated audits. Specific CAATs and their use are shown in the table below.

Writing and execution of various computer techniques are performed by auditors at intermediate and senior levels. Decisions about the use of a particular CAAT are made in conjunction with the business auditors.

CAATs are used during data center and integrated audits. Each time a CAAT is considered, all of the alternatives are evaluated and compared to existing manual audit procedures. The major criteria are audit quality, coverage, and efficiency.

CAAT	Software	Vendor	Objective
Custom audit software	COBOL/ CULPRIT	IBM/Cullinet	Assist in compliance and substantive testing.
Generalized audit software	EDP AUDITOR	Cullinet	Evaluate data center operations. Determine statistical sampling.
Utility programs	(e.g., IEHLIST)	IBM/DEC	Acquire data on system software.
	ACF2	SKK	Evaluate data security.
	GUARDIAN	On-Line Software	Evaluate data security.
Program comparison	Source Compare	Coopers & Lybrand	Evaluate controls over application program changes.
Test data	N/A	N/A	Test program procedures for compliance.
Generalized and micro software	LOTUS 1-2-3	Lotus Development Corp.	Assist in compliance and substantive testing.

Specialized Audit Software. Audit software written in COBOL (Common Business Oriented Language) and CULPRIT has been used to accomplish various audit objectives. In a recent audit of the Real Estate and Mortgage Department, software was written to assist in compliance testing. The customer file was read to ensure that all customer records contained a tax identification number. Additionally, the loan file was searched for any nonaccrual loans. This created audit efficiencies because the existing procedure was for the auditor to request a listing of the files from the programmers and examine that listing manually. Barring any major changes to the real estate and mortgage system, the software will be run annually to help in compliance testing.

Specialized audit software has also been used in substantive testing. Two particular uses are recalculation of transactions and production of audit confirmations. For example, recalculating the trial balance helped substantiate the general ledger account balances and ensure that transactions were properly classified. The procedure has been to calculate transactions manually to determine if they were properly classified on the balance sheet.

Software has also been written for Treasury Department audits to test the programmed procedures of interest calculations on various financial instruments. Without this software, there would have been difficulty in testing this manually.

For audits of the various loan departments, as well as audits of demand deposit accounts, software has been written to extract customer balances for confirmations.

Software written to test programmed procedures requires time-consuming development. However, its use in subsequent years has increased audit efficiency.

Generalized Audit Software. The generalized audit software package, EDP AUDITOR, includes several routines. As an example, two of those routines were selected for use during audits. The SMF routine is used to verify that abended jobs were properly corrected and resubmitted, as well as to verify that only authorized batch jobs were executed. The statistical sampling routine was used to select a random sample of transactions in an integrated audit.

In one use of the EDP AUDITOR SMF routine during a data center audit, it was discovered that it had been decided not to record the record type for abended jobs. There was also a problem in verifying that only authorized production jobs were executed, since it was difficult to distinguish between test and production jobs due to job naming standards. As a result, the auditor could only match jobs from job schedules to the SMF output, rather than the more appropriate matching of SMF output to job schedules.

At the conclusion of the audit, the audit team decided to use the EDP AUDITOR SMF routine again in the next year to evaluate the efficiency of computer operations.

The random selection routine of EDP AUDITOR has been applied to the audits of Income and Expense, and the Balance Sheet. During the Income and Expense audit, transactions were selected at random, using EDP AUDITOR, to verify supporting documentation. Accounts were also selected at random for the Balance Sheet audit to reconcile chosen accounts to supporting documentation.

Utility Programs. Utilities, part of the operating system and security software packages, are used extensively. In the DEC and IBM environments, these utilities are used primarily to read the system software files to obtain information about the operating system. This has helped confirm the auditors understanding of the operating system environment.

The utilities in ACF2 and GUARDIAN security software are used to evaluate data security controls. Using ACF2 and GUARDIAN, reports are produced listing the various attributes of logonids, the rules protecting specific application files, security over on-line transactions, and security options installed on the system.

Program Comparison. To ensure that modifications to application programs are properly approved, program comparison is done during data center and integrated audits. A copy of the source library made during the prior year's data center audit is matched against a copy of the current version of the source library using Coopers & Lybrand's Source Compare program. Each line of program code is compared to the prior version. Any differences are indicated, showing that the program was changed. Approval of all such changes should be documented on a Change Control form. This indicates whether change control procedures are being followed.

Test Data. Test data is a technique used on a limited basis in integrated audits. Test data enables testing of controls by using data developed by the audit department as input to the production system. An important aspect of its use is to assemble a representative sample of transactions to test all possible conditions. This technique has been used in a Trust Department audit to test programmed procedures.

Generalized Microcomputer Software. Microcomputer (PC) software is used to test key aspects of the commercial loan function in the Real Estate Division. This particular application was designed to use both PC Lotus-based software and conventional programs. The description indicates some of the areas of microcomputer use in audits.

1. *Program 1 (PC).* Program I uses Lotus to recalculate interest accruals. The source interest bills were recomputed and compared to the AFS Trial Balance. Any differences were noted in the last column. (No exceptions were noted.) This reperformance and testing of a programmed procedure shows automation of an area that had not been tested previously.
2. *Program II (PC).* This programmed procedure had been reperformed manually in previous audits. Due to the variety of interest rates, not all types had been tested. Using Lotus, all interest rate formulas were recomputed. In addition, approximately two days were saved on the audit due to the automation of the programmed procedure test.
3. *Program III (PC).* This program combined several types of compliance testing and evaluated relationships between various fields listed on the report. For example, it uses items that are extracted by Programs IV and V. As a result of this programmed

procedure testing, an exception was noted that resulted in an audit report comment.

4. *Programs IV and V (PC).* Using a PC-based portfolio position report, a copy of the disk was interrogated, matched, and sorted by dollar amount. This data was then used for input to other audit software, and used in the loan documentation review. Previously, this step was done manually. Automating this procedure saved two days, as well as making other steps easier.
5. *Program VI (PC).* This checklist increased efficiency during the loan documentation review. In addition, automating the form used makes it possible to produce reports for particular fields listed on the checklist, and to report exceptions.
6. *Program VII (PC).* Loan-to-value ratios were recomputed using Lotus. Comments were included for clarification. The procedure automated a previously manual workpaper. Calculations required were entered once to the spreadsheet; using it, the entire loan-to-value column was computed and printed with ease.
7. *Program VIII.* This audit software identified all transactions with an effective date greater than the posting date. Loss of interest income was calculated, and 27 days of interest were identified as not collected.

Processing and Security Concerns

Recently, the General Auditor commissioned a worldwide review of the Audit Department's policies and procedures relating to their own data access capabilities, EDP general controls, and purchase/lease/inventory of computer equipment and software. As a result of the review, additional policies and procedures have either been put in place or are being finalized, including:

- Formalized procedures defining how system and data access should be requested, approved, and monitored.
- Documented procedures to outline the program change process for programs that reside on the data center mainframes.
- Formal backup and recovery procedures for audit software and files maintained at the various data centers.
- Documented procedures concerning the controls over program libraries, and maintenance of PC programs, report writers, and other software products.
- Formalized data security procedures for the department's personal PC files and PC use, especially to control the off-loading of files and programs from mainframes.

Future Advanced CAATs

The department has identified advanced CAATs to be used in the future. Those that have been applied successfully to date will be continued; others are now being envisioned to make the best use of future technology.

One area that would be particularly helpful is developing a continuous audit process. Using audit software, it would capture data and transactions, identify unusual conditions, and analyze results on an on-line real-time basis.

Another future area of emphasis already identified is developing more sophisticated analytical software tools to assist in the process of allocating audit resources to areas of increase audit risk. Existing microcomputer-based risk analysis software helps in the identification of those areas. Future emphasis will also be given to developing and enhancing computerized risk assessment models.

As Manufacturers Hanover makes extensive investments in computer resources and telecommunications networks, there will naturally be increased logical access auditing. This area will be addressed through a more widespread use of audit software. Lastly, the Audit Department has identified various areas where additional efficiencies can be created through more extensive use of microcomputers. These include electronic permanent files, plus automating all workpapers, audit programs, and audit reporting.

CASE STUDY: JOHNSON & JOHNSON

Company Description

Johnson & Johnson, based in New Brunswick, N.J., manufactures and markets a wide range of health care, consumer, and pharmaceutical products. Gross revenues for 1986 were over $7 billion. Products in the health care sector range from sterile operating room supplies and instruments to intraocular replacement lenses for cataract patients. Pharmaceutical products cover a broad spectrum, including family planning, therapeutic agents, and veterinary products. Products within the consumer sector include over-the-counter analgesics, infant care, and feminine hygiene products.

The company is represented in markets worldwide, covering six continents, and employs over 70,000 people. Since its founding 100 years ago, the company has followed a philosophy of decentralized management, which characterizes the structure, operations, and management style of the operating units.

As a result of this decentralized philosophy, the company has over 200 operating units throughout the world. The management of each operating unit has direct responsibility for that unit's conduct of business. In keeping with a decentralized philosophy, corporate headquarters provides very broad policies, rather than specific detailed procedures. The definition of operating methods and procedures is under management control at each operating unit. This decentralized control permits local management to tailor each subsidiary to meet the particular needs of the local market.

Computer hardware throughout the corporation is 95 percent IBM, covering the entire range of the IBM product line. The range starts with the IBM System 34 minicomputer and goes up through the IBM 3090 series mainframes used at several of the larger subsidiaries. In all, there are over 160 computer installations throughout the corporation.

Just as the definition of methods and procedures is under control of local management, the same is true of computer systems. The selection of computer systems is entirely under the control of local management to permit tailoring those systems to the needs of their businesses.

The majority of systems in use throughout the corporation were developed in-house. There is a trend toward installing software packages as the cost of system development becomes prohibitive and recruiting qualified information systems professionals becomes more and more difficult. There are virtually no "common" systems in use, with the exception of a Human Resource Payroll System recently installed for all U.S.-based, salaried employees.

As a result of this decentralized philosophy, each information systems environment throughout the corporation is unique. The hardware configuration, as well as the individual application systems, varies from one operating unit to the next. In fact, the very character of the information systems varies. Some subsidiaries have traditional batch systems, while others have installed and applied the latest technology.

Some subsidiaries have just recently installed their first computer systems and are experiencing the impact of such a change. On the other hand, some of the more established subsidiaries, which have more mature systems in place, are trying to adapt to new technologies and attitudes in an environment difficult to change.

In essence, this philosophy of decentralization permits the corporation to tailor its business to the needs of local markets. It also produces unique information systems environments. The difference between these environments and systems, and the range of technologies employed, present particular problems, as well as opportunities, for the internal auditor.

The Internal Audit Department

The Corporate Internal Audit Department at Johnson & Johnson has been in existence for over 35 years. The Director of Internal Audit reports to the

Corporate Treasurer and to the Audit Committee of the Board of Directors. The Audit Committee is composed entirely of outside directors. This reporting structure gives the department close contact with executive corporate management, while ensuring the independence necessary for the department to function effectively.

The Department's Audit Objectives

The mission of the Corporate Internal Audit Department is clearly stated. It is "to assist company management in establishing and maintaining adequate systems of internal control." The primary responsibility for internal control rests with company management. This responsibility is reflected in corporate policies and is a direct result of decentralized philosophy. Since the management of each subsidiary has complete control over the selection and definition of systems and procedures, that same management has complete responsibility for the design and maintenance of internal control systems.

The Corporate Internal Audit Department accomplishes its mission through direct audit services, as well as indirect service activities. Direct services are formal audits; these include recurring reviews, pre-implementation system reviews, and special request audits. A recurring review includes a review of major financial transaction cycles (revenue, production, disbursements), as well as review of major financial statement areas, such as cash and fixed assets.

If an operating unit under review has a computer installation, then a data center audit is performed as part of the review. A data center audit is always performed as an integral part of the recurring review in order to assess the total control environment, including the interrelationship of manual and computer controls.

The field work may be performed by an information systems (IS) auditor or a generalist auditor (one whose primary background is in financial auditing). In fact, almost all data center reviews of IBM System 34 through System 38 installations are performed by generalist auditors. This integration of computer and traditional audit skills at the staff level allows greater audit coverage, increased flexibility in assignment scheduling, and development of the skills that will be needed by future financial professionals.

Since the mission of the Corporate Internal Audit Department is to assist company management, other activities of a more general and indirect nature are undertaken. One such activity is the publication and maintenance of an Internal Control Handbook. This publication describes, for each functional area of the finance and MIS organizations, the objectives of a sound system of internal control. These publications are distributed to the CFO and MIS director of each operating unit, throughout the corporation.

Another example of a support activity performed by the Corporate Internal Audit Department was the development of the History File Analysis software for IBM System 34 and System 36 installations. These installations are often characterized by a small MIS staff, resulting in a problem in the area of segregation of duties.

Although the hardware in this case provides detailed logging facilities (History File), the logs produced are so voluminous and in such awkward format that their review as a control procedure was impractical. In the course of audit work at these installations, a way to summarize the information contained in these logs was developed to facilitate an efficient and effective review of computer activity.

In addition, software routines were added to point out the use of powerful utility programs and report on conditions such as password security violations. Once this package was documented and tested, it was distributed to all System 34 installations within the corporation. This software permits an after-the-fact review of computer processing activity, and thus compensates for the inadequate segregation of duties.

More recent advances in information system technology have given rise to a new set of internal control issues, requiring a related response from the Corporate Internal Audit Department. Some of the issues generated by the application of these new technologies include access to company data by third parties such as hospitals, physicians, and customers. The proliferation of personal computers with their variety of applications has changed the location of data storage and, as such, has changed the location for required control procedures. The complexity of newer technologies requires greater computer literacy among all auditors and a greater level of detailed technical knowledge among information systems auditors. Finally, the added speed of computer-related technological change has made all operating units that much more dynamic. The need for an up-to-date information base and continual audit risk assessment is greater than ever.

These advances in technology, however, represent solutions as well as problems. The same PC that causes audit concern can be a powerful audit tool. The same complex computer installations and systems that challenge the auditor's knowledge also present an opportunity to develop equally complex audit approaches and tools. These complex environments present an opportunity to place greater reliance on computerized systems, reduce traditional manual audit testing, and, in so doing, develop state-of-the-art audit professionals.

To respond to this changing technology and properly fulfill its mission, the Corporate Internal Audit Department recognized the need for a technical support function. The function's purpose is two-fold. It supports nonaudit activities, such as helping ensure that the Internal Control Handbook addresses increasingly technical topics, which it must do to remain relevant.

The technical support function is also responsible for the development and maintenance of audit programs, audit software, and training of 10 information systems auditors and 45 generalist auditors. While this function currently consists of only two full-time individuals, the benefits derived over the past two years are very apparent.

In summary, the Corporate Internal Audit Department fulfills its mission in a dynamic high-technology environment by:

- Continually assessing audit risk, using an in-house-developed risk assessment data base, coupled with direct access to the financial results of all operating units.
- Visiting every operating unit at least once every three years, based on audit risk.
- Integrating data center reviews with traditional financial audits to assess the total control environment.
- Cross-training IS and generalist auditors to increase overall staff skill levels and further support the integrated approach.
- Performing pre-implementation reviews whenever possible to ensure that new systems are controlled and auditable.
- Using technical support staff to maintain required audit skills and develop a pool of talent for the corporation.
- Providing assistance to corporate management through the publication of the Internal Control Handbook and by consulting on control methodologies for new technologies.

Advanced Computer Auditing: A Detailed Study of Johnson & Johnson Hospital Services

It is difficult to present a single example that depicts the internal audit philosophy and resulting actions described above. Rather, the following detailed study of one operating unit at Johnson & Johnson was chosen to demonstrate application of the advanced computer auditing practices followed by the Corporate Internal Audit Department. That operating unit is Johnson & Johnson Hospital Services (JJHS).

Company Description. JJHS was created in 1983 to develop and implement corporate marketing programs on behalf of Johnson & Johnson professional companies. These programs make it easier for customers to do business with Johnson & Johnson; they respond to the needs of hospitals, multihospital systems, alternative sites, and distributors to reduce costs. The strategy is to perform order entry, distribution, invoicing, and collection for the professional health care companies of Johnson & Johnson. A national eight-center distribution network handles most of the company products and supports the system.

To achieve its objective, the company implemented an Information Management System (IMS) data base system with on-line, real-time updating and operating features, capable of handling over 15,000 customers, thousands of products, and many complex customer-specific pricing terms. The heart of the process is the COACT® On-Line Procurement System. This heavily modified package will permit direct order entry from hospitals or distributors, computer-to-computer, automated, or telephone with immediate confirmation.

Audit Concerns. With a high volume of transactions and system complexity, the primary audit concerns were for the system to include appropriate internal accounting controls from the outset, and that it be auditable. Specifically, these concerns were the following:

1. The programs, when operational, must operate according to management's intentions. Therefore, control must be exercised to ensure that user requirements were met, that appropriate testing was done, that all exceptions are followed up and resolved appropriately, and that only authorized and tested programs are made operational.
2. The MIS environment must be able to ensure ongoing system integrity, meaning that controls must be in place to ensure the propriety of program changes, program and file security, consistent operations, and appropriate implementation and maintenance of system software. Included in the environmental considerations was the concern that adequate contingency planning be done.
3. Appropriate user controls must be in place to ensure that day-to-day processing is complete and accurate and that only valid processing takes place. Of particular importance is that sufficient controls be in place to ensure proper interface processing between Hospital Services and the respective domestic companies.
4. Appropriate control reports must be produced and data on file accessible to the auditors.

Audit Approach. From the start, Hospital Services Management agreed that the Corporate Internal Audit Department would review the entire system development process on a pre-implementation basis to provide a measure of comfort that the system was being implemented in a controlled manner. The Corporate Internal Audit Department, in turn, provided management with the specific control objectives forming the basis of the pre-implementation review.

The audit approach itself consisted of the following:

- Financial internal auditors obtained and recorded an understanding of control procedures at Hospital Services and over the interfaces with domestic companies. IS auditors obtained and recorded an understanding of the key programmed procedures and tied this understanding back to the documentation created by generalist auditors.
- IS auditors performed specific audits of the integrity control environment: security, data base administration, system software, and program change control.
- The audit team reviewed the scope of the company's test plan, detailed test plans, and test results.
- General control software (details provided below) was used to provide the details necessary to evaluate the general controls.
- The external auditors reviewed the work of the corporate internal auditors, following Statement of Auditing Standards (SAS) No. 9, *The Effect of an Internal Audit Function on the Scope of the Independent Auditor's Examination.*

Audit Techniques Available. Techniques available were the following:

1. *Integrated test facility (ITF)*—Involves Hospital Services including "dummy" records in its files that the auditors could review to ensure the propriety of processing.
2. *Test deck/test cases*—Involves submission and evaluation of test transactions. Two variations of this were considered: test cases prepared by Hospital Services as part of the normal testing processing and test cases prepared by internal audit to simulate actual processing.
3. *Audit software*—Three types were available:
   - *General control software*—Coopers & Lybrand Software (SMF Analyzer, SLAPS, Source Compare, Core Image Compare, and PARMLIB Analyzer) along with system utilities (ACF2/DECOMPILE) were available to extract information with which to evaluate general controls.
   - *Data base software*—IMS Analyzer was available to extract information regarding the data base structure and content.

- *Application software*—AUDITPAK II and the option to develop customized retrieval software were available to extract application information with which to substantiate balances.

Audit Techniques Selected. The Corporate Internal Audit Department chose test cases, general control software, and data base software for use in the course of the audit. The reasons for selecting these techniques were:

1. *Test cases.* The company's plan from the beginning was to rely on detailed testing by the user, in the form of test cases (a test deck), to ensure that the system was operating properly. The plan was for each user to prepare those test cases necessary to test out each and every functional element of the system; this resulted in several hundred test cases.

   The auditors determined that the test plan was complete in that all business conditions were being tested. They then determined that the test cases actually tested all programmed procedures. Having done this, they determined that a review of user testing—making sure that all cases were submitted, that errors were researched and resolved properly, that they were documented properly, and that proper approvals were obtained—was an appropriate substitute for creating a test deck of their own.

   This testing was performed over approximately six months, with the auditors involved in reviewing the process on a continuing basis. No significant problems were uncovered at the time, and no such problems have surfaced to date.

2. *General control software.* It was felt that controls in this complex environment would be impossible to verify without software. The software techniques used were:

   - PARMLIB Analyzer to obtain an understanding of the system configuration and components.
   - SLAPS to determine which programs were changed.
   - Source Compare and Core Image Compare to compare current source and object modules to control copies to determine changes, and compare source against object to ensure consistency.
   - SMF Analyzer to extract information regarding programs executed and file accesses.
   - ACF2 utility program, which was used to decompile the ACF2 rules to allow for evaluation of security procedures.

3. *Data base software*. The IMS Analyzer was used to provide the data base structure and extract information regarding access paths and logical relationships.

The techniques selected are summarized below, grouped under the respective general control category:

Implementation Controls

- Test cases
- Source Compare
- Core Image Compare
- IMS Analyzer

Program and File Security

- ACF2 utility
- IMS Analyzer
- SMF Analyzer

Computer Operations

- Test cases
- PARMLIB Analyzer

System Software

- ACF2 utility
- PARMLIB Analyzer

Audit Techniques Not Selected. An ITF and application software were not used. The ITF was not selected because:

- The manpower and skill level required were prohibitive.
- There would be a detrimental impact on system overhead.
- The ITF would be difficult to test fully and maintain.
- To test the ITF fully, test cases would have to be developed in any event, so that test cases were a better choice.

Application software was not considered necessary, since the system was designed with sufficient controls to warrant reliance. Sufficient audit reports, which such software would produce, were designed into the system.

Processing Concerns. The major processing concerns were:

- *Developing skills to use software*. Internal Audit asked the external auditors to train the staff doing the Hospital Services audit. A two-day program was developed covering SMF, SLAPS, Core Image Compare, and Source Compare.

- *Timing of software execution.* Initially, the internal auditors needed the information to decide exactly when to execute the software; they did not want to do it too early or too late. The solution was giving them a better understanding of the development schedules, which was obtained after several meetings with management.
- *Documentation of results.* Initially, internal auditors had questions regarding the results of Core Image Compare (e.g., how to read, interpret, and evaluate results). Coopers & Lybrand training, plus time spent by the Corporate Internal Audit Department's technical person, resolved questions.

Security Concerns. The security concerns related to the protection of the audit software itself and the distribution of the results of applying such software. How to protect and rely on software was a critical question. The choice was to install the software each time it was to be executed or to leave it on the system in a protected library. The risk of leaving it on the system did not appear too great because the ACF2 protection was adequate. Also, the auditee did not have access to the code, which made changing the programs almost impossible. Therefore, the Corporate Internal Audit Department chose to leave the software on the system. No unauthorized accesses to these programs were uncovered, through reviewing either SMF data or ACF2 data.

Another question regarding security was whether results of using the system utilities could be relied on. The internal auditors chose to decompile ACF2 rules using system utilities. The assumption was made that the utility program was not tampered with, since the auditee did not know ahead of time that such software would be used.

Efficiency. The efficiency of the methods selected was evaluated as follows:

1. *Test deck/test cases.* This technique was very efficient for several reasons. First, the Corporate Internal Audit Department's time was spent reviewing the detail work performed by the company rather than performing that work. Second, the objectives of both the Corporate Internal Audit Department and the company were accomplished without duplication of effort. Last, this testing was included in operational system testing, resulting in no additional impact on the company.

2. *Audit software.* While there existed no basis for comparison, the perception was that the information technology control, data base, and system utility software approach was more efficient than the traditional compliance or validation approach. Once installed, the software was executed quickly with minimal problems.

Effectiveness. The combination of techniques proved very effective. The system went live without problems; subsequent audits indicated no problems as well. Additionally, the audit was completed one month prior to live operation. Finally, management responded favorably to the auditors' role.

Problems Encountered. Certain problems were encountered with respect to each technique:

1. *Test deck/test cases.* Problems revolved around waiting for the company staff to complete the cases, then ensuring close coordination with them to review results in a timely manner. Another issue was ensuring audit staff continuity due to the time involved in the process and the need to have a detailed knowledge of the system. These problems were overcome because the Corporate Internal Audit Department was kept current as to the status of the testing and committed to keep the same staff on the project for the duration.
2. *Audit software.* The problems with audit software revolved around acquiring the necessary expertise, staff continuity, and timing of the work. The expertise was acquired through training and support provided by Coopers & Lybrand. Staff continuity, needed due to the detailed knowledge of the system required to audit it, was attained because of the Corporate Internal Audit Department's commitment to keep the required staff on the engagement. To assure the timeliness of the work—a tight window in which to execute the software and evaluate the results—the Corporate Internal Audit Department kept up-to-date about the project's status. The department fostered a good relationship with management that resulted in effective communication between the Corporate Internal Audit Department and the company.

Advantages and Disadvantages. The advantage of the test deck/test case technique was that the testing was done of the actual system rather than around the system. Also, the detail work was done by the company, maximizing the work of the Corporate Internal Audit Department in terms of leverage. The advantages of the audit software were the following:

1. Control concerns in the technical environment were presented in a quantitative manner.
2. Changes in system configuration were identified rapidly.
3. The technical approach was readily accepted and appreciated by management.
4. The in-depth technical knowledge obtained will form the basis of future audit efforts.
5. The technical capabilities of the EDP internal audit staff were increased.

The disadvantages of the test deck approach was that it was overly dependent on company personnel. The disadvantage of the audit software was that too much paper was generated and staffing flexibility was reduced. The ACF2 review specifically was time-consuming and required a detailed knowledge of ACF2. The audit software is segmented into specific products and thus requires close supervision to ensure that problems are not "falling through the cracks."

Changes for the Future

Based on the Hospital Services audit, the Corporate Internal Audit Department has made the following changes:

- Tailored audit programs have been developed that combine manual and computerized control testing objectives and criteria. This reduces dependence on internal coordination and reduces risk of testing "falling through the cracks."
- A technical support function has been established within IS auditing to train staff, maintain softwre, and assist in problem resolution. This function reduces dependence on company personnel and increases the skill level of all IS auditors, thus reducing dependency on specific staff to accomplish certain tasks or provide required continuity.
- A new continuing audit approach has been initiated, rather than one massive audit once per year. This reduces risk through more frequent monitoring, provides greater staffing flexibility and more hands-on training to more staff, and minimizes the impact on company personnel.

Future Requirements

The primary item on the list of future requirements is developing a menu-driven, user-friendly system where the auditor specifies, via menus, what software should be executed and what processing criteria apply. Thus, the first menu would be a list of all audit software products available, with the subsequent screens asking for the details relating to each software product. A second item to be considered should be an expert system designed to analyze the specifics of the system and generate test cases. A third item should be the development of an ACF2 Analyzer to reduce dependence on system utilities and specific staff personnel. Fourth, the software should produce more exception reporting.

APPENDIX **D**

Interviews With Perpetrators of Computer Fraud

COMPUTER-RELATED FRAUD AND ABUSE IN GOVERNMENT AGENCIES

In view of the number and size of computer systems used by the U.S. government, the problems of computer fraud and abuse are well-known to the agencies concerned. Various studies have been undertaken as a result. Of particular interest to EDP auditors are two studies, "Computer-Related Fraud and Abuse in Government Agencies" and the follow-up "Computer-Related Fraud in Government Agencies: Perpetrator Interviews," both conducted by the Department of Health and Human Services (HHS).

This appendix presents an overview of the first study and excerpts from the interviews held and the questions asked in the second study.[1] This material has been extracted from the HHS report and provides a fascinating glimpse into the motivations and methods of actual perpetrators of computer fraud and abuse, It also indicates the need for ongoing education of system personnel about controls and their purpose, as well as the importance of access controls. (See Chapter 31, "Logical Access Controls" for more information on these key controls.) The insights provided by these studies are invaluable for understanding these issues.

Findings

In 1982, the President's Council on Integrity and Efficiency (PCIE), concerned about growing incidences of computer-related fraud and abuse, commissioned the Inspector General of HHS to study the problem. The resulting perspective on the nature and scope of computer-related fraud and abuse, and on what the Inspector General (IG) community should do to deal with the problem, was presented in a report issued in June 1983.

The HHS Inspector General surveyed federal agencies about cases of computer-related fraud and abuse identified from January 1978 through March 1982. That survey obtained 172 cases (69 fraud and 103 abuse) and analyzed them for perpetrator characteristics, techniques of perpetration, losses, methods of detection, and controls. The resulting report, "Computer-Related Fraud and Abuse in Government Agencies," included the following findings:

- Fraud cases primarily involved theft of cash or diversion of assets, usually through input manipulation in benefit or payroll systems.

---

[1] Permission to print these excerpts has been granted by the Inspector General of HHS, who wishes to acknowledge the work of John I. Molnar, project manager for the interview-based study.

Most abuse cases involved use of computer time for outside business or entertainment.

- Most perpetrators were federal, nonsupervisory employees. Four out of five of the fraud perpetrators earned $20,000 a year or less. Two thirds of the fraud perpetrators were functional users of the computer system, rather than data processing personnel.
- Confirmed losses ranged up to $177,383 per case, although actual losses were thought to be higher in many cases.
- Operating personnel found over half of the frauds and over two-thirds of the abuses. More important, half of the cases were detected by accident, twice the incidence of detection through either controls or audits/reviews.

The report recommended that the IG community upgrade its expertise through computer training and awareness programs and that controls in automated systems be given especially close scrutiny. Because some survey responses were incomplete, the PCIE requested that the study be extended, with particular attention to specifics about controls in the victimized system environments.

Objectives of the Study

The PCIE asked the HHS Inspector General to expand on the original study by interviewing the identified perpetrators. The objective was to determine what the perpetrators would tell about their crimes and the vulnerabilities in government computer systems. Specific study questions included:

- Who were the perpetrators?
- What jobs did they have?
- How was the crime committed?
- Why was the crime committed?
- What was the work environment?

Scope and Methodology

First, perpetrators of the 69 computer-related fraud cases from the original study had to be identified, because that study, to preserve confidentiality and encourage cooperation, had not done so. It used only data descriptive of the crime. The agencies were able to identify perpetrators of 60 of the original 69 cases.

The HHS Inspector General was able to locate the perpetrators of 39 cases and interview 29 perpetrators of 21 of those cases. Of the others, nine cases were not prosecuted; seven perpetrators refused to be interviewed; and two cases were still open.

Because more cases had occurred since the original study two years earlier, the IG community was requested to identify all subsequent computer-related fraud cases. That yielded 18 additional perpetrators, of whom 17 were interviewed (one refused). Perpetrators in three of these newer cases were interviewed during their presentencing period.

In total, 46 perpetrators were interviewed (29 original and 17 new). They were involved in 39 cases of computer-related fraud, involving seven federal agencies including:

- Department of Agriculture
- Department of Defense
- Department of Health and Human Services
- Department of Justice
- Department of Labor
- Department of the Treasury
- Veterans Administration

The findings of this study are based largely on discussions with these 46 perpetrators. In addition, other sources of information were used in the analysis. The 46 discussions do not represent a statistically valid sample of government computer-related fraud cases. Instead, they represent the voluntary comments of perpetrators identified for this study and are presented to add new insights to the understanding of this relatively new type of crime. Following is the information developed in response to the specific study questions, grouped using the questions and responses as headings.

Who Were the Perpetrators?

"When I got out of the Navy I was job hopping. I took the PACE test to find a secure government job and was hired as a casework representative. I was promoted and knew I had a career."—A federal caseworker.

Perpetrators Were Employees, Not Outsiders. People using computers to defraud the government could be anywhere, given current technology. However, as was found in the original study, virtually all perpetrators were employees of an agency administering a federal program. With virtually all of the computer-related frauds committed by employees, two related points can be made: (1) Since none of the perpetrators who had gained access to the government computer system was from outside the agency, none was a beneficiary, client, or hacker; (2) all the perpetrators were authorized users, i.e., it was a necessary part of their jobs either to query, enter, or modify data in the computer system or to direct the operation of the computer system.

Just over half of the perpetrators were federal employees. The remaining were from state (16 percent), local (16 percent), and private (12 percent) agencies. The private sector employees were under contract to a government agency to administer a federal program or manage an automated system; all acted independently, rather than as part of a corporate scheme. Many of the perpetrators had co-conspirators who were not employees, but none of those personnel gained direct access to the computer.

The one perpetrator who was not an agency employee was a health care provider. A terminal was placed at his facility by the fiscal intermediary to expedite the submission of state Medicaid claims.

Perpetrators Were Young, Good Employees. Perpetrators appeared to be the younger employees of the agency. Their median age was 30 at the time they committed the crimes. In comparison, the average age of federal employees is about 40.

Three quarters of the perpetrators said they had attended college. A third had at least a bachelor's degree, with some having done postgraduate work. Two thirds had from one to four years of college, and some had attained an associate degree. Many of those who did not attend college had attended classes in business or computer academies.

During meetings with the perpetrators, they were asked about their job performance ratings. In general, they reported that they were good employees; only two noted unsatisfactory performance appraisals. Two thirds had received above average, excellent, or outstanding ratings, and one third reported average or satisfactory performance evaluations. It was not uncommon for the perpetrator to be considered one of the better employees in the office—the one to whom other employees went with problems. Many were also "students of the computer system" and were called upon to assist others. Additionally, a quarter of the perpetrators said that they had received awards for their performance. Ironically, four of those award recipients received their award for designing or implementing the computer system they ultimately stole from. For example, a programmer with a federal agency working on a payroll system got a cash award in 1981 when he set up the electronic funds transfer for his agency's payroll system. In 1982, he used that same system to steal to support his cocaine habit.

Another indicator of the perpetrators' success with the agencies is that about three quarters had been promoted or advanced in job responsibilities while at the agency.

Based on discussions with the perpetrators, most of them had sought permanent government employment. For example, for a third this was the job they sought after getting out of school. Another third had consciously sought a permanent government job after having worked elsewhere.

Although they were among the younger employees of the agencies, they had spent an average of over five years with the agency before they began to commit the crimes. Time on the job before the crime ranged from one year to 20 years and varied by type of employee. While federal employees had been with their agency for an average of six and a half years when they committed their crime, this figure dropped to five years for state employees and three for employees of local public agencies.

Some Had Criminal Records. One of the most surprising findings was that almost one-quarter of the perpetrators had prior criminal records when hired by a government agency. While a few admitted that they had hidden that fact from their employer, others were hired under special programs for ex-felons or their employment was an acknowledged condition of probation. The earlier crimes of the perpetrators ranged from rape and armed robbery to white-collar crimes of embezzlement and forgery. For some, the computer-related fraud was their second crime; for others, it was but one in a series of criminal activities. While 18 percent of the federal employee perpetrators had previous criminal records, this figure was as high as 43 percent for state and local employees. None of the private employees had a former criminal record.

Time on the job before the fraud was committed varied between those with a criminal record and those without one. Only 14 percent of those without criminal records committed their computer-related fraud within one year of being hired, as compared with 40 percent of those with a criminal record. Similarly, the median length of employment with the victimized agency for ex-offenders was only three years, in contrast to six years for those without a criminal record. Two-thirds of the ex-offenders were in the specific job where they committed the crime for less than one year, compared with only one-third of those without prior records. Apparently, the opportunity to commit fraud was seized more quickly by those with prior records. Carla and James are two such perpetrators.

> When Carla was interviewed, she was in a Federal prison. This was her third time in jail. In the early 1970s, she was sentenced to three years in a state prison for forgery and was later convicted of welfare fraud in the mid-1970s. In fact, she was on probation for welfare fraud when she was hired by a county welfare agency as a clerk-typist in their data

center. An A.A. degree in accounting, hard work, and good evaluations won her a data center supervisory position within one year.

At about this time, she met James, a data input technician working on the same program. James had been hired under a special program for ex-offenders. He had been arrested and convicted at least five times in the six years prior to being hired. The charges included theft of government property, credit card theft, forgery (27 counts), and five arms violations. During the interview, he readily admitted that he was a career criminal. During his first year on the job, he too had been promoted, but he also acquired a drug addiction that could not be financed by his $10,000 salary.

Together, James and Carla developed a plan to steal to support his drug habit and supplement her salary. Four months, fifty cases, and $120,000 later they were caught by a computer match.

What Jobs Did They Have?

"I didn't need to sit at a terminal to do my job. I just filled out forms. In keypunching, they never check anything. They just entered what was on the form."—A federal voucher clerk.

Perpetrators Had a Broad Range of Jobs. The perpetrators held a wide variety of jobs, ranging from secretaries to senior program managers and from entry level clerks to highly trained systems analysts.

Caseworker was the most commonly occupied job type (35 percent). This is a relatively discrete group of employees in entitlement programs who determine eligibility and the amount of the payments to be made to program beneficiaries. Most of these employees met directly with the public, but some made decisions based on the case files. None were in supervisory positions.

Computer support or technical personnel was the next most frequently held job type (28 percent). These are both professional and support staff whose raison d'etre was the computer system. About half could best be characterized as data entry technicians, that is, nonsupervisory employees who sat at video terminals and entered data into the system. They usually made no evaluation of or decisions on the data; they just entered it. The remaining technicians were involved with the overall computer operations. Three were computer professionals who either designed and wrote programs or supervised the operation of large management information systems. The others were data center support personnel performing such functions as loading decks of cards, hanging tapes, or managing hard-copy output.

The third most common position (26 percent) was clerical, including employees whose primary responsibility was to review and process paper, such as case files, payroll forms, or vouchers and bills for goods or services rendered to the agency. As a normal part of their job they were functional users of the computer, but they did not spend all of their time at a terminal.

Of the remaining five perpetrators, four were line managers heading up major management information systems or financial operations, and one was a health care provider.

Direct Computer Access Not Universal. To perform their jobs, all the perpetrators needed to modify data in the system or have access to the computer itself. Not all actually sat at a terminal or worked on a computer; just under half performed their jobs through the creation of input documents. These documents were occasionally reviewed; they were then submitted to technicians who entered the data. This is particularly true for the caseworkers; only two of the 16 loaded data directly into the computer. Many caseworkers did have query-only access to the computer system to review case status. For example, in benefit program field offices caseworkers have query-only computer terminals to review the status of specific cases. To change a case, they must complete a form, which is reviewed by one technician and submitted to another technician to be entered into the computer system.

Most Worked for Benefit Programs. Just over three-quarters of the perpetrators worked for benefit programs that issued funds and were in a position to issue those funds. About half of these employees worked for federally administered entitlement programs such as Social Security or the black lung program. A third worked for state or locally administered grant programs such as food stamps or unemployment insurance. The remainder were employees of private companies managing financial transactions for the Medicaid or Medicare programs.

The remaining perpetrators worked in administrative or staff positions, most often in various parts of payroll operations.

How Were the Crimes Perpetrated?

"I brought the screen up with a phony ID. I created a phony beneficiary and a phony claim using my mother's Social Security number. I just keyed it in."—A private agency clerk.

Most Perpetrators Issued Funds. The 46 perpetrators interviewed were involved in 39 different criminal cases. In four instances, two perpetrators per case were interviewed and in one case, four were interviewed. Accordingly, the following analysis of specific computer-related frauds is based on 39 cases.

In 85 percent of the cases, the perpetrators caused negotiable financial instruments to be issued, most frequently U.S. Treasury checks. Checks were also caused to be issued against state agencies and private financial organizations; a few cases involved issuances of food stamp coupons, which were usually converted to cash at about 75 cents for a dollar's worth.

The cases that did not involve negotiable financial documents included:

- Restoration of annual leave.
- Modification of income tax deductions.
- Taking funds that had been returned to the agency.
- Sale of false ID cards.
- Sale of information.

Virtually All Were "Data Diddlers." "Data diddling" is a common term for a crime committed by an employee by manipulating data before or during the input process or during output from the computer system. Examples are changing the name, address, or bank account of a beneficiary to that of the perpetrator's co-conspirator or erasing the history of a payment so that a duplicate check is issued.

Over 90 percent of the cases involved data diddling. This is consistent with the finding in the original study that most cases involved manipulation of data. Almost all the cases involved manipulating input to the data system, but a few involved the manipulation during both the input and output processes. These cases involved food stamp issuance, and output data manipulation was necessary to bypass controls, such as separation of duties, and to conceal the fact that illegal stamps were issued.

Half of the cases of input manipulation were not committed with "hands on" computer access. The perpetrators, because they had substantial knowledge of the system, were able to create documents that were later entered into the system by another person. The perpetrators' documents thus modified the data in the system to cause the illegal transactions.

The three cases that could not be described as data diddling were all committed by computer experts. In one instance, data from a criminal justice information computer system was sold. The two other cases were technical computer crimes, often referred to as "Trojan horses," in which someone places a small, illegal computer program within a larger normal operating program. The small program is difficult to detect and generates the illegal transactions when the larger program is run.

In one of these cases, the names and addresses of three friends of a federal programmer were inserted in place of three employees in the agency's payroll. After the program was run, the sub-program was deleted so that the checks went to the perpetrators' friends, but a review of the computer tape showed that checks were issued to the employees. The second "Trojan horse" case was quite similar. A technical consultant from a private company working on a federal benefit program caused his wife's name and address to be inserted in place of those of a beneficiary when the program to issue the entitlement check was run.

Three Schemes Predominate. The crimes committed were dictated by the purpose of the computer system on which the perpetrator worked. Virtually all cases involved the manipulation of data in either ongoing or one-time payment systems. Ongoing payment schemes occur in benefit program systems where a person or family is eligible for a specific benefit such as Social Security, unemployment insurance, or a paycheck. Once eligibility is established, funds are issued on a regular basis.

One-time payment schemes occur in financial systems designed to issue funds to a vendor, provider, or beneficiary in response to a specific bill or voucher for goods or services. In these payment systems, perpetrators had two options: They could create unauthorized files or records or manipulate existing ones.

Three predominant schemes used by perpetrators accounted for 35 of the 39 cases. The most common scheme—manipulation of data on existing cases in an ongoing payment system—accounted for almost half of the crimes. In Social Security or other entitlement programs, a valid beneficiary already existed in the program data base. When the beneficiary died or lost eligibility, the perpetrator redirected the check to himself or to a co-conspirator. In other instances, perpetrators caused duplicate payments to be issued to relatives who were valid cases on the system. A third way of taking advantage of existing cases was to reactivate dormant cases and have the benefits sent to a co-conspirator. Following is a common example of this scheme:

> Bill, a caseworker, got a notification that a beneficiary had died. Instead of terminating that person's eligibility, he went to a bank and opened an account in that beneficiary's name (and Social Security number). He then simply completed an input form that changed the address so that the check would be sent to his bank via direct deposit. Bill then periodically drew money out of that account. Bill didn't have to do very much modification to the case file in the computer. All he did was change the routing of the check.

The second type of scheme, which was used in about one-quarter of the cases, involved the creation of false claims in a one-time payment system, with payments sent to co-conspirators. Most frequently, perpetrators authorized a payment to a co-conspirator for bogus bills, such as a purchase order or reimbursement to beneficiaries for medical services. For example:

> Tom was a voucher examiner. His job was to review bills for completeness and then give them to data entry technicians to be loaded into the system so that payment could be made. One day Tom started submitting bogus bills to the technicians. They were just like real bills from doctors and physical therapists because there was MD or PT after every name. That was one of the edits in the system. However, the names and addresses were not those of real medical professionals; they were Tom's friends. Over 18 months they stole $250,000.

In the third common scheme, false records were created and added to files in ongoing payment programs. This was more difficult than the other schemes because of the documentation required to establish eligibility. In some cases, the perpetrators used the identities of co-conspirators; in others they created false identities. For example:

> Some employees used both versions of this scheme with a food stamp program. First they had friends come to the office and apply for food stamps. They needed real Social Security numbers and matching names because that was a control in the system. Once they had the real names and numbers, they put false income data on the application and their friends became eligible for benefits.
>
> When the Cuban and Haitian boatlift people began arriving, the eligibility system broke down. The newcomers became eligible for benefits but didn't have Social Security numbers. In order to bypass the Social Security number control, the program officials adopted a system of pseudo-Social Security numbers that could be issued in each office. The perpetrators didn't need their friends' names or numbers now; they could just create false beneficiaries with pseudo-numbers. And they did.

In the schemes that involved ongoing payment systems, often perpetrators would periodically terminate their illegal cases or claims to prevent detection. For example, cases were terminated to avoid a quality control audit of cases or a programmatic requirement for a periodic, face-to-face recertification of the case. Other perpetrators kept bogus cases going for a specific number of months—usually three to six.

It was also common in an entitlement program for the perpetrator to initiate the periodic payments with a large payment. These are typical of an adjustment in benefits caused by retroactive eligibility or to account for previous underpayments. This was often not a separate act but was done at the time the perpetrator initially modified or created the case.

Most Took Steps to Cover Up Their Crime. To cover up their crime, in almost half of the cases the perpetrators destroyed the hard-copy evidence of their crime. This occurred most often when the perpetrator, such as a caseworker, did not have direct access to the computer. Those perpetrators destroyed the input documents they had given to the input technicians. But some perpetrators also had to destroy computer output evidence of their crime, such as printouts or alerts produced by a screen or edit in the system. A perpetrator who had worked for a federal agency said, "At first I was really nervous. I had to put the case file in my briefcase and walk out of the building. When I got home I burned it. When I did it and realized how easy it was, I knew how bad the system was."

A few perpetrators reported that they did not have to worry about destroying evidence of their crime. Instead, they relied on virtually nonexistent filing systems or on routine, periodic destruction of hard copy. Some perpetrators also used the computer to cover up their crime. For example, they reported that they were able to delete the record of their illegal transaction from the system or they relied on routine purging of transactions.

Most Used Co-Conspirators. Original study survey data indicated that most of the perpetrators (75 percent) acted alone. However, based on these interviews, three quarters of the computer-related fraud cases involved co-conspirators. Beyond the psychological value of providing moral support, co-conspirators served other specific needs. Most often they were from outside the agency and provided a false ID and address and/or received and cashed checks. In some cases, fellow employees conspired in the crime, usually in situations in which it was necessary to bypass controls, such as separation of duties. In only a few cases, a perpetrator used both internal and external co-conspirators.

Most of those who did not use co-conspirators felt very strongly that this was the only way that they could commit the crime. One senior level manager summed it up when he said, "I couldn't have done it if I had had to involve someone else." These perpetrators were generally older employees, and, interestingly, 60 percent of those who had acted alone had received awards, compared with only 20 percent of those who used co-conspirators. All but one of the perpetrators with a former criminal record used co-conspirators.

Only a Few Had to Bypass ID and Password Controls. Almost half of the perpetrators said that the computer systems did not require them to use an identification number and/or password to get data into the system, for two reasons. First, as already noted, many perpetrators did not need direct access to the computer system to commit their crime. (However, some of these perpetrators did have to forge a supervisor's signature on the data entry document.) Second, some perpetrators worked on systems that simply did not require ID or password controls for each user. This would typically occur where a bank of terminals was brought on-line at the beginning of the day and shut down in the evneing. During the day any number of staff had access to the system.

In the remaining cases, nine perpetrators used their own ID and/or password to commit the crime, while only 11 had to make up or steal an ID number. When perpetrators used their own ID/password, it was usually on systems that did not record the ID with the transactions, so there was no permanent record of who made the data entry.

Those who needed another ID/password identification to commit their crime did not seem to have too much difficulty getting it. Some just sat at the terminal during their free time and made up possible identifying combinations until they found a valid one. In two cases, any three alpha characters would serve as an identifier and all the employees knew it. In three other offices, the ID number was simply an employee's initials, so the perpetrators just stole another worker's ID.

Frequency, Duration, and Loss Varied Greatly. The number of times the perpetrators committed their criminal acts ranged from one to 200, dictated in part by the scheme they used. For example, if the perpetrator created or manipulated data in an entitlement program, that one criminal act would yield a monthly check as long as the case was active. However, if the perpetrator created false bills in a voucher payment system, that crime would usually yield only one check. One perpetrator made only four unauthorized entries into a benefit program computer and got over $100,000. Another entered 55 false bills into a state bill payment system and only got $1,000. The median frequency for committing the criminal act was eight times, which demonstrates how efficient it is to use a computer to commit a crime and how infrequently the perpetrators needed to exploit the vulnerabilities in the system.

The duration of the crime also affected the number of times the illegal act was committed. The time from the first illegal act until the perpetrator was caught, or voluntarily stopped prior to being caught, ranged from one month to 72 months. The median duration was six months.

The reported amount of direct financial loss to the government agency ranged from no loss to $350,000, with an average loss per case of $45,000. Eighteen percent of the cases involved losses greater than $100,000, somewhat higher than the 7 percent reported in the original study. There were two cases of no dollar loss, one in which information was sold and the other in which a false ID was issued for immigration purposes. Although none of the perpetrators admitted to stealing more than was identified in their case as submitted to the court, some implied that more was stolen.

Why Did They Commit the Crime?

"I had personal problems because I was $20,000 in debt. But I had also worked my butt off for them and they passed me over for a promotion. I was good and deserved more. I decided to get back at them."—A federal program manager.

Perpetrators Stole Under Stress. Because eight perpetrators refused to admit to having committed a crime, the HHS Inspector General was not able to discuss their motives. Consequently, the analysis of motives is based on 38 discussions. Three quarters of the perpetrators reported that they were responding to a specific situational stress when they committed their crime. Most of these stole money because of a specific family problem such as medical bills, potential eviction or loss of a home, or loss of spousal income. Others reported that specific debts caused them to steal, and a few said they stole to support a drug habit.

Still others reported their primary reason was because they were disgruntled. Some were angry at the organization, while others were seeking revenge on an immediate supervisor. A systems analyst for a private company confided: "I had given my soul to that company and I got burned. That company ended up being my life and I got caught in the stigma of this lousy contract with the government. They wouldn't transfer me out. I had to show them." Furthermore, a third of those who stole because of a specific personal problem noted that they were also unhappy employees, which made it easier for them to commit their crime.

Although most perpetrators started stealing to meet a specific need or in response to other stresses, few stopped voluntarily once that need was met. Only one in six of the perpetrators stopped voluntarily.

Temptation and Boredom Influenced Others. A quarter of the perpetrators reported committing their crime because an opportunity presented itself rather than because of some driving problem. In some cases, it was a specific event such as funds being returned to the office or the accidental discovery of a vulnerable procedure in the system. For others, it was due to boredom or free time. The perpetrators, often sitting at a terminal, would play with the system or play beat the system in their idle time until they won the game. For example:

Connie, a terminal operator for a state program, enjoyed exploring the system. She worked in the reimbursement section and found that there was an emergency payment program with no screens for payments under $1,000. "When it started I was playing with the terminal on a break. I typed in my friend's name and then I hit return; it was processed. I could have cancelled it, but I didn't."

Only Some Feared Being Caught. Perpetrators reported that a significant contributing factor was that they did not fear being caught or punished. Over half said that they did not even think about the consequences of their actions; they acted on impulse or they just did not care. One programmer said, "The drugs were in control. I didn't even think about being caught."

Most of those who realized they might lose their job, go to jail, or be forced to pay restitution felt that the chances of being caught were minimal. The primary factor was that most felt that management was not sensitive to crime from the inside, so they were not being watched.

What Was the Work Environment?

"Everyone had an ID number and there was a password to bring the system up. But the codes and ID numbers were on the wall, so everyone and anyone could see them. No one cared."—A state claims examiner.

Controls Seen as Weak. Not surprisingly, most perpetrators rated computer security and internal controls in their offices as weak and not a significant barrier to their crime. While over 80 percent were able to identify specific examples of computer security, three-quarters of those said it was weak.

The most common examples of security noted by the perpetrators were various types of access controls. Most systems required personal ID codes and/or passwords that perpetrators easily found ways to bypass (or they did not need direct access to the system). Usually, the access code gave the user full access. In only a few cases was the user limited to specific files or types of transactions.

Other common controls noted were screens, edits, or alerts built into the system. Generally, these features would limit the amount of checks that could be issued or would send a hard-copy message back to the office that a specific, atypical transaction had been initiated. A third form of control noted by the perpetrators was separation of duties. In such instances, people who made eligibility or payment decisions were not permitted to do data entry.

While access controls, screens, and separation of duties were designed into most computer systems, poor implementation at the user level often undermined their effectiveness. Access controls were often simplistic or were bypassed in daily practice in the interest of productivity. For example, it was not uncommon for ID numbers to be the users' initials or any three digits. Also, passwords and operating codes were often issued in memos or manuals. Terminals, once brought on-line by an authorized operator, were often left on when the operator left the terminal. Edits and screens in the system were well-known to all system users and the perpetrators usually just steered clear of them. A few reported that it was not uncommon, when a backlog or special event arose, for managers to lift the edits or screens to speed up the input process.

The security feature of separation of duties was breached when, because of staffing changes, a person was trained in both input and output duties or when terminals were simply left unattended after being brought on-line. For example, some offices have separate terminals for query-only and input. A number of caseworker perpetrators, who had query-only authority, said it was easy to just walk in and sit down at an input terminal and enter an illegal transaction.

Perpetrators Were Aware of Other Crimes. Another factor that influenced the perpetrators was their perception that the system was vulnerable. Two-thirds reported that they were aware of other crimes "like theirs." Half said they knew of specific crimes. In the wake of a computer crime, it was common for the modus operandi of the perpetrator to be spread by rumor. In a few instances, the crime seemed to pervade the office. This was particularly true when supervisors were part of the scheme. For instance, a supervisor in one food stamp office recruited workers to be part of a crime by showing them how to commit it. Four perpetrators from one case were interviewed, but it was estimated that as many as 30 people were involved. In another office, the number was estimated at 14.

Perpetrators Said Supervision Was Weak. The perpetrators frequently volunteered that "no one was watching me," when discussing how and why their crime was committed. These reports of weak supervision fell into two categories.

First were weaknesses associated with more traditional forms of supervision. Perpetrators reported that supervisors did not review their work either because they were trusted employees, because their supervisor was too overloaded to review everything, or simply because work generally was not reviewed. If and when work was reviewed, it was reviewed for productivity and for errors. Employee crime appeared to be a low priority at best.

The second form of weak supervision was of a more technical nature.

Some perpetrators reported that their supervisor knew what their job was, but not how they actually did it at the computer terminal. Often, supervisors began working at the agency when the job was done manually and never learned how it was done on the automated system. Perpetrators were able to take advantage of such supervisory naiveté. One perpetrator reported, "One of the largest problems you have is that managers have no knowledge of the systems. I finished my project three months ahead of time and my supervisor didn't know." Another perpetrator who was paying bogus bills to friends said, "My supervisor didn't know anything about the system. Those old ladies watched me all day and never caught me."

How Would Perpetrators Strengthen the Systems?

"I would impress people with the idea of computer security or any security. We knew no one was watching."—A federal caseworker.

During discussions with the perpetrators, they were asked what could have prevented them from committing their crime or how they would eliminate the vulnerabilities in the computer system they had exploited. Following are their more commonly cited recommendations.

Random Case Validation. Perpetrators who modified existing cases or created false ones said they exploited the fact that cases were not verified. When case files were reviewed, it was just a paper review. No one actually spoke to the beneficiary. In fact, one of the major problems perpetrators had in concealing their crimes was dealing with periodic case recertifications. It was common for a perpetrator to terminate a false case when a recertification notice went out. Perpetrators recommend that supervisors randomly, openly, and on an ad hoc basis contact beneficiaries to verify their existence and the status of their case. It appears that a very small sample, with only a telephone inquiry, would have raised the risk of detection sufficiently to preclude some of the crimes.

Rotate Caseload. Some perpetrators were able to conceal their crime and control their bogus cases because they were permanently assigned a specific caseload. Case assignments are often based on alphabetical order or the end digit in the beneficiary's ID number. Perpetrators recommended rotating caseloads to ensure that one person does not have permanent control of a case.

Identify Workers With Their Transactions in the Data Base. Perpetrators noted that they were able to enter bogus data into the system anonymously.

Most systems that the perpetrators worked on did not identify the input technician and/or caseworker with the transaction. Consequently, the perpetrators felt that the system "wasn't being watched." The perpetrators recommended that the system identify the person who authorizes and/or inputs each transaction.

Limit Access Within the System. Perpetrators noted that they were often able to commit or cover up their crime by using override or force codes in the system. Such codes give the opportunity to delete data from the system or to bypass edits and screens. Perpetrators recommended that system users' access be limited to only the codes or types of transactions they need to do their job and suggest that this be controlled by each user's ID and password.

Enforce Security Features. Some perpetrators were able to committ their crimes despite computer security features specifically designed to prevent such crimes. Sometimes, computer controls were bypassed to promote office efficiencies; in other situations, they were not in effect because of benign neglect. Perpetrators recommend that the purpose and value of computer system controls be stressed to first-line managers and that people in charge of computer security periodically evaluate the implementation of specific controls.

Conclusions and Recommendations

Investigations of computer-related fraud cases are generally limited to the facts necessary to prosecute the alleged perpetrators. The findings from the interviews with perpetrators add to earlier findings reported by Inspectors General based on data in their files. For example, interviews reported the involvement of co-conspirators in many more cases than the IG files suggested. Similarly, interviews provided more descriptive information on how the crimes were perpetrated and on the effectiveness, or lack thereof, of system controls.

Debrief Perpetrators Routinely. Law enforcement officials and criminologists often interview people convicted of economic crimes to identify the characteristics of a subset of perpetrators. Because computer fraud is a relatively new area of economic crime, such interviews of perpetrators will add to the growing body of knowledge in this area. Findings from interviews can be used by management and Inspectors General to prevent additional fraud cases. The HHS Inspector General recommends, therefore, that:

- Inspectors General routinely debrief perpetrators of computer fraud to identify the specific vulnerabilities in their computer systems.
- Inspectors General provide feedback to management on the findings from perpetrator interviews and ensure that controls are instituted to correct vulnerabilities.
- Inspectors General, program managers, and systems security officers include perpetrator case histories in training on computer crime and computer security, both to heighten awareness and to act as a deterrent.

Strengthen Automated System Controls. Perpetrators reported that the existing controls in the victimized systems were weak and easily bypassed. IDs and passwords were simplistic and/or public knowledge and gave the user access to the whole system, rather than only to the applications or transactions necessary for the user's job. A number of the victimized systems did not identify or maintain a record of the specific individual who authorized or entered data, creating an atmosphere of anonymity that severely hampered later review or investigation. Screens and edits were easily circumvented by users or lifted by management in the interest of productivity. These findings suggest the need to implement additional controls to strengthen the integrity of automated systems and prevent the perception that "no one is watching." The HHS Inspector General therefore recommends that:

- All payment systems be capable of enforcing personal accountability, by including such features as personal identification and authentication, and audit trails.
- Access controls in such systems limit user access to only the programs, records, or transactions required by the user's job responsibility.
- Management periodically review the adequacy and implementation of all automated system controls and security features, as required by Office of Management and Budget (OMB) Circulars A-71 (TM-1)[2] and A-123.

Guidance to State, Local, and Private Agencies. Federal agencies have a substantial investment in state, local, and private computer systems, both because the federal government finances most of the development and maintenance costs of such systems and because those systems control the allocation of federal funds. Yet these systems appear to be vulnerable. About

[2] This circular was superseded by OMB Circular A-130 (Dec. 12, 1985).

half of the perpetrators worked for state, local, or private agencies that were administering federal programs. It is recommended that:

- Federal agencies reevaluate their guidance to state, local, and private administering agencies regarding computer security and controls.
- Vulnerabilities in state, local, or private agencies' computer systems be addressed with the same vigor as those in federal systems.

Training and Awareness of Line Managers. The original study observed that IG investigators were not fully aware of internal control procedures for automated systems. Nor were they aware of specific vulnerabilities in their agency's computer systems. Training in these areas was recommended. It appears that a similar lack of sensitivity to controls and potential vulnerabilities exists among line program managers. The potential for employee crime has not been stressed, and some managers see system controls more as impediments to productivity than necessary security features. It is recommended that:

- IGs and/or system security officers provide training and awareness programs targeted to line program managers.
- Procedures be established for "advertising" the existence of internal and system controls to indicate that "someone is indeed watching."

Review Personnel Security Procedures. In the course of locating the perpetrators, the HHS Inspector General learned that one in five had a prior criminal record. Some were hired by the agencies under special placement programs for ex-felons. In light of the findings of the studies it is recommended that:

- Inspectors General and management reevaluate agency personnel security policies and clearance practices for people in positions of trust, including all positions with access to payroll, benefit records, and other payment data.

These recommendations can be applied to organizations everywhere. It is not just the government that has vulnerable security over its computer systems.

Glossary

AAA American Accounting Association.

abend *Ab*normal *end* of task. Termination of a computer task when an error state prevents the completion of the task.

abort In a computer system, controlled termination of a processing activity when it cannot or should not continue.

ACB Application control block (IMS/VS). When an application program is scheduled for execution, IMS/VS must first have the DBD and PSB control blocks available. These control blocks are put into an IMS/VS internal format called ACB.

ACB Application control block (VSAM). The operating system obtains the information needed to read from or write to a VSAM data set from an ACB.

ACBGEN The IMS/VS utility used to merge the DBD and PSB in the internal ACB format. An ACBGEN is required for IMS/VS DC (Data Communication) applications and is optional for IMS/VS batch applications.

accelerated depreciation A depreciation accounting method where depreciable costs are deducted in greater amounts during the beginning years of an asset's economic life and decreased each year thereafter.

access The way the computer obtains data so that particular data can be located and made available for processing.

access control A control designed to prevent unauthorized access to data or use of system functions and programs, preventing unauthorized changes.

access method Any of the data management techniques (sequential, indexed-sequential, or direct) available for transferring data between storage and input/output devices.

access method services A multifunction service program that defines VSAM files and allocates space for them, converts indexed-sequential files to key-sequential files with indexes, modifies file attributes in the catalog, reorganizes files, facilitates data portability between operating systems, creates backup copies of files and indexes, and lists the records of the files and catalogs.

access path Sequence of hardware and software components significant to access control. Any component capable of enforcing access restrictions (e.g., ACF2) or any component that could be used to bypass an access restriction should be considered part of the access path. The access path can also be defined as the path through which a user requests travels, including the telecommunications software, transaction processing software, application program, and so forth.

account balance The difference in dollars between the total debits and the total credits in an account.

accountability The existence of a record that permits the identification of an individual who performed some specific activity (e.g., an update to a data file or an attempted breach of security) so that responsibility for that activity can be established.

accounting cycle The complete sequence of reporting and summarizing procedures performed on financial data.

accounting equation Assets equal liabilities plus owner's equity (A = L + OE).

accounting period The time covered by an operating statement. One year is the accounting period for much financial reporting; financial statements are prepared by many organizations for each quarter of the year as well as for each month.

accounting system A set of forms, records, instruction manuals, flowcharts, equipment, and programs that reports the financial activities of an organization.

accounts payable Amounts that a company owes its creditors for goods and services purchased on open account.

accounts receivable Amounts that a company expects to collect from its customers for goods and services sold on open account.

accounts receivable ledger A listing of accounts that includes a detailed summary of activities for each customer. The total of this subsidiary ledger agrees with the general ledger controlling account, accounts receivable.

accrual basis A method of accounting where revenue is recorded in the period it is earned and expenses are recorded in the period incurred, regardless of when cash is received or disbursed.

accrued expenses Expenses that have accumulated at the end of the accounting period but are payable at a future date.

accrued revenue (unrecorded revenue) Revenue earned in the current accounting period but not yet received.

accumulated depreciation A contra-asset (liability) account shown as a deduction from the related fixed asset account in the balance sheet. Depreciation charged throughout the useful life of an asset is recorded in this account.

ACD Automatic call distributor; used in telecommunications.

ACF2 An access control software package originally produced by SKK Cambridge Systems Group for protecting and monitoring access to computer systems.

acoustic coupler A simple kind of modem that uses sound waves to transmit data over the public telephone network via a conventional telephone handset and a cradle the handset fits into.

active file A fixed and related group of computerized records whose expiration date falls after its processing date.

address, disk Specifies physical location of machine-readable data on the magnetic storage device.

address, memory The location of a particular byte within the computer's memory.

address, space The collection of all the addresses (real or virtual) assigned to a particular computer task.

adjusted trial balance A listing of all ledger account balances after the amounts have been changed to include the adjusting entries made at the end of the period.

adjusting entries Journal postings required at the end of the period to update the accounts before financial statements are prepared. Primarily, adjusting entries serve to apportion transactions properly between the accounting periods affected and to record any revenue earned or expenses incurred that have not been recorded before the end of the period.

after-closing trial balance A trial balance prepared after all closing entries have been made. Consists of accounts for assets, liabilities, and owner's equity.

aging of accounts receivable An analysis of individual customers' uncollected account records according to the length of time amounts due are outstanding. Groups are usually formulated as follows: current, past due 1-30 days, past due 31-60 days, past due 61-90 days, more than 90 days past due. A step in estimating the total uncollectible portion of accounts receivable.

AICPA American Institute of Certified Public Accountants.

ALE Annual Loss Exposure. The estimated yearly dollar loss time. The estimated probability of its occurrence in a year.

algebra, Boolean *See* Boolean algebra.

ALGOL A high-level programming language, most often used in nonbusiness applications, that expresses programs by algorithms.

algorithm A step-by-step process designed for problem solving. Governing rules, as well as the steps themselves, are finite in number.

ALI American Law Institute.

allocate To grant a resource to, or reserve it for, a job or task, such as allocated disk space for data to be stored on as it is updated.

allowance for doubtful accounts An asset valuation account that compares the total number of receivables with that portion estimated to be uncollectible.

alphanumeric (also called **alphameric**) The alphabetic, numeric, and symbolic character elements used by computers to describe data.

alternate routing In a computer system, another communications path used if the primary path is not available. There may be one or more possible paths.

ALU Arithmetic logic unit. A basic part of the central processing unit of the computer.

American Standard Code for Information Interchange *See* ASCII.

amortization The systematic write-off, to expense, of the cost of an intangible asset over the period of its economic usefulness.

amplitude modulation With respect to communications techniques, one of three ways of modifying a sine wave signal so it can carry data. The sine wave, or carrier, is modified in accordance with the information to be transmitted.

analog computer Processes data that is represented as measures of physical variables.

analog transmission Sending a continuously variable signal over communication lines as opposed to sending the discretely variable signal of digital.

analytical engine The machine designed by Charles Babbage in 1830 to calculate mathematical processes automatically while storing their intermediate results. Essentially a precursor to the modern computer.

analytical review A type of accounting study intended to corroborate the logical interrelationship among accounts and to identify and explain all significant changes and abnormalities.

ANSI American National Standards Institute.

APF Authorized program facility. A system facility whereby access to restricted system functions is controlled.

APL A Programming Language. A high-level programming language used for mathematical applications.

application program A specific task-oriented program, such as an accounts payable processing program, supplied or designed to suit individual user needs.

appropriation of retained earnings. The transfer of a portion of earned surplus to a separate account by order of the board of directors to indicate that portion's unavailability for dividends.

arithmetic logic unit. *See* ALU.

ARQ *A*utomatic *R*e*Q*uest for repetition. A system employing an error-detecting code, structured so that any transmission error included in a signal initiates a retransmission of the character incorrectly received.

Artificial Intelligence (AI) A broad term regarding advanced computer systems that includes the development of natural languages for programming and addressing computers, and systems that can simulate human capabilities such as learning and analysis, and alphanumeric character and voice recognition.

ASB Auditing Standards Board.

ASCII American Standard Code for Information Interchange. A 128-character, seven-bit code for data transfer adopted by the American Standards Association to achieve compatibility between data devices.

ASP Asymmetric multiprocessing system. An extension to the IBM System/360 Operating System that allows multiple CPUs to share resources. Renamed in 1972 as JES/3.

Assembler (also called **Assembly**) A low-level programming language, designed for a particular computer model or type, in which instructions are written alphanumerically and represent specific machine and memory functions.

asset turnover Sales divided by total assets.

assets Economic resources (things of value) owned by a business that are expected to benefit future operations. Current assets are cash and other assets expected to be converted into cash within one year or the current operating cycle (whichever is longer).

asynchronous transmission (also called **start-stop transmission**) Transmission in which each data character is individually synchronized, usually by the use of start and stop elements. The intervals between transmitted characters may not be of equal length.

ATM Automated teller machine.

attributes Set of access rights authorized to a user or a set of access types (read, write) associated with a system resource. These are stored in tables on the system.

audit equation Knowledge plus corroboration equals understanding of the subject matter.

audit opinion The report issued by certified public accountants after an audit, or examination of the financial statements, of an organization. Expresses a judgment on the fairness and accuracy of the financial statements and indicates the nature and limits of the responsibility being assumed by the independent auditors.

audit program A list of steps to be performed during an examination. It controls the nature, extent, and timing of procedures performed during the examination.

audit report A written declaration issued by a certified public accountant (CPA) that expresses an independent professional opinion on the fairness and reliability of the financial statements of a business.

audit risk The chance that the auditor will issue an unqualified opinion on financial statements that are materially misstated.

audit trail In computer systems, a step-by-step history of a transaction, especially a transaction with security sensitivity. Includes source documents, electronic logs, and records of accesses to restricted files.

auditing The principal activity of a CPA. An independent examination of the accounting records and other business-related evidence to support the expression of an impartial, informed opinion about the reliability of the financial statements.

AudSEC Auditing Standards Executive Committee.

authentication The process of validating a claimed identity.

authorization The act of first comparing a proposed transaction with plans, conditions, constraints, or general knowledge of what constitutes propriety and then deciding whether or not the transaction is valid and in accord with management intentions.

authorized Having the delegated authority to perform an activity.

authorized program facility *See* APF.

automatic call distributor *See* ACD.

automatic request for repetition *See* ARQ.

average-cost Total cost of goods available for sale divided by the number of units available for sale. A method of inventory valuation.

background Processing lower priority jobs or tasks when computer resources are not otherwise needed for higher priority jobs.

backup Any duplicate of a primary resource function, such as a copy of a computer program or a data file. This standby is used in case of loss or failure of the primary resource.

bad debt A receivable (or a portion thereof) that has been determined to be uncollectible and is charged as an expense of the accounting period.

BAL Basic Assembler Language. An assembly language used to write computer programs.

balance sheet An organization's statement of financial position, presenting assets, liabilities, and owner's equity as they exist on a specific date.

bandwidth The range of frequencies available for signaling. The differences are expressed in cycles per second (hertz) between the highest and lowest frequencies of a band. The wider the bandwidth, the greater the data flow in a given period.

bar code The arrangement of black stripes and spaces on products that is read by an optical scanner to identify the products and/or their prices.

baseband signaling A communications transmission technique where digitally encoded information remains in its original frequency (such as amplitude) during transmission over a communications channel.

BASIC Beginner's All-purpose Symbolic Instruction Code. A high-level procedure-oriented programming language. Developed as a teaching tool at Dartmouth University, BASIC is easy to learn and use.

Basic Assembler Language *See* BAL.

batch In computer operations, the processing of a group of related transactions or other items at planned intervals. Large cyclic processing needs, such as payroll and inventory, benefit from this individual processing of application programs. In many systems, batches are processed overnight or during periods of off-peak usage.

baud Unit of signaling speed for data transmission. If each signal event represents only one bit condition, baud rate is the same as bits per second. When each signal event represents an amount other than one bit, then baud rate does not equal bits per second. A 300 baud rate transmits 30 characters per second. A 9,600 baud rate can send a full data screen in two seconds.

Beginner's All-purpose Symbolic Instruction Code *See* BASIC.

beginning inventory Goods on hand and available for sale at the start of the accounting period.

bidirectional logical relationship In a data base, when the two possible paths between the structural element connection of a data base are defined. For example, in IBM's Information Management System (IMS), definition of the logical relationship of both paths can be from the physical parent through the logical child to the logical parent and from the logical parent through the logical child to the physical parent. (Differs from a unidirectional logical relationship in that both paths are defined.)

binary digit The smallest unit of information in a two-part system, the binary digit represents either the mark or space of an on or off (1 or 0) condition. The way in which data is stored in a computer system.

binary synchronous transmission (BISYNC) A uniform discipline using a defined set of control characters and control character sequences for synchronized transmission of binary coded data between stations in a data communications system.

bit (b) Contraction of binary digit.

BLP *See* bypass label processing

board A printed circuit board that is a subcomponent of computer hardware.

book value The net amount at which an asset is shown in the accounting records. For depreciable assets, book value equals cost minus accumulated depreciation.

Boolean algebra A set of logical rules that establishes relationships between statements. Those statements form a binary system where their combination of statements is either true or false.

Boolean search capability In IBM's Information Management System (IMS) data base software packages, portions of information can be labeled and retrieved using the logic capabilities of Boolean algebra.

bootstrap (boot) A program that brings another program (often the operating system) into operation to run the computer. May be called the initial program load (IPL).

bpi Bits per inch. Relates to the density of data on a magnetic storage medium like tape.

BPI Bytes per inch (equal to 8 bpi).

bps Bits per second. Relates to the speed of data transfer.

BPS Bytes per second (equal to 8 bps).

branch A decision location in the computer's processing flow or a departure from the normal processing route within a program. A branch may occur as the result of a condition test, depending on the results of that test (*see* test).

broadband With respect to communications, a subdividable portion of the data transfer frequency spectrum.

BSC Binary synchronous communications.

budget With respect to capital assets, used in evaluating proposed investments in capital assets and the financing of these investments. With respect to cash accounting, a forecast of cash receipts and cash disbursements expected for a future period, as well as cash balances and cash requirements within future periods.

buffer The computer's temporary storage area used to compensate for a difference in rate of data flow when transmitting data from one device to another, such as from a computer to a printer.

bug A mistake or error in a computer program.

burst To separate on the perforated line the continuous multi-part stationery of computer printers into separate sheets after printing.

bus An information path used as a common connection between several similar or different devices. Used frequently in microprocessors as a simple path for transferring data, control, and addressing information.

business entity An organization—of any size—that enters into economic activity whose transactions must be recorded, summarized, and reported as separate functions in the community.

bypass label processing (BLP) An option used in job control language statements to instruct the operating system not to check volume/data set labels.

CAD Computer-aided design.

CAE Computer-aided engineering.

call Transfer of program control from one routine (the calling program) to another (the called program) usually with the intention of returning control to the calling program, to bring the second routine into use during processing of the first.

CAM Computer-aided manufacture.

capital assets Stocks, bonds, and rental property not used in a trade or business.

card reader A computer input device that identifies the hole pattern in punched cards and translates the characters represented by those holes into an electronic form understood by the computer.

carrier, communications common A company that furnishes communications services to the general public, regulated by appropriate local, state, or federal agencies. The term includes truckers and movers, bus lines, and airlines but is also used to refer to telecommunications companies.

carrier system With respect to communications, a way to obtain a number of channels over a single path by first modulating each channel on a different frequency and then demodulating at the receiving point to restore the signals to their original form.

CASE Computer-aided software engineering.

cash basis An accounting system in which revenue and expenses are recorded when received and paid, regardless of the period they apply to. This system fails to match revenue with related expenses and does not meet generally accepted accounting principles (GAAP). Used for individual income tax returns and in accounting records of many professional firms and small service-type enterprises.

cash flow statement A statement showing the sources of cash receipts and the purpose of cash payments during an accounting period. This information is useful for explaining changes in the balance of the cash account, but it is not a substitute for an income statement.

catalog The collection of data set indexes (data set name, I/O unit, and volume serial number) maintained by data management. One way a computer system keeps track of stored data.

cathode ray tube *See* CRT.

CATV Cable television.

CCITT Consultative Committee on International Telephone and Telegraph.

central processing unit *See* CPU.

centralization In a computer system, when the main processing activity is done in one geographic location (often called the home office or the computer center).

centralized accounting A technique in which the branches of a company send information on transactions to the home office, which maintains the financial records for the entire company.

certified information systems auditor (CISA) A professional certification sponsored by the EDP Auditors Association.

certified public accountant (CPA) An independent professional accountant registered and licensed by a state to offer auditing and accounting services to clients.

change accumulation log The file created by the IMS Data Base Change Accumulation facility that contains only the information from the log data sets necessary for recovery. The utility eliminates all non-data base records and combines all data base records that update the same segment.

channel A path for electrical transmission between two or more points. Also referred to as a circuit, line, or link.

channel, analog A channel on which the information transmitted can take any value between the limits defined by the channel. Most voice channels are analog channels.

channel, voice-grade A channel suitable for transmission of speech, digital or analog data, or facsimile, generally with a frequency range of about 300 to 3,400 cycles per second.

channel to channel *See* CTC.

character Letter, number, punctuation, or other sign contained in a message. There may be characters for special symbols and some control functions in a computer system.

character distortion With respect to data communications, distortion caused by transients that, as a result of the modulation, are present in the data transmission channel. Depending on transmission qualities, unreliable data may be transmitted.

chart of accounts A systematic listing of account names and numbers that applies to a specific accounting entity.

check digit In computerized data, a numeric value computed to provide assurance that the original value has not been altered (and is, therefore, possible erroneous) in storage, construction, or transmission.

check register A simplified version of the cash payments journal used for recording cash payments when a voucher is being used.

child segment In a hierarchical data base, a segment immediately below another segment in the hierarchy. A child segment has only one parent segment.

chip The miniature wafer on which circuit elements, which carry electronic impulses understood by the computer, have been imprinted.

CICA Canadian Institute of Chartered Accountants.

CICS Customer Information Control System. An IBM communications system used for production applications in a mainframe environment.

circuit A conducting path through which an electronic current passes. With respect to two-wire circuitry, where a circuit is formed by two conductors that are insulated from each other. The two conductors can be used as either a one-way transmission path, a half-duplex path, or a duplex path. With respect to four-wire circuitry, where a communication path with four wires (two for each direction of transmission) links separated sending and receiving devices.

CISA *See* certified information systems auditor.

closing entries Journal postings made at the end of the period to close temporary accounts (revenue, expense, and drawing accounts) and transfer balances to a capital account.

CMS Conversational Monitor System. An IBM on-line interactive system product used for application development.

COBOL Common Business Oriented Language. A high-level procedure-oriented programming language used for many business applications.

code A system of symbols representing words or instructions to the computer and used to convert, transmit, or store data. As a verb, to write a program. With respect to command codes in data base applications, may be used to modify the function code of a call, the segment qualification, and the establishment of parentage (*see* parentage).

command A job control statement or a message, sent to the computer system, that initiates a processing task.

Common Business Oriented Language *See* COBOL.

communications Transmitting data or information between locations, often between two or more computers.

comparative financial statement Financial statement data that covers two or more successive periods and is placed in adjacent columns to facilitate a study of changes.

compare In a computer program, a function where two or more items are examined to reveal their relationship.

compile The act of translating a high-level language source program into an object module or program written in machine language. A compiler is a program that translates a source program into an object module after checking its syntax and produces a listing of the source program with diagnostics that may affect the source program's execution.

component percentage The relationship of any financial statement item to a total including that item. For example, each type of asset as a percentage of total assets.

composition Here, the set of characters that may be used to create a valid password.

concatenated fields A string of fields. Data sets can also be concatenated, or run together.

conditioning With respect to data communications, the addition of equipment to a leased voice-grade communications channel to reduce distortion.

confidentiality In general, the concept that confidential computerized files or information will remain so. In an audit, assuring the client that, except for disclosure required by law and custom, information shared with the auditor will go no further without the client's permission.

consolidated financial statements Reports that present the economic position and operating results of a group of affiliated corporations as if the group represented a single unified business.

constant With respect to computer systems, a value that does not change during program execution.

contention With respect to computer systems, when different users try to access the same system resources. With respect to communications, a method of line control in which the terminals request to transmit. If the channel in question is free, transmission goes ahead; if it is not free, the terminal waits until it is free. A queue of contention requests may be built up by the computer in a set sequence or in the same sequence in which requests are made.

contingency plan Management policy and procedures designed to maintain or restore computer operations, possible at an alternate data center, in the event of emergencies, system failure, or disaster.

contingent liabilities Recorded obligations that relate to past events but may arise on occurrence of a future event deemed possible but not probable.

contra-account A ledger account that is deducted from, or offset against, a related account in the financial statement, such as allowance for doubtful accounts. A contra-asset account is one with a credit balance that is offset against, or deducted from, an asset account to produce the proper balance sheet valuation for the asset.

contribution margin Sales less variable costs.

contribution margin ratio The percentage of sales available to cover fixed expenses and yield a net income.

control (or controlling) account A general ledger account supported by detailed information in a subsidiary ledger.

control character In computerized data, an alphanumeric character whose occurrence in a particular context initiates, modifies, or stops a control operation, such as "carriage return" or "enter."

control logic (or structure) The order of the computer's processing functions.

control program (CP) The independent program that operates to schedule and supervise the execution of programs in the computer system.

control read-only memory *See* CROM.

control section (CSECT) The part of a computer program specified by the programmer to be a relocatable unit, all elements of which are to be loaded into adjoining storage locations for execution. Usually given a name; if not, it is known as a private code. A CSECT is sometimes called a section definition.

control statement In computer programming, a command that directs the logical sequence of processing operations.

control total A total, generated manually or by computer, used to check the processing results.

control unit The part of the central processing unit that holds computer instruction codes and whose functions include decoding instructions, initiating operations, and monitoring system operations.

controls The methods, policies, and procedures adopted within an organization to ensure the safeguarding of assets, the accuracy and reliability of data, the promotion of administrative efficiency, and the adherence to management standards and intentions.

controls, application (also called **input, processing, output**) Methods of ensuring that only complete, accurate, and valid data is entered and updated in a computer system; that processing accomplishes the correct task; that processing results meet expectations; and that data is maintained.

controls, general (also called **information technology** or **IT controls**) Controls over the EDP system operations as a whole, including the design, security, and use of computer programs; the security of data files; and controls over access. Consists of system software and related manual procedures.

conversational mode (also called **interactive**) A computer processing technique that involves step-by-step interaction between the user at a terminal, by means of keyboard and display, and a computer.

Conversational Monitoring System *See* CMS.

copyright An exclusive right inferred by authorship and ensured by the federal government (Copyright Act of 1977) to protect the production and sale of literary or artistic material for a certain period of years. Can also refer to software.

core Main memory within the computer.

cost accounting A specialized field of accounting concerned with determining and controlling the cost of particular products or processes.

cost center An organizational unit, such as the personnel department, that incurs expenses or costs but does not directly generate revenue.

cost of goods manufactured Cost of units of finished product completed during a period. Beginning inventory of goods in process, plus cost of raw material used, plus direct labor and factory overhead, minus ending inventory of goods in process equals cost of goods manufactured.

cost of goods sold A computation appearing as a separate section of an income statement showing the cost of goods sold during the period. Computed by first adding net delivered cost of merchandise purchased to beginning inventory (to obtain cost of goods available for sale) and then deducting the amount of the ending inventory from this total.

cost of inventory The price paid for the inventory plus the cost of bringing the goods to the point where they are offered for sale.

cost principle (historic cost) An accounting policy whereby assets are recorded at their original cost to the organization.

cost revenue analysis A method of studying the response of revenue and costs to variations in business volume.

CP *See* control program.

CPA *See* certified public accountant.

CP/M Control program/microcomputers. One of the first widely used operating systems for microcomputers.

cps Characters per second.

CPU Central processing unit. The part of the computer housing the electronic circuits that control the hardware, arithmetic logic unit, and main memory. Functions include decoding the instructions that control the electronic circuits, performing arithmetic and logic operations, and monitoring machine performance.

CRC *See* cyclic redundancy check.

credit An amount entered on the right-hand side of an account. A credit is used to record a decrease in an asset and an increase in a liability or in owner's equity.

credit agency An organization, such as Dun & Bradstreet, Inc. or TRW Credit, that gathers credit data on individuals and business concerns and distributes the information to its clients for a fee.

credit memorandum A document issued to show a reduction in the amount owed by a customer because of goods returned, a defect in the goods returned, or an error.

CROM Control read-only memory. The programming embodied in the read-only memory (ROM) is used to control the processing of operations or the function of a microprocessor.

cross-foot To add footed columns across to obtain a total. This total is checked against the accumulated total for a column.

CRT Cathode ray tube. A television-like vacuum tube unit used for information entry and display. Terminals including such displays are frequently called CRTs. This is an I/O device.

cryptographic key A data item used to encrypt or decrypt data so that only those having the key can perform these processes. (The Data Encryption Standard (DES) uses a secret 64-bit number.)

CSECT *See* control section.

CSMA/CD(CA) Carrier sense multiple access LAN with collision detection (collision avoidance).

CTC Channel to channel. A communications term relating to data transmission.

current ratio Current assets divided by current liabilities. A measure of short-run debt-paying ability.

current-value accounting The valuation of assets and measurement of income in terms of current values rather than historical cost. An approach designed to avoid the distortion of financial statements by inflation.

cursor A movable shape (often a bar or rectangle) that marks the place on a computer terminal screen where the next character entered will be displayed.

Customer Information Control System *See* CICS.

cycle billing A system of billing customers at various dates during the month to avoid concentration of work at month-end.

cyclic redundancy check(CRC) An error detection scheme for computer systems in which a check character is generated by first dividing all the serialized bits in a block of data by a predetermined binary number and then using the remainder as the check character.

cylinder A unit of storage on a disk, composed of tracks. In a disk pack, the set of all tracks with the same nominal distance from the center of the axis of rotation.

data Facts and information that can be communicated and manipulated. In relation to a computer program, the input that a program and its instructions perform on and that determines the results of processing.

data base A systematic collection of data elements organized according to a specific design that can be hierarchical or relational.

data base administrator (DBA) The individual responsible for both the design of the data base, including the structure and contents, and the access capabilities of application programs and users to the data base. Additional responsibilities include operation, performance, integrity, and security of the data base.

data base definition (DBD) Describes structure (hierarchy), sequence, key fields, update rules, and so forth of a computerized data base. In IBM's Information Management System (IMS), the DBD can describe a physical or a logical data base.

data base management system (DBMS) A system software product that aids in controlling and using the data needed by application programs. A DBMS can help create and maintain a well-organized data base.

data base record The single occurrence of a root segment and all its dependent segments.

data communications The movement of data between geographically separate locations via public and/or private electrical transmission systems.

data definition statement (DD statement) An IBM operating system job control statement that describes the data set to be associated with a particular job step.

data dictionary A data structure listing and defining the contents of the data base.

data element The smallest unit of addressable information in a data base. A field in a data base segment.

data element dictionary (DED) A file listing data element specifications, definitions, descriptions, and other information as developed for a particular application.

Data Encryption Standard (DES) The cryptographic standard most commonly used in EDP. It is specified in the U.S. National Bureau of Standards Federal Information Processing Standards Publications (FIPS PUB) Nos. 46, 74, and 81.

data entry Placing data into a computer system through a data input device, such as a keyboard, a diskette, or a card reader.

Data Language/1 *See* DL/1.

data processing The computerized preparation of documents and the flow of data contained in these documents through the major steps of recording, classifying, and summarizing.

data set A group of related computerized records.

data set group In IBM's Information Management System (IMS), the partitioning of the data base record type into subtrees of segment types, and the storing of instances of each subtree in a separate group.

data set name (DSNAME, DSN) The DSNAME is the name of a data set, or group of related records (a file).

data transmissions The technique, and its related technology, used in sending data between geographically separated locations or devices over a communications channel.

dataphone The communications equipment furnished by AT&T for data communication services.

DBA *See* data base administrator.

DBD *See* data base definition.

DBMS *See* data base management system.

DD statement *See* data definition statement.

debit An amount entered on the left-hand side of an account. A debit is used to record an increase in an asset and a decrease in a liability or in owner's equity.

debit memorandum A document issued by a buyer to show a decrease in the amount previously recorded as owed to a seller. May also be ussed by a seller to increase the amount previously recorded as receivable from a customer.

debug To find and eliminate program errors or computer system malfunctions. Debugging programs means locating errors.

decentralization Distributing computer processing among the different data centers of a geographically diversified organization.

decentralized accounting system A system in which each branch of a company maintains its own complete set of accounting records.

decision support system (DSS) A system that helps provide information needed by management to run a business. DSSs are becoming critical to the success of many organizations.

deck A group of related punch cards; it is analogous to a file.

decryption The process of transforming encrypted data back into its original form.

DED *See* data element dictionary.

default Failure to pay interest on, or principal of, a promissory note at the due date. In a computer system, a default or a default value is automatically chosen by the program from the alternatives when the user does not specify a choice.

deferred charge An expenditure expected to yield benefits for several accounting periods and therefore be capitalized and written off during the periods benefited.

deferred revenue An obligation to render services or deliver goods in the future because of advance receipt of payment.

density With respect to data storage, the number of elements per unit length, area, or volume, such as characters or bits per inch on magnetic tape.

depletion Allocating the cost of a natural resource to the units removed as the resource is mined, pumped, cut, or otherwise consumed.

depreciable cost The cost of an asset minus the estimated residual or salvage value.

depreciation The systematic allocation of the cost of an asset to expense during the periods of its useful life.

DES *See* Data Encryption Standard.

dial-up terminal A remote terminal that is connected to a telecommunications line where the connection between the terminal and the computer is initiated at the remote terminal. Several remote terminals may share the single telecommunications line connected to the computer.

dibit A set of two bits. In four-phase modulation, each possible dibit is encoded as one of four possible states: 00, 01, 10, 11.

digit In the binary system, a numeric character representing the integers 1 or 0.

digit portion (byte) The four right-most bit positions in a byte. Also called the numeric portion.

digital computer A device that processes data, represented in discrete form, in the on/off, 1/0 condition. Generically, computer usually refers to a digital computer.

digital data Information represented by a code or characters, such as numbers or letters, consisting of a sequence of discrete elements, rather than the continuous wave-like sequence of analog data.

digital signal A discontinuous signal where the various states come at discrete intervals. *Compare with* analog transmission.

direct access device (also called **direct access storage device—DASD)** A peripheral hardware unit that provides the capability to access and/or manipulate data as required without having to access all preceding records to reach it. (In sequential access, as in tape, all records must be read to reach the one required.)

direct address pointer Contains the address of the physical storage location of a related segment in a computer system data base. A component of the segment prefix.

direct charge-off method A method of accounting for uncollectible receivables in which no expense is recognized until individual accounts are determined to be worthless. At that point the account receivable is written off with an offsetting debit to uncollectible accounts expense. Fails to match revenue and related expenses.

direct labor Employees' wages directly related to production.

directory A computerized index of all system and user files currently maintained by the computer system.

disclosure principle Financial statements should disclose all material and relevant information about the financial position and operating results of a business. The notes accompanying financial statements are an important means of disclosure.

discontinued operations The operations (revenue and expenses) of a company segment that has been eliminated, rendered obsolete, or sold.

discount With respect to cash sales accounting, a price reduction offered by manufacturers and wholesalers to encourge customers to pay invoices within a specified discount period.

discount rate The required rate of return used by an investor to discount future cash flows to their present value.

discounted cash flows The present value of expected future cash flows.

disk *See* magnetic disk.

disk drive A type of direct access storage device that uses magnetic disks as the storage medium, and physically reads from, or writes to, the data stored on the magnetic disk.

disk operating system *See* DOS.

diskette (also called **floppy disk**) A flexible magnetic storage medium. The flexible plastic disk is housed in a rigid protective cardboard or plastic cover. Most microcomputers use diskettes.

distributed processing A computer system whose processing is spread among the different data centers of an organization.

DL/1 Data Language/1. The interface between the user program and IBM's Information Management System (IMS).

documentation All the charts, forms, tapes, reports, and other business papers that guide and describe the working of a company's system of accounting and internal control. A complete and accurate description and authorization of a transaction and each operation a transaction passes through. In computer terminology, the written description of a system or program and how it operates.

DOS Disk operating system. A disk-resident operating system that provides operating system capabilities for computing systems of 16K and larger.

dot-matrix A two-dimensional representation of characters that is arranged by combining dots into rows and columns. A dot-matrix that represents graphic characters is used for a computer terminal and can be reproduced on hard copy using a dot-matrix printer.

double declining balance depreciation The most widely used version of declining balance depreciation. The rate is double the straight-line rate.

double-entry method In recording financial transactions, the total dollar amount of debits must equal the total dollar amount of credits.

down time The time that the computer system is unavailable for processing, usually calculated as a percentage of total time available for processing.

DSN *See* data set name.

DSNAME *See* data set name.

dump (also called **file dump, core dump,** or **memory dump**) To write, in a condensed manner, the contents of a computer file or memory location. A process often used to find problems (bugs).

duplex transmission (also called **full-duplex transmission**) With respect to communications, simultaneous two-way independent transmission in both directions. *Compare with* half-duplex transmission.

dynamic processing In a multiprogramming system, swapping jobs among different system resources (memory locations and peripherals) according to priorities during execution.

EBCDIC Extended Binary-Coded Decimal Interchange Code. An eight-bit coded set of characters used for data representation.

edit To prepare data for future computer operations, including programmed procedures that inspect data for accuracy, add or delete items, and do format checks on data contents.

EDP Auditors Association/EDP Auditors Foundation (EDPAA/EDPAF) Founded in 1969 and 1976 respectively, these professional associations established the CISA (certified information systems auditor) designation and examination.

EFT Electronic Funds Transfer

electronic journal A chronological file that records the processing activities of a computer system and is maintained and stored by the system.

electronic mail Written messages, such as letters or memos, sent and delivered by computer communications links from person to person.

employee's individual earnings record A record maintained for each employee summarizing gross earnings, deductions, net pay, and other payroll information.

employee's withholding exemption certificate (W-4) A federal form prepared by the employee and given to the employer stating the number of withholding exemptions claimed. Used in determining the amount of income tax to be withheld from the employee's pay.

employer's quarterly federal tax return (941) A report prepared every three months by the employer to provide the federal government with a record of all wages paid, amounts withheld, and amounts of tax on both employees and employer.

encryption Scrambling computerized information to secure data by using special algorithms for transmission or other purposes. Passwords are stored within the system and are often encrypted, so that even when unauthorized access of their file takes place, they cannot be read or understood.

ending inventory Goods still on hand and available for sale to customers at the close of the accounting period.

equity method An accounting method used when one corporation's investment in another is large enough to influence the policies of the investee. The investor recognizes as investment income its proportionate share of the investee's net income, rather than considering dividends received as income.

execute When the computer system performs operations it is directed to do by the program instructions.

expenditure With respect to capital, the amount of cash or property paid for assets incurred for the benefit of future periods.

expenses The cost of the goods and services used up in obtaining revenue. Sometimes referred to as expired costs.

expert system A system that uses software to hold and work with the knowledge of experts, making it possible to apply that knowledge to a particular transaction or situation. Used for decision support, expert systems are taking an increasingly important role in today's organizations. Also referred to as artificial intelligence (AI), these systems, today, are actually expert systems, not true AI.

expiration date With respect to a computer file, the date after which the computer system no longer automatically protects the file from being overwritten by other data.

expired password A password that is due to be changed at the first available opportunity. The only function of an expired password is to permit a user or a responsible official (e.g., a security officer) to sign on and create another password. Once a new password has been created, the user can resume normal activities using the new password.

Extended Binary-Coded Decimal Interchange Code *See* EBCDIC.

extraordinary items Transactions and events that are both unusual and infrequent, such as a sale of a major asset, noted in financial statements.

factory overhead All costs incurred in the manufacturing process other than the cost of raw material and direct labor, such as insurance, depreciation of machinery, and supervisors' salaries.

FASB *See* Financial Accounting Standards Board.

FCC Federal Communications Commission.

federal employment compensation tax A tax imposed on the employer by the Federal Unemployment Tax Act (FUTA) and based on the amount of payrolls. Designed to provide temporary payments to unemployed persons.

Federal Insurance Contribution Act tax *See* FICA tax.

feedback System output. Includes control operations' output returned to the input side of computer processing to evaluate the system conformation's effectiveness.

fiber optics A method of transmitting signals using light in a glass filament cable.

FICA tax A tax proposed by the Federal Insurance Contribution Act on both employer and employees. Used to finance the Social Security program.

field In a data base, the smallest unit of data that can be named and directed. A string of fields is a concatenated field or a record. In a record, such as an invoice, the physical area assigned to categorized data, such as a customer account number.

field signature In a data base, defines the interpretation of a unique data unit according to application program specifications.

FIFO *See* first-in, first-out.

file A collection of records stored in computerized form, often on magnetic storage media. Files may be created, located, queried, updated, displayed, scratched, backed up, printed, named, and classified by type.

Financial Accounting Standards Board (FASB) An independent group that conducts research in accounting and that issues authoritative statements as to proper reporting of financial information. Formerly the Accounting Principles Board (APB).

financial forecast A plan of operations for a future period with expected results expressed in dollars.

financial statement order Sequence of accounts in the ledger: balance sheet accounts first (assets, liabilities, and owner's equity), followed by income statement accounts (revenue and expenses).

financial statements Reports that summarize the financial position and operating results of a business (balance sheet and income statement).

finished goods inventory Completed manufactured products that are available for sale.

firmware Permanent computer instructions encoded into the circuits of semiconductor chips. A type of read-only memory.

first-in, first-out (FIFO) In inventory accounting, the cost of goods sold based on the assumption that the first merchandise acquired is the first merchandise sold, and that the ending inventory consists of the most recently acquired goods. In data processing, a queuing technique where the next item to be handled is the item that has been in the queue the longest.

fiscal year Any 12-month accounting period adopted by a business.

fixed cost A cost that does not change with variations in the level of output.

flag In programming, a predetermined piece of data that marks an expected or special event during processing.

flexible budget A budget or series of budgets that cover a variety of production levels.

floppy disk *See* diskette.

flowchart A diagram of the movement of transactions, computer functions, media, and/or operations within a system. The processing flow is represented by symbolic shapes for operation, device, data file, and so on to depict the system or program.

FOB Free on board. With respect to FOB destination, when the seller incurs the cost of shipping the goods to the buyer and retains title to the goods while they are en route. With respect to FOB shipping point, when the buyer incurs the cost of shipping the goods, and title to the goods passes to the buyer at the time of shipment.

footing The total of amounts in a column.

format The spatial organization of data (characters, fields, records, files) whether they may be printed, displayed, or stored.

FORTRAN *FOR*mula *TRAN*slation. A high-level programming language that uses arithmetic formulas to express computer programs.

fraud Dishonest acts intended to deceive. May involve the theft of assets and falsification of records and statements.

free on board *See* FOB.

frequency-division multiplex With respect to communications, a multiplex system in which the available transmission frequency range is divided into narrower bands, each used for a separate channel.

frequency modulation With respect to communications, one of three ways of modifying a sine wave signal to make it carry information. The sine wave, or carrier, is modified in accordance with the information to be transmitted.

full (absorption) costing The traditional method of product costing in which both fixed and variable manufacturing costs are treated as product costs and charged to inventories.

full-duplex transmission *See* duplex transmission.

function The special activity or purpose of a task; a processing operation for which a computer has hardware and/or software facilities.

function code A data base call element that specifies the action to be taken on the data base.

GAAP *See* generally accepted accounting principles.

GAAS *See* generally accepted auditing standards.

gain With respect to capital, the amount of excess proceeds realized on the sale or exchange of a capital asset over its book value.

GAO General Accounting Office. A government audit agency that reports to Congress.

general and administrative expenses Expenses of the general offices, accounting department, personnel office, credit and collection department, and activities other than the selling of goods. A subdivision of operating expenses.

general ledger The recorded collection of accounts where all of an organization's financial transactions are classified, either in detail or in summary form from a subsidiary ledger.

generalized sequential access method *See* GSAM.

generally accepted accounting principles (GAAP) Standards or guidelines for the preparation of financial statements to achieve the objectives of understandability, reliability, and comparability. Also used as criteria for judging acceptability of accounting methods. Those accounting principles that have received substantial authoritative support, such as the approval of the Financial Accounting Standards Board, the American Institute of Certified Public Accountants, or the Securities and Exchange Commission.

generally accepted auditing standards (GAAS) Quality guidelines issued by the American Institute of Certified Public Accountants regarding the conduct and report of the field work and audit of a public accountant.

goods in process (work in process) inventory Inventory consisting of partially finished products at various stages of completion in the manufacturing process.

gross earnings Total amount earned by an employee before deductions such as Social Security taxes, federal income tax withheld, and any voluntary deductions.

gross income All income and gains from whatever source derived unless specifically excluded by law, such as interest on state and municipal bonds.

gross price method A policy of recording invoices at the gross amount before cash discounts and of recording cash discounts taken in accounts called Purchase Discounts and Sales Discounts.

gross profit method A way to estimate the cost of ending inventory, based on the assumption that the rate of gross profit remains approximately the same from year to year.

gross profit on sales Revenue from sales minus cost of goods sold.

GSAM Generalized sequential access method. An IBM Information Management System (IMS/VS) method that allows sequential OS/VS data sets to be accessed as IMS/VS data bases.

hacking An unauthorized attempt at accessing a computer system. The term is most often used in relation to a person who attempts to enter a system from a remote location by circumventing network access controls. Typically, hackers are individuals who spend an inordinate amount of time working on computers for other than professional purposes; they usually are fairly young and often still in school.

half-duplex transmission With respect to communications, an independent transmission that may flow in either direction but in only one direction at a time. *Compare with* duplex transmission.

hard copy Computer reports, files, and documents printed on paper and visually readable.

hardware The actual equipment of a computer system. Describes components of the machine including electronic circuitry, peripherals, and processor.

hash totals The addition of any numeric data existing for all documents in the batch, that can be checked against the total of the same numeric data fields for items processed.

HASP Houston Automatic Spooling Program. A computer program that provides supplementary management functions, such as the control of job flow that is part of job management, ordering of task processing that is part of task management, as well as data management and spooling. Renamed in 1972 as JES/2.

HDAM Hierarchical direct access method. An IMS/VS data base access method of organizing the data using a randomizing routine to store and locate root segments. HDAM is efficient for a data base that will have primarily direct access.

HDLC High-level data link control.

hertz A unit of frequency equal to one cycle per second.

HIDAM Hierarchical indexed direct access method. An IMS/VS data base access method using an index to access the root segments in the HDAM data base. HIDAM is the access method that is most efficient for an approximately equal amount of direct and sequential processing.

hierarchical direct access method *See* HDAM.

hierarchical indexed direct access method *See* HIDAM.

hierarchical indexed sequential access method *See* HISAM.

hierarchical sequential access method *See* HSAM.

hierarchy A structured set of computerized data.

Hierarchy: Input-Processing-Output *See* HIPO.

high-level language Programming language closely related to the English language or human mathematical expressions. High-level languages do not reflect the structure of a specific computer. COBOL, FORTRAN, BASIC, ALGOL, and PL/1 are high-level languages.

HIPO Hierarchy: Input-Processing-Output. A flowcharting technique used during program design and development; also used to document program function.

HISAM Hierarchical indexed sequential access method. An IMS/VS data base access method that stores segments in hierarchic sequence with an index to locate root segments. HISAM is used for direct access of data base records by root keys, sequential access of data base records, and sequential access of dependent segments.

historical cost An asset's cost at its acquisition. Includes actual cost and associated costs, such as shipping and installation.

holding gains The change in an asset's current value (whether an increase or a decrease) during the current period.

host computer The primary computer in a distributed or multiple computer system. Data base access and access to the network are controlled by the host computer. Synonymous with host processor.

host language The programming mechanism that functions with DL/1 to access IBM's Information Management System (IMS) data bases.

Houston Automatic Spooling Program *See* HASP.

HSAM Hierarchical sequential access method. An IMS/VS data base access method to retrieve the root segments in the same sequence as they were stored in the data base. HSAM is used for data bases that are processed sequentially. They cannot be updated.

hybrid computer Using digital and analog technology, can process discrete and variable data in the same machine.

IAPC *See* International Auditing Practices Committee.

IBG *See* interblock gap.

IC *See* integrated circuit.

identifier (ID) A character string used to uniquely name and identify a person or system component, used for both identification and control purposes.

IEEE Institute of Electrical and Electronic Engineers.

IFAC *See* International Federation of Accountants.

IIA *See* Institute of Internal Auditors; Insurance Institute of America.

IMS *See* Information Management System.

income statement A report used to evaluate the performance of a business by matching its revenue and related expenses for a particular accounting period. Shows the net income or net loss.

income summary account The summary account in the ledger to which revenue and expense accounts are posted for closing at the end of the period. The balance (credit balance for net income, debit balance for a net loss) is transferred to the owner's capital account.

index A table used to locate the records of an indexed sequential data set.

index data base Contains HIDAM (hierarchic indexed direct access method) root segment keys, which are used to index the retrieval of the physical HIDAM root segment.

indexed sequential access method *See* ISAM.

indirect labor Employee wages that are not directly related to production.

individual accountability Measures by which the identity of a user can be positively associated with regard to access to machines, time, method, type of access, and work performed; records used to determine which individual performed a task.

Information Management System (IMS) A general purpose IBM system product that allows users to access a computer-maintained data base through remote terminals.

initial machine load (IML) The processes that load the system microcode from diskette to control storage.

initial password A password whose function is to permit a user to sign on and create another secret password for future use.

initial program load (IPL) (also called a **bootstrap** or **boot program**) A program that brings another program (often the operating sytem) into operation to run the computer.

initialize With respect to a magnetic disk, the process of establishing the disk areas that will store files.

input Information/data received by the computer environment from the external environment or another area within the computer environment. The process of entering information to the computer.

input device Equipment, such as a tape drive or a disk drive, used to enter data/information to the magnetic storage of a computer system.

input media The physical tool that data can be recorded on in machine-readable format for entry into a computer system.

input/output *See* I/O.

input, processing, output *See* controls, application.

inquiry processing Direct, on-line access to a computer file, providing immediate reference to its contents and resulting in a response to the requested information.

installment basis of accounting A method of recognizing income from installment sales that is based on collections rather than date of sale. Acceptable for income tax purposes but ordinarily not for other accounting purposes.

Institute of Internal Auditors (IIA) Formed in 1941 to promote professionalism and education. Activities include sponsoring seminars, conferences, research, and *The Internal Auditor*, a monthly professional journal. Also sponsors CIA (certified internal auditor) certification.

Insurance Institute of America (IIA) Founded in 1909, the IIA offers educational programs and professional certification for the property-liability insurance business.

intangible assets Those assets used in the operation of a business that have no physical substance and are noncurrent.

integrated circuit (IC) A combination of interconnected electronic circuit elements, components that are manufactured together and otherwise inseparable, on a single unit.

integrity With respect to data, its accuracy, quality, validity, and safety from unauthorized use.

information technology controls *See* controls, general.

interactive A computer system that involves responses or prompts between the user and the computer, such as an automated teller machine. Often called a conversational system.

interblock gap (IBG) The space between units of data on magnetic storage media where no data is recorded.

interest A charge made for the use of money. The formula for computing interest is: principal × rate of interest × time = interest (P × R × T = I).

interface The place, or boundary, of two or more computer systems, devices, or processes that permits this interaction to occur.

interim statements Financial reports prepared at intervals of less than one year, such as quarterly and monthly statements.

internal auditing An activity carried on in organizations by an in-house professional staff to investigate and evaluate the system of internal controls on a year-round basis. Also, evaluating the efficiency of individiual departments within the organization.

internal control All measures used by a business to guard against errors, waste, or fraud and to assure the reliability of accounting data. Designed to aid in the efficient operation of a business and to encourage compliance with company policies.

International Auditing Practices Committee (IAPC) Established by the International

Federation of Accountants to develop guidelines regarding generally accepted auditing practices and audit responses.

International Federation of Accountants (IFAC) Serves to promote a coordinated worldwide accounting profession, including coordinated auditing standards.

interpreter A programming language processor that translates and executes source code into machine code serially (that is, one instruction at a time with instructions processed immediately).

intersection data With respect to the hierarchical relationship of data in a data base, when a logical child is retrieved, the data returned into the I/O area can include the logical parent concatenated key, physical segment data, and logical parent data, in that order. The physical segment data is said to be intersection data.

inventory Goods acquired or produced for sale in the regular operation of a business. Goods in which a business deals.

inverted data base A logical data base that permits the processing of segments in a physical hierarchy in an "upward" fashion.

invoice An itemized statement of goods being bought or sold. Shows quantities, prices, and credit terms. Serves as the basis for an entry in the accounting records of both seller and buyer because it evidences the transfer of ownership of goods.

I/O Input/output. Devices that can be used for input and/or output.

I/O area (segment I/O area) As a result of a call, this area can contain the segment(s) retrieved, the segment(s) to be replaced, the segment(s) to be inserted, or the segment(s) to be deleted.

IPL *See* initial program load.

ISAM Indexed sequential access method. An access method that allows records to be stored and retrieved using a key.

ISDN Integrated services digital network.

JCL *See* job control language.

JES Job entry subsystem. A system facility that provides I/O spooling functions, job class scheduling, remote job entry capability, and managing. The primary job entry subsystem used by Multiple Virtual Storage (MVS).

job A set of data that completely defines a unit of work for a computer. A job usually includes programs, linkages, files, and instructions to the operating system.

job control language (JCL) Any one of the control statements in the input job stream that identifies a job or defines its requirements.

job entry subsystem *See* JES.

job-order costing system An accounting method that assigns the costs of raw material, direct labor, and factory overhead to a specific job.

job step In a computer system, a unit of work associated with one processing program. A job consists of one or more job steps.

journal A chronological record of transactions, showing for each transaction the debits and credits to be entered in specific ledger accounts. With respect to cash receipts, used only to record all cash received. With respect to cash payments, a special journal used to record all payments of cash. With respect to computer systems, the logging of data for an informational trail.

journal entry A financial transaction translated into its debit and credit components, and an explanation of the transaction. In systems, can be computerized.

journalize To state a transaction and enter it in a journal.

K Stands for 1,024; in computers, usually bytes.

key In cryptography, a symbol or sequence of symbols that controls the operation of encryption and decryption.

key entry *See* data entry.

key field A field used by the computer to locate data.

labor rate variance The difference between the standard labor rate and the actual rate, multiplied by the actual hours.

LAN Local area network.

language In the computer environment, a set of alphabetic, numeric, and symbolic character elements used with a rule structure to communicate between people and machines.

language translator A computer program that changes the source code of one computer language into the source code of another.

last-in, first-out (LIFO) A method of computing the cost of goods sold by using the prices paid for the most recently acquired units. Ending inventory is valued on the basis of prices paid for the units first acquired.

LATA Local access and transport area.

LCD Liquid crystal display.

LED Light-emitting diode.

ledger A book, file, or other record containing all the separate accounts of a business. In systems, can be computerized.

length The minimum and maximum number of characters allowed for a particular data element, or other input such as a password.

level A number representing the vertical position at which segments are contained within a data base. It also represents the level of dependency.

liabilities Debts or obligations of a business. The claims of creditors against its assets.

library In computer terms, a library is a collection of similar files, such as data sets contained on tape and/or disks, stored together in a common area. Typical uses are to store a group of source programs or a group of load modules. In a library, each program is called a member. Libraries are also called partitioned data sets (PDS).

LIFO *See* last-in, first-out.

line printer Used for high-speed printing on continuous forms.

linkage editor A utility program that takes as its input object modules and produces a machine language load module.

linkedit The act of combining an object program with needed read/write or other specialized functions to create a computer-executable program (or load module). This procedure is performed by a computer program called a linkage editor.

load Moving data or programs from a storage device to the computer's memory for processing.

load library A partitioned data set used for storing load modules for later retrieval.

load module The results of the linkedit process.The load module is fully executable by the computer.

log With respect to computer systems, to record an event or a transaction. May include the time and duration of the event; often a log is recorded on a computerized journal.

log-in (logon) To begin a session, usually in a mainframe or minicomputer environment, by identifying an authorized user and a password that permits access to the computer's resources.

log-out (logoff) To end a session, usually in a mainframe or minicomputer environment, when the authorized user has finished working with the computer's resources.

logic error In computer programming, when an error in processing occurs even though the program is syntactically correct.

logical data base A data base containing segments that are involved in logical relationships. Many logical data bases (representing different hierarchical views) can be defined for one physical data base. One logical data base can be defined to view several physical data bases. The segments in a logical data base must be defined in at least one physical data base. A logical data base must have a corresponding logical data base definition.

logical terminal A name that is related to a physical terminal. One physical terminal can have one or more logical terminals associated with it. The user can reference the logical terminal in the construction and transmission of messages without concern for such things as physical terminal address. If the physical terminal becomes inoperative, the logical terminals associated with it can be dynamically reassigned to another physical terminal.

long-term capital gains and losses Gains and losses resulting from sale of capital assets owned for more than a specific period (nine months in 1977 and one year thereafter).

longitudinal redundancy check (LRC) A system of error control based on the formation of a block check using a preset formula. The formula is applied in the same manner to each character. In a simple case, the LRC is created by forming a parity check on each bit position of all the characters in the block. For example, the first bit of the LRC character creates odd parity among the one-bit positions of the characters in the block.

loop checking A method of checking the accuracy of data transmission. The received data is returned to the sending unit for comparison with the original data, which has been stored there for this purpose. May be referred to as message and/or information feedback.

loss With respect to capital, the deficit resulting from the sale or exchange of a capital asset for less than its cost.

low-level language Computer programming language designed to reflect the structure of a specific computer. Provides each object code instruction with a source code instruction. Assembly is a low-level language.

lower of aggregate cost or market The total cost of marketable securities owned is compared with the market value determined at the balance sheet date. The lower of these two aggregate figures is the amount used to value the asset in the balance sheet. The method presently required by Financial Accounting Standards Board rules for valuation of marketable securities.

lower-of-cost-or-market A method of inventory pricing in which goods are valued at original cost or replacement cost (market), whichever is lower.

LRC *See* longitudinal redundancy check.

machine language A code that is understood and used directly by a computer.

macro instruction A general term used to collectively describe an instruction statement, the corresponding instruction definition, the resulting assembly language statements, the machine language instructions, and other data produced from the assembly language statements. A set of machine language instructions for commonly used routines. An example is DIVIDE, a common macro, whose one descriptive word adds the set of instructions stored in memory so that the program performs division.

magnetic disk With respect to computer storage, the rotating platters that data is written to and read from. The data is recorded on the magnetic surface in bit patterns that run in the tracks within cylinders on the surface of the disk.

magnetic ink character recognition (MICR) A computer input technique that translates characters printed in magnetic ink into bit patterns understood by the computer.

magnetic tape With respect to computer storage, the magnetically coated plastic ribbon that data is written to and read from. The data is recorded in bit patterns that correspond to the channels on the tape's surface.

mainframe In reference to a computer environment, a large general purpose computer consisting of control unit, arithmetic unit, and main storage. Because of its size, this hardware unit can process and store tremendous amounts of data.

maintenance, file Altering computerized records by updating them to keep their contents current, adding new records, and adjusting storage organization as required and indexes as changes occur.

maintenance, program Altering computer programs to reflect new processing requirements or fluctuating processing requirements, and documenting these changes.

management information system *See* MIS.

manual processing Noncomputerized, nonautomated manipulation of data.

manufacturing account A summary account used in closing the accounts of a manufacturing business. All costs used in computing the cost of goods manufactured are transferred into the account, which is then closed to the income summary.

margin of safety Amount by which actual sales exceed the break-even point.

master budget A report that combines the overall financial and operating plan of an organization.

master file In a computer, the most currently accurate and authorative permanent or semi-permanent computerized record of information maintained over an extended period. Standing data is a term (sometimes) used to refer to the master file data.

master terminal A logical terminal that has complete control of the IBM Information Management System (IMS) communications facilities, message scheduling, and data base operation.

matching principle To measure income, the revenue earned during an accounting period is compared with the expenses incurred in generating this revenue.

material price variance The difference between the standard price and the actual price of material used, multiplied by the standard quantity.

materiality An auditing concept regarding the relative importance of an amount or item. An item is considered as not material when it is not significant enough to influence decisions or have an effect on the financial statements.

member The generic name for a computerized file in a computer system's library.

memory The unit or component of a computer that can receive, contain, and output data. Main memory stores programs during program execution. Secondary memory, or storage, is usually held on a peripheral device.

menu A list of options, or items, displayed on a terminal from which a user can choose. The selection initiates the next task performed by the computer.

menu driven A program, usually in an interactive computer system, controlled by the selections made by the user from a menu.

message switching With respect to communications, the technique of receiving a message, storing it until the proper outgoing line is available, and then re-transmitting. No direct connection between the incoming and outgoing lines is set up, as it is in line-switching.

microcomputer A small computer built around a microprocessor. The relatively small expense of a microcomputer allows home users and business professionals access to low-cost computer resources.

microprocessor An integrated circuit device that contains the miniaturized circuitry to perform arithmetic, logic, and control operations. Popularly called a "computer on a chip."

microwave Any electromagnetic wave in the radio-frequency spectrum above 890 megacycles per second.

million instructions per second *See* MIPS.

minicomputer General all-purpose computer designed for an office environment and ranging in price from $20,000 to more than $200,000. Memory size and processing speed fall between a microcomputer and a medium-sized mainframe.

MIPS Million instructions per second. Used when describing the computing speed of some computers.

MIS Management information system. Computer applications designed to support management with appropriate and timely information for analysis and to support their control function.

mnemonic With respect to computer systems, programming language symbols that represent computer operations and are rendered easier to remember through an English-like name that is pronounceable.

modem A contraction of modulator-demodulator. A hardware peripheral device. The term may be used when the modulator and the demodulator are associated in the same signal-conversion equipment. *See* modulation.

modulation The process by which some characteristic of one wave is varied in accordance with another wave or signal. This technique is used in data sets and modems to make business machine signals compatible with communications facilities.

module A separate independent subset of instructions within a computer program, a module can be written, compiled, and tested before being linked with the remaining parts of the program.

monetary items With respect to changes in price levels, monetary items include assets representing claims to a fixed number of dollars, such as cash and receivables, and all liabilities. Monetary items are not restated when preparing general purchasing power financial statements.

multidrop line (also called **multipoint**) With respect to communications, a line or a circuit interconnecting several computer stations within a network.

multiple occurrence of a segment In IBM's Information Management System (IMS) when more than one occurrence of a segment exists within the same data base record. Also known as a twin.

multiplex, multichannel Use of a common communications channel to make two or more channels. This is achieved either by splitting the frequency band transmitted by the common channel into narrower bands, each of which is used to constitute a distinct channel (frequency-division multiplex) or by allocating the common channel in turn to constitute different intermittent channels (time-division multiplex).

multiplexer A device that uses several communication channels at the same time, a multiplexer can transmit and receive messages and control the communication lines so that multiple users can access a system.

multiprocessing (also called **parallel processing**) In a computer system, two or more processors linked by an operating system that share data and peripheral devices and can execute multiple programs simultaneously.

multiprogramming A computer operation that provides for two or more application programs to execute simultaneously from a single computer resource. A typical multiprogramming operation is a time-sharing system.

negative confirmation With respect to data communications, a type of confirmation that requests the recipient to respond only if in disagreement with the information provided.

net assets Assets minus liabilities. Equal to owner's equity.

net income Revenue earned above the related expenses for a given period.

net present value The excess of the present value of the net cash flows expected from an investment over the amount to be invested.

net price method A policy of recording purchase invoices at amounts net of (reduced by) cash discounts.

net realizable value The prospective selling price minus anticipated selling expenses. Inventory should not be carried at more than net realizable value.

net tangible assets Total of all assets (except the intangibles) minus liabilities.

network Linking two or more computers, at different geographical locations, with data communications technology to provide the sharing of computer resources.

nibble Half a byte (four consecutive bits).

NIST National Institute of Standards and Technology. A part of the U.S. Department of Commerce that issues standards and publications.

noise Random electrical signals, introduced by circuit components or natural disturbances, that tend to degrade the performance of a communications channel.

noncurrent account Any balance sheet account other than a current asset or a current liability. Noncurrent accounts include long-term investments, plant assets, intangible assets, long-term liabilities, and stockholder's equity accounts.

notes payable Formal written obligations to pay a stipulated amount of money, usually with interest, at a specific future date.

notes receivable Receivables (assets) evidenced by a formal written promise to pay a certain amount of money, usually with interest, at a future date.

object program (also called **object module**) The result of compiling a source program. Not a fully executable program, an object program is used by the linkedit program to create a load module.

obsolescence The process of becoming out of date and less efficient than newer types of equipment. In accounting, a major factor limiting the useful life of most depreciable assets.

OCR Optical character recognition. A computer input technique that translates printed graphic characters (may be handwritten) into bit patterns. The newer bit patterns aare compared with bit patterns held in memory to determine which known character the graphic character resembles.

OEM Original equipment manufacturer. Describes a purchaser, or customer, who buys a product from another manufacturer to be used as an element in the purchaser's own salable product. For example, an organization that gathers the hardware and software resources that compose a ready-to-perform computer system and then sells the complete system as a single package.

off-line Computer operations and devices not directly and continually controlled by a system's CPU. Types of input such as punched cards are considered elements of an off-line system because a manual operation is required between initial recording of data on the card and actual processing of data.

office automation As computer resources become increasingly affordable, the concept of a paperless office that relies on computer technology to store records in machine-readable form, manipulate documents through word processors, and transfer data through communications carriers.

one-way encryption A way of encrypting data so that the original data cannot be decrypted.

on-line A processing term that categorizes operations under direct, immediate control of the CPU. Interactive and real-time systems are among those classified as on-line systems.

operand The function code in a computer instruction that tells the computer which instruction to perform.

operating cycle The average period from the purchase of merchandise to its sale and conversion back to cash.

operating expenses Includes selling, general, and administrative expenses. Deducted from gross profit on sales to determine net income.

operating system Software that controls the execution of computer programs and that may provide scheduling, debugging, input/output control, accounting, compilation, storage assignment, data management, and related services. *See also* DOS.

opinion, adverse A judgment that the financial statements do not present fairly what they purport to present. It is required when the auditor has sufficient evidence for believing that the statements are misleading.

opinion, disclaimer of Used if the auditor does not have enough evidence to form an opinion either because the scope of the auditor's examination was seriously limited or because there are major and pervasive uncertainties that cannot be resolved.

opinion, piecemeal The complement of a qualified opinion, that is, a qualified opinion gives an opinion on the financial statements as a whole and makes exceptions for certain items, while a piecemeal opinion disclaims or is adverse on the financial statements as a whole and gives an opinion on certain items. (No longer permitted.)

opinion, qualified An opinion containing a modified phrase for one of four basic reasons: departures from generally accepted accounting principles, departures from consistent application of accounting principles, limitations of the scope of the examination, and uncertainties affecting the financial statements that cannot be resolved. The first three use the term "except for"; the fourth, "subject to."

optical character recognition *See* OCR.

Orange Book The Department of Defense publication titled "Trusted Computer System Evaluation Criteria," which is known by the color of its cover. It is a standard for review of information security.

original equipment manufacturer *See* OEM.

output Data/information produced by computer processing, such as graphic display on a terminal and hard copy.

output device Peripheral equipment, such as a printer or tape drive, that translates the machine code produced by a computer system into a form that can be used outside the system.

output media The form on which data is displayed, printed, or punched, including terminal display and microfilm.

owned data The concept of users being responsible for, or "owning," their data.

owner's equity The excess of assets over liabilities. The amount of an owner's net investment in a business plus profits from successful operations that have been retained in the business.

PABX Private automatic branch exchange.

package With respect to computer software, an application-specific program or set of programs that is mass-marketed and usually mass-produced.

packet switching A method of transmitting data where messages are broken up into a number of packets that are transmitted independently and subsequently regrouped at a receiving point.

page That portion of a program swapped between secondary computer storage and primary computer storage (memory) during program execution.

paging The interchange of a page between primary and secondary computer storage. Since main memory cannot hold the larger quantity of data that a storage device can, paging maximizes memory storage space by keeping on hand only the data currently required.

par value The legal capital of a corporation. Also the face amount of a share of capital stock. Represents the minimum amount per share to be invested in the corporation when shares are originally issued.

parallel conversion An installment technique whereby a new computer system is run concurrently with the old system until the new system has been proven.

parallel processing *See* multiprocessing.

parallel transmission Simultaneous transmission of the bits making up a character or byte, either over separate communications channels or on different carrier frequencies on the channel.

parameter (PARM) A variable that is given a constant value for a specified computer application and that may denote the application. A paramater establishes limits, selects options, or otherwise controls the behavior of a computer system.

parent Any data base segment that has one or more dependent segments. *See* child segment.

parent company A corporation that owns a controlling interest in another company.

parentage In a data base, a state of positioning that allows the user to control the processing of dependent (lower level) segments.

parity bit Addition of noninformation bits to data, making the sum in a grouping of bits either always even or always odd. This permits detection of bit groupings that contain errors. It may be applied to characters, blocks, or any convenient bit grouping.

parity check A horizontal parity check exists when a parity check is applied to the group of certain bits from every character in a block (also called longitudinal redundancy check). A vertical parity check exists when a parity check is applied to the group that is all bits in one character (also called vertical redundancy check). An even or odd parity check tests whether the value of digits in a group of binary digits is even (even parity check) or odd (odd parity check).

PARM *See* parameter.

PARM field The parameter or PARM field on the JCL execute (EXEC) statement allows variable information to be passed to a program at execution time. The maximum number of characters that may be passed is 100. Many IBM products use this field to pass program options, such as compiler option. IMS batch system uses this field to pass the name of the IMS application program to process and the program specification block (PSB) to be used.

partition That part of computer memory assigned to a program during execution.

partitioned data set *See* PDS.

partnership An association of two or more persons to carry on, as co-owners, a business for profit.

PASCAL A high-level programming language, rigidly structured.

passphrase (1) A group of words or character strings used as a password. The words are usually joined by a non-space character. (2) A sequence of characters, longer than the password, that is converted to the password used by the system to authenticate the user.

password A confidential character string used to authenticate an identity or prevent unauthorized accesses. Knowledge of the password is considered proof of authorization to use the assigned capabilities. There are two types of passwords: One is associated with a user ID and serves to confirm that the person entering the user ID is really that particular user. *See* personal password. The second is associated with the use of system resources and normally identifies one of a number of users who are allowed to perform the function. (*See* resource password).

password administrator A person who has the responsibility for administering the password aspects of the security program.

path Any hierarchical path in a data base.

payback period The length of time necessary to recover the cost of an investment through the cash flows generated by that investment. Payback period is one criterion used in making capital budgeting decisions.

payroll record A record listing the names of employees during a given pay period, the rates of pay, time worked, gross earnings, deductions for taxes and any other amounts withheld, and net pay.

payroll register A form of payroll record showing, for each pay period, all payroll information for employees (individually and in total).

PBX Private branch exchange.

PCB Program communication block. A part of a program specification block (PSB), the PCB communicates a data base definition name to DL/1 and specifies allowed processing options that can be performed on the data base by an application program. Also indicates the segments that can be affected by the specified processing options. Segments in a data base can be masked from application program view by not specifying them in the PCB. Also used by IMS/VS DC (Data Communication) to transmit messages between the terminal and application program.

PCB mask An interface between DL/1 and the application program. Exists in the application program and contains data base definition name, segment level retrieved, status code, processing options, segment name, key length, number of sensitive segments, and the key feedback area.

PCM Pulse code modulation.

PDS Partitioned data set. Independent groups of sequentially organized records, called members, are in direct access storage. Each number has a name stored in a directory that is part of the data set and contains the location of the member's starting point. PDSs are generally used to store programs. As a result, many are often referred to as libraries.

percentage of completion method An accounting method for long-term contracts, when the percentage of costs incurred to the estimate of total costs is multiplied by the estimate of total profit. This process determines an amount of revenue earned to date for recognition in the current accounting period.

performance monitor With respect to system software, a program that tracks and records the speed, reliability, and other service levels delivered by a computer system.

period costs Costs that are charged to expense during the period in which they are incurred. Generally include costs associated with selling and administrative functions.

periodic inventory system A method of accounting whereby a physical count is taken and the goods on hand are priced at regular intervals.

peripheral A hardware unit that is separated from the CPU and provides input, output, or storage capabilities when used in conjunction with a computer.

perpetual inventory system A system of accounting for merchandise, it provides a continuous record showing the quantity and cost of all goods on hand.

personal password A password known only to one individual that is used to authenticate that person's identity.

phase modulation With respect to communications, one of three ways of modifying a sine wave signal to make it carry information. The sine wave, or carrier, is changed in accordance with the information to be transmitted.

physical inventory The process of counting and pricing the merchandise on hand at a given date, usually the end of the accounting period.

physical terminal A hardware device used to enter or record messages being sent or received over communications lines. A physical terminal can be defined as many logical terminals.

PL/1 Programming Language/1. A high-level programming language designed by IBM to incorporate the features of COBOL and FORTRAN.

plant and equipment (fixed assets) Long-lived assets used in the operation of a business.

plug compatible With respect to computer equipment, hardware designed and distributed by one manufacturer that can be connected to, and operate with, the hardware of a different manufacturer to create one integrated computer system.

pointer With respect to a data base, indicates the location of an item of data.

polling A means of controlling communication lines. The communication control device calls the terminals under its control as a means of permitting them to transmit information. Polling is an alternative to contention; it makes sure that no terminal is kept waiting for a long time.

polling list The polling signal is usually sent under program control. The program refers to a polling list that exists for each channel and tells the sequence in which the terminals are to be polled.

polynomial checking An error detection code designed to discover if any data has been altered during transmission, thereby causing the receiving end to have erroneous data. A mathematical operation is performed on the data by the sender and repeated by the receiver. If the results are the same, then the data is unaltered.

port An interface between a peripheral device and the CPU. Usually a physical connection point such as a multiple-pin electrical connector or a cable ending that data passes through when entering or exiting the CPU.

POS Point of sale. The terminal that replaces the cash register in a retail business.

positive confirmation A type of confirmation that requests the recipient to respond in any event.

posting The process of transferring information from the journal to individual accounts in the ledger.

POTS Plain old telephone system. A colloquialism referring to the traditional voice network.

prefix With respect to data base processing, the control portion of a segment.

prepaid expenses Payments that are made in the current accounting period and benefit the current and future accounting periods. The amount applicable to future periods is classified as an asset on the balance sheet.

present value The amount of money today that is considered equivalent to a cash inflow or outflow expected to take place in the future. The present value of money is always less than the future amount, since money on hand today can be invested to become the equivalent of a larger amount in the future.

price/earnings ratio Market price of a share of common stock divided by annual earnings per share.

pricing the inventory The assignment of an appropriate dollar value to each item of merchandise determined to be on hand at the time of taking a physical count of inventory.

prime An area containing data and related track indexes. Prime areas exist for all indexed sequential data sets.

printed circuit board The plastic and bonded copper board that has etched electrical conductor patterns, integrated circuitry soldered and mounted in place, and edge connectors lined up along one side of the board to connect with external circuitry. Most modern technology has all electronic circuitry on printed circuit boards.

printer A peripheral output device that records on paper the information from computer systems.

prior period adjustments Gains or losses of material amounts that constitute adjustment of prior years' reported earnings and are recorded directly in the retained earnings account.

privileges Set of access rights authorized and allowed to a user and permitted by the access control system.

pro forma statement A statement that presents the effects of specific hypothetical conditions or prospective transactions on historical financial statements.

process cost system A method of cost accounting, used mainly in continuous mass production, in which costs are assigned to processes or operations and averaged over units produced.

processing options Specified in program specifications block (PSB) generation to indicate the processing that an application can perform on a segment in IBM's Information Management System (IMS).

processing regions In IBM's Information Management System (IMS) the four processing regions are Control Region, Batch Processing Region, Batch Message Processing Region, and Message Processing Region.

product costs Costs that are directly related to work in process and finished goods inventory, such as costs of direct material, direct labor, and overhead.

profit center A unit of a business that produces revenue that can be identified with the unit.

profit-volume formula Sales equal variable expenses plus fixed expenses plus net income.

program A set of related instructions that, when followed and executed by a computer, perform operations or tasks. Application programs, user programs, system programs, source programs, and object programs are all software programs.

program communication block *See* PCB.

program development The activities involved in creating workable, applicable programs. Includes writing, coding, debugging, and testing.

program specification block *See* PSB.

program temporary fix *See* PTF.

programmable read-only memory *See* PROM.

Programming Language/1 *See* PL/1.

programming specification The phase during program design that describes the function, structure, input, output, and storage requirements of the program.

PROM Programmable read-only memory. Typically, a semiconductor memory chip that is programmed after it is manufactured. The programming is normally accomplished through physical or electrical techniques.

prompt With respect to an interactive computer system, a message sent to the user from the computer system and displayed on a video peripheral unit. The message is usually a question, the response to which initiates the computer's next task.

PSB Program specification block. With respect to an Information Management System (IMS) data base, contains one or more program communication blocks (PCBs) that indicate segments and how data can be processed by an application program.

PTF Program temporary fix. When a problem is identified in vendor-provided programs, the vendor, such as IBM, first provides a PTF to temporarily overcome the problem. These PTFs are often implemented using a ZAP with a PTF serial number for identification. Most vendors distribute their software in object code format.

public switched network With respect to communications, any switching system that provides circuit switching to many customers. It includes these four networks: Telex, TWX, telephone, and Broadband Exchange.

punched card A rectangle of cardboard in which holes can be placed in specific patterns that represent data. These hole patterns are read by a device that translates a pattern into information understood by the computer. The holes can also be punched by a computer for subsequent input, as they are for utility bills.

purchase journal A special journal used exclusively to record purchases for merchandise on credit.

purchase method Accounting for a business combination by recording assets at current market values as indicated by the price paid in the acquisition.

purchase order A serially numbered document sent by the purchasing department of a business to a supplier or vendor for ordering material or services.

purchase returns and allowances An account used by the buying company to record the cost of unsatisfactory merchandise returned to the supplier. Also used for a downward adjustment of the purchase price of merchandise because of some defect in the goods.

purchases An account used to record the cost of merchandise purchased for sale to customers.

query A message that requests a programmed search of available data for a specific item when sent to a computer system. Also may be the facility in a data base that allows data to be viewed by a user but not manipulated and therefore changed.

queue With respect to computer systems, the first in, first out waiting line that prioritizes programs awaiting processing, including files and records.

RACF An IBM access control software product for protecting and monitoring access to computer resources.

RAM Random access memory. An internal memory component, usually a semiconductor, that data can be read from and written to. Data is transferred from a disk or diskette to RAM during processing. Since a semiconductor is volatile, data can be lost from RAM if electrical power is interrupted during processing.

randomizing module A user-supplied routine that converts a root segment key to root segment address. Required for hierarchical direct access method (HDAM) data bases only.

rate of corporate earnings Usually expressed as the percentage relationship of net income to sales. Can also be reflected by comparing net income with total assets or stockholder's equity.

rate of return on investment. The overall test of management's ability to earn a satisfactory return on the assets under its control. Numerous variations of the return on investment (ROI) concept are used, such as return on total assets and return on total equities.

raw (direct) material inventory Raw material or purchased components that are available for production and will become part of the finished product.

read-only memory *See* ROM.

read/write head With respect to magnetic tape and disk drive units, the mechanism that reads data from the tape or disk and/or writes data to the tape or disk.

real-time processing An interactive on-line computer system that produces results, inititated by an operator at a terminal, in a very short time to allow tasks to be started and finished almost immediately, with immediate update of files concerned.

realization Income recognition when both the earning process is virtually complete and goods and services have been exchanged.

receiving report An internal form that is prepared by the receiving department for each incoming shipment and shows the quantity and condition of goods received.

reciprocal accounts Offsetting accounts maintained by the home office and a branch. The home office maintains an account (with a debit balance) summarizing its investment in the branch. The branch maintains a home office account (with a credit balance).

record A unit of related data items. The group of data fields that can be accessed by a program and contains the complete set of information on a particular item, such as a payroll master file record that would contain employee name, number, address, rate of pay, etc.

recovery The restoration of computing capabilities and facilities after a system failure.

recovery of accounts receivable The collection of accounts receivable previously written off as worthless.

referback A job control language (JCL) statement that refers back to a previous step/statement for information, such as a data set name, to be used at a new point in the processing sequence.

remote access Communication with a computer by terminal stations or computers at a location other than the computer.

remote job entry *See* RJE.

replacement cost The estimated currrent cost of replacing goods in inventory or goods sold during the period. In financial statements, large corporations must disclose historical and current replacement costs of inventories and cost of goods sold.

report Computer processing output formatted to be easily read and understood by the user.

Report Program Generator *See* RPG.

research and development (R&D) expenses Expenditures intended to lead to new products or to improve existing products.

residual (salvage) value The portion of an asset's cost expected to be recovered through sale or trade-in of the asset at the end of its useful life.

resource Facilities used by the system to process data including data sets, terminals, transactions, main storage, CPU, and other input/output devices.

resource password A password associated with a specific system function, program, or group of data which is distributed to all those authorized to access that function, program, or group of data (e.g., a transaction code that must be entered along with a transaction before it can be processed).

resource security Access restrictions tied to particular hardware or software resources such as terminals, menus, functions, or files. Access to a particular system resource is limited to particular user IDs or a particular set of other system resources (e.g., access to a field within a file is limited to one particular program).

responsibility accounting A cost accounting system that establishes centers of responsibility throughout an organization by allocating costs and revenue to each center. This approach provides the organization with information on the performance of each center and the proficiency of the person to whom authority for the center has been assigned.

retail method A way of estimating inventory in a retail store. The method is based on the assumption that the cost of goods on hand bears the same percentage relationship to retail prices as does the cost of all goods available for sale to the original retail prices.

retained earnings That portion of stockholder's equity resulting from profits earned and retained in the business.

return on investment (ROI) A percentage that expresses the relationship between investment and profit. Computed by dividing the organization's net income by investment or owner's equity.

revenue The price of goods sold and services rendered by a business. Equal to the inflow of cash and receivables in exchange for services rendered or goods delivered during the period.

RJE Remote job entry. With respect to computer system with locations geographically separate from the main computer center, submitting batch processing jobs via a data communications link.

robotics A general term that includes the design and construction of automated, programmable equipment that can perform physical operations (such as production work and mechanical tasks) involving three-dimensional movement.

ROI *See* return on investment.

ROM Read-only memory. Preprogrammed memory circuitry that can be read from, but not written to (altered). Usually programmed during manufacturing, routines such as loading the computer and language translators are stored in this form.

root segments The highest level, or topmost segment, of data base system hierarchy. Always a parent in Information Management System (IMS).

routing The assignment of the communications path by which a message or telephone call reaches its destination.

routing indicator An address, or group of characters, in the heading of a message, the routing indicator defines the final circuit or terminal to which the message has to be delivered.

RPG Report Program Generator. A high-level, commercially oriented programming language specifically designed for writing application programs that meet business data processing requirements, such as management reports.

rules A data base definition specification that controls inserting, replacing, and deleting segments involved in logical relationships. Rules are also the foundation of many expert systems, which use those rules to apply the knowledge in the knowledge base (somewhat like a data base) to the problem at hand.

rules data base A system file that contains all of the access privileges, including restrictions, and attributes for users and the resources they seek to access.

run A popular, idiomatic expression for program execution.

sales The revenue account credited with the sales price of goods sold during the accounting period.

sales journal A special journal used exclusively to record sales of merchandise on credit.

sales returns and allowance An account used by the selling company to record the sales price of goods returned by customers. Also used for a downward adjustment of the sales price allowed to the customer because of some defect in the goods.

sample With respect to auditing, choosing a portion of available data to represent or reflect the validity, accuracy, etc., of financial statements to be reported in the audit report.

SAP Statements on Auditing Procedure. Now called Statements on Auditing Standards. *See* SAS.

SAS Statements on Auditing Standards. Released by the American Institute of Certified Public Accountants to guide external audits conducted by public accountants.

save In a computer system, a command or operation that moves recently entered data from temporary memory storage to a permanent file or storage medium such as a disk or tape.

scoresheet A listing of all items, large and small, that the auditor believes could or should be adjusted.

scratch With respect to a computer file, to delete or make unavailable.

SDLC *See* Synchronous Data Link Control; system development life cycle.

search field A search field defined in a data base definition is used to access a data base through segment search arguments to qualify non-key fields.

Securities and Exchange Commission (SEC) A government agency that reviews various financial reports of corporations that offer securities for sale to the public. Works closely with the Financial Accounting Standards Board and the American Institute of Certified Public Accountants to improve financial reporting practices.

security administrator Person who is responsible for managing the security procedures.

security policy The set of standards and requirements that defines how an organization manages, protects, and distributes sensitive data.

segment The primary unit of information in a data base. In Information Management System (IMS), composed of a prefix and data element (possibly key fields, intersection data, and concatenated information). A dependent segment in a data base is one that has a parent (*see* parent; child) and is independent of the parent segment as well as of any higher level segments in its hierarchical path. All segments are considered logical segments in a logical data base definition (DBD). A physical segment is any segment defined in a physical DBD except a virtual segment.

segment key field Defined in a data base definition and used to communicate with other data base facilities, such as IBM's Information Management System DL/1; a means to process data base segments.

segment level In IBM's Information Management System (IMS), data base structure can have up to 15 levels in a hierarchical structure. Segment level 1 is the root or base level; segment levels 2–15 are for lower level segments.

segment name Defined by the SEGM statement in an IBM Information Management System (IMS) data base definition generation (DBDGEN). References a logical relationship in a logical data base definition.

segment pairing When the same segment data in a data base exists or is available in more than one logical view, the segments are said to be paired.

segment search argument *See* SSA.

segment sensitivity Described by a SENSEG statement of the program communication block (PCB) in IBM's Information Management System (IMS). Indicates which segments are available to an application program. Segment data that is available to one application or group of applications but not available to other applications is said to be owned data.

segment type *See* segment name.

selling expenses Expenses of marketing the product, such as advertising, salaries, and delivery of merchandise to customers. A subdivision of operating expenses.

semiconductor An electronic device that conducts electricity by utilizing the atomic instability of silicon when combined with phosphorous. A semiconductor can limit the flow of electricity to one direction. Circuitry that uses semiconductors is called solid state.

semivariable costs Costs that respond to changes in volume of output by less than a proportionate amount.

serial numbering of documents The assignment of an unbroken sequence of numbers to a given class of documents, such as checks or invoices, so that the omission or loss of a document will be readily apparent.

SFAS Statements of Financial Accounting Standards. Issued by the Financial Accounting Standards Board, statements of standards governing the preparation of financial reports.

SHISAM Simple hierarchical indexed sequential access method. A hierarchical indexed sequential access method (HISAM) data base that contains only root segments.

SHSAM Simple hierarchical sequential access method. A hierarchical sequential access method (HSAM) data base that contains only root segments.

sign-on The procedure performed at a computer terminal while it is in initial mode. This procedure may include the sign-on commands (or command) and a password only, or it may include other user-specified security data.

silicon-on-sapphire *See* SOS.

simple hierarchical indexed sequential access method *See* SHISAM.

simple hierarchical sequential access method *See* SHSAM.

simplex mode Operation of a communications channel in one direction only, with no capability for reversing.

simulation With respect to mathematics, a model of a future event created by using current and historical data. In regard to computer systems, a programming technique whereby one computer system's operation can be imitated by a different computer.

SMDR Station message detail recording.

SMF System Management Facility. An IBM control program that provides the means for gathering and recording information that can be used to evaluate the extent of computer system usage.

SMP/4 System Modification Program. An IBM service aid for controlling modifications to an operating system. A later version of this program is SMP/E.

SNA Systems Network Architecture. Both an IBM system product and a concept that defines the internal architecture of a computer's communications system.

Social Security taxes FICA and FUTA taxes based on payrolls and intended to provide funds for operating benefit programs in which monthly retirement payments and Medicare benefits are paid to qualified workers in covered industries, as well as benefits to the family of a worker who dies before reaching retirement age.

software Computer programs that direct computer processing and can be stored and manipulated by a computer system.

SOP Statement of Position.

sort The rearrangement of computerized data into groups according to specific criteria, such as ascending, descending, numeric, or alphabetic sequence.

SOS Silicon-on-sapphire. An integrated circuit fabrication technology that uses a sapphire substrate or base on which to build silicon-based semiconductors/integrated circuits.

source and allocation of funds *See* statement of changes in financial position.

source document The initial, or original, recording of data before it is introduced to a computer system.

source program A version of a computer program written in human-readable statements. In this state, a program can be reviewed, analyzed, updated, and read by a compiler. It must be compiled and linkedited before it can be executed by the computer.

specific identification method A method of pricing inventory by identifying the units in the ending inventory in terms of specific purchases.

spool Simultaneous peripheral operations on-line. Sending data from one computer storage area to another storage area with a different speed capability, such as from a high-speed device to a slow-speed device, where an intermediate device, such as a buffer, exists between the transfer source and the destination.

SSA Segment search argument. In IBM's Information Management System (IMS) data base structure, SSAs are a component of a call and are used (through Boolean logic, relational values) to obtain a desired position in a data base. Can be a segment name only.

standard cost A formulated estimate of future cost that should be incurred under conditions expected to prevail. It establishes a measure from which current results can be compared and deviations and inefficiencies can be observed. Standard cost is usually expressed per unit.

standing data (also called **master file data**) In a computer system, the most currently accurate and authoritative permanent or semi-permanent computerized record of information maintained over an extended period.

start element With respect to data communications, the first element of a character used to permit synchronization in certain serial transmissions.

statement A computer operation command written in a high-level programming language that translates into a low-level language instruction and initiates the processing operation.

statement of account A monthly statement, sent by a company to a customer, showing charges for sales during the month, credits for payments received on goods returned, and the balance receivable from the customer at the end of the month.

statement of changes in financial position (also called **source and allocation of funds**) A financial statement showing the sources and uses of working capital during the accounting period. In addition, this statement shows financing and investing activities, such as exchange transactions, that do not directly affect working capital.

statement of retained earnings A financial statement that presents the variation in retained earnings for the year being reported on.

Statements on Auditing Procedure Now called Statements on Auditing Standards. *See* SAS.

Statements on Auditing Standards *See* SAS.

status code A code that can be used by an application program to discover the results of a function call. The code may be found in the program communication block mask (PCB mask). IBM's Information Management System (IMS) returns a code indicating the results of the call using a status code.

steplib A data definition statement in job control language in which a private library (where a program resides) is specified.

stock Transferable units of ownership in a corporation. Refers to both common and preferred stock.

storage An area in a computer system where the bit patterns that represent data are held before, during, and after processing. Primary storage is considered main memory.

storage device A hardware unit that can receive, retain, and output data.

store and forward With respect to communications, the process of message handling used in a message switching system. (*See* message switching.)

straight-line depreciation A method of depreciation that allocates the cost of an asset (minus any residual value) equally to each year of its useful life.

structured design A specific technique for designing computer software, using the tools and techniques originally defined by Yourdon.

subroutine A sequenced set of statements that may be used in one or more computer programs and at one or more points in a computer program. Subroutines can be referenced by a program, so that they do not have to be written in full within the program each time they are used.

subsidiary company A corporation in which a controlling stock interest is held by another corporation.

subsidiary ledger A supplementary record used to provide detailed information for a control account in the general ledger. The total of accounts in a subsidiary ledger equals the balance of the related control account in the general ledger.

substantiation *See* validation.

sum-of-the-years'-digits depreciation An accelerated method of depreciation. The depreciable cost is multiplied each year by a fraction, the numerator of which is the remaining years of useful life (as of the beginning of the current year) and the denominator of which is the sum of the years of useful life.

supervisor As applied to the computer operating system, a routine executed either in response to a requirement for altering or interrupting the flow of operations through the CPU, or for performance of input/output operations. Also may be the medium through which the use of resources is coordinated and the flow of operations through the CPU is maintained.

SVC Routine The operating system routine that receives control to process a specific supervisor call.

symbolic language A programming language that uses numeric words or symbols to represent operations and memory addresses. High-level and low-level languages as known are virtually all symbolic languages.

symbolic pointer Used mainly to construct logical relationships in a HISAM data base or between HDAM or HIDAM and HISAM. These pointers are user data fields and do not exist in a prefix: The fields must, however, be physically concatenated at the beginning of the segment data. This type of pointer is required for HISAM logical relationships because DL/1 must use ISAM to index through the data base, beginning at the root level (thus, the concatenated key). Symbolic pointers are optional in HDAM or HIDAM.

Synchronous Data Link Control (SDLC) A uniform data communications discipline using synchronous data transmission techniques for the transfer of data between stations in a point-to-point, multipoint, or loop arrangement.

synchronous transmission With respect to data communications, transmission in which data characters and bits are transmitted at a fixed rate with the transmitter and receiver synchronized. This method eliminates the need for start-stop elements, providing greater efficiency.

syntactical error A violation of the rules governing statement formats of computer programming. A syntactical error in a program prevents the program from executing correctly, if it executes at all.

sysout With respect to IBM's job control language (JCL), an indicator used in data definition statements to signify that a data set is to be written to a system output unit.

system An integrated set of elements designed to direct, cooperatively, the control and management of computer processing functions.

system development life cycle (SDLC) The organizational arrangements and procedures involved in developing new computer applications or modifying existing systems or programs.

System Management Facility *See* SMF.

System Modification Program *See* SMP.

system software Computer programs and related routines that control the processing of computer hardware and non-user-related functions.

Systems Network Architecture *See* SNA.

table With respect to computer programs, a table, like a dictionary, is a collection of data items where an item can be identified by an assigned label, by its positional relationship to other items in the collection, or by other elements that unambiguously identify that item.

tangible plant assets Long-lived assets used in the operation of the business and possessing physical substance, such as land and buildings.

tape *See* magnetic tape.

tape management system (TMS) A specialized system software tool that lists the computer resource allocations needed in a specified job run, including individual reels of tape.

target segment In IBM's Information Management System Virtual Storage (IMS/VS), the segment that the secondary index points to (*See* index data base.)

task A unit of work or an instruction performed by a computer. May include larger functions, such as payroll processing, or an operation, such as data input/output.

telco Telephone company.

telecommunications (TC) With respect to data communications, a general term applied to data that is transmitted by electrical, optical, or acoustical means between separate computing facilities.

teleprocessing (TP) A form of information handling in which a data processing system utilizes communications facilities. (Originally, but no longer, an IBM trademark.)

Teletype Trademark of Teletype Corporation, usually referring to a series of different types of teleprinter equipment, such as tape punches, reperforators, and page printers, utilized for communications systems.

terminal Any device capable of sending and/or receiving information over a communications channel. CRTs are often used as operator terminals.

test With respect to data accuracy, the comparison of data values during program processing to determine their "truthfulness."

text processing *See* word processing.

tie line A private-line communications channel of the kind provided by communications common carriers for linking two or more points together.

time-sharing A multiprogramming system that provides multiple users, at different geographic locations, on-line access to a central computer resource. The computer's resources are divided among the users in individual slices of time.

time slice In a multiprogramming system, the amount of processing time devoted to a job or specific processing resource in relation to the entire duration of all computer processing activities.

TOP SECRET Access control software produced by CGA Software Products Group to protect and monitor access to computer systems.

total manufacturing costs The total cost of raw material used, direct labor, and factory overhead cost for a given period without regard to whether products are completed.

TP *See* teleprocessing.

track The path on a magnetic storage medium, tape or disk, that data is recorded on. On a magnetic tape, parallel tracks run the length of the tape; on a magnetic disk, these tracks circle the area of the disk.

transaction file A group of one or more computerized records, usually transient in nature, containing current business activity and processed with an associated master file. Transaction files are sometimes accumulated during the day and processed in batch production overnight or during off-peak processing periods.

transactions Business events that can be measured in money and are entered in the accounting records.

transcription The translated copy of human-readable source documents to machine-readable tape, disk, diskette, or punched cards.

transistor A semiconductor device that, for computer applications, performs nearly all the functions of an electronic tube, especially amplification and switching. Invented in 1948 at Bell Laboratories.

transmit To send data from one location to one or more receiving locations, often over public telephone lines.

trap door A computer program that adds an entry or exit into the system, often for the purpose of inserting additional processing steps to an authorized program.

Trojan horse A computer program that seems to be or actually is useful but that contains unauthorized code that may compromise security.

trusted A component is said to be ''trusted'' if it can be relied on to enforce the defined security requirements.

trusted identification forwarding An identification method used in networks whereby the sending host can verify that an authorized user on its system is attempting to access another host. The sending host transmits the required user authentication information to the receiving host. The receiving host can then verify that the user is validated for access to its system. This process may be transparent to the user.

turnaround time The elapsed time between input and output results during which computer processing takes place.

turnkey A computer system delivered to the purchaser by the vendor ready to begin operations by installing the equipment with its software in the prepared environment and turning it on.

twin (also called **physical twin**) In a data base, the multiple occurrences of physical segments within the same physical parent.

uncollectible accounts expense The expense caused by failure of customers to pay amounts owed to the company. Also, the ledger account used to show the estimated uncollectible credit sales for the year.

unidirectional logical relationship In IBM's Information Management System (IMS), only one path of a logical relationship is defined: from the physical parent through the logical child to the logical parent. There is no segment pairing involved. (*See* bidirectional logical relationship; segment pairing.)

units-of-output depreciation A depreciation method in which cost (minus residual value) is divided by the estimated units of lifetime output. The unit depreciation cost is multiplied by the actual units of output each year to compute the annual depreciation expense.

universal product code A type of bar code used in marking merchandise for identification in pricing and description at point-of-sale equipment.

UNIX™ A real-time, multitasking, multiuser operating system. A registered trademark of AT&T Information Systems.

unrealized losses and gains An unrealized loss results from writing down marketable securities to a market value below cost. An unrealized gain results from restoring a former write-down because of a recovery in market price. Securities cannot be written up above aggregate cost. Unrealized losses and gains on marketable securities classified as current assets are included in determining the year's net income.

update A computer processing activity whose function is to incorporate new versions of data into current data; includes adding, deleting, and replacing data.

useful life Normal life of an asset, determined by its usefulness to its owner.

user friendly Describes computer products that are conversational, free of technical jargon, and easy to use and learn.

user ID User identification. A unique identifier assigned to each authorized computer user.

utilities A type of system software function; usually routines that are frequently required by the system during normal processing operations. Sort programs are considered utilities, for one example.

utility program *See* utilities.

validation (also called **substantiation**) The act of establishing the truth, accuracy, or relevance of an amount or fact by corroborating it through reperformance, vouching, confirmation, or reconciliation. In computer programs, procedures or routines can validate data as it is entered.

valuation account An account, such as allowance for doubtful accounts, with a credit balance, which is offset against an asset account to produce the proper balance sheet value for an asset.

valuation allowance for marketable securities Used to reduce the carrying value of marketable securities from cost to a market value below cost. Adjusted at each balance sheet date.

value added networks Federal Communication Commission (FCC) term for packet switching network services, such as Telenet and Tymnet, deemed to have offered a communication facility not previously available.

vaporware A derogatory term for hardware or software that has been announced by a vendor but is not available for sale.

variable (direct) costing A method of cost accounting that treats only raw material, direct labor, and overhead that varies directly with the level of production as product costs. These are charged to inventory. The fixed component of overhead is recognized as a period cost.

variable costs Costs that vary proportionately with volume of output.

variable length segment IBM's Information Management System Virtual Storage (IMS/VS) capability that allows a segment to vary in length between a minimum and maximum specified in the data base definition.

VDT Visual Display Terminal. A terminal with a screen.

VDU Visual (or Video) Display Unit. A terminal with a screen.

verify To check that data has been entered into the computer system accurately. For example, data entered through the keyboard, or keyed, is checked for correctness.

videotex An interactive, transactional computer system used to receive information, send electronic mail, order goods and services from on-line catalogs, and do banking through a central computer containing complex data bases. Access is via a videotex terminal or a personal or home computer with a modem.

view The appearance of a hierarchy to an application program. The data base definition and program specification block define the way the data looks and is structured.

Virtual Machine *See* VM.

virtual storage access method *See* VSAM.

virus Code designed to copy itself onto a file within a computer's operating system. Each time the affected program is executed, the virus embeds itself onto an uninfected program. The virus may further propagate through communication networks, such as bulletin board systems, and spread to other users.

VM Virtual Machine. An IBM system product for on-line time-sharing applications, where multiple users, including remote users, access a functional simulation of a complete computing system and its related devices.

voice synthesizer A computer output device that translates data in digital form to human-audible form, similar to that of a human voice.

volume A method of naming or defining a single computer disk or reel of magnetic tape. For tape, a volume defines a single reel of tape and the volume name is usually a serial number. For disk storage, the volume is a single unit (logically and sometimes physically).

volume header The label that names the data files on the volume or a subsection of the volume.

voucher A document prepared to authorize and describe an expenditure.

voucher register A special journal used to record all liabilities that have been approved for payment.

voucher system A method of controlling expenditures and the payment of liabilities. Requires that every liability be recorded as soon as it is incurred, and that checks be issued only in payment of approved liabilities.

VSAM Virtual storage access method. An access method for the direct or sequential processing of fixed variable length records on direct access storage devices.

WATS Wide area telephone service.

weakness With respect to a control, the inconsistent or improper operation of that control, rendering it deficient.

Wide Area Network (WAN) A type of formal communications network covering an expanded geographical area (e.g., city to city).

word processing (also called **text processing**) Using computer technology, such as a keyboard, terminal, and software, to facilitate the storage, input, editing, and revision of printed documentation.

working capital The difference between current assets and current liabilities. This amount represents the net amount of capital available for current use in a business.

working papers (also called **workpapers**) With respect to auditing, the forms, schedules, flowcharts, analyses, and correspondence prepared and collected during an examination that serve as the basis for the audit report.

work sheet A large columnar sheet designed to arrange all the accounting data required at the end of the period in convenient form. Facilitates preparation of financial statements.

WORM Write once read many. An unerasable, high-density optical storage device.

writing off an account receivable The removal of an account receivable from the accounting records because it is considered uncollectible and therefore is no longer regarded as an asset. The offsetting debit is to the allowance for doubtful accounts.

Xenix A licensed version of the AT&T Information Systems operating system, UNIX™.

XMT In computer systems, the abbreviation for transmit.

year-end adjustment At the close of a fiscal period, modifications made to add any unrecorded or nonroutine transactions, such as accruals, inventory changes, policy changes, or reclassification, to a ledger account. Not usually a correction.

ZAP A generic term used to define a type of program that can alter data and programs directly, bypassing controls. Because of this ability, the ZAP and SuperZAP programs must be secured from casual or unauthorized use.

zone portion The four left-most positions in a byte.

Bibliography

Ahituv, Niv, and Seev Neumann. *Principles of Information Systems for Management*. Dubuque, Iowa: William C. Brown Co., 1982.

Albrecht, W. Steve, et al. *Evaluating the Effectiveness of Internal Audit Departments*. Altamonte Springs, Fla.: Institute of Internal Auditors, 1986.

———. *Deterring Fraud: The Internal Auditor's Perspective*. Altamonte Springs, Fla.: Institute of Internal Auditors, 1984.

American Bar Association. *Report on Computer Crime*. Washington, D.C.: Section on Criminal Justice, 1984.

American Institute of Certified Public Accountants. *Codification of Statements on Auditing Standards*. New York: American Institute of Certified Public Accountants, 1988.

———. *Audit Procedure Study: Auditor's Use of Microcomputers*. New York: American Institute of Certified Public Accountants, 1986.

———. *Audit Guide: Audits of Service-Center-Produced Records*. Rev. ed. New York: American Institute of Certified Public Accountants, 1985.

———. *International Auditing Guideline: Auditing in an EDP Environment*. New York: American Institute of Certified Public Accountants, 1984.

———. *International Auditing Guideline: Computer-Assisted Audit Techniques*. New York: American Institute of Certified Public Accountants, 1984.

———. *MAS Technical Consulting Practice Aid: Assisting Clients in Software Contract Negotiations*. New York: American Institute of Certified Public Accountants, 1984.

———. *MAS Technical Consulting Practice Aid: EDP Engagement: Software Package Evaluation & Selection*. New York: American Institute of Certified Public Accountants, 1984.

———. *Report on the Study of EDP-Related Fraud in the Banking and Insurance Industry*. New York: American Institute of Certified Public Accountants, 1984.

———. *Statement on Auditing Standards No. 48; The Effects of Computer Processing on the Examination of Financial Statements*. New York: American Institute of Certified Public Accountants, 1984.

———. *Computer Services Guideline: Audit and Control Considerations in an On-Line Environment*. New York: American Institute of Certified Public Accountants, 1983.

———. *Computer Services Guideline: Management, Control & Audit EDP Systems*. New York: American Institute of Certified Public Accountants, 1983.

———. *MAS Technical Consulting Practice Aid: EDP Engagement System Planning and General Design*. New York: American Institute of Certified Public Accountants, 1982.

———. *Computer Services Guideline: Audit and Control Considerations in a Minicomputer Environment*. New York: American Institute of Certified Public Accountants, 1981.

———. *Audit Approaches for a Computerized Inventory System*. New York: American Institute of Certified Public Accountants, 1980.

———. *Audit and Accounting Guide: Computer-Assisted Audit Techniques*. New York: American Institute of Certified Public Accountants, 1979.

———. *Guidelines to Assess Computerized General Ledger and Financial Reporting Systems for Use in CPA firms*. New York: American Institute of Certified Public Accountants, 1979.

———. *Audit Considerations in Electronic Fund Transfer Systems*. New York: American Institute of Certified Public Accountants, 1978.

———. *The Auditor's Study and Evaluation of Internal Control in EDP System*. New York: American Institute of Certified Public Accountants, 1977.

Andriole, Stephen J. *Interactive Computer-Based Systems*. Princeton, N.J.: Petrocelli Books, 1983.

Arevalo, Claire B. *Effective Writing: A Handbook for Accountants*. Englewood Cliffs, N.J.: Prentice-Hall, 1984.

Arkin, Herbert. *Handbook of Sampling for Auditing and Accounting*. 3d ed. New York: McGraw-Hill Book Company, 1984.

———. *Sampling Methods for the Auditor: An Advanced Treatment*. New York: McGraw-Hill, 1982.

Atre, Shakuntala. *DBMS for the Eighties*. Wellesley, Mass.: QED Information Sciences, 1983.

Auerbach Publishers, Inc. *EDP Auditing*. Pennsauken, N.J.: Auerbach Publishers, 1988.

———. *Practical Data Base Management*. Reston, VA.: Reston Publishing Co., 1982.

Aumiaux, M. *Microprocessor Systems*. New York: John Wiley & Sons, 1982.

Banahan, Mike, and Andy Rutter. *The Unix™ Operating System Book*. New York: John Wiley & Sons, 1983.

Bank Administration Institute. *Statement of Principle and Standards for Internal Auditing in the Banking Industry*. Park Ridge, Ill.: Bank Administration Institute (undated).

Barefield, Russell M., and S. Mark Young. *Internal Auditing in a Just-in-Time Manufacturing Environment*. Altamonte Springs, Fla.: Institute of Internal Auditors, 1988.

Barret, Michael J., et al. *A Common Body of Professional Knowledge for Internal Auditors: A Research Study*. Altamonte Springs, Fla.: Institute of Internal Auditors, 1985.

Beizer, Boris *Software Testing Techniques*. New York: Van Nostrand Reinhold (Electrical-Computer Science and Engineering Series), 1982.

Bently, T., and I. Forkner. *Making Information Systems Work for You: An MIS Guide for Business and Professional People*. Old Tappan, N.J.: Prentice-Hall, 1983.

Benton, C. *The Database Guide: How to Select, Organize and Implement Database Systems for Microcomputers*. Bowie, Md.: Robert J. Brady Co., 1984.

Berry, Leonard Eugene. *Coordinating Total Audit Coverage: Trends and Practices*. Altamonte Springs, Fla.: Institute of Internal Auditors, 1984.

Bigelow, R., and S. Nycum. *Your Computer and the Law*. 2d ed. Reston, Va.: Reston Publishing Co., 1984.

Bjorner and Jones. *Formal Specification and Software Development*. Englewood Cliffs, N.J.: Prentice-Hall, 1982.

Boritz, J. Efrim. *Planning for the Internal Audit Function*. Altamonte Springs, Fla.: Institute of Internal Auditors, 1983.

Bradley, J. *Introduction to Data Base Management in Business*. New York: Holt, Rinehart and Winston, 1983.

Brill, Alan E. *Building Controls Into Structured Systems*. New York: Yourdon, Inc., 1983.

Brink, Victor Z., and Mortimer Dittenhofer. *Case Studies in Internal Auditing*. Altamonte Springs, Fla.: Institute of Internal Auditors, 1985.

Brink, Victor Z., and Herbert Witt. *Modern Internal Auditing: Appraising Operations and Controls*. 4th ed. New York: John Wiley & Sons, 1982.

British Computer Society. *Control and Audit of Minicomputer Systems: A Report of British Computer Society Auditing by Computer Specialist Group*. New York: John Wiley & Sons, 1981.

Bromage, Mary C. *Writing Audit Reports*. 2d ed. New York: McGraw-Hill Book Company, 1984.

Brooner, Ernie. *Microcomputer Data-Base Management*. Indianapolis, Ind.: Sams & Co., 1982.

Bruce, Phillip, and Sam M. Pederson. *The Software Development Project: Planning and Management*. New York: John Wiley & Sons, 1982.

Burton, John C., Russell E. Palmer, and Robert S. Kay, ed. *Handbook of Accounting and Auditing*. Boston, Mass.: Warren, Gorham & Lamont, 1988.

Byers, Robert A. *Everyman's Database Primer*. Reston, Va.: Reston Publishing Co., 1983.

California CPA Society's Committee on Electronic Data Processing. *Audit Implications of Small Business Computers*. Carol Stream, Ill.: EDP Auditors Foundation, Inc., 1987.

California Society of Certified Public Accountants. *A Computer Impact Series Report Prepared by the Committee on Electronic Data Processing*. Palo Alto, Cal.: California Society of Certified Public Accountants (undated).

Caron, Paul F. *Developing the Internal Auditor's Leadership Skills*. Altamonte Springs, Fla.: Institute of Internal Auditors, 1983.

Chereb, D. *Business Simulation: Forecasting with Micrcomputers*. Old Tappan, N.J.: Prentice-Hall, 1983.

Chorafas, Dimitris N. *Databases for Networks and Minicomputers*. Princeton, N.J.: Petrocelli Books, 1982.

Christian, Kaare. *The UNIX™ Operating System*. New York: John Wiley & Sons, 1983.

Christie, L., and L. Christie. *The Encyclopedia of Microcomputer Terminology: A Sourcebook for Business and Professional People*. Old Tappan, N.J.: Prentice-Hall, 1984.

Ciliberti, Anthony N. *Bank Internal Auditing Manual*. Boston, Mass.: Warren, Gorham & Lamont, 1986.

Collins, G., and G. Blay. *Structured Systems Development Techniques: Strategic Planning to System Testing*. New York: John Wiley & Sons, 1983.

The Computer and Business Equipment Manufacturers Association. *Privacy and Security: A Bibliography*. Washington, D.C.: The Computer and Business Equipment Manufacturers Association, 1982.

Computers, Control and Information Theory Abstract Newsletter. Springfield, Va.: U.S. Department of Commerce, National Technical Information Service, 1988.

Condon, R. *Data Processing Systems Analysis and Design*. 3d ed. Reston, Va.: Reston Publishing Co., 1982.

The Congressional Research Service Review. Washington, D.C.: Library of Congress, Congressional Research Service, 1988.

Cortada. James W. *An Annotated Bibliography on the History of Data Processing*. Westport, Conn.: Greenwood Press, 1983.

Courtemanche, Gil. *The New Internal Auditing*. Altamonte Springs, Fla.: Institute of Internal Auditors, 1986.

Dallas, Dennis A., and S. Rao Vallabhaneni. *Auditing Program Libraries for Change Controls*. Altamonte Springs, Fla.: Institute of Internal Auditors, 1986.

Daniels, Alan, and Don Yeates. *Design and Analysis of Software Systems*. Princeton, N.J.: Petrocelli Books, 1983.

Danning, Dorothy E. *Cryptography and Protection*. Reading, Mass.: Addison-Wesley Publishing Co. (Computer Science Series), 1982.

Date, C. J. *Database: A User's Guide*. Reading, Mass.: Addison-Wesley Publishing Co., 1983.

———. *Auditing and EDP*. 2d ed. New York: American Institute of Certified Public Accountants, 1983.

Davis, James R., and Barry E. Cushing. *Accounting Information Systems: A Book of Readings*. Reading, Mass.: Addison-Wesley, 1982.

Davis, Keagle W., and William E. Perry. *Auditing Computer Applications: A Basic Systematic Approach*. New York: John Wiley & Sons, 1982.

Defliese, P. L., H. R. Jaenicke, J. D. Sullivan, and R. A. Gnospelius. *Montgomery's Auditing*. 10th ed. New York: John Wiley & Sons, 1985.

DeMarco, Tom. *Controlling Software Projects: Management Measurement and Estimation*. New York: Yourdon, Inc., 1982.

Deutsch, Michael S. *Software Verification and Validation: Realistic Project Approaches*. Englewood Cliffs, N.J.: Prentice-Hall, 1982.

Dickinson, Brian. *Developing Structured Systems: A Methodology Using Structured Techniques*. New York: Yourdon, Inc., 1981.

Digest of Public General Bills and Resolutions. Washington, D.C.: Library of Congress, Congressional Research Service, 1988.

Directory of Computer Software. Springfield, Va.: U.S. Department of Commerce, National Technical Information Service, 1988.

Directory of Computerized Datafiles. Springfield, Va.: U.S. Department of Commerce, National Technical Information Service, 1988.

Dittenhofer, Mortimer A., and Rebecca J. Klemm. *Ethics and the Internal Auditor*. Altamonte Springs, Fla.: Institute of Internal Auditors, 1983.

Eaton, J., and J. Snithers. *This Is It: A Manager's Guide to Information Technology*. London, England: Philip Allan Publishers, Ltd., 1982.

EDP Auditors Foundation, Inc. *Certification Program for EDP Auditors*. Hanover Park, Ill.: EDP Auditors Foundation, Inc. (undated).

———. *Advanced Computer Assisted Audit Techniques*. Carol Stream, Ill.: EDP Auditors Foundation, Inc., 1987.

———. *General Standards for Information Systems Auditing*. Carol Stream, Ill.: EDP Auditors Foundation, Inc., 1987.

———. *The EDP Auditor Journal of the EDP Auditors Foundation*. Carol Stream, Ill.: EDP Auditors Foundation, Inc., 1983.

———. *Control Objectives*. Steamwood, Ill.: EDP Auditors Foundation, 1980.

Edwards, Chris. *Developing Microcomputerbased Business Systems*. Englewood Cliffs, N.J.: Prentice-Hall, 1983.

Enger, Norman L., and Paul W. Howerton. *Computer Security: A Management Audit Approach*. New York: American Management Associations, 1980.

Fernandez, Eduardo B., et al. *Database Security and Integrity*. Reading, Mass.: Addison-Wesley Publishing Co. (International Business Machines Systems Programming Series), 1981.

Ferngold, Carl. *Introduction to Data Processing*. Dubuque, Iowa: William C. Brown, 1975.

Flavin, Matt. *Fundamental Concepts of Information Modeling*. New York: Yourdon, Inc., 1981.

Franta, W. R., et al. *Formal Methods of Program Verification and Specification*. Englewood Cliffs, N.J.: Prentice-Hall, 1982.

Froehlich, Allan F. *Managing the Data Center*. Belmont, Cal.: Lifetime Learning Publications, 1982.

Galland, Frank J. *Dictionary of Computering: Data Communications, Hardware and Software Basics*. New York: John Wiley & Sons, 1982.

Gallegos, Richardson, and Birthrick. *Audit and Control of Information Systems*. Carol Stream, Ill.: EDP Auditors Foundation, Inc., 1987.

Glasson, B. C. *EDP Development Guidelines*. Wellesley, Mass.: QED Information Sciences, Inc., 1984.

Goldberg, Robert, and Harold Lorin. *The Economics of Information Processing (Volume I: Management Perspectives; Volume II: Operation, Programming and Software Models)*. New York: John Wiley & Sons, 1982.

Gremillion, Lee L. *Managing MIS Implementation*. Ann Arbor, Mich.: University Microfilms International Res Press, 1982.

Hampton, J. *Financial Management Concepts Using Spreadsheet Applications*. Reston, Va.: Reston Publishing Co., 1984.

Harmeyer, W. James, et al. *Conducting Internal Audit Interviews*. Altamonte Springs, Fla.: Institute of Internal Auditors, 1984.

Harvard Business Review. *Catching Up With the Computer Revolution*. New York: John Wiley & Sons, 1983.

Heeschen, Paul E., and Lawrence B. Sawyer. *Internal Auditor's Handbook*. Altamonte Springs, Fla.: Institute of Internal Auditors, 1984.

Highland, Harold Joseph. *Protecting Your Microcomputer System*. New York: John Wiley & Sons, 1984.

Hodge, B., R. Fleck, and C. Honess. *Management Information Systems*. Reston, Va.: Reston Publishing Co., 1984.

Holstrum, Gary L., et al. *Audit Evidence in the Year 2000*. Altamonte Springs, Fla.: Institute of Internal Auditors, 1988.

Horton, F. *Information Resources Management*. Old Tappan, N.J.: Prentice-Hall, 1984.

House, William C., ed. *Decision Support Systems*. Princeton, N.J.: Petrocelli Books, 1983.

Hoyle, J., and R. Scott. *Practical Case to Auditing: A Systems Approach*. Reston, Va.: Reston Publishing Co., 1982.

Inmon, William H. *Management Control of Data Processing: Preventing Management-by-Crisis*. Englewood Cliffs, N.J.: Prentice-Hall, 1983.

Inmon, William H., and L. Jeanne Friedman. *Design Review Methodology for a Database Environment*. Englewood Cliffs, N.J.: Prentice-Hall, 1982.

Institute of Electrical and Electronic Engineers. *Advances in Software Technology*. New York: Institute of Electrical and Electronic Engineers, 1981.

Institute of Internal Auditors. *Management and Control of End-User Computing*. Altamonte Springs, Fla.: Institute of Internal Auditors, 1988.

———. *Telecommunications Management, Control, and Audit*. Altamonte Springs, Fla.: Institute of Internal Auditors, 1987.

———. *End-User Computing Guide*. Altamonte Springs, Fla.: Institute of Internal Auditors, 1986.

———. *System Development Audit Review Guide*. Altamonte Springs, Fla.: Institute of Internal Auditors, 1986.

———. *Common Body of Knowledge for Internal Auditors*. Altamonte Springs, Fla.: Institute of Internal Auditors, 1984.

———. *Quality Assurance Review Manual for Internal Auditing*. Altamonte Springs, Fla.: Institute of Internal Auditors, 1984.

———, AICPA, and the Canadian Institute of Chartered Accountants. *Report of the Joint Data Base Task Force*. Altamonte Springs, Fla.; Institute of Internal Auditors, 1983.

———. *How to Acquire and Use Generalized Audit Software*. Altamonte Springs, Fla.: Institute of Internal Auditors, 1979.

———. *Standards for the Professional Practice of Internal Auditing*. Altamonte Springs, Fla.: Institute of Internal Auditors, 1978.

———. *Systems Auditability and Control Study*. 3 vols. Altamonte Springs, Fla.: Institute of Internal Auditors, 1978.

———. *Systems Auditability and Control—Audit Practices*. Altamonte Springs, Fla.: Institute of Internal Auditors, 1977.

———. *Systems Auditability and Control—Control Practices*. Altamonte Springs, Fla.: Institute of Internal Auditors, 1977.

International Business Machines Corporation. *Data Security Controls and Procedures: A Philosophy for DP Installations*. Pub. No. G320-5649. White Plains, N.Y.: International Business Machines, 1977.

———. *Management Controls and Data Processing*. Pub. No. GF20-0006. White Plains, N.Y.: International Business Machines, 1976.

———. *Managing the Data Processing Organization*. Pub. No. GE19-5208. White Plains, N.Y.: International Business Machines, 1976.

———. *Auditability Information Catalog*. Pub. No. GB21-9883. White Plains, N.Y.: International Business Machines, 1975.

———. *The Considerations of Physical Security in a Computer Environment*. Pub. No. GB20-2700. White Plains, N.Y.: International Business Machines, 1972.

Johnson, K. P., and H. R. Jaenicke. *Evaluating Internal Control: Concepts, Guidelines, Procedures, Documentation*. New York: John Wiley & Sons, 1980.

Jones, Seymore, and M. Bruce Cohen. *The Emerging Business: Managing for Growth*. New York: John Wiley & Sons, 1983.

Kacmar, C. *On-Line Systems Design and Implementation (Using ANS COBOL and Command Level CICS)*. Reston, Va.: Reston Publishing Co., 1984.

Klien, M. *Data Communications With IBM Microcomputers*. Bowie, Md.: Robert J. Brady Co., 1984.

Koshy, G. *Local Area Computer Networks*. Reston, Va.: Reston Publishing Co., 1984.

Kowalczyk, David S. *Cadmus' Operational Auditing*. Altamonte Springs, Fla.: Institute of Internal Auditors, 1987.

Kropatkin, Philip. *Management and the Audit Network*. Altamonte Springs, Fla.: Wiley/Ronald Press and the Institute of Internal Auditors, 1987.

———. *Audit Logic: A Guide to Successful Audits*. New York: John Wiley & Sons, 1984.

Krueger, Charles A. *Use of Ratio Analysis by the Internal Auditor*. Altamonte Springs, Fla.: Institute of Internal Auditors, 1986.

Kuong, Javier F. *Computer Security, Auditing and Controls: Text and Readings*. Wellesley Hills, Mass.: Management Advisory Publications, 1974.

Kurshan, B., and B. Healy. *Computer Fundamentals*. Reston Va.: Reston Publishing Co., 1984.

Law Enforcement Assistance Administration. *Criminal Justice Resource Manual on Computer Crime*. Washington, D.C.: Office of Justice Assistance, Research, and Statistics, U.S. Department of Justice, 1987.

Leibholz, Stephen W., and Louis D. Wilson. *User's Guide to Computer Crime: Its Commission, Detection and Prevention*. Radnor, Pa.: Chilton Book Co., 1974.

Leiss, Ernst L. *Principles of Data Security*. New York: Plenum Publishing Corp., 1982.

Lemieux, Richard N., et al. *Customer Satisfaction Audit: A Management Perspective*. Altamonte Springs, Fla.: Institute of Internal Auditors, 1985.

Lobel, Jerome. *Foiling the System Breakers*. New York: McGraw-Hill, Inc., 1986.

Long, L. *Managers' Guide to Computers and Information Systems*. Englewood Cliffs, N.J.: Prentice-Hall, 1983.

———. *Data Processing Documentation and Procedures Manual*. Reston, Va.: Reston Publishing Co., 1982.

Longworth, G. *Management Handbook of Computer Operations*. New York: John Wiley & Sons, 1982.

Macron, T. *Microcomputers in Large Organizations*. Old Tappan, N.J.: Prentice-Hall, 1983.

Mair, William C., Keagle W. Davis, and Donald Wood. *Computer Control and Audit*. 2d ed. Altamonte Springs, Fla.: Institute of Internal Auditors, 1978.

———. *EDP Controls and Audit*. Altamonte Springs, Fla.: Institute of Internal Auditors, 1976.

———. *Microcomputer-Based Information and Decision Support Systems*. Reston, Va.: Reston Publishing Co., 1983.

Major Legislation of the Congress. Washington, D.C.: Library of Congress, Congressional Research Service, 1988.

Maniak, Angela. *Presenting Audit Results: Logic, Content, and Form*. Altamonte Springs, Fla.: Institute of Internal Auditors, 1985.

Martin, James. *Managing the Database Environment*. Englewood Cliffs, N.J.: Prentice-Hall, 1983.

———. *Strategic Data Planning Methodologies*. Englewood Cliffs, N.J.: Prentice-Hall, 1982.

———. *Computer Networks and Distributed Processing: Software, Techniques and Architecture*. Englewood Cliffs, N.J.: Prentice-Hall, 1981.

———. *Design and Strategy for Distributed DP,* Englewood Cliffs, N.J.: Prentice-Hall, 1981.

———. *Security, Accuracy and Privacy in Computer Systems*. Englewood Cliffs, N.J.: Prentice-Hall, 1973.

McClure, Carma. *Managing Software Development and Maintenance*. New York: Van Nostrand Reinhold, 1981.

McLeod, Raymond, and Irvine Forkner. *Computerized Business Information Systems: An Introduction to Data Processing*. 2d ed. New York: John Wiley & Sons, 1982.

McNichols, C. *Microcromputer-Based Data Analysis*. Reston, Va.: Reston Publishing Co., 1984.

McRae, T. W. *Statistical Sampling for Audit and Control*. New York: John Wiley & Sons, 1974.

Meigs, Walter, John Larsen, and Robert F. Meigs. *Principles of Auditing*. 8th ed. Homewood, Ill.: Richard D. Irwin, 1985.

Metropolis, Edby N., et al. *A History of Computing in the 20th Century*. New York: Academic Press, Harcourt Brace Jovanovich, 1980.

Moeller, Robert R. *Artificial Intelligence*. Atlamonte Springs, Fla.: Institute of Internal Auditors, 1987.

Morris, Michael F., and Paul Roth. *Computer Performance Evaluation: Tools and Techniques for Effective Analysis*. New York: Van Nostrand Reinhold Co., 1981.

Morris, Richard M., III. *Developing a Charter for Internal Audit Function*. Altamonte Springs, Fla.: Institute of Internal Auditors, 1983.

Mullins, C., and T. West. *Harnessing Information Technologies*. Old Tappan, N.J.: Prentice-Hall, 1984.

Narvaez, Christopher R., et al. *A Model for Preacquisition Audits of Financial Institutions*. Altamonte Springs, Fla.: Institute of Internal Auditors, 1984.

National Institute of Standards and Technology.* *Data Encryption Standard*. FIPS Pub. No. 46. Washington, D.C.,: National Technical Information Services, 1988.

———. *Software Documentation*. Washington, D.C.: Government Printing Office, 1982.

———. *Automatic Data Processing Risk Assessment*. NBSIR 77-1228. Washington, D.C.: Government Printing Office, 1979. (Check with National Institute of Standards and Technology for availability.)

———. *An Analysis of Computer Security Safeguards for Detecting and Preventing International Computer Misuse*. National Bureau of Standards Special Publication 500-25. Washington, D.C.: Government Printing Office, 1978. (Check with National Institute of Standards and Technology for availability.)

———. *EFT in the United States: The Final Report of the National Commission*

* Formerly National Bureau of Standards.

of Electronic Funds Transfer, October 28, 1977, Washington, D.C. 052-003-00475-5. Washington, D.C.: Government Printing Office, 1977.

———. *The Use of Passwords for Controlled Access to Computer Resources*. Washington, D.C.: Government Printing Office, 1977. (Check with National Institute of Standards and Technology for availability.)

———. *Glossary for Computer System Security*. FIPS Pub. No. 39. Washington, D.C.: National Technical Information Services, 1976.

———. *Approaches to Privacy and Security in Computer Systems*. SD Catalog No. C13, 10:404. Washington, D.C.: Government Printing Office, 1974 (Check with National Institute of Standards and Technology for availability.)

———. *Guidelines for ADP Physical Security and Risk Management*. FIP Pub. No. 31. Washington, D.C.: National Technical Information Services, 1974.

Newman, Maurice S. *Accounting Estimates by Computer Sampling*. New York: John Wiley & Sons, 1982.

Nilles, J. *Micros and Modems: Telecommunicating With Personal Computers*. Reston, Va.: Reston Publishing Co., 1983.

Page, John, and Paul Hooper. *Accounting and Information Systems*. 2d ed. Reston, Va.: Reston Publishing Co., 1982.

Parikh, Girish. *Techniques of Program and System Maintenance*. Boston, Mass.: Little, Brown & Co., 1982.

Parker, Donn B. *Manager's Guide to Computer Security*. Reston, Va.: Reston Publishing Co., 1983.

———. *Computer Security*. Reston, Va.: Reston Publishing Co., 1981.

———. *Computer Security Management*. Reston, Va.: Reston Publishing Co., 1981.

———. *Computer Abuse Assessment and Control Study Final Report*. Menlo Park, Cal.: SRI International, March 1979.

———. *Ethical Conflicts in Computer Science and Technology*. Arlington, Va.: AFIPS Press, 1979.

———. *Crime by Computer*. New York: Charles Scribner's Sons, 1976.

Paz, Lawrence W. *Integrating the Internal Auditor into EDP*. Altamonte Springs, Fla.: Institute of Internal Auditors, 1983.

Perry, William E. *Ensuring Database Integrity*. New York: John Wiley & Sons, 1983.

———. *Improving Audit Productivity*. New York: John Wiley & Sons, 1983.

———. *Managing Systems Maintenance*. Wellesley, Mass.: QED Information Sciences, 1983.

———. *The Accountant's Guide to Computer Systems*. New York: John Wiley & Sons, 1982.

———. *Computer Control and Security: A Guide for Managers and Systems Analysts*. New York: John Wiley & Sons, 1981.

———. *Planning EDP Audits*. Carol Stream, Ill.: EDP Auditors Foundation, 1981.

———. *Selecting EDP Audit Areas*. Carol Stream, Ill.: Auditors Foundation, 1980.

Peters, Paul, and Anton Meijer. *Computer Network Architectures*. Rockville, Md.: Computer Science Press, 1983.

Pfleeger, Charles P. *Machine Organization: An Introduction to the Structure and Programming of Computing Systems*. New York: John Wiley & Sons, 1982.

Plagman, Bernard K., and Steven J. Ross. *Audit and Control of Systems Programming Activities*. Altamonte Springs, Fla.: Institute of Internal Auditors, 1985.

Ralston, Anthony, ed. *Encyclopedia of Computer Science and Engineering*. 2d ed. New York: Van Nostrand Reinhold, 1982.

Randall, R. *Microcomputers in Small Business*. Old Tappan, N.J., Prentice-Hall, 1982.

Ratliff, Richard L., et al. *Internal Auditing: Principles and Techniques*. Altamonte Springs, Fla.: Institute of Internal Auditors, 1988.

Romney, Marshall B., and James V. Hansen. *Data Communications: Concepts and Controls*. Altamonte Springs, Fla.: Institute of Internal Auditors, 1986.

Rosenthal, S. *Rosenthal's Computer Glossary*. Old Tappan, N.J. Prentice-Hall., 1984.

Rotch, W., and B. Allen. *Cases in Management Accounting and Control Systems*. Reston, Va.: Reston Publishing Co., 1983.

Rothberg, Gabriel B. *Structured EDP Auditing*. Carol Stream, Ill.: EDP Auditors Foundation, Inc., 1983.

Ryan, Jody L. "Expert Systems in the Future: The Redistribution of Power." *Journal of Systems Management,* Vol. 39, No. 4. Cleveland, Ohio: Association for Systems Management, 1988.

Salton, G., and M. McGill. *Introduction to Modern Information Retrieval*. New York: McGraw-Hill Book Co., 1983.

Sardinas, Joseph, and John G. Burch. *EDP Auditing: A Primer*. New York: John Wiley & Sons, 1981.

Sawyer, Lawrence B. *Elements of Management-Oriented Auditing*. Altamonte Springs, Fla.: Institute of Internal Auditors, 1984.

Schmittroth, Jr., John, ed. *Encyclopedia of Information Systems and Services*. Detroit: Gale Research Co., 1982.

Schweitzer, J. *Protecting Information in the Electronic Workplace: A Guide for Managers*. Reston, Va.: Reston Publishing Co., 1983.

Scott, R., et al. *Auditing: A Systems Approach*. Reston, Va.: Reston Publishing Co., 1982.

Seitz, N. *Business Forecasting: Concepts and Microcomputer Applications*. Reston, Va.: Reston Publishing Co., 1984.

Sharifi, Mohsen, and Badie Farah. *Integrated Case Studies in Accounting & Information Systems*. Englewood Cliffs, N.J.: Prentice-Hall, 1987.

Sippl, Charles J., and Roger J. Sippl. *Computer Dictionary and Handbook*. 3d ed. Indianapolis, Ind.: Sams & Co., 1980.

Sorkin, Horton L., and Donald E. Ricketts. *Quantitative Techniques for Internal Auditing*. Altamonte Springs, Fla.: Institute of Internal Auditors, 1983.

Squires, T. *Security in Systems Design*. New York: John Wiley & Sons, 1981.

———. *Computer Security: The Personal Aspect*. New York: John Wiley & Sons, 1980.

Stringer, Kenneth W., and Trevor R. Stewart. *Statistical Techniques for Analytical Review in Auditing*. New York: John Wiley & Sons, 1986.

Svanks, Maija I. *Integrity Analysis: A Methodology for EDP Audit and Data Quality Assurance*. Carol Stream, Ill.: EDP Auditors Foundation, Inc., 1988.

Talbot, James Reid. *Computer Security*. New York: John Wiley & Sons, 1981.

Taylor, D. H., and G. W. Glezen. *Auditing: Integrated Concepts and Procedures*. New York: John Wiley & Sons, 1982.

Tricker, R. I., and Richard Boland. *Management Information and Control Systems*. 2d ed. New York: John Wiley & Sons, 1982.

USX Corporation. *End-Use Computing Guide*. Altamonte Springs, Fla.: Institute of Internal Auditors, 1986.

Vaillancourt, Pauline M. *International Directory of Acronyms in Library, Information and Computer Sciences*. New York: R. R. Bowker Co., 1980.

Vallabhaneni, S. Rao. *Auditing the Maintenance of Software*. Englewood Cliffs: N.J.: Prentice-Hall, 1987.

———. *Auditing of Purchased Software: Acquisition, Adaption, and Installation*. Altamonte Springs, Fla.: Institute of Internal Auditors, 1985.

———. *Auditing Operational Application Systems on Large Computers: A Step-by-Step Approach*. Carol Stream, Ill.: EDP Auditors Foundation, Inc., 1985.

Wallace, Wanda A. *A Time Series Analysis of the Effect of Internal Audit Activities on External Audit Fees*. Altamonte Springs, Fla.: Institute of Internal Auditors, 1984.

———. *Handbook of Internal Accounting Controls*. Englewood Cliffs, N.J.: Prentice-Hall, Inc., 1984.

Walsh M. *Database and Data Communications Systems: A Guide for Managers*. Reston, Va.: Reston Publishing Co., 1983.

———. *Information Management Systems/Virtual Storage*. Reston, Va.: Reston Publishing Co., 1983.

Weber, R. *EDP Auditing: Conceptual Foundations and Practice*. New York: McGraw-Hill Book Co., 1982.

Weil, Ulric. *Information Systems in the Eighties: Products, Markets and Vendors*. Englewood Cliffs, N.J.: Prentice-Hall, 1982.

Weis, S. *Computer Applications Guide for Accountants*. Reston, Va.: Reston Publishing Co., 1984.

Westermeier, ed. *EDP and the Law*. Parkridge, Ill.: Data Processing Management Association, 1981.

Wetherbe, James C. *Executive's Guide to Computer-Based Information Systems*. Englewood Cliffs, N.J.: Prentice-Hall, 1983.

White, Kenneth R., and James A. Xander. *Survey of Internal Auditing: Trends and Practices*. Altamonte Springs, Fla.: Institute of Internal Auditors, 1984.

White, Richard, et al. "The Role of the Internal Auditor in the Deterrence, Detection, and Reporting of Fraudulent Financial Reporting," and "Control and Internal Auditing." *IIA Reports on Fraud*. Altamonte Springs, Fla.: Institute of Internal Auditors, 1985.

Wilkins, Barry J. *The Internal Auditor's Information Security Handbook*. Altamonte Springs, Fla.: Institute of Internal Auditors, 1979.

Wilkinson, Joseph W. *Accounting and Information Systems*. New York: John Wiley & Sons, 1982.

Wood, M. B. *Introducing Computer Security*. New York: John Wiley & Sons, 1982.

Woolfe, Roger. *Videotex: The New Television-Telephone Information Services*. New York: John Wiley & Sons, 1980.

Index

[Chapter numbers are boldface and are followed by a colon; lightface numbers after the colon refer to pages within the chapter.]

A

[*Chapter numbers are boldface and are followed by a colon; lightface numbers after the colon refer to pages within the chapter.*]

[Chapter numbers are boldface and are followed by a colon; lightface numbers after the colon refer to pages within the chapter.]

[Chapter numbers are boldface and are followed by a colon; lightface numbers after the colon refer to pages within the chapter.]

[Chapter numbers are boldface and are followed by a colon; lightface numbers after the colon refer to pages within the chapter.]

[*Chapter numbers are boldface and are followed by a colon; lightface numbers after the colon refer to pages within the chapter.*]

[*Chapter numbers are boldface and are followed by a colon; lightface numbers after the colon refer to pages within the chapter.*]

[Chapter numbers are boldface and are followed by a colon; lightface numbers after the colon refer to pages within the chapter.]

[Chapter numbers are boldface and are followed by a colon; lightface numbers after the colon refer to pages within the chapter.]

E

[Chapter numbers are boldface and are followed by a colon; lightface numbers after the colon refer to pages within the chapter.]

F

[*Chapter numbers are boldface and are followed by a colon; lightface numbers after the colon refer to pages within the chapter.*]

[*Chapter numbers are boldface and are followed by a colon; lightface numbers after the colon refer to pages within the chapter.*]

[Chapter numbers are boldface and are followed by a colon; lightface numbers after the colon refer to pages within the chapter.]

I

[*Chapter numbers are boldface and are followed by a colon; lightface numbers after the colon refer to pages within the chapter.*]

[*Chapter numbers are boldface and are followed by a colon; lightface numbers after the colon refer to pages within the chapter.*]

[*Chapter numbers are boldface and are followed by a colon; lightface numbers after the colon refer to pages within the chapter.*]

[Chapter numbers are boldface and are followed by a colon; lightface numbers after the colon refer to pages within the chapter.]

N

[*Chapter numbers are boldface and are followed by a colon; lightface numbers after the colon refer to pages within the chapter.*]

[*Chapter numbers are boldface and are followed by a colon; lightface numbers after the colon refer to pages within the chapter.*]

[*Chapter numbers are boldface and are followed by a colon; lightface numbers after the colon refer to pages within the chapter.*]

Q

R

[*Chapter numbers are boldface and are followed by a colon; lightface numbers after the colon refer to pages within the chapter.*]

[Chapter numbers are boldface and are followed by a colon; lightface numbers after the colon refer to pages within the chapter.]

S

[Chapter numbers are boldface and are followed by a colon; lightface numbers after the colon refer to pages within the chapter.]

[Chapter numbers are boldface and are followed by a colon; lightface numbers after the colon refer to pages within the chapter.]

[Chapter numbers are boldface and are followed by a colon; lightface numbers after the colon refer to pages within the chapter.]

[Chapter numbers are boldface and are followed by a colon; lightface numbers after the colon refer to pages within the chapter.]

U

V

[Chapter numbers are boldface and are followed by a colon; lightface numbers after the colon refer to pages within the chapter.]